The GALE
ENCYCLOPEDIA *of*
MENTAL HEALTH

SECOND EDITION

The GALE ENCYCLOPEDIA of MENTAL HEALTH

SECOND EDITION

VOLUME

1

A – L

LAURIE J. FUNDUKIAN AND JEFFREY WILSON, EDITORS

GALE
CENGAGE Learning

Detroit • New York • San Francisco • New Haven, Conn • Waterville, Maine • London

Gale Encyclopedia of Mental Health, Second Edition

Project Editors
Laurie J. Fundukian, Jeffrey Wilson

Editorial
Jacqueline Longe, Brigham Narins

Production Technology
Luann Brennan, Paul Lewon

Editorial Systems Support
Andrea Lopeman

Rights and Acquisitions
Margaret Abendroth, Emma Hull, Ron
Montgomery, Robbie Robertson

Imaging and Multimedia
Lezlie Light, Robyn V. Young

Product Design
Pamela Galbreath

Composition and Electronic Prepress
Evi Seoud

Manufacturing
Wendy Blurton

Indexing
Factiva Inc.

LIBRARY OF CONGRESS CATALOGING-IN-PUBLICATION DATA

The Gale encyclopedia of mental health, second edition / Laurie J. Fundukian and Jeffrey
Wilson, editors.
      p. cm.
            Includes bibliographical references and index.
            ISBN 978-1-4144-2987-8 (set hardcover: alk. paper)–
            ISBN 978-1-4144-2988-5 (vol. 1 hardcover: alk. paper)–
            ISBN 978-1-4144-2989-2 (vol. 2 hardcover: alk. paper)–
            1. Psychiatry–Encyclopedias.
            2. Mental illness–Encyclopedias.
            Fundukian, Laurie J., 1970- Wilson, Jeffrey, 1971- Title: Encyclopedia of
mental health.
RC437.G36 2008
616.89003–dc22   2007026137

This title is also available as an e-book.
ISBN-13: 978-1-4144-2990-8 (set); ISBN-10: 1-4144-2990-8 (set).
Contact your Gale sales representative for ordering information.

CONTENTS

ALPHABETICAL LIST OF ENTRIES

Kaufman Short Neurological
  Assessment Procedure
Kava kava
Kleine-Levin Syndrome
Kleptomania

L

Lamotrigine
Late-life Depression
Lavender
Learning disorders
Light therapy
Lithium carbonate
Lorazepam
Loxapine
Luria-Nebraska
  Neuropsychological Battery

M

Magnetic resonance imaging
Magnetic seizure therapy
Major depressive disorder
Male orgasmic disorder
Malingering
Managed care
Manic episode
Maprotiline
Marital and family therapists
Mathematics disorder
Matrix model
Medication-induced movement
  disorders
Meditation
Memantine
Mental health courts
Mental retardation
Mesoridazine
Methadone
Methamphetamine
Methylphenidate
Mini-mental state examination
Minnesota Multiphasic
  Personality Inventory
Mirtazapine
Mixed episode
Mixed receptive-expressive
  language disorder
Modeling
Molindone

Monoamine oxidase inhibitors
  MAOIs
Movement disorders
Multisystemic therapy

N

Naltrexone
Narcissistic personality disorder
Narcolepsy
Nefazodone
Negative symptoms
Neglect
Neuroleptic malignant syndrome
Neuropsychiatry/Behavioral
  Neurology
Neuropsychological testing
Neurosis
Neurotransmitters
Nicotine and related disorders
Nightmare disorder
Nortriptyline
Nutrition and mental health
Nutrition counseling

O

Obesity
Obsession
Obsessive-compulsive disorder
Obsessive-compulsive personality
  disorder
Olanzapine
Opioids and related disorders
Oppositional defiant disorder
Origin of mental illnesses
Oxazepam

P

Pain disorder
Panic attack
Panic disorder
Paranoia
Paranoid personality disorder
Paraphilias
Parent management training
Paroxetine
Passionflower
Pathological gambling disorder
Paxil and Paxil CR

Pedophilia
Peer groups
Pemoline
Perphenazine
Personality disorders
Person-centered therapy
Pervasive developmental
  disorders
Phencyclidine and related
  disorders
Phenelzine
Phonological disorder
Pica
Pick's disease
Pimozide
Play therapy
Polysomnography
Polysubstance dependence
Positive symptoms
Positron emission tomography
Postpartum depression
Post-traumatic stress disorder
Premature ejaculation
Premenstrual Syndrome
Process addiction
Propranolol
Protriptyline
Pseudocyesis
Psychiatrist
Psychoanalysis
Psychodynamic psychotherapy
Psychologist
Psychosis
Psychosurgery
Psychotherapy
Psychotherapy integration
Pyromania

Q

Quazepam
Quetiapine

R

Rage (road rage)
Rational emotive therapy
Reactive attachment disorder of
  infancy or early childhood
Reading disorder
Reinforcement
Relapse and relapse prevention

PLEASE READ—IMPORTANT INFORMATION

The *Gale Encyclopedia of Mental Health* is a health reference product designed to inform and educate readers about mental health, mental disorders and psychiatry. Gale believes the product to be comprehensive, but not necessarily definitive. It is intended to supplement, not replace, consultation with a physician or other healthcare practitioners. While Gale has made substantial efforts to provide information that is accurate, comprehensive, and up-to-date, Gale makes no representations or warranties of any kind, including without limitation, warranties of merchantability or fitness for a particular purpose, nor does it guarantee the accuracy, comprehensiveness, or timeliness of the information contained in this product. Readers should be aware that the universe of medical knowledge is constantly growing and changing, and that differences of opinion exist among authorities. Readers are also advised to seek professional diagnosis and treatment for any medical condition, and to discuss information obtained from this book with their healthcare provider.

INTRODUCTION

The *Gale Encyclopedia of Mental Health* is a valuable source of information for anyone who wants to learn more about mental health, disorders, drugs and treatments. This collection of approximately 450 entries provides in-depth coverage of specific disorders recognized by the American Psychiatric Association (as well as some disorders not formally recognized as distinct disorders), diagnostic procedures and techniques, therapies, psychiatric medications, and biographies of several key people who are recognized for their important work in the field of mental health. In addition, entries have been included to facilitate understanding of related topics, such as Advance directives, Crisis housing, and Neurotransmitters.

This encyclopedia minimizes medical jargon and uses language that laypersons can understand, while still providing thorough coverage that will benefit health science students as well.

Entries follow a standardized format that provides information at a glance. Rubrics include:

Disorders

- Definition
- Description
- Causes and symptoms
- Demographics
- Diagnosis
- Treatments
- Prognosis
- Prevention
- Resources

Medications

- Definition
- Purpose
- Description
- Recommended dosage
- Precautions
- Side effects
- Interactions
- Resources

INCLUSION CRITERIA

A preliminary list of mental disorders and related topics was compiled from a wide variety of sources, including professional medical guides and textbooks, as well as consumer guides and encyclopedias. The advisory board, made up of professionals from a variety of health care fields including psychology, psychiatry, pharmacy, and social work, evaluated the topics and made suggestions for inclusion. Final selection of topics to include was made by the advisory board in conjunction with the Gale editors.

ABOUT THE CONTRIBUTORS

The essays were compiled by experienced medical writers, including physicians, pharmacists, and psychologists. The advisors reviewed the completed essays to ensure that they are appropriate, up-to-date, and accurate.

HOW TO USE THIS BOOK

The *Gale Encyclopedia of Mental Health* has been designed with ready reference in mind.

- Straight **alphabetical arrangement** of topics allows users to locate information quickly.

- **Bold-faced terms** within entries direct the reader to related articles.

- **Cross-references** placed throughout the encyclopedia direct readers from alternate names, drug brand names, and related topics to entries.

- A list of **key terms** is provided where appropriate to define unfamiliar terms or concepts. A **glossary** of key terms is also included at the back of Volume II.
- The **Resources** sections direct readers to additional sources of information on a topic.

- Valuable **contact information** for organizations and support groups is included with many of the disorder entries.
- A comprehensive **general index** guides readers to all topics mentioned in the text.

GRAPHICS

The *Gale Encyclopedia of Mental Health* contains approximately 120 illustrations, photos, and tables.

ADVISORY BOARD

Several experts in mental health have provided invaluable assistance in the formulation of this encyclopedia. The editors would like to thank for their time and their contributions.

Abnormal involuntary movement scale

Definition

The Abnormal Involuntary Movement Scale (AIMS) is a rating scale that was designed in the 1970s to measure involuntary movements known as **tardive dyskinesia** (TD). TD is a disorder that sometimes develops as a side effect of long-term treatment with neuroleptic (antipsychotic) medications.

Purpose

Tardive dyskinesia is a syndrome characterized by abnormal involuntary movements of the patient's face, mouth, trunk, or limbs, which affects 20–30% of patients who have been treated for months or years with neuroleptic medications. Patients who are older, are heavy smokers, or have diabetes mellitus are at higher risk of developing TD. The movements of the patient's limbs and trunk are sometimes called choreathetoid, which means a dance-like movement that repeats itself and has no rhythm. The AIMS test is used not only to detect tardive dyskinesia but also to follow the severity of a patient's TD over time. It is a valuable tool for clinicians who are monitoring the effects of long-term treatment with neuroleptic medications and also for researchers studying the effects of these drugs. The AIMS test is given every three to six months to monitor the patient for the development of TD. For most patients, TD develops three months after the initiation of neuroleptic therapy; in elderly patients, however, TD can develop after as little as one month.

Precautions

The AIMS test was originally developed for administration by trained clinicians. People who are not health care professionals, however, can also be taught to administer the test by completing a training seminar.

Description

The entire test can be completed in about 10 minutes. The AIMS test has a total of twelve items rating involuntary movements of various areas of the patient's body. These items are rated on a five-point scale of severity from 0–4. The scale is rated from 0 (none), 1 (minimal), 2 (mild), 3 (moderate), 4 (severe). Two of the 12 items refer to dental care. The patient must be calm and sitting in a firm chair that does not have arms, and the patient cannot have anything in his or her mouth. The clinician asks the patient about the condition of his or her teeth and dentures, or if he or she is having any pain or discomfort from dentures.

The remaining 10 items refer to body movements themselves. In this section of the test, the clinician or rater asks the patient about body movements. The rater also looks at the patient in order to note any unusual movements first-hand. The patient is asked if he or she has noticed any unusual movements of the mouth, face, hands or feet. If the patient says yes, the clinician then asks if the movements annoy the patient or interfere with daily activities. Next, the patient is observed for any movements while sitting in the chair with feet flat on the floor, knees separated slightly with the hands on the knees. The patient is asked to open his or her mouth and stick out the tongue twice while the rater watches. The patient is then asked to tap his or her thumb with each finger very rapidly for 10–15 seconds, the right hand first and then the left hand. Again the rater observes the patient's face and legs for any abnormal movements.

After the face and hands have been tested, the patient is then asked to flex (bend) and extend one arm at a time. The patient is then asked to stand up so that the rater can observe the entire body for movements. Next, the patient is asked to extend both arms in front of the body with the palms facing downward. The trunk, legs and mouth are again observed for signs of TD. The patient then walks a few paces, while his or her gait and hands are observed by the rater twice.

Results

The total score on the AIMS test is not reported to the patient. A rating of 2 or higher on the AIMS scale, however, is evidence of TD. If the patient has mild TD in two areas or moderate movements in one area, then he or she should be given a **diagnosis** of TD. The AIMS test is considered extremely reliable when it is given by experienced raters.

If the patient's score on the AIMS test suggests the diagnosis of TD, the clinician must consider whether the patient still needs to be on an antipsychotic medication. This question should be discussed with the patient and his or her family. If the patient requires ongoing treatment with antipsychotic drugs, the dose can often be lowered. A lower dosage should result in a lower level of TD symptoms. Another option is to place the patient on a trial dosage of clozapine (Clozaril), a newer antipsychotic medication that has fewer side effects than the older neuroleptics.

See also Medication-induced movement disorders; Schizophrenia.

Resources

BOOKS

American Psychiatric Association. *Diagnostic and Statistical Manual of Mental Disorders.* 4th edition, text revised. Washington, DC: American Psychiatric Association, 2000.

Blacker, Deborah, M.D., Sc.D. "Psychiatric Rating Scales." In *Comprehensive Textbook of Psychiatry,* edited by Benjamin J. Sadock, M.D. and Virginia A. Sadock, M.D. 7th edition. Philadelphia: Lippincott Williams and Wilkins, 2000.

Mischoulon, David, and Maurizio Fava. "Diagnostic Rating Scales and Psychiatric Instruments." In *Psychiatry Update and Board Preparation,* edited by Thomas A. Stern, M.D. and John B. Herman, M.D. New York: McGraw Hill, 2000.

PERIODICALS

Gervin, Maurice, M.R.C. Psych, and others. "Spontaneous Abnormal Involuntary Movements in First-Episode Schizophrenia and Schizophreniform Disorder: Baseline Rate in a Group of Patients From an Irish Catchment Area." *American Journal of Psychiatry* (September 1998): 1202-1206.

Jeste, Dilip V., M.D., and others. "Incidence of Tardive Dyskinesia in Early Stages of Low Dose Treatment With Typical Neuroleptics in Older Patients." *American Journal of Psychiatry* (February 1999): 309-311.

Ondo, William G., M.D., and others. "Tetrabenazine Treatment for Tardive Dyskinesia: Assessment by Randomized Videotape Protocol." *American Journal of Psychiatry* (August 1999): 1279-1281.

ORGANIZATIONS

National Alliance for Research on Schizophrenia and Depression (NARSAD). 60 Cutter Mill Road, Suite 404, Great Neck, NY 11021. (516) 829-0091. <www.mhsource.com>.

National Institute of Mental Health (NIMH). 6001 Executive Boulevard, Room 8184, Bethesda, MD, 20892-9663. (301) 443-4513. <http://www.nimh.nih.gov>.

Susan Hobbs, M.D.

Abuse

Definition

Abuse is a complex psychosocial problem that affects large numbers of adults as well as children throughout the world. It is listed in the *Diagnostic and Statistic Manual of Mental Disorders,* the fourth edition, text revision (*DSM-IV-TR*) under the heading of "Other Conditions That May Be a Focus of Clinical Attention." Although abuse was initially defined with regard to children when it first received sustained attention in the 1950s, clinicians and researchers now recognize that adults can suffer abuse under a number of different circumstances. Abuse refers to harmful or injurious treatment of another human being that may include physical, sexual, verbal, psychological/emotional, intellectual, or spiritual maltreatment. Abuse may coexist with **neglect**, which is defined as failure to meet a dependent person's basic physical and medical needs, emotional deprivation, and/or desertion. Neglect is sometimes described as passive abuse.

The costs of abuse to society run into billions of dollars annually in the United States alone. They include not only the direct costs of immediate medical and psychiatric treatment of abused people but also the indirect costs of learning difficulties, interrupted education, workplace absenteeism, and long-term health problems of abuse survivors.

Types of abuse

Physical

Physical abuse refers to striking or beating another person with the hands or an object, but may include assault with a knife, gun, or other weapon. Physical abuse also includes such behaviors as locking someone in a closet or other small space, depriving someone of sleep, and burning, gagging, or tying someone up. Physical abuse of infants or children may include shaking them, dropping them on the floor, or throwing them against the wall or other hard object.

Sexual

Sexual abuse refers to inappropriate sexual contact between a child or adult and a person who has some kind of family or professional authority over that child or adult. Sexual abuse may include verbal remarks, fondling or kissing, or attempted or completed intercourse. Sexual contact between a child and a biological relative is known as incest, although some therapists extend the term to cover sexual contact between a child and any trusted caregiver, including relatives by marriage. Girls are more likely than boys to be abused sexually. According to a conservative estimate, 38% of girls and 16% of boys are sexually abused before their eighteenth birthday.

Verbal

Verbal abuse refers to regular and consistent belittling, name-calling, labeling, or ridicule of a person. It may also include spoken threats. It is one of the most difficult forms of abuse to prove because it does not leave physical scars or other evidence, but it is nonetheless hurtful. Verbal abuse may occur in schools or workplaces as well as in families.

Emotional/psychological

Emotional/psychological abuse covers a variety of behaviors that hurt or injure others even though no physical contact may be involved. In fact, emotional abuse is a stronger predictor than physical abuse of the likelihood of **suicide** attempts in later life. One form of emotional abuse involves the destruction of someone's pet or valued possession in order to cause pain. Another abusive behavior is emotional blackmail, such as threatening to commit suicide unless the other person does what is wanted. Other behaviors in this category include the silent treatment, shaming or humiliating people in front of others, or punishing them for receiving an award or honor.

Intellectual/spiritual

Intellectual/spiritual abuse refers to such behaviors as punishing people for having different intellectual interests or religious beliefs from others in the family, preventing them from attending worship services, ridiculing their opinions, and the like.

Child abuse

Child abuse first attracted national attention in the United States in the 1950s, when a Denver pediatrician named C. Henry Kempe began publishing his findings regarding x-ray evidence of intentional injuries to small children. Kempe's research was followed by numerous investigations of other signs of child abuse and neglect, including **learning disorders**, malnutrition, failure to thrive, conduct disorders, emotional retardation, and sexually transmitted diseases in very young children.

Experts believe that child abuse in the United States is still significantly underreported. In 2004, there were an estimated 1,490 child deaths from abuse or neglect in the United States, indicating a rate of two children for every 100,000 in the population. In recent years, the rate of maltreatment and child abuse appears to have decreased and was reported in 2004 to be 11.9 children for every thousand in the United States. The forms of abuse included neglect, physical abuse, sexual abuse, and emotional or psychological abuse. Of the children who survive abuse, an estimated 20% have permanent physical injury. Children with birth defects, developmental delays, or chronic illnesses are at higher risk of being abused by parents or other caregivers.

Abused adults

The women's movement of the 1970s led not only to greater recognition of domestic violence and other forms of abuse of adults, but also to research into the factors in the wider society that perpetuate abusive attitudes and behaviors. Women are more likely than men to be the targets of abuse in adult life, and one in four women will experience domestic violence in her lifetime.

Domestic violence

Domestic violence refers to the physical, emotional, and sexual abuse of a spouse or domestic partner. Early research into the problem of wife battering focused on middle-class couples, but it has since been recognized that spouse abuse occurs among couples of any socioeconomic status. In addition, domestic violence also occurs among gay and lesbian couples. It is estimated that four million women in the United States are involved in abusive marriages or relationships; moreover, a significant percentage of female murder victims are killed by their spouses or partners rather than by strangers.

Domestic violence illustrates the tendency of abusive people to attack anyone they perceive as vulnerable: most men who batter women also abuse their children; some battered women abuse their children; and abusive humans are frequently cruel to animals.

Elder abuse

Elder abuse has also become a subject of national concern in the last two decades. As older adults live longer, many become dependent for years on adult caregivers, who may be either their own adult children or nursing home personnel. Care of the elderly can be extremely stressful, especially if the older adult has **dementia**. Elder abuse may include physical hitting or slapping; withholding food or medications; tying them to a chair or bed; neglecting to bathe them or help them to the toilet; taking their personal possessions, including money or property; and restricting or cutting off their contacts with friends and relatives.

Abusive professional relationships

Adults can also be abused by sexually exploitative doctors, therapists, clergy, and other helping professionals. Although instances of this type of abuse were dismissed prior to the 1980s as consensual participation in sexual activity, most professionals now recognize that these cases actually reflect the practitioner's abuse of social and educational power. About 85% of sexual abuse cases in the professions involve male practitioners and female clients; another 12% involve male practitioners and male clients; and the remaining 3% involve female practitioners and either male or female clients. Ironically, many of these abusive relationships hurt women who sought professional help in order to deal with the effects of childhood abuse.

Stalking

Stalking, or the repeated pursuit or surveillance of another person by physical or electronic means, is now defined as a crime in all 50 states. Many cases of stalking are extensions of domestic violence, in that the stalker (usually a male) attempts to track down a wife or girlfriend who left him. However, stalkers may also be casual acquaintances, workplace colleagues, or even total strangers. Stalking may include a number of abusive behaviors, including forced entry into a person's home, destruction of cars or other personal property, anonymous letters to a person's friends or employer, or repeated phone calls, letters, or e-mails. About 80% of stalking cases reported to police involve men stalking women.

Workplace bullying

Workplace **bullying** is, like stalking, increasingly recognized as interpersonal abuse. It should not be confused with sexual harassment or racial discrimination. Workplace bullying refers to verbal abuse of other workers, interfering with their work, withholding equipment or other resources they need to do their job, or invading their personal space, including touching them in a controlling manner. Half of all workplace bullies are women, and the majority (81%) are bosses or supervisors.

Causes of abuse

The causes of interpersonal abuse are complex and overlapping. Some of the most important factors are:

- early learning experiences: This factor is sometimes described as the "life cycle" of abuse. Many abusive parents were themselves abused as children and have learned to see hurtful behavior as normal childrearing. At the other end of the life cycle, some adults who abuse their elderly parent are paying back the parent for abusing them in their early years.
- ignorance of developmental timetables: Some parents have unrealistic expectations of children in terms of the appropriate age for toilet training, feeding themselves, and similar milestones; they may attack their children for not meeting these expectations.
- economic stress: Many caregivers cannot afford part-time day care for children or dependent elderly parents, which would relieve some of their emotional strain. Even middle-class families can be financially stressed if they find themselves responsible for the costs of caring for elderly parents before their own children are financially independent.
- lack of social support or social resources: Caregivers who have the support of an extended family, religious group, or close friends and neighbors are less likely to lose their self-control under stress.

- substance abuse: Alcohol and mood-altering drugs do not cause abuse directly, but they weaken or remove a person's inhibitions against violence toward others. In addition, the cost of a drug habit often gives a person with a substance addiction another reason for resenting the needs of the dependent person. A majority of workplace bullies are substance addicts.
- mental disorders: Depression, personality disorders, dissociative disorders, and anxiety disorders can all affect parents' ability to care for their children appropriately. A small percentage of abusive parents or spouses are psychotic.
- belief systems: Many men still think that they have a "right" to a relationship with a woman; and many people regard parents' rights over children as absolute.
- the role of bystanders: Research in the social sciences has shown that one factor that encourages abusers to continue their hurtful behavior is discovering that people who know about or suspect the abuse are reluctant to get involved. In most cases, bystanders are afraid of possible physical, social, or legal consequences for reporting abuse. The result, however, is that many abusers come to see themselves as invulnerable.

Aftereffects

Abuse affects all dimensions of human development and existence.

Physical and neurobiological

In addition to such direct results of trauma as broken bones or ruptured internal organs, physically abused children often display retarded physical growth and poor coordination. Malnutrition may slow the development of the **brain** as well as produce such dietary deficiency diseases as rickets. In both children and adults, repeated trauma produces changes in the neurochemistry of the brain that affect memory formation. Instead of memories being formed in the normal way, which allows them to be modified by later experiences and integrated into a person's ongoing life, traumatic memories are stored as chaotic fragments of emotion and sensation that are sealed off from ordinary consciousness. These traumatic memories may then erupt from time to time in the form of flashbacks.

Cognitive and emotional

Abused children develop distorted patterns of cognition (knowing) because they are stressed emotionally by abuse. As adults, they may experience cognitive distortions that make it hard for them to distinguish between normal occurrences and abnormal ones, or between important matters and relatively trivial ones. They often misinterpret other people's behavior and refuse to trust them. Emotional distortions include such patterns as being unable to handle strong feelings, or being unusually tolerant of behavior from others that most people would protest.

Social and educational

The cognitive and emotional aftereffects of abuse have a powerful impact on adult educational, social, and occupational functioning. Children who are abused are often in physical and emotional pain at school; they cannot concentrate on schoolwork, and consequently fall behind in their grades. They often find it hard to make or keep friends, and may be victimized by bullies or become bullies themselves. In adult life, abuse survivors are at risk of repeating childhood patterns through forming relationships with abusive spouses, employers, or professionals. Even though survivors may consciously want to avoid further abuse, they are often unconsciously attracted to people who remind them of their family of origin. Abused adults are also likely to fail to complete their educations, or they accept employment that is significantly below their actual level of ability.

Treatment

Treatment of the aftereffects of abuse must be tailored to the needs of the specific individual, but usually involves a variety of long-term considerations that may include legal concerns, geographical relocation, and housing or employment as well as immediate medical or psychiatric care.

Medical and psychiatric

In addition to requiring immediate treatment for physical injuries, abused children and adults often need long-term **psychotherapy** in order to recover from specific mental disorders and to learn new ways of dealing with distorted thoughts and feelings. This approach to therapy is known as cognitive restructuring. Specific mental disorders that have been linked to childhood abuse include major depression, **bulimia nervosa**, **social phobia**, Munchausen syndrome by proxy, **generalized anxiety disorder**, **post-traumatic stress disorder**, **borderline personality disorder**, **dissociative amnesia**, and **dissociative identity disorder**. Abused adults may develop post-traumatic stress disorder, major depression, or substance abuse disorders. At present, researchers are focusing on genetic factors as a partial explanation of the fact that some people appear to react more intensely than others to being abused.

KEY TERMS

Cognitive restructuring—An approach to psychotherapy that focuses on helping patients examine distorted patterns of perceiving and thinking in order to change their emotional responses to people and situations.

Dementia—A group of symptoms (syndrome) associated with a progressive loss of memory and other intellectual functions that is serious enough to interfere with a person's ability to perform the tasks of daily life. Dementia impairs memory, alters personality, leads to deterioration in personal grooming, impairs reasoning ability, and causes disorientation.

Flashback—The reemergence of a traumatic memory as a vivid recollection of sounds, images, and sensations associated with the trauma. Those having the flashbacks typically feel as if they are reliving the event.

Incest—Unlawful sexual contact between people who are biologically related. Many therapists, however, use the term to refer to inappropriate sexual contact between any members of a family, including stepparents and stepsiblings.

Stalking—The intentional pursuit or surveillance of another person, usually with the intent of forcing that person into a dating or marriage relationship. Stalking is now punishable as a crime in all 50 states.

Legal considerations

Medical professionals and, increasingly, religious professionals, are required by law to report child abuse to law enforcement officials, usually a child protection agency. Physicians are granted immunity from lawsuits for making such reports.

Adults in abusive situations may encounter a variety of responses from law enforcement or the criminal justice system. In general, cases of spouse abuse, stalking, and sexual abuse by professionals are taken more seriously than they were two or three decades ago. Many communities now require police officers to arrest aggressors in domestic violence situations, and a growing number of small towns as well as cities have shelters for family members fleeing violent households. All major medical, educational, and legal professional societies, as well as mainstream religious bodies, have adopted strict codes of ethics, and have procedures in place for reporting cases of abuse by their members.

Prevention

Prevention of abuse requires long-term social changes in attitudes toward violence, gender roles, and the relationship of the family to other institutions. Research in the structure and function of the brain may help to develop more effective treatments for the aftereffects of abuse and possibly new approaches to help break the intergenerational cycle of abuse. At present, preventive measures include protective removal of children or elders from abusive households, legal penalties for abusive spouses and professionals, and education of the public about the nature and causes of abuse.

Resources

BOOKS

American Psychiatric Association. *Diagnostic and Statistical Manual of Mental Disorders*. 4th ed., Text rev. Washington, D.C.: American Psychiatric Association, 2000.

Baumeister, Roy F., PhD. *Evil: Inside Human Violence and Cruelty*. New York: W. H. Freeman and Company, 1999.

Beers, Mark H., MD. "Chapter 41: Behavior Disorders in Dementia." *The Merck Manual of Geriatrics*, Mark H. Beers, MD, and Robert Berkow, MD, eds. Whitehouse Station, NJ: Merck Research Laboratories, 2000.

"Child Abuse and Neglect." Section 19, Chapter 264 in *The Merck Manual of Diagnosis and Therapy*, Mark H. Beers, MD, and Robert Berkow, MD, eds. Whitehouse Station, NJ: Merck Research Laboratories, 1999.

Herman, Judith, MD. *Trauma and Recovery*. 2nd ed., revised. New York: Basic Books, 1997.

Marcantonio, Edward, MD. "Dementia." Chapter 40 in *The Merck Manual of Geriatrics*, Mark H. Beers, MD, and Robert Berkow, MD, eds. Whitehouse Station, NJ: Merck Research Laboratories, 2000.

Morris, Virginia. *How to Care for Aging Parents*. New York: Workman Publishing, 1996.

Rutter, Peter, MD. *Sex in the Forbidden Zone: When Men in Power—Therapists, Doctors, Clergy, Teachers, and Others—Betray Women's Trust*. New York: Jeremy P. Tarcher, 1989.

Stout, Martha, PhD. *The Myth of Sanity: Tales of Multiple Personality in Everyday Life*. New York: Penguin Books, 2001.

Walker, Lenore E., PhD. *The Battered Woman*. New York: Harper & Row, 1979.

Weitzman, Susan, PhD. *"Not to People Like Us": Hidden Abuse in Upscale Marriages*. New York: Basic Books, 2000.

PERIODICALS

Carter, Ann. "Abuse of Older Adults." *Clinical Reference Systems Annual* (2000): 12.

Gibb, Brandon E., and others. "Childhood Maltreatment and College Students' Current Suicidal Ideation: A Test of the Hopelessness Theory." *Suicide and Life-Threatening Behavior* 31 (2001): 405–15.

Lieb, Roselind. "Parental Psychopathology, Parenting Styles, and the Risk of Social Phobia in Offspring: A Prospective-Longitudinal Community Study." *Journal of the American Medical Association* 284 (December 13, 2000): 2855.

Plunkett, A., and others. "Suicide Risk Following Child Sexual Abuse." *Ambulatory Pediatrics* 1 (September–October 2001): 262–66.

Redford, Jennifer. "Are Sexual Abuse and Bulimia Linked?" *Physician Assistant* 25 (March 2001): 21.

Steiger, Howard, and others. "Association of Serotonin and Cortisol Indices with Childhood Abuse in Bulimia Nervosa." *Archives of General Psychiatry* 58 (September 2001): 837.

Strayhorn, Joseph M., Jr. "Self-Control: Theory and Research." *Journal of the American Academy of Child and Adolescent Psychiatry* 41 (January 2002): 7–16.

Van der Kolk, Bessel. "The Body Keeps the Score: Memory and the Evolving Psychobiology of PTSD." *Harvard Review of Psychiatry* 1 (1994): 253–65.

ORGANIZATIONS

American Academy of Child and Adolescent Psychiatry. 3615 Wisconsin Avenue, NW, Washington, DC 20016-3007. Telephone: (202) 966-7300. Fax: (202) 966-2891. <www.aacap.org>.

C. Henry Kempe National Center for the Prevention and Treatment of Child Abuse and Neglect. 1205 Oneida Street, Denver, CO 80220. Telephone: (303) 321-3963.

National Coalition Against Domestic Violence. 1120 Lincoln Street, Suite 1603, Denver, CO, 80203, Telephone: (303) 839-1852, Fax: (303) 831-9251, TTY: (303) 839-1681. <http://www.ncadv.org>.

National Institute of Mental Health. 6001 Executive Boulevard, Room 8184, MSC 9663, Bethesda, MD 20892-9663. Telephone: (301) 443-4513. <www.nimh.nih.gov>.

OTHER

Campaign Against Workplace Bullying. P. O. Box 1886, Benicia, CA 94510. <www.bullybusters.org>.

Child Welfare Information Gateway. "Child Abuse and Neglect Fatalities: Statistics and Interventions." 2006. <http://www.childwelfare.gov/pubs/factsheets/fatality.pdf>.

National Library of Medicine. National Institutes of Health. "Domestic Violence." <http://www.nlm.nih.gov/medlineplus/domesticviolence.html>.

U.S. Department of Health and Human Services, Administration on Children, Youth and Families. *Child Maltreatment 2004* (Washington, D.C.: U.S. Government Printing Office, 2006). <http://www.acf.hhs.gov/programs/cb/pubs/cm04/cm04.pdf>.

Rebecca Frey, PhD
Emily Jane Willingham, PhD

Acne excoriee *see* **Dermatotillomania**

Acupressure *see* **Bodywork therapies**

Acupuncture

Definition

Acupuncture, one of the main forms of therapy in traditional Chinese medicine (TCM), has been practiced for at least 2,500 years. In acupuncture, certain points on the body associated with energy channels or meridians are stimulated by the insertion of fine needles. Unlike the hollow hypodermic needles used in mainstream medicine to give injections or draw blood, acupuncture needles are solid. The points can be needled between 15 and 90 degrees in range relative to the skin's surface, depending on treatment.

Acupuncture is thought to restore health by removing energy imbalances and blockages in the body. Practitioners of TCM believe that there is a vital force or energy called *qi* (pronounced "chee") that flows through the body, and between the skin surface and the internal organs, along channels or pathways called meridians. There are 12 major and eight minor meridians. Qi regulates the spiritual, emotional, mental, and physical harmony of the body by keeping the forces of yin and yang in balance. Yang is a principle of heat, activity, brightness, outwardness, while yin represents coldness, passivity, darkness, interiority, etc. TCM does not try to eliminate either yin or yang, but to keep them in harmonious balance. Acupuncture may be used to raise or lower the level of yin or yang in a specific part of the body in order to restore the energy balance.

Acupuncture was virtually unknown in the United States prior to President Nixon's trip to China in 1972. A reporter for the *New York Times* named James Reston wrote a story for the newspaper about the doctors in Beijing who used acupuncture to relieve his pain following abdominal surgery. By 1993, Americans were making 12 million visits per year to acupuncturists, and spending $500 million annually on acupuncture treatments. By 1995, there were an estimated 10,000 certified acupuncturists practicing in the United States; as of 2000, there were 20,000. About a third of the credentialed acupuncturists in the United States are MDs.

Acupuncture's record of success has been sufficiently impressive to stimulate a number of research projects investigating its mechanisms as well as its efficacy. Research has been funded not only by the National Center for Complementary and Alternative Medicine (NCCAM), but also by the National Institute on Alcohol **Abuse** and Alcoholism (NIAAA), the National Institute of Dental Research, the National Institute of Neurological Disorders and **Stroke** (NINDS), and the

National Institute on Drug Abuse. In 1997 a consensus panel of the National Institutes of Health (NIH) presented a landmark report in which it described acupuncture as a sufficiently promising form of treatment to merit further study. In 2000, the British Medical Association (BMA) recommended that acupuncture should be made more readily available through the National Health Service (NHS), and that family doctors should be trained in some of its techniques.

Purpose

The purpose of acupuncture in TCM is the rebalancing of opposing energy forces in different parts of the body. In Western terms, acupuncture is used most commonly as an adjunctive treatment for the relief of chronic or acute pain. In the United States, acupuncture is most widely used to treat pain associated with musculoskeletal disorders, but it has also been used in the treatment of **substance abuse**, and to relieve nausea and vomiting. A study done in 2001 showed that acupuncture was highly effective in stopping the intense vomiting associated with a condition in pregnant women known as hyperemesis gravidarum. In the past several years, acupuncture has been tried with a new patient population, namely children with **chronic pain** syndromes. One study of 30 young patients with disorders ranging from migraine headaches to endometriosis found that 70% felt that their symptoms had been relieved by acupuncture, and described themselves as "pleased" by the results of treatment. In addition to these disorders, acupuncture has been used in the United States to treat asthma, infertility, **depression**, **anxiety**, HIV infection, fibromyalgia, menstrual cramps, carpal tunnel syndrome, tennis elbow, pitcher's shoulder, chronic **fatigue** syndrome, and postoperative pain. It has even been used in veterinary medicine to treat chronic pain and prevent epileptic convulsions in animals. As of 2002, NCCAM is sponsoring research regarding the effectiveness of acupuncture in the rehabilitation of stroke patients.

The exact Western medicine mechanism by which acupuncture works is not known. Western researchers have suggested three basic explanations of acupuncture's efficacy in pain relief:

- Western studies have found evidence that the traditional acupuncture points conduct electromagnetic signals. Stimulating the acupuncture points causes these signals to be relayed to the brain at a higher than normal rate. These signals in turn cause the brain to release pain-relieving chemicals known as endorphins, and immune system cells to weak or injured parts of the body.

- Other studies have shown that acupuncture activates the release of opioids into the central nervous system. Opioids are also analgesic, or pain-relieving compounds.
- Acupuncture appears to alter the chemical balance of the brain itself by modifying the production and release of neurotransmitters and neurohormones. Acupuncture has been documented to affect certain involuntary body functions, including immune reactions, blood pressure, and body temperature.

In addition to its efficacy in relieving pain and other chronic conditions, acupuncture has gained in popularity because of several additional advantages:

- It lacks the side effects associated with many medications and surgical treatments in Western medicine.
- It is highly cost-effective; it may be used early in the course of a disease, potentially saving the patient the cost of hospitalizations, laboratory tests, and high-priced drugs.
- It can easily be combined with other forms of therapy, including psychotherapy.
- It is noninvasive.
- It carries relatively few risks.

Precautions

Although the risk of infection in acupuncture is minimal, patients should make sure that the acupuncturist uses sterile disposable needles. In the United States, the Food and Drug Administration (FDA) mandates the use of sterilized needles made from nontoxic materials. The needles must be clearly labeled as having their use restricted to qualified practitioners.

Patients should also inquire about the practitioner's credentials. Since acupuncture is now taught in over forty accredited medical schools and osteopathic colleges in the United States, patients who would prefer to be treated by an MD or an osteopath can obtain a list of licensed physicians who practice acupuncture in their area from the American Academy of Medical Acupuncture. With regard to non-physician acupuncturists, 31 states have established training standards that acupuncturists must meet in order to be licensed in those states. In Great Britain, practitioners must qualify by passing a course offered by the British Acupuncture Accreditation Board.

Patients seeking acupuncture treatment should provide the practitioner with the same information about their health conditions and other forms of treatment that they would give their primary care doctor. This information should include other alternative and complementary therapies, especially herbal remedies.

Acupuncture should not be used to treat severe traumatic injuries and other emergency conditions requiring immediate surgery. In addition, it does not appear to be useful in **smoking cessation** programs.

As is true with other forms of medical treatment, a minority of patients do not respond to acupuncture. The reasons for nonresponsiveness are not known at the present stage of research.

Description

In traditional Chinese medicine, acupuncture treatment begins with a thorough physical examination in which the practitioner evaluates the patient's skin color, vocal tone, and tongue color and coating. The practitioner then takes the patient's pulse at six locations and three depth levels on each wrist. These 36 pulse measurements will tell the practitioner where the qi in the patient's body might be blocked or unbalanced. After collecting this information, the acupuncturist will then identify the patterns of energy disturbance and the acupuncture points that should be stimulated to unblock the qi or restore harmony. Up to 10 or 12 acupuncture needles will be inserted at strategic points along the relevant meridians. In traditional Chinese practice, the needles are twirled or rotated as they are inserted. Many patients feel nothing at all during this procedure, although others experience a prickling or mild aching sensation, and still others a feeling of warmth or heaviness.

The practitioner may combine acupuncture with moxibustion to increase the effectiveness of the treatment. Moxibustion is a technique in which the acupuncturist lights a small piece of wormwood, called a moxa, above the acupuncture point above the skin. When the patient begins to feel the warmth from the burning herb, it is removed. Cupping is another technique that is a method of stimulation of acupuncture points by applying suction through a metal, wood, or glass jar, and in which a partial vacuum has been created. Producing blood congestion at the site, the site is thus stimulated. The method is used for lower back pain, sprains, soft tissue injuries, as well as relieving fluid from the lungs in chronic bronchitis.

In addition to the traditional Chinese techniques of acupuncture, the following are also used in the United States:

- Electroacupuncture. In this form of acupuncture, the traditional acupuncture points are stimulated by an electronic device instead of a needle.
- Japanese meridian acupuncture. Japanese acupuncture uses thinner, smaller needles, and focuses on the meridians rather than on specific points along their course.

- Korean hand acupuncture. Traditional Korean medicine regards the hand as a "map" of the entire body, such that any part of the body can be treated by stimulating the corresponding point on the hand.
- Western medical acupuncture. Western physicians trained in this style of acupuncture insert needles into so-called trigger points in sore muscles, as well as into the traditional points used in Chinese medicine.
- Ear acupuncture. This technique regards the ear as having acupuncture points that correspond to other parts of the body. Ear acupuncture is often used to treat substance abuse and chronic pain syndromes.

A standard acupuncture treatment takes between 45 minutes to an hour and costs between $40 and $100, although initial appointments often cost more. Chronic conditions usually require 10 treatment sessions, but acute conditions or minor illnesses may require only one or two visits. Follow-up visits are often scheduled for patients with chronic pain. About 70–80% of health insurers in the United States reimbursed patients for acupuncture treatments.

Preparation

Apart from a medical history and physical examination, no specific preparation is required for an acupuncture treatment. In addition to using sterile needles, licensed acupuncturists will wipe the skin over each acupuncture point with an antiseptic solution before inserting the needle.

Aftercare

No particular aftercare is required, as the needles should not draw blood when properly inserted. Many patients experience a feeling of relaxation or even a pleasant drowsiness after the treatment. Some patients report feeling energized.

Risks

Several American and British reports have concluded that the risks to the patient from an acupuncture treatment are minimal. Most complications from acupuncture fall into one of three categories: infections, most often from improperly sterilized needles; bruising or minor soft tissue injury; and injuries to muscle tissue. Serious side effects with sterilized needles are rare, although cases of pneumothorax and cardiac tamponade have been reported in the European literature. One American pediatrician estimates that the risk of serious injury from acupuncture performed by a licensed practitioner ranges between 1:10,000 and 1:100,000—or about the same degree of risk as a negative reaction to penicillin.

KEY TERMS

Cardiac tamponade—A condition in which blood leaking into the membrane surrounding the heart puts pressure on the heart muscle, preventing complete filling of the heart's chambers and normal heartbeat.

Electroacupuncture—A variation of acupuncture in which the practitioner stimulates the traditional acupuncture points electronically.

Endorphins—A group of peptide compounds released by the body in response to stress or traumatic injury. Endorphins react with opiate receptors in the brain to reduce or relieve pain.

Hyperemesis gravidarum—Uncontrollable nausea and vomiting associated with pregnancy. Acupuncture appears to be an effective treatment for women with this condition.

Meridians—In traditional Chinese medicine, a network of pathways or channels that convey qi (also sometimes spelled "ki"), or vital energy, through the body.

Moxibustion—A technique in traditional Chinese medicine that involves burning a *Moxa*, or cone of dried wormwood leaves, close to the skin to relieve pain. When used with acupuncture, the cone is placed on top of the needle at an acupuncture point and burned

Neurotransmitter—A chemical in the brain that transmits messages between neurons, or nerve cells.

Opioids—Substances that reduce pain and may induce sleep. Some opioids are endogenous, which means that they are produced within the human body. Other opioids are produced by plants or formulated synthetically in the laboratory.

Pneumothorax—A condition in which air or gas is present in the chest cavity.

Qi—The Chinese term for energy, life force, or vital force.

Yin and yang—In traditional Chinese medicine and philosophy, a pair of opposing forces whose harmonious balance in the body is necessary to good health.

Normal results

Normal results from acupuncture are relief of pain and/or improvement of the condition being treated.

Abnormal results

Abnormal results from acupuncture include infection, a severe side effect, or worsening of the condition being treated.

Resources

BOOKS

Pelletier, Kenneth R., MD. "Acupuncture: From the Yellow Emperor to Magnetic Resonance Imaging (MRI)." Chapter 5 in *The Best Alternative Medicine*. New York: Simon and Schuster, 2002.

Reid, Daniel P. *Chinese Herbal Medicine*. Boston, MA: Shambhala, 1993.

Svoboda, Robert, and Arnie Lade. *Tao and Dharma: Chinese Medicine and Ayurveda*. Twin Lakes, WI: Lotus Press, 1995.

PERIODICALS

Cerrato, Paul L. "New Studies on Acupuncture and Emesis (Acupuncture for Relief of Nausea and Vomiting Caused by Chemotherapy)." *Contemporary OB/GYN* 46 (April 2001): 749.

Kemper, Kathi J., and others. "On Pins and Needles? Pediatric Pain: Patients' Experience with Acupuncture." *Pediatrics* 105 (April 2000): 620–633.

Kirchgatterer, Andreas. "Cardiac Tamponade Following Acupuncture." *Chest* 117 (May 2000): 1510–1511.

Nwabudike, Lawrence C., and Constantin Ionescu-Tirgoviste. "Acupuncture in the Treatment of Diabetic Peripheral Neuropathy." *Diabetes* 49 (May 2000): 628.

Silvert, Mark. "Acupuncture Wins BMA Approval (British Medical Association)." *British Medical Journal* 321 (July 1, 2000): 637–639.

Vickers, Andrew. "Acupuncture (ABC of Complementary Medicine)." *British Medical Journal* 319 (October 9, 1999): 704-708.

ORGANIZATIONS

American Academy of Medical Acupuncture/Medical Acupuncture Research Organization. 5820 Wilshire Boulevard, Suite 500, Los Angeles, CA 90036. Telephone: (800) 521-2262 or (323) 937-5514. Fax: (323) 937-0959. <www.medicalacupuncture.org>.

American Association of Oriental Medicine. 433 Front Street, Catasauqua, PA 18032. Telephone: (610) 266-1433. Fax: (610) 264-2768. <www.aaom.org>.

National Center for Complementary and Alternative Medicine (NCCAM) Clearinghouse. P.O. Box 7923, Gaithersburg, MD 20898. Telephone: (888) 644-6226. TTY: (866) 464-3615. Fax: (866) 464-3616. <www.nccam.nih.gov>.

OTHER

National Center for Complementary and Alternative Medicine (NCCAM). Fact Sheets. *Acupuncture Information and Resources.* <www.nccam.nih.gov/fcp/factsheets/acupuncture>.

Rebecca J. Frey, Ph.D.

Acute stress disorder

Definition

Acute **stress** disorder (ASD) is an **anxiety** disorder characterized by a cluster of dissociative and anxiety symptoms that occur within a month of a traumatic stressor. It is a relatively new diagnostic category and was added to the fourth edition of the ***Diagnostic and Statistical Manual of Mental Disorders (DSM-IV)*** in 1994 to distinguish time-limited reactions to trauma from the farther-reaching and longer-lasting **post-traumatic stress disorder** (PTSD). Published by the American Psychiatric Association, the *DSM* contains diagnostic criteria, research findings, and treatment information for mental disorders. It is the primary reference for mental health professionals in the United States.

Description

ASD, like PTSD, begins with exposure to an extremely traumatic, horrifying, or terrifying event. Unlike PTSD, however, ASD emerges sooner and abates more quickly; it is also marked by more dissociative symptoms. If left untreated, however, ASD is likely to progress to PTSD. Because the two share many symptoms, some researchers and clinicians question the validity of maintaining separate diagnostic categories. Others explain them as two phases of an extended reaction to traumatic stress.

Causes and symptoms

Causes

The immediate cause of ASD is exposure to trauma—an extreme stressor involving a threat to life or the prospect of serious injury; witnessing an event that involves the death or serious injury of another person; or learning of the violent death or serious injury of a family member or close friend. The trauma's impact is determined by its cause, scope, and extent. Natural disasters (floods, earthquakes, hurricanes, etc.) or accidents (plane crashes, workplace explosions) are less traumatic than human

acts of intentional cruelty or terrorism. Terrorist-inflicted trauma appears to produce particularly high rates of ASD and PTSD in survivors and bystanders.

Although most people define trauma in terms of events such as war, terrorist attacks, and other events that result in vast loss of life, the leading cause of stress-related mental disorders in the United States is motor vehicle accidents. Most Americans will be involved in a traffic accident at some point in their lives, and 25% of the population will be involved in accidents resulting in serious injuries. The National Comorbidity Survey of 1995 found that 9% of survivors of serious motor vehicle accidents developed ASD or PTSD.

Several factors influence a person's risk of developing ASD after trauma:

- Age—Older adults are less likely to develop ASD, possibly because they have had more experience coping with painful or stressful events.
- Previous exposure—People who were abused or experienced trauma as children are more likely to develop ASD (or PTSD) as adults, because these may produce long-lasting biochemical changes in the central nervous system.
- Biological vulnerability—Twin studies indicate that certain abnormalities in brain hormone levels and brain structure are inherited, and that these increase a person's susceptibility to ASD following exposure to trauma.
- Support networks—People who have a network of close friends and relatives are less likely to develop ASD.
- Perception and interpretation—People who feel inappropriate responsibility for the trauma, regard the event as punishment for personal wrongdoing, or have generally negative or pessimistic worldviews are more likely to develop ASD than those who do not personalize the trauma or are able to maintain a balanced view of life.

Symptoms

Acute stress disorder may be diagnosed in patients who lived through or witnessed a traumatic event to which they responded with intense fear, horror, or helplessness, and are currently experiencing three or more of the following dissociative symptoms:

- psychic numbing
- being dazed or less aware of surroundings
- derealization
- depersonalization
- dissociative amnesia

Other symptoms that indicate ASD are:

- Reexperiencing the trauma in recurrent dreams, images, thoughts, illusions, or flashbacks; or intense distress when exposed to reminders of the trauma.

- A marked tendency to avoid people, places, objects, conversations, and other stimuli reminiscent of the trauma (many people who develop ASD after a traffic accident, for example, refuse to drive a car for a period of time).

- Hyperarousal or anxiety, including sleep problems, irritability, inability to concentrate, an unusually intense startle response, hypervigilance, and physical restlessness (pacing the floor, fidgeting, etc.).

- Significantly impaired social functions and/or the inability to do necessary tasks, including seeking help.

- Symptoms last for a minimum of two days and a maximum of four weeks, and occur within four weeks of the traumatic event.

- The symptoms are not caused by a substance (medication or drug of abuse) or by a general medical condition; do not meet the criteria of a brief psychotic disorder; and do not represent the worsening of a mental disorder that the person had before the traumatic event.

People with ASD may also show symptoms of **depression** including difficulty enjoying activities that they previously found pleasurable; difficulty in concentrating; and survivor's guilt at having survived an accident or escaping serious injury when others did not. The *DSM-IV-TR* (revised edition published in 2000) notes that people diagnosed with ASD "often perceive themselves to have greater responsibility for the consequences of the trauma than is warranted," and may feel that they will not live out their normal lifespans. Many symptoms of ASD are also found in patients with PTSD.

Demographics

Acute responses to traumatic stressors are far more widespread in the general United States population than was first thought in 1980, when PTSD was introduced as a diagnostic category in the *DSM-III*. The National Comorbidity Survey, a major epidemiological study conducted between 1990 and 1992, estimated that the lifetime prevalence among adult Americans is 7.8%, with women (10.4%) twice as likely as men (5%) to be diagnosed with trauma-related stress disorders at some point in their lives. These figures represent only a small proportion of adults who have experienced at least one traumatic event—60.7% of men and 51.2% of women respectively. More than 10% of the men and 6% of the women reported experiencing four or more types of trauma in their lives.

The prevalence of ASD by itself in the general United States population is not known. A few studies of people exposed to traumatic events found rates of ASD between 14% and 33%. Some groups are at greater risk of developing ASD or PTSD, including people living in depressed urban areas or on Native American reservations (23%) and victims of violent crimes (58%).

Diagnosis

ASD symptoms develop within a month after the traumatic event; it is still unknown, however, why some trauma survivors develop symptoms more rapidly than others. Delayed symptoms are often triggered by a situation that resembles the original trauma.

ASD is usually diagnosed by matching the patient's symptoms to the *DSM-IV-TR* criteria. The patient may also meet the criteria for a major depressive episode or **major depressive disorder**. A person who has been exposed to a traumatic stressor and has developed symptoms that do not meet the criteria for ASD may be diagnosed as having an adjustment disorder.

There are no diagnostic interviews or questionnaires in widespread use for diagnosing ASD, although screening instruments specific to the disorder are being developed. A group of Australian clinicians has developed a 19-item Acute Stress Disorder Scale, which appears to be effective in diagnosing ASD but frequently makes false-positive predictions of PTSD. The authors of the scale recommend that its use should be followed by a careful clinical evaluation.

Treatments

Therapy for ASD requires the use of several treatment modalities because the disorder affects systems of belief and meaning, interpersonal relationships, and occupational functioning as well as physical well-being.

Medications

Medications are usually limited to those necessary for treating individual symptoms. **Clonidine** is given for hyperarousal; **propranolol, clonazepam**, or **alprazolam** for anxiety and panic reactions; **fluoxetine** for avoidance symptoms; and **trazodone** or topiramate for **insomnia** and nightmares. **Antidepressants** may be prescribed if ASD progresses to PTSD. These medications may include **selective serotonin reuptake inhibitors (SSRIs)**, monoamine oxidase inhibitors (MAOIs), or tricyclic antidepressants.

Psychotherapy

Cognitive behavioral therapy, exposure therapy, therapeutic writing (journaling), and supportive therapy have been found effective in treating ASD. One variant of cognitive behavioral therapy called psychoeducational therapy appears to be three to four times as effective as supportive therapy in preventing ASD from progressing to PTSD. This treatment combines cognitive restructuring of the traumatic event with exposure to disturbing images and techniques for anxiety management. In addition, it can help patients identify and reinforce positive aspects of their experience. For example, some people find new strengths or talents within themselves in times of crisis, or discover new spiritual resources.

Group and family therapies also appear to help patients with ASD reinforce effective strategies for coping with the trauma, and may reduce the risk of social isolation as a reaction to the trauma. They give patients opportunities to describe what happened and how they responded; they also let patients receive warmth and caring from their listeners, and help put memories of the event into a coherent narrative, allowing them to integrate the trauma into their overall lives.

Critical incident stress management (CISM) is a comprehensive crisis-intervention system in which a team of specially trained practitioners comes to the site of a traumatic event and provides several different forms of assistance, including one-on-one crisis support; crisis management briefing, which is a 45–75-minute intervention for groups of people affected by the traumatic event; and critical incident stress debriefing, which is a structured group discussion of the event. CISM appears to be particularly helpful in preventing burnout and ASD in emergency service personnel, rescue personnel, police, and other caregivers who are involved in treating survivors of a traumatic event.

Alternative and complementary treatments

Many mainstream practitioners recommend holistic or naturopathic approaches to recovery from ASD, including good nutrition with appropriate dietary supplements and regular exercise. **Yoga** and some forms of body work or massage therapy are helpful in treating the muscular soreness and stiffness that is often a side effect of the anxiety and insomnia related to ASD. Hydrotherapy is often helpful for post-traumatic muscular aches and cramps. A skilled naturopath may also recommend peppermint or other herbal preparations to calm the patient's digestive tract. In addition, prayer, **meditation**, or counseling with a spiritual advisor have been found to be helpful in treating patients with ASD whose belief systems have been affected by the traumatic event.

Diagnosis and treatment of ASD in children

Very little is known about the prevalence of ASD or PTSD in children, and even less is known how effectively medications and **psychotherapy** treat these disorders in this age group. There are as yet no standardized screens or diagnostic interviews in widespread use for assessing either ASD or PTSD in children, although a Child Post-traumatic Stress Reaction Index was published in 1992. One preliminary study recommends the cautious use of low doses of **imipramine** for treating children with ASD, but notes that research in this area has barely begun.

Prognosis

Untreated ASD is highly likely to progress to PTSD in children as well as in adults. One team of Australian researchers found that 80% of persons diagnosed with ASD met criteria for PTSD six months later; 75% met criteria for PTSD two years after the traumatic event.

Clinicians in Norway have compiled a list of four "early response" variables that appear to be effective predictors of ASD's progressing to PTSD:

- the degree of the patient's sleep disturbance
- a strong startle reaction
- the degree of the patient's social withdrawal
- fear or phobia related to the site of the traumatic event

In addition to developing PTSD, people diagnosed with ASD are at increased risk of developing a major depressive disorder, particularly if their emotional responses to the trauma were marked by intense despair and hopelessness. Other sequelae may include neglect of personal needs for health or safety; and impulsive or needlessly risky behavior.

Prevention

Some forms of trauma, such as natural disasters and accidents, can never be completely eliminated from human life. Traumas caused by human intention would require major social changes to reduce their frequency and severity, but given the increasing prevalence of trauma-related stress disorders around the world, these long-term changes are worth the effort. In the short run, educating people—particularly those in the helping professions—about the signs of critical incident stress may prevent some cases of exposure to

KEY TERMS

Adjustment disorder—A disorder defined by the development of significant emotional or behavioral symptoms in response to a stressful event or series of events. Symptoms may include depressed mood, anxiety, and impairment of social and occupational functioning.

Depersonalization—A dissociative symptom in which the patient feels that his or her body is unreal, changing, or dissolving.

Derealization—A dissociative symptom in which the external environment is perceived as unreal or dreamlike.

Dissociation—A reaction to trauma in which the mind splits off certain aspects of the traumatic event from conscious awareness. Dissociation can affect the patient's memory, sense of reality, and sense of identity.

Dissociative amnesia—A dissociative disorder characterized by loss of memory for a period or periods of time in the patient's life. May occur as a result of a traumatic event.

Exposure therapy—A form of cognitive-behavioral therapy in which patients suffering from phobias are exposed to their feared objects or situations while accompanied by the therapist. The length of exposure is gradually increased until the association between the feared situation and the patient's experienced panic symptoms is no longer present.

Flashback—The re-emergence of a traumatic memory as a vivid recollection of sounds, images, and sensations associated with the trauma. The person having the flashback typically feels as if he or she is reliving the event.

Hyperarousal—A symptom of traumatic stress characterized by abnormally intense reactions to stimuli. A heightened startle response is one sign of hyperarousal.

Hypervigilance—A state of abnormally intense wariness or watchfulness that is found in survivors of trauma or long-term abuse. Hypervigilance is sometimes described as "being on red alert all the time."

Personalization—The tendency to refer large-scale events or general patterns of events to the self in inappropriate ways. For example, a person who regards the loss of a friend or relative in an accident as punishment for having quarreled with them before the accident is said to be personalizing the event. Personalization increases a person's risk of developing ASD or PTSD after a traumatic event.

Psychic numbing—An inability to respond emotionally with normal intensity to people or situations; this affects positive emotions as well as fear or anger.

Sequela (plural, sequelae)—An abnormal condition resulting from a previous disease or disorder. An episode of depression is a common sequela of acute stress disorder.

Supportive—An approach to psychotherapy that seeks to encourage the patient or offer emotional support to him or her, as distinct from insight-oriented or educational approaches to treatment.

Survivor's guilt—A psychological reaction in trauma survivors that takes the form of guilt feelings for having survived or escaped a trauma without serious injury when others did not.

Therapeutic writing—A treatment technique in which patients are asked to set down in writing an account of the traumatic event and their emotional responses to it.

---

trauma from developing into ASD and progressing to full-blown PTSD.

Resources

BOOKS

"Acute Stress Disorder." Section 15, Chapter 187. In *The Merck Manual of Diagnosis and Therapy*, edited by Mark H. Beers, MD, and Robert Berkow, MD. Whitehouse Station, NJ: Merck Research Laboratories, 2001.

American Psychiatric Association. *Diagnostic and Statistical Manual of Mental Disorders*. 4th edition, text revised. Washington, DC: American Psychiatric Association, 2000.

Herman, Judith, MD. *Trauma and Recovery*. 2nd ed., revised. New York: Basic Books, 1997.

Pelletier, Kenneth R., MD. *The Best Alternative Medicine*. New York: Simon & Schuster, 2002.

PERIODICALS

Bowles, Stephen V. "Acute and Post-Traumatic Stress Disorder After Spontaneous Abortion." *American Family Physician* 61 (March 2000): 1689-1696.

Bryant, R. A. "The Acute Stress Disorder Scale: A Tool for Predicting Post-Traumatic Stress Disorder."

Australian Journal of Emergency Management (Winter 1999): 13-15.

Butler, Dennis J. "Post-Traumatic Stress Reactions Following Motor Vehicle Accidents." *American Family Physician* 60 (August 1999): 524-531.

Harbert, Kenneth. "Acute Traumatic Stress: Helping Patients Regain Control." *Clinician Reviews* 12 (January 2002): 42-56.

Marshall, R. D., R. Spitzer, and M. R. Liebowitz. "Review and Critique of the New DSM-IV Diagnosis of Acute Stress Disorder." *American Journal of Psychiatry* 156 (1999): 1677-1685.

Robert, Rhonda. "Imipramine Treatment in Pediatric Burn Patients with Symptoms of Acute Stress Disorder: A Pilot Study." *Journal of the American Academy of Child and Adolescent Psychiatry* 38 (July 1999): 1129-1136.

van der Kolk, Bessel. "The Body Keeps the Score: Memory and the Evolving Psychobiology of PTSD." *Harvard Review of Psychiatry* 1 (1994): 253-265.

ORGANIZATIONS

American Academy of Experts in Traumatic Stress. 368 Veterans Memorial Highway, Commack, NY 11725. Telephone: (631) 543-2217. Fax: (631) 543-6977. <www.aaets.org>.

Anxiety Disorders Association of America. 11900 Parklawn Dr., Ste. 100, Rockville, MD 20852. Telephone: (301) 231-9350.

International Society for Traumatic Stress Studies. 60 Revere Drive, Suite 500, Northbrook, IL 60062. Telephone: (847) 480-9028. Fax: (847) 480-9282. <www.istss.org>.

National Institute of Mental Health. 6001 Executive Boulevard, Room 8184, MSC 9663, Bethesda, MD 20892-9663. Telephone: (301) 443-4513. <www.nimh.nih.gov>.

Society for Traumatic Stress Studies. 60 Revere Dr., Ste. 500, Northbrook, IL 60062. Telephone: (708) 480-9080.

Rebecca J. Frey, Ph.D.

Adapin *see* **Doxepin**

Addiction

Definition

Most definitions refer to addiction as the compulsive need to use a habit-forming substance, or an irresistible urge to engage in a behavior. Two other important defining features of addiction are tolerance, the increasing need for more of the substance to obtain the same effect, and withdrawal, the unpleasant symptoms that arise when an addict is prevented from using the chosen substance or engaging in the behavior. **Relapse** and mood modification are also features.

Description

The term addiction has come to refer to a wide and complex range of behaviors. While addiction most commonly refers to compulsive use of substances, including alcohol, prescription and illegal drugs, cigarettes, and food, it is also associated with compulsive behaviors involving activities such as work, exercise, shopping, sex, using the Internet, and gambling.

Causes and symptoms

Causes

The most prevalent model of addiction today is the so-called disease model. This model, first introduced in the late 1940s by E. M. Jellinek, was adopted in 1956 by the American Medical Association. Since that time, the disease model of alcoholism and drug addiction has been well accepted throughout the world. Some experts argue that addiction is better understood as learned behavior and is modifiable through "unlearning" the negative behaviors and then learning new, positive behaviors.

Disease model adherents believe that the **compulsion** to use is genetically and physiologically based and that, while the disease can be arrested, it is progressive and chronic, and fatal if unchecked. Twin studies have shown that there is a strong heritable component to addiction, although, as with most diseases, environmental factors can also play a role.

Symptoms

The initial positive consequences of substance use or a potentially addictive behavior are what initially "hook" a person, who may then become addicted. People with substance use disorders or behavioral addiction describe feelings of euphoria or release of tension when using the substance or engaging in the activity of choice. Many experts believe that these substances and activities affect **neurotransmitters** in the **brain**. The primary pathway involved in the development and persistence of these disorders of addiction is the brain reward pathway, or mesolimbic pathway, which operates via a neurotransmitter called **dopamine**. The dopamine pathways may interact with other neurotransmitters, including opioid pathways. These neuronal pathways have been identified as underlying both substance use disorders and behavioral addictions.

As a person with an addiction continues to use a substance or engage in a behavior, his or her body adjusts to the substance and tolerance develops. Increasing amounts of the substance are needed to produce the same effect. In some case, levels of substances that a person with a substance use disorder routinely ingests might be lethal to someone who has not built up a tolerance.

Over time, physical symptoms of dependence strengthen. Failure to use a substance or engage in a behavior can lead to withdrawal symptoms, which can vary depending on the substance or behavior involved. For some drugs, these symptoms can include flu-like aches and pains, digestive upset, and, in severe cases, **seizures**, and hallucinatory sensations, such as the feeling of bugs crawling on the skin. Organ damage, including the brain and liver, can lead to serious and even fatal illness as well as mental symptoms such as **dementia**. Severe disruption of social and family relationships, and of the ability to maintain a steady job, are also symptoms of the addictive process.

Demographics

According to a 2006 national survey of adolescents, 14.9% of the high-school students surveyed reported having used an illicit drug in the previous month. A 2003 report showed that adolescents and young adults were most likely to have engaged in illicit drug use in the previous month, with the peak occurring 18- to 20-year-old age range; however, drug use among adolescents declined by 17% from 2001 to 2004. In spite of the decline, 19.5 million Americans, about 8.2% of the population, were current users of an illicit drug in 2003. Drugs used included marijuana/hashish, **cocaine** (including crack), heroin, hallucinogens, inhalants, or prescription-type psychotherapeutics used nonmedically, and the opiates Vicodin and OxyContin have emerged as drugs of concern for their use among high-school students. The most commonly used illicit drug in the United States is marijuana.

Addiction is more common among men than women, and the ratio of men to women using drugs other than alcohol is even higher. **Substance abuse** is higher among the unemployed and the less educated. Most illicit drug users are white.

Diagnosis

Substance **abuse** and dependence are among the psychological disorders categorized as major clinical syndromes (known as "Axis 1") in the American Psychiatric Association's **Diagnostic and Statistical Manual of Mental Disorders** (*DSM-IV-TR*). Alcohol, classified as a depressant, is the most frequently abused psychoactive substance. Alcohol abuse and dependence affect more than 20 million Americans— about 13% of the adult population. An alcoholic has

been defined as a person whose drinking impairs his or her life adjustment, affecting health, personal relationships, and/or work.

When blood alcohol level reaches 0.08%, a person is considered legally intoxicated in most states. Judgment and other rational processes are impaired, as are motor coordination, speech, and vision. Alcohol abuse, according to the *DSM-IV-TR*, progresses through a series of stages from social drinking to chronic alcoholism. Danger signs that indicate the probable onset of a drinking problem include frequent desire to drink, increasing alcohol consumption, memory lapses (blackouts), and morning drinking. Other symptoms include attempts to hide alcohol from family and colleagues, and attempts to drink in secret. Among the most acute reactions to alcohol are four conditions referred to as alcoholic psychoses: alcohol idiosyncratic intoxication (an acute reaction in persons with an abnormally low tolerance for alcohol); alcohol withdrawal **delirium** (delirium tremens); **hallucinations**; and Korsakoff's **psychosis**, an irreversible brain disorder involving severe memory loss.

Other substance abuse disorders are diagnosed by looking for patterns of compulsive use, frequency of use, increasing tolerance, and withdrawal symptoms when the substance is unavailable or the individual tries to stop using.

Treatments

Pharmacologic

Addictions are notoriously difficult to treat. Physical addictions alter a person's brain chemistry in ways that make it difficult to be exposed to the addictive substance again without relapsing. Some medications, such as Antabuse (**disulfiram**), have shown limited effectiveness in treating alcohol addiction. Substitute medications, such as **methadone**, a drug that blocks the euphoric effect of opiates, have also shown mixed results. When an addicted individual is using a substance to self-medicate for **depression**, **anxiety**, and other psychological symptoms, prescription medications can be an effective treatment.

Psychological and psychosocial

It is a commonly held belief by many professionals that people with addictive disorders cannot be treated effectively by conventional outpatient **psychotherapy**. Substance abusers are often presumed to have severe personality problems and to be very resistant to treatment, to lack the motivation to change, or to be just too much trouble in an outpatient office setting. Unfortunately, these beliefs may create a self-fulfilling prophecy. Many of the negative behaviors and personality problems associated with chronic substance use disappear when use of the substance stops. While some substance abusers do, in fact, have other mental disorders, they represent only a minority of the addicted population.

Most treatment for addictive behaviors is provided not by practicing clinicians (psychiatrists, psychologists, and **social workers**), but rather by specialized addiction treatment programs and clinics. These programs rely upon confrontational tactics and re-education as their primary approaches, often employing former or recovering addicts to treat newly admitted addicts.

Some addicts are helped by the combination of individual, group, and family treatment. In family treatment (or **family therapy**), "enabling behaviors" can be addressed and changed. Enabling behaviors are the actions of family members who assist the addict in maintaining active addiction, including providing money, food, and shelter. Residential settings may be effective in initially assisting the addicted individual to stay away from the many "cues," including people, places, and things, that formed the setting for their substance use.

During the past several decades, alternatives to the complete abstinence model (the generally accepted model in the United States) have arisen. Controlled use programs allow addicted individuals to reduce their use without committing to complete abstinence. This alternative is highly controversial. The generally accepted position is that only by complete abstinence can an addicted individual recover. The effectiveness of addiction treatment based on behavioral and other psychotherapeutic methods, however, is well documented. Among these are motivation-enhancing strategies, relapse-prevention strategies using cognitive-behavioral approaches, solution-oriented and other brief therapy techniques, and harm-reduction approaches.

Self-help groups such as Alcoholics Anonymous and Narcotics Anonymous have also developed widespread popularity. The approach of one addict helping another to stay "clean," without professional **intervention**, has had tremendous acceptance in the United States and other countries.

Prognosis

Relapse and recidivism are, unfortunately, very common. Interestingly, a classic study shows that people addicted to different substances show very similar patterns of relapse. Whatever the addictive substances, data show that about two-thirds of all relapses occur within the first 90 days following treatment.

Many consider recovery to be an ongoing, lifelong process. Because the use of addictive substances alters brain chemistry, cravings can persist for many years. For this reason, the prevailing belief is that recovery is only possible by commitment to complete abstinence from all substance use.

Prevention

Prevention approaches are most effectively targeted at young teenagers between the ages of 11 and 13. It is during these years that most young people are likely to experiment with drugs and alcohol. Hence, reducing experimentation during this critical period holds promise for reducing the number of adults with addictive disease. Effective prevention programs focus on addressing the concerns of young people with regard to the effects of drugs. Training older adolescents to help younger adolescents resist peer pressure has shown considerable effectiveness in preventing experimentation.

See also Alcohol and related disorders; Amphetamines and related disorders; Antianxiety drugs and abuse-related disorders; Barbiturates; Caffeine and related disorders; Cannabis and related disorders; Denial; Disease concept of chemical dependency; Dual diagnosis; Hypnotics and related disorders; Internet addiction disorder; Nicotine and related disorders; Opioids and related disorders; Relapse and relapse prevention; Sedatives and related drugs; Self-help groups; Substance abuse and related disorders; Support groups; Wernicke-Korsakoff syndrome.

Resources

BOOKS

American Psychiatric Association. *Diagnostic and Statistical Manual of Mental Disorders.* 4th ed., text rev. Washington, D.C.: American Psychiatric Association, 2000.

Hurley, Jennifer A., ed. *Addiction: Opposing Viewpoints.* San Diego, CA: Greenhaven Press, 2000.

Kaplan, Harold I., MD., and Benjamin J. Sadock, MD. *Synopsis of Psychiatry:Behavioral Sciences/Clinical Psychiatry.* 8th ed. Baltimore, MD: Lippincott Williams and Wilkins, 1998.

Marlatt, G. Alan, and Judith R. Gordon, eds. *Relapse Prevention.* New York: The Guilford Press, 1985.

Wekesser, Carol, ed. *Chemical Dependency: Opposing Viewpoints.* San Diego, CA: Greenhaven Press, 1997.

PERIODICALS

Grant, Jon E., JD, MD, MPH, Judson A. Brewer, MD, Ph.D., and Marc N. Potenza, MD, Ph.D. "The Neurobiology of substance and behavioral addictions." *CNS Spectrums* 11 (2006): 924–30.

Franken, Ingmar H. A., Jan Booij, and Wim van den Brink. "The role of dopamine in human addiction: From reward to motivated attention." *European Journal of Pharmacology* 526 (2005): 199–206.

Kienast, T., and A. Heinz. "Dopamine and the diseased brain." *CNS & Neurological Disorders-Drug Targets* 5 (2006): 109–31.

Lobo, Daniela S.S., M.D., Ph.D., and James L. Kennedy, MD, F.R.C.P.C. "The genetics of gambling and behavioral addictions." *CNS Spectrums* 11 (2006): 931–9.

Pallanti, Stefano, M.D., Ph.D. "From impulse-control disorders toward behavioral addictions." *CNS Spectrums* 11 (2006): 921—2.

Washton, Arnold M. "Why psychologists should know how to treat substance use disorders." *NYS Psychologist* January 2002: 9–13.

ORGANIZATIONS

National Institute on Drug Abuse (NIDA). U.S. Department of Health and Human Services, 5600 Fishers Ln., Rockville, MD 20857. <http://www.nida.nih.gov>.

National Library of Medicine. "Drug Abuse." <http://www.nlm.nih.gov/medlineplus/drugabuse.html>.

Barbara S. Sternberg, Ph.D.
Emily Jane Willingham, Ph.D.

Adjustment disorders

Definition

Adjustment disorders are a group of disorders in which a person's psychological response to a stressor elicits symptoms that warrant clinical attention. This uniting feature of the adjustment disorders can manifest as emotional distress that exceeds what is an expected norm or by notable impairment of the person's functioning in the world, socially, academically, and/or occupationally.

Description

Often, a person experiences a stressful event as one that changes his or her world in some fundamental way. An adjustment disorder represents significant difficulty in adjusting to the new reality. Subsets of this disorder make up the most frequent psychiatric diagnoses among mentally ill populations, with features that include **depression** and **anxiety**. Many clinicians believe that it is difficult to discern a difference between a reaction to **stress** that falls within a population norm and when the line has been crossed into symptoms warranting a **diagnosis** of adjustment disorder. This difficulty, according to some experts, lies in the presentation of disorders in the *Diagnostic and Statistical Manual of Mental Disorders-IV, Text Revision* (also known as the DSM-IV-TR) as a dichotomy between what happens in the mind and what occurs physically in the body. Research results increasingly support that the dichotomy may not be tenable.

The DSM-IV-TR lists six subtypes of adjustment disorder, generally based on what feature best characterizes the person's symptoms. These six subtypes are adjustment disorder with depressed mood, with anxiety, with mixed anxiety and depressed mood, with disturbance of conduct, with disturbance of emotions and conduct, or adjustment disorder unspecified. This last subtype is applied when one of the other five simply does not fit the manifestations.

The criteria for these disorders also include time parameters. One of the criteria for diagnosing an adjustment disorder is that it is an acute response, lasting six or fewer months. However, in some special cases, the response can be chronic, lasting longer than six months, usually when the stressor has lasting consequences.

The stressful events that precipitate an adjustment disorder vary widely. They may include the loss of a job; the end of a romantic relationship; a life transition such as a career change or retirement; or a serious accident or sickness. Some are acute "one-time" stressors, such as relocating to a new area, while others are chronic, such as caring for a child with **mental retardation**.

In spite of the disagreement among professionals about the validity of the diagnosis of adjustment disorder, many researchers consider the category useful for two reasons: (1) an adjustment disorder may be an early sign of a major mental disorder and allow for early treatment and **intervention**; and (2) adjustment disorders are "situational" or "reactive" and do not imply that the patient has an underlying **brain** disease.

Causes and symptoms

Causes

In the initial edition of the DSM-IV, the identifiable stressor was described as being "psychosocial," a category that excludes physical illnesses and natural disasters. In the *DSM-IV-TR*, the word "psychosocial" was deleted to make the point that any stressful event can lead to an adjustment disorder. It is important to recognize, however, that while adjustment disorders are triggered by external stressors, the symptoms result from the person's interpretation of and adaptation to the stressful event or circumstances.

Beliefs, perceptions, fears, and expectations influence the development of an adjustment disorder.

People with chronic physical illnesses appear to have an increased risk of developing adjustment disorders, particularly one with depressed mood. This connection has been demonstrated among cancer patients. The relationship between **chronic pain** (as is commonly experienced by cancer patients) and depressive symptoms is still being studied.

Symptoms

Unlike many other disorders categorized in the DMS-IV-TR, adjustment disorders do not have an accompanying clearly delineated symptom profile, which has led to its being perceived as a "transitional" diagnosis, awaiting the manifestation of symptoms more clearly related to some other, better-defined disorder. This ambiguity arises from the difficulty in establishing what defines a reaction within the norms of a population. The *DSM-IV-TR* states that the symptoms of an adjustment disorder must appear within three months of a stressor; and that they must meet at least one of the following criteria: (1) the distress is greater than what would be expected in response to that particular stressor; or (2) the patient experiences significant impairment in social relationships or in occupational or academic settings. Moreover, the symptoms cannot represent bereavement, as normally experienced after the death of a loved one and cannot be an exacerbation of another, preexisting disorder and does not meet the criteria for another disorder.

Each of the six subtypes of adjustment disorder is characterized by its own predominant symptoms:

- With depressed mood: The chief manifestations are feelings of sadness and depression, with a sense of accompanying hopelessness. The patient may be tearful and have uncontrollable bouts of crying.
- With anxiety: The patient is troubled by feelings of apprehension, nervousness, and worry. He or she may also feel jittery and unable to control his or her thoughts of doom. Children with this subtype may express fears of separation from parents or other significant people, and refuse to go to sleep alone or attend school.
- With mixed anxiety and depressed mood: The patient has a combination of symptoms from the previous two subtypes.
- With disturbance of conduct: This subtype involves such noticeable behavioral changes as shoplifting, truancy, reckless driving, aggressive outbursts, or sexual promiscuity. The patient disregards the rights of others or previously followed rules of conduct with little concern, guilt or remorse.
- With mixed disturbance of emotions and conduct: The patient exhibits sudden changes in behavior combined with feelings of depression or anxiety. He or she may feel or express guilt about the behavior, but then repeat it shortly thereafter.
- Unspecified: This subtype covers patients who are adjusting poorly to stress but who do not fit into the other categories. These patients may complain of physical illness and pull away from social contact.

Adjustment disorders may lead to **suicide** or suicidal thinking. They may also complicate the treatment of other diseases when, for instance, a sufferer loses interest in taking medication as prescribed or adhering to **diets** or exercise regimens.

An adjustment disorder can occur at any stage of life.

Demographics

Even though this disorder is so commonly diagnosed, there have been few large-scale epidemiological studies targeting adjustment disorders. Adjustment disorder appears to be fairly common in the American population; recent figures estimate that 5–20% of adults seeking outpatient psychological treatment have one of the subtypes of this disorder. As many as 70% of children in psychiatric inpatient settings may be diagnosed with an adjustment disorder. In a questionnaire sent to child psychiatrists in the early 1990s, 55% admitted to giving children the diagnosis of an adjustment disorder to avoid the **stigma** associated with other disorders.

Women are diagnosed with adjustment disorder twice as often as men, and diagnosis is also more frequent in females among adolescents.

There are no current studies of differences in the frequency of adjustment disorder in different racial or ethnic groups. There is, however, some potential for bias in diagnosis, particularly when the diagnostic criteria concern abnormal responses to stressors. The *DSM-IV-TR* specifies that clinicians must take a patient's cultural background into account when evaluating his or her responses to stressors.

Diagnosis

Adjustment disorders are almost always diagnosed as the result of an interview with a **psychiatrist**. The psychiatrist will take a history, including identification of the stressor that has triggered the adjustment disorder, and evaluate the patient's responses to the stressor. The patient's primary physician may give him or her a thorough physical examination to rule out a previously undiagnosed medical illness.

The American Psychiatric Association considers adjustment disorder to be a residual category, meaning that the diagnosis is given only when an individual does not meet the criteria for a major mental disorder. For example, if a person fits the more stringent criteria for **major depressive disorder**, the diagnosis of adjustment disorder is not given. If the patient is diagnosed with an adjustment disorder but continues to have symptoms for more than six months after the stressor and its consequences have ceased, the diagnosis is changed to another mental disorder. The one exception to this time limit is situations in which the stressor itself is chronic or has enduring consequences. In that case, the adjustment disorder would be considered chronic and the diagnosis could stand beyond six months.

The lack of a diagnostic checklist distinguishes adjustment disorders from either **post-traumatic stress disorder** or **acute stress disorder**. All three require the presence of a stressor, but the latter two define the extreme stressor and specific patterns of symptoms. With adjustment disorder, the stressor may be any event that is significant to the patient, and the disorder may take very different forms in different patients.

Adjustment disorders must also be distinguished from **personality disorders**, which are caused by enduring personality traits that are inflexible and cause impairment. A personality disorder that has not yet surfaced may be made worse by a stressor and may mimic an adjustment disorder. A clinician must separate relatively stable traits in a patient's personality from passing disturbances. In some cases, however, the patient may be given both diagnoses. Again, it is important for psychiatrists to be sensitive to the role of cultural factors in the presentation of the patient's symptoms.

If the stressor is a physical illness, diagnosis is further complicated. It is important to recognize the difference between an adjustment disorder and the direct physiological effects of a general medical condition (e.g. the usual temporary functional impairment associated with chemotherapy). This distinction can be clarified through communication with the patient's physician or by education about the medical condition and its treatment. For some individuals, however, both may occur and reinforce each other.

Treatments

There have been few research studies of significant scope to compare the efficacy of different treatments for adjustment disorder. The relative lack of outcome studies is partially due to the lack of specificity in the diagnosis itself. Because there is such variability in the types of stressors involved in adjustment disorders, it has proven difficult to design effective studies. As a result, there is no consensus regarding the most effective treatments for adjustment disorder.

Psychological and social interventions

There are, however, guidelines for effective treatment of people with adjustment disorders. Effective treatments include stress-reduction approaches; therapies that teach coping strategies for stressors that cannot be reduced or removed; and those that help patients build support networks of friends, family, and people in similar circumstances. **Psychodynamic psychotherapy** may be helpful in clarifying and interpreting the meaning of the stressor for a particular patient. For example, if the person has cancer, he or she may become more dependent on others, which may be threatening for people who place a high value on self-sufficiency. By exploring those feelings, the patient can then begin to recognize all that is not lost and regain a sense of self-worth.

Therapies that encourage the patient to express the fear, anxiety, rage, helplessness, and hopelessness of dealing with the stressful situation may be helpful. These approaches include journaling, certain types of art therapy, and movement or dance therapy. **Support groups** and **group therapy** allow patients to gain perspective on the adversity and establish relationships with others who share their problem. Psychoeducation and medical crisis counseling can assist individuals and families facing stress caused by a medical illness.

Such types of brief therapy as **family therapy**, **cognitive-behavioral therapy**, solution-focused therapy, and **interpersonal therapy** have all met with some success in treating adjustment disorder.

Medications

Clinicians do not agree on the role of medications in treating adjustment disorder. Some argue that medication is not necessary for adjustment disorders because of their brief duration. In addition, they maintain that medications may be counterproductive by undercutting the patient's sense of responsibility and his or her motivation to find effective solutions. At the other end of the spectrum, other clinicians maintain that medication by itself is the best form of treatment, particularly for patients with medical conditions, those who are terminally ill, and those resistant to **psychotherapy**. Others advocate a middle ground of treatment that combines medication and psychotherapy.

Alternative therapies

Spiritual and religious counseling can be helpful, particularly for people coping with existential issues related to physical illness.

Some herbal remedies appear to be helpful to some patients with adjustment disorders. For adjustment disorder with anxiety, a randomized controlled trial found that the 91 patients receiving Euphytose (an herbal preparation containing a combination of plant extracts including Crataegus, Ballota, Passiflora, Valeriana, Cola, and Paullinia) showed significant improvement over the 91 patients taking a placebo. There have been no reported follow-up studies confirming these findings.

Prognosis

Most adults who are diagnosed with adjustment disorder have a favorable prognosis. For most people, an adjustment disorder is temporary and will either resolve by itself or respond to treatment. For some, however, the stressor will remain chronic and the symptoms may worsen. Still other patients may develop a major depressive disorder even in the absence of an additional stressor.

Studies have been conducted to follow up on patients five years after their initial diagnosis. At that time, 71% of adults were completely well with no residual symptoms, while 21% had developed a major depressive disorder or alcoholism. For children aged 8–13, adjustment disorder did not predict future psychiatric disturbances. For adolescents, the prognosis is grimmer. After five years, 43% had developed a major psychiatric disorder, often of far greater severity. These disorders included **schizophrenia**, **schizoaffective disorder**, major depression, substance use disorders, or personality disorders. In contrast with adults, the adolescents' behavioral symptoms and the type of adjustment disorder predicted future mental disorders.

Researchers have noted that once an adjustment disorder is diagnosed, psychotherapy, medication, or both can prevent the development of a more serious mental disorder. Effective treatment is critical, as adjustment disorder is associated with an increased risk of suicide attempts, completed suicide, **substance abuse**, and various unexplained physical complaints. Patients with chronic stressors may require ongoing treatment for continued symptom management. While

patients may not become symptom-free, treatment can halt the progression toward a more serious mental disorder by enhancing the patient's ability to cope.

Prevention

In many cases, there is little possibility of preventing the stressors that trigger adjustment disorders. One preventive strategy that is helpful to many patients, however, is learning to be proactive in managing ordinary life stress, and maximizing their problem-solving abilities when they are not in crisis. In addition, the general availability of counseling following a large-scale stressful event may ameliorate some stress responses.

See also Anxiety-reduction techniques; Bodywork therapies; Cognitive retraining techniques; Generalized anxiety disorder; Cognitive problem-solving skills training.

KEY TERMS

Cognitive-behavioral therapy—An approach to psychotherapy that emphasizes the correction of distorted thinking patterns and changing one's behaviors accordingly.

Group therapy—Group interaction designed to provide support, correction through feedback, constructive criticism, and a forum for consultation and reference.

Interpersonal therapy—An approach that includes psychoeducation about the sick role, and emphasis on the present and improving interpersonal dynamics and relationships. Interpersonal therapy is effective in treating adjustment disorders related to physical illness.

Psychosocial—A term that refers to the emotional and social aspects of psychological disorders.

Solution-focused therapy—A type of therapy that involves concrete goals and an emphasis on future direction rather than past experiences.

Stressor—A stimulus or event that provokes a stress response in an organism. Stressors can be categorized as acute or chronic, and as external or internal to the organism.

Support group—A group whose primary purpose is the provision of empathy and emotional support for its members. Support groups are less formal and less goal-directed than group therapy.

Resources

BOOKS

American Psychiatric Association. *Diagnostic and Statistical Manual of Mental Disorders.* 4th ed., Text rev. Washington, D.C.: American Psychiatric Association, 2000.

Araoz, Daniel L., and Marie Carrese. *Solution-Oriented Brief Therapy for Adjustment Disorders: A Guide for Providers Under Managed Care.* New York: Brunner/Mazel, 1996.

Gabbard, Glen O., MD. "Adjustment Disorders." *Treatment of Psychiatric Disorders,* written by James. J. Strain, MD, Anwarul Karim, MD, and Angela Cartagena Rochas, MA. 3rd ed, Vol. 2. Washington, D.C.: American Psychiatric Press, 2001.

Nicholi, Armand, ed. *The New Harvard Guide to Psychiatry.* Cambridge, MA: Harvard University Press, 1988.

PERIODICALS

Angelino, Andrew F., and Glenn J. Treisman. "Major Depression and Demoralization in Cancer Patients: Diagnostic and Treatment Considerations." *Supportive Cancer Care* (November 2000): 344–49.

Casey, P., and others. "Can Adjustment Disorder and Depressive Episode Be Distinguished?" *Journal of Affective Disorders* 92 (2006): 291–97.

Grassi, Luigi, and others. "Psychosomatic Characterization of Adjustment Disorders in the Medical Setting: Some Suggestions for DSM-V." *Journal of Affective Disorders* (2006).

Jones, Rick, and others. "Outcome for Adjustment Disorder with Depressed Mood: Comparison with Other Mood Disorders." *Journal of Affective Disorders* (1999): 55.

Pelkonen, Mirjami, and others. "Adolescent Adjustment Disorder: Precipitant Stressors and Distress Symptoms of 89 Outpatients." *European Psychiatry* (2006).

Strain, James J., and others. "Adjustment Disorder: A Multisite Study of its Utilization and Interventions in the Consultation-Liaison Psychiatry Setting." *General Hospital Psychiatry* (1998): 20.

ORGANIZATIONS

National Institute of Mental Health. 6001 Executive Boulevard, Rm. 8184, MSC 9663, Bethesda, MD 20892-9663. Telephone: (301) 443-4513. <http://nimh.nih.gov>.

OTHER

National Cancer Institute. National Institutes of Health. "The Adjustment Disorders." <http://www.cancer.gov/cancertopics/pdq/supportivecare/adjustment/HealthProfessional/page4>.

National Library of Medicine. National Institutes of Health. <http://www.nlm.nih.gov/medlineplus/ency/article/000932.htm>.

Holly Scherstuhl, M.Ed.
Emily Jane Willingham, PhD

Adrenaline

Definition

Adrenaline (also known as epinephrine) is a hormone and neurotransmitter the sympathetic nervous system releases as part of the body's "fight-or-flight" response. Adrenaline increases blood and oxygen flow to the muscles, releases stored energy from the liver and fat cells, and prepares the body for quick action.

Synthesis

Epinephrine is an amine hormone. It is produced and released by a region in the central part of the adrenal gland called the adrenal medulla. In a multi-step process, enzymes convert the amino acid tyrosine into the chemical L-dopa, which is converted to **dopamine** and then converted to norepinephrine. Epinephrine is synthesized from norepinephrine (noradrenaline) and released into the bloodstream.

Together, epinephrine and norepinephrine are known as the catecholamines. Epinephrine makes up about 80% of the catecholamines that are released as part of the body's **stress** response.

Mechanisms of action

When the body is confronted with a dangerous or stressful situation (such as a test for which someone has not studied or an encounter with a dangerous-looking individual), the fight-or-flight response is initiated. In order to act quickly, the body diverts energy away from areas where it is not needed to those where it is most required, such as the heart and muscles.

When the body senses a threat, the hypothalamus in the **brain** releases nerve signals to the adrenal medulla to release epinephrine and norepinephrine.

When released, the epinephrine circulates around the body through the bloodstream until it reaches its target organs—the heart, blood vessels, liver, and fat cells. The hormone binds to two different types of receptors: alpha-adrenergic and beta-adrenergic receptors. Each of these receptors triggers a different action within cells. Alpha receptors initiate smooth muscle contraction and blood vessel constriction, whereas beta receptors stimulate the heart muscle.

The release of epinephrine causes the following reactions in the body:

- The heart beats faster, pumping additional blood throughout the body, and especially to the muscles, in preparation for action.
- Blood vessels constrict, raising the blood pressure.

- Small tubes in the lungs called bronchioles dilate to send more oxygen throughout the body.
- Glycogen (the stored form of glucose) is broken down into glucose in the liver and released.
- Fat stores are released from adipose tissue to be used for energy.
- Blood flow slows to the digestive tract, skin, and kidneys, where it is not needed as much.

History

The first people to identify the effects of epinephrine were British physician George Oliver (1841–1915) and endocrinologist Edward Albert Sharpey-Schafer (1850–1935). In 1894, they discovered that injecting an extract from the adrenal gland into the bloodstream of an animal raised its blood pressure. Then in 1901, Japanese chemist Jokichi Takamine (1854–1922) isolated and purified epinephrine from the adrenal medulla and patented it. British pharmacologist Henry Dale (1875–1968) began using the name adrenaline for the hormone.

Medication and adrenaline

Epinephrine can be isolated from the adrenal glands of animals and used for medical purposes. It can be injected into the heart to restart the heartbeats of people who are experiencing cardiac arrest. It can open the bronchioles of the lungs in people with asthma, or in those who have had severe allergic responses to food, medications, or other substances. Drugs called beta-blockers are often given to patients to reduce **anxiety**. These drugs block beta-adrenergic receptors, slowing the heart rate and lowering blood pressure.

Adrenaline addiction

Some people may experience a drug-like high from participating in behaviors that trigger the body's fight-or-flight response. These people are sometimes referred to as "adrenaline junkies" or "adrenaline addicts". For example, people who seek thrills, such as skydivers, mountain climbers, and extreme skiers, experience a rush of adrenaline from the knowledge that their actions could result in severe injury or even death. Compulsive gamblers often cite the reason for their **addiction** as less the desire to win than the physical rush they get from playing. Some people who steal feel that same type of adrenaline rush from the idea that they might be apprehended. The heightened sense of awareness, increased heartbeat, and rapid breathing that occur when the adrenal medulla releases adrenaline is similar to the high people experience when taking drugs, and it can be similarly addictive.

KEY TERMS

Adrenaline (epinephrine)—A hormone and neurotransmitter released by the adrenal gland as part of the body's fight-or-flight response.

Adrenaline addiction—A drug-like response some people experience from participating in activities (such as skydiving or gambling) that trigger adrenaline release.

Beta-blockers—Drugs that block beta-adrenergic receptors to reduce the actions of epinephrine, thereby lowering the heart rate and blood pressure.

Bronchioles—Tiny tubes in the lungs.

Catecholamines—A class of hormones that includes epinephrine and norepinephrine, which are involved in the fight-or-flight response.

Enzymes—Proteins that trigger chemical reactions in the body.

Glycogen—The form of the sugar, glucose, that is stored in the liver and muscles.

Norepinephrine (noradrenaline)—A hormone produced by the adrenal gland, along with epinephrine, as part of the fight-or-flight response.

Tyrosine—The amino acid from which epinephrine is synthesized.

Resources

BOOKS

Church, Matt. *Adrenaline Junkies and Serotonin Seekers: Balance Your Brain Chemistry to Maximize Energy, Stamina, Mental Sharpness, and Emotional Well-Being.* Berkeley, CA: Ulysses Press, 2004.

Goldstein, David S. *Adrenaline and the Inner World: An Introduction to Scientific Integrative Medicine.* Baltimore, MD: The Johns Hopkins University Press, 2006.

Meyer, Jerrold S., and Linda F. Quenzer. *Psychopharmacology: Drugs, the Brain and Behavior.* Sunderland, MA: Sinauer Associates, 2004.

ORGANIZATIONS

Adrenaline Addicts Anonymous. 350 South Center Street, Number 500, Reno, NV 89501. <http://www.adrenaline addicts.org/>.

American Psychiatric Association. 1000 Wilson Boulevard, Suite 1825, Arlington, VA 22209-3901. Telephone: (703) 907-7300. <http://www.psych.org>.

National Alliance on Mental Illness. 2107 Wilson Boulevard, Suite 300, Arlington, VA 22201-3042. Telephone: (800) 950-6264. <http://www.nami.org>.

National Institute of Mental Health. 6001 Executive Boulevard, Room 8184, MSC 9663, Bethesda, MD 20892-9663. Telephone: (866) 615-6464. <http://www.nimh.nih.gov>.

Stephanie N. Watson

Advance directives

Definition

An advance directive is a written document in which people clearly specify how medical decisions affecting them are to be made if they are unable to make them or authorize a specific person to make such decisions for them. These documents are sometimes called "living wills." Psychiatric advance directives serve the same purpose as general medical advance directives, but are written by mental health consumers as a set of directions for others to follow prior to the onset of a period in which their decision making is impaired or an incapacitating crisis arises.

Description

According to the National Mental Health Association (NMHA), it has become increasingly accepted over the past 30 years that consumers of mental health services know which treatments work best for them, and their opinions have become increasingly valued by those providing services. However, when mental health consumers become unable to make decisions or to give **informed consent** for treatments offered, others (including family, friends, judges, or care providers) make the decisions for them in crisis. In these kinds of crisis situations, advance directives may be beneficial for people receiving care, because the advance directive is a legal document that may protect them from unwanted treatment or **involuntary hospitalization**. Many states have passed laws related to advance directives and psychiatric advance directives. In some cases, the laws detail the content of these psychiatric advance directives, which may include instructions about antipsychotic medication, **electroconvulsive therapy**, or hospital admission, and the naming of people who can act as surrogate decision makers if necessary.

Psychiatric advance directives usually fall into two categories: instruction directives and agent-driven directives.

Instruction directives

An instruction directive is a written document that specifies which treatments individuals do and do not want, in the case that they become unable to make decisions about their care. These documents may indicate the affected individual's preferences about many aspects of treatment, including:

• people who should be contacted at a time of psychiatric crisis
• activities that reduce (and heighten) anxiety for the individual
• effective alternatives to restraint or seclusion for the individual
• acceptable and unacceptable medications and dosages
• other interventions that might be considered during a time of crisis (such as electroconvulsive therapy)

Agent-driven directives

An agent-driven directive may also be called a durable power of attorney. This directive is a signed, dated, and witnessed document that authorizes a designated person (usually a family member or close friend) to act as an agent or proxy. This empowers the proxy to make medical decisions for patients when they are deemed unable to make these decisions for themselves. Such a power of attorney frequently includes the person's stated preferences in regard to treatment. Several states do not allow any of the following people to act as a person's proxy:

• the person's physician, or other health care provider
• the staff of health care facilities that is providing the person's care
• guardians (often called conservators) of the person's financial affairs
• employees of federal agencies financially responsible for a person's care
• any person that serves as agent or proxy for 10 people or more. The person who is to act as the proxy should be familiar with the individual's expressed wishes about care, and should understand how to work within the mental health system.

These two distinct documents may, in some cases, be combined into one form.

Special concerns

In the United States, each state has laws about general medical advance directives and how those laws apply to psychiatric advance directives; a few states exclude psychiatric advance directives from their statutes. The specific form the advance directive should take, the language it should use, and the number of witnesses required to make the document legal and binding vary from state to state. In general, according to the National Mental Health Association, physicians and other health care professionals are expected to comply with the instructions of an advance directive, as long as those instructions are within the guidelines of accepted medical practice. It is recommended that people speak to their attorneys or physicians to ensure that their wishes are communicated in a form that is legally acceptable in their state.

Some other considerations associated with advance directives center on how they are implemented and whether or not a person who wants to complete one actually does so. Various solutions have been proposed to address these problems, including a proposal for video-based advance directives in which patients would produce videotapes documenting their directives. In addition, even though as many as two-thirds of people with mental illness report that they would complete a psychiatric advance directive, only 4–13% of outpatients receiving mental health treatment through public sector resources report having done so. One proposal put forward to address this disconnect is the implementation of facilitated psychiatric advance directives involving a guided discussion and review of choices for completing an advance directive. One study assessing the efficacy of this approach found that completion of psychiatric advance directives in the group that received the facilitated **intervention** was 61%, compared to the 3% of participants who did not receive facilitated intervention.

Resources

BOOKS

Clayman, Charles A., M.D. *American Medical Association Home Medical Encyclopedia*. New York: Random House, 1989.

Doukas, David J., and William Reichel. *Planning for Uncertainty, A Guide to Living Wills and Other Advance Directives for Health Care*. Baltimore, MD: Johns Hopkins University Press, 1993.

National Mental Health Association. *Psychiatric Advance Directives Issue Summary. Mental Health America,* 2002.

PERIODICALS

Moseley, Ray, Aram Dobalian, and Robert Hatch. "The Problem with Advance Directives: Maybe It Is the Medium, Not the Message." *Archives of Gerontology and Geriatrics* 41 (2005): 211–19.

Srebnik, Debra S., and others. "The Content and Clinical Utility of Psychiatric Advance Directives." *Psychiatric Services* 56 (2005): 592–98.

Swanson, Jeffrey W., and others. "Facilitated Psychiatric Advance Directives: A Randomized Trial of an Intervention to Foster Advance Treatment Planning among Persons with Severe Mental Illness." *American Journal of Psychiatry* 163 (2006): 1943–51.

ORGANIZATIONS

Advance Directive Training Project. Resource Center. Albany, NY. Telephone: (518) 463-9242. <www.peer-resource.org>.

American Psychiatric Association. 1400 K Street NW, Washington, DC 20005. Telephone: (888) 357-7924. Fax: (202) 682-6850. Web site: <http://www.psych.org/>.

Judge David L. Bazelon Center for Mental Health Law. Washington, DC. Telephone: (202) 467-5730. <www.bazelon.org/advdir.html>.

Mental Health America. (Produces a *Psychiatric Advance Directives Toolkit*). Telephone: (800) 969-6642.

National Association of Protection and Advocacy Systems. Washington DC. Telephone: (202) 408-9514. <www.protectionandadvocacy.com>.

OTHER

Caring Connections. Part of the National Hospice and Palliative Care Organiation. Toll-free helpline: (800) 658-8898 (also available in Spanish at Telephone: (877) 658-8896). <http://www.caringinfo.org/i4a/pages/index.cfm?pageid = 1>.

National Library of Medicine. National Institutes of Health. "Advance Directives." <http://www.nlm.nih.gov/medlineplus/advancedirectives.html>.

Joan Schonbeck, RN
Emily Jane Willingham, PhD

Affect

Definition

Affect is a psychological term for an observable expression of emotion.

Description

A person's affect is the expression of emotion or feelings displayed to others through facial expressions, hand gestures, voice tone, and other emotional signs such as laughter or tears. Individual affect fluctuates according to emotional state. What is considered a normal range of affect, called the *broad affect*, varies from culture to culture, and even within a culture. Certain individuals may gesture prolifically while talking, and display dramatic facial expressions in reaction to social situations or other stimuli. Others may show little outward response to social environments or interactions, expressing a narrow range of emotions to the outside world.

People with psychological disorders may display variations in their affect. A *restricted* or *constricted affect* describes a mild restriction in the range or intensity of display of feelings. As the reduction in display of emotion becomes more severe, the term *blunted affect* may be applied. The absence of any exhibition of emotions is described as *flat affect* where the voice is monotone, the face expressionless, and the body immobile. *Labile affect* describes emotional instability or dramatic mood swings. When the outward display of emotion is out of context for the situation, such as laughter while describing pain or sadness, the affect is termed "inappropriate."

See also Borderline personality disorder; Depression and depressive disorders; Major depressive disorder; Schizophrenia.

Example of a crowd situation, which may cause anxiety, perhaps leading to agoraphobia. *(bildgentur-online/begsteiger/Alamy)*

Agoraphobia

Definition

Agoraphobia is an **anxiety** disorder characterized by intense fear related to being in situations from which escape might be difficult or embarrassing (i.e., being on a bus or train), or in which help might not be available in the event of a **panic attack** or panic symptoms. Panic is defined as extreme and unreasonable fear and anxiety.

According to the handbook used by mental health professionals to diagnose mental disorders, the ***Diagnostic and Statistical Manual of Mental Disorders***, fourth edition, text revision, also known as the *DSM-IV-TR,* patients with agoraphobia are typically afraid of such symptoms as feeling dizzy, having an attack of diarrhea, fainting, or "going crazy."

The word "agoraphobia" comes from two Greek words that mean "fear" (phobos) and "marketplace" (agora). The anxiety associated with agoraphobia leads to avoidance of situations that involve being outside one's home alone, being in crowds, being on a bridge, or traveling by car or public transportation. Agoraphobia may intensify to the point that it interferes with a person's ability to take a job outside the home or to carry out such ordinary errands and activities as shopping for groceries or going out to a movie.

Description

The close association in agoraphobia between fear of being outside one's home and fear of having panic symptoms is reflected in *DSM-IV-TR* classification of two separate disorders: **panic disorder** (PD) with agoraphobia, and agoraphobia without PD. PD is essentially characterized by sudden attacks of fear and panic. There may be no known reason for the occurrence of panic attacks; they are frequently triggered by fear-producing events or thoughts, such as driving or being in an elevator. PD is believed to be due to an abnormal activation of the body's hormonal system, causing a sudden "fight-or-flight" response.

The chief distinction between PD with agoraphobia and agoraphobia without PD is that patients who are diagnosed with PD with agoraphobia meet all criteria for PD; in agoraphobia without PD, patients are afraid of panic-like symptoms in public places, rather than full-blown panic attacks.

People with agoraphobia appear to have two distinct types of anxiety—panic, and the anticipatory anxiety related to fear of future panic attacks. Patients with agoraphobia are sometimes able to endure being in the situations they fear by "gritting their teeth," or by having a friend or relative accompany them.

In the United States' diagnostic system, the symptoms of agoraphobia can be similar to those of specific phobia and **social phobia**. In agoraphobia and specific phobia, the focus is fear itself; with social phobia, the person's focus is on how others are perceiving him/her. Patients diagnosed with agoraphobia tend to be more afraid of their own internal physical sensations and similar cues than of the reactions of others per se. In cases of specific phobia, the person fears very specific situations, whereas in agoraphobia, the person generally fears a variety of situations (being outside of the home alone or traveling on public transportation, for example). An example of a patient diagnosed with a specific phobia rather than agoraphobia would be the person whose fear is triggered only by being in a bus, rather than a car or taxi. The fear of the bus is more specific than the fear of traveling on public transportation in general, which may be experienced by a person with agoraphobia. The *DSM-IV-TR* remarks that the differential **diagnosis** of agoraphobia "can be difficult because all of these conditions are characterized by avoidance of specific situations."

Causes and symptoms

Causes

Currently, the causes of agoraphobia are complex and not completely understood. Research indicates several factors can contribute to the condition.

GENETIC. It has been known for some years that **anxiety disorders** tend to run in families. Recent research has confirmed earlier hypotheses that there is a genetic component to agoraphobia, and that it can be separated from susceptibility to PD. In 2001, a team of Yale geneticists reported the discovery of a genetic locus on human chomosome 3 that governs a person's risk of developing agoraphobia. PD was found to be associated with two loci: one on human chromosome 1 and the other on chromosome 11q. The researchers concluded that agoraphobia and PD are common; they are both inheritable anxiety disorders that share some, but not all, of their genetic loci for susceptibility.

INNATE TEMPERAMENT. A number of researchers have pointed to inborn temperament as a broad vulnerability factor in the development of anxiety and mood disorders. In other words, a person's natural disposition or temperament may become a factor in developing a number of mood or anxiety disorders. Some people seem more sensitive throughout their lives to events, but upbringing and life history are also important factors in determining who will develop these disorders. Children who manifest what is known as "behavioral inhibition" (a group of behaviors that are displayed when the child is confronted with a new situation or unfamiliar people) in early infancy are at increased risk for developing more than one anxiety disorder in adult life—particularly if the inhibition remains over time. These behaviors include moving around, crying, and general irritability, followed by withdrawing, seeking comfort from a familiar person, and stopping what one is doing when one notices the new person or situation. Children of depressed or anxious parents are more likely to develop behavioral inhibition.

PHYSIOLOGICAL REACTIONS TO ILLNESS. Another factor in the development of PD and agoraphobia appears to be a history of respiratory disease. Some researchers have hypothesized that repeated episodes of respiratory disease would predispose a child to PD by making breathing difficult and lowering the threshold for feeling suffocated. It is also possible that respiratory diseases could generate fearful beliefs in the child's mind that would lead him or her to exaggerate the significance of respiratory symptoms.

LIFE EVENTS. About 42% of patients diagnosed with agoraphobia report histories of real or feared separation from their parents or other caretakers in childhood. This statistic has been interpreted to mean that agoraphobia in adults is the aftermath of unresolved childhood separation anxiety. The fact that many patients diagnosed with agoraphobia report that their first episode occurred after the death of a loved one, and the observation that other people with agorophobia feel safe in going out as long as someone is with them, have been taken as supportive evidence of the separation anxiety hypothesis.

LEARNED BEHAVIOR. There are also theories about human learning that explain agoraphobia. It is thought that a person's initial experience of panic-like symptoms in a specific situation—for example, being alone in a subway station—may lead the person to associate physical symptoms of panic with all subway stations. Avoiding all subway stations would then reduce the level of the person's discomfort. Unfortunately, the avoidance strengthens the phobia because the person is unlikely to have the opportunity to test whether subway stations actually cause uncomfortable physical sensations. One treatment modality—exposure therapy—is based on the premise that phobias can be "unlearned" by reversing the pattern of avoidance.

SOCIAL FACTORS RELATED TO GENDER. Gender role socialization has been suggested as an explanation for the fact that the majority of patients with agoraphobia are women. One form of this hypothesis maintains that some parents still teach girls to be fearful and timid about venturing out in public. Another version relates agoraphobia to the mother-daughter relationship, maintaining that mothers tend to give daughters mixed messages about becoming separate individuals. As a result, girls grow up with a more fragile sense of self, and may stay within the physical boundaries of their home because they lack a firm sense of their internal psychological boundaries.

Symptoms

The symptoms of an episode of agoraphobia may include any or all of the following:

- trembling
- breaking out in sweat
- heart palpitations
- paresthesias (tingling or "pins and needles" sensations in the hands or feet)
- nausea
- fatigue
- rapid pulse or breathing rate
- a sense of impending doom

In most cases, the person with agoraphobia feels some relief from the symptoms after he or she has left the precipitating situation or returned home.

Demographics

In general, phobias are the most common mental disorders in the general United States population, affecting about 7% of adults, or 6.4 million Americans. Agoraphobia is one of the most common phobias, affecting between 2.7% and 5.8% of American adults. The onset of symptoms is most likely to occur between age 15 and age 35. The lifetime prevalence of agoraphobia is estimated at 5%–12%. Like most phobias, agoraphobia is two to four times more common in women than in men.

The incidence of agoraphobia appears to be similar across races and ethnic groups in the United States.

Diagnosis

The differential diagnosis of agoraphobia is described differently in *DSM-IV-TR* and in *ICD-10*, the European diagnostic maunual. The U.S. diagnostic manual specifies that agoraphobia must be defined in relation to PD, and that the diagnoses of **specific phobias** and social phobias are the next to consider. The *DSM-IV-TR* also specifies that the patient's symptoms must not be related to **substance abuse**; and if they are related to a general medical condition, they must have excessive symptoms usually associated with that condition. For example, a person with Crohn's disease has realistic concerns about an attack of diarrhea in a public place and should not be diagnosed with agoraphobia unless the fear of losing bowel control is clearly exaggerated. The *DSM-IV-TR* does not require a person to experience agoraphobia within a set number of circumstances in order to meet the diagnostic criteria.

In contrast, the European diagnostic manual primarily distinguishes between agoraphobia and delusional or obsessive disorders, and depressive episodes. In addition, *ICD-10* specifies that the patient's anxiety must be restricted to or occur primarily within two out of four specific situations: in crowds, in public places, while traveling alone, or while traveling away from home. The primary area of agreement between the American and European diagnostic manuals is that both specify avoidance of the feared situation as a diagnostic criterion.

Diagnosis of agoraphobia is usually made by a physician after careful exclusion of other mental disorders and physical conditions or diseases that might be related to the patient's fears. Head injury, pneumonia, and withdrawal from certain medications can produce some of the symptoms of a panic attack. In addition, the physician may ask about caffeine intake as a possible dietary factor. Currently, there are no laboratory tests or diagnostic **imaging studies** that can be used to diagnose agoraphobia.

Furthermore, there are no widely used diagnostic interviews or screening instruments specifically for agoraphobia. Dutch researchers have developed a self-report questionnaire that promises to be helpful to doctors treating people with agoraphobia. The test is called the Agoraphobic Self-Statements Questionnaire, or ASQ, and is intended to evaluate thinking processes in patients with agoraphobia, as distinct from their emotional responses.

Treatments

Treatment of agoraphobia usually consists of medication plus **cognitive-behavioral therapy** (CBT). The physician may also recommend an alternative form of treatment for the anxiety symptoms associated with agoraphobia. Some patients may be advised to cut down on or give up coffee or tea, as the caffeine in these beverages can be contribute to their panic symptoms.

Medications

Medications that have been used with patients diagnosed with agoraphobia include the benzodiazepine tranquilizers, the MAO inhibitors (MAOIs), tricyclic **antidepressants** (TCAs), and the selective serotonin uptake inhibitors, or **SSRIs**. In the past few years, the SSRIs have come to be regarded as the first-choice medication treatment because they have fewer side effects. The **benzodiazepines** have the disadvantage of increasing the symptoms of agoraphobia when they are withdrawn, as well as interfering with CBT.

Associationism—A theory about human learning that explains complex psychological phenomena in terms of coincidental relationships. For example, a person with agoraphobia who is afraid of riding in a car may have had a panic attack in a car on one occasion and has learned to associate cars with the physical symptoms of a panic attack.

Ayurvedic medicine—The traditional medical system of India. Ayurvedic treatments include diet, exercises, herbal treatments, meditation, massage, breathing techniques, and exposure to sunlight.

Behavioral inhibition—A set of behaviors that appear in early infancy that are displayed when the child is confronted with a new situation or unfamiliar people. These behaviors include moving around, crying, and general irritability, followed by withdrawing, and seeking comfort from a familiar person. These behaviors are associated with an increased risk of social phobia and panic disorder in later life. Behavioral inhibition in children appears to be linked to anxiety and mood disorders in their parents.

Cognitive restructuring—An approach to psychotherapy that focuses on helping the patient examine distorted patterns of perceiving and thinking in order to change their emotional responses to people and situations.

Exposure therapy—A form of cognitive-behavioral therapy in which patients with phobias are exposed to their feared objects or situations while accompanied by the therapist. The length of exposure is gradually increased until the association between the feared situation and the patient's experienced panic symptoms is no longer present.

Paresthesia—An abnormal sensation of tingling or "pins and needles." Paresthesia is a common panic-like symptom associated with agoraphobia.

Phobia—Irrational fear of places, things, or situations that lead to avoidance.

Simple phobia—An older term for specific phobia.

Specific phobia—A type of phobia in which the object or situation that arouses fear is clearly identifiable and limited. An older term for specific phobia is simple phobia.

(Benzodiazepines can decrease mental sharpness, making it difficult for patients taking these medications to focus in therapy sessions.) The MAOIs require patients to follow certain dietary guidelines. For example, they must exclude aged cheeses, red wine, and certain types of beans. TCAs may produce such side effects as blurred vision, constipation, dry mouth, and drowsiness.

Psychotherapy

CBT is regarded as the most effective psychotherapeutic treatment for agoraphobia. The specific CBT approach that seems to work best with agoraphobia is exposure therapy. Exposure therapy is based on undoing the association that the patient originally formed between the panic symptoms and the feared situation. By being repeatedly exposed to the feared location or situation, the patient gradually learns that he or she is not in danger, and the anxiety symptoms fade away. The therapist typically explains the procedure of exposure therapy to the patient and reassures him or her that the exposure can be stopped at any time that his or her limits of toleration have been reached. The patient is then exposed in the course of a number of treatment sessions to the feared situation, usually for a slightly longer period each time. A typical course of exposure therapy takes about 12 weeks.

On the other hand, one group of German researchers reported good results in treating patients with agoraphobia with individual high-density exposure therapy. The patients were exposed to their respective feared situations for an entire day for two to three weeks. One year later, the patients had maintained their improvement.

Exposure treatment for agoraphobia may be combined with cognitive restructuring. This form of cognitive behavioral therapy teaches patients to observe the thoughts that they have in the feared situation, such as, "I'll die if I have to go into that railroad station," and replace these thoughts with positive statements. In this example, the patient with agoraphobia might say to him- or herself, "I'll be just fine when I go in there to buy my ticket."

Although insight-oriented therapies have generally been considered relatively ineffective in treating agoraphobia, a recent trial of brief **psychodynamic psychotherapy** in patients with PD with agoraphobia indicates that this form of treatment may also be beneficial. Of the 21 patients who participated in the

24-session course of treatment (twice weekly for 12 weeks), 16 experienced remission of their agoraphobia. There were no relapses at six-month follow-up.

Alternative and complementary treatments

Patients diagnosed with agoraphobia have reported that alternative therapies, such as **hypnotherapy** and music therapy, were helpful in relieving symptoms of anxiety and panic. Ayurvedic medicine, **yoga**, religious practice, and guided imagery **meditation** have also been helpful.

Prognosis

The prognosis for untreated agoraphobia is considered poor by most European as well as most American physicians. The *DSM-IV-TR* remarks that little is known about the course of agoraphobia without PD, but that anecdotal evidence indicates that it may persist for years with patients becoming increasingly impaired. The *ICD-10* refers to agoraphobia as "the most incapacitating of the phobic disorders," to the point that some patients become completely housebound. With proper treatment, however, 90% of patients diagnosed with agoraphobia can recover and resume a normal life.

Prevention

The genetic factors that appear to be implicated in the development of agoraphobia cannot be prevented. On the other hand, recent recognition of the link between anxiety and mood disorders in parents and vulnerability to phobic disorders in their children may help to identify children at risk and to develop appropriate preventive strategies for them.

Resources

BOOKS

American Psychiatric Association. *Diagnostic and Statistical Manual of Mental Disorders*. 4th edition, text revised. Washington, DC: American Psychiatric Association, 2000.

Freeman, Arthur, James Pretzer, Barbara Fleming, and Karen M. Simon. *Clinical Applications of Cognitive Therapy (2nd ed.)*. New York: Kluwer Academic/Plenum Publishers, 2004.

Pelletier, Kenneth R., MD. "CAM Therapies for Specific Conditions: Anxiety." *The Best Alternative Medicine*, Part II. New York: Simon and Schuster, 2002.

Starcevic, Vladan. *Anxiety Disorders in Adults: A Clinical Guide*. New York: Oxford University Press, 2005.

World Health Organization (WHO). *The ICD-10 Classification of Mental and Behavioural Disorders*. Geneva: WHO, 1992.

PERIODICALS

Churchill, Rachel, Furukawa, Toshi A., and Watanabe, Norio. "Psychotherapy plus Antidepressant for Panic Disorder With or Without Agoraphobia: Systematic Review." *British Journal of Psychiatry* 188.4 (April 2006): 305–312.

Roy-Byrne, Peter P., Michelle G. Craske, and Murray B. Stein. "Panic Disorder." *Lancet* 368.9540 (September 2006): 1023–1032.

ORGANIZATIONS

Anxiety Disorders Association of America. 11900 Parklawn Drive, Suite 100, Rockville, MD 20852-2624. Telephone: (301) 231-9350. <www.adaa.org>.

Ayurvedic and Naturopathic Medical Clinic. 2115 112th Ave NE, Bellevue, WA 98004. Telephone: (425) 453-8022. <www.ayurvedicscience.com>.

Freedom From Fear. 308 Seaview Avenue, Staten Island, NY 10305. Telephone: (718) 351-1717. <www.freedomfromfear.com>.

National Mental Health Association. 1021 Prince Street, Alexandria, VA 22314-2971. Telephone: (800) 969-6642. <www.nmha.org>.

OTHER

National Institute of Mental Health (NIMH). *Anxiety Disorders*. NIH Publication No. 00-3879 (2000). <www.nimh.nih.gov/anxiety/anxiety.cfm>.

Rebecca Frey, Ph.D.
Ruth M. Wienclaw, Ph.D.

AIMS *see* **Abnormal involuntary movement scale**

Akineton *see* **Biperiden**

Alcohol-induced persisting amnestic disorder *see* **Wernicke-Korsakoff syndrome**

Alcohol and related disorders

Definition

Alcoholism is defined as alcohol-seeking and -consumption behavior that is harmful. Long-term and uncontrollable harmful consumption can cause alcohol-related disorders that include **antisocial personality disorder**, mood disorders (bipolar and major **depression**) and **anxiety disorders**.

Description

Alcoholism is the popular term for the disorder recognized by the American Psychiatric Association (APA) as alcohol dependence. The hallmarks of this disorder are **addiction** to alcohol, inability to stop

An Alcoholics Anonymous meeting. *(Hank Morgan/Photo Researchers, Inc)*

drinking, and repeated interpersonal, school, or work-related problems that can be directly attributed to the use of alcohol. Alcoholism can have serious consequences, affecting an individual's health and personal life, as well as affecting society at large.

Alcohol dependence is a complex disorder that includes the social and interpersonal issues mentioned above, and includes biological elements, as well. These elements are related to tolerance and withdrawal, cognitive (thinking) problems that include craving, and behavioral abnormalities including the impaired ability to stop drinking. Withdrawal is a term that refers to the symptoms that occur when a person dependent on a substance stops taking that substance for a period of time; withdrawal symptoms vary in type and severity depending on the substance, but alcohol withdrawal symptoms can include shaking, irritability, and nausea. Tolerance is a reduced response to the alcohol consumed and can be acute or chronic. Acute tolerance occurs during a single episode of drinking and is greater when blood alcohol concentration rises. Chronic tolerance occurs over the long term when there is greater resistance to the intoxicating effects

of alcohol, and, as a result, the affected person has to drink more to achieve the desired effect.

The APA also recognizes another alcohol-use disorder called alcohol **abuse**. Alcohol abuse is similar to dependence in that the use of alcohol is impairing the affected person's ability to achieve goals and fulfill responsibilities, and his or her interpersonal relationships are affected by the alcohol abuse. However, unlike a person with dependence, a person diagnosed with alcohol abuse does not experience tolerance or, when not drinking, withdrawal symptoms. People who abuse alcohol can become dependent on the substance over time.

Alcohol-related disorders are groups of disorders that can result in persons who are long-term users of alcohol. These disorders can affect the person's metabolism, gastrointestinal tract, nervous system, bone marrow (the matter in bones that forms essential blood cells) and can cause endocrine (hormone) problems. Additionally, alcoholism can result in nutritional deficiencies. Some common alcohol-related medical disorders include vitamin deficiencies, alterations in sugar and fat levels in blood, hepatitis, fatty liver, cirrhosis, esophagitis (inflammation of the esophagus), gastritis (inflammation of the lining of the stomach), **dementia**, abnormal heart rates and rhythms, lowered platelets (cells important for forming a clot), leukopenia (decrease in the number of white blood cells that are important for body defenses and immunity), and testicular atrophy (shrinking of the testicles). Persons with **anxiety**, depression, or **bipolar disorder** may consume alcohol for temporary relief from their symptoms. Others, such as persons with antisocial personality disorder, may use alcohol in a way that may become part of a **dual diagnosis** of criminality and substance dependence.

Demographics

The lifetime prevalence of alcohol abuse in the general population is thought to be between 13.7% and 23.5%. The disorder is more common in males than in females. Alcoholism and alcohol abuse affect 20% or more of adult hospitalized and ambulatory patients (those receiving care on an outpatient basis). Alcoholism can develop in people of all races and socioeconomic classes. Approximately two-thirds of Americans 18 years and older drink alcohol. The annual cost of alcohol abuse in the United States is $185 billion. Alcoholism ranks third in the United States as a preventable disease, and alcohol is related to approximately 20,000 deaths each year.

Causes and symptoms

Causes

The cause of alcoholism is related to behavioral, biological, and genetic factors.

Behaviorally, alcohol consumption is related to internal or external feedback. Internal feedback is the internal state a person experiences during and after alcohol consumption. External feedback is made up of the cues that other people send the person when he or she drinks. Internal states pertaining to alcohol can include shame or hangover. Alcohol-related external cues can include reprimands, criticism, or encouragement. People may drink to the point of dependence because of peer pressure, acceptance in a peer group, or because drinking is related to specific moods (easygoing, relaxed, calm, sociable) that are related to the formation of intimate relationships.

Biologically, repeated use of alcohol can impair the **brain** levels of a "pleasure" neurotransmitter called **dopamine**. **Neurotransmitters** are chemicals in the brain that pass impulses from one nerve cell to the next. When a person is dependent on alcohol, his or her brain areas that produce dopamine become depleted and the individual can no longer enjoy the pleasures of everyday life—his or her brain chemistry is rearranged to depend on alcohol for transient euphoria (state of happiness).

Genetic studies have suggested that the GABA-A receptor alpha2 subunit gene (GABRA2) and alcohol dehydrogenase (ADH) genes increase the risk for alcohol dependence. The GABRA genes are related to a receptor for gamma-amino butyric acid (GABA), a chemical in the central nervous system that is believed to mediate some of the physiological effects of alcohol. ADH is a chemical involved in the oxidation of alcohol in the body. These genes related to alcohol abuse can be passed from parents to their children.

Other genetic studies have demonstrated that close relatives of an alcoholic are four times more likely to become alcoholics themselves. Furthermore, this risk holds true even for children who were adopted away from their biological families at birth and raised in a non-alcoholic adoptive family, with no knowledge of their biological family's difficulties with alcohol.

Symptoms

ALCOHOL DEPENDENCE. Individuals who are alcohol-dependent compulsively drink ethanol (the chemical name for alcohol) to the level of intoxication. Intoxication occurs at blood alcohol levels of 50 to 150 mg/dl and is characterized by euphoria at first, and then if blood concentrations of alcohol continue to rise, a person can become explosively combative. Neurologically, acute intoxication causes impaired thinking, lack of coordination, slow or irregular eye movements, and impaired vision. As the person repeatedly drinks, the body develops a reduced response to ethanol called tolerance.

People with chronic tolerance may appear to be sober (not intoxicated) even after consumption of alcohol that could cause death in non-drinkers. People with alcohol dependence may also develop alcoholic blackouts after large amounts of ethanol consumption. These blackouts are typically characterized by **amnesia** (loss of memory) lasting several hours without impaired consciousness. In other words, people experiencing blackouts appear to be conscious, but will not remember their actions during the blackouts after the intoxication has worn off.

People with alcohol dependence also develop alcohol withdrawal (a state of non-drinking) syndrome. The nervous system adapts to chronic ethanol exposure by increasing the activity of nerve-cell mechanisms that counteract alcohol's depressant effects. Therefore, when drinking is abruptly reduced, the affected person develops disordered perceptions, **seizures**, and tremor (often accompanied by irritability, nausea, and vomiting). Tremor of the hands known as "morning shakes," usually occurs in the morning due to overnight abstinence. The most serious manifestation of alcohol withdrawal syndrome is **delirium** tremens, which occurs in approximately 5% of people dependent on alcohol. Delirium tremens consists of agitation, disorientation, **insomnia**, **hallucinations**, **delusions**, intense sweating, fever, and increased heart rate (tachycardia). This state is a medical emergency because it can be fatal, and affected persons must be immediately hospitalized and treated with medications that control vital physiological functions.

The APA publishes a manual for mental health professionals called the ***Diagnostic and Statistical Manual of Mental Disorders***, also known as the *DSM*. This manual lists criteria that each disorder must meet for **diagnosis**. The criteria are symptoms that must be present so that the diagnosis can be made. Alcohol dependence can be diagnosed if three or more of the following symptoms are present within a 12-month period:

- tolerance
- withdrawal
- drinking alcohol in larger amounts and over a longer period of time than was planned
- Continued desire or attempts to stop alcohol use
- preoccupation with, and great deal of time spent seeking alcohol
- drinking is the focal point of person's life (using takes up most of the person's time)
- continued use despite health problems related to drinking (such as liver damage)

ALCOHOL ABUSE. In order for a person to be diagnosed with alcohol abuse, one of the following four criteria must be met within a 12-month period. Because of drinking, a person repeatedly:

- fails to live up to his or her most important responsibilities at home, school, or work
- physically endangers him- or herself, or others (for example, by drinking and driving)
- gets into trouble with the law
- experiences difficulties in relationships or jobs

Diagnosis

The diagnosis of alcoholism can either be based on medical and/or psychological conditions. With a long-term history of abusive drinking, medical conditions can result, and these could lead the physician to suspect a patient's alcoholism. These medical conditions may include organ complications such as: cirrhosis (liver), hepatitis (liver), pancreatitis (pancreas), peripheral neuropathy (nervous system), or cardiomyopathy (heart). Additionally, recurrent trauma, resulting in bone fractures, **fatigue**, depression, sexual dysfunction, fluctuating blood pressure, and **sleep disorders** may prompt the clinician to further assess for alcoholism.

Psychological diagnosis can be accomplished through a clinical interview and history (biopsychosocial assessment), and from a choice of many standardized alcohol use tests. The biopsychosocial assessment is an extensive interview conducted by the clinician. During the interview, the clinician will ask the patient about many areas of life, including childhood, education, and medical history. One very simple tool for beginning the diagnosis of alcoholism is called the CAGE questionnaire. It consists of four questions, with the first letters of each key word spelling out the word CAGE:

- Have you ever tried to *Cut* down on your drinking?
- Have you ever been *Annoyed* by anyone's comments about your drinking?
- Have you ever felt *Guilty* about your drinking?
- Do you ever need an *Eye-opener* (a morning drink of alcohol) to start the day?

Other, longer lists of questions exist to help determine the severity and effects of a person's alcohol use. Given the recent research pointing to a genetic basis for alcoholism, the doctor will also attempt to ascertain whether anyone else in the person's family has ever suffered from alcoholism.

Diagnosis is sometimes facilitated when family members call the attention of a physician to a loved one's difficulties with alcohol.

Treatments

Comprehensive treatment for alcohol dependence has two components: **detoxification** and rehabilitation.

Detoxification

The goal of detoxification is to rid the patient's body of the toxic effects of alcohol. Because the person's body has become accustomed to alcohol, the person will need to be supported as he or she goes through withdrawal. Withdrawal will be different for different patients, depending on the severity of the alcoholism, as measured by the quantity of alcohol ingested daily and the length of time the patient has been dependent on alcohol. Withdrawal symptoms can range from mild to life-threatening. Mild withdrawal symptoms include nausea, achiness, diarrhea, difficulty sleeping, sweatiness, anxiety, and trembling. This phase begins between five and eight hours after the last drink, and is over in about three to five days. More severe effects of withdrawal can include hallucinations (in which a patient sees, hears, or feels something that is not actually real), seizures, a strong craving for alcohol, confusion, fever, fast heart rate, high blood pressure, and delirium (a fluctuating level of consciousness). Severe withdrawal can involve delirium tremens, which involve fever, delirium, intense sweating, and tremors. Patients at highest risk for delirium tremens are those with other medical problems, including malnutrition, liver disease, or Wernicke's encephalopathy. Delirium tremens usually begins about three to five days after the patient's last drink, progressing from the more mild symptoms to the more severe, and may last a number of days.

Patients going through mild withdrawal are simply monitored carefully to make sure that more severe symptoms do not develop. No medications are necessary, however. Treatment of a patient with more severe effects of withdrawal may require the use of sedative medications to relieve the discomfort of withdrawal and to avoid the potentially life-threatening complications of high blood pressure, fast heart rate, and seizures. Benzodiazapines are medications that ease tension by slowing down the central nervous system and may be helpful in those patients experiencing hallucinations. Because of the patient's nausea, fluids may need to be given through a vein (intravenously), along with some necessary sugars and salts. It is crucial that thiamine be included in the fluids, because thiamine is usually quite low in patients with alcohol dependence, and deficiency of thiamine is responsible for Wernick's encephalopathy.

Rehabilitation

After cessation of drinking has been accomplished, the next steps involve helping the patient stay healthy and avoid relapsing. (**Relapse** occurs when a patient returns to old behaviors that he or she was trying to change.) This phase of treatment is referred to as rehabilitation. The best programs incorporate the family into the therapy, because the family has undoubtedly been severely affected by the patient's drinking. Some therapists believe that family members, in an effort to deal with their loved one's drinking problem, sometimes develop patterns of behavior that unintentionally support or "enable"

the patient's drinking. This situation is referred to as "co-dependence," and must be addressed in order to treat a person's alcoholism successfully.

PSYCHOLOGICAL THERAPIES. **Psychotherapy** helps affected persons to anticipate, understand, recognize, and prevent relapse. Behavioral therapy approaches typically include community-centered **support groups**, meetings such as Alcoholics Anonymous (AA), **cognitive-behavioral therapy** (CBT), and Motivated Enhancement Therapy (MET). CBT focuses on teaching alcoholics recognition and coping skills for craving states and high-risk situations that precipitate or trigger relapsing behaviors. MET can motivate patients to use their personal resources to initiate changes in behavior. Many people recovering from substance dependence find peer-led support groups helpful in helping them avoid relapse.

MEDICATIONS. Two medications, **naltrexone** (ReVia) and acamprosate (Campral), can help decrease craving states in alcoholics. A version of naltrexone, called **vivitrol**, can be injected by a healthcare professional once a month to help reduce an individual's urge to drink. In combination with psychotherapy, these medications can help reduce relapse. Another medication called **disulfiram** (Antabuse) affects the metabolism of alcohol and causes unpleasant effects in patients who consume alcohol while taking the medication. Antabuse should only be taken by people who are committed to recovery and understand that they are to avoid all contact with alcohol or alcohol-containing products. People who have alcohol dependence along with other disorders, such as depression, can work with their physicians to determine if medication might be a feasible treatment option for them.

ADDITIONAL TREATMENTS. Alternative treatments can be a helpful adjunct for the alcoholic patient, once the medical danger of withdrawal has passed. Because many alcoholics have very stressful lives (whether because of or leading to the alcoholism is sometimes a matter of debate), many of the treatments for alcoholism involve managing and relieving **stress**. These include massage, **meditation**, and **hypnotherapy**. The malnutrition of long-term alcohol use is addressed by nutrition-oriented practitioners and dietitians with careful attention to a healthy diet and the use of nutritional supplements such as vitamins A, B complex, and C, as well as certain fatty acids, amino acids, zinc, magnesium, and selenium. **Acupuncture** is believed to decrease both withdrawal symptoms and to help improve a patient's chances for continued recovery from alcoholism.

KEY TERMS

Antisocial personality disorder—Disorder characterized by behavior pattern of disregard for others' rights. People with this disorder often deceive and manipulate, or their behavior might include aggression to people or animals or property destruction, for example. This disorder has also been called sociopathy or psychopathy.

Blackout—A period of loss of consciousness or memory.

Delirium tremens—Serious alcohol withdrawal symptoms that must be treated in a hospital and that may include shaking, delirium, and hallucinations.

Detoxification—A process in which the body is allowed to free itself of a drug while the symptoms of withdrawal are treated. It is the primary step in any treatment program for drug or alcohol abuse.

Euphoria—A feeling or state of well-being or elation.

Intoxication—Condition of being drunk.

Relapse—A person experiences a relapse when he or she re-engages in a behavior that is harmful and that he or she was trying to change or eliminate. Relapse is a common occurrence after treatment for many disorders, including addictions and eating disorders.

Thiamine—A B-vitamin that is essential to normal metabolism and nerve function, and whose absorption is affected by alcoholism.

Tolerance—Progressive decrease in the effectiveness of a drug with long-term use.

Wernicke's encephalopathy—Group of symptoms that appears in people who are dependent on alcohol. The syndrome is due to a thiamine deficiency, and severely affects one's memory, preventing new learning from taking place.

Withdrawal—Symptoms experienced by a person who has become physically dependent on a drug, experienced when the drug use is discontinued.

Prognosis

Most persons who use alcohol start to drink during adolescence or early adulthood. Approximately 50% of male drinkers have alcohol-related problems such as fighting, blackouts, or legal problems during their early drinking years, usually late teens or early twenties. People who cannot control their drinking behaviors will tend to accumulate drinking-related problems and

become dependent on alcohol. Although many alcoholics can maintain sobriety with psychotherapeutic interventions alone, research indicates that medications such as disulfiram, in combination with psychotherapy, can be very effective for achieving sobriety.

Prevention

Good prevention includes education and a knowledge of family (genetic) propensity. If alcohol dependence is present in a close family member, then relatives should know and be discouraged to drink beverages that contain alcohol. Education of older children and young teenagers concerning the negative effects and consequences of drinking alcohol may help to decrease or recognize problems before start or worsen.

Resources

BOOKS

Brozner, Elaine. *New Research on Alcohol Abuse And Alcoholism.* New York: Nova Science Publishers, 2006.

Dodes, Lance M. *The Heart of Addiction: A New Approach to Understanding and Managing Alcoholism and Other Addictive Behaviors.* New York: Harper, 2002.

Johnson, Bankole A., Pedro Ruiz, and Marc Galanter, eds. *Handbook of Clinical Alcoholism Treatment.* Baltimore, MD: Lippincott Williams & Wilkins 2003.

ORGANIZATIONS

Alcoholics Anonymous. P.O. Box 459, New York, NY 10163. Telephone: (212) 870-3400. <http://www.alcoholics-anonymous.org/>

National Institute on Alcohol Abuse and Alcoholism. National Institutes of Health. 5635 Fishers Lane Bethesda, MD 20892-9304. <http://www.niaaa.nih.gov/>

Substance Abuse and Mental Health Services Administration (SAMHSA). 1 Choke Cherry Road, Rockville, MD, 20857. Telephone: (800) 729-6686. <http://ncadi.samhsa.gov/>

Laith Farid Gulli, MD
Michael Mooney, M.A.,CAC,CCS
Tanya Bivins, B.S.N.,RN
Bill Asenjo, MS,CRC
Stephanie N. Watson

Alcoholics Anonymous *see* **Self-help groups**

Alprazolam

Definition

Alprazolam is a tranquilizer. It belongs to a group of drugs called **benzodiazepines**. In the United States alprazolam is sold under brand name Xanax.

Purpose

The United States Food and Drug Administration (FDA) has approved alprazolam to treat **anxiety**, **panic disorder**, and anxiety associated with **depression**. Occasionally alprazolam is used to treat alcohol withdrawal, but it is not FDA-approved for this use, and is not normally the first drug tried in treating alcohol withdrawal symptoms.

Description

Alprazolam is classified as a benzodiazepine. Benzodiazepines are sedative-hypnotic drugs that help to relieve nervousness, tension, and other anxiety symptoms by slowing the central nervous system. To do this, they block the effects of a specific chemical involved in the transmission of nerve impulses in the **brain**, decreasing the excitement level of the nerve cells.

All benzodiazepines cause sedation, including drowsiness and reduced mental alertness. However, one benefit of alprazolam is that it causes somewhat less drowsiness than many other benzodiazepine drugs.

Alprazolam comes in 0.25-mg, 0.5-mg, 1-mg and 2-mg tablets, and 1-mg/ml solution.

Recommended dosage

The recommended initial adult dose for anxiety is 0.25–0.5 mg taken three times daily. This dosage may be increased every three to four days to a maximum total of 4 mg daily. Dosage for alcohol withdrawal usually totals from 2–2.5 mg daily given in several small doses throughout the day.

The starting dose for treating panic disorder is 0.5 mg three times daily. This dosage may be increased every three to four days until the total daily dosage ranges from 2–10 mg. The total amount should be divided in at least three even daily doses. Average doses for anxiety associated with depression range from 2.5–3 mg daily divided into even doses.

Precautions

Alprazolam should not be used by patients who are pregnant, have narrow angle glaucoma, take ketoconazole or itraconazole, or those who are allergic to this or any other benzodiazepine drug. The dose of alprazolam must be carefully regulated and individualized in the elderly (over age 60), people with liver or kidney disease, and those taking other medications used to treat mental disorders.

Because alprazolam is a nervous system and respiratory depressant, it should not be taken with other similar depressants, such as alcohol, other **sedatives**, sleeping pills, or tranquilizers. People taking this drug, should not drive, operate dangerous machinery, or engage in hazardous activities that require mental alertness at least until they see how the drug affects them.

Alprazolam should be used under close physician supervision in patients with history of **substance abuse**. Like other benzodiazepines, alprazolam can be habit-forming. Risk and severity of dependence appears greater in patients taking doses larger than 4 mg daily. However, smaller doses may cause dependence if alprazolam is taken longer than 12 weeks.

Suddenly discontinuing alprazolam after several weeks may cause uncomfortable symptoms of withdrawal. Withdrawal symptoms in people who have taken alprazolam three months or longer may include **seizures**, anxiety, nervousness, and headache. Patients should discuss with their doctor how to gradually discontinue alprazolam use to avoid such symptoms.

Side effects

The most common side effects of alprazolam include sedation, dizziness, drowsiness, **insomnia**, and nervousness. The intensity of these side effects usually declines gradually and subsides in about eight weeks. A drop in blood pressure and an increase in heart rate may also occur in people who are taking alprazolam.

Decreased sex drive, menstrual disorders, and both weight gain and weight loss has been associated with use of alprazolam. People who experience the side effects of stomach upset, nausea, vomiting, and dry mouth should eat frequent, small meals and/or chew sugarless gum. Alprazolam has been associated with both diarrhea and constipation, as well as tremor, muscle cramps, vision disturbances, and rash.

Interactions

Alprazolam interacts with a long list of other medications. Anyone starting this drug should review the other medications they are taking with their physician and pharmacist for possible interactions. The most severe interactions occur with antifungal medications, such as ketoconazole, itraconazole, and fluconazole. These are associated with alprazolam toxicity (excessive sedation, **fatigue**, slurred speech, slowed reactions and other types of psychomotor impairment).

Estrogens (female hormones), erythromycin (an antibiotic), **fluoxetine** (Prozac, Sarafem), cimetidine (Tagamet), isoniazid, and **disulfiram** (Antabuse) can increase the effects of alprazolam. Carbamazepine can make alprazolam less effective. When alprazolam is

KEY TERMS

Benzodiazepines—A group of central nervous system depressants used to relieve anxiety or to induce sleep.

Glaucoma—A group of eye diseases characterized by increased pressure within the eye significant enough to damage eye tissue and structures. If untreated, glaucoma results in blindness.

combined with other sedative drugs (tranquilizers, sleeping pills) or alcohol, its depressants effects are more intense. These combinations should be avoided.

Resources

BOOKS

Kay, Jerald. *Psychiatry: Behavioral Science and Clinical Essentials.* Philadelphia: W. B. Saunders Company, 2000.

Lacy, Charles F. *Drug Information Handbook.* Hudson, OH: Lexi-Comp, Inc. 2002.

Pharmacia and Upjohn Company Staff. *Product Information: Xanax, alprazolam.* Kalamazoo, MI: Pharmacia and Upjohn Company, 1999.

Ajna Hamidovic, Pharm.D.

Alzheimer's disease

Definition

Alzheimer's disease, or AD, is a progressive, incurable disease of the **brain** caused by the degeneration and eventual death of neurons (nerve cells) in several areas of the brain.

Description

Patients with AD first lose such mental functions as short-term memory and the ability to learn new things. In the later stages of AD they gradually lose control over their sense of orientation, their emotions, and other aspects of behavior. End-stage AD is characterized by loss of control of body functions, an increased likelihood of **seizures**, loss of the ability to eat or swallow, and eventual death from infection or malnutrition. Alzheimer's disease is the most common cause of **dementia** (loss of cognitive abilities) in people aged 65 and older; it is thought to be responsible for 50%–70% of cases of dementia in the United States.

A nurse works with a patient with Alzheimer's *(AP Images)*

Alzheimer's disease was first identified in 1906 by a German **psychiatrist** and neuroanatomist named Alois Alzheimer. He was studying slides prepared from the brain of a fifty-one-year-old woman, known as Frau D., who had died after several years of dementia with symptoms that did not fit the definition of any brain disorder known at the time. Alzheimer was the first to describe the plaques and neurofibrillary tangles that are now used to identify AD at autopsy. Plaques are clumps or clusters of dead or dying nerve cells and other cellular debris found in the brains of patients with Alzheimer's disease. Neurofibrillary tangles are the accumulations of twisted protein fragments found inside nerve cells in the brains of patients with AD. Because dementia had been associated with elderly people and Frau D. had been middle-aged, AD was first known as presenile dementia, and was thought to be a very rare disorder. It was not until the early 1950s that researchers at St. Elizabeth's Hospital in Washington, D.C., came to recognize that AD is the single most common cause of dementia in adults.

Alzheimer's disease is now considered a very serious public health problem because of the growing numbers of people who are affected by it, the increasing length of their lives, and the direct and indirect costs of their care. It is estimated that 4.5 million people in the United States had AD as of 2006. About 5% of people between the ages of 65 and 74, and almost 50% of people aged 85 and older, have AD. The number of cases of AD is expected to more than triple by 2050. The direct and indirect costs of caring for Americans with AD is estimated to be at least $100 billion annually.

Types of Alzheimer's disease

There are two different types of Alzheimer's disease.

FAMILIAL AD. Familial AD is a rare form of Alzheimer's disease found in fewer than 10% of AD patients. It develops before the age of 65, and is caused by gene mutations on chromosomes 1, 14 or 21.

SPORADIC OR LATE-ONSET AD. Sporadic or late-onset AD is the most common form of the disease; its symptoms usually begin to appear after age 65. The cause of this type of AD is unknown. Having a particular form of the APOE gene, located on chromosome 19, increases the risk of this type of AD.

Stages

Health care professionals use the term "insidious" to describe AD, which means that it is very gradual in onset. Many times people recognize the first symptoms of the disorder in a friend or family member only in hindsight. In addition, the present generation of people old enough to be at risk for AD is the first generation in history to know what the **diagnosis** means; there are therefore very powerful emotional reasons for attributing the early signs of AD to normal aging, job **stress**, adjusting to retirement, and other less troubling factors. The insidious onset of AD is a characteristic, however, that allows doctors to distinguish it from other causes of dementia, including **vascular dementia**.

EARLY-STAGE ALZHEIMER'S. Early-stage Alzheimer's disease may begin almost imperceptibly. The first symptoms usually include short-term memory loss, temporary episodes of spatial disorientation, groping for words while one is speaking, minor problems with arithmetic, and small errors of judgment. For example, the person may light a stove burner under a saucepan before noticing that he has forgotten to put the food or water in the pan first, or he may have difficulty balancing a checkbook as quickly as he used to. At this stage in the disease, however, the patient can usually keep up with most activities of daily life. Although some persons at this point can still operate a motor vehicle safely, it is advisable to consult a physician about possible impairment behind the wheel. Many patients with early-stage AD voluntarily give up their driver's licenses for their own safety and that of other drivers on the roads.

MIDDLE-STAGE ALZHEIMER'S. In the middle stage, which typically begins two to three years after onset, the person begins to lose awareness of his or her cognitive deficits. Memory lapses are more frequent and the person begins to have more severe problems with language. Unlike early-stage AD, the problems caused by loss of cognitive functioning are impossible to ignore. The middle stage of AD is the point at which the behavioral and psychiatric symptoms that are so stressful to caregivers often begin—the agitation, wandering, temper outbursts, **depression**, and disorientation. The patient is at high risk for falls and similar accidents. In addition, the patient becomes increasingly unable to understand simple instructions or to follow a conversation, and begins to lose his or her basic sense of personal identity.

END-STAGE ALZHEIMER'S. End-stage Alzheimer's disease is marked by the loss of the ability to walk and eventually even to sit up. Patients may be able to use a wheelchair for awhile, but eventually become completely bedridden. They lose bladder and bowel control. When the disease begins to affect the patient's brain stem, the basic processes of digestion, respiration, and excretion shut down. Patients usually stop eating at this point and sleep most of the time. The hands and feet begin to feel cold, the breathing becomes shallow, and the patient is generally unresponsive to caregivers. Eventually the patient's breathing simply stops.

Causes and symptoms

Causes

Evidence has accumulated that Alzheimer's disease is multifactorial—that is, it is caused by a combination of several genetic and environmental factors.

GENETIC. Early-onset AD is caused by a defect in one of three genes known as APP, presenilin-1 (PS1), and presenilin-2 (PS2). The APP gene is found on chromosome 21. People with Down syndrome, who have three copies of chromosome 21, develop an Alzheimer's type dementia if they live longer than 40 years of age. A family history of Down syndrome is associated with a greater risk of developing early-onset AD. Mutations of the APP gene are associated with an onset of AD between the ages of 55 and 60.

The PS1 gene is found on chromosome 14, and the PS2 gene is found on chromosome 1. Mutations in these genes are associated with an onset of AD between 30 and 50 years.

The APP, PS1 and PS2 gene mutations are very rare, and only account for about 5% of all cases of AD.

Genetic research indicates that late-onset Alzheimer's disease is a polygenic disorder; that is, its development is influenced by more than one gene. It has been known since 1993 that a specific form of a gene for apolipoprotein E (APOE4) on human chromosome 19 is a genetic risk factor for late-onset AD. People who inherit the APOE4 gene from both parents have a greater chance of developing AD than those who inherit the gene from only one parent. About 65% of people with AD have at least one copy of the APOE4 gene. One of the remaining puzzles about this particular gene, however, is that it is not a consistent marker for AD. In other words, some people who have the APOE4 gene do not develop AD, and some who do not have the gene do develop the disorder. Researchers are working on identifying other genes that may also influence people's susceptibility to AD.

Familial Alzheimer's disease appears to be related to abnormal genes on human chromosomes 21 and 14.

NEUROBIOLOGICAL. Investigators since Alois Alzheimer's time have studied the abnormalities found at autopsy in the brains of patients with AD. One abnormality is plaques, or clumps, of a sticky protein called beta amyloid. Beta amyloid is formed when a substance called amyloid precursor protein, or APP, fails to be metabolized properly in the body. After beta amyloid is formed, pieces of it then stick to one another and gradually build up into plaques. The other abnormal finding is neurofibrillary tangles, which are twisted threads of a protein called tau that form inside nerve cells. If the tau protein is damaged by the addition of molecules of phosphorus, a process called hyperphosphorylation, it forms filaments that twist around each other to form the neurofibrillary tangles. Research suggests that the abnormal tau protein may be caused by increases in amyloid. As the plaques and tangles accumulate in the brain, they cause the nerve cells to wither and eventually die. As the nerve cells die, the affected parts of the brain start to shrink in size. It is still not known, however, whether the plaques and tangles are causes of AD or results of it.

Another nervous system abnormality in AD is the lowered level of **neurotransmitters** produced by the cells in the brain. Neurotransmitters are chemicals that carry nerve impulses across the small gaps (synapses) between nerve cells. The neurotransmitters affected by Alzheimer's include serotonin, norepinephrine, and acetylcholine. Many of the behavioral and psychiatric problems associated with AD are thought to result from the inadequate supply of these neurotransmitters.

ENVIRONMENTAL. Researchers have been studying the possibility that certain chemicals or other toxins in the environment may have a role in causing or triggering AD. The environmental factors that have been considered include aluminum, zinc, toxins in contaminated food, viruses, and a history of head trauma.

RISK FACTORS. A number of factors have been identified that increase a person's risk of developing Alzheimer's:

- Age. The risk of developing AD rises after age 65, and rises sharply after age 75. While 1% of the population has AD at age 65, almost 50% of those over 85 have it.
- Sex. Women are more likely to develop AD than men. However, it is not known whether women are more susceptible to the disorder or more likely to develop it because they live longer than men, on average.
- Family history of AD.
- Having Down syndrome.
- History of head injury.
- Substances in the environment. Higher-than-average amounts of aluminum have been found in the brains of patients with AD. Some researchers in the late 1990s thought that exposure to aluminum might be a risk factor for the disorder. It now appears that the levels of aluminum in the brains of patients are a result rather than a cause of AD.
- Low occupational attainment and education level. Studies have found a clear correlation between employment in jobs that are not mentally challenging and an increased risk of AD. In addition, taking less rather than more challenging jobs as one grows older is associated with a higher risk of AD.
- High systolic blood pressure.
- High blood cholesterol levels. When both high systolic blood pressure and high cholesterol are present, the risk of developing AD increases by a factor of 3.5.
- Mild cognitive impairment (MCI). Mild cognitive impairment is a transitional decline in cognitive functioning that precedes the onset of AD. MCI is characterized primarily by memory loss while other cognitive functions remain intact. Persons with MCI are at higher risk for AD than people who do not develop the condition; 12% of people with mild cognitive impairment develop Alzheimer's disease each year, compared with 1–2% per year of people without MCI. After four years, 40% of people diagnosed with mild cognitive impairment have clear symptoms of Alzheimer's disease.
- Diet. Researchers suspect that a high-cholesterol, high-fat diet may be implicated in the onset of AD. High levels of an amino acid called homocysteine may also be a risk factor for late-onset AD.

Symptoms

The symptoms of AD can be grouped into three categories: cognitive deficits, or losses of brain function related to memory and learning; behavioral and psychiatric symptoms of dementia, or BPSD; and problems with activities of daily life, or ADLs.

COGNITIVE DEFICITS. There are four major symptoms of loss of cognitive capacities in AD:

- Amnesia. Amnesia refers to memory impairment; however, loss of short-term memory also means that the patient loses his or her sense of time as well.
- Aphasia. Aphasia refers to loss of language function. The person may not remember the names of objects and may use words like "thing" or "it" instead; they may echo what other people say or repeat a word or phrase over and over. On occasion the person may lose the ability to speak except for curse words.
- Apraxia. Apraxia is the loss of the ability to perform voluntary movements in the absence of paralysis. For example, person with apraxia may have trouble putting on a hospital gown or brushing his or her teeth.
- Agnosia. Agnosia comes from a Greek word that means "to not know", and refers to inability to recognize familiar places and people. Patients with agnosia may even fail to recognize their own face in a mirror.

NEUROPSYCHIATRIC SYMPTOMS. Symptoms associated with BPSD include:

- Depression. Depression associated with AD is thought to result from the lowered production of the neurotransmitter serotonin. Depression in AD can be treated with medication, usually with one of the selective serotonin reuptake inhibitors, or SSRIs.
- Delusions. A delusion is a false belief that a person maintains even when presented with contrary evidence. For example, patients with AD may say that a person is stealing their things when they cannot remember where they have put them. Suspicions of other people caused by delusions can sometimes be treated with medication.
- Wandering. This behavior may result from becoming disoriented and getting lost, but sometimes people with AD wander for no apparent reason. The Alzheimer's Association in Chicago has a Safe Return Hotline that can be contacted for information about registering a patient with AD. If the registered patient should wander from home, the Safe Return Hotline can help identify the patient and return him or her to their family or nursing home.
- Hallucinations. Like delusions, hallucinations in AD patients are thought to be related to the deterioration of the patient's brain tissue. In a hallucination, the patient has a sensory experience that is real to him or her but not to other people. Hallucinations can affect any of the senses, but most are either visual or auditory. For example, a patient with AD may say that he or she sees little Martians in the corner of the room,

or that he or she hears the voice of a long-dead parent calling to them. Hallucinations are sometimes caused by medications that the patient may be taking.

- Aggression. Aggression refers to hitting, shoving, pushing, or threatening behavior.
- Agitation. Agitation refers to emotionally excited behavior (screaming, shouting, cursing, pacing, fidgeting, etc.) that is disruptive or unsafe. Agitation may result from the changes in the patient's brain tissue, or it may be a symptom of depression associated with Alzheimer's disease.

For most of the twentieth century, studies of patients with AD focused on the cognitive symptoms of the disorder. It was not until the 1980s and 1990s that researchers began to look more closely at the behavioral and psychiatric symptoms of AD. Such methods of standardized assessment of these symptoms as the neuropsychiatric inventory are very recent developments.

PROBLEMS WITH ACTIVITIES OF DAILY LIVING (ADLS). Needing help with ADLs, or personal care activities that are part of everyday living, is among the earliest symptoms of AD. The functions that are often affected include:

- eating, including simple cooking and washing dishes
- bathing, showering, or shaving
- grooming and dressing in clothing appropriate to the weather and activity
- toileting
- other aspects of personal hygiene (brushing teeth or cleaning dentures, washing hair, etc.)
- shopping for groceries and other necessary items

Health care professionals usually assess the ADLs of a patient diagnosed with AD in order to determine what type of care is needed.

Demographics

Some demographic statistics in the developed countries have already been cited in the context of risk factors for AD and public health concerns related to the disorder.

AD is thought to be less prevalent in non-Western developed countries such as Japan, and in less industrialized countries such as India and Nigeria. However, relatively little is known about the demographics of AD and other forms of dementia in the developing countries. Alzheimer's Disease International, which is based in London, supports a group of researchers called the 10/66 Dementia Research Group. The 10/66 group is trying to correct the global imbalance of

AD research; as of 2001, fewer than 10% of all population-based research studies of AD and related forms of dementia have been directed toward the 66% of people with these disorders who live outside the developed countries.

Diagnosis

Currently, the diagnosis of AD is essentially a process of exclusion. A skilled physician can diagnose probable AD with 90% accuracy, but the diagnosis can only be confirmed post mortem (after death), by performing an autopsy and examining the patient's brain tissue.

Diagnostic evaluation of AD

At present, the diagnostic process includes the following components:

- Clinical interview. In the absence of laboratory tests or imaging studies that can provide definite diagnoses, the physician must rely on his or her clinical judgment. In evaluating the patient, the doctor will assess signs of cognitive impairment other than short-term memory loss. In most cases, the doctor will ask a family member or close friend of the patient about the suddenness of symptom onset and the length of time that the patient seems to have been impaired.
- Physical examination. The patient will be given a complete physical and have blood and urine samples taken to rule out vitamin deficiencies, head trauma, tertiary syphilis, thyroid disorders, and other possible causes of dementia. The doctor will also review all the medications that the patient is taking (including alternative remedies) in order to exclude reversible dementia caused by drug interactions.
- Neurological examination. In early AD, the neurological findings are usually normal. If the patient appears to have had a stroke, he or she will be referred for a more thorough assessment by a neurologist.
- Tests of cognitive function. The patient will be given the mini-mental status examination (MMSE) and such other tests of cognitive function as the clock test or verbal fluency tests. The MMSE is a screening test and should not be used by itself to make the diagnosis of AD. In addition, the MMSE is not very sensitive in detecting cognitive impairment in people who previously functioned at a high level and were well educated. It is possible for a well-educated person to score a perfect 30 on the MMSE and still have cognitive impairment. The clock test is a test in which patients are asked to draw a clock face. Sometimes, patients will also be asked to include a specific time on the clock, such as 3:20. Patients with AD often draw the face of the clock with numbers out of order, or all of the hour markers in a portion of the clock face instead of evenly spaced around the face, and often have difficulty adding the clock hands.

- Neuropsychiatric evaluation. A neuropsychiatric examination may be given to determine the pattern of the patient's cognitive impairment and probe his or her level of functioning more deeply. The patient may be asked to write a sample check, to describe how they answer the phone, to interpret sample traffic signs, and to look at a shopping list and pick out the items on the list from a display.
- Diagnostic imaging. Imaging studies are useful in detecting such causes of dementia as a previously undiagnosed brain tumor or abnormal brain structure. Scans can show doctors that certain areas of the brain have lost tissue (as happens in AD), and can strengthen a physician's suspicion of a patient's AD diagnosis, but scans cannot diagnose AD on their own. Scans are used more to rule out other possible diagnoses and to confirm a suspected diagnosis. CT (computed tomography) scans are commonly performed, as well as MRI (magnetic resonance imaging) scans in patients who are having problems with gait or balance. PET (positron emission tomography) and SPECT (single photon emission computed tomography) scans can be used to evaluate patterns of glucose (sugar) metabolism in the brain and to differentiate the patterns that are characteristic of Alzheimer's from those associated with vascular dementia and Pick's disease. PET scans are more precise than SPECT scans, but their cost may be prohibitive.

Ethical considerations

A blood test can determine whether a person has the APOE4 gene. However, since APOE4 is only a risk factor for AD rather than a cause, the test cannot determine whether a person will develop AD. The National Institute on Aging does not recommend using the test to screen people for AD. One reason is that the test results are not conclusive—some people who eventually develop AD do not carry this gene, and some people who carry the gene do not develop AD. Another important reason is that there are ethical implications of testing for a disease that presently has no cure, in terms of the psychological consequences for patients and their families and the possible loss of health insurance and job opportunities for people found to be carrying the gene. These considerations may change, however, if researchers discover better treatments for

Acetylcholine—A naturally occurring chemical in the body that transmits nerve impulses from cell to cell. Generally, it has opposite effects from dopamine and norepinephrine; it causes blood vessels to dilate, lowers blood pressure, and slows the heartbeat. Central nervous system well-being is dependent on a balance among acetylcholine, dopamine, serotonin, and norepinephrine.

Agitation—Excessive restlessness or emotional disturbance that is often associated with anxiety or psychosis. Agitation may be associated with middle-stage Alzheimer's disease.

Agnosia—Loss of the ability to recognize familiar people, places, and objects.

Amygdala—An almond-shaped brain structure in the limbic system that is activated in stressful situations to trigger the emotion of fear. It is thought that the emotional overreactions in Alzheimer's patients are related to the destruction of neurons in the amygdala.

Amyloid—A waxy translucent substance composed mostly of protein, that forms plaques (abnormal deposits) in the brain during the progression of Alzheimer's disease.

Aphasia—Loss of language abilities.

Apolipoprotein E—A protein that transports cholesterol through the body. One form of this protein, APOE4, is associated with a 60% risk of late-onset AD.

Apraxia—Inability to perform purposeful movements that is not caused by paralysis or loss of feeling.

Beta amyloid protein—A starchy substance that builds up in the brains of people with AD to form the plaques that are characteristic of the disease. Beta amyloid is formed when amyloid precursor protein, or APP, is not broken down properly by the body.

Bleomycin hydrolase—An enzyme involved in the body's processing of amyloid precursor protein. If the gene that governs production of BH mutates, the APP accumulates, producing the plaques in the brains of patients with AD.

Brain stem—The part of the brain that is continuous with the spinal cord and controls most basic life functions. It is the last part of the brain that is destroyed by Alzheimer's disease.

Cholinesterase inhibitors—A group of medications given to slow the progression of Alzheimer's disease.

Delirium—A disturbance of consciousness marked by confusion, difficulty paying attention, delusions, hallucinations, or restlessness. It can be distinguished from dementia by its relatively sudden onset and variation in the severity of the symptoms.

Dementia—A group of symptoms (syndrome) associated with a progressive loss of memory and other intellectual functions that is serious enough to interfere with a person's ability to perform the tasks of daily life. Dementia impairs memory, alters personality, leads to deterioration in personal grooming, impairs reasoning ability, and causes disorientation.

primary dementia, more effective preventive methods, or more reliable genetic markers for AD.

Treatments

At present the mainstay of Alzheimer's treatment is medication, both to slow symptom progression and to manage the behavioral and psychiatric symptoms of AD.

Medications to slow symptom progression

The medications most commonly given to delay the progression of symptoms in AD are a group of drugs called cholinesterase inhibitors. These drugs were approved by the FDA over a decade ago. They work by slowing down the body's destruction of the neurotransmitter acetylcholine.

The cholinesterase inhibitors include:

• Tacrine (Cognex). This drug is the oldest cholinesterase inhibitor in use. It is used less often than newer

agents because it must be taken four times a day and may cause liver damage.

• Donepezil (Aricept). This drug is the one used most commonly as of 2002 to treat AD. It has fewer side effects than tacrine and can be given in one daily dose.

• Rivastigmine (Exelon). This drug is taken twice daily.

• Galantamine (Reminyl). This is the newest cholinesterase inhibitor, approved in late 2001. It acts on an additional acetylcholine receptor.

None of these medications provides more than modest benefits to patients with AD: they slow the progression of symptoms for about six months to a year in one-third to one-half of patients with AD. In addition, the cholinesterase inhibitors have side effects, most commonly nausea, vomiting, diarrhea, muscle cramps, and sleep disturbances.

Another medication that has recently been approved for AD is **memantine** (Namenda). Meman-

Down syndrome—A genetic disorder characterized by an extra chromosome 21 (trisomy 21), mental retardation, and susceptibility to early-onset Alzheimer's disease.

Gingko—A shade tree native to China with fan-shaped leaves and fleshy seeds with edible kernels. Gingko extract is being studied as a possible complementary or adjunctive treatment for Alzheimer's disease.

Hallucination—False sensory perceptions. A person experiencing a hallucination may "hear" sounds or "see" people or objects that are not really present. Hallucinations can also affect the senses of smell, touch, and taste.

Hippocampus—A part of the brain that is involved in memory formation and learning. The hippocampus is shaped like a curved ridge and belongs to an organ system called the limbic system.

Insidious—Proceeding gradually and inconspicuously but with serious effect.

Mild cognitive impairment (MCI)—A transitional phase of memory loss in older people that precedes dementia or Alzheimer's disease.

Neurofibrillary tangles—Accumulations of twisted protein fragments found inside the nerve cells in the brains of patients with Alzheimer's disease.

Neurotransmitters—Chemicals that carry nerve impulses from one nerve cell to another. Alzheimer's disease causes a drop in the production of several important neurotransmitters.

Plaques—Clumps or clusters of beta amyloid fragments, dead or dying nerve cells, and other cellular debris, found in the brains of patients with Alzheimer's disease.

Polygenic—A trait or disorder that is determined by a group of genes acting together. Most human characteristics, including height, weight, and general body build, are polygenic. Schizophrenia and late-onset Alzheimer's disease are considered polygenic disorders.

Post mortem—After death. The definitive diagnosis of Alzheimer's disease can be made only after the patient's death.

Presenile dementia—An older name for Alzheimer's disease.

Pseudodementia—A term for a depression with symptoms resembling those of dementia. The term "dementia of depression" is now preferred.

Systolic—Referring to the rhythmic contraction of the heart (systole), when the blood in the chambers of the heart is forced out. Systolic blood pressure is blood pressure measured during this phase.

Tau protein—A protein that is involved in maintaining the internal structure of nerve cells. The tau protein is damaged in Alzheimer's disease and ends up forming the neurofibrillary tangles.

tine is thought to regulate the activity of a neurotransmitter called glutamate. When used alone or together with donezapil, it appears to help AD patients to function better cognitively.

Because brain inflammation may contribute to AD, researchers are studying nonsteroidal anti-inflammatory drugs, such as celecoxib (Celebrex) and naproxen (Aleve), to see whether they can slow the onset of AD. Recent studies have shown that naproxen and another anti-inflammatory nonsteroid drug, rofecoxib (Vioxx) do not, however, slow the progression of AD in people who have already developed AD.

Medications for BPSD

Medications are also prescribed to manage the behavioral and psychiatric symptoms of AD, which are often quite stressful for caregivers if the patient is being cared for at home. These medications are usually prescribed for specific symptoms:

- Delusions: Antipsychotic drugs, usually haloperidol (Haldol) or risperidone (Risperdal).
- Agitation: Short-term anti-anxiety drugs, usually lorazepam (Ativan) or buspirone (BuSpar).
- Depression: One of the selective serotonin reuptake inhibitors (SSRIs), at half the dosage for a young adult.
- Pain: Acetaminophen or a very low dose of codeine.

In general, older patients require lower dosages than those given to younger adults. Patients with AD are also more susceptible to the side effects of medications. For these reasons, physicians often recommend making changes in the patient's environment to reduce the behavioral symptoms before trying medications.

Alternative and complementary treatments

Some complementary therapies have been shown to benefit patients with Alzheimer's.

NATUROPATHY. A naturopathic approach to AD includes supplementing antioxidant vitamins (vitamins A, E, and C) in the patient's diet, along with adding carotenoids, small amounts of selenium and zinc, and thiamine. Research shows that vitamin E can slow the progression of some symptoms of AD by about seven months. Currently, research is being done to find out whether vitamin E can prevent or delay AD in patients who have MCI. Botanical supplements that have been said to improve cognitive function include an extract made from *Gingko biloba*, a tree that is native to China. GBE, or gingko biloba extract, is the most frequently used herbal medicine in Europe. It is available in Germany by prescription and in an over-the-counter form, and has been approved by the German Commission E for dementia-related memory loss. Gingko extract is thought to work in a manner similar to the cholinesterase inhibitors. At present, the National Center for Complementary and Alternative Medicine (NCCAM) is conducting studies of gingko extract as a treatment for Alzheimer's.

MUSIC THERAPY. Music therapy has been found to calm agitated patients with AD, to improve mood, and to enhance long-term memory. Old familiar songs are particularly effective in improving recall. In other studies, music therapy has been shown to reduce sensations of **chronic pain** in patients with AD.

Prognosis

There is no cure for Alzheimer's disease. The prognosis is progressive loss of mental and bodily functions leading to death within seven to ten years. Some patients, however, die within three years of diagnosis and others may survive for as long as fifteen.

Prevention

Researchers are considering several different strategies to prevent AD. A vaccine to prevent the formation of beta amyloid plaques was initially tested in animals, but **clinical trials** in humans were stopped because of dangerous side effects. Research on new treatment approaches continues.

See also Dementia; Mini mental state examination (MMSE).

Resources

BOOKS

American Psychiatric Association. *Diagnostic and Statistical Manual of Mental Disorders*. 4th edition, text revised. Washington, DC: American Psychiatric Association, 2000.

Butcher, James N., Susan Mineka, and Jill M. Hooley, *Abnormal Psychology*. Boston, MA: Pearson Education, Inc., 2007.

Keck, David. *Forgetting Whose We Are: Alzheimer's Disease and the Love of God*. Nashville, TN: Abingdon Press, 1996.

Mace, Nancy L., and Peter V. Rabins. *The 36-Hour Day*. Revised and updated edition. New York: Warner Books, Inc., 2001; by arrangement with The Johns Hopkins University Press.

Pelletier, Kenneth R., MD. *The Best Alternative Medicine*. Part II. "CAM Therapies for Specific Conditions: Alzheimer's Disease." New York: Simon and Schuster, 2002.

Shenk, David. *The Forgetting: Alzheimer's: Portrait of an Epidemic*. New York: Doubleday, 2001.

PERIODICALS

Aisen, P. S., J. Schmeidler, and G. M. Pasinetti. "Randomized Pilot Study of Nimesulide Treatment in Alzheimer's Disease." *Neurology* 58 (April 9, 2002): 1050-1054.

Bone, Kerry. "Gingko and Alzheimer's Disease." *Townsend Letter for Doctors and Patients* (January 2001): 27.

Delargarza, V.W., MD. "Pharmacologic Treatment of Alzheimer's Disease: An Update." *American Family Physician* 68, no. 7 (October 1, 2003): 1365-1372.

Desai, P. P., H. C. Hendrie, R. M. Evans, and others. "Genetic Variation in Apolipoprotein D Affects the Risk of Alzheimer's Disease in African Americans." *American Journal of Human Genetics* 69 (October 2001): 416.

Editorial Commentary. "Neuropsychiatric Phenomena in Alzheimer's Disease." *Journal of Neurology, Neurosurgery and Psychiatry* 71 (December 2001): 715.

"Head Injury Linked to Increased Risk of Alzheimer's Disease." *FDA Consumer* 35 (January-February 2001): 8.

Holmes, C., H. Smith, R. Ganderton, and others. "Psychosis and Aggression in Alzheimer's Disease: The Effect of Dopamine Receptor Gene Variation." *Journal of Neurology, Neurosurgery and Psychiatry* 71 (December 2001): 777-779.

in't Veld, Bas A., Annemieke Ruitenberg, Albert Hofman, and others. "Nonsteroidal Anti-inflammatory Drugs and the Risk of Alzheimer's Disease." *New England Journal of Medicine* 345 (November 22, 2001): 1515-1521.

Khosh, Farhang. "Naturopathic Approach to Alzheimer's Disease." *Townsend Letter for Doctors and Patients* (July 2001): 22-24.

Kim, S. Y., J. H. Karlawish, E. D. Caine. "Current State of Research on Decision-Making Competence of Cognitively Impaired Elderly Persons." *American Journal of Geriartic Psychiatry* 10 (March-April 2002): 151-165.

Kivipelto, M., and others. "Midlife Vascular Risk Factors and Alzheimer's Disease in Later Life: Longitudinal, Population-Based Study." *British Medical Journal* 322 (June 16, 2001): 1447-1451.

Langbart, C. "Diagnosing and Treating Alzheimer's Disease: A Practitioner's Overview." *Journal of the American Academy of Nurse Practitioners* 14 (March 2002): 103-109.

Luedecking-Zimmer, E., S. T. DeKosky, M. I. Kamboh. "Candidate Genes for Late-Onset Alzheimer's Disease on Chromosome 12." *American Journal of Human Genetics* 69 (October 2001): 518.

Olin, J. T., I. R. Katz, B. S. Meyers, and others. "Provisional Diagnostic Criteria for Depression of Alzheimer Disease: Rationale and Background." *American Journal of Geriatric Psychiatry* 10 (March-April 2002): 129-141.

Shigenobu, K., M. Ikeda, R. Fukuhara, and others. "Reducing the Burden of Caring for Alzheimer's Disease Through the Amelioration of 'Delusions of Theft' by Drug Therapy." *International Journal of Geriatric Psychiatry* 17 (March 2002): 211-217.

Silverman, Daniel H. S., Gary W. Small, Carol Y. Chang, and others. "Positron Emission Tomography in Evaluation of Dementia: Regional Brain Metabolism and Long-Term Outcome." *Journal of the American Medical Association* 286 (November 7, 2001): 2120.

Sloane, P. D., S. Zimmerman, C. Suchindran, and others. "The Public Health Impact of Alzheimer's Disease, 2000-2050: Potential Implication of Treatment Advances." *Annual Review of Public Health* 23 (2002): 213-231.

Walsh, D. M., I. Klyubin, J. V. Fadeeva, and others. "Naturally Secreted Oligomers of Amyloid Beta Protein Potently Inhibit Hippocampal Long-Term Potentiation in Vivo." *Nature* 416 (April 4, 2002): 535-539.

ORGANIZATIONS

Alzheimer's Association. 919 North Michigan Avenue, Suite 1100, Chicago, IL 60611-1676. Telephone: (800) 272-3900 or (312) 335-8700. Fax: (312) 335-1110. <www.alz.org>.

Alzheimer's Disease Education and Referral (ADEAR) Center. P. O. Box 8250, Silver Spring, MD 20907-8250. Telephone: (800) 438-4380. <www.alzheimers.org>.

Alzheimer's Disease International. 45–46 Lower Marsh, London SE1 7RG, UK. Telephone: (+44) 20-7620-3011. Fax: (+44) 20-7401-7351. <www.alz.co.uk>.

National Center for Complementary and Alternative Medicine (NCCAM) Clearinghouse. P.O. Box 7923, Gaithersburg, MD 20898. Telephone: (888) 644-6226. TTY: (866) 464-3615. Fax: (866) 464-3616. <www.nccam.nih.gov>.

National Institute of Mental Health. 6001 Executive Boulevard, Room 8184, MSC 9663, Bethesda, MD 20892-9663. Telephone: (301) 443-4513. <www.nimh.nih.gov>.

National Institute of Neurological Disorders and Stroke (NINDS). Building 31, Room 8A06, 9000 Rockville Pike, Bethesda, MD 20892. Telephone: (301) 496-5751. <www.ninds.nih.gov>.

OTHER

Alzheimer's Association. *Alzheimer's Disease Fact Sheet.* (June 2, 2004).

Alzheimer's Disease Education and Referral (ADEAR) Center. *Alzheimer's Disease Genetics Fact Sheet* NIH Publication No. 03-3431. (August, 2004).

Alzheimer's Disease Education and Referral (ADEAR) Center. *Alzheimer's Disease Fact Sheet* NIH Publication No. 06-3431. (July, 2006).

Safe Return Hotline. (888) 572-8566. This hotline provides information about registering a patient with AD with the Alzheimer's Association as a means of identification in the event that he or she wanders away from home.

Rebecca Frey, Ph.D.
Ruvanee Pietersz Vilhauer, PhD

Amantadine

Definition

Amantadine is a synthetic antiviral agent that also has strong antiparkinsonian properties. It is sold in the United States under the brand name Symmetrel, and is also available under its generic name.

Purpose

Amantadine is used to treat a group of side effects (called parkinsonian side effects) that include tremors, difficulty walking, and slack muscle tone. These side effects may occur in patients who are taking antipsychotic medications used to treat mental disorders such as **schizophrenia**. An unrelated use of amantadine is in the treatment of viral infections of some strains of influenza A.

Description

Some medicines, called antipsychotic drugs, that are used to treat schizophrenia and other mental disorders can cause side effects similar to the symptoms of Parkinson's disease. The patient does not have Parkinson's disease, but may experience shaking in muscles while at rest, difficulty with voluntary movements, and poor muscle tone.

One way to eliminate these undesirable side effects is to stop taking the antipsychotic medicine. Unfortunately, the symptoms of the original mental disorder usually come back, so in most cases simply stopping the antipsychotic medication is not a reasonable option. Some drugs that control the symptoms of Parkinson's disease such as amantadine also control the parkinsonian side effects of antipsychotic medicines.

Amantadine works by restoring the chemical balance between **dopamine** and acetylcholine, two neurotransmitter chemicals in the **brain**. Taking amantadine along with the antipsychotic medicine helps to control symptoms of the mental disorder, while reducing parkinsonian side effects. Amantadine is in the same family of drugs (commonly known as anticholinergic drugs) as **biperiden** and **trihexyphenidyl**.

Recommended dosage

Amantadine is available in 100-mg tablets and capsules, as well as a syrup containing 50 mg of amantadine in each teaspoonful. For the treatment of drug-induced parkinsonian side effects, amantadine is usually given in a dose of 100 mg orally twice a day. Some patients may need a total daily dose as high as 300 mg. Patients who are taking other antiparkinsonian drugs at the same time may require lower daily doses of amantadine (e.g., 100 mg daily).

People with kidney disease or who are on hemodialysis must have their doses lowered. In these patients, doses may range from 100 mg daily to as little as 200 mg every seven days.

Precautions

Amantadine increases the amount of the neurotransmitter dopamine (a central nervous system stimulant) in the brain. Because of this, patients with a history of epilepsy or other seizure disorders should be carefully monitored while taking this drug. This is especially true in the elderly and in patients with kidney disease. Amantadine may cause visual disturbances and affect mental alertness and coordination. People should not operate dangerous machinery or motor vehicles while taking this drug.

Side effects

Five to ten percent of patients taking amantadine may experience the following nervous system side effects:

- dizziness or lightheadedness
- insomnia
- nervousness or anxiety
- impaired concentration

One to five percent of patients taking amantadine may experience the following nervous system side effects:

- irritability or agitation
- depression
- confusion
- lack of coordination
- sleepiness or nightmares
- fatigue
- headache

In addition, up to 1% of patients may experience **hallucinations**, euphoria (excitement), extreme forgetfulness, aggressive behavior, personality changes, or **seizures**. Seizures are the most serious of all the side effects associated with amantadine.

KEY TERMS

Acetylcholine—A naturally occurring chemical in the body that transmits nerve impulses from cell to cell. Generally, it has opposite effects from dopamine and norepinephrine; it causes blood vessels to dilate, lowers blood pressure, and slows the heartbeat. Central nervous system well-being is dependent on a balance among acetylcholine, dopamine, serotonin, and norepinephrine.

Anticholinergic—Related to the ability of a drug to block the nervous system chemical acetylcholine. When acetylcholine is blocked, patients often experience dry mouth and skin, increased heart rate, blurred vision, and difficulty in urinating. In severe cases, blocking acetylcholine may cloud thinking and cause delirium.

Dopamine—A chemical in brain tissue that serves to transmit nerve impulses (is a neurotransmitter) and helps to regulate movement and emotions.

Neurotransmitter—A chemical in the brain that transmits messages between neurons, or nerve cells.

Parkinsonian—Related to symptoms associated with Parkinson's disease, a nervous system disorder characterized by abnormal muscle movement of the tongue, face, and neck, inability to walk or move quickly, walking in a shuffling manner, restlessness, and/or tremors.

Gastrointestinal side effects may also occur in patients taking amantadine. Up to 10% of people taking this drug experience nausea and up to 5% have dry mouth, loss of appetite, constipation, and vomiting. In most situations, amantadine may be continued and these side effects treated symptomatically.

Between 1% and 5% of patients taking amantadine have also reported a bluish coloring of their skin (usually on the legs) that is associated with enlargement of the blood vessels (called livedo reticularis). This side effect usually appears within one month to one year of starting the drug and subsides within weeks to months after the drug is discontinued. People who think they may be experiencing this or other side effects from any medication should tell their physicians.

Interactions

Taking amantadine along with other drugs used to treat parkinsonian side effects may cause increased confusion or even hallucinations. The combination of amantadine and central nervous system stimulants (e.g., **amphetamines** or decongestants) may cause increased central nervous stimulation or increase the likelihood of seizures.

Resources

BOOKS

American Society of Health-System Pharmacists. *AHFS Drug Information 2002*. Bethesda, MD: American Society of Health-System Pharmacists, 2002.

PERIODICALS

Graham, Karen A., and others. "Double-Blind, Placebo-Controlled Investigation of Amantadine for Weight Loss in Subjects Who Gained Weight with Olanzapine." *American Journal of Psychiatry* 162. 9 (September 2005): 1744–46.

Martinez-Martin, Pablo, and others. "Impact of Fatigue in Parkinson's Disease: The Fatigue Impact Scale for Daily Use (D-FIS)." *Quality of Life Research: An International Journal of Quality of Life Aspects of Treatment, Care and Rehabilitation* 15. 4 (May 2006): 597–606.

Silver, Henry, and others. "A Double-Blind, Cross-Over Comparison of the Effects of Amantadine or Placebo on Visuomotor and Cognitive Function Medicated Schizophrenia Patients." *International Clinical Psychopharmacology* 20. 6 (November 2005): 319–26.

OTHER

Endo Pharmaceuticals, Inc. *SYMMETREL (Amantadine Hydrochloride, USP) Tablets and Syrup: Package Insert.* <http://www.endo.com/PDF/symmetrel_pack_insert.pdf>.

Jack Raber, Pharm.D.
Ruth A. Wienclaw, PhD

Ambien *see* **Zolpidem**

Amitriptyline

Definition

Amitriptyline is a medication used to treat various forms of **depression**, pain associated with the nerves (neuropathic pain), and to prevent migraine headaches. It is sold in the United States under the brand names Elavil and Endep.

Purpose

Amitriptyline helps relieve depression and pain. This medication, usually given at bedtime, also helps patients sleep better.

Description

This medication is one of several tricyclic **antidepressants**, so-called because of the three-ring chemical structure common to these drugs. Amitriptyline acts to block reabsorption of **neurotransmitters** (chemicals that transmit nerve messages in the **brain**). Amitriptyline and the other tricyclic antidepressants are primarily used to treat mental depression but are increasingly being replaced by a newer and more effective group of antidepressant drugs called **selective serotonin reuptake inhibitors** (**SSRIs**). Amitriptyline is sometimes prescribed to help treat pain associated with cancer. In addition, it is sometimes prescribed for various types of **chronic pain**. Tablets are available in 10, 25, 50, 70, and 150 mg.

Recommended dosage

The usual adult dose for pain management ranges from 10 mg to 150 mg at bedtime. Patients are generally started on a low dose and the amount may be increased as needed. Side effects, such as a dry mouth and drowsiness, may make it difficult to increase the dose in older adults. Bedtime dosing helps the patient sleep. Doctors generally prescribe 75–150 mg for depression. It is given at bedtime or in divided doses during the day. It may take 30 days for the patient to feel less depressed. Pain relief is usually noticed sooner than the mood change. Teens and older adults usually receive a lower dose. If the nightly dose is missed, it should not be taken the next morning. Taking amitriptyline during waking hours could result in noticeable side effects. Patients should check with their doctors if the daily dose is missed. Those on more than one dose per day should take a missed dose as soon as it is remembered but should not take two doses at the same time. While amitriptyline is usually administered orally, injectable amitriptyline is available. It should not be used in this form long-term; patients should switch to tablets as soon as possible.

Precautions

Patients should not stop taking this medication suddenly. The dose should gradually be decreased, then discontinued. If the drug is stopped abruptly, the patient may experience headache, nausea, or discomfort throughout the body, and a worsening of original symptoms. The effects of the medication last for three to seven days after it has been stopped, and older patients usually are more prone to some side effects such as drowsiness, dizziness, mental confusion, blurry vision, dry mouth, difficulty urinating, and constipation. Taking a lower dose may help resolve these problems. Patients may need to stop this medication before surgery.

Amitriptyline should not be given to anyone with allergies to the drug or to patients recovering from a heart attack. Patients taking the monoamine oxidase inhibitors (MAOIs), Parnate (**tranylcypromine**) and Nardil (phenelzine)—different types of antidepressants—should not use amitriptyline in combination. It should be administered with caution to patients with glaucoma, **seizures**, urinary retention, overactive thyroid, poor liver or kidney function, alcoholism, asthma, digestive disorders, enlarged prostate, seizures, or heart disease. This medication should not be given to children under 12 years of age. Pregnant women should discuss the risks and benefits of this medication with their doctors, as fetal deformities have been associated with taking this drug during pregnancy. Women should not breastfeed while using amitriptyline.

Side effects

Common side effects include dry mouth, drowsiness, constipation, and dizziness or lightheadedness when standing. Patients can suck on ice cubes or sugarless hard candy to combat the dry mouth. Increased fiber in the diet and additional fluids may help relieve constipation. Dizziness is usually caused by a drop in blood pressure when suddenly changing position. Patients should slowly rise from a sitting or lying position if dizziness is noticed. Amitriptyline may increase the risk of falls in older adults. Patients should not drive or operate machinery or appliances while under the influence of this drug. Alcohol and other central nervous system depressants can increase drowsiness. Amitriptyline may also produce blurry vision, irregular or fast heartbeat, high or low blood pressure, palpitations, and an increase or decrease in a diabetic patient's blood sugar levels. Patients' skin may become more sensitive to the sun and thus direct sunlight should be avoided by wearing protective clothing and the application of sunscreen with a protective factor of 15 or higher.

Amitriptyline may increase appetite, cause weight gain, or produce an unpleasant taste in the mouth. It may also cause diarrhea, vomiting, or heartburn. Taking this medication with food may decrease digestive side effects. Other less likely side effects include muscle tremors, nervousness, impaired sexual function, sweating, rash, itching, hair loss, ringing in the ears, or changes in the makeup of the patient's blood. Patients with **schizophrenia** may develop an increase in psychiatric symptoms.

Interactions

Patients should always tell all doctors and dentists that they are taking this medication. It may decrease the effectiveness of some drugs used to treat high blood pressure and should not be taken with other antidepressants, epinephrine and other adrenaline-type drugs, or **methylphenidate**. Patients should not take over-the-counter medications without checking with their doctors. For instance, amitriptyline should not be taken with Tagamet (cimetidine) or Neosynephrine. Patients taking amitriptyline should avoid the dietary supplements St. John's wort, belladonna, henbane, and scopolia. Black tea may decrease the absorption of this drug. Patients should ingest the drug and tea at least two hours apart.

See also Depression and depressive disorders; Pharmacotherapy.

Resources

BOOKS

Consumer Reports Staff. *Consumer Reports Complete Drug Reference.* 2002 ed. Denver: Micromedex Thomson Healthcare, 2001.

Ellsworth, Allan J., and others. *Mosby's Medical Drug Reference, 2001–2002.* St. Louis: Mosby, 2001.

PERIODICALS

Berger, A., S. Mercadante, and G. Oster. "Use of Antiepileptics and Tricyclic Antidepressants in Cancer Patients with Neuropathic Pain." *European Journal of Cancer Care* 15.2 (May 2006): 138–45.

Frese, A., and S. Evers. "Pharmacologic Treatment of Central Post-Stroke Pain." *Clinical Journal of Pain* 22.3 (March 2006): 252–60.

Mayers, Andrew G., and David S. Baldwin. "Antidepressants and Their Effect on Sleep." *Human*

Psychopharmacology: Clinical and Experimental 20.8 (December 2005): 533–59.

Miyasaki, J. M., and others. "Practice Parameter: Evaluation and Treatment of Depression, Psychosis, and Dementia in Parkinson Disease (an Evidence-Based Review): Report of the Quality Standards Subcommittee of the American Academy of Neurology." *Neurology* 66.7 (April 2006): 996–1002.

Sterr, Andrea, and others. "Electroencephalographic Abnormalities Associated with Antidepressant Treatment: A Comparison of Mirtazapine, Venlafaxine, Citalopram, Reboxetine, and Amitriptyline." *Journal of Clinical Psychiatry* 67.2 (February 2006): 325–26.

Veldhuijzen, D. S., and others. "Acute and Subchronic Effects of Amitriptyline on Processing Capacity in Neuropathic Pain Patients Using Visual Event-Related Potentials: Preliminary Findings." *Psychopharmacology* 183.4 (2006): 462–70.

Weber-Hamann, B., and others. "Resistin and Adiponectin in Major Depression: The Association with Free Cortisol and Effects of Antidepressant Treatment." *Journal of Psychiatric Research* 41.3–4 (April–June 2007): 344–50.

Yousefi, Pouran, and John Coffey. "For Fibromyalgia, Which Treatments Are the Most Effective?" *Journal of Family Practice* 54.12 (December 2005): 1094–95.

OTHER

Elavil (amitriptyline HCl Tablets and Injection): Package Insert. <http://www.fda.gov/MedWatch/SAFETY/2003/03Jul_PI/Elavil_PI.pdf>.

Mark Mitchell, MD
Ruth A. Wienclaw, PhD

Amnesia

Definition

Amnesia is a partial or total loss of memory.

Description

There are numerous causes of amnesia, including **stroke**, injury to the **brain**, surgery, alcoholism, encephalitis (inflammation of the brain), and **electroconvulsive therapy**. (Electroconvulsive therapy, or ECT, is a treatment for various mental disorders in which electricity is sent to the brain through electrodes.)

Contrary to the popular notion of amnesia—in which a person suffers a severe blow to the head, for example, and cannot recall his or her past life and experiences—the principal symptom of amnesia is the inability to retain new information, beginning at the point at which the amnesia began. The capacity to recall past experiences may vary, depending on the severity of the amnesia.

There are two types of amnesia: retrograde and anterograde. Retrograde amnesia refers to the loss of memory of one's past and can vary from person to person. Some sufferers retain virtually full recall of things that happened prior to the onset of amnesia; others forget only their recent past, and still others lose all memory of their past lives. Anterograde amnesia refers to the inability to recall events or facts introduced since the amnesia began.

The diagnostic manual used by clinicians, called the ***Diagnostic and Statistical Manual of Mental Disorders*** (DSM), lists three classifications of **amnestic disorders**, described below.

Amnestic disorder due to a general medical condition

The memory loss of amnestic disorder due to a general medical condition can be transient or chronic. This disorder can manifest as retrograde or anterograde loss. For **diagnosis**, the person must experience impairment of social or occupational functioning that differs from their normal levels, and the memory loss cannot occur as part of **dementia** or **delirium**. The medical condition responsible must be confirmed by patient history or by physical exam or lab results.

Substance-induced persisting amnestic disorder

Substance-induced persisting amnestic disorder can occur with use of alcohol, **sedatives**, hypnotics, or anxiolytics. Methotrexate, a chemotherapy drug, can induce it, as can some toxins, including lead, mercury, carbon monoxide, insecticides, or industrial solvents. There are subtypes, including alcohol-induced persisting amnestic disorder. In the alcohol-induced form, the symptoms of **Wernicke-Korsakoff syndrome** may manifest as a result of the thiamine deficiency. Full recovery is not the norm with alcohol-induced amnestic disorder but is possible when caused by other drugs. The diagnostic criteria for the substance-induced form of amnestic disorder are similar to those for that induced by a general medical condition, except that the history should show exposure to the substance involved.

Amnestic disorder not otherwise specified

If the characteristics of the amnesia do not fit either of the above categories, the disorder is then classified as amnestic disorder not otherwise specified, generally because the causative agent/event is not known.

Dissociative amnesia

Dissociative amnesia is part of a different group of disorders, the **dissociative disorders**. It manifests as an inability to remember information that is personally important, but possibly traumatic or stressful. It was previously called Psychogenic amnesia. The memory impairment in this disorder is reversible, and memory loss can be of several types. It can be localized, in which the missing memory covers a defined period of time, or it can be selective, so that only bits and pieces of a situation are recalled. There are also three less common types: generalized (memories covering a lifetime are missing); continuous (memories are missing from a specific time period up to the present); and systematized (only memories from specific categories of information are missing, such as the names of family members). This disorder can arise in a person of any age.

Amnesia is not always obvious to the casual observer—motor skills such as tying shoelaces and bike riding are retained, as is the ability to read and comprehend the meaning of words. Because of this phenomenon, researchers have suggested that there is more than one area of the brain used to store memory. General knowledge and perceptual skills may be stored in a memory separate from the one used to store personal facts.

Childhood amnesia, a term coined by Anna Freud in the late 1940s, refers to the fact that most people cannot recall childhood experiences during the first three to five years of life. It has been suggested that this type of amnesia occurs because children and adults organize memories in different ways. The differences are based on the brain's physical development and communication among the different areas of the brain involved in developing memory. Others believe children begin remembering facts and events once they have accumulated enough experience to be able to relate experiences to each other.

See also Amnestic disorders; Dissociative amnesia; Dissociative fugue.

Resources

BOOKS

American Psychiatric Association. *Diagnostic and Statistical Manual of Mental Disorders,* 4th ed., Text rev. Washington, D.C.: American Psychiatric Association, 2000.

OTHER

Martin, Peter R., Charles, K. Singleton, and Susanne Hiller-Sturmhoefel. National Institute of Alcohol Abuse and Alcoholism. "The Role of Thiamine Deficiency in Alcoholic Brain Disease." <http://pubs.niaaa.nih.gov/publications/arh27-2/134-142.htm> (2006).
National Institute on Alcohol Abuse and Alcoholism. "Alcohol's Damaging Effects on the Brain." <http://pubs.niaaa.nih.gov/publications/aa63/aa63.htm>.

National Institute of Neurological Disorders and Stroke. "Wernicke-Korsakoff Syndrome Information Page." <http://www.ninds.nih.gov/disorders/wernicke_korsakoff/wernicke-korsakoff.htm>.

Emily Jane Willingham, PhD

Amnestic disorders

Definition

The amnestic disorders are a group of disorders that involve loss of memories previously established, loss of the ability to create new memories, or loss of the ability to learn new information. As defined by the mental health professional's handbook, the *Diagnostic and Statistical Manual of Mental Disorders*, fourth edition, text revision (2000), also known as *DSM-IV-TR*, the amnestic disorders result from two basic causes: general medical conditions that produce memory disturbances; and exposure to a chemical (drug of **abuse**, medication, or environmental toxin). An amnestic disorder whose cause cannot be definitely established may be given the **diagnosis** of amnestic disorder not otherwise specified.

Description

The amnestic disorders are characterized by problems with memory function. There is a range of symptoms associated with the amnestic disorders, as well as differences in the severity of symptoms. Some people experience difficulty recalling events that happened or facts that they learned before the onset of the amnestic disorder. This type of **amnesia** is called retrograde amnesia. Other people experience the inability to learn new facts or retain new memories, which is called anterograde amnesia. People with amnestic disorders do not usually forget all of their personal history and their identity, although memory loss of this degree of severity occurs in rare instances in patients with **dissociative disorders**.

Causes and symptoms

Causes

In general, amnestic disorders are caused by structural or chemical damage to parts of the **brain**. Problems remembering previously learned information vary widely according to the location and the severity of brain damage. The ability to learn and remember new information, however, is always affected in an amnestic disorder.

Amnestic disorder due to a general medical condition can be caused by head trauma, tumors, **stroke**, or cerebrovascular disease (disease affecting the blood vessels in the brain). Substance-induced amnestic disorder can be caused by alcoholism, long-term heavy drug use, or exposure to such toxins as lead, mercury, carbon monoxide, and certain insecticides. In cases of amnestic disorder caused by alcoholism, it is thought that the root of the disorder is a vitamin deficiency that is commonly associated with alcoholism, known as Korsakoff's syndrome. The causes of transient global amnesia, or TGA, are unclear.

Symptoms

In addition to problems with information recall and the formation of new memories, people with amnestic disorders are often disoriented with respect to time and space, which means that they are unable to tell an examiner where they are or what day of the week it is. Most patients with amnestic disorders lack insight into their loss of memory, which means that they will deny that there is anything wrong with their memory in spite of evidence to the contrary. Others will admit that they have a memory problem but have no apparent emotional reaction to their condition. Some persons with amnestic disorders undergo a personality change; they may appear apathetic or bland, as if the distinctive features of their personality have been washed out of them.

Some people experiencing amnestic disorders confabulate, which means that they fill in memory gaps with false information that they believe to be true. Confabulation should not be confused with intentional lying. It is much more common in patients with temporary amnestic disorders than it is in people with long-term amnestic disorders.

Transient global amnesia (TGA) is characterized by episodes during which the patient is unable to create new memories or learn new information, and sometimes is unable to recall past memories. The episodes occur suddenly and are generally short. Patients with TGA often appear confused or bewildered.

Demographics

The overall incidence of the amnestic disorders is difficult to estimate. Amnestic disorders related to head injuries may affect people in any age group. Alcohol-induced amnestic disorder is most common in people over the age of 40 with histories of prolonged heavy alcohol use. Amnestic disorders resulting from the abuse of drugs other than alcohol are most common in people between the ages of 20 and 40. Transient global amnesia usually appears in people over 50. Only 3% of people who experience transient global amnesia have symptoms that recur within a year.

Diagnosis

Amnestic disorders may be self-reported, if the patient has retained insight into his or her memory problems. More often, however, the disorder is diagnosed because a friend, relative, employer, or acquaintance of the patient has become concerned about the memory loss or recognizes that the patient is confabulating, and takes the patient to a doctor for evaluation. Patients who are disoriented, or whose amnesia is associated with head trauma or **substance abuse**, may be taken to a hospital emergency room.

The doctor will first examine the patient for signs or symptoms of traumatic injury, substance abuse, or a general medical condition. He or she may order **imaging studies** to identify specific areas of brain injury, or laboratory tests of blood and urine samples to determine exposure to environmental toxins or recent consumption of alcohol or drugs of abuse. If general medical conditions and substance abuse are ruled out, the doctor may administer a brief test of the patient's cognitive status, such as the **mini-mental state examination** or MMSE. The MMSE is often used to evaluate a patient for **dementia**, which is characterized by several disturbances in cognitive functioning (speech problems, problems in recognizing a person's face, etc.) that are not present in amnestic disorders. The doctor may also test the patient's ability to repeat a string of numbers (the so-called digit span test) in order to rule out **delirium**. Patients with an amnestic disorder can usually pay attention well enough to repeat a sequence of numbers whereas patients with delirium have difficulty focusing or shifting their attention. In some cases the patient may also be examined by a neurologist (a doctor who specializes in disorders of the central nervous system).

If there is no evidence of a medical condition or substance use that would explain the patient's memory problems, the doctor may test the patient's memory several times in order to rule out **malingering** or a **factitious disorder**. Patients who are faking the symptoms of an amnestic disorder will usually give inconsistent answers to memory tests if they are tested more than once.

DSM-IV-TR specifies three general categories of amnestic disorders. These are: amnestic disorder due to a general medical condition, substance-induced persisting amnestic disorder, and amnestic disorder not otherwise specified. The basic criterion for diagnosing an amnestic disorder is the development of problems remembering information or events that the patient previously knew, or inability to learn new information or remember new events. In addition, the memory

KEY TERMS

Anterograde amnesia—Amnesia for events that occurred after a physical injury or emotional trauma but before the present moment.

Confabulation—In psychiatry, the filling-in of gaps in memory with false information that the patient believes to be true. It is not deliberate telling of lies.

Delirium—A disturbance of consciousness marked by confusion, difficulty paying attention, delusions, hallucinations, or restlessness.

Dementia—A group of symptoms (syndrome) associated with a progressive loss of memory and other intellectual functions that is serious enough to interfere with a person's ability to perform the tasks of daily life. Dementia impairs memory, alters personality, leads to deterioration in personal grooming, impairs reasoning ability, and causes disorientation.

Dissociation—A reaction to trauma in which the mind splits off certain aspects of the traumatic event from conscious awareness. Dissociation can affect the patient's memory, sense of reality, and sense of identity.

Factitious disorder—A type of mental disturbance in which patients intentionally act physically or men-

tally ill without obvious benefits. It is distinguished from malingering by the absence of an obvious motive, and from conversion disorder by intentional production of symptoms.

Hypnotic—A type of medication that induces sleep.

Korsakoff's syndrome—A disorder of the central nervous system resulting from long-term thiamin deficiency. It is characterized by amnesia, confusion, confabulation, and unsteady gait; and is most commonly seen in alcoholics.

Malingering—Knowingly pretending to be physically or mentally ill to avoid some unpleasant duty or responsibility, or for economic benefit.

Orientation—In psychiatry, the ability to locate oneself in one's environment with respect to time, place and people.

Retrograde amnesia—Amnesia for events that occurred before a traumatic injury.

Thiamin—A B-vitamin that is essential to normal metabolism and nerve function, and whose absorption is affected by alcoholism.

disturbance must be sufficiently severe to affect the patient's social and occupational functioning, and to represent a noticeable decline from the patient's previous level of functioning. *DSM-IV-TR* also specifies that the memory problems cannot occur only during delirium, dementia, substance use or withdrawal.

Treatments

There are no treatments that have been proved effective in most cases of amnestic disorder. Many patients recover slowly over time, and sometimes recover memories that were formed before the onset of the amnestic disorder. Patients generally recover from transient global amnesia without treatment. In people judged to have the signs that often lead to alcohol-induced persisting amnestic disorder, treatment with thiamin may stop the disorder from developing.

Prognosis

Amnestic disorders caused by alcoholism do not generally improve significantly over time, although in a small number of cases the patient's condition improves completely. In many cases the symptoms are severe, and in some cases warrant long-term care

for the patient to make sure his or her daily needs are met. Other substance-induced amnestic disorders have a variable rate of recovery, although in many cases full recovery does eventually occur. Transient global amnesia usually resolves fully.

Prevention

Amnestic disorders resulting from trauma are not generally considered preventable. Avoiding exposure to environmental toxins, refraining from abuse of alcohol or other substances, and maintaining a balanced diet may help to prevent some forms of amnestic disorders.

See also Dissociative amnesia.

Resources

BOOKS

American Psychiatric Association. *Diagnostic and Statistical Manual of Mental Disorders*. 4th ed. text revised. Washington DC: American Psychiatric Association, 2000.

Sadock, Benjamin J. and Virginia A. Sadock, eds. *Comprehensive Textbook of Psychiatry*. 7th ed. Vol. 2. Philadelphia: Lippincott Williams & Wilkins, 2000.

PERIODICALS

Corridan, Brian J., S. N. Mary Leung, I. Harri Jenkins. "A Case of Sleeping and Forgetting." *The Lancet* 357, no. 9255 (February 17, 2001): 524.

Jernigan, Terry L., Arne L. Ostergaard. "When Alcoholism Affects Memory Functions." *Alcohol Health & Research World* 19 no. 2 (Spring 1995): 104-108.

Kesler, Roman, Richard Zweifler. "Confusion and Memory Loss." *Patient Care* 34. 4 (February 29, 2000): 117.

Weiner, Richard D. "Retrograde Amnesia With Electroconvulsive Therapy." *Archives of General Psychiatry* 57. 6 (June 2000): 591.

ORGANIZATIONS

American Academy of Child and Adolescent Psychiatry. P. O. Box 96106, Washington, D.C. 20090. Telephone: (800) 333-7636. <www.aacap.org>.

Tish Davidson, A.M.

Amobarbitol *see* **Barbiturates**

Amoxapine

Definition

Amoxapine is an oral dibenzoxazepine-derivative tricyclic antidepressant. Formerly sold in the United States under the brand name Asendin, it is now manufactured and sold only under its generic name.

Purpose

Amoxapine is used primarily to treat **depression** and to treat the combination of symptoms of **anxiety** and depression. Like most **antidepressants** of this chemical and pharmacological class, amoxapine has also been used in limited numbers of patients to treat **panic disorder, obsessive-compulsive disorder, attention deficit/ hyperactivity disorder, enuresis** (bed-wetting), eating disorders such as **bulimia nervosa, cocaine** dependency, and the depressive phase of bipolar (manic-depressive) disorder. It has also been used to support **smoking cessation** programs.

Description

Tricyclic antidepressants act to change the balance of naturally occurring chemicals in the **brain** that regulate the transmission of nerve impulses between cells. Amoxapine acts primarily by increasing the concentration of norepinephrine and serotonin (both chemicals that stimulate nerve cells) and, to a lesser extent, by blocking the action of another brain chemical, acetylcholine. Amoxapine shares most of the properties of other tricyclic antidepressants, such as **amitriptyline, clomipramine, desipramine, imipramine, nortriptyline, protriptyline,** and **trimipramine.** Studies comparing amoxapine with these other drugs have shown that amoxapine is no more or less effective than other antidepressants of its type. Its choice for treatment is as much a function of physician preference as any other factor.

The therapeutic effects of amoxapine, like other antidepressants, appear slowly. Maximum benefit is often not evident for at least two weeks after starting the drug. People taking amoxapine should be aware of this and continue taking the drug as directed even if they do not see immediate improvement.

Recommended dosage

As with any antidepressant, amoxapine must be adjusted by the physician to produce the desired therapeutic effect. Amoxapine is available as 25-mg, 50-mg, 100-mg, and 150-mg oral tablets. Therapy is usually started at 100 to 150 mg per day and increased to 200 to 300 mg daily by the end of the first week. If no improvement is seen at this dose after two weeks, the physician may increase the dose up to 400 mg per day in outpatients and up to 600 mg per day in hospitalized patients. Doses up to 300 mg may be given in single or divided doses. Doses of more than 300 mg per day should be divided in two or three doses daily.

Because of changes in drug metabolism of older patients, starting at about age 60, the initial dose of amoxapine should be adjusted downward to 50 to 75 mg per day and increased to 100 to 150 mg daily by the end of the first week. Some older patients may require up to 300 mg daily, but doses should never be increased beyond that.

Precautions

Like all tricyclic antidepressants, amoxapine should be used cautiously and with close physician supervision in people, especially the elderly, who have benign prostatic hypertrophy, urinary retention, and glaucoma, especially angle-closure glaucoma (the most severe form). Before starting treatment, people with these conditions should discuss the relative risks and benefits of treatment with their doctors to help determine if amoxapine is the right antidepressant for them.

A common problem with tricyclic antidepressants is sedation (drowsiness, lack of physical and mental alertness). This side effect is especially noticeable early in therapy. In most patients, sedation decreases or disappears entirely with time, but until then patients taking amoxapine should not perform hazardous activities requiring mental alertness or coordination.

The sedative effect is increased when amoxapine is taken with other central nervous system depressants, such as alcoholic beverages, sleeping medications, other **sedatives**, or antihistamines. It may be dangerous to take amoxapine in combination with these substances. Amoxapine may increase the possibility of having **seizures**. Patients should tell their physician if they have a history of seizures, including seizures brought on by the **abuse** of drugs or alcohol. These people should use amoxapine only with caution and be closely monitored by their physician.

Amoxapine may increase heart rate and **stress** on the heart. It may be dangerous for people with cardiovascular disease, especially those who have recently had a heart attack, to take this drug or other antidepressants in the same pharmacological class. In rare cases where patients with cardiovascular disease must receive amoxapine, they should be monitored closely for cardiac rhythm disturbances and signs of cardiac stress or damage.

Side effects

Amoxapine shares side effects common to all tricyclic antidepressants. The most frequent of these are dry mouth, constipation, urinary retention, increased heart rate, sedation, irritability, dizziness, and decreased coordination. As with most side effects associated with tricyclic antidepressants, the intensity is highest at the beginning of therapy and tends to decrease with continued use.

Dry mouth, if severe to the point of causing difficulty speaking or swallowing, may be managed by dosage reduction or temporary discontinuation of the drug. Patients may also chew sugarless gum or suck on sugarless candy in order to increase the flow of saliva. Some artificial saliva products may give temporary relief.

Men with prostate enlargement who take amoxapine may be especially likely to have problems with urinary retention. Symptoms include having difficulty starting a urine flow and more difficulty than usual passing urine. In most cases, urinary retention is managed with dose reduction or by switching to another type of antidepressant. In extreme cases, patients may require treatment with bethanechol, a drug that reverses this particular side effect. People who think they may be experiencing any side effects from this or any other medication should tell their physicians.

Interactions

Dangerously high blood pressure has resulted from the combination of tricyclic antidepressants,

such as amoxapine, and members of another class of antidepressants known as monoamine oxidase inhibitors (MAOI). Because of this, amoxapine should never be taken in combination with MAOIs. Patient taking any MAOIs, for example Nardil (**phenelzine** sulfate) or Parmate (**tranylcypromine** sulfate), should stop the MAOI then wait at least 14 days before starting amoxapine or any other tricyclic antidepressant. The same holds true when discontinuing amoxapine and starting an MAOI.

Amoxapine may decrease the blood pressure–lowering effects of **clonidine**. Patients who take both drugs should be monitored for loss of blood-pressure control and the dose of clonidine increased as needed.

The sedative effects of amoxapine are increased by other central nervous system depressants such as alcohol, sedatives, sleeping medications, or medications used for other mental disorders such as **schizophrenia**. The anticholinergic effects of amoxapine are additive with other anticholinergic drugs such as **benztropine**, **biperiden**, **trihexyphenidyl**, and antihistamines.

See also Neurotransmitters.

Resources

BOOKS

American Society of Health-System Pharmacists. *AHFS Drug Information 2002*. Bethesda: American Society of Health-System Pharmacists, 2002.

DeVane, C. Lindsay, Pharm.D. "Drug Therapy for Mood Disorders." In *Fundamentals of Monitoring Psychoactive Drug Therapy*. Baltimore: Williams and Wilkins, 1990.

Jack Raber, Pharm.D.

Amphetamine sulfate. *(David Hoffman Photo Library/Alamy)*

Amphetamines

Definition

Amphetamines are a group of drugs that stimulate the central nervous system. Some of the brand names of amphetamines sold in the United States are Dexedrine, Biphetamine, Dexampex, Ferndex, Oxydess II, Spancap No. 1, Desoxyn, and Methampex. Some generic names of amphetamines include amphetamine, dextroamphetamine, and **methamphetamine**.

Purpose

Amphetamines stimulate the nervous system and are used in the treatment of **depression**, **obesity**, attention deficit disorders such as **attention deficit/hyperactivity disorder** (ADHD), and **narcolepsy**, a disorder that causes individuals to fall asleep at inappropriate times during the day. Amphetamines produce considerable side effects and are especially toxic in large quantities. Amphetamines are commonly abused as recreational drugs and are highly addictive.

Description

Amphetamines are usually given orally and their effects can last for hours. Amphetamines produce their effects by altering chemicals that transmit nerve messages in the body.

Recommended dosage

Stimulants approved by the U.S. Food and Drug Administration (FDA) for treatment of ADHD are **methylphenidate** (which occurs under several trade names, including Ritalin), mixed amphetamine salts (trade name Adderall), and dextroamphetamine (trade

name Dexedrine). These comparatively short-acting stimulants necessitate several doses through the day to maintain appropriate levels. Some long-acting forms are available, such as Ritalin LA and Adderall XR, and there is also a transdermal patch (trade name Daytrana) for delivery of methylphenidate through the skin.

The typical dose for amphetamines in the treatment of narcolepsy in adults ranges from 5 mg to 60 mg per day. These daily doses are usually divided into at least two small doses taken during the day. Doses usually start on the low end of the range and are increased until the desired effects occur. Children over the age of 12 years with narcolepsy receive 10 mg per day initially. Children between the ages of six and 12 years start with 5 mg per day. The typical dose for adults with obesity ranges from 5 mg to 30 mg per day given in divided doses. The medication is usually given about one-half hour to one hour before meals.

Precautions

Stimulant use in children with ADHD has been associated in some studies with sudden death in a small number of cases, leading to widespread concern; however, subsequent studies have found no difference in sudden death rates among children taking stimulants for ADHD and the general population using no medication. Use of these medications is not recommended for people who have known heart disease.

Another stimulant-related concern is the effects of these drugs on growth rate. Studies do indicate that while a child is taking stimulants, growth rate can slow. Some practitioners may recommend "drug holidays," in which the child stops taking the drug when circumstances require less focus or self-discipline, such as over a summer vacation. Studies indicate that the adverse effects on growth rate are eliminated by these drug holidays.

One of the drugs that has been used to treat ADHD, **pemoline** (trade name Cylert) is not recommended as a first-line approach to ADHD because of the potential for serious side effects related to the liver.

People who are taking amphetamines should not stop taking these drugs suddenly. The dose should be lowered gradually and then discontinued. Amphetamines should only be used while under the supervision of a physician. People should generally take the drug early in the day so that it does not interfere with sleep at night. Hazardous activities should be avoided until the person's condition has been stabilized with medication. The effects of amphetamine can last up to 20 hours after the medication has last been taken. Amphetamine therapy given to women for medical reasons does not present a significant risk of congenital disorders to the developing fetus. In such cases, a mild withdrawal in the newborn may occur. However, illicit use of amphetamines for nonmedical reasons presents a significant risk to the fetus and the newborn because of uncontrolled doses. Methamphetamine use during pregnancy, for example, has been associated with fetal growth retardation, premature birth, and heart and **brain** abnormalities.

Amphetamines are highly addictive and should be used only if alternative approaches have failed. They should be used with great caution in children under three years of age, in anyone with a history of slightly elevated blood pressure, people with neurological tics, and in individuals with Tourette's syndrome. Individuals with a history of an overactive thyroid should not take amphetamines, nor should those with moderate-to-severe high blood pressure, the eye disease called glaucoma, severe arteriosclerosis (hardening of the arteries), or psychotic symptoms (**hallucinations** and **delusions**). Individuals with a history of drug **abuse**, psychological agitation, or cardiovascular system disease should also not receive amphetamine therapy. In addition, patients who have taken a type of antidepressant called monoamine oxidase inhibitors (MAOIs) within the last 14 days should not receive amphetamines. MAOIs include **phenelzine** (Nardil) and **tranylcypromine** (Parnate).

Side effects

The most common side effects that are associated with amphetamines include the development of an irregular heartbeat, increased heart rate or blood pressure, dizziness, **insomnia**, restlessness, headache, shakiness, dry mouth, metallic taste, diarrhea, constipation, and weight loss. Other side effects can include

KEY TERMS

Anticonvulsant drugs—Medications that relieve or prevent seizures.

Arteriosclerosis—A thickening, hardening, and loss of elasticity of the walls of the arteries.

Attention deficit disorder—A condition that mostly affects children and involves the inability to concentrate on various tasks.

Congenital—Present at birth.

Glaucoma—A group of eye diseases characterized by increased pressure within the eye significant enough to damage eye tissue and structures. If untreated, glaucoma results in blindness.

Monoamine oxidase inhibitors (MAOIs)—A group of antidepressant drugs that decreases the activity of monoamine oxidase, a neurotransmitter in the brain that affects mood.

Tic—A sudden involuntary behavior that is difficult or impossible for the person to suppress. Tics may be either motor (related to movement) or vocal, and may become more pronounced under stress.

Tourette's syndrome—A neurological disorder characterized by multiple involuntary movements and uncontrollable vocalizations called tics that come and go over years, usually beginning in childhood and becoming chronic. Sometimes the tics include inappropriate language.

Tricyclic antidepressants—Antidepressant medications that have the common characteristic of a three-ring nucleus in their chemical structure. Imipramine and amitriptyline are examples of tricyclic antidepressants.

changes in sexual drive, nausea, vomiting, allergic reactions, chills, depression, irritability, and other problems involving the digestive system. High doses, whether for medical purposes or illicit ones, can cause **addiction**, dependence, increased aggression, and, in some cases, psychotic episodes.

Interactions

Patients taking amphetamines should always tell their physicians and dentists that they are using this medication. Patients should consult their physicians before taking any over-the-counter medications while taking amphetamines. The interaction between over-the-counter cold medications with amphetamine, for instance, is particularly dangerous because this combination can significantly increase blood pressure. Such cold medications should be avoided when using amphetamines unless a physician has carefully analyzed the combination.

The combination of amphetamines and antacids slows down the ability of the body to eliminate the amphetamine. Furazolidone (Furoxone) combined with amphetamine can significantly increase blood pressure. Sodium bicarbonate can reduce the amount of amphetamine eliminated from the body, thereby dangerously increasing amphetamine levels in the body. Certain medications taken to control high blood pressure, including guanadrel (Hylorel) and guanethidine (Ismelin), MAOIs, and selegiline (Eldepryl) should not be used in conjunction with amphetamines. In addition, antihistamines, anticonvulsant drugs, and tricyclic **antidepressants** including **desipramine** (Norpramin) and **imipramine** (Tofranil) should not be combined with amphetamines.

See also Attention deficit/hyperactivity disorder; Tic disorders.

Resources

BOOKS

Consumer Reports staff. *Consumer Reports Complete Drug Reference.* 2002 ed. Denver: Micromedex Thomson Healthcare, 2001.

Ellsworth, Allan J., and others. *Mosby's Medical Drug Reference, 2001–2002.* St. Louis: Mosby, 2001.

Hardman, Joel G., and Lee E. Limbird, eds. *Goodman & Gilman's The Pharmacological Basis of Therapeutics.* 10th ed. New York: McGraw-Hill, 2001.

Mosby's GenRx staff. *Mosby's GenRx.* 9th ed. St. Louis: Mosby, 1999.

Venes, Donald, and Clayton L. Thomas. *Taber's Cyclopedic Medical Dictionary.* 19th ed. Philadelphia: F. A. Davis, 2001.

PERIODICALS

Lopez, Frank A. "ADHD: New Pharmacological Treatments on the Horizon." *Developmental and Behavioral Pediatrics* 27 (2006): 410–16.

Pliszka, Steven R. "Pharmacologic Treatment of Attention-Deficit/Hyperactivity Disorder: Efficacy, Safety, and Mechanisms of Action." *Neuropsychological Reviews* (2007). doi: 10.1007/s11065-006-9017-3.

Sulzer, David, and others. "Mechanisms of Neurotransmitter Release by Amphetamines: A Review." *Progress in Neurobiology* 75 (2005): 406–33.

OTHER

National Library of Medicine. National Institutes of Health. "Amphetamines." Updated links to news and information. <http://www.nlm.nih.gov/medlineplus/druginfo/uspdi/202031.html>.

National Library of Medicine. National Institutes of Health. Information about prescription amphetamines. "Amphetamines, systemic." <http://www.nlm.nih.gov/medlineplus/druginfo/uspdi/202031.html>.

Mark Mitchell, MD
Emily Jane Willingham, PhD

Amphetamines and related disorders

Definition

Amphetamines are a group of powerful and highly addictive substances that dramatically affect the central nervous system. They induce a feeling of well-being and improve alertness, attention, and performance on various cognitive and motor tasks. Closely related are the so-called substitute amphetamines, which include MDMA, also known as **ecstasy** and **methamphetamine**. Finally, some over-the-counter drugs used as **appetite suppressants** also have amphetamine-like action. Amphetamine-related disorders refer to the effects of **abuse**, dependence, and acute intoxication stemming from inappropriate amphetamine and amphetamine-related drug usage.

Description

Several amphetamines are currently available in the United States, including dextroamphetamine (Dexedrine) and **methylphenidate** (Ritalin). These Schedule II stimulants (those the U.S. Drug Enforcement Agency considers to have medical usefulness and a high potential for abuse), known to be highly addictive, require a triplicate prescription that cannot be refilled. Amphetamines are also known as sympathomimetics, stimulants, and psychostimulants. Methamphetamine, the most common illegally produced amphetamine, goes by the street name of "speed," "meth," or "chalk." When it is smoked, it is called "ice," "crystal," "crank," or "glass." Methamphetamine is a white, odorless, bitter-tasting crystalline powder that dissolves in water or alcohol.

The leaves of the East African bush *Catha edulis* can be chewed for their stimulant effects. This drug, cathinone or Khat, has an effect on most of the central nervous system, in addition to providing the other properties of amphetamines. Also, manufacture of methamphetamine in illegal laboratories has increased dramatically in recent years, leading to stricter laws governing the sale of products containing ephedrine or pseudoephedrine, the primary components of this drug.

Amphetamines intended for medical use were first used in nasal decongestants and bronchial inhalers. Early in the 1900s, they were also used to treat several medical and psychiatric conditions, including attention-deficit disorders, **obesity**, **depression**, and **narcolepsy** (a rare condition in which individuals fall asleep at dangerous and inappropriate moments and cannot maintain normal alertness). They are still used to treat these disorders today.

In the 1970s, governmental agencies initiated restrictions increasing the difficulty of obtaining amphetamines legally through prescription. During this same time period, a drug chemically related to the amphetamines began to be produced. This so-called designer drug, best known as "ecstasy," but also as MDMA, XTC, and Adam, has behavioral effects that combine amphetamine-like and hallucinogen-like properties.

The structure of amphetamines differs significantly from that of **cocaine**, even though both are stimulants with similar behavioral and physiological effects. Like cocaine, amphetamine results in an accumulation of the neurotransmitter **dopamine** in the prefrontal cortex. It is this excessive dopamine concentration that appears to produce the stimulation and feelings of euphoria experienced by the user. Cocaine is much more quickly metabolized and removed from the body, whereas amphetamines have a much longer duration of action. A large percentage of the drug remains unchanged in the body, leading to prolonged stimulant effects.

The handbook that mental health professionals use to diagnose mental disorders is the ***Diagnostic and Statistical Manual of Mental Disorders,*** also known as the *DSM*. The 2000 edition of this manual (the fourth edition, text revision, also known as *DSM-IV-TR*) describes four separate amphetamine-related disorders. These are:

- amphetamine dependence: Refers to chronic or episodic binges (known as "speed runs"), with brief drug-free periods of time in between use.

- amphetamine abuse: Less severe than dependence. Individuals diagnosed with amphetamine abuse have milder but nevertheless still substantial problems due to their drug usage.

- amphetamine intoxication: Refers to serious maladaptive behavioral or psychological changes that develop during, or shortly after, use of an amphetamine or related substance.

- amphetamine withdrawal: Refers to symptoms that develop within a few hours to several days after

reducing or stopping heavy and prolonged amphetamine use. Withdrawal symptoms are, in general, opposite to those seen during intoxication, and include fatigue, vivid and unpleasant dreams, insomnia or hypersomnia (too much sleep), increased appetite, and agitation or slowing down.

Causes and symptoms

Causes

All amphetamines are rapidly absorbed when taken orally, and even more rapidly absorbed when smoked, snorted, or injected. Tolerance develops with both standard and designer amphetamines, leading to the need for increasing doses by the user.

Amphetamines, such as dextroamphetamine, methamphetamine, and methylphenidate, produce their primary effects by causing the release of catecholamines, especially the nerve-signaling molecule or neurotransmitter dopamine, in the **brain**. These effects are particularly strong in areas of the brain associated with pleasure, specifically, the cerebral cortex and the limbic system, known as the "reward pathway." The effect on this pathway is probably responsible for the addictive quality of the amphetamines.

MDMA causes the release of the **neurotransmitters** dopamine and serotonin and the neurohormone norepinephrine. Serotonin is responsible for producing the hallucinogenic effects of the drug.

Symptoms

According to the *DSM-IV-TR,* symptoms of heavy, chronic, or episodic use of amphetamine, known as amphetamine dependence, can be very serious. Amphetamine dependence is characterized by compulsive drug-seeking and drug use, leading to functional and molecular changes in the brain. Aggressive or violent behavior may occur, especially when high doses are ingested. Individuals may develop **anxiety** or paranoid ideas, also with the possibility of experiencing terrifying psychotic episodes that resemble **schizophrenia**, with visual or auditory **hallucinations**, **delusions** such as the sensation of insects creeping on the skin (known as "formication"), hyperactivity, hypersexuality, confusion, and incoherence. Amphetamine-induced **psychosis** differs from true psychosis in that despite other symptoms, the disorganized thinking that is a hallmark of schizophrenia tends to be absent. Amphetamine dependence consistently affects relationships at home, school, and/or work.

Amphetamine abuse is less serious than dependence, but can cause milder versions of the symptoms described above, as well as problems with family, school, and work. Legal problems may stem from aggressive behavior while using, or from obtaining drugs illegally. Individuals may continue to use despite the awareness that usage negatively impacts all areas of their lives.

Acute amphetamine intoxication begins with a "high" feeling that may be followed by feelings of euphoria. Users experience enhanced energy, becoming more outgoing and talkative, and more alert. Other symptoms include anxiety, tension, grandiosity, repetitive behavior, anger, fighting, and impaired judgment.

In both acute and chronic intoxication, individuals may experience dulled feelings, along with fatigue or sadness, and social withdrawal. These behavioral and psychological changes are accompanied by other signs and symptoms including increased or irregular heartbeat, dilation of the pupils, elevated or lowered blood pressure, heavy perspiring or chills, nausea and/ or vomiting, motor agitation or retardation, muscle weakness, respiratory depression, chest pain, and eventually confusion, **seizures**, coma, or a variety of cardiovascular problems, including **stroke**. With amphetamine overdoses, death can result if treatment is not received immediately. Long-term abuse can lead to memory loss as well, and contributes to increased transmission of hepatitis and HIV/AIDS. Impaired social and work functioning is another hallmark of both acute and chronic intoxication.

Following amphetamine intoxication, a "crash" occurs with symptoms of anxiety, shakiness, depressed mood, lethargy, fatigue, nightmares, headache, perspiring, muscle cramps, stomach cramps, and increased appetite. Withdrawal symptoms usually peak in two to four days and are gone within one week. The most serious withdrawal symptom is depression, possibly very severe and leading to suicidal thoughts.

Use of so-called designer amphetamines, such as MDMA, leads to similar symptoms. Users also report a sense of feeling unusual closeness with other people and enhanced personal comfort. They describe seeing an increased luminescence of objects in the environment, although these hallucinogenic effects are less than those caused by other hallucinogens, such as LSD. Some psychotherapists have suggested further research into the possible use of designer amphetamines in conjunction with **psychotherapy**. This idea is highly controversial, however.

As with other amphetamines, use of MDMA produces cardiovascular effects of increased blood pressure, heart rate, and heart oxygen consumption. People with pre-existing heart disease are at increased risk of cardiovascular catastrophe resulting from MDMA use. MDMA is not processed and removed from the body quickly and remains active for a long period of time. As a result, toxicity may rise dramatically when users take multiple doses over brief time periods, leading to harmful reactions such as dehydration, hyperthermia, and seizures.

MDMA tablets often contain other drugs, such as ephedrine, a stimulant, and dextromethorphan, a cough suppressant with PCP-like effects at high doses. These additives increase the harmful effects of MDMA. They also appear also to have toxic effects on the brain's serotonin system. In tests of learning and memory, people who use MDMA perform more poorly than people who do not use. Research with primates shows that MDMA can cause long-lasting brain damage. Exposure to MDMA during the period of pregnancy in which the fetal brain is developing is associated with learning deficits that last into adulthood.

Demographics

Amphetamine dependence and abuse occur at all levels of society, most commonly among 18- to 30-year-olds. Intravenous use is more common among individuals from lower socioeconomic groups, and has a male-to-female ratio of three or four to one. Among people who do not use intravenously users, males and females are relatively equally divided.

Of greatest recent concern has been the rise in the use of methamphetamine, although in some areas, this increase has leveled off in recent years. The lifetime prevalence of methamphetamine abuse among U.S. students in grade 12 fell from 6.2% of respondents to 4.5% over two years in one recent government survey. However, in some metropolitan areas, including Atlanta, Denver, Honolulu, and Phoenix, use has increased, and there was a 15% increase in methamphetamine treatment admissions in St. Louis from 2004 to 2005. In some parts of Texas, this drug has replaced crack as a drug of choice. Another national survey found that 10.4 million Americans age 12 or older had tried methamphetamine at least once in their lives. The problem seems to be particularly concerning in Western states, although it is spreading quickly in the South and Midwest, being reported as the fastest-growing problem in metropolitan Atlanta in 2006.

Diagnosis

Classic amphetamines

Four classic amphetamine-related diagnostic categories are listed in the *DSM-IV-TR*. These are:

- amphetamine dependence
- amphetamine abuse

- amphetamine intoxication
- amphetamine withdrawal

Amphetamine dependence refers to chronic or episodic use of amphetamines, involving drug binges known as "speed runs." These episodes are punctuated by brief, drug-free periods. Aggressive or violent behavior is associated with amphetamine dependence, particularly when high doses are ingested. Intense but temporary anxiety may occur, as well as paranoid ideas and psychotic behavior resembling schizophrenia. Increased tolerance and withdrawal symptoms are part of the diagnostic picture. Conversely, some individuals with amphetamine dependence become sensitized to the drug, experiencing increasingly greater stimulation, and other negative mental or neurological effects, even from small doses.

Amphetamine abuse, while not as serious as amphetamine dependence, can also cause multiple problems. Legal difficulties are common, in addition to increased arguments with family and friends. If tolerance or withdrawal occur, amphetamine dependence is diagnosed.

Amphetamine intoxication refers to serious behavioral or psychological changes that develop during, or shortly after, use of amphetamine. Intoxication begins with a "high" feeling, followed by euphoria, enhanced energy, talkativeness, hyperactivity, restlessness, hypervigilance indicated by an individual's extreme sensitivity, and closely observant of everything in the environment. Other symptoms are anxiety, tension, repetitive behavior, anger, fighting, and impaired judgment. With chronic intoxication, there may be fatigue or sadness and withdrawal from others. Other signs and symptoms of intoxication are increased heart rate, dilation of the pupils, elevated or lowered blood pressure, perspiration or chills, nausea or vomiting, weight loss, cardiac irregularities, and, eventually, confusion, seizures, coma, or death.

During amphetamine withdrawal, intense symptoms of depression are typical. Additional diagnostic symptoms are fatigue, vivid and unpleasant dreams, insomnia or sleeping too much, increased appetite, and agitation.

Treatments

According to the National Institute on Drug Abuse (NIDA), the most effective treatments for amphetamine **addiction** are cognitive-behavioral interventions. These are psychotherapeutic approaches that help individuals learn to identify and change their problematic patterns of thoughts and beliefs. As a result of changed thoughts and beliefs, feelings become more manageable and less painful. Interventions also help individuals increase their skills for coping with life's stressors. Amphetamine recovery groups, and Narcotics Anonymous also appear to help.

No specific medications are known to exist that are helpful for treating amphetamine dependence. On occasion, antidepressant medications can help combat the depressive symptoms frequently experienced by people who are newly abstinent from amphetamine use.

Overdoses of amphetamines are treated in established ways in emergency rooms. Because hyperthermia (elevated body temperature) and convulsions are common, emergency room treatment focuses on reducing body temperature and administering anticonvulsant medications.

Acute methamphetamine intoxication is often handled by observation in a safe, quiet environment. When extreme anxiety or panic is part of the reaction, treatment with antianxiety medications may be helpful. In cases of methamphetamine-induced psychoses, short-term use of antipsychotic medications is usually successful.

Prognosis

Classic amphetamines

According to the *DSM-IV-TR,* some individuals who develop abuse or dependence on amphetamines initiate use in an attempt to control their weight. Others become introduced through the illegal market. Dependence can occur very quickly when the substance is used intravenously or is smoked. The few long-term data available show a tendency for people who have been dependent on amphetamines to decrease or stop using them after 8 to 10 years. This may result from the development of adverse mental and physical effects that emerge with long-term dependence. Few data are available on the long-term course of abuse.

Designer amphetamines

The NIDA reports that studies provide direct evidence that chronic use of MDMA causes brain damage in humans. Using advanced brain imaging techniques, one study found that MDMA harms neurons that release serotonin. Serotonin plays an important role in regulating memory and other mental functions.

In a related study, researchers found that people who heavily use MDMA have memory problems that persist for at least two weeks after stopping use of the drug. Both studies strongly suggest that the extent of damage is directly related to the amount of MDMA used.

KEY TERMS

Amphetamine abuse—An amphetamine problem in which the user experiences negative consequences from the use, but has not reached the point of dependence.

Amphetamine dependence—The most serious type of amphetamine problem.

Amphetamine intoxication—The effects on the body that develop during or shortly after amphetamine use.

Amphetamine withdrawal—Symptoms that develop shortly after reducing or stopping heavy amphetamine use.

Amphetamines—A group of powerful and highly addictive substances that stimulate the central nervous system. Amphetamines may be prescribed for various medical conditions, but are often purchased illicitly and abused.

Catecholamine—A group of neurotransmitters synthesized from the amino acid tyrosine and released by the hypothalamic-pituitary-adrenal system in the brain in response to acute stress. The catecholamines include dopamine, serotonin, norepinephrine, and epinephrine.

Catha edulis—Leaves of an East African bush that can be chewed for their stimulant effect.

Designer amphetamines—Substances close in chemical structure to classic amphetamines that provide both stimulant and hallucinogenic effects.

Dopamine—A chemical in brain tissue that serves to transmit nerve impulses (is a neurotransmitter) and helps to regulate movement and emotions. Large amounts of dopamine are released following ingestion of amphetamines.

Ecstasy—Best known of the so-called designer amphetamines, also known as MDMA. It produces both stimulant and hallucinogenic effects.

Ephedrine—An amphetamine-like substance used as a nasal decongestant.

Formication—The sensation of bugs creeping on the skin.

Hyperthermia—Elevated body temperature resulting from ingestion of amphetamines.

Methamphetamine—The most common illegally produced amphetamine.

Serotonin—A widely distributed neurotransmitter that is found in blood platelets, the lining of the digestive tract, and the brain, and that works in combination with norepinephrine. It causes very powerful contractions of smooth muscle, and is associated with mood, attention, emotions, and sleep. Low levels of serotonin are associated with depression. Large amounts of serotonin are released after ingestion of MDMA.

"Speed run"—The episodic bingeing on amphetamines.

Prevention

In 1999, NIDA began a program known as the "Club Drug Initiative" in response to recent increases in abuse of MDMA and other drugs used in similar environments. This ongoing program seeks to increase awareness of the dangers of these drugs among teens, young adults, parents, and community members.

Research indicates a pervasive perception among users that MDMA is a "fun" drug with minimal risks. This myth might point to the main reason for the widespread increase in the drug's abuse. The Club Drug Initiative seeks to make the dangers of MDMA use far better known. Evidence of the program's initial success with this initiative might be seen in what is considered a growing perception by high school seniors that MDMA is a dangerous drug.

See also Addiction; Appetite suppressants; Cognitve-behavioral therapy; Disease concept of chemical dependency; Narcolepsy; Obesity; Relapse and relapse prevention; Self-help groups; Support groups.

Resources

BOOKS

American Psychiatric Association. *Diagnostic and Statistical Manual of Mental Disorders.* 4th ed., Text rev. Washington, D.C.: American Psychiatric Association, 2000.

Kaplan, Harold I., MD, and Benjamin J. Sadock, MD. *Synopsis of Psychiatry: Behavioral Sciences/Clinical Psychiatry.* 8th ed. Baltimore, MD: Lippincott Williams and Wilkins, 1998.

PERIODICALS

Sulzer, David, and others. "Mechanisms of Neurotransmitter Release by Amphetamines: A Review." *Progress in Neurobiology* 75 (2005): 406–33.

ORGANIZATIONS

Narcotics Anonymous (NA). P.O. Box 9999, Van Nuys, CA 91409. Telephone: (818) 780-3951.

National Institute on Drug Abuse (NIDA). U.S. Department of Health and Human Services, 5600 Fishers Lane, Rockville, MD 20857. Telephone: (301) 443-6245. <http://www.nida.nih.gov>.

NIDA. Club Drug Initiative. <http://www.clubdrugs.org>.

OTHER

National Institute on Drug Abuse. NIDA Infofacts: *Methamphetamine*. 2006. <http://www.nida.nih.gov/Infofacts/methamphetamine.html>.

National Institute on Drug Abuse. NIDA Research Report. *Methamphetamine Abuse and Addiction*: NIH Publication No. 06-4210, Sept. 2006. <http://www.nida.nih.gov/ResearchReports/methamph/methamph.html>.

National Library of Medicine. National Institutes of Health. "Amphetamines." Updated links to news and information. <http://www.nlm.nih.gov/medlineplus/druginfo/uspdi/202031.html>.

National Library of Medicine. National Institutes of Health. Information about prescription amphetamines. "Amphetamines, systemic." <http://www.nlm.nih.gov/medlineplus/druginfo/uspdi/202031.html>.

National Survey on Drug Use and Health. "The NSDUH Report: Methamphetamine." 2007. <http://oas.samhsa.gov/2k6/meth/meth.htm>.

U.S. Food and Drug Administration. "Some Cold Medicines Move Behind Counter." *FDA Consumer Magazine* July–Aug. (2006). <http://www.fda.gov/fdac/features/2006/406_meth.html>.

Barbara S. Sternberg, PhD
Emily Jane Willingham, PhD

Anafranil *see* **Clomipramine**

Anorexia nervosa

Definition

Anorexia nervosa (AN) is an eating disorder characterized by an intense fear of gaining weight and becoming fat. Because of this fear, the affected individual starves herself or himself, and the person's weight falls to about 85% (or less) of the normal weight for age and height.

Description

AN affects females more commonly than males—90% of those affected are female. Typically, the disorder begins when an adolescent or young woman of normal or slightly overweight stature decides to diet. As weight falls, the intensity and **obsession** with dieting increases. Affected persons may also increase physical exertion or exercise as weight decreases to lose more pounds. An affected person develops peculiar rules concerning exercise and eating. Weight loss and avoidance of food is equated in these patients with a sense of accomplishment and success. Weight gain is viewed as a sign of weakness ("succumbing to eating") and as failure. Eventually, the affected person becomes increasingly focused on losing weight and devotes most efforts to dieting and exercise.

Anorexia nervosa is a complex eating disorder that has biological, psychological, and social consequences for those who suffer from it. When diagnosed early, the prognosis for AN is good.

Demographics

AN is considered to be a rare illness. The prevalence even in high-risk groups and high-risk situations is approximately 0.5–1%. Partial disorders (diagnosed when symptoms are present, but do not meet the full criteria as established in the *DSM*) are more commonly seen in psychological practice. The incidence (number of new cases) of AN has increased during the last 50 years due to increased societal concerns regarding body shape, weight, and appearance. Some occupations such as ballet dancing and fashion modeling may predispose persons to develop AN, due to preoccupation with physical appearance. This disorder usually affects women more than men in a ratio of about one to 10.

Causes and symptoms

Causes

The exact causes of AN are not currently known, but the current thinking about AN is that it is caused by multiple factors. There are several models that can identify risk factors and psychological conditions that predispose persons to develop AN. The predisposing risk factors include:

- female gender
- perfectionism
- personality factors, including being eager to please other persons and high expectations for oneself
- family history of eating disorders
- living in an industrialized society
- difficulty communicating negative emotions such as anger or fear
- difficulty resolving problems or conflict
- low self-esteem

Research indicates that genetic factors play a role in more than half of anorexia cases. Genetic factors

Self-portrait done by a girl while in treatment for anorexia nervosa. *(Photo Researchers, Inc.)*

can also predispose an individual to behaviors that make her susceptible to AN, such as perfectionism, **obsessive-compulsive disorder**, and **anxiety**.

Specialists in **family therapy** have demonstrated that dysfunctional family relationships and impaired family interaction can contribute to the development of AN. Mothers of persons with AN tend to be intrusive, perfectionistic, overprotective, and have a fear of separation. Fathers of AN-affected individuals are often described as passive, withdrawn, moody, emotionally constricted, obsessive, and ineffective. Sociocultural factors include the messages given by society and the culture about women's roles and the thinness ideal for women's bodies. Developmental causes can include adolescent "acting out" or fear of adulthood transition. In addition, there appears to be a genetic correlation, because AN occurs more commonly in biological relatives of persons who have this disorder.

Precipitating factors are often related to the developmental transitions common in adolescence. The onset of menstruation may be threatening in that it represents maturation or growing up. During this time in development, females gain weight as part of the developmental process, and this gain may cause a decrease in self-esteem. Development of AN could be a way that the adolescent retreats back to childhood so as not to be burdened by maturity and physical concerns. Autonomy and independence struggles during adolescence may be acted out by developing AN. Some adolescents may develop AN because of their ambivalence about adulthood or because of loneliness, isolation, and abandonment they feel.

Symptoms

Most of the physical symptoms associated with AN are secondary to starvation. The **brain** is affected—there is evidence to suggest alterations in brain size, neurotransmitter balance, and hormonal secretion signals originating from the brain. **Neurotransmitters** are the chemicals in the brain that transmit messages from nerve cell to nerve cell. Hormonal secretion signals modulate sex organ activity. Thus, when these signals are not functioning properly, the sex organs are affected. Significant weight loss (and loss in body fat, in particular) inhibits the production of estrogen, which is necessary for menstruation. AN patients experience a loss of menstrual periods, known as amenorrhea. Additionally, other physiologic systems are affected by the starvation. AN patients often have electrolyte (sodium and potassium ion) imbalance and blood cell abnormalities affecting both white and red blood cells. Heart function is also compromised and a person affected with AN may develop congestive heart failure (a chronic weakening of the heart due to work overload), slow heart rate (bradycardia), and abnormal rates and rhythms (arrhythmias). The gastrointestinal tract is also affected, and a person with AN usually exhibits diminished gastric motility (movement) and delayed gastric emptying. These abnormalities may cause symptoms of bloating and constipation. In addition, bone growth is affected by starvation, and over the long term, AN patients can develop osteoporosis, a bone loss disease.

Physically, persons with AN can exhibit cold hands and feet, dry skin, hair loss, headaches, fainting, dizziness, and lethargy (loss of energy). Individuals with AN may also develop lanugo (a fine downy hair normally seen in infants) on the face or back. Psychologically, these persons may have an inability to concentrate, due to the problems with cognitive functioning caused by starvation. Additionally, they may be irritable, depressed, and socially withdrawn, and they obsessively avoid food. Persons affected with AN may also have lowered body temperature (hypothermia), and lowered blood pressure, heart rate, glucose and white blood cells (cells that help fight against infection). They may also have a loss of muscle mass.

In order to diagnose AN, a patient's symptoms must meet the symptom criteria established in the professional's handbook, the *Diagnostic and Statistical Manual of Mental Disorders*, also called the *DSM*. These symptoms include:

- refusal to maintain normal body weight, resulting in a weight that is less than 85% of the expected weight
- an intense fear of gaining weight, even if the affected person is underweight.
- distorted body image, obsession with body weight as key factor in self-evaluation, or denial of the seriousness of the low body weight
- amenorrhea

Diagnosis

Initial assessment usually includes a careful interview and history (clinical evaluation). A weight history, menstrual history, and description of daily food intake are important during initial evaluation. Risk factors and family history are also vital in suspected cases. Laboratory results can reveal anemia (low red blood cell count in the blood), lowered white blood cells, pulse, blood pressure, and body temperature. The decreased temperature in extremities may cause a slight red-purple discoloration in limbs (acrocyanosis). There are two psychological questionnaires that can be administered to aid in **diagnosis**, called the Eating Attitudes Test (EAT) and Eating Disorders Inventory (EDI). The disadvantage of these tests is that they may produce false-positive results, which means that a test result may indicate that the test taker has anorexia, when, actually, she or he does not.

Treatments

Persons affected with AN are often in denial, in that they do not see themselves as thin or in need of professional help. Education is important, as is engagement on the part of the patient—a connection from the patient to her treatment, so that she agrees to be actively involved. Engagement is a necessary but difficult task in the treatment of AN. If the affected person's medical condition has deteriorated, **hospitalization** may be required. Initially, treatment objectives are focused on reversing behavioral abnormalities and nutritional deficiencies. Emotional support and reassurance that eating and caloric restoration will not make the person overweight are essential components during initial treatment sessions. Psychosocial (both psychological and social) issues and family dysfunction are also addressed, which may reduce the risk of relapsing behaviors. (Relapsing behaviors occur when an individual goes back to the old patterns that he or she is trying to eliminate.) At present, there is no standardized psychotherapeutic treatment model to address the multifactorial problems associated with AN. **Cognitive-behavioral therapy** (CBT) may help to improve and modify irrational perceptions and overemphasis of weight gain. Current treatment usually begins with behavioral interventions and should include family therapy (if age appropriate). **Psychodynamic psychotherapy** (also called exploratory **psychotherapy**) is often helpful in the treatment of AN. There are no medications to treat AN. Treatment for this disorder is often long term.

Prognosis

If this disorder is not successfully diagnosed or treated, the affected person may die of malnutrition

KEY TERMS

Amenorrhea—Absence of menstrual periods.

Anemia—Condition that results when there is a deficiency of oxygen in the blood. Can cause fatigue and impair mental functions.

False-positive—A test result that is positive for a specific condition or disorder, but this result is inaccurate.

Lanugo—Downy hair, usually associated with infants, that sometimes develops on the face and back of people affected by anorexia nervosa.

and multi-organ complications. The mortality rate among anorexia patients is between 6% and 20%. However, early diagnosis and appropriate treatment interventions are correlated with a favorable outcome.

Research results concerning outcome of specific AN treatments are inconsistent. Some results, however, have been validated. The prognosis appears to be more positive for persons who are young at onset of the disorder, and/or who have experienced a low number of disorder-related hospitalizations. The prognosis is not as positive for persons with long duration illness, very low body weight, and persistent family dysfunction. Additionally, the clinical outcome can be complicated by comorbid, or co-occurring or concurrent, disorders (without any causal relationship to AN) such as **depression**, anxiety, and **substance abuse**.

Prevention

A nurturing and healthy family environment during developing years is particularly important. Recognition of the clinical signs with immediate treatment can possibly prevent disorder progression, and, as stated, early diagnosis and treatment are correlated with a favorable outcome.

Resources

BOOKS

Lock, James, and others. *Treatment Manual for Anorexia Nervosa: A Family-Based Approach.* New ed. New York: The Guilford Press, 2002.

Scaglius, Fernanda Baeza, and others, contributors. *Anorexia Nervosa And Bulimia Nervosa: New Research.* Nova Science Publishers, 2006.

ORGANIZATIONS

National Alliance on Mental Illness, Colonial Place Three, 2107 Wilson Blvd., Suite 300, Arlington, VA 22201-3042. Telephone: (703) 524-7600. <http://www.nami.org/>.

National Association of Anorexia Nervosa and Associated Disorders, P.O. Box 7, Highland Park, IL 60035. Hotline: (847) 831-3438. <http://www.anad.org>.

Laith Farid Gulli, MD
Catherine Seeley, CSW
Nicole Mallory, MS,PA-C
Stephanie N. Watson

Anosognosia

Definition

Anosognosia is a disorder in which a person who has suffered **brain** injury or damage is unaware of sensory, perceptual, motor, affective, or cognitive deficits.

Description

The term anosognosia was first adopted by J. Babinski in 1914, to refer to a lack of knowledge, awareness, or recognition, of deficits, observed in patients with neurological impairments. The term is derived from the roots *a* (without), *noso* (illness), and *gnosia* (knowledge). The terms anosognosia, impaired awareness, unawareness of deficits, and lack of insight are sometimes used interchangeably in the scientific literature. Some researchers also use the term anosognosia interchangeably with the term **denial** of illness, which is a condition in which patients do not acknowledge that they have a deficit or disease. Others, however, distinguish anosognosia from denial of illness based on its primary etiology. Anosognosia is thought to be due primarily to a neurological lesion. Denial of illness, on the other hand, is thought to be due primarily to a psychological process in which a patient tries to manage the distressing emotions related to having the illness or disability.

Some researchers have suggested that denial of illness and anosognosia can co-occur in patients with brain injury. Efforts to distinguish between the two syndromes have revealed that brain injury patients with denial of illness and brain injury patients with anosognosia react differently when confronted with information about their deficits. Patients who deny their deficits show an implicit or partial awareness of these deficits, become angry or resistant when confronted with information about the deficits, and struggle actively when asked to perform tasks after being confronted with such information. Patients with anosognosia, on the other hand, do not have information about their deficits, are perplexed when given feedback about their functional or behavioral deficits, and are cautiously willing or indifferent when asked to perform tasks with this new information about themselves.

Anosognosia can include unawareness of many different kinds of deficits, such as blindness, aphasia, **amnesia**, paralysis, and weakness of limbs. The first detailed description of anosognosia, provided by C. von Monakow in 1885, was of a man who was unaware of being blind after damage to the cortex of the brain. In 1889, G. Anton described a case of a man who, after damage to the right side of his brain, was unaware of that he was unable to move his left limbs, that he was blind in his left eye, and that he could not feel anything on his left side.

Patients with anosognosia often appear unaware of deficits even when these deficits are clearly evident. Anosognosic patients with hemiplegia (paralysis on one side of the body) might, for example, reply in the affirmative when asked if they can walk. When asked to raise their arms, they might raise only the unimpaired arm, but insist that both arms are raised. When confronted with the truth, they often admit to it, but then shortly afterwards, appear once again unaware of their deficits. Patients with anosognosia sometimes fabricate information to explain their deficits. For example, when a patient with paralysis of the left side is asked to move his left arm, he might explain his inability to do so by stating that because he is right-handed, his left side is weaker than his right. Confabulations can sometimes be illogical or bizarre. For example, a patient, when shown his paralyzed left arm, might insist that the arm belongs to someone else. Patients with anosognosia may not be motivated to engage in rehabilitation therapy because they do not recognize that they have deficits.

Anosognosia can be selective. A patient may admit to one kind of deficit, such as blindness in one visual field, but appear unaware of another deficit, such as paralysis of a limb. Anosognosia can also vary in degree. In its most extreme form, patients may completely deny a deficit, or fail to recognize it. In less extreme forms, patients may minimize the deficit or appear unconcerned about it, a condition referred to as anosodiaphoria.

Causes and symptoms

Causes

Scientists still have a poor understanding of anosognosia and its causes. Many different kinds of theories have been proposed to account for anosognosia. For many years after anosognosia was first described, researchers thought of it as a psychological phenom-

KEY TERMS

Aphasia—The loss of the ability to speak or understand language, due to brain injury or disease.

Amnesia—Memory loss.

Confabulation—The filling in of gaps in memory with false or imagined details.

Hemiplegia—Paralysis of one side of the body.

Lesion—An injured, diseased, or damaged area.

Vestibular system—The body system that helps to maintain balance and orient the body.

enon arising from, for example, an attempt to cope with the **stress** of having a disability. However, other researchers pointed out that a psychological account does not explain why most cases of anosognosia are seen in patients with damage to the right hemisphere, and why ansosognosic patients sometimes deny one kind of disability but admit to being aware of others. Another kind of theory suggests that anosognosia may be the result of damage to areas and processes in the brain that represent the position, movement and sensation of different parts of the body. According to this type of theory, if, for example, a part of the brain that represents the left arm is damaged, the person may no longer be aware of an inability to move the left arm. Attentional theories, posed by some researchers, propose that anosognosia is due, not to a problem with representing a particular body area, but an inability to direct attention to a particular part of the body. Other theories focus on the fact that damage to the right hemisphere of the brain affects the ability to perceive and express emotions, and suggest that such damage may in part explain why anosognosic patients appear unconcerned about their deficits. Yet others have suggested that anosognosia arises when normal connections between the two hemispheres of the brain are lost.

Demographics

Although there are no reports of exact percentages, the majority of patients with acquired brain injuries are thought to show some unawareness of their deficits. Most research, however, has not attempted to distinguish between anosognosia and denial of illness in these patients. Lesions in the right hemisphere of the brain appear to be more likely to result in anosognosia than lesions in the left hemisphere.

Treatments

Cases of anosognosia often resolve themselves over time. In long-term cases, cognitive therapy may help patients cope with their impaired function, but may not relieve the anosognosia. Researchers have found that caloric reflex testing—stimulating the vestibular system by squirting cold water into one ear—temporarily removes the anosognosia in some patients. The reasons for this temporary effect are unknown.

See also Anton's syndrome; Confabulation; Unilateral neglect.

Resources

BOOKS

Butcher, James N., Susan Mineka, and Jill. M. Hooley. *Abnormal Psychology*. Boston, MA: Pearson Education, 2007.

Hirstein, William. *Brain Fiction: Self-Deception and the Riddle of Confabulation*. Cambridge, MA: MIT Press. 2005.

PERIODICALS

Kortee, Kathleen B., and Stephen T. Wegener. "Denial of Illness in Medical Rehabilitation Populations: Theory, Research and Definition." *Rehabilitation Psychology* 49. 3 (2004): 187–99.

Kortte, Kathleen Bechtold, Stephen T. Wegener, and Kathleen Chwalisz. "Anosognosia and Denial: Their Relationship to Coping and Depression in Acquired Brain Injury." *Rehabilitation Psychology* 48. 3 (2003): 131–36.

Vuilleumier, Patrik. "Anosognosia: The Neurology of Beliefs and Uncertainties." *Cortex* 40 (2004): 9–17.

Ruvanee Pietersz Vilhauer, PhD

Antabuse *see* **Disulfiram**

▌Anti-anxiety drugs and abuse

Definition

Anti-anxiety drugs, or "anxiolytics," are powerful central nervous system (CNS) depressants that can slow normal **brain** function. They are often prescribed to reduce feelings of tension and **anxiety**, and/or to bring about sleep. Anti-anxiety medications are among the most abused drugs in the United States, obtained both legally, via prescription, and illegally, through the black market. These drugs are also known as **sedatives**.

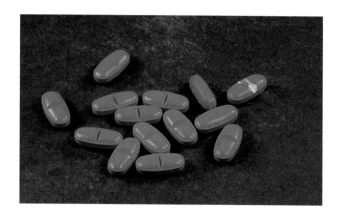

Rohypnol tablets. *(David Hoffman Photo Library/Alamy)*

Description

The drugs associated with this class of substance-related disorders are the **benzodiazepines** (e.g. **diazepam** [Valium], **chlordiazepoxide** [Librium], **alprazolam** [Xanax], **triazolam** [Halcion], and **estazolam** [ProSom]), the **barbiturates** (e.g., Seconal and pentobarbital [Nembutal]), and barbiturate-like substances including Quaalude, Equanil, and Doriden. Any of these drugs is capable of producing either wakeful relief from tension, or sleep, depending upon dosage. Some nonpsychiatric uses of anti-anxiety medications include treatment and prevention of **seizures**, or as muscle relaxants, anesthetics, and drugs to make other anesthetics work more effectively (known as "adjuvants").

Although the types of central nervous system depressants work differently, they all produce a pleasant drowsy or calming effect. If used over a long period of time, tolerance develops, and larger doses are needed to achieve the initial effects. Continued use can lead both to physical dependence, and when use is reduced or stopped to withdrawal symptoms. When combined with each other or other CNS depressants, such as alcohol, the effects are additive.

In addition to the drugs available in the United States by prescription, there are three other drugs that are predominantly central nervous system depressants with significant potential for **abuse**. These are:

- gamma hydroxybutyrate (GHB)
- flunitrazepam (Rohypnol)
- ketamine

GHB has been abused in the United States since about 1990, for its euphoric, sedative, and anabolic (bodybuilding) effects. It was widely available over the counter in health food stores until 1992. Bodybuilders used it to aid in reducing percentage of body fat, and to build muscle. Street names for GHB include "Liquid ecstasy," "soap," "easy lay," and "Georgia home boy."

Rohypnol has been of particular concern during the last few years because of its abuse in date rape. When mixed with alcohol, Rohypnol can incapacitate its victims and prevent them from resisting sexual assault. It can also lead to anterograde **amnesia**, in which individuals cannot remember what they experienced while under the influence. Rohypnol can be lethal when mixed with alcohol and/or other depressants. Rohypnol is not available by prescription in the United States, and it is illegal to import it. Even so, illegal use of Rohypnol started appearing in the United States in the early 1990s, where it became known as "rophies," "roofies," "roach," and "rope."

Ketamine is an anesthetic used predominately by veterinarians to treat animals. It can be injected or snorted. Ketamine goes by the street names of "Special K," or "Vitamin K." At certain doses, ketamine can cause dreamlike states and **hallucinations**. It has become particularly common in club and rave (large, all-night dance marathon) settings, and has also been used as a date-rape drug. At high doses, it can cause **delirium**, amnesia, impaired motor functioning, high blood pressure, and **depression**. It can also cause potentially fatal respiratory problems.

Causes and symptoms

Causes

Anti-anxiety drugs can be taken orally to bring about a general calming or drowsy effect, usually experienced as pleasant. Abuse of anti-anxiety medication can develop with prolonged use, as tolerance grows relatively quickly. Increasing amounts of the drug are then needed to produce the initial effect. It is possible to become addicted to anti-anxiety drugs even when they are medically prescribed.

A second cause of anti-anxiety drug abuse is the use of anti-anxiety drugs when combined with other drugs, such as **cocaine**. It is not uncommon for an addict to pair the use of a stimulant, such as cocaine or **methamphetamine**, with a CNS depressant. This allows the user to feel alert for an extended period of time, and then be able to "come down" from the high, and even fall asleep.

Symptoms

Even when prescribed for medical reasons, an individual taking central nervous system depressants usually feels sleepy and uncoordinated during the first few days of treatment. As the body adjusts to the effects of the drug, these feelings begin to disappear. If the drug is used long term, the body develops tolerance, and increasing doses are needed to obtain the desired effect of general calming or drowsiness.

The use of anti-anxiety drugs can pose extreme danger when taken along with other medications that cause CNS depression, such as prescription pain medicines, some over-the-counter cold and allergy medications, or alcohol. Use of additional depressants can slow breathing and respiration, and can even lead to death.

Withdrawal from anti-anxiety medications can be dangerous if not done under medical supervision. The safest method of withdrawal involves a gradual reduction of dosage. Abrupt withdrawal from these medications can lead to seizures due to sudden increase in brain activity.

Demographics

According to the 2005 National Survey on Drug Use and Health, 20% of people 12 years of age and older have at some point in their life used prescription-type psychotherapeutic drugs (including anti-anxiety medications) for recreational purposes, although only 6.2% admitted to having done so in the month before the survey was taken. Of these, the highest rate of abuse occurred in people 18–25 (30.3%), followed by those in the 26 and older age bracket (19.3%). In general, males were more likely to abuse prescription-type drugs than females (21.9% versus 18.3%). By race, American Indians or Alaska natives were the most likely to engage in this form of drug abuse (29.0%), while African Americans were the least likely to do so (12.6%).

Diagnosis

The manual used by mental health professionals to diagnose mental illnesses, the **Diagnostic and Statistical Manual of Mental Disorders**, (the fourth edition, text revision or *DSM-IV-TR*,) includes specific diagnostic criteria for four types of anti-anxiety medication abuse. These are:

- dependence
- abuse
- intoxication
- withdrawal

Substance dependence, the more severe form of **addiction**, is a group of cognitive, behavioral, and physiological symptoms associated with the continued use of the substance, and includes both tolerance and withdrawal symptoms. Abuse is a less severe form of addiction that may also result in risky behavior, such as driving while under the influence. For example, an individual with an abuse disorder may miss work or school, or get into arguments with parents or spouse about substance use. Such problems can easily escalate into full-blown dependence.

Intoxication refers to the presence of clinically significant problem behaviors or psychological changes, such as inappropriate sexual or aggressive behavior, mood swings, impaired judgment, or impaired social or work functioning, that develop during or shortly after use of an anti-anxiety medication. As with other CNS depressants such as alcohol, these behaviors may be accompanied by slurred speech, unsteady gait, memory or attention problems, poor coordination, and eventually, stupor or coma. Memory impairment is relatively common, especially a kind known as anterograde amnesia that resembles alcoholic blackouts.

Withdrawal is a characteristic syndrome that develops when use of anti-anxiety medication is severely reduced or stopped abruptly. It is similar to abrupt cessation of heavy alcohol use. Symptoms may include increases in heart rate, respiratory rate, blood pressure or body temperature, sweating, hand tremor, **insomnia**, anxiety, nausea, and restlessness. Seizures may occur in perhaps as many as 20–30% of individuals undergoing untreated withdrawal. In the more severe forms of withdrawal, hallucinations and delirium can occur. Withdrawal symptoms are generally the opposite of the acute effects experience by first-time users of the drugs. Length of withdrawal varies depending upon the drug, and may last as few as 10 hours, or as long as three to four weeks. The longer the substance has been taken, and the higher the dosages used, the more likely that withdrawal will be severe.

Treatments

According to the National Institute on Drug Abuse (NIDA), successful treatment for anti-anxiety medication addiction needs to incorporate several components. Counseling, particularly cognitive-behavior counseling, focuses on helping addicted individuals identify and change behaviors, attitudes, and beliefs that contributed to their drug usage. Combined with prescribed medications to make withdrawal safer and easier, counseling can help the addicted individual eventually make a full recovery. Often, it takes multiple courses of treatment before full recovery can be achieved. Various levels of care, from outpatient to residential care for up to 18 months, are available, depending upon need. Narcotics Anonymous also offers ongoing recovery support.

Prognosis

The most typical course, according to the *DSM-IV-TR* involves teens or young people in their early 20s who may escalate occasional use of anti-anxiety medications to the point at which they develop problems such as abuse or dependence. This is particularly likely for individuals who also abuse other substances. An initial pattern of use at parties can eventually lead to daily use and high degrees of tolerance.

A second course, observed somewhat less frequently, involves individuals who initially obtain medications by prescription, usually for treatment of anxiety or insomnia. Though the vast majority of people who use medications as prescribed do not go on to develop **substance abuse** problems, a small minority do. Again, tolerance develops and the need for higher dosages to reach the initial effects occurs. Individuals may justify their continued use on the basis of the original symptoms, but active substance seeking becomes increasingly part of the picture. Others at higher risk are those with alcohol dependence who might be given prescription anti-anxiety medications to reduce their anxiety or insomnia.

Prevention

Health-care professionals play a very important role in preventing and detecting abuse of prescription drugs. Primary care physicians, nurse practitioners and pharmacists can all play a role.

It is estimated by NIDA that approximately 70% of all Americans visit a health-care provider at least once every two years. Thus, health-care providers are in a unique position not only to prescribe medications as appropriate, but also to identify prescription drug abuse when it exists and recommend appropriate treatment for recovery. Screening for substance abuse should be incorporated into routine history-taking, or if a patient presents with symptoms associated with problem drug use.

Over time, providers should be alert to any increases in the amount of medication being used, which may be a sign of tolerance. They should also be aware that individuals addicted to prescription medications may engage in "doctor shopping," that is, going from provider to provider in an effort to obtain multiple prescriptions of their abused drug.

Pharmacists can play a role in preventing prescription drug abuse as well. They should provide information and advice about the correct way to take prescribed medications, and be alert to drug interactions. They can also play a role in detecting prescription fraud by noticing suspicious-looking prescription forms.

KEY TERMS

Abuse—Substance abuse is a milder form of addiction than substance dependence. Generally, people who have been diagnosed with substance abuse do not experience the tolerance or withdrawal symptoms—the signs of physiological dependence—that people dependent on a substance experience.

Anxiolytic—A preparation or substance given to relieve anxiety; a tranquilizer.

Barbiturates—A class of medications (including Seconal and Nembutal) that causes sedation and drowsiness. They may be prescribed legally, but may also be used as drugs of abuse.

Benzodiazepines—A group of central nervous system depressants used to relieve anxiety or to induce sleep.

Dependence—The adaptation of neurons and other physical processes to the use of a drug, followed by withdrawal symptoms when the drug is removed; physiological and/or psychological addiction.

GHB—GHB, or gamma hydroxybutyrate, is a central nervous system depressant that has been abused in the United States for euphoric, sedative, bodybuilding, and date-rape purposes.

Intoxication—The presence of significant problem behaviors or psychological changes following ingestion of a substance.

Ketamine—An anesthetic used predominately by veterinarians to treat animals that can be used as a date-rape drug.

Rohypnol—Rohypnol, or flunitrazepam, is a central nervous system depressant that is not legal in the United States, but is used as a date-rape drug.

Sedative—A medication that induces relaxation and sleep.

Tranquilizer—A medication that induces a feeling of calm and relaxation.

Withdrawal—Symptoms experienced by a person who has become physically dependent on a drug, experienced when the drug use is discontinued.

See also Addiction; Anxiety and anxiety disorders; Anxiety-reduction techniques; Barbiturates; Buspirone; Chlordiazepoxide; Clonazepam; Clorazepine; Cognitive-behavioral therapy; Diazepam; Disease concept of chemical dependency; Estazolam;

Flurazepam; Fluvoxamine; Hypnotics and related disorders; Insomnia; Lorazepam; Sedatives and related drugs; Substance abuse and related disorders; Support groups; Triazolam; Zolpidem.

Resources

BOOKS

American Psychiatric Association. *American Psychiatric Association Diagnostic and Statistical Manual of Mental Disorders.* 4th ed., text rev. Washington, D.C.: American Psychiatric Association, 2000.

PERIODICALS

Carter, Lawrence P., and others. "Relative Abuse Liability of GHB in Humans: A Comparison of Psychomotor, Subjective, and Cognitive Effects of Supratherapeutic Doses of Triazolam, Pentobarbital, and GHB." *Neuropsychopharmacology* 31.11 (November 2006): 2537–51.

de Wit, Harriet, and others. "Evaluation of the Abuse Potential of Pagoclone, a Partial GABA-Sub(A) Agonist." *Journal of Clinical Psychopharmacology* 26.3 (June 2006): 268–73.

Kurtz, Steven P., and others. "Prescription Drug Abuse Among Ecstasy Users in Miami." *Journal of Addictive Diseases* 24.4 (2005): 1–16.

Mintzer, Miriam Z., and R. R. Griffiths. "An Abuse Liability Comparison of Flunitrazepam and Triazolam in Sedative Drug Abusers." *Behavioural Pharmacology* 16.7 (November 2005): 579–84.

ORGANIZATIONS

American Council for Drug Education, 136 E. 64th St., New York, NY 10021.

Narcotics Anonymous, P.O. Box 9999, Van Nuys, CA 91409. Telephone: (818) 780-3951.

National Institute on Drug Abuse (NIDA). U.S. Department of Health and Human Services. 5600 Fishers Lane, Rockville, MD 20857 <http://www.nida.nih.gov>.

OTHER

U.S. Department of Health and Human Services, Office of Applied Statistics. *2005 National Survey on Drug Use and Health.* <http://www.oas.samhsa.gov/nsduhLatest.htm>.

Barbara S. Sternberg, PhD
Ruth A. Wienclaw, PhD

Antidepressants

Definition

Antidepressants are medications that are used primarily to treat **depression**. Antidepressant drugs are also sometimes used to treat other psychological disorders, such as **anxiety disorders** and eating disorders. Because they are thought to increase the effectiveness of some pain medications, they are sometimes used in the treatment of migraine-type headaches. They are also used as a component of **smoking cessation** programs, and in the treatment of fibromyalgia and some types of **sleep disorders**.

Description

Antidepressant drugs can be used to treat depression and other disorders. A person with depression has symptoms that last for at least two weeks. These symptoms can include feelings of sadness, emptiness, guilt, or worthlessness, loss of interest in previously pleasurable activities, changes in eating and sleeping patterns, **fatigue**, lethargy or agitation, difficulty concentrating, and suicidal thoughts. Antidepressant drugs are not the only treatment for depression; **psychotherapy** and other treatments are also independently effective in alleviating depression. Antidepressant drugs, if prescribed, are often used in combination with these other treatments.

The type of antidepressant medication prescribed depends on the particular array of symptoms a patient displays or reports. There are several different types of antidepressant drugs. All of them work by altering the level or activity of **neurotransmitters** in the **brain**. Neurotransmitters are chemicals that are released by neurons, or nerve cells. They attach to other neurons and activate them in various ways. Although antidepressant drugs affect communication between neurons within hours after these drugs are ingested, symptoms of depression usually improve only after a few weeks of taking the medication. Some people notice improvement in symptoms after only two weeks, but many people notice a benefit only after six to eight weeks of using the medication. The reason for this delayed effect of antidepressants is not entirely clear. One theory is related to the finding that the changes in neurotransmitter activity caused by antidepressants increase the release of other chemicals, called neurotrophins, in the brain. In the normal brain, neurotrophins help neurons to grow and connect to other neurons. People with depression sometimes have shrinkage of neurons in parts of the brain. When more neurotrophins are present, neurons in these areas of the brain can grow.

The main classes of antidepressant drugs are tricyclics, monoamine oxidase inhibitors (MAOIs), **selective serotonin reuptake inhibitors (SSRIs)**, and atypical antidepressants. A patient who does not improve with one type of antidepressant drug may sometimes be helped by another type of antidepressant, because different drugs work in different ways.

Tricyclic antidepressants

The first class of drugs used to treat depression, from the 1960s through the 1980s, was that of tricyclic antidepressants. Tricyclic antidepressants work by preventing neurons from reabsorbing the neurotransmitters serotonin, **dopamine**, and norepinephrine, after they are released. This means that the neurotransmitters are able to remain in the gaps between neurons for a longer period of time, thus continuing to activate the neurons that receive them. Tricyclic antidepressants can have side effects because they can prevent nerve cells from functioning normally, and because they can prevent additional neurotransmitters from working effectively. For example, they block the activity of histamine, a neurotransmitter that is involved in keeping people alert and awake. They also block the activity of acetylcholine, a neurotransmitter that is involved in many automatic bodily activities. Tricyclic antidepressants include **imipramine** (trade name Tofranil), **amitriptyline** (trade names Elavil, Endep), **clomipramine** (trade name Anafranil), **doxepin** (trade names Sinequan, Adapin), **desipramine** (trade name Norpramin), **nortriptyline** (trade name Pamelor), **protriptyline** (trade name Vivactil), and **trimipramine** (trade name Surmontil).

MAOIs

The monoamine oxidase inhibitors are drugs that prevent neurotransmitters such as dopamine, serotonin and norepinephrine from being broken down into inactive chemicals. This means that, when MAOIs are used, more of these neurotransmitters are available to send messages in the brain. MAOIs can have potentially serious side effects because they also prevent the amino acid tyramine from being broken down. Tyramine is a chemical that the body needs, and it is found in foods like aged cheese, smoked and pickled meats and fish, and raisins. If tyramine that is ingested cannot be broken down, it can accumulate in the body, causing increased blood pressure and possibly strokes. The MAOIs include isocarboxazid (trade name Marplan), **phenelzine** (trade name Nardil), and **tranylcypromine** (trade name Parnate).

SSRIs

The selective serotonin reuptake inhibitors are drugs that work by preventing neurons from reabsorbing serotonin after it is released, so that the effect of serotonin on adjoining neurons is prolonged. The SSRIs include **citalopram** (trade name Celexa), escitalopram (trade name Lexapro), **fluoxetine** (trade name

Prozac), **fluvoxamine** (trade name Luvox), **paroxetine** (trade name **Paxil**), and **sertraline** (trade name Zoloft).

Atypical antidepressants

The atypical antidepressants are a miscellaneous collection of drugs. One of these drugs, **bupropion** (trade name Wellbutrin), prevents dopamine, and to some extent, norepinephrine, from being reabsorbed by neurons, so that these neurotransmitters are able to have a more prolonged effect. Another drug, **venlafaxine** (trade name Effexor), prevents serotonin, and to a smaller extent, norepinephrine and dopamine, from being reabsorbed. Other atypical antidepressants include **mirtazapine** (trade name Remeron), **trazodone** (trade name Desyrel) and duloxetine (trade name Cymbalta).

Recommended dosage

The dosage of antidepressants depends on the particular drug being prescribed, and other factors such as the age of the patient, the patient's body chemistry, and the patient's body weight. Patients are usually started on a low dose to minimize side effects, and the dose is gradually increased over time to a level that is therapeutic. Newer antidepressants, however, may be started at the therapeutic dosage level.

Precautions

In 2005, the U.S. Food and Drug Administration warned that SSRI drugs may increase suicidal thoughts in children and adolescents. It urged health-care practitioners and families of patients to carefully monitor people, of any age, who take these drugs. The National Institutes of Health is currently carrying out research to study the nature of the association between suicidal thoughts and antidepressant drugs. Canadian researchers at McGill University also found that adults over age 50 who take SSRIs are at double the risk of bone fractures.

Antidepressants can precipitate mania in people who are susceptible to **bipolar disorder**. Therefore, a health-care practitioner typically takes a detailed history of a patient before prescribing antidepressants. Various medical problems may affect the effectiveness or risks of antidepressants. These include, but are not limited to, angina, headaches, epilepsy, recent heart attacks or **stroke**, kidney disease, and diabetes. Some antidepressants may affect a fetus, therefore pregnant women should inform their doctors about their condition before antidepressants are prescribed. Patients taking tricyclic antidepressants should carefully

---

KEY TERMS

Anxiety disorder—A type of psychological disorder characterized by unrealistic, irrational fear or intense anxiety.

Eating disorder—A type of psychological disorder characterized by disturbances in eating patterns, extreme concern about weight gain and unhealthy efforts to control weight.

Sleeping disorders—Disorders in which people experience disturbances of sleep.

Fibromyalgia—A condition in which a person experiences chronic pain in the muscles and soft tissues around joints.

Mania—A state in which a person experiences intense excitement and euphoria.

Stroke—A temporary loss of normal blood flow to an area of the brain, caused by blockage or rupture of a blood vessel.

---

adhere to the dietary restrictions provided by their doctor, in order to avoid potentially serious side effects. Patients who stop taking antidepressants may experience withdrawal symptoms if the drugs are abruptly discontinued.

Side effects

People who take antidepressants may experience side effects. Different people experience different side effects. Such side effects may include dry mouth, constipation, nausea, bladder problems, sexual problems, blurred vision, dizziness, daytime drowsiness, **insomnia**, increased heart rate, headache, nervousness, and agitation. The newer antidepressants are thought to have fewer and less troublesome side effects than the tricyclic antidepressants and the MAOIs.

Interactions

Antidepressants may result in dangerous side effects if taken in combination with other medications. There can also be dangerous side effects if different types of antidepressants are combined with each other. Patients should inform their doctor about all other medications and herbal supplements they are taking before antidepressant drugs are prescribed. Alcohol or other recreational drugs may decrease the effectiveness of antidepressants. Antidepressants may increase the intoxicating effect of alcohol.

Resources

BOOKS

American Psychiatric Association. *Diagnostical and Statistical Manual of Mental Disorders,* 4th edition, Text revision. Washington, D.C.:American Psychiatric Association, 2000.

Diamond, Ronald, J. *Instant Psychopharmacology.* 2nd edition. New York: W.W. Norton and Company, 2002.

Dunbar, Katherine Read, ed. *Antidepressants.* Farmington Hills, MI: Greenhaven Press, 2006.

Kalat, James W. *Biological Psychology.* 9th edition. Belmont, CA: Thomson Wadsworth, 2007.

OTHER

"New NIMH Research Strives to Understand How Antidepressants May Be Associated with Suicidal Thoughts and Actions." National Institutes of Health. 2006. <http://www.nih.gov/news/pr/nov2006/nimh-13.htm> (January 12, 2006).

"Medications." National Institutes of Mental Health. 2002. <http://www.nimh.nih.gov/publicat/medicate.cfm> (January 12, 2006).

"Drug Information: Antidepressants, Monoamine Oxidase (MAO) Inhibitor (Systemic)." Medline Plus. 2005. <http://www.nlm.nih.gov/medlineplus/druginfo/uspdi/202054.html> (January 2006).

"Drug Information: Antidepressants, Tricyclic (Systemic)." Medline Plus. 2005. <http://www.nlm.nih.gov/medli neplus/druginfo/uspdi/202055.html> (January 2006).

"Daily Use of Antidepressants Associated with Increased Risk of Fracture in Older Adults" Newswise. <http://www.newswise.com/articles/view/526667/> (January 2007).

Ruvanee Pietersz Vilhauer, Ph.D.

Antisocial personality disorder

Definition

Also known as psychopathy, sociopathy, or dissocial personality disorder, antisocial personality disorder (APD) is a **diagnosis** applied to persons who routinely behave with little or no regard for the rights, safety, or feelings of others. This pattern of behavior is seen in children or young adolescents and can persist into adulthood.

The most recent edition of the ***Diagnostic and Statistical Manual of Mental Disorders,*** (the fourth edition, text revision or *DSM-IV-TR*) classifies APD as one of four "Cluster B Personality Disorders" along with borderline, histrionic, and narcissistic **personality disorders**.

Description

Men or women diagnosed with this personality disorder demonstrate few emotions beyond contempt for other people. Their lack of empathy is often combined with an inflated sense of self-worth and a superficial charm that tends to mask an inner indifference to the needs or feelings of others. Some studies indicate that people with APD can only mimic the emotions associated with committed love relationships and friendships that most people feel naturally.

People reared by parents with antisocial personality disorder or **substance abuse** disorders are more likely to develop APD than members of the general population. People with the disorder may be homeless, living in poverty, suffering from a concurrent substance **abuse** disorder, or piling up extensive criminal records, as antisocial personality disorder is associated with low socioeconomic status and urban backgrounds. Highly intelligent individuals with APD, however, may not come to the attention of the criminal justice or mental health care systems and may be underrepresented in diagnostic statistics.

Some legal experts and mental health professionals do not think that APD should be classified as a mental disorder on the grounds that the classification appears to excuse unethical, illegal, or immoral behavior. Despite these concerns, juries in the United States have consistently demonstrated that they do not regard a diagnosis of APD as exempting a person from prosecution or punishment for crimes committed.

Furthermore, some experts disagree with the categorization by the American Psychiatric Association (APA) of antisocial personality disorder. The APA considers the term "psychopathy" as another, synonymous name for APD. However, some experts make a distinction between psychopathy and APD. Dr. Robert Hare, an authority on psychopathy and the originator of the **Hare Psychopathy Checklist**, claims that all psychopaths have APD but not all individuals diagnosed with APD are psychopaths. Recent reports have made this distinction even clearer, suggesting that there is emotional deficit component of psychopathy that is not necessarily present in people with APD. One expert review comments that only 25% of people diagnosed with APD or the putatively related "conduct disorder" will show psychopathic tendencies.

Causes and symptoms

Causes

Studies of adopted children indicate that both genetic and environmental factors influence the development of APD, with heritability estimates ranging from 44% to 72%. Both biological and adopted children of people diagnosed with the disorder have an increased risk of developing it. Children born to parents diagnosed with APD but adopted into other families resemble their biological more than their adoptive parents in this regard. The environment of the adoptive home, however, may lower the child's risk of developing APD.

Researchers have linked antisocial personality disorder to childhood physical or sexual abuse, neurological disorders (which are often undiagnosed), and low IQ. Some experts have recently questioned the link between psychopathy, which these experts distinguish from APD, and early environmental trauma. As with other personality disorders, no one has identified any specific cause or causes of antisocial personality disorder. Indeed, one group with the U.S. National Institute of Mental Health has stated that "there are many developmental routes to an elevated risk for antisocial behavior." Persons diagnosed with APD also have an increased incidence of **somatization disorder** and substance-related disorders.

The *DSM-IV-TR* adds that persons who show signs of **conduct disorder** with accompanying attention-deficit/hyperactivity disorder before the age of 10 have a greater chance of being diagnosed with APD as adults than do other children. The manual notes that abuse or **neglect** combined with erratic parenting or inconsistent discipline appears to increase the risk that a child diagnosed with conduct disorder will develop APD as an adult.

Brain imaging studies have identified some specific characteristics in the brains of people diagnosed with APD that suggest dysfunction of structures in the frontal and temporal lobes of the brain.

Symptoms

The central characteristic of antisocial personality disorder is an extreme disregard for the rights of other people. Individuals with APD lie and cheat to gain money or power. Their disregard for authority often leads to arrest and imprisonment. Because they have little regard for others and may act impulsively, they are frequently involved in fights. They show loyalty to few if any other people and are likely to seek power over others in order to satisfy sexual desires or economic needs.

People with APD often become effective "con artists." Those with well-developed verbal abilities can often charm and fool their victims, including unsuspecting or inexperienced therapists. People with

APD have no respect for what others regard as societal norms or legal constraints. They may quit jobs on short notice, move to another city, or end relationships without warning and without what others would consider good reason. Criminal activities typically include theft, selling illegal drugs, and check fraud. Because persons with antisocial personality disorder make "looking out for number one" their highest priority, they are quick to exploit others. They commonly rationalize these actions by dismissing their victims as weak, stupid, or unwary.

Some work has been done on the relationship between what are called "minor physical anomalies" and the presence of various disorders, including aggression disorders and psychopathy. The presence of these features—which include low-seated ears and adherent ear lobes—is associated with developmental derailments in the fetus at the end of the third trimester of pregnancy, and they have been linked with the development of conduct disorder and violence in adulthood. Studies directly examining their association, if any, with psychopathy or APD are lacking. Birth complications are known risk factors for violent, antisocial behaviors.

Demographics

APD is estimated to affect 3% of males and 1% of females in the general population of the United States. Mental health professionals may diagnose 3–30% of the population in clinical settings as having the disorder. The percentages may be even higher among prison inmates or persons in treatment for substance abuse. By some estimates, three-quarters of the prison population may meet the diagnostic criteria for APD.

Diagnosis

The diagnosis of antisocial personality disorder is usually based on a combination of a careful medical as well as psychiatric history and an interview with the patient. The doctor will look for recurrent or repetitive patterns of antisocial behavior. He or she may use a diagnostic questionnaire for APD, such as the Hare Psychopathy Checklist-Revised or the self-reporting Psychopathic Personality Inventory, if the patient's history suggests the diagnosis. A person aged 18 years or older with a childhood history of disregard for the rights of others can be diagnosed as having APD if he or she gives evidence of three of the following seven behaviors associated with disregard for others:

- Fails to conform to social norms, as indicated by frequently performing illegal acts or pursuing illegal occupations.

- Deceives and manipulates others for selfish reasons, often in order to obtain money, sex, drugs, or power. This behavior may involve repeated lying, conning, or the use of false names.
- Fails to plan ahead or displays impulsive behavior, as indicated by a long succession of short-term jobs or frequent changes of address.
- Engages in repeated fights or assaults as a consequence of irritability and aggressiveness.
- Exhibits reckless disregard for safety of self or others.
- Shows a consistent pattern of irresponsible behavior, including failure to find and keep a job for a sustained length of time and refusal to pay bills or honor debts.
- Shows no evidence of sadness, regret or remorse for actions that have hurt others.

To meet *DSM-IV-TR* criteria for APD, a person must also have had some symptoms of conduct disorder before age 15. An adult 18 years or older who does not meet all the criteria for APD may be given a diagnosis of conduct disorder.

Antisocial behavior may appear in other mental disorders as well as in APD. These conditions must be distinguished from true APD. For instance, it is not uncommon for a person with a substance abuse disorder to lie to others in order to obtain money for drugs or alcohol. But unless indications of antisocial behavior were present during the person's childhood, he or she would not be diagnosed with antisocial personality disorder. People who meet the criteria for a substance abuse disorder as well as APD would be given a **dual diagnosis**.

Treatments

Antisocial personality disorder is highly unresponsive to any form of treatment, in part because persons with APD rarely seek treatment voluntarily. If they do seek help, it is usually in an attempt to find relief from **depression** or other forms of emotional distress. Although there are medications that are effective in treating some of the symptoms of the disorder, noncompliance with medication regimens or abuse of the drugs prevents the widespread use of these medications. The most successful treatment programs for APD are long-term structured residential settings in which the patient systematically earns privileges as he or she modifies behavior. In other words, if a person diagnosed with APD is placed in an environment in which they cannot victimize others, their behavior may improve. It is unlikely, however, that they would maintain good behavior if they left the disciplined environment.

If some form of individual **psychotherapy** is provided along with **behavior modification** techniques, the therapist's primary task is to establish a relationship with the patient, who has usually had very few healthy relationships in his or her life and is unable to trust others. The patient should be given the opportunity to establish positive relationships with as many people as possible and be encouraged to join **self-help groups** or prosocial organizations.

Unfortunately, these approaches are rarely if ever effective. Many persons with APD use therapy sessions to learn how to turn "the system" to their advantage. Their pervasive pattern of manipulation and deceit extends to all aspects of their life, including therapy. Generally, their behavior must be controlled in a setting where they know they have no chance of getting around the rules.

Prognosis

APD can follow a chronic and unremitting course from childhood or early adolescence into adult life.

The impulsiveness that characterizes the disorder often leads to a jail sentence or an early death through accident, homicide, or **suicide**. There is some evidence that the worst behaviors that define APD diminish by midlife; the more overtly aggressive symptoms of the disorder occur less frequently in older patients. This improvement is especially true of criminal behavior but may apply to other antisocial acts as well.

Prevention

Measures intended to prevent antisocial personality disorder must begin with interventions in early childhood, before youths are at risk for developing conduct disorder. Preventive strategies include education for parenthood and other programs intended to lower the incidence of child abuse; Big Brother/Big Sister and similar mentoring programs to provide children at risk with adult role models of responsible and prosocial behavior; and further research into the genetic factors involved in APD.

Resources

BOOKS

American Psychiatric Association. *Diagnostic and Statistical Manual of Mental Disorders,* 4th ed., Text rev. Washington D.C.: American Psychiatric Association, 2000.

Black, Donald, W., with C. Lindon Larson. *Bad Boys, Bad Men: Confronting Antisocial Personality Disorder.* New York: Oxford University Press, 1999.

Cleckley, Hervey. *The Mask of Sanity,* 5th ed. Augusta, GA: Emily S. Cleckley, 1988.

Hare, Robert D. *Without Conscience: The Disturbing World of the Psychopaths Among Us.* New York: The Guilford Press, 1993.

Lykken, David T. *The Antisocial Personalities.* Hillsdale, NJ: Lawrence Erlbaum Associates, 1995.

Simon, Robert I. *Bad Men Do What Good Men Dream: A Forensic Psychiatrist Illuminates the Darker Side of Human Behavior.* Washington D.C.: American Psychiatric Press, 1996.

PERIODICALS

Abbott, Alison. "Into the Mind of a Killer." *Nature* 410 (2001): 296–98.

OTHER

Hare, Robert D. "Dr. Robert Hare's Page for the Study of Psychopaths." <http://www.hare.org> (January 29, 2002).

National Library of Medicine. National Institutes of Health. "Antisocial Personality Disorder." <http://www.nlm. nih.gov/medlineplus/ency/article/000921.htm>.

Dean A. Haycock, PhD
Emily Jane Willingham, PhD

Anxiety and anxiety disorders

Definition

Anxiety is a mood characterized by apprehension and associated bodily symptoms of tension (e.g., tense muscles, fast breathing, rapid heart beat). When anxious, the individual anticipates threat, danger, or misfortune. Such fears may be real or imagined, come from either an internal or external source, and may be identifiable or vague. Anxiety is a prominent feature in a group of disorders collectively called anxiety disorders, including **panic disorder** (with or without **agoraphobia**), agoraphobia without panic disorder, **specific phobias**, **social phobia**, **obsessive-compulsive disorder** (OCD), **post-traumatic stress disorder** (PTSD), **acute stress disorder**, **generalized anxiety disorder**, anxiety disorder due to a general medical condition, and **substance-induced anxiety disorder**.

Description

Stimulated by real or imagined dangers, anxiety afflicts people of all ages and social backgrounds. When the anxiety results from irrational fears, it can disrupt or disable normal life. Some researchers believe anxiety is synonymous with fear, occurring in varying degrees and in situations in which people feel threatened by some danger. Others describe anxiety as an unpleasant emotion caused by unidentifiable dangers or dangers that, in reality, pose no threat. Unlike fear, which is caused by realistic, known dangers, anxiety can be more difficult to identify and to alleviate.

Rather than attempting to formulate a strict definition of anxiety, most psychologists simply make the distinction between normal anxiety and neurotic anxiety, or anxiety disorders. Normal (sometimes called objective) anxiety occurs when people react appropriately to the situation causing the anxiety. For example, many people experience stage fright—the fear of speaking in public in front of large groups of people. And most people feel anxious on the first day at a new job for any number of reasons. They are uncertain how they will be received by coworkers, they may be unfamiliar with their duties, or they may be unsure they made the correct decision in taking the job. There is little, if any, real danger posed by either situation, yet each can stimulate intense feelings of anxiety that can affect or derail a person's desires or obligations. However, despite these feelings and any accompanying physiological responses, most people carry on and eventually adapt. In contrast, anxiety that is characteristic of anxiety disorders is disproportionately intense. Anxious feelings interfere with a person's ability to carry out normal or desired activities. Sigmund Freud described neurotic anxiety as a danger signal. In his id-ego-superego scheme of human behavior, anxiety occurs when unconscious sexual or aggressive tendencies conflict with physical or moral limitations.

According to the most recent edition of the *Diagnostic and Statistical Manual of Mental Disorders,* (the fourth edition, text revision or *DSM-IV-TR*), the following disorders are considered anxiety disorders:

• Panic disorder without agoraphobia—A person with this disorder has recurrent panic attacks and worries about experiencing more attacks, but agoraphobia is not present. Panic attacks are sudden attacks of intense fear or apprehension during which the person may experience shortness of breath, increased heart rate, choking, and/or a fear of losing control. Agoraphobia is anxiety about places or situations from which escape might be difficult, or in which help might not be available.

• Panic disorder with agoraphobia—A person with this disorder experiences recurrent panic attacks but also has agoraphobia. The anxiety about certain places or situations may lead to avoidance of those places or situations.

• Agoraphobia without history of panic disorder—The person with this disorder has agoraphobia and experiences paniclike symptoms but does not experience recurring panic attacks.

• Specific phobias—A person diagnosed with a specific phobia experiences extreme anxiety when he or she is exposed to a particular object or situation. The feared stimuli may include: particular animals (dogs, spiders, snakes, etc.), situations (crossing bridges, driving through tunnels), storms, heights, and many others.

• Social phobia—A person with social phobia fears social situations or situations in which he or she is expected to perform. These situations may include eating in public or speaking in public, for example.

• Obsessive-compulsive disorder—A person with this disorder feels anxiety in the presence of a certain stimulus or situation, and feels compelled to perform an act (a compulsion) to neutralize the anxiety. For example, upon touching a doorknob, a person may feel compelled to wash his or her hands four times, or more.

• Post-traumatic stress disorder—This disorder may be diagnosed after a person has experienced a traumatic event, and long after the event, the person still mentally reexperiences the event along with the same feelings of anxiety that the original event produced.

• Acute stress disorder—Disorder with similar symptoms to post-traumatic stress disorder, but is experienced immediately after the traumatic event. If this disorder persists longer than one month, the diagnosis may be changed to post-traumatic stress disorder.

• Generalized anxiety disorder—A person who has experienced six months or more of persistent and excessive worry and anxiety may receive this diagnosis.

• Anxiety due to a general medical condition—Anxiety that the clinician deems is caused by a medical condition.

• Substance-induced anxiety disorder—Symptoms of anxiety that are caused by a drug, a medication, or a toxin.

• Anxiety disorder not otherwise specified—This diagnosis may be given when a patient's symptoms do not meet the exact criteria for each of the above disorders as specified by *DSM-IV-TR.*

Currently, there is debate over the conceptualization and diagnostic criteria for several specific anxiety disorders. The diagnostic criteria of the *DSM-IV-TR* assume that the cluster of disorders characterized as "anxiety disorders" all have in common a pathological anxiety. However, not all clinicians and theorists agree that this is true. In addition, some believe that anxiety disorders can be further broken down into subtypes or that other the category should be widened to include other disorders (e.g., **hypochondriasis**, **avoidant personality disorder**).

Resources

BOOKS

Amen, Daniel G. *Change Your Brain, Change Your Life: The Breakthrough Program for Conquering Anxiety, Depression, Obsessiveness, Anger, and Impulsiveness.* New York: Crown Publishing Group, 2000.

American Psychiatric Association. *Diagnostic and Statistical Manual of Mental Disorders,* 4th ed., Text revision. Washington D.C.: American Psychiatric Association, 2000.

Morris, Tracy L. and John S. March, eds. *Anxiety Disorders in Children and Adolescents,* 2nd ed. New York: The Guildford Press, 2004.

Starcevic, Vladan. *Anxiety Disorders in Adults: A Clinical Guide.* New York: Oxford University Press, 2005.

VandenBos, Gary R., ed. *APA Dictionary of Psychology.* Washington D.C.: American Psychological Association, 2007.

Veeraraghavan, Vimala and Shalini Singh. *Anxiety Disorders: Psychological Assessment and Treatment.* Thousand Oaks, CA: Sage Publications, 2002.

Ruth A. Wienclaw, PhD

Anxiety reduction techniques

Definition

Anxiety reduction techniques are learned skills that can be used by an individual to help overcome anxiety and its associated mental and physical symptoms, including tension, worry, and nervousness. These techniques include relaxation, visualization and imagery, diaphragmatic breathing, **stress** inoculation, and **meditation**.

Relaxation or progressive relaxation

This anxiety reduction technique is based on the premise that anxiety and stress are associated with muscle tension. When one achieves deep muscle relaxation, muscle tension is reduced, and this relaxed state is incompatible with anxiety.

Visualization and imagery

This anxiety reduction technique aids the person in making a mental image of what he or she wants to accomplish. For example, an individual might wish to release worries or concerns, or create a relaxing image to escape momentarily from a stressful event.

Diaphragmatic breathing

This technique involves teaching a person to breathe sufficient amounts of air to help his or her blood fill with oxygen and be purified properly. In this technique, the individual breathes deeply from the diaphragm, which is located low in the chest, near the abdomen.

Stress inoculation

Self-talk, or the things that people tell themselves about stressful situations, can be habitual. For example, a person may take an ordinary event and automatically magnify its importance. Stress inoculation training is a type of therapy that teaches clients to cope with anxiety and stressful situations by learning more functional patterns of self-talk.

Meditation

In this anxiety reduction technique, an individual is trained to focus his or her attention on one thing at a time.

Purpose

The goal of learning and implementing anxiety reduction techniques is to help reduce the intensity of anxiety that an individual feels. These techniques are also helpful in teaching people how to relax and manage stress. Many of the techniques are used in combination with each other. For example, a person may be taught diaphragmatic breathing while also engaging in relaxation techniques, a visualization and imagery exercise, and/or meditation.

Relaxation or progressive relaxation

Relaxation has been used to help women during childbirth and people with **chronic pain**. Relaxation has also been used to treat muscle tension, muscle spasms, neck and back pain, and to decrease perspiration and respiratory rates. Furthermore, relaxation can help with **fatigue**, **depression**, **insomnia**, irritable bowel syndrome, high blood pressure, mild phobias, and **stuttering**.

Visualization and imagery

Visualization and imagery techniques have been helpful in treating general or specific anxiety, headaches, and muscle tension and spasms. They are also useful in reducing or eliminating pain, and in the recovery from illnesses and injuries. Visualization and imagery techniques have also been used by athletes to help them achieve peak performance.

Diaphragmatic breathing

Diaphragmatic breathing has been found to help people reduce anxiety, depression, irritability, muscle tension, circulation, and fatigue.

Stress inoculation

Stress inoculation has been helpful in reducing interpersonal and general anxiety. For example, these techniques may be used when a person has an upcoming job interview, speech, or test. Stress inoculation has also been used to treat phobias, fear of heights, and chronic anger problems.

Meditation

Meditation has been used to treat and prevent high blood pressure, heart disease, strokes, migraine headaches, immunization diseases, obsessive thinking, attention problems, anxiety, depression, and anger difficulties.

Description

These various techniques are often practiced and demonstrated in therapy sessions with a trained professional. In addition, the person learning the techniques would need to continue to practice them on a regular basis, outside of the therapy sessions.

Relaxation or progressive relaxation

In progressive relaxation, an individual is instructed to tighten and then relax various muscles. He or she either lies down or sits in a chair with his/her head supported. Each muscle group (such as face muscles, arm muscles, leg muscles, etc.) is tensed for five to seven seconds and then relaxed for 20 to 30 seconds. This helps the person recognize the feeling of tense and relaxed muscles. This entire procedure is repeated one to five times, and usually starts with the face muscles and moves downward to the foot muscles. When relaxation is used with chronic pain and childbirth, the techniques focus the person's attention on breathing and relaxing muscles as a distraction from the pain. For mastery, relaxation techniques are typically practiced every day for one to two weeks. A person may engage in these techniques anywhere from 15 minutes to an hour per session. Sometimes, the individual will record and replay instructions on tightening and relaxing various muscle groups until he or she becomes familiar with the muscle groups and establishes a comfortable routine.

Visualization and imagery

The basic premise behind visualization and imagery is that one's thoughts become reality. For example, if an individual thinks anxious thoughts, then he or she will become tense. The principle of visualization and imagery is that a person can use his or her imagination to be persuaded to feel a certain way or do anything that is physically possible to do. There are three basic types of visualization: programmed, receptive, and guided visualization.

In programmed visualization, the person creates a vivid image including sight, taste, sound, and smell. The individual then imagines a goal he or she wants to attain or some type of healing that is desired. In the visualization, the goal is achieved, or the healing occurs.

An idea underlying both receptive visualization and guided visualization is that the person is seeking an answer to a life question or resolution to an issue, and the answer or resolution is within the person, but is buried or inaccessible because of fear, doubt, or anxiety. These techniques are similar to dream interpretation and free association techniques used in **psychoanalysis** or psychodynamic therapy. For example, an individual may wonder whether he should remain in his current job. A proponent of these techniques would maintain that "deep down," below the level of conscious thought, the man knows what he really wants to do, but he is not allowing himself to listen to his desires or to act—he is blocking the message his subconscious is sending him. The goal of these techniques is to enable the person to relax and focus enough to receive that message, so that he or she can do what needs to be done. In receptive visualization, the individual creates a peaceful scene in his or her mind. After the image is formed, the person asks a question and waits for the answer. To continue the example above, the man imagines a beach, and he asks himself the question, "Should I leave my job?" He continues to relax and remain in the scene, and he may "hear" an answer blowing in the breeze or "see" a boat sailing away, which may be symbolic of his wish to leave his job.

In guided visualization, the person creates a very vivid image, as in programmed visualization, but omits some important elements. The person then waits for the subconscious to supply the missing pieces. For example, a computer programmer may wonder if she should stay in her present job or return to school for an advanced degree. In engaging in guided visualization, she may visualize her cubicle at work, the pictures on her desk, the feel of her desk chair, the sounds of people outside her cubicle typing and talking, but she will omit an element from the scene. In this case, she may omit her computer. She will then wait to see what her subconscious uses to replace her computer. This woman may find in her visualization that her computer has been replaced by books, which may represent her desire to return to school.

Visualization and imagery exercises work best when a person is relaxed. Visualization and imagery exercises are typically practiced two to three times a day for 10 to 20 minutes at a time. How quickly an individual will see results can vary. Many times people report immediate symptom relief. However, the personal goals a person sets, the power of a his or her imagination, and willingness to practice can all influence how rapidly benefits can be obtained. Some people find it helpful to tape record and replay detailed descriptions of what they want to visualize or imagine.

Diaphragmatic breathing

Diaphragmatic breathing can typically be learned in minutes; however, the benefits may not be recognized until after several months of persistent practice. When breathing from the diaphragm, clients are often told to lie down on a rug or blanket, with their legs slightly apart, arms to the sides not touching the body, with their eyes closed. Attention is brought to the breathing by placing one hand on the chest and the other hand on the abdomen area. The client is then instructed to breathe in through the nose and exhale out the mouth. Each time the client breathes in, he or she should try to breathe deeper. This should be practiced for a minimum of five minutes once or twice a day. Over a few weeks of practice, the time period engaged in diaphragmatic breathing should be increased to 20 minutes and the activity can be performed while lying down, sitting, or standing.

Stress inoculation

As people go about their daily lives, they often have thoughts in which they are talking to themselves. Stress inoculation involves this self-talk in helping clients decrease their anxiety and stress. Stress inoculation therapy works on the basis of turning the client's own thought patterns into a "vaccine" against stress-induced anxiety. The first step is to develop a list of stressful situations and arrange them from least to most stressful. Once anxiety-producing situations are identified, the client is taught to curb the anxiety-provoking thoughts and replace them with more positive coping thoughts. Once these new thoughts are learned, they can be tried out in real situations. The time it takes to replace old habitual thoughts with new thoughts can vary depending on the amount of practice and commitment to make this change.

Meditation

There are various forms of meditation. Depending on the type used, the individual focuses his or her attention in slightly different ways. For example, Zen meditation focuses on breathing, whereas in transcendental meditation, the person makes a sound or says a mantra selected to keep all other images and problems from intruding on his or her thoughts. With practice, a person can reach a meditative state and obtain its benefits within a few minutes.

Aftercare

After a person has learned and practiced anxiety reduction techniques, he or she may need additional instruction from a trained professional. Having a trained professional review these techniques can help reinforce what the person has already learned and been practicing. Furthermore, the person may identify aspects of the techniques that he or she is doing incorrectly, areas that need more attention or focus, and alternative methods of engaging in the techniques.

Risks

There are minimal risks associated with these techniques, but some physical problems have occurred. For example, precautions should be taken when doing progressive relaxation and tensing the neck and back. Excessive tightening can create muscle or spinal damage. Additionally, tightening various muscle groups, such as the toes or feet, could result in muscle cramps. If physical problems occur, such as difficulty taking deep breaths, unusual muscle pain, or an increased level of anxiety, then the individual should seek assistance from a physician.

Normal results

In general, after engaging in these anxiety reduction techniques, many people report an increased sense of well-being and relaxation. People have a greater sense of control, and confidence in their coping abilities. This results in a decreased need to fear or avoid stressful situations.

Relaxation or progressive relaxation

Progressive relaxation can be useful in reducing muscle tension. Engaging in relaxation may help to improve a person's energy level, depression, and anxiety, as well as the ability to retrieve information from memory.

Visualization and imagery

By engaging in the positive thinking often associated with visualization and imagery, a person can create a clearer image of what he or she wants to accomplish. By repeating the image again and again, the individual comes to expect what he or she wants will occur. As a result, the person will often begin to act in a way more consistent with accomplishing the goal.

Diaphragmatic breathing

Sufficient amounts of air reach the lungs, which purifies and oxygenates the blood. Waste products in the blood are removed, and organs and tissues become nourished.

Stress inoculation

A person will have more realistic views of stressful and anxiety-producing situations in his or her life. The individual will be able to relax away tension by effectively thinking useful coping thoughts rather than negative interpretations of situations.

Meditation

As people learn to meditate, they often discover that they have some control over the thoughts that come to their minds, as opposed to feeling as though thoughts "pop" into their heads. Many people begin

ROLLO MAY (1909-1994)

Rollo May was the second of six children and the eldest son of Earl Tuttle, a Young Men's Christian Associations field secretary, and Matie Boughton May, a homemaker. May grew up in Michigan in a family that had "more than its share of troubles." He later described his parents as "austere disciplinarians and anti-intellectuals" and portrayed their relationship as "discordant" and the precursor for his interest in psychology and counseling. His oldest sister was frequently psychotic and spent time in mental hospitals.

His lectures on counseling and personality adjustment were published as his first book, *The Art of Counseling: How to Gain and Give Mental Health* (1939), which was well regarded. May studied psychology at Columbia University in New York City. While working on his dissertation in 1942 and still counseling, May was diagnosed with tuberculosis. His personal struggle against death solidified his views on existentialism. While recuperating in upstate New York for almost two years, May wrote *The Meaning of Anxiety* (1950), which he considered the "watershed" event of his career. He stressed that anxiety can be a positive, motivating force for social and personal devel-

opment, and that people can use their inner resources for life choices. In 1953 May published his second book, *Man's Search for Himself*. Written in laymen's terms, it was a popular and critical success and established May as a leader of American existentialism.

By the early 1960s May had become a leader in challenging behaviorism and psychoanalysis. He "defected" from biological determinism by stressing unique conscious elements in individual psychology. After moving to California in 1975, he resumed his private practice as a therapist. He also served in various capacities at the Saybrook Institute of the California School of Professional Psychology. More books and ideas followed: *Power and Innocence: A Search for the Sources of Violence* (1972), *The Courage to Create* (1975), *My Quest for Beauty* (1985), and *The Cry for Myth* (1991). May was a prolific writer and thinker who wrote more than fifteen books, many of which are directly related to his personal life and growth as a person. He was the recipient of the American Psychological Association's Gold Medal for his distinguished career in psychology, Phi Beta Kappa's Ralph Waldo Emerson Award, and the Whole Life Humanitarian Award.

to recognize dysfunctional patterns of thought and perceptions that have influenced their lives. Additionally, many people report a greater ability to manage their emotions and gain a greater sense of stability. When a person meditates, he or she often suppresses the activity of the sympathetic nervous system, the part of the nervous system that activates the body for emergencies and activities. Meditation also lowers a person's metabolism, heart, and breathing rates. Additionally, meditation decreases the chemical in the body often associated with stress.

Abnormal results

Once a person begins to implement these anxiety reduction techniques effectively, he or she may discover old or hidden psychological pain. The individual may feel angry, frightened, or depressed, and it may be beneficial for him or her to talk to a friend, mental health professional, or meditation teacher.

Some people have difficulty with various aspects of the different techniques. For example, an individual may feel restless when first learning how to meditate, or may feel as though a thousand thoughts are running through his or her mind. However, with practice and assistance from a trained professional, these difficulties will subside. People who feel frustrated or discouraged

may simply need to find ways to make the practice of these techniques more comfortable. As is the case with many other skills, effectively reducing anxiety with these techniques requires patience and practice. If an individual does not consistently practice these techniques, the benefits will probably not be obtained.

Resources

BOOKS

Bourne, Edmund J. *The Anxiety and Phobia Workbook*. 4th ed. Oakland, CA: New Harbinger Publications, 2005.

Donaghy, Marie, Rosemary A. Payne and Keith Bellamy. *Relaxation Techniques: A Practical Handbook for the Health Care Professional*. Oxford: Churchill Livingstone, 2005.

Smith, Jonathan C. *Stress Management: A Comprehensive Handbook of Techniques and Strategies*. New York: Springer Publishing Company, 2002.

Veeraraghavan, Vimala and Shalini Singh. *Anxiety Disorders: Psychological Assessment and Treatment*. Thousand Oaks, CA: Sage Publications, 2002.

Wolpe, Joseph. *Practices Without Principles*. Washington D.C.: American Psychological Association, 2006.

PERIODICALS

Arch, Joanna J. and Michelle G. Craske. "Mechanisms of Mindfulness: Emotion Regulation Following a Focused Breathing Induction." *Behaviour Research and Therapy* 44.12 (December. 2006): 1849–58.

Bornas, Xavier, and others. "Changes in Heart Rate Variability of Flight Phobics During a Paced Breathing Task and Exposure to Fearful Stimuli." *International Journal of Clinical and Health Psychology* 6.3 (September 2006): 549–63.

Hunt, Melissa, and others. "The Role of Imagery in the Maintenance and Treatment of Snake Fear." *Journal of Behavior Therapy and Experimental Psychiatry* 37.4 (December 2006): 283–298.

Lundgren, Jesper, Sven G. Carlsson, and Ulf Berggren. "Relaxation Versus Cognitive Therapies for Dental Fear—A Psychophysiological Approach." *Health Psychology* 25.3 (May 2006): 267–73.

Meuret, Alicia E., Thomas Ritz, Frank H. Wilhelm, and Walton T. Roth. "Voluntary Hyperventilation in the Treatment of Panic Disorder—Functions of Hyperventilation, Their Implications for Breathing Training, and Recommendations for Standardization." *Clinical Psychology Review* 25.3 (May 2005): 285–306.

Rausch, Sarah M., Sandra E. Gramling, and Stephen M. Auerbach. "Effects of a Single Session of Large-Group Meditation and Progressive Muscle Relaxation Training on Stress Reduction, Reactivity, and Recovery." *International Journal of Stress Management* 13.3 (August 2006): 273–90.

Roth, Walton T. "Physiological Markers for Anxiety: Panic Disorder and Phobias." *International Journal of Psychophysiology* 58.2–3 (November–December 2005): 190–98.

ORGANIZATIONS

American Psychiatric Association, 1400 K Street NW, Washington, DC 20005. <http://www.psych.org>.

American Psychological Association, 750 1st St. NE, Washington, DC 20002. Telephone: (202) 336-5500. <http://www.apa.org>.

Anxiety Disorders Association of America. 11900 Parklawn Drive, Suite 100, Rockville, MD 20852. Telephone: (301) 231-9350. <http://www.adaa.org>.

The National Institute of Mental Health, 5600 Fischers Lane, Room 15C05, Rockville, MD 20857. Telephone: (301) 443-4513. <http://www.nimh.nih.gov/>.

The National Mental Health Association. 1201 Prince Street, Alexandria, VA 22314-2971.

Keith Beard, Psy.D.
Ruth A. Wienclaw, PhD

Apathy

Definition

Apathy can be defined as an absence or suppression of emotion, feeling, concern or passion. Further, apathy is an indifference to things generally found to be exciting or moving.

Description

A strong connection exists between apathy and mental disorders. Apathy is one of the hallmark symptoms of **schizophrenia**. Many people with schizophrenia express little interest in the events surrounding them. Apathy can also occur in **depression and depressive disorders**. For example, people who are depressed and have **major depressive disorder** or **dysthymic disorder** often feel numb to events occurring around them, and do not derive pleasure from experiences that they once found enjoyable.

The World Health Organization (WHO) defines health as an optimal state of being that maximizes one's potential for physical, mental, emotional and spiritual growth. It does not confine health to physical parameters or measures. Passion, interest and action are needed for optimal mental and emotional health. Persons who are apathetic would seem to fall short of the WHO definition of health.

All people may experience periods of apathy. Disappointment and dejection are elements of life, and apathy is a normal way for humans to cope with such stresses—to be able to "shrug off" disappointments enables people to move forward and try other activities and achieve new goals. When the stresses pass, the apparent apathy also disappears. A period of apathy can also be viewed as a normal and transient phase through which many adolescents pass.

It is important to note, however, that long-term apathy and detachment are not normal.

Treatment

Transient apathy can be overcome. Friends and professionals may be able to assist individuals to develop an interest in their surroundings. Attitude is important. Persons who desire to overcome apathy have much higher odds of succeeding than do persons lacking a positive attitude.

Other than support, no specific treatment is needed for apathy associated with adolescence, unless other, more troubling disorders are also present.

The treatment of more persistent apathy (in a depressive disorder, for example), or the apathy that is characteristic of schizophrenia, may respond to treatment for the primary disorder.

DEPRESSION. For **depressive disorders**, a number of **antidepressants** may be effective, including tricyclic antidepressants, monoamine oxidase inhibitors (MAOIs) and **selective serotonin reuptake inhibitors (SSRIs)**. The tricyclic antidepressants include **amitriptyline** (Elavil), **imipramine** (Tofranil), and **nortriptyline** (Aventyl,

Pamelor). MAOIs include **tranylcypromine** (Parnate) and **phenelzine** (Nardil). The most commonly prescribed SSRIs are **fluoxetine** (Prozac), **sertraline** (Zoloft), **paroxetine (Paxil)**, **fluvoxamine** (Luvox), and **citalopram** (Celexa).

SCHIZOPHRENIA. For schizophrenia, the primary goal is to treat the more prominent symptoms (**positive symptoms**) of the disorder, such as the thought disorder and **hallucinations** that patients experience. Atypical antipsychotics are newer medications introduced in the 1990s that have been found to be effective for the treatment of schizophrenia. These medications include **clozapine** (Clozaril), **risperidone** (Risperdal), **quetiapine** (Seroquel), **ziprasidone** (Geodon), and **olanzapine** (Zyprexa). These newer drugs are more effective in treating the **negative symptoms** of schizophrenia (such as empathy) and have fewer side effects than the older antipsychotics. Most atypical antipsychotics, however, do have weight gain as a side effect; and patients taking clozapine must have their blood monitored periodically for signs of agranulocytosis, or a drop in the number of white blood cells.

Resources

BOOKS

Gelder, Michael, Richard Mayou, and Philip Cowen. *Shorter Oxford Textbook of Psychiatry.* 4th ed. New York: Oxford University Press, 2001.

Wilson, Josephine F. *Biological Foundations of Human Behavior.* New York: Harcourt, 2002.

PERIODICALS

Adams, K. B. "Depressive symptoms, depletion, or developmental change? Withdrawal, apathy, and lack of vigor in the Geriatric Depression Scale." *Gerontologist* 41, no. 6 (2001): 768-777.

Carota A., F. Staub, and J. Bogousslavsky. "Emotions, behaviours and mood changes in stroke." *Current Opinions in Neurology* 15, no. 1 (2002): 57-69.

Kalechstein, A. D., T. F. Newton, and A. H. Leavengood. "Apathy syndrome in cocaine dependence." *Psychiatry Resident* 109, no. 1 (2002): 97-100.

Landes, A. M., S. D. Sperry, M. E. Strauss, and D. S. Geldmacher. "Apathy in Alzheimer's disease." *Journal of the American Geriatric Society* 49, no. 12 (2001): 1700-1707.

Ramirez, S. M., H. Glover, C. Ohlde, R. Mercer, P. Goodnick, C. Hamlin, and M. I. Perez-Rivera. "Relationship of numbing to alexithymia, apathy, and depression." *Psychological Reports* 88, no. 1 (2001): 189-200.

Starkstein, S. E., G. Petracca, E. Chemerinski, and J. Kremer. "Syndromic validity of apathy in Alzheimer's disease." *American Journal of Psychiatry* 158, no. 6 (2001): 872-877.

ORGANIZATIONS

American Psychiatric Association. 1400 K Street NW, Washington, DC 20005. Telephone: (888) 357-7924. Fax: (202) 682-6850.

American Psychological Association. 750 First Street NW, Washington, DC, 20002-4242. Telephone: (800) 374-2721 or (202) 336-5500. Web site: <http://www.apa.org/>.

L. Fleming Fallon, Jr., M.D., Dr.P.H.

Appetite suppressants

Definition

Appetite-suppressant medications are drugs that promote weight loss by decreasing appetite or increasing the sensation of fullness.

Description

Obesity is a disease that affects millions of American adults, adolescents, and children, posing serious health risks. Medical professionals generally consider obesity to be a chronic illness requiring life-long treatment and management. It is often grouped with other chronic conditions, such as high blood pressure and diabetes, as a condition that can be controlled but not cured. One is considered obese if 20% over ideal body weight, according to standard height-weight charts, or if one's Body Mass Index, or BMI, (a ratio of height to weight, indicaating the amount of fat tissue in the body) exceeds 30%.

The most important strategies for managing obesity are not medications but rather, a healthy diet coupled with moderate exercise. As in other chronic conditions, the use of prescription medications may assist in managing the condition for some individuals but it is never the sole treatment for obesity, nor is it ever considered a cure.

The class of medications used most often for weight loss are commonly referred to as "appetite suppressants." These medications promote weight loss by helping to diminish appetite, and/or by increasing the subjective feeling of fullness. They work by increasing serotonin or catecholamines, two **neurotransmitters** (chemicals) in the **brain** that affect both mood and appetite.

Several prescription medications are currently approved for treatment of obesity. In general, the effects of these medications are modest, leading to an average initial weight loss of between 5 and 22 lbs (2.3–10 kg); though studies show that weight returns after cessation of the drugs. There is considerable individual difference in response to these medications; some people experience greater weight loss than others. The goal of prescribing weight loss medication is to help the medically at-risk obese patient "jump-start" their weight loss effort and lose 10% or more of their starting body weight. When this can be accomplished, it usually leads to a reduction in risk for obesity-related illnesses, such as high blood pressure, heart disease and diabetes. Weight loss tends to be greatest during the first few weeks or months of treatment, leveling off after about six months. Research suggests that if a patient does not lose at least four pounds during the first four weeks on a particular medication, that medication is unlikely to be effective over the long run. Few studies have addressed safety or effectiveness of medications taken for more than a few months at a time. Little data exists on the long term effectiveness of the drugs.

All but two of the prescription appetite suppressants in the United States have been approved by the U.S. Food and Drug Administration (FDA), for short-term use only. Short-term use generally means a few weeks or months at the longest. One appetite suppressant medication was approved for longer-term use within the past decade, but that drug, dexfenfluramine (Redux) was withdrawn from the market because of unacceptable risks associated with its use.

Another medication was approved within the past few years for longer-term use, up to a year and possibly longer, in significantly obese patients. This drug, an appetite suppressant, is called sibutramine (Meridia). Individuals with a history of heart disease, irregular heartbeat, high blood pressure, or history of **stroke** should not take sibutramine. All patients taking this medication should have their blood pressure monitored regularly.

A relatively new drug, orlistat (Xenical), was approved in 1999 by the FDA for at least a year or longer, as well. Orlistat is not an appetite suppressant, but rather, a member of a new class of anti-obesity drugs known as "lipase inhibitors." These medications work by preventing enzymes in the gastrointestinal tract from breaking down dietary fats into smaller molecules that can be absorbed by the body. The result is that fat absorbed from food is decreased by about 30%. This effectively reduces the calories absorbed by the body by 30%, aiding in weight loss.

While the FDA regulates how a medication can be advertised or promoted by the manufacturer, these regulations do not constrain physicians from prescribing them as they believe appropriate. This practice of prescribing medications for conditions other than those

for which they were approved, or at different dosages, or for different lengths of time, is known as "off-label" use. Many of the prescription medications available for weight management are used in an "off-label" manner.

Most of the side effects of prescription medications for weight loss are mild; but some very serious complications have been reported in recent years. They were so serious that two medications were voluntarily removed from the market by the manufacturers in 1997. These two medications, fenfluramine (Pondimin), and dexfenfluramine (Redux), were shown to be associated with a rare but very serious and potentially fatal disorder known as primary pulmonary hypertension (PPH), a disease of the lungs. Forty-five percent of patients with PPH die within four years of **diagnosis**.

Medications for weight loss

Prescription medications

Prescription medications currently prescribed for weight loss include:

- Generic name: Dexfenfluramine (Trade name: Redux) (withdrawn)
- Generic name: Diethylpropion (Trade names: Tenuate, Tenuate dospan)
- Generic name: Fenfluramine (Trade name: Pondimin) (withdrawn)
- Generic name: Mazindole (Trade name: Sanorex)
- Generic name: Orlistat (Trade name: Xenical)
- Generic name: Phendimetrazine (Trade names: Bontril, Plegine, Prelu-2, X-Troxine)
- Generic name: Phentermine (Trade name: Adipex-P, Fastin, Ionamin, Oby-trim)
- Generic name: Sibutramine (Trade name: Meridia)

Some antidepressant medications have been studied for use as possible appetite depressants, because they frequently depress appetite in the early weeks and months of use. Research indicates, however, that while individuals may lose weight initially during antidepressant treatment, a tendency to lose only modest amounts of weight arises after six months. Furthermore, most patients who lose weight early in antidepressant medication treatment tend to regain the weight while still using the medication.

Amphetamines and similar medications were frequently prescribed in the United States, during the 1960s and 70s, as appetite suppressants. However, because of their addictive potential, they are not prescribed today for weight control, except by a remainder of "diet doctors" who defy political correctness and continue to distribute them.

SINGLE DRUG TREATMENT. The medications listed are currently used, except where noted, to treat obesity. In general, these medications are modestly effective, especially when used in conjunction with a healthy diet and moderate exercise. Average weight losses between five to 22 lbs (2.3–10 kg) can be expected beyond those seen with non-drug obesity treatments, when only a low calorie and exerise regimen are followed. There is considerable individual variation in response to weight-loss medications; some people experience more weight loss than others.

COMBINED DRUG TREATMENT. Combined drug treatment using fenfluramine and phentermine ("fen/phen") is no longer available due to the withdrawal of fenfluramine from the market. There is little information about the safety or effectiveness of other prescription drug combinations for weight loss. Until further research is conducted on safety or effectiveness, using combinations of medications for weight loss is not advised unless a patient is participating in a research study.

POTENTIAL BENEFITS OF APPETITE SUPPRESSANT TREATMENT. Short-term use of appetite suppressant medications has been shown to modestly reduce health risks for obese individuals. Studies have found that these medications can lower blood pressure, blood cholesterol, blood fats (triglycerides), and decrease insulin resistance (the body's ability to utilize blood sugar). Long-term studies need to be conducted to determine if weight loss assisted by appetite suppressant medications can improve health long-term.

POTENTIAL RISKS OF APPETITE SUPPRESSANT TREATMENT. All prescription medications used to treat obesity, with the exception of orlistat, are controlled substances. This means that doctors need to follow rigid guidelines when prescribing them. Although **abuse** and dependence are uncommon with non-amphetamine appetite suppressant medications, doctors need to exercise caution when prescribing them, especially for patients with a history of alcohol or drug abuse.

DEVELOPMENT OF TOLERANCE. Studies of appetite suppressant medications indicate that an individual's weight tends to level off after four to six months of treatment. While some patients and doctors may be concerned that this indicates growing tolerance to the medications, the leveling off may indicate that the medication has reached its limit of effectiveness. Current research is not clear regarding whether weight gained with continued medication is due to drug tolerance, or to reduced effectiveness of the medication over time.

SIDE EFFECTS. Because obesity is a condition affecting millions of Americans, many of whom are basically healthy, the side effects of using powerful medications such as appetite suppressants are of great concern. Most side effects of these medications are mild and diminish as treatment continues. Rarely, serious and even fatal outcomes have been reported. The FDA approved appetite suppressant medications that affect serotonin (fenfluramine and dexfenfluramine) have been withdrawn from the market. Medications that affect catecholamine levels (such as phentermine, dietylpropion, and mazindol) may cause symptoms of sleeplessness, nervousness, and euphoria.

Primary pulmonary hypertension (PPH) is a rare but potentially fatal disease that affects the blood vessels in the lungs and causes death within four years in 45% of its victims. Patients who use the appetite suppressant medications that are prescribed for a use of three months are at increased risk of developing this condition if used longer. Estimates are that between one in 22,000 and one in 44,000 individuals will develop the disorder each year. While the risk of developing PPH is very small, doctors and patients should be aware of this potentially deadly complication when they consider the risks and benefits of using appetite suppressant medications for long-term treatment of obesity. Patients taking appetite suppressants should contact their doctors if they experience shortness of breath, chest pain, faintness, or swelling in the lower legs and ankles. The vast majority of cases of PPH related to appetite suppressant use have occurred in patients taking fenfluarmine or dexfenfluramine, either alone or in combination with each other or other drugs, such as phentermine. There have been only a few cases of PPH reported among patients taking phentermine alone, although the possibility that phentermine alone may be associated with PPH cannot be ruled out at this time.

Animal research has suggested that appetite suppressant medications affecting the neurotransmitter serotonin, such as fenfluramine and dexfenfluramine, can damage the central nervous system. These findings have not been reported in humans. Some patients have reported **depression** or memory loss when using appetite suppressant medications alone or in combination, but it is not known if these problems are actually caused by the medications or by other factors.

Over-the-counter appetite suppressants

In addition to the numerous prescription medications for weight loss, a few over-the-counter agents are marketed for weight loss. The most common, phenylpropanalomine, is an appetite suppressant that is distantly related to the amphetamines. Like the amphetamines, this drug has the side effect of increased blood pressure and heart rate, and thus should not be used by anyone with hypertension or heart disease. Other over-the-counter medications contain fiber or bulking agents, and presumably work by increasing the sensation of fullness. Some preparations contain the anesthetic benzocaine. This agent numbs the mouth and may make eating less appealing temporarily. No evidence exists that any of these medications is effective in producing significant weight loss.

See also Amphetamines and related disorders; Diets; Anorexia nervosa; Bulimia nervosa; Obesity; Self-help groups; Support groups.

Resources

BOOKS

Hales, Dianne, and Robert E Hales, MD. *Caring for the Mind: The Comprehensive Guide to Mental Health.* New York: Bantam Books, 1995.

Kaplan, Harold I., MD, and Benjamin J Sadock, MD. *Synopsis of Psychiatry.* 8th edition. Lippincott Williams and Wilkins, 1998.

PERIODICALS

National Institute of Diabetes and Digestive and Kidney Diseases (NIDDK) of the National Institutes of Health (NIH). *Prescription Medications for the Treatment of Obesity,* MSI-WCIN019, Weight-control information network. 2001.

National Institute of Diabetes and Digestive and Kidney Diseases (NIDDK) of the National Institutes of Health (NIH). *Questions About Appetite Suppressant Medication Treatment,* MSI-WCIN020, Weight-control information network. 2001.

U. S. Food and Drug Administration. *FDA Approves Orlistat for Obesity, Food and Drug Administration* FDA Talk Paper, April 26, 1999.

ORGANIZATIONS

Weight-control Information Network. 1 Win Way, Bethesda, MD 20892-3665. Telephone: (202) 828-1025. <www.niddk.nih.gov/health/nutrit/win.htm>.

Overeaters Anonymous, 4025 Spencer Street, Suite 203, Torrance, CA 90503. Telephone: (310) 618-8835. <http://www.overeatersanonymous.org/>.

OTHER

CBS News. "Diet Drug Meridia Under Fire." (May 29, 2002). <http://www.cbsnews.com>.

Barbara S. Sternberg, Ph.D.

Aprepitant

Purpose

Aprepitant (brand name Emend) is a drug used to prevent stomachaches and vomiting in persons receiving cancer-killing medicines (chemotherapy) or who have received medicines to prevent pain during surgery (anesthesia). The drug also affects substances in the part of the **brain** also associated with emotions, which has led scientists to question whether aprepitant could be used to treat certain mental disorders, particularly major **depression**.

Description

Aprepitant is classified as a substance P neurokin-1 (NK-1) receptor antagonist. This means it blocks proteins called NK-1 receptors, which sit on cells in the brain region linked to gastrointestinal problems and the body's response to **stress**, **anxiety**, and depression. The receptors attach or bind to a naturally occurring chemical called substance P, which is found in higher amounts in persons with depression. Blocking the NK-1 receptors causes a decrease in the normal action of substance P that would be mediated by the NK-1 receptor

Scientists have theorized that aprepitant could possibly become a unique antidepressant. In 1998, researchers reported that more than half of patients with depression who took aprepitant had an improvement in mood. The study involved 213 people who took the drug for six weeks. The scientists also discovered that the medicine worked as well as **paroxetine** (**Paxil**) in reducing anxiety.

In 2001, however, a larger trial involving 700 patients with mild to moderate depression failed to show that aprepitant worked any better than existing antidepressant medications. Additional studies also failed. In 2003, Merck & Company, the manufacturer of aprepitant, said it would no longer pursue the drug as a treatment for depression. The decision came just a few months after aprepitant received United States Food and Drug Administration (FDA) approval as a preventive for chemotherapy-related stomach upset.

Some researchers still investigate aprepitant as a possible treatment for depression, but the results continue to be disappointing. In 2006, research concluded that aprepitant did not reduce depression symptoms any better than the placebo.

Recommended dosage

Aprepitant is only approved to prevent nausea and vomiting in persons receiving chemotherapy or who have just had surgery. It comes in capsule form, and is taken by mouth with or without food.

Chemotherapy-related nausea and vomiting

Those receiving chemotherapy take aprepitant for three days, in combination with other drugs. The general recommended dose is as follows:

- Day 1: 125 mg by mouth one hour before receiving chemotherapy
- Day 2: 80 mg by mouth in the morning
- Day 3: 80 mg by mouth in the morning

Post-operative nausea and vomiting

Aprepitant is given alone to prevent upset stomach and vomiting that can occur after surgery. The recommended dosage is 40 mg, taken by mouth, within three hours before receiving anesthesia.

Precautions

Aprepitant is well tolerated in those with mild to moderate liver disease. No aprepitant studies have been conducted in persons with severe liver disease. The drug has not been tested in people under age 18.

The FDA classifies a drug according to how it may affect a developing fetus. Aprepitant is in category B. Animal studies have shown that the drug does not harm a developing fetus, but the drug has not been studied in pregnant women. It is unclear whether the drug passes into breast milk. Women who are pregnant or breastfeeding should talk to their doctor before taking this drug.

Side effects

Studies of more than 3,000 people show that aprepitant is generally well tolerated. The most common side effects in persons taking 80–125 mg aprepitant to prevent chemotherapy-related nausea and vomiting are:

- constipation
- diarrhea
- dizziness
- extreme tiredness
- hair loss
- headache
- hiccups
- loss of appetite
- stomachaches and pains
- weakness

The most common side effects in persons taking 40 mg aprepitant to prevent nausea and vomiting after an operation are:

- constipation
- headache
- itching
- fever
- low blood pressure
- stomachaches

The following symptoms are rare, but require immediate medical attention:

- breathing difficulty
- hives
- hoarseness (rough, scratchy voice)
- skin rash
- swelling of the face, throat, tongue, lips, hands, or lower legs and feet
- trouble swallowing

KEY TERMS

Anesthesia—Medicines that block pain signals from traveling along the nerves to the brain. Anesthesia is often given before surgery so the patient does not feel any pain during the procedure.

Chemotherapy—The use of medicines to kill cancer cells.

Receptor—A molecule, such as a protein, on a cell's surface that attaches to a specific substance.

Substance P—A naturally occurring chemical found throughout the brain, spinal cord, and nervous system.

Aprepitant has been linked to tumor development in laboratory animals. It is unclear if the medicine increases the risk of tumors in humans.

Interactions

Serious, life-threatening reactions can occur if aprepitant is taken with any of the following drugs:

- astemizole (Hismanal)
- cisapride (Propulsid)
- pimozide (Orap)
- terfenadine (Seldane)

Aprepitant can increase levels of certain chemotherapy drugs in the blood. Patients who take aprepitant with any of the following drugs should be very carefully monitored by a doctor:

- docetaxel (Taxotere)
- etoposide (Etopophos, Vepesid)
- ifosfamide (Mitoxana)
- imatinib (Gleevec)
- irinotecan (Campto)
- paclitaxel (Taxol)
- vinblastine (Velbe)
- vincristine (Oncovin)
- vinorelbine (Navelbine)

Aprepitant may make birth control pills less effective. An additional form of birth control should be used when taking aprepitant and for a month after the last dose.

Those who take aprepitant with the blood thinner warfarin should be closely monitored by a doctor. Taking the two drugs together can affect blood-clotting time. Blood tests are needed to determine whether the dosage of warfarin needs to be adjusted.

Aprepitant can cause increased levels of dexamethasone (Decadron) and methylprednisolone (Medrol) in the blood. Patients may need their dosages decreased if taken with aprepitant.

Aprepitant should be used with caution when taking the following drugs, which can increase the risk of side effects:

- alprazolam (Xanax)
- midazolam (Versed)
- triazolam (Halcion)

Resources

BOOKS

Karch, Amy M. *2007 Lippincott's Nursing Drug Guide*. Philadelphia: Lippincott Williams & Wilkins, 2007.

ORGANIZATIONS

Mental Health America. 2000 N. Beauregard Street, 6th Floor. Alexandria, VA 22311. Telephone: (800) 969-6MHA (6642). <http://www.nmha.org>.

National Alliance on Mental Illness. 2107 Wilson Boulevard, Suite 300, Arlington, VA 22201-3042. Telephone: (703) 524-7600. <http://www.nami.org>.

National Institute of Mental Health. 6001 Executive Boulevard, Room 8184, MSC 9663, Bethesda, MD 20892-9663. Telephone: (301) 443-4513. <http://www.nimh.nih.gov>.

Kelli Miller Stacy

Aricept *see* **Donepezil**

Aripiprazole

Purpose

Aripiprazole (brand name Abilify) is a newer generation antipsychotic medication. It was approved by the U.S. Food & Drug Administration (FDA) in 2002 to treat **schizophrenia** symptoms. The symptoms of schizophrenia include **hallucinations**, **delusions**, **paranoia**, and social withdrawal.

The drug is also FDA–approved as a therapy for people with bipolar disorder who have had episodes of acute mania or mixed episodes of mania and **depression**, but who have subsequently been stabilized for at least six weeks.

Aripiprazole can be used short-term to treat acute psychotic and manic states and agitation in **dementia**, as well as long-term to treat chronic psychotic disorders, such as schizophrenia. In the past, these conditions were typically treated with conventional antipsychotic drugs, such as phenothiazine, thioxanthene, and butyrophenone neuroleptics.

Although aripiprazole is primarily indicated for the treatment of adults, some studies have indicated that it also may be effective for children and adolescents with **bipolar disorder**. In the few studies that have been conducted, the drug was well tolerated in this population; however, researchers say that a lower dose is appropriate in younger patients.

Description

Aripiprazole is part of a class of drugs called atypical antipsychotics. This class, which also includes **clozapine**, **olanzapine**, **quetiapine**, **risperidone**, and **ziprasidone**, are called "atypical" because of their relatively lower risk of certain types of adverse side effects compared to traditional antipsychotic drugs.

The exact mechanism by which aripiprazole and other atypical antipsychotic drugs work is unknown. Scientists believe that schizophrenia is caused by an imbalance of **dopamine** in the **brain**. Dopamine is a neurotransmitter that affects movement and balance. The theory is that aripiprazole acts as a partial agonist and antagonist, meaning that it binds to dopamine receptors in the brain and partially activates these receptors, while preventing dopamine from binding to them and fully activating them. Conventional antipsychotic drugs, by comparison, act as full antagonists. These drugs completely block dopamine receptors and significantly interfere with dopamine transmission, which can cause severe movement side effects. Aripiprazole also affects another neurotransmitter, serotonin, which is involved in regulating mood, and which is also imbalanced in people with schizophrenia.

Although studies suggest that aripiprazole works well to treat psychotic conditions such as schizophrenia, very little research has been conducted comparing its effectiveness with that of conventional antipsychotic drugs.

Recommended Dosage

Aripiprazole is only available by prescription. It is taken once a day by mouth as either a tablet or an oral solution. The oral solution is designed for older patients who have difficulty swallowing a tablet. Tablets range from 2 mg to 30 mg strengths. The oral solution is available in a 1-mg/mL solution. Aripiprazole can be taken with or without food. Some patients start out on a low dose, and then their doctor increases the dose after approximately two weeks.

Precautions

Women who are pregnant, who intend to become pregnant, or who are nursing should ask their doctor before taking this drug. Aripiprazole may increase the risk for diabetes, and people who develop extreme thirst, frequent urination, or other diabetes symptoms while taking the drug should see a doctor for assessment.

Because of potential interactions, people who are taking aripiprazole should tell their doctor if they have or are taking medications for any of the following conditions:

- Alzheimer's disease
- Anxiety
- Depression
- Diabetes
- Heart disease or heart failure
- High or low blood pressure
- Human immunodeficiency virus (HIV)
- Irritable bowel disease
- Mental illness
- Parkinson's disease
- Seizures
- Stroke or mini–stroke
- Surgery
- Ulcers

Because this medication may cause drowsiness and can impair judgment and motor skills, people who take it should take precautions when operating a motor vehicle or machinery. Alcohol can increase the sedative effects, and is not advised for people who are taking aripiprazole. Also, people who take this drug should use caution when exercising, because aripiprazole can affect the body's ability to regulate temperature, potentially leading to overheating and dehydration.

Side Effects

Aripiprazole and other atypical antipsychotic drugs tend to cause fewer neurological side effects than the older antipsychotic drugs. In particular, they have a lower risk of extrapyramidal symptoms, a group of involuntary muscle **movement disorders**. However, the drug does have side effects.

The most common side effects with aripiprazole are:

- anxiety
- constipation

KEY TERMS

Atypical antipsychotic—A class of newer-generation antipsychotic medications that are used to treat schizophrenia and other psychotic disorders.

Bipolar disorder—A brain disorder that causes extreme emotional shifts, or mood swings.

Delusions—A condition in which a person experiences beliefs that are untrue.

Dementia—A loss of mental ability, often occurring with age, that can interfere with a person's ability to think clearly and function independently.

Dopamine—A chemical messenger in the brain that regulates movement and balance.

Extrapyramidal—Related to the motor system in the brain. Extrapyramidal symptoms affect movement and coordination.

Hallucinations—Seeing, hearing, feeling, smelling, or tasting things that do not exist.

Mania—A mood disorder in which a person may become impulsive or irritable, and may exercise extremely poor judgment.

Neuroleptic malignant syndrome—A rare response to certain antipsychotic drugs, which can raise the body temperature to potentially life-threatening levels.

Serotonin—A chemical messenger in the brain that affects mood and emotion.

Paranoia—Condition in which a person has an irrational suspicion about another person or situation.

Partial agonist—A substance that partially activates a receptor in the brain, while blocking the neurotransmitter for that receptor from binding to it.

Schizophrenia—A mental disorder in which a person experiences hallucinations and delusions, and displays unusual behavior.

- difficulty sleeping
- dizziness
- drowsiness
- headache
- nausea
- nervousness
- numbness
- tremor

- vomiting
- weight gain

This drug can increase the risk for a rare condition called neuroleptic malignant syndrome (NML). This condition, which is sometimes caused by drugs that interfere with the dopamine pathway, can raise body temperatures to potentially life-threatening levels.

Aripiprazole is not approved for the treatment of **psychosis** in elderly patients with dementia. The FDA in 2005 released a public health advisory warning patients and doctors against using aripiprazole and other atypical antipsychotics off-label. In studies, these drugs significantly increased the risk of death in older patients with dementia compared to placebo. Most of the deaths were associated with heart failure or infections such as pneumonia. Atypical antipsychotics also have been associated with an increased risk for stroke in elderly patients with dementia-related psychosis.

Interactions

Aripiprazole can have potentially dangerous interactions with the following drugs:

- famotidine
- valproate
- lithium
- dextromethorphan
- warfarin
- omeprazole
- lorazepam

Resources

BOOKS

Beers, Mark H. *The Merck Manual of Medical Information: 2nd Home Edition.* New York, NY: Pocket, 2004.

Mondimore, Francis Mark. *Bipolar Disorder: A Guide for Patients and Families,* 2nd edition. Baltimore, MD: The Johns Hopkins University Press, 2006.

Stahl, Stephen M. *Essential Psychopharmacology: The Prescriber's Guide: Antipsychotics and Mood Stabilizers.* New York, NY: Cambridge University Press, 2006.

Torrey, E. Fuller. *Surviving Schizophrenia: A Manual for Families, Patients, and Providers.* 5th edition. New York, NY: Harper Collins Publishers, 2006.

ORGANIZATIONS

American Psychiatric Association. 1000 Wilson Boulevard, Suite 1825, Arlington, VA 22209-3901. Telephone: (703) 907-7300. < http://www.psych.org/>.

National Alliance on Mental Illness. 2107 Wilson Blvd., Suite 300, Arlington, VA 22201-3042. Telephone: (800) 950-6264. <http://www.nami.org>.

National Institute of Mental Health. 6001 Executive Boulevard, Room 8184, MSC 9663 Bethesda, MD 20892-9663. Telephone: (866)615-6464. <http://www.nimh.nih.gov/>.

The Mental Health Research Association. 60 Cutter Mill Road, Suite 404, Great Neck, NY 11021. Telephone: (800) 829-8289. <narsad.org>.

Stephanie N. Watson

Aromatherapy

Definition

Aromatherapy is a holistic treatment based on the external use of essential aromatic plant oils to maintain and promote physical, physiological, and spiritual well-being. The essential oils may be used in massage, added to a warm bath, used to moisten a compress that is applied to the affected part of the body, added to a vaporizer for inhalation, or diffused throughout a room.

The term aromatherapy (*aromatherapie* in the original French) was coined in 1928 by a French chemist, René Maurice Gattefossé, to describe the therapeutic use of aromatic substances (essential oils) in wound healing. Gattefossé discovered the healing properties of essential plant oils accidentally; after burning his hand in a laboratory accident, he found that **lavender** oil healed his burns in a very short time. He then experimented with plant oils in treating soldiers wounded in World War I, and found that there were several essential oils that speeded physical healing. As the practice of aromatherapy expanded, it came to incorporate a holistic emphasis on healing or invigorating all levels of a person's being. In the United States and Great Britain, the contemporary practice of aromatherapy is often associated with naturopathy and Western herbal medicine. In Great Britain, aromatherapy is one of the most frequently used forms of alternative medicine; in the United States, many hospital-affiliated centers for the study of complementary and alternative medicine (CAM) offer aromatherapy as well as other alternative approaches. Aromatherapy has also been added to holistic nursing board examinations in the United States within the last few years.

Purpose

One of the basic concepts of mind/body medicine is that a positive frame of mind helps to keep people in good health. Aromatherapists maintain that essential oils derived from plants help people to slow down, relax from **stress**, and enjoy the sensory experiences of massage, warm water, and pleasant smells. Aromatherapy is thought to improve a person's mental outlook and sense of well-being by affecting the limbic system via the olfactory nerve, or the sense of smell. The limbic system is the area of the **brain** that regulates emotions. Relaxing and pleasant smells stimulate emotional responses of pleasure and relaxation. From a holistic perspective, aromatherapy is a form of preventive health care. Most aromatherapists believe that aromatherapy should not be used as a substitute for mainstream medical or psychiatric care, but as an adjunct to it.

Aromatherapy is considered to be a useful complementary treatment for the relief of **depression**, **anxiety**, **insomnia**, **panic disorder**, stress-related physical disorders, menstrual cramps, and some gastrointestinal complaints. For example, peppermint oil calms gastrointestinal spasms when ingested, or taken by mouth. A recent Scottish study found that aromatherapy has a measurably calming effect on the symptoms of **dementia** in elderly people.

Aromatherapy can be used by itself, or combined with Swedish massage, shiatsu, acupressure, reflexology, or **light therapy** to reinforce the positive results of these treatments.

Although there are professional aromatherapists as well as practitioners of holistic medicine who offer aromatherapy among their other services, people can also use aromatherapy at home as part of self-care. There are many guides to the various techniques of aromatherapy and the proper use of essential plant oils available in inexpensive paperback editions.

Precautions

People who are interested in using essential oils at home should be careful to purchase them from reliable sources. The U. S. Food and Drug Administration (FDA) does not regulate the manufacture of essential plant oils. Consequently, instances of consumer fraud have been reported. In the case of essential oils, the most common form of fraud is substitution of synthetic compounds for natural essential oils, which are expensive to produce.

Another precaution is to avoid applying essential oils directly to the skin as a form of perfume. Some essential oils such as oil of orange or oil of peppermint are irritating to the skin if applied full-strength. When essential oils are used in massage, they are always diluted in a carrier oil.

A final precaution is to avoid taking essential oils internally without a consultation with a physician or naturopathist. Possible exceptions may be peppermint oil and aloe vera.

Description

Essential plant oils are prepared for use in aromatherapy in several different ways. Most are prepared by steam distillation, a process in which the flowers, leaves, or other plant parts are heated by steam from boiling water. The vapors that result then pass through a condenser that separates the scented water from the essential oil, which is siphoned off into a separate container. Other methods of extracting essential oils include expression, or squeezing, which is limited to citrus oils; *enfleurage*, in which flower petals are placed on a bed of purified fat that soaks up the essential oils; and maceration, in which the plant parts are crushed and covered with warm vegetable oil that absorbs the essential oils.

There are several different techniques for the use of essential oils in aromatherapy:

- Massage: This is the technique that most people associate with aromatherapy. For use in massage, essential oils are mixed with a vegetable carrier oil, usually wheatgerm, avocado, olive, safflower, grapeseed, or soya bean oil. A ratio that is commonly recommended is 2.5–5% essential oil to 95–97.5% carrier oil.
- Full-body baths: In this technique, the essential oil is added to a tubful of warm (but not hot) water as the water is running. The dosage of essential oil is usually 5–10 drops per bath.
- Hand or foot baths: These are often recommended to treat arthritis or skin disorders of the hands or feet as well as sore muscles. The hands or feet are soaked for 10–15 minutes in a basin of warm water to which 5–7 drops of essential oil have been added.
- Inhalations: This technique is used to treat sinus problems or such nasal allergies as hay fever. Two cups of water are brought to a boil and then allowed to cool for 5–10 minutes. Two to five drops of essential oil are added to the steaming water, and the person leans over the container and inhales the fragrant vapors for 5–10 minutes.
- Diffusion: This technique requires the use of a special nebulizer to disperse microscopic droplets of essential oil into the air, or a clay diffuser that allows the oil to evaporate into the air when it is warmed by a small votive candle or electric bulb. Diffusion is recommended for treating emotional upsets.

- Compresses: These are made by soaking four or five layers of cotton cloth in a solution of warm water and essential oil, wringing out the cloth so that it is moist but not dripping, and applying it to the affected part of the body. The compress is then covered with a layer of plastic wrap, followed by a pre-warmed towel, and kept in place for one or two hours. Aromatherapy compresses are used to treat wounds, sprains, bruises, sore muscles, menstrual cramps, and respiratory congestion.
- Aromatic salves: Salves are made by melting together 1 1/4 cup of vegetable oil and 1 oz of beeswax in a double boiler over medium heat, and adding the desired combination of essential oils.
- Internal use: Some essential oils such as oil of peppermint and cinnamon can be used to make teas or mouthwashes, or mixed with a glass of honey and water. The dose depends on the oil, but a physician, naturopathist, or other practitioner should be consulted.

Preparation

Aromatherapists recommend the use of fresh oils and oil mixtures in the techniques described above. Both essential oils and vegetable carrier oils deteriorate over time and should not be kept longer than one or two months; thus, it is best to mix only small quantities of massage oils or salves at any one time.

No special preparation for an aromatherapy treatment is required on the patient's part.

Aftercare

Aromatherapy does not require any particular form of aftercare, although many patients like to rest quietly for a few minutes after a bath or massage with essential oils.

Risks

There are no risks involved in external aromatherapy when essential oils are diluted as recommended. Not all essential oils, however, should be taken internally. Benzoin and other essential oils derived from tree resins should not be used internally.

A few cases have been reported of dissociative episodes triggered by fragrances associated with traumatic experiences. Patients in treatment for **post-traumatic stress disorder** (PTSD) or any of the **dissociative disorders** should consult their therapist before they use aromatherapy.

KEY TERMS

Carrier—A vegetable oil such as safflower, olive, grapeseed, or wheatgerm oil used to dilute essential oils for massage.

Enfleurage—A technique for extracting essential oils from flower petals by placing them on a layer of purified fat.

Essential oil—The product of special ducts or cells in the tissues of aromatic plants (or the sap of certain trees) that gives the plant its characteristic aroma and therapeutic properties. Essential oils are sometimes called volatile oils because they evaporate readily at room temperature.

Limbic system—A group of structures in the brain that includes the amygdala, hippocampus, olfactory bulbs, and hypothalamus. The limbic system is associated with homeostasis and the regulation and arousal of emotions.

Maceration—A technique for extracting essential oils from plant leaves and stems by crushing the plant parts and soaking them in warm vegetable oil.

Olfactory nerve—The cranial nerve that regulates the sense of smell.

Normal results

Normal results from aromatherapy include a sense of relaxation, relief from tension, and improved well-being.

Abnormal results

Abnormal results include skin irritations or other allergic reactions to essential oils, and the development of traumatic memories associated with specific smells.

Resources

BOOKS

Pelletier, Kenneth R., M.D. *The Best Alternative Medicine.* New York: Simon and Schuster, 2002.

Price, Shirley. *Practical Aromatherapy.* Second edition, revised. London, UK: Thorsons, 1994.

PERIODICALS

Buckle, J. "The Role of Aromatherapy in Nursing Care." *Nursing Clinics of North America* 36 (March 2001): 57-72.

Ilmberger, I., E. Heuberger, C. Mahrhofer, and others. "The Influence of Essential Oils on Human Attention: Alertness." *Chemistry and the Senses* 3 (March 2001): 239-245.

Simpson, N., and K. Roman. "Complementary Medicine Use in Children: Extent and Reasons." *British Journal of General Practice* 51 (November 2001): 914-916.

Smallwood, J., R. Brown, F. Coulter, and others. "Aromatherapy and Behaviour Disturbances in Dementia: A Randomized Controlled Trial." *International Journal of Geriatric Psychiatry* 16 (October 2001): 1010-1013.

ORGANIZATIONS

American Association of Naturopathic Physicians. 601 Valley Street, Suite 105, Seattle, WA 98109. Telephone: (206) 298-0126. <www.naturopathic.org>.

International Aromatherapy and Herb Association. 3541 West Acapulco Lane. Phoenix, AZ 85053-4625. Telephone: (602) 938-4439. <www.aztec.asu.edu./iaha/>.

National Association for Holistic Aromatherapy (NAHA). 4509 Interlake Avenue North, #233, Seattle, WA 98103-6773. Telephone: (888) ASK-NAHA or (206) 547-2164. <www.naha.org>.

Rebecca J. Frey, Ph.D.

Art therapy *see* **Creative therapies**
Artane *see* **Trihexyphenidyl**
Asendin *see* **Amoxapine**

Asperger's disorder

Definition

Asperger's disorder, which is also called Asperger's syndrome (AS) or autistic psychopathy, belongs to a group of childhood disorders known as **pervasive developmental disorders** (PDDs) or autistic spectrum disorders. The essential features of Asperger's disorder are severe social interaction impairment and restricted, repetitive patterns of behavior and activities. It is similar to **autism**, but children with AS do not have the same difficulties in acquiring language that children with autism have.

In the mental health professional's diagnostic handbook, the *Diagnostic and Statistical Manual of Mental Disorders* fourth edition text revised, or *DSM-IV-TR*, Asperger's disorder is classified as a developmental disorder of childhood.

Description

AS was first described by Hans Asperger, an Austrian **psychiatrist**, in 1944. Asperger's work was unavailable in English before the mid-1970s; as a result, AS was often unrecognized in English-speaking countries until the late 1980s. Before *DSM-IV* (published in 1994) there was no officially agreed-upon definition of AS. In the words of ICD-10, the European equivalent of the *DSM-IV*, AS is "a disorder of uncertain nosological validity." (Nosological refers to the classification of diseases.) There are three major reasons for this lack of clarity: differences between the diagnostic criteria used in Europe and those used in the United States; the fact that some of the diagnostic criteria depend on the observer's interpretation rather than objective measurements; and the fact that the clinical picture of AS changes as the child grows older.

Asperger's disorder is one of the milder pervasive developmental disorders. Children with AS learn to talk at the usual age and often have above-average verbal skills. They have normal or above-normal intelligence and the ability to feed or dress themselves and take care of their other daily needs. The distinguishing features of AS are problems with social interaction, particularly reciprocating and empathizing with the feelings of others; difficulties with nonverbal communication (such as facial expressions); peculiar speech habits that include repeated words or phrases and a flat, emotionless vocal tone; an apparent lack of "common sense" a fascination with obscure or limited subjects (for example, the parts of a clock or small machine, railroad schedules, astronomical data, etc.) often to the exclusion of other interests; clumsy and awkward physical movements; and odd or eccentric behaviors (hand wringing or finger flapping; swaying or other repetitive whole-body movements; watching spinning objects for long periods of time).

Causes and symptoms

Causes

There is some indication that AS runs in families, particularly in families with histories of **depression** and **bipolar disorder**. Asperger noted that his initial group of patients had fathers with AS symptoms. Knowledge of the genetic profile of the disorder, however, is quite limited as of 2002.

In addition, about 50% of AS patients have a history of oxygen deprivation during the birth process, which has led to the hypothesis that the disorder is caused by damage to **brain** tissue before or during childbirth. Another cause that has been suggested is an organic defect in the functioning of the brain.

As of 2002, there is no known connection between Asperger's disorder and childhood trauma, abuse or **neglect**.

Symptoms

In young children, the symptoms of AS typically include problems picking up social cues and understanding the basics of interacting with other children. The child may want friendships but find him- or herself unable to make friends.

Most children with AS are diagnosed during the elementary school years because the symptoms of the disorder become more apparent at this point. They include:

- Poor pragmatic language skills. This phrase means that the child does not use the right tone or volume of voice for a specific context, and does not understand that using humorous or slang expressions also depends on social context.
- Problems with hand-eye coordination and other visual skills.
- Problems making eye contact with others.
- Learning difficulties, which may range from mild to severe.
- Tendency to become absorbed in a particular topic and not know when others are bored with conversation about it. At this stage in their education, children with AS are likely to be labeled as "nerds."
- Repetitive behaviors. These include such behaviors as counting a group of coins or marbles over and over; reciting the same song or poem several times; buttoning and unbuttoning a jacket repeatedly; etc.

Adolescence is one of the most painful periods of life for young people with AS, because social interactions are more complex in this age group and require more subtle social skills. Some boys with AS become frustrated trying to relate to their peers and may become aggressive. Both boys and girls with the disorder are often quite naive for their age and easily manipulated by "street-wise" classmates. They are also more vulnerable than most youngsters to peer pressure.

Little research has been done regarding adults with AS. Some have serious difficulties with social and occupational functioning, but others are able to finish their schooling, join the workforce, and marry and have families.

Demographics

Although the incidence of AS has been variously estimated between 0.024% and 0.36% of the general population in North America and northern Europe, further research is required to determine its true rate of occurrence—especially because the diagnostic criteria have been defined so recently. In addition, no research regarding the incidence of AS has been done on the populations of developing countries, and nothing is known about the incidence of the disorder in different racial or ethnic groups.

With regard to gender differences, AS appears to be much more common in boys. Dr. Asperger's first patients were all boys, but girls have been diagnosed with AS since the 1980s. One Swedish study found the male/female ratio to be 4:1; however, the World Health Organization's ICD-10 classification gives the male to female ratio as 8 to 1.

Diagnosis

As of early 2002, there are no blood tests or brain scans that can be used to diagnose AS. Until *DSM-IV* (1994), there was no "official" list of symptoms for the disorder, which made its **diagnosis** both difficult and inexact. Although most children with AS are diagnosed between five and nine years of age, many are not diagnosed until adulthood. Misdiagnoses are common; AS has been confused with such other neurological disorders as Tourette's syndrome, or with attention-deficit disorder (ADD), **oppositional defiant disorder** (ODD), or **obsessive-compulsive disorder** (OCD). Some researchers think that AS may overlap with some types of learning disability, such as the nonverbal learning disability (NLD) syndrome identified in 1989.

The inclusion of AS as a separate diagnostic category in *DSM-IV* was justified on the basis of a large international field trial of over a thousand children and adolescents. Nevertheless, the diagnosis of AS is also complicated by confusion with such other diagnostic categories as "high-functioning (IQ higher than 70) autism" or HFA, and "schizoid personality disorder of childhood." Unlike **schizoid personality disorder** of childhood, AS is not an unchanging set of personality traits—AS has a developmental dimension. AS is distinguished from HFA by the following characteristics:

- later onset of symptoms (usually around three years of age).
- early development of grammatical speech; the AS child's verbal IQ (scores on verbal sections of standardized intelligence tests) is usually higher than performance IQ (how well the child performs in school). The reverse is usually true for autistic children.
- less severe deficiencies in social and communication skills.
- presence of intense interest in one or two topics.
- physical clumsiness and lack of coordination

- family is more likely to have a history of the disorder.
- lower frequency of neurological disorders.
- more positive outcome in later life.

DSM-IV-TR criteria for Asperger's disorder

The *DSM-IV-TR* specifies the following diagnostic criteria for AS:

- The child's social interactions are impaired in at least two of the following ways: markedly limited use of nonverbal communication (facial expressions, for example); lack of age-appropriate peer relationships; failure to share enjoyment, interests, or accomplishment with others; lack of reciprocity (turn-taking) in social interactions.
- The child's behavior, interests, and activities are characterized by repetitive or rigid patterns, such as an abnormal preoccupation with one or two topics, or with parts of objects; repetitive physical movements; or rigid insistence on certain routines and rituals.
- The patient's social, occupational, or educational functioning is significantly impaired.
- The child has normal age-appropriate language skills.
- The child has normal age-appropriate cognitive skills, self-help abilities, and curiosity about the environment.
- The child does not meet criteria for another specific PDD or schizophrenia.

To establish the diagnosis, the child psychiatrist or **psychologist** would observe the child, and would interview parents, possibly teachers, and the affected child (depending on the child's age), and would gather a comprehensive medical and social history.

Other diagnostic scales and checklists

Other instruments that have been used to identify children with AS include Gillberg's criteria, a six-item list compiled by a Swedish researcher that specifies problems in social interaction, a preoccupying narrow interest, forcing routines and interests on the self or others, speech and language problems, nonverbal communication problems, and physical clumsiness; and the Australian Scale for Asperger's Syndrome, a detailed multi-item questionnaire developed in 1996.

Brain imaging findings

As of 2002, only a few structural abnormalities of the brain have been linked to AS. Findings include abnormally large folds in the brain tissue in the left frontal region, abnormally small folds in the operculum (a lid-like structure composed of portions of three adjoining brain lobes), and damage to the left temporal lobe (a part of the brain containing a sensory area associated with hearing). The first single photon emission tomography (SPECT) study of an AS patient found a lower-than-normal supply of blood to the left parietal area of the brain, an area associated with bodily sensations. Brain **imaging studies** on a larger sample of AS patients is the next stage of research.

Treatments

There is no cure for AS and no prescribed treatment regimen for all AS patients. Specific treatments are based on the individual's symptom pattern.

Medications

Many children with AS do not require any medication. For those who do, the drugs that are recommended most often include psychostimulants (**methylphenidate, pemoline**), **clonidine**, or one of the tricyclic **antidepressants** (TCAs) for hyperactivity or inattention; **beta blockers**, neuroleptics (antipsychotic medications), or lithium (**lithium carbonate**) for anger or aggression; **selective serotonin reuptake inhibitors** (**SSRIs**) or TCAs for rituals (repetitive behaviors) and preoccupations; and SSRIs or TCAs for **anxiety** symptoms. One alternative herbal remedy that has been tried with AS patients is **St. John's wort**.

Psychotherapy

AS patients often benefit from individual **psychotherapy**, particularly during adolescence, in order to cope with depression and other painful feelings related to their social difficulties. Many children with AS are also helped by **group therapy**, which brings them together with others facing the same challenges. There are therapy groups for parents as well.

Therapists who are experienced in treating children with Asperger's disorder have found that the child should be allowed to proceed slowly in forming an emotional bond with the therapist. Too much emotional intensity at the beginning may be more than the child can handle. Behavioral approaches seem to work best with these children. **Play therapy** can be helpful in teaching the child to recognize social cues as well as lowering the level of emotional tension.

Adults with AS are most likely to benefit from individual therapy using a cognitive-behavioral approach, although many also attend group therapy. Some adults have been helped by working with speech therapists on their pragmatic language skills. A relatively new approach called behavioral coaching has been used to help adults with AS learn to organize and set priorities for their daily activities.

Educational considerations

Most AS patients have normal or above-normal intelligence, and are able to complete their education up through the graduate or professional school level. Many are unusually skilled in music or good in subjects requiring rote memorization. On the other hand, the verbal skills of children with AS frequently cause difficulties with teachers, who may not understand why these "bright" children have social and communication problems. Some AS children are dyslexic; others have difficulty with writing or mathematics. In some cases, AS children have been mistakenly put in special programs either for children with much lower levels of functioning, or for children with conduct disorders. AS children do best in structured learning situations in which they learn problem-solving and social skills as well as academic subjects. They frequently need protection from the teasing and **bullying** of other children, and often become hypersensitive to criticism by their teenage years. One approach that has been found helpful at the high-school level is to pair the adolescent with AS with a slightly older teenager who can serve as a mentor. The mentor can "clue in" the younger adolescent about the slang, dress code, cliques, and other "facts of life" at the local high school.

Employment

Adults with AS are productively employed in a wide variety of fields, including the learned professions. They do best, however, in jobs with regular routines or occupations that allow them to work in isolation. In large companies, employers or supervisors and workplace colleagues may need some information about AS in order to understand the new employee's "eccentricities."

Prognosis

AS is a lifelong but stable condition. The prognosis for children with AS is generally good as far as intellectual development is concerned, although few school districts as of 2002 are equipped to meet the special social needs of this group of children. Adults with AS appear to be at greater risk of depression than the general population. In addition, some researchers believe that people with AS have an increased risk of a psychotic episode (a period of

KEY TERMS

Autistic psychopathy—Hans Asperger's original name for the condition now known as Asperger's disorder. It is still used occasionally as a synonym for the disorder.

DSM—Abbreviation for the *Diagnostic and Statistical Manual of Mental Disorders,* a handbook for mental health professionals that includes lists of symptoms that indicate specific diagnoses. The text is periodically revised, and the latest version was published in 2000 and is called *DSM-IV-TR,* for Fourth Edition, Text Revised.

Gillberg's criteria—A six-item checklist for AS developed by Christopher Gillberg, a Swedish researcher. It is widely used in Europe as a diagnostic tool.

High-functioning autism (HFA)—A subcategory of autistic disorder consisting of children diagnosed with IQs of 70 or higher. Children with AS are often misdiagnosed as having HFA.

Nonverbal learning disability (NLD)—A learning disability syndrome identified in 1989 that may overlap with some of the symptoms of AS.

Pervasive developmental disorders (PDDs)—A category of childhood disorders that includes Asperger's syndrome and Rett's disorder. The PDDs are sometimes referred to collectively as autistic spectrum disorders.

Semantic-pragmatic disorder—A term that refers to the difficulty that children with AS and some forms of autism have with pragmatic language skills. Pragmatic language skills include knowing the proper tone of voice for a given context, using humor appropriately, making eye contact with a conversation partner, maintaining the appropriate volume of one's voice, etc.

time during which the affected person loses touch with reality) in adolescence or adult life.

Prevention

Effective prevention of Asperger's disorder awaits further genetic mapping together with ongoing research in the structures and functioning of the brain. The only practical preventive strategy as of 2002 is better protection of the fetus against oxygen deprivation during childbirth.

Resources

BOOKS

American Psychiatric Association. *Diagnostic and Statistical Manual of Mental Disorders.* 4th edition, text revised. Washington, DC: American Psychiatric Association, 2000.

"Psychiatric Conditions in Childhood and Adolescence." Section 19, Chapter 274. In *The Merck Manual of Diagnosis and Therapy,* edited by Mark H. Beers, M.D., and Robert Berkow, M.D. Whitehouse Station, NJ: Merck Research Laboratories, 1999.

Thoene, Jess G., ed. *Physicians' Guide to Rare Diseases.* Montvale, NJ: Dowden Publishing Company, 1995.

World Health Organization (WHO). *The ICD-10 Classification of Mental and Behavioural Disorders.* Geneva: WHO, 1992.

PERIODICALS

Bishop, D. V. M. "Autism, Asperger's Syndrome & Semantic-Pragmatic Disorder: Where Are the Boundaries?" *British Journal of Disorders of Communication* 24 (1989): 107-121.

Gillberg, C. "The Neurobiology of Infantile Autism." *Journal of Child Psychology and Psychiatry* 29 (1988): 257-266.

ORGANIZATIONS

Autism Research Institute. 4182 Adams Avenue, San Diego, CA 92116.

Families of Adults Afflicted with Asperger's Syndrome (FAAAS). P.O. Box 514, Centerville, MA 02632. <www.faaas.org>.

National Association of Rare Disorders (NORD). P.O. Box 8923, New Fairfield, CT 06812-8923. Telephone: (800) 999-NORD or (203) 746-6518.

Yale-LDA Social Learning Disabilities Project. Yale Child Study Center, New Haven, CT. The Project is looking for study subjects with PDDs between the ages of 8 and 24, including AS patients. Contact person: Sanno Zack at (203) 785-3488 or Sanno.Zack@yale.edu. <www.info.med.Yale.edu/chldstdy/autism>.

OTHER

American Academy of Child & Adolescent Psychiatry (AACAP). "Asperger's Disorder." AACAP Facts For Families Pamphlet #69. Washington, DC: American Academy of Child & Adolescent Psychiatry, 1999.

Rebecca J. Frey, Ph.D.

Assertive community treatment

Definition

Assertive community treatment (ACT) combines multiple types of help—including medication, counseling, education, legal and financial support—provided by community-based, mobile teams to people with severe mental illnesses.

Purpose

ACT is aimed at older teenagers and adults with a severe mental illness that greatly impacts their ability to care for themselves and function at home and at work. The intensive program is designed to help those with serious, long-term mental illness including, but not limited to, **schizophrenia**. ACT combines medication, counseling, rehabilitation, education, legal and financial support, and family assistance.

Description

Arnold Marx, MD, Leonard Stein, MD, and Mary Ann Test, Ph.D., pioneered the ACT program in the late 1960s in Madison, Wisconsin, as an alternative to admission to a psychiatric institution. While working at Mendota State Hospital, the trio noticed that patients who got better in the hospital often became sick again when reentering the community. They proposed that a round-the-clock program outside the hospital could provide the same ongoing support and therapy. In 1972, they put their theory to the test and formally launched ACT. Today, the program is offered in certain U.S. states and throughout Canada and England.

Because ACT provides care outside of the doctor's office, usually in the comfort of the patient's home, the community-based program is sometimes referred to as a hospital without walls. The cornerstone of each ACT program is a diverse team of nearly a dozen different health care specialists, including doctors, nurses, and counselors. The program provides support and care 24 hours a day, seven days a week, all year long.

Project leaders, called case managers, usually have fewer than 10 patients, which allows for highly individualized care. A patient is considered a client of the ACT team. ACT is different from other **community mental health** center (CMHC) services. The ACT team comes to the client, while CMHC patients must go to a clinic. Those who participate in ACT receive more personalized attention, and may be in contact with the ACT team daily, as opposed to weekly or monthly. The ACT team provides all necessary care, including **substance abuse** treatment and rehabilitation. CMHC services often refer clients to an outside specialist.

Key features

ACT has three key features: treatment, rehabilitation, and support services.

- Treatment may involve antipsychotic and antidepressant medicines, substance abuse therapy, coun-

seling, and possible admission to a hospital for closer monitoring.

- The rehabilitation arm of the program helps the patient find volunteer work and paid employment and provides support for continuing education. Specialists teach patients new behaviors, such as how to structure schedules and perform daily activities.
- The support services advise patients on how to find legal and financial support, housing, transportation, and other services. Family members are taught how to cope with their loved one's illness and are provided with education materials. According to the Schizophrenia Patient Outcomes Research Team (PORT) study, funded by the National Institute of Mental Health and the Agency for Health Care Policy and Research, fewer than one in 10 families of persons with schizophrenia receives such education and support.

ACT may also be referred to as the Program of Assertive Community Treatment or PACT. Many organizations use the terms interchangeably. Other names for ACT include community support programs (CSP) and mobile treatment teams (MTT).

Goals

ACT may benefit those with schizophrenia, **schizoaffective disorder**, and **bipolar disorder**. PORT recommends ACT as an effective treatment for schizophrenia and persons with serious mental illness.

ACT is targeted to persons with very severe mental illness that has led to repeated hospital and emergency room visits, **homelessness**, or jail time. According to the National Jail Association, about 700,000 persons with mental illness are incarcerated every year. ACT programs have helped such criminal offenders meet their legal obligations while providing medical support and rehabilitation services.

The ACT program has several goals:

- relieve or cure symptoms of the disorder.
- reduce or prevent repeated, severe episodes associated with the disorder.
- enhance the quality of life.
- improve functioning at work and in social settings.
- encourage independence and teach necessary self-care skills.
- reduce the burden of care on a patient's family by providing education and support.

Effectiveness

Studies have shown that ACT and similar programs greatly reduce the number of hospital stays among those with severe mental illness. One study

KEY TERMS

Antidepressant—A drug used to treat depression.

Antipsychotic—A drug used to treat serious mental disorders that cause hallucinations or delusions.

Bipolar disorder—A mental illness marked by alternating periods of excitement and depression. Also called manic-depressive disorder.

Delusion—A false belief that persists.

Hallucination—Seeing or hearing something that does not really exist.

Substance abuse—Overuse of a drug or alcohol, which leads to addiction.

found that ACT not only reduced overall hospital admissions, it also decreased the length of the hospital stays. ACT has been shown to improve patient functioning and encourage patients to stick to their treatment routines. The benefits are reported to be particularly marked among those with a coexisting mental disorder and substance abuse problem, perhaps because such patients are at higher risk of **hospitalization** and complications.

Compared to those who are admitted to an institution, ACT clients have fewer symptoms, more positive social interactions, and spend less time unemployed. Experts say anywhere between 20–40% of people with the most severe and persistent mental illnesses would benefit from ACT.

Availability

There are a limited number of ACT teams in the United States. As of January 2007, only Delaware, Idaho, Missouri, Rhode Island, Texas, and Wisconsin offered statewide programs. However, 19 other states offered test, or pilot, programs.

Because there are so many specialists on an ACT team, it can be costly. Some argue that the expense is justified, particularly when compared to the cost of an extended hospital stay. According to the National Alliance on Mental Illness, ACT costs each participant between $9,000 and $14,000 a year, while hospital costs for an extended stay can exceed $100,000.

Resources

ORGANIZATIONS

Assertive Community Treatment Association. Suite 102, 810 E. Grand River Avenue, Brighton, MI 48116. Telephone: (810) 227-1859. <http:// www.actassociation.org>.

National Alliance on Mental Illness. 2107 Wilson Blvd., Suite 300, Arlington, VA 22201-3042. Telephone: (703) 524-7600. <http://www.nami.org>.

National Mental Health Information Center. P.O. Box 42557, Washington, DC 20015. Telephone: (800) 789-2647. <http://mentalhealth.samhsa.gov>.

Kelli Miller Stacy

Assertiveness training

Definition

Assertiveness training is a form of behavior therapy designed to help people stand up for themselves—to empower themselves, in more contemporary terms. Assertiveness is a response that seeks to maintain an appropriate balance between passivity and aggression. Assertive responses promote fairness and equality in human interactions, based on a positive sense of respect for self and others.

Assertiveness training has a decades-long history in mental health and personal growth groups, going back to the women's movement of the 1970s. The approach was introduced to encourage women to stand up for themselves appropriately in their interactions with others, particularly as they moved into graduate education and the workplace in greater numbers. The original association of assertiveness training with the women's movement in the United States grew out of the discovery of many women in the movement that they were hampered by their inability to be assertive. Today, assertiveness training is used as part of communication training in settings as diverse as schools, corporate boardrooms, and psychiatric hospitals, for programs as varied as **substance abuse** treatment, **social skills training**, vocational programs, and responding to harassment.

Purpose

The purpose of assertiveness training is to teach persons appropriate strategies for identifying and acting on their desires, needs, and opinions while remaining respectful of others. This form of training is tailored to the needs of specific participants and the situations they find particularly challenging. Assertiveness training is a broad approach that can be applied to many different personal, academic, health care, and work situations.

Learning to communicate in a clear and honest fashion usually improves relationships within one's

Recruits at a police training school act out a scenario. Role play is one form of assertiveness training. *(Homer Sykes/Alamy)*

life. Women in particular have often been taught to hide their real feelings and preferences, and to try to get their way by manipulation or other indirect means. Specific areas of **intervention** and change in assertiveness training include conflict resolution, realistic goal-setting, and **stress** management. In addition to emotional and psychological benefits, taking a more active approach to self-determination has been shown to have positive outcomes in many personal choices related to health, including being assertive in risky sexual situations; abstaining from using drugs or alcohol; and assuming responsibility for self-care if one has a chronic illness like diabetes or cancer.

Precautions

There are a few precautions with assertiveness training. One potential caution would be to remain within assertive responses, rather than become aggressive in standing up for oneself. Some participants in assertiveness training programs who are just learning the techniques of appropriate assertiveness may "overdo" their new behaviors and come across as aggressive rather than assertive. Such overcompensa-

tion would most likely disappear with continued practice of the techniques.

One additional precaution about assertiveness training is that it should not be regarded as the equivalent of martial arts training or similar physical self-defense techniques. It is important to distinguish between contexts or situations in which verbal assertiveness is appropriate and useful, and those in which it is irrelevant. In some situations, a person's decision to leave the situation or seek help because they sense danger is preferable to an encounter with a criminal.

Description

Assertiveness training is often included within other programs, but "stand-alone" programs in self-assertion are often given in women's centers or college counseling centers. Corporate programs for new personnel sometimes offer assertiveness training as part of communication or teamwork groups, or as part of a program on sexual harassment.

Assertiveness training typically begins with an information-gathering exercise in which participants are asked to think about and list the areas in their life in which they have difficulty asserting themselves. Very often they will notice specific situations or patterns of behavior that they want to focus on during the course. The next stage in assertive training is usually role-plays designed to help participants practice clearer and more direct forms of communicating with others. The role-plays allow for practice and repetition of the new techniques, helping each person learn assertive responses by acting on them. Feedback is provided to improve the response, and the role-play is repeated. Eventually, each person is asked to practice assertive techniques in everyday life, outside the training setting. Role-plays usually incorporate specific problems for individual participants, such as difficulty speaking up to an overbearing boss; setting limits to intrusive friends; or stating a clear preference about dinner to one's spouse. Role-plays often include examples of aggressive and passive responses, in addition to the assertive responses, to help participants distinguish between these extremes as they learn a new set of behaviors.

Assertiveness training promotes the use of "I" statements as a way to help individuals express their feelings and reactions to others. A commonly used model of an "I" statement is "when you _____, I feel _____", to help the participant describe what they see the other person as doing, and how they feel about that action. "I" statements are often contrasted with "you" statements, which are usually not received well by others. For example, "When you are two hours late getting home from work, I feel both anxious and angry," is a less accusing communication than "You are a selfish and inconsiderate jerk for not telling me you would be two hours late." Prompts are often used to help participants learn new communication styles. This approach helps participants learn new ways of expressing themselves as well as how it feels to be assertive.

Learning specific techniques and perspectives, such as self-observation skills, awareness of personal preferences and assuming personal responsibility are important components of the assertiveness training process. Role-play and practice help with self-observation, while making lists can be a helpful technique for exploring personal preferences for those who may not have a good sense of their own needs and desires. Participants may be asked to list anything from their ten favorite movies or pieces of music to their favorite foods, places they would like to visit, subjects that interest them, and so on.

Preparation

Preparation for assertiveness training varies from person to person. For some participants, no preparation is needed before practicing the techniques; for others, however, individual counseling or therapy may help prepare the individual for assertiveness training. For participants who may be more shy and feel uncomfortable saying "no" or speaking up for themselves, a brief course of individual therapy will help to prepare them psychologically and emotionally to use assertive techniques.

Aftercare

Aftercare can involve ongoing supportive therapy, again based on the individual's level of comfort in using the assertive techniques. For those who are comfortable using the techniques on their own, a supportive social network or occasional participation in a support group will be enough to help maintain the new behavioral patterns. The ultimate goal is for each participant to self-monitor effectively his or her use of assertive techniques on an ongoing basis.

Risks

There are minimal risks associated with assertiveness training. Personal relationships may be affected if those around the participant have difficulty accepting the changes in their friend or family member. This risk, however, is no greater than that associated with any other life change.

Another potential risk is that of overcompensating in the early stages of training by being too aggressive. With appropriate feedback, participants can usually learn to modify and improve their responses.

People who are very shy or self-conscious, or who were harshly treated as children, may also experience **anxiety** during the training as they work toward speaking up and otherwise changing their behaviors. The anxiety may be uncomfortable, but should decrease as the person becomes more comfortable with the techniques and receives encouragement from others in the program.

Normal results

An enhanced sense of well-being and more positive self-esteem are typical results from assertiveness training. Many participants report that they feel better about themselves and more capable of handling the stresses of daily life. In addition, people who have participated in assertiveness training have a better sense of boundaries, and are able to set appropriate and healthy limits with others. Being able to set appropriate limits (such as saying "no") helps people to avoid feeling victimized by others.

A healthy sense of self-determination and respect for others is the ultimate outcome of assertiveness training. Such a balance helps each person work better with others, and make appropriate decisions for themselves.

Abnormal results

Unusual results may include becoming too aggressive in setting boundaries, as if the individual is overcompensating. With appropriate training, role-play, and feedback, this response can be re-learned. Alternatively, for very shy individuals, a heightened sense of anxiety may be experienced when using the techniques initially. The nervousness or anxiety is usually due to the individual's concern about others' reactions to their assertive responses. Over time, the anxiety will usually decrease.

See also Behavior modification; Gender issues in mental health.

Resources

BOOKS

Alberti, R., and M. Emmons. *Your Perfect Right: Assertiveness and Equality in Your Life and Relationships.* 8th edition. Atascadero, CA: Impact Publishers, Inc., 2001.

Butler, Pamela E., Ph.D. *Self-Assertion for Women.* Second edition, revised. New York: HarperCollins, 1992.

de Becker, Gavin. *The Gift of Fear: Survival Signals That Protect Us from Violence.* New York: Little, Brown, and Company, 1998.

Shaevitz, Marjorie Hansen. *The Confident Woman: Learn the Rules of the Game.* New York: Harmony Books, 1999.

Smith, M. *When I Say No, I Feel Guilty.* Bantam, 1975.

PERIODICALS

Weinhardt, L. S., M. P. Carey, K. B. Carey, and R. N. Verdecias. "Increasing assertiveness skills to reduce HIV risk among women living with a severe and persistent mental illness." *Journal of Consulting & Clinical Psychology* Vol. 66, no. 4 (Aug. 1998): 680-684.

Deanna Pledge, Ph.D.

Assessment and diagnosis

Definition

Psychological assessment is the process of gathering and evaluating data about a patient's symptoms, mental state, behaviors, and background. Using these data, a **diagnosis** of the disease or disorder is made.

Purpose

The purpose of psychological assessment is to reduce and organize the data concerning a patient so that a diagnosis and recommendation for a course of treatment can be made. The psychological assessment (also called the biopsychosocial or psychiatric assessment) gathers information to diagnose any mental disorder that the person may have; it is the first step in treating a diagnosed disorder. The process typically starts with a chief complaint or presenting problem—this is usually what prompts the person to seek help. A complete psychological assessment should include:

- biopsychosocial history
- neurological assessment
- psychological testing (if applicable)
- physical examination (if required by a psychiatrist)
- brain imaging (if necessary)

Once complete, the assessment will help establish either a tentative or definitive diagnosis. With this information, the clinician can inform the patient of the results, and treatment can begin.

Precautions

Accurate information gathering and objective notes are essential for psychological assessment. However, these can be difficult to obtain if the person is not willing to disclose all necessary information, either out of embarrassment or through **denial** that symptoms of a mental problem even exist.

Description

The American Psychological Association Code of Ethics states that a psychologist's assessments must be based on evidence "sufficient to substantiate their findings," usually including a direct examination of the patient. If an examination of the patient is not possible, the **psychologist** must note this explicitly in his or her conclusions or recommendations.

The psychological assessment, an extremely effective and accepted diagnostic tool, is a structured interview that has several parts:

- identifying information
- chief complaint (presenting problem)
- history of present illness
- past medical and psychological history
- personal history
- family history
- substance abuse history
- mental status examination (MSE)

Before beginning, the clinician should introduce himself or herself and attempt to make the person comfortable in a professional setting. A common fluency in language or competent translator is essential for information gathering and questioning.

Identifying information

These are general and emotionally neutral questions that usually include name, age, occupation, and marital status.

Chief complaint (presenting problem)

This consists of questions such as "Why are you seeking psychological help today?" that reveal past mental disorders and/or the symptoms that made the person seek **psychotherapy**. The patient's responses can also help the clinician ask pertinent questions during other parts of the interview, and can help clarify the presence of symptoms.

History of present illness

The patient describes the onset of signs and symptoms that comprise the current mental problem.

Past medical and psychological history

Because medical problems—including thyroid disease, Parkinson's disease, head trauma, and brain infections—can cause psychological symptoms, a thorough medical history must be taken. The interviewer also asks about previous psychological/psychiatric treatment, including **hospitalization**, outpatient or substance **abuse** treatment, and medication prescribed for mental disorders. The treatment's duration, effectiveness, and outcome is also noted.

Personal history

This portion of the assessment provides information on the patient's entire life, beginning with prenatal development, including maternal abortions, nutrition, and drug use during pregnancy; birth trauma; and birth order. The patient's life is then discussed in distinct phases:

EARLY CHILDHOOD (INFANCY–THREE YEARS). Questions include information about temperament, walking, talking, toilet training, nutrition and feeding, family relationships, behavioral problems, hospitalization, and separation from early childhood caregivers.

MIDDLE CHILDHOOD (THREE–11 YEARS). Pertinent information will be gathered concerning learning, relationship with peers and family, behavioral problems, and general personality development.

ADOLESCENCE (12–18 YEARS). Information typically includes school history, behavioral problems, and sexual development.

ADULTHOOD. This section details the patient's education, sexual history, relationships and/or marriages, peer relationships, occupation, and current circumstances.

Family history

Family history is crucially important since many mental disorders can be inherited genetically. Additionally, family interactions may affect the patient's symptoms and disorder.

Substance use history

This portion of the psychological assessment details information on the patient's use of both illicit drugs (opiates, **cocaine**, alcohol, marijuana, hallucinogens, and depressants) and legally prescribed medications, as well as **nicotine** and caffeine. Questions usually focus on age of first use, age of last use, period of heaviest use, usage within the past 30 days, frequency, quantity, and route of usage. Tolerance and dependence, if present, are noted, as are the patient's treatment history, any medical complications (e.g., AIDS), and legal problems associated with usage (e.g., driving or operating a vehicle or machine while impaired).

Mental Status Examination (MSE)

This assesses the patient's mental state, and begins by evaluating:

- Appearance: hygiene, general appearance, grooming, and attire.
- Behavior: abnormal movements, hyperactivity and eye contact with the interviewer.
- Speech: fluency, rate, clarity, and tone, all of which may indicate the patient's mental state. A fast-talking person, for example, may be anxious. Speech can also reveal intoxication or impairment as well as problems in the mouth (e.g., dentures, cleft palate) or speech impairment.

KEY TERMS

Affect—The expression of emotion displayed to others through facial expressions, hand gestures, tone of voice, etc. Types of affect include flat (inanimate, no expression), blunted (minimally responsive), inappropriate (incongruous expressions of emotion relative to the content of a conversation), and labile (sudden and abrupt changes in type and intensity of emotion).

Assessment—In the context of psychological assessment (a structured interview), assessment is information-gathering to diagnose a mental disorder.

Biopsychosocial history—A history of significant past and current experiences that influence client behaviors, including medical, educational, employment, and interpersonal experiences. Alcohol or drug use and involvement with the legal system are also assessed in a biopsychosocial history.

Delusion—A false belief that is resistant to reason or contrary to actual fact. A patient may be convinced, for example, that someone is trying to poison him or her, or that he or she has a fatal illness despite evidence to the contrary.

Dependence—The adaptation of neurons and other physical processes to the use of a drug, followed by withdrawal symptoms when the drug is removed; physiological and/or psychological addiction.

Hallucinations—False sensory perceptions. A person experiencing a hallucination may "hear" sounds or "see" people or objects that are not really present. Hallucinations can also affect the senses of smell, touch, and taste.

Phobia—Irrational fear of places, things, or situations that lead to avoidance.

Psychotropic drug—Medication that has an effect on the mind, brain, behavior, perceptions, or emotions. Psychotropic medications are used to treat mental illnesses because they affect a patient's moods and perceptions.

Tolerance—Progressive decrease in the effectiveness of a drug with long-term use.

The examiner then goes on to assess other aspects of the patient's mental state, such as mood, thought process, and cognition, beginning with a question such as that suggested in the *Merck Manual of Geriatrics:* "I would like to ask you some questions about your feelings, your thinking, and your memory as a routine part of the examination. Is that all right with you?"

Mood and affect

These outward manifestations of the patient's mental state are important indicators. The clinician can ask the patient to describe his or her current mood ("How do you feel? Are you happy? Sad? Angry?"). The patient's affect, or emotional state, however, is observed and interpreted by the clinician throughout the interview, and described in standardized terms, such as excitable, flat, inappropriate, or labile (rapidly shifting).

Thought process and content

Thought process (or form) indicates whether or not the interviewee is properly oriented to time and place. Thought content reveals how connected, coherent, and logical the patient's thoughts are. The interviewer may ask the patient to identify themselves and loved ones, to name the current date, and/or to describe the route taken to the examiner's location. The

patient's responses to questions can indicate disturbances in thought, such as circumstantial thinking (circuitous, persistent storytelling), tangential thinking (response not pertinent to the question) black/white (extreme) thinking, and impoverished (minimally responsive) thinking. Disturbed thought content can also indicate **delusions**, **hallucinations**, phobias, and obsessions. In addition, the examiner may question the patient about suicidal and/or homicidal thoughts.

Cognition

Cognition refers to the patient's attention, awareness, memory (long-, intermediate-, and short-term), general knowledge, abstract thinking ability, insight, and judgment. The interviewer may ask the patient to spell a word forward and backward, identify the current president, read and/or write something, compare two objects, and explain the meaning of common sayings.

Preparation

An evaluation session appointment is made with a qualified mental health practitioner. A specialist (someone specializing in anxiety/depressive disorders, pain management, **hypnotherapy**, or chemical dependency, for example) may be sought or recommended. A private, quiet, nonthreatening, environment is recommended to ensure comfort and confidentiality.

Aftercare

Aftercare depends on the results of the evaluation. Treatment may be initiated and/or further tests may be required to confirm the diagnosis.

Risks

There are no known risks involved. A person seeking a mental health evaluation does so for a reason and may learn of an existing or potential mental problem.

Normal results

The patient does not require psychological therapy or psychotropic drug (medications beneficial to treat certain mental disorders) treatment.

Abnormal results

The person has a mental disorder that may require psychotherapy or a combination of psychotherapy and medications.

Resources

BOOKS

Andreasen, Nancy C., and Donald W. Black.*Introductory Textbook of Psychiatry*. 3rd ed. Washington, D.C.: American Psychiatric Publishing, 2001.
VandenBos, Gary R., ed. *APA Dictionary of Psychology*. Washington, D.C.: American Psychological Association, 2007.

Laith Farid Gulli, MD
Bilal Nasser, MD
Robert Ramirez

Ativan *see* **Lorazepam**

Attachment disorder *see* **Reactive attachment disorder of infancy or early childhood**

Attention deficit/hyperactivity disorder

Definition

Attention deficit/hyperactivity disorder (ADHD) is a developmental disorder characterized by distractibility, hyperactivity, impulsive behaviors, and the inability to remain focused on tasks or activities.

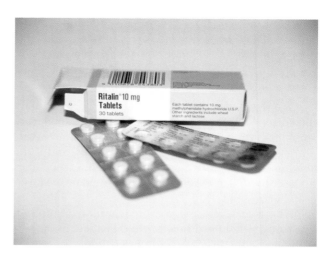

Ritalin pills. *(Tracy Dominey/Photo Researchers, Inc)*

Description

ADHD was first described in 1845. The estimated prevalence of ADHD, also known as hyperkinetic disorder (HKD) outside of the United States, is 8% to 10% of children. Although difficult to assess in infancy and toddlerhood, signs of ADHD may begin to appear as early as age two or three, but the symptom picture changes as adolescence approaches. Many symptoms, particularly hyperactivity, diminish in early adulthood; however, up to 70% of individuals with ADHD experience persistent impulsivity and problems focusing attention throughout their adult lives. Inattention is the most frequent persistent symptom in adults with ADHD.

Causes and symptoms

Causes

The causes of ADHD are thought to be an interaction of environment and genes. Heredity plays a major role in the development of ADHD. A number of genes considered to confer susceptibility to ADHD have been identified, and some researchers have suggested that ADHD may arise from several different combinations of these susceptibility genes and environmental factors. These genes primarily involve the signaling proteins active in the brain's **dopamine** (a nerve-signaling molecule) pathways, supporting the prevailing theory that the signaling of dopamine and other **neurotransmitters** is responsible for the symptoms of the disorder. **Brain** imaging results also support this idea. These studies have identified distinct differences in dopamine processing and uptake in the brains of people with ADHD compared to those of people without the disorder. Some researchers see a link between ADHD and **obsessive-compulsive disorder** (OCD) in heredity studies of families, and children with an ADHD parent or sibling are more likely to develop the disorder themselves. Studies of identical twins point to a heritability rate as high as 91%.

Some environmental factors have been strongly linked to ADHD. Studies have found that maternal smoking during pregnancy can increase a child's overall risk of ADHD by two-and-a-half times, and if the child is a girl, the risk can be as much as 4.6 times higher. Low birth weight also has been identified as a risk factor, and lead exposure has been linked to ADHD; lead levels above a predetermined cutoff in one study were linked to a fourfold increase in the risk of having ADHD. Traumatic brain injury or neurological disorders may also trigger ADHD symptoms.

Symptoms

The **diagnosis** of ADHD requires the presence of at least six of the following symptoms of inattention, or six or more symptoms of hyperactivity and impulsivity combined:

Inattention:

- fails to pay close attention to detail or makes careless mistakes in schoolwork or other activities
- has difficulty sustaining attention in tasks or activities
- does not appear to listen when spoken to
- does not follow through on instructions and does not finish tasks
- has difficulty organizing tasks and activities
- avoids or dislikes tasks that require sustained mental effort (e.g., homework)
- is easily distracted
- is forgetful in daily activities

Hyperactivity:

- fidgets with hands or feet or squirms in seat
- does not remain seated when expected to
- runs or climbs excessively when inappropriate (in adolescents and adults, feelings of restlessness)
- has difficulty playing quietly
- is constantly on the move
- talks excessively

Impulsivity:

- blurts out answers before the question has been completed
- has difficulty waiting turns
- interrupts and/or intrudes on others

Further criteria to establish a diagnosis also require that some symptoms develop before age seven, and that they significantly impair functioning in two or more settings (e.g., home and school) for a period of at least six months.

Many individuals with ADHD have symptoms from all three of the above categories. Some children, however, have behavior patterns in which inattention dominates, or hyperactivity and impulsivity dominate. For this reason, ADHD can be further categorized, or subdivided, into three subtypes. Children who have at least six symptoms from both of the inattention and hyperactivity–impulsivity categories may be diagnosed with ADHD, combined type. Children who meet the symptom criteria for inattention, but not for hyperactivity–impulsivity, are diagnosed with attention deficit/hyperactivity disorder, predominantly inattentive type, commonly called attention deficit disorder (ADD). Children with predominantly attentive type may go undiagnosed until negative academic consequences arise; children who daydream are much less noticeable than children who are in constant, impulsive motion. Children who experience more symptoms from the hyperactivity and impulsivity categories, but fewer than six symptoms of inattention may be diagnosed with ADHD, predominantly hyperactive–impulsive type.

Diagnosis

The first step in determining if a child has ADHD is to consult with a pediatrician. The pediatrician can make an initial evaluation of the child's developmental maturity compared to other children in the same age group, using guidelines for the diagnosis and evaluation of ADHD provided by the American Academy of Pediatrics. The physician should also perform a comprehensive physical examination to rule out any organic causes of ADHD symptoms, such as an overactive thyroid or vision or hearing problems.

If no organic problem can be found, a **psychologist**, **psychiatrist**, neurologist/pediatric neurologist, neuropsychologist, developmental pediatrician, or learning specialist is typically consulted to perform a comprehensive ADHD assessment. A complete medical, family, social, psychiatric, and educational history is compiled from existing medical and school records and from interviews with parents and teachers. Interviews may also be conducted with the children, depending on their age. Along with these interviews, several clinical questionnaires may also be used, such as the Conners' Rating Scales (Teacher's Questionnaire and Parent's Questionnaire), Child Behavior Checklist (CBCL), and the Achenbach Child Behavior

Checklist. These inventories provide valuable information on the child's behavior in different settings and situations. In addition, the Wender Utah Rating Scale has been adapted for use in diagnosing ADHD in adults, as has the Conners' Adult ADHD rating scale.

It is important to note that mental disorders such as **depression** and **anxiety** disorder can cause symptoms similar to ADHD: Depression can cause attention problems, and anxiety can cause symptoms similar to hyperactivity. A complete and comprehensive psychological assessment is critical to differentiate ADHD from other possible mood and behavioral disorders. **Bipolar disorder**, for example, may be misdiagnosed as ADHD.

Federal law requires a public school to assess children when ADHD is suspected and there are observable effects on their schoolwork and interactions with peers. A pediatrician can also provide a referral to a psychologist or pediatric specialist for ADHD assessment. Parents should check with their insurance plans to see if these services are covered if they choose to pursue a private evaluation.

Treatment

Therapy that addresses both psychological and social issues (called psychosocial therapy), usually combined with medications, is the treatment approach of choice to alleviate ADHD symptoms. This combination has proved to be the most effective treatment approach to ADHD.

Medications

For 70 years, psychostimulant medication has been used to treat symptoms of ADHD, and stimulants are still considered the first-line medication for treatment of ADHD. It may seem paradoxical to treat a disorder of hyperactivity with a stimulant medication, but people with ADHD typically experience a calming effect from stimulants. Stimulants approved by the U.S. Food and Drug Administration (FDA) for treatment of ADHD are **methylphenidate** (which occurs under several trade names, including Ritalin), mixed amphetamine salts (trade name Adderall), and dextroamphetamine (trade name Dexedrine). These stimulants are comparatively short acting, requiring several doses during a day to maintain appropriate levels. Some long-acting forms are available, such as Ritalin LA and Adderall XR, and a transdermal patch (trade name Daytrana) is also available for delivery of methylphenidate through the skin.

Stimulant use in children with ADHD has been associated in some studies with sudden death in a small number of cases, leading to widespread concern; however, subsequent studies have found no difference in sudden death rates among children taking stimulants for ADHD and the general population using no medication. Use of these medications is not recommended for people who have known heart disease.

Another stimulant-related side effect of concern is the effect these drugs have on growth rate. Studies do indicate that while a child is taking stimulants, growth rate can slow. Some practitioners may recommend "drug holidays," in which the child stops taking the drug when circumstances require less focus or self-discipline, such as over a summer vacation. Studies indicate that the adverse effects on growth rate are eliminated by these drug holidays.

One of the drugs that has been used to treat ADHD, **pemoline** (trade name Cylert) is not recommended as a first-line approach to ADHD because of the potential for serious side effects related to the liver.

More minor side effects associated with stimulant-based treatment include decreased appetite, **insomnia**, increased anxiety, and irritability.

Some newer drugs for treating ADHD have also come on the market. Among these is atomoxetine (trade name, Strattera), which inhibits reuptake of noradrenaline, a nerve-signaling molecule. This drug is the only nonstimulant drug treatment for ADHD that is approved by the FDA. It is suggested as an alternative for children who cannot tolerate standard psychostimulant therapy.

Another drug, modafinil, had stirred up a great deal of interest because it was effective in treating ADHD in a couple of double-blind, placebo-controlled trials, but the FDA recently declined approval of the drug for clinical use.

Other prescription drugs used in the treatment of ADHD are not FDA-approved for that purpose and therefore their use in treating this disorder is "off-label." These drugs include tricyclic **antidepressants** such as **imipramine**, the antidepressant buproprion, and guanfacine, a mimic of a specific form of neurotransmitter (nerve-signaling molecule). All of these drugs have shown some effectiveness in various studies but are not specifically approved for treatment of ADHD.

Psychosocial therapies

Drug therapy may control the symptoms of ADHD, but most experts recommend that drug therapy accompany concerted efforts involving behavioral therapy to address the underlying causes. **Behavior modification** therapy uses a reward system to reinforce good behavior and task completion and can be implemented both in the classroom and at home. A tangible reward such as a sticker may be given to children every time they complete a task or behave in an acceptable manner. A chart may be used to display the stickers and visually illustrate their progress. When a certain number of stickers are collected, the child may trade them in for a bigger reward such as a trip to the zoo or a day at the beach. The reward system stays in place until the good behavior becomes ingrained. Behavioral therapy is often the first-line approach to treatment in preschool-age children diagnosed with ADHD.

A variation of this technique, **cognitive-behavioral therapy**, may work for some children to decrease impulsive behavior by getting the child to recognize the connection between thoughts and behavior, and to change behavior by changing negative thinking patterns.

Individual **psychotherapy** can help children with ADHD build self-esteem, provide a place to discuss worries and anxieties, and help them to gain insight into behavior and feelings.

Family therapy may also be beneficial to help parents and family members develop coping skills and to work through feelings of guilt or anger they may be experiencing.

Children with ADHD perform better within a familiar, consistent, and structured routine with positive reinforcements for good behavior and real consequences for bad behavior. Family, friends, and caretakers should all be educated on the special needs and behaviors of children with ADHD so that they can act consistently. Communication between parents and teachers is especially critical to ensuring that children with ADHD have appropriate learning environments.

Other important therapies for children with ADHD can include **social skills training**, in which the children learn appropriate social interactions from behaviors that are modeled for them.

Alternative treatment

A number of alternative treatments exist for ADHD. Although there is a lack of controlled studies to prove their efficacy, proponents report that they are successful in controlling symptoms in some ADHD patients. Some of the more popular alternative treatments include:

- EEG (electroencephalograph) biofeedback. By measuring brain wave activity and teaching patients with ADHD which type of brain wave is associated with attention, EEG biofeedback attempts to train patients to generate the desired brain wave activity.
- limited sugar intake. However, data indicate that this method does not actually reduce symptoms.
- relaxation training.

Prognosis

If untreated, ADHD negatively affects the social and educational performance of children with ADHD and can seriously damage their sense of self-esteem. Children with ADHD have impaired relationships with their peers and may be looked upon as social outcasts. They may be perceived as slow learners or troublemakers in the classroom. Siblings and even parents may develop resentful feelings toward a child with ADHD.

Some children with ADHD also develop **conduct disorder** problems. For those adolescents who have both ADHD and a conduct disorder, up to 25% go on to develop **antisocial personality disorder** and criminal behavior, **substance abuse**, and a high rate of **suicide** attempts that can be symptomatic of that disorder. Children diagnosed with ADHD are also more likely to have a learning disorder, a mood disorder such as depression, or an anxiety disorder.

Approximately 70–80% of patients with ADHD treated with stimulant medication experience significant relief from symptoms, at least in the short term. Approximately half of children with ADHD seem to "outgrow" the disorder in adolescence or early adulthood; the other half will retain some or all symptoms of ADHD as adults. With early identification and **intervention**, careful **compliance** with a treatment program, and a supportive and nurturing home and school environment, children with ADHD can and do flourish socially and academically.

Resources

BOOKS

American Psychiatric Association. *Diagnostic and Statistical Manual of Mental Disorders*. 4th ed., Text revised. Washington, D.C.: American Psychiatric Press, 2000.

Arnold, L. Eugene. *Contemporary Diagnosis and Management of Attention Deficit/Hyperactivity Disorder*. Newtown: Handbooks in Health Care Company, 2000.

Boyles, Nancy S. *Parenting a Child with Attention Deficit/Hyperactivity Disorder*. New York: Contemporary Books, 1999.

Fowler, Rick, and Jerilyn Fowler. *Honey, Are You Listening? Attention Deficit/Hyperacitivity Disorder and Your Marriage*. Gainsville: Fair Havens Publications, 2002.

Goldman, Lee, and J. Claude Bennett, eds. *Cecil Textbook of Medicine*. 21st ed. Saint Louis: Harcourt Health Sciences Group, 2000.

Jones, Clare B. *Sourcebook for Children with Attention Deficit Disorder*. San Antonio: Communication Skill Builders/Therapy Skill Builders, 1998.

Morrison, Jaydene. *Coping with ADD-ADHD: Attention-Deficit Disorder–Attention Deficit Hyperactivity Disorder*. New York: Rosen Publishing Group, 2000.

Munden, Alison. *ADHD Handbook: A Guide for Parents and Professionals*. Philadelphia: Taylor and Francis, 1999.

Noble, John. *Textbook of Primary Care Medicine*. Saint Louis: Mosby, Incorporated, 2001.

Osman, Betty B. *Learning Disabilities and ADHD: A Family Guide to Living and Learning Together*. New York: John Wiley and Sons, 1997.

Tasman, Allan, Jerald Kay, MD, and Jeffrey A. Lieberman, MD, eds. *Psychiatry*. 1st ed. W. B. Saunders Company, 1997.

PERIODICALS

Forssberg, Hans, and others. "Altered Pattern of Brain Dopamine Synthesis in Male Adolescents with Attention Deficit Hyperactivity Disorder." *Behavioral and Brain Functions* (2006).

Lopez, Frank A. "ADHD: New Pharmacological Treatments on the Horizon." *Developmental and Behavioral Pediatrics* 27 (2006): 410–16.

Miller, Bernhard W., and others. "Neuropsychological Assessment of Adult Patients with Attention-Deficit/Hyperactivity Disorder." *European Archives of Pyschiatry and Clinical Neuroscience* (2007).

Pliszka, Steven R. "Pharmacologic Treatment of Attention-Deficit/Hyperactivity Disorder: Efficacy, Safety, and Mechanisms of Action." *Neuropsychological Reviews* (2007).

Thapar, Anita, and others. "Gene–Environment Interaction in Attention-Deficit Hyperactivity Disorder and the Importance of a Developmental Perspective." *British Journal of Psychiatry* 190 (2007): 1–3.

Tillett, Tanya. "Adding Up to ADHD: Effects of Early Exposures." *Environmental Health Perspectives* 114 (2006): A715.

ORGANIZATIONS

American Academy of Child and Adolescent Psychiatry (AACAP). 3615 Wisconsin Ave. NW, Washington, DC 20016. Telephone: (202) 966-7300. <http://www.aacap.org>.

Attention Deficit Disorder Association (ADDA). 1788 Second Street, Suite 200, Highland Park, IL 60035. Telephone: (847) 432-ADDA. <http://www.add.org>.

Children and Adults with Attention Deficit Disorder (CHADD). 8181 Professional Place, Suite 201, Landover, MD 20785. CHADD National Call Center: (800) 233-4050. Web site: <http://chadd.org>.

OTHER

National Institute of Mental Health. National Institutes of Health. "Attention-Deficit/Hyperactivity Disorder." <http://www.nimh.nih.gov/publicat/adhd.cfm>.

National Library of Medicine. National Institutes of Health. "Attention-Deficit/Hyperactivity Disorder." <http://www.nlm.nih.gov/medlineplus/attentiondeficithyperactivitydisorder.html>.

Paula Anne Ford-Martin, MA
Laith Farid Gulli, MD
Nicole Mallory, MS, PA-C
Emily Jane Willingham, PhD

Autism

Definition

The term "autism" refers to a cluster of conditions appearing early in childhood. All involve severe impairments in social interaction, communication, and patterns of rigid, repetitive behaviors. To be considered a manifestation of an autistic disorder, some of these impairments must be exhibited before the age of three.

The reference book used by mental health professionals to diagnose mental disorders is the *Diagnostic and Statistical Manual of Mental Disorders*, also known as the *DSM*. The 2000 edition of this reference book (the Fourth Edition Text Revision known as *DSM-IV-TR*) places autism in a category called **pervasive developmental disorders**. All of these disorders are characterized by ongoing problems with mutual social interaction and communication, or the presence of stereotyped, repetitive behaviors and unusual interests, and activities. People diagnosed with these disorders are affected in many ways for their entire lives.

Description

Because autism is a spectrum disorder, each child diagnosed with an autistic disorder differs from every other in the suite of symptoms they display and the characteristics and intensity of those symptoms; thus, general descriptions of autistic behavior and characteristics do not apply equally to every child. Still, the common impairments in social interaction and communication, and patterns of rigid, repetitive behaviors can make it possible to recognize children with these disorders, who may differ markedly from neurotypical children in many ways.

Many parents of autistic children sense that something is not quite right even when their children are infants. The infants may have feeding problems, dislike being changed or bathed, or fuss over any change in routine. They may hold their bodies rigid, making it difficult for parents to cuddle them. Or, they may fail to anticipate being lifted, lying passively while the parent reaches for them, rather than holding their arms up in return. Most parents of autistic children become aware of the atypicality of these and other behaviors only gradually.

Impairments in social interaction are usually among the earliest symptoms to develop. The most common social impairment is a kind of indifference to other people, or aloofness, even towards parents and close caregivers. The baby may fail to respond to his or her name being called and may show very little facial expression unless extremely angry, upset, or happy. Babies with autism may resist being touched and appear to be lost in their own world. Between seven and 10 months of age, most infants often resist being separated from a parent or well-known caregiver, but these infants who are later diagnosed with autism may show no emotion when picked up by a stranger.

Other children with autism may be very passive, although less resistant to efforts by others to interact. However, they may not initiate social interaction themselves. Still others may attempt to engage with adults and peers but in ways that strike others as inappropriate or odd.

Because autistic children can be extremely sensitive to change, any change within the family situation can be potentially traumatic to the autistic child. A move, divorce, birth of a sibling, or other stressors that occur in the lives of most families may evoke a more extreme reaction from an autistic child.

In adolescence and adulthood, some higher-functioning people with autistic disorders may appear overly formal and polite. They may appear to react with little spontaneity, as if social interaction does not come naturally or easily to them, as though they are trying to follow a pre-determined set of rules.

Some people with autism have normal intelligence, and some may exhibit special talents in areas such as music or memory. However, persons people with autism can have mental or emotional problems that co-exist with their autism. Some of these other disorders include impulse control disorders, **obsessive-compulsive disorder**, mood and **anxiety disorders**, and **mental retardation**.

Causes and symptoms

Causes

PSYCHOLOGICAL AND FAMILY FACTORS. Although Henry Maudsley, in the late 1800s, was the first **psychiatrist** to focus on very young children with mental disorders, it was the psychiatrist Leo Kanner who coined the phrase "early infantile autism" in 1943. Kanner believed that the parents of children with autistic behaviors were emotionally cold and intellectually distant. He coined the term "refrigerator parents" to describe them. His belief that parental personality and behavior played a powerful role in the development of autistic behaviors left a devastating legacy of guilt and self-blame among parents of autistic children that continues to this day. Recent studies are unequivocal, however, in demonstrating that parents of autistic children are no different from parents of healthy children in their personalities or parenting behaviors. In fact, many families with an autistic child also have one or more neurotypical children.

NEUROLOGICAL AND BIOLOGICAL FACTORS. While there is no single neurological abnormality found in children with autistic disorders, some research using non-invasive **brain** imaging techniques such as **magnetic resonance imaging** (MRI) has demonstrated notable differences between the brains of people with autism and neurotypical brains. Several of the brain areas being researched are known to control emotion and the expression of emotion. These areas include the temporal lobe (large lobe of each side of the brain that contains a sensory area associated with hearing), the limbic system, the cerebellum, the frontal lobe, the amygdala, and the brain stem, which regulates homeostasis (body temperature and heart rate). Among other findings, the brains of some but not all children with autism are abnormally large, and abnormalities in head growth may be manifest even in infancy. Studies also have identified differences between people with and without autism and brain chemical concentrations, volume, and distribution of gray and white matter (nerve cell bodies and their axons), and hemispheric connectivity. There are still no imaging techniques that can be used as definitive diagnostic approaches. Recent research has focused particularly on the temporal lobe because of the finding that previously healthy people who sustain temporal lobe damage may develop autistic-like symptoms. In animal research, when the temporal lobe is damaged, social behavior declines, and restless, repetitive motor behaviors are common.

Although some research initially indicated an association between many events at birth and autism, subsequent studies have not supported many of these findings. There also has not been substantiation of a finding that meconium (the product of the fetal bowel) in amniotic fluid might have linked to autism. Some studies have found a link between maternal age over 35 years and autism and use of medication during pregnancy and autism. Factors related to intrauterine growth and fetal distress (Apgar score lower than 5) may be related to the development of autism. Many studies suggest that in utero (i.e., prenatal) events and genetics play a mixed role in the development of autism.

ALLERGIES, INFECTIONS, AND IMMUNIZATIONS. Some professionals believe that autistic symptoms may be caused by allergies to particular fungi, viral infections, and various foods. No controlled studies have supported these beliefs, but some parents and professionals report improvement when allergens and/or certain foods are eliminated from the diet.

Viral infections of the mother, such as rubella, or of the young child, such as encephalitis, mumps, and measles, occasionally appear to cause autistic disorders. The common childhood immunization series known as MMR (measles, mumps, rubella) has recently come under scrutiny as a possible cause of some autistic conditions; however, no further clinical, animal, or epidemiological studies have supported this finding.

Very rarely, autism is associated with hereditary disorders, such as tuberous sclerosis or fragile X syndrome, which is the leading cause of mental retardation.

Symptoms

DSM-IV-TR specifies three diagnostic categories, each with four components, that are used to make a diagnosis of autistic disorder. These diagnostic categories are impairments in social interaction, communication, and particular patterns of behavior. More information about the individual diagnostic categories and components follows.

SOCIAL INTERACTION. Qualitative impairment in social interaction, as demonstrated by at least two of the following:

- impairment in the use of nonverbal behaviors such as eye contact, facial expression, body posture, and gestures used for social interaction
- failure to develop age-appropriate peer relationships
- lack of attempts to share pleasure, activities, interests, or achievements with other people (e.g., by failing to bring items of interest to a parent, or pointing out animals or objects)
- inability to respond to social situations or other people's emotions with empathy or a concerned attitude

COMMUNICATION. Qualitative impairments in communicating in at least one of the following four areas:

- lack of, or delay in development of spoken language, without attempts to communicate through alternative means such as gestures or mime
- in individuals who do speak, severe impairment in the ability to initiate or sustain a conversation with others
- repetitive and stereotyped use of language, or use of words in unusual, idiosyncratic ways
- failure to show imaginative play, such as make-believe or social imitative play appropriate to developmental level

BEHAVIOR. Restricted, repetitive, and stereotyped patterns of behavior, interests, and activities, as demonstrated by at least one of the following:

- unusual and overly absorbing preoccupation with one or more interests or activities
- a need for rigid adherence to specific routines or rituals in daily life
- stereotyped and repetitive motor behaviors using parts of the body such as fingers, hands, or the whole body
- persistent preoccupation with parts of objects

Demographics

Autistic disorders strike families of all ethnic and socioeconomic backgrounds. Men are affected more frequently than women by a ratio as high as 4:1. In recent years, autism rates appear to have spiked, according to some reports by as much as several hundred percent. It is difficult for epidemiologists to determine whether or not this rise is attributable to better diagnosis and greater general awareness of symptoms or to a genuine increase in cases. Some recent studies have concluded that there is not a true increase in the incidence of autism and that broader criteria and increased awareness on the part of doctors explain the increase. Early studies suggested a prevalence rate of four to 10 cases per 10,000 children. The most recent studies have suggested a much higher prevalence, as high as 60 cases for every 10,000 children, or between three and six cases per 1,000. Rates reported in different studies can vary based on the population being assessed.

Autism recurs in siblings at a rate of 2–8%, higher than its prevalence in the general population but considerably less than would be expected if it were attributable to a single gene. Studies of monozygotic (identical) and dizygotic (fraternal) twins show a 60% concordance rate for identical twins and a rate of 0% for fraternal twins, indicating that autism has a strong heritable element.

Diagnosis

Because young infants are so limited in their range of behavior, autistic disorders are generally discovered gradually, and rarely diagnosed before the age of two or three. Parents may not realize that their baby's behavior is different from that of other infants until he or she reaches an age where a wide range of behaviors are typically displayed. Most doctors may attempt to reassure concerned parents of infants under two years that their children are "normal," or will "grow out of" a disturbing behavior, because many children do. At the time that speech and language usually develop, parents are more likely to observe that their autistic child is not at the same level as other children the same age. Once the child is old enough to play with other children, it becomes more apparent that the autistic child either is not interested in doing so, or does so in unusual ways that differ from most children of the same age. Motor development may also appear unusual, with repetitive motions such as spinning, self-injurious behaviors such as headbanging, and rocking back and forth, giving the parents strong clues that their child behaves differently from others.

The child who continues to display unusual behaviors at about the age of two years would most likely receive a referral from the pediatrician to a child psychiatrist, developmental pediatrician, or early **intervention** program with a multi-disciplinary staff including psychiatrists, psychologists, and **social workers**. These professionals would be the ones to diagnose autistic disorder, and, ideally, offer an early intervention program simultaneously. To reach a diagnosis, the professional(s) would observe the child both with and without parents present, interview the parents about the pregnancy, birth, siblings, family history, and early behaviors, and possibly administer an assessment like the Bayley scales of infant development.

Differential diagnosis

Differential diagnosis is the process of distinguishing one disorder from other similar disorders. Because there are currently no medical tests (such as a blood test) to detect autism, the diagnosis is often established by ruling out other disorders and clarifying the distinguishing characteristics of autism disorder versus other pervasive developmental disorders, such as Asperger syndrome.

MENTAL RETARDATION. Mental retardation is present with autism in about 70% of cases. What distinguishes children with mental retardation who do not have autistic symptoms from those who do is evenness of development. Children with mental retardation tend to exhibit a more even level of functioning in all areas, whereas autistic children tend to exhibit extreme variability within areas and between areas. Children with autistic disorders show uneven development in areas such as motor, language, and social skills. A child with autism may have high-level cognitive functioning in one area, but low-level cognitive functioning in another area, for example. Or a child with autism may exhibit delayed cognitive development, but normal motor skills development. For this reason, autism is often referred to as a "spectrum disorder" because of the large spectrum or range of variability in symptoms and functioning. Also, many children with mental retardation relate well to people and enjoy social connection, which is rare for autistic children.

LANGUAGE DISORDER. Children with autistic disorders may appear similar in some ways to children with language disorders. Unlike autistic children, however, children with language disorders exhibit neurotypical responses to most people, situations, and objects. They make eye contact and show interest in peer and adult relationships.

CHILDHOOD SCHIZOPHRENIA. Schizophrenia is a disturbance of emotion and thought processes that rarely occurs in young children. When it does, it is characterized by **hallucinations** and delusions—seeing and hearing things that are not there, for example.

These are not symptoms that appear among autistic children.

DEGENERATIVE ORGANIC BRAIN DISORDER. This is an extremely rare condition that may at first appear similar to autistic disorders. In degenerative organic brain disorder, the child begins to develop normally, but over time, speech, language, motor skills and other age-appropriate behaviors disintegrate and do not return. The disintegration is progressive. In children with autistic disorders, some children may begin to develop words and language and then lose them at around eighteen months. However, with appropriate education, these skills can be relearned and surpassed by the autistic child.

Treatments

Autistic disorders cannot be cured, but children who have these disorders can make considerable progress in all areas of life. Depending upon the level of intellectual function, it is possible for some children with autism to become functioning, semi-independent or independent adults capable of working and enjoying some social relationships. Parenting a child with autism can be extremely challenging, however, and many families find **support groups** to be helpful. Both medication and psychosocial therapies (therapies that address both psychological and social issues) can help ameliorate troubling symptoms. Education is key for helping these children learn socially acceptable behaviors, decreasing odd mannerisms and behaviors, and increasing appropriate verbal and non-verbal language skills.

Education

Most educational programs for children with autistic disorders involve small, specialized classes with teachers specially trained to work with autistic children, although schools generally make efforts to "mainstream" children with special needs as much as possible, using classrooms aides and other resources. Research has shown that autistic children need regular, daily structure and routine, and they maintain their skills best when there are not frequent disruptions of their daily school program.

One method that has been used extensively both within the classroom and at home is a **behavior modification** method known as Applied Behavior Analysis, or ABA. Specially trained teachers break down large goals into small steps that are taught and repeated until the child masters each one. Slowly, step by step, more appropriate patterns of behavior and communication are formed or shaped in this way.

Positive **reinforcement** is used in many forms, such as praise (for those children who are motivated by it), time permitted to engage in a favorite activity, or a small favored food item. For ABA to be most effective, parents need to be trained to use these same skills to continue the work at home.

Medications

Although no one drug is helpful to children with autistic disorders, several medications are currently used, along with education, to reduce severe temper tantrums and destructive aggression, self-injurious behaviors, hyperactivity, and unusual, repetitive behaviors. Medications may also help the autistic child become more receptive to learning and relating to others. Some of the medications commonly used include **risperidone** (Risperdal), and **haloperidol** (Haldol). Although there are side effects associated with these medications, careful dosing and use of other medications to counteract side effects often enable the autistic child to function more effectively.

Non-conventional treatments

One non-conventional and experimental treatment for autism is the use of secretin, a hormone produced in the small intestine that stimulates the pancreas to release sodium bicarbonate and other digestive enzymes. Studies have found no improvement from secretin administration in autism in general, although it may effect some improvement in a specific population subset.

Another experimental treatment involves *Candida albicans*, the technical term for a common yeast that is found in the human body. Some scientists believe that an overgrowth of this yeast may cause or worsen autism. Some reports indicate that children treated with anti-yeast medications improve in eye contact, social abilities, language skills, concentration, and sleep, and that they show a reduction in aggressive and hyperactive behavior.

An additional non-conventional treatment being researched for autism is a nutritional supplement, vitamin B_6. Some experts believe that vitamin B_6 holds promise for reducing autistic symptoms and helping autistic children progress in all areas. It may be combined with magnesium and the combination appears to have no known side effects. Improvements attributed to these supplements in some studies include enhanced language, eye-contact, and behaviors, as well as more normal brain activity and improved immune system functioning.

These treatments remain outside mainstream medicine, however, and research is ongoing as to their efficacy. Parents interested in these therapies may wish to discuss them with their child's health care team.

Prognosis

Autistic disorders follow a continuous course throughout life. Autistic individuals with higher levels of intelligence may become able to work and live independently or, more frequently, semi-independently. This is especially true for those with IQ scores of 70 or higher. One in six children with autism becomes a well-adjusted adult. Another one out of six achieves a fair degree of adjustment in adult life. Others may never be able to leave the structured environment of home or, later, special group home placement. During adolescence, sexual feelings emerge that a teen with autism may find difficult to handle appropriately. Supervision throughout life is needed for the majority of individuals diagnosed with these disorders.

Prevention

At present, no specific means of preventing autistic disorders exist. Because of an elevated likelihood of giving birth to more than one autistic child exists, genetic counseling is recommended.

Resources

BOOKS

American Psychiatric Association. *Diagnostic and Statistical Manual of Mental Disorders*. 4th ed., text rev. Washington, D.C.: American Psychiatric Association, 2000.

Hamilton, Lynn, *Facing Autism*. Colorado Springs, CO: WaterBrook Press, 2000.

Kaplan, Harold, MD, and Benjamin Sadock, MD. *Synopsis of Psychiatry*. 8th ed., rev. Baltimore, MD: Lippincott Williams and Wilkins, 1998.

Powers, Michael, Psy.D., ed. *Children with Autism: A Parent's Guide*. 2nd ed. Bethesda, MD.: Woodbine House, 2000.

Wing, Lorna, MD. *The Autistic Spectrum*. Berkeley, CA: Ulysses Press, 2001.

PERIODICALS

Hultman, Christina M., Par Sparen, and Sven Cnattingius, "Perinatal risk factors for infantile autism." *Epidemiology* 13 (2002): 417–23.

Lainhart, Janet E. "Advances in autism neuroimaging research for the clinician and the geneticist." *American Journal of Medical Genetics Part C* 142C (2006): 33–39.

Larsson, Heidi J., and others. "Risk factors for autism: perinatal factors, parental psychiatric history, and socioeconomic status." *American Journal of Epidemiology* 161 (2005): 916–25.

Maimburg, R.D., and M. Vaeth. "Perinatal risk factors and infantile autism." *Acta Psychiatry Scandinavia* 114 (2006): 257–64.

Muhle, Rebecca, Stephanie V. Trentacoste, and Isabelle, MD Rapin. "The genetics of autism." *Pediatrics* 113 (2004): e472–e486.

Taylor, B. "Vaccines and the changing epidemiology of autism." *Child: Care, Health, and Development* 32 (2006): 511–9.

ORGANIZATIONS

American Psychiatric Association. 1400 K Street NW, Washington, DC 20005.

Autism Network International, P.O. Box 448, Syracuse, NY 13210-0448. <http://www.students.uiuc.edu/-bordner/ani/>.

The Autism Society of America. 7910 Woodmont Avenue, Suite 300, Bethesda, MD 20814-3015. <http://www.autism-society.org>.

Families for Early Autism Treatment (F.E.A.T.). P.O. Box 255722, Sacramento, CA 95865-1536. <http://www.feat.org>.

Families Working Together. 12400 Cypress Avenue, Space 20, Chino, CA 91710. <http://www.ucddfam.com>.

Barbara S. Sternberg, Ph.D.
Emily Jane Willingham, Ph.D.

Aventyl *see* **Nortriptyline**

Aversion therapy

Definition

Aversion therapy is a form of behavior therapy in which an aversive stimulus (causing a strong feeling of dislike or disgust) is paired with an undesirable behavior in order to reduce or eliminate that behavior.

Purpose

As with other behavior therapies, aversion therapy is a treatment grounded in learning theory—one of its basic principles being that all behavior is learned and that undesirable behaviors can be unlearned under the right circumstances. Aversion therapy is an application of the branch of learning theory called classical conditioning. Within this model of learning, an undesirable behavior, such as a deviant sexual act, is matched with an unpleasant (aversive) stimulus. The unpleasant feelings or sensations become associated with that behavior, and the behavior will decrease in frequency or stop altogether. Aversion therapy differs from those types of behavior therapy based on principles of operant conditioning. In operant therapy, the aversive stimulus, usually called punishment, is presented after the behavior rather than together with it.

The goal of aversion therapy has been to decrease or eliminate undesirable behaviors. Treatment focuses on changing a specific behavior itself, unlike insight-oriented approaches that focus on uncovering unconscious motives in order to produce change. The behaviors for which aversion therapy has been tried as a treatment include such addictions as alcohol **abuse**, drug abuse, and smoking; pathological gambling; **paraphilias**; and more benign habits—including writer's cramp. Most controversially, this approach has been attempted as a way to "cure" homosexuality. Both the type of behavior to be changed and the characteristics of the aversive stimulus influence the treatment—which may be administered in either outpatient or inpatient settings as a self-sufficient **intervention** or as part of a multimodal program. Under some circumstances, aversion therapy may be self-administered.

Precautions

A variety of aversive stimuli have been used as part of this approach, including chemical and pharmacological stimulants, as well as electric shock. Foul odors, nasty tastes, and loud noises have been employed as aversive stimuli somewhat less frequently. The chemicals and medications generate very unpleasant and often physically painful responses. This type of aversive stimulation may be risky for people with heart or lung problems because of the possibility of making the medical conditions worse. Patients with these conditions should be cleared by their doctors first. Often, however, the more intrusive aversive stimuli are administered within inpatient settings under medical supervision. An uncomfortable but safe level of electric (sometimes called faradic) shock is often preferred to chemical and pharmacological aversants because of the risks that these substances involve.

In addition to the health precautions mentioned above, there are ethical concerns surrounding the use of aversive stimuli. There are additional problems with patient acceptance and negative public perception of procedures using aversants. Aversion treatment that makes use of powerful substances customarily (and intentionally) causes extremely uncomfortable consequences, including nausea and vomiting. These effects may lead to poor **compliance** with treatment, high dropout rates, potentially hostile and aggressive patients, and public relations problems. Social critics and members of the general public alike often consider this type of treatment punitive and morally objectionable. Although the scenes were exaggerated in the disturbing parts of the Stanley Kubrick film *A Clockwork Orange,* they depicted the use of aversion therapy to reform the criminal protagonist and provide a powerful example of society's perception of this treatment.

Parents and other advocates for people with **mental retardation** and developmental disabilities have been particularly vocal in their condemnation of behavior therapy that uses aversive procedures in general. Aversive procedures are used within a variety of **behavior modification** strategies and the term is sometimes confused with the more specific technique of aversion therapy. Aversive procedures are usually based on an operant conditioning model that involves punishment. Advocates for special patient populations believe that all aversive procedures are punitive, coercive, and use unnecessary amounts of control and manipulation to modify behavior. They call for therapists to stop using aversive stimuli, noting that positive, nonaversive, behavioral-change strategies are available. These strategies are at least as, if not more, effective than aversive procedures.

In general, there are not very many studies in the scientific literature that produce strong evidence of the effectiveness of aversion therapy. Some studies indicate that aversion therapy for smokers may be somewhat effective, but a significant problem with the approach in smokers is compliance with the therapy, as is the case with most attempts at aversion therapy. Overall, in programs addressing substance use disorders, the results with aversion therapy do not compare favorably with therapies focusing on positive reward.

Description

According to the American Psychiatric Association, aversion therapy should be practiced only in very specialized centers.

KEY TERMS

Aversion—A strong feeling of dislike or disgust. Aversion therapy makes use of this feeling to reduce or eliminate an undesirable behavior. Chemicals or medications used to produce unpleasant effects are called aversants.

Classical conditioning—A process used in psychology in which a previously neutral stimulus eventually produces a specific response by being paired repeatedly with another stimulus that produces that response. The best-known example of classical conditioning is Pavlov's dogs, who were conditioned to salivate when they heard a bell ring (the previously neutral stimulus) because the sound had been paired repeatedly with their feeding time.

Compliance—In medicine or psychiatry, cooperation with a treatment plan or schedule of medications.

Detoxification—A process in which the body is allowed to free itself of a drug while the symptoms of withdrawal are treated. It is the primary step in any treatment program for drug or alcohol abuse.

Emetic—A medication intended to cause vomiting. Emetics are sometimes used in aversion therapy in place of electric shock. Their most common use in mainstream medicine is in treating accidental poisoning.

Faradic—A type of discontinuous alternating electric current sometimes used in aversion therapy. It is named for Michael Faraday, an eminent British physicist.

Stimulus—Something that incites or moves a person to thought, emotion, or action. In mainstream psychotherapy, a stimulus can be anything from a certain picture or image to smell, sound, word, or idea. In aversion therapy, the stimulus is typically a mild electric shock or a medication that produces unpleasant results.

Risks

Patients with cardiac, pulmonary, or gastrointestinal problems may experience a worsening of their symptoms, depending upon the characteristics and strength of the aversive stimuli. Some therapists have reported that patients undergoing aversion therapy, especially treatment that uses powerful chemical or pharmacological aversive stimuli, have become negative and aggressive.

Outcomes

Depending upon the objectives established at the beginning of treatment, patients successfully completing a course of aversion therapy may see a reduction or cessation of the undesirable behavior.

Some clinicians have reported that patients undergoing aversive treatment using electric shocks have experienced increased **anxiety** and anxiety-related symptoms that may interfere with the conditioning process, as well as lead to decreased acceptance of the treatment. As indicated above, a few clinicians have reported a worrisome increase in hostility among patients receiving aversion therapy, especially those undergoing treatment using chemical aversants. Although aversion therapy has some adherents, lack of rigorous outcome studies demonstrating its effectiveness, along with the ethical objections mentioned earlier, have generated numerous opponents among clinicians as well as the general public. These opponents point out that less intrusive alternative treatments, such as **covert sensitization**, are available.

Resources

BOOKS

American Psychiatric Association. *Practice Guidelines for the Treatment of Psychiatric Disorders*. Washington, D.C.: American Psychiatric Association, 2000.

Colman, Andrew. *A Dictionary of Psychology*. New York: Oxford University, 2001.

Committee on the Social and Economic Impact of Gambling. *Pathological Gambling: A Critical Review*. Washington, D.C.: Committee on the Social and Economic Impact of Gambling, 1999.

Kaplan, Harold, and Benjamin Sadock, eds. *Synopsis of Psychiatry*. 8th ed. Baltimore: Williams and Wilkins, 1998.

Plaud, Joseph, and Georg Eifert, eds. *From Behavior Theory to Behavior Therapy*. Boston: Allyn and Bacon, 1998.

PERIODICALS

Howard, M. "Pharmacological Aversion Treatment of Alcohol Abuse." *American Journal of Drug and Alcohol Abuse* 27. 3 (2001): 561–85.

ORGANIZATIONS

Association for Advancement of Behavior Therapy. 305 Seventh Avenue, 16th Floor, New York, NY 10001-6008. <http://www.aabt.org>.

OTHER

Kleber, Herbert D., et al. *Practice Guideline for Treatment of Patients with Substance Use Disorders*, 2nd ed. (2006). Available online through the American Psychiatric Association: <http://www.psych.org/psych_pract/treatg/pg/SUD2ePG_04-28-06.pdf>.

John Garrison, PhD
Emily Jane Willingham, PhD

Avoidant personality disorder

Definition

Avoidant personality disorder is characterized by hypersensitivity to rejection and criticism, desire for uncritical acceptance by others, social withdrawal despite a desire for affection and acceptance, and low self-esteem. The behavior patterns associated with avoidant personality disorder are persistent and severe, impairing the ability to work with others or maintain social relationships.

Description

People who are diagnosed with avoidant personality disorder desire to be in relationships with others but lack the skills and confidence that are necessary in social interactions. In order to protect themselves from anticipated criticism or ridicule, they withdraw from other people. This avoidance of interaction tends to isolate them from meaningful relationships, and serves to reinforce their nervousness and awkwardness in social situations.

The behavior of people with avoidant personality disorder is characterized by social withdrawal, shyness, distrustfulness, and emotional distance. These people tend to be very cautious when they speak, and they convey a general impression of awkwardness in their manner. Most are highly self-conscious and self-critical about their problems relating to others.

Avoidant personalities can be categorized into four types:

- Shy/social phobic avoidants: Use withdrawal mechanisms to manage social anxiety. Shy avoidants have difficulty forming relationships with others and may be seriously isolated. Social phobic avoidants frequently are more symbolic in their withdrawal, and tend to express their avoidance particularly in situations where they are asked to perform in public. Shy/social phobic avoidants are usually perceived as self-conscious or introverted by others.
- "Mingles" avoidants: Appear to be "normal" and well-related in most situations. Although they can form new relationships, they find it difficult to sustain them over time for a variety of reasons including fear of success, desire to fail, and inability to settle down.
- "Seven year itch" avoidants: Although this type is able to form relationships, they are unable to maintain them over time. They may be able to commit fully at first, but become restless over time and leave the relationship.

- Dependent/codependent avoidants: This type of avoidant appears to want to start new relationships but are unable to sever ties to old relationships (e.g., living with one's parents) that are necessary to make that possible.

Causes and symptoms

Causes

The cause of avoidant personality disorder is not clearly defined, and may be influenced by a combination of social, genetic, and biological factors. Avoidant personality traits typically appear in childhood, with signs of excessive shyness and fear when the child confronts new people and situations. These characteristics are also developmentally appropriate emotions for children, however, and do not necessarily mean that a pattern of avoidant personality disorder will continue into adulthood. When shyness, unfounded fear of rejection, hypersensitivity to criticism, and a pattern of social avoidance persist and intensify through adolescence and young adulthood, a **diagnosis** of avoidant personality disorder is often indicated.

Many persons diagnosed with avoidant personality disorder have had painful early experiences of chronic parental criticism and rejection. The need to bond with the rejecting parents makes the avoidant person hungry for relationships but their longing gradually develops into a defensive shell of self-protection against repeated parental criticisms. Ridicule or rejection by peers further reinforces the young person's pattern of social withdrawal and contributes to their fear of social contact.

Symptoms

The most recent edition of the ***Diagnostic and Statistical Manual of Mental Disorders,*** (the fourth edition, text revision or *DSM-IV-TR*) specifies seven diagnostic criteria for avoidant personality disorder:

- The person avoids occupational activities that require significant interpersonal contact. Job interviews or promotions may be turned down because the person's own perceptions of his or her abilities do not match the job description.
- The person is reluctant to participate in social involvement without clear assurance that he or she will be accepted. People with this disorder assume other people are not safe to trust until proven otherwise. Others must offer repeated support and encouragement in order to persuade them to participate in a social event.

- The person fears being shamed or ridiculed in close relationships. As a result, people with this disorder become overly alert to behavioral cues that may indicate disapproval or rejection. They will flee a situation in which they believe that others might turn against them.
- The person is preoccupied with being criticized or rejected. Much mental and physical energy is spent brooding about and avoiding situations perceived as "dangerous."
- The person is inhibited in unfamiliar social situations due to feelings of inadequacy. Low self-esteem undermines his or her confidence in meeting and conversing with new acquaintances.
- The person regards him- or herself as socially inept. This self-disparagement is especially apparent when the person must make social contacts with strangers. People with avoidant personality disorder perceive themselves as unappealing or inferior to others.
- The person is reluctant to take social risks, in order to avoid possible humiliation. Avoidant people seek interactions that promise the greatest amount of acceptance while minimizing the likelihood of embarrassment or rejection. They might go to a school dance, for example, but remain in one corner chatting with close friends rather than going out on the dance floor with someone they do not know well.

Demographics

Avoidant personality disorder appears to be as frequent in males as in females. It affects between 0.5% and 1.0% of adults in the general North American population, but it has been diagnosed in approximately 10% of clinical outpatients.

Diagnosis

Many individuals exhibit some avoidant behaviors at one point or another in their lives. Occasional feelings of self-doubt and fear in new and unfamiliar social or personal relationships are not unusual, nor are they unhealthy, as these situations may trigger feelings of inadequacy and the wish to hide from social contact in even the most self-confident individuals. An example would be the anxious hesitancy of a new immigrant in a country with a different language and strange customs. Avoidant characteristics are regarded as meeting the diagnostic criteria for a personality disorder only when: they begin to have a long-term negative impact on the affected person; they lead to functional impairment by significantly altering occupational choice or lifestyle, or otherwise impinging on quality of life; and cause significant emotional distress.

Avoidant personality disorder can occur in conjunction with other social phobias, mood and **anxiety disorders**, and **personality disorders**. The diagnosis may be complicated by the fact that avoidant personality disorder may be either the cause or result of other mood and anxiety disorders. For example, individuals who have **major depressive disorder** may begin to withdraw from social situations and experience feelings of worthlessness, symptoms that are also prominent features of avoidant personality disorder. On the other hand, the insecurity and isolation that are symptoms of avoidant personality disorder can trigger feelings of **depression**.

The characteristics of avoidant personality disorder may resemble those found in both schizoid and schizotypal personality disorders. Persons with these disorders are prone to social isolation. Those diagnosed with avoidant personality disorder, however, differ from those with schizoid or schizotypal disorder, because they want to have relationships with others but are prevented by their social inadequacies. Persons diagnosed with schizoid and schizotypal personality disorders, on the other hand, usually prefer social isolation.

Personality disorders are usually diagnosed following a complete medical history and an interview with the patient. Although there are no laboratory tests for personality disorders, the doctor may give the patient a physical examination to rule out the possibility that a general medical condition is affecting the patient's behavior. For example, people with disorders of the digestive tract may avoid social occasions for fear of a sudden attack of diarrhea or the need to vomit. If the interview with the patient suggests a diagnosis of avoidant personality disorder, the doctor may administer a diagnostic questionnaire or another type of assessment tool.

Assessment tools helpful in diagnosing avoidant personality disorder include:

- Minnesota Multiphasic Personality Inventory (MMPI)
- Millon Clinical Multiaxial Inventory (MCMI)
- Rorschach Psychodiagnostic Test
- Thematic Apperception Test (TAT)

In diagnosis, it is important to distinguish between the fear of relating that characterizes avoidant personality disorder from the inability to form relationships that characterizes schizoid patients. Similarly, it is important to distinguish between the fear of relationship characteristic of the avoidant personality and a healthy, natural desire to be alone.

Treatments

The general goal of treatment in avoidant personality disorder is improvement of self-esteem and confidence. As the patient's self-confidence and social skills improve, he or she will become more resilient to potential or real criticism by others.

Psychodynamically oriented therapies

These approaches are usually supportive; the therapist empathizes with the patient's strong sense of shame and inadequacy in order to create a relationship of trust. Therapy usually moves slowly at first because persons with avoidant personality disorder are mistrustful of others. Treatment that probes into their emotional state too quickly may result in more protective withdrawal by the patient. As trust is established and the patient feels safer discussing details of his or her situation, he or she may be able to draw important connections between their deeply felt sense of shame and their behavior in social situations.

Cognitive-behavioral therapy

Cognitive-behavioral therapy (CBT) may be helpful in treating individuals with avoidant personality disorder. This approach assumes that faulty thinking patterns underlie the personality disorder, and therefore focuses on changing distorted cognitive patterns by examining the validity of the assumptions behind them. If a patient feels he is inferior to his peers, unlikable, and socially unacceptable, a cognitive therapist would test the reality of these assumptions by asking the patient to name friends and family who enjoy his company, or to describe past social encounters that were fulfilling to him. By showing the patient that others value his company and that social situations can be enjoyable, the irrationality of his social fears and insecurities are exposed. This process is known as "cognitive restructuring."

Group therapy

Group therapy may provide patients with avoidant personality disorder with social experiences that expose them to feedback from others in a safe, controlled environment. They may, however, be reluctant to enter group therapy due to their fear of social rejection. An empathetic environment in the group setting can help each member overcome his or her social anxieties. **Social skills training** can also be incorporated into group therapy to enhance social awareness and feedback.

KEY TERMS

Cognitive restructuring—An approach to psychotherapy that focuses on helping patients examine distorted patterns of perception and thought in order to change their emotional responses to people and situations.

Monoamine oxidase inhibitors (MAOIs)—A group of antidepressant drugs that decreases the activity of monoamine oxidase, a neurotransmitter found in the brain that affects mood. MAOIs are also used in the treatment of avoidant personality disorder.

Supportive—An approach to psychotherapy that seeks to encourage the patient or offer emotional support to him or her, as distinct from insight-oriented or educational approaches to treatment.

Family and marital therapy

Family or couple therapy can be helpful for a patient who wants to break out of a family pattern that reinforces the avoidant behavior. The focus of marital therapy would include attempting to break the cycle of rejection, criticism or ridicule that typically characterizes most avoidant marriages. Other strategies include helping the couple to develop constructive ways of relating to one another without shame.

Medications

The use of monoamine oxidase inhibitors (MAOIs) has proven useful in helping patients with avoidant personality disorder to control symptoms of social unease and experience initial success. The major drawback of these medications is limitations on the patient's diet. People taking MAOIs must avoid foods containing a substance known as tyramine, which is found in most cheeses, liver, red wines, sherry, vermouth, beans with broad pods, soy sauce, sauerkraut, and meat extracts.

Prognosis

Higher-functioning persons with avoidant personality disorder can generally be expected to improve their social awareness and improve their social skills to some degree. But because of the significant social fear and deep-seated feelings of inferiority, these patterns usually do not change dramatically. Lower-functioning persons are likely to drop out of treatment if they become too anxious.

Prevention

Since avoidant personality disorder usually originates in the patient's family of origin, the only known preventive measure is a nurturing, emotionally stimulating, and expressive family environment.

Resources

BOOKS

American Psychiatric Association. *Diagnostic and Statistical Manual of Mental Disorders,* 4th ed., Text revision. Washington D.C.: American Psychiatric Association, 2000.

Freeman, Arthur, James Pretzer, Barbara Fleming, and Karen M. Simon. *Clinical Applications of Cognitive Therapy,* 2nd ed. New York: Kluwer Academic/Plenum Publishers, 2004.

Kantor, Martin. *Distancing: Avoidant Personality Disorder,* Revised and expanded. Westport, CT: Praeger, 2003.

Newman, Cory F., and Randy Fingerhut. "Psychotherapy for Avoidant Personality Disorder." *Oxford Textbook of Psychotherapy.* New York: Oxford University Press, 2005, 311–19.

Rasmussen, Paul R. *The Personality-Guided Cognitive-Behavioral Therapy.* Washington D.C.: American Psychological Association, 2005.

Silverstein, Marshall L. *Disorders of the Self: A Personality-Guided Approach.* Washington D.C.: American Psychological Association, 2007.

VandenBos, Gary R., ed. *APA Dictionary of Psychology.* Washington D.C.: American Psychological Association, 2007.

PERIODICALS

Emmelkamp, Paul M., Ank Benner, Antoinette Kuipers, Guus A. Feiertag, Harrie C. Koster, and Franske J. van Apeldoorn. "Comparison of Brief Dynamic and Cognitive-Behavioural Therapies in Avoidant Personality Disorder." *British Journal of Psychiatry* 189. 1 (July 2006): 60–64.

Gude, Tore, Sigmund Karterud, Geir Pedersen, and Erik Falkum. "The Quality of the Diagnostic and Statistical Manual of Mental Disorders, Fourth Edition Dependent Personality Disorder Prototype." *Comprehensive Psychiatry* 47.6 (November–December 2006): 456–62.

Herbert, James D. "Social Skills Training Augments the Effectiveness of Cognitive Behavioral Group Therapy for Social Anxiety Disorder." *Behavior Therapy* 36.2 (Spring 2005): 125–38.

Hopwood, C. J., L. C. Morey, J. G. Gunderson A. E. Skodol, M. T. Shea, C. M. Grilo, and,T. H.McGlashan. "Hierarchical Relationships Between Borderline, Schizotypal, Avoidant and Obsessive-Compulsive Personality Disorders." *Acta Psychiatrica Scandinavica* 113. 5 (May 2006): 430–39.

Hummelen, Benjamin, Theresa Wilberg, Geir Pedersen, and Sigmund Karterud. "An Investigation of the Validity of the Diagnostic and Statistical Manual of Mental Disorders, Fourth Edition Avoidant Personality Disorder Construct as a Prototype Category and the Psychometric Properties of the Diagnostic Criteria." *Comprehensive Psychiatry* 47.5 (September–October 2006): 376–83.

Huprich, Steven K. "Differentiating Avoidant and Depressive Personality Disorders." *Journal of Personality Disorders* 19.6 (December 2005): 659–73.

Huprich, Steven K., Mark Zimmerman, and Iwona Chelminski. "Disentangling Depressive Personality Disorder from Avoidant, Borderline, and Obsessive-Compulsive Personality Disorders." *Comprehensive Psychiatry* 47.4 (July–August 2006): 298–306.

Ralevski, E., and others. "Avoidant Personality Disorder and Social Phobia: Distinct Enough to Be Separate Disorders?" *Acta Psychiatrica Scandinavica* 112.3 (September 2005): 208–14.

ORGANIZATIONS

American Psychiatric Association. 1400 K Street NW, Washington DC 20005. <http://www.psych.org>.

Gary Gilles, MA
Paula Ford-Martin, MA
Ruth A. Wienclaw, PhD

B

Barbiturates

Definition

Barbiturates are a large class of drugs, consisting of many different brand-name products with generic equivalents, which are used primarily for mild sedation, general anesthesia, and as a treatment for some types of epilepsy. One barbiturate, butalbital, exists only as a component of headache preparations that also include acetaminophen and sometimes caffeine. The most common members of the barbiturate family are phenobarbital (Luminal), pentobarbital (Nembutal), amobarbital (Amytal), secobarbital (Seconal), thiopental (Pentothal, Sodium Pentothal, also colloquially known as "truth serum"), methohexital (Brevital), and butalbital (a component of Fiorinal and Fioricet). They exist in numerous formulations and strengths.

Purpose

Barbiturates are used to sedate patients prior to surgery as well as to produce general anesthesia, to treat some forms of epilepsy, and to treat simple and migraine headache. These drugs are highly addictive and are often abused as recreational drugs. Although still commercially available, barbiturates such as secobarbital, pentobarbital, and amobarbital are no longer routinely recommended for the treatment of **insomnia** because of their ability to cause dependence, tolerance, and withdrawal. In general, barbiturates lose their efficacy when they are used to treat insomnia on a daily basis for more than two weeks. These drugs also have significant side effects when taken in large doses and can cause respiratory failure and death. Newer and safer medicines are now available for the treatment of insomnia.

Description

The therapeutic effects of barbiturates as a class of drugs are all related to their ability to depress the central nervous system, producing sedation. At high enough doses and with certain preparations, they can induce sleep. All barbiturates also have anticonvulsant properties although phenobarbital is the preferred barbiturate to treat epilepsy because it can produce anticonvulsant effects at levels low enough not to cause extreme sedation or sleep.

Recommended dosage

The typical dose of phenobarbital for use as an anticonvulsant in adults is 60–250 mg per day. When a series of serious **seizures** known as status epilepticus occurs, adults are usually first given 300–800 mg intravenously (directly into the vein) followed by 120–240 mg every 20 minutes up to a maximum of 1,000–2,000 mg. For sedation, adults are given 30–120 mg per day divided into two or three doses. For sedation before surgery, 100–200 mg are given in an intramuscular injection (a shot) about one hour before the surgery.

The typical dose for an anticonvulsant effect for children must be determined by the doctor, but the usual dose ranges from about 0.45 mg to 2.7 mg per pound (or 1 to 6 mg per kg) per day. For anesthesia before surgery in children, 0.45 mg to 1.35 mg per pound (1 mg to 3 mg per kg) of body weight is given about one hour before the surgery.

The typical dose of butalbital, as a component of headache preparations such as Fiorinal or Fioricet, is 50–100 mg administered every four to six hours as needed.

Precautions

Children who are hyperactive should not receive phenobarbital or other barbiturates. Paradoxically, some children become stimulated and hyperactive after receiving barbiturates.

The use of barbiturates in the elderly (over age 65) should be watched closely. Elderly patients must be carefully monitored for confusion, agitation, **delirium**, and excitement if they take barbiturates. Barbiturates should be avoided in elderly patients who are receiving drugs for other mental disorders such as **schizophrenia** or **depression**.

Women should be aware that barbiturate use can make hormonal birth control pills containing estrogen less effective. Women should not use barbiturates during pregnancy unless they are necessary to control seizures. In these cases, they should take the minimum amount required to control the seizures. Barbiturate use by pregnant women has been associated with increased risk of fetal damage, newborn bleeding problems, bleeding during childbirth, and, if occurring in the final three months of gestation, dependency in the newborn with attendant withdrawal effects after birth. One study has found a potential link between barbiturate use during pregnancy and **brain** tumors in the infant. Women who are breast-feeding should not take barbiturates because these drugs enter the breast milk and may cause serious side effects in the nursing baby.

Long-term barbiturate use should be avoided unless there is a strong medical need, as in the case of epilepsy, because of the potential for **addiction**, dependence, tolerance, and withdrawal. People should not drive, operate heavy equipment, or perform other hazardous activities requiring mental alertness while taking barbiturates.

Side effects

The most common side effect of barbiturate use is drowsiness. Less common side effects include agitation, confusion, breathing difficulties, abnormally low blood pressure, nausea, vomiting, constipation, lowered body temperature, decreased heart rate, movement difficulty, nightmares, **anxiety**, nervousness, mental depression, and dizziness. Rare but reported side effects include fever, headache, anemia, allergic reactions, and liver damage.

Interactions

Patients should always tell their doctor and dentist when they are taking barbiturates. Barbiturates should generally not be taken with other drugs used to treat mental disorders. In addition, patients should inform their healthcare providers about any health or medical problems, especially a history or alcohol or drug **abuse**, problems with anemia, asthma, diabetes, hyperthyroid, or kidney or liver disease, among others.

There are a number of drugs that barbiturates should not be combined with because the barbiturates may increase the rate of breakdown of these drugs, thus reducing their availability to the body. These

KEY TERMS

Addiction—A compulsive need for, and use of, a habit-forming substance or behavior.

Anticonvulsant—A medication used to control the abnormal electrical activity in the brain that causes seizures.

Corticosteroids—Any one of a number of hormonal steroid compounds that are derived from the adrenal gland.

Delirium—A disturbance of consciousness marked by confusion, difficulty paying attention, delusions, hallucinations, or restlessness.

Dependence—The adaptation of neurons and other physical processes to the use of a drug, followed by withdrawal symptoms when the drug is removed; physiological and/or psychological addiction.

Hyperactivity—Behavior disturbances, usually in children and adolescents, that involve impulsiveness, low levels of concentration, and distractibility.

Intramuscular—An injection that is given into a muscle.

Monoamine oxidase inhibitors (MAOIs)—A group of antidepressant drugs that decrease the activity of monoamine oxidase, a neurotransmitter found in the brain that affects mood.

Status epilepticus—Series of grand mal epileptic seizures that may occur when the patient is asleep or awake and involves diminished consciousness.

Tolerance—Progressive decrease in the effectiveness of a drug with long-term use.

Withdrawal—Symptoms experienced by a person who has become physically dependent on a drug, occurring when the drug use is discontinued.

drugs include oral corticosteroids such as predisolone, methylprednisolone, prednisone, or dexamethasone, estrogen and oral contraceptives, blood-thinning medications such as warfarin (Coumadin), the antibiotic doxycycline (Vibramycin), and anticonvulsants such as phenytoin (Dilantin).

Barbiturates should not be combined with alcohol because the combination produces additive depressant effects in the central nervous system.

Barbiturates may lower the amount of absorption of the vitamins D and K.

Resources

BOOKS

Consumer Reports Staff. *Consumer Reports Complete Drug Reference,* 2002 ed. Denver: Micromedex Thomson Healthcare, 2001.

Ellsworth, Allan J., and others. *Mosby's Medical Drug Reference, 2001–2002.* St. Louis: Mosby, 2001.

Hardman, Joel G., and Lee E. Limbird, eds. *Goodman & Gilman's The Pharmacological Basis of Therapeutics,* 10th ed. New York: McGraw-Hill, 2001.

Mosby's GenRx Staff. *Mosby's GenRx,* 9th ed. St. Louis: Mosby, 1999.

Venes, Donald, and Clayton L. Thomas. *Taber's Cyclopedic Medical Dictionary,* 19th ed. Philadelphia: F. A. Davis, 2001.

OTHER

Cooper, Jeffrey S. "Toxicity, Sedative-Hypnotics." <http://www.emedicine.com/emerg/topic525.htm>.

National Library of Medicine. National Institutes of Health. "Barbiturates, Systemic." <http://www.nlm.nih.gov/medlineplus/druginfo/uspdi/202081.html>.

Mark Mitchell, MD
Emily Jane Willingham, PhD

Beck Depression Inventory

Definition

The Beck **Depression** Inventory (BDI) is a series of 21 self-reported questions developed to measure the intensity, severity, and depth of depressive symptoms in patients aged 13–80. A shorter form is composed of seven questions and is designed for administration by primary care providers.

Purpose

The BDI was first developed by Aaron T. Beck, a pioneer in cognitive therapy. Its purpose is to detect, assess, and monitor changes in depressive symptoms among people in a mental health care setting.

Precautions

The BDI is designed for use by trained professionals. It should be administered by a knowledgeable mental health professional who is trained in its use and interpretation.

Description

The BDI was developed in 1961, adapted in 1969, and copyrighted in 1979. A second version of the inventory (BDI-II) was developed and published in 1996 to reflect revisions in the fourth edition, text revision of the *Diagnostic and Statistical Manual of Mental Disorders* (*DSM-IV-TR*), a handbook that mental health professionals use to diagnose mental disorders.

The long form of the BDI is composed of 21 questions or items, each with four possible responses. Each response is assigned a score ranging from zero to three, indicating the severity of the symptom that the patient has experienced over the past two weeks. A version designed for use by primary care providers (BDI-PC) is composed of seven self-reported items.

Individual questions of the BDI assess mood, pessimism, sense of failure, self-dissatisfaction, guilt, punishment, self-dislike, self-accusation, suicidal ideas, crying, irritability, social withdrawal, body image, work difficulties, **insomnia**, **fatigue**, appetite, weight loss, bodily preoccupation, and loss of libido. The first 13 items assess symptoms that are psychological in nature, while items 14 to 21 assess more physical symptoms.

The BDI is also used to detect depressive symptoms in a primary care setting. The BDI usually takes between five and ten minutes to complete as part of a psychological or medical examination.

Results

The sum of all BDI item scores indicates the severity of depression. The test is scored differently for the general population and for individuals who have been clinically diagnosed with depression. For the general population, a score of 21 or over represents depression. For people who have been clinically diagnosed, scores from 0 to 9 represent minimal depressive symptoms, scores of 10 to 16 indicate mild depression, scores of 17 to 29 indicate moderate depression, and scores of 30 to 63 indicate severe depression. The BDI can distinguish between different subtypes of **depressive disorders**, such as major depression and dysthymia (a less severe form of depression).

The BDI has been extensively tested for content validity, concurrent validity, and construct validity. The BDI has content validity (the extent to which items of a test are representative of that which is to be measured) because it was constructed from a consensus among clinicians about depressive symptoms displayed by psychiatric patients. Concurrent validity is a measure of the extent to which a test concurs with already existing standards; at least 35 studies have shown concurrent validity between the BDI and such measures of depression as the Hamilton Depression Rating Scale and the Minnesota Multiphasic Personality Inventory-D. Tests for construct validity (the degree to which a test measures an internal construct or variable) have shown the BDI to be related to medical symptoms, **anxiety**, **stress**, loneliness, sleep patterns, alcoholism, suicidal behaviors, and adjustment among youth.

Factor analysis, a statistical method used to determine underlying relationships between variables, has also supported the validity of the BDI. The BDI can be interpreted as one syndrome (depression) composed of three factors: negative attitudes toward self, performance impairment, and somatic (bodily) disturbance.

The BDI has also been extensively tested for reliability, following established standards for psychological tests published in 1985. Internal consistency has been successfully estimated by over 25 studies in many populations. The BDI has been shown to be valid and reliable, with results corresponding to clinician ratings of depression in more than 90% of all cases.

Higher BDI scores have been shown in a few studies to be inversely related to educational attainment; the BDI, however, does not consistently correlate with sex, race, or age.

See also Cognitive-behavioral therapy.

Resources

BOOKS

American Psychiatric Association. *Diagnostic and Statistical Manual of Mental Disorders*. 4th ed., Text rev. Washington, D.C.: American Psychiatric Association, 2000.

Clark, David A., Aaron T. Beck, and Brad A. Alford. *Scientific Foundations of Cognitive Theory and Therapy of Depression*. New York: John Wiley & Sons, 2003.

Nezu, Arthur, George F. Ronan, and Elizabeth A. Meadows, eds. *Practitioner's Guide to Empirically Based Measures of Depression*. New York: Springer Publishing Company, 2006.

Tolman, Anton O. *Depression In Adults: The Latest Assessment And Treatment Strategies*. Kansas City, MO: Compact Clinicals, 2005.

VandenBos, Gary R., ed. *APA Dictionary of Psychology*. Washington, D.C.: American Psychological Association, 2006.

PERIODICALS

Carlbring, Per, and others. "Internet vs. Paper and Pencil Administration of Questionnaires Commonly Used in Panic/Agoraphobia Research." *Computers in Human Behavior* 23.3 (May 2007): 1421–34.

Mehl, Matthias R. "The Lay Assessment of Subclinical Depression in Daily Life." *Psychological Assessment* 18.3 (September 2006): 340–45.

Poole, Helen, Ros Bramwell, and Peter Murphy. "Factor Structure of the Beck Depression Inventory-II Patients with Chronic Pain." *Clinical Journal of Pain* 22.9 (November–December 2006): 790–98.

Snijders, A. H., M. M. Robertson, and M. Orth. "Beck Depression Inventory Is a Useful Screening Tool for Major Depressive Disorder in Gilles de la Tourette Syndrome." *Journal of Neurology, Neurosurgery & Psychiatry* 77.6 (June 2006): 787–89.

Solomon, Ari, and others. "Taxometric Investigation of Unipolar Depression in a Large Community Sample." *Psychological Medicine* 36.7 (July 2006): 973–85.

ORGANIZATIONS

American Psychiatric Association. 1400 K Street NW, Washington, DC 20005. <http://www.psych.org>.

The Center for Mental Health Services Knowledge Exchange Network (KEN). U.S. Department of Health and Human Services. Telephone: (800) 789-2647. <http://www.mentalhealth.org>.

National Alliance for the Mentally Ill (NAMI). Colonial Place 3, 2107 Wilson Boulevard, Suite 300, Arlington VA 22201-3042. Telephone: (703) 524-7600 or (800) 950-6264. <http://www.nami.org>.

National Depressive and Manic Depressive Association (NDMDA). 730 N. Franklin Street, Suite 501, Chicago IL 60601-3526. Telephone: (314) 642-0049 or (800) 826-3632. <http://www.ndmda.org>.

National Institute of Mental Health. 6001 Executive Boulevard, Room 8184, MSC 9663, Bethesda, MD 20892-9663. Telephone: (301) 443-4513. <http://www.nimh.nih.gov>.

Substance Abuse and Mental Health Services Administration (SAMHSA). Center for Mental Health Services (CMHS), Department of Health and Human Services. 5600 Fishers Lane, Rockville MD 20857. <http://www.samhsa.org>.

Michael Polgar, PhD
Ruth A. Wienclaw, PhD

Bedwetting *see* **Enuresis**

Behavior modification

Definition

Behavior modification is a treatment approach, based on the principles of operant conditioning, that replaces undesirable behaviors with more desirable ones through positive or negative **reinforcement**.

B.F. SKINNER (1894–1956)

B. F. Skinner was born in Susquehanna, Pennsylvania. Skinner became interested in behavioristic psychology after reading the works of John Watson and Ivan Pavlov. He entered Harvard University as a graduate student in psychology in 1928 and received his degree three years later. While at Harvard, he laid the foundation for a new system of behavioral analysis through his research in the field of animal learning, utilizing unique experimental equipment of his own design.

His most successful and well-known apparatus, known as the Skinner Box, was a cage in which a laboratory rat could, by pressing on a bar, activate a mechanism that would drop a food pellet into the cage. Another device recorded each press of the bar, producing a permanent record of experimental results without the presence of a tester. Skinner analyzed the rats' bar-pressing behavior by varying his patterns of reinforcement (feeding) to learn their responses to different schedules (including random ones). Using this box to study how rats "operated on" their environment led Skinner to formulate the principle of operant conditioning—applicable to a wide range of both human and animal behaviors—through which an experimenter can gradually shape the behavior of a subject by manipulating its responses through reinforcement or lack of it. In contrast to Pavlovian, or response, conditioning, which depends on an outside stimulus, Skinner's operant conditioning depends on the subject's responses themselves. Skinner introduced the concept of operant conditioning to the public in his first book, *The Behavior of Organisms* (1938). His ideas eventually became so influential that the American Psychological Association created a separate division of studies related to them (Division 25: "The Experimental Analysis of Behavior"), and four journals of behaviorist research were established.

Skinner's work was also influential in the clinical treatment of mental and emotional disorders. In the late 1940s he began to develop the behavior modification method, in which subjects receive a series of small rewards for desired behavior. Considered a useful technique for psychologists and psychiatrists with deeply disturbed patients, behavior modification has also been widely used by the general population in overcoming obesity, shyness, speech defects, addiction to smoking, and other problems. Extending his ideas to the realm of philosophy, Skinner concluded that all behavior was the result of either positive or negative reinforcement, and thus the existence of free will was merely an illusion. To explore the social ramifications of his behaviorist principles, he wrote the novel *Walden Two* (1948), which depicted a utopian society in which all reinforcement was positive. While detractors of this controversial work regarded its vision of social control through strict positive reinforcement as totalitarian, the 1967 founding of the Twin Oaks Community in Virginia was inspired by Skinner's ideas. Skinner elaborated further on his ideas about positive social control in his book *Beyond Freedom and Dignity* (1971), which critiques the notion of human autonomy, arguing that many actions ascribed to free will are performed due to necessity.

Purpose

Behavior modification is used to treat a variety of problems in both adults and children. It has been successfully used to treat **obsessive-compulsive disorder** (OCD), **attention deficit/hyperactivity disorder** (ADHD), phobias, **enuresis** (bed-wetting), **anxiety** disorder, and **separation anxiety disorder**, among others.

Description

Behavior modification is based on the principles of operant conditioning, which were developed by American behaviorist B. F. Skinner (1904–1990). Skinner formulated the concept of operant conditioning, through which behavior could be shaped by reinforcement or lack of it. Skinner considered his concept applicable to a wide range of both human and animal behaviors and introduced operant conditioning to the general public in his 1938 book, *The Behavior of Organisms*. It is distinguished by a focus on behavior and its consequences. Other related forms of therapy, such as **cognitive-behavioral therapy**, may take in to account internal motivation and feelings as well.

One behavior modification technique that is widely used is positive reinforcement, which encourages certain behaviors through a system of rewards. In behavior therapy, it is common for the therapist to draw up a contract with the client establishing the terms of the reward system. The system can consist of goals, rewards, and consequences. In addition to being practiced either consciously or unconsciously by educators and parents in general, this system also has come in to widespread use as a systematic approach for addressing behaviors in children with attention deficit/hyperactivity disorder.

Behavior modification can also discourage unwanted behavior, through either negative reinforcement or punishment. Negative reinforcement refers to a behavior that, when its elimination depends on a response, the behavior will increase the rate of recurrence or likelihood of that response. Punishment is the application of an adversive or unpleasant stimulus in reaction to a particular behavior. For children, this could be the removal of television privileges when they disobey their parents or teachers. The removal of reinforcement altogether is called extinction. Extinction eliminates the incentive for unwanted behavior by withholding the expected response. A widespread parenting technique based on extinction is the time-out, in which a child is separated from the group when he or she misbehaves. This technique removes the expected reward of parental attention.

Results

Normal results are that undesirable behaviors are replaced with more desirable ones.

See also Aversion theraphy; Cognitive-behavioral therapy; Token economy system.

Resources

BOOKS

Martin, Garry. *Behavior Modification: What It Is and How to Do It.* Englewood Cliffs, NJ: Prentice-Hall, 1988.

OTHER

Association for Behavioral and Cognitive Therapies. 305 Seventh Avenue, Floor 16. New York, NY 10001. Telephone: (212) 647-1890. <http://www.aabt.org/>.

"Attention-Deficit/Hyperactivity Disorder." Bethesda (MD): National Institute of Mental Health, National Institutes of Health, U.S. Department of Health and Human Services; (2006). NIH publication No. 3572. Available online at <http://www.nimh.nih.gov/publicat/adhd.cfm>.

Emily Jane Willingham, PhD

Behavior therapy *see* **Cognitive-behavioral therapy**

Behavioral addiction *see* **Process addiction**

Behavioral self-control training *see* **Self-control strategies**

Benadryl *see* **Diphenhydramine**

Bender Gestalt Test

Definition

The Bender Gestalt Test, or the Bender Visual Motor Gestalt Test, is a psychological assessment instrument used to evaluate visual-motor functioning and visual perception skills in both children and adults. Scores on the test are used to identify possible organic **brain** damage and the degree maturation of the nervous system. The Bender Gestalt was developed by **psychiatrist** Lauretta Bender in the late nineteenth century.

Purpose

The Bender Gestalt Test is used to evaluate visual maturity, visual motor integration skills, style of responding, reaction to frustration, ability to correct mistakes, planning and organizational skills, and motivation. Copying figures requires fine motor skills, the ability to discriminate between visual stimuli, the capacity to integrate visual skills with motor skills, and the ability to shift attention from the original design to what is being drawn.

Precautions

The Bender Gestalt Test should not be administered to an individual with severe visual impairment unless his or her vision has been adequately corrected with eyeglasses. Additionally, the test should not be given to an examinee with a severe motor impairment, as the impairment would affect his or her ability to draw the geometric figures correctly. The test scores might thereby be distorted.

The Bender Gestalt Test has been criticized for being used to assess problems with organic factors in the brain. This criticism stems from the lack of specific signs on the Bender Gestalt Test that are definitively associated with brain injury, **mental retardation**, and other physiological disorders. Therefore, when making a **diagnosis** of brain injury, the Bender Gestalt Test should never be used in isolation. When making a diagnosis, results from the Bender Gestalt Test should be used in conjunction with other medical, developmental, educational, psychological, and neuropsychological information.

Finally, psychometric testing requires administration and evaluation by a clinically trained examiner. If a scoring system is used, the examiner should carefully evaluate its reliability and validity, as well as the normative sample being used. A normative sample is a group within a population who takes a test and represents the larger population. This group's scores on a test are then be used to create "norms" with which the scores of test takers are compared.

Description

The Bender Gestalt Test is an individually administered pencil and paper test used to make a diagnosis of brain injury. There are nine geometric figures drawn in black. These figures are presented to the examinee one at a time; then, the examinee is asked to copy the figure on a blank sheet of paper. Examinees are allowed to erase, but cannot use any mechanical aids (such as rulers). The popularity of this test among clinicians is most likely the short amount of time it takes to administer and score. The average amount of time to complete the test is five to ten minutes.

The Bender Gestalt Test lends itself to several variations in administration. One method requires that the examinee view each card for five seconds, after which the card is removed. The examinee draws the figure from memory. Another variation involves having the examinee draw the figures by following the standard procedure. The examinee is then given a clean sheet of paper and asked to draw as many figures as he or she can recall. Last, the test is given to a group, rather than to an individual (i.e., standard administration). It should be noted that these variations were not part of the original test.

Results

A scoring system does not have to be used to interpret performance on the Bender Gestalt Test; however, there are several reliable and valid scoring systems available. Many of the available scoring systems focus on specific-type difficulties experienced by the test taker. These difficulties may indicate poor visual-motor abilities that include:

- angular difficulty: This includes increasing, decreasing, distorting, or omitting an angle in a figure.
- bizarre doodling: This involves adding peculiar components to the drawing that have no relationship to the original Bender Gestalt figure.
- closure difficulty: This occurs when the examinee has difficulty closing open spaces on a figure, or connecting various parts of the figure. This results in a gap in the copied figure.
- cohesion: This involves drawing a part of a figure larger or smaller than shown on the original figure and out of proportion with the rest of the figure. This error may also include drawing a figure or part of a figure significantly out of proportion with other figures that have been drawn.
- collision: This involves crowding the designs or allowing the end of one design to overlap or touch a part of another design.
- contamination: This occurs when a previous figure, or part of a figure, influences the examinee in adequate completion of the current figure. For example, an examinee may combine two different Bender Gestalt figures.

- fragmentation: This involves destroying part of the figure by not completing or breaking up the figures in ways that entirely lose the original design.
- impotence: This occurs when the examinee draws a figure inaccurately and seems to recognize the error, then, he or she makes several unsuccessful attempts to improve the drawing.
- irregular line quality or lack of motor coordination: This involves drawing rough lines, particularly when the examinee shows a tremor motion, during the drawing of the figure.
- line extension: This involves adding or extending a part of the copied figure that was not on the original figure.
- omission: This involves failing to adequately connect the parts of a figure or reproducing only parts of a figure.
- overlapping difficulty: This includes problems in drawing portions of the figures that overlap, simplifying the drawing at the point that it overlaps, sketching or redrawing the overlapping portions, or otherwise distorting the figure at the point at which it overlaps.
- perseveration: This includes increasing, prolonging, or continuing the number of units in a figure. For example, an examinee may draw significantly more dots or circles than shown on the original figure.
- retrogression: This involves substituting more primitive figures for the original design—for example, substituting solid lines or loops for circles, dashes for dots, dots for circles, circles for dots, or filling in circles. There must be evidence that the examinee is capable of drawing more mature figures.
- rotation: This involves rotating a figure or part of a figure by 45° or more. This error is also scored when the examinee rotates the stimulus card that is being copied.
- scribbling: This involves drawing primitive lines that have no relationship to the original Bender Gestalt figure.
- simplification: This involves replacing a part of the figure with a more simplified figure. This error is not due to maturation. Drawings that are primitive in terms of maturation would be categorized under "Retrogression."
- superimposition of design: This involves drawing one or more of the figures on top of each other.
- workover: This involves reinforcing, increased pressure, or overworking a line or lines in a whole or part of a figure.

KEY TERMS

Psychometric testing—Pertaining to testing and measurement of mental or psychological abilities. Psychometric tests convert an individual's psychological traits and attributes into a numerical estimation or evaluation.

Additionally, observing the examinee's behavior while drawing the figures can provide the examiner with an informal evaluation and data that can supplement the formal evaluation of the examinee's visual and perceptual functioning. For example, if an examinee takes a large amount of time to complete the geometric figures, it may suggest a slow, methodical approach to tasks, compulsive tendencies, or depressive symptoms. If an examinee rapidly completes the test, this could indicate an impulsive style.

Resources

BOOKS

Hutt, M. L. *The Hutt Adaptation of the Bender Gestalt Test.* New York: Grune and Stratton, 1985.

Kaufman, Alan, S., and Elizabeth O. Lichtenberger. *Assessing Adolescent and Adult Intelligence.* Boston: Allyn and Bacon, 2001.

Koppitz, E. M. *The Bender Gestalt Test for Young Children.* Vol. 2. New York: Grune and Stratton, 1975.

Pascal, G. R., and B. J. Suttell. *The Bender Gestalt Test: Quantification and Validation for Adults.* New York: Grune and Stratton, 1951.

Sattler, Jerome M. "Assessment of visual-motor perception and motor proficiency." In *Assessment of Children: Behavioral and Clinical Applications.* 4th ed. San Diego: Jerome M. Sattler, Publisher, Inc., 2002.

Watkins, E. O. *The Watkins Bender Gestalt Scoring System.* Novato, CA: Academic Therapy, 1976.

PERIODICALS

Piotrowski, C. "A Review of the Clinical and Research Use of the Bender Gestalt Test." *Perceptual and Motor Skills* 81 (1995): 1272-1274.

Benzodiazepines

Definition

Benzodiazepines belong to a class of drugs with sedative and hypnotic properties. The principal use of this class of drugs is to produce drowsiness and enable sleep, although they are among the most commonly

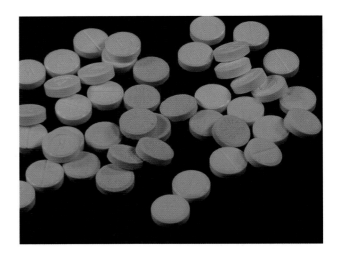

Generic benzodiazepam tablets. *(David Hoffman Photo Library/ Alamy)*

prescribed drugs for producing anti-anxiety effects. Benzodiazepines are also widely prescribed for muscle spasticity, convulsive disorders, pre-surgical sedation, involuntary **movement disorders**, and **detoxification** from alcohol and other substances. The action of benzodiazepines result is primarily from effects on the central nervous system. However, the benzodiazepines are not simply neuronal depressants, they have a complex pharmacological profile such that the clinical usefulness of individual drugs varies widely.

Description

While the selectivity of unique benzodiazepine drugs allows them to have therapeutic potential for various conditions, this class of drugs has a common sedative profile. The sedative properties of benzodiazepines progress through a continuum from sedation to hypnosis to stupor. The sedation component is associated with memory impairment and retrograde **amnesia** for events that occur while under the effects of the drug. Benzodiazepines increase total sleep time. Benzodiazepine use is associated with refreshing sleep even though not all stages of sleep are affected equally. Other effects of benzodiazepines that can be produced at non-sedative doses are muscle relaxation, anti-seizure activity, and analgesia. The anti-anxiety effects of benzodiazepines relieve the excessive or exaggerated debilitating generalized worry about everyday life events.

Mechanism of action

Benzodiazepines affect a key neurotransmitter in the **brain** called gamma-amino butyric acid (GABA). This neurotransmitter has an inhibitory effect on neurons. Benzodiazepines enhance the affinity of the recognition site on the GABA receptor for GABA, resulting in an increase in GABA-mediated inhibition. Activation of the GABA receptor complex is thought to be responsible for producing the therapeutic anti-anxiety effects of benzodiazepines and for mediating many of the side effects of these drugs.

In addition to benzodiazepines, other drugs affect the GABA receptor complex, which serves as a primary site of action of benzodiazepines, **barbiturates**, and other sedative-hypnotics, such as alcohol. Benzodiazepines and barbiturates act on separate binding sites on the receptor to enhance the inhibitory action of GABA. They do so by altering the receptor so that it has a greater binding affinity for GABA. Ethanol modifies the receptor by altering its membrane environment so that it has increased affinity for GABA and the other sedative-hypnotic drugs. Benzodiazepines, barbiturates, and ethanol all have related actions on a common receptor type (GABA receptors), which explains their pharmacologic synergy and the therapeutic benefit of benzodiazepines in alcohol detoxification.

Side effects

Benzodiazepines are central nervous system depressants, and the major side effects of these drugs are an extension of their actions. However, paradoxical effects such as increased **anxiety**, hostility, irritability, vivid dreams, psychoses, and confusion have been reported as side effects of this class of drugs. Other acute side effects include skin rash, nausea, headache, vertigo, and irregular menses. Long-term treatment can result in both tolerance (a decrease in efficacy to a repeated dose) and dependence (real or perceived reliance on the drug to function).

Tolerance to all of the actions of benzodiazepines can develop. Tolerance to the hypnotic effects develops rapidly, which is beneficial against daytime anxiety but makes management of **insomnia** difficult. Initial relief of insomnia is followed by a gradual loss of efficacy. Tolerance to the anxiolytic effect develops more slowly than tolerance to the hypnotic effects, but benzodiazepines often lose their efficacy after four to six months of regular use. Benzodiazepine therapy is often continued to suppress withdrawal symptoms. Dosage escalation maintains tolerance and dependence, and patients may have difficulty discontinuing drug therapy. Thus, after long-term use of benzodiazepines (or ethanol), there is a decrease in the efficacy of GABA receptors, presumably as a result of tolerance. When benzodiazepines or ethanol are abruptly discontinued, this decreased inhibitory neurotransmis-

---

KEY TERMS

Barbiturate—General neuronal depressant.

Central nervous system—The brain and spinal cord.

Gamma amino butyric acid (GABA)—A chemical messenger in the brain that provides neuronal inhibition.

Hypnotic—A drug that produces drowsiness and facilitates the onset and maintenance of sleep.

Neurotransmitters—Chemical messengers that transmit signals between nerves.

Sedative—A drug that decreases activity and calms the recipient.

---

sion is unmasked, leading to withdrawal symptoms such as anxiety, insomnia, autonomic hyperactivity (for example, increased heart rate and dilated pupils), and, possibly, **seizures**. Withdrawal symptoms emerge with rapid dose reduction or abrupt discontinuation of the drug.

Long-term use of benzodiazepines may also result in psychologic dependence or "overreliance" on the drug, including a loss of self-confidence and drug-seeking behavior. Patients may be reluctant to discontinue the drug because of anticipatory anxiety.

Interactions

Additive effects with other central nervous system depressants (for example, barbiturates, or ethanol) are the primary drug interactions observed with benzodiazepines.

Resources

BOOKS

American Psychiatric Association. *Diagnostic and Statistical Manual of Mental Disorders.* 4th ed., Text rev. Washington, D.C.: American Psychiatric Association, 2000.

Doble, Adam, Ian Martin, and David J. Nutt. *Calming the Brain: Benzodiazepines and Related Drugs from Laboratory to Clinic.* London: Taylor and Francis, 2004.

Hardman, Joel Griffith, Lee E. Limbird, and Alfred G. Gilman. *Goodman & Gilman's The Pharmacological Basis of Therapeutics.* New York: McGraw-Hill, 2001.

Andrew J. Bean, PhD

Benztropine

Definition

Benztropine is classified as an antiparkinsonian agent. It is sold in the United States under the brand name Cogentin and is also available under its generic name.

Purpose

Benztropine is used to treat a group of side effects (called parkinsonian side effects) that include tremors, difficulty walking, and slack muscle tone. These side effects may occur in patients who are taking antipsychotic medications used to treat mental disorders such as **schizophrenia**.

Description

Some medicines, called antipsychotic drugs, that are used to treat schizophrenia and other mental disorders can cause side effects that are similar to the symptoms of Parkinson's disease. Patients do not have Parkinson's disease, but they may experience shaking in muscles while at rest, difficulty with voluntary movements, and poor muscle tone. These symptoms are similar to the symptoms of Parkinson's disease.

One way to eliminate these undesirable side effects is to stop taking the antipsychotic medicine. Unfortunately, the symptoms of the original mental disorder usually come back, so simply stopping the antipsychotic medication is not a reasonable option in most cases. Some drugs that control the symptoms of Parkinson's disease, such as benztropine, also control the parkinsonian side effects of antipsychotic medicines.

Benztropine works by restoring the chemical balance between **dopamine** and acetylcholine, two neurotransmitter chemicals in the **brain**. Taking benztropine along with the antipsychotic medicine helps to control symptoms of the mental disorder, while reducing parkinsonian side effects. Benztropine is in the same family of drugs (commonly known as anticholinergic drugs) as **biperiden** and **trihexyphenidyl**.

Recommended dosage

Benztropine is available in 0.5-, 1.0-, and 2.0-mg tablets and in an injectable form containing 2 mg of drug in each 2 mL glass container. For the treatment of tremors, poor muscle tone, and similar side effects, benztropine should be started at a dose of 1 to 2 mg orally. In cases of severe side effects, benztropine can be given as an intramuscular injection two to three times daily or as needed. Parkinson-like side effects caused by antipsychotic drugs may come and go, so benztropine may not be needed on a regular basis. Benztropine may also be prescribed to prevent these side effects before they actually occur. This is called a prophylactic (preventative) therapy.

Precautions

Benztropine should never be used in children under age three. It should be used cautiously and with close physician supervision in older children and in the elderly. Like all anticholinergic drugs, benztropine decreases the body's ability to sweat and cool itself. People who are unaccustomed to being outside in hot weather should take care to stay as cool as possible and drink extra fluids. People who are chronically ill, have a central nervous system disease, or who work outside during hot weather may need to avoid taking benztropine.

People who have the following medical problems may experience increased negative side effects when taking benztropine. Those who have these problems should discuss their conditions with their physician before starting the drug:

- glaucoma, especially closed-angle glaucoma
- intestinal obstruction
- prostate enlargement
- urinary bladder obstruction

Although rare, some patients experience euphoria while taking benztropine and may **abuse** it for this reason. Euphoria can occur at doses only two to four times the normal daily dose. Patients with a history of drug abuse should be observed carefully for benztropine abuse.

Side effects

Although benztropine helps to control the side effects of antipsychotic drugs, it can produce side effects of its own. A person taking benztropine may have some of the following reactions, which may vary in intensity:

- dry mouth
- dry skin
- blurred vision
- nausea or vomiting
- constipation
- disorientation
- drowsiness
- irritability
- increased heart rate
- urinary retention

KEY TERMS

Acetylcholine—A naturally occurring chemical in the body that transmits nerve impulses from cell to cell. Generally, it has opposite effects from dopamine and norepinephrine; it causes blood vessels to dilate, lowers blood pressure, and slows the heartbeat. Central nervous system well-being is dependent on a balance among acetylcholine, dopamine, serotonin, and norepinephrine.

Anticholinergic—Related to the ability of a drug to block the nervous system chemical acetylcholine. When acetylcholine is blocked, patients often experience dry mouth and skin, increased heart rate, blurred vision, and difficulty urinating. In severe cases, blocking acetylcholine may cloud thinking and cause delirium.

Catheterization—Placing a tube in the bladder so that it can be emptied of urine.

Dopamine—A chemical in brain tissue that serves to transmit nerve impulses (is a neurotransmitter) and helps to regulate movement and emotions.

Neurotransmitter—A chemical in the brain that transmits messages between neurons, or nerve cells.

Parkinsonian—Related to symptoms associated with Parkinson's disease, a nervous system disorder characterized by abnormal muscle movement of the tongue, face, and neck, inability to walk or move quickly, walking in a shuffling manner, restlessness, and/or tremors.

Dry mouth, if severe to the point of causing difficulty speaking or swallowing, may be managed by reducing or temporarily discontinuing benztropine. Chewing sugarless gum or sucking on sugarless candy may also help to increase the flow of saliva. Some artificial saliva products may give temporary relief.

Men with prostate enlargement may be especially prone to urinary retention. Symptoms of this problem include having difficulty starting a urine flow and more difficulty passing urine than usual. This side effect may be severe and require discontinuation of the drug. Urinary retention may require catheterization. People who think they may be experiencing any side effects from this or any other medication should tell their physicians.

Patients who take an overdose of benztropine are treated with forced vomiting, removal of stomach contents and stomach washing, activated charcoal, and respiratory support if needed. They are also given physostigmine, an antidote for anticholinergic drug poisoning.

Interactions

When drugs such as benztropine are taken with **antidepressants** such as **amitriptyline, imipramine, trimipramine, desipramine, nortriptyline, protriptyline, amoxapine,** and **doxepin** or with many antihistamines that also have anticholinergic properties, the effects and side effects of benztropine are usually intensified.

Drugs such as benztropine decrease the speed with which food moves through the stomach and intestines. Because of this, the absorption of other drugs being taken may be enhanced by benztropine. Patients receiving benztropine should be alerted to unusual responses to other drugs they might be taking and report any changes to their physicians.

Resources

BOOKS

American Society of Health-System Pharmacists. *AHFS Drug Information 2002*. Bethesda: American Society of Health-System Pharmacists, 2002.

Preston, John D., John H. O'Neal, and Mary C. Talaga. *Handbook of Clinical Psychopharmacology for Therapists*. 4th ed. Oakland, CA: New Harbinger Publications, 2004.

PERIODICALS

de Leon, Jose. "Benztropine Equivalents for Antimuscarinic Medication." *American Journal of Psychiatry* 162.3 (March. 2005): 627.

Penetar, David M., and others. "Benztropine Pretreatment Does Not Affect Responses to Acute Cocaine Administration in Human Volunteers." *Human Psychopharmacology: Clinical and Experimental* 21.8 (Dec. 2006): 549–59.

Jack Raber, Pharm.D.
Ruth A. Wienclaw, PhD

Bereavement

Definition

Bereavement is the experience a person has when a loved one dies.

Description

Bereavement usually refers to the experience of losing a loved one to death. **Grief** refers to the reaction people have to loss or bereavement. Most people can expect to be bereaved at some point in their lifetimes.

Many people are bereaved each year. In 2003, for example, nearly 2.5 million U.S. citizens died, leaving behind many millions of bereaved individuals.

Bereavement is thus a common and normal part of life, and is not a psychiatric disorder. People who have normal, uncomplicated reactions to bereavement usually adjust to their loss over time and do not need clinical **intervention**. However, research indicates that bereavement is one of the most stressful experiences faced by people. The fourth edition of the *Diagnostic and Statistical Manual of Mental Disorders (DSM-IV)* lists bereavement as a condition that may be a focus of clinical attention, even though it is not considered a disorder. Bereavement is associated with a high risk of psychological distress, social isolation, physical illness, and death.

Many researchers agree that bereaved people go through different phases after the loss of a loved one. In the avoidance phase, people may have difficulty understanding and coming to grips with the reality of the situation. They may experience shock, numbness, disbelief, and **denial**. In the confrontation phase, people realize the reality of their loss, and they typically have intense negative feelings such as deep sadness, guilt, helplessness, panic, confusion, powerlessness, anger, rage, and despair. They may blame themselves or others for the loss, feel that life is unjust, and experience a sense of disillusionment and a loss of faith. In the accommodation phase, people gradually adjust to their loss. People do not necessarily go through these phases in an orderly fashion. Instead they may move back and forth between them over time.

Painful feelings typically continue for many months after bereavement, but they diminish in intensity over time, eventually becoming episodic. Such feelings may reemerge in more acute forms on memorable occasions such as anniversaries and holidays, and when especially poignant memories of the deceased are recalled. While negative feelings associated with bereavement typically do not completely disappear over time, they become less debilitating and overwhelming. Successful adjustment to the loss is marked by the ability to manage these feelings effectively as they wax and wane.

Not all feelings and experiences associated with bereavement are negative. Some bereaved people feel positive emotions such as relief that the deceased is no longer suffering, particularly after a lengthy illness. Over time, some people find that bereavement, though a difficult experience, is also a time of personal growth. They may develop a new appreciation for life and come to have an increased sense of self-esteem as they master new tasks and adjust to the experience of carrying on independently from the loved one they lost.

Adapting to loss involves recognizing and accepting the life changes that follow the loss. Finding ways to focus on the positive aspects of life and trying to find meaning in the loss are helpful coping strategies. Bereaved people often continue to have some form of relationship with the deceased person. Attachment to physical reminders of the deceased is common, especially in the initial period after bereavement. People often maintain a continuing bond with the deceased person through their religious or spiritual faith. Spiritual connections with the deceased may take the form of praying to the deceased or sensing the presence of the deceased in one's life. Many cultures endorse preserving bonds with the dead through commemorative festivals and rituals. For example, the Day of the Dead celebration in Mexico allows the bereaved to celebrate the lives of the deceased.

In the initial months of bereavement, people often have symptoms that are characteristic of clinical **depression**, such as sadness, **insomnia**, loss of appetite, and weight loss. However, because these kinds of symptoms are normal and expected reactions to loss, a **diagnosis** of **major depressive disorder**, or clinical depression, is not generally given unless these symptoms are present to a significant degree two months after the loss of the loved one. Although grief may produce permanent changes in bereaved people, most people are able to accept their loss over time, see that there is still potential for having satisfying relationships with people, be productive, enjoy activities, have a sense of self-esteem, and find meaning and purpose in their lives. A small minority of bereaved people, however, experience pathological grief reactions that may need clinical intervention. Pathological reactions are more common among people who suffer traumatic losses, such as the violent death of a loved one, and among people who are excessively dependent on the deceased. Some may experience major depressive disorder or **post-traumatic stress disorder** (PTSD). Major depressive disorder is generally diagnosed only after two months have passed since the loss, and only if the bereaved person experiences persistent feelings of guilt that are not limited to guilt about the death of the loved one, thoughts of death that are unrelated to the death of the loved one, feelings of unworthiness, feeling slowed down, and being unable to perform normal activities. Post-traumatic **stress** disorder may be diagnosed if the bereaved person experienced the violent or traumatic death of a loved one, has recollections of the death that are recurrent and disturbing, avoids situations that are reminiscent of the death, and has marked irritability and difficulty sleeping and concentrating. In one study, researchers found that 9% of bereaved people met the criteria for major depressive disorder four months after their loss, and 5.7% met the criteria for post-traumatic stress disorder. Some scientists have proposed that the term "complicated grief disorder" be applied to describe additional cases in which people experience pathological reactions after bereavement. In one study, 10% of bereaved people studied met the criteria for complicated grief disorder. Complicated grief disorder is not listed in the *DSM-IV*, but scientists have proposed that it be included in the next edition. Complicated grief disorder has also been referred to as atypical grief, abnormal grief, pathologic grief, and pathologic mourning. Unlike people who experience normal bereavement, people who experience complicated grief disorder remain in a chronic state of mourning. They are unable to accept their loss and to make the adjustments needed to live effectively and productively without the loved one. They feel an intense yearning for the person they lost, experience persistent distressing thoughts about the deceased, and feel bitter and agitated about their loss. Although these kinds of reactions are common and normal in people in the initial months following the loss of a loved one, persistence of such symptoms beyond six months may be indicative of a pathological condition that may not resolve naturally. People who have difficulties with attachment to others, feel unprepared for the death of the loved one, and feel unsupported after the loss are at particularly high risk for complicated grief disorder. **Psychotherapy**, medications, and participation in **support groups** may be helpful in reducing the chronic, dysfunctional levels of grief that such people experience.

It is important to note that the reactions to bereavement can vary a great deal. Reactions are influenced by the personalities of the bereaved, their relationship to the deceased, the manner of death, and the cultural background of the bereaved. There are considerable differences between cultural groups in the ways that bereavement is expressed and in the duration of normal bereavement. Variations in bereavement reactions should be taken into account when trying to determine whether the particular response of a bereaved person is normal or pathological.

Many community organizations offer support to the bereaved. These include hospitals, social service agencies, funeral homes, hospices, YMCAs, and religious organizations such as churches, synagogues, and mosques.

See also Grief.

Resources

BOOKS

American Psychiatric Association. *Diagnostic and Statistical Manual of Mental Disorders*. 4th ed., text rev. Washington, D.C.: American Psychiatric Association, 2000.

Hooyman, Nancy R., and Betty J. Kramer. *Living Through Loss: Interventions Across the Life Span*. New York: Columbia University Press, 2006.

Lendrum, Susan and Gabrielle Syme. *Gift of Tears: A Practical Approach to Loss and Bereavement in Counselling and Psychotherapy*. 2d ed. New York: Brunner-Routledge, 2004.

PERIODICALS

Dutton, Yulia Chentsova, and Sidney Zisook. "Adaptation to Bereavement." *Death Studies* 29 (2005): 877–903.

"JAMA Patient Page: Grief." *The Journal of the American Medical Association* 23.21 (June 2005). <http://jama.ama-assn.org/cgi/content/full/293/21/2686>.

Zhang, Baohui, Areej El-Jawahri, and Holly G. Prigerson. "Update on Bereavement Research: Evidence-Based Guidelines for the Diagnosis and Treatment of Complicated Bereavement." *Journal of Palliative Medicine* 9.5 (2006): 1188–1203.

ORGANIZATIONS

American Hospice Foundation. 2120 L Street NW, Suite 200, Washington, D.C. 20037. Telephone: (202) 223-0204. <http://www.americanhospice.org>.

American Psychiatric Association. 1000 Wilson Boulevard, Suite 1825, Arlington, VA 22209-3901. Telephone: (703) 907-7300. <http://www.psych.org>.

Dougy Center for Grieving Children. P.O. Box 86552, Portland, OR 97286. Telephone: (503) 775-5683. <http://www.dougy.org>.

Mental Health America. 2000 N. Beauregard Street, 6th Floor Alexandria, VA 22311. Telephone: (703) 684-7722, (800) 969-6MHA (6642). <http://www.nmha.org>.

National Institute of Mental Health (NIMH). 6001 Executive Boulevard, Room 8184, MSC 9663, Bethesda, MD 20892-9663. (866) 615-6464. <http://www.nimh.nih.gov>.

TAPS (Tragedy Assistance Program for Survivors), Inc. 2001 S Street NW, Suite 300, Washington, D.C. 20009. Telephone: (800) 959-TAPS. <http://www.taps.org>.

The Compassionate Friends, Inc. P. O. Box 3696, Oak Brook, IL 60522-3696. Telephone: (877) 969-0010, (630) 990-0010. <http://www.compassionatefriends.org>.

Ruvanee Pietersz Vilhauer, PhD

Beta blockers

Definition

Beta blockers, also known as beta antagonists, are a class of drugs that were first developed for the treatment of certain heart conditions and hypertension. Later, beta blockers were also found to be useful in glaucoma, migraine, and some psychiatric disorders such as performance **anxiety**, tremors secondary to lithium, and **movement disorders** that are caused by some drugs used in the treatment of **psychosis**. There are a number of beta blockers approved for use in the United States, including acebutolol, bisoprolol, nadolol, proproanolol, and metoprolol, which have various trade names. **Propranolol** is the most commonly used in psychiatric practice.

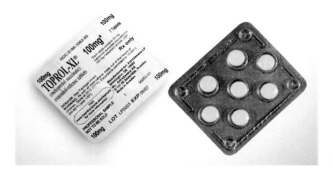

Toprol-xl (metoprolol succinate), a beta blocker used to treat angina and hypertension. *(John Kaprielian/Photo Researchers, Inc)*

Purpose

Beta blockers are proven effective in the treatment of performance anxiety, lithium-induced tremors, and neuroleptic-induced akathesia (a physical condition caused by certain antipsychotic drugs). Beta blockers have sometimes been used with **benzodiazepines** in treating alcohol withdrawal.

Description

Beta blockers act on that part of the central nervous system that controls mental alertness, lung function, heart rate, and blood vessels. Although there is more than one mechanism by which beta blockers work in anxiety states, the most beneficial result probably arises from the fact that beta blockers slow the heart to a normal rate and rhythm. Therefore, persons with performance anxiety do not experience the usual chest tightness and rapid heart rate that is associated with such acts as public speaking or acting.

Certain antipsychotic medications known as neuroleptics can cause an unwanted effect called akathesia, which is the inability to sit, stand still, or remain inactive. Patients are restless, and in severe cases, may pace constantly and forcefully and repeatedly stomp their feet. Beta blockers can sometimes treat this condition with a lower incidence of side effects than other drugs.

Recommended dosage

Propranolol is available in several different forms. Tablets are available, as are an oral solution and an injectable form. Dosage varies considerably depended on the reason for taking the drug and the age of the person. A physician will determine the appropriate dosage, although some examples are given below.

For one-time usage to treat performance anxiety, a single dose ranging from 10–40 mg taken a half hour before the performance (e.g., public speaking) is typical.

For lithium-induced tremors that cannot be controlled by reducing caffeine intake or administering the dosage of lithium at bedtime, propranolol at a dose of 20–160 mg daily can be given in two or three evenly divided doses.

For akathesia caused by antipsychotic medications, propranolol can be administered at doses of 10–30 mg three times daily.

Precautions

Because of their ability to narrow airways, beta blockers, especially propranolol, should not be taken by people with asthma and chronic obstructive pulmonary disease (COPD). If there is an urgent need to use beta blockers in persons with respiratory problems, atenolol or metoprolol are the beta blockers of choice because they are less likely to have this side effect, although even these drugs should also be used with caution. Patients with congestive heart failure, or certain cardiac conduction abnormalities such as a heart block, should also receive these drugs with caution.

Beta blockers should be used with close physician monitoring in people with diabetes, since the symptoms of low blood sugar (increased heart rate, lightheadedness, and abnormal perspiration) may be not be recognized by patients.

KEY TERMS

Akathesia—Agitated or restless movement, usually affecting the legs. Movement is accompanied by a sense of discomfort and an inability to sit, stand still, or remain inactive for periods of time. Akathisia is a common side effect of some neuroleptic (antipsychotic) medications.

Benzodiazepines—A group of central nervous system depressants used to relieve anxiety or to induce sleep.

Tremor—Involuntary shaking of the hands and arms.

Side effects

Beta blockers can cause undesired decreases in blood pressure and are typically not given if blood pressure is 90/60 mm Hg or less.

Beta blockers can also cause an undesired drop in heart rate. People whose resting heart rate is less than 55 beats per minute should not take beta blockers.

Occasionally, beta blockers can cause rash, weakness, nausea, vomiting, and stomach discomfort.

Interactions

Each medication in the class of beta blockers has the potential to interact with a multitude of other medications. Anyone starting beta-blocker therapy should review the other medications they are taking with their physician and pharmacist for possible interactions. Patients should always inform all their healthcare providers, including dentists, that they are taking beta blockers.

Resources

BOOKS

Kaplan, Harold. *Comprehensive Textbook of Psychiatry.* Philadelphia: Lippincott Williams and Wilkins, 1995.

Kay, Jerald. *Psychiatry: Behavioral Science and Clinical Essentials.* Philadelphia: W. B. Saunders Company, 2000.

OTHER

National Library of Medicine. National Institutes of Health. "Beta-adrenergic Blocking Agents (systemic)." <http://www.nlm.nih.gov/medlineplus/druginfo/uspdi/202087.html>.

Ajna Hamidovic, Pharm.D.
Emily Jane Willingham, PhD

Bibliotherapy

Definition

Bibliotherapy is a form of therapy in which structured readings are used as an adjunct to **psychotherapy**. Such readings can be used to reinforce learning or insights gained in the therapeutic session or to give individuals additional professional resources to help in personal growth and development.

Purpose

The goal of bibliotherapy is to broaden and deepen the client's understanding of the particular problem that requires treatment. The written materials may educate the client about the disorder itself or be used to increase the client's acceptance of a proposed treatment. Many people find that the opportunity to read about their problem outside the therapist's office facilitates active participation in their treatment and promotes a stronger sense of personal responsibility for recovery. In addition, many are relieved to find that others have had the same disorder or problem and have coped successfully with or recovered from it. From the therapist's standpoint, providing clients with specific information or assignments to be completed outside regular in-office sessions speeds the progress of therapy.

The goals of bibliotherapy include the following:

- provide information or insight
- stimulate discussion about problems
- communicate new values or attitudes
- create awareness of the existence of the problem in the wider population
- provide potential solutions to problems

Bibliotherapy has been applied in a variety of settings to many kinds of people with psychological problems. Practitioners have reported successful use of bibliotherapy in treating people with eating disorders, **anxiety** and mood disorders, **agoraphobia**, alcohol and **substance abuse**, and stress-related physical disorders.

Precautions

Bibliotherapy is an adjunct to psychotherapy. It is not intended as a replacement for psychotherapy or as a self-help treatment. In addition, bibliotherapy is not likely to be useful with clients who have thought disorders, psychoses, limited intellectual ability, dyslexia, or active resistance to treatment.

KEY TERMS

Adjunct—A form of treatment that is not strictly necessary but is helpful to a therapy regimen.

Cognitive-behavioral therapy—An approach to psychotherapy that emphasizes the correction of distorted thinking patterns and changing one's behaviors accordingly.

Dyslexia—A type of reading disorder.

Regimen—A regulated course of treatment for a medical or mental disorder.

Description

In most settings, bibliotherapy is used as an adjunct to more traditional forms of psychotherapy. Practitioners of cognitive-behavioral therapies are among the most enthusiastic supporters of bibliotherapy, particularly in the development of individualized treatment protocols, including workbooks, for specific disorders. For example, clients with eating disorders, especially **bulimia nervosa**, often benefit from receiving educational information appropriate to their stage of recovery, such as books or articles about cultural biases regarding weight, attractiveness, and dieting. This information helps clients better understand the rationale for their treatment and to work on new skills or behavioral changes more effectively.

Aftercare

Unlike many standard forms of psychotherapy, bibliotherapeutic approaches often include specific examples of ways to deal with relapses or setbacks. As long as the clients keep these materials, they have easy access to resources for getting back on track.

Risks

People who use self-help manuals without professional guidance run the risk of misapplying techniques or misdiagnosing their problems.

Normal results

As with any form of treatment, bibliotherapy is effective only if it actively engages the client's desire for and belief in recovery. For many people, additional information or workbooks can be used in private to reinforce their commitment to getting better. People who lack the time or finances to attend regular psychotherapy sessions at a practitioner's office often find that bibliotherapy can bridge the gap between infre-

quent appointments. Further, the nature of the disorder itself may sometimes preclude in-office treatment, such as for people suffering from agoraphobia. Current research indicates that a bibliotherapeutic approach can be highly effective in helping people with agoraphobia better understand and cope with their symptoms.

Resources

BOOKS

Hipsky, Shellie Jacobs. *The Drama Discovery Curriculum: Bibliotherapy and Theater Games for Students with Emotional and Behavioral Challenges.* Lancaster, PA: Proactive Publications, 2006.

VandenBos, Gary R. ed. *APA Dictionary of Psychology.* Washington, D.C.: American Psychological Association, 2006.

White, John R. "Introduction." *Cognitive-Behavioral Group Therapy for Specific Problems and Populations,* John R. White and Arthur S. Freeman, eds. Washington, D.C.: American Psychological Association, 2002.

PERIODICALS

Carlbring, Per, and others. "An Open Study of Internet-Based Bibliotherapy with Minimal Therapist Contact via Email for Social Phobia." *Clinical Psychologist* 10.1 (March 2006): 30–38.

Febbraro, Greg A. R. "An Investigation Into the Effectiveness of Bibliotherapy and Minimal Contact Interventions in the Treatment of Panic Attacks." *Journal of Clinical Psychology* 61.6 (June 2005): 763–79.

Floyd, Mark, and others. "Two-Year Follow-Up of Bibliotherapy and Individual Cognitive Therapy for Depressed Older Adults." *Behavior Modification* 30.3 (May 2006): 281–94.

Foster, Tom. "Read All About It: Guided Bibliotherapy for Depression in Adults." *Irish Journal of Psychological Medicine* 23.3 (September 2006): 111–13.

Frieswijk, Nynke, and others. "The Effectiveness of a Bibliotherapy in Increasing the Self-Management Ability of Slightly to Moderately Frail Older People." *Patient Education and Counseling* 61.2 (May 2006): 219–27.

Heath, Melissa Allen, and others. "Bibliotherapy: A Resource to Facilitate Emotional Healing and Growth." *School Psychology International* 26.5 (December 2005): 563–80.

Lyneham, Heidi J., and Ronald M. Rapee. "Evaluation of Therapist-Supported Parent-Implemented CBT for Anxiety Disorders in Rural Children." *Behaviour Research and Therapy* 44.9 (September 2006): 1287–1300.

Norcross, John C. "Integrating Self-Help Into Psychotherapy: 16 Practical Suggestions." *Professional Psychology: Research and Practice* 37.6 (December. 2006): 683–93.

Pehrsson, Dale E., and P. A. McMillen. "Bibliotherapy Evaluation Tool: Grounding Counselors in the Therapeutic Use of Literature." *Arts in Psychotherapy* 32.1 (2005): 47–59.

Rapee, Ronald M., Maree J. Abbott, and Heidi J. Lyneham. "Bibliotherapy for Children With Anxiety Disorders Using Written Materials for Parents: A Randomized Controlled Trial." *Journal of Consulting and Clinical Psychology* 74.3 (June 2006): 436–44.

Reeves, T., and J. M. Stace. "Improving Patient Access and Choice: Assisted Bibliotherapy for Mild to Moderate Stress/Anxiety in Primary Care." *Journal of Psychiatric and Mental Health Nursing* 12.3 (June 2005): 341–46.

Scogin, Forrest, and others. "Evidence-Based Psychotherapies for Depression in Older Adults." *Clinical Psychology: Science and Practice* 12.3 (Fall 2005): 222–37.

Vos, Theo, and others. "Assessing Cost-Effectiveness in Mental Health: Helping Policy-Makers Prioritize and Plan Health Services." *Australian and New Zealand Journal of Psychiatry* 39.8 (August. 2005): 701–12.

Jane A. Fitzgerald, PhD
Ruth A. Wienclaw, PhD

College students, a demographic known to engage in binge drinking, at a bar. *(Alex Segre/Alamy)*

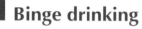

Binge drinking

Definition

Binge drinking refers to the practice of drinking alcoholic beverages to the point of intoxication. However, there is no universally accepted definition for the term with regard to amount of alcohol or rate of drinking. Some researchers prefer the phrase "episodic heavy drinking," in part because of the multiple and varied definitions for the word "binge" itself, which may refer to a bout of drinking lasting several days.

The National Institute on Alcohol **Abuse** and Alcoholism defines binge drinking as "a pattern of drinking alcohol that brings blood alcohol content to 0.08% or above." For men of average weight, this means five drinks in about two hours; for women, four drinks.

Description

Binge drinking begins with exposure to drinking and feeling the high that results. Abuse of alcohol begins with the desire to reach that state of feeling high again and again.

Binge drinking can take many forms, but its essence is drinking to get drunk. The factors involved in binge drinking are similar to those of drinking alcohol in the first place and can be characterized as social and psychological in nature. Binge drinkers report they engage in the practice for social reasons of status, to fit in with a drinking culture, and because of peer pressure. Others may drink as an escapist mechanism from **stress** or problems in life.

Risk factors and demographics

Both personality traits and genetics contribute to a susceptibility to abuse alcohol. Lonely, shy, or depressed people are at risk, as are those with hostile or self-destructive tendencies. Children of alcoholics are at higher risk of alcoholism themselves. This fact may result from both familial patterns and genetics alike.

The pattern of alcohol consumption known as binge drinking is most often associated with college students, with good reason. In a survey, 44% of U.S. college students reported the behavior in the last two weeks before the survey was taken, and half of these reports included three or more occasions in that time period. More than 50% of the men surveyed drank five or more drinks and 40% of the women drank at least four drinks in a row. Additional risk factors were residing in a sorority or fraternity and having engaged in binge drinking in high school.

Health consequences

A single episode of binge drinking can result in loss of coordination and impaired cognitive function and, at higher doses, loss of consciousness. At very high doses, death can occur, usually associated with severely slowed breathing. Passing out from alcohol often functions as a fail-safe, making it impossible to drink more and risking death. Thus, binge drinking is especially dangerous, because very high blood levels of alcohol can be achieved by drinking a lot in a short period of time.

Binge drinking may be a precursor to alcohol dependence. Frequent bouts of drinking can induce tolerance, which means more alcohol needs to be taken to achieve a particular level of intoxication. Physical dependence on alcohol occurs when the body doesn't function normally without alcohol, resulting in a withdrawal syndrome.

Drinking to intoxication also increases the likelihood of participating in other high-risk behaviors such as driving under the influence, engaging in unsafe sex, and other accidents that can accompany the poor muscular and physical control that occurs with drunkenness. Intoxication can also trigger aggression and violence. Thus, binge drinking increases the chance of physical injury, property damage, and run-ins with law enforcement officials. For pregnant women, binge drinking can directly harm the fetus.

Other unwanted effects are associated with the aftereffects of a bout of heavy drinking. Binge drinkers are more likely to miss school or work or be less productive in their workaday lives. They also may suffer the consequences of inappropriate interpersonal behavior, losing friends, and making enemies.

Prevention

Education is the primary method by which to curb binge drinking. Based on the incidence of binge drinking in college students, targeting that population is an obvious place to start. Colleges and universities have engaged in drinking awareness and prevention programs that may begin as early as freshman orientation.

Other modes of education are more general, in schools, workplaces, and the mainstream media. Healthcare providers and social service workers can dispense advice in meetings with patients and clients. For young people, evidence shows that parental influence and family values and mores are very powerful determinants of drinking behavior.

Another point of prevention is at the point of sale. Approaches that focus on places of drinking, bars and restaurants, have proved to have some effect. Changing atmospheric characteristics such as lighting and music can affect patron behavior including how much and how fast drinks are consumed. Wait staff can diminish the effects of drinking by attending to serving drinks at a slower rate, offering food or non-alcoholic drink alternatives, and finally refusing service to intoxicated customers and making sure drinkers don't drive.

KEY TERMS

Alcohol—An organic chemical and the active agent in beer, wine, and liquor; chemically known as ethanol.

Alcoholism—Chronic and compulsive use of alcohol that interferes with everyday life as with work and personal relationships.

Anxiolytic drug—A drug that decreases feelings of anxiety or panic.

Intoxication—The state that occurs with high doses of alcohol, characterized by loss of coordination and uninhibited behavior; drunkenness.

Physical dependence—An altered physiological state produced by repeated administration of a drug such that continued presence of the drug is required to prevent withdrawal.

Tolerance—The physical state produced when, with repeated dosing, a drug produces a smaller effect or a higher dose is requited to achieve the same effect.

Withdrawal—A syndrome of ill effects that occurs when administration of a dependence-producing drug ceases.

Diagnosis and treatment

If physical dependence on alcohol has occurred in a person who experiences binge drinking, medical treatment is warranted to manage the withdrawal syndrome. These include prescribing anxiolytic drugs (used to control symptoms of **anxiety**) and close supervision by a physician.

Short of physical dependence, counseling may be required to address the underlying reasons for abusing alcohol. The counseling may be directed by a physician or by one of many groups such as Alcoholics Anonymous that have a proven track record of helping those with drinking problems.

Resources

BOOKS

"Alcohol." *The Merck Manual of Diagnosis and Therapy, Professional Edition.* 18th ed. Ed. Mark H. Beers. Whitehouse Station, NJ: Merck & Co., 2005.

OTHER

"Binge Drinking." *ICAP Blue Book.* International Center for Alcohol Policies, 2005. <http://www.icap.org/portals/0/download/all_pdfs/blue_book/Module_06_Binge_Drinking.pdf>.

"Fact Sheet: Binge Drinking on College Campuses." *Alcohol Policies Project*. Center for Science in the Public Interest, 2000. <http://www.cspinet.org/booze/collfact1.htm>.

National Institute on Alcohol Abuse and Alcoholism. <http://www.niaaa.nih.gov>.

Jill U. Adams

Binge eating

Description

Binge eating is a form of overeating in which a person ingests a large amount of food during a discrete period of time (within one or two hours, for example) and experiences feelings of being out of control and unable to stop eating during the episode. In practice, the duration of a binge may vary greatly from one event to the next, making it difficult to define the number of binges occurring in a given day. Binge eating often occurs in the absence of hunger and is characterized by eating very rapidly; eating alone (due to embarrassment over the amount being eaten); and having strong negative feelings, such as guilt, shame and **depression**, following the binge. Typically, a binge episode ends only when all the desirable binge foods have been consumed or when the person feels too full to continue eating.

While binge eating is a symptom of **bulimia nervosa**, it differs from this disorder in that behaviors intended to get rid of the food (fasting, excessive exercise, or using laxatives or inducing vomiting to "purge" the food from the system) are present among those with bulimia, but are generally absent among binge eaters. Binge eating may also occur in **anorexia nervosa**.

The clinician's diagnostic handbook, the ***Diagnostic and Statistical Manual of Mental Disorders*** (fourth edition, text revised, published in 2000) subsumes binge eating under the **diagnosis** of eating disorders not otherwise specified. Binge eating disorder is, however, under consideration as a separate diagnostic category, pending further study.

Symptoms and treatments

Binge eating episodes may occur in response to strong negative emotions, such as depression or **anxiety**, or to less defined feelings of distress or tension. The act of bingeing seems to alleviate these uncomfortable feelings temporarily and binge eaters typically

A girl binge eating. *(Bubbles Photolibrary/Alamy)*

describe themselves as "numb" or "spaced out" while engaged in these behaviors. Some people report that binges are related to the ingestion of certain "trigger foods," usually carbohydrates, but regardless of the stimulus, the feeling of eating without being able to control one's intake is a frightening experience for most people. The aftermath of a binge often includes an overwhelming sense of self-disgust, depression and anxiety.

While people who binge eat are clearly at high risk for becoming overweight, there are important differences between simple **obesity** and binge eating. People who binge eat are far more likely to report significant mood problems, especially depression, and to report greater dissatisfaction with their weight and shape than are comparably obese persons. They are also more likely to describe themselves as experiencing personal problems and work difficulties and to be hypersensitive to the thoughts and opinions of others. Like people with bulimia nervosa, they also have an increased likelihood of being diagnosed with major depression, substance-related disorders, and **personality disorders**, yet the overall rates of recovery for binge eating disorders are actually more favorable than those obtained in bulimia.

Binge eating is not common among the general public, but it is prevalent among persons attending weight loss clinics, where as many as half of the participants may fit this description. Both males and females develop binge-eating problems, but the rate of occurrence is 1.5 times greater among women. Age of onset is usually adolescence through young adulthood and the course of the disorder is often marked by a long history of on-again, off-again dieting.

As is the case with other forms of eating disorders, identification of specific causes for binge eating has been difficult. Since many people report relief from painful or uncomfortable mental states while bingeing, the behavior offers short-term emotional relief, making it likely to be repeated. Some investigators have considered genetic influences and personality variables. Still others have suggested that the "culture of thinness" in western societies contributes to the tendency toward harsh self-evaluation characterizing binge-eaters who then turn to food for solace.

At present, the most effective treatment approach to reducing the incidence of binge eating appears to be **cognitive-behavioral therapy** (CBT). The goal of this therapy is the development of skills for effectively coping with emotional distress rather than seeking to numb or disguise troubling feelings. This therapy focuses on helping the affected individual to decrease the binge eating behavior by recognizing the connection between thoughts and behavior, and to change behavior by changing negative thinking patterns. Follow-up research has been very encouraging, documenting both a decrease in depressive symptoms and a corresponding likelihood of healthy weight loss as the individual achieves better control of eating behaviors.

Resources

BOOKS

American Psychiatric Association. *Diagnostic and Statistical Manual of Mental Disorders.* 4th edition, text revised. Washington, DC: American Psychiatric Association, 2000.

Bowers, Wayne A. "Eating Disorders." In *Cognitive-Behavioral Group Therapy,* edited by John R. White and Arthur S. Freeman. Washington, D.C.: American Psychological Association, 2000.

Striegel-Moore, Ruth H., and Linda Smolak, eds. *Eating Disorders: Innovative Directions in Research and Practice.* Washington DC: American Psychological Association, 2001.

Thompson, J. Kevin, and others. *Exacting Beauty: Theory, Assessment, and Treatment.* Washington, DC: American Psychological Association, 1999.

Tobin, David L. *Coping Strategies Therapy for Bulimia Nervosa.* Washington, D.C.: American Psychological Association, 2000.

Jane A. Fitzgerald, Ph.D.

Biofeedback

Definition

Biofeedback is a technique that uses monitoring instruments to measure and feed back information about muscle tension, heart rate, sweat responses, skin temperature, or **brain** activity.

Terms associated with biofeedback include applied psychophysiology or behavioral physiology. It is also viewed as a mind-body therapy method used in complementary and alternative medicine. Biofeedback is an important part of understanding the relationship between physical state and thoughts, feelings, and behaviors.

Purpose

The purpose of biofeedback is to enhance an individual's awareness of physical reactions to physical, emotional, or psychological **stress**, and their ability to influence their own physiological responses. The overall purpose is to develop self-regulation skills that play a role in improving health and well-being.

Biofeedback has been used as a part of a comprehensive treatment approach with a number of conditions, including **chronic pain**, irritable bowel syndrome (IBS), temporomandibular joint disorder (TMJ), Raynaud's syndrome, epilepsy, **attention deficit/hyperactivity disorder** (ADHD), **anxiety**, migraine headaches, **depression**, traumatic brain injury, and **sleep disorders**. There is some support for using biofeedback in the treatment of diabetes when self-monitoring of blood glucose levels is maintained and within the context of regular physician consultation and supervision.

Biofeedback has been a useful tool in helping individuals with urinary incontinence regain bladder control by controlling the muscles used in urination. Sensors are placed in the vaginal or anal canal to help individuals learn when the muscles are properly contracted. A recent study found that this type of biofeedback treatment was safe, effective, and well liked by women patients 55 years and older.

Conditions related to stress are also treated using biofeedback, such as certain types of headaches, high

Biofeedback training. A woman monitors the patient, who is connected with wires on his head to the equipment. *(Custom Medical Stock Photo, Inc. Reproduced by permission.)*

blood pressure, bruxism or teeth grinding, **post-traumatic stress disorder** (PTSD), eating disorders, **substance abuse**, and some **anxiety disorders**. In treatment of stress-related conditions, biofeedback is often used in combination with relaxation training. Sometimes, biofeedback is used to help individuals learn how to experience deeper relaxation, such as in childbirth education programs or general stress management. This is referred to as biofeedback-assisted relaxation training. Even for individuals who can achieve relaxation through other strategies such as **meditation** or relaxation, biofeedback can be a valuable added technique. Biofeedback offers special advantages, such as allowing the clinician to track closely the places where an individual tenses up and helps the individual learn what thoughts and feelings are associated with the tension.

Precautions

Biofeedback depends on the motivation and active participation of an individual. Thus, it may not be suitable for individuals with low motivation who are not willing to take a highly active role in treatment, such as those who have depression. Also, since biofeedback focuses on initiating behavioral changes, individuals inclined to examine their past to alleviate problems and symptoms may benefit more from other treatment types, such as **psychotherapy**. Individuals with cognitive impairment may be unable to remain engaged in the treatment, depending on their level of functioning. Also, individuals with a pacemaker or other implanted electrical devices should inform their health care professional before entering biofeedback training, as certain types of bio-

feedback sensors may interfere with the devices. Patients with specific pain symptoms in which the cause is unknown should have a thorough medical examination to rule out any serious underlying disease before starting biofeedback training. Biofeedback can be used in combination with conventional therapies; however, while it can be used in combination with conventional medical treatment for illnesses such as cancer and diabetes, it should not replace those treatments.

Research on the success of biofeedback in treating certain conditions is inconclusive or needs to be validated. Some research studies use a small number of participants, which makes it difficult to generalize the results to a larger population. Also, many conditions have different subtypes with a variety of psychological, social, and physical causes. This fact, combined with research design concerns, makes it difficult to compare research studies. For example, while most studies have reported positive outcomes in the treatment of alcohol **abuse** and dependence, problems with methods and statistical analyses have called study results into question. Also, its effectiveness in treating opiate abuse or dependence has not been consistently shown, as with its use in treating menopausal hot flashes, and there are limitations in studies relating to its use in cancer treatment. Continued research is needed to further evaluate and improve different biofeedback techniques for various conditions.

Description

According to the Association for Applied Psychophysiology and Biofeedback, the technique was developed in the early 1970s by psychologists and physicians. These techniques continue to be used by psychologists, physicians, nurses, and other health care professionals such as physical therapists. Prior to beginning any biofeedback training, individuals may need a comprehensive psychological, educational, and/or medical assessment. Biofeedback can be used in conjunction with nonmedical treatments, such as psychotherapy, **cognitive-behavioral therapy**, and behavioral treatment strategies.

How biofeedback works

Biofeedback utilizes electronic sensors, or electrodes, attached to various parts of the body to detect changes in physical responses. Signals then inform the individual of these changes by means of visual or auditory signals such as a light display or a series of beeps. While the individual views or listens to feedback, he or she begins to recognize thoughts, feelings, and mental images that influence his or her physical reactions. By monitoring this mind-body connection, the individual can use the same thoughts, feelings, and mental images as cues or reminders to become more relaxed, or to change heartbeat, brain wave patterns, body temperature, and other body functions. The individual uses trial-and-error to change the signals change in the desired direction. For example, individuals trying to control their blood pressure levels may see a light flash whenever the pressure drops below a certain level. They may then try to remember what their thoughts and feelings were at the moment and deliberately maintain them to keep the blood pressure level low.

Through training, the individual learns to control the targeted physical response and, over time, is able to recognize what is required to reduce problematic symptoms. Eventually, the external biofeedback becomes unnecessary as the individual learns to perceive internal physical responses and make the desired changes. The individual then has a powerful, portable, and self-administered treatment tool to deal with problematic symptoms.

Three stages of biofeedback training

- Awareness of the problematic physical response: Individuals may complete a psychophysiological stress profile (PSP) to identify how their bodies respond to a variety of stressors and determine their ability to overcome undesired physical reactions. This involves a period of rest, stress, and recovery. For example, various sensors are attached to various parts of the body, and a baseline measurement lasting from two to four minutes records physical responses. The individual then goes through a standard set of stressors (such as rapid math calculations or running in place) each lasting from two to four minutes. This is followed by another relaxation period to determine the length of the recovery period.
- Using signals from the biofeedback equipment to control physical responses: The individual is assisted in reaching certain goals related to managing a specific physical response.
- Transferring control from biofeedback equipment or the health care professional: Individuals learn to identify triggers that alert them to implement their new-found self-regulation skills.

Types of biofeedback equipment

- Electromyograph (EMG): Sensors (or electrodes) placed on the skin on pertinent parts of the body monitor electrical activity in muscles, specifically tension. This is the most frequently used biofeedback

method in the treatment of various neurologic disorders such as stroke, cerebral palsy, traumatic brain injury, and multiple sclerosis. In children and adolescents, EMG may be used to treat tension headaches, enuresis, and encopresis. In treating TMJ or bruxism, EMG sensors are placed on jaw muscles. Chronic stress is treated by monitoring muscle tension in various places on the body.

- Galvanic skin response (GSR): Sensors on the fingers monitor perspiration or sweating. This is also referred to as obtaining a skin conductance level (SCL). GSR may be used in the treatment of anxiety, fears or phobias, stress, and sleep problems.
- Temperature or thermal sensors: Sensors monitor body temperature and changes in blood flow. Changes in hand temperature, for example, can indicate relaxation when there is increased blood flow to the skin. Temperature biofeedback may be useful for treating migraine headache, Raynaud's disorder, and anxiety disorders.
- Heart rate sensors: A pulse monitor placed on the fingertip monitors pulse rate. Increases in heart rate are associated with emotional arousal, such as being angry or fearful. Decreases in heart rate are associated with relaxation.
- Capnometry (CAP): Respiratory sensors monitor oxygen intake and carbon dioxide output. This differentiates correct breathing from problematic breathing practices. Breath control training may be used to treat panic attacks, asthma, and a variety of stress-related conditions.
- Electroencephalographs (EEG) or neurofeedback: Sensors attached to the scalp monitor brain wave activity in different parts of the brain. It may be used to treat conditions with proven or suspected impact on brain wave patterns such as seizure disorders or epilepsy, ADHD, learning disabilities, migraine headaches, traumatic brain injury, and sleep disorders.

Biofeedback is geared toward whatever a person finds most appealing and understandable and provided in several formats such as auditory, visual, or multimedia. Audio feedback, that may take the form of changes in one and pitch, is useful because visual attention is not necessary. Visual feedback can be provided in various forms such as bar or line graphs on a computer screen. Initially, it was thought that—over time—computer signals could become boring or visually unappealing. In response to this, Barry Bittman developed Mindscope in 1992 that displays video scenes with realistic sounds on a high-definition television set connected to a computer. Physical responses detected by the biofeedback equipment control an engaging audiovisual environment of beautiful and realistic scenes. Clarity, perspective, motion, and sounds improve as the individual deepens their relaxation. For children and adolescents, this may be described as a "video game for the body." Visual displays for EMG biofeedback may include sports such as basketball, baseball, and golf, where the individual plays against the computer.

The setting in which biofeedback training takes place can vary. Sometimes the clinician, client, and equipment are in the same room. Sometimes the client may sit in comfortable seating in a semi-dark, quiet room while the clinician is in another room with the equipment. In this arrangement, the clinician and client may communicate using an intercom.

In some cases, children and adolescents may reach the desired level of control in three to five sessions. Depending on the condition, biofeedback training may require a series of sessions for several days or weeks. In general, it may take 10 or 15 sessions at the lower end to 40 or 50 sessions at the higher end.

Preparation

Biofeedback is most successful when individuals are motivated to learn. It is useful for people who have difficulty relaxing, even when they make efforts to do so. A receptive and open attitude, or "passive volition," is important for attaining desired responses rather than actively focusing attaining them. It is important that individuals are willing to practice regularly at home to apply the skill to everyday life. Establishing a foundation of trust and confidence in the health care professional is an important component of biofeedback training.

Before beginning biofeedback training, an initial consultation will be conducted to record medical history, treatment background, and biofeedback goals. The procedure will be explained to provide a clear understanding of how and why the training will be helpful. The individual may be shown the equipment and told where they will be placed and how they work.

Before electrodes are placed on the body, the skin surface must be adequately prepared by using alcohol preparation pads to remove oils, makeup, and dead skin cells that may interfere with the biofeedback signal. An electrode paste is then applied to the sensor, or a small adhesive pad is used to adhere the sensor to the skin. Heart rate, temperature, and GSR monitors may be placed on the fingertip with a Velcro or elastic band. With CAP, the tip of a small, flexible, plastic tube is positioned in the nostril using tape. An individual may be taught several forms of biofeedback

initially, then the training may be tailored to the individual's preference.

The biofeedback trainer must have technical skill, an understanding of basic anatomy and physiology, knowledge of various conditions, and familiarity with computer hardware and software. The American Psychological Association views biofeedback as a proficiency area, master's and doctoral level training programs are available through a variety of sources, and certification is available through the Biofeedback Certification Institute of America.

Aftercare

One or two follow-up sessions may be arranged two to four months after the initial set of appointments. In this way, long-term progress can be assessed, support can be provided, and adjustments can be made, if needed.

Risks

There are no known side effects with properly administered biofeedback. Problems may occur if biofeedback is used to treat certain conditions where the use of biofeedback is not advised.

Normal results

A normal result may be indicated by achieving the desired changes in muscle tension, heart rate, sweat activity, respiration rate, temperate change, and brainwave activity. Health care professionals may use various criteria or normal values that have been developed for some biofeedback equipment. These values indicate levels that can be expected from normal physiological functioning or relaxation. Importantly, an individual learns to control their physical reactions, which may lead to feelings of empowerment and confidence.

Abnormal results

Unusual results may arise from a number of factors, including poor sensor or electrode contact with the skin and interference from other electrical signals or "noise." Some equipment may react to room temperature conditions, especially when the room is very hot or very cold. Although inexpensive monitoring equipment is available, such as watches that monitor heartbeat and handheld GSR devices, their results may not be accurate.

See also Anxiety and anxiety disorders; Substance abuse and related disorders.

Resources

BOOKS

Culbert, Timothy P. "Biofeedback with Children and Adolescents." In *Innovative Psychotherapy Techniques in Child and Adolescent Therapy.*, edited by C. Schaefer. 2nd ed. New York: John Wiley and Sons, 1999.

Di Franco, Joyce T. "Biofeedback." In *Childbirth Education: Practice, Research and Theory*, edited by F. H. Nichols and S. S. Humenick. 2nd ed. Philadelphia: W.B. Saunders, 2000.

Schwartz, Mark S., and Associates. *Biofeedback: A Practitioner's Guide.* New York: Guilford, 1987.

Spencer, John W., and J. J. Jacobs. *Complementary/Alternative Medicine: An Evidence-Based Approach.* Baltimore: Mosby, 1999.

Stoyva, Johann M., and Thomas H. Budzynski. "Biofeedback Methods in the Treatment of Anxiety and Stress Disorders." In *Principles and Practice of Stress Management,* edited by P. M. Lehrer and R. L. Woolfolk. 2nd ed. New York: Guilford Press, 1993.

PERIODICALS

American Psychological Association. "HCFA will cover biofeedback for incontinence." *Monitor on Psychology* 31, no.11 (December 2000).

Burgio, Kathryn L., Julie L. Locher, Patricia S. Goode, M. Hardin, B. Joan McDowell, and Dorothy C. Dombrowski. "Behavioral vs. Drug Treatment for Urge Urinary Incontinence in Older Women: A Randomized Controlled Trial." *JAMA, The Journal of the American Medical Association* 280.23 (December 1998): 1995-2000.

ORGANIZATIONS

Association for Applied Psychotherapy and Biofeedback. 10200 W. 44th Avenue, Suite 304, Wheat Ridge, CO 80033-2840. Telephone: (303) 422-8436. <http://www.aapb.org>.

Biofeedback Certification Institute of America. 1022 W. 44th Avenue, Suite 310, Wheat Ridge, CO 80033. Telephone: (303) 420-2902. <http://www.bcia.org>.

Joneis Thomas, Ph.D.

Biperiden

Definition

Biperiden is classified as an antiparkinsonian agent. It is sold in the United States under the brand name of Akineton.

Purpose

Biperiden is used to treat a group of side effects (called parkinsonian side effects) that include tremors, difficulty walking, and slack muscle tone. These side effects may occur in patients who are taking antipsychotic medications used to treat mental disorders such as **schizophrenia**.

Description

Some medicines, called antipsychotic drugs, that are used to treat schizophrenia and other mental disorders can cause side effects that are similar to the symptoms of Parkinson's disease. The patient does not have Parkinson's disease, but he or she may experience shaking in muscles while at rest, difficulty with voluntary movements, and poor muscle tone. These symptoms are similar to the symptoms of Parkinson's disease.

One way to eliminate these undesirable side effects is to stop taking the antipsychotic medicine. Unfortunately, the symptoms of the original mental disorder usually come back, so in most cases simply stopping the antipsychotic medication is not a reasonable option. Some drugs such as biperiden that control the symptoms of Parkinson's disease also control the parkinsonian side effects of antipsychotic medicines.

Biperiden works by restoring the chemical balance between **dopamine** and acetylcholine, two neurotransmitter chemicals in the **brain**. Taking biperiden along with the antipsychotic medicine helps to control symptoms of the mental disorder, while reducing parkinsonian side effects. Biperiden is in the same family of drugs (commonly known as anticholinergic drugs) as **benztropine**, **amantadine**, and **trihexyphenidyl**.

Recommended dosage

Biperiden is available in 2-mg tablets. For the treatment of tremor, poor muscle tone, and similar parkinsonian side effects, the dose of biperiden is 2 mg orally one to three times daily. Parkinson-like side effects caused by antipsychotic drugs may come and go, so biperiden may not be needed on a regular basis. Biperiden may also be prescribed to prevent these side effects before they actually occur. This is called as prophylactic (preventative) therapy.

Precautions

Biperiden should never be used in children under age three. It should be used cautiously and with close physician supervision in older children and in the elderly. Biperiden, like all anticholinergic drugs, decreases sweating and the body's ability to cool itself. People who are unaccustomed to being outside in hot weather should take care to stay as cool as possible and drink extra fluids. People who are chronically ill, have a central nervous system disease, or who work outside during hot weather may need to avoid taking biperiden.

People who have the following medical problems may experience increased negative side effects when taking biperiden. Anyone with these problems should discuss their condition with their physician before starting the drug:

- glaucoma, especially closed-angle glaucoma
- intestinal obstruction
- prostate enlargement
- urinary bladder obstruction

Although rare, some patients experience euphoria while taking biperiden and may **abuse** it for this reason. Euphoria can occur at doses only two to four times the normal daily dose. Patients with a history of drug abuse should be observed carefully for biperiden abuse.

Side effects

Although biperiden helps control the side effects of antipsychotic drugs, it can produce side effects of its own. A person taking biperiden may have some of the following side effects, which may vary in intensity:

- dry mouth
- dry skin
- blurred vision
- nausea or vomiting
- constipation
- disorientation
- drowsiness
- irritability
- increased heart rate
- urinary retention

Dry mouth, if severe to the point of causing difficulty in speaking or swallowing, may be managed by dosage reduction or temporary discontinuation of the drug. Chewing sugarless gum or sucking on sugarless candy may also help to increase the flow of saliva. Some artificial saliva products may give temporary relief.

Men with prostate enlargement may be especially prone to urinary retention. Symptoms of this problem include having difficulty starting a urine flow and more difficulty passing urine than usual. This side effect may be severe and require discontinuation of the drug. Urinary retention may require catheterization. People who think they may be experiencing any side effects from this or any other medication should tell their physicians.

Patients who take an overdose of biperiden are treated with forced vomiting, removal of stomach contents and stomach washing, activated charcoal, and respiratory support if needed. They are also given physostigmine, an antidote for anticholinergic drug poisoning.

Interactions

When drugs such as biperiden are taken with **antidepressants** such as **amitriptyline**, **imipramine**, **trimipramine**, **desipramine**, **nortriptyline**, **protriptyline**, **amoxapine**, and **doxepin**, as well as with many antihistamines that also have anticholinergic properties, the effects of biperiden are usually intensified.

Drugs such as biperiden decrease the speed with which food moves through the stomach and intestines. Because of this, it is possible that the absorption of some drugs may be enhanced by biperiden. Patients receiving biperiden should be observed for unusual responses to other drugs they might be taking.

KEY TERMS

Acetylcholine—A naturally occurring chemical in the body that transmits nerve impulses from cell to cell. Generally, it has opposite effects from dopamine and norepinephrine; it causes blood vessels to dilate, lowers blood pressure, and slows the heartbeat. Central nervous system well-being is dependent on a balance among acetylcholine, dopamine, serotonin, and norepinephrine.

Anticholinergic—Related to the ability of a drug to block the nervous system chemical acetylcholine. When acetylcholine is blocked, patients often experience dry mouth and skin, increased heart rate, blurred vision, and difficulty in urinating. In severe cases, blocking acetylcholine may cloud thinking and cause delirium.

Catheterization—Placing a tube in the bladder so that it can be emptied of urine.

Dopamine—A chemical in brain tissue that serves to transmit nerve impulses (is a neurotransmitter) and helps to regulate movement and emotions.

Neurotransmitter—A chemical in the brain that transmits messages between neurons, or nerve cells.

Parkinsonian—Related to symptoms associated with Parkinson's disease, a nervous system disorder characterized by abnormal muscle movement of the tongue, face, and neck, inability to walk or move quickly, walking in a shuffling manner, restlessness, and/or tremors.

Resources

BOOKS

American Society of Health-System Pharmacists. *AHFS Drug Information 2002*. Bethesda: American Society of Health-System Pharmacists, 2002.

DeVane, C. Lindsay, Pharm.D. "Drug Therapy for Psychoses" In *Fundamentals of Monitoring Psychoactive Drug Therapy*. Baltimore: Williams and Wilkins, 1990.

Jack Raber, Pharm.D.

Biphetamine *see* **Amphetamines**

Bipolar disorder

Definition

Bipolar, or manic-depressive, disorder is a mood disorder that causes radical emotional changes and mood swings, from manic highs to depressive lows. The majority of bipolar individuals experience alternating episodes of mania (an elevated or euphoric mood or irritable state) and **depression**.

Description

In the United States alone, bipolar disorder afflicts an estimated 5% of the general population, or almost 15 million people. According to a 2006 study, bipolar disorder costs the U.S. workplace as much as $14 billion a year, lost to the average 65.5 workdays each worker with bipolar disorder missed annually. The average age of onset of bipolar disorder is from adolescence through the early twenties. However, because of the complexity of the disorder, a correct **diagnosis** can be delayed for several years or more. There also has been a new recognition of new-onset bipolar disorder in later life, which occurs among the elderly at rates of about 1% and appears to be more prevalent among elderly men than elderly women.

The Diagnostic and Statistical Manual of Mental Disorders, fourth edition text revised (*DSM-IV-TR*), the diagnostic standard for mental health professionals in the United States, defines four separate categories of bipolar disorder: bipolar I, bipolar II, cyclothymia, and bipolar not otherwise specified (NOS).

Bipolar I disorder is characterized by manic episodes, the "high" of the manic-depressive cycle. A bipolar patient experiencing mania often has feelings of self-importance, elation, talkativeness, increased sociability, and a desire to embark on goal-oriented activities, coupled with the characteristics of irritability, impatience, impulsiveness, hyperactivity, and a decreased need for sleep. Usually this manic period is followed by a period of depression, although a few bipolar I individuals may not experience a major depressive episode. Mixed states, in which both manic or hypomanic symptoms and depressive symptoms occur at the same time, also frequently occur with bipolar I patients (for example, depression with the racing thoughts of mania). In addition, dysphoric mania (mania characterized by anger and irritability) is common.

Bipolar II disorder is characterized by major depressive episodes alternating with episodes of **hypomania**, a milder form of mania. Bipolar depression may be difficult to distinguish from unipolar depression (depression without mania, as found in **major depressive disorder**). Patients with bipolar depression tend to have extremely low energy, retarded mental and physical processes, and more profound **fatigue** (for example, hypersomnia—a sleep disorder marked by a need for excessive sleep or sleepiness when awake) than people with unipolar depression.

Cyclothymia refers to the cycling of hypomanic episodes with depression that does not reach major depressive proportions. One-third of patients with cyclothymia will develop bipolar I or II disorder later in life.

A phenomenon known as rapid cycling occurs in up to 20% of bipolar I and II patients. In rapid cycling, manic and depressive episodes must alternate frequently—at least four times in twelve months—to meet the diagnostic definition. In some cases of "ultra-rapid cycling," the patient may bounce between manic and depressive states several times within a 24-hour period. This condition is very hard to distinguish from mixed states.

Bipolar NOS is a category for bipolar states that do not clearly fit into the bipolar I, II, or cyclothymia diagnoses.

Causes and symptoms

Causes

The root causes of bipolar disorder have not been clearly defined, but studies suggest a strong heritable component. The most recent research has identified areas on four different chromosomes (6, 13, 18, and 22) that may carry genes whose protein products confer susceptibility to bipolar disorder. A study from 2006 suggests that inclusion of symptoms of common comorbidities of bipolar disorder and a measurement of social functioning might help researchers pinpoint more closely the genes involved in the development of these disorders.

Studies of the underlying genetics of bipolar disorders also have closely focused on genes related to the regulation of **dopamine**, a neurotransmitter (nerve-signaling molecule) that is involved generally in mood disorders. Recent studies examining the genes expressed in dopamine neurons (nerve cells) in different parts of the **brain** have shown that the parts of the brain known to be involved in mood disorders such as bipolar disorder exhibit different patterns of gene expression from other neurons. The area of the brain most closely associated with dopamine's involvement in bipolar disorders is the ventral tegmental area, which plays a role in the brain's dopamine-based reward system and in regulation of addictive or emotional behaviors.

Symptoms

Symptoms of bipolar depressive episodes include low energy levels, feelings of despair, difficulty con-

centrating, extreme fatigue, and psychomotor retardation (slowed mental and physical capabilities). Manic episodes are characterized by feelings of euphoria, lack of inhibitions, racing thoughts, diminished need for sleep, talkativeness, risk taking, and irritability. In extreme cases, mania can induce **hallucinations** and other psychotic symptoms such as grandiose **delusions** (ideas that the person affected is extremely important or has some unrecognized talent or insight).

Comorbidities

A large percentage of people diagnosed with bipolar disorder also experience comorbidities, with one study finding that 67% of patients with bipolar disorder had a comorbidity and 76% who had bipolar II disorder also had a comorbidity. Overall, 65% of all bipolar patients will have a comorbidity, including **anxiety disorders**, **attention deficit/hyperactivity disorder**, and substance and alcohol **abuse**. Suicidal ideation (thinking seriously about attempting **suicide**) and suicide are relatively common. The type of comorbidity can vary based on sex; women are more likely to have an eating disorder comorbidity or **post-traumatic stress disorder** (PTSD) as a comorbidity.

Demographics

The disorder is more common among women than men. Women have been observed at increased risk of developing subsequent episodes in the period immediately following childbirth, the postpartum period. The average age at onset in a recent large study was the same for men and women: 17.2 years. Men with bipolar disorder are more likely than women to have a history of violence and to have experienced legal problems, and women are more likely than men to have made a suicide attempt. In the survey of U.S. workers from 2006, twice as many women as men met the criteria for bipolar disorder, but there were no distinctions based on ethnicity.

Diagnosis

Bipolar disorder is usually diagnosed and treated by a **psychiatrist** and/or a **psychologist** with medical assistance. In addition to an interview, several clinical inventories or scales may be used to assess the patient's mental status and determine the presence of bipolar symptoms. These include the Millon Clinical Multiaxial Inventory III (MCMI-III), **Minnesota Multiphasic Personality Inventory** II (MMPI-2), the Internal State Scale (ISS), the Self-Report Manic Inventory (SRMI), and the Young Mania Rating Scale (YMRS). The tests are verbal and/or written and are administered in both hospital and outpatient settings.

Psychologists and psychiatrists typically use the criteria listed in the *DSM-IV-TR* as a guideline for diagnosis of bipolar disorder and other mental illnesses. The *DSM-IV-TR* describes a **manic episode** as an abnormally elevated or irritable mood lasting a period of at least one week that is distinguished by at least three of the mania symptoms: inflated self-esteem, decreased need for sleep, talkativeness, racing thoughts, distractibility, increase in goal-directed activity, or excessive involvement in pleasurable activities that have a high potential for painful consequences. If the mood of the patient is irritable and not elevated, four of the symptoms are required.

Although many clinicians find the criteria too rigid, a hypomanic diagnosis requires a duration of at least four days with at least three of the symptoms indicated for manic episodes (four if mood is irritable and not elevated). *DSM-IV-TR* notes that, unlike manic episodes, hypomanic episodes do not cause a marked impairment in social or occupational functioning, do not require **hospitalization**, and do not have psychotic features (no delusions or hallucinations). In addition, because hypomanic episodes are characterized by high energy and goal-directed activities and often result in a positive outcome, or are perceived in a positive manner by the patient, bipolar II disorder can go undiagnosed.

Bipolar symptoms often manifest differently in children and adolescents than they appear in adults. Manic episodes in these age groups are typically characterized by more psychotic features than in adults, which may lead to a misdiagnosis of **schizophrenia**. Children and adolescents also tend toward irritability and aggressiveness instead of elation. Further, symptoms tend to be chronic, or ongoing, rather than acute, or episodic. Bipolar children are easily distracted, impulsive, and hyperactive, which can lead to a misdiagnosis of ADHD. Furthermore, their aggression often leads to violence, which may be misdiagnosed as a **conduct disorder**.

Substance abuse, thyroid disease, and use of prescription or over-the-counter medication can mask or mimic the presence of bipolar disorder. In cases of substance abuse, the patient must ordinarily undergo a period of **detoxification** and abstinence before a mood disorder is diagnosed and treatment begins.

Treatments

Bipolar disorder is usually treated with both medical and psychosocial interventions. Psychosocial therapies address both psychological and social issues.

Medical interventions

A combination of mood-stabilizing agents with **antidepressants**, antipsychotics, and anticonvulsants is used to regulate manic and depressive episodes.

MOOD-STABILIZING AGENTS. Mood-stabilizing agents such as lithium, **carbamazepine**, and **valproic acid** (valproate) are prescribed to regulate the manic highs and lows of bipolar disorder:

- Lithium (lithium carbonate, Cibalith-S, Eskalith, Lithane, Lithobid, Lithonate, Lithotabs) is one of the oldest and most frequently prescribed drugs available for the treatment of bipolar mania and depression. Because the drug takes four to ten days to reach a therapeutic level in the bloodstream, it is sometimes prescribed in conjunction with neuroleptics (other psychiatric drugs) and/or benzodiazepines (medications that ease tension by slowing down the central nervous system) to provide more immediate relief of a manic episode. Lithium has also been shown to be effective in regulating bipolar depression, but it is not recommended for mixed mania. Lithium may not be an effective long-term treatment option for rapid cyclers, who typically develop a tolerance for it or may not respond to it. Possible side effects of the drug include weight gain, thirst, nausea, and hand tremors. Prolonged lithium use may also cause hyperthyroidism (a disease of the thyroid marked by heart palpitations, nervousness, the presence of goiter, sweating, and a wide array of other symptoms).

- Carbamazepine (Tegretol, Atretol) is an anticonvulsant drug (a drug to treat seizures) usually prescribed in conjunction with other mood-stabilizing agents. The drug is often used to treat bipolar patients who have not responded well to lithium therapy. Blurred vision and abnormal eye movement are two possible side effects of carbamazepine therapy. It may also result in a reduction in red blood cells (anemia), which if left untreated can be life threatening (as in aplastic anemia). Signs to watch for and report immediately to a doctor include easy bruising, tiny purple dots or spots on the skin, or mouth sores.

- Valproic acid (divalproex sodium, or Depakote; valproate, or Depakene) is one of the few drugs available that has been proven effective in treating rapid cycling bipolar and mixed-states patients. Valproate is prescribed alone or in combination with carbamazepine and/or lithium. Stomach cramps, indigestion, diarrhea, hair loss, appetite loss, nausea, and unusual weight loss or gain are some of the common side effects of valproate. This drug can cause severe damage to the liver and pancreas, with the greatest risk of liver damage in children under age two years and in people taking two or more medications to prevent seizures or people with certain metabolic disorders. Warning signs that warrant an immediate call to the doctor include severe fatigue, nausea, vomiting, facial swelling, or loss of appetite.

ANTIDEPRESSANTS. Although mania receives more attention, the reality is that people with bipolar disorder spend more time in depressive episodes, making antidepressant treatment seem like a logical choice. However, research indicates that antidepressants, including **selective serotonin reuptake inhibitors (SSRIs)** and tricyclic antidepressants, may stimulate manic episodes in some bipolar patients. Tricyclic antidepressants used to treat unipolar depression may trigger rapid cycling in bipolar patients and are, therefore, not a preferred treatment option for bipolar depression. Antidepressants that may be used to treat bipolar depression include:

- SSRIs, such as fluoxetine (Prozac), sertraline (Zoloft), and paroxetine (Paxil), regulate depression by regulating levels of serotonin, a neurotransmitter. Anxiety, diarrhea, drowsiness, headache, sweating, nausea, sexual problems, and insomnia are all possible side effects of SSRIs.

- Monoamine oxidase inhibitors (also called MAOIs), such as tranylcypromine (Parnate) and phenelzine (Nardil), block the action of monoamine oxidase (MAO), an enzyme in the central nervous system. Patients taking certain kinds of MAOIs must cut foods high in tyramine (found in aged cheeses and meats) out of their diets, although use of a newer, more selective form of MAOI, selegiline, delivered via a low-dose transdermal patch, does not generally require dietary adjustment.

- Bupropion (Wellbutrin) is a heterocyclic antidepressant. The exact neurochemical mechanism of the drug is not known, but it has been effective in regulating bipolar depression in some patients. Side effects of bupropion include agitation, anxiety, confusion, tremor, dry mouth, fast or irregular heartbeat, headache, and insomnia. It now comes with a warning about its use in teenagers and children because some research indicates an increased risk of suicidal ideation and suicide attempts in young people taking this type of antidepressant. Its use in people under age 18 is not recommended.

- Lamotrigine is an antiepileptic that has shown some promise in treating bipolar I depression. Its dosage will vary based on whether or not the person is also taking other drugs, such as valproic acid. This drug is associated with a rare incidence of the development of a serious rash, and the risk of the rash increases if the person is also taking valproic acid. Children are more susceptible to this adverse, possibly life-threatening rash. Women who are pregnant should discuss carefully with their doctor whether or not to use lamotrigine. Studies have shown that fetal exposure in the first trimester of pregnancy increases the chances of cleft lip or cleft palate.

ADJUNCT TREATMENTS. These adjunct treatments are used in conjunction with a long-term pharmaceutical treatment plan:

- Long-acting benzodiazepines (medications that ease tension by slowing the central nervous system) such as clonazepam (Klonapin) and alprazolam (Xanax) are used for rapid treatment of manic symptoms to calm and sedate patients until mania or hypomania have waned and mood-stabilizing agents can take effect. Sedation is a common effect, and clumsiness, lightheadedness, and slurred speech are other possible side effects of benzodiazepines.

- Neuroleptics (antipsychotic medications) such as chlorpromazine (Thorazine) and haloperidol (Haldol) are also used to control mania while a mood stabilizer such as lithium or valproate takes effect. Because neuroleptic side effects can be severe (difficulty in speaking or swallowing, paralysis of the eyes, loss of balance control, muscle spasms, severe restlessness, stiffness of arms and legs, tremors in fingers and hands, twisting movements of body, and weakness of arms and legs), benzodiazepines are generally preferred over neuroleptics.

- Electroconvulsive therapy (ECT) has a high success rate for treating both unipolar and bipolar depression, and mania. However, because of the convenience of drug treatment and the stigma sometimes attached to ECT therapy, ECT is usually employed after all pharmaceutical treatment options have been explored. ECT is given under anesthesia and patients are given a muscle relaxant medication to prevent convulsions. The treatment consists of a series of electrical pulses that move into the brain through electrodes on the patient's head. Although the exact mechanisms behind the success of ECT therapy are not known, it is believed that this electrical current alters the electrochemical processes of the brain, consequently relieving depression. Headaches, muscle soreness, nausea, and confusion are possible side effects immediately following an ECT procedure. Temporary memory loss has also been reported in ECT patients. In bipolar patients, ECT is often used in conjunction with drug therapy.

- Calcium channel blockers (nimodipine, or Nimotop), typically used to treat angina and hypotension (low blood pressure), have been found effective, in a few small studies, for treating rapid cyclers. Calcium channel blockers stop the excess calcium buildup in cells that is thought to be a cause of bipolar disorder. They are usually used in conjunction with other drug therapies such as carbamazepine or lithium.

Clozapine (Clozaril) is an antipsychotic medication used to control manic episodes in patients who have not responded to typical mood-stabilizing agents. The drug has also been a useful prophylactic, or preventative treatment, in some bipolar patients. Common side effects of clozapine include tachycardia (rapid heart rate), hypotension, constipation, and weight gain. Agranulocytosis, a potentially serious but reversible condition in which the white blood cells that typically fight infection in the body are destroyed, is a possible side effect of clozapine. Patients treated with the drug should undergo weekly blood tests to monitor white blood cell counts.

Risperidone (Risperdal) is an antipsychotic medication that has been successful in controlling mania. The side effects of risperidone are mild compared to many other antipsychotics (constipation, coughing, diarrhea, dry mouth, headache, heartburn, increased length of sleep and dream activity, nausea, runny nose, sore throat, fatigue, and weight gain). However, because of a risk of death in older people with **dementia** who take antipsychotics, risperidone is not approved by the FDA for treatment of behavioral disorders in older adults with dementia.

Repeated **transcranial magnetic stimulation (rTMS)** is a newer treatment for the depressive phase of bipolar disorder. In rTMS, a large magnet is placed on the patient's head and magnetic fields of different frequency are generated to stimulate the left front cortex of the brain. Unlike ECT, rTMS requires no anesthesia and does not induce seizures.

Psychosocial interventions

Because bipolar disorder is thought to be biological in nature, psychological therapy is recommended as a companion to, but not a substitute for, pharmaceutical treatment of the disease. **Psychotherapy**, such as **cognitive-behavioral therapy**, can be a useful tool in helping patients and their families adjust to the disorder, in encouraging **compliance** to a medication regimen, and in reducing the risk of suicide. Also, educative counseling is recommended for the patient and family.

In educative counseling, patients (and their families) learn of the high rates of social dysfunction and marital discord associated with this disorder. Patients also learn how their treatment will progress, which factors can affect treatment, and what kind of follow-up after treatment will be implemented. Genetic counseling should be a part of **family education** programs because this disorder is more prevalent among first-degree relatives of individuals with the disorder.

Social support for individuals with bipolar disorder is also important. Some people with the disorder, as well as their families, may find **support groups** helpful.

Alternative treatment

General recommendations include maintaining a calm environment, avoiding over-stimulation, getting plenty of rest, exercising regularly, and maintaining a proper diet. Some Chinese herbs may soften mood swings, but care must be taken (and good communication with the physician is essential) when combining herbal therapies with medications. **Biofeedback** is effective in helping some patients control symptoms such as irritability, poor self-control, racing thoughts, and sleep problems.

Prognosis

While most patients will show some positive response to treatment, response varies widely, from full recovery to complete unresponsiveness to all drugs and/or ECT therapy. Drug therapies frequently need adjustment to achieve the maximum benefit for the patient. Bipolar disorder is a chronic recurrent illness in over 90% of those afflicted, and one that requires lifelong observation and treatment after diagnosis. Patients with untreated or inadequately treated bipolar disorder have a suicide rate of 15–25% and a nine-year decrease in life expectancy. With proper treatment, the life expectancy of the bipolar patient increases by nearly seven years and work productivity increases by ten years.

Prevention

The ongoing medical management of bipolar disorder is critical to preventing **relapse** (recurrence) of manic episodes. Even in carefully controlled treatment programs, bipolar patients may experience recurring episodes of the disorder. Patient education in the form of psychotherapy or **self-help groups** is crucial for training bipolar patients to recognize signs of mania and depression and to take an active part in their treatment program.

KEY TERMS

Anticonvulsant medication—A medication that prevents convulsions or seizures; often prescribed in the treatment of epilepsy. Several anticonvulsant medications have been found effective in the treatment of bipolar disorder.

Antipsychotic medication—A medication used to treat psychotic symptoms of schizophrenia such as hallucinations, delusions, and delirium. May be used to treat symptoms in other disorders as well.

Benzodiazepines—A group of central nervous system depressants used to relieve anxiety or to induce sleep.

ECT—Electroconvulsive therapy is sometimes used to treat depression or mania when pharmaceutical treatment fails.

Hypomania—A milder form of mania that is characteristic of bipolar II disorder.

Mania—An elevated or euphoric mood or irritable state that is characteristic of bipolar I disorder. This state is characterized by mental and physical hyperactivity, disorganization of behavior, and inappropriate elevation of mood.

Mixed mania/mixed state—A mental state in which symptoms of both depression and mania occur simultaneously.

Neurotransmitter—A chemical in the brain that transmits messages between neurons, or nerve cells. Changes in the levels of certain neurotransmitters, such as serotonin, norepinephrine, and dopamine, are thought to be related to bipolar disorder.

Psychomotor retardation—Slowed mental and physical processes characteristic of a bipolar depressive episode.

Resources

BOOKS

American Psychiatric Association. *Diagnostic and Statistical Manual of Mental Disorders.* 4th ed., Text rev. Washington, D.C.: American Psychiatric Association, 2000.

Maxmen, Jerrold S., and Nicholas G. Ward. "Mood Disorders." In *Essential Psychopathology and Its Treatment.* 2nd ed. New York: W. W. Norton, 1995.

Tasman, Allan, Jerald Kay, MD, and Jeffrey A. Lieberman, MD, eds. *Psychiatry,* 1st ed. Philadelphia: W. B. Saunders, 1997.

Whybrow, Peter C. *A Mood Apart.* New York: Harper Collins, 1997.

PERIODICALS

Greene, James G. "Gene Expression Profiles of Brain Dopamine Neurons and Relevance to Neuropsychatric Disease." *Journal of Physiology* 575 (2006): 411–16.

Hoblyn, Jennifer. "Bipolar Disorder in Later Life." *Geriatrics* 59 (2004): 41–44.

Keck, P., S. McElroy, and L. Arnold. "Advances in the Pathophysiology and Treatment of Psychiatric Disorders: Implications for Internal Medicine." *Medical clinics of North America* 85.3 (2001).

Kilzieh, N., and H. Akiskal. "Rapid-cycling Bipolar Disorder: An Overview of Research and Clinical Experience." *Psychiatric Clinics of North America* 22.3 (1999).

Nierenberg, Andrew A., and others "Systematic Treatment Enhancement Program for Bipolar Disorder (STEP-BD): A Clinical View." *Journal of Clinical Psychiatry* 67.11 (2006).

Schulze, Thomas G., and others. "What Is Familial about Familial Bipolar Disorder?" *Archives of General Psychiatry* 63 (2006): 1368–76.

ORGANIZATIONS

American Psychiatric Association. 1400 K Street NW, Washington, DC 20005. Telephone: (888) 357-7924. <http://www.psych.org>.

Child and Adolescent Bipolar Foundation. 1000 Skokie Boulevard, Suite 570, Wilmette, IL 60091. E-mail: cabf@bpkids.org. <http://www.bpkids.org/site/PageServer>.

Depression and Bipolar Support Alliance. 730 N. Franklin Street, Suite 501, Chicago, IL 60610-7224. Telephone: (800) 826-3632. Fax: (312) 642-7243. <http://www.dbsalliance .org/site/PageServer?pagename = home>.

National Alliance for the Mentally Ill (NAMI). Colonial Place Three, 2107 Wilson Boulevard, Suite 300, Arlington, VA 22201-3042. Telephone: (800) 950-6264. <http://www.nami.org>.

National Depressive and Manic-Depressive Association (NDMDA). 730 N. Franklin St., Suite 501, Chicago, IL 60610. Telephone: (800) 826-3632. <http://www.ndmda. org>.

National Institute of Mental Health, Mental Health Public Inquiries. 5600 Fishers Lane, Room 15C-05, Rockville, MD 20857. Telephone: (888) 826-9438. <http://www. nimh.nih.gov>.

OTHER

"Bipolar Disorder." National Library of Medicine, National Institutes of Health. <http://www.nlm.nih.gov/medlineplus/bipolardisorder.html>.

"Bupropion." National Library of Medicine, National Institutes of Health. <http://www.nlm.nih.gov/medlineplus/druginfo/medmaster/a695033.html>.

"Drug Information: Carbamazepine." National Library of Medicine, National Institutes of Health. <http://www.nlm.nih.gov/medlineplus/print/druginfo/medmaster/a682237.html>.

"Lamotrigine." National Library of Medicine, National Institutes of Health. <http://www.nlm.nih.gov/medlineplus/druginfo/medmaster/a695007.html>.

"Patient Information Sheet: Lamotrigine (marketed as Lamictal)." U.S. Food and Drug Administration. <http://www.fda.gov/cder/drug/InfoSheets/patient/lamotriginePIS.htm>.

"Patient Information Sheet: Risperidone Tablets (marketed as Risperdal)." U.S. Food and Drug Administration. <http://www.fda.gov/cder/drug/InfoSheets/patient/risperidonePIS.htm>.

"Risperidone." National Library of Medicine, National Institutes of Health. <http://www.nlm.nih.gov/medlineplus/druginfo/medmaster/a694015.html>.

"Valproic Acid." National Library of Medicine, National Institutes of Health. <http://www.nlm.nih.gov/medlineplus/druginfo/medmaster/a682412.html>.

Paula Anne Ford-Martin, MA
Laith Farid Gulli, MD
Nicole Mallory, MS, PA-C
Emily Jane Willingham, PhD

A teenage girl cries over a pimple. In body dysmorphic disorder, excessive preoccupation with minor or imagined faults can cause a marked decline in a patient's day to day life. *(mediacolor's/Alamy)*

Body dysmorphic disorder

Definition

Body dysmorphic disorder (BDD) is defined by the *Diagnostic and Statistical Manual of Mental Disorders (DSM-IV-TR)* (a handbook for mental health professionals) as a condition marked by excessive preoccupation with an imaginary or minor defect in a facial feature or localized part of the body. The diagnostic criteria specify that the condition must be sufficiently severe to cause a decline in the patient's social, occupational, or educational functioning. The most common cause of this decline is the time lost to obsessing about the "defect." The *DSM-IV-TR* assigns BDD to the larger category of somatoform disorders, which are disorders characterized by physical complaints that appear to be medical in origin but that cannot be explained in terms of a physical disease, the results of **substance abuse**, or by another mental disorder.

Although cases of BDD have been reported in the psychiatric literature from a number of different countries for over a century, the disorder was first defined as a formal diagnostic category by the *DSM-III-R* in 1987. The word "dysmorphic" comes from two Greek words, *dys*, which means "bad," or "ugly;" and, *morphos,* that means "shape," or "form." BDD was previously known as dysmorphophobia.

Description

BDD is characterized by an unusually exaggerated degree of worry or concern about a specific part of the face or body, rather than the general size or shape of the body. It is distinguished from **anorexia nervosa** and **bulimia nervosa** because patients with these disorders are preoccupied with their overall weight and body shape. For example, an adolescent who obsesses that her breasts are too large and wants to have plastic surgery to reduce their size but is otherwise unconcerned about her weight and is eating normally might be diagnosed with BDD, but not with anorexia or bulimia. Studies have found that between 40% and 76% of people with BDD seek out nonpsychiatric treatments such as cosmetic surgery or dermatological treatments, and the rates of people with BDD among all cosmetic surgery patients range from 7% to 15%; rates are similar in dermatological practices.

Since the first publication of *DSM-IV* in 1994, some psychiatrists have suggested that a subtype of BDD exists, which they term muscle dysmorphia. Muscle dysmorphia is marked by excessive concern with one's muscularity and/or fitness. Persons with muscle dysmorphia spend unusual amounts of time working out in gyms or exercising rather than obsessing about a feature such as the skin or nose. Muscle dysmorphia is more prevalent among males. To accommodate muscle dysmorphia as a classification, the *DSM-IV-TR* has added references regarding body build and excessive weightlifting to DSM-IV's description of BDD.

BDD and muscle dysmorphia can both be described as disorders resulting from the patient's distorted body image. Body image refers to the mental picture individuals have of their outward appearance, including size, shape, and form. It has two major components: how the people perceive their physical appearance, and how they feel about their body. Significant distortions in self-perception can lead to intense dissatisfaction with one's body and dysfunctional behaviors aimed at improving one's appearance. Some patients with BDD are aware that their concerns are excessive; others do not have this degree of insight. About 50% of patients diagnosed with BDD also meet the criteria for a **delusional disorder**, which is characterized by beliefs that are not based in reality.

The usual age of onset of BDD is adolescence; the average age of patients diagnosed with the disorder is 17.

BDD has a high rate of comorbidity, which means that people diagnosed with the disorder are highly likely to have been diagnosed with another psychiatric disorder, most commonly major **depression**, **social phobia**, or **obsessive-compulsive disorder** (OCD).

Causes and symptoms

Causes

The causes of BDD fall into two major categories, neurobiological and psychosocial.

NEUROBIOLOGICAL CAUSES. Research indicates that patients diagnosed with BDD have serotonin levels that are lower than normal. Serotonin is a neurotransmitter—a chemical produced by the **brain** that helps to transmit nerve impulses across the junctions between nerve cells. Low serotonin levels are associated with depression and other mood disorders.

PSYCHOSOCIAL CAUSES. A young person's family of origin has a powerful influence on his or her vulnerability to BDD. Children whose parents are themselves obsessed with appearance, dieting, and/or bodybuilding, or who are highly critical of their children's looks, are at greater risk of developing BDD.

An additional factor in some young people is a history of childhood trauma or abuse. Buried feelings about the abuse or traumatic incident emerge in the form of **obsession** about a part of the face or body. This "reassignment" of emotions from the unacknowledged true cause to another issue is called displacement. For example, an adolescent who frequently felt overwhelmed in childhood by physically abusive parents may develop a preoccupation at the high school level with muscular strength and power.

Another important factor in the development of BDD is the influence of the mass media in developed countries, particularly the role of advertising in spreading images of physically "perfect" men and women. Impressionable children and adolescents absorb the message that anything short of physical perfection is unacceptable. They may then develop distorted perceptions of their own faces and bodies.

Symptoms

The central symptom of BDD is excessive concern with a specific facial feature or body part. The parts of the body most frequently involved are the skin, hair, nose, teeth, breasts, eyes, and even eyebrows, but any feature can be a focus of the obsession.

Other symptoms of body dysmorphic disorder include:

- Ritualistic behavior. Ritualistic behavior refers to actions that the patient performs to manage anxiety and that take up excessive amounts of his or her time. Patients are typically upset if someone or something interferes with or interrupts their ritual. In the context of BDD, ritualistic behaviors may include exercise or makeup routines, assuming specific poses or postures in front of a mirror, or skinpicking.
- Camouflaging the "problem" feature or body part with makeup, hats, or clothing. Camouflaging appears to be the single most common symptom among patients with BDD, occurring in 94%.
- Abnormal behavior around mirrors, car bumpers, large windows, or similar reflecting surfaces. A majority of patients diagnosed with BDD frequently check their appearance in mirrors or spend long periods of time doing so. A minority, however, react in the opposite fashion and avoid mirrors whenever possible.
- Frequent requests for reassurance from others about their appearance.
- Frequently comparing one's appearance to others.
- Avoiding activities outside the home, including school and social events.

BDD patients have high rates of self-destructive behavior, including performing surgery on themselves at home (liposuction followed by skin stapling, sawing down teeth, and removing facial scars with sandpaper) and attempted or completed **suicide**. Many are unable to remain in school, form healthy relationships, or keep steady jobs. In one group of 100 patients diagnosed with BDD, 48% had been hospitalized for psychiatric reasons, and 30% had made at least one suicide attempt.

The loss of functioning resulting from BDD can have serious consequences for the patient's future.

Adolescents with BDD often cut school and may be reluctant to participate in sports, join church- or civic-sponsored youth groups, or hold part-time or summer jobs. One study found that 32% of participants had missed work for at least a week in the previous month because of their BDD, while 32% of those still in school had missed classes for a week. Adults with muscle dysmorphia have been known to turn down job promotions to have more time to work out in their gym or fitness center. The economic consequences of BDD also include overspending on cosmetics, clothing, or plastic surgery.

Demographics

As mentioned earlier, BDD is primarily a disorder of young people. Its true incidence in the general population is unknown; however, among the nonclinical, general population, the rate is between 0.7% and 1.1%, and in the narrower student general population, rates range between 2% and 13%. Among psychiatric patients, rates are around 13%. The *DSM-IV-TR* gives a range of 5–40% for patients in clinical mental health settings diagnosed with anxiety or **depressive disorders** to be diagnosed with BDD. There have not been significant interactions between ethnicity and gender identified in the few studies examining these factors and BDD. At least one study has found that there appears to be a heritable aspect to BDD, with a higher rate among families of people who have the disorder than among the general population.

Diagnosis

The **diagnosis** of BDD in children and adolescents is often made by physicians in family practice because they are more likely to have developed long-term relationships of trust with the young people. With adults, it is often specialists in dermatology, cosmetic dentistry, or plastic surgery who may suspect that the patient has BDD because of frequent requests for repeated or unnecessary procedures. The diagnosis is made on the basis of the patient's history together with the physician's observations of the patient's overall mood and conversation patterns. People with BDD often come across to others as generally anxious and worried. In addition, the patient's dress or clothing styles, attempting to hide the "problem" feature, may suggest a diagnosis of BDD.

Several questionnaires are used for assessing the presence of BDD. Researchers sometimes use a semi-structured interview called the BDD Data Form to collect information about the disorder from patients. This form includes demographic information, information about body areas of concern and the history

and course of the illness, and the patient's history of **hospitalization** or suicide attempts, if any. Another diagnostic questionnaire frequently used to identify BDD patients is the Structured Clinical Interview for DSM-III-R Disorders, or SCID-II. Other questionnaires also used in assessments are the Yale-Brown Obsessive Compulsive Scale Modified for Body Dysmorphic Disorder and the Body Dysmorphic Disorder Examination.

There are no brain **imaging studies** or laboratory tests as of 2007 that can be used to diagnose BDD. Some studies using brain imaging have identified some characteristics similar to those seen in obsessive-compulsive disorder, although studies are not in complete agreement on this.

Treatments

The standard treatment regimen for body dysmorphic disorder is a combination of medications and **psychotherapy**. Surgical, dental, or dermatologic treatments have been found ineffective and in some cases may exacerbate symptoms. In one study, cosmetic surgeons reported that 40% of their patients with BDD had made legal or physical threats against them.

Medications

The medications most frequently prescribed for patients with BDD are the **selective serotonin reuptake inhibitors** (SSRIs), most commonly **fluoxetine** (Prozac) or **sertraline** (Zoloft). Other **SSRIs** that have been used with this group of patients include **fluoxamine** (Luvox) and **paroxetine** (**Paxil**). As of 2006, the only one of these medications that is FDA-approved for use in children is fluoxetine.

The relatively high rate of positive responses to SSRIs among BDD patients led to the hypothesis that the disorder has a neurobiological component related to serotonin levels in the body. An associated finding is that patients with BDD require higher dosages of SSRI medications to be effective than patients who are being treated for depression with these drugs.

Psychotherapy

The most effective approach to psychotherapy with BDD patients is **cognitive-behavioral therapy**, of which cognitive restructuring is one component. Because the disorder is related to **delusions** about one's appearance, cognitive-oriented therapy that challenges inaccurate self-perceptions is more effective than purely supportive approaches. Relaxation techniques also work well with BDD patients when they are combined with cognitive restructuring.

KEY TERMS

Body image—A term that refers to a person's inner picture of his or her outward appearance. It has two components: perceptions of the appearance of one's body, and emotional responses to those perceptions.

Comorbidity—Association or presence of two or more mental disorders in the same patient. A disorder that is said to have a high degree of comorbidity is likely to occur in patients diagnosed with other disorders that may share or reinforce some of its symptoms.

Delusion—A false belief that is resistant to reason or contrary to actual fact. Common delusions include delusions of persecution, delusions about one's importance (sometimes called delusions of grandeur), or delusions of being controlled by others. In BDD, the delusion is related to the patient's perception of his or her body.

Displacement—A psychological process in which feelings originating from one source are expressed outwardly in terms of concern or preoccupation with an issue or problem that the patient considers more acceptable. In some BDD patients, obsession about the body includes displaced feelings, often related to a history of childhood abuse.

Muscle dysmorphia—A subtype of BDD, described as excessive preoccupation with muscularity and bodybuilding to the point of interference with social, educational, or occupational functioning.

Neurotransmitter—A chemical produced by the brain that helps to transmit nerve impulses across the junctions between nerve cells.

Serotonin—A widely distributed neurotransmitter that is found in blood platelets, the lining of the digestive tract, and the brain, and that works in combination with norepinephrine. It causes very powerful contractions of smooth muscle, and is associated with mood, attention, emotions, and sleep. Low levels of serotonin are associated with depression.

Somatoform disorders—A group of psychiatric disorders in the *DSM-IV-TR* classification that are characterized by external physical symptoms or complaints. BDD is classified as a somatoform disorder.

Prognosis

The *DSM-IV-TR* notes that the disorder "has a fairly continuous course, with few symptom-free intervals, although the intensity of symptoms may wax and wane over time."

Prevention

Given the pervasive influence of the mass media in contemporary Western societies, the best preventive strategy involves challenging those afflicted with the disorder and who consequently have unrealistic images of attractive people. Parents, teachers, primary health care professionals, and other adults who work with young people can point out and discuss the pitfalls of trying to look "perfect." In addition, parents or other adults can educate themselves about BDD and its symptoms, and pay attention to any warning signs in their children's dress or behavior. They also can modulate their own behaviors of pointing out or highlighting physical "imperfections" in themselves or in their children because there is a link between parents with such concerns and children with BDD.

See also Aromatherapy; Yoga.

Resources

BOOKS

American Psychiatric Association. *Diagnostic and Statistical Manual of Mental Disorders.* 4th ed., Text rev. Washington, D.C.: American Psychiatric Association, 2000.

Beers, Mark H., MD, and Robert Berkow, MD, eds. "Body Dysmorphic Disorder," Section 15, Chapter 186. *The Merck Manual of Diagnosis and Therapy.* Whitehouse Station, NJ: Merck Research Laboratories, 1999.

Johnston, Joni E., Psy D. *Appearance Obsession: Learning to Love the Way You Look.* Deerfield Beach, FL: Health Communications, 1994.

Peiss, Kathy. *Hope in a Jar: The Making of America's Beauty Culture.* New York: Henry Holt and Company, 1998.

Rodin, Judith, PhD. *Body Traps: Breaking the Binds That Keep You from Feeling Good About Your Body.* New York: William Morrow, 1992.

PERIODICALS

Albertini, Ralph S. "Thirty-Three Cases of Body Dysmorphic Disorder in Children and Adolescents." *Journal of the American Academy of Child and Adolescent Psychiatry* 38 (1999): 528–44.

"BDD Patients Resorting to Self-Surgery." *Cosmetic Surgery Times* 3 (2000): 29.

Carey, Paul, and others. "SPECT imaging of body dysmorphic disorder." *Journal of Neuropsychiatry Clinical Neuroscience* 16 (2004): 357–59.

Chung, Bryan. "Muscle Dysmorphia: A Critical Review of the Proposed Criteria." *Perspectives in Biology and Medicine* 44 (2001): 565–74.

Crerand, Canice E., and others. "Nonpsychiatric Medical Treatment of Body Dysmorphic Disorder." *Psychosomatics* 46 (2005): 549–55.

Jesitus, John. "Fixing the Cracks in the Mirror: Identifying, Treating Disorder in Pediatric Patients May Take More Than Dermatologic Treatments Alone." *Dermatology Times* 22 (2001): 740–42.

Kirchner, Jeffrey T. "Treatment of Patients with Body Dysmorphic Disorder." *American Family Physician* 61 (2000): 1837–43.

Leone, James E., Edward J. Sedory, and Kimberly A. Gray. "Recognition and Treatment of Muscle Dysmorphia and Related Body Image Disorders." *Journal of Athletic Training* 40 (2005): 352–59.

Mason, Staci. "Demystifying Muscle Dysmorphia." *IDEA Health & Fitness Source* 19 (2001): 71–77.

Phillips, K. A., and S. L. McElroy. "Personality Disorders and Traits in Patients with Body Dysmorphic Disorder." *Comparative Psychiatry* 41 (2000): 229–36.

Phillips, Katharine A., and others. "Demographic Characteristics, Phenomenology, Comorbidity, and Family History in 200 Individuals with Body Dysmorphic Disorder." *Psychosomatics* 46 (2005): 317–26.

Pope, Courtney G., and others. "Clinical Features of Muscle Dysmorphia Among Males with Body Dysmorphic Disorder." *Body Image* 2 (2005): 395–400.

Slaughter, James R. "In Pursuit of Perfection: A Primary Care Physician's Guide to Body Dysmorphic Disorder." *American Family Physician* 60 (1999): 569–80.

ORGANIZATIONS

American Academy of Child and Adolescent Psychiatry. 3615 Wisconsin Avenue, NW, Washington, D.C. 20016-3007. Telephone: (202) 966-7300. Fax: (202) 966-2891. <http://www.aacap.org>.

National Institute of Mental Health. 6001 Executive Boulevard, Room 8184, MSC 9663, Bethesda, MD 20892-9663. Telephone: (301) 443-4513. <http://www.nimh.nih.gov>.

Rebecca Frey, PhD
Emily Jane Willingham, PhD

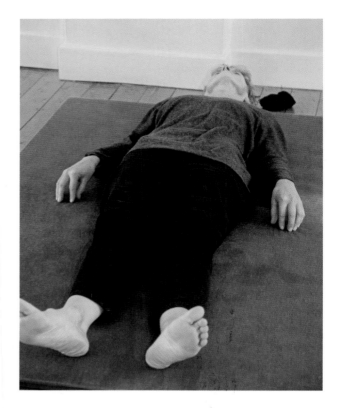

A woman experiencing feldenkreis treatment. *(Libby Welch/ Alamy)*

Bodywork therapies

Definition

Bodywork therapies is a general term that refers to a group of body-based approaches to treatment that emphasize manipulation and realignment of the body's structure in order to improve its function as well as the client's mental outlook. These therapies typically combine a relatively passive phase, in which the client receives deep-tissue bodywork or postural correction from an experienced instructor or practitioner, and a more active period of movement education, in which the client practices sitting, standing, and moving about with better alignment of the body and greater ease of motion.

Bodywork should not be equated with massage simply speaking. Massage therapy is one form of bodywork, but in massage therapy, the practitioner uses oil or lotion to reduce the friction between his or her hands and the client's skin. In most forms of body work, little if any lubrication is used, as the goal of this type of hands-on treatment is to warm, relax and stretch the fascia (a band or sheath of connective tissue that covers, supports, or connects the muscles and the internal organs) and underlying layers of tissue.

Purpose

The purpose of bodywork therapy is the correction of problems in the client's overall posture, connective tissue, and/or musculature in order to bring about greater ease of movement, less discomfort, and a higher level of energy in daily activity. Some forms of bodywork have as a secondary purpose the healing or prevention of repetitive **stress** injuries, particularly for people whose occupations require intensive use of specific parts of the body (such as dancers, musicians, professional athletes, opera singers, etc.) Bodywork may also heal or prevent specific musculoskeletal problems, such as lower back pain or neck pain.

Bodywork therapies are holistic in that they stress increased self-awareness and intelligent use of one's body as one of the goals of treatment. Some of these therapies use verbal discussion, visualization or guided imagery along with movement education to help clients break old patterns of moving and feeling. Although most bodywork therapists do not address mental disorders directly in their work with clients, they are often knowledgeable about the applications of bodywork to such specific emotions as depession, anger, or fear.

Although some bodywork therapies, such as Rolfing or Hellerwork, offer programs structured around a specific number or sequence of lessons, all therapies of this type emphasize individualized treatment and respect for the uniqueness of each individual's body. Bodywork instructors or practitioners typically work with clients on a one-to-one basis, as distinct from a group or classroom approach.

Precautions

Persons who are seriously ill, acutely feverish, or who have a contagious infection should wait until they have recovered before beginning a course of bodywork. As a rule, types of bodywork that involve intensive manipulation or stretching of the deeper layers of body tissue are not suitable for persons who have undergone recent surgery or have recently experienced severe injury. In the case of Tragerwork, shiatsu, and trigger point therapy, clients should inform the therapist of any open wounds, bruises, or fractures so that the affected part of the body can be avoided during treatment. Craniosacral therapy, the Feldenkrais method, and the Alexander technique involve gentle touch and do not require any special precautions.

Persons who are recovering from abuse or receiving treatment for any post-traumatic syndrome or dissociative disorder should consult their therapist before undertaking bodywork. Although bodywork is frequently recommended as an adjunctive treatment for these disorders, it can also trigger flashbacks if the bodywork therapist touches a part of the patient's body associated with the abuse or trauma. Many bodywork therapists, however, are well informed about post-traumatic symptoms and disorders, and able to adjust their treatments accordingly.

Description

The following are brief descriptions of some of the more popular bodywork therapies.

Alexander technique

The Alexander technique was developed by an Australian actor named F. Matthias Alexander (1869-1955), who had voice problems that were not helped by any available medical treatments. Alexander decided to set up a number of mirrors so that he could watch himself during a performance from different angles. He found that he was holding his head and neck too far forward, and that these unconscious patterns were the source of the tension in his body that was harming his voice. He then developed a method for teaching others to observe the patterns of tension and stress in their posture and movement, and to correct these patterns with a combination of hands-on guidance and visualization exercises. The Alexander technique is included in the curricula of the Juilliard School of Music and many other drama and music schools around the world, because performing artists are particularly vulnerable to repetitive stress injuries if they hold or move their bodies incorrectly.

In an Alexander technique session, the client works one-on-one with an instructor who uses verbal explanations as well as guided movement. The sessions are usually referred to as "explorations" and last about 30 minutes. Although most clients see positive changes after only two or three sessions, teachers of the technique recommend a course of 20–30 sessions so that new movement skills can be learned and changes maintained.

Rolfing

Rolfing, which is also called Rolf therapy or structural integration, is a holistic system of bodywork that uses deep manipulation of the body's soft tissue to realign and balance the body's myofascial (muscular and connective tissue) structure. It was developed by Ida Rolf (1896-1979), a biochemist who became interested in the structure of the human body after an accident damaged her health. She studied with an osteopath as well as with practitioners of other forms of alternative medicine, and developed her own technique of body movement that she called structural integration. Rolfing is an approach that seeks to counteract the effects of gravity, which tends to pull the body out of alignment over time and cause the connective tissues to stiffen and contract.

Rolfing treatment begins with the so-called "Basic Ten," a series of ten sessions each lasting 60–90 minutes, spaced a week or longer apart. After a period of integration, the client may undertake advanced treatment sessions. "Tune-up" sessions are recommended every six months. In Rolfing sessions, the practitioner uses his or her fingers, hands, knuckles, or elbows to rework the connective tissue over the client's entire body. The deep tissues are worked until they become pliable, which allows the muscles to lengthen and return to their proper alignment. Rolfing treatments are done on a massage table, with the client wearing only undergarments.

Hellerwork

Hellerwork is a bodywork therapy developed by Joseph Heller, a former NASA engineer who became a certified Rolfer in 1972 and started his own version of structural integration, called Hellerwork, in 1979. Heller describes his program as "a powerful system of somatic education and structural bodywork" based on a series of eleven sessions. Hellerwork is somewhat similar to Rolfing in that it begins with manipulation of the deep tissues of the body. Heller, however, decided that physical realignment of the body by itself is insufficient, so he extended his system to include movement education and "self-awareness facilitated through dialogue."

The bodywork aspect of Hellerwork is intended to release the tension that exists in the fascia, which is the sheath or layer of connective tissue that covers, supports, or connects the muscles and internal organs of the body. Fascia is flexible and moist in its normal state, but the effects of gravity and ongoing physical stresses lead to misalignments that cause the fascia to become stiff and rigid. The first hour of a Hellerwork session is devoted to deep connective tissue bodywork in which the Hellerwork practitioner uses his or her hands to release tension in the client's fascia. The bodywork is followed by movement education, which includes the use of video feedback to help clients learn movement patterns that will help to keep their bodies in proper alignment. The third component of Hellerwork is verbal dialogue, which is intended to help clients become more aware of the relationships between their emotions and attitudes and their body.

Tragerwork

Trager psychophysical integration, which is often called simply Tragerwork, was developed by Milton Trager (1908-1977), a man who was born with a spinal deformity and earned a medical degree in his middle age after working out an approach to healing **chronic pain**. Tragerwork is based on the theory that many illnesses are caused by tension patterns that are held in the unconscious mind as much as in the tissues of the body; clients are advised to think of Tragerwork sessions as "learning experiences" rather than "treatments." Tragerwork sessions are divided into bodywork, which is referred to as tablework, and an exercise period. Trager practitioners use their hands during tablework to perform a variety of gentle motions—rocking, shaking, vibrating, and gentle stretching—intended to help the client release their patterns of tension by experiencing how it feels to move freely and effortlessly on one's own. Following the tablework, clients are taught how to perform simple dance-like exercises called Mentastics, for practice at home. Tragerwork sessions take between 60–90 minutes, while clients are advised to spent 10–15 minutes three times a day doing the Mentastics exercises.

Feldenkrais method

The Feldenkrais method, like Hellerwork, refers to its approach as "somatic education." Developed by Moshe Feldenkrais (1904-1984), a scientist and engineer who was also a judo instructor, the Feldenkrais method consists of two major applications—Awareness Through Movement (ATM) lessons, a set of verbally directed exercise lessons intended to engage the client's intelligence as well as physical perception; and Functional Integration (FI), in which a Feldenkrais practitioner works with the client one-on-one, guiding him or her through a series of movements that alter habitual patterns and convey new learning directly to the neuromuscular system. Functional Integration is done with the client fully clothed, lying or sitting on a low padded table.

Perhaps the most distinctive feature of the Feldenkrais method is its emphasis on new patterns of thinking, attention, cognition, and imagination as byproducts of new patterns of physical movement. It is the most intellectually oriented of the various bodywork therapies, and has been described by one observer as "an unusual melding of motor development, biomechanics, psychology, and martial arts." The Feldenkrais method is the form of bodywork that has been most extensively studied by mainstream medical researchers.

Trigger point therapy

Trigger point therapy, which is sometimes called myotherapy, is a treatment for pain relief in the musculoskeletal system based on the application of pressure to trigger points in the client's body. Trigger points are defined as hypersensitive spots or areas in the muscles that cause pain when subjected to stress, whether the stress is an occupational injury, a disease, or emotional stress. Trigger points are not necessarily in the same location where the client feels pain.

Myotherapy is a two-step process. In the first step, the therapist locates the client's trigger points and applies pressure to them. This step relieves pain and also relaxes the muscles associated with it. In the second part of the therapy session, the client learns a series of exercises that progressively stretch the muscles that have been relaxed by the therapist's pressure. Most clients need fewer than 10 sessions to benefit from myotherapy. One distinctive feature of trigger point therapy is that clients are asked to bring a relative or trusted friend to learn the pressure technique and the client's personal trigger points. This "buddy system" helps the client to maintain the benefits of the therapy in the event of a **relapse**.

Shiatsu

Shiatsu is the oldest form of bodywork therapy, having been practiced for centuries in Japan as part of traditional medical practice. It is also the type of bodywork most commonly requested by clients in Western countries as well as in East Asia. The word *shiatsu* itself is a combination of two Japanese words that mean "pressure" and "finger." Shiatsu resembles acupuncture in its use of the basic concepts of ki, the vital energy that flows throughout the body, and the meridians, or 12 major pathways that channel ki to the various organs of the body. In Asian terms, shiatsu works by unblocking and rebalancing the distribution of ki in the body. In the categories of Western medicine, shiatsu may stimulate the release of endorphins, which are chemical compounds that block the receptors in the **brain** that perceive pain.

A shiatsu treatment begins with the practitioner's assessment of the client's basic state of health, including posture, vocal tone, complexion color, and condition of hair. This evaluation is used together with ongoing information about the client's energy level gained through the actual bodywork. The shiatsu practitioner works with the client lying fully clothed on a futon. The practitioner seeks out the meridians in the client's body through finger pressure, and stimulates points along the meridians known as tsubos. The tsubos are centers of high energy where the ki tends to collect. Pressure on the tsubos results in a release of energy that rebalances the energy level throughout the body.

Craniosacral therapy

Craniosacral therapy, or CST, is a form of treatment that originated with William Sutherland, an American osteopath of the 1930s who theorized that the manipulative techniques that osteopaths were taught could be applied to the skull. Sutherland knew from his medical training that the skull is not a single piece of bone, but consists of several bones that meet at seams; and that the cerebrospinal fluid that bathes the brain and spinal cord has a natural rise-and-fall rhythm. Sutherland experimented with gentle manipulation of the skull in order to correct imbalances in the distribution of the cerebrospinal fluid. Contemporary craniosacral therapists practice manipulation not only of the skull, but of the meningeal membranes that cover the brain and the spinal cord, and sometimes of the facial bones. Many practitioners of CST are also osteopaths, or DOs.

In CST, the patient lies on a massage table while the therapist gently palpates, or presses, the skull and spine. If the practitioner is also an osteopath, he or she will take a complete medical history as well. The therapist also "listens" to the cranial rhythmic impulse, or rhythmic pulsation of the cerebrospinal fluid, with his or her hands. Interruptions of the normal flow by abnormalities caused by tension or by injuries are diagnostic clues to the practitioner. Once he or she has identified the cause of the abnormal rhythm, the skull and spinal column are gently manipulated to restore the natural rhythm of the cranial impulse. Craniosacral therapy appears to be particularly useful in treating physical disorders of the head, including migraine headaches, ringing in the ears, sinus problems, and injuries of the head, neck, and spine. In addition, patients rarely require extended periods of CST treatments.

Preparation

Bodywork usually requires little preparation on the client's or patient's part, except for partial undressing for Rolfing, trigger point therapy, and Hellerwork.

Aftercare

Aftercare for shiatsu, trigger point therapy, and craniosacral therapy involves a brief period of rest after the treatment.

Some bodywork approaches involve various types of long-term aftercare. Rolfing clients return for advanced treatments or tune-ups after a period of integrating the changes in their bodies resulting frm the Basic Ten sessions. Tragerwork clients are taught Mentastics exercises to be done at home.

The Alexander technique and the Feldenkrais approach assume that clients will continue to practice their movement and postural changes for the rest of their lives. Trigger point therapy clients are asked to involve friends or relatives who can help them maintain the benefits of the therapy after the treatment sessions are over.

Risks

The deep tissue massage and manipulation in Rolfing and Hellerwork are uncomfortable for many people, particularly the first few sessions. There are, however, no serious risks of physical injury from any form of bodywork that is administered by a trained practitioner of the specific treatment. As mentioned, however, bodywork therapies that involve intensive manipulation or stretching of the deeper layers of body tissue are not suitable for persons who have undergone recent surgery or have recently suffered severe injury.

Normal results

Normal results from bodywork include deep relaxation, improved posture, greater ease and spontaneity of movement, greater range of motion for certain joints, greater understanding of the structures and functions of the body and their relationship to emotions, and release of negative emotions.

Many persons also report healing or improvement of specific conditions, including migraine headaches, repetitive stress injuries, osteoarthritis, **insomnia**, sprains and bruises, sports injuries, stress-related illnesses, sciatica, postpregnancy problems, menstrual cramps, temporomandibular joint disorders, lower back pain, whiplash injuries, disorders of the immune system, asthma, **depression**, digestive problems, chronic **fatigue**, and painful scar tissue. The Alexander technique has been reported to ease the process of childbirth by improving the mother's postural alignment prior to delivery.

Some studies of the Feldenkrais method have found that its positive effects on subjects' self-esteem, mood, and **anxiety** sympoms are more significant than its effects on body function.

Abnormal results

Abnormal results from bodywork therapies would include serious physical injury or trauma-based psychological reactions.

See also Acupuncture; Energy therapies.

KEY TERMS

Bodywork—Any technique involving hands-on massage or manipulation of the body.

Endorphins—A group of peptide compounds released by the body in response to stress or traumatic injury. Endorphins react with opiate receptors in the brain to reduce or relieve pain sensations. Shiatsu is thought to work by stimulating the release of endorphins.

Fascia (plural, fasciae)—A band or sheath of connective tissue that covers, supports, or connects the muscles and the internal organs.

Ki—The Japanese spelling of qi, the traditional Chinese term for vital energy or the life force.

Meridians—In traditional Chinese medicine, a network of pathways or channels that convey qi (also sometimes spelled "ki"), or vital energy, through the body.

Movement education—A term that refers to the active phase of bodywork, in which clients learn to move with greater freedom and to maintain the proper alignment of their bodies.

Repetitive stress injury (RSI)—A type of injury to the musculoskeletal and nervous systems associated with occupational strain or overuse of a specific part of the body. Bodywork therapies are often recommended to people suffering from RSIs.

Somatic education—A term used in both Hellerwork and the Feldenkrais method to describe the integration of bodywork with self-awareness, intelligence, and imagination.

Structural integration—The term used to describe the method and philosophy of life associated with Rolfing. Its fundamental concept is the vertical line.

Tsubo—In shiatsu, a center of high energy located along one of the body's meridians. Stimulation of the tsubos during a shiatsu treatment is thought to rebalance the flow of vital energy in the body.

Resources

BOOKS

Pelletier, Kenneth R., MD. *The Best Alternative Medicine.* New York: Simon and Schuster, 2002.

PERIODICALS

Dunn, P. A., and D. K. Rogers. "Feldenkrais Sensory Imagery and Forward Reach." *Perception and Motor Skills* 91 (December 2000): 755-757.

Hornung, S. "An ABC of Alternative Medicine: Heller-work." *Health Visit* 59 (December 1986): 387-388.

Huntley, A., and E. Ernst. "Complementary and Alternative Therapies for Treating Multiple Sclerosis Symptoms: A Systematic Review." *Complementary Therapies in Medicine* 8 (June 2000): 97-105.

Johnson, S. K., and others. "A Controlled Investigation of Bodywork in Multiple Sclerosis." *Journal of Alternative and Complementary Medicine* 5 (June 1999): 237-243.

Mackereth, P. "Tough Places to be Tender: Contracting for Happy or 'Good Enough' Endings in Therapeutic Massage/Bodywork?" *Complementary Therapies in Nursing and Midwifery* 6 (August 2000): 111-115.

Perron, Wendy. "Guide to Bodywork Approaches." *Dance Magazine* 74 (November 2000): 12-15.

Stallibrass, C., and M. Hampson. "The Alexander Technique: Its Application in Midwifery and the Results of Preliminary Research Into Parkinson's." *Complementary Therapies in Nursing and Midwifery* 7 (February 2001): 13-18.

ORGANIZATIONS

Bonnie Prudden Pain Erasure Clinic and School for Physical Fitness and Myotherapy. P.O. Box 65240. Tucson, AZ 85728. Telephone: (520) 529-3979. Fax: (520) 529-6679. <www.bonnieprudden.com>.

Cranial Academy. 3500 DePauw Boulevard, Indianapolis, IN 46268. Telephone: (317) 879-0713.

Craniosacral Therapy Association of the United Kingdom. Monomark House, 27 Old Gloucester Street, London, WC1N 3XX. Telephone: 07000-784-735. <www.craniosacral.co.uk/>.

Feldenkrais Guild of North America. 3611 S.W. Hood Avenue, Suite 100, Portland, OR 97201. Telephone: (800) 775-2118 or (503) 221-6612. Fax: (503) 221-6616. <www.feldenkrais.com>.

The Guild for Structural Integration. 209 Canyon Blvd. P.O. Box 1868. Boulder, CO 80306-1868. Telephone: (303) 449-5903. (800) 530-8875. <www.rolfguild.org.>.

Hellerwork. 406 Berry St. Mt. Shasta, CA 96067. Telephone: (530) 926-2500. <www.hellerwork.com>.

International School of Shiatsu. 10 South Clinton Street, Doylestown, PA 18901. Telephone: (215) 340-9918. Fax: (215) 340-9181. <www.shiatsubo.com.>.

The Society of Teachers of the Alexander Technique. <www.stat.org.uk>.

The Trager Institute. 21 Locust Avenue, Mill Valley, CA 94941-2806. Telephone: (415) 388-2688. Fax: (415) 388-2710. <www.trager.com.>.

OTHER

National Certification Board for Therapeutic Massage and Bodywork. 8201 Greensboro Drive, Suite 300. McLean, VA 22102. Telephone: (703) 610-9015.

NIH National Center for Complementary and Alternative Medicine (NCCAM) Clearinghouse. P. O. Box 8218, Silver Spring, MD 20907-8218. TTY/TDY: (888) 644-6226. Fax: (301) 495-4957. Web site: <http://www.nccam.nih.gov>.

Borderline personality disorder

Definition

Borderline personality disorder (BPD) is a mental disorder characterized by disturbed and unstable interpersonal relationships and self-image, along with impulsive behavior, unstable mood, and suicidal behavior.

Description

Individuals with BPD have a history of unstable interpersonal relationships. They have difficulty interpreting reality and view significant people in their lives as either completely flawless or extremely unfair and uncaring (a phenomenon known as "splitting"). These alternating feelings of idealization and devaluation are one major feature of borderline personality disorder. Because borderline patients set up such excessive and unrealistic expectations for others, they are inevitably disappointed when their expectations are not realized.

The term "borderline" was originally used by **psychologist** Adolf Stern in the 1930s to describe patients whose condition bordered somewhere between **psychosis** and **neurosis**, although today, the term "borderline" used in this sense is considered a misnomer. The term is better applicable today in describing the borderline states of consciousness these patients sometimes feel when they experience dissociative symptoms (a feeling of disconnection from oneself). The syndrome itself is considered a complex disorder, rather than one lying on a border between psychosis and neurosis.

Causes and symptoms

Causes

In about 24% of cases, there is a history of childhood sex abuse, and in about one-third of cases, there is a history of severe abuse of some kind. Thus, abuse is considered a risk factor, but it is an environmental contributor thought to interact with a genetic basis. Twin studies have suggested that at least some features of this disorder are highly heritable. Mood instability and impulsivity are about 50% heritable, and studies of BPD specifically suggest a similar level of heritability. The root biological cause may be disruptions in signaling pathways involving serotonin, a nerve signaling molecule, but more studies are necessary to confirm the biological basis.

The feelings of inadequacy and self-loathing that arise from situations of abuse or **neglect** may contribute to the development of a borderline personality. It has also been theorized that these patients try to compensate for the care they were denied in childhood through the idealized demands they now make on themselves and on others as adults.

Symptoms

The handbook used by mental health professionals to diagnose mental disorders is the ***Diagnostic and Statistical Manual of Mental Disorders (DSM)***. The 2000 edition of this manual (fourth edition, text revised) is known as the *DSM-IV-TR*. Published by the American Psychiatric Association, the *DSM* contains diagnostic criteria, research findings, and treatment information for mental disorders. It is the primary reference for mental health professionals in the United States. BPD was first listed as a disorder in the third edition *DSM-III*, which was published in 1980, and has been revised in subsequent editions.

The *DSM-IV-TR* requires that at least five of the following criteria (or symptoms) be present in an individual for a **diagnosis** of BPD, although some researchers suggest that criteria from each of three dimensions (groupings) should actually be met:

DIMENSION: AFFECTIVE (MOOD-RELATED) SYMPTOMS.

- Unstable mood caused by brief but intense episodes of depression, irritability, or anxiety. These episodes are generally much briefer than the highs and lows of bipolar disorder. The strongest tendency is to outbursts of anger. The level of mood instability can be a strong predictor of whether or not suicide will be attempted.
- Chronic feelings of emptiness.
- Inappropriate and intense anger, or difficulty controlling anger displayed through temper outbursts, physical fights, and/or sarcasm.

DIMENSION: IMPULSIVE SYMPTOMS.

- Impulsive behavior in at least two areas (e.g., spending, sex, substance abuse, reckless driving, binge eating).
- Recurrent suicidal behavior, gestures, or threats, or recurring acts of self-mutilation (such as cutting or burning oneself). This behavior results from the combination of impulsivity and rapidly and intensely changeable mood.
- Pattern of unstable and intense interpersonal relationships, characterized by alternating between idealization and devaluation ("love-hate" relationships).

DIMENSION: INTERPERSONAL SYMPTOMS.

- Extreme, persistently unstable self-image and sense of self.
- Frantic efforts to avoid real or perceived abandonment.

In addition, there is a cognitive criterion for diagnosis that includes stress-related **paranoia** that passes fairly quickly and/or severe dissociative symptoms—feeling disconnected from oneself, as if one is an observer of one's own actions; sometimes occurs with flashbacks. One study found that about 40% of patients with BPD reported having semipsychotic thoughts. The rate in another study was 27% of patients. A different study also found that the presence of psychotic symptoms can be a predictor of self-harm in patients who have **personality disorders**.

Some patients with BPD are mistakenly diagnosed with bipolar disorder or with **schizophrenia**. BPD can be distinguished from bipolar disorder based on the brevity of the extreme mood swings, which typically last only hours, rather than days or weeks. In spite of the fact that auditory **hallucinations** can occur in people with BPD, it is distinguished from schizophrenia because the patient with BPD knows the hallucinations are not real, whereas the patient with schizophrenia does not.

Demographics

Borderline personality disorder accounts for 30–60% of all personality disorders and is present in approximately 1% of the general population, a frequency similar to that of schizophrenia. The disorder appears to affect women more frequently than men; as many as 80% of all patients receiving therapy are female, but this sex bias is not as obvious in samples from community populations. The characteristic of suicidality (thinking about or attempting suicide) is less prominent in traditional societies that experience little cultural change from one generation to the next, but is increasing in modern societies and in societies experiencing rapid change.

Diagnosis

Borderline personality disorder typically first appears in early adulthood, with the usual age of onset around 18 years. Although the disorder may occur in adolescence, it may be difficult to diagnose, since borderline symptoms such as impulsive and experimental behaviors, insecurity, and mood swings are common—even developmentally appropriate—occurrences at this age.

Assessment is based first on determination of whether or not the person meets at least five of the nine *DSM-IV-TR* criteria. The next step typically involves completion of a personality assessment, which involves interviewing the patient, but also can involve querying family members or friends, with the patient's agreement. Last, the symptoms of BPD that suggest the diagnosis must have been present consistently over time.

Borderline symptoms may also be the result of chronic substance abuse and/or medical conditions (specifically, disorders of the central nervous system). These should be ruled out before making the diagnosis of borderline personality disorder.

BPD commonly occurs with mood disorders (i.e., depression and anxiety), **post-traumatic stress disorder** (PTSD), eating disorders, **attention deficit/hyperactivity disorder** (ADHD), and other personality disorders. Another accompanying comorbidity may be substance use disorder. It has also been suggested by some researchers that borderline personality disorder is not a true pathological condition in and of itself, but rather a number of overlapping personality disorders; it is, however, commonly recognized as a separate and distinct disorder by the American Psychiatric Association and by most mental health professionals. It is diagnosed by interviewing the patient and matching symptoms to the *DSM-IV-TR* criteria. Supplementary testing may also be necessary.

Treatment

Individuals with borderline personality disorder seek psychiatric help and **hospitalization** at a much higher rate than people with other personality disorders, probably because of their fear of abandonment and their need to seek idealized interpersonal relationships. These patients represent the highest percentage of diagnosed personality disorders (up to 60%).

Providing effective therapy for the borderline personality patient is a necessary, but difficult, challenge. The therapist-patient relationship is subject to the same inappropriate and unrealistic demands that borderline personalities place on all their significant interpersonal relationships. They are chronic "treatment seekers" who become easily frustrated with their therapist if they feel they are not receiving adequate attention or empathy, and symptomatic anger, impulsivity, and self-destructive behavior can impede the therapist-patient relationship. However, their fear of abandonment and of ending the therapy relationship may actually cause them to discontinue treatment as soon as progress is made.

Psychotherapy, typically in the form of **cognitive-behavioral therapy**, is usually the treatment of choice for borderline personalities. Dialectical behavior therapy (DBT), a cognitive-behavioral technique, has emerged as an effective therapy for borderline personalities with suicidal tendencies. The treatment focuses on giving the borderline patient self-confidence and coping tools for life outside of treatment through a combination of **social skills training**, mood-awareness and meditative exercises, and education about the disorder. **Group therapy** is also an option for some borderline patients, although some may feel threatened by the idea of "sharing" a therapist with others.

Medication is not considered a first-line treatment choice but may be useful in treating some symptoms of the disorder and/or the mood disorders that have been diagnosed in conjunction with BPD. Some patients with BPD may find themselves taking several different medications, each designed to address one of the main manifestations of BPD, but there are no data from **clinical trials** supporting such a regimen.

Prognosis

The disorder usually peaks in young adulthood and frequently stabilizes after age 30. In 75% of cases, normal function will have returned by age 35 to 40, and in 90% of cases, function will be normal by age 50. Unfortunately, the remaining 10% fall into the group of patients who die as a result of suicide. Approximately 75–80% of borderline patients attempt or threaten suicide, and between 8–10% are successful. Managing this highly prevalent suicidality is one of the greatest therapeutic challenges in BPD. The behavior peaks usually when the patient is in the mid-20s, but most of the completed suicides actually occur among patients older than 30 years, usually in patients who have experienced no recovery after many treatment attempts. If the borderline patient suffers from depressive disorder, the risk of suicide is much higher. For this reason, swift diagnosis and appropriate interventions are critical. Self-harming behaviors are generally not considered to be attempted suicide but instead to serve as a relief from an extreme emotional state.

Prevention

Prevention recommendations are scarce. Given the genetic basis of the disorder, current technologies do not allow preventions targeting that aspect of its etiology. The only known prevention would be to ensure a safe and nurturing environment during childhood.

See also Dissociation/Dissociative disorders.

Resources

BOOKS

Linehan, Marsha. *Cognitive-Behavioral Treatment of Borderline Personality Disorder*. New York: Guilford Press, 1993.

Linehan, Marsha. *Skills Training Manual for Treating Borderline Personality Disorder*. New York: Guilford Press, 1993.

Moskovitz, Richard A. *Lost in the Mirror: An Inside Look at Borderline Personality Disorder*. Dallas, TX: Taylor Publishing, 1996.

Tasman, Allan, Jerald Kay, and Jeffrey A. Lieberman, eds. *Psychiatry*. Philadelphia: W. B. Saunders Company, 1997.

PERIODICALS

Gurvits, I., H. Koenigsberg, and L. Siever. "Neurotransmitter Dysfunction in Patients with Borderline Personality Disorder." *Psychiatric Clinics of North America* 23.1 (March 2000): 27–40.

Paris, Joel. "Borderline Personality Disorder." *Canadian Medical Association Journal* 172 (2005): 1579–83.

Soloff, P. "Psychopharmacology of Borderline Personality Disorder." *Psychiatric Clinics of North America* 23.1 (March 2000): 169–92.

ORGANIZATIONS

American Psychiatric Association. 1400 K Street NW, Washington, DC 20005. <http://www.psych.org>.

BPD Central, National Alliance for the Mentally Ill. 200 N. Glebe Road, Suite 1015, Arlington, VA 22203-3754. Telephone: (800) 950-6264. Web site: <http://www.bpdcentral.com>.

OTHER

National Institute of Mental Health. National Institutes of Health. "Borderline Personality Disorder." NIH publication 01-4928. (2006) <http://www.nimh.nih.gov/publicat/bpd.cfm>.

Laith Farid Gulli, MD
Linda Hesson, MA, Psy.S., L.L.P., C.A.C.
Micheal Mooney, MA., C.A.C, C.C.S.
Emily Jane Willingham, PhD

Brain

Definition

The brain is the part of the central nervous system located in the skull. It controls the mental processes and physical actions of a human being.

Description

The brain, along with the spinal cord and network of nerves, controls information flow throughout the body, voluntary actions such as walking, reading, and talking, and involuntary reactions such as breathing and digestion.

The human brain is a soft, shiny, grayish-white, mushroom-shaped structure. The brain of an average adult weighs about 3 lb (1.4 kg). At birth, the average infant's brain weighs 13.7 oz (390 g); by age 15, it has nearly reached full adult size. The brain is protected by the skull and a three-layered membrane called the meninges. The brain's surface is covered with many bright red arteries and bluish veins that penetrate inward. Glucose, oxygen, and certain ions pass easily across the blood-brain barrier into the brain, although other substances, such as antibiotics, do not.

The four principal sections of the human brain are: the brain stem, the diencephalon, the cerebrum (divided into two large paired cerebral hemispheres), and the cerebellum.

The brain stem

The brain stem connects the brain with the spinal cord. Every message transmitted between the brain and spinal cord passes through the medulla oblongata—a part of the brain stem—via nerve fibers. The fibers on the right side of the medulla cross to the left and those on the left cross to the right. As a result, each side of the brain controls the opposite side of the body. The medulla regulates the heartbeat, breathing rate, and blood-vessel diameters; it also helps coordinate swallowing, vomiting, hiccupping, coughing, and sneezing.

Another brain stem component, the pons (meaning "bridge"), conducts messages between the spinal cord and the rest of the brain, and between the different parts of the brain. The midbrain conveys impulses between the cerebral cortex, pons, and spinal cord and also contains visual and audio reflex centers involving the movement of the eyeballs and head.

Twelve pairs of cranial nerves originate in the underside of the brain, mostly from the brain stem. They leave the skull through openings and extend as peripheral nerves to their destinations. Among these cranial nerves are the olfactory nerves that bring messages about smell and the optic nerves that conduct visual information.

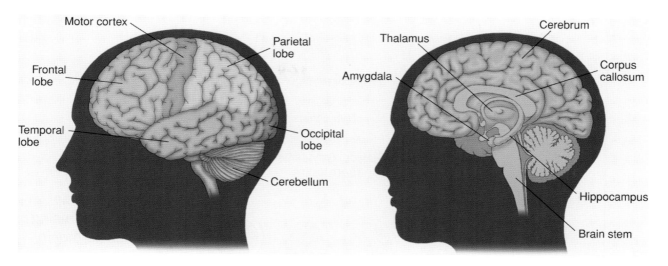

Diagram showing the anatomy of the human brain: Exterior view showing the lobes (on left) and the interior sections (right). *(Frank Forney)*

The diencephalon

The diencephalon lies above the brain stem and embodies the thalamus and hypothalamus. The thalamus is an important relay station for sensory information, interpreting sound, smell, taste, pain, pressure, temperature, and touch; it also regulates some emotions and memory. The hypothalamus controls a number of body functions, such as heartbeat and digestion, and helps regulate the endocrine system (hormonal system) and body temperature. The hypothalamus signals hunger and thirst and also helps regulate sleep, anger, and aggression.

The cerebrum

Constituting nearly 90% of the brain's weight, the cerebrum is divided into specific areas that interpret sensory impulses. For example, spoken and written languages are transmitted to a part of the cerebrum called Wernicke's area where meaning is constructed. Motor areas control muscle movements. Broca's area translates thoughts into speech, and coordinates the muscles needed for speaking. Impulses from other motor areas direct hand muscles for writing and eye muscles for physical movement necessary for reading. The cerebrum is divided into left and right hemispheres. A deep fissure separates the two, with the corpus callosum, a large bundle of fibers, connecting them.

By studying patients whose corpora callosa had been destroyed, scientists realized that differences existed between the left and right sides of the cerebral cortex. The left side of the brain functions mainly in speech, logic, writing, and arithmetic. The right side, on the other hand, is more concerned with imagination, art, symbols, and spatial relations. For most right-handed people (and many left-handed people as well), the left half of the brain is dominant.

The cerebrum's outer layer, the cerebral cortex, is composed of gray matter, which is made up of nerve cell bodies. About 0.08 in (2 mm) thick with a surface area about 5 sq. ft (0.5 sq m), it's nearly half the size of an office desk (if it were spread out flat). White matter, composed of nerve fibers covered with myelin sheaths, lies beneath the gray matter. During embryonic development, the gray matter grows faster than the white and folds in on itself, giving the brain its characteristic wrinkles, called convolutions, or gyri; the grooves between them are known as sulci.

The cerebellum

The cerebellum is located below the cerebrum and behind the brain stem. It is butterfly shaped, with the "wings" known as the cerebellar hemispheres; the two halves are connected by the vermis. The cerebellum coordinates many neuromuscular functions, such as balance and coordination. Disorders related to damage of the cerebellum often result in ataxia (problems with coordination), dysarthria (unclear speech resulting from problems controlling the muscles used in speaking), and nystagmus (uncontrollable jerking of the eyeballs). A brain tumor that is relatively common in children known as medulloblastoma grows in the cerebellum.

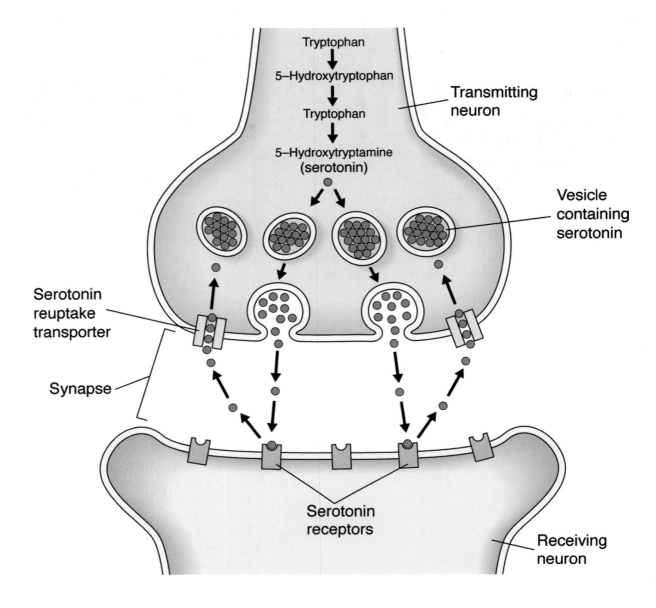

Tryptophan

5–Hydroxytryptophan

Tryptophan

5–Hydroxytryptamine
(serotonin)

**Transmitting
neuron**

**Vesicle
containing
serotonin**

**Serotonin
reuptake
transporter**

Synapse

**Serotonin
receptors**

**Receiving
neuron**

Diagram showing transmitting and receiving neurons and the role of serotonin in communication between neurons. *(Frank Forney)*

Studying the brain

Neurons carry information through the nervous system in the form of brief electrical impulses called action potentials. When an impulse reaches the end of an axon, **neurotransmitters** are released at junctions called synapses. The neurotransmitters are chemicals that bind to receptors on the receiving neurons, triggering the continuation of the impulse. Fifty different neurotransmitters have been discovered since the first was identified in 1920. By studying the chemical effects of neurotransmitters in the brain, scientists have developed treatments for mental disorders and are learning more about how drugs affect the brain.

Computerized brain imaging

Technology provides useful tools for researching the brain and helping patients with brain disorders. An electroencephalogram (EEG) records brain waves, which are produced by electrical activity in the brain. It is obtained by positioning electrodes on the head and amplifying the waves with an electroencephalograph.

EEGs are valuable in diagnosing brain diseases such as epilepsy and tumors.

Scientists use several other techniques to study and understand the brain and diagnose disorders.

MAGNETIC RESONANCE IMAGING (MRI). Using a magnetic field to display the living brain at various depths, MRI can produce very clear and detailed pictures of brain structures. These images, which often appear as cross-sectional slices, are obtained by altering the main magnetic field of a specific brain area. MRI is particularly valuable in diagnosing damage to soft tissues, such as areas affected by head trauma or **stroke**. This is crucial when early **diagnosis** improves the chances of successful treatment. MRI also reveals tumors and other types of brain lesions.

POSITRON EMISSION TOMOGRAPHY (PET). During this test, a technician injects the patient with a small amount of a substance, such as glucose, that is marked with a radioactive tag. By tracking the radioactive substance as it travels to the brain, physicians can see almost immediately where glucose is consumed in the brain. This indicates brain activity, an important factor in diagnosing epilepsy, **Alzheimer's disease**, or Parkinson's disease. PET is also valuable in locating tumors and brain areas that have been affected by a stroke or blood clot.

POSITRON EMISSION TOMOGRAPHY (PET) AND FDDNP. Researchers have developed a molecule, abbreviated FDDNP, that binds to the plaques and protein tangles that characterize Alzheimer's disease in the brain. This molecule also is fluorescent, and after injection of a solution of FDDNP into a patient, clinicians can use PET to capture an image of the brain showing where it has bound and is fluorescing. In this way, they can distinguish a brain even with mild cognitive impairment compared to a brain with no cognitive impairment and also can distinguish mild impairment from Alzheimer's disease.

MAGNETOENCEPHALOGRAPHY (MEG). Magnetoencephalography measures the electromagnetic fields created between neurons as electrochemical information is passed along. Of all brain-scanning methods, MEG provides the most accurate indicator of nerve cell activity, which can be measured in milliseconds. By combining an MRI with MEG, clinicians can get a noninvasive look at the brain that is especially useful in diagnosing epilepsy or migraines, for example. MEG also helps identify specific brain areas involved with different tasks. Any movement by the patient—wiggling the toes, for example—appears on the computer screen immediately as concentric colored rings. This pinpoints brain signals even before the toes are

actually wiggled. Researchers foresee that these techniques could someday help paralysis victims move by supplying information on how to stimulate their muscles or indicating the signals needed to control an artificial limb.

COMPUTED AXIAL TOMOGRAPHY (CAT OR CT) SCAN. This type of scan uses X-rays to produce a picture of the targeted area of the body in cross sections. Clinicians may use a dye that creates a contrast between tissues to highlight a specific area of interest for the scan. In the brain, this type of scan can be used to identify an area of stroke or hemorrhage, causes of headache, and causes of lost sensory or motor function. This test may also be used in the diagnosis of other disorders involving the brain, including **delirium**, **dementia**, and **schizophrenia**.

See also Addiction; Nutrition and mental health.

Resources

BOOKS

Bear, Mark F., Barry W. Connors, and Michael A. Paradiso. *Neuroscience: Exploring the Brain.* Baltimore: Williams and Wilkins, 1996.

Burstein, John. *The Mind by Slim Goodbody.* Minneapolis, MN: Fairview Press, 1996.

Carey, Joseph, ed. *Brain Facts.* Washington, D.C.: Society for Neuroscience, 1993.

Greenfield, Susan A., ed. *The Human Mind Explained: An Owner's Guide to the Mysteries of the Mind.* New York: Henry Holt, 1996.

Howard, Pierce J. *The Owner's Manual for the Brain: Everyday Applications from Mind-Brain Research.* Austin, TX: Leornian Press, 1994.

Jackson, Carolyn, ed. *How Things Work: The Brain.* Alexandria, VA: Time-Life Books, 1990.

KEY TERMS

Corpus callosum—(plural, corpora callosa) A thick bundle of nerve fibers lying deep in the brain that connects the two cerebral hemispheres and coordinates their functions.

Meninges—A membrane covering the brain and spinal cord that consists of three layers: the pia mater, the innermost layer; the arachnoid, in the middle; and the dura mater, the outermost layer.

Myelin sheaths—A fatty layer around nerve cells that aids the transmission of nerve impulses.

Peripheral nerve—A nerve in a distant location from the brain that receives information in the form of an impulse from the brain and spinal cord.

PERIODICAL

Small, Gary W., and others. "PET of brain amyloid and tau in mild cognitive impairment." *The New England Journal of Medicine* 355 (2006): 2652–2663.

OTHER

The Mind. Alexandria, VA: PBS Video, 1988. (Series of nine 1-hour videocassettes.)

National Library of Medicine. "Cranial CT Scan." <http://www.nlm.nih.gov/medlineplus/ency/article/003786.htm>.

The Nature of the Nerve Impulse. Films for the Humanities and Sciences, 1994-95. (Videocassette.)

Laith Farid Gulli, M.D.

Breathing-related sleep disorder

Definition

Breathing-related sleep disorder is marked by sleep disruption from abnormal breathing during sleep. The most common complaint of individuals with breathing-related sleep disorder is excessive daytime sleepiness, brought on by frequent interruptions of nocturnal, or nighttime, sleep. A less frequent complaint is **insomnia** or inability to sleep. About two-thirds with this disorder experience daytime sleepiness and one-third from an inability to sleep.

Mental health professionals use the ***Diagnostic and Statistical Manual of Mental Disorders***, also known as the *DSM* to diagnose mental disorders. In the 2000 edition of this manual (the fourth edition, text revision, also known as *DSM-IV-TR*), breathing-related sleep disorder is listed as one of several different primary **sleep disorders**. Within the category of primary sleep disorders, it is classified as one of the dyssomnias, which are characterized by irregularities in the quality, timing, and amount of sleep.

The *DSM-IV-TR* lists three types of breathing-related sleep disorder: obstructive sleep apnea syndrome (the most common type), central sleep apnea syndrome, and central alveolar hypoventilation syndrome.

Description

The most common feature of any breathing-related sleep disorder is interruption of the person's sleep, leading to excessive daytime sleepiness. When the regular nighttime sleep of individuals is frequently interrupted, sleepiness at other times of the day is the usual result. People with breathing-related sleep dis-

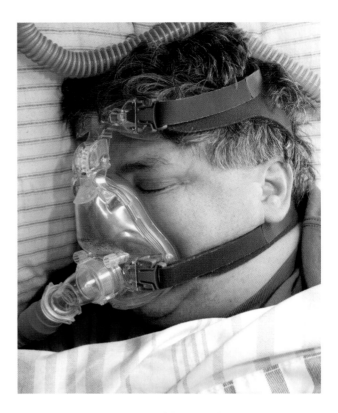

An individual undergoes the CPAP test for sleep apnea.
(Custom Medical Stock Photo, Inc. Reproduced by permission.)

order often find that they feel sleepy during relaxing activities such as reading or watching a movie. With extreme cases, those with this condition may feel so sleepy that they fall asleep during activities that require alertness, such as talking, walking, or driving.

Other people with breathing-related sleep disorder report having insomnia, or the inability to sleep. Patients also find that their sleep does not refresh them; they may awaken frequently during sleep, or have difficulty breathing while sleeping or lying down.

The two sleep apnea syndromes that are listed as subtypes of breathing-related sleep disorder are characterized by episodes of airway blockage or breathing cessation during sleep. Sleep apnea is potentially deadly. Central alveolar hypoventilation syndrome is distinguished from the other two subtypes of breathing-related sleep disorder by the fact that shallow breathing causes the reduced oxygen content of the blood. The alveoli, which are the tiny air sacs in the lung tissue, cannot oxygenate the blood efficiently because those with this disorder are not breathing deeply enough. Shallow breathing often occurs when people are awake and is common in severely overweight individuals.

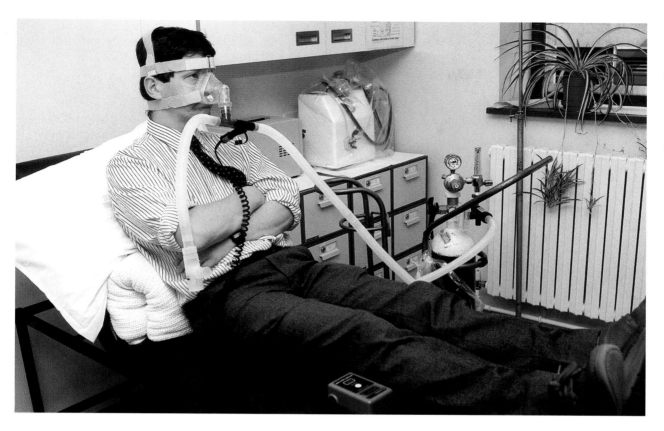

Patient wearing CPAP (continuous positive airway pressure) system, which can monitor such conditions as sleep apnea.
(Medical-on-Line/Alamy)

Causes and symptoms

Causes

Many people with the obstructive sleep apnea syndrome subtype of breathing-related sleep disorder are overweight. The symptoms often grow worse as their weight increases. People who have obstructive sleep apnea and are not overweight often have breathing passages that are narrowed by swollen tonsils, abnormally large adenoids, or other abnormalities of the various structures of the mouth and throat. The fundamental underlying cause appears to be a narrow or collapsible airway with a loss of muscle tone in the airway during sleep.

Central sleep apnea syndrome is often associated with cardiac or neurological conditions affecting airflow regulation. It is a disorder that occurs most frequently in elderly patients.

Patients diagnosed with central alveolar hypoventilation syndrome experience a breathing impairment related to abnormally low arterial oxygen levels.

Symptoms

Obstructive sleep apnea syndrome, which is the most common type of breathing-related sleep disorder, is marked by frequent episodes of upper airway obstruction during sleep. Patients with this syndrome alternate between loud snores or gasps and silent periods that usually last for 20–30 seconds. The snoring is caused by the partial blockage of the airway. The silent periods are caused by complete obstruction of the airway, which makes the patient's breathing stop. These periods of breathing cessation can last between 10 seconds and one minute.

Obstructive sleep apnea syndrome is also common in children with enlarged tonsils. The symptoms of any breathing-related sleep disorder in children are often subtle and more difficult to diagnose. Children under five years are more likely to demonstrate nighttime symptoms such as apnea and breathing difficulties. Children over five years are more likely to demonstrate daytime symptoms such as sleepiness and attention difficulties.

People with central sleep apnea syndrome experience periods when the oxygenation of blood in the lungs temporarily stops during sleep, but they do not suffer airway obstruction. Although these patients may snore, their snoring is usually mild and not a major complaint.

Central alveolar hypoventilation syndrome is characterized by excessive sleepiness and insomnia.

Demographics

As of 2007, it has been estimated that between 7 and 18 million Americans have some kind of breathing-related sleep disorder. Rates are higher among people who are overweight, obese, or elderly. The majority of patients with the obstructive sleep apnea type of breathing-related sleep disorder are overweight, middle-aged males. Four percent of middle-aged men and 2% of middle-aged women meet the criteria for obstructive sleep apnea. Among children the male-to-female ratio is 1:1. Prevalence of breathing-related sleep disorder among children peaks between two and eight years of age.

Diagnosis

A **diagnosis** of breathing-related sleep disorder usually requires a thorough physical examination of the patient. The patient may be referred to an otorhinolaryngologist (a doctor who specializes in disorders of the ear, nose, and throat) for a detailed evaluation of the upper respiratory tract. The physical examination is followed by observation of the patient in a sleep clinic or laboratory. Breathing patterns, including episodes of snoring and apnea, are evaluated when the patient is connected to a device called a polysomnogram. The polysomnogram uses a set of electrodes to measure several different body functions associated with sleep, including heart rate, eye movements, **brain** waves, muscle activity, breathing, changes in blood oxygen concentration, and body position. Interviews are also conducted with the patients and their partners.

To meet criteria for the diagnosis of breathing-related sleep disorder, patients must experience interruptions of sleep leading to insomnia or excessive sleepiness that have been determined to result from one of the following sleep-related breathing conditions: obstructive sleep apnea syndrome, central sleep apnea syndrome, or central alveolar hypoventilation syndrome.

The disturbance in sleep must also not be attributed to another mental disorder or by a general medical condition not related to breathing.

The disturbance in sleep must not be due to the direct effects on the body of a prescription medication or drug of **abuse**.

Treatments

Weight loss is a key to effective treatment of overweight people with breathing-related sleep disorder. It is often considered the first step in treating any disorder involving sleep apnea. Increased exercise and reduced-calorie **diets** are the most important components of an effective weight loss regimen.

Another approach to addressing sleep apnea is a postural change during sleep, called "positional therapy." The U.S. Food and Drug Administration (FDA) has approved a pillow that is supposed to aid in preventing the sleeper from assuming a supine (on the back) position, a position that may worsen sleep apnea. In addition, postural alarms are also being marketed to warn the sleeper, but many people try home-based approaches to ensuring that they do not flip onto their backs during sleep. One study has found that sleeping on the back with the torso elevated may result in reduced apneas, but recommended that patients trying this option use foam pillows rather than soft pillows, which can push the chin onto the chest and worsen apnea.

Oral appliances may be effective for people who have mild apnea. The most common of these is the mandibular advancement device (also called MAD), which pushes the lower jaw forward, keeping the airway open.

Continuous positive airway pressure therapy, also known as CPAP therapy, is a popular form of treatment for the obstructive sleep apnea subtype of breathing-related sleep disorder. CPAP therapy, which has been in use since 1981, involves the use of a high-pressure blower that delivers continuous air flow to a mask worn by the patient during sleep. The airflow from the CPAP blower is often very effective in reducing or eliminating sleep apnea episodes. CPAP treatment is, however, inconvenient and somewhat noisy for anyone who must share a bedroom with the patient. Patients do not always comply with this form of treatment; a 2004 study indicated that about 25% of patients who are treated with CPAP therapy stop using it within a year. A couple of alternative forms of CPAP may improve **compliance** by improving comfort, including bi-level positive airway pressure, which has two sets of air pressures that it delivers, one for exhalation and one for inhalation, to make using the device more comfortable. Also, a more recent introduction is the C-Flex, which provides flexible positive airway pressure, alternating pressures for inhalation and exhalation on a breath-by-breath basis. The company that produces the C-Flex received FDA permission to market its product in 2004. CPAPs, as medical devices, must be obtained through a doctor's prescription.

There are no medications that directly target sleep apnea.

Surgery to relieve airway obstruction may be performed in some cases. If the airway obstruction is related to anatomical structures that narrow the airway, surgical reshaping of the soft palate and uvula (a small, conical-shaped piece of tissue attached to the middle of the soft palate) may be performed. Another surgical procedure that is sometimes conducted on very obese patients with obstructive sleep apnea is a tracheostomy, or an artificial opening made in the windpipe. This operation has a number of unpleasant side effects, however, and so is usually reserved for patients whose breathing-related disorder is life-threatening.

Patients with sleep apnea are advised to abstain from alcohol and sedative medications, which are often given to patients who display any type of sleeping irregularities. Alcohol and **sedatives** often increase the likelihood of upper airway problems during sleep.

Prognosis

Breathing-related sleep disorder often has a gradual long-term progression and a chronic course. For this reason, many people have the disorder for years before seeking treatment. For many, symptoms worsen during middle age, causing people to seek treatment at that point.

Successful treatment of other conditions, such as **obesity**, the common cardiovascular and cerebrovascular comorbidities, or enlarged tonsils in children, often aids in the treatment of breathing-related sleep disorder. Weight loss often leads to spontaneous resolution of the disorder. Because **depression** has been found at high rates among people with sleep apnea (as high as 64% in some studies), any assessments should evaluate for the presence of depression to aid in improving the prognosis.

Prevention

Because overweight people are more likely to develop the more common obstructive sleep apnea type of breathing-related sleep disorder, a good preventive measure is effective weight management. Good general health and treatment of related physio-

---

KEY TERMS

Alveolar—Pertaining to alveoli, which are tiny air sacs at the ends of the small air passages in the lungs.

Apnea—A brief suspension or interruption of breathing.

Dyssomnia—A type of sleep disorder characterized by a problem with the amount, quality, or timing of the patient's sleep.

Hypoventilation—An abnormally low level of blood oxygenation in the lungs.

Polysomnogram—A machine that is used to diagnose sleep disorders by measuring and recording a variety of body functions related to sleep, including heart rate, eye movements, brain waves, muscle activity, breathing, changes in blood oxygen concentration, and body position.

Syndrome—A group of symptoms that together characterize a disease or disorder.

Tracheostomy—A surgical procedure in which an artificial opening is made in the patient's windpipe to relieve airway obstruction.

---

logical conditions are also effective in preventing the disorder.

See also Circadian rhythm sleep disorder; Obesity.

Resources

BOOKS

American Psychiatric Association. *Diagnostic and Statistical Manual of Mental Disorders*. 4th ed., Text rev. Washington, D.C.: American Psychiatric Association, 2000.

Buysse, Daniel J., Charles M. Morin, and Charles F. Reynolds III. "Sleep Disorders." *Treatments of Psychiatric Disorders*, edited by Glen O. Gabbard. 2nd ed. Washington, D.C.: American Psychiatric Press.

Hobson, J. Allan, and Rosalia Silvestri. "Sleep and Its Disorders." *The Harvard Guide to Psychiatry*, edited by Armand M. Nicholi, Jr., MD. Cambridge, MA: Belknap Press of Harvard University Press, 1999.

Saskin, Paul. "Obstructive Sleep Apnea: Treatment Options, Efficacy, and Effects." *Understanding Sleep: The Evaluation and Treatment of Sleep Disorders*, edited by Mark R. Pressman, PhD, and William C. Orr, PhD. Washington, D.C.: American Psychological Association, 1997.

Thorpy, Michael J., MD, and Jan Yager, PhD. *The Encyclopedia of Sleep and Sleep Disorders*. 2nd ed. New York: Facts on File, 2001.

ORGANIZATIONS

American Sleep Apnea Association. 1424 K Street NW, Suite 302, Washington DC 20005. <http://www.sleepapnea.org>.

American Sleep Disorders Association. 6301 Bandel Road NW, Suite 101, Rochester, MN 55901. <http://www.asda.org>.

National Center on Sleep Disorders Research. <http://www.nhlbi.nih.gov/about/ncsdr/index.htm>.

National Sleep Foundation. 1522 K Street, NW, Suite 500, Washington, DC 20005. Telephone: (202) 347-3471. <http://www.sleepfoundation.org/>.

PERIODICALS

Aloia, Mark S., and others. "Treatment Adherence and Outcomes in Flexible vs. Standard Continuous Positive Airway Pressure Therapy." *Chest* 127 (2005): 2085–93.

Dauvilliers, Yves, and A. Buguet. "Hypersomnia." *Dialogues in Clinical Neuroscience* 7 (2005): 347–56.

Haba-Rubio, José. "Psychiatric Aspects of Organic Sleep Disorders." *Dialogues in Clinical Neuroscience* 7 (2005): 335–46.

Lloberes, Patricia, and others. "Predictive Factors of Quality-of-life Improvement and Continuous Positive Airway Pressure Use in Patients with Sleep Apnea-Hypopnea Syndrome: Study at 1 Year." *Chest* 126.4 (2004): 1241–47.

OTHER

National Heart, Lung, and Blood Institute. "Sleep Apnea." <http://www.nhlbi.nih.gov/health/dci/Diseases/SleepApnea/SleepApnea_WhatIs.html>.

"Breathing-related Sleep Disorders." *Emedicine.com.* This Web site offers pictures of CPAP devices and detailed information about testing and surgical options. <http://www.emedicine.com/med/topic3130.htm>.

Ali Fahmy, PhD
Emily Jane Willingham, PhD

Brief psychotic disorder

Definition

Brief psychotic disorder is a short-term psychiatric disorder lasting between one day and one month, with complete remission and return to full functioning following the episode. In brief psychotic disorder, the individual experiences at least one symptom of **psychosis**: incoherence, **delusions**, **hallucinations**, and/or grossly disorganized or catatonic behavior.

The cause of the symptoms helps to determine whether or not the person is described as having brief psychotic disorder. If the psychotic symptoms appear as a result of a physical disease, a reaction to medica-tion, or intoxication with drugs or alcohol, then the unusual behaviors are not classified as brief psychotic disorder. If hallucinations, delusions, or other psychotic symptoms occur at the same time that an individual is experiencing major clinical **depression** or bipolar (manic-depressive) disorder, then the brief psychotic disorder **diagnosis** is not given. The decision rules that allow the clinician to identify this cluster of symptoms as brief psychotic disorder are outlined in the *Diagnostic and Statistical Manual of Mental Disorders* Fourth Edition Text Revision, produced by the American Psychiatric Association. This manual is referred to by most mental health professionals as *DSM-IV-TR.*

Description

Positive symptoms

The person experiencing brief psychotic disorder always has one or more "positive" psychotic symptoms. The psychotic symptoms are not positive in the everyday sense of something being good or useful. Positive in this context is used with the medical meaning: a factor is present that is not normally expected, or a normal type of behavior is experienced in its most extreme form. **Positive symptoms** of psychosis include hallucinations, delusions, strange bodily movements or lack of movements (catatonic behavior), peculiar speech, and bizarre or primitive behavior.

HALLUCINATIONS. Hallucinations involve experiencing sensations that have no corresponding objective reality. Hallucinations can occur in various forms that parallel the human senses. Visual hallucinations involve the sense of sight, or "seeing things." Auditory hallucinations generally involve hearing voices, and are the most common of the hallucinations. Sometimes, a hallucination can include both voices and some visual experience; mental health professionals describe this as an "auditory-visual hallucination." Smelling nonexistent smells or feeling things on or under one's skin that do not actually exist are forms of somatic hallucinations. Somatic comes from *soma,* the Greek word for body; thus, somatic hallucinations are bodily hallucinations.

DELUSIONS. Delusions are also a classic psychotic feature. Delusions are strongly held irrational and unrealistic beliefs that are extremely difficult to change, even when the person is exposed to evidence that contradicts the delusion. The layperson typically thinks of delusions as being paranoid, or persecutory, wherein the delusional person is excessively suspicious and continually feels at the mercy of conspirators who are "out to get" him or her. However, delusions can also be unjustified beliefs that are grandiose, involve elaborate love fantasies (called erotomanic delusions), or extreme and irrational jealousy. Grandiose delusions are persistent irrational beliefs that somehow exaggerate the person's importance, such as believing oneself to be a famous person, or having an enviable position such as being the Prime Minister or President. Often grandiose delusions take on religious overtones; for instance, a person might become convinced that she is the Virgin Mary. Furthermore, delusions can also be somatic. Somatic delusions are erroneous but strongly held beliefs about the characteristics or functioning of one's body; an example is a mental health consumer who refuses to eat because of a conviction that the throat muscles are completely paralyzed and that only liquids can be swallowed, when there is no actual physical reason to be unable to swallow.

OTHER PSYCHOTIC SYMPTOMS. Other psychotic symptoms that may occur in brief psychotic disorder are strange bodily movements or lack of movements (catatonic behavior), peculiar speech, and bizarre or childlike behavior. Catatonic behavior or **catatonia** involves both possible extremes related to movement. Catalepsy is the motionless aspect of catatonia—a person with catalepsy may remain fixed in the same position for hours on end. Rapid or persistently repeated movements, frequent grimacing and strange facial expressions, and unusual gestures are the opposite end of the catatonia phenomenon. Peculiar speech is also seen in some cases of brief psychotic disorder. Speech distortions can involve words mixed together in no coherent order, responses that are irrelevant and strange in the context of the conversation in which they occur, or echolalia, the repetition of another person's exact spoken words, repeated either immediately after the speaker or after a delay of minutes or hours. Bizarre behavior can range from childlike behaviors such as skipping, singing, or hopping in inappropriate circumstances to unusual practices such as hoarding food or covering one's head and clothing with aluminum foil wrappings.

Of course, not all of these psychotic symptoms will be observed simultaneously in the person with brief psychotic disorder. Any constellation of these positive psychotic symptoms that occurs for one entire day up to one month is considered to be brief psychotic disorder, unless there is some other syndrome or biological cause that caused the symptoms to appear.

Causes and symptoms

Causes

Brief psychotic disorder is not a simple or consistent disorder with a single cause. Because many phe-

nomena can prompt a short-term experience of psychotic symptoms, there are several ways of viewing the causes of the disorder.

AN EARLY PHASE OF SCHIZOPHRENIA. Because of the similarities between brief psychotic disorder, **schizophreniform disorder**, and **schizophrenia**, many clinicians have come to think of brief psychotic disorder as being the precursor to a lengthier psychotic disorder. Although this can only be identified retrospectively, brief psychotic disorder is often the diagnosis that was originally used when an individual (who later develops schizophrenia) experiences a first psychotic break from more typical functioning.

A STRESS RESPONSE. At times, under severe **stress**, temporary psychotic reactions may appear. The source of stress can be from typical events encountered by many people in the course of a lifetime, such as being widowed or divorced. The severe stress may be more unusual, such as being in combat, enduring a natural disaster, or being taken hostage. The person generally returns to a normal method of functioning when the stress decreases or more support is available, or better coping skills are learned.

POSTPARTUM PSYCHOSIS. In some susceptible women, dramatic hormonal changes in childbirth and shortly afterward can result in a form of brief psychotic disorder often referred to as postpartum psychosis. Unfortunately, postpartum conditions are often misidentified and improperly treated. In many cases of a mother killing her infant or committing **suicide**, postpartum psychosis is involved.

DEFENSE MECHANISM IN PERSONALITY DISORDER. Persons with **personality disorders** appear to be more susceptible to developing brief psychotic reactions in response to stress. Individuals with personality disorders have not developed effective adult mechanisms for coping with life. When life becomes more demanding and difficult than can be tolerated, the person may lapse into a brief psychotic state.

CULTURALLY DEFINED DISORDER. Culture is a very important factor in understanding mental health and psychological disturbance, and brief psychotic disorder is an excellent example. The types of behavior that occur during brief psychotic disorder are very much shaped by the expectations and traditions of the individual's culture. In many cultures, there are some forms of mental disorders that meet criteria for brief psychotic disorder and manifest with symptoms that are peculiar to that culture or community. Individuals within the group exhibit similar behavior, which may be attributed to a particular cause or stimulus, such as cabin fever, witchcraft, or spiritual possession, or may be the result of a culturally specific phobia, such as the fear of sinning among religious communities or the fear of being cold in tropical climates. The *DSM-IV-TR* terms disorders unique to certain societies or groups to be culture-bound. An example of a culture-bound syndrome is *koro,* a syndrome observed in Japan and some other areas of Asia but not elsewhere. Koro is an **obsession** to the point of delusion with the possibility that the genitals will retract or shrink into the body and cause death.

Conversely, while culture shapes the form a psychotic reaction may take, culture also determines what is *not* to be considered psychotic. Behaviors that in one culture would be thought of as bizarre or psychotic may be acceptable in another. For example, some cultural groups and religions view "speaking in tongues" as a valuable expression of the gifts of God, whereas viewed out of context, the unrecognizable speech patterns might be viewed as psychotic. If the behaviors shown are culturally acceptable in the person's society or religion, and happen in an approved setting such as a religious service, then brief psychotic disorder would not be diagnosed.

Symptoms

The *DSM-IV-TR* provides three major criteria for brief psychotic disorder:

- At least one positive symptom of psychosis, from the following symptoms: delusions; hallucinations; disorganized speech which is strange, peculiar, difficult to comprehend; disorganized (bizarre or childlike) behavior; or catatonic behavior.
- Limited duration. The psychotic symptoms have occurred for at least one day but less than one month. There is an eventual return to normal level of functioning.
- The symptoms are not biologically influenced or attributable to another disorder. In other words, the symptoms cannot be occurring as part of a mood disorder, schizoaffective disorder, or schizophrenia, and they cannot be due to intoxication with drugs or alcohol. Further, the symptoms cannot be an adverse reaction to a medication, and they cannot be caused by a physical injury or medical illness.

Demographics

The actual rate of brief psychotic disorder is unknown, although it appears to be fairly rare in the United States and other developed countries. While psychotic reactions that occur and subside in under a month are more common in developing nations, the mental disorders wherein psychotic symptoms last longer than one month are more prevalent in developed countries. The disorder appears to be more common in adolescents and young adults than in those of middle age or older.

Diagnosis

Using the *DSM-IV-TR* criteria makes identification of the disorder relatively clear-cut. However, an unusual aspect to this diagnosis is the emphasis on the length of time that symptoms have been evident. Most mental health disorder diagnoses do not include the duration of the symptoms as part of their definitions. However, the length of time the person has had psychotic symptoms is one of the major distinctions among three different psychotic disorders. Brief psychotic disorder involves the shortest duration of suffering psychotic symptoms: one day to one month. Schizophreniform disorder also involves the individual showing signs of psychosis, but for a longer period (one month or more, but less than six months). Schizophrenia is diagnosed in individuals who have evidenced psychotic symptoms that are not associated with physical disease, mood disorder, or intoxication, for six months or longer. Another complicating factor in making the diagnosis is the context in which the psychotic symptoms are experienced. If the psychotic-like behaviors evidenced are acceptable in the person's culture or religion and these behaviors happen in a traditionally expected context such as a religious service or **meditation**, then brief psychotic disorder would not be diagnosed.

The disorder is usually diagnosed by obtaining information in interview from the client and possibly from immediate family. Also, the diagnostician would be likely to perform a semistructured interview called a mental status examination, which examines the person's ability to concentrate, to remember, to realistically understand the situation, and to think logically.

Treatments

Antipsychotic medications are very effective in ending a brief psychotic episode. A number of different antipsychotics are used for the purpose of terminating acute psychotic episodes. **Haloperidol** (Haldol) is most commonly used if the psychotic symptoms are accompanied by agitation. Agitation is a state of frantic activity that is often accompanied by anger or fearfulness; when in an agitated state, the client is more likely to cause harm to self or others. In agitated psychotic states, the haloperidol is often given as an injection, accompanied by other medications that decrease **anxiety (lorazepam,** also known as Ativan) and slow behavior (**diphenhydramine**, also known as Benadryl). If the client is not agitated, usually a newer-generation antipsychotic is used, given daily as tablets, capsules or liquid, for a lengthier period of time. The antipsychotic that would be used is likely to be one of the following: **olanzapine** (Zyprexa), **quetiapine** (Seroquel), or **risperidone** (Risperdal). Hormones may also be prescribed for postpartum psychosis. Supportive therapy may also prove helpful in some situations, in decreasing the client's anxiety and educating the client about the psychiatric illness. In culture-bound syndromes, the most effective treatment is often the one that is societally expected; for example, bathing in a river viewed as sacred might be a usual method of curing the psychotic-like state, in a particular culture.

Prognosis

The prognosis is fairly positive in brief psychotic disorder because by its own definition, a return to normal functioning is expected. If there is a major life event as a stress or an unusual traumatic experience that initiated the episode, chances are very good that there will be no recurrence. If there is not a particular triggering event or if the episode occurred in an individual with a personality disorder, the likelihood of recurrence is higher. If an episode is a recurrence without a specific triggering event, then the beginnings of the development of schizophrenia or **bipolar disorder** may be at hand, in which case the prognosis is poor. In the individual with personality disorder, the pattern may recur in response to stress, so that there are intermittent experiences of brief psychotic disorder over the course of a lifetime.

Prevention

In women who have experienced brief postpartum psychosis, one prevention option is to forgo having additional children. If a postpartum psychosis has occurred in the past, in subsequent pregnancies the physician may be proactive in prescribing an antipsychotic medication regimen to be taken in the postpartum period in order to prevent psychotic symptoms from recurring. In many cases severe stressors can be a trigger for brief psychotic disorder. Therefore, in response to identifiable extreme stressors, such as natural disasters or terrorist attacks, strong social support and immediate postcrisis counseling could possibly prevent the development of brief psychotic disorder in susceptible persons.

See also Borderline personality disorder; Delirium; Dementia; Postpartum depression; Post-traumatic

---

stress disorder; Schizotypal personality disorder; Substance abuse.

Resources

BOOKS

American Psychiatric Association. *Diagnostic and Statistical Manual of Mental Disorders,* 4th ed., Text rev. Washington, D.C.: American Psychiatric Association, 2000.

First, Michael B., and Allan Tasman. *Clinical Guide to the Diagnosis and Treatment of Mental Disorders.* New York: John Wiley & Sons, 2006.

Marneros, Andreas, and Frank Pillmann. *Acute and Transient Psychoses.* New York: Cambridge University Press, 2004.

VandenBos, Gary R., ed. *APA Dictionary of Psychology.* Washington, D.C.: American Psychological Association, 2006.

PERIODICALS

Amini, Homayoun, and others. "Diagnostic Stability in Patients with First-Episode Psychosis." *Australasian Psychiatry* 13.4 (December 2005): 388–92.

Correll, Christoph U., and others. "Prospective Study of Adolescents with Subsyndromal Psychosis: Characteristics and Outcome." *Journal of Child and Adolescent Psychopharmacology* 15.3 (2005): 418–33.

Kalaitzi, C. K., and D. Sakkas. "Brief Psychotic Disorder Associated with Sturge-Weber Syndrome." *European Psychiatry* 20.4 (June 2005): 356–57.

Rufino, Armanda, C. T. B. F., Ricardo R. Uchida, José A. A. Vilela, João M. A. Marques, Antonio W. Zuardi, and Cristina M. Del-Ben. "Stability of the Diagnosis of First-Episode Psychosis Made in an Emergency Setting." *General Hospital Psychiatry* 27.3 (May--June 2005): 189--93.

Thangadurai, P., R. Gopalakrishnan, S. Kurian, and K. S. Jacob. "Diagnostic Stability and Status of Acute and Transient Psychotic Disorders." *British Journal of Psychiatry* 188.3 (March 2006): 293.

Deborah Rosch Eifert, PhD
Ruth A. Wienclaw, PhD

Bulimia nervosa

Definition

Bulimia nervosa is an eating disorder characterized by **binge eating** and engaging in inappropriate ways of counteracting the bingeing (using laxatives, for example) to prevent weight gain. The word "bulimia" is the Latin form of the Greek word *boulimia*, which means "extreme hunger." A binge is consuming a larger amount of food within a limited period of time than most people would eat in similar circumstances. Most people with bulimia report feelings of loss of control associated with bingeing, and some have mildly dissociative experiences in the course of a binge, which means that they feel disconnected from themselves and from reality when they binge.

The handbook for mental health professionals to aid in **diagnosis** is the ***Diagnostic and Statistical Manual of Mental Disorders***, also known as the *DSM-IV-TR*. It categorizes bulimia nervosa as an eating disorder, along with **anorexia nervosa**.

Description

Bulimia nervosa is classified into two subtypes according to the methods used by the patient to prevent weight gain after a binge. The purging subtype of bulimia is characterized by the use of self-induced vomiting, laxatives, enemas, or diuretics (pills that induce urination); in the nonpurging subtype, fasting or overexercising is used to compensate for binge eating.

The onset of bulimia nervosa is most common in late adolescence or early adult life. Dieting efforts and body dissatisfaction, however, often occur in the teenage years. For these reasons, it is often described as a developmental disorder. Genetic researchers have identified specific genes linked to susceptibility to eating disorders, and the environmental primary factor in the development of bulimia nervosa is **stress** related to

A bulimic young woman crouching over a toilet bowl in order to self-induce vomiting. *(Cristina Pedrazzini/Photo Researchers, Inc)*

the onset of puberty. Girls who have strongly negative feelings about their bodies in response to puberty are at high risk for developing bulimia.

The binge eating associated with bulimia begins most often after a period of strict dieting. Most people with bulimia develop purging behaviors in response to the bingeing. Vomiting is used by 80–90% of patients diagnosed with bulimia. The personal accounts of recovered bulimics suggest that most "discover" vomiting independently as a way of ridding themselves of the food rather than learning about it from other adolescents. Vomiting is often done to relieve an uncomfortable sensation of fullness in the stomach following a binge as well as to prevent absorption of the calories in the food. Vomiting is frequently induced by touching the gag reflex at the back of the throat with the fingers or a toothbrush, but a minority of patients use syrup of ipecac to induce vomiting. About one-third of bulimics use laxatives after binge eating to empty the digestive tract, and a minority use diuretics or enemas. Purging behaviors lead to a series of digestive and metabolic disturbances that then reinforce the behaviors.

A small proportion of bulimics exercise excessively or fast after a binge instead of purging.

Patients with bulimia may come to the attention of a **psychiatrist** because they develop medical or dental complications of the eating disorder. In some cases, the adolescent's dentist is the "case finder." In many cases, however, the person with bulimia seeks help.

Causes and symptoms

Causes

Bulimia nervosa is understood to be a complex disorder with multiple factors contributing to its development. Studies suggest an interaction among genetics, familial factors, and social pressures in the development of an eating disorder.

GENETICS. Several studies have obtained results pointing to a genetic understructure for eating disorders, including bulimia. Studies investigating the relationship between characteristics of bulimia in families and their correlation with patterns of gene expression have linked bulimia to genes on human chromosome 10.

FAMILIAL FACTORS. A number of recent studies point to the interpersonal relationships in the family of origin (the patient's family while growing up) as a factor in the later development of bulimia. People with bulimia are more likely than people with anorexia to have been sexually abused in childhood; studies have found that abnormalities in blood levels of serotonin (a neurotransmitter associated with mood disorders) and cortisol (the primary stress hormone in humans) in bulimic patients with a history of childhood sexual **abuse** resemble those in patients with **post-traumatic stress disorder** (PTSD). Post-traumatic stress disorder is a mental disorder that can develop after someone has experienced a traumatic event (horrors of war, for example) and is unable to put that event behind him or her—the disorder is characterized by very realistic flashbacks of the traumatic event.

A history of eating conflicts and struggles over food in the family of origin is also a risk factor for the development of bulimia nervosa. Personal accounts by recovered bulimics frequently note that one or both parents were preoccupied with food or dieting. Fathers appear to be as influential as mothers in this regard. A recent study focusing on girls suggests that the influence of the father may be related to the father's own concerns and body preoccupations and that this influence may be stronger as a child gets older. Other risk factors identified in a 2007 study, which followed the children from birth, were a low activity level in early childhood and rapid eating in later childhood. In addition, and not surprisingly, peer and parental teasing about body weight or shape also increase risk.

An additional risk factor for early-onset bulimia is interest in or preparation for a sport or occupation that requires strict weight control, such as gymnastics, figure skating, horse jockeying, wrestling, or modeling.

SOCIOCULTURAL CAUSES. Emphasis in the mass media on slenderness in women as the primary criterion of beauty and desirability is commonly noted in studies of bulimia. Historians of fashion have remarked that the standard of female attractiveness has changed over the past half century in the direction of greater slenderness; some have commented that Marilyn Monroe would be considered "fat" by contemporary standards. The ideal female figure is not only unattainable by the vast majority of women, but is lighter than the standards associated with good health by insurance companies. In 1965 the average model weighed 8% less than the average American woman; by 2001, she weighed 25% less. Recent news reports have focused on this **obsession** with thinness in the fashion industry because of the deaths of several models from eating disorders. One major fashion group in Spain went so far as to set a minimum body mass index for models on its catwalks in 2006 after a model died during a show in South America of causes apparently related to an eating disorder. In the United States, magazine covers feature razor-thin actresses with alarmed questions about their weight and health splashed across the covers, sending a mixed message.

Another factor mentioned by intellectual historians is the centuries-old split in Western philosophy between mind and body. Instead of regarding a human person as a unified whole consisting of body, soul, and mind, Western thought since Plato has tended to divide human nature in a dualistic fashion between the life of the mind and the needs of the body. Furthermore, this division was associated with gender symbolism in such a way that the life of the mind was associated with masculinity and the needs of the body with femininity. The physical dimension of human life was correlated with men's physical, legal, and economic domination of women. Although this dualistic pattern of symbolic thought is no longer a conscious part of the Western mindset, it appears to influence Western culture on a subconscious level.

A number of different theories have been put forward to explain the connections between familial and social factors and bulimia. Some of these theories include:

- Bulimia results from a conflict between mother and daughter about nurturing and dependency. Girls are typically weaned earlier than boys and fed less. The bulimic's bingeing and purging represent a conflict between wanting comfort and believing that she does not deserve it.

- Bulimia develops when an adolescent displaces larger conflicts about being a woman in a hypersexualized society onto food. Many writers have commented about the contradictory demands placed on women in contemporary society—for example, to be sexually appealing yet "untouchable" at the same time. Controlling body size and food intake becomes a simplified solution to a very complex problem of personal identity and moral standards.
- Bulimia is an obsession with food that the culture encourages to protect men from competition from intellectually liberated women. Women who are spending hours each day thinking about food, or bingeing and purging, do not have the emotional and intellectual energy to take their rightful places in the learned professions and the business world.
- Bulimia expresses a fear of fat rooted in childhood memories of mother's size relative to one's own.
- Bulimia results from intensified competition among women for professional achievement (getting a desirable job or a promotion, or being accepted into graduate or professional school) as well as personal success (getting a husband), because studies have indicated that businesses and graduate programs discriminate against overweight applicants.
- Bulimia results from attempts to control emotional chaos in one's interpersonal relationships by imposing rigid controls on food intake.

Nutrition experts have pointed to the easy availability of foods high in processed carbohydrates in developed countries as a social factor that contributes to the incidence of bulimia. One study found that subjects who were given two slices of standard mass-produced white bread with some jelly had their levels of serotonin increased temporarily by 450%. This finding suggests that bulimics who binge on ice cream, bread, cookies, pizza, and fast food items that are high in processed carbohydrates are simply manipulating their neurochemistry in a highly efficient manner. The incidence of bulimia may be lower in developing countries because **diets** that are high in vegetables and whole-grain products but low in processed carbohydrates do not affect serotonin levels in the **brain** as rapidly or as effectively.

Symptoms

The *DSM-IV-TR* specifies that bingeing and the inappropriate attempts to compensate for it must occur twice a week for three months on average to meet the diagnostic criteria for bulimia nervosa.

A second criterion of bulimia nervosa is exaggerated concern with body shape and weight. Bulimia can be distinguished from **body dysmorphic disorder** (BDD) by the fact that people with BDD usually focus on a specific physical feature—most commonly a facial feature—rather than overall shape and weight. Bulimics do, however, resemble patients with BDD in that they have distorted body images.

Bulimia is associated with a number of physical symptoms. Binge eating by itself rarely causes serious medical complications, but it is associated with nausea, abdominal distension and cramping, slowed digestion, and weight gain.

Self-induced vomiting, on the other hand, may have serious medical consequences, including:

- Erosion of tooth enamel, particularly on the molars and maxillary incisors. Loss of tooth enamel is irreversible.
- Enlargement of the salivary glands.
- Scars and calloused areas on the knuckles from contact with the teeth.
- Irritation of the throat and esophagus from contact with stomach acid.
- Tearing of mucous membranes in the upper gastrointestinal tract or perforation of the esophagus and stomach wall. Perforation of part of the digestive tract is a rare complication of bulimia but is potentially fatal.
- Electrolyte imbalances. The loss of fluids from repeated vomiting and laxative abuse can deplete the body's stores of hydrogen chloride, potassium, sodium, and magnesium. Hypokalemia (abnormally low levels of potassium in the blood) is a potential medical emergency that can lead to muscle cramps, seizures, and heart arrhythmias.

Other physical symptoms associated with bulimia include irregular menstrual periods or amenorrhea; petechiae (pinhead-sized bruises from capillaries ruptured by increased pressure due to vomiting) in the skin around the eyes, and rectal prolapse (the lowering of the rectum from its usual position).

Demographics

Bulimia nervosa affects between 1% and 3% of women in the developed countries; its prevalence is thought to have increased markedly since 1970. The rates are similar across cultures as otherwise different as the United States, Japan, the United Kingdom, Australia, South Africa, Canada, France, Germany, and Israel. About 80% to 90% of patients with bulimia are female.

The average age at onset of bulimia nervosa appears to be dropping in the developed countries.

A study of eating disorders in Rochester, Minnesota, over the 50 years between 1935 and 1985 indicated that the incidence rates for women over 20 remained fairly constant, but there was a significant rise for women between 15 and 20 years of age. The average age at onset among women with bulimia was 14 and among men, 18.

Homosexual men appear to be as vulnerable to developing bulimia as heterosexual women, while lesbians are less vulnerable.

Recent studies indicate that bulimia in the United States is no longer primarily a disorder of Caucasian women; the rates among African American and Hispanic women have risen faster than the rate of bulimia for the female population as a whole. One report indicates that the chief difference between African American and Caucasian bulimics in the United States is that the African American patients are less likely to eat restricted diets between episodes of binge eating.

Diagnosis

The diagnosis of bulimia nervosa is made on the basis of a physical examination, a psychiatric assessment, the patient's eating history, and the findings of laboratory studies. Patients who do not meet the full criteria for bulimia nervosa may be given the diagnosis of subsyndromal bulimia or of an eating disorder not otherwise specified (EDNOS).

Physical examination

Patients suspected of having bulimia nervosa should be given a complete physical examination because the disorder has so many potential medical complications. In addition, most bulimics are close to normal weight or only slightly overweight, and so do not look outwardly different from most people of their sex in their age group. The examination should include not only vital signs and an assessment of the patient's height and weight relative to age, but also checking for such signs of bulimia as general hair loss, abdominal soreness, swelling of the parotid glands, telltale scars on the back of the hand, petechiae, edema, and teeth that look ragged or "moth-eaten."

Psychiatric assessment

Psychiatric assessment of patients with bulimia usually includes four components:

- a thorough history of body weight, eating patterns, diets, typical daily food intake, methods of purging (if used), and concept of ideal weight.

- a history of the patient's significant relationships with parents, siblings, and peers, including present or past physical, emotional, or sexual abuse.

- a history of previous psychiatric treatment (if any) and assessment of comorbid (occurring at the same time as the bulimia) mood, anxiety, substance abuse, or personality disorders.

- administration of standardized instruments that measure attitudes toward eating, body size, and weight. Common tests for eating disorders include the Eating Disorder Examination; the Eating Disorder Inventory; the Eating Attitude Test, or EAT; and the Kids' Eating Disorder Survey (KEDS).

Laboratory findings

Laboratory tests ordered for patients suspected of having bulimia usually include a complete blood cell count, blood serum chemistry, thyroid tests, and urinalysis. If necessary, the doctor may also order a chest x ray and an electrocardiogram (EKG). Typical findings in patients with bulimia include low levels of chloride and potassium in the blood, and higher than normal levels of amylase, a digestive enzyme found in saliva.

Treatments

Treatment for bulimia nervosa typically involves several therapy approaches. It is, however, complicated by several factors.

First, patients diagnosed with bulimia nervosa frequently have coexisting psychiatric disorders that typically include major **depression, dysthymic disorder, anxiety disorders**, substance abuse disorders, or personality disorders. In the case of depression, the mood disorder may either precede or follow the onset of bulimia, and, with bulimia, the prevalence of depression is 40–70%. With regard to substance abuse, about 30% of patients diagnosed with bulimia nervosa abuse either alcohol or stimulants over the course of the eating disorder. The personality disorders most often diagnosed in bulimics are the so-called Cluster B disorders—borderline, narcissistic, histrionic, and antisocial. **Borderline personality disorder** is a disorder characterized by stormy interpersonal relationships, unstable self-image, and impulsive behavior. People with **narcissistic personality disorder** believe that they are extremely important and are unable to have empathy for others. Individuals with **histrionic personality disorder** seek attention almost constantly and are very emotional. **Antisocial personality disorder** is characterized by a behavior pattern of a disregard for others' rights—people with this disorder often deceive and manipulate others. Although patients may have both bulimia nervosa and anorexia nervosa, a number of clinicians have noted that patients with predominate bulimia tend to develop impulsive and unstable personality disturbances whereas patients with predominate anorexia tend to be more obsessional and perfectionistic. Estimates of the prevalence of personality disorders among patients with bulimia range between 2% and 50%. The clinician must then decide whether to treat the eating disorder and the comorbid conditions concurrently or sequentially. It is generally agreed, however, that a substance abuse disorder, if present, must be treated before the bulimia can be effectively managed. It is also generally agreed that mood disorders and bulimia can be treated concurrently, often using antidepressant medication along with therapy.

Second, the limitations on treatment imposed by **managed care** complicate the treatment of bulimia nervosa. When the disorder first received attention in the 1970s, patients with bulimia were often hospitalized until the most significant physical symptoms of the disorder could be treated. Few patients with bulimia are hospitalized today, however, with the exception of medical emergencies related to electrolyte imbalances and gastrointestinal injuries associated with the eating disorder. Most treatment protocols for bulimia nervosa now reflect cost-containment measures.

Medications

The most common medications given to patients are **antidepressants**, because bulimia is so closely associated with depression. Short-term medication trials have reported that tricyclic antidepressants—desipramine, **imipramine**, and amitriptyline—reduce episodes of binge eating by 47–91% and vomiting by 45–78%. The monoamine oxidase inhibitors are not recommended as initial medications for patients diagnosed with bulimia because of their side effects. The most promising results have been obtained with the **selective serotonin reuptake inhibitors**, or **SSRIs**. **Fluoxetine** (Prozac) was approved in 1998 by the Food and Drug Administration (FDA) for the treatment of bulimia nervosa. Effective dosages of fluoxetine are higher for the treatment of bulimia than they are for the treatment of depression. Although a combination of medication and **cognitive-behavioral therapy** is more effective in treating most patients with bulimia than medication alone, one team of researchers reported success in treating some bulimics who had not responded to **psychotherapy** with fluoxetine by itself.

Ondansetron (Zofran), a drug that was originally developed to control nausea from chemotherapy and radiation therapy for cancer, blocks serotonin reuptake and also works to inhibit vomiting. It has shown some benefit in ameliorating symptoms of bulimia nervosa.

In addition to antidepressant or antinausea medications, such acid-reducing medications as cimetidine and ranitidine, or antacids, may be given to patients with bulimia to relieve discomfort in the digestive tract associated with irritation caused by stomach acid.

Psychotherapy

Cognitive-behavioral therapy (CBT) is regarded as the most successful psychotherapeutic approach to bulimia nervosa. CBT is intended to interrupt the faulty thinking processes associated with bulimia, such as preoccupations with food and weight, black-white thinking ("all or nothing" thinking, or thinking thoughts only at extreme ends of a spectrum), and low self-esteem, as well as such behaviors as the binge-purge cycle. Patients are first helped to regain control over their food intake by keeping food diaries and receiving feedback about their meal plans, symptom triggers, nutritional balance, and so on. They are then taught to challenge rigid thought patterns by receiving **assertiveness training** and practice in identifying and expressing their feelings in words rather than through distorted eating patterns. About 50% of bulimic patients treated with CBT are able to stop bingeing and purging. Of the remaining half, some show partial improvement and a small minority do not respond at all.

Family therapy is sometimes recommended as an additional mode of treatment for patients with bulimia who come from severely troubled or food-obsessed families that increase their risk of relapsing.

Other mainstream therapies

Medical nutrition therapy, or MNT, is a recognized component of the treatment of eating disorders. Effective MNT for patients with bulimia involves an understanding of cognitive-behavioral therapy as well as the registered dietitian's usual role of assisting the physician with monitoring the patient's physical symptoms, laboratory values, and vital signs. In the treatment of bulimia, the dietitian's specialized knowledge of nutrition may be quite helpful in dealing with the myths about food and fad diets that many bulimic patients believe. The dietitian's most important task, however, is helping the patient to normalize her or his eating patterns to break the deprivation/bingeing cycle that is characteristic of bulimia nervosa. Calorie intake is usually based on retaining the patient's weight to prevent hunger, because hunger increases susceptibility to bingeing.

KEY TERMS

Binge—An excessive amount of food consumed in a short period of time. Usually, while a person binge eats, he or she feels disconnected from reality, and feels unable to stop. The bingeing may temporarily relieve depression or anxiety, but after the binge, the person usually feels guilty and depressed.

Body image—A term that refers to a person's inner picture of his or her outward appearance. It has two components: perceptions of the appearance of one's body, and emotional responses to those perceptions.

Comorbidity—Association or presence of two or more mental disorders in the same patient. A disorder that is said to have a high degree of comorbidity is likely to occur in patients diagnosed with other disorders that may share or reinforce some of its symptoms.

Cortisol—A steroid hormone released by the cortex (outer portion) of the adrenal gland when a person is under stress.

Diuretic—A medication or substance given to increase the amount of urine excreted.

Dysthymic disorder—A mood disorder that is less severe than depression but usually more chronic.

Electrolytes—Substances or elements that dissociate into electrically charged particles (ions) when dissolved in the blood. The electrolytes in human blood include potassium, magnesium, and chloride.

Hypokalemia—Abnormally low levels of potassium in the blood. Hypokalemia is a potential medical emergency, as it can lead to disturbances in of the heart rhythm. Muscle cramps and pain are a common symptom of hypokalemia in bulimic patients.

Incisors—The four teeth in the front of each jaw in humans. The incisors of patients with bulimia frequently show signs of erosion from stomach acid.

Ipecac—The dried root of *Caephalis ipecacuanha*, a South American plant. Given in syrup form, ipecac is most commonly used to induce vomiting in cases of accidental poisoning.

Petechiae—Pinpoint-sized hemorrhages in the skin or a mucous membrane. In bulimia, petechiae may appear in the skin around the eyes as a result of increased pressure in the capillaries caused by vomiting.

Purging—Inappropriate actions taken to prevent weight gain, often after bingeing, including self-induced vomiting or the misuse of laxatives, diuretics, enemas, or other medications.

Serotonin—A widely distributed neurotransmitter that is found in blood platelets, the lining of the digestive tract, and the brain, and that works in combination with norepinephrine. It causes very powerful contractions of smooth muscle, and is associated with mood, attention, emotions, and sleep. Low levels of serotonin are associated with depression.

One study from upstate New York found that bright **light therapy** (regular exposure to ultraviolet light), of the type frequently prescribed for **seasonal affective disorder** (SAD), appears to be effective in reducing binge eating in patients diagnosed with bulimia. It also significantly relieved depressive symptoms, as measured by the patients' scores on the **Beck Depression Inventory**. As of 2007, no further studies addressing the effect of bright light on binge eating have been published.

Alternative and complementary treatments

Alternative therapies that have been shown to be helpful for some patients in relieving the anxiety and muscular soreness associated with bulimia nervosa include **acupuncture**, massage therapy, hydrotherapy, and shiatsu.

Herbal remedies that have been used to calm digestive upsets in bulimic patients include teas made from **chamomile** or peppermint. Peppermint helps to soothe the intestines by slowing down the rate of smooth muscle contractions (peristalsis). Chamomile has been used to help expel gas from the digestive tract, a common complaint of bulimics. Both herbs have a wide margin of safety.

Some bulimic patients have responded well to **yoga** because its emphasis on focused breathing and **meditation** calls attention to and challenges the distorted thought patterns that characterize bulimia. In addition, the stretching and bending movements that are part of a yoga practice help to displace negative thoughts focused on the body's outward appearance with positive appreciation of its strength and agility. Last, because yoga is noncompetitive, it allows bulimics to explore the uniqueness of their bodies rather than constantly comparing themselves to other people.

Prognosis

The prognosis of bulimia depends on several factors, including age at onset, types of purging behaviors used (if any), and the presence of other psychiatric conditions or disorders. In many cases, the disorder becomes a chronic (long-term) condition; 20–50% of patients have symptoms for at least five years in spite of treatment. The usual pattern is an alternation between periods of remission and new episodes of bingeing. Patients whose periods of remission last for a year or longer have a better prognosis; patients diagnosed with major depression or a personality disorder have a less favorable prognosis. Overall, however, the prognosis for full recovery from bulimia nervosa is considered relatively poor compared to other eating disorders.

Bulimia nervosa appears to produce changes in the functioning of the serotonin system in the brain. A team of researchers at the University of Pittsburgh who compared brain images taken by **positron emission tomography** (PET) from bulimic women who had been in remission for a year or longer with brain images from healthy women found that the recovered bulimics did not have a normal age-related decline in serotonin binding. Because serotonin helps to regulate mood, appetite, and impulse control, the study may help to explain why some women may be more susceptible to developing bulimia than others.

Prevention

Although a genetic link to bulimia has been identified, there are currently no gene-based preventive measures. With regard to family influences, the overwhelming majority of studies have found that the most important preventive measure that can be taken is the establishment of healthful eating patterns and attitudes toward food in the family of origin.

See also Nutrition counseling.

Resources

BOOKS

American Psychiatric Association. *Diagnostic and Statistical Manual of Mental Disorders*. 4th ed., Text rev. Washington, D.C.: American Psychiatric Association, 2000.

"Bulimia Nervosa." Section 15, Chapter 196. *The Merck Manual of Diagnosis and Therapy*, edited by Mark H. Beers, MD, and Robert Berkow, MD. Whitehouse Station, NJ: Merck Research Laboratories, 2001.

Chernin, Kim. *The Obsession: Reflections on the Tyranny of Slenderness*. Revised edition. New York: HarperPerennial Editions, 1994.

Eichenbaum, Luise, and Susie Orbach. *Understanding Women: A Feminist Psychoanalytic Approach*. New York: Basic Books, Publishers, 1983.

Hornbacher, Marya. *Wasted: A Memoir of Anorexia and Bulimia*. New York: HarperPerennial Editions, 1999.

Newmark, Gretchen Rose. "Overcoming Eating Disorders." In *Living Yoga: A Comprehensive Guide for Daily Life*, edited by Georg Feuerstein and Stephan Bodia. New York: Jeremy P. Tarcher/Perigee, 1993.

Rodin, Judith, PhD. *Body Traps: Breaking the Binds That Keep You from Feeling Good About Your Body*. New York: William Morrow, 1992.

Roth, Geneen. *When Food is Love*. New York: Penguin Books, 1992.

Wolf, Naomi. *The Beauty Myth: How Images of Beauty Are Used Against Women*. New York: Anchor Books, 1992.

PERIODICALS

Agras, Stewart W., and others. "Childhood Risk Factors for Thin Body Preoccupation and Social Pressure to be Thin." *Journal of the American Academy of Child and Adolescent Psychiatry* 46 (2007): 171–78.

Bulik, Cynthia M. "Exploring the Gene–Environment Nexus in Eating Disorders." *Journal of Psychiatry and Neuroscience* 30 (2005): 335–39.

Bulik, C. M., and others. "Twin Studies of Eating Disorders: A Review." *International Journal of Eating Disorders* 27 (2000): 1–20.

Eliot, A. W., and C. W. Baker. "Eating Disordered Adolescent Males." *Adolescence* 36 (Fall 2001): 535–43.

Fairburn, Christopher C. "The Natural Course of Bulimia Nervosa and Binge Eating Disorder in Young Women." *Journal of the American Medical Association* 284 (October 18, 2000): 1906.

Hay, Phillipa J., and Josué Bacaltchuk. "Bulimia Nervosa: Review of Treatments." *British Medical Journal* 303 (July 7, 2001): 33–37.

Kaye, Walter H., Guido K. Frank, Carolyn C. Meltzer, and others. "Altered Serotonin 2A Receptor Activity in Women Who Have Recovered from Bulimia Nervosa." *American Journal of Psychiatry* 158 (July 2001): 1152–55.

Kotler, Lisa A., Patricia Cohen, Mark Davies, and others. "Longitudinal Relationships Between Childhood, Adolescent, and Adult Eating Disorders." *Journal of the American Academy of Child and Adolescent Psychiatry* 40 (December 2001): 1434–40.

"Light Therapy for Bulimia." *Family Practice News* 10 (February 1, 2000): 32.

Little, J. W. "Eating Disorders: Dental Implications." *Oral Surgery, Oral Medicine, Oral Pathology, Oral Radiology, and Endodontics* 93 (February 2002): 138–43.

McGilley, Beth M., and Tamara L. Pryor. "Assessment and Treatment of Bulimia Nervosa." *American Family Physician* 57 (June 1998): 1339.

Miller, Karl E. "Cognitive Behavior Treatment of Bulimia Nervosa." *American Family Physician* 63 (February 1, 2001): 536.

"Position of the American Dietetic Association: Nutrition Intervention in the Treatment of Anorexia Nervosa, Bulimia Nervosa, and Eating Disorders Not Otherwise Specified." *Journal of the American Dietetic Association* 101 (July 2001): 810–28.

Romano, Steven J., Katherine A. Halmi, Neena P. Sankar, and others. "A Placebo-Controlled Study of Fluoxetine in Continued Treatment of Bulimia Nervosa After Successful Acute Fluoxetine Treatment." *American Journal of Psychiatry* 159 (January 2002): 96–102.

Steiger, Howard, Lise Gauvin, Mimi Israel, and others. "Association of Serotonin and Cortisol Indices with Childhood Abuse in Bulimia Nervosa." *Archives of General Psychiatry* 58 (September 2001): 837.

Vink, T., A. Hinney, A. A. van Elburg, and others. "Association Between an Agouti-Related Protein Gene Polymorphism and Anorexia Nervosa." *Molecular Psychiatry* 6 (May 2001): 325–28.

Walling, Anne D. "Anti-Nausea Drug Promising in Treatment of Bulimia Nervosa." *American Family Physician* 62 (September 1, 2000): 1156.

ORGANIZATIONS

Academy for Eating Disorders, Montefiore Medical School, Adolescent Medicine. 111 East 210th Street, Bronx, NY 10467. Telephone: (718) 920-6782.

American Academy of Child and Adolescent Psychiatry. 3615 Wisconsin Avenue N.W., Washington, DC 20016-3007. Telephone: (202) 966-7300. Fax: (202) 966-2891. <http://www.aacap.org>.

American Anorexia/Bulimia Association. 165 W. 46th Street, Suite 1108, New York, NY 10036. Telephone: (212) 575-6200.

American Dietetic Association. Telephone: (800) 877-1600. <http://www.eatright.org>.

Anorexia Nervosa and Related Eating Disorders, Inc. (ANRED). P.O. Box 5102, Eugene, OR 97405. Telephone: (541) 344-1144. <http://www.anred.com>.

Center for the Study of Anorexia and Bulimia. 1 W. 91st St., New York, NY 10024. Telephone: (212) 595-3449.

OTHER

"Bulima Nervosa." U.S. Department of Health and Human Services. <http://www.womenshealth.gov/faq/Easy-read/bulnervosa-etr.htm>.

Rebecca Frey, PhD
Emily Jane Willingham, PhD

Bullying

Definition

Bullying is a persistent pattern of threatening, harassing, or aggressive behavior directed toward another person or persons who are perceived as smaller, weaker, or less powerful. Although often thought of as a childhood phenomenon, bullying can occur wherever people interact, most notably observable in the workplace and in the home. Bullying is also called harassment.

Description

"Kids will be kids," the saying goes, so warning signs of bullying are often overlooked as a natural part of childhood. However, although playground bullies have been around since time immemorial, such behavior should neither be considered acceptable nor excusable. Bullying is a form of abuse and violence, and the tragic Columbine High School massacre in 1999 underscores the potential dangers of unchecked bullying.

There are many forms of bullying. Bullies may intimidate or harass their victims physically through hitting, pushing, or other physical violence; verbally through such actions as threats or name calling; or psychologically through spreading rumors, making sexual comments or gestures, or excluding the victim from desired activities. Such behavior does not need to occur in person: Cyberbullying is a persistent pattern of threatening, harassing, or aggressive behavior carried out online.

There are many reasons to stop bullying. Bullying interferes with school performance, and children who are afraid of being bullied are more likely to miss school or drop out. Bullied children frequently experience developmental harm and fail to reach their full physiological, social, and academic potentials. Children who are bullied grow increasingly insecure and anxious, and have persistently decreased self-esteem and greater **depression** than their peers, often even as adults. Children have even been known to commit **suicide** as a result of being bullied.

People who are bullies as children often become bullies as adults. Bullying behavior in the home is called child abuse or spousal abuse. Bullying also occurs in prisons and in churches.

Recently, attention has been turned to the topic of bullying in the workplace (sometimes called harassment), where bosses and organizational peers bully those whom they perceive as their inferiors or weaker

A young boy faces bullying from older and bigger kids. *(Gideon Mendel/Alamy)*

than they. Those bullied at work often become perceived as ineffective, thus abrogating their career success and influencing their earning potential. Victims of workplace bullying often change jobs in search of a less hostile environment because organizations are frequently not sensitive to the issue of workplace bullying or equipped to adequately or justly deal with it.

Demographics

Bullying in children

Bullying among children is a persistent and substantial problem. According to a study published in 2001 by the Kaiser Family Foundation and Nickelodeon Television, 55% of 8–11-year-olds and 68% of 12–15-year-olds said that bullying is a "big problem" for people their age. Seventy-four percent of the 8–11-year-olds and 86% of the 12–15-year-olds also reported that children were bullied or teased at their school. Children at greatest risk of being bullied are those who are perceived as social isolates or outcasts by their peers, have a history of changing schools, have poor social skills and a desire to fit in "at any cost," are

defenseless, or are viewed by their peers as being different.

A study of more than 16,000 children in the sixth through tenth grades conducted for the National Institute of Child Health and Human Development found that bullying is a common problem in the United States and requires serious attention. Nearly 60% of the children responding to the survey reported that they had been victims of rumors. More than 50% of the children reported that they had been the victims of sexual harassment.

The National Center for Education Statistics (NCES) of the U.S. Department of Education found that white, non-Hispanic children were more likely to report being the victims of bullying than black or other non-Hispanic children. Younger children were more likely to report being bullied than older children, and children attending schools with gangs were more likely to report being bullied than children in schools without a major gang presence. No differences were found in these patterns between public and private schools. Fewer children reported bullying in schools that were supervised by police officers, security officers, or staff hallway monitors. Victims of bullying were more likely to be criminally victimized at school than were other children. Victims of bullying were more afraid of being attacked both at school and elsewhere and more likely to avoid certain areas of school (for example, the cafeteria, hallways or stairs, or restrooms) or activities where bullying was more likely to take place. Significantly, victims of bullies were more likely to report that they carried weapons to school for protection.

Children who are identified as bullies by the time they are eight years of age are six times more likely than other children to have a criminal conviction by the time they are 24 years old. Bullying behavior may also be accompanied by other inappropriate behavior, including criminal, delinquent, or gang behavior.

Bullying in the workplace

Although research has been conducted on bullying in Europe for some time, the topic has only recently become of interest in the United States. There are no "official" figures currently available for incidents of bullying in the workplace. However, the nonprofit Workplace Bullying Institute conducted an informal survey of 1,000 self-selected volunteer respondents. Although it cannot be assumed that the volunteers answering the survey are representative of individuals in the workplace in general, the results do give food for thought concerning the prevalence of workplace bullying.

In the survey, 80% of the women and 20% of the men reported having been bullied at work. Sixty-one percent of the victims of workplace bullying said that the behavior was ongoing. The survey also found that 70% of victims of workplace bullying lose their jobs: 37% of the victims were fired or involuntarily terminated and 16% of the victims transferred to another position within the same organization. On the other hand, the survey found that only 4% of bullies stopped their aggressive or harassing actions after punishment and that only 9% of workplace bullies were transferred, fired, or involuntarily terminated. Contrary to the cartoon portrait of male bullies, the survey showed that 50% of workplace bullying was done by women victimizing other women. Men bullying women accounted for only 30% of bullying, while men bullying men accounted for 12% of workplace bullying and women bullying men accounted for 8%. The figure with women bullying other women is particularly interesting because such same-sex harassment (with the exception of sexual harassment) is usually outside the scope of antidiscrimination laws and is typically not tracked.

Causes and symptoms

As of this writing, there is no evidence to support the theory that there is a genetic component to bullying behavior. Particularly in children, it is most often theorized that bullying is a result of the bully copying the actions of role models who bully others. This frequently happens when bullies come from a home in which one parent bullies another or one or both parents bully the children. When such behavior is modeled for children with personality traits such as lack of impulse control or aggression, they are particularly prone to bullying behavior, which is often continued into adulthood.

Bullying in children

According to the U.S. Department of Health and Human Services, children with dominant personalities and who are more impulsive and active are more prone to becoming bullies than children without these traits. Bullies also often have a history of emotional or behavioral problems. Victims of bullying, on the other hand, tend to be more anxious, insecure, and socially isolated than their peers, and often lack age-appropriate social skills. The probability of victimization can be compounded when the victim has low self-esteem due to physical characteristics (for example, the victim believes her/himself to be unattractive or is outside the normal range for height or weight) or problems (for example, health problems or physical or mental disability).

Warning signs and factors that may indicate risk for being or becoming a bully include:

- lack of impulse control (frequent loss of temper, extreme impulsiveness, easily frustrated, extreme mood swings)
- family factors (abuse or violence within the family, substance or alcohol abuse within the family, overly permissive parenting, lack of clear limits, inadequate parental supervision, harsh/corporal punishment, child abuse, inconsistent parenting)
- behavioral symptoms (gang affiliation, name calling or abusive language, carrying a weapon, hurting animals, alcohol or drug abuse, making serious threats, vandalizing or damaging property, frequent physical fighting)

Symptoms that a child may be being bullied include:

- social withdrawal or isolation (few or no friends; feeling isolated, sad, and alone; feeling picked on or persecuted; feeling rejected or not liked; having poor social skills)

- somatic complaints (frequent complaints about illness; displaying victim body language, including hanging head, hunching shoulders, and avoiding eye contact)
- avoidant behavior (not wanting to go to school; skips classes or skips school)
- affective reactions (crying easily; having mood swings; talking about hopelessness, running away, or suicide)
- physical clues (bringing home damaged possessions or reports that belongings were "lost")
- behavior changes (changes in eating or sleeping patterns)
- aggressive behavior (threatening violence to self or others, taking or attempting to take weapon to school)

Each child will react to bullying in a different manner, and some children will react with only a few of these symptoms. This, however, does not mean that bullying is not severe or that **intervention** is not needed.

Bullying in the workplace

Bullying in the workplace is usually motivated by political rather than personal reasons. Workers compete over scarce resources such as promotions, raises, and the corner office or other honors. In an attempt to climb the ladder of success, some individuals do what they can to not only present themselves in a good light to their superiors, but to make one or more coworkers seem unworthy or inept. Bullying bosses demonstrate poor leadership styles and poor motivational skills, frequently attempting to further either their own or the company's agenda through harassment, belittling, or other negative behaviors.

Common tactics used by bullies in the workplace include:

- discounting/belittling victim in public (making statements such as "that's silly" in response to victim's ideas, disregarding evidence of satisfactory or superlative work done by victim, taking credit for victim's work)
- false accusations (rumors about victim, lies about victim's performance)
- harassment (verbal putdowns based on gender, race, disability)
- isolating behaviors (encouraging others to turn against victim, socially or physically isolating the victim from others)
- nonverbal aggression (staring, glaring, silent treatment)
- sabotages victim's work

- unequal treatment (retaliating against victim who files a complaint, making up arbitrary rules for victim to follow, assigning undesirable work as a punishment, making unreasonable/unreachable goals or deadlines for victim, performing a constructive discharge of duties)

Diagnosis

Bullying in itself is not a mental disorder, although aggressive or harassing behavior may be symptomatic of a number of disorders, particularly **antisocial personality disorder** and schizoid behavior. There are, however, a number of criteria to help determine if someone is a bully. First, to qualify as bullying, the bully's behavior must be intended to cause physical or psychological harm to the other person. Second, bullying behavior is not an isolated incident but results in a consistent pattern of such behavior over time. Third, bullying occurs where there is an imbalance of power whereby the bully has more physical or psychological power than the victim. Harassing behavior is not considered to be bullying if it occurs between individuals of equal strength and status or if it is a one-time event.

Bullying behavior in children can include any of the following behaviors:

- dominance (enjoying feeling powerful and in control, seeking to dominate or manipulate others, being a poor winner or loser)
- lack of empathy (deriving satisfaction from the fears, pain, or discomfort of others; enjoying conflict between others; displaying intolerance and prejudice toward others)
- negative emotions or violence (displaying uncontrolled anger or a pattern of impulsive and chronic hitting, intimidating, or aggressive behavior)
- lack of responsibility (blaming others for his/her problems)
- other behaviors (using drugs or alcohol, or being a gang member; hiding bullying behavior from adults; having a history of discipline problems)

Victims of bullying—whether children or adults—may need to be assessed and treated for an **anxiety** disorder if they need help responding to or recovering from bullying.

Treatments and prevention

If bullying behavior is symptomatic of an underlying mental disorder such as antisocial personality disorder, treatment and prevention should be guided by and address the underlying disorder. For situations in which bullying behavior is not part of a pattern associated with an underlying mental disorder, treatment and establishing organizational or familial processes for dealing with it are required.

Bullying in children

To help keep a child from becoming a bully, it is important to be a role model for nonviolent behavior. Parents should also clearly communicate to the child that bullying behavior is not acceptable, and clear limits should be established for acceptable behavior and consequences for ignoring the limits should be defined. Teaching good social skills—including efficacious conflict resolution skills and anger management skills—can also help potential bullies learn alternative, socially acceptable behaviors. If the child persists in bullying behavior or if the parent(s) suspect that their child is a bully, help can be sought from mental health professionals and school counselors. Taking the child to a child **psychologist** and participating in **family therapy** as appropriate can help teach a bully better interpersonal skills. Contacting the school counselor or a child psychologist is also an appropriate step in helping the victims of bullies.

If parents suspect that their child may be being bullied, they should make sure that he or she understands that the problem is not his or her fault and that he or she does not have to face the situation alone. Parents can discuss ways to deal with bullies, including walking away, being assertive, and getting help. Parents should also encourage the child to report bullying behavior to a teacher, counselor, or other trusted adult. However, parents should not try to resolve the situation themselves but should contact the school to report the behavior and for recommendations for further assistance.

Bullying in the workplace

Bullying in the workplace can be minimized if the organization develops and enforces anti-harassment policies and procedures. These should include a stated definition on what constitutes harassment, creating and implementing a disciplinary system to punish the bully rather than the victim, and instituting a formal grievance system to report workplace bullying. Other measures that can be taken include inclusiveness and harassment training, awareness training to educate employees on how to spot bullying behavior, and offering courses in conflict resolution, anger management, or **assertiveness training**.

Bullies are not the only ones needing help. The intention of a bully is to harm the other person; victims, therefore, may experience a number of negative

---

KEY TERMS

Antisocial personality disorder—A personality disorder characterized by aggressive, impulsive, or even violent actions that violate the established rules or conventions of a society.

Anxiety disorder—A group of mood disorders characterized by apprehension and associated bodily symptoms of tension (such as tense muscles, fast breathing, rapid heart beat). When anxious, the individual anticipates threat, danger, or misfortune. Anxiety disorders include panic disorder (with or without agoraphobia), agoraphobia without panic disorder, specific phobias, social phobia, obsessive-compulsive disorder (OCD), post-traumatic stress disorder (PTSD), acute stress disorder, generalized anxiety disorder, anxiety disorder due to a general medical condition, and substance-induced anxiety disorder.

Representative sample—A subset of the overall population of interest that is chosen so that it accurately displays the same essential characteristics of the larger population in the same proportion.

---

consequences from being the victim of a bully. If the behavior associated with being a victim persists after the bullying situation has been resolved or if the situation continues without just resolution, victims should be assessed for depression and/or an anxiety disorder if their symptoms warrant, and receive the appropriate treatment.

Resources

BOOKS

Einarsen, Ståle, Helge Hoel, Dieter Zapf, and Cary L. Cooper, eds. *Bullying and Emotional Abuse in the Workplace: International Perspectives in Research and Practice.* New York: Taylor and Francis, 2003.

Espelage, Dorothy L., and Susan M. Swearer, eds. *Bullying in American Schools: A Social-Ecological Perspective on Prevention and Intervention.* Mahwah, NJ: Lawrence Erlbaum Associates, 2003.

Geffner, Robert A, Marti Tamm Loring, and Corinna Young, eds. *Bullying Behavior: Current Issues, Research, and Interventions.* Binghamton, New York: Haworth Maltreatment and Trauma Press, 2002.

Needham, Andrea. *Workplace Bullying: The Costly Business Secret.* New York: Penguin Global, 2004.

O'Moore, Mona, and Stephen Minton. *Dealing with Bullying in Schools: A Training Manual for Teachers, Parents and Other Professionals.* London: Paul Chapman Publishing, 2004.

Rigby, Ken. *New Perspectives on Bullying*. London: Jessica Kingsley Publishers, 2002.

VandenBos, Gary R.,ed. *APA Dictionary of Psychology*. Washington, D.C.: American Psychological Association, 2007.

PERIODICALS

Ahmed, Eliza, and Valerie Braithwaite. "Forgiveness, Reconciliation, and Shame: Three Key Variables in Reducing School Bullying." *Journal of Social Issues* 62.2 (2006): 347–70.

Bowling, Nathan A., and Terry A. Beehr. "Workplace Harassment from the Victim's Perspective: A Theoretical Model and Meta-Analysis." *Journal of Applied Psychology* 91.5 (2006): 998–1012.

Chan, John H. F. "Systemic Patterns in Bullying and Victimization." *School Psychology International* 27.3 (2006): 352–369.

Cossa, Mario. "How Rude!: Using Sociodrama in the Investigation of Bullying and Harassing Behavior and in Teaching Civility in Educational Communities." *Journal of Group Psychotherapy, Psychodrama and Sociometry* 58.4 (2006): 182–94.

Heydenberk, Roberta A., Warren R. Heydenberk, and Vera Tzenova. "Conflict Resolution and Bully Prevention: Skills for School Success." *Conflict Resolution Quarterly* 24.1 (2006): 55–69.

Kim, Young Shin, Bennett L. Leventhal, Yun-Joo Koh, Alan Hubbard, and W. Thomas Boyce. "School Bullying and Youth Violence: Causes or Consequences of Psychopathologic Behavior?" *Archives of General Psychiatry* 63.9 (2006): 1035–41.

Ledley, Deborah Roth, and others. "The Relationship Between Childhood Teasing and Later Interpersonal Functioning." *Journal of Psychopathology and Behavioral Assessment* 28.1 (2006): 33–40.

Lee, Raymond T., and Céleste M. Brotheridge. "When Prey Turns Predatory: Workplace Bullying as a Predictor of Counteraggression/Bullying, Coping, and Well-Being." *European Journal of Work and Organizational Psychology* 15.3 (2006): 352–77.

Lewis, Sian E. "Recognition of Workplace Bullying: A Qualitative Study of Women Targets in the Public Sector." *Journal of Community and Applied Social Psychology* 16.2 (2006): 119–35.

Lutgen-Sandvik, Pamela. "Take This Job and . . . : Quitting and Other Forms of Resistance to Workplace Bullying." *Communication Monographs* 73.4 (2006): 406–33.

Moayed, Farman A., Nancy Daraiseh, Richard Shell, and Sam Salem. "Workplace Bullying: A Systematic Review of Risk Factors and Outcomes." *Theoretical Issues in Ergonomics Science* 7.3 (2006): 311–27.

Nickel, Marius K., and others. "Influence of Family Therapy on Bullying Behaviour, Cortisol Secretion, Anger, and Quality of Life in Bullying Male Adolescents: A Randomized, Prospective, Controlled Study." *Canadian Journal of Psychiatry* 51.6 (2006): 355–62.

Parkins, Irina Sumajin, and Harold D. Fishbein. "The Influence of Personality on Workplace Bullying and Discrimination." *Journal of Applied Social Psychology* 36.10 (2006): 2554–77.

Patchin, Justin W., and Sameer Hinduja. "Bullies Move Beyond the Schoolyard: A Preliminary Look at Cyberbullying." *Youth Violence and Juvenile Justice* 4.2 (2006): 148–69.

Peskin, Melissa Fleschler, Susan R. Tortolero, and Christine M. Markham. "Bullying and Victimization Among Black and Hispanic Adolescents." *Adolescence* 41.163 (2006): 467–84.

Phillips, Debby A. "Punking and Bullying: Strategies in Middle School, High School, and Beyond." *Journal of Interpersonal Violence* 22.2 (2007): 158–78.

Twemlow, Stuart W., Peter Fonagy, Frank C. Sacco, and John R. Brethour Jr. "Teachers Who Bully Students: A Hidden Trauma." *International Journal of Social Psychiatry* 52.3 (2006): 187–98.

ORGANIZATIONS

American Academy of Child and Adolescent Psychiatry. 3615 Wisconsin Avenue N.W., Washington, DC 20016-3007. Telephone: (202) 966-7300. <http://www.aacap.org>.

Mental Health America. 2000 N. Beauregard Street, 6th Floor, Alexandria, VA 22311. Telephone: (800) 969-6642. TTY: (800) 433-5959. <http://www.nmha.org>.

National Institute of Child Health and Human Development. P.O. Box 3006, Rockville, MD 20847. Telephone: (800) 370-2943. TTY: Telephone: (888) 320-6942. <http://www.nichd.nih.gov>.

National Institute of Mental Health (NIMH), Public Information and Communications Branch. 6001 Executive Boulevard, Room 8184, MSC 9663, Bethesda, MD 20892-9663. Telephone: (866) 615-6464. TTY: (866) 415-8051. <http://www.nimh.nih.gov>.

National Mental Health Information Center. P.O. Box 42557, Washington, DC 20015. Telephone: (800) 789-2647. TDD: (866) 889-2647. <http://mentalhealth. samhsa.gov>.

National Youth Violence Prevention Resource Center. P.O. Box 10809, Rockville, MD 20849-0809. Telephone: (866) 723-3968. TTY: (888) 503-3952. <http://www. safeyouth.org>.

U.S. Human Resources and Service Administration, Stop Bullying Now! <http://www.stopbullyingnow.hrsa.gov>.

Workplace Bullying Institute. Telephone: (360) 656-6630. <http://www .bullyinginstitute.org>.

Ruth A. Wienclaw, PhD

Bupropion

Definition

Bupropion is an antidepressant drug used to elevate mood and promote recovery of a normal range of emotions in patients with **depressive disorders**. In addition, bupropion is used to as an aid in **smoking cessation** treatment. In the United States, bupropion is sold as an antidepressant under the brand name Wellbutrin. As a smoking cessation treatment, the drug is marketed under the brand name Zyban.

Purpose

Bupropion is principally known as an antidepressant drug used to promote recovery of depressed patients. It also has therapeutic uses in smoking cessation treatment, **panic disorder**, and **attention deficit/ hyperactivity disorder** (ADHD).

Description

Bupropion is a nontricyclic antidepressant drug. Tricyclic **antidepressants**, which have a three-ring chemical structure, may cause troublesome side effects including sedation, dizziness, fainting, and weight gain. Until the 1980s, such drugs were the mainstay of the pharmacological treatment of **depression**. Bupropion was one of the first antidepressants with a significantly different chemical structure to be developed by pharmaceutical researchers seeking drugs effective in treating depression but without the unwanted actions of the tricyclic antidepressants.

The exact way that bupropion works in the **brain** is not understood. Its mechanism of action appears to be different from that of most other antidepressant drugs, although bupropion does act on some of the same **neurotransmitters** and neurotransmission pathways. Neurotransmitters are naturally occurring chemicals that regulate the transmission of nerve impulses from one cell to another. Mental well-being is partially dependent on maintaining the proper balance among the various neurotransmitters in the brain. Bupropion may restore normal emotional feelings by counteracting abnormalities of neurotransmission that occur in depressive disorders.

In contrast to the drowsiness frequently caused by other antidepressants, bupropion is a mild stimulant. Bupropion is also less likely to cause weight gain and adverse effects on blood pressure and the heart. However, it is more likely to trigger epileptic **seizures**.

Recommended dosage

The usual adult dose of bupropion (Wellbutrin) is 100 mg, taken three times per day, with at least six hours between doses. The extended release form of the drug (Wellbutrin SR) is taken as 150 mg twice a day with at least eight hours between doses. For smoking cessation, bupropion (Zyban) is taken as 150 mg extended release tablets twice a day, with at least eight hours between doses. Bupropion treatment should be started at a lower dose, then gradually increased to a therapeutic dosage, as directed by the physician. Generally, the total dosage should not exceed 300 mg per day, except as directed by the physician.

The therapeutic effects of bupropion, like other antidepressants, appear slowly. Maximum benefit is often not evident for several weeks after starting the drug. People taking bupropion should be aware of this and continue taking the drug as directed even if they do not see immediate improvement in mood.

Since higher doses of bupropion increase the risk of seizures, no more than 150 mg should be given at any one time, and the total daily dosage should not be increased by more than 100 mg every three days. Increasing the dosage gradually also minimizes agitation, restlessness, and **insomnia** that may occur.

Healthy elderly patients do not appear to be more sensitive to side effects of bupropion than younger adults and do not require reduced doses. Certain medical conditions, especially liver and kidney disease, may necessitate dose reduction. Although bupropion has been taken by children and adolescents under age 18, it has not been systematically studied in these age groups.

Precautions

Bupropion is more likely to trigger epileptic seizures than other antidepressants. The drug should not be given to patients who have a history of epilepsy, take other medication to help control seizures, or have some other condition associated with seizures, such as head trauma or alcoholism. Nevertheless, in fewer than 1% of healthy people taking bupropion at the recommended dose have seizures. The possibility of seizures is increased at higher doses and following a sudden increase in dose. Patients should minimize alcohol intake while taking bupropion, since alcohol consumption increases the chance of seizures.

Because of the possibility of overdose, potentially suicidal patients should be given only small quantities of the drug at one time. Increases in blood pressure have occurred in patients taking bupropion along with **nicotine** treatment for smoking cessation. Monitoring blood pressure is recommended in such cases. Excessive stimulation, agitation, insomnia, and **anxiety** have been troublesome side effects for some patients, especially when treatment is first begun or when the dose is increased. Such adverse effects may be less intense and less frequent when the dose is increased gradually.

It has not been determined whether bupropion is safe to take during pregnancy. Pregnant women

KEY TERMS

Antipsychotic drug—A medication used to treat psychotic symptoms of schizophrenia such as hallucinations, delusions, and delirium. May be used to treat symptoms in other disorders, as well.

Epilepsy—A neurological disorder characterized by the onset of seizures. Seizures are caused by a disturbance in the electrical activity in the brain and can cause loss of consciousness, muscle spasms, rhythmic movements, abnormal sensory experiences, or altered mental states.

Neurotransmission—The conduction of a nerve impulse along a chain of nerve cells, which occurs when a cell in the chain secretes a chemical substance, called a neurotransmitter, onto a subsequent cell.

Neurotransmitter—A chemical in the brain that transmits messages between neurons, or nerve cells.

Parkinson's disease—A disease of the nervous system most common in people over age 60, characterized by a shuffling gait, trembling of the fingers and hands, and muscle stiffness.

should take bupropion only if necessary. The drug is secreted in breast milk. Women taking bupropion should consult their physicians about breast-feeding.

Side effects

Bupropion is a mild stimulant and may cause insomnia, agitation, confusion, restlessness, and anxiety. These effects may be more pronounced at the beginning of therapy and after dose increases. Headache, dizziness, and tremor may occur. Despite stimulating effects, bupropion may also cause sedation.

Weight loss is more common with bupropion than weight gain, but both have been reported. Excessive sweating, dry mouth, sore throat, nausea, vomiting, decreased appetite, constipation, blurred vision, and rapid heart rate may occur.

Interactions

Bupropion should not be administered along with other medications that lower the seizure threshold, such as **steroids** and the asthma medication theophylline. Many psychiatric medications also lower the seizure threshold. Monoamine oxidase inhibitors

(MAOIs), another type of antidepressant medication, should not be taken with bupropion. Adverse effects may increase in patients taking levodopa and other medications for Parkinson's disease along with bupropion. Patients should inform their doctors about all other medications they are taking before starting this drug.

Nicotine patch therapy may be administered concurrently with bupropion in smoking cessation treatment. If this is done, blood pressure must be monitored, since increased blood pressure has been reported with this combination of medications.

Certain drugs, especially those eliminated by the liver, may interfere with the elimination of bupropion from the body, causing higher blood levels and increased side effects. Conversely, bupropion may retard the elimination of other medicines, including many antidepressants, antipsychotic drugs, and heart medications, resulting in higher blood levels and potentially increased side effects.

Resources

BOOKS

Preston, John D., John H. O'Neal, and Mary C. Talaga. *Handbook of Clinical Psychopharmacology for Therapists,* 4th ed. Oakland, CA: New Harbinger Publications, 2004.

PERIODICALS

Gonzales, David, and others. "Varenicline, an $\alpha4\beta2$ Nicotinic Acetylcholine Receptor Partial Agonist, vs. Sustained-Release Bupropion and Placebo for Smoking Cessation: A Randomized Controlled Trial." *Journal of the American Medical Association* 296.1 (July 2006): 47–55.

Ingersoll, Karen S., and Jessye Cohen. "Combination Treatment for Nicotine Dependence: State of the Science." *Substance Use and Misuse* 40.13–14 (2005): 1923–43.

Little, John T., and others. "Bupropion and Venlafaxine Responders Differ in Pretreatment Regional Cerebral Metabolism in Unipolar Depression." *Biological Psychiatry* 57.3 (February 2005): 220–28.

Thase, Michael E., and others. "Remission Rates Following Antidepressant Therapy With Bupropion or Selective Serotonin Reuptake Inhibitors: A Meta-Analysis of Original Data From 7 Randomized Controlled Trials." *Journal of Clinical Psychiatry* 66.8 (August 2005): 974–81.

Richard Kapit, M.D.
Ruth A. Wienclaw, Ph.D.

BuSpar *see* **Buspirone**

Buspirone

Definition

Buspirone is an antianxiety (anxiolytic) drug sold in the United States under the brand name BuSpar. It is also available under its generic name. Buspirone is used for the treatment of generalized **anxiety disorders** and for short-term relief of symptoms of **anxiety**.

Description

Buspirone's mechanism of action is unclear but probably involves actions on such central nervous system chemicals as **dopamine**, serotonin, acetylcholine, and norepinephrine. These chemicals are called **neurotransmitters** and are involved in the transmission of nervous impulses from cell to cell. Mental wellbeing is partially dependent on maintaining a balance among different neurotransmitters.

Buspirone's actions are different from the common class of **sedatives** called **benzodiazepines**. The primary actions of benzodiazepines are to reduce anxiety, relax skeletal muscles, and induce sleep. The earliest drugs in this class were **chlordiazepoxide** (Librium) and **diazepam** (Valium). The mechanism of buspirone's action is also different from **barbiturates** such as phenobarbital. Unlike benzodiazepines, buspirone has no anticonvulsant or muscle-relaxant properties, and unlike benzodiazepines or barbiturates it does not have strong sedative properties. If **insomnia** is a component of the patient's anxiety disorder, a sedative/hypnotic drug may be taken along with buspirone at bedtime. Buspirone also diminishes anger and hostility for most people. Unlike benzodiazepines, which may aggravate anger and hostility in some patients (especially older patients), buspirone may help patients with anxiety who also have a history of aggression.

The benefits of buspirone take a long time to become evident. Unlike benzodiazepines, where onset of action and time to maximum benefit are short, patients must take buspirone for three to four weeks before feeling the maximum benefit of the drug. In some cases, four to six weeks of treatment may be required. Patients should be aware of this and continue to take the drug as prescribed even if they think they are not seeing any improvement.

Buspirone is available in 5-, 10-, 15-, and 30-mg tablets.

Recommended dosage

The usual starting dose of buspirone is 10 to 15 mg per day. This total amount is divided into two or three doses. For example, a dose of 5 mg may be given two or three times per day to make a total dose of 10 to 15 mg per day. The dose may be increased in increments of 5 mg daily every two to four days. Most patients will respond to a dose of 15 to 30 mg daily. Patients should not take a total dose of more than 60 mg daily. When patients are receiving certain other drugs in addition to buspirone, starting doses of buspirone may need to be lowered (e.g., 2.5 mg twice daily), and any dosage increases should be done with caution and under close physician supervision. Dosages may need to be reduced in patients with kidney or liver problems.

Precautions

Buspirone is less sedating (it causes less drowsiness and mental sluggishness) than other antianxiety drugs. However, some patients may still experience drowsiness and mental impairment. Because it is impossible to predict which patients may experience sedation with buspirone, those starting this drug should not drive or operate dangerous machinery until they know how the drug will affect them.

Patients who have been taking benzodiazepines for a long time should be gradually withdrawn from them while they are being switched over to buspirone. They should also be observed for symptoms of benzodiazepine withdrawal.

Patients with kidney damage should take buspirone with caution in close consultation with their physician. They may require a lower dosage of buspirone to prevent buildup of the drug in the body. Patients with severe kidney disease should not take buspirone. Patients with liver damage should likewise be monitored for a buildup of buspirone and have their doses lowered if necessary.

Side effects

The most common side effects associated with buspirone involve the nervous system. Ten percent of patients may experience dizziness, drowsiness, and headache, and another 5% may experience **fatigue**, nervousness, insomnia, and light-headedness. Patients may also experience excitement, **depression**, anger, hostility, confusion, nightmares, or other **sleep disorders**, lack of coordination, tremor, and numbness of the extremities. Although buspirone is considered nonsedating, some patients will experience drowsiness and lack of mental alertness at higher doses and especially early in therapy. In most patients, these side effects decrease with time.

The following side effects have also been associated with buspirone:

- nausea (up to 8% of patients)
- dry mouth, abdominal distress, gastric distress, diarrhea, and constipation (up to 5% of patients)
- rapid heart rate and palpitations (up to 2% of patients)
- blurred vision (up to 2% of patients)
- increased or decreased appetite
- flatulence
- nonspecific chest pain
- rash
- irregular menstrual periods and/or breakthrough bleeding

Interactions

Dangerously high blood pressure has resulted from the combination of buspirone and members of another class of **antidepressants** known as monoamine oxidase inhibitors (MAOIs). Because of this, buspirone should never be taken in combination with MAOIs. Patient taking any MAOIs, such as Nardil (**phenelzine** sulfate) or Parmate (**tranylcypromine** sulfate), should stop the MAOIs then wait at least 10 days before starting buspirone. The same holds true when discontinuing buspirone and starting an MAOIs.

Certain drugs may inhibit the enzyme system in the liver that breaks down buspirone. Examples of drugs that might inhibit this system are erythromycin, a broad-spectrum antibiotic; itraconazole, an oral antifungal agent; and **nefazodone**, an antidepressant. When these drugs are combined with buspirone, buspirone concentrations may increase to the point of toxicity (poisoning). These combinations should either be avoided or doses of buspirone decreased to compensate for this interaction.

Resources

BOOKS

American Society of Health-System Pharmacists. *AHFS Drug Information 2002*. Bethesda: American Society of Health-System Pharmacists, 2002.

Preston, John D., John H. O'Neal, and Mary C Talaga. *Handbook of Clinical Psychopharmacology for Therapists*, 4th ed. Oakland, CA: New Harbinger Publications, 2004.

KEY TERMS

Acetylcholine—A naturally occurring chemical in the body that transmits nerve impulses from cell to cell. Generally, it has opposite effects from dopamine and norepinephrine; it causes blood vessels to dilate, lowers blood pressure, and slows the heartbeat. Central nervous system well-being is dependent on a balance among acetylcholine, dopamine, serotonin, and norepinephrine.

Anxiolytic—A preparation or substance given to relieve anxiety; a tranquilizer.

Benzodiazepines—A group of central nervous system depressants used to relieve anxiety or to induce sleep.

Dopamine—A chemical in brain tissue that serves to transmit nerve impulses (is a neurotransmitter) and helps to regulate movement and emotions.

Norepinephrine—A neurotransmitter in the brain that acts to constrict blood vessels and raise blood pressure. It works in combination with serotonin.

Serotonin—A widely distributed neurotransmitter that that works in combination with norepinephrine and is found in blood platelets, the lining of the digestive tract, and the brain. It causes very powerful contractions of smooth muscle, and is associated with mood, attention, emotions, and sleep. Low levels of serotonin are associated with depression.

PERIODICALS

Baldwin, David S., and Claire Polkinghorn. "Evidence-Based Pharmacotherapy of Generalized Anxiety Disorder." *International Journal of Neuropsychopharmacology* 8.2 (June 2005): 293–302.

Buydens-Branchey, Laure, Marc Branchey, and Christine Reel-Brander. "Efficacy of Buspirone in the Treatment of Opioid Withdrawal." *Journal of Clinical Psychopharmacology* 25.3 (June 2005): 230–36.

Helvink, Badalin, and Suzanne Holroyd. "Buspirone for Stereotypic Movements in Elderly With Cognitive Impairment." *Journal of Neuropsychiatry and Clinical Neurosciences* 18.2 (Spring 2006): 242–44.

McRae, Aimee L., Kathleen T. Brady, and Rickey E. Carter. "Buspirone for Treatment of Marijuana Dependence: A Pilot Study." *The American Journal on Addictions* 15.5 (September–October 2006): 404.

Quitkin, Frederick, and others. "Medication Augmentation After the Failure of SSRIs for Depression." *New England Journal of Medicine* 354.12 (March 2006): 1243–52.

Verster, Joris C., Dieuwke S. Veldhuijzen, and Edmund R
Volkerts. "Is It Safe to Drive a Car When Treated with
Anxiolytics? Evidence from On-the-Road Driving
Studies During Normal Traffic." *Current Psychiatry
Reviews* 1.2 (June 2005): 215–25.

Jack Raber, Pharm.D.
Ruth A. Wienclaw, PhD

C

Caffeine-related disorders

Definition

Caffeine is a white, bitter crystalline alkaloid derived from coffee or tea. It belongs to a class of compounds called xanthines, its chemical formula being 1,3,7-trimethylxanthine. Caffeine is classified together with **cocaine** and **amphetamines** as an analeptic, or central nervous system stimulant. Coffee is the most abundant source of caffeine, although caffeine is also found in tea, cocoa, and cola beverages as well as in over-the-counter and prescription medications for pain relief.

In the clinician's handbook for diagnosing mental disorders (the ***Diagnostic and Statistical Manual of Mental Disorders***, known as the *DSM-IV-TR*), caffeine-related disorders are classified under the rubric of substance-related disorders. *DSM-IV-TR* specifies four caffeine-related disorders: caffeine intoxication, caffeine-induced **anxiety** disorder, caffeine-induced sleep disorder, and caffeine-related disorder not otherwise specified. A fifth, caffeine withdrawal, is listed under the heading of "Criteria Sets and Axes Provided for Further Study."

Caffeine-related disorders are often unrecognized for a number of reasons:

- Caffeine has a "low profile" as a drug of abuse. Consumption of drinks containing caffeine is unregulated by law and is nearly universal in the United States; one well-known textbook of pharmacology refers to caffeine as "the most widely used psychoactive drug in the world." In many countries, coffee is a social lubricant as well as a stimulant; the "coffee break" is a common office ritual, and many people find it difficult to imagine eating a meal in a fine restaurant without having coffee at some point during the meal. It is estimated that 10–12 billion pounds of coffee are consumed worldwide each year.

- People often underestimate the amount of caffeine they consume on a daily basis because they think of caffeine only in connection with coffee as a beverage. Tea, cocoa, and some types of soft drink, including root beer and orange soda as well as cola beverages, also contain significant amounts of caffeine. In one British case study, a teenager who was hospitalized with muscle weakness, nausea, vomiting, diarrhea, and weight loss was found to have caffeine intoxication caused by drinking 8 liters (about 2 gallons) of cola on a daily basis for the previous two years. She had been consuming over a gram of caffeine per day. Chocolate bars and coffee-flavored yogurt or ice cream are additional sources of measurable amounts of caffeine.

- Caffeine has some legitimate medical uses in athletic training and in the relief of tension-type headaches. It is available in over-the-counter (OTC) preparations containing aspirin or acetaminophen for pain relief as well as in such OTC stimulants as NoDoz and Vivarin.

- Caffeine is less likely to produce the same degree of physical or psychological dependence as other drugs of abuse. Few coffee or tea drinkers report loss of control over caffeine intake, or significant difficulty in reducing or stopping consumption of beverages and food items containing caffeine.

- The symptoms of caffeine intoxication are easy to confuse with those of an anxiety disorder.

The *DSM-TR-IV* states that it is unclear as of 2000 whether the tolerance, withdrawal symptoms, and "some aspects of dependence on caffeine" seen in some people who drink large amounts of coffee "are associated with clinically significant impairment that meets the criteria for **Substance Abuse** or Substance Dependence." On the other hand, a research team at Johns Hopkins regards caffeine as a model drug for understanding substance abuse and dependence. The team maintains that 9%–30% of caffeine consumers in the United States may be caffeine-dependent according to *DSM* criteria for substance dependency.

Description

Pharmacological aspects of caffeine

An outline of the effects of caffeine on the central nervous system (CNS) and other organ systems of the body may be helpful in understanding its potential for physical dependence. When a person drinks a beverage containing caffeine (or eats coffee-flavored ice cream), the caffeine is absorbed from the digestive tract without being broken down. It is rapidly distributed throughout the tissues of the body by means of the bloodstream. If a pregnant woman drinks a cup of coffee or tea, the caffeine in the drink will cross the placental barrier and enter the baby's bloodstream.

When the caffeine reaches the **brain**, it increases the secretion of norepinephrine, a neurotransmitter that is associated with the so-called fight or flight **stress** response. The rise in norepinephrine levels and the increased activity of the neurons, or nerve cells, in many other areas of the brain helps to explain why the symptoms of caffeine intoxication resemble the symptoms of a **panic attack**.

The effects of caffeine are thought to occur as a result of competitive antagonism at adenosine receptors. Adenosine is a water-soluble compound of adenine and ribose; it functions to modulate the activities of nerve cells and produces a mild sedative effect when it activates certain types of adenosine receptors. Caffeine competes with adenosine to bind at these receptors and counteracts the sedative effects of the adenosine. If the person stops drinking coffee, the adenosine has no competition for activating its usual receptors and may produce a sedative effect that is experienced as **fatigue** or drowsiness.

Caffeine content of food items and OTC preparations

The caffeine content of various food items and medications is as follows:

- brewed coffee, 8-oz cup: 135–150 mg
- instant coffee, 8-oz cup: 95 mg.
- powdered cappuccino beverage, 8-oz cup: 45–60 mg
- tea brewed from leaves or bag, 8-oz cup: 50 mg
- iced tea from mix, 8-oz glass: 25–45 mg
- Snapple iced tea, 8-oz glass: 21 mg
- Mountain Dew, 8-oz glass: 38 mg
- Dr. Pepper, 8-oz. glass: 28 mg
- diet cola, 8-oz glass: 31 mg
- root beer, 8-oz glass: 16 mg
- coffee ice cream, 8-oz serving: 60–85 mg
- coffee yogurt, 8-oz serving: 45 mg.
- dark chocolate candy bar, 1.5 oz: 31 mg
- NoDoz, regular strength, 1 tablet: 100 mg
- NoDoz, maximum strength, 1 tablet: 200 mg
- Excedrin, 2 tablets: 130 mg

Caffeine can produce a range of physical symptoms following ingestion of as little as 100 mg, although amounts of 250 mg or higher are usually needed to produce symptoms that meet the criteria of caffeine intoxication.

Caffeine intoxication

To meet *DSM-IV-TR* criteria for caffeine intoxication, a person must develop five or more of the twelve symptoms identified, the symptoms must cause significant distress or impair the person's social or occupational functioning; and the symptoms must not be caused by a medical disorder or better accounted for by an anxiety disorder or other mental disorder.

Because people develop tolerance to caffeine fairly quickly with habitual use, caffeine intoxication is most likely to occur in those who consume caffeine infrequently or who have recently increased their intake significantly.

Caffeine-induced anxiety and sleep disorders

DSM-IV-TR criteria for caffeine-induced anxiety and **sleep disorders** specify that the symptoms of anxiety and **insomnia** respectively must be more severe than the symptoms associated with caffeine intoxication. In addition, the anxiety or insomnia must be severe enough to require separate clinical attention.

Causes and symptoms

Causes

The immediate cause of caffeine intoxication and other caffeine-related disorders is consumption of an amount of caffeine sufficient to produce the symptoms specified by *DSM-IV-TR* as criteria for the disorder. The precise amount of caffeine necessary to produce symptoms varies from person to person depending on body size and degree of tolerance to caffeine. Tolerance of the stimulating effects of caffeine builds up rapidly in humans; mild withdrawal symptoms have been reported in persons who were drinking as little as one to two cups of coffee per day.

Some people may find it easier than others to consume large doses of caffeine because they are insensitive to its taste. Caffeine tastes bitter to most adults, which may serve to limit their consumption of coffee and other caffeinated beverages. Slightly more than 30% of the American population, however, has an inherited inability to taste caffeine.

Symptoms

The symptoms of caffeine intoxication include:

- restlessness
- nervousness
- excitement
- insomnia
- flushed face
- diuresis (increased urinary output)
- gastrointestinal disturbance
- muscle twitching
- talking or thinking in a rambling manner
- tachycardia (speeded-up heartbeat) or disturbances of heart rhythm
- periods of inexhaustibility
- psychomotor agitation

People have reported ringing in the ears or seeing flashes of light at doses of caffeine above 250 mg. Profuse sweating and diarrhea have also been reported. Doses of caffeine higher than 10 g may produce respiratory failure, **seizures**, and eventually death.

Side effects and complications

High short-term consumption of caffeine can produce or worsen gastrointestinal problems, occasionally leading to peptic ulcers or hematemesis (vomiting blood).

In addition to the symptoms produced by high short-term doses, long-term consumption of caffeine has been associated with fertility problems and with bone loss in women leading to osteoporosis in old age. Some studies have found that pregnant women who consume more than 150 mg per day of caffeine have an increased risk of miscarriage and low birth weight babies, but the findings are complicated by the fact that most women who drink large amounts of coffee during pregnancy are also heavy smokers. Some researchers believe that long-term consumption of caffeine is implicated in cardiovascular diseases, but acknowledge that further research is required.

On the other hand, moderate doses of caffeine improve athletic performance as well as alertness. Caffeine in small doses can relieve tension headaches, and one study found that a combination of ibuprofen and caffeine was more effective in relieving tension head-

aches than either ibuprofen alone or a placebo. Coffee consumption also appears to lower the risk of alcoholic and nonalcoholic cirrhosis of the liver.

Drug interactions

Caffeine is often combined with aspirin or acetaminophen in over-the-counter and prescription analgesics (pain relievers). It can also be combined with ibuprofen. On the other hand, certain groups of drugs should not be combined with caffeine or taken with beverages containing caffeine. Oral contraceptives, cimetidine (Tagamet), mexiletine (Mexitil), and **disulfiram** (Antabuse) interfere with the breakdown of caffeine in the body. Caffeine interferes with the body's absorption of iron, and with drugs that regulate heart rhythm, including quinidine and **propranolol** (Inderal). Caffeine may produce serious side effects when taken together with monoamine oxidase inhibitors or with certain decongestant medications.

Combinations of ephedra and caffeine have been used in weight-loss programs because they produce greater weight loss than can be achieved by caloric restriction alone. Major studies are underway as of 2001 at Harvard and Vanderbilt to determine the safety of these regimens.

Practitioners of homeopathy have traditionally advised patients not to drink beverages containing caffeine in the belief that caffeine "antidotes" homeopathic remedies. Contemporary homeopaths disagree on the antidoting effects of caffeine, observing that homeopathy is used widely and effectively in Europe and that Europeans tend to drink strong espresso coffee more frequently than Americans.

Demographics

The general population of the United States has a high level of caffeine consumption, with an average intake of 200 mg per day. About 85% of the population uses caffeine in any given year. Among adults in the United States, about 30% consume 500 mg or more each day. These figures are lower, however, than the figures for Sweden, the United Kingdom, and other parts of Europe, where the average daily consumption of caffeine is 400 mg or higher. In developing countries, the average consumption of caffeine is much lower—about 50 mg per day.

In the United States, levels of caffeine consumption among all races and ethnic groups are related to age, with usage beginning in the late teens and rising until the early 30s. Caffeine consumption tapers off in adults over 40 and decreases in adults over 65.

Caffeine intake is higher among males than among females in North America.

Diagnosis

Diagnosis of a caffeine-related disorder is usually based on the patient's recent history, a physical examination, or laboratory analysis of body fluids. In addition to medical evidence, the examiner will rule out other mental disorders, particularly manic episodes, **generalized anxiety disorder**, **panic disorder**, amphetamine intoxication, or withdrawal from **sedatives**, tranquilizers, sleep medications, or **nicotine**. All of these disorders or syndromes may produce symptoms resembling those of caffeine intoxication. In most cases the temporal relationship of the symptoms to high levels of caffeine intake establishes the diagnosis.

In some cases, the examiner may consider the possibility of **depression** during the differential diagnosis, as many people with depression and eating disorders self-medicate with caffeine.

Treatments

Treatment of caffeine-related disorders involves lowering consumption levels or abstaining from beverages containing caffeine. Some people experience mild withdrawal symptoms that include headaches, irritability, and occasionally nausea, but these usually resolve quickly.

Caffeine consumption has the advantage of having relatively weak (compared to alcohol or cigarettes) social **reinforcement**, in the sense that one can easily choose a noncaffeinated or decaffeinated beverage in a restaurant or at a party without attracting comment. Thus physical dependence on caffeine is less complicated by the social factors that reinforce nicotine and other drug habits.

Prognosis

With the exception of acute episodes of caffeinism, people recover from caffeine intoxication without great difficulty.

Prevention

Prevention of caffeine-related disorders requires awareness of the caffeine content of caffeinated beverages, OTC drugs, and other sources of caffeine; monitoring one's daily intake; and substituting decaffeinated coffee, tea, or soft drinks for the caffeinated versions of these beverages.

KEY TERMS

Adenosine—A compound that serves to modulate the activities of nerve cells (neurons) and to produce a mild sedative effect when it activates certain types of adenosine receptors. Caffeine is thought to produce its stimulating effect by competing with adenosine for activation of these receptors.

Analeptic—A substance that acts as a stimulant of the central nervous system. Caffeine is classified as an analeptic.

Caffeinism—A disorder caused by ingesting very high doses of caffeine (10g or more per day) and characterized by seizures and respiratory failure.

Dependence—The adaptation of neurons and other physical processes to the use of a drug, followed by withdrawal symptoms when the drug is removed; physiological and/or psychological addiction.

Hematemesis—Vomiting blood. Hematemesis is a symptom that sometimes occurs with gastrointestinal ulcers made worse by high levels of caffeine consumption.

Norepinephrine—A catecholamine neurotransmitter that acts to constrict blood vessels, raise blood pressure, and dilate the bronchi of the respiratory system. Caffeine increases the secretion of norepinephrine.

Reinforcement—A term that refers to the ability of a drug or substance to produce effects that will make the user want to take it again.

Tolerance—Progressive decrease in the effectiveness of a drug with long-term use.

Withdrawal—Symptoms experienced by a person who has become physically dependent on a drug, experienced when the drug use is discontinued.

Xanthine—A class of crystalline nitrogenous compounds that includes caffeine, which is 1,3,7-trimethylxanthine.

Resources

BOOKS

American Psychiatric Association. *Diagnostic and Statistical Manual of Mental Disorders.* 4th edition, text revised. Washington, DC: American Psychiatric Association, 2000.

"Anxiety Due to a Physical Disorder or a Substance." Section 15, Chapter 187. In *The Merck Manual of Diagnosis and Therapy*, edited by Mark H. Beers, MD, and

Robert Berkow, MD. Whitehouse Station, NJ: Merck Research Laboratories, 1999.

Murray, Michael, ND, and Joseph Pizzorno, ND. *Encyclopedia of Natural Medicine.* Rocklin, CA: Prima Publishing, 1991.

O'Brien, Charles P. "Drug Addiction and Drug Abuse." Chapter 24 in *Goodman & Gilman's The Pharmacological Basis of Therapeutics,* edited by J. G. Hardman and L. E. Limbird. 9th edition. New York and St. Louis, MO: McGraw-Hill, 1996.

Pelletier, Kenneth R., MD. "Naturopathic Medicine." Chapter 7, in *The Best Alternative Medicine.* New York: Simon & Schuster, 2002.

PERIODICALS

Breslin, P. A. S., C. D. Tharp, and D. R. Reed. "Selective Taste Blindness to Caffeine and Sucrose Octa Acetate: Novel Bimodal Taste Distributions Unrelated to PROP and PTC." *American Journal of Human Genetics* 69 (October 2001): 507.

"Caffeine Toxicity from Cola Consumption." *Internal Medicine Journal* 31 (2001): 317–318.

Corrao, G. "Coffee, Caffeine, and the Risk of Liver Cirrhosis." *Annals of Epidemiology* 11 (October 2001): 458–465.

De Valck, E., and R. Cluydts. "Slow-Release Caffeine as a Countermeasure to Driver Sleepiness Induced by Partial Sleep Deprivation." *Journal of Sleep Research* 10 (September 2001): 203–209.

Diamond, S., T. K. Balm, and F. G. Freitag. "Ibuprofen Plus Caffeine in the Treatment of Tension-Type Headache." *Clinical Pharmacology and Therapeutics* 68 (2000): 312–319.

Griffiths, R. R., and A. L. Chausmer. "Caffeine as a Model Drug of Dependence: Recent Developments in Understanding Caffeine Withdrawal, the Caffeine Dependence Syndrome, and Caffeine Negative Reinforcement." *Nihon Shinkei Seishin Yakurigaku Zasshi* 20 (November 2000): 223–231.

MacFadyen, L., D. Eadie, and T. McGowan. "Community Pharmacists' Experience of Over-the-Counter Medicine Misuse in Scotland." *Journal of Research in Social Health* 121 (September 2001): 185–192.

Preboth, Monica. "Effect of Caffeine on Exercise Performance." *American Family Physician* 61 (May 2000): 628.

Rapurl, P. B., J. C. Gallagher, H. K. Kinyarnu, and others. "Caffeine Intake Increases the Rate of Bone Loss in Elderly Women and Interacts with Vitamin D Receptor Genotypes." *American Journal of Clinical Nutrition* 74 (2001): 694–700.

Rumpler, William, James Seale, Beverly Clevidence, and others. "Oolong Tea Increases Metabolic Rate and Fat Oxidation in Men." *Journal of Nutrition* 131 (November 2001): 2848–2852.

Sardao, V. A., P. J. Oliveira, and A. J. Moreno. "Caffeine Enhances the Calcium-Dependent Cardiac Mitochondrial Permeability Transition: Relevance for Caffeine Toxicity." *Toxicology and Applied Pharmacology* 179 (February 2002): 50–56.

ORGANIZATIONS

American College of Sports Medicine. P. O. Box 1440, Indianapolis, IN 46206-1440. Telephone: (317) 637-9200.

American Dietetic Association. Telephone: (800) 877-1600. <www.eatright.org>.

Center for Science in the Public Interest (CSPI). <www.cspinet.org>.

Rebecca J. Frey, Ph.D.

Cannabis and related disorders

Definition

Cannabis, more commonly called marijuana, refers to the several varieties of *Cannabis sativa*, or Indian hemp plant, that contains the psychoactive drug delta-9-tetrahydrocannabinol (THC). Cannabis-related disorders refer to problems associated with the use of substances derived from this plant.

Description

Cannabis—in the form of marijuana, hashish (a dried resinous material that seeps from cannabis leaves and is more potent than marijuana), or other cannabinoids—is considered the most commonly used illegal substance in the world. Its effects have been known for thousands of years, and were described as early as the fifth century B.C., when the Greek historian Herodotus told of a tribe of nomads who, after inhaling the smoke of roasted hemp seeds, emerged from their tent excited and shouting for joy.

Cannabis is the abbreviation for the Latin name for the hemp plant—*Cannabis sativa*. All parts of the plant contain psychoactive substances, with THC making up the highest percentage. The most potent parts are the flowering tops and the dried, blackish-brown residue that comes from the leaves known as hashish, or "hash."

There are more than 200 slang terms for marijuana, including "pot," "herb," "weed," "Mary Jane," "grass," "tea," and "ganja." It is usually chopped and/or shredded and rolled into a cigarette, or "joint," or placed in a pipe (sometimes called a "bong") and smoked. An alternative method of using marijuana involves adding it to foods and eating it, such as baking it into brownies. It can also be brewed as a tea. Marijuana has appeared in the form of "blunts"—cigarettes emptied of their tobacco content and filled with a combination of marijuana and another drug such as crack **cocaine.**

A teenage boy smoking a cannibis cigarette. *(ImageState/Alamy)*

Between 1840 and 1900, European and American medical journals published numerous articles on the therapeutic uses of marijuana. It was recommended as an appetite stimulant, muscle relaxant, painkiller, sedative, and anticonvulsant. As late as 1913, Sir William Osler recommended it highly for treatment of migraine. Public opinion changed, however, in the early 1900s, as alternative medications such as aspirin, opiates, and **barbiturates** became available. In 1937, the United States passed the Marijuana Tax Act, which made the drug essentially impossible to obtain for medical purposes.

By the year 2000, the debate over the use of marijuana as a medicine continued. THC is known to successfully treat nausea caused by cancer treatment drugs, stimulate the appetites of persons diagnosed with acquired immune deficiency syndrome (AIDS), and possibly assist in the treatment of glaucoma. Its use as a medicinal agent is still, however, highly controversial. Although the states of Arizona and California passed laws in 1996 making it legal for physicians to prescribe marijuana in the form of cigarettes for treatment of the diseases listed above, governmental agencies continue to oppose strongly its use as a medicine, and doctors who do prescribe it may find their licenses at risk.

Cannabis-related disorders reflect the problematic use of cannabis products to varying degrees. These disorders include:

- Cannabis dependence: The compulsive need to use the drug, coupled with problems associated with chronic drug use.
- Cannabis abuse: Periodic use that may cause legal problems, problems at work, home, or school, or danger when driving.

- Cannabis intoxication: The direct effects of acute cannabis use and reactions that accompany it such as feeling "high," euphoria, sleepiness, lethargy, impairment in short-term memory, stimulated appetite, impaired judgment, distorted sensory perceptions, impaired motor performance, and other symptoms.

Causes and symptoms

Causes

Cannabis-related disorders share many of the same root causes with other addictive substances. The initial desire for a "high," combined with the widely held perception that cannabis use is not dangerous, often leads to experimentation in the teen years.

Recent research challenges the notion that cannabis use is not physically addictive. According to the National Institute of Drug Abuse (NIDA), daily cannabis users experience withdrawal symptoms including irritability, stomach pain, aggression, and **anxiety**. Many frequent cannabis users are believed to continue using in order to avoid these unpleasant symptoms. Long-term use may lead to changes in the **brain** similar to those seen with long-term use of other addictive substances. It is believed that the greater availability, higher potency, and lower price for cannabis in recent years all contribute to the increase in cannabis-related disorders.

Beginning in the 1990s, researchers began to discover that cannabis-like compounds are naturally produced in various parts of the human body. These compounds, called "endocannabinoids," appear to suppress inflammation and other responses of the immune system. One of these endocannabinoids—anandamide—appears to help regulate the early stages of pregnancy.

Symptoms

CANNABIS DEPENDENCE AND ABUSE. The handbook used by mental health professionals to diagnose mental disorders is the ***Diagnostic and Statistical Manual of Mental Disorders***, also known as the *DSM-IV-TR*. This manual states that the central features of cannabis dependence are compulsive use, tolerance of its effects, and withdrawal symptoms. Use may interfere with family, school, and work, and may cause legal problems.

Regular cannabis smokers may show many of the same respiratory symptoms as tobacco smokers. These include daily cough and phlegm, chronic bronchitis, and more frequent chest colds. Continued use can lead to abnormal functioning of the lung tissue, which may be injured or destroyed by the cannabis smoke.

Recent research indicates that smoking marijuana has the potential to cause severe increases in heart rate and blood pressure, particularly if combined with cocaine use. Even with marijuana use alone, however, the heart rate of subjects increased an average of 29 beats per minute when smoking marijuana.

A study of heavy marijuana users has shown that critical skills related to attention, memory, and learning can be impaired, even after use is discontinued for at least 24 hours. Heavy users, compared to light users, made more errors on tasks and had more difficulty sustaining attention and shifting attention when required. They also had more difficulty registering, processing, and using information. These findings suggest that the greater impairment in mental functioning among heavy users is most likely due to an alteration of brain activity directly produced by the marijuana use.

Recent studies have found that babies born to mothers who used marijuana during pregnancy were smaller than those born to nonusing mothers. Smaller babies are more likely to develop health problems. Additionally, nursing mothers who use marijuana pass some of the THC to the baby in their breast milk. Research shows that use of marijuana during the first month of breastfeeding can impair an infant's motor development.

Cannabis abuse is characterized by less frequent use and less severe problems. However, as with cannabis dependence, abuse can interfere with performance at school or work, cause legal problems, and interfere with motor activities such as driving or operating machinery.

CANNABIS INTOXICATION. Cannabis intoxication refers to the occurrence of problematic behaviors or psychological changes that develop during, or shortly after, cannabis use. Intoxication usually starts with a "high" feeling followed by euphoria, inappropriate laughter, and feelings of grandiosity. Other symptoms include sedation, lethargy, impaired short-term memory, difficulty with motor tasks, impaired judgment, distorted sensory perceptions, and the feeling that time is passing unusually slowly. Sometimes severe anxiety, feelings of **depression**, or social withdrawal may occur. Along with these symptoms, common signs of cannabis intoxication include reddening of the membranes around the eyes, increased appetite, dry mouth, and increased heart rate.

Demographics

The NIDA conducts an annual nationwide study of twelfth-, tenth-, and eighth-grade students and young adults. This study is known as the *Monitoring the Future Study*, or *MTF*. Results show that after a decade of decreased use in the 1980s, marijuana use among students began to rise in the early 1990s. Data show that, between 1998 and 1999, marijuana use continued to increase among twelfth and tenth graders. For twelfth graders, the lifetime rate (use of marijuana at least one or more times) is higher than for any year since 1987. However, these rates remain well below those seen in the late 1970s and early 1980s. Daily marijuana use among students in all three grades also showed a slight increase.

Another method by which the government measures marijuana use is the *Community Epidemiology Work Group*, or *CEWG*. This method examines rates of emergency room admissions related to marijuana use in 20 major metropolitan areas. In 1998, use of marijuana showed an upward trend in most of the areas monitored, with the largest increases occurring in Dallas, Boston, Denver, San Diego, and Atlanta. The highest percentage increase in emergency room visits related to marijuana was among 12- to 17-year-olds.

Treatment data for marijuana abuse increased in six of the metropolitan areas surveyed but remained stable elsewhere. Marijuana treatment admissions were highest in Denver, Miami, New Orleans, and Minneapolis/St. Paul. Half of the admissions in Minneapolis/St. Paul were under the age of 18 years.

Marijuana remains the most commonly used illicit drug in the United States. As with most other illicit drugs, cannabis use disorders appear more often in males and is most common among people between the ages of 18 and 30 years.

An estimated 2.1 million people started using marijuana in 1998. According to data from a study released in the late 1990s called the *National Household Survey on Drug Abuse*, or *NHSDA*, more than 72 million Americans ages 12 years and older (33%) tried marijuana at least once during their lifetime, while almost 18.7 million (8.6%) used marijuana in the previous year. This represents a considerable increase since 1985, when 56.5 million Americans (29.4%) had tried marijuana at least once in their life, and 26.1 million (13.6%) had used marijuana within the past year.

Diagnosis

Diagnosis of cannabis-related disorders is made in a number of ways. Intoxication is easiest to diagnose because of clinically observable signs, including reddened eye membranes, increased appetite, dry mouth, and increased heart rate. It is also diagnosed by the presence of problematic behavioral or psychological changes such as impaired motor coordination, judgment, anxiety, euphoria, and social withdrawal. Occasionally, panic attacks may occur, and there may be impairment of short-term memory. Lowered immune system resistance, lowered testosterone levels in males, and chromosomal damage may also occur. Psychologically, chronic use of marijuana has been associated with a loss of ambition known as the "amotivational syndrome."

Cannabis use is often paired with the use of other addictive substances, especially **nicotine**, alcohol, and cocaine. Marijuana may be mixed and smoked with opiates, **phencyclidine** (PCP or angel dust), or hallucinogenic drugs. Individuals who regularly use cannabis often report physical and mental lethargy and an inability to experience pleasure when not intoxicated (known as anhedonia). If taken in sufficiently high dosages, cannabinoids have psychoactive effects similar to hallucinogens such as lysergic acid diethylamide (LSD), and individuals using high doses may experience adverse effects that resemble hallucinogen-induced "bad trips." Paranoid ideation is another possible effect of heavy use, and, occasionally, **hallucinations** and **delusions** occur. Highly intoxicated individuals may feel as if they are outside their body (depersonalization) or as if what they are experiencing isn't real (derealization). Fatal traffic accidents are more common among individuals testing positive for cannabis use.

Urine tests can usually identify metabolites of cannabinoids. Because cannabinoids are fat soluble, they remain in the body for extended periods. Individuals who have used cannabis may show positive urine tests for as long as two to four weeks after using.

Examination of the nasopharynx and bronchial lining may also show clinical changes due to cannabis use. Marijuana smoke is known to contain even larger amounts of carcinogens than tobacco smoke. Sometimes cannabis use is associated with weight gain.

Treatments

Treatment options for individuals with cannabis-related disorders are identical to those available for people with alcohol and other **substance abuse** disorders. The goal of treatment is abstinence. Treatment approaches range from in-patient **hospitalization**, drug and alcohol rehabilitation facilities, and various out-patient programs. Twelve-step programs such as Narcotics Anonymous are also treatment options. For heavy users experiencing withdrawal symptoms, treatment with anti-anxiety and/or antidepressant medication may assist in the treatment process.

Prognosis

According to the *DSM-IV-TR*, cannabis dependence and abuse tend to develop over a period of time.

It may, however, develop more rapidly among young people with other emotional problems. Most people who become dependent begin using regularly. Gradually, over time, both frequency and amount increase. With chronic use, there can sometimes be a decrease in or loss of the pleasurable effects of the substance, along with increased feelings of anxiety and/or depression. As with alcohol and nicotine, cannabis use tends to begin early in the course of substance abuse and many people later go on to develop dependence on other illicit substances. Because of this, cannabis has been referred to as a "gateway" drug, although this view remains highly controversial. There is much that remains unknown about the social, psychological, and neurochemical basis of drug use progression, and it is unclear whether marijuana use actually causes individuals to go on to use other illicit substances.

One long-term effects of chronic use has been termed the "amotivational syndrome." This refers to the observations that many heavy, chronic users seem unambitious in relation to school and/or career.

Prevention

Many drug education programs focus strongly on discouraging marijuana experimentation among young teenagers. Recent research reported by the NIDA indicates that high-sensation-seekers—that is, individuals who seek out new, emotionally intense experiences and are willing to take risks to obtain these experiences—are at greater risk for using marijuana and other drugs, and for using them at an earlier age. As a result, the NIDA developed a series of public service announcements (PSAs) for national television. These PSAs were dramatic and attention getting, and were aired during programs that would appeal to high sensation-seekers, such as action-oriented television shows. These PSAs were aired in a limited television area and the results monitored. Marijuana use declined substantially among teens during the PSA campaigns, and long-term effects were shown for several months afterwards. In one county, marijuana use decreased by 38%, and in another, by 26.7%.

Drug education programs such as the "D.A.R.E." (Drug Awareness and Resistance Education) programs target fifth graders. These and other antidrug programs focus on peer pressure resistance and the use of older teens who oppose drug use as models of a drug-free lifestyle. These programs show mixed results.

KEY TERMS

Amotivational syndrome—Loss of ambition associated with chronic cannabis (marijuana) use.

Anandamide—One type of endocannabinoid that appears to help regulate early pregnancy.

Cannabis—The collective name for several varieties of Indian hemp plant. Also known as marijuana.

Cannabis abuse—Periodic use of cannabis, less serious than dependence, but still capable of causing problems for the user.

Cannabis dependence—The compulsive need to use cannabis, leading to problems.

Cannabis intoxication—The direct effects of acute cannabis use and the reactions that accompany those effects.

Delta-9-tetrahydrocannabinol (THC)—The primary active ingredient in marijuana.

Endocannabinoids—Cannabis-like compounds produced naturally in the human body.

Hashish—The dark, blackish resinous material that exudes from the leaves of the Indian hemp plant.

Marijuana—The dried and shredded or chopped leaves of the Indian hemp plant.

See also Addiction; Disease concept of chemical dependency; Dual diagnosis; Nicotine and related disorders; Opioids and related disorders; Relapse and relapse prevention; Self-help groups; Substance abuse and related disorders; Support groups.

Resources

BOOKS

American Psychiatric Association. *Diagnostic and Statistical Manual of Mental Disorders*. 4th edition, text revised. Washington, DC: American Psychiatric Association, 2000.

Hurley, Jennifer A., ed. *Addiction: Opposing Viewpoints*. San Diego, CA: Greenhaven Press, 2000.

Kaplan, Harold I., M.D., and Benjamin J. Sadock, M.D. *Synopsis of Psychiatry: Behavioral Sciences/Clinical Psychiatry*. 8th edition. Baltimore, MD: Lippincott Williams and Wilkins, 1998.

Wekesser, Carol, ed. *Chemical Dependency: Opposing Viewpoints*. San Diego, CA: Greenhaven Press, 1997.

PERIODICALS

NIDA Notes Volume 14, Number 4, November, 1999.
NIDA Notes Volume 15, Number 1, March 2000.
NIDA Notes Volume 16, Number 4, October 2001.
NIDA Notes volume 15, Number 3, August 2000.
NIDA Infofax, "Marijuana," 13551.

ORGANIZATIONS

American Council for Drug Education. 136 E. 64th St., NY, NY 10021.

Narcotics Anonymous. PO box 9999, Van Nuys, CA 91409. Telephone: (818) 780-3951.

National Institute on Drug Abuse (NIDA). US Department of Health and Human Services, 5600 Fishers Ln., Rockville, MD 20857. <http://www.nida.nih.gov>

National Organization for the Reform of Marijuana Laws (NORML). 2001 S St. NW, Suite 640, Washington, DC 20009. Telephone: (202) 483-5500.

Barbara S. Sternberg, Ph.D.

Capgras syndrome

Definition

Capgras syndrome (CS) is a relatively rare delusion of negative identification in which the patient believes that an individual or individuals well-known to him or her is an almost identical physiological double.

Description

Named for the French **psychiatrist** Jean Capgras in 1923, CS is also known as the "illusion of doubles" and the "illusion of false recognition." Although the object of the delusion is typically a person with whom the patient is either particularly familiar or has an emotional tie, cases have been reported of the delusion being extended to pets and even inanimate objects, such as letters or a teacup. The term "syndrome"—a group of symptoms characterizing a disorder—as applied to CS is misleading; CS is more accurately described as a symptom associated with multiple physiological and psychological disorders.

Demographics

Reported cases of CS have focused on adults, although a few cases have been reported with younger adults. It was once thought that CS is a disorder occurring only in women. However, cases have also been reported in men.

CS is related to numerous underlying causes including central nervous system disorders, **dementia**, and **psychosis**. The demographics of CS vary with the underlying cause.

Causes and Symptoms

The literature is divided as to whether CS is psychological or physiological in nature. Historically, CS was thought to be a purely psychological condition. More recently, however, the focus has shifted, and CS is now considered by many clinicians to be a disorder of the central nervous system. It is estimated that between 21% and 40% of CS cases stem from physiological disorders including dementia, head trauma, epilepsy, and cerebrovascular disease. Neuroimaging data suggest a link between CS and abnormalities of the right hemisphere of the **brain**. In fact, the literature supports the conclusion that CS can be a symptom of virtually any central nervous system disorder.

CS has been observed in association with various systemic illnesses including vitamin B-12 deficiency, chicken encephalitis, and diseases of the thyroid, parathyroid, and liver. CS has also been found associated with the use of various drugs, including morphine and **diazepam** (Valium). CS has been observed following transient physiological disturbances such as pneumocystis pneumonia in an HIV-positive patient, migraine headache, overdose of a bronchial dilator containing **adrenaline** and adropinemethonitrate, and interictal psychosis of epilepsy.

Diagnosis

Most clinicians regard CS as a symptom associated with numerous underlying causes rather than a syndrome in the classical sense of the term. **Diagnosis** should be based on psychological and personality testing as well as neuroradiological testing to determine the underlying cause rather than relying purely on behavioral descriptions.

CS can occur at any time during a psychosis and is not currently considered to be an essential element of any psychological disorder. It is impossible to predict the occurrence of CS based on the course of the overall psychopathology.

Treatments

CS is typically treated with a combination of antipsychotic medication and supportive psychological therapy in which stronger areas of mental and behavioral processes are used to overcome weaker areas of functioning. Patients presenting with CS stemming from psychosis have been found to improve on **pimozide** even when nonresponsive to **haloperidol**. CS stemming from physiological causes is best treated by treating the underlying disorder.

Prognosis

The symptoms of CS have been found in most, but not all, cases to clear shortly after the remission of the psychosis. In the case of **depression**, however, the

---

KEY TERMS

Central nervous system—The brain and spinal cord.

Delusion—A false idea held despite all evidence to the contrary.

Dementia—Deterioration of intellect, reasoning ability, memory, and will resulting from organic brain disease.

Interictal—Occurring between seizures.

Psychosis—A mental illness that markedly interferes with the patient's ability to deal with the demands of everyday life. Psychosis is characterized by loss of contact with reality, often accompanied by delusions and hallucinations.

---

symptoms of CS persist longer than those of other syndromes of doubles (syndrome of Frégoli, syndrome of intermetamorphosis, syndrome of subjective doubles). The symptoms of CS invariably recur when there is a **relapse** of the basic psychotic condition with which they were associated.

Prevention

CS is an uncommon occurrence associated with a range of disorders both psychological and physiological in nature. Prevention of CS is actually a question of preventing the underlying disorder resulting in CS. There are no investigations under way concerning the prevention of CS.

Resources

BOOKS

Fewtrell, David, and Kieron O'Connor. "Capgras syndrome and delusions of misidentification." in *Clinical Phenomenology and Cognitive Psychology*. New York: Routledge, 1995.

PERIODICALS

Doran, John M. "The Capgras Syndrome: Neurological/ Neuropsychological Perspectives." *Neurolpsychology* 4, no. 1(January 1990): 29-42.

Ruth A. Wienclaw, Ph.D.

Carbamazepine

Definition

Carbamazepine is an anticonvulsant that is structurally related to tricyclic **antidepressants** such as **amitriptyline** and **imipramine**. In the United States, carbamazepine is sold under the trade names Tegretol and Carbatrol.

Purpose

Carbamazepine is effective in the treatment of psychomotor and grand mal **seizures** and a type of facial pain called trigeminal neuralgia and, in combination with other drugs, for psychiatric disorders such as mania and extreme aggression. Carbamazepine is also occasionally used to control pain in persons with cancer.

Description

Carbamazepine was first marketed as an antiseizure medication and as a first-line treatment for trigeminal neuralgia. Because it was later noted to be effective in patients with certain psychiatric disorders, psychiatrists began combining it with other drugs such as lithium and major tranquilizers in severe cases of bipolar disease and aggressive behavior that could not be managed with single-drug therapy.

Carbamazepine is available in 100-mg chewable tablets, 200-mg capsules, and a suspension at 100 mg per 5 ml of liquid.

Recommended dosage

When used to treat seizure disorders or psychiatric disease, the recommended initial dosage of carbamazepine is 200 mg two times each day. If needed, the daily dosage may be increased by 200 mg once each week. Total daily dosages should not exceed 1,000 mg in children between the ages of 12 and 15 years. Total daily dosages for adults should not exceed 1,200 mg. Carbamazepine should be taken with meals.

Precautions

Carbamazepine should be used with caution in persons who also experience other types of seizure disorders such as atypical absence seizures. Among such individuals, carbamazepine usage has been associated with an increased risk of initiating, rather than controlling, generalized convulsions.

Carbamazepine should never be discontinued abruptly unless another treatment for seizures is initiated at the same time. If this does not happen, acute withdrawal of carbamazepine may result in seizures.

Patients should be alert for signs and symptoms of bone marrow toxicity such as fever, sore throat, infection, mouth sores, easy bruising, or bleeding which occurs just under the skin.

Because carbamazepine may affect mental alertness, especially early in therapy, patients receiving this drug should be cautioned about operating dangerous machinery or driving a car until the drug's effects can be fully evaluated.

Side effects

The most commonly reported adverse reactions to carbamazepine include dizziness, drowsiness, unsteadiness, nausea, and vomiting. These are more common when therapy is just beginning.

Carbamazepine has been reported to cause aplastic anemia. This is a form of anemia that generally does not respond to treatment. The bone marrow of persons with aplastic anemia does not produce adequate amounts of red blood cells, white blood cells, and platelets. Blood counts should be monitored for individuals using this drug. Some people with previously diagnosed **depression** of the bone marrow should not take carbamazepine.

Carbamazepine may cause birth defects and should be avoided by women who are pregnant. An effective contraceptive method should be used while taking carbamazepine. It is important to note that this medication may decrease the effectiveness of oral contraceptives. The drug can cross into breast milk and should be avoided by women who are breast-feeding. Carbamazepine may also cause a skin rash or sensitivity to the sun.

Interactions

Blood levels of carbamazepine may be reduced when it is used in combination with other drugs such as phenobarbitol, phenytoin or primidone. This means that inadequate amounts of carbamazepine are available to the body, limiting the ability of the drug to control seizure activity or treat psychiatric disease. Carbamazepine also causes reductions in the blood levels of the following drugs when they are used simultaneously: phenytoin, warfarin, doxycycline, **haloperidol**, **valproic acid**, and theophylline.

The simultaneous administration of carbamazepine with erythromycin, cimetidine, propoxyohene, isoniacid, **fluoxetine** and calcium channel blockers such as nifedipine and verapamil may increase the blood level of carbamazepine to a toxic range.

The simultaneous use of carbamazepine and oral contraceptives may increase the possibility that the oral contraceptive will not be effective in preventing pregnancy. Some physicians recommend that a different

Carbamazepine

KEY TERMS

Absence seizure—An epileptic seizure characterized by a sudden, momentary loss of consciousness, occasionally accompanied by some minor, jerky movements in the neck or upper arms, a twitching of the face, or a loss of muscle tone.

Aplastic anemia—A form of anemia in which the bone marrow does not produce adequate amounts of peripheral blood components such as red cells, white cells, and platelets.

Bipolar disorder—A mental disorder characterized by dramatic and sometimes rapid mood swings, resulting in both manic and depressive episodes; formerly called manic-depressive disorder.

Convulsion—A violent, involuntary contraction or series of contractions of muscles.

Grand mal seizure—A seizure characterized by a sudden loss of consciousness that is immediately followed by generalized convulsions. Such a seizure is usually preceded by a sensory experience, called an aura, which provides a warning as to an impending convulsion.

Psychomotor seizure—A seizure characterized by electrical activity that is characterized by variable degrees of loss of consciousness and often accompanied by bizarre behavior.

method of contraception be used while carbamazepine is being taken.

People taking carbamazepine should not drink grapefruit juice. Grapefruit juice slows the breakdown of carbamazepine, increasing the concentration of carbamazepine in the bloodstream.

Due to the potential of many interactions with other drugs, individuals should consult with a physician or pharmacist prior to starting any new medications either bought over the counter or initiated by another physician.

Resources

BOOKS

El-Mallakh, Rif S. "Lithium and Antiepileptic Drugs in Bipolar Depression." *Bipolar Depression: A Comprehensive Guide.* Washington, D.C.: American Psychiatric Publishing, 2006: 147–66.

Foreman, John C., and Torben Johansen. *Textbook of Receptor Pharmacology*, 2nd ed. Boca Raton, FL: CRC Press, 2002.

Page, Clive P., and Michael Murphy. *Integrated Pharmacology*. St. Louis: Mosby-Year Book, 2002.

Preston, John D., John H. O'Neal, and Mary C. Talaga. *Handbook of Clinical Psychopharmacology for Therapists*, 4th ed. Oakland, CA: New Harbinger Publications, 2004.

PERIODICALS

Bowden, Charles L., and Nancy U. Karren. "Anticonvulsants in Bipolar Disorder." *Australian and New Zealand Journal of Psychiatry* 40.5 (May 2006): 386–93.

Cepeda, M. Soledad, and John T. Farrar. "Economic Evaluation of Oral Treatments for Neuropathic Pain." *Journal of Pain* 7.2 (Feb. 2006): 119–28.

DeBattista, Charles, and Alan F. Schatzberg. "Psychotropic Dosing and Monitoring Guidelines." *Primary Psychiatry* 13.6 (June 2006): 61–81.

El-Mallakh, Rif, Richard H. Weisler, Mark H. Townsend, and Lawrence D. Ginsberg. "Bipolar II Disorder: Current and Future Treatment Options." *Annals of Clinical Psychiatry* 18.4 (Oct.–Dec. 2006): 259–66.

Gamble, C., P. R. Williamson, D. W. Chadwick, and A. G. Marson. "A Meta-Analysis of Individual Patient Responses to Lamotrigine or Carbamazepine Monotherapy." *Neurology* 66.9 (May 2006): 1310–17.

Gayatri, N. A., and, J. H. Livingston. "Aggravation of Epilepsy by Anti-Epileptic Drugs." *Developmental Medicine and Child Neurology* 48.5 (May 2006): 394–98.

Ginsberg, Lawrence D. "Carbamazepine Extended-Release Capsules Use in Bipolar Disorder: Efficacy and Safety in Adult Patients." *Annals of Clinical Psychiatry* 18 (Supplement 1) (May 2006): 9–14.

Ginsberg, Lawrence D. "Outcomes and Length of Treatment with Carbamazepine Extended-Release Capsules in Bipolar Disorder." *Annals of Clinical Psychiatry* 18 (Supplement 1) (May 2006): 15–18.

Ginsberg, Lawrence D. "Predictors of Response to Carbamazepine Extended-Release Capsules Treatment in Bipolar Disorder." *Annals of Clinical Psychiatry* 18 (Supplement 1) (May 2006): 23–26.

Ginsberg, Lawrence D. "Safety of Carbamazepine Extended-Release Capsules in Bipolar Disorder Polypharmacy." *Annals of Clinical Psychiatry* 18 (Supplement 1) (May 2006): 19–22.

Nasrallah, Henry A., Terence A. Ketter, and Amir H. Kalali. "Carbamazepine and Valproate for The Treatment of Bipolar Disorder: A Review of the Literature." *Journal of Affective Disorders* 95.1–3 (Oct. 2006): 69–78.

Zhang, Zhang-Jin, and others. "Adjunctive Herbal Medicine with Carbamazepine for Bipolar Disorders: A Double-Blind, Randomized, Placebo-Controlled Study." *Journal of Psychiatric Research* 41.3–4 (2007): 360–69.

OTHER

American Academy of Clinical Toxicology. 777 East Park Drive, P.O. Box 8820, Harrisburg, PA 17105-8820. Telephone: (717) 558-7750. Fax: (717) 558-7845. Web site: <http://www.clintox.org/index.html>.

American Psychiatric Association. 1400 K Street NW, Washington, DC 20005. Telephone: (888) 357-7924. Fax: (202) 682-6850. Web site: <http://www.psych.org/>.

American Society for Clinical Pharmacology and Therapeutics. 528 North Washington Street, Alexandria, VA 22314. Telephone: (703) 836-6981. Fax: (703) 836-5223.

American Society for Pharmacology and Experimental Therapeutics. 9650 Rockville Pike, Bethesda, MD 20814-3995. Telephone: (301) 530-7060. Fax: (301) 530-7061. Web site: <http://www.aspet.org/>.

L. Fleming Fallon, Jr., MD, Dr.P.H.
Ruth A. Wienclaw, PhD

CASE *see* **Clinical Assessment Scales for the Elderly**

Case management

Definition

Case management is a system for managing and delivering health care with the goal of improving the quality and continuity of care and decreasing health care costs. Case management includes coordinating all necessary medical and mental health care as well as any associated support services.

Purpose

Case management tries to enhance access to care and improve the continuity and efficiency of services. Depending on the specific setting and locale, case managers are responsible for a variety of tasks, ranging from linking clients to services to actually providing intensive clinical or rehabilitative services themselves. Other core functions include outreach to engage clients in services, assessing individual needs, arranging requisite support services (such as housing, benefit programs, job training), monitoring medication and use of services, and advocating for client rights and entitlements.

Case management is not a time-limited service, but is intended to be ongoing, providing clients whatever they need whenever they need it, for as long as necessary.

Historical background

Over the past 50 years, there have been fundamental changes in the system of mental health care in America. In the 1950s, mental health care for people with severe and persistent mental illnesses (like **schizophrenia**, **bipolar disorder**, severe **depression**, and **schizoaffective disorder**) was provided almost exclusively by large public mental hospitals. Created as part of a reform movement, these state hospitals provided a wide range of basic life supports in addition to mental health treatment, including housing, meals, clothing, and laundry services, and varying degrees of social and **vocational rehabilitation**.

During the latter half of the same decade, the introduction of neuroleptic medication provided symptomatic management of seriously disabling psychoses. This breakthrough, and other subsequent reforms in mental health policy (including the introduction of Medicare and Medicaid in 1965 and the Supplemental Security Income [SSI] program in 1974), provided incentives for policy makers to discharge patients to the community and transfer state mental health expenditures to the federal government.

These advances—coupled with new procedural safeguards for involuntary patients, court decisions establishing the right to treatment in the least restrictive setting, and changed philosophies of care—led to widespread **deinstitutionalization**. In 1955, there were 559,000 people in state hospitals; by 1980, that number had dropped to 132,000. According to the most recent data from the U.S. Center for Mental Health Services, although the number of mental health organizations providing 24-hour services (hospital inpatient and residential treatment) more than doubled in the United States from 1970 to 1998, the number of psychiatric beds provided by these organizations decreased by half.

As a result of deinstitutionalization policies, the number of patients discharged from hospitals has risen, and the average length of stay for newly admitted patients has decreased. An increasing number of patients are never admitted at all, but are diverted to a more complex and decentralized system of community-based care. Case management was designed to remedy the confusion created by multiple care providers in different settings, and to assure accessibility, continuity of care, and accountability for individuals with long-term disabling mental illnesses.

Models of case management

The two models of case management mentioned most often in the mental health literature are assertive community treatment (ACT) and intensive case management. A third model, clinical case management, refers to a program where the case manager assigned to a client also functions as their primary therapist.

Assertive community treatment

The ACT model originated in an inpatient research unit at Mendota State Hospital in Madison,

Wisconsin, in the late 1960s. The program's architects, Arnold Marx, MD, Leonard Stein, MD, and Mary Ann Test, PhD, sought to create a "hospital without walls." In this model, teams of 10–12 professionals—including case managers, a **psychiatrist**, nurses, **social workers**, and vocational specialists—are assigned ongoing responsibility 24 hours a day, 7 days a week, 365 days a year, for a caseload of approximately 10 clients with severe and persistent mental illnesses.

ACT uses multidisciplinary teams with low client-to-staff ratios, emphasizes assertive outreach, provides in-vivo services (in the client's own setting), emphasizes assisting clients in managing their illness, assists with activities of daily living (ADL) skills, and emphasizes relationship building, emotional support, **crisis intervention** (as necessary), and an orientation, whenever possible, toward providing clients with services rather than linking them to other providers.

Compared to other psychosocial interventions the program has a remarkably strong evidence base. Twenty-five randomized controlled **clinical trials** have demonstrated that these programs reduce **hospitalization**, **homelessness**, and inappropriate hospitalization; increase housing stability; control psychiatric symptoms; and improve quality of life, especially among individuals who are high users of mental health services. The ACT model has been implemented in 33 states.

Intensive case management

Intensive case management practices are typically targeted to individuals with the greatest service needs, including individuals with a history of multiple hospitalizations, people dually diagnosed with **substance abuse** problems, individuals with mental illness who have been involved with the criminal justice system, and individuals who are both homeless and severely mentally ill.

In 2000, Richard Schaedle and Irwin Epstein conducted a survey of 22 experts and found that although intensive case management shares many critical ingredients with ACT programs, its elements are not as clearly articulated. Another distinction between intensive case management and ACT appears to be that the latter relies more heavily on a team versus individual approach. In addition, intensive case managers are more likely to "broker" treatment and rehabilitation services rather than provide them directly. Finally, intensive case management programs are more likely to focus on client strengths, empowering clients to fully participate in all treatment decisions.

Clinical case management

A meta-analytic study comparing ACT and clinical case management found that although the generic approach resulted in increased hospital admissions, it significantly decreased the length of stay. This suggests that the overall impact of clinical case management is positive. Consistent with prior research, the study concluded that both ACT and high-quality clinical case management should be essential features of any mental health service system. One of the greatest tragedies of deinstitutionalization has been that most families often become de facto case managers for their family members, without any training or support.

Case management for children and adolescents

Case management is also used to coordinate care for children with serious emotional disturbances—diagnosed mental health problems that substantially disrupt a child's ability to function socially, academically, and emotionally. Although not a formal **diagnosis** in the ***Diagnostic and Statistical Manual of Mental Disorders (DSM),*** the handbook published by the American Psychiatric Association and used by mental health professionals to diagnose mental disorders, the term "serious emotional disturbance" is commonly used by states and the federal government to identify children with the greatest service needs. Although the limited research on case management for children and youth with serious emotional disturbances has been primarily focused on service use rather than clinical outcomes, there is growing evidence that case management is an effective **intervention** for this population.

Case management models used for children vary considerably. One model, called "wraparound," helps families develop a plan to address the child's individual needs across multiple life domains (home and school, for example). Research on the effectiveness of this model is still in an early stage. Another model, known as the children and youth intensive case management or expanded broker model, had been evaluated in two controlled studies. Findings suggest that this broker/advocacy model results in behavioral improvements and fewer days in hospital settings.

Conclusion

In recent years, many case management programs have expanded their teams to successfully utilize consumers as peer counselors and family members as outreach workers. The programs have also been adapted to serve older individuals with severe and persistent mental illnesses. While the ACT model offers the

KEY TERMS

Medicaid—A program jointly funded by state and federal governments that reimburses hospitals and physicians for the care of individuals who cannot pay for their own medical expenses. These individuals may be in low-income households or may have chronic disabilities.

Medicare—A federally funded health insurance program for individuals aged 65 and older, and certain categories of younger people with disabilities.

Meta-analysis—The statistical analysis of a large collection of analyses from individual studies for the purpose of integrating the findings.

Neuroleptic—Another name for the older antipsychotic medications, such as haloperidol (Haldol) and chlorpromazine (Thorazine).

Psychosis (plural: psychoses)—A severe state that is characterized by loss of contact with reality and deterioration in normal social functioning; examples are schizophrenia and paranoia. Psychosis is usually one feature of an overarching disorder, not a disorder in itself.

Supplemental Security Income—A federal program that provides cash to meet basic needs for food, shelter, and clothing for aged, blind, and disabled individuals who have little or no income.

strongest evidential base for its effectiveness, research into the clinical and service system outcomes of this and other models of case management is ongoing.

The effectiveness of any case management program depends upon the availability of high-quality treatment and support services in a given community, the structure and coordination of the service system, and on the ability of an individual or family to pay for care either through private insurance or (more often) through public benefit and entitlement programs. With recent policy directives from the Centers for Medicaid and Medicare Services (formerly the Health Care Financing Administration or HCFA) promoting the use of Medicaid funds for ACT, more states are funding case management through Medicaid. Although some policy makers express concern about costs, the savings realized from keeping patients out of jails, hospitals, and emergency rooms usually offsets the expense of these programs. Compared to traditional outpatient programs, case management also offers a level of care that is far more comprehensive and humane for a disabled population.

Resources

BOOKS

Cesta, Toni G., Hussein A. Tahan, and Lois F. Fink. *The Case Manager's Survival Guide: Winning Strategies for Clinical Practice.* 2nd ed. St. Louis: Mosby Publishing, 2002.

Mullahy, Catherine. *The Case Manager's Handbook.* 3rd ed. Boston: Jones and Bartlett Publishers, 2004.

Nathan, Peter E., and Jack M. Gorman, eds. *A Guide to Treatments that Work.* 2nd ed. New York: Oxford University Press, 2002.

Roessler, Richard T., and Stanford E. Rubin, eds. *Case Management and Rehabilitation Counseling: Procedures and Techniques.* 4th ed. Austin, TX: PRO-ED, 2006.

Summers, Nancy. *Fundamentals of Case Management Practice: Skills for the Human Services.* 2nd ed. Belmont, CA: Wadsworth Publishing, 2005.

PERIODICALS

Angell, Beth, and Colleen Mahoney. "Reconceptualizing the Case Management Relationship in Intensive Treatment: A Study of Staff Perceptions and Experiences." *Administration and Policy in Mental Health and Mental Health Services Research* 34.2 (Mar. 2007): 172–88.

Buck, Page Walker, and Leslie B. Alexander. "Neglected Voices: Consumers with Serious Mental Illness Speak About Intensive Case Management." *Administration and Policy in Mental Health and Mental Health Services Research* 33.4 (July 2006): 470–81.

Coviello, Donna M., and others. "The Effectiveness of Outreach Case Management in Re-Enrolling Discharged Methadone Patients." *Drug and Alcohol Dependence* 85.1 (Oct. 2006): 56–65.

Hsieh, Chang-Ming. "Using Client Satisfaction to Improve Case Management Services for the Elderly." *Research on Social Work Practice* 16.6 (Nov. 2006): 605–12.

King, Robert. "Intensive Case Management: A Critical Re-Appraisal of the Scientific Evidence for Effectiveness." *Administration and Policy in Mental Health and Mental Health Services Research* 33.5 (Sept. 2006): 529–35.

Rosenthal, David A., and others. "A Survey of Current Disability Management Practice: Emerging Trends and Implications for Certification." *Rehabilitation Counseling Bulletin* 50.2 (Winter 2007): 76–86.

Sells, Dave, and others. "The Treatment Relationship in Peer-Based and Regular Case Management for Clients With Severe Mental Illness." *Psychiatric Services* 57.8 (Aug. 2006): 1179–84.

OTHER

PACT Across America. National Alliance for the Mentally Ill. "Assertive Community Treatment (ACT)" (accessed April 7, 2002). <http://www.nami.org/about/pact.htm>.

Irene S. Levine, PhD
Ruth A. Wienclaw, PhD

CAT *see* **Children's Apperception Test**
CAT scan *see* **Computed tomography**
Catapres *see* **Clonidine**

Catatonia

Definition

Catatonia is a disturbance of motor behavior that can have either a psychological or neurological cause. Its most well-known form involves a rigid, immobile position that is held by a person for a considerable length of time—often days, weeks, or longer. It can also refer to agitated, purposeless motor activity that is not stimulated by something in the environment. A less extreme form of catatonia involves very slowed motor activity. Often, the physical posture of a catatonic individual is unusual and/or inappropriate, and the individual may hold a posture if placed in it by someone else. According to the handbook used by mental health professionals to diagnose mental disorders, the ***Diagnostic and Statistical Manual of Mental Disorders***, the 4th edition, text revision, also known as the *DSM-IV-TR*, some 5–9% of all psychiatric inpatients show some catatonic symptoms. Of these, 25–50% are associated with mood disorders, 10–15% are associated with **schizophrenia**, and the remainder are associated with other mental disorders.

Description

Catatonia is described in the *DSM-IV-TR*, as having what may seem like contradictory symptoms. It can be characterized by immobility, a rigid positioning of the body held for a considerable length of time. Patients diagnosed with a catatonic disorder may maintain their body position for hours, days, weeks or even months at a time. However, it also can manifest as excessive movement, such as frantic running up and down a flight of stairs. A person in a semi-immobile catatonic state may allow a postural change and then "freeze" in the new posture, or may resist attempts at change. There may be a complete lack of verbalization, or echolalia (repeating or echoing heard phrases or sentences). This apparent paradoxical presentation of symptoms may have its root in the fact that catatonia has a variety of causes. In fact, some experts argue that catatonia, rather than being a discrete and describable classification, may instead be a collection of various illnesses without common specificities. It has been associated with a laundry list of disorders, including psychotic disorders, **depressive disorders**, dementias, and reactive disorders. It is, however, currently classified into a handful of types in the *DSM-IV-TR*.

Types of catatonia

CATATONIC SCHIZOPHRENIA. As with all types of schizophrenia, the catatonic type involves a marked

disturbance in all spheres of life. The individual shows disturbances in thinking, feeling, and behavior. A patient may be unable to maintain intimate relationships or to train for and sustain employment.

The catatonic type of schizophrenia is characterized by severe psychomotor disturbance. Individuals with this disorder show extreme immobility. They may stay in the same position for hours, days, weeks, or longer. The position they assume may be unusual and appear uncomfortable to the observer. If another person moves part of the catatonic individual's body, such as a limb, he or she may maintain the position into which they are placed, a condition known as "waxy flexibility." Sometimes catatonia presents itself as excessive motor activity, but the activity seems purposeless, and does not appear to fit with what is happening in the environment. In its most severe forms, whether stupor or agitation, the individual may need close supervision to keep from injuring him- or herself, or others.

DEPRESSION WITH CATATONIC FEATURES. Individuals who are severely depressed may show disturbances of motor behavior that are similar to that of catatonic schizophrenics, as previously described. They may be essentially immobile, or exhibit excessive but random-seeming motor activity. Extreme negativism, elective mutism (choosing not to speak), peculiar movements, mimicking words or phrases (known as "echolalia") or mimicking movements (known as "echopraxia") may also be part of the picture. Again, in its most extreme forms, catatonic stupor (not moving for hours, days, weeks, or longer), and catatonic activity (random-seeming activity) may necessitate supervision so that the individual does not hurt him- or herself, or others. Catatonic behaviors may also be seen in persons with other mood disorders, such as manic or mixed-mood states; these are also known as bipolar I and bipolar II disorders.

CATATONIC DISORDER DUE TO GENERAL MEDICAL CONDITION. Individuals with catatonia due to a medical condition may show symptoms similar to persons with catatonic schizophrenia and catatonic **depression**. However, the cause is believed to be physiological. Certain neurologic diseases, such as encephalitis, may cause catatonic symptoms that can be either temporary or lasting.

See also Affect; Bipolar disorders; Catatonic disorder; Hypomanic episode; Major depressive disorder; Manic episode; Mood disorders; Schizophrenia.

Resources

BOOKS

American Psychiatric Association. *Diagnostic and Statistical Manual of Mental Disorders.* 4th ed., Text rev. Washington, D.C.: American Psychiatric Association, 2000.

Kaplan, Harold I., MD, and Benjamin J. Sadock, MD. *Synopsis of Psychiatry: Behavioral Sciences/Clinical Psychiatry,* 8th ed. Baltimore, MD: Lippincott Williams and Wilkins, 1998.

PERIODICALS

Penland, Heath R., Natalie Weder, and Rajesh R. Tampi. "The Catatonic Dilemma Expanded." *Annals of General Psychiatry* 5 (2006): 14. An open-access publication available at: <http://www.annals-general-psychiatry.com/content/5/1/14>.

Barbara Sternberg, PhD
Emily Jane Willingham, PhD

Catatonic disorders

Definition

Catatonic disorders are a group of symptoms characterized by disturbances in motor (muscular movement) behavior that may have either a psychological or a physiological basis. The condition itself is called **catatonia**.

Catatonic symptoms were first described by the **psychiatrist** Karl Ludwig Kahlbaum in 1874. Kahlbaum described catatonia as a disorder characterized by unusual motor symptoms. His description of individuals with catatonic behaviors remains accurate to this day. Kahlbaum carefully documented the symp-

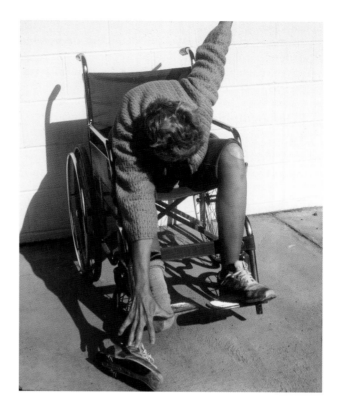

A patient with catatonic schizophrenia. *(Photo Researchers)*

toms and the course of the illness, providing a natural history of this unusual disorder.

Description

The ***Diagnostic and Statistical Manual of Mental Disorders***, fourth edition, text revision (also known as the *DSM-IV-TR*) describes catatonia as having what may seem like contradictory symptoms. It can be characterized by immobility, a rigid positioning of the body held for a considerable length of time. Patients diagnosed with a catatonic disorder may maintain their body position for hours, days, weeks, or even months at a time. However, catatonia also can manifest as excessive movement, such as frantic running up and down a flight of stairs. People in semi-immobile catatonic states may allow a postural change and then "freeze" in the new posture, or may resist attempts at change. They may display a complete lack of verbalization, or echolalia (repeating or echoing heard phrases or sentences). This apparent paradoxical presentation of symptoms may have its root in the fact that catatonia has a variety of causes. In fact, some experts argue that, rather than being a discrete and describable classification, catatonia may instead be a collection of various illnesses without common specificities. It has been associated with a laundry list of disorders, including psychotic disorders, **depressive disorders**, dementias, and reactive disorders. It is, however, currently classified into a handful of types in the *DSM-IV-TR*.

Demographics

Rates of catatonia are extremely variable and have generally been recorded based on the accompanying co-morbidity or underlying cause. For example, the range of prevalence of catatonic **schizophrenia** is 7% to 17%. Studies also seem to suggest that diagnoses of catatonic schizophrenia has decreased dramatically over time. No one is sure what underlies this apparent decrease, although some explanations include changes in the definition of catatonia, improvement in approaches to care, and simple underdiagnosis. In patients with affective disorders (disorders related to the emotion or mood displayed to others), symptoms of catatonia occur in 13% to 31%, with higher prevalence among people with **bipolar disorder**.

DSM-IV types of catatonic disorder

CATATONIC SCHIZOPHRENIA. A characteristic of disorders now classified under the schizophrenia umbrella is severe disturbance in motor behavior. Individuals with catatonic schizophrenia often show extreme immobility. They may stay in the same position for hours, days, weeks, or longer. The position they assume may be unusual and appear uncomfortable to the observer; for example, the person with catatonic schizophrenia may stand on one leg like a stork, or hold one arm outstretched for a long time. If an observer moves a hand or limb of the catatonic person's body, he or she may maintain the new position. This condition is known as waxy flexibility. In other situations, a person with catatonic schizophrenia may be extremely active, but the activity appears bizarre, purposeless, and unconnected to the situation or surroundings. Catatonic stupor is characterized by slowed motor activity, often to the point of being motionless and appearing unaware of surroundings. Patients may exhibit negativism, which means that they resist all attempts to be moved, or all instructions or requests to move, without any apparent motivation.

DEPRESSION WITH CATATONIC FEATURES. People who are severely depressed may show disturbances of motor behavior resembling those of patients diagnosed with catatonic schizophrenia. These people with **depression** may remain virtually motionless, or move around in an extremely vigorous but apparently random fashion. Other parts of the symptomatic picture may include extreme negativism, elective mutism (choosing not to speak), peculiar movements, and echolalia or echopraxia (imitating another person's movements). These behaviors may require caregivers to supervise patients to ensure they do not harm themselves or others.

MOOD DISORDERS AND CATATONIA. Catatonic behaviors may also occur in people with other mood disorders. People experiencing manic or mixed mood states (a simultaneous combination of manic and depressive symptoms) may at times exhibit either the immobility or agitated random activity seen in catatonia. A severely depressed person may experience intense emotional pain from simply moving a finger. Even getting up out of a chair can be a painful chore that may take hours for an individual with severe depression. As the depression begins to lift, the catatonic symptoms diminish.

CATATONIC DISORDER DUE TO A GENERAL MEDICAL CONDITION. People with catatonic disorder due to a medical condition show symptoms similar to those of catatonic schizophrenia and catatonic depression, except that the cause is believed to be related to an underlying medical condition. Neurological diseases such as encephalitis may cause catatonic symptoms that can be temporary or lasting. Overall, at least 35 distinct medical and neurological illnesses have been associated with catatonia; in addition to encephalitis as a common causative agent, others include structural damage to the central nervous system, metabolic disturbances, **seizures**, and exposure to some drugs.

Causes and symptoms

Causes

Although the initiating factors of catatonia can vary greatly, research has identified common underlying mechanisms in some cases. For example, there may be imbalances or problems in regulating signaling among nerves in the central nervous system, involving **neurotransmitters** (nerve signaling molecules) like **dopamine** and serotonin. In addition, some brain **imaging studies** have found an enlarged cerebral cortex and reduced cerebellum in some people with catatonia, although this is not a consistent finding. People who have emerged from catatonic states report having had intense emotions, including uncontrollable **anxiety** and literally paralyzing fear. Others also report having experienced depression, euphoria, or aggression while in the catatonic state.

Symptoms

CATATONIC SCHIZOPHRENIA. Catatonic schizophrenia manifests with prominent motor symptoms and abnormalities. These symptoms, as given in the *DSM-IV-TR*, include:

- catalepsy, or motionlessness maintained over a long period of time
- catatonic excitement, marked by agitation and seemingly pointless movement
- catatonic stupor, with markedly slowed motor activity, often to the point of immobility and seeming unawareness of the environment
- catatonic rigidity, in which a rigid position is assumed and held against all outside efforts to change it
- catatonic posturing, in which a bizarre or inappropriate posture is assumed and maintained over a long period of time
- waxy flexibility, in which a limb or other body part of a catatonic person can be moved into another position that is then maintained. The body part feels to an observer as if it were made of wax.
- akinesia, or absence of physical movement

DEPRESSION WITH CATATONIC FEATURES. Within the category of mood disorders, catatonic symptoms are most commonly associated with bipolar I disorder. Bipolar I disorder is a mood disorder involving periods of mania interspersed with depressive episodes. Symptoms of catatonic excitement, such as random activity unrelated to the environment or repetition of words, phrases, and movements may occur during manic phases. Catatonic immobility may appear during the most severe phase of the depressive cycle. The actual catatonic symptoms are indistinguishable from those seen in catatonic schizophrenia. It is also possible for catatonic symptoms to occur in conjunction with other mood disorders, including bipolar II disorder (involving a milder form of mania called **hypomania**), mixed disorders (involving simultaneous mania and depression), and major depressive disorders.

CATATONIC DISORDER DUE TO GENERAL MEDICAL CONDITION. Symptoms of catatonic disorder caused by medical conditions are indistinguishable from those that occur in schizophrenia and mood disorders. Unlike persons with schizophrenia, however, those with catatonic symptoms due to a medical condition demonstrate greater insight and awareness into their illness and symptoms. They have periods of clear thinking, and their **affect** (emotional response) is generally appropriate to the circumstances. Neither of these conditions is true of patients with schizophrenia or severe depression.

Demographics

According to the *DSM-IV-TR*, between 5% and 9% of all psychiatric inpatients show some catatonic symptoms. Of these, 25–50% are associated with mood disorders, 10–15% are associated with schizo-

phrenia, and the remainder are associated with other mental disorders. Catatonic symptoms can also occur in a wide variety of general medical conditions, including infectious, metabolic, and neurological disorders. They may also appear as side effects of various medications, including several drugs of **abuse**.

Diagnosis

Important diagnostic distinctions must be made to determine the cause of catatonic symptoms. Catatonic schizophrenia is diagnosed when the patient's other symptoms include thought disorder, inappropriate affect, and a history of peculiar behavior and dysfunctional relationships. Catatonic symptoms associated with a mood disorder are diagnosed when patients have a prior history of mood disorder, or after careful psychiatric evaluation. Medical tests are necessary to determine the cause of catatonic symptoms caused by infectious diseases, metabolic abnormalities, or neurological conditions. Patients should be asked about recent use of both prescribed and illicit drugs to determine whether the symptoms are drug-related.

Treatments

Treatment for catatonic symptoms can rely on drug-based approaches or on **electroconvulsive therapy** (ECT). **Benzodiazepines** (for example, **lorazepam**) have often been the first-line treatment approach, although response to this therapy varies a great deal. One study has found that use of lorazepam was not effective in treating chronic catatonia, and there are other concerns about using benzodiazepines, including the fact that withdrawal from these drugs has itself been associated with inducing catatonia.

Other drugs that have been applied in cases of catatonia include antipsychotics. As with benzodiazepines, there are some concerns that the attempted cure could also be causative; these drugs have also been associated with precipitating catatonic episodes. On the flip side, the perceived reduction in rates of catatonic schizophrenia has accompanied the introduction and increasing use of these drugs. Other drugs, such as lithium or **amantadine**, have shown unpredictable success and elicited variable responses.

ECT, or electroconvulsive therapy, elicits negative reactions from many people, as it involves the administration of an electric shock to the brain to essentially cause a seizure. However, many psychiatrists maintain that it is a safe and effective approach and is the "ultimate treatment" for catatonia, especially if patients only partially respond to drug therapy.

KEY TERMS

Akinesia—Absence of physical movement.

Catalepsy—An abnormal condition characterized by postural rigidity and mental stupor, associated with certain mental disorders.

Catatonic disorder—A severe disturbance of motor behavior characterized by either extreme immobility or stupor, or by random and purposeless activity.

Catatonic schizophrenia—A subtype of a severe mental disorder that affects thinking, feeling, and behavior, and that is also characterized by catatonic behaviors—either extreme stupor or random, purposeless activity.

Dopamine—A chemical in brain tissue that serves to transmit nerve impulses (a neurotransmitter) and helps to regulate movement and emotions.

Echolalia—Meaningless repetition of words or phrases spoken by another.

Echopraxia—Imitation of another person's physical movements in a repetitious or senseless manner.

Hypomania—A milder form of mania which is characteristic of bipolar II disorder.

Mutism—Inability to speak due to conscious refusal or psychological inhibition.

Serotonin—A widely distributed neurotransmitter that is found in blood platelets, the lining of the digestive tract, and the brain, and that works in combination with norepinephrine. It causes very powerful contractions of smooth muscle, and is associated with mood, attention, emotions, and sleep. Low levels of serotonin are associated with depression.

Stupor—A trance-like state that causes a person to appear numb to his or her environment.

Waxy flexibility—A condition in which a person's body part, usually a limb, can be moved by others into different positions, where it remains for long periods of time.

Prognosis

The prognosis for a person with catatonia varies with the cause underlying the disorder. With disorders such as alcohol-use disorder or affective disorder, the prognosis for resolution is relatively good; however, when catatonia accompanies schizophrenia, there is an association with earlier and higher levels of mortality. In one review, the authors ranked the associated disorder with the relative prognosis from best to worst, as follows: depression with catatonia, periodic catatonia, cycloid psychoses with catatonia, bipolar disorder with catatonia, catatonic schizophrenia, and non-catatonic schizophrenia. The choice of treatment also can influence prognosis.

Prevention

There are no specific preventive measures for most causes of catatonia. Infectious disease can sometimes be prevented. Catatonic symptoms caused by medications or drugs of abuse can be reversed by suspending use of the drug.

See also Affect; Bipolar disorders; Hypomanic episode; Major depressive disorder; Mania; Manic episode; Mood disorders; Schizophrenia.

Resources

BOOKS

American Psychiatric Association. *Diagnostic and Statistical Manual of Mental Disorders.* 4th ed., Text rev. Washington, D.C.: American Psychiatric Association, 2000.

Kaplan, Harold I., MD, and Benjamin J. Sadock, MD. *Synopsis of Psychiatry: Behavioral Sciences/Clinical Psychiatry.* 8th ed. Baltimore, MD: Lippincott Williams and Wilkins, 1998.

Sacks, Oliver. *Awakenings.* New York: HarperPerennial, 1990.

PERIODICALS

Carroll, B. T. "Kahlbaum's Catatonia Revisited." *Psychiatry and Clinical Neuroscience* 55.5 (Oct. 2001): 431–36.

Penland, Heath R., Natalie Weder, and Rajesh R. Tampi. "The Catatonic Dilemma Expanded." *Annals of General Psychiatry* 5 (2006): 14. An open-access publication available at: <http://www.annals-general-psychiatry.com/content/5/1/14>.

Pfuhlmann, B., and G. Stober. "The Different Conceptions of Catatonia: Historical Overview and Critical Discussion." *European Archives of Psychiatry and Clinical Neruoscience* 251, Supplement 1 (2001): 14–17.

Sarkstein, S. E., J. C. Golar, and A. Hodgkiss. "Karl Ludwig Kahlbaum's Concept of Catatonia." *History of Psychiatry* 6.22, part 2 (June 1995): 201–207.

ORGANIZATIONS

American Psychiatric Association. 1400 K Street NW, Washington, DC 20002. Telephone: (202) 336-5500.

Mental Illness Foundation. 420 Lexington Avenue, Suite 2104, New York, NY 10170. Telephone: (212) 682-4699.

National Alliance for the Mentally Ill (NAMI). 2101 Wilson Boulevard, Suite 302, Arlington, VA 22201.

National Mental Health Association. 1021 Prince Street, Alexandria, VA, 22314. Telephone: (703) 684-7722.

Barbara Sternberg, PhD
Emily Jane Willingham, PhD

CATIE

Purpose

The Clinical Antipsychotic Trials of Intervention Effectiveness (CATIE) Schizophrenia Study is a clinical trial funded by the National Institute of Mental Health and coordinated by the University of North Carolina at Chapel Hill. The purpose of the study is to evaluate the effectiveness and side effects of newer antipsychotic drugs (sometimes referred to as atypical antipsychotics) in comparison to conventional antipsychotic drugs in the treatment of **schizophrenia.** One of the purposes of the study was to help doctors maximize the benefits of antipsychotic drugs while minimizing their negative side effects.

Description

Atypical antipsychotic medications frequently have fewer serious adverse side effects than conventional antipsychotics. The CATIE study was an attempt to scientifically investigate the effectiveness of the newer drugs in comparison with the conventional antipsychotic drug **perphenazine** (Trilafon). All drugs used in the CATIE study had been previously approved by the U.S. Food and Drug Administration (FDA). The atypical antipsychotic drugs under investigation in the study were:

- clozapine (Clozaril)
- olanzapine (Zyprexa)
- quetiapine (Seroquel)
- risperidone (Risperdal)
- ziprasidone (Geodon)

Aripiprazole (Abilify), another atypical antipsychotic drug, was not approved by the FDA in time to be included in the study. No placebos were used in the study.

All of the drugs evaluated in the CATIE study had already undergone **clinical trials** by the representative pharmaceutical companies in order to get FDA approval to market each drug. Although these studies were appropriately rigorous to earn FDA approval, they typically had a limited number of participants, tested only two or three drugs per study, and lasted only four to eight weeks.

As opposed to the clinical trials previously conducted by the pharmaceutical companies, the CATIE study lasted for 18 months and used over 1,400 participants. This more in-depth study allowed researchers to study drug actions and side effects in more depth as well as examine more long-term effects of their use.

Although the pharmaceutical companies donated the medications for the study and advised the researchers concerned of optimal doses, they had no other input into the design, implementation, analysis, or interpretation of the study results.

The CATIE study was open to participants from 18 to 65 years of age who had been diagnosed with schizophrenia using the *Diagnostic and Statistical Manual of Mental Disorders*, Fourth Edition, Text Revision (*DSM-IV-TR*), and who were able to use oral medications. Of the 1,460 patients who were enrolled in the CATIE study, 74% were male, 40% were non-white, and 12% were Hispanic. The mean (average) age of CATIE participants was 40.6 years. The average length of time participants had been schizophrenic was 14.4 years. Participants in the study came from 57 different clinical sites across the country and reflect the range of people in the United States suffering from schizophrenia.

Study participants were randomly assigned to the experimental treatments in a double-blind study. This means that the doctors administering the drugs were not able to choose which medication their patients received, and that neither the researchers, administering physicians, or patients knew which treatment the patients were receiving. This study design helped ensure that preconceived expectations about the effectiveness of any of the drugs did not affect the outcome of the study. Patients were randomly assigned to either one of the atypical antipsychotics or the control conventional antipsychotic. Patients continued on the assigned drug for 18 months or until the drug failed to continue to control their symptoms or produced intolerable side effects, or the patients decided to stop the medication or withdraw from the study.

Previous research has shown that patients taking antipsychotic medication are better off than those not taking such medication. Previous research has also found that staying on antipsychotic medication is critical to controlling the symptoms of schizophrenia and presenting a **relapse**. Therefore, one of the primary measures of success in the CATIE study was how long patients benefited from the medication to which they were assigned and how long before they decided it needed to be changed. When patients decided that the medication was not effective, researchers recorded the reasons the medication was stopped (e.g., the medication no longer controlled the symptoms, the side effects were intolerable). Other data collected included the effects of the medications on the symptoms of schizophrenia and level of the patient's functioning on the medication.

Findings of the study

The study found that the conventional antipsychotic generally was equally effective and tolerated as well as the newer, more expensive, atypical antipsychotic medications. Of the atypical antipsychotics, olanzapine performed somewhat better than the other drugs in the study. Patients on this drug were less likely to be hospitalized for psychotic relapse and tended to stay on their medication longer than patients taking other antipsychotic drugs in the study. However, patients on olanzapine also tended to gain significant weight and experience other metabolic changes associated with diabetes than did patients taking the other drugs in the study.

Nearly 75% of the patients in the CATIE study switched to a different medication during the course of the study. Participants who stopped taking the medication for any reason were given the opportunity to continue in the study in one of two ways. In the "efficacy pathway," patients who discontinued an atypical antipsychotic because it was not sufficiently effective were randomly assigned to receive another atypical antipsychotic to help determine what treatment should be chosen for such patients. In the "tolerability pathway," patients who discontinued their medication because of side effects were allowed to receive another medication in order to help determine the next best choice for patients who experience adverse side effects with an atypical antipsychotic. The conventional antipsychotic (perphenazine) was not included in this second phase of the study because researchers had not expected the conventional medication to work as well as the newer drugs when they designed the study.

Most of the participants in the Phase II efficacy pathway study had not benefited from their first antipsychotic medication and had worse symptoms than at the beginning of the study. These participants also tended to have worse symptoms than those participants in the tolerability pathway study. Clozapine was very effective for this group and worked significantly better than the other atypical antipsychotics. Forty-four percent of participants in this part of the study were able to stay on their medication for the remainder of the study. Participants on the efficacy pathway stayed on their medication for an average of 10 months as opposed to three months for those taking the other atypical antipsychotics. In addition, most of these participants had greater symptom relief than participants taking the other medications.

As in Phase I of the study, in the tolerability pathway of the Phase II study, a high rate (74%) of patients stopped taking their medication. However, 35% of the Phase II participants in the tolerability study who took olanzapine or risperidone continued taking their medication until the end of the study. Only 23% of participants taking ziprasidone and 16% of participants taking quetiapine in the Phase I study were able to continue throughout the entire 18 months.

The results of the Phase II study show that the choice of a different medication for patients who stop taking an antipsychotic medication depends on why they stopped taking the first medication. Participants who stopped taking their antipsychotic medication in Phase I because it was not adequately controlling their symptoms were more likely to stay on their medication if they were switched to olanzapine or risperidone rather than quetiapine or ziprasidone. There was no difference between the four medications tested in Phase II, however, for participants who had stopped taking their Phase I medication because they experienced adverse side effects.

The CATIE study has several major implications. First, the results of Phase I of the study show that it is worthwhile to start patients on less expensive conventional antipsychotic medications before trying the atypicals. Specifically, physicians and patients should consider perphenazine as an alterative to atypical antipsychotics both because of its similar effectiveness and its lower price.

The CATIE study results can also be used to help select a different antipsychotic medication for those patients who were not successfully treated on another antipsychotic. The results of the Phase II study show that the reason for stopping the first medication should be considered when choosing another medication.

The study results also show that clozapine is often a good choice of medication for patients who did not respond well to other antipsychotic medications. In Phase II of the study, clozapine was more effective in controlling symptoms than the other atypical antipsychotics under evaluation. For patients whose symptoms are not well controlled on clozapine, olanzapine and risperidone tend to be more effective than ziprasidone or quetiapine. However, the side effects of these drugs must be taken into account.

The CATIE study did not reveal a clear path of next treatment for those patients who had discontinued use of an antipsychotic due to adverse side effects. In such cases, it is important to balance the degree of symptom control from the drug with the nature of its side effects. For example, olanzapine tended to result in considerable weight gain and metabolic problems, whereas ziprasidone consistently resulted in weight loss and improvement of metabolic disorders. Of the drugs tested, risperidone had the least adverse side effects.

KEY TERMS

Atypical antisychotic—A newer antipsychotic drug that is less likely to cause significant adverse side effects than conventional antipsychotic medications. Atypical antipsychotics are also called novel antipsychotics or second-generation antipsychotics.

Clinical trial—A controlled scientific experiment designed to investigate the effectiveness of a drug or treatment in curing or lessening the symptoms of a disease or disorder.

Double-blind study—A research study in which neither the participants nor the professional administering the drug or treatment know whether they are receiving the experimental treatment or a placebo or control treatment.

Placebo—A preparation without pharmacological effect that is given in place of a drug in clinical trials to determine the effectiveness of the drug under study; a "sugar pill."

Resources

BOOKS

American Psychiatric Association. *Diagnostic and Statistical Manual of Mental Disorders.* 4th ed., Text rev. Washington, D.C.: American Psychiatric Association, 2000.

VandenBos, Gary R., ed. *APA Dictionary of Psychology.* Washington, D.C.: American Psychological Association, 2007.

PERIODICALS

Davis, S. M., G. G. Koch, C. E. Davis, and L. M. LaVange. "Statistical Approaches to Effectiveness Measurement and Outcome-Driven Re-Randomizations in the Clinical Antipsychotic Trials of Intervention Effectiveness (CATIE) Studies." *Schizophrenia Bulletin* 29.1 (2003): 73–80.

Essock, S. M., and others. "Effectiveness of Switching Antipsychotic Medications." *American Journal of Psychiatry* 163.12 (Dec. 2006): 2090–95.

Keefe, R. S., and others. "Neurocognitive Assessment in the Clinical Antipsychotic Trials of Intervention Effectiveness (CATIE) Project Schizophrenia Trial: Development, Methodology, and Rationale." *Schizophrenia Bulletin* 291 (2003): 45–55.

Lieberman, J. A., and others. "Effectiveness of Antipsychotic Drugs in Patients with Chronic Schizophrenia." *New England Journal of Medicine* 353.12 (Sep. 22, 2005): 1209–23.

Lieberman, J. A., and T. S. Stroup. "Guest Editors' Introduction: What Can Large Pragmatic Clinical Trials Do for Public Mental Health Care?" *Schizophrenia Bulletin* 29.1 (2003): 1–6.

McEvoy, J. P., and others. "Effectiveness of Clozapine Versus Olanzapine, Quetiapine, and Risperidone in Patients with Chronic Schizophrenia Who Did Not Respond to Prior Atypical Antipsychotic Treatment." *American Journal of Psychiatry* 163.4 (Apr. 2006): 600–610.

Rosenheck, R., J. Doyle, D. Leslie, and A. Fontana. "Changing Environments and Alternative Perspectives in Evaluating the Cost-Effectiveness of New Antipsychotic Drugs." *Schizophrenia Bulletin* 29.1 (2003): 81–93.

Rosenheck, R. A., and others. "Cost-Effectiveness of Second-Generation Antipsychotics and Perphenazine in a Randomized Trial of Treatment for Chronic Schizophrenia." *American Journal of Psychiatry* 163.12 (Dec. 2006): 2080–89.

Schneider, L. S., and others. "Clinical Antipsychotic Trials of Intervention Effectiveness (CATIE): Alzheimer's Disease Trial." *Schizophrenia Bulletin* 29.1 (2003): 57–72.

Schneider, L. S., and others. "Effectiveness of Atypical Antipsychotic Drugs in Patients with Alzheimer's Disease." *New England Journal of Medicine* 355.125 (Oct. 2006): 1525–38.

Sernyak, M. J., D. Leslie, and R. Rosenheck. "Use of System-Wide Outcomes Monitoring Data to Compare the Effectiveness of Atypical Neuroleptic Medications." *American Journal of Psychiatry* 160.2 (Feb. 2003): 310–15.

Stroup, T. S., and P. S. Appelbaum. "Evaluation of 'Subject Advocate' Procedures in the Clinical Antipsychotic Trials of Intervention Effectiveness (CATIE) Schizophrenia Study." *Schizophrenia Bulletin* 32.1 (Jan. 2006): 147–52.

Stroup, T. S., and others. "Effectiveness of Olanzapine, Quetiapine, Risperidone, and Ziprasidone in Patients With Chronic Schizophrenia Following Discontinuation of a Previous Atypical Antipsychotic." *American Journal of Psychiatry* 163.4 (Apr. 2006): 611–22.

Stroup, T. S., and others. "The National Institute of Mental Health Clinical Antipsychotic Trials of Intervention Effectiveness (CATIE) Project: Schizophrenia Trial Design and Protocol Development." *Schizophrenia Bulletin* 29.1 (2003): 15–31.

Swartz, M. S., and others. "Assessing Clinical and Functional Outcomes in the Clinical Antipsychotic Trials of Intervention Effectiveness (CATIE) Schizophrenia Trial." *Schizophrenia Bulletin* 29.1 (2003): 33–43.

OTHER

CATIE. *CATIE: Clinical Antipsychotic Trials of Intervention Effectiveness Schizophrenia Study,* 2003. <http://www.catie.unc.edu/schizophrenia>.

National Institutes of Health. *CATIE Schizophrenia Trial,* 2006. <http://www.clinicaltrials.gov/ct/show/NCT00014001?order=1>.

Ruth A. Wienclaw, PhD

Causes of mental illness *see* **Origin of mental illnesses**

Celexa *see* **Citalopram**

Chamomile

Definition

Chamomile is a plant that has been used since ancient Egypt in a variety of healing applications. Chamomile is a native of the Old World; it is related to the daisy family, having strongly scented foliage and flowers with white petals and yellow centers. The name chamomile is derived from two Greek words that mean "ground" and "apple," because chamomile leaves smell somewhat like apples, and because the plant grows close to the ground.

There are two varieties of chamomile commonly used in herbal preparations for internal use and for **aromatherapy**. One is called Roman chamomile (*Anthemis nobilis*), with contemporary sources in Belgium and southern England. Roman chamomile grows to a height of 9 in (23 cm) or less, and is frequently used as a ground cover along garden paths because of its pleasant apple scent. German chamomile (*Matricaria recutita*) is grown extensively in Germany, Hungary, and parts of the former Soviet Union. German chamomile grows to a height of about 3 ft (1 m) and is the variety most commonly cultivated in the United States, where it is used medicinally.

Purpose

Chamomile has been used internally for a wide variety of complaints. The traditional German description of chamomile is *alles zutraut*, which means that the plant "is good for everything."

Chamomile has been used internally for the following purposes:

- antispasmodic: A preparation given to relieve intestinal cramping and relax the smooth muscles of the internal organs. Chamomile is used as an antispasmodic to relieve digestive disorders, menstrual cramps, premenstrual syndrome (PMS), headache, and other stress-related disorders.
- anthelminthic: Chamomile has been used to expel parasitic worms from the digestive tract.
- carminative: Chamomile is given to help expel gas from the intestines.
- sedative: Perhaps the most frequent internal use of chamomile is in teas prepared to relieve anxiety and insomnia.
- anti-inflammatory: Roman chamomile has been used to soothe the discomfort of gingivitis (inflamed gums), earache, and arthritis. German chamomile is used in Europe to treat oral mucosities in cancer patients following chemotherapy treatment.

Dried chamomile flowers. (*Geoffrey Kidd/Alamy*)

- antiseptic: Chamomile has mild antibacterial properties, and is sometimes used as a mouthwash or eyewash. It can be applied to compresses to treat bruises or small cuts.
- other: Mexican Americans, especially the elderly, have been reported to use chamomile for the treatment of asthma and urinary incontinence. It is one of the two most popular herbs in use among this population.

The external uses of chamomile include blending its essential oil with **lavender** or rose for scenting perfumes, candles, creams, or other aromatherapy products intended to calm or relax the user. Chamomile is considered a middle note in perfumery, which means that its scent lasts somewhat longer than those of top notes but is less long lasting than scents extracted from resinous or gum-bearing plants. Chamomile is also a popular ingredient in shampoos, rinses, and similar products to add highlights to blonde or light brown hair.

Other external uses of chamomile include topical preparations for the treatment of bruises, scrapes, skin irritations, and joint pain. The antibacterial and anti-inflammatory properties of chamomile make it a widely used external treatment for acne, arthritis, burns, ulcerated areas of skin, and even diaper rash.

The German E Commission, regarded as an authority on herbal treatments, has recommended chamomile to "combat inflammation, stimulate the regeneration of cell tissue, and promote the healing of refractory wounds and skin ulcers."

Description

The flowers are the part of the chamomile plant that are harvested for both internal and external use. Chamomile flowers can be dried and used directly for teas and homemade topical preparations, but they are also available commercially in prepackaged tea bags and in capsule form. The essential oil of chamomile is pressed from the leaves as well as the flowers of the plant; it costs about $22–$35 for 5 ml. Chamomile is also available as a liquid extract.

The chemically active components of chamomile include alpha bisabobol, chamozulene, polyines, tannin, coumarin, flavonoids, and apigenin. However, no single factor has been credited with all the major healing properties of whole chamomile; it is assumed that the various components work together to produce the plant's beneficial effects.

Recommended dosage

Children may be given 1–2 ml of a glycerine preparation of German chamomile three times a day for colic; or 2–4 oz (57–100 g) of tea, one to three times a day, depending on the child's weight.

Adults may take a tea made from 0.7–1 oz (2–3 g) of dried chamomile steeped in hot water, three to four times daily for relief of heartburn, gas, or stomach cramps. Alternately, adults may take 5 ml of 1:5 dilution of chamomile tincture three times daily.

For use as a mouthwash, one may prepare a tea from 0.7–1 oz (2–3 g) of dried chamomile flowers, allow the tea to cool, and then gargle as often as desired. To soothe an irritated upper respiratory tract during cold season, adults may pour a few drops of essential oil of chamomile on top of steaming water and inhale the fragrant vapors.

For relief of eczema, insect bites, and other skin irritations, adults may add 4 oz (110 g) of dried chamomile flowers to a warm bath. Topical ointments containing 3–10% chamomile may be used for psoriasis, eczema, or dry, irritated skin.

Precautions

Because chamomile is related botanically to the ragweed plant, persons who are highly allergic to ragweed should use chamomile with caution.

KEY TERMS

Anthelminthic—A type of medication given to expel or eliminate intestinal worms.

Antispasmodic—A medication or preparation given to relieve muscle or digestive cramps.

Carminative—A substance or preparation that relieves digestive gas.

Essential oil—The product of special ducts or cells in the tissues of aromatic plants (or the sap of certain trees) that gives the plant its characteristic aroma and therapeutic properties. Essential oils are sometimes called volatile oils because they evaporate readily at room temperature.

Flavonoids—Plant pigments that have a variety of effects on human physiology. Some of these pigments have anti-inflammatory, anti-carcinogenic, and antioxidant effects, for example.

Middle note—A term used in perfumery and aromatherapy to designate essential oils whose odors emerge later than top notes but evaporate more rapidly than bottom notes. Chamomile is considered a middle note in aromatherapy.

Tannin—An astringent compound found in chamomile, oak bark, and certain other plants. Tannin in large quantities can interfere with iron absorption.

Topical—A type of medication or preparation intended for use on the skin or external surface of the body. Chamomile is commonly used in topical preparations for acne, open skin irritations, and similar conditions because of its antibacterial properties.

Chamomile is generally safe to drink when prepared using the recommended quantity of dried flowers. Highly concentrated tea made from Roman chamomile has been reported to cause nausea; this reaction is caused by a compound found in Roman chamomile called anthemic acid.

Women who are pregnant or lactating should not use chamomile.

Persons taking warfarin or similar blood-thinning medications should use chamomile only after consulting their physician, as it may intensify the effects of anticoagulant drugs.

Side effects

Chamomile can cause allergic reactions in people who are sensitive to ragweed.

Interactions

Chamomile can increase the effects of anticoagulant medications. In addition, its tannin content may interfere with iron absorption. Chamomile may also add to the effects of **benzodiazepines**, including valium, Ativan, and Versed. No other noteworthy medication interactions have been reported.

Resources

BOOKS

PDR for Herbal Medicines. Montvale, NJ: Medical Economics Company, 1998.

Pelletier, Kenneth R., MD. "Western Herbal Medicine: Nature's Green Pharmacy." Chapter 6 in *The Best Alternative Medicine.* New York: Simon and Schuster, 2002.

Price, Shirley. *Practical Aromatherapy.* Second edition, revised. London, UK: Thorsons, 1994.

PERIODICALS

Bone, Kerry. "Safety Issues in Herbal Medicine: Adulteration, Adverse Reactions and Organ Toxicities." *Townsend Letter for Doctors and Patients* (October 2001): 142.

Loera, Jose A., Sandra A. Black, Kyriakos S. Markides, and others. "The Use of Herbal Medicines by Older Mexican Americans." *Journals of Gerontology,* Series A (November 2001): M714-M718.

Miller, Lucinda G. "Herbal Medicinals." *Archives of Internal Medicine* 158 (November 1998): 2200-2211.

OTHER

American Botanical Council. PO Box 144345. Austin, TX 78714-4345. <www.herbalgram.org>.

National Association for Holistic Aromatherapy (NAHA). 4509 Interlake Avenue North, #233, Seattle, WA 98103-6773. (888) ASK-NAHA or (206) 547-2164. <www.naha.org.>.

Rebecca J. Frey, Ph.D.

Child abuse *see* Abuse

Child Depression Inventory

Definition

The Child **Depression** Inventory (CDI) is a symptom-oriented instrument for assessing depression in children between the ages of seven and 17 years. The basic CDI consists of 27 items, but a 10-item short form is also available for use as a screener.

Purpose

The CDI was first published by Maria Kovacs in 1992. It was developed because depression in young children is often difficult to diagnose, and also because depression was regarded as an adult disorder until the 1970s. It was thought that children's nervous systems were not sufficiently mature to manifest the neurochemical changes in **brain** function associated with depression.

In 2002 the National Institute of Mental Health (NIMH) estimated that as many as 2.5% of children and 8.3% of adolescents under the age of 18 in the United States have depression. A study sponsored by the NIMH of 9- to 17-year-olds found that 6% developed depression in a six-month period, with 4.9% diagnosed as having major depression. Research also indicates that children and adolescents experience the onset of depression at earlier ages than previous generations, are more likely to experience recurrences, and are more likely to experience severe depression as adults.

The CDI is intended to detect and evaluate the symptoms of a **major depressive disorder** or **dysthymic disorder** in children or adolescents, and to distinguish between children with those disorders and children with other psychiatric conditions. The CDI can be administered repeatedly in order to measure changes in the depression over time and to evaluate the results of treatment for **depressive disorders**. It is regarded as adequate for assessing the severity of the depressive symptoms.

The CDI has also been used in research studies of the epidemiology of depression in children as well as studies of dissociative symptoms and post-traumatic syndromes in children. It has been rated as having adequate to excellent psychometric properties by research psychologists.

Precautions

The CDI shares certain drawbacks with other self-report measures used in children, namely that children do not have the same level of ability as adults to understand and report strong internal emotions. On the other hand, children have the same ability as adults to modify their answers on the CDI and similar tests to reflect what they think are the desired answers rather than what they actually feel. This phenomenon is variously known as "faking good" or "faking bad," depending on the bias of the modified answers. Some researchers have also observed that children who do not have age-appropriate reading skills may receive an inaccurate **diagnosis** on the basis of their CDI score.

KEY TERMS

Dysthymic disorder—A mood disorder that is less severe than depression but usually more chronic. Dysthymic disorder is diagnosed in children and adolescents when a depressed mood persists for a least one year and is accompanied by at least two other symptoms of major depression.

Epidemiology—The study of the causes, incidence, transmission, and control of diseases.

Frequency distribution—In statistics, the correspondence between a set of frequencies and the set of categories used to classify the group being tested.

Psychometric—Pertaining to testing and measurement of mental or psychological abilities. Psychometric tests convert an individual's psychological traits and attributes into a numerical estimation or evaluation.

Self-rated—A term in psychological testing that means that the person taking the test is the one who decides whether a question applies to them and records the answer, as distinct from an examiner's evaluating and recording answers.

Standard deviation—A measure of variability in a set of scores. The standard deviations are based on a comparison to others in the same age group. Standardizing the scores in this way allows scores across age groups to be compared.

The results of the CDI should be evaluated only by a trained professional **psychologist** or **psychiatrist**, not by a parent, teacher, or school nurse.

Because depressive symptoms fluctuate somewhat in children as well as in adults, the author of the test recommends retesting children who score positive on the CDI, with a two- to four-week interval between the test and the retest. A child who screens positive on the CDI should receive a comprehensive diagnostic evaluation by a licensed mental health professional. The evaluation should include interviews with the child or adolescent; the parents or other caregivers; and, when possible, such other observers as teachers, social service personnel, or the child's primary care physician.

Description

The CDI is self-rated, which means that the child or adolescent being evaluated records their answers to the questions on the test sheet, as distinct from giving verbal answers to questions that are then analyzed and recorded by the examiner. Other self-rated instruments for assessing depression in children include the **Beck Depression Inventory** (BDI) and the Weinberg Screening Affective Scale (WSAS).

Each question on the CDI consists of three possible responses; the child or adolescent being evaluated selects the response that most closely describes him or her over the preceding two weeks. The CDI is designed to make quantitative measurements of the following symptoms of depression: mood disturbances; capacity for enjoyment; depressed self-evaluation; disturbances in behavior toward other people; and vegetative symptoms, which include **fatigue**, oversleeping, having difficulty with activities requiring effort, and other symptoms of passivity or inactivity.

Results

The test administrator totals the responses and plots them onto a profile form. A score that falls below a cutoff point, or is 1.0 to 2.0 standard deviations above the mean, is considered to be positive for depression.

Resources

BOOKS

"Psychiatric Conditions in Childhood and Adolescence." Section 19, Chapter 274 in *The Merck Manual of Diagnosis and Therapy,* edited by Mark H. Beers, MD, and Robert Berkow, MD. Whitehouse Station, NJ: Merck Research Laboratories, 1999.

PERIODICALS

Finch, A. J., and others. "Children's Depression Inventory: Reliability Over Repeated Administrations." *Journal of Clinical Child Psychology* 16 (1987): 339-341.

Liss, Heidi, Vicky Phares, and Laura Liljequist. "Symptom Endorsement Differences on the Children's Depression Inventory with Children and Adolescents on an Inpatient Unit." *Journal of Personality Assessment* 76: 396-411.

Michael, Kurt D. "Reliability of Children's Self-Reported Internalizing Symptoms Over Short- to Medium-Length Time Intervals." *Journal of the American Academy of Child and Adolescent Psychiatry* 37 (February 1998): 205-212.

ORGANIZATIONS

American Academy of Child and Adolescent Psychiatry. 3615 Wisconsin Avenue, NW, Washington, DC 20016. Telephone: (202) 966-7300. <www.aacap.org>.

American Psychological Association. 750 First Street, NE, Washington, DC 20002. Telephone: (202) 336-5500. <www.apa.org>.

National Depressive and Manic-Depressive Association. 730 North Franklin Street, Suite 501, Chicago, IL 60610-3526. Telephone: (800) 826-3632. <www.ndmda.org>.

OTHER

National Institute of Mental Health (NIMH). *Depression in Children and Adolescents: A Fact Sheet for Physicians.* <www.nimh.nih.gov/publicat/depchildres fact.cfm>.

Texas A & M University at Corpus Christi and the Corpus Christi Independent School District. *School Nurse Reference Sheet—Depression.* <www.ecdc.tamucc.edu? HELP/depression>.

Rebecca J. Frey, Ph.D.

Childhood disintegrative disorder

Definition

Childhood disintegrative disorder (CDD) is a developmental disorder that resembles **autism**. It is characterized by at least two years of normal development, followed by loss of language, social skills, and motor skills before age ten. Other names for childhood disintegrative disorder are Heller's syndrome, **dementia** infantilis, and disintegrative **psychosis**

Description

Thomas Heller, an Austrian educator, first described childhood disintegrative disorder in 1908. It is a complex disorder that affects many different areas of the child'sdevelopment. It is grouped with the **pervasive developmental disorders** (PDDs) and is related to the better known and more common disorder of autism.

Initially CDD was considered strictly a medical disorder and was believed to have identifiable medical causes. After researchers reviewed the reported cases of CDD, however, no specific medical or neurological cause was found to account for all occurrences of the disorder. For that reason, CDD was included in the fourth edition of the **Diagnostic and Statistical Manual of Mental Disorders**, or *DSM-IV*, in 1994. The *Diagnostic and Statistical Manual* is the standard reference work consulted by mental health professionals in the United States and Canada.

Causes and symptoms

Causes

The cause of childhood disintegrative disorder is unknown. Research findings suggest, however, that it may arise in the neurobiology of the **brain**. About half the children diagnosed with CDD have an abnormal electroencephalogram (EEG). EEGs measure the electrical activity in the brain generated by nerve transmission (brain waves). CDD is also sometimes associated with **seizures**, another indication that the neurobiology of the brain may be involved. CDD is occasionally associated with such diagnosed medical disorders of the brain as leukodystrophy and Schilder's disease; but no one disease, brain defect, disorder, or condition can account for all symptoms and all cases. Research is hampered by the rarity of this disorder.

Symptoms

Children with CDD have at least two years of normal development in all areas—language understanding, speech, skill in the use of large and small muscles, and social development. After this period of normal growth, the child begins to lose the skills he or she has acquired. This loss usually takes place between ages three and four, but it can happen any time up to age ten.

The loss of skills may be gradual, but more often occurs rapidly over a period of six to nine months. The transition may begin with unexplained changes in behavior, such as **anxiety**, unprovoked anger, or agitation. Behavioral changes are followed by loss of communication, social, and motor skills. Children may stop speaking or revert to single words. They often lose bowel or bladder control and withdraw into themselves, rejecting social interaction with adults or other children. They may perform repetitious activities and often have trouble moving from one activity to the next.

In this way CDD resembles autism. In autism, however, previously acquired skills are not usually lost. According to the *Handbook of Autism and Pervasive Developmental Disorders*, virtually all children with CDD lose speech and social skills. About 90% lose self-help skills (the ability to feed, wash, and toilet themselves); and about the same number develop non-specific overactivity. After a time, the regression stops, but the child does not usually regain the skills that were lost.

Demographics

CDD is a rare disease, much less common than autism. About one in 100,000 children are thought to have CDD. It is possible, however, that the disorder is underdiagnosed. For a long time, it was thought that CDD occurred equally among boys and girls. Newer research suggests that it is about four times more common in boys, and that many girls who were diagnosed with CDD actually had Rett's disorder, a disorder that shares many of the symptoms of CDD but occurs almost always in girls.

Diagnosis

CDD is most commonly diagnosed when the parents of the affected child consult the pediatrician about the child's loss of previously acquired skills. The doctor will first give the child a medical examination to rule out epilepsy or other medical conditions. The child's head may also be x rayed to rule out head trauma or a brain tumor. Following the medical examinations and tests, the child will be referred to a **psychiatrist** who specializes in treating children and adolescents. The psychiatrist will then make the differential **diagnosis** of CDD.

To be diagnosed with CDD, a child must show loss or regression in at least two of the areas listed below. Usually regression occurs in more than two areas. These are:

- receptive language skills (language understanding)
- expressive language skills (spoken language)
- social or self-help skills
- play with peers
- motor skills
- bowel or bladder control, if previously established

Children with CDD are unable to start conversations with other people and often do not communicate with nonverbal signals (smiles, gestures, nodding the head, etc.) either. They also lose interest in playing games and in relationships with other people. They may engage in strange repetitive behavior, such as bobbing the head up and down, or other repeated movements. These changes must not be caused by a general medical condition or another diagnosed mental disorder.

CDD must be differentiated from autism and such other specific pervasive developmental disorders as Rett's disease. It also must be differentiated from **schizophrenia**. One of the differences between CDD and other PDDs is that to be diagnosed with CDD, a child must develop normally for at least two years before loss of skills occurs, and the loss must occur before age ten. Parents' reports of the child's development, records in baby books, medical records kept by the child's pediatrician, and home movies are often used to document normal development through the first two years of life.

Treatments

Treatment for CDD is very similar to treatment for autism. The emphasis falls on early and intense educational interventions. Most treatment is behavior-based and highly structured. Educating the parents so that they can support the child's treatments at home is usually part of the overall treatment plan. Speech and

---

KEY TERMS

Autism—A developmental disability that appears early in life, in which normal brain development is disrupted and social and communication skills are retarded, sometimes severely.

Dementia infantilis—Another term for childhood disintegrative disorder, used more frequently in the European medical literature. The Latin name literally means "early childhood dementia."

Leukodystrophy—A disturbance of the white matter of the brain.

Schilder's disease—A disturbance of the white matter of the brain that causes blindness, deafness, and mental deterioration.

Sensory integration therapy—A treatment that was originally designed for children with autism. Sensory integration therapy is often performed by occupational or physical therapists; its goal is to help the child with autism or CDD process information acquired through the senses (hearing, touch, taste, and smell as well as sight) more effectively.

---

language therapy, occupational therapy, social skills development, and sensory integration therapy may all be used according to the needs of the individual child

Families with a child who has CDD often find themselves highly stressed. Practical demands on caregivers are high, and CDD takes an emotional toll on family members. Finding appropriate providers with experience delivering services for a child with CDD is sometimes difficult, especially outside large cities. **Support groups** for families can help reduce their isolation and frustration. Because CDD is rare, autism support groups and organizations include families of children with CDD in their services.

Prognosis

The prognosis for children with CDD is very poor; it is worse than the prognosis for children with autism. Once skills are lost, they are not usually regained. Only about 20% of children diagnosed with the disorder reacquire the ability to speak in sentences. Most adults with CDD remain dependent on full-time caregivers or are institutionalized.

Prevention

Since the causes of CDD are unknown, there are no known ways to prevent this disorder.

Resources

BOOKS

American Psychiatric Association *Diagnostic and Statistical Manual of Mental Disorders*. 4th ed. text revised. Washington DC: American Psychiatric Association, 2000.

Hales, Robert E., Stuart C. Yudofsky, and John A. Talbot. *The American Psychiatric Press Textbook of Psychiatry*. 3rd ed. Washington, DC: American Psychiatric Press, 2000.

Sadock, Benjamin J., and Virginia A. Sadock, eds. *Comprehensive Textbook of Psychiatry*. 7th edition. Vol. 2. Philadelphia: Lippincott Williams and Wilkins, 2000.

ORGANIZATIONS

Autism Society of America. 7910 Woodmont Avenue, Suite 300, Bethesda, MD 20814-3067. (301) 657-0881 or 800-3 AUTISM. <http://www.autism-society.org>.

National Association of Rare Disorders (NORD). P.O. Box 8923, New Fairfield, CT 06812-8923. (800) 999-NORD or (203) 746-6518.

Tish Davidson, A.M.

Children's Apperception Test

Definition

The Children's Apperception Test, often abbreviated as CAT, is an individually administered projective personality test appropriate for children aged 3–10 years.

Purpose

The CAT is intended to measure the personality traits, attitudes, and psychodynamic processes evident in prepubertal children. By presenting a series of pictures and asking a child to describe the situations and make up stories about the people or animals in the pictures, an examiner can elicit this information about the child.

The CAT was originally developed to assess psychosexual conflicts related to certain stages of a child's development. Examples of these conflicts include relationship issues, sibling rivalry, and aggression. Today, the CAT is more often used as an assessment technique in clinical evaluation. Clinical diagnoses can be based in part on the CAT and other projective techniques.

Precautions

A **psychologist** or other professional person who is administering the CAT must be trained in its usage and interpretation, and be familiar with the psychological theories underlying the pictures. Because of the subjective nature of interpreting and analyzing CAT results, caution should be used in drawing conclusions from the test results. Most clinical psychologists recommend using the CAT in conjunction with other psychological tests designed for children.

The CAT is frequently criticized for its lack of objective scoring, its reliance on the scorer's own scoring method and bias, and the lack of accepted evidence for its reliability (consistency of results) and validity (effectiveness in measuring what it was designed to measure). For example, no clear evidence exists that the test measures needs, conflicts, or other processes related to human motivations in a valid and reliable way.

Older children between 7 and 10 years old may feel that the animal pictures in the original version of the CAT are too childish for them. They may respond better to the pictures of human beings available in the Children's Apperception Test-Human Figures (CAT-H), a version of the CAT in which human beings replace animals in the pictures.

Description

The CAT was developed in 1949 by Leopold Bellak and Sonya Sorel Bellak. It was an offshoot of the widely used **Thematic Apperception Test** (TAT), which was based on Henry Murray's need-based theory of personality. Bellak and Bellak developed the CAT because they saw a need for an apperception test specifically designed for children. The most recent revision of the CAT was published in 1993.

The original CAT featured ten pictures of animals in such human social contexts as playing games or sleeping in a bed. Today, this version is known as the CAT or the CAT-A (for animal). Animals were chosen for the pictures because it was believed that young children relate better to animals than humans. Each picture is presented by a test administrator in the form of a card. The test is always administered to an individual child; it should never be given in group form. The test is not timed but normally takes 20–30 minutes. It should be given in a quiet room in which the administrator and the child will not be disturbed by other people or activities.

The second version of the CAT, the CAT-H, was developed in 1965 by Bellak and Bellak. The CAT-H includes ten pictures of human beings in the same situations as the animals in the original CAT. The CAT-H was designed for the same age group as the

KEY TERMS

Apperception—The process of understanding through linkage with previous experience. The term was coined by one of the authors of the TAT to underscore the fact that people don't "perceive" the story cards in a vacuum; rather, they construct their stories on the basis of past experiences as well as present personality traits.

Defense—An unconscious mental process that protects the conscious mind from unacceptable or painful thoughts, impulses, or desires. Examples of defenses include denial, rationalization, projection, and repression. Some defenses are considered to represent lower levels of maturation than others; thus identifying a child's defenses may be helpful in evaluating his or her level of psychological maturity.

Ego—In Freudian psychology, the conscious, rational part of the mind that experiences and reacts to the outside world.

Projective test—A psychological test in which the test taker responds to or provides ambiguous, abstract, or unstructured stimuli, often in the form of pictures or drawings.

Psychodynamic—Referring to the motivational forces, unconscious as well as conscious, that form human attitudes and behavior.

Psychosexual conflicts—In Freudian categories, internal conflicts related to problems at a particular stage of childhood development. Freud associated each developmental stage with a particular part of the human body, such as the mouth or the phallus.

Reliability—The ability of a test to yield consistent, repeatable results.

Sibling rivalry—Competition among brothers and sisters in a nuclear family. It is considered to be an important influence in shaping the personalities of children who grow up in middle-class Western societies but less relevant in traditional African and Asian cultures.

Superego—According to Freud, the part of the mind that represents traditional parental and societal values. The superego is the source of guilt feelings.

Validity—The ability of a test to measure accurately what it claims to measure.

CAT-A but appeals especially to children aged 7–10, who may prefer pictures of humans to pictures of animals.

The pictures on the CAT were chosen to draw out children's fantasies and encourage story telling. Descriptions of the ten pictures are as follows: baby chicks seated around a table with an adult chicken appearing in the background; a large bear and a baby bear playing tug-of-war; a lion sitting on a throne being watched by a mouse through a peephole; a mother kangaroo with a joey (baby kangaroo) in her pouch and an older joey beside her; two baby bears sleeping on a small bed in front of a larger bed containing two bulges; a cave in which two large bears are lying down next to a baby bear; a ferocious tiger leaping toward a monkey who is trying to climb a tree; two adult monkeys sitting on a sofa while another adult monkey talks to a baby monkey; a rabbit sitting on a child's bed viewed through a doorway; and a puppy being spanked by an adult dog in front of a bathroom. The cards in the human version substitute human adults and children for the animals but the situations are the same. Gender identity, however, is more ambiguous in the animal pictures

than in the human ones. The ambiguity of gender can allow for children to relate to all the child animals in the pictures rather than just the human beings of their own sex.

The pictures are meant to encourage the children to tell stories related to competition, illness, injuries, body image, family life, and school situations. The CAT test manual suggests that the administrator should consider the following variables when analyzing a child's story about a particular card: the protagonist (main character) of the story; the primary needs of the protagonist; and the relationship of the main character to his or her personal environment. The pictures also draw out a child's anxieties, fears, and psychological defenses.

One theoretical basis for the CAT and other apperception tests is Murray's theory of personality. Murray is credited with clarifying the concept of human needs. He believed that a person's needs affect the way in which he or she interacts with the environment. The pictures on the CAT often address the manner in which individuals interact with their environment in terms of need fulfillment. Murray developed the TAT, in order to assess the relative strength of a person's needs. The needs that Murray particularly emphasized include the need for achievement and the need for recognition.

Because the primary content of the CAT consists of pictures, it is widely used in countries outside the United States.

Results

Scoring of the CAT is not based on objective scales; it must be performed by a trained test administrator or scorer. The scorer's interpretation should take into account the following variables: the story's primary theme; the story's hero or heroine; the needs or drives of the hero or heroine; the environment in which the story takes place; the child's perception of the figures in the picture; the main conflicts in the story; the anxieties and defenses expressed in the story; the function of the child's superego; and the integration of the child's ego.

Consider, for example, the card in which a ferocious tiger leaps toward a monkey who is trying to climb a tree. A child may talk about his or her fears of aggression or punishment. The monkey may be described as a hero escaping punishment from the evil tiger. This story line may represent the child's perceived need to escape punishment from an angry parent or a bully. Conversely, a child may perceive the picture in a relatively harmless way, perhaps seeing the monkey and tiger playing an innocent game.

A projective test like the CAT allows for a wide variety of acceptable responses. There is no "incorrect" response to the pictures. The scorer is responsible for interpreting the child's responses in a coherent way in order to make the test useful as a clinical assessment technique. It is recommended practice for the administrator to obtain the child's personal and medical history before giving the CAT, in order to provide a context for what might otherwise appear to be abnormal responses. For example, it would be normal under the circumstances for a child whose pet has just died to tell stories that include themes of **grief** or loss even though most children would not respond to the cards in that way.

A person scoring the CAT has considerable flexibility in interpretation. He or she can use the analysis of a child's responses to support a psychological **diagnosis**, provide a basis for a clinical evaluation, or gain insight into the child's internal psychological structure.

See also Rorschach technique.

Resources

BOOKS

Groth-Marnat, Gary. *Handbook of Psychological Assessment.* 3rd edition. New York: John Wiley and Sons, 1997.

Kline, Paul. *The Handbook of Psychological Testing.* New York: Routledge, 1999.

Maddox, Taddy. *Tests.* Austin, TX: Pro-ed, 1997.

Suzuki, Lisa A., Joseph G. Ponterotto, and Paul J. Meller. *Handbook of Multicultural Assessment.* San Francisco: Jossey-Bass, 2001.

Ali Fahmy, Ph.D.

Chloral hydrate

Definition

Chloral hydrate is a drug used to help sedate persons before and after surgery, to help relieve **anxiety** or tension, and to promote sleep in individuals with **insomnia**. It is sold in the United States under the brand names Aquachloral®, Aquachloral Supprettes®, and Noctec®. It is also available under its generic name.

Purpose

Because of its calming effect, chloral hydrate is primarily used to help sedate persons before and after surgery, especially children. It is also used to help people with sleep difficulties fall asleep. Chloral hydrate can be used to help calm tense or nervous persons as well.

Description

Chloral hydrate is classified as a sedative-hypnotic drug. The mechanism by which this drug works is not completely understood. It is believed that a chemical produced by chloral hydrate, called trichloroethanol, causes a mild depressive effect on the **brain**.

Recommended dosage

Chloral hydrate is available in oral and suppository forms. The oral form includes both capsules and syrup. Adults usually receive 500–1,000 mg taken 15–30 minutes before bedtime or one to two hours before surgery. These dosages are for hypnotic effects. For sedative effects, 250 mg is usually taken three times daily after meals. Total daily dosage should not be more than 2 g (2,000 mg). The hypnotic dose for children is usually 50 mg for every kilogram of body weight. The maximum amount per single dose is 1 g.

Daily dosage is usually divided into several smaller doses and taken throughout the day. The sedative dose is typically one-half of the hypnotic dose. The syrup form should be combined with a half glass of fruit juice or water. The capsules should be taken with a full glass of water or juice to help prevent stomach upset.

The typical dose using suppositories is 500 to 1,000 mg at bedtime for adults to address trouble sleeping, and 325 mg three times a day for daytime sedation in adults. For children in preparation for a medical procedure, the dose is calculated based on body weight, usually at 50 mg per kilogram. Children also may receive this as light sedation before an electroencephalograph test, in which case the dose is usually 25 mg per kilogram of body weight.

Precautions

The treating doctor needs to check the progress of any patients taking this drug for more than a few days to ensure significant side effects are not developing. Patients should not stop taking chloral hydrate suddenly. Instead, the dosage should be gradually decreased over time. Chloral hydrate can produce increased effects when combined with other central nervous depressants such as alcohol, antihistamines, and tranquilizers, resulting in significant drowsiness. This drug can sometimes cause persons to become drowsy, light-headed, or dizzy, and should generally not be used in patients with a history of severe kidney disease, severe liver disease, or those with a history of significant heart disease.

Chloral hydrate should be used with great caution only where necessary in persons with a history of heart disease, people with gastrointestinal problems or porphyria, those with a history of drug **abuse**, and in the elderly. It should be used with caution in pregnant women and in women who are nursing. Chloral hydrate, like most drugs, can be taken in excess to the point of overdose. Signs of overdose include difficulty in swallowing, extreme weakness, confusion, **seizures**, extreme drowsiness, low body temperature, staggering, changes in heart rate, and breathing problems.

Side effects

Uncommon but serious side effects of chloral hydrate use include skin rash or hives. Even more rare side effects include confusion, hallucination, and excessive excitement. The development of any of these side effects should be promptly reported to a doctor.

Less serious but more common side effects of chloral hydrate use include nausea, stomach pain,

KEY TERMS

Hydrated—A substance combined chemically with water.

Hypnotic—A type of medication that induces sleep.

Porphyria—A group of disorders that arise from changes in the metabolism of porphyrin, a naturally occurring compound in the body, and that are characterized by acute abdominal pain and neurological problems.

Sedative—A medication that induces relaxation and sleep.

and vomiting. Less common and not particularly serious side effects include diarrhea, light-headedness, drowsiness, and clumsiness.

Interactions

Because of additive depressant effects on the central nervous system, this drug should not be combined with alcohol as the combination can lead to significant drowsiness. Likewise, chloral hydrate should not be combined with tricyclic **antidepressants** or with the blood-thinning drug called warfarin. The prescribing physician should be made aware of any drugs or medications you are taking.

Resources

BOOKS

Consumer Reports Staff. *Consumer Reports Complete Drug Reference,* 2002 ed. Denver: Micromedex Thomson Healthcare, 2001.

Ellsworth, Allan J., and others. *Mosby's Medical Drug Reference.* 2001–2002 ed. St. Louis: Mosby, 2001.

Hardman, Joel G., Lee E. Limbird, eds. *Goodman & Gilman's The Pharmacological Basis of Therapeutics,* 10th ed. New York: McGraw-Hill, 2001.

Mosby's GenRx Staff. *Mosby's GenRx,* 9th ed. St. Louis: Mosby, 1999.

Venes, Donald, and others, eds. *Taber's Cyclopedic Medical Dictionary,* 19th ed. Philadelphia: F. A. Davis, 2001.

OTHER

National Library of Medicine. National Institutes of Health. "Chloral Hydrate." <http://www.nlm.nih.gov/medline plus/druginfo/medmaster/a682201.html>.

National Library of Medicine. National Institutes of Health. "Chloral Hydrate (Systemic)." <http://www.nlm.nih.gov/medlineplus/druginfo/medmaster/a682201.html>.

Mark Mitchell, MD
Emily Jane Willingham, PhD

Chlordiazepoxide

Definition

Chlordiazepoxide is used for the treatment of **anxiety** and also to control agitation brought on by alcohol withdrawal. It is a member of the benzodiazepine family of compounds, which slow the central nervous system to ease tension or nervousness. In the United States, it is sold under the trade names of Librium® and Librax®, and as Limbitrol® when in combination with another drug, **amitriptyline**.

Purpose

Chlordiazepoxide is used for the short-term relief of symptoms of anxiety and the management of **anxiety disorders**. It is also used for treating symptoms of withdrawal from acute alcoholism and alcoholic intoxication. One drug therapy combines this drug with amitriptyline to treat **depression** that accompanies anxiety or tension.

Description

Chlordiazepoxide is useful when treating anxiety for short periods of time. It has sedative properties that are useful for these brief periods of use. In addition, it is occasionally used to stimulate appetites and is a weak analgesic. Its precise mechanism of action is unknown, and several hours are needed for peak levels of the drug to be achieved. Chlordiazepoxide is available in 5-, 10-, and 25-mg capsules.

Recommended dosage

The recommended dosage varies with **diagnosis**. The lowest possible dosage that provides relief from symptoms should be used as the drug has a high potential to cause physiological and psychological dependence. When used in adults for the treatment of moderate anxiety, the usual oral dosage is 5–10 mg three or four times per day. When used for the treatment of more severe **anxiety and anxiety disorders**, the usual oral dosage is 20–25 mg three or four times per day. When used by older persons, or to relieve symptoms of preoperative apprehension or anxiety, the usual oral dosage is 5 mg two to four times per day. If used as a preoperative medication, the usual dosage is 50–100 mg via intramuscular (IM) injection. When used to treat symptoms of acute alcoholism, the usual initial oral dosage is 50–100 mg, repeated as needed until agitation is adequately controlled. The recommended maximum dosage is 300 mg per day. The usual dosage for children is 5 mg two to four times per day.

Precautions

Persons with suicidal tendencies should be closely monitored, as chlordiazepoxide may lower the threshold for action in attempting **suicide**. The drug has a high potential to cause physiological or psychological dependence.

In the last few years, there have been cases in which pills originating overseas but sold over the counter in the United States have contained chlordiazepoxide. A case from 2001 involved ingredients shipped from China for pill manufacture in California, and another case from 2006 involved pills from Brazil. Both resulted in warnings to consumers by the U.S. Food and Drug Administration (FDA). In the more recent case, the products—marketed as dietary/weight loss supplements under the names Emagrece Sim and Herbathin—were available for sale over the Internet and imported and distributed by a Florida company. Because of the serious possibility of interactions with medication and vitamins and the lack of quality control, taking these pills can be dangerous. The FDA advises consumers who have these products to return them to the distributor.

Side effects

Other than physiological and psychological dependence, few adverse effects have been reported. The most commonly reported include drowsiness, confusion, and movement difficulties. These are most common among older persons. Occasionally, transient loss of consciousness has been reported.

Other adverse effects include edema (abnormal accumulation of fluid in bodily tissues), minor menstrual irregularities, nausea, constipation and, infrequently, changes in libido (sex drive). Also, chlordiazepoxide may impair mental or physical skills needed to perform complex motor tasks. For this reason, persons using this drug are advised not to drive automobiles or operate machinery.

This drug is known to increase the risk birth defects in the fetus when taken during the first three months of pregnancy, and it also can cause dependency in the developing baby that can result in withdrawal symptoms following birth. Chlordiazepoxide passes into the breast milk and can cause breathing trouble and slow heartbeat in babies.

Interactions

Chlordiazepoxide may increase the effect of alcohol or other substances that depress central nervous

KEY TERMS

Analgesic—A substance that provides relief from pain.

Edema—Abnormal accumulation of fluid in the interstitial spaces of bodily tissue.

Libido—Psychic energy or instinctual drive associated with sexual desire, pleasure, or creativity.

Porphyria—A group of disorders that arise from changes in the metabolism of porphyrin, a naturally occurring compound in the body, and that are characterized by acute abdominal pain and neurological problems.

Porphyrin—Any iron- or magnesium-free pyrrole derivative occurring in many plant and animal tissues.

system functions. For this reason, they should not be used at the same time. A small number of reports of interaction with oral anticoagulants have been received, and it may exacerbate porphyria, which is a group of inherited disorders in which there is abnormally increased production of substances called porphyrins. Any medications, prescribed or over the counter, should be brought to the attention of a doctor or pharmacist.

See also Addiction; Alcohol and related disorders; Anti-anxiety drugs and abuse-related disorders; Pharmacotherapy.

Resources

BOOKS

Adams, Michael, and Norman Holland. *Core Concepts in Pharmacology*. Philadelphia: Lippincott-Raven, 1998.

Albers, Lawrence J., MD, Rhoda K. Hahn, MD, and Christopher Reist, MD. *Handbook of Psychiatric Drugs. 2001–2002*. Laguna Hills, CA: Current Clinical Strategies Publishing, 2001.

Foreman, John C., and Torben Johansen. *Textbook of Receptor Pharmacology,* 2nd ed. Boca Raton, FL: CRC Press, 2002.

Page, Clive P., and Michael Murphy. *Integrated Pharmacology*. St. Louis: Mosby-Year Book, 2002.

Von Boxtel, Chris J., Budiono Santoso, and I. Ralph Edwards. *Drug Benefits and Risks: International Textbook of Clinical Pharmacology*. New York: John Wiley & Sons, 2001.

PERIODICALS

Alexopoulou A., A. Michael, and S. P. Dourakis. "Acute Thrombocytopenic Purpura in a Patient Treated with Chlordiazepoxide and Clidinium." *Archives of Internal Medicine* 161.14 (2001): 1778–79.

ORGANIZATIONS

American Academy of Clinical Toxicology. 777 East Park Drive, PO Box 8820, Harrisburg, PA 17105-8820. Telephone: (717) 558-7750. Fax: (717) 558-7845. Web site: <http://www.clintox.org/index.html>.

American Academy of Family Physicians. 11400 Tomahawk Creek Parkway, Leawood, KS 66211-2672. Telephone: (913) 906-6000. Web site: <http://www.aafp.org>.

American Medical Association. 515 N. State Street, Chicago, IL 60610. Telephone: (312) 464-5000. Web site: <http://www.ama-assn.org>.

American Psychiatric Association. 1400 K Street NW, Washington, DC 20005. Telephone: (888) 357-7924. Fax: (202) 682-6850. Web site: <http://www.psych.org>.

American Society for Clinical Pharmacology and Therapeutics. 528 North Washington Street, Alexandria, VA 22314. Telephone: (703) 836-6981. Fax: (703) 836-5223. Web site: <http://www.ascpt.org>.

American Society for Pharmacology and Experimental Therapeutics. 9650 Rockville Pike, Bethesda, MD 20814-3995. Telephone: (301) 530-7060. Fax: (301) 530-7061. Web site: <http://www.aspet.org>.

OTHER

National Library of Medicine. National Institutes of Health. "Chlordiazepoxide." <http://www.nlm.nih.gov/medlineplus/druginfo/medmaster/a682078.html>.

National Library of Medicine. National Institutes of Health. "Chlordiazepoxide and Amitryptiline." <http://www.nlm.nih.gov/medlineplus/druginfo/uspdi/202129.html>.

U.S. Food and Drug Administration. "FDA News: FDA Warns Consumers About Brazilian Diet pills Found to Contain Active Drug Ingredients. Emagrece Sim and Herbathin Dietary Supplements May be Harmful." (2006). <http://www.fda.gov/bbs/topics/news/2006/NEW01298.html>.

U.S. Food and Drug Administration. Label Information for Limbitrol®. < http://www.fda.gov/cder/foi/label/2001/16949S33lbl.pdf>.

L.Fleming Fallon, Jr.,MD,Dr.P.H.
Emily Jane Willingham, PhD

Chlorpromazine

Definition

Chlorpromazine is an antipsychotic drug. It is a member of the phenothiazine family of compounds and is used to alleviate the symptoms and signs of **psychosis**. Psychosis is a form of severe mental illness characterized by loss of contact with reality, **hallucinations**, **delusions**, agitation, and unusual behavior.

HEINZ EDGAR LEHMANN
(1911–1999)

Heinz Edgar Lehmann was a German born Canadian psychiatrist best known for his use of chlorpromazine for the treatment of schizophrenia in 1950s. Born in Berlin, Germany, he was educated at the University of Freiburg, the University of Marburg, the University of Vienna, and the University of Berlin. He emigrated to Canada in 1937. In 1947, he was appointed Clinical Director of Montreal's Douglas Hospital. From 1971 to 1975, he was the Chair of the McGill University Department of Psychiatry. In 1976, he was made an Officer of the Order of Canada. In 1970, he was made a Fellow of the Royal Society of Canada. He was inducted into the Canadian Medical Hall of Fame in 1998. In 1999, the Canadian College of Neuropsychopharmacology established the Heinz Lehmann Award in his honor, given in recognition of outstanding contributions to research in neuropsychopharmacology in Canada.

In the United States, chlorpromazine is also sold under the brand name Thorazine®.

Purpose

Chlorpromazine is principally used to reduce the signs and symptoms of psychosis. For this purpose, the drug is used in **schizophrenia** and the manic phase of bipolar (formerly manic-depressive) disorder. The drug is also used in the management of severe behavioral disorders with aggression, combativeness, or excessive excitability. Chlorpromazine may sometimes be used as a sedative in nonpsychotic patients with excessive **anxiety** and agitation. In addition, the drug has been used to relieve nausea, vomiting, and persistent hiccups.

Description

Chlorpromazine was the first antipsychotic drug. It is not an exaggeration to say that the development of this medication began a revolution in the treatment of severe mental illness, which continues to this day. Patients with schizophrenia and other psychoses, who once would have been considered hopelessly untreatable and relegated to the back wards of state institutions, are today often able, as a result of treatment with chlorpromazine or similar medications, to live in the community and lead fuller lives.

The discovery of chlorpromazine resulted from efforts of pharmaceutical researchers in the first half of the twentieth century to develop sedative medications. Several drugs of a chemical class known as phenothiazines were investigated and shown to be effective **sedatives**, but they had little effect on agitated patients with psychosis. A new phenothiazine drug, chlorpromazine, was synthesized in France in 1950 and was tested on such patients. In 1952, two French psychiatrists, Delay and Deniker, announced that the drug exerted a specific effect in diminishing the symptoms and signs of psychosis in patients with severe mental illnesses.

The mechanism of action of chlorpromazine occurs primarily through its interactions with proteins on the cell that take messages from **dopamine**, a nerve signaling molecule, and send them to other cells.

Chlorpromazine, when sold under the name Thorazine®, is available in many forms: tablets of 10, 25, 50, 100, and 200 mg; spansules (sustained release capsules) of 30, 75, and 150 mg; ampules for injection of 25 and 50 mg; a multidose vial of 10 mL of 25 mg/mL; syrup 10mg/5mL, 4 fl oz.; and suppositories of 25 and 100 mg. Generic chlorpromazine manufacturers may supply a somewhat different set of dosages and products.

Recommended dosage

For acutely disturbed adult patients diagnosed with a psychosis, such as schizophrenia or mania, the usual daily dosage ranges from 100 mg to 1000 mg per day. Some patients may require a higher dosage. There is great variation in individual dosage requirements for chlorpromazine and for other antipsychotic medications. It is usually advisable to begin with a lower dosage, and increase the dosage until sufficient reduction of symptoms is achieved. Maximum reduction of symptoms may take many weeks of continued treatment. Because of the possibility of side effects, which may be severe, lower dosages should be used in outpatients, children, the elderly, and patients with serious health problems. For nonpsychotic patients with excessive anxiety or agitation, amounts used are generally less than 200 mg per day, divided among two or three doses.

For nausea and vomiting in adults, the usual dosage is 10–25 mg every four to six hours as needed, given by injection. Alternatively, doses of 50–100 mg may be given rectally. Persistent hiccups may be treated with 25–50 mg three or four times per day, orally or by injection.

Precautions

Elderly patients (those over age 65), especially women, and patients receiving long-term antipsychotic treatment are prone to develop **tardive dyskinesia**. This syndrome consists of involuntary, uncoordinated movements that may not disappear or may only partially improve after the drug is stopped. Tardive dyskinesia involves involuntary movements of the tongue, jaw, mouth or face or other groups of skeletal muscles and may also appear after chlorpromazine use has stopped. There is no known effective treatment for tardive dyskinesia, although gradual (but rarely complete) improvement may occur over a long period. The need for long-term antipsychotic medication should be weighed against the risk of developing tardive dyskinesia, which increases with duration of treatment.

Neuroleptic malignant syndrome (NMS), a dangerous condition with high fever, muscular rigidity, rapid pulse, sweating, and altered mental state, may occur with antipsychotic medication. NMS requires immediate medical treatment.

Phenothiazine drugs, such as chlorpromazine, may cause sedation and may interfere with driving and other tasks requiring alertness. They may increase the effects of alcohol and sedatives. The adverse effects of chlorpromazine may be increased in people with diseases of the heart, liver, or kidney, or other debilitating illnesses. Phenothiazines may lower the seizure threshold, making it more likely that a seizure will occur in people who have a history of **seizures**. People with epilepsy may require adjustment of their antiseizure medications. Chlorpromazine may cause acute muscle spasms, particularly of the head and neck, and sudden decreases of blood pressure. Patients may need to be hospitalized during the initial phase of treatment, particularly when receiving high doses or treatment by injection.

Chlorpromazine reduces the body's ability to sweat, thus interfering with the regulation of body temperature. This may be a problem for some people in very hot weather. The problem most commonly occurs in elderly people in hot buildings without air conditioning. Body temperature may reach fatal levels. People taking chlorpromazine should be aware of the possibility of developing hyperthermia (high body temperature) in very hot weather. They should seek cool places in very hot weather.

Children may be especially susceptible to neurologic reactions to phenothiazines, such as muscle spasms. Elderly patients may be particularly sensitive to sedation, low blood pressure, and other side effects. These patients should start with lower doses and increase their dosage gradually under physician supervision. Chlorpromazine may decrease salivation in older patients, predisposing to tooth decay, gum dis-ease, and mouth infections. Candy and other sugary foods should be limited, and oral hygiene should be maintained.

Chlorpromazine, like all phenothiazines, should not be taken by pregnant women because they harm the developing fetus. Breast-feeding is not recommended while taking the drug. Phenothiazines are secreted in breast milk and may cause harm to nursing infants.

Side effects

Chlorpromazine and other phenothiazines may cause many side effects. The following more common side effects are grouped by the body system affected:

- cardiovascular: Decreases of blood pressure, especially on arising, which may cause dizziness or fainting; rapid heart rate and changes in heart rhythm and electrocardiogram.
- nervous system: Sedation, muscle spasms of the head and neck, muscle rigidity, restlessness, tremors, slowed movement, shuffling gait, increased seizure tendency.
- digestive system: Dry mouth, nausea, constipation, abnormal liver tests.
- autonomic: Blurred vision, nasal congestion, reduced sweating, difficulty urinating, problems with ejaculation, impotence.
- hormonal: Lactation, breast enlargement.
- skin: Rashes, sensitivity to sunlight.
- body as a whole: Weight gain.

Interactions

Chlorpromazine interacts with a long list of other medications. Anyone starting this drug should review the other medications they are taking with their physician and pharmacist for possible interactions. Chlorpromazine and other phenothiazines may intensify the effects of drugs causing sedation, including alcohol, **barbiturates**, narcotic pain medications, minor tranquilizers, and antihistamines. Similarly, chlorpromazine may cause excessive reductions of blood pressure in patients taking other medicines that lower blood pressure. Chlorpromazine may also intensify side effects of drugs that also cause blurred vision, dry mouth, diminished sweating in hot weather, and constipation. Many other antipsychotics and **antidepressants** cause such effects.

Chlorpromazine may enhance the effects of medications that lower the seizure threshold, such as steroid drugs, the asthma medication theophylline, and many other psychiatric drugs. Patients with epilepsy may require dosage adjustments of their antiseizure medications. The effectiveness of medications for Parkinson's

KEY TERMS

Antipsychotic drug—A medication used to treat psychotic symptoms of schizophrenia such as hallucinations, delusions, and delirium. May be used to treat symptoms in other disorders as well.

Dopamine—A chemical in brain tissue that serves to transmit nerve impulses (is a neurotransmitter) and helps to regulate movement and emotions.

Epilepsy—A neurological disorder characterized by the onset of seizures. Seizures are caused by a disturbance in the electrical activity in the brain and can cause loss of consciousness, muscle spasms, rhythmic movements, abnormal sensory experiences, or altered mental states.

Neurotransmission—The conduction of a nerve impulse along a chain of nerve cells, which occurs when one cell in the chain secretes a chemical substance, called a neurotransmitter, onto a subsequent cell.

Neurotransmitter—A chemical in the brain that transmits messages between neurons, or nerve cells.

Parkinson's disease—A disease of the nervous system most common in people over 60, characterized by a shuffling gait, trembling of the fingers and hands, and muscle stiffness.

Phenothiazine—A class of drugs widely used in the treatment of psychosis.

disease may be reduced by chlorpromazine and other antipsychotics. The likelihood of changes in heart rhythm may be increased when the drug is taken with other medications that have the same effect, including other antipsychotic drugs, antidepressants, certain heart medicines, and erythromycin.

Certain drugs that are eliminated by the liver may interfere with the elimination of chlorpromazine from the body, causing higher blood levels and increased side effects. Chlorpromazine may retard the elimination of other medicines, including many antidepressants, antipsychotic drugs, and heart medications, resulting in higher levels of these other medications and possibly increased side effects.

Resources

BOOKS

American Society of Health-System Pharmacists, Inc. *AHFS Drug Information*, Gerald K. McEvoy, Pharm.D., ed. Bethesda, MD: American Society of Health-System Pharmacists, 2001.

Medical Economics Staff. *Physicians' Desk Reference*, 55th ed. Montvale, NJ: Medical Economics Company, 2001.

Nissen, David, ed. *Mosby's GenRx*, 11th ed. St. Louis: Mosby, 2001.

OTHER

National Library of Medicine. National Institutes of Health. "Chlorpromazine." <http://www.nlm.nih.gov/medline plus/druginfo/medmaster/a682040.html>.

National Library of Medicine. National Institutes of Health. "Chlorpromazine Overdose." <http://www.nlm.nih. gov/medlineplus/ency/article/002608.htm>.

Rosenbloom, Michael. "Chlorpromazine and the Psycho-pharmacologic Revolution." *Journal of the American Medical Association* 287 (2002): 1860–1861. <http:// jama.ama-assn.org/cgi/content/full/287/14/1860>.

Richard Kapit, MD
Emily Jane Willingham, PhD

Chronic motor or vocal tic disorder *see* **Tic disorders**

Chronic pain

Definition

Chronic **pain disorder** has no clear physical cause, or occurs with illnesses that do not explain the pain. It is described in the mental-health handbook, ***Diagnostic and Statistical Manual of Mental Disorders*** (*DSM*). The pain is severe enough to need treatment, lasts more than six months, and includes psychological factors. The National Institute of Neurological Disorders and **Stroke** states that chronic pain lasts longer than the average expected time for any given condition. Furthermore, acute pain alerts the nervous system to protect against injury, but chronic pain is useless because the injury is gone.

Description

Chronic pain is different for each individual. It can be continuous or it can come and go. It is described as burning, tingling, shooting, electrical, or an ache, with numbness. Other patients report stiffness, discomfort, soreness, and tightness.

Incidence/Prevalence

Up to 40% of the American population may experience chronic pain. There is inadequate data available about the rates of pain, because the definition has changed within the American Psychiatric Association (APA).

The Chronic Pain Network reports tens of millions of people with low-back pain and arthritis, many with a five-year pain history and pain occurring six days a week. In 2003, 38 million Americans reported chronic back pain, 36 million had migraines, 19.3 million reported arthritis, 3.1 million had diabetic neuropathy, 1.4 million reported cancer pain, and 0.5 million reported HIV/AIDS-related pain.

American Pain Society (APS) president C. Richard Chapman, PhD, states that only 25% of the 23 million patients who have surgery every year get pain relief. There are 65 million injuries per year and millions more cases where disease causes pain. Over 40% of pain patients in the moderate-to-severe range cannot find relief and only 30% of cancer-pain patients are relieved.

Causes and symptoms

Causes

Multiple causes of many types can cause pain. The most common noncancer pain types are back and neck, fibromyalgia, headache, arthritis, and neurologically based pain.

Symptoms

The symptoms of chronic pain disorder, as described by the APA, include at least one of the following:

- depression and anxiety
- negative or distorted thinking
- problems with social relationships
- disability or reduced ability to participate in usual daily activities
- increased pain that requires treatment
- insomnia and fatigue

Demographics

Women are twice as likely as men to have chronic pain and adults aged 40–50 are the most affected.

Possible risk factors

The risk factors recognized for chronic pain disorder by the APA include:

- one's parents or siblings experiencing it
- depression or alcohol abuse occurring in one's family
- being pain-prone and having a usual behavior pattern of self-sacrifice, self-defeating behavior, and abusive interactions
- demonstrating underlying severe depression
- being a hard-working, rigid, obsessive, or perfectionistic individual

Complications

Complications stemming from chronic pain disorder can include **suicide**, anger and depression, anxiety, and **substance abuse** and **addiction** and/or alcohol abuse. Substance and alcohol abuse can often be a self-medicating behavior used to mask the pain experience and to remove pain behaviors as well as feelings of anxiety, anger, and depression arising from the frustration of unrelieved pain. The patient may overuse prescription medications, use medications for off-label purposes, or seek illegal substances. This may be especially true if the patient lives among unsupportive or abusive others. Suicide may be an act of ending pain permanently or the accidental result of drug overdose or alcohol poisoning.

Associated conditions

These include secondary gain, substance use, dependent or **histrionic personality disorder**, major depression in 25–50% of cases, and dysthymia (milder depression) in 60–100% of chronic-pain cases.

Diagnosis

A **psychiatrist** first determines if the pain is medical. If so, then there is no pain disorder. If not, then the psychiatrist determines whether the pain is pretended. If this is the case, the **diagnosis** is either **malingering** for rewards such as narcotics, or a **factitious disorder** that rewards the patient for acting sick.

A pain disorder includes pain that occurs in at least one place in the body and needs treatment, as well as psychological factors, significant distress, and pain that is not better explained by mood, anxiety, or **psychosis**.

Psychological measures

The psychiatrist uses several methods to find the severity of pain and the role of psychological factors. These include standardized and informal interviews, pain-rating scales, and visual scales where the patient marks a place on a line to show the amount of pain, or chooses a picture of a facial expression to represent the degree of pain.

The simplest test for pain is to ask the patient how much pain they are feeling on a scale of 1 to 10. On this scale, 1 is the least amount of pain and 10 is the most or worst pain ever felt. Other tests used are the McGill Pain Questionnaire and the West Haven-Yale Multidimensional Pain Inventory.

Treatments

The goal of treatment is controlling and managing pain in order for the patient to be able to function in daily life. In 2007, the American Chronic Pain Association (ACPA) concluded that: "An essential concept in pain management is that each person is different and will respond differently to situations, interventions, and medications. It is important for the person with pain, family members, and others to avoid quick judgments based on what they hear or read about medications. The best place to get advice about medications is from the health care provider."

Multidisciplinary approach

Patients should seek interested, well-qualified health care professionals and work with them to find solutions effective for their unique pain experiences. This may include physicians, medical specialists, nurse practitioners, alternative therapists, mental health professionals, physical therapists, chiropractors, massage therapists, a personal trainer; and a pastor, rabbi, or spiritual mentor.

Several methods of treatment can work together to manage chronic pain. This combined treatment can be different and require unique "doses," according to individual needs. It is not one-size-fits-all, and medication alone is often not the total solution.

Patients should learn everything possible about their unique pain in order to understand it. Learning should be with the intent of accepting, targeting, and effectively treating the pain. Patients and families can investigate through public, university, and hospital libraries; Internet research databases; pain-related discussion boards; and online and in-person **support groups** of encouraging, like-minded people. In addition, it is vital to stay up-to-date concerning the progress of *Decade of Pain Control and Research*, which was declared January 1, 2001 by the U.S. Congress.

Medications

Medication schedules can be tricky, but they are important. The ACPA promotes the use of a long-term daily pain reliever supplemented by a short-term fast-acting drug for flare-ups.

Depression often occurs with pain. In using **opioids** (narcotics), potential pain relief must be considered in the light of the side effects of nausea and constipation. Long-term narcotic use presents the risk of drug dependency. Pain-modifying drugs like **amitriptyline** affect the **brain** with doses lower than those given for depression. This resulting untreated depression can

then result in increased pain. Other **antidepressants** may also be prescribed. Further, anticonvulsant drugs can be used off-label in pain trigger point injections. This involves the injection of a cocktail of steroid and anesthetic combinations at the body's affected pressure points to relieve painfully contracted tissues.

Psychological and social interventions

Chronic pain treatment may require individual or group **psychotherapy**; family, behavioral, physical, or occupational therapy; or **biofeedback**. Treatment for insomnia may require relaxation training and education about good sleep habits.

Cognitive-behavioral therapy

Cognitive-behavioral therapy (CBT) educates patients about the pain-and-tension cycle, teaching them how to manage pain and distress, and about the effects of their medications. It helps patients to change their thinking about pain. Patients are taught to identify and modify negative or distorted thought patterns, such as the helplessness and hopelessness of depression. Within CBT, progressive muscle relaxation, deep breathing, visual imagery, hypnosis, and biofeedback are all useful treatments. Pain diaries are useful for charting patterns of pain so patients can identify what affects it, and help determine how well medication are working.

Behavior modification

Behavior modification is taught to the patients and families so that usual activity and non-pain behaviors are encouraged and the pain behaviors of passiveness, inactivity, and medication dependency are removed.

Alternative therapies

Other treatments include **acupuncture**, electrical stimulation acupuncture, transcutaneous electrical nerve stimulation, massage, nerve blocks, surgery, **meditation**, exercise, **yoga**, music, poetry, and art therapy.

Other management

Organization

The Asian concept of feng shui says that unhealthy layouts of homes and workspaces causes **stress**. If spaces are difficult to maneuver or are cluttered and dim, then pain may increase and last longer. Spaces are best arranged for openness and convenience. Pain patients can also eliminate unnecessary tasks, break big jobs into smaller steps, take breaks, use schedules, and enlist help to reduce stress and pain.

KEY TERMS

Ankylosing spondylitis—A spinal arthritis that begins in the low back and can spread upwards to the skull.

Feng shui—The Chinese method of arranging of objects to increase positive energy flow.

Secondary gain—The advantage gained by having symptoms.

Yoga—A form of stretching and breathing mediation.

Laughter

That laughter is good medicine was demonstrated by journalist and medical professor Norman Cousins as he used planned bouts of laughter to treat himself, with his doctor's collaboration, for the debilitating pain of ankylosing spondylitis.

Prognosis

The prognosis for total relief of pain symptoms is not good in cases of chronic pain disorder. The usual pattern includes flare-ups between periods of moderate or less-severe pain. The prognosis is best if a patient can keep working. Unemployment leads to isolation, inactivity, and negative thinking, which results in more pain. If there is **reinforcement** of pain behavior by disability payments, gaining attention, or abuse of addictive drugs, relief of chromic pain is less likely. Recent studies show that cognitive-behavioral therapy along with antidepressants is the most effective treatment.

Prevention

Pain disorder may be prevented by early **intervention** at the beginning of pain. When pain becomes chronic, it is important to find help with using strategies to manage the pain before inactivity, immobility, and depression appear. Most pain patients see their own doctor first, and the doctor may refer them to a psychiatrist or pain clinic. This does not mean that the doctor does not believe the pain is real. It means that he or she needs to work with other professionals in order to relieve the pain.

Resources

PERIODICALS

Flor, H., and C. Hermann. "Neuropsychotherapy for Chronic Pain. Changing Pain Memories by Behavioral Interventions." *Verhaltenstherapie* 16.2 (2006): 86–94.

Gallagher, Rollin M., Maripat Welz-Bosna, and Arnold Gammaitoni. "Assessment of Dosing Frequency of Sustained-release Opioid Preparations in Patients with Chronic Nonmalignant Pain." *Pain Medicine* 8.1 (2007): 71–74.

"Hospitals Get Better at Pain Management, Often Led by Clinical Nurse Specialists." *Hospitals and Health Networks* 80.11 (2006): 94.

McWilliams, A. Lachlan, R. Goodwin, and B. Cox. "Depression and Anxiety Associated with Three Pain Conditions: Results from a Nationally Representative Sample." *The Journal of the International Association for the Study of Pain* 111 (2004): 77–83.

Monina, E., G. Falzetti, V. Firetto, L. Mariani, and C. A. Caputi. "Behavioural Evaluation in Patients Affected by Chronic Pain: A Preliminary Study." *The Journal of Headache and Pain* 7.6 (2006): 395–402.

Naughton, Felix, Polly Ashworth, and Suzanne M. Skevington. "Does Sleep Quality Predict Pain-related Disability in Chronic Pain Patients?" *PAIN. The Journal of the International Association for the Study of Pain* 127.3 (2007): 243–52.

Osborne, Travis L., and others. "Psychosocial Factors Associated with Pain intensity, Pain-related Interference, and Psychological Functioning in Persons with Multiple Sclerosis and Pain." *PAIN. The Journal of the International Association for the Study of Pain* 7.102 (2007): 52–62.

Phillips, Donald M. "JCAHO Pain Management Standards Are Unveiled." *Journal of the American Medical Association* 284.4 (2000): 428–9

Smith, Blair H., Gary J. Macfarlane, and Nicola Torrance. "Epidemiology of Chronic Pain, from the Laboratory to the Bus Stop: Time to Add Understanding of Biological Mechanisms to the Study of Risk Factors in Population-based Research?" *PAIN. The Journal of the International Association for the Study of Pain* 127, 1–2 (2007): 5–10.

ORGANIZATIONS

American Chronic Pain Association. P.O. Box 850, Rocklin, CA 95677-0850. Telephone: (800) 533-3231.

American Pain Society. 4700 W. Lake Avenue, Glenview, IL 60025-1485. Telephone: (847) 375-4715. <http://www.ampainsoc. org>.

American Psychiatric Association. 1000 Wilson Boulevard, Suite 1825, Arlington, VA. 22209-3901. Telephone: (703) 907-7300 <http://www.psych.org>.

Chronic Pain Network. <http://www.chronicpainnetwork. com>.

National Institute of Neurological Disorders and Stroke. P.O. Box 5801, Bethesda, MD 20824. Telephone: (800) 352-9424. <http://www.ninds.nih.gov>.

UCLA History of Pain Project, The John C. Liebeskind History of Pain Collection. <http://www.library.ucla. edu/libraries/biomed/his/pain.html>.

OTHER

Masuda, A., M. Hattenmaru, and C. Tei. "Repeated Thermal Therapy Improves Outcomes in Patients with Chronic Pain." *International Congress Series. 18th World Congress.* Kobe, Japan. (2005).

National Institutes of Health. Statement by National Institutes of Health, U.S. Department of Health and Human Services, on An Update of NIH Pain Research and Related Program Initiatives, before Statement for the Record, Subcommittee on Health, Committee on Energy and Commerce, U.S. House of Representatives. (Dec. 8, 2005).

Patty Inglish, MS

Cigarettes *see* **Nicotine and related disorders**

Circadian rhythm sleep disorder

Definition

Circadian rhythm sleep disorder is a persistent or recurring pattern of sleep disruption resulting either from an altered sleep-wake schedule or an inequality between a person's natural sleep-wake cycle and the sleep-related demands placed on him or her. The term circadian rhythm refers to a person's internal sleep and wake-related rhythms that occur throughout a 24-hour period. The sleep disruption leads to **insomnia** or excessive sleepiness during the day, resulting in impaired functioning.

The Fourth Edition Text Revision of the ***Diagnostic and Statistical Manual of Mental Disorders*** (*DSM-IV-TR*, a handbook used by mental health professionals to diagnose mental disorders) defines circadian rhythm sleep disorder as one of several primary **sleep disorders**. Within the category of primary sleep disorders, it is classified as one of the dyssomnias, characterized by irregularities in an individual's quality, timing, and amount of sleep. In earlier versions of the *DSM*, the disorder is called sleep-wake schedule disorder.

Description

Circadian rhythm sleep disorder involves an alteration of an individual's circadian system or a mismatch between a person's natural, or endogenous, circadian system and the external, or exogenous, demands placed on it. It can lead to insomnia at certain times of the day or excessive sleepiness throughout the day. The insomnia or excessive sleepiness

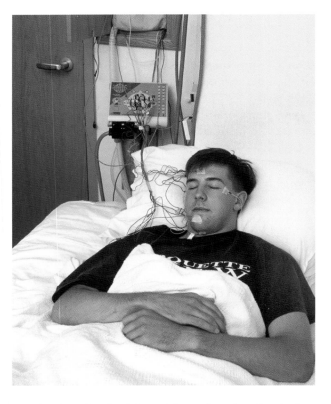

A patient in a sleeping lab participates in a circadian rhythm experiment. *(Hank Morgan/Photo Researchers, Inc)*

results in impaired functioning in social, occupational, or other environments.

The *DSM-IV-TR* lists four types of circadian rhythm sleep disorder: delayed sleep phase type, jet lag type, shift work type, and unspecified type.

Causes and symptoms

Causes

The delayed sleep phase type of circadian rhythm sleep disorder is marked by a delay of the sleep-wake cycle as it relates to the demands of society. It is often due to a psychosocial stressor (an event in a person's environment that causes **stress** or discomfort), especially for adolescents. The delayed sleep-wake cycle leads to chronic sleep deprivation and habitually late sleeping hours. Individuals with this type often have difficulty changing their sleeping patterns to an earlier and more socially acceptable time. Their actual sleep, once it begins, is normal. It is the timing of their sleeping and waking that is persistently delayed.

The jet lag type of circadian rhythm sleep disorder is characterized by disruptions arising from a mismatch between a person's circadian cycle and the cycle required by a different time zone. The more time zones that are traveled, the greater the disruption. Eastbound travel, in which sleep-wake hours are advanced, typically causes more problems than westbound travel, in which sleep-wake hours are delayed. People who travel often and cross many time zones when they travel are most susceptible to this type.

The shift work type of circadian rhythm sleep disorder is distinguished by disruptions due to a conflict between a person's endogenous circadian cycle and the cycle required by shift work. Individuals who work the night shift often experience this problem, especially those people who switch to a normal sleep schedule on days off. Also, people who work rotating shifts experience this problem because of the changing sleep-wake schedules they experience. The disruptions caused by shift work result in inconsistent circadian schedules and an inability to consistently adjust to the changes.

The unspecified type of circadian rhythm sleep disorder is characterized by a pattern of sleep-wake disturbance and circadian mismatch that is not due to the causes of the other three types. Examples of other causes include irregular sleep-wake patterns and non-24-hour sleep-wake patterns. If an individual's sleep-wake pattern is based on a period of time of slightly more than 24 hours, their circadian rhythm can become progressively delayed.

Symptoms

Individuals with the delayed sleep phase type of the disorder exhibit habitually late sleep hours and an inability to consistently change their sleeping schedule. They often show sleepiness during the desired wake period of their days. Their actual phase of sleep is normal. Once they fall asleep, they stay asleep for a normal period of time, albeit a period of time that starts and stops at an abnormally late time.

Individuals with the jet lag type of circadian rhythm sleep disorder demonstrate sleepiness during the desired wake portion of the day due to the change in time zone. They have difficulty sleeping during the desired sleep portion of the day. They also have difficulty altering their sleep-wake schedule to one appropriate to the new time zone.

Individuals with the shift work type of the disorder feel sleepy or fall asleep during the desired wake period, which includes the time spent at work. People with rotating shift schedules, especially schedules that gradually change, exhibit sleep disturbance and wake period sleepiness. Insufficient sleep time, family and social expectations, and alcohol use worsen this problem.

Individuals with the unspecified type of circadian rhythm sleep disorder also exhibit daytime and evening sleepiness or insomnia, especially those people who have a non-24-hour sleep pattern. People with irregular sleep patterns have difficulty knowing when they will fall asleep and wake up.

Demographics

The delayed sleep phase type of the disorder usually begins during adolescence and can continue without treatment through adulthood. People with this type may have a family history of delayed sleep phase. The delayed sleep phase type of the disorder is thought to impact up to 4% of adults and up to 7% of adolescents.

The shift work and jet lag types of the disorder often result in more severe symptoms for late-middle-aged and elderly people. It is estimated that up to 60% of night shift workers have the shift work type of circadian rhythm sleep disorder.

Diagnosis

In order to diagnose circadian rhythm sleep disorder, patients are often asked for records of their sleep and wake times in order to determine if a **diagnosis** is warranted. Interviews and direct observation in a sleep lab may also be utilized. A diagnosis requires a pattern of sleep disruption caused by a mismatch between a person's circadian sleep-wake pattern and the pattern required by that person's environment. The disruption can be persistent or recurrent and leads to impaired functioning, often in a social or occupational context.

To differentiate circadian rhythm sleep disorder from other diagnoses, the sleep disruption must not occur exclusively during the cause of another sleep disorder or other disorder. The disturbance in sleep must not be due to the direct physiological effects of a substance, whether used for medication or **abuse**, or to a general medical condition.

The delayed sleep phase type of the disorder requires a persistent pattern of delayed sleeping and awakening and an inability to change the pattern. The jet lag type requires sleepiness and wakefulness at inappropriate times relative to the local time zone; there must be repeated travel more than one time zone away. The shift work type requires excessive sleepiness during the desired wake period and an inability to sleep during the desired sleep period, both due to changing shift work or night shift work.

Diagnosis of any type of circadian rhythm sleep disorder must be distinguished from normal adjustments a person makes in reaction to a schedule change. The sleep disruptions must be persistent and recurring and lead to social or occupational problems. People who prefer unusually late or early sleep schedules or people adjusting to a new sleep schedule should not receive this diagnosis unless they meet the other criteria.

Treatments

Treatment of the delayed sleep phase type depends on the severity of the case. Mild cases may be addressed by an individual simply adhering to strict sleep and wake times. Severe cases may require incremental changes in sleep time, where a person sleeps 15 to 30 minutes earlier each day until an appropriate pattern is reached. Other methods of altering delayed sleep patterns include prescribing a night of sleep deprivation or the use of chronotherapy, a method in which sleep is delayed for three hours each night until the sleep pattern is rotated around the clock.

Often, treatment is ignored for persons with the jet lag type because people eventually return to their regular time zone and normal sleep-wake cycle and no longer exhibit symptoms. For people who travel often, it is preferable to adjust to the new time zone by sleeping at times appropriate to that zone if they intend to be there for one week or longer. **Diets** that target jet lag are also effective for some people, and **light therapy**, which involves exposure to a lighted device to simulate daytime, may be helpful to some people to adjust to new time zones.

People with the shift work type of the disorder benefit most from a non-changing work schedule. If rotating or changing shifts are unavoidable, rotations that occur in a clockwise direction, where shifts get progressively later and later, are preferable to those in a counter-clockwise direction. Also, when attempting to sleep, it is a good idea to create a comfortable sleeping environment by eliminating daytime noise and light.

Prognosis

Individuals with delayed sleep phase type often have great difficulty changing their sleep patterns and when they are able to change their circadian cycle, they have difficulty maintaining the changes.

People with jet lag type or shift work type can reduce symptoms often by simply decreasing the amount of travel or returning to a normal work schedule. When these changes are not possible, these individuals have trouble making the constant adjustments required to sleep and wake. People with the shift work type often report a reversal of symptoms two weeks after returning to a normal work and sleep schedule.

Prevention

Because circadian rhythm sleep disorder is usually related to environmental stressors, avoidance of these stressors (such as long-distance travel, shift work, and sleep-disrupting lifestyles) can prevent the disorder from beginning or continuing. People who are able to adhere strictly to a normal sleep-wake schedule can also offset circadian rhythm-related problems.

See also Breathing-related sleep disorder; Sleep disorders.

Resources

BOOKS

American Psychiatric Association. *Diagnostic and Statistical Manual of Mental Disorders.* 4th edition, text revised. Washington, DC: American Psychiatric Association, 2000.

Buysse, Daniel J., Charles M. Morin, and Charles F. Reynolds III. "Sleep Disorders." In *Treatments of Psychiatric Disorders,* edited by Glen O. Gabbard. 2nd edition. Washington, DC: American Psychiatric Press, 1995.

Hobson, J. Allan, and Rosalia Silvestri. "Sleep and Its Disorders." In *The Harvard Guide to Psychiatry,* edited by Armand M. Nicholi, Jr., M.D. Cambridge, MA: Belknap Press of Harvard University Press, 1999.

Thorpy, Michael J., M.D., and Jan Yager, Ph.D. *The Encyclopedia of Sleep and Sleep Disorders.* 2nd edition. New York: Facts on File, 2001.

ORGANIZATIONS

American Sleep Disorders Association. 6301 Bandel Road NW, Suite 101, Rochester, MN 55901. <http://www.asda.org>.

Ali Fahmy, Ph.D.

Citalopram

Definition

Citalopram is a selective serotonin reuptake inhibitor (SSRI) antidepressant drug that is sold in the United States under brand name Celexa.

Purpose

Citalopram is approved by the United States Food and Drug Administration (FDA) for the treatment of **depression**. It appears to be very effective in the treatment of **panic disorder** and is being evaluated for the treatment of **obsessive-compulsive disorder**, alcohol **abuse**, headache, **post-traumatic stress disorder**, and **premenstrual syndrome**.

Description

Serotonin is a **brain** chemical that carries nerve impulses from one nerve cell to another. Researchers think that depression and certain other mental disorders may be caused, in part, because there is not enough serotonin being released and transmitted in the brain. Like the other SSRI **antidepressants**, **fluoxetine** (Prozac), **sertraline** (Zoloft), and **paroxetine (Paxil)**, citalopram increases the level of brain serotonin (also known as 5-HT). Increased serotonin levels in the brain may be beneficial in patients with obsessive-compulsive dirder, alcoholism, certain types of headaches, post-traumatic **stress** disorder (PTSD), pre-menstrual tension and mood swings, and panic disorder.

Citalopram is available in 20-mg, 40-mg, and 60-mg tablets.

Recommended dosage

The daily dosage of citalopram for depression ranges from 20–60 mg. The initial dosage is usually 20 mg per day. This dosage may then be increased to 40 mg per day at an interval of no less than one week. Most patients experience relief from depression at this dosage and do not require more than 40 mg per day. The dosage is taken once daily, either in the morning or in the evening.

Patients who are being treated for panic disorder receive doses ranging from 20–60 mg daily. A dosage of 20–30 mg daily appears to be optimal for the treatment of most panic disorders.

Precautions

Patients who are allergic to citalopram, any other SSRI drug, or any component of the preparation should not take citalopram.

Patients with liver problems and elderly patients (over age 65) need to take smaller amounts of the drug. Dosage for these patients should start at 20 mg but can be increased to 40 mg daily if needed. Patients with kidney problems do not need dosage adjustments. Patients with history of mania, **suicide** attempts, or seizure disorders should start citalopram with caution and only under close physician supervision. There is no clinical data available on the use of citalopram in children and adolescents.

Side effects

More than 15% of patients develop **insomnia** while taking citalopram. Nausea and dry mouth occur in about 20% patients being treated with citalopram. Patients also experience tremor, **anxiety**, agitation, yawning, headaches, dizziness, restlessness, and sedation with citalopram therapy. These side effects usually diminish or disappear with continued use of the drug, although it may take up to four weeks for this to occur.

A drop in blood pressure and increased heart rate have been associated with citalopram use. In general, patients do not experience weight gain or loss after starting citalopram.

Sexual dysfunction, which includes decreased sex drive in women and difficulty ejaculating in men, is also associated with the use of citalopram. In some patients, it may take up to 12 weeks for these side effects to disappear. In some patients these sexual side effects never resolve. If sexual side effects continue, the dose of citalopram may be reduced, patients can also have drug holidays where the weekend dose is either decreased or skipped, or they can discuss with their physician the risks and benefits of switching to another antidepressant.

Interactions

Citlopram interacts with a long list of other medications. Anyone starting this drug should review the other medications they are taking with their physician and pharmacist for possible interactions. Patients should always inform all their health care providers, including dentists, that they are taking citalopram.

Certain antifungal medications such as itraconazole, fluconazole, ketoconazole, as well as the antibiotic erythromycin, can increase the levels of citalopram in the body. This can cause increased side effects. Levomethadyl, a medication used to treat opioid dependence, may cause toxicity to the heart if used together with citalopram.

Serious side effects called serotonin syndrome have resulted from the combination of antidepressants such as citalopram and members of another class of antidepressants known as monoamine oxidase inhibitors (MAOIs). Serotonin syndrome usually consists of at least three of the following symptoms: diarrhea, fever, sweatiness, mood or behavior changes, overactive reflexes, fast heart rate, restlessness, shivering or shaking. Because of this, citalopram should never be taken in combination with MAOIs. MAOIs include isocarboxazid, nialamide, pargyline, selegiline, **phenelzine**, procarbazine, iproniazid, and clorgyline. Patient taking any MAOIs, should stop the MAOI then wait at least 14 days before starting citalopram or any other antidepressant. The same holds true when discontinuing citalopram and starting an MAOI.

Buspirone, an anti-anxiety medication, should not be used together with citalopram. Ginkgo and **St. John's Wort**, herbal supplements that are common in the United States, should not be taken together with citalopram.

Resources

BOOKS

Forest Pharmaceuticals, Inc. Staff. *Product Information: Celexa, citalopram*. St. Louis, MO: Forest Pharmaceuticals, Inc., 2001.

Lacy, Charles F. *Drug Information Handbook*. Lexi-Comp, Inc. 2002.

PERIODICALS

Lepola, Ulla. "A Controlled, Prospective, One-Year Trial of Citalopram in the Treatment of Panic Disorder." *Journal of Clinical Psychiatry* 59 (1998): 528-534.

Ajna Hamidovic, Pharm.D.

Client-centered therapy *see* **Person-centered therapy**

Clinical antipsychotic trials of intervention effectiveness *see* **CATIE study**

Clinical Assessment Scales for the Elderly

Definition

The Clinical Assessment Scales for the Elderly, often abbreviated as CASE, is a diagnostic tool used to determine the presence of mental disorders and other conditions in elderly adults.

Purpose

The CASE is used to determine the presence of mental disorders in an elderly person as defined by the *Diagnostic and Statistical Manual of Mental Disorders*, fourth edition, text revision (2000), which is also called *DSM-IV-TR*. The *DSM-IV-TR* is the basic reference work consulted by mental health professionals when making a **diagnosis**. The CASE, which is used with adults between the ages of 55 and 90, consists of a self-report form in which the person answers questions about himself or herself related to various scales. If the elderly adult is unable to complete the form because of cognitive or physical deficiencies, an other-rating form is provided for use by a knowledgeable caregiver, such as a spouse, child, or health-care worker.

The CASE is not always used specifically for diagnosing mental disorders. It may be administered simply as a general assessment tool to gain insight about an elderly person. It may serve as a neurological screening tool to rule out other problems. The test makers also claim that it can be used as an early screening tool for **dementia**, opening the door for elderly adults to receive medications to slow the progress of **Alzheimer's disease**.

Description

The Clinical Assessment Scales for the Elderly were written by Cecil Reynolds and Erin Bigler. The most recent version of the test was published in 2001. The CASE consists of 10 clinical scales that measure the following: **Anxiety**; Cognitive Competence; **Depression**; Fear of Aging; Obsessive-Compulsiveness; **Paranoia**; Psychoticism; Somatization; Mania; and **Substance Abuse**. The degree to which an elderly person exhibits symptoms in these areas can help a mental health professional with the process of differential diagnosis for a mental disorder.

The CASE also includes three validity scales. These are helpful in evaluating the consistency of a person's responses and whether the person is faking his or her answers.

KEY TERMS

Alzheimer's disease—An incurable dementia marked by the loss of cognitive ability and memory over a period of 10–15 years. Usually affects elderly people.

Dementia—A group of symptoms (syndrome) associated with a progressive loss of memory and other intellectual functions that is serious enough to interfere with a person's ability to perform the tasks of daily life. Dementia impairs memory, alters personality, leads to deterioration in personal grooming, impairs reasoning ability, and causes disorientation.

Reliability—The ability of a test to yield consistent, repeatable results.

Standardization—The administration of a test to a sample group of people for the purpose of establishing test norms.

Validity—The ability of a test to measure accurately what it claims to measure.

The person who is completing the CASE, whether using the self-rating or the other-rating form, responds to the test's written items. The test usually takes 20–40 minutes to finish, but it is not timed. People are generally given as much time as they need to complete it.

A shorter version of the test, called the Clinical Assessment Scales for the Elderly-Short Form (CASE-SF) is also available. The CASE-SF takes about 20 minutes to complete and includes all 10 of the clinical scales.

Results

Scoring for the CASE is relatively simple. Scores are calculated for each scale and then compared to age-appropriate scores to determine the presence or severity of symptoms. For example, if a person scores high on the Depression scale, this information could be used as part of an overall diagnosis for a *DSM-IV-TR* depressive disorder. A person scoring high in Psychoticism may have a psychotic disorder. For any specific *DSM-IV-TR* diagnosis to be made, however, all of the required criteria for that disorder must be met. The results from the CASE may satisfy only some of the requirements.

The Fear of Aging scale assesses the person's degree of apprehension or concern about the aging process. It is not necessarily related to a particular

DSM-IV-TR disorder. Information about a person's fear of aging, however, may be helpful during the diagnostic process. It may also be useful information for a psychotherapist or other counselor, to understand the patient's concerns or to measure progress in therapy.

The CASE was standardized using a sample of 2,000 adults in the United States, 1,000 for each of the two test forms. The test has been shown to have good reliability and validity. For example, scores from the CASE Depression scale have been shown to correlate very well with scores on the widely used **Beck Depression Inventory**, or BDI.

See also Figure drawings; House-Tree-Person Test.

Resources

BOOKS

American Psychiatric Association. *Diagnostic and Statistical Manual of Mental Disorders,* 4th ed., Text rev. Washington, D.C.: American Psychiatric Association, 2000.

Reynolds, Cecil R., and Erin D. Bigler. *Clinical Assessment Scales for the Elderly.* San Antonio, TX: The Psychological Corporation, 2001.

Ali Fahmy, PhD
Emily Jane Willingham, PhD

Clinical trials

Definition

A clinical trial is a controlled scientific experiment designed to determine the effectiveness of a treatment in curing or lessening the symptoms of a disease or disorder.

Description

Clinical trials typically are used to assess the effectiveness of a new treatment in comparison with the current standard of care or an existing treatment for a disease or disorder. For example, before a new drug is approved by the U.S. Food and Drug Administration (FDA) for release and use in the United States, the drug must first undergo rigorous testing to determine (a) whether or not it is effective in treating the disorder, and (b) what side effects may result from the drug use that make it inadvisable or dangerous to some or all potential patients.

A child participates in a clinical research trial. *(Geoff Tompkinson/Photo Researchers, Inc)*

Clinical trials are research studies designed according to professional standards using scientific methods. In clinical trials, as many variables as possible are controlled to determine the effects of the drug or treatment option. For example, a simple experiment to test the effectiveness of a new drug for epilepsy might include the following steps. First, researchers typically randomly divide the research subjects into two groups: one group that receives the new drug and the other group that receives the conventional drug or treatment. The group receiving the new drug is called the experimental group and the group receiving no treatment or conventional treatment is called the control group. Researchers then collect baseline data on the symptoms of the subjects prior to treatment, such as number and frequency of **seizures**. This phase of the experiment is called the pretest. After the pretest data are collected, the researchers give the new drug (the independent variable) to the experimental group while not changing the treatment of the control group. After an appropriate amount of time for the drug to take effect, the subjects are tested again using the same criteria as were used for the pretest to determine any difference between the two groups as a result of the drug (dependent variable). When all the data are collected, they are statistically analyzed to determine if there is a reasonable basis to say that the effects of the new drug are significantly different from the effects of the old treatment (or no treatment) and not due to chance variations. This basic research design can be made more complicated to simultaneously answer multiple research questions, such as what dose of the new medication is most effective, whether increasing dosage levels of the medication results in more side effects, whether the drug is effective for some demographic groups but not others (e.g., only works well on adult females but not on adult males), or to compare several treatments at once.

KEY TERMS

Control group—A group in a research study that does not receive the experimental treatment. For example, in an experiment testing the effectiveness of a new drug, the control group might receive the current drug of choice while the experimental group receives the new drug under investigation.

Dependent variable—The outcome variable in an experiment. For example, in a test of the effects of a new drug for the treatment of a disease, the effects of the drug on the disease (i.e., the change in symptoms after taking the drug) would be the dependent variable.

Double-blind study—A research study in which neither the participants nor the professional administering the drug or treatment know whether they are receiving the experimental treatment or a placebo or control treatment.

Experimental group—The group of participants in a research study who receive the experimental treatment or drug under investigation.

Independent variable—The variable in an experiment that is manipulated by researchers in order to determine its effects. For example, in a test of the

effects of a new drug on the treatment of a disease, whether or not the subjects received the new drug would be the independent variable.

Informed consent—A legal document prepared as an agreement for treatment or nontreatment that requires physicians to disclose the benefits, risks, and alternatives of the treatment. Informed consent allows fully informed, rational patients to be involved in the choices about their health.

Placebo—A preparation without pharmacological effect that is given in place of a drug in clinical trials to determine the effectiveness of the drug under study; a "sugar pill."

Randomization—The process of randomly assigning participants in an experiment to the various conditions (i.e., experimental and control groups) so that each individual has an equal chance of being assigned to any of the groups. Randomization helps ensure that each of the groups is roughly the same and that the results are due to the treatment, not to the makeup of the groups.

Research subject—A participant in a research experiment or clinical trial.

There are several general types of clinical trials:

- treatment trials that test the relative effectiveness of new drugs or treatments or combinations of drugs and/or treatments
- prevention trials that investigate ways to prevent a disease in individuals who have not previously had it or to prevent its return in individuals who have previously had the condition
- diagnostic trials that seek to find better ways for diagnosing a disorder or illness
- screening trials to determine the best way to detect a disease or disorder
- quality-of-life trials that investigate how to make life easier or more normal for those with a chronic illness

Clinical trials typically have four phases. In Phase I, the experimental drug or treatment is tested on a small group of people to investigate its safety, determine a recommended dosage or range, and identify potential side effects. In Phase II, the experimental drug or treatment is tested on a larger group of people to further determine its effectiveness and safety. Phase III clinical trials examine the drug or treatment from an even wider perspective. The experimental drug or

treatment is given to large groups of people to confirm the findings of the previous studies on a larger population. Phase III clinical trials are also often used to compare the relative effectiveness of treatments and gather safety information. Finally, Phase IV clinical trials are run after a drug has been marketed. At this time a drug may undergo further studies to examine its risks, benefits, and optimal use.

Considerations before entering a clinical trial as a subject

Clinical trials are necessary to help ensure the safety and effectiveness of a drug or treatment before it is put into general use. In addition, joining a clinical trial as a research subject may be of potential benefit to patients who have exhausted available treatment options without success. Clinical trials give patients the opportunity to try a new drug or treatment that may help their condition when conventional methods have failed. However, certain things must be considered before joining a clinical trial as a subject.

First, there is no guarantee that subjects in clinical trials will receive the new drug or treatment. They may be randomly placed in the control group where they receive a placebo or conventional treatment rather than the new drug or treatment. There is no way to tell whether or not one will be in the experimental group or the control group. Frequently, even researchers or people administrating the treatment do not know which group the subject is in (this is called a double-blind study) so that their expectations will not unintentionally bias the results. Therefore, all other available treatment options should typically be tried before joining a clinical trial as a subject.

In addition, there is always the possibility of encountering unknown negative side effects from the new drug or treatment. For this reason, subjects in clinical trials are required to read, understand, and sign **informed consent** documents. The decision to join a clinical trial as a subject should always be made in conjunction with one's health care provider in order to reduce the risk of negative side effects from the treatment.

Resources

BOOKS

VandenBos, Gary R., ed. *APA Dictionary of Psychology.* Washington, D.C.: American Psychological Association, 2007.

ORGANIZATIONS

National Institutes of Health. <http://www.clinicaltrials.gov>.

Pharmaceutical Research and Manufacturers of America (PhRMA). <http://www.phrma.org>.

Ruth A. Wienclaw, PhD

Clomipramine

Definition

Clomipramine is an antidepressant drug used primarily to alleviate obsessions and compulsions in patients with **obsessive-compulsive disorder**. Clomipramine is also used in the treatment of **depressive disorders** and in a number of other psychiatric and medical conditions. In the United States, the drug has also been known by the brand name Anafranil.

Purpose

Clomipramine is principally used in the treatment of the obsessions and compulsions of obsessive-compulsive disorder (OCD), when these symptoms greatly disrupt the patient's daily activities. Obsessions are repetitive thoughts and impulses, and compulsions are repetitive behaviors. Patients with OCD find these experiences inappropriate, distressing, and time-consuming.

Clomipramine may also be used in the treatment of depressive disorders, especially when associated with obsessions and compulsions, and in **panic disorder**, pain management, sleep attacks (**narcolepsy** and cataplexy), and **anorexia nervosa**. The drug may help to reduce compulsive behaviors in a variety of disorders with such symptoms, including **trichotillomania** (hair pulling), onychophagia (nail biting), Tourette's disorder (tics and vocalizations), and childhood **autism**.

Description

Clomipramine is one of the tricyclic **antidepressants**, so-called because of the three-ring chemical structure common to these drugs. In the 1940s and 1950s, pharmaceutical researchers synthesized a number of new compounds for possible medical use as antihistamines and **sedatives**. After testing in animal experiments, a few of these substances were selected for human study. One potential drug, a tricyclic compound called **imipramine**, was not useful in calming agitation, but it had a striking effect in improving the mood of certain patients with **depression**.

Since the discovery of imipramine, many other tricyclic antidepressants have been developed with somewhat different pharmacological activities and side effect profiles. Within this group of drugs, clomipramine is exceptionally potent in affecting levels of serotonin in the **brain**. In this action, it is similar to serotonin-selective antidepressant drugs, like **fluoxetine** (Prozac), which act specifically on serotonin levels and are effective in OCD. Serotonin is a messenger chemical (neurotransmitter) involved in transmitting signals between nerve cells. Clomipramine reduces the effects on serotonin transmission in depression and OCD symptoms.

Recommended dosage

For adults, clomipramine is administered in dosages up to a maximum of 250 mg per day. Starting with a dose of 25 mg, the dosage is increased during the first two weeks to 100 mg per day. If needed, it is further increased gradually over the next several weeks. The initial dose is low to avoid side effects, and it is increased slowly to permit the patient to develop tolerance or adapt to side effects that may occur.

KEY TERMS

Autonomic—The part of the nervous system that governs the heart, involuntary muscles, and glands.

Cataplexy—A symptom of narcolepsy marked by a sudden episode of muscle weakness triggered by strong emotions. The muscle weakness may cause the person's knees to buckle, or the head to drop. In severe cases, the patient may become paralyzed for a few seconds or minutes.

Epilepsy—A neurological disorder characterized by the onset of seizures. Seizures are caused by a disturbance in the electrical activity in the brain and can cause loss of consciousness, muscle spasms, rhythmic movements, abnormal sensory experiences, or altered mental states.

Kilogram—A metric unit of weight. It equals 2.2 lbs.

Monoamine oxidase (MAO) inhibitors—A group of antidepressant drugs that decreases the activity of monoamine oxidase, a neurotransmitter found in the brain that affects mood.

Neurotransmitter—A chemical in the brain that transmits messages between neurons, or nerve cells.

Serotonin—A widely distributed neurotransmitter that is found in blood platelets, the lining of the digestive tract, and the brain, and that works in combination with norepinephrine. It causes very powerful contractions of smooth muscle, and is associated with mood, attention, emotions, and sleep. Low levels of serotonin are associated with depression.

Older patients (over age 65), children, and adolescents are more sensitive to the side effects and toxicities of tricyclic antidepressants such as clomipramine. The maximum daily dose is usually lower for elderly patients than for younger adults. For children and adolescents, the maximum recommended daily dose is the lesser of 100 mg or 3 mg per kg of body weight.

Precautions

Seizures are the most important risk associated with clomipramine. Among patients taking the drug for six months or more, more than 1% may experience seizures. The risk of seizure increases with larger doses, and seizures have been reported to occur following abrupt discontinuation of the medication. Caution and physician supervision is required if the patient has a history of epilepsy or some other condition associated with seizures, such as brain damage or alcoholism.

Clomipramine and other tricyclic antidepressants often cause drowsiness. Activities requiring alertness, such as driving, should be avoided until patients understand how the drug affects them. Dizziness or lightheadedness may occur on arising from a seated position, due to sudden decreases in blood pressure. Fainting may also occur. Some patients, especially men with prostate enlargement, may experience difficulty urinating. Glaucoma may be worsened. Sensitivity to ultraviolet light may increase, and sunburns may occur more easily.

Tricyclic antidepressants, including clomipramine, should be used with caution and physician supervision in patients with heart disease, because of the possibility of adverse effects on heart rhythm. Adverse effects on the heart occur frequently when tricyclics are taken in overdose. Only small quantities of these drugs should be given to patients who may be suicidal.

Tricyclic antidepressants may cause dry mouth, due to decreased saliva, possibly contributing to the development of tooth decay, gum disease, and mouth infections. Patients should avoid sweets, sugary beverages, and chewing gum containing sugar.

It has not been determined whether clomipramine is safe to take during pregnancy, and the patient's need for this medicine should be balanced against the possibility of harm to the fetus. Tricyclic antidepressants may be secreted in breast milk, and may cause sedation and depress the breathing of a nursing infant.

Side effects

Clomipramine may cause many side effects. Initially, the side effects of tricyclic drugs may be more pronounced, but sensitivity often decreases with continued treatment.

The following more common side effects are grouped by the body system affected:

- cardiovascular: Decreases of blood pressure upon arising, which may cause dizziness or fainting, increases of blood pressure, rapid heart rate, pounding heart, altered heart rhythm.
- nervous system: Sedation, dizziness, headache, confusion, nervousness, restlessness, sleep difficulties, numbness, tingling sensations, tremors, twitches, increased seizure tendency.

- digestive system: Dry mouth, nausea, loss of appetite, indigestion, and constipation.
- autonomic: Blurred vision, increased sweating.
- genital/urinary: Difficulty urinating, menstrual pain, ejaculatory difficulty, impotence, decreased sex drive.
- skin: Rashes, sensitivity to sunlight.
- body as a whole: Fatigue, weight gain, flushing.

Less commonly, tricyclic drugs may cause adverse effects on almost any organ or system of the body, particularly the blood, hormones, kidney, and liver. Patients should consult their physicians if symptoms develop or bodily changes appear.

Interactions

Tricyclic antidepressants, such as clomipramine, may interact with many other drugs. Patients should inform their physicians about all other drugs they are taking before starting treatment.

Clomipramine may intensify the effects of other drugs that act on serotonin levels, possibly producing serotonin syndrome, a rare but dangerous condition with fever, sweating, tremors, and changes in mental state. Drugs that may interact this way include other antidepressants, especially selective serotonin reuptake inhibitor (SSRI) drugs and monoamine oxidase (MAO) inhibitors. These drugs should not be taken within two weeks of taking clomipramine. Other drugs to avoid include lithium, **alprazolam** (Xanax), fenfluramine (Pondimin), amphetamine, dextromethorphan (used in cough suppressants), meperidine (Demerol), and tramadol (Ultram).

Tricyclic drugs may intensify the effects of other drugs causing sedation, including alcohol, **barbiturates**, narcotic pain medications, minor tranquilizers, and antihistamines. Tricyclics may cause excessive reductions of blood pressure in patients taking blood pressure medicine, especially upon standing from a sitting or reclined position. Conversely, these drugs may interfere with the pressure-reducing effects of certain other blood pressure medicines and may necessitate an adjustment in dosage. Tricyclics may interact with thyroid medications to produce abnormalities of heart rhythm. Concurrent use of tricyclic antidepressants with other psychiatric medicines may result in intensification of certain side effects.

Certain drugs may interfere with the elimination of tricyclic antidepressants from the body, causing higher blood levels and increased side effects. This effect may occur with cimetidine (Tagamet), other antidepressants, **methylphenidate** (Ritalin, Concerta), and some antipsychotic medications.

Resources

BOOKS

Maina, Giuseppe, Umberto Albert, and Filippo Bogetto. "Obsessive-Compulsive Disorder Resistant to Pharmacological Treatment." *Obsessive Compulsive Disorder Research*. Hauppauge, NY: Nova Biomedical Books, 2005, 171–99.

Preston, John D., John H. O'Neal, and Mary C. Talaga. *Handbook of Clinical Psychopharmacology for Therapists,* 4th ed. Oakland, CA: New Harbinger Publications, 2004.

Simpson, H. Blair, and Michael R. Liebowitz. "Combining Pharmacotherapy and Cognitive-Behavioral Therapy in the Treatment of OCD." *Concepts and Controversies in Obsessive-Compulsive Disorder*. New York: Springer Science, (2005) 359–76.

PERIODICALS

Anderson, Shawanda W., and Marvin B. Booker. "Cognitive Behavioral Therapy Versus Psychosurgery for Refractory Obsessive-Compulsive Disorder." *Journal of Neuropsychiatry and Clinical Neurosciences* 18.1 (Winter 2006): 129.

Fineberg, Naomi A., and Tim M. Gale. "Evidence-Based Pharmacotherapy of Obsessive-Compulsive Disorder." *International Journal of Neuropsychopharmacology* 8.1 (Mar. 2005): 107–29.

Foa, Edna B., and others. "Randomized, Placebo-Controlled Trial of Exposure and Ritual Prevention, Clomipramine, and Their Combination in the Treatment of Obsessive-Compulsive Disorder." *American Journal of Psychiatry* 162.1 (Jan. 2005): 151–61.

Shavitt, Roseli G., and others. "Clinical Features Associated with Treatment Response in Obsessive-Compulsive Disorder." *Comprehensive Psychiatry* 47.4 (Jul.–Aug. 2006): 276–81.

Simpson, Helen Blair, and others. "Response Versus Remission in Obsessive-Compulsive Disorder." *Journal of Clinical Psychiatry* 67.2 (Feb. 2006): 269–76.

Richard Kapit, MD
Ruth A. Wienclaw, PhD

Clonazepam

Definition

Clonazepam belongs to a group of drugs called benzodiazapines. **Benzodiazepines** are medications that help relieve nervousness, tension, symptoms of **anxiety**, and some types of **seizures** by slowing the central nervous system. In the United States, clonazepam is sold under brand name Klonopin.

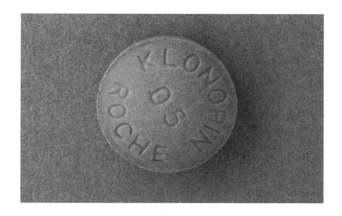

A clonazepam tablet (klonopin). *(Custom Medical Stock Photo, Inc. Reproduced by Permission.)*

Purpose

Although clonazepam is approved by the U.S. Food and Drug Administration (FDA) for the treatment of **panic disorder** and some types of epilepsy, it is also used to treat **social phobia**, mania, and **post-traumatic stress disorder**.

Description

Clonazepam belongs to a group of drugs called benzodiazepines. Benzodiazepines are sedative-hypnotic drugs that help to relieve nervousness, tension, anxiety symptoms, and seizures by slowing the central nervous system. To do this, they block the effects of a specific chemical involved in the transmission of nerve impulses in the **brain**, decreasing the excitement level of the nerve cells.

When clonazepam is used to treat panic disorder, it is more sedating than **alprazolam**, another benzodiazepine drug used to treat panic disorder. However, unlike alprazolam, clonazepam may trigger depressive episodes in patients with a previous history of **depression**. In people who experience social phobia, treatment with clonazepam reduces the rate of depression. The use of clonazepam for social phobia is considered an off-label use—a use that is legal, but not specifically approved by the FDA.

Clonazepam comes in 0.5 mg-, 1.0 mg-, and 2.0 mg-tablets.

Recommended dosage

For panic disorder, the initial recommended dose is 0.25 mg twice daily. This dose can be increased every three days in increments of 0.125–0.25 mg twice daily. The target dose for panic disorder is 1.0 mg per day, although some people benefit from doses up to a maximum of 4.0 mg per day. When a person stops taking clonazepam, the drug should be gradually discontinued by decreasing the dose by 0.125 mg twice daily every three days.

Although clonazepam is not FDA-approved for the treatment of post-traumatic stress disorder, doses in the range of 0.25–3.0 mg daily appear to help treat symptoms of this disorder. Daily dosages for the treatment of social phobia range from 1.0–2.5 mg, while the dosage to control mania may be as high as 10.0 mg daily.

Precautions

Women who are pregnant should not use clonazepam, because it may harm the developing fetus. Clonazepam should never be taken by people who have had an allergic reaction to it or another benzodiazepine drug such as **diazepam** (Valium). People with narrow-angle glaucoma or severe liver disease should not take clonazepam. People who have kidney disease may need to take a reduced dosage of the drug. Saliva production may increase while taking clonazepam. Because of this, people with respiratory disease or an impaired gag reflex should use clonazepam with close physician supervision.

Because clonazepam is a nervous system depressant, it should not be taken with other such depressants, such as alcohol, other **sedatives**, sleeping pills, or tranquilizers. People taking clonazepam may feel unusually drowsy and mentally sluggish when they first start taking the drug. They should not drive, operate dangerous machinery, or engage in hazardous activities that require mental alertness until they see how clonazepam affects them. This excessive sedation usually goes away after a short time on the drug.

People who have underlying depression should be closely monitored while taking clonazepam, especially if they are at risk for attempting **suicide**.

Side effects

The main side effects of clonazepam are sedation, dizziness, impaired coordination, depression, and **fatigue**. Some people experience decreased sex drive while taking clonazepam.

A small number of people develop sinus problems and upper respiratory tract infections while taking clonazepam. One of the side effects of clonazepam may be increased salivation. This may cause some people to start coughing while taking clonazepam. Clonazepam may also cause anorexia and dry mouth. It may cause either constipation or diarrhea.

There are a few reports of clonazepam causing menstrual irregularities or blurred vision.

Interactions

Clonazepam may increase the sedative effects of other drugs that depress the central nervous system such as certain strong pain medicines (opiates such as codeine, oxycodone, hydromorphone) and antihistamines (found in many cold and allergy medications). The sedative effect is also increased if clonazepam is taken with alcohol.

Disulfiram (Antabuse), a medication used to treat alcohol dependence, increases the effect of clonazepam. Medications that make clonazepam ineffective include phenobarbital, phenytoin, **carbamazepine**, theophylline, rifampin, and rifabutin.

Resources

BOOKS

Lacy, Charles F. *Drug Information Handbook*. Hudson, OH: Lexi-Comp, 2002.

Preston, John D., John H. O'Neal, and Mary C. Talaga. *Handbook of Clinical Psychopharmacology for Therapists*, 4th ed. Oakland, CA: New Harbinger Publications, 2004.

PERIODICALS

Nardi, Antonio E., and Giampaolo Perna. "Clonazepam in the Treatment of Psychiatric Disorders: An Update." *International Clinical Psychopharmacology* 21.3 (May 2006): 131–42.

Paparrigopoulos, Thomas J. "REM Sleep Behaviour Disorder: Clinical Profiles and Pathophysiology." *International Review of Psychiatry* 17.4 (Aug. 2005): 293–300.

Ajna Hamidovic, Pharm.D.
Ruth A. Wienclaw, PhD

Clonidine

Definition

Clonidine belongs to a class of drugs called central alpha-adrenergic agonists. In the United States, clonidine tablets are sold under the brand name Catapres and clonidine skin patches are sold under the brand name Catapres-TTS. The tablets are also available generically. There is also an injectable form that is administered directly into the spinal cord for the treatment of postoperative pain.

Purpose

Clonidine tablets and patches are approved by the U.S. Food and Drug Administration (FDA) for the treatment of high blood pressure. In addition, clonidine has been found to be useful in the treatment of alcohol, opiate, and **nicotine** withdrawal syndromes, **attention deficit/hyperactivity disorder** (ADHD), and Tourette's syndrome, which is one of the **tic disorders**.

Description

Clonidine was synthesized in 1960s and was initially tested as a nasal decongestant. In the United States, clonidine was first used to treat hypertension although it has also been investigated for treatment of different neuropsychiatric disorders. Clonidine works on specific nerve cells in the **brain** that are responsible for lowering blood pressure, slowing heart rate, and decreasing the body's reaction to the withdrawal of chemicals like alcohol, opiates, **cocaine**, and nicotine. Because of this, clonidine is often used to treat the symptoms of drug, alcohol, and nicotine withdrawal.

Clonidine is beneficial in opiate withdrawal because it treats symptoms that are commonly associated with that condition (watery eyes and nose, diarrhea, irritability). For this condition, clonidine is often used alone. For the treatment of alcohol withdrawal, clonidine is usually combined with benzodiazepine tranquilizers such as Librium, Valium, Xanax, or Ativan.

Several studies of treatment for **smoking cessation** showed patients treated with clonidine had decreased nicotine craving. Clonidine skin patches appear to be more effective than tablets in this condition. Both dermal patches and tablets are effective in the treatment of Tourette's syndrome and ADHD.

Clonidine tablets are available in 0.1 mg, 0.2 mg, and 0.3 mg strengths. Clonidine skin patches are available in 0.1 mg, 0.2 mg, and 0.3 mg per day patches. Each patch lasts seven days.

Recommended dosage

Dosages of 0.4–0.6 mg have been used for the treatment of alcohol withdrawal. Total daily dosage for the treatment of opiate withdrawal range between 0.5 and 1.4 mg, depending on the stage as well as the severity of withdrawal symptoms. If the clonidine patch is used to treat nicotine withdrawal symptoms, dosages that deliver 0.1–0.2 mg daily are used. For oral therapy (tablets), a total dosage of 0.2–0.4 mg daily is taken in divided doses.

Pediatric doses of clonidine are calculated based on the child's body weight. Clonidine dosage for ADHD in children is 5 micrograms per kilogram of body weight per day orally in four divided doses. Children who require a daily dosage of 0.2 mg usually can use the 0.3 mg dermal patch. If ADHD is associated with sleep disturbances, low to moderate doses of clonidine can be taken at bedtime. Oral doses in children with Tourette's syndrome range from 3–6 micrograms per kilogram of body weight per day divided into two to four even doses.

Precautions

Clonidine should not be used by people who have a known allergy to this drug. If a person has underlying **depression**, clonidine should be used with caution and under close physician supervision.

Clonidine should not be abruptly withdrawn, but rather slowly decreased over several days to avoid withdrawal symptoms. Withdrawal symptoms include an increase in blood pressure, irritability, nervousness, **insomnia**, and headache. Because of the possibility of withdrawal, clonidine should not be used in patients who are unwilling or unable to follow the prescribing information

Clonidine should be used only with caution and close physician supervision in patients with chronic renal failure, coronary artery disease, and in patients with preexisting eye problems. People with kidney disease may need to take a reduced dosage. Clonidine should not be used by pregnant women, except in the rare case where the benefits of taking clonidine outweigh the risks to the developing fetus.

Side effects

The most common side effect associated with clonidine is dizziness accompanying sudden changes in position such as standing up rapidly. In order to avoid this, patients should stand up slowly. People using the dermal patch may develop rash, hair loss, a burning sensation on the skin, or other skin irritations where

the patch is applied. Switching to tablets may not completely eliminate these skin problems.

Clonidine can cause dry mouth, constipation, nausea, daytime sleepiness, weakness, and lethargy. These side effects may take several weeks to disappear. In some cases, these side effects can be eliminated with dosage readjustment. In addition, clonidine may cause eye dryness, loss of sex drive, and decreased sexual activity.

If patients experience weight gain in the beginning of therapy, they can expect this side effect to decline over a period of several days to weeks.

Interactions

Clonidine's blood pressure–lowering effects may be enhanced by other drugs that also lower blood pressure. Conversely, the blood pressure–lowering effects of clonidine may be negated by many **antidepressants**.

Resources

BOOKS

Lacy, Charles F. *Drug Information Handbook*. Hudson, OH: Lexi-Comp, 2002.

Preston, John D., John H. O'Neal, and Mary C. Talaga. *Handbook of Clinical Psychopharmacology for Therapists,* 4th ed. Oakland, CA: New Harbinger Publications, 2004.

PERIODICALS

Favrat, B., and others. "Opioid Antagonist Detoxification Under Anaesthesia Versus Traditional Clonidine Detoxification Combined with an Additional Week of Psychosocial Support: A Randomised Clinical Trial." *Drug and Alcohol Dependence* 81.2 (Feb. 2006): 109–16.

Friemoth, Jerry. "What Is the Most Effective Treatment For ADHD in Children?" *Journal of Family Practice* 54.2 (Feb. 2005): 166–68.

Marsch, Lisa A., and others. "Comparison of Pharmacological Treatments for Opioid-Dependent Adolescents: A Randomized Controlled Trial." *Archives of General Psychiatry* 62.10 (Oct. 2005): 1157–64.

Ponizovsky, Alexander M., and others. "Well-Being, Psychosocial Factors, and Side-Effects Among Heroin-Dependent Inpatients After Detoxification Using Buprenorphine Versus Clonidine." *Addictive Behaviors* 31.11 (Nov. 2006): 2002–2013.

Schnoes, Connie J., and others. "Pediatric Prescribing Practices for Clonidine and Other Pharmacologic Agents for Children With Sleep Disturbance." *Clinical Pediatrics* 45.3 (Apr. 2006): 229–38.

Ajna Hamidovic, Pharm.D.
Ruth A. Wienclaw, PhD

Clorazepate

Definition

Clorazepate is a medication that belongs to a family of drugs called benzodiazepines—a group of pharmacologically active compounds used to produce a calming effect by relieving **anxiety** and tension. In the United States, clorazepate is sold under brand names Tranxene and Gen-XENE.

Purpose

Clorazepate is used for the treatment of anxiety and alcohol withdrawal. Moreover, clorazepate is an adjunct in the management of partial **seizures**.

Description

Clorazepate binds to different sites in the **brain**, causing them to shift into a state that is less excitable. It is very effective in treating **anxiety and anxiety disorders**. Moreover, anxiety associated with undergoing surgical procedures is controlled with clorazepate. Clorazepate alone is not efficacious in treating seizures; however, if used along with other standard seizure medications, such as phenobarbital, primidone, phenytoin, **carbamazepine**, and **valproic acid**, better seizure control may be achieved. Convulsions and anxiety associated with alcohol withdrawal are controlled with clorazepate.

Clorazepate is available in two different formulations. Clorazepate tablets come in 3.75 mg, 7.5 mg, and 15.0 mg doses, while slow-release tablets, administered once daily, are available in 11.25 mg and 22.5 mg strengths. Capsules are available in 3.75 mg, 7.5 mg, and 15.0 mg strengths.

Recommended dosage

If used for anxiety, the dose of clorazepate usually ranges anywhere from 15 mg to 60 mg daily in divided dose intervals. Usually, however, the average dose is 30 mg daily given in two to four doses. If slow-release formulation is used, the dose of either 11.25 mg or 22.5 mg is usually administered at bedtime. Slow-release products should not be used to initiate therapy.

Doses of clorazepate for the management of seizures differ in adult and pediatric populations. Patients who are nine to 12 years of age should be started on 3.75–7.5 mg twice daily. This dose should be increased by no more than 3.75 mg weekly. The maximum dose per day is 60 mg administered in two to three divided doses. Children older than 12 and adults should receive 7.5 mg two to three times daily. This can be increased to a higher dose by adding 7.5 mg at weekly intervals. The total daily dose should not exceed 90 mg daily administered in two to three doses. In patients undergoing alcohol withdrawal, the first dose is 30 mg. Treatment is continued with 15 mg two to four times daily for the maximum dose of 90 mg in one day. Once maximum dose is achieved, the dose is gradually decreased over subsequent days.

Precautions

Pregnant women should not take clorazepate. Patients who have narrow-angle glaucoma should not take clorazepate, as this may worsen their condition. Clorazepate should not be used in patients younger than nine years of age.

If **depression** coexists with anxiety, clorazepate should be used with caution as suicidal tendencies may be present. (One of the side effects with this medication is depression; if a patient has an underlying problem with depression, that problem can be exacerbated with clorazepate.) Patients should be cautioned against engaging in hazardous occupations requiring mental alertness, since clorazepate causes drowsiness and dizziness. Abrupt discontinuation of clorazepate has been associated with withdrawal symptoms and seizures. Hence, doses of clorazepate should be slowly decreased in patients who have been taking clorazepate continuously over several weeks. Other withdrawal symptoms may include nervousness, **insomnia**, irritability, diarrhea, and muscle aches. The doses for elderly

KEY TERMS

Benzodiazepines—A group of central nervous system depressants used to relieve anxiety or to induce sleep.

Glaucoma—A group of eye diseases characterized by increased pressure within the eye significant enough to damage eye tissue and structures. If untreated, glaucoma results in blindness.

patients, as well as patients with liver or kidney problems, may need to be decreased.

Side effects

The most common side effects include drowsiness, dizziness, and confusion. There are a few reports about behavioral changes associated with the use of clorazepate and they include rage, depression, irritability, and aggression.

Other side effects include vision disturbances—such as blurred and double vision—decreased libido, nausea, vomiting, either decreased or increased appetite, and diarrhea or constipation. In a few cases, clorazepate has been associated with liver toxicity where patients developed jaundice or fever. It is also known to cause a rash.

Interactions

Simultaneous use of clorazepate and dong quai, a Chinese herb, has been associated with excessive muscle relaxation and central nervous system depression. Other herbs that should not be used with clorazepate include **ginkgo biloba** and **kava kava**.

Omeprazole, a medication used to treat heartburn, should not be used together with clorazepate. Medicines to treat disorders associated with increased acid secretions—such as ranitidine, sucralfate, and pantoprazole—are not contraindicated with clorazepate. **Valerian**, an herb used as a sleep aid, binds to the same receptors in the brain as clorazepate; thus, the desired effects of clorazepate may not be seen in patients taking it and valerian at the same time.

Clorazepate may increase the effects of other drugs that cause drowsiness. These drugs include antihistamines (such as Benadryl), **sedatives** (usually used to treat insomnia), pain relievers, anxiety and seizure medicines, and muscle relaxants. Alcohol combined with clorazepate also causes excessive drowsiness.

See also Alcohol and related disorders; Antianxiety drugs and abuse-related disorders; Depression and depressive disorders.

Resources

BOOKS

Preston, John D., John H. O'Neal, and Mary C. Talaga. *Handbook of Clinical Psychopharmacology for Therapists,* 4th ed. Oakland, CA: New Harbinger Publications, 2004.

PERIODICALS

Lelong-Boulouard, Véronique, and others. "Interactions of Buprenorphine and Dipotassium Clorazepate on Anxiety and Memory Functions in the Mouse." *Drug and Alcohol Dependence* 85.2 (Nov. 2006): 103–13.

Millan, Mark J., and others. "Anxiolytic Properties of Agomelatine, an Antidepressant with Melatoninergic and Serotonergic Properties: Role of 5-HT-Sub (2C) Receptor Blockade." *Psychopharmacology* 177.4 (Feb. 2005): 1–12.

Quentin, Thomas, and others. "Clorazepate Affects Cell Surface Regulation of δ and κ Opioid Receptors, Thereby Altering Buprenorphine-Induced Adaptation in the Rat Brain." *Brain Research* 1063.1 (Nov. 2005): 84–95.

Rowlett, James K., and others. "Anti-Conflict Effects of Benzodiazepines in Rhesus Monkeys: Relationship with Therapeutic Doses in Humans and Role of GABA-Sub(A) Receptors." *Psychopharmacology* 184.2 (Jan. 2006): 201–11.

Ajna Hamidovic, Pharm.D.
Ruth A. Wienclaw, PhD

Clozapine

Definition

Clozapine is an antipsychotic drug used to alleviate the symptoms and signs of schizophrenia—a form of severe mental illness—that is characterized by loss of contact with reality, **hallucinations**, **delusions**, and unusual behavior. In the United States, the drug is also known by the brand name Clozaril.

Purpose

Clozapine is principally used to reduce the signs and symptoms of severe schizophrenic illness. The drug is intended for use in patients with severe **schizophrenia** who have not responded to any other antipsychotic drug. Clozapine is also used in patients with

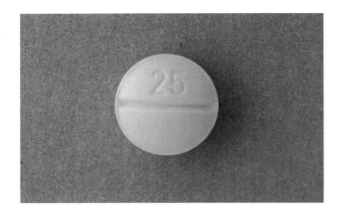

Clozapine tablet. *(Custom Medical Stock Photo, Inc. Reproduced by permission.)*

severe schizophrenia when other antipsychotic medications have caused intolerable side effects.

Description

Clozapine is considered an atypical antipsychotic drug. Atypical antipsychotics differ from typical antipsychotics in their effectiveness in schizophrenia and their profile of side effects. Clozapine may reduce the signs and symptoms of schizophrenia in a large proportion of patients with treatment-resistant schizophrenia who do not respond to typical antipsychotics. Moreover, the drug is less likely than typical antipsychotics to cause **tardive dyskinesia** and other extrapyramidal side effects. Tardive dyskinesia is a syndrome of involuntary, uncoordinated movements that may not disappear or may only partially improve after the drug is stopped. Tardive dyskinesia involves involuntary movements of the tongue, jaw, mouth or face, or other groups of skeletal muscles. The incidence of tardive dyskinesia increases with increasing age and with increasing dosage. It may also appear after the use of the antipsychotic has stopped. Women are at greater risk than men for developing tardive dyskinesia. There is no known effective treatment for this syndrome, although gradual (but rarely complete) improvement may occur over a long period.

Clozapine was the first atypical antipsychotic drug to be developed. In the late 1980s, clozapine was tested in severely ill patients with schizophrenia who had been treated with a typical antipsychotic drug but had not shown much improvement. A significant proportion of these patients improved as a result of treatment with clozapine.

The superiority of clozapine in patients resistant to treatment is considered an important advance, but the drug is not without problems. Clozapine is gener-

ally considered the most toxic of the antipsychotic drugs. It causes agranulocytosis, a life-threatening depletion of white blood cells, in 1–2% of patients. It also causes epileptic **seizures** and adverse effects on the heart and blood pressure more frequently than other antipsychotic medicines. Clozapine is usually reserved for the most severely ill patients with schizophrenia who have not responded to other treatments. Other atypical antipsychotic drugs have been developed in recent years, and they are considered safer to use than clozapine.

The mechanisms of action of antipsychotic drugs are not completely understood. The effect of clozapine is believed to be related to its actions in blocking neurotransmission due to the **neurotransmitters dopamine** and serotonin in a region of the **brain** called the limbic system, which is involved with emotions and motivation. The actions of clozapine may target the limbic system more specifically than those of typical antipsychotic drugs.

Recently, the effectiveness of clozapine was evaluated in the Clinical Antipsychotic Trials of **Intervention** Effectiveness (CATIE) Schizophrenia Study. This study evaluated the effectiveness and side effects of newer antipsychotic drugs (sometimes referred to as atypical antipsychotics)—including clozapine—in comparison to a conventional antipsychotic drug in the treatment of schizophrenia.

In Phase I of the study it was found that the newer antipsychotic medications—including clozapine—were not significantly more effective than the less expensive, conventional antipsychotic medications. In Phase II of the study, it was found that participants who had not benefited from their first antipsychotic medication tended to be effectively treated by clozapine. It was further found that for these patients, clozapine worked significantly better than other atypical antipsychotics. The conventional antipsychotic, however, was not included in this phase of the study.

The study results also showed that clozapine is often a good choice of medication for patients who did not respond well to other antipsychotic medications. It was more effective in controlling symptoms than the other atypical antipsychotics under evaluation. For patients whose symptoms are not well-controlled on clozapine, **olanzapine** and **risperidone** tended to be more effective than **ziprasidone** or **quetiapine**.

Recommended dosage

Clozapine is available as 25 mg and 100 mg tablets. The usual dosage of clozapine is 300–600 mg per day; however, some patients may require daily dosages of up to 900 mg. To minimize side effects, the initial dose of clozapine is 12.5 mg (one-half tablet) twice a day, and the dose is increased by 25–50 mg each day, until the dose reaches 300–450 mg per day. The daily dosage of the drug is then determined based on the individual patient's response, but increases should not exceed 100 mg once or twice a week.

Precautions

Clozapine may cause agranulocytosis, a life-threatening depletion of white blood cells. The blood cells affected by clozapine defend the body against infections by bacteria and other microorganisms, and patients with agranulocytosis are subject to severe infections. Clozapine treatment is reserved for the most severely ill patients with schizophrenia who have not responded to other treatments. Clozapine is available only through a distribution system that assures close monitoring of white blood cells. Patients must have white blood cell counts determined before starting treatment, then once every week for the first six months, once every other week after that, and once a week for the first month after clozapine treatment is stopped.

Clozapine may cause epileptic seizures in about 5% of patients. The frequency of seizures goes up as the dose of the drug is increased. Patients who experience seizures on clozapine should usually discontinue the drug or reduce the dose. Neuroleptic malignant syndrome (NMS), a dangerous condition with high fever, muscular rigidity, rapid pulse, sweating, and altered mental state, may occur with all antipsychotic medications, including clozapine. NMS requires immediate medical treatment.

Clozapine frequently causes sedation and may interfere with driving and other tasks requiring alertness. The drug may increase the effects of alcohol and **sedatives**. Clozapine may cause low blood pressure and sudden drops in blood pressure on standing up, which may cause dizziness or fainting. Elevated heart rate may occur in 25% of patients; this effect may be a serious risk for patients with heart disease. Clozapine-induced fever, unrelated to any illness, may occur. The fever usually subsides within a few days, but it may require discontinuing the drug.

The safety and effectiveness of clozapine in children under 16 years old have not been established. Elderly patients may be particularly sensitive to sedation, low blood pressure, and other side effects. The drug should be used with caution in older patients. Clozapine should be used in pregnant women only when strictly necessary. The drug has not been adequately studied in pregnancy. In animal studies, however, clozapine has not produced harmful effects on the fetus. Clozapine may be secreted in breast milk, and breast-feeding may not be advisable.

Side effects

Clozapine may cause many side effects. The following side effects are grouped by the body system affected:

- cardiovascular: decreases of blood pressure, especially on arising from a seated or lying position, which may cause dizziness or fainting; rapid heart rate; changes in heart rhythm; and electrocardiogram
- nervous system: sedation, increased seizure tendency
- digestive system: increased appetite, excessive salivation, nausea, constipation, abnormal liver tests, elevated blood sugar
- autonomic: blurred vision, exacerbation of glaucoma, dry mouth, nasal congestion, decreased sweating, difficulty urinating, particularly in men with enlarged prostate
- skin: rashes
- body as a whole: weight gain, fever

Interactions

Clozapine may interact with many other drugs. Patients should inform their physicians about all other drugs they are taking before starting treatment. Because of the risk of agranulocytosis, clozapine should not be given along with medications that suppress production of blood cells.

Clozapine may intensify the effects of drugs causing sedation, including alcohol, **barbiturates**, narcotic pain medications, minor tranquilizers, and antihistamines. Similarly, clozapine may cause excessive reductions of blood pressure in patients taking other medicines that lower blood pressure. Clozapine may also intensify side effects of drugs that cause blurred vision, dry mouth, diminished sweating in hot weather, and constipation. Many other antipsychotics and **antidepressants** cause such side effects.

Clozapine may increase the effects of other medications that also lower seizure threshold (make it more likely to have seizures), such as steroid drugs, the asthma medication theophylline, and many other psychiatric drugs. Patients with epilepsy may require adjustment in their dosage of antiseizure medications. Lithium may increase the risk of seizures and other nervous system adverse effects when given with clozapine.

KEY TERMS

Agranulocytosis—A blood disorder characterized by a reduction in the number of circulating white blood cells (granulocytes). White blood cells defend the body against infections. Agranulocytosis is a potential side effect of some of the newer antipsychotic medications used to treat schizophrenia.

Antipsychotic drug—A medication used to treat psychotic symptoms of schizophrenia such as hallucinations, delusions, and delirium. These drugs may be used to treat symptoms in other disorders, as well.

Autonomic—The part of the nervous system that governs the heart, involuntary muscles, and glands.

Epilepsy—A neurological disorder characterized by the onset of seizures. Seizures are caused by a disturbance in the electrical activity in the brain and can cause loss of consciousness, muscle spasms, rhythmic movements, abnormal sensory experiences, or altered mental states.

Extrapyramidal side effects—A group of neurological side effects including muscle spasms, involuntary movements, and symptoms that resemble Parkinson's disease (also called drug-induced parkinsonism).

Parkinson's disease—A disease of the nervous system most common in people over 60, characterized by a shuffling gait, trembling of the fingers and hands, and muscle stiffness.

Tardive dyskinesia—A condition that involves involuntary movements of the tongue, jaw, mouth or face, or other groups of skeletal muscles. The condition usually occurs either late in antipsychotic therapy or even after the therapy is discontinued. It may be irreversible.

Certain drugs that are eliminated by the liver may interfere with the elimination of clozapine from the body, causing higher blood levels and increased side effects. Conversely, clozapine may interfere with the elimination of other drugs that are eliminated by the liver. Antidepressants that affect brain serotonin levels may increase blood levels of clozapine, possibly causing increased side effects.

Resources

BOOKS

Preston, John D., John H. O'Neal, and Mary C. Talaga. *Handbook of Clinical Psychopharmacology for Therapists.* 4th ed. Oakland, CA: New Harbinger Publications, 2004.

Taylor, David, Robert Kerwin, and Carol Paton. *The Maudsley 2005–2006 Prescribing Guidelines.* New York: Taylor and Francis, 2005.

PERIODICALS

Brunette, Mary F., and others. "Clozapine Use and Relapses of Substance Use Disorder Among Patients With Co-occurring Schizophrenia and Substance Use Disorders." *Schizophrenia Bulletin* 32.4 (Oct. 2006): 637–43.

Essock, S. M., and others. "Effectiveness of Switching Antipsychotic Medications." *American Journal of Psychiatry* 163.12 (Dec. 2006): 2090–95.

Lamberti, J. Steven, and others. "Prevalence of the Metabolic Syndrome Among Patients Receiving Clozapine." *American Journal of Psychiatry* 163.7 (July 2006): 1273–76.

Lieberman, J. A., and others. "Effectiveness of Antipsychotic Drugs in Patients with Chronic Schizophrenia." *New England Journal of Medicine* 353.12 (Sept. 22, 2005): 1209–23.

Luchins, Daniel J. "In the Aftermath of CATIE: How Should Administrators Value Atypical Antipsychotic Medications?" *Administration and Policy in Mental Health and Mental Health Services Research* 33.5 (Sept. 2006): 541–43.

McEvoy, J. P., and others. "Effectiveness of Clozapine Versus Olanzapine, Quetiapine, and Risperidone in Patients with Chronic Schizophrenia Who Did Not Respond to Prior Atypical Antipsychotic Treatment." *American Journal of Psychiatry* 163.4 (Apr. 2006): 600–610.

Miodownik, Chanoch, and others. "The Effect of Sudden Clozapine Discontinuation on Management of Schizophrenic Patients: A Retrospective Controlled Study." *Journal of Clinical Psychiatry* 67.8 (Aug. 2006): 1204–1208.

Rocha, Fábio Lopes, and Cláudia Hara. "Benefits of Combining Aripiprazole to Clozapine: Three Case Reports." *Progress in Neuro-Psychopharmacology and Biological Psychiatry* 30.6 (July 2006): 1167–69.

Shaw, Philip, and Judith L. Rapoport. "Decision Making About Children With Psychotic Symptoms: Using the Best Evidence in Choosing a Treatment." *Journal of the American Academy of Child and Adolescent Psychiatry* 45.11 (Nov. 2006): 1381–86.

Shaw, Philip, and others. "Childhood-Onset Schizophrenia: A Double-Blind, Randomized Clozapine-Olanzapine Comparison." *Archives of General Psychiatry* 63.7 (July 2006): 721–30.

OTHER

CATIE. *CATIE: Clinical Antipsychotic Trials of Intervention Effectiveness Schizophrenia Study.* 2003. <http://www.catie.unc.edu/schizophrenia>.

National Institutes of Health. *CATIE Schizophrenia Trial.* 2006. <http://www.clinicaltrials.gov/ct/show/NCT00014001?order=1>.

Richard Kapit, MD
Ruth A. Wienclaw, PhD

Clozaril *see* **Clozapine**

Cocaine and related disorders

Definition

Cocaine is extracted from the coca plant, which grows in Central and South America. The substance is processed into many forms for use as an illegal drug of **abuse**. Cocaine is dangerously addictive, and users of the drug experience a "high"—a feeling of euphoria or intense happiness, along with hypervigilance, increased sensitivity, irritablity or anger, impaired judgment, and **anxiety**.

Forms of the drug

In its most common form, cocaine is a whitish crystalline powder that produces feelings of euphoria when ingested. In powder form, cocaine is known by such street names as "coke," "blow," "C," "flake," "snow" and "toot." It is most commonly inhaled or snorted. It may also be dissolved in water and injected.

Crack is a form of cocaine that can be smoked and that produces an immediate, more intense, and more short-lived high. It comes in off-white chunks or chips called "rocks."

In addition to their stand-alone use, both cocaine and crack are often mixed with other substances. Cocaine may be mixed with methcathinone to create a "wildcat." Cigars may be hollowed out and filled with a mixture of crack and marijuana. Either cocaine or crack used in conjunction with heroin is called a "speedball." Cocaine used together with alcohol represents the most common fatal two-drug combination.

Description

Cocaine-related disorders is a very broad topic. According to the mental health clinician's handbook, ***Diagnostic and Statistical Manual of Mental Disorders***, fourth edition, text revised (also known as the *DSM-IV-TR*), the broad category of cocaine-related disorders can be subdivided into two categories: cocaine use disorders and cocaine-induced disorders. Cocaine use disorders include cocaine dependence and cocaine abuse. Cocaine-induced disorders include:

- cocaine intoxication
- cocaine withdrawal
- cocaine intoxication delirium
- cocaine-induced psychotic disorder, with delusions
- cocaine-induced psychotic disorder, with hallucinations
- cocaine-induced mood disorder
- cocaine-induced anxiety disorder
- cocaine-induced sexual dysfunction
- cocaine-induced sleep disorder
- cocaine-related disorder not otherwise specified

Cocaine use disorders

COCAINE ABUSE. For the cocaine abuser, the use of the substance leads to maladaptive behavior over a 12-month period. The person may fail to meet responsibilities at school, work, or home. The cocaine abuse impairs the affected person's judgment, and he or she puts him- or herself in physical danger to use the substance. For example, the individual may use cocaine in an unsafe environment. The person who abuses cocaine may be arrested or charged with possession of the substance, yet will continue to use cocaine despite all of the personal and legal problems that may result.

COCAINE DEPENDENCE. Cocaine dependence is even more serious than cocaine abuse. Dependence is a maladaptive behavior that, over a three-month period, has caused the affected individual to experience tolerance for and withdrawal symptoms from cocaine. Tolerance is the need to increase the amount of cocaine intake to achieve the same desired effect. In other words, someone who is dependent on cocaine needs more cocaine to produce the same "high" that a lesser amount produced in the past. The dependent person also experiences cocaine withdrawal. Withdrawal symptoms develop within hours or days after cocaine use that has been heavy and prolonged and then abruptly stopped. The symptoms include irritable mood and two or more of the following symptoms: **fatigue**, nightmares, difficulty sleeping or too much sleep, elevated appetite, agitation (restlessness), or slowed physical movements. The onset of withdrawal symptoms can cause a person to use more cocaine to avoid these painful and uncomfortable symptoms. The dependent person uses larger amounts of cocaine for longer periods of time than intended. He or she cannot cut back on the use of the substance, often has a difficult time resisting cocaine when it is available, and may abandon work or school to spend more time acquiring and planning to acquire more cocaine. The individual continues to use the cocaine despite the negative effects it has on family life, work and school.

Cocaine-induced disorders

COCAINE INTOXICATION. Cocaine intoxication occurs after recent cocaine use. The person experiences a feeling of intense happiness, hypervigilance, increased sensitivity, irritability or anger, with impaired judgement, and anxiety. The intoxication impairs the person's ability to function at work, school, or in social situations. Two or more of the following symptoms are present immediately after the use of the cocaine:

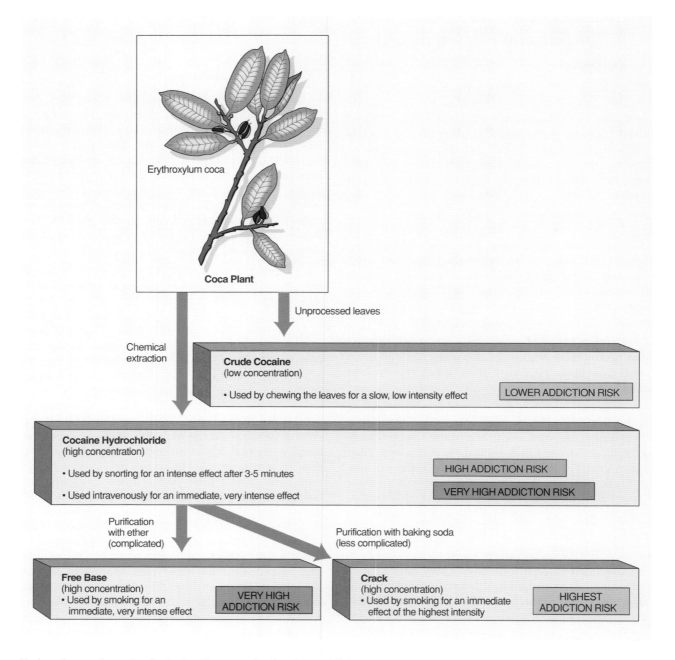

Various forms of cocaine (including the coca plant) and the addiciton risks associated with them. *(Chart by Hans & Cassidy)*

- enlarged pupils
- elevated heart rate
- elevated or lowered blood pressure
- chills and increased sweating
- nausea or vomiting
- weight loss
- agitation or slowed movements
- weak muscles

- chest pain
- coma
- confusion
- irregular heartbeat
- depressed respiration
- seizures
- odd postures
- odd movements

COCAINE WITHDRAWAL. As mentioned, withdrawal symptoms develop within hours or days after cocaine use that has been heavy and prolonged and then abruptly stopped. The symptoms include irritable mood and two or more of the following symptoms: fatigue, nightmares, difficulty sleeping or too much sleep, elevated appetite, agitation (restlessness), or slowed physical movements.

COCAINE-INDUCED DELIRIUM. According to the *DSM-IV-TR*, several criteria must be met in order for a health care professional to establish the **diagnosis** of cocaine-induced delirium. Patients have a disturbance of their level of consciousness or awareness, evidenced by drowsiness or an inability to concentrate or pay attention. Patients also experience a change in their cognition (ability to think) evidenced by a deficit in their language or their memory. For example, these patients may forget where they have placed an item, or their speech is confusing. These symptoms have rapid onset within hours or days of using cocaine and the symptoms fluctuate throughout the course of the day. These findings cannot be explained by **dementia** (state of impaired thought processes and memory that can be caused by various diseases and conditions) and the doctor must not be able to recognize some other physical reason that can account for the symptoms other than cocaine intoxication.

COCAINE-INDUCED PSYCHOTIC DISORDER, WITH DELUSIONS. The person with this disorder has experienced intoxication or withdrawal from cocaine within a month from the time he or she begins to experience delusions (beliefs that the person continues to maintain, despite evidence to the contrary). In order for this state to be considered cocaine-induced psychotic disorder, these symptoms cannot be due to another condition or substance.

COCAINE-INDUCED PSYCHOTIC DISORDER, WITH HALLUCINATIONS. This condition is the same as cocaine-induced psychotic disorder with delusions, except that this affected individual experiences hallucinations instead of delusions. Hallucinations can be described as hearing and seeing things that are not real.

COCAINE-INDUCED MOOD DISORDER. The person with this disorder has experienced intoxication or withdrawal from cocaine within a month from the time he or she begins to experience depressed, elevated, or irritable mood with **apathy** (lack of empathy for others, and lack of showing a broad range of appropriate emotions).

COCAINE-INDUCED ANXIETY DISORDER. The person this disorder has experienced intoxication or withdrawal from cocaine within a month from the time he or

she begins to experience anxiety, panic attacks, obsessions, or compulsions. Panic attacks are discrete episodes of intense anxiety. Persons affected with panic attacks may experience accelerated heart rate, shaking or trembling, sweating, shortness of breath, or fear of going crazy or losing control, as well as other symptoms. An **obsession** is an unwelcome, uncontrollable, persistent idea, thought, image, or emotion that a person cannot help thinking even though it creates significant distress or anxiety. A **compulsion** is a repetitive, excessive, meaningless activity or mental exercise which a person performs in an attempt to avoid distress or worry.

COCAINE-INDUCED SEXUAL DYSFUNCTION. The person with this disorder has experienced intoxication or withdrawal from cocaine within a month from the time he or she begins to experience sexual difficulties, and these difficulties are deemed by the clinician to be due directly to the cocaine use. Substance-induced sexual difficulties can range from impaired desire, impaired arousal, impaired orgasm, or sexual pain.

COCAINE-INDUCED SLEEP DISORDER. This disorder is characterized by difficulty sleeping (**insomnia**) during intoxication or increased sleep duration when patients are in withdrawal.

COCAINE-RELATED DISORDER NOT OTHERWISE SPECIFIED. This classification is reserved for clinicians to use when a cocaine disorder that the clinician sees does not fit into any of the above categories.

Causes and symptoms

Causes

BIOCHEMICAL/PHYSIOLOGICAL CAUSES. Twin studies have demonstrated that there is a higher rate of cocaine abuse in identical twins as compared to fraternal twins. This indicates that genetic factors contribute to the development of cocaine abuse. This finding also indicates, however, that unique environmental factors contribute to the development of cocaine abuse, as well. (If genes alone determined who would develop cocaine dependence, 100% of the identical twins with the predisposing genes would develop the disorder. However, because the results show only a relationship, or a correlation, between genetics and cocaine use among twins, these results indicate that other factors must be at work, as well.) Studies have also shown that disorders like **attention deficit/hyperactivity disorder** (ADHD), **conduct disorder**, and **antisocial personality disorder** all have genetic components, and since patients who abuse cocaine have a high incidence of these diagnoses, they may also be genetically predisposed to abusing cocaine.

REINFORCEMENT. Learning and conditioning also play a unique role in the perpetuation of cocaine abuse. Each inhalation and injection of cocaine causes pleasurable feelings that reinforce the drug-taking procedure. In addition, the patient's environment also plays a role in cueing and reinforcing the experience in the patient's mind. The association between cocaine and environment is so strong that many people recovering from cocaine addiction report that being in an area where they used drugs brings back memories of the experience and makes them crave drugs. Specific areas of the brain are thought to be involved in cocaine craving, including the amygdala (a part of the brain that controls aggression and emotional reactivity), and the prefrontal cortex (a part of the brain that regulates anger, aggression, and the brain's assessment of fear, threats, and danger).

Symptoms

The following list is a summary of the acute (short-term) physical and psychological effects of cocaine on the body:

- blood vessels constrict
- elevated heart rate
- elevated blood pressure
- a feeling of intense happiness
- elevated energy level
- a state of increased alertness and sensory sensitivity
- elevated anxiety
- panic attacks
- elevated self-esteem
- diminished appetite
- spontaneous ejaculation and heightened sexual arousal
- psychosis (loss of contact with reality)

The following list is a summary of the chronic (long-term) physical and psychological effects of cocaine on the body:

- depressed mood
- irritability
- physical agitation
- decreased motivation
- difficulty sleeping
- hypervigilance
- elevated anxiety
- panic attacks
- hallucinations
- psychosis

Demographics

The patterns of cocaine abuse in the United States have changed much over the past thirty years. The patterns have also been changing in other parts of the world as well, including South America and Western Europe. In the United States, several studies have attempted to track drug abuse in many different populations. The studies include: the Monitoring the Future Study (MTF); the National Household Survey on Drug Abuse (NHSDA); the Drug Abuse Warning Network (DAWN), which gets reports from Emergency Rooms and medical examiners' offices on drug-related cases and deaths; and Arrestee Drug Abuse Monitoring (ADAM), which gets information on urine samples obtained from people who have been arrested.

In the annual MTF study, cocaine use among high school seniors had declined from 13.1% in 1985 to 3.1% in 1992—the lowest it had been since 1975 when the survey was first implemented. The rate of cocaine use began to rise again and peaked at 5.5% in 1997. The NHSDA found that the levels of cocaine use declined over the same time period. The decline in the rates has been thought to be due in part to education about the risks of cocaine abuse.

The incidence of new crack cocaine users has also decreased. There was a minimal decline in the numbers of excessive cocaine users between the years 1985 and 1997. The Epidemiologic Catchment Area (ECA) studies done in the early 1980s combined cocaine dependence with cocaine abuse and found that one-month to six-month prevalence rates for cocaine abuse and dependence were low or could not be measured. The lifetime rate of cocaine abuse was 0.2%.

A 1997 study from The National Institute on Drug Abuse indicates that among outpatients who abuse substances, 55% abuse cocaine.

Cocaine abuse affects both genders and many different populations across the United States. Males are one-and-a-half to two times more likely to abuse cocaine than females. Cocaine began as a drug of the upper classes in the 1970s; now the socioeconomic status of cocaine users has shifted. Cocaine is more likely to be abused by the economically disadvantaged because it is easy for them to get, and it is inexpensive ($10 for a small bag of crack cocaine). These factors have led to increased violence (because people who are cocaine dependent often will become involved in illegal activity, such as drug dealing, in order to acquire funds for their habit) and higher rates of acquired immune deficiency (AIDS) among disadvantaged populations.

Diagnosis

If a mental health clinician suspects cocaine use, he or she may ask the patient specifically about swallowing, injecting, or smoking the substance. Urine and blood testing will also be conducted to determine the presence of the substance. Doctors may also talk to friends or relatives concerning the patient's drug use, especially for cases in which the physician suspects that the patient is not being entirely honest about substance use. The clinician may also investigate a patient's legal history for drug arrests that may give clues to periods of **substance abuse** to which the patient will not admit.

Differential diagnosis

Differential diagnosis is the process of distinguishing one condition from other, similar conditions. The cocaine abuse disorder is easily confused with other substance abuse disorders and various forms of mental illness.

The symptoms of cocaine intoxication, such as increased talkativeness, poor sleep, and the intense feelings of happiness are similar to the symptoms for **bipolar disorder**, so the urine toxification screening test may play a key role in the diagnosis. Patients with cocaine intoxication with hallucinations and delusions can be mistaken for schizophrenic patients instead, further emphasizing the importance of the urine and blood screens. As part of establishing the diagnosis, the physician must also rule out PCP (**phencyclidine**) intoxication and Cushing's disease (an endocrine disorder of excessive cortisol production). Withdrawal symptoms are similar to those of the patient with major **depression**. For this reason, the clinician may ask the patient about his or her mood during times of abstinence from drug use to discern if any true mood disorders are present. If cocaine use is causing depression, the depression should resolve within a couple of weeks of stopping drug use.

Laboratory testing

The breakdown products of cocaine remain in the urine. The length of time that they remain depends on the dose of cocaine, but most doses would not remain in the urine longer than a few days. Cocaine can also be found in other bodily fluids such as blood, saliva, sweat, and hair, and these provide better estimates as to recent cocaine use. The hair can hold evidence that a patient has been using drugs for weeks to months. Positron emission tomography (PET) and single-photon emission **computed tomography** (SPECT) are different kinds of **imaging studies**. Both kinds of scans look at the amount of blood that is flowing to the brain.

When these images are taken of the brains of people who abuse cocaine, the resulting scans have revealed abnormalities in certain sections of the brain. The brains of people addicted to cocaine shrink, or atrophy.

Neuropsychological assessment

Neuropsychological testing is also an important tool for examining the effects of toxic substances on brain functioning. Some physicians may use neuropsychological assessments to reveal patients' cognitive and physical impairment after cocaine use. Neuropsychological testing assesses brain functioning through structured and systematic behavioral observation. Neuropsychological tests are designed to examine a variety of cognitive abilities, including speed of information processing, attention, memory, and language. An example of a task that a physician might ask the patient to complete as part of a neuropsychological examination is to name as many words beginning with a particular letter as the patient can in one minute. Patients who abuse cocaine often have difficulty completing tasks, such as the one described, that require concentration and memory.

Treatments

Psychological and social interventions

TREATMENT SETTINGS. Not all patients who abuse cocaine need to resort to long-term treatment. Treatment length varies with the degree that a person is dependent on the substance. If the patient has other psychiatric conditions such as major depression or **schizophrenia** or has significant medical complications of cocaine abuse, then he or she is more likely to require higher-intensity treatment. Residential programs/therapeutic communities may be helpful, particularly in more severe cases. Patients typically spend six to 12 months in such programs, which may also include vocational training and other features. The availability of such treatment, as well as medical insurance's ability to cover treatment, are all issues that affect the patient's access to treatment.

PSYCHOTHERAPY. A wide range of behavioral interventions have been successfully used to treat cocaine addiction. The approach used must be tailored to the specific needs of each individual patient, however.

Contingency management rewards drug abstinence (confirmed by urine testing) with points or vouchers which patients can exchange for such things as an evening out or membership in a gym. **Cognitive-behavioral therapy** helps users learn to recognize and avoid situations most likely to lead to cocaine use and to develop healthier ways to cope with stressful situations.

Supportive therapy helps patients to modify their behavior by preventing **relapse** by taking actions such as staying away from drug-using friends and from neighborhoods or situations where cocaine is abundant.

Self-help groups like Narcotics Anonymous (NA) or Cocaine Anonymous (CA) are helpful for many recovering substance abusers. CA is a twelve-step program for cocaine abusers modeled after Alcoholics Anonymous (AA). **Support groups** and **group therapy** led by a therapist can be helpful because other addicts can share coping and relapse-prevention strategies. The group's support can help patients face devastating changes and life issues. Some experts recommend that patients be cocaine-free for at least two weeks before participating in a group, but other experts argue that a two-week waiting period is unnecessary and counterproductive. Group counseling sessions led by drug counselors who are in recovery themselves are also useful for some people overcoming their addictions. These group counseling sessions differ from group therapy in that the people in a counseling group are constantly changing.

The National Institute of Drug Abuse conducted a study comparing different forms of **psychotherapy**: patients who had both group drug counseling and individual drug counseling had improved outcomes. Patients who had cognitive-behavioral therapy stayed in treatment longer.

Medications

Many medications—greater than twenty—have been tested but none have been found to reduce the intensity of withdrawal. **Dopamine** agonists like **amantadine** and bromocriptine and tricyclic **antidepressants** such as **desipramine** have failed in studies to help treat symptoms of cocaine withdrawal or intoxication.

Alternative therapy

Alternative techniques, such as **acupuncture**, EEG **biofeedback**, and visualization, may be useful in treating addiction when combined with conventional treatment approaches.

Prognosis

Not all cocaine abusers become dependent on the drug. However, even someone who only uses occasionally can experience the harmful effects (interpersonal relationship conflicts, work or school difficulties, etc.) of using cocaine, and even occasional use is enough to addict. In the course of a person's battle with cocaine abuse, he or she may vary the forms of the drug that he or she uses. A person may use the inhaled form at one time and the injected form at another, for example.

Many studies of short-term outpatient treatment over a six-month to two-year period indicate that people addicted to cocaine have a better chance of recovering than people who are addicted to heroin. A study of veterans who participated in an inpatient or day hospital treatment program that lasted 28 days, revealed that about 60% of people who were abstinent at four months were able to maintain their abstinence at seven months.

Having a good social support network greatly improves the prognosis for recovery from cocaine abuse and dependence.

Prevention

Efforts to prevent cocaine abuse, as well as any substance abuse, begin with prevention programs that are based in schools, in the workplace, heath care clinics, criminal justice systems, and public housing. Programs such as Students Taught Awareness (STAR) are cost effective and have reduced the rates of substance abuse in the schools. These school-based programs also foster parental involvement and education about substance abuse issues. The juvenile justice system also implements drug prevention programs. Even many workplaces provide drug screening and treatment and counseling for those who test positive. Employers may also provide workshops on substance abuse prevention. The United States Department of Housing and Urban Development (HUD) also sponsors drug prevention programs.

See also Addiction; Detoxification; Disease concept of chemical dependency.

Resources

BOOKS

American Psychiatric Association. *Diagnostic and Statistical Manual of Mental Disorders*. 4th edition, text revised. Washington, DC: American Psychiatric Association, 2000.

Jaffe, Jerome H., M.D. "Cocaine-Related Disorders." In *Comprehensive Textbook of Psychiatry*, edited by Benjamin J. Sadock, M.D. and Virginia A. Sadock, M.D. 7th edition. Philadelphia: Lippincott Williams and Wilkins, 2000.

Matthews, John. "Substance-Related Disorders: Cocaine and Narcotics." In *Psychiatry Update and Board Preparation*, edited by Thomas A. Stern, M.D. and John B. Herman, M.D. New York: McGraw Hill, 2000.

PERIODICALS

Adinoff, Byron, M.D. and others. "Limbic Response to Procaine in Cocaine Addicted Subjects." *American Journal of Psychiatry* (March 2001): 390-398.

Held, Gale A., M.P.A. "Linkages Between Substance Abuse Prevention and Other Human Services Literature Review." *National Institute on Drug Abuse (NIDA)* (June 1998).

Jacobsen, Leslie K., M.D. and others. "Quantitative Morphology of the Caudate and Putamen in Patients With Cocaine Dependence." *American Journal of Psychiatry* (March 2000): 486-489.

Kampman, Kyle M., M.D. and others. "Amantadine in the Treatment of Cocaine-Dependent Patients With Severe Withdrawal Symptoms." *American Journal of Psychiatry* (December 2000): 2052-2054.

ORGANIZATIONS

National Institute on Drug Abuse (NIDA). 6001 Executive Boulevard, Room 5213, Bethesda, MD, 20892-9561. (301) 443-1124. <http://www.nida.nih.gov>.

The American Academy of Addiction Psychiatry (AAAP). 7301 Mission Road, Suite 252, Prairie Village, KS, 66208. (913) 262-6161. <http://www.aaap.org>.

Cocaine Anonymous World Services (CAWS). 3740 Overland Ave. Ste. C, Los Angeles, CA, 90034. (310) 559-5833. <http://www.ca.org>.

OTHER

Leshner, Alan Ph.D. "Cocaine Abuse and Addiction." *National Institute on Drug Abuse Research Report Series* NIH Publication Number 99-4342, Washington, D.C. Supt.of doc. U.S. Government Printing Offices, 1999.

Susan Hobbs, M.D.
Peter Gregutt

Cogentin *see* **Benztropine**

Cognex *see* **Tacrine**

Cognistat

Definition

The Cognistat is a standardized neurobehavioral screening test. It is a test that examines neurological (**brain** and central nervous system) health in relation to a person's behavior.

Purpose

As a screening test, the Cognistat may be administered to identify basic strengths and weaknesses so that further tests (if necessary) can be selected, and the data provided by the Cognistat can then be used as preliminary data against which scores from other tests given may be compared. Cognistat results have been used in a number of arenas, most notably in behavioral medicine. For example, Cognistat results may be useful to track cognitive decline (decreased thinking and reasoning abilities) in patients with organic brain disorders, to develop helpful strategies for cognitive problems associated with **schizophrenia**, and to help distinguish among terminally ill cancer patients those with **depression** and **anxiety** versus those with cognitive impairment.

Precautions

The Cognistat is more sensitive than many similar tests, but considers a limited sample of behavior at a brief point in time. Thus, its results are not generalizable and should not be viewed as conclusive indicators of the areas being assessed. It is important that the examiner be properly trained in the use of the test. Test takers may be affected by test-related discomfort or performance anxiety. This may be particularly true when prior to testing, the examinee was not fully aware of his or her deficits, especially deficits that become more apparent as testing progresses. The test's reliability has not been fully documented. Further research and standardization data is needed.

Description

The Cognistat usually takes less than 45 minutes to complete, and the test explores, quantifies, and describes performance in central areas of brain-behavior relations: level of consciousness, orientation, attention, language, constructional ability, memory, calculations and reasoning. The sub-areas of language are spontaneous speech, comprehension, repetition, and naming. The sub-areas of reasoning are similarities and judgment. Exploration occurs through interactive behavioral tasks that rely on perception, cognitive processing, and motor skills. The test is more quickly administered to higher than lower functioning individuals by providing a difficult screening item at the beginning of each section. Only when a screening item is missed are the metric, or more remedial, items applied, usually from easiest to most difficult within that section.

The test begins with the examiner asking general questions of the test taker (name, address, age, etc.), and while these questions are being answered, the examiner is subjectively assessing the test taker's level of consciousness. Then, the examiner asks general questions to confirm the test taker's level of orientation, meaning that the test taker is correctly oriented to place and time—he or she knows what day it is and where he or she is. To test the examinee's attention and memory, the test taker will be asked to repeat a series of digits and the first part of a verbal memory task will be given. (This task will be asked about again later in the test.)

The language section begins with a sample of spontaneous speech derived by asking for a description of a detailed line drawing. The language comprehension section requires responses to simple commands that involve manipulation of common objects placed before the examinee. In the language repetition subtest, the test taker is asked to repeat short phrases and simple sentences. In naming, the last of the language subtests, the screening item differs in form from the metric (easier) items. In the screening item, the examiner holds up an object and asks the test taker to name its four major parts, as the examiner points to them one after another. If the test taker fails, he or she is asked to name eight separate objects, one after another represented by line drawings.

In the next section, constructional ability, the screening item is a visual memory task wherein a stimulus sheet is presented for ten seconds, and the examinee is asked to draw the stimuli from memory. The test taker is then asked to assemble plastic tiles into designs, one after another, as each is shown on a card. Faster completion yields greater points. After the constructional items, the test taker is asked to recall the verbal memory items presented earlier. For items he or she cannot recall, the examiner provides prompts, or clues.

The calculations section is composed of simple verbal mathematics, and is followed by the reasoning section, which includes two subtests. The first consists of associative thinking items known as similarities. In similarities items, the examinee is asked to explain how two concepts are alike. Greater points are awarded if

their concept is abstract rather than concrete. The final subtest on the Cognistat is the judgment subtest of the reasoning section. In the judgment subtest, the examinee is asked to answer questions that demonstrate practical judgment in solving basic problem scenarios. Scores for this subtest are weighted based on their appropriateness. There is only one fully appropriate response to each item.

The test booklet provides space for listing medications, and for noting comments about any physical deficits and the examinee's impression of his or her own performance.

Results

When test administration is complete, the examiner tallies the points earned in each section, and plots them on the cognitive status profile located on the front of the test booklet. On the profile, numerical scores are described to fall within the normal or impaired range. The impaired range is broken down into mild, moderate and severe. An individual's scores can also be compared to standardization group data, and their profile may be compared to five case study profiles presented in the test guide. The few items that do not allow for quantitative analysis—the sample of spontaneous speech, for example—are factored into the interpretation of results by the examiner. There is no mechanism for transforming raw scores into percentiles or standard scores, and the test is not designed to generate one main score.

Resources

BOOKS

The Northern California Neurobehavioral Group, Inc. *Manual for the Neurobehavioral Cognitive Status Examination.* Fairfax, CA.

PERIODICALS

Kiernan, R., J. Mueller, W. Langston, and C. Van Dyke. "The Neurobehavioral Cognitive Status Examination: A brief but differentiated approach to cognitive assessment." *Annals of Internal Medicine* 107 (1987): 481-485.

Logue, P., L. Tupler, C. D'Amico, and F. Schmitt. "The Neurobehavioral Cognitive Status Examination: Psychometric properties in use with psychiatric inpatients." *Journal of Clinical Psychology* 49 (Jan. 1993): 80-89.

Geoffrey G. Grimm, Ph.D., LPC

Cognitive-behavioral therapy

Definition

Cognitive therapy is a psychosocial (both psychological and social) therapy that assumes that faulty thought patterns (called cognitive patterns) cause maladaptive behavior and emotional responses. The treatment focuses on changing thoughts to solve psychological and personality problems. Behavior therapy is also a goal-oriented, therapeutic approach, and it treats emotional and behavioral disorders as maladaptive learned responses that can be replaced by healthier ones with appropriate training. Cognitive-behavioral therapy (CBT) integrates features of **behavior modification** into the traditional cognitive restructuring approach.

Purpose

CBT attempts to change clients' unhealthy behavior or thought processes through cognitive restructuring (examining assumptions behind the thought patterns) and through the use of behavior therapy techniques.

CBT is a treatment option for a number of mental disorders, including **depression, dissociative identity disorder**, eating disorders, **generalized anxiety disorder, hypochondriasis, insomnia, obsessive-compulsive disorder**, and **panic disorder** without **agoraphobia**.

Precautions

CBT may not be appropriate for all patients. Patients with significant cognitive impairments (patients with traumatic **brain** injury or organic brain disease, for example) and individuals who are not willing to take an active role in the treatment process are not usually good candidates.

Description

Origins of the two approaches

Psychologist Aaron Beck developed cognitive therapy in the 1960s. The treatment is based on the principle that maladaptive behavior (ineffective, self-defeating behavior) is triggered by inappropriate or irrational thinking patterns, called automatic thoughts. Instead of reacting to the reality of a situation, an individual automatically reacts to his or her own distorted view of the situation. Cognitive therapy strives to change these thought patterns (also known as cognitive distortions), by examining the rationality and validity of the assumptions behind them. This process is termed cognitive restructuring.

Behavior therapy focuses on observable behavior and its modification in the present, in sharp contrast to the psychoanalytic method of Sigmund Freud (1856–1939), which focuses on unconscious mental processes and their roots in the past. Behavior therapy was developed during the 1950s by researchers and therapists who were critical of the prevailing psychodynamic treatment methods. The therapy drew on a variety of theories and research, including the classical conditioning principles of the Russian physiologist Ivan Pavlov (1849–1936), the work of American B. F. Skinner (1904–1990), and the work of **psychiatrist** Joseph Wolpe (1915–1997). Pavlov became famous for experiments in which dogs were trained to salivate at the sound of a bell, and Skinner pioneered the concept of operant conditioning, in which behavior is modified by changing the response it elicits. Wolpe is probably best known for his work in the areas of desensitization and **assertiveness training**. By the 1970s, behavior therapy enjoyed widespread popularity as a treatment approach. Since the 1980s, many therapists have begun to use CBT to change clients' unhealthy behavior by replacing negative or self-defeating thought patterns with more positive ones.

The combined approach

In CBT, the therapist works with the patient to identify the thoughts that are causing distress, and employs behavioral therapy techniques to alter the resulting behavior. Patients may have certain fundamental core beliefs, known as schemas, that are flawed and are having a negative impact on the patient's behavior and functioning.

For example, a patient with depression may develop a **social phobia** because he is convinced that he is uninteresting and impossible to love. A cognitive-behavioral therapist would test this assumption by asking the patient to name family and friends who care for him and enjoy his company. By showing the patient that others value him, the therapist exposes the irrationality of the patient's assumption and also provides a new model of thought for the patient to change his previous behavior pattern (i.e., I am an interesting and likeable person, therefore I should not have any problem making new social acquaintances). Additional behavioral techniques such as conditioning (the use of positive and/or negative reinforcements to encourage desired behavior) and **systematic desensitization** (gradual exposure to anxiety-producing situations to extinguish the fear response) may then be used to gradually reintroduce the patient to social situations.

CBT is usually administered in an outpatient setting (clinic or doctor's office) by a specially trained therapist. Therapy may be in either individual or group sessions. Therapists are psychologists (PhD, PsyD, EdD, or MA degree), clinical **social workers** (M.S.W., D.S.W., or L.S.W. degree), counselors (MA or MS degree), or psychiatrists (MD trained in psychiatry).

Techniques

Therapists use several different techniques in the course of CBT to help patients examine and change thoughts and behaviors. These include:

- Validity testing. The therapist asks the patient to defend his or her thoughts and beliefs. If the patient cannot produce objective evidence supporting his or her assumptions, the invalidity, or faulty nature, is exposed.
- Cognitive rehearsal. The patient is asked to imagine a difficult situation he or she has encountered in the past, and then works with the therapist to practice how to cope successfully with the problem. When the patient is confronted with a similar situation again, the rehearsed behavior will be drawn on to manage it.
- Guided discovery. The therapist asks the patient a series of questions designed to guide the patient towards the discovery of his or her cognitive distortions.
- Writing in a journal. Patients keep a detailed written diary of situations that arise in everyday life, the thoughts and emotions surrounding them, and the behaviors that accompany them. The therapist and patient then review the journal together to discover maladaptive thought patterns and how these thoughts impact behavior.
- Homework. To encourage self-discovery and reinforce insights made in therapy, the therapist may ask the patient to do homework assignments. These

may include note-taking during the session, journaling, review of an audiotape of the patient session, or reading books or articles appropriate to the therapy. They may also be more behaviorally focused, applying a newly learned strategy or coping mechanism to a situation, and then recording the results for the next therapy session.

- Modeling. Role-playing exercises allow the therapist to act out appropriate reactions to different situations. The patient can then model this behavior.
- Systematic positive reinforcement. Human behavior is routinely motivated and rewarded by positive reinforcement, and a more specialized version of this phenomenon (systematic positive reinforcement) is used by behavior-oriented therapists. Rules are established that specify particular behaviors that are to be reinforced, and a reward system is set up. With children, this sometimes takes the form of tokens that may be accumulated and later exchanged for certain privileges. Just as providing reinforcement strengthens behaviors, withholding it weakens them. Eradicating undesirable behavior by deliberately withholding reinforcement is another popular treatment method called extinction. For example, a child who habitually shouts to attract attention may be ignored unless he or she speaks in a conversational tone.
- Aversive conditioning. This technique employs the principles of classical conditioning to lessen the appeal of a behavior that is difficult to change because it is either very habitual or temporarily rewarding. The client is exposed to an unpleasant stimulus while engaged in or thinking about the behavior in question. Eventually the behavior itself becomes associated with unpleasant rather than pleasant feelings. One treatment method used with alcoholics is the administration of a nausea-inducing drug together with an alcoholic beverage to produce an aversion to the taste and smell of alcohol by having it become associated with nausea. Studies investigating use of these aversive conditioning approaches have not identified a high level of therapeutic effectiveness. According to the American Psychiatric Association, aversion therapy should be practiced only in very specialized centers. In counterconditioning, a maladaptive response is weakened by the strengthening of a response that is incompatible with it. A well-known type of counterconditioning is systematic desensitization, which counteracts the anxiety connected with a particular behavior or situation by inducing a relaxed response to it instead. This method is often used in the treatment of people who are afraid of flying.

Preparation

Because CBT is a collaborative effort between therapist and patient, a comfortable working relationship is critical to successful treatment. Individuals interested in CBT should schedule a consultation session with their prospective therapist before starting treatment. The consultation session is similar to an interview session, and it allows both patient and therapist to get to know one another. During the consultation, the therapist gathers information to make an initial assessment of the patient and to recommend both direction and goals for treatment. The patient has the opportunity to learn about the therapist's professional credentials, his/her approach to treatment, and other relevant issues.

In some managed-care settings, an intake interview is required before a patient can meet with a therapist. The intake interview is typically performed by a psychiatric nurse, counselor, or social worker, either face-to-face or over the phone. It is used to gather a brief background on treatment history and make a preliminary evaluation of the patient before assigning them to a therapist.

Results

Because CBT is employed for such a broad spectrum of illnesses and is often used in conjunction with medications and other treatment interventions, it is difficult to measure overall success rates for the therapy. However, several studies have indicated that CBT:

- may reduce the rate of rehospitalization and improve social and occupational functioning for bipolar disorder patients, when combined with pharmacotherapy (treatment with medication)
- is an effective treatment for patients with bulimia nervosa
- can help generalized anxiety patients manage their worry, when combined with relaxation exercises
- is helpful in treating hypochondriasis
- may be effective for treating depression, especially when combined with pharmacotherapy, and may also prevent depression in at-risk children
- is one of the first-line treatments for obsessive-compulsive disorder
- that focuses on education and provides some exposure and coping skills is effective for treating panic disorder without agoraphobia
- is effective for helping to treat insomnia, and its effects may be sustained longer than the effects of medications alone

See also Aversion therapy; Behavior modification; Cognitive problem-solving skills training; Cognitive retraining techniques; Covert sensitization; Exposure treatment; Rational emotive therapy; Systematic desensitization.

Resources

BOOKS

Alford, B. A., and A. T. Beck. *The Integrative Power of Cognitive Therapy.* New York: Guilford, 1997.

Beck, A. T. *Prisoners of Hate: The Cognitive Basis of Anger, Hostility, and Violence.* New York: HarperCollins Publishers, 1999.

Craighead, Linda W. *Cognitive and Behavioral Interventions: An Empirical Approach to Mental Health Problems.* Boston: Allyn and Bacon, 1994.

Nathan, Peter E., and Jack M. Gorman. *A Guide to Treatments that Work,* 2nd ed. New York: Oxford University Press, 2002.

Weishaar, Marjorie. "Cognitive Therapy." *Encyclopedia of Mental Health,* Ed. Howard S. Friedman. San Diego: Academic Press, 1998.

Wolpe, Joseph. *The Practice of Behavior Therapy.* Tarrytown, NY: Pergamon Press, 1996.

PERIODICALS

Rupke, Stuart J., David Blecke, and Marjorie Renfrow. "Cognitive Therapy for Depression." *American Family Physician* 73 (2006): 83–85. Also available online at: <http://www.aafp.org/afp/20060101/83.html>.

OTHER

American Academy of Family Physicians. "Cognitive Therapy." Available online at: <http://familydoctor.org/882.xml>.

Kleber, Herbert D., and others. *Practice Guideline for Treatment of Patients with Substance Use Disorders,* 2nd ed. (2006). Available online through the American Psychiatric Association at: <http://www.psych.org/psych_pract/treatg/pg/SUD2ePG_04-28-06.pdf>.

National Alliance on Mental Illness. "Cognitive-Behavioral Therapy." Available online at: <http://www.nami.org/Template.cfm?Section = About_Treatments_and_Supports&template=/ContentManagement/ContentDisplay.cfm&ContentID=7952>.

Paula Ford-Martin, MS
Emily Jane Willingham, PhD

Cognitive problem-solving skills training

Definition

Cognitive problem-solving skills training (CPSST) attempts to decrease a child's inappropriate or disruptive behaviors by teaching the child new skills for approaching situations that previously provoked negative behavior. Using both cognitive and behavioral techniques and focusing on the child more than on the parents or the family unit, CPSST helps the child gain the ability to self-manage thoughts and feelings and interact appropriately with others by developing new perspectives and solutions. The basis of the treatment is the underlying principle that children lacking constructive ways to address the environment have problematic behaviors; teaching these children ways to positively problem-solve and challenge dysfunctional thoughts improves functioning.

Purpose

The goal of CPSST is to reduce or terminate inappropriate, dysfunctional behaviors by expanding the "behavioral repertoire," including ways of cognitive processing. The behavioral repertoire is the range of ways of behaving that an individual possesses. In children with **conduct disorder**, **intermittent explosive disorder**, oppositional-defiant disorder, antisocial behaviors, aggressive acting-out, or **attention deficit/ hyperactivity disorder** with disruptive behavior, the number of ways of interpreting reality and responding to the world are limited and involve negative responses. Although CPSST originally focused on children with problem behaviors or poor relationships with others, it has generalized to a variety of different disorders in children and adults (most of the treatment research is supporting its use in children).

Description

The therapist conducts individual CPSST sessions with the child, once a week for 45 minutes to an hour, typically for several months to a year. The cognitive portion of the treatment involves changing faulty or narrow views of daily situations, confronting irrational interpretations of others' actions, challenging unhelpful assumptions that typically underlie the individual's problem behaviors, and generating alternative solutions to problems. For example, meeting with a child who has received a school suspension for becoming physically enraged at a teacher, the therapist starts by exploring the situation with the child, asking what thoughts and feelings were experienced. The child might state, "My teacher hates me. I'm always getting sent to the principal and she yells at me all the time." The therapist helps the child see some faulty ways of thinking by asking what the child has seen or experienced in the classroom previous to this incident, thus exploring the supporting evidence for the "my teacher hates me" notion. Questions would be ones that could confirm or disconfirm the assumptions, or

that identify the precipitants of the teacher disciplining the child. The therapist tries to help the child shift his or her perceptions so that, instead of seeing the student-teacher negative interactions as something external to the self, the child comes to see his or her part in the problem. This discussion also helps the child to discern opportunities to influence the outcome of the interactions. When the child makes a global, stable, and negative attribution about why the interactions with the teacher are negative—where the attitude of the teacher is the cause of the problems—the child loses the sense of having any efficacy and is liable to show poorer behavior. By changing the child's perceptions and examining different options for the child's responses in that situation, however, the child can identify ways that changing his or her own behavior could improve the outcome.

The behavioral aspect of CPSST involves **modeling** of more positive behaviors, role-playing challenging situations, and rewarding improvement in behavior, as well as providing corrective feedback on alternative (and more appropriate) ways of handling situations when undesirable behavior occurs. In each session, the child is coached on problem-solving techniques including brainstorming a number of possible solutions to difficulties, evaluating solutions, and planning the steps involving in gaining a desired goal (also called "means-end thinking"). For instance, if the child in the above example felt that the teacher's accusations were unfair, the therapist would help to come up with some options for the child to use in the event of a similar situation (such as visualizing a calming scene, using a mediator to work out the conflict, or avoiding the behaviors that precipitate a trip to the principal's office). The options generated would be discussed and evaluated as to how practical they are and how to implement them.

The child is given therapy homework of implementing these newer ways of thinking and behaving in specific types of problematic situations in school, with peers, or at home. The child might be asked to keep track of negative, externalizing thoughts by keeping a log of them for several days. The therapist would ask the child to conduct an experiment—try one of the new options and compare the results. Typically, the between-sessions work begins with the conditions that appear the easiest in which to successfully use the updated ways of thinking and behaving, gradually progressing to more complex or challenging circumstances. The child would get rewarded for trying the new techniques with praise, hugs, or earning points towards something desired.

Although the bulk of the sessions involve the individual child and the therapist, the parents are brought

KEY TERMS

Behavior modification—An approach to therapy based on the principles of operant conditioning. Behavior modification seeks to replace undesirable behaviors with preferable behaviors through the use of positive or negative reinforcement.

Cognitive-behavioral therapy—An approach to psychotherapy that emphasizes the correction of distorted thinking patterns and changing one's behaviors accordingly.

Response-contingent learning—A principle that suggests that the consequences of a behavior determine whether it will increase or decrease in frequency. Behaviors that bring about desired responses tend to decrease, while those that either remove the chance to obtain a desirable outcome, or those that cause some unpleasant or painful consequence, tend to decrease.

Social learning—Learning by observing others' responses and acquiring those responses through imitation of the role model(s).

into the therapy for a portion of the work. The parents observe the therapist and the child as they practice the new skills and are educated on how to assist the child outside the sessions. Parents learn how to correctly remind the child to use the CPSST techniques for problem solving in daily living and assist the child with the steps involved in applying these skills. Parents are also coached on how to promote the positive behaviors by rewarding their occurrence with praise, extra attention, points toward obtaining a reward desired by the child, stickers or other small indicators of positive behavior, additional privileges, or hugs (and other affectionate gestures). The scientific term for the rewarding of desired behavior is "positive reinforcement" referring to consequences that cause the desired target behavior to increase.

In research studies of outcomes, CPSST has been found to be effective in changing children's behavior. Changes in behavior have been shown to persist long-term (to a year) after completion of treatment. Success in altering undesirable behaviors is enhanced when CPSST is combined with **parent management training**. Parent management training is the in-depth education of parents or other primary caretakers in applying behavioral techniques such as positive **reinforcement** or time away from reinforcement opportunities in their parenting.

Risks

Inappropriate or inept application of cognitive-behavioral techniques such as those used in CPSST may intensify the problem. CPSST should be undertaken with a behavioral health professional (**psychologist**, **psychiatrist**, or clinical social worker) with experience in CPSST. Parents should seek therapists with good credentials, skills, and training.

Results

While individual results vary, problematic behaviors are reduced or eliminated in many children.

See also Behavior modification; Token economy system.

Resources

BOOKS

D'Zurilla, T. J., and A. M. Nezu. *Problem Solving Therapy: A Social Competence Approach to Clinical Intervention,* 2nd ed. New York: Springer Publishing Company, 1999.

Hendren, R. L. *Disruptive Behavior Disorders in Children and Adolescents.* Review of Psychiatry Series, Vol. 18, No. 2. Washington D.C.: American Psychiatric Press, 1999.

Kazdin, A.E. "Treatment of Conduct Disorders." *Conduct Disorders in Childhood and Adolescence.* Ed. J. Hill and B. Maughan. Cambridge, UK: Cambridge University Press, 2001. 408–409.

PERIODICALS

Gilbert, S. "Solution-Focused Treatment: A Model for Managed Care Success." *The Counselor* 15.5 (1997): 23–25.

Kazdin, Alan E., T. Siegel, and D. Bass. "Cognitive Problem-Solving Skills Training and Parent Management Training in the Treatment of Antisocial Behavior in Children." *Journal of Consulting and Clinical Psychology* 60 (1992): 733–47.

Matthews, W. J. "Brief Therapy: A Problem Solving Model of Change." *The Counselor* 17.4 (1999): 29–32.

Thomas, Christopher R. "Evidence-Based Practice for Conduct Disorder Symptoms." *Journal of the American Academy of Child and Adolescent Psychiatry* 45 (2006): 109–14.

ORGANIZATIONS

Association for the Advancement of Behavior Therapy. 305 Seventh Avenue, 16th Floor, New York, NY 10001-60008. Telephone: (212) 647-1890.

The American Institute for Cognitive Therapy. 136 East 57th Street, Suite 1101, New York, NY 10022. Telephone: (212) 308-2440. Web site: <http://www.cognitive therapynyc.com/child.asp>

Deborah RoschEifert, PhD
Emily Jane Willingham, PhD

Cognitive remediation

Definition

Cognitive remediation is a teaching process that targets areas of neuropsychological functioning involved in learning and basic day-to-day functioning. This terminology can be confusing because some researchers use the phrase "cognitive remediation" to refer to environmental adjustments meant to ease cognitive requirements. In this article, the term refers to a treatment approach designed to address cognitive deficits through neural rehabilitation. This approach relies on the idea, demonstrated in many recent studies of humans and primates, that the **brain** can circumvent damage or loss through repetition of the same activity.

Purpose

The goals of cognitive remediation are to bolster specific cognitive capacities that are weak. It is distinguished from a compensatory approach that seeks to get around a cognitive deficit by use of compensating strategies, such as using a notebook as a memory support in memory loss. Cognitive remediation has been applied in those who have had a traumatic brain injury (a **stroke**, tumor, or head injury), in those who have learning disabilities, and in people who have **schizophrenia**. For people with brain injury, remediation typically targets the following neuropsychological functions: attention and concentration, memory, planning, monitoring one's work or behavior, and making adjustments based on feedback. Remediation is also used to help children and adults cope with learning disabilities. Learning disabilities can interfere with progress in reading; in understanding and communicating through spoken language; in writing; in arithmetic; in understanding such nonverbal information as telling time or understanding visual information; and in comprehending social interactions and cues. Difficulties with concentration, problem solving, organization, identifying errors, and using feedback effectively are also areas that can be treated with cognitive remediation. People with schizophrenia sometimes exhibit cognitive impairment, and cognitive remediation therapy has shown promise in addressing these losses.

Description

Individuals who have had a traumatic brain injury will work with a remediator using computer programs that target one area at a time, such as attention. The individual is then helped to generalize what is learned from the program to real life. This **intervention** is usually done at a hospital, although it is not limited to clinical settings. Remediation for this group of people is considered helpful but not curative. It is typically practiced by a neuropsychologist.

Remediation for individuals with learning disabilities aims to bolster a particular area of learning or adaptation, such as in academics or socialization. Although the intervention varies according to the disability and the individual's profile of strengths and weaknesses, the remediator will make use of the person's stronger capacities to bolster the weaker ones. For example, the person might need help with written language because he frequently omits words from his sentences. Once it has been determined that the person's oral language (both receptive and expressive) is adequate and that the motor aspect of writing is intact, the remediator has an idea of the person's strengths and weaknesses in the area of writing. In this case, the remediator makes use of the person's stronger auditory (hearing-related) skills to build up the capacity to translate spoken language into written (visual) language. Specifically, the remediator might read aloud a sentence written by the student (with omissions) and ask the student to identify the mistakes that he hears. The person identifies an omission that he hears and then is shown on paper the place where the word is missing. In this way, he can learn to identify errors visually that he can already identify through the auditory modality of listening. This particular exercise fosters visual awareness of errors, which is a symptom or outcome of the deeper problem of translating language from oral to visual form.

This process can also be achieved with computer-assisted tasks. These methods focus on gradually increasing the difficulty level and complexity of cognitive functions being applied.

The process then continues with diminishing degrees of assistance. Specifically, after the student becomes more skillful in matching visual omissions with the auditory ones read by the remediator, the person himself begins to read the sentences aloud and identify the words that are missing from the sentences on the page. In the next step, he would begin to read his work silently with the same kind of scrutiny as in the previous exercise. In this manner, remediation fosters both learning and internalizing a cognitive capacity.

Cognitive remediation sessions for learning disabilities usually take place twice a week. This type of

KEY TERMS

Auditory—Pertaining to the sense of hearing.

Cognitive—Pertaining to the mental processes of memory, perception, judgment, and reasoning.

Compensatory—Counterbalancing or offsetting. A compensatory strategy is one that makes up for or balances a weakness in some area of functioning.

Modality—One of the primary forms of sensation, as vision, touch, or hearing.

Socialization—An ongoing process in which a person learns and internalizes the values and behavior patterns of his or her culture and social group.

intervention is practiced by psychologists, neuropsychologists, special educators, and learning specialists. The depth and breadth of the intervention will vary according to the remediator's professional training and his or her particular area of expertise. Some professionals specialize in working with certain types of learning disabilities; some, like psychologists, may incorporate their understanding of emotional difficulties within their work as a cognitive remediator.

Cognitive remediation can also take a strategy-oriented approach, in which the patient practices tasks that require strategizing.

Preparation

Before remediation can begin, the person being treated must receive a neuropsychological or in-depth psychological evaluation in order to identify the underlying neuropsychological capacities (i.e., language, memory, attention, visual perception, visual spatial abilities, motor abilities) that are interfering with acquiring the skills that are needed. The evaluation is also intended to rule out emotional difficulties as the primary cause of learning problems. Children with learning disabilities frequently experience feelings of inadequacy and low self-esteem that need to be addressed. If psychological difficulties, however, are the main reason for a person's academic struggles, he or she should be treated with **psychotherapy** rather than cognitive remediation.

Typical results

When remediation is targeting the problem area accurately, and the individual is actively engaging in the process, then progress should be evident in the skill area targeted, in the person's awareness of his or her area of difficulty, and in his or her awareness of some techniques and strategies that are helpful.

See also Learning disorders.

Resources

BOOKS

Gaddes, William H., and Dorothy Edgell. *Learning Disabilities and Brain Function: A Neuropsychological Approach*, 3rd ed. New York: Springer-Verlag, 1994.

Johnson, Doris J., and Helmer Myklebust. *Learning Disabilities, Educational Principles and Practices*. New York: Grune and Stratton, 1967.

Rothstein, Arden, PhD, Lawrence Benjamin, PhD, Melvin Crosby, PhD, and Katie Eisenstadt, PhD. *Learning Disorders, an Integration of Neuropsychological and Psychoanalytic Considerations*. Connecticut: International Universities Press, 1988.

PERIODICALS

Wexler, Bruce E., and Morris D. Bell. "Cognitive Remediation and Vocational Rehabilitation for Schizophrenia." *Schizophrenia Bulletin* 31 (2005): 931–41.

OTHER

LDOnLine. A Web site addressing learning disabilities and ADHD. <www.ldonline.org>.

Susan Fine, Psy.D.
Emily Jane Willingham, PhD

Cognitive retraining

Definition

Cognitive retraining is a therapeutic strategy that seeks to improve or restore a person's cognitive skills. These skills include paying attention, remembering, organizing, reasoning and understanding, problem solving, decision making, and higher level cognitive abilities. These skills are all interrelated. Cognitive retraining is one aspect of cognitive rehabilitation, a comprehensive approach to restoring such skills after **brain** injury or other disability.

Purpose

The purpose of cognitive retraining is the reduction of cognitive problems associated with brain injury, other disabilities or disorders, and/or aging. The overall purpose of the therapy is to decrease the everyday problems faced by individuals with cognitive difficulties, thereby improving the quality of their lives.

Precautions

The extent to which a person with a brain injury can recover from or compensate for cognitive problems varies with the person and their injury. Therapy must be tailored to each individual's needs and abilities. Some cognitive retraining techniques require higher levels of skill, and therefore would be more suitable for persons who have made some progress in their recovery. In addition, a person's moods and emotions have an effect on their cognitive skills. Someone who is depressed, for example, may need **psychotherapy** and/or medication before he or she can engage in and benefit from cognitive retraining. Some persons with brain injuries may find it difficult to transfer a skill learned in one setting, such as a clinic, to another setting, such as their home. Although a specific individual may show some improvement on training tasks, his or her cognitive skills may not be considered improved or restored unless there is some evidence that the skills have been transferred to everyday settings and can be maintained over time.

Description

The techniques of cognitive retraining are best known for their use with persons who have had a brain injury. However, cognitive retraining has also been used to treat **dementia**, **schizophrenia**, attention-deficit disorder, learning disabilities, **obsessive-compulsive disorder**, and cognitive changes associated with aging. Professionals from a variety of fields, such as psychology, psychiatry, occupational therapy, and **speech-language pathology**, may be involved in cognitive retraining.

Cognitive retraining includes a considerable amount of repetitive practice that targets the skills of interest. In fact, repetition is essential for the newly retrained skills to become automatic. Regular feedback is another important element of cognitive retraining, as is the use of rewards, such as money. Retraining usually begins with simpler skills and proceeds to more complicated skills. The therapist may address cognitive skills while the person is practicing real-life tasks, in an effort to improve their performance of these tasks. In fact, practicing skills in the ways and settings they will be used in real life is critical to the success of retraining efforts. The length of time for cognitive training varies according to the type and extent of the injury and the type of retraining skills used. For example, retraining memory may take months or years. In contrast, it may take only a few days or weeks to retrain someone to organize his or her home or workplace.

The use of computerization for cognitive retraining has become an increasingly common practice. In particular, researchers have focused on developing a "mixed-reality" system, producing a virtual reality environment for the person undergoing rehabilitation. This system, called in one study a "Human Experience Modeler," places the patient in a context similar to reality—such as home or work—except that the stimuli can be controlled and the patient's experiences captured with automated feedback provided. These approaches have shown some promising success in pilot studies.

Types of cognitive retraining

- Attention and concentration retraining. This type of cognitive retraining aims to improve several abilities, including focusing attention, dividing attention, maintaining attention while reducing the effects of boredom and fatigue, and resisting distraction. Attention has been considered the foundation of other more complicated cognitive skills, and therefore an important skill for cognitive retraining. This area of cognitive retraining has been widely researched, and has been shown to improve patients' abilities in various tasks related to attention.

- Memory retraining. Memory retraining involves teaching the patient several strategies that can be used to recall certain types of information. For example, rhymes may be used as a memory aid. A series of numbers, such as a phone number with an area code, may be broken down into smaller groups. A person may be taught to go through each letter of the alphabet until he or she remembers someone's name. Both memory and organization problems are common and often disabling after head injury.

- Organizational skills retraining. This approach is used when the person has difficulty keeping track of or finding items, doing tasks in a set order, and/or doing something in a timely manner. Strategies may include having one identified place for an item ("a place for everything and everything in its place"). In addition, the person can be taught to keep the items that are used most frequently closer to him or her (the front or the lower shelves of a cabinet, drawer, closet, or desk, for example). Items that are often used together (such as comb and brush, toothbrush and toothpaste) are placed beside each other. Items may be put into categories (allocating decorations to a specific holiday, such as the Fourth of July or Thanksgiving, for example). These strategies help individuals function better in their home or work environment.

- Reasoning. Reasoning refers to the ability to connect and organize information in a logical, rational way.

Reasoning retraining techniques include: listing the facts or reality of a situation; excluding irrelevant facts or details; putting the steps to solve a problem in a logical order; and avoiding irrational thinking, such as jumping to conclusions based on incomplete information, or focusing on the negative aspects of the situation and ignoring the positive. When the person can connect relevant information in a logical way, they are better able to understand or comprehend it.

- Problem solving. Problem-solving retraining aims to help people define a problem; come up with possible solutions to it; discuss the solution(s) with others and listen to their advice; review the various possible solutions from many perspectives; and evaluate whether the problem was solved after going through these steps. This sequence may be repeated several times until the problem is solved. This process is referred to as "SOLVE," from the first letter of the name of each step: Specify; Options; Listen; Vary; and Evaluate. The "SOLVE" technique is more appropriate for use with individuals at a higher level of functioning.

- Decision making. Decision-making retraining is used when a person must choose among a number of options. The goal of this retraining is to help him or her consider the decision thoroughly before taking any action. The considerations may range from such practical matters as money, people, rules and policies, to personality issues.

- Executive skills. Executive skills retraining refers to teaching individuals how to monitor themselves, control their thinking and actions, think in advance, set goals, manage time, act in socially acceptable ways, and transfer skills to new situations. These are higher-level cognitive skills. Charts and videotapes may be used to monitor behavior, and a variety of questions, tasks, and games may be used in retraining these skills.

Preparation

Cognitive retraining usually takes place in a quiet room without distractions. It is also important for the person to feel relaxed and calm while they are being retrained in cognitive skills. Engaging in cognitive retraining is not recommended when someone is emotional distressed, e.g., after the recent loss of a loved one. The therapist usually evaluates the person's level of cognitive skills and the extent of their cognitive problems before retraining begins. This evaluation provides a way to monitor improvement by comparing the patient's skill levels during and after retraining to his or her skill levels before retraining. Cognitive

KEY TERMS

Cognitive—Pertaining to the mental processes of memory, perception, judgment, and reasoning.

Executive skills—Higher-level cognitive skills that are used when a person makes and carries out plans, organizes and performs complex tasks, etc.

retraining requires patience and persistence on the part of everyone involved.

Aftercare

The therapist will try to promote the transfer of skills learned using cognitive retraining techniques to the settings of the patient's everyday life. Training may be continued until the patient's skills are improved, transferred to, and maintained in real world activities.

Risks

It is important for the therapist, patient, and the patient's friends or family members not to assume that improvement on training exercises and tests automatically leads to transfer of the skills to real-life settings.

Typical results

Cognitive retraining may be considered successful if performance on a behavior related to a particular cognitive skill has improved. It is ultimately successful if it helps the injured person improve his or her functioning and meet his or her needs in real-life situations and settings.

See also Attention-deficit/hyperactivity disorder; Dementia; Learning disabilities; Schizophrenia.

Resources

BOOKS

Mateer, Catherine A., and Sarah Raskin. "Cognitive Rehabilitation." *Rehabilitation of the Adult and Child with Traumatic Brain Injury,* 3rd ed. M. Rosenthal, E. R. Griffith, J. S. Kreutzer, and B. Pentland, eds. Philadelphia: F. A. Davis, 1999.

Parente, Rick, and D. Herrmann. *Retraining Cognition: Techniques and Applications.* Gaithersburg, MD: Aspen, 1996.

Ylvisaker, Mark, and Timothy J. Feeney. *Collaborative Brain Injury Intervention.* San Diego: Singular, 1998.

PERIODICALS

Buhlmann, Ulrike, and others. "Cognitive Retraining for Organizational Impairment in Obsessive-Compulsive Disorder." *Psychiatry Research* 144 (2006): 109–16.

Fidopiastis, C.M., and others. "Human Experience Modeler: Context-Driven Cognitive Retraining to Facilitate Transfer of Learning." *CyberPsychology and Behavior* 9 (2006): 183–87.

OTHER

American Brain Tumor Association. "Becoming Well Again through Cognitive Retraining." (2006) Available online at: <http://www.abta.org/wellagain2.php>.

Joneis Thomas, PhD
Emily Jane Willingham, PhD

Cognitive self-regulation *see* **Self-control strategies**

Cognitive therapy *see* **Cognitive-behavioral therapy**

Communication skills and disorders

Definition

Communication skills are the skills needed to use language (spoken, written, signed, or otherwise communicated) to interact with others, and communication disorders are problems related to the development of these skills.

Description

Language employs symbols—words, gestures, or spoken sounds—to represent objects and ideas. Communication of language begins with spoken sounds combined with gestures, relying on two different types of skills. Children first acquire the skills to receive communications; that is, the ability to listen and understand what they hear (supported by accompanying gestures). Next, they begin experimenting with expressing themselves through speaking and gesturing. Speaking begins as repetitive syllables, followed by words, phrases, and sentences. Later, children learn the skills of reading and writing, which are the written forms of communication. Although milestones are described for development of these skills, many children begin speaking significantly earlier or later than the milestone date. Parents should refrain from attaching too much significance to either deviation from the average. When a child's deviation from the average does cause the parents concern, they can contact a pediatrician or other professional for advice.

Spoken language problems are referred to using a number of designations, including language delay, language disability, or a specific type of language disability. In general, experts distinguish between those people who seem to be slow in developing spoken language (language delay) and those who seem to have difficulty achieving a milestone of spoken language (language disorders). Language disorders include **stuttering**; articulation disorders, such as substituting one sound for another (tandy for candy), omitting a sound (canny for candy), or distorting a sound (shlip for sip); and voice disorders, such as inappropriate pitch, volume, or quality. Causes can be related to hearing, nerve/muscle disorders, head injury, viral diseases, **mental retardation**, drug **abuse**, or cleft lip or palate.

The *Diagnostic and Statistical Manual of Mental Disorders,* fourth edition, text revision (also known as the *DSM-IV-TR*), published by the American Psychiatric Association, lists the following disorders as communication disorders:

- Expressive language disorder: Disorder characterized by impairment in expressive language development.
- Mixed receptive-expressive language disorder: Impairment in both receptive and expressive language development. The affected child has a more difficult time understanding and expressing language as compared to peers.
- Phonological disorder: Inability to use expected speech sounds appropriate for the child's age and dialect.
- Stuttering: Unexpected disturbances in the normal patterns and flow of speech.
- Communication disorder not otherwise specified: This may be diagnosed when a child has an irregularity in speech or a difficulty (in voice or pitch, etc.) but the child's symptoms do not exactly match any of the specific categories of impairment that the *DSM* recognizes.

See also Speech-language pathology.

Resources

BOOKS

American Psychiatric Association. *Diagnostic and Statistical Manual of Mental Disorders,* 4th ed., Text rev. Washington D.C.: American Psychiatric Association, 2000.

PERIODICALS

Cowley, Geoffrey. "The Language Explosion." *Newsweek* 129 (Spring–Summer 1997): 16–22.

ORGANIZATIONS

American Speech-Language-Hearing Association. 10801 Rockville Pike, Rockville, MD 20852. Telephone: (800) 638-8255. <http://www.asha.org>.

The Childhood Apraxia of Speech Association of North America. <http://www.apraxia-kids.org/>.

National Institute on Deafness and Other Communication Disorders, National Institutes of Health. Bethesda, MD, 20892. <http://www.nidcd.nih.gov/>. This agency also has a Web site, "What is voice, what is speech, what is language?" at: <http://www.nidcd.nih.gov/health/voice/whatis_vsl.htm>.

The National Institutes of Health. <http://health.nih.gov/result.asp/612>.

Emily Jane Willingham, PhD

Community mental health

Definition

Community mental health is a decentralized pattern of mental health or other services for people with mental illnesses. Community-based care is designed to supplement and decrease the need for more costly inpatient mental health care delivered in hospitals. Community mental health care may be more accessible and responsive to local needs because it is based in a variety of community settings rather than aggregating and isolating patients and patient care in central hospitals. Community mental health assessment, which has grown into a science called psychiatric epidemiology, is a field of research measuring rates of mental disorder upon which mental health care systems can be developed and evaluated.

Community mental health centers

In the United States, an increase in community mental health care delivery began in the 1960s when President John F. Kennedy signed the 1963 Community Mental Health Centers (CMHC) Act (Public Law #88-164). Growing community mental health capacities were intended to complement and mirror trends toward fewer hospital stays and shorter visits for mental illness. This restructuring of mental health service delivery has occurred in the context of evolving fiscal responsibilities, however. The goals and practices of community mental health have been complicated and revised by economic and political changes.

The National Institute of Mental Health (NIMH) initially developed a CMHC program in the 1960s. CMHCs were designed to provide comprehensive services for people with mental illness, locate these services closer to home, and provide an umbrella of integrated services for a catchment area of 125,000-250,000 people. CMHCs were designed to provide prevention, early treatment, and continuity of care in communities, promoting social integration of people with mental health needs.

Competing public interests

At the outset, CMHCs were providing outpatient care to people with less severe, episodic, or acute mental health problems. In the 1980s, more people with serious mental illness began using CMHCs, due in part to **deinstitutionalization**, and following the redirection and capping of federal funds for local mental health care. With growing awareness of the homeless mentally ill, state-funded CMHCs faced new challenges, and their work became fragmented according to catchment areas of responsibility, leaving some urban centers overburdened, while others maintained locally funded operations, limiting responsibility for their area only.

The growth of local community mental health centers was an example of competing governmental interests and authorities. Growing numbers of CMHCs were mandated federally and to be funded by local communities, bypassing state control. This growth in outpatient capacity was later used to complement decreases in inpatient hospital care, or deinstitutionalization, which reduced the costs of diminishing and state-funded mental hospitals.

Policies to improve public mental health care

Community mental health centers were the first of several programmatic attempts to improve mental health care in the latter part of the twentieth century. A second was when the federal government recommended Community Support Programs (CSPs) in 1977–1978 in response to problems associated with deinstitutionalization. CSPs focused on providing direct care and rehabilitation for the chronically mentally ill. However federal support for mental health care and CMHCs in particular was reduced in 1980–1981, with the repeal of the Mental Health Systems Act and the federal budgeting actions that cut funding and provided it instead through block grants to states.

A third initiative has been to expand the national capacity for children's mental health care under the Child and Adolescent Service System Program (CASSP), beginning in the 1980s. Principles for this system of care included a continuum of services, including mental health. The expansion of mental health classification systems and the **Diagnostic and Statistical**

Manual of Mental Disorders, or *DSM*, has helped identify and treat a growing number of children and youth. A fourth initiative was a joint effort by the Robert Wood Johnson Foundation and the department of Housing and Urban Development. Their Program on Chronic Mental Illness (PCMI) promoted the integration of regional mental health authorities in nine cities. Coordinated local mental health systems run by local mental health authorities remain an important goal of mental health policy. As this program ended, another program, Access to Community Care and Effective Services and Supports (ACCESS) began in 1993, ending in 1998. This nine-state demonstration project targeted homeless populations with mental illness.

Finally, many private and public health systems have moved towards managed mental health care, which has become also known as behavioral health care. This form of cost containment is a constellation of organizational reforms, financing systems, and regulatory techniques. **Managed care,** which began its expansion throughout health care in the 1990s, provided mental health care policy new challenges. While federal health policy and medical assistance provide reimbursement for mental health care and for people with mental illness, the regulation of these systems has grown increasingly complex.

The United States Department of Health and Human Services has developed the Comprehensive Community Mental Health Services Program for Children and Their Families with the goal of improving the delivery of mental health services to families with children and adolescents who have serious emotional disturbances. According to their information, as many as two-thirds of children and adolescents in the United States do not receive the mental health services they need. This fraction in absolute numbers translates to as many as 6.3 million children. The program is designed to bring together various children's mental health programs into a single plan or system of care, led by the family. Grants from this program, which was first authorized in 1992, target improvements and expansions of such systems.

Resources

BOOKS

Aneshensel, Carol, and Jo Phelan, eds. *Handbook of the Sociology of Mental Health.* New York: Kluwer Academic, 1999.

Scheid, Teresa, and Allan Horwitz, eds. *Handbook for the Study of Mental Health.* New York: Cambridge University Press, 1999.

PERIODICALS

Grob, Gerald. "Government and Mental Health Policy: A Structural Analysis." *Milbank Quarterly* 72.3 (1994): 471–500.

Rothbard, Aileen B., So-Young Min, Eri Kino, and Yin-Ling Irene Wong. "Long-Term Effectiveness of the ACCESS Program Linking Community Mental Health Services to Homeless Persons with Serious Mental Illness." *The Journal of Behavioral Health and Services and Research* 31 (2004): 441–49.

ORGANIZATIONS

American Psychiatric Association. 1400 K Street NW, Washington, DC 20005. <http://www.psych.org>.

American Sociological Association. 1307 New York Ave., Washington, DC 20005-4701. <http://www.asanet.org>.

National Institute of Mental Health. 6001 Executive Boulevard, Rm. 8184, MSC 9663, Bethesda, MD 20892-9663. (301) 443-4513. <http://www.nimh.nih.gov>. This agency also maintains a Web site with information about how to locate community mental health services locally. It is available at: <http://www.nimh.nih.gov/healthinformation/gettinghelp.cfm>.

Substance Abuse and Mental Health Services Administration (SAMHSA), Center for Mental Health Services (CMHS), Department of Health and Human Services. 5600 Fishers Lane, Rockville MD 20857. <http://www.samhsa.org>.

Michael Polgar, PhD
Emily Jane Willingham, PhD

Compliance

Definition

Compliance with appropriate, recommended, and prescribed mental health treatments simply means that a person is following a doctor's orders. Compliance is more likely when there is agreement and confidence regarding the medical **diagnosis** and prognosis. Compliance is complicated by uncertainty about the nature of an illness and/or the effects of certain treatments, particularly medications. Some practitioners argue that the concept of "compliance" is paternalistic and does not include the patient enough in the decision-making process. Many recent studies have focused more on the concept of shared decision making with a strong relationship between the patient and practitioner. Either way, the nature of this relationship can be a strong determinant of how well a patient adheres to an agreed-upon course.

In everyday usage, the term compliance means deference and obedience, elevating the authority of medical expertise. Alternatively, adherence to medical advice refers to a somewhat more informed and equitable decision by a consumer to stick with appropriate medical treatment. In any case, a mental health treatment cannot be effective or even evaluated if a consumer does not follow a doctor's orders. A mental health treatment that is effective for one disorder may not be beneficial for other disorders, and diagnoses may evolve over time, complicating the issue of compliance.

Health providers and consumers

From a health provider's viewpoint, for medical treatments to have their desired effects, complying or conforming to treatments is absolutely necessary. The concept of medication management reflects this idea that the provider is responsible and in control, while the consumer is a docile body who is incapacitated by disease or condition. From the perspective of health consumers, adherence to medical treatment is enhanced when there is a good health-care relationship and when consumers openly share their health beliefs and experience of illness with their provider.

Problems with compliance

In mental health care, uncertainty about compliance is a challenging source of variation in the effectiveness of treatments. Noncompliance can represent a significant risk and cost to the medical system. For providers, partial compliance or discontinuation of medications represents the difficulty of maintaining treatment successes over time. Problems with compliance are often attributed to the consumer, but may also reflect the appropriateness of a medication or treatment.

Compliance rates

Rates of compliance with mental health appointments are the greatest challenge (estimated in one hospital at 91%), while medication noncompliance is the second most challenging problem in the treatment of persons with mental illness. Mental health medication compliance can be determined by questioning patients, counting pills or prescriptions, and through drug monitoring with urine, blood, or other test measures. Overall, recent research estimates compliance to be 58%. Patients who report lower rates are often considered unreliable indicators of compliance, while physicians report higher rates. Compliance with antidepressant medications is higher, on average (65%). Mental health medication compliance rates are only somewhat lower than medication compliance in other types of health care, which have been estimated at 76%.

Explaining variation in compliance

Research in psychiatry, psychology, and sociology provides many explanations for variations in compliance. In psychiatry, clinical problems such as drug or alcohol **abuse** are sometimes used to explain noncompliance. Patients may also discontinue taking medications because of unwanted side effects. Health beliefs and patient-provider relationships are also recognized. In psychology and sociology, health beliefs and behaviors (in context of family, work, etc.) may enhance or limit compliance. If an individual's family member supports medication compliance, and the individual believes in the medicine's benefits, compliance may be enhanced (similar to a placebo effect). If an individual feels that a medicine makes him or her drowsy and affects work, compliance may be reduced. People who have limited access to or trust in doctors or medical science, and people whose faith precludes them from certain types of medical care, are less likely to comply with treatment recommendations.

To a large extent, patient compliance is a direct reflection of the quality of the doctor-patient relationship. When provider and consumer achieve a successful treatment alliance, as is advocated as part of the shared decision-making approach, and when the treatment is practical and beneficial for both the provider and the consumer, cooperation reduces concerns about treatment for both parties. When consumers are empowered and motivated to improve their health with the help of a doctor, compliance or adherence to treatment is higher. When there is distrust, disagreement, or misunderstanding involved, as when mental health status is uncertain or treatment side effects are unwelcome, compliance is lower. One British study found that patients with mental disorders were likely to prefer the form of treatment recommended by psychiatrists with whom they had good relationships, even if the treatment itself was painful. Some patients preferred **electroconvulsive therapy** (ECT) to tranquilizers for **depression** because they had built up trusting relationships with the doctors who used ECT, and perceived the doctors who recommended medications as **bullying** and condescending. Because noncompliant consumers are less likely to continue in care, they are also less likely to find helpful providers or successful treatments. Thus, noncompliance with treatment may become a self-fulfilling cycle.

Compliance is higher when treatments, including medications, help consumers feel better, when a family supports the treatment, and when taking medication prevents **relapse** of symptoms. However, as mentioned, people may be distressed by potential side effects of any medication, including those psychiatric medications that limit functioning. Limited functioning through drowsiness, also a problem of the older generation of antihistamines, is the best example. It is an effect of many medicines, particularly those for mental disorders. Other unwelcome side effects of various psychiatric medications include weight gain, involuntary movements such as muscle twitching, and impaired coordination. Consumers may feel embarrassed about taking medication, especially medications for illnesses that have a strong social **stigma** associated with them; may have difficulty getting a prescription for medication; and may have financial problems paying for treatment or medication. In some cases, when a patient is noncompliant or perceived to be at odds with treatment recommendations, they may risk losing autonomy over medical decisions. When at risk to self or others, people who are medication noncompliant may be pressured or forced to take medication at the risk of being involuntarily hospitalized.

Multiple challenges in mental health care

Compliance rates reflect the proportion of individuals in treatment who have the highest possibility of successful treatment. Noncompliance rates reflect those individuals who have either discontinued or avoided treatment, and thus have lower probabilities of treatment success. Sometimes patients do not want to get rid of their symptoms (mania, for example), or patients may not consider their experiences (symptoms) to be indicative of a disorder. In addition, successful mental health care is hampered by the fact that many people with mental health problems either do not use or lack access to mental health care.

The National Co-morbidity Survey found that only 40% of individuals with serious mental illness receive any treatment in a given year, and 39% of this group receives minimally adequate care. This means that merely 15% of all people in need receive minimally adequate care. Therefore, compliance with treatment is part of a larger national challenge to provide quality mental health care and to use it well.

Resources

BOOKS

Horwitz, Allan. *Creating Mental Illness*. Chicago: University of Chicago Press, 2002.

Pescosolido, Bernice, Carol Boyer, and Keri Lubell. "The Social Dynamics of Responding to Mental Health Problems." *Handbook for the Study of Mental Health*. T. Scheid, and A. Horwitz, eds. New York: Cambridge University Press. 1999.

Pescosolido, Bernice, and Carol Boyer. "How Do People Come to Use Mental Health Services?" *Handbook of the Sociology of Mental Health*. C. Aneshensel and J. Phelan, eds. New York: Kluwer Academic, 1999.

PERIODICALS

Adams, Jared R., and, Robert E. Drake. "Shared Decision-Making and Evidence-Based Practice." *Community Mental Health Journal* 42 (2006): 87–105.

Bebbington, P. E. "The Contend and Context of Compliance." *International Clinical Psychopharmacology* 9 (Jan. 1995): 41–50.

Centorrino, Franca, Miguel Hernan, Giuseppa Drago-Ferrante, and others. "Factors Associated with Noncompliance with Psychiatric Outpatient Visits." *Psychiatric Services* 52 (March 2001): 378–80.

Cramer, Joyce, and Robert Rosenheck. "Compliance with Medication Regimens for Mental and Physical Disorders." *Psychiatric Services* 49 (Feb. 1998): 196–201.

Helbling, Josef, Vladeta Ajdacic-Gross, Christoph Lauber, Ruth Weyermann, Tom Burns, and Wulf Rossler. "Attitudes to Antipsychotic Drugs and their Side Effects: A Comparison Between General Practitioners and the General Population." *BioMed Central Psychiatry* 6 (2006): 42.

Wang, Philip, Olga Demler, and Ronald Kessler. "Adequacy of Treatment for Serious Mental Illness in the United States." *American Journal of Public Health* 92.1 (2002): 92–98.

ORGANIZATIONS

American Psychiatric Association. 1400 K Street NW, Washington, DC 20005. <http://www.psych.org>.

American Sociological Association. 1307 New York Ave., Washington, DC 20005-4701. <http://www.asanet.org>.

National Institute of Mental Health. 6001 Executive Boulevard, Rm. 8184, MSC 9663, Bethesda, MD 20892-9663. Telephone: (301) 443-4513. <http://www.nimh.nih.gov>.

Substance Abuse and Mental Health Services Administration (SAMHSA), Center for Mental Health Services (CMHS), Department of Health and Human Services. 5600 Fishers Lane, Rockville MD 20857. <http://www.samhsa.org>.

Michael Polgar, PhD
Emily Jane Willingham, PhD

Compulsion

Definition

A compulsion is a behavior or mental act performed to help reduce **anxiety** or distress.

Description

Compulsions are not voluntary activities and are not performed for pleasure. Instead, a person with a compulsion feels the need to engage in a particular behavior to relieve the **stress** and discomfort which would become overwhelming if the activity were not performed in a specific, repeated manner. Examples of compulsive motor activities are washing hands until raw, repeatedly checking the security of a locked door, and arranging and rearranging items in a set order. Some examples of compulsory mental acts are counting or silently repeating specific words. If a person troubled by compulsions is unable to perform such activities, stress and discomfort increase. The performance of the acts relieves distress, but only temporarily.

Often, compulsions are not acts that could logically be expected to relieve or prevent the fears that inspire them. For example, a person might feel compelled to count numbers in a certain order to "undo" the perceived damage or threat that follows a thought or behavior. Or a person might check to make sure a door is locked every few minutes. Compulsions, in some cases, are attempts to undo obsessions and are usually not successful.

See also Obsession; Obsessive-compulsive disorder.

Resources

BOOKS

VandenBos, Gary R. (ed). *APA Dictionary of Psychology.* Washington, DC: American Psychological Association, 2007.

Dean A. Haycock, Ph.D.
Ruth A. Wienclaw, Ph.D.

Compulsive gambling *see* **Pathological gambling disorder**

Compulsive skin picking *see* **Dermatotillomania**

Computed tomography

Definition

Computed tomography scanning, also called CT scan, CAT scan, or computerized axial tomography, is a diagnostic tool that provides views of internal body structures using x rays. In the field of mental health, a CT scan may be used when a patient seeks medical help for symptoms that could possibly be caused by a **brain** tumor. These symptoms may include headaches, emotional abnormalities, or intellectual or memory problems. In these cases, a CT scan may be performed to "rule out" a tumor, so that other tests can be performed in order to establish an accurate **diagnosis**.

Purpose

CT scans are used to image bone, soft tissues, and air. Since the 1990s, CT equipment has become more affordable and available. CT scans have become the imaging exam of choice for the diagnoses of most solid tumors. Because the computerized image is sharp, focused, and three-dimensional, many structures can be better differentiated (visualized) when compared with standard x rays.

Common indications for CT scans include:

- Sinus studies. The CT scan can show details of sinusitis, bone fractures, and the presence of bony tumor involvement. Physicians may order a CT scan of the sinuses to provide an accurate map for surgery.
- Brain studies. Brain CT scans can detect hematomas (blood clotted mass), tumors, strokes, aneurysms (a blood vessel that ruptures), and degenerative or infected brain tissue. The introduction of CT scanning, especially spiral CT, has helped reduce the need for more invasive procedures such as cerebral angiography (inserting a wire through an artery to where it will reach brain vessels for visualization in real time).
- Body scans. CT scans of the chest, abdomen, spine, and extremities can detect the presence of tumors, enlarged lymph nodes, abnormal collection of fluid, and vertebral disc disease. These scans can also be helpful in evaluating the extent of bone breakdown in osteoporosis.
- Heart and aorta scans. CT scans can focus on the thoracic (chest) or abdominal aorta to locate aneurysms and other possible aortic diseases. A newer type of CT scan, called electron beam CT, can be used to detect calcium buildup in arteries. Because it is a new technology, it is not yet widely used and its indications are not yet well-defined.

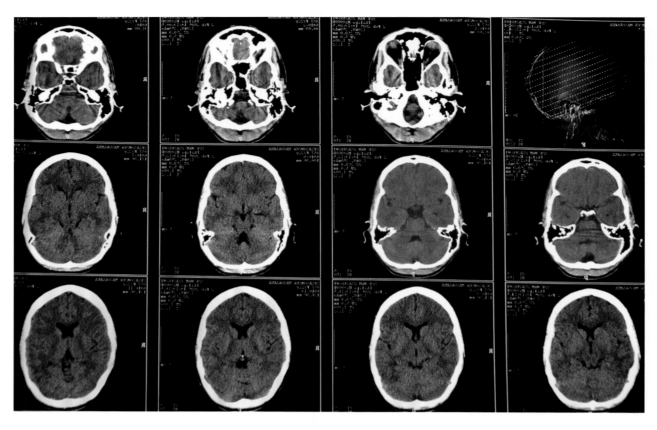

CT scan of a human brain. *(Konrad Zelazowski/Alamy)*

• Chest scans. CT scans of the chest are useful in distinguishing tumors and in detailing accumulation of fluid in chest infections.

Precautions

Pregnant women or those who could possibly be pregnant should not have a CT scan, particularly a full body or abdominal scan, unless the diagnostic benefits outweigh the risks. If the exam is necessary for obstetric purposes, technologists are instructed not to repeat films if there are errors. Pregnant patients receiving a CT scan or any x ray exam away from the abdominal area may be protected by a lead apron; most radiation, known as scatter, travels through the body, however, and is not totally blocked by the apron.

Contrast agents are often used in CT exams, though some types of tumors are better seen without it. Patients should discuss the use of contrast agents with their doctor, and should be asked to sign a consent form prior to the administration of contrast. One of the common contrast agents, iodine, can cause allergic reactions. Patients who are known to be allergic to iodine or shellfish should inform the physician prior to the CT scan; a combination of medications can be given to such patients before the scan to prevent or minimize the reaction. Contrast agents may also put patients with diabetes at risk of kidney failure, particularly those taking the medication glucophage.

Description

Computed tomography, is a combination of focused x-ray beams and the computerized production of an image. Introduced in the early 1970s, this radiologic procedure has advanced rapidly and is now widely used, sometimes in the place of standard x rays.

CT equipment

A CT scan may be performed in a hospital or outpatient imaging center. Although the equipment looks large and intimidating, it is very sophisticated and fairly comfortable. The patient is asked to lie on a gantry, or narrow table, that slides into the center of the scanner. The scanner looks like a doughnut and is round in the middle, which allows the x-ray beam to rotate around the patient. The scanner section may also be tilted slightly to allow for certain cross-sectional angles.

CT procedure

The gantry moves very slightly as the precise adjustments for each sectional image are made. A technologist watches the procedure from a window and views the images on a computer screen. Generally, patients are alone during the procedure, though exceptions are sometimes made for pediatric patients. Communication is possible via an intercom system.

It is essential that the patient lie very still during the procedure to prevent motion blurring. In some studies, such as chest CTs, the patient will be asked to hold his or her breath during image capture.

Following the procedure, films of the images are usually printed for the radiologist and referring physician to review. A radiologist can also interpret CT exams on the computer screen. The procedure time will vary in length depending on the area being imaged. Average study times are from 30 to 60 minutes. Some patients may be concerned about claustrophobia (a feeling of being "closed in") but the width of the "doughnut" portion of the scanner is such that many patients can be reassured of openness. Doctors may consider giving **sedatives** to patients who have severe claustrophobia or difficulty lying still (such as small children).

The CT image

While traditional x-ray machines image organs in two dimensions, often resulting in organs in the front of the body being superimposed over those in the back, CT scans allow for a more three-dimensional effect. CT images can be likened to slices in a loaf of bread. Precise sections of the body can be located and imaged as cross-sectional views. The screen before the technologist shows a computer's analysis of each section detected by the x-ray beam. Thus, various densities of tissue can be easily distinguished.

Contrast agents

Contrast agents are often used in CT exams and in other radiology procedures to illuminate certain details of anatomy more clearly. Some contrasts are natural, such as air or water. A water-based contrast agent is sometimes administered for specific diagnostic purposes. Barium sulfate is commonly used in gastroenterology procedures. The patient may drink this contrast or receive it in an enema. Oral or rectal contrast is usually given when examining the abdomen or cells, but not when scanning the brain or chest. Iodine is the most widely used intravenous contrast agent and is given through an intravenous needle.

If contrast agents are used in the CT exam, these will be administered several minutes before the study begins. Patients undergoing abdominal CT may be asked to drink a contrast medium. Some patients may experience a salty taste, flushing of the face, warmth or slight nausea, or hives from an intravenous contrast injection. Technologists and radiologists have the equipment and training to help patients through these minor reactions and to handle more severe reactions. Severe reactions to contrast are rare, but do occur.

Newer types of CT scans

The spiral CT scan, also called a helical CT, is a newer version of CT. This type of scan is continuous in motion and allows for the continuous re-creation of images. For example, traditional CT allows the technologist to take slices at very small and precise intervals one after the other. Spiral CT allows for a continuous flow of images, without stopping the scanner to move to the next image slice. A major advantage of spiral CT is the ability to reconstruct images anywhere along the length of the study area. Because the procedure is faster, patients are required to lie still for shorter periods of time. The ability to image contrast more rapidly after it is injected, when it is at its highest level, is another advantage of spiral CT's high speed.

Electron beam CT scans are another newer type of CT technology that can be used to detect calcium buildup in arteries. These calcium deposits are potential risk factors for coronary artery disease. Electron beam CT scans take pictures much more quickly than conventional CTs, and are therefore better able to produce clear images of the heart as it pumps blood. Because it is a newer and expensive test, electron beam CT scanning is not widely used.

Some facilities will have spiral, electron, and conventional CT available. Although spiral is more advantageous for many applications, conventional CT is still a superior and precise method for imaging many tissues and structures. The physician will evaluate which type of CT works best for the specific exam purpose.

Preparation

If a contrast medium is administered, the patient may be asked to fast for about four to six hours prior to the procedure. Patients will usually be given a gown (like a typical hospital gown) to be worn during the procedure. All metal and jewelry should be removed to avoid artifacts on the film. Depending on the type of study, patients may also be required to remove dentures.

Aftercare

Generally, no aftercare is required following a CT scan. Immediately following the exam, the technologist will continue to watch the patient for possible adverse contrast reactions. Patients are instructed to advise the technologist of any symptoms, particularly respiratory difficulty. The site of contrast injection will be bandaged and may feel tender following the exam.

Risks

Radiation exposure from a CT scan is similar to, though higher than, that of a conventional x ray. Although this is a risk to pregnant women, the risk for other adults is minimal and should produce no effects. Severe contrast reactions are rare, but they are a risk of many CT procedures.

Normal results

Normal findings on a CT exam show bone, the most dense tissue, as white areas. Tissues and fat will show as various shades of gray, and fluids will be gray or black. Air will also look black. Intravenous, oral, and rectal contrast appear as white areas. The radiologist can determine if tissues and organs appear normal by the sensitivity of the gray shadows.

Abnormal results

Abnormal results may show different characteristics of tissues within organs. Accumulations of blood or other fluids where they do not belong may be detected. Radiologists can differentiate among types of tumors throughout the body by viewing details of their makeup.

Sinus studies

The increasing availability and lowered cost of CT scanning has lead to its increased use in sinus studies, either as a replacement for a sinus x ray or as a follow-up to an abnormal sinus radiograph. The sensitivity of CT allows for the location of areas of sinus infection, particularly chronic infection. Sinus tumors will show as shades of gray indicating the difference in their density from that of normal tissues in the area.

Brain studies

The precise differences in density allowed by CT scan can clearly show tumors, strokes, or lesions in the brain area as altered densities. These lighter or darker areas on the image may indicate a tumor or hematoma within the brain and skull area. Different types of tumors can be identified by the presence of edema (fluid), by the tissue's density, or by studying blood

---

KEY TERMS

Aneurysm—A symptomless bulging of a weak arterial wall that can rupture, leading to stroke.

Cerebral ateriography—A procedure that allows a wire to be inserted in blood vessels in the brain which generates an image of diseases in these arteries.

Contrast (agent, medium)—A substance injected into the body that illuminates certain structures that would otherwise be hard to see on the radiograph (film).

Gantry—A name for the couch or table used in a CT scan. The patient lies on the gantry while it slides into the x-ray scanner.

Hematoma—An accumulation of blood, often clotted, in a body tissue or organ, usually caused by a break or tear in a blood vessel.

Metastasis—Secondary cancer, or cancer that has spread from one body organ or tissue to another.

Osteoporosis—A loss of bone minerals.

Radiologist—A medical doctor specially trained in radiology (x ray) interpretation and its use in the diagnosis of disease and injury.

Spiral CT—Also referred to as helical CT, this method allows for continuous 360-degree x-ray image capture.

Thoracic—Refers to the chest area. The thorax runs between the abdomen and neck and is encased in the ribs.

---

vessel location and activity. The speed and convenience of CT often allows for detection of hemorrhage (bleeding) before symptoms even occur.

Body scans

The body CT scan can identify abnormal body structures and organs. A CT scan may indicate tumors or cysts, enlarged lymph nodes, abnormal collections of fluids, blood, fat, or cancer metastasis. Tumors resulting from metastasis (movement of the cancer from the primary site of cancer growth to a distant site) are different in makeup than primary (original) tumors.

Chest scans

In addition to those findings that may indicate aortic aneurysms (rupture of the largest artery in the body), chest CT studies can show other problems in

---

the heart and lungs, and distinguish between an aortic aneurysm and a tumor adjacent to the aorta. CT will not only show differences between air, water, tissues and bone, but will also assign numerical values to the various densities. Coin-sized lesions in the lungs may be indicative of tuberculosis or tumors. CT will help distinguish among the two. Enlarged lymph nodes in the chest area may indicate Hodgkin's disease (a blood disorder).

Resources

BOOKS

Abeloff, M. *Clinical Oncology,* 2nd Ed. Orlando, Florida: Churchill Livingstone, Inc., 2000.
Springhouse Corporation. *Illustrated Guide to Diagnostic Tests.* Springhouse, PA: Springhouse Corporation, 1998.

PERIODICALS

Holbert, J. M. "Role of Spiral Computed Tomography in the Diagnosis of Pulmonary Embolism in the Emergency Department." *Annals of Emergency Medicine* (May 1999): 520-28.

ORGANIZATIONS

American College of Radiology. 1891 Preston White Drive, Reston, VA 22091. Telephone: (800) ACR-LINE. <http://www.acr.org>.

Laith Farid Gulli, M.D.
Teresa G. Norris, R.N.

A bully threatens a smaller boy. Violent behavior is one symptom of conduct disorder. *(Don Hammond/Design Pics/ Corbis)*

Conduct disorder

Definition

Conduct disorder is a childhood behavior disorder characterized by aggressive and destructive activities that cause disruptions in the child's natural environments such as home, school, church, or the neighborhood. The overriding feature of conduct disorder is the repetitive and persistent pattern of behaviors that violate societal norms and the rights of other people. It is one of the most prevalent categories of mental health problems of children in this country, with rates estimated at 9% for males and 2% for females.

Description

The specific behaviors used to produce a **diagnosis** of conduct disorder fall into four groups: aggressive conduct that causes or threatens physical harm to other people or animals, nonaggressive behavior that causes property loss or damage, deceitfulness or theft, and serious violations of rules. Two subtypes of conduct disorder can be delineated based on the age that symptoms first appear. Childhood-onset type is appropriate for children showing at least one of the behaviors in question before the age of 10. Adolescent onset type is defined by the absence of any conduct disorder criteria before the age of 10. Severity may be described as mild, moderate or severe, depending on the number of problems exhibited and their impact on other people.

A youngster who shows symptoms (most often aggression) before age 10 may also exhibit oppositional behavior and peer relationship problems. When they also show persistent conduct disorder and then develop adult **antisocial personality disorder**, they should be distinguished from an individual who had no symptoms of conduct disorder before age 10. The childhood type is more highly associated with heightened aggression, male gender, **oppositional defiant disorder**, and a family history of antisocial behavior.

The individual behaviors that can be observed when conduct disorder is diagnosed may be both common, problematic, and chronic. They tend to occur frequently and are distressingly consistent across time, settings, and families. Not surprisingly, these children function poorly in a variety of places. In fact, the behaviors clustered within the term "conduct disorder" account for a majority of clinical referrals, classroom detentions or other sanctions, being asked to stop participating in numerous activities, and can be extremely difficult (even impossible) for parents to manage.

The negative consequences of conduct disorder, particularly childhood onset, may include illicit drug use, dropping out of school, violent behavior, severe family conflict, and frequent delinquent acts. Such behaviors often result in the child's eventual placement out of the home, in special education and/or the juvenile justice system. There is evidence that the rates of disruptive behavior disorders may be as high as 50% in youth in public sectors of care such as juvenile justice, alcohol and drug services, schools for youths with serious emotional disturbances, child welfare, and mental health.

The financial costs of crime and correction for repeated juvenile offenses by youth with conduct disorder are extensive. The social costs include citizens' fear of such behavior, loss of a sense of safety, and disruptions in classrooms that interfere with other children's opportunity to learn. The costs to the child and his or her family are enormous in terms of the emotional and other resources needed to address the consequences of the constellation of symptoms that define conduct disorder.

Causes

There is no known cause for conduct disorder. The frustrating behavior of youngsters with conduct disorder frequently leads to blaming, labeling and other unproductive activities. Children who are "acting out" do not inspire sympathy or the benefit of the doubt. They are often ostracized by other children. Parents of such children are often blamed as poor disciplinarians or bad parents. As a result, parents of children with conduct disorder may be reluctant to engage with schools or other authorities. At the same time, there is a strong correlation between children diagnosed with conduct disorder and a significant level of family dysfunction, poor parenting practices, an overemphasis on coercion and hostile communication patterns, verbal and physical aggression and a history of maltreatment.

There is a suggestion of an, as yet, unidentified genetic component to what has generally been viewed as a behavioral disorder. One study with adopted children in the mid-1990s looked at the relationship between birth parents with antisocial personality dis-

order, and adverse adoptive home environments. When these two adverse conditions occurred, there was significantly increased aggressiveness and conduct disorder in the adopted children. That was not the case if there was no indication of antisocial personality disorder in the birth parents. This finding has important implications for prevention and **intervention** of conduct disorders and its associated conditions of **substance abuse** and aggressiveness.

Diagnosis

The ***Diagnostic and Statistical Manual of Mental Disorders*** (also known as the *DSM-IV-TR*) indicates that for conduct disorder to be diagnosed, the patient has repeatedly violated rules, age-appropriate social norms and the rights of others for a period of at least twelve months. This is shown by three or more of the following behaviors, with at least one having taken place in the previous six months: agression to people or animals, property destruction, lying or theft, and serious rule violations.

Aggression to people or animals includes:

- engaging in frequent bullying or threatening
- often starting fights
- using a weapon that could cause serious injury (gun, knife, club, broken glass)
- showing physical cruelty to people
- showing physical cruelty to animals
- engaging in theft with confrontation (armed robbery, extortion, mugging, purse snatching)
- forcing sex upon someone

Property destruction includes:

- deliberately setting fires to cause serious damage
- deliberately destroying the property of others by means other than fire setting

Lying or theft includes:

- breaking into building, car, or house belonging to someone else
- frequently lying or breaking promises for gain or to avoid obligations (called "conning")
- stealing valuables without confrontation (burglary, forgery, shop lifting)

Serious rule violations include:

- beginning before age 13, frequently staying out at night against parents' wishes
- running away from parents overnight twice or more or once if for an extended period
- engaging in frequent truancy beginning before the age of 13

Mild severity would mean there are few problems with conduct beyond those needed to make a diagnosis and all of the problems cause little harm to other people. Moderate severity means the number and effect of the conduct problems is between the extremes of mild and severe. Severe is indicated if there are many more conduct symptoms than are needed to make the diagnosis (more than three in the previous twelve months or more than one in the previous six months), or, the behaviors cause other people considerable harm.

It is generally diagnosed when somebody, often a child in school, comes to the attention of authorities (school, law enforcement, and others) most often because of behavior. The person might then be referred to a **psychiatrist** or **psychologist** for **assessment and diagnosis**. It is unlikely that any sort of specific test is given; rather, the individual would have to meet the criteria in the *DSM-IV-TR*. Usually there is a history of acting out in school, neighborhood, home, and other social settings. Court-ordered treatment would likely occur if the person comes to the attention of the police and if a crime is involved. A judge might order treatment as an alternative to jail, or before a sentence is served.

Treatments

Earlier treatments of youth with conduct disorder relied on legal processes to either declare a child in need of supervision or treatment and thus able to be placed in residential settings established for this purpose. While residential placements may still be used, recent treatment models have relied less on such restrictive procedures. The increased visibility and sophistication of the consumer movement, comprised of families of children and youth with mental health disorders, is bringing pressure to bear on treatment providers to stop blaming families, stop removing children from their families for services, focus instead on strengths and assets in both the child and his or her family, and to use community-based interventions in several domains in which the child and family live.

Community-based interventions are sometimes called wrap-around services to describe the intention that they will be brought to the child's natural environment in a comprehensive and flexible way. The idea is to target a range of child, parent, family and social system factors associated with a child's behavioral problems. This approach has been successful in modifying antisocial behavior, rates of restrictive placement, and in reducing the cost of services.

Another treatment that has been used with some success is the *Child Cognitive Behavioral Treatment*

and Skills Training which trains children with conduct disorder in anger-coping, peer coping, and problem-solving skills.

Parent Management Training and **family therapy** are also used to treat conduct disorder. Parents learn to apply behavioral principles effectively, how to play with their children, and how to teach and coach the child to use new skills.

Medication is sometimes used and may be effective in controlling aggression. Generally, a variety of treatment modes are used to address such a complex disorder. Severe antisocial behavior on the part of the child and adverse parenting practices may suggest that the family will stop treatment before it can be effective, or before meaningful change can result.

Prognosis

Early identification and appropriate and innovative treatment will improve the course of conduct disorder and possibly prevent a host of negative outcomes that are often a consequence of the behaviors associated with it. Unfortunately, the **stigma** of treatment and the undiagnosed problems of many parents are still significant enough that families whose children could benefit from treatment, never find their way to a treatment setting. Instead their children come into contact with the juvenile and criminal justice system.

Prevention

Prognosis may best be improved by prevention of conduct disorder before it becomes so resistant to treatment. Research is being conducted on what early interventions hold the greatest promise. It incorporates several components such as child tutoring, classroom intervention, peer training, social-cognitive skills training, parent training, and family problem solving.

Other studies have included early parent or family interventions, school based interventions and community interventions. Again, these include a variety of elements as suggested before, including parent training that includes education about normal child development, child problem solving, and family **communication skills** training. Research is still needed to determine where and when to target specific preventive interventions.

Resources

BOOKS

American Psychiatric Association. *Diagnostic and Statistical Manual of Mental Disorders*. 4th edition, text revised. Washington, DC: American Psychiatric Association Publishing, Inc. 2000.

Kazdin, Alan E., ed. *Encyclopedia of Psychology.* Vol. 2. Washington, D.C.: Oxford University Press, 2000.

Morrison, James M.D. *DSM-IV Made Easy: The Clinician's Guide to Diagnosis.* New York, The Guilford Press, 1995.

PERIODICALS

Bennett, Kathryn J. PhD, and David Offord, MD. "Screening for Conduct Problems: Does Predictive Accuracy of Conduct Disorder Symptoms Improve with Age?" *Journal of the American Academy of Child and Adolescent Psychiatry* 40, no. 12 (2001).

Biederman, Joseph M.D., Eric Mick, ScD, Stephen V. Faraone, PhD, and Melissa Burback, B.A. "Patterns of Remission and Symptom Decline in Conduct Disorder: A four-Year Prospective Study of an ADHD Sample." *Journal of the American Academy of Child and Adolescent Psychiatry* 40, no. 3 (2001).

Cadoret, Remi J., MD, William R. Yates, MD, Ed Troughton, George Woodworth, PhD, and Mark A. Stewart, MD. "Genetic-Environmental Interaction in the Genesis of Aggressivity and Conduct Disorders." *Archives of General Psychiatry* 52, no. 11 (1995).

Garland, Ann F. PhD, Richard Hough, PhD, Kristen McCabe, PhD, May Yeh, PhD, Patricia Wood, MPH, MA, and Gregory Aarons, PhD. "Prevalence of Psychiatric Disorders in Youths Across Five Sectors of Care." *Journal of the American Academy of Child and Adolescent Psychiatry* 40, no. 4 (2001).

ORGANIZATIONS

American Academy of Child and Adolescent Psychiatry. 3615 Wisconsin Ave. NW, Washington, DC 20016. <http://www.aacap.org>.

Federation of Families for Children's Mental Health. 1101 King St., Suite 420, Alexandria, VA 22314. <http://www.ffcmh.org>.

Judy Leaver, M.A.

Conners' Rating Scales-Revised

Definition

Developed by C. Keith Conners, Ph.D., the Conners' Rating Scales–Revised (CRS-R) are paper and pencil screening questionnaires designed to be completed by parents and teachers to assist in evaluating children for **attention deficit/hyperactivity disorder** (ADHD).

Purpose

The CSR-R is used as part of a comprehensive examination and are designed to be easily administered and scored. Both the long and short versions are tools to assist in determining whether children between the ages of three and 17 years might have ADHD.

Precautions

Those who administer the CRS-R should have a good understanding of psychological testing and its limitations. Although the CRS-R can be readily administered and scored by a nonprofessional, the ultimate responsibility for interpretation lies with a seasoned professional. As with all psychological evaluation instruments, the CRS-R is not perfect. One runs the risk of obtaining false positives (incorrectly diagnosing the disorder) or false negatives (failing to identify the disorder). Therefore, the information obtained from completed forms should not be used in isolation. It should be one piece of a complex evaluation that includes a clinical interview with the child, other diagnostic measures such as a computerized continuous performance test, and patient self-report—for those old enough and with sufficient reading ability to do so.

Previous versions of the Conners' scales were criticized by those claiming disparity between results obtained in different ethnic groups. The most recent version should dispel this concern, since they were "normed" using data from more than 8,000 subjects crossing all cultural and ethnic boundaries. The technical manual for CRS-R even contains separate normative information for specific ethnic groups. However, when age and sex are taken into account there were either no differences or insignificant differences. Statistically, a difference of two or three T-score points would be insignificant.

Description

The CRS-Rs are available in long and short versions for both parents and teachers. The long version for parents contains 80 items while the long version for teachers contains 59 items. The parents' short version contains 27 items and the teachers' short version has 28. The forms are multi-paged, and numbers circled on the front or back page are automatically transferred to a middle section for use by the clinician. The clinician transfers the circled scores into appropriate scales on the middle form and totals each scale at the bottom of the page. The parent version contains scales A through N. The teacher version is similar but lacks scale G (psychosomatic) contained on the parent version.

Results

After transferring the raw scores to the various scales and totaling them, the total of each scale (A–N) is transferred to another form designed to graphically portray the results. The clinician must be careful to transpose the raw scores to the correct age group column within each major scale. For example, column 1 is used for ages three to five, column 2 for ages six to eight,

Normed—Describes a process used in the developmental stages of a test instrument. The new test is first given to a cross-section of a population for which it is designed. The scores, placements, rankings, etc., of these persons then become the source for all future comparisons (norm group). When a new subject takes the test, his/her score, placement, ranking, etc., is determined based upon comparison with or deviation from the norm group.

Psychosomatic—Physical disorder originating in, or aggravated by, the psychic or emotional processes of the individual.

column 3 for ages nine to 11, etc. Each of these column scores can then be converted to a T-score. T-scores are standardized scores with a mean of 50 and a standard deviation of 10. These can be further converted to percentile scores as needed.

As a rule, T-scores above 60 are cause for concern and have interpretive value. Interpretable scores range from a low T-score of 61 (mildly atypical) to above 70 (markedly atypical). However, again, this information should not be used in isolation to make a **diagnosis**.

See also Attention deficit/hyperactivity disorder.

Resources

BOOKS

Conners' Rating Scales-Revised Technical Manual. North Tonawanda, New York: Multi Health Systems, 2000.

ORGANIZATIONS

Center for Mental Health Services. Office of Consumer, Family, and Public Information, 5600 Fishers Lane, Room 15-105 Rockville, MD 20857. (301) 443-2792.
Children and Adults with Attention Deficit Disorders (CH.A.D.D.). 499 NW 70th Avenue, Suite 109, Plantation, FL 33317. (305) 587-3700. (800) 233-4050 <www.chadd.org>.

Jack H. Booth, Psy.D.

Conversion disorder

Definition

Conversion disorder is defined by the *Diagnostic and Statistical Manual of Mental Disorders*, fourth edition, text revision, also known as the *DSM-IV-TR*

as a mental disorder whose central feature is the appearance of symptoms affecting the patient's senses or voluntary movements that suggest a neurological or general medical disease or condition. Somatoform disorders are marked by persistent physical symptoms that cannot be fully explained by a medical condition, **substance abuse**, or other mental disorder, but rather seem to stem from psychological issues or conflicts. The *DSM-IV-TR* classifies conversion disorder as one of the somatoform disorders, first classified as a group of mental disorders by the *DSM III* in 1980. Other terms that have sometimes been used for conversion disorder include pseudoneurologic syndrome, hysterical **neurosis**, and psychogenic disorder.

Conversion disorder is a major reason for visits to primary care practitioners. One study of health care utilization estimated that 25–72% of office visits to primary care doctors involved psychological distress that takes the form of somatic (physical) symptoms. Another study estimated that at least 10% of all medical treatments and diagnostic services were ordered for patients with no evidence of organic disease. Conversion disorder carries a high economic price tag. Patients who convert their emotional problems into physical symptoms spend nine times as much for health care as people who do not somatosize; and 82% of adults with conversion disorder stop working because of their symptoms. The annual bill for conversion disorder in the United States comes to $20 billion, not counting absenteeism from work and disability payments.

Description

Conversion disorder has a complicated history that helps to explain the number of different names for it. Two eminent neurologists of the nineteenth century, Jean-Martin Charcot in Paris, France, and Josef Breuer in Vienna, Austria, were investigating what was then called hysteria, a disorder primarily affecting women (the term "hysteria" comes from the Greek word for uterus or womb). Women diagnosed with hysteria had frequent emotional outbursts and a variety of neurologic symptoms, including paralysis, fainting spells, convulsions, and temporary loss of sight or hearing. Pierre Janet (one of Charcot's students), and Breuer independently came to the same conclusion about the cause of hysteria—that it resulted from psychological trauma. Janet, in fact, coined the term "dissociation" to describe the altered state of consciousness experienced by many patients who were diagnosed with hysteria.

The next stage in the study of conversion disorder was research into the causes of "combat neurosis" in World

War I (1914–1918) and World War II (1939–1945). Many of the symptoms observed in "shell-shocked" soldiers were identical to those of "hysterical" women. Two of the techniques still used in the treatment of conversion disorder, hypnosis and narcotherapy, were introduced as therapies for combat veterans. The various terms used by successive editions of the *DSM* and the *ICD* (the European equivalent of *DSM*) for conversion disorder reflect its association with hysteria and **dissociation**. The first edition of the *DSM* (1952) used the term "conversion reaction." The *DSM-II* (1968) called the disorder "hysterical neurosis (conversion type)," and the *DSM-III* (1980), *DSM-III-R* (1987), and *DSM-IV* (1994) have all used the term "conversion disorder." *ICD-10* refers to it as "dissociative (conversion) disorder."

DSM-IV-TR (2000) specifies six criteria for the **diagnosis** of conversion disorder. They are:

- The patient has one or more symptoms or deficits affecting the senses or voluntary movement that suggest a neurological or general medical disorder.

- The onset or worsening of the symptoms was preceded by conflicts or stressors in the patient's life.

- The symptom is not faked or produced intentionally.

- The symptom cannot be fully explained as the result of a general medical disorder, substance intake, or a behavior related to the patient's culture.

- The symptom is severe enough to interfere with the patient's schooling, employment, or social relationships, or is serious enough to require a medical evaluation.

- The symptom is not limited to pain or sexual dysfunction, does not occur only in the context of somatization disorder, and is not better accounted for by another mental disorder.

The *DSM-IV-TR* lists four subtypes of conversion disorder: conversion disorder with motor symptom or deficit; with sensory symptom or deficit; with **seizures** or convulsions; and with mixed presentation.

Although conversion disorder is most commonly found in individuals, it sometimes occurs in groups. One such instance occurred in 1997 in a group of three young men and six adolescent women of the Embera, an indigenous tribe in Colombia. The young people believed that they had been put under a spell or curse and developed dissociative symptoms that were not helped by antipsychotic medications or traditional herbal remedies. They were cured when shamans from their ethnic group came to visit them. The episode was attributed to psychological **stress** resulting from rapid cultural change.

Another example of group conversion disorder occurred in Iran in 1992. Ten girls out of a classroom of 26 became unable to walk or move normally following tetanus inoculations. Although the local physicians were able to treat the girls successfully, public health programs to immunize people against tetanus suffered an immediate negative impact. One explanation of group conversion disorder is that an individual who is susceptible to the disorder is typically more affected by suggestion and easier to hypnotize than the average person.

Causes and symptoms

Causes

The immediate cause of conversion disorder is a stressful event or situation that leads the patient to develop bodily symptoms as symbolic expressions of a long-standing psychological conflict or problem. One **psychiatrist** has defined the symptoms as "a code that conceals the message from the sender as well as from the receiver."

Two terms that are used in connection with the causes of conversion disorder are primary gain and secondary gain. Primary gain refers to the lessening of the **anxiety** and communication of the unconscious wish that the patient derives from the symptom(s). Secondary gain refers to the interference with daily tasks, removal from the uncomfortable situation, or increased attention from significant others that the patient obtains as a result of the symptom(s).

Physical, emotional, or sexual **abuse** can be a contributing cause of conversion disorder in both adults and children. In a study of 34 children who developed pseudoseizures, 32% had a history of **depression** or sexual abuse, and 44% had recently experienced a parental divorce, death, or violent quarrel. At least one study, however, has found no consistent association between dissociation and sexual or physical abuse. In the adult population, conversion disorder may be associated with mobbing, a term that originated among European psychiatrists and industrial psychologists to describe psychological abuse in the workplace. One American woman who quit her job because of mobbing was unable to walk for several months. Adult males sometimes develop conversion disorder during military basic training. Conversion disorder may also develop in adults as a long-delayed aftereffect of childhood abuse. A team of surgeons reported on the case of a patient who went into a psychogenic coma following a throat operation. The surgeons found that she had been repeatedly raped as a child by her father, who stifled her cries by smothering her with a pillow.

Symptoms

In general, symptoms of conversion disorder are not under the patient's conscious control, and are frequently mysterious and frightening to the patient. The symptoms usually have an acute onset, but sometimes worsen gradually.

The most frequent forms of conversion disorder in Western countries include:

- pseudoparalysis. In pseudoparalysis, the patient loses the use of half of his/her body or of a single limb. The weakness does not follow anatomical patterns and is often inconsistent upon repeat examination.
- pseudosensory syndromes. Patients with these syndromes often complain of numbness or lack of sensation in various parts of their bodies. The loss of sensation typically follows the patient's notion of their anatomy, rather than known characteristics of the human nervous system.
- pseudoseizures. These are the most difficult symptoms of conversion disorder to distinguish from their organic equivalents. Between 5% and 35% of patients with pseudoseizures also have epilepsy. Electroencephalograms (EEGs) and the measurement of serum prolactin levels are useful in distinguishing pseudoseizures from epileptic seizures.
- pseudocoma. Pseudocoma is also difficult to diagnose. Because true coma may indicate a life-threatening condition, patients must be given standard treatments for coma until the diagnosis can be established.
- psychogenic movement disorders. These can mimic myoclonus, parkinsonism, dystonia, dyskinesia, and tremor. Doctors sometimes give patients with suspected psychogenic movement disorders a placebo medication to determine whether the movements are psychogenic or the result of an organic disorder.
- pseudoblindness. Pseudoblindness is one of the most common forms of conversion disorder related to vision. Placing a mirror in front of the patient and tilting it from side to side can often be used to determine pseudoblindness, because humans tend to follow the reflection of their eyes.
- pseudodiplopia. Pseudodiplopia, or seeing double, can usually be diagnosed by examining the patient's eyes.
- pseudoptosis. Ptosis, or drooping of the upper eyelid, is a common symptom of myasthenia gravis and a few other disorders. Some people can cause their eyelids to droop voluntarily with practice. The diagnosis can be made on the basis of the eyebrow; in true ptosis, the eyebrows are lifted, whereas in pseudoptosis they are lowered.
- hysterical aphonia. Aphonia refers to loss of the ability to produce sounds. In hysterical aphonia, the patient's cough and whisper are normal, and examination of the throat reveals normal movement of the vocal cords.

Psychiatrists working in various parts of the Middle East and Asia report that the symptoms of conversion disorder as listed by the *DSM-IV* and the *ICD-10* do not fit well with the symptoms of the disorder most frequently encountered in their patient populations.

Demographics

The lifetime prevalence rates of conversion disorder in the general population are estimated to fall between 2.5 and 500 per 100,000 people. Differences among estimates reflect differences in the method of diagnosis as well as regional population differences. In terms of clinical populations, conversion disorder is diagnosed in 5–14% of general hospital patients; 1–3% of outpatient referrals to psychiatrists; and 5–25% of psychiatric outpatients. The frequency among clinical populations overall is reported between 20 and 120 per 100,000 patients.

Among adults, women diagnosed with conversion disorder outnumber men by a 2:1 to 10:1 ratio; among children, however, the gender ratio is closer to 1:1. Less-educated people and those of lower socioeconomic status are more likely to develop conversion disorder; race by itself does not appear to be a factor. There is, however, a major difference between the populations of developing and developed countries. In developing countries, the prevalence of conversion disorder may run as high as 31%.

Diagnosis

Conversion disorder is one of the few mental disorders that appears to be overdiagnosed, particularly in emergency departments. There are numerous instances of serious neurologic illness that were initially misdiagnosed as conversion disorder. Newer techniques of diagnostic imaging have helped to lower the rate of medical errors. In addition, functional MRI has identified specific areas of the **brain** that show differential activation in cases of conversion disorder, and imaging findings may eventually be useful in distinguishing conversion disorder.

Diagnostic issues

Diagnosis of conversion disorder is complicated by its coexistence with physical illness in as many as 60% of patients. Alternatively explained, a diagnosis of conversion disorder does not exclude the possibility of a concurrent organic disease. The examining doctor will usually order a mental health evaluation when conversion disorder is suspected, as well as x-rays, other **imaging studies** that may be useful, and appropriate laboratory tests. The doctor will also take a thorough patient history that will include the presence of recent stressors in the patient's life, as well as a history of abuse. Children and adolescents are usually asked about their school experiences, one question they are asked is whether a recent change of school or an experience related to school may have intensified academic pressure.

In addition, there are a number of bedside tests that doctors can use to distinguish between symptoms of conversion disorder and symptoms caused by physical diseases. These may include the drop test, in which a "paralyzed" arm is dropped over the patient's face. In conversion disorder, the arm will not strike the face. Other tests include applying a mildly painful stimulus to a "weak" or "numb" part of the body. The patient's pulse rate will typically rise in cases of conversion disorder, and he or she will usually pull back the limb that is being touched.

Factors suggesting a diagnosis of conversion disorder

The doctor can also use a list of factors known to be associated with conversion disorder to assess the likelihood that a specific patient may have the disorder:

- age. Conversion disorder is rarely seen in children younger than six years or adults over 35 years.
- sex. The female:male ratio for the disorder ranges between 2:1 and 10:1. It is thought that higher rates of conversion disorder in women may reflect the greater vulnerability of females to abuse.
- residence. People who live in rural areas are more likely to develop conversion disorder than those who live in cities.
- level of education. Conversion disorder occurs less often among sophisticated or highly educated people.
- family history. Children sometimes develop conversion disorder from observing their parents' reactions to stressors. This process is known as social modeling.
- a recent stressful change or event in the patient's life.

An additional feature suggesting conversion disorder is the presence of *la belle indifférence*. The French phrase refers to an attitude of relative unconcern on the patient's part about the symptoms or their implications. La belle indifférence is, however, much more common in adults with conversion disorder than in children or adolescents. Patients in these younger age groups are much more likely to react to their symptoms with fear or hopelessness. A recent review of the published reports of la belle indifférence found that this feature was not useful in discriminating conversion disorder from physically based disease because of muddy definitions and application of it in diagnosis.

Medical conditions that mimic conversion symptoms

It is important for the doctor to rule out serious medical disorders in patients who appear to have conversion symptoms. At least one study has found an approximately 4% rate of misdiagnosis of an actual physical problem as a conversion disorder. The following disorders must be considered in the differential diagnosis:

- multiple sclerosis (blindness resulting from optic neuritis)
- myasthenia gravis (muscle weakness)
- periodic paralysis (muscle weakness)
- myopathies (muscle weakness)
- polymyositis (muscle weakness)
- Guillain-Barré syndrome (motor and sensory symptoms)

Treatments

Patients diagnosed with conversion disorder frequently benefit from a team approach to treatment and from a combination of treatment modalities. A team approach is particularly beneficial if the patient has a history of abuse, or if he or she is being treated for a concurrent physical condition or illness.

Medications

While there are no drugs for the direct treatment of conversion disorder, medications are sometimes given to patients to treat the anxiety or depression that may be associated with conversion disorder.

Psychotherapy

Psychodynamic psychotherapy is sometimes used with children and adolescents to help them gain insight into their symptoms. Cognitive-behavioral approaches have also been tried, with good results. **Family therapy** is often recommended for younger

KEY TERMS

Aphonia—Inability to speak caused by a functional disturbance of the voice box or vocal cords.

(la) Belle indifférence—A psychiatric symptom sometimes found in patients with conversion disorder, in which the patient shows a surprising lack of concern about the nature or implications of his/her physical symptom(s).

Conversion—In psychiatry, a process in which a repressed feeling, impulse, thought, or memory emerges in the form of a bodily symptom.

Diplopia—A disorder of vision in which a single object appears double. Diplopia is sometimes called double vision.

Dyskinesia—Difficulty in performing voluntary muscular movements.

Dystonia—A neurological disorder characterized by involuntary muscle spasms. The spasms can cause a painful twisting of the body and difficulty walking or moving.

Electroencephalogram (EEG)—A test that measures the electrical activity of the brain by means of electrodes placed on the scalp or in the brain itself.

Factitious disorder—A type of mental disturbance in which patients intentionally act physically or mentally ill without obvious benefits. It is distinguished from malingering by the absence of an obvious motive, and from conversion disorder by intentional production of symptoms.

Hysteria—In nineteenth-century psychiatric use, a neurotic disorder characterized by violent emotional outbursts and disturbances of the sensory and motor (movement-related) functions. The term "hysterical neurosis" is still used by some psychiatrists as a synonym for conversion disorder.

Malingering—Knowingly pretending to be physically or mentally ill to avoid some unpleasant duty or responsibility, or for economic benefit.

Myoclonus—An abrupt spasm or twitching in a muscle or group of muscles.

Narcotherapy—A form of psychotherapy that involves the administration of a drug that makes the patient drowsy.

Primary gain—In psychiatry, the principal psychological reason for the development of a patient's symptoms. In conversion disorder, the primary gain from the symptom is the reduction of anxiety and the exclusion of an inner conflict from conscious awareness.

Pseudoseizure—A fit that resembles an epileptic seizure but is not associated with abnormal electrical discharges in the patient's brain.

Psychogenic—Originating in the mind, or in a mental process or condition. The term "psychogenic" is sometimes used as a synonym for "conversion."

Ptosis—Drooping of the upper eyelid.

Secondary gain—A term that refers to other benefits that a patient obtains from a conversion symptom. For example, a patient's loss of function in an arm might require other family members to do the patient's share of household chores; or they might give the patient more attention and sympathy than he or she usually receives.

Shaman—In certain indigenous tribes or groups, a person who acts as an intermediary between the natural and supernatural worlds. Shamans are regarded as having the power or ability to cure illnesses.

Social modeling—A process of learning behavioral and emotional-response patterns from observing one's parents or other adults. Some researchers think that social modeling plays a part in the development of conversion disorder in children.

Somatoform disorders—A group of psychiatric disorders in the *DSM-IV-TR* classification that are characterized by external physical symptoms or complaints that are related to psychological problems rather than organic illness. Conversion disorder is classified as a somatoform disorder.

Stressor—A stimulus or event that provokes a stress response in an organism. Stressors can be categorized as acute or chronic, and as external or internal to the organism.

patients whose symptoms may be related to family dysfunction. **Group therapy** appears to be particularly useful in helping adolescents to learn social skills and coping strategies, and to decrease their dependency on their families.

Inpatient treatment

Hospitalization is sometimes recommended for children with conversion disorders who are not helped by outpatient treatment. Inpatient treatment also allows for a more complete assessment of possible coexisting organic disorders, and for the child to improve his or her level of functioning outside of an abusive or otherwise dysfunctional home environment.

Alternative and complementary therapies

Alternative and complementary therapies that have been shown to be helpful in the treatment of conversion disorder include hypnosis, relaxation techniques, visualization, and **biofeedback**.

Prognosis

The prognosis for recovery from conversion disorder is highly favorable. Patients who have clearly identifiable stressors in their lives, acute onset of symptoms, and a short interval between symptom onset and treatment have the best prognosis. Of patients hospitalized for the disorder, over half recover within two weeks. Between 20% and 25% will **relapse** within a year. The individual symptoms of conversion disorder are usually self-limited and do not lead to lasting disabilities; however, patients with hysterical aphonia, paralysis, or visual disturbances, have better prognoses for full recovery than those with tremor or pseudoseizures.

Prevention

The incidence of conversion disorder in adults is likely to continue to decline with rising levels of formal education and the spread of basic information about human psychology. Prevention of conversion disorder in children and adolescents depends on better strategies for preventing abuse.

See also Abuse.

Resources

BOOKS

American Psychiatric Association. *Diagnostic and Statistical Manual of Mental Disorders.* 4th ed., Text rev. Washington D.C.: American Psychiatric Association, 2000.
"Conversion Disorder." *The Merck Manual of Diagnosis and Therapy,* Mark H. Beers, MD and Robert Berkow, MD, eds. Whitehouse Station, NJ: Merck Research Laboratories, 1999.
Dorland's Pocket Medical Dictionary, 25th ed. Philadelphia: W. B. Saunders Company, 1995.
Davenport, Noa, PhD, Ruth D. Schwartz, and Gail P. Elliott. *Mobbing: Emotional Abuse in the American Workplace.* Ames, IA: Civil Society Publishing, 1999.
Herman, Judith, MD. *Trauma and Recovery,* 2nd ed., revised. New York: Basic Books, 1997.
Pelletier, Kenneth R., MD. "Sound Mind, Sound Body: MindBody Medicine Comes of Age." Chapter 2 in *The*

Best Alternative Medicine. New York: Simon and Schuster, 2002.
World Health Organization (WHO). *The ICD-10 Classification of Mental and Behavioural Disorders.* Geneva: WHO, 1992.

PERIODICALS

Al-Sharbati, M. M., N. Viernes, A. Al-Hussaini, and others. "A Case of Bilateral Ptosis with Unsteady Gait: Suggestibility and Culture in Conversion Disorder." *International Journal of Psychiatry in Medicine* 31 (2001): 225–32.
Campo, John V. "Negative Reinforcement and Behavioral Management of Conversion Disorder." *Journal of the American Academy of Child and Adolescent Psychiatry* 39 (June 2000): 787–90.
Crimlisk, Helen L., and others. "Slater Revisited: 6-Year Follow-Up of Patients with Medically Unexplained Motor Symptoms." *British Medical Journal* 316 (Feb. 21, 1998): 582-86.
Glick, T. H., T. P. Workman, and S. V. Gaufberg. "Suspected Conversion Disorder: Foreseeable Risks and Avoidable Errors." *Academy of Emergency Medicine* 7 (Nov. 2000): 1272–77.
Haghighi, S. S., and S. Meyer. "Psychogenic Paraplegia in a Patient with Normal Electrophysiologic Findings." *Spinal Cord* 39 (Dec. 2001): 664–67.
Isaac, Mohan, and Chand, Prabhat K. "Dissociative and Conversion Disorders: Defining Boundaries." *Current Opinions in Psychiatry* 19 (2006): 61–66.
Meyers, Timothy J., Bruce W. Jafek, and Arlen D. Meyers. "Recurrent Psychogenic Coma Following Tracheal Stenosis Repair." *Archives of Otolaryngology—Head & Neck Surgery* 125 (Nov. 1999): 1267.
Moene, F. C., E. H. Landberg, K. A. Hoogduin, and others. "Organic Syndromes Diagnosed as Conversion Disorder: Identification and Frequency in a Study of 85 Patients." *Journal of Psychosomatic Research* w49 (July 2000): 7–12.
Mori, S., S. Fujieda, T. Yamamoto, and others. "Psychogenic Hearing Loss with Panic Anxiety Attack After the Onset of Acute Inner Ear Disorder." *ORL Journal of Otorhinolaryngology and Related Specialties* 64 (Jan.-Feb. 2002): 41–44.
Pineros, Marion, Diego Rosselli, Claudia Calderon. "An Epidemic of Collective Conversion and Dissociation Disorder in an Indigenous Group of Colombia: Its Relation to Cultural Change." *Social Science & Medicine* 46 (June 1998): 1425–28.
Shalbani, Aziz, and Marwan N. Sabbagh. "Pseudoneurologic Syndromes: Recognition and Diagnoses." *American Family Physician* 57 (May 15, 1998): 207–12.
Stone, Jon, and others. "Systematic Review of Misdiagnosis of Conversion Symptom and 'Hysteria'" *British Medical Journal* (2005).
Stone, Jon, Roger Smyth, Alan Carson, Charles Warlow, and Michael Sharpe. "La Belle Indifference in Conversion Symptoms and Hysteria." *British Journal of Psychiatry* 188 (2006): 204–209.

Syed, E. U., and others. "Conversion Disorder: Difficulties in Diagnosis Using DSM-IV/ICD-10." *Journal of the Pakistani Medical Association* 51 (April 2001): 143–45.

Wyllie, Elaine, John P. Glazer, Selim Benbadis, and others. "Psychiatric Features of Children and Adults with Pseudoseizures." *Archives of Pediatrics & Adolescent Medicine* 153 (March 1999): 244–48.

Yasamy, M. T., A. Bahramnezhad, H. Ziaaddini. "Post-vaccination Mass Psychogenic Illness in an Iranian Rural School." *Eastern Mediterranean Health Journal* 5 (July 1999): 710–16.

ORGANIZATIONS

American Academy of Child and Adolescent Psychiatry. 3615 Wisconsin Avenue, NW, Washington, DC 20016-3007. Telephone: (202) 966-7300. Fax: (202) 966-2891. <www.aacap.org>.

National Institute of Mental Health. 6001 Executive Boulevard, Room 8184, MSC 9663, Bethesda, MD 20892-9663. (301) 443-4513. <www.nimh.nih.gov>.

Rebecca J. Frey, PhD
Emily Jane Willingham, PhD

Co-occurring disorders/dual diagnosis

Definition

Co-occurring disorders are sets of mental illnesses that appear together in a single individual. They include a **substance abuse** disorder with at least one other Axis I or Axis II mental illness. The five Axes are standard diagnostic categories established by the American Psychiatric Association (APA). In co-occurring disorders, an Axis I substance **abuse** disorder is always present simultaneously with at least one other mental health disorder from Axis I or II. Another name for co-occurring disorders is **dual diagnosis**, although this may include several diagnoses and not only two (dual). Dual **diagnosis** in this case means "more than one." Yet another name given this condition is co-morbidity, with morbidity meaning "illness."

Description

The term substance abuse includes substance-use disorders on a continuum from experimentation, to regular use, to drug dependence and **addiction**. Substances include prescription drugs, over-the-counter medications, marijuana, **cocaine**, heroin, mescaline (peyote), glues (sniffing), spray-can aerosols (huffing), and other categories. Substance abuse is the usual

co-occurring disorder among adults with severe mental disorders (SMDs) such as **bipolar disorder**, other psychoses, and **depression**.

Depression itself is the most common mental illness coexisting with physical disorders. Further, depression often occurs among patients with substance abuse, whereas substance abuse can coexist with **anxiety**, **post-traumatic stress disorder** (PTSD), **personality disorders**, and eating disorders. Co-occurring disorders result in serious problems such as higher rates of illness **relapse** than in cases of only one mental illness; increased numbers of hospitalizations; and higher risks for violence, incarceration, **homelessness**, **suicide**, and exposure to major infections such as HIV and hepatitis.

Incidence/Prevalence

According to statistics compiled by the U.S. Substance Abuse and Mental Health Services Administration (SAMHSA), 10 million Americans or more will develop at least one mental illness together with a substance abuse disorder in any one-year period. The APA has learned that 7% of the American population, or 21 million people, have a full-blown **psychosis** at any given time. Co-occurring disorders affect a full 50% of all individuals that have severe mental disorders such as psychoses. Kessler, et al., recently found in a controlled study that 55% of the general population may experience one mental illness, 22% from two, and 23% from three co-occurring disorders. This translates to 69 million Americans having three co-occurring disorders.

SAMSHA has found that the prevalence of co-occurring disorders has increased during the last three decades. Named in the early 1980s, dual diagnoses considered most likely to occur among either youth and young adults with **schizophrenia** or people with bipolar disorder, all of whom showed a history of drug abuse and/or alcohol abuse. The medical opinion was that a person's entrance into the drug culture was the cause of another mental illness. Currently, it is thought that one or more mental disorders occur first, followed by drugs or alcohol used in self-medicating behavior used to cover unwanted mental symptoms.

Demographics

Children of alcoholics and of drug-addicted individuals are more likely to have co-occurring disorders than America's general population. In addition, patients with depression are more at risk for substance abuse and alcohol abuse disorders than people having no mental illness. In addition, the U.S. Department of Health and

Human Services has found that people who have received public assistance under welfare reform programs experienced an average of three or four SMDs in addition to substance abuse, without receiving adequate treatment. The affected homeless population suffers similar circumstances, while youth and the aged are also affected by co-occurring disorders.

Among youth, disruptive behavior disorders occur more frequently with than without substance abuse disorders. Older adults with depression or anxiety are at higher risk for substance and alcohol abuse than middle-aged adults. Seniors may be grieving losses of family, friends, and employment. They may drink or misuse drugs to rid themselves of pain and the complications of poverty. Co-occurring disorders complicate the management of any memory problems they may have, slowing metabolism, arthritis, hypertension, diabetes, Alzheimer's disease and other dementias, and various additional health problems. Further, because women generally outlive men, co-occurring disorders and related physical problems are more prevalently becoming the maladies of older women. However, they also affect veterans and people with eating disorders.

Substance or alcohol abuse may co-occur with eating disorders, because such patients self-medicate feelings of shame, anxiety, extreme hunger, and self-hate commonly experienced in eating disorders. This further complicates their recovery. Finally, many military veterans experience anxiety, depression, and/or post-traumatic **stress** disorder (PTSD) at the same time they have a history of substance abuse or alcoholism. Unfortunately, assessment, treatment, and prevention services for veterans have been inadequate.

Diagnosis

Careful assessment by a licensed professional and therapeutic team is necessary to plan effective treatment strategies. This begins with a detailed medical history and clinical interviews of the patient and family members to establish related health and behavioral patterns and substance or alcohol abuse history. Because **denial** is an inherent aspect of the problem, a battery of psychiatric tests can uncover mental illnesses. These tests include the **Minnesota Multiphasic Personality Inventory** (MMPI), Rorschach and other inkblot tests, other personality and projective tests, the Wechsler intelligence scales, and others. A number of substance abuse checklists can help determine substance and alcohol-related disorders.

Treatment

Despite evidence of the high prevalence of dual diagnoses, the U.S. mental health and substance abuse systems have run separate programs, causing confusion. Failure to combine services for coordinated treatment means prolonged suffering and expense for patients, families, insurance companies, the U.S. health care system, and public assistance and disability programs. In light of welfare reform and health care improvements, the 1990s provided many programs for these patients, often more holistic and supported by federal funding for targeting ex-offenders and welfare-to-work populations.

The key factors in an integrated treatment program are (1) treatment must be approached in stages; (2) assertive outreach leads to higher client retention rates; (3) motivational interventions accompanied by education, counseling, and social support; (4) viewing recovery as a long-term, community-based process; (5) effecting a comprehensive strategy; and (6) a successful program must be culturally sensitive and culturally competent.

Investigators such as Roszak, Sacks, and Watkins have found recently that for many dual diagnosis patients, the criminal justice system is their last stop. Many jailed youth fail to be diagnosed. Their behavior mandated their incarceration and mental health assessment was not considered. The juvenile and adult justice systems have become the treatment provider, but treatment is not always an option. Two-thirds (67%) of incarcerated youth with substance abuse disorders have one or more additional mental illnesses. The coexistence of a **conduct disorder** and/or attention deficit–type disorders with substance abuse results in a serious disability. However, a dual diagnosis patient in the criminal justice system may never receive psychiatric evaluation or treatment.

A specific problem with treatments for dual diagnoses is that most mental health treatments are designed, tested, and validated through controlled studies of individuals who have only one mental diagnosis. These treatments may not be as effective when there are two or more mental disorders. However, individually prescribed treatment plans have been successful in using these specific components:

- planned therapeutic interventions: The client is engaged and persuaded to participate in rehabilitation. In planned group and individual therapies, the patients are given coping skills and support toward managing their illnesses.
- psychological counseling: This includes both cognitive (thinking) and behavioral skills to change negative thinking patterns and unwanted behaviors. It can include role-playing and homework.
- social counseling: This includes support groups, group therapy, and family therapy facilitated by professionals.

KEY TERMS

Axis—One of five diagnostic categories of the American Psychiatric Association that are used for mental health diagnoses. Axis I describes the clinical syndrome or major diagnosis; Axis II lists developmental disorders or mental retardation and personality disorders; Axis III lists physical disorders; Axis IV includes the severity of psychosocial stressors for the individual; and Axis V describes an individual's highest level of functioning currently and in the past 12 months.

Co-occurring disorders—Sets of mental illnesses—usually substance abuse and at least one other Axis I or Axis II disorder—that appear together in a single individual. Also called dual diagnosis or co-morbidity disorders.

Intervention—A confrontation of a substance abuser by a group of interested people that propose immediate medical treatment. An intervention is also a method of treatment used in therapy.

Substance abuse—Illicit, inaccurate, or recreational use of either prescription or illegal drugs. Alcohol can also be abused as a substance but has its own category, alcohol abuse.

Welfare-to-Work—Several American public reforms of the late 1990s and early 2000s, designed to move individuals from public assistance to paying jobs.

It includes diversity and sensitivity training and cultural competency instruction.

- health-related education: This helps clients commit to managing their illnesses. It requires an acceptance of and commitment to a long-term supervised recovery process.

- aggressive follow-up: A treatment team provides intensive, frequent patient follow-up with meetings in the patient's workplace and home as well as in the case manager's office.

- comprehensive treatment: This holistic treatment targets education, health, employment, personal behavior patterns, stress management, peer networks, family, housing, financial skills, spiritual life, and other aspects.

Additional considerations

Alcoholics Anonymous, Al-Anon, Narcotics Anonymous, and similar 12-step programs frequently supplement treatment for substance abuse and co-occurring disorders. However, their success cannot be quantitatively validated, because they are anonymous. Further, the direct confrontation of an engagement

intervention and that of ongoing 12-step programs can be too threatening for mental health patients. The primary care physician or therapist must decide the most appropriate strategies for each patient.

The use of psychiatric drugs to alter mood or behavior is understandably controversial in substance abuse recovery, so treatments such as support groups for co-occurring disorders can be more effective than drug therapies.

Prognosis

The prognosis for co-occurring disorders depends on the prognosis of the separate disorders occurring in a specific patient, along with the combined effects of those disorders. Dual diagnoses usually present a worse overall health outlook than a single mental illness. Early preventative education, screening, assessment, diagnosis, and treatment are vital to the health of a person suffering from or at risk for co-occurring disorders. Appropriate health promotion education is useful and necessary in alerting the general populations to the risks and signs of co-occurring disorders and in helping themselves maintain good mental hygiene.

Resources

BOOKS

American Psychological Association. *Diagnostic and Statistical Manual of Mental Disorders.* 4th ed., Text rev. Washington, D.C.: American Psychiatric Association, 2000.

Sacks, Stanley, PhD, and Richard K. Ries, MD. *Treatment Improvement Protocol (TIP) Series 42. Substance Abuse Treatment for Persons with Co-occurring Disorders.* U.S. Department of Health and Human Service. Public Health Service. Substance Abuse and Mental Health Services Administration, 2005.

PERIODICALS

Kessler, Ronald C., PhD; Wai Tat Chiu, AM; Olga Demler, MA, MS; and Ellen E. Walters, MS. "Prevalence, Severity, and Comorbidity of 12-month DSM-IV Disorders in the National Comorbidity Survey Replication." *Archive of General Psychiatry* 62 (2005): 617–627.

Roszak, Dennis J. "Mental Illness Starts Early in Life, but Treatment Often Begins Decades Later." *Hospitals & Health Networks* 79.7 (2005): 130.

Saxena, Shekhar, and Jose Manoel Bertolote. "Co-occurring Depression & Physical Disorders: Need for an Adequate Response from the Health Care System." *Indian Journal of Medical Research.* 122.4 (2005): 273–276.

Watkins, Katherine E., Sarah B. Hunter, and others. "Prevalence and Characteristics of Clients with Co-occurring Disorders in Outpatient Substance Abuse

Treatment." *American Journal of Drug and Alcohol Abuse* 30.4 (2004): 749–764.

ORGANIZATIONS

American Psychiatric Association. 1000 Wilson Boulevard, Suite 1825, Arlington, VA 22209-3901. <http://www.psych.org>.

Double Trouble In Recovery. c/o Mental Health Empowerment Project. 271 Central Avenue, Albany, NY 12209. Telephone: (518) 434-1393

Dual Disorders Anonymous. P.O. Box 681264, Schaumburg, IL 60168. Telephone: (847) 781-1553.

Dual Recovery Anonymous. P.O. Box 218232, Nashville, TN 37221. Telephone: (887) 883-2332.

National Alliance for the Mentally Ill (NAMI). 2107 Wilson Boulevard, Suite 300, Arlington, VA 22201. <http://www.nami.org>.

Mental Health America. 1021 Prince Street, Alexandria, VA 22314. <http://www.nmha.org>.

Patty Inglish, MS

Couples therapy

Definition

Couples therapy is a form of psychological therapy used to treat relationship distress for one or both individuals in the relationship, as well as the couple as a pair.

Purpose

The purpose of couples therapy is to restore a better level of functioning in couples who experience relationship distress. The reasons for distress can include poor **communication skills**, incompatibility, or a broad spectrum of psychological disorders that include domestic violence, alcoholism, **depression**, **anxiety**, and **schizophrenia**. The focus of couples therapy is to identify the presence of dissatisfaction and distress in the relationship and to devise and implement a treatment plan with objectives designed to improve or alleviate the presenting symptoms and restore the relationship to a better and healthier level of functioning. Couples therapy can assist persons who are having complaints of intimacy, sexual, and communication difficulties.

Precautions

Couples who seek treatment should consult for services from a mental health practitioner who specializes in this area.

A couple attending a therapy session. *(Photofusion Picture Library/Alamy)*

Patients should be advised that being honest, providing all necessary information, cooperating, keeping appointments, arriving on time, and desiring change and improvement sincerely are all imperative to increase the chance of successful outcome. Additionally, a willingness to work with the process of treatment is essential.

Description

Couples therapy sessions differ according to the chosen model or philosophy behind the therapy. There are several models for treating couples with relationship difficulties. These commonly used strategies include psychoanalytic couples therapy, object relations couple therapy, ego analytical couples therapy, behavioral couples therapy, integrative behavioral couples therapy, and cognitive-behavioral couples therapy. Some therapies focus on education and prevention.

Psychoanalytical couples therapy

Psychoanalytic therapy attempts to uncover unresolved childhood conflicts with parental figures and how these behaviors are part of the current relationship problems. The psychoanalytic approach tends to develop an understanding of present-day interpersonal interactions in connection with early development. The success in personal development of early stages dictates the future behavior of interpersonal relationships. The essential core of this model deals with the process of separation and individuation (becoming a separate, distinct self) from mother-child interactions during childhood. A critical part of this model is introjection. The process of introjection includes introjects (infant processing versions) of the love object (mother).

The developmental process of introjection forms the basis an unconscious representation of others (objects) and is vital for development of a separate and defined sense of self. The psychoanalytic approach analyzes marital relations and mate selection as originating from parent-child relationship during developmental stages of the child.

Object relations couple therapy

The object relations model creates an environment of neutrality and impartiality to understand the distortions and intrapsychic (internalized) conflicts that each partner contributes to the relationship in the form of dysfunctional behaviors. This model proposes that there is a complementary personality fit between couples that is unconscious and fulfills certain needs. This model supports the thought that a "mothering figure" is the central motivation for selection and attachment of a mate. Choosing a mothering figure induces further repression (nondevelopment) of portions of personality that were not well developed (called "lost parts"). This repression causes relationship difficulties.

Ego analytic couples therapy

Ego analytical approaches use methods to foster the ability to communicate important feelings in the couple's relationship. This model proposes that dysfunction originates from the patients' inability to recognize intolerance and invalidation of sensitivities and problems in a relationship. According to this model, there are two major categories of problems. The first category of problems relates to dysfunction brought into the relationship from early childhood trauma and experiences. The second involves the patient's reaction to difficulties and a sense of unentitlement (a personal feeling that one does not deserve something). A patient's shame and guilt are major factors precipitating the thoughts of unentitlement.

Behavioral marital therapy

Behavioral marital therapists tend to improve relationships between a couple by increasing positive exchanges and decreasing the frequency of negative and punishing interactions. This model focuses on the influence that environment has in creating and maintaining relationship behavior. Behavior exchange between partners is flowing continuously and prior histories can affect relationship interactions. Behavior therapy in general is based on the idea that when certain behaviors are rewarded, they are reinforced. The amount of rewards (positive reinforcers) received

in relation to the amount of aversive behavior is linked to an individual's sense of relationship dissatisfaction.

Integrative behavioral couples therapy

Integrative behaviorists help couples by improving behavior exchange, communication, and the couples' abilities for problem-solving skills. The integrative behavioral therapy approach examines functioning of the couple and is more flexible and individualized to specific problems in the relationship than behavior marital therapy. This approach examines problems and interactions that are repetitious (acts that are repeatedly done causing relationship problems).

Cognitive behavior marital therapy

The cognitive-approach therapist educates and increases awareness concerning perceptions, assumptions, attributions or standards of interaction between the couple. The central theme for understanding marital discourse using **cognitive-behavioral therapy** is based on the behavioral marital therapy model. A couple's emotional and behavioral dysfunction are related to inappropriate information processing (possibly "jumping to conclusions," for example) and negative cognitive appraisals. This model attempts to discover the negative types of thinking that drive negative behaviors that cause relationship distress.

Emotionally focused therapy

Emotionally focused therapy assists patients to acknowledge, assess, and express emotions that are related to distress. This model views emotion and cognition (thinking) as interdependent, and sees emotion as a primary "driver" of interpersonal expression. The primary theme of emotionally focused therapy is that couple distress stems from unexpressed and unacknowledged emotional needs. The dysfunction arises from negative interactions from emotions that have been withheld from disclosure from each partner.

Structural strategic marital therapy

Structural strategic therapists will challenge existing negative perceptions and present alternative possibilities and behaviors. These alternate behaviors encourage positive perceptions by role playing. This model views relationship progression in developmental stages. According to this model, the couple's distress reflects difficulties in coping mechanisms related to life changes, which can be either environmental or personal. Despite relationship dissatisfaction, the couple will tend to resist change, maintaining status quo, and attempting baseline functioning to keep the system going.

Educational and preventive couples therapy

There are several programs designed for therapists to use with married and soon-to-be-married couples with the goal of establishing good communication early in the relationship. These programs, some of which have proven efficacy, focus on open communication, listening skills, and relationship training. Among these are the PREP program, which has been used since 1989 and is practiced by mental health professionals, laypersons, and clergy in 28 countries. It can have a secular or a religious basis. Other programs with strong research backing are the Couples Communication and the PAIRS programs. The Couples Communication Program involves an "awareness wheel" and a "listening wheel" that helps couples trace their issues and learn how to listen to one another. The Practical Application of Intimate Relationship Skills (PAIRS) program explores a couple's past emotional issues and the ways in which these have shaped their current interaction. Similarly to other programs, the focus is on listening and tackling problems.

Preparation

Couples should be informed that cooperation is vital for the process and they should have a desire to modify and/or change dysfunctional behaviors. Honesty and emotional openness is a necessary component for treatment. Results cannot be guaranteed. The psychotherapist would typically provide an extensive assessment process during the initial appointment. This couples assessment process usually includes in-depth information gathering concerning the presenting problem. It also includes, in the form an interview, an assessment of occupations, schooling, employment, childhood development, parental history, **substance abuse**, and religion; and relational, medical, legal, and past psychological history. After collecting the background information the psychotherapist can then devise the best course of treatment. Further psychological tests and measurements may be indicated initially or as the need arises during the treatment process.

Aftercare

Treatment usually takes several months or longer. Once the couple has developed adequate skills and has displayed an improved level of functioning that is satisfactory to both parties, then treatment can be terminated. The couple should be alert to the return to the behaviors that they are trying to change or

eliminate. These are called relapsing behaviors, and relapse-prevention behaviors can help keep them at bay. Patients are encouraged to return to treatment if **relapse** symptoms appear. Follow-up visits and long-term psychological therapy can be arranged between parties if this is mutually decided as necessary and beneficial.

Risks

The major risk of couples therapy is lack of improvement or return to dysfunctional behaviors. These tend not to occur unless there is a breakdown in skills learned and developed during treatment, or one person is resistant to long-term change.

Normal results

A normal progression of couples therapy is relief from symptomatic behaviors that cause marital discourse, distress, and difficulties. The couple is restored to healthier interactions and behaviors are adjusted to produce a happier balance of mutually appropriate interactions. Patients who are sincere and reasonable with a willingness to change tend to produce better outcomes. Patients usually develop skills and increased awareness that promotes healthier relationship interactions.

Abnormal results

There are no known abnormal results from couples therapy. At worst, patients do not get better because they cannot break away from self-induced, self-defeating behaviors that precipitate marital dysfunction and distress. The problems are not worsened if treatment is provided by a trained mental health practitioner in this specialty.

Resources

BOOKS

Noble, John, and others. *Textbook of Primary Care Medicine,* 3rd ed. Mosby, 2001.

Tasman, Allan, and others. *Psychiatry.* Philadelphia: W. B. Saunders Company, 1997.

PERIODICALS

Hampson, R. B, C. C. Prince, and W. R. Beavers. "Marital Therapy: Qualities of Couples who Fare Better or Worse in Treatment." *Journal of Marital and Family Therapy* 25.4 (Oct. 1999): 411–24.

ORGANIZATIONS

The American Association for Marriage and Family Therapy. 1133 15th Street NW, Suite 30, Washington, DC 20005. Telephone: (202) 452-0109. Fax: (202) 223-2329. Web site: <http:/www.aamft.org>.

OTHER

American Psychology Association, Psychology Matters. "Marital Education Programs Keep Couples Together." (2004) Available online at: <http://www.psychologymatters.org/maritaled.html>.

Gordon, Lori. "The PAIRS Program." Information available online at: <http://www.PAIRS.com>.

Markman, H.J., and Scott Stanley. "The PREP Program." Information available online at: <http://www.PREPinc.com>.

Miller, Sherod. "Couples Communication Program." Information available online at: <http://www.couplecommunication.com>.

Laith Farid Gulli, M.D.
Kathleen Berrisford, MSCSW,CAC
Emily Jane Willingham, PhD

Covert sensitization

Definition

Covert sensitization is a form of behavior therapy in which an undesirable behavior is paired with an unpleasant image in order to eliminate that behavior.

Purpose

As with other **behavior modification** therapies, covert sensitization is a treatment grounded in learning theory—one of the basic tenets being that all behavior is learned and that undesirable behaviors can be unlearned under the right circumstances. Covert sensitization is one of a group of behavior therapy procedures classified as covert conditioning, in which an aversive stimulus in the form of a nausea-or anxiety-producing image is paired with an undesirable behavior to change that behavior. It is best understood as a mixture of both the classical and the operant conditioning categories of learning. Based on research begun in the 1960s, psychologists Joseph Cautela and Albert Kearney published the 1986 classic *The Covert Conditioning Handbook*, which remains a definitive treatise on the subject.

The goal of covert sensitization is to directly eliminate the undesirable behavior itself, unlike insight-oriented psychotherapies that focus on uncovering unconscious motives in order to produce change. The behaviors targeted for modification are often referred to as "maladaptive approach behaviors," which includes behaviors such as alcohol **abuse**, drug abuse, and smoking; pathological gambling; overeating; sexual deviations, and sexually based nuisance behaviors such as obscene phone calling. The type of behavior to be changed and the characteristics of the aversive imagery to be used influence the treatment, which is usually administered in an outpatient setting either by itself or as a component of a multimodal program. Self-administered homework assignments are almost always part of the treatment package. Some therapists incorporate covert sensitization with hypnosis in the belief that outcome is enhanced.

Description

The patient being treated with covert sensitization can expect a fairly standard set of procedures. The therapist begins by assessing the problem behavior, and will most likely measure frequency, severity, and the environment in which it occurs. Depending upon the type of behavior to be changed, some therapists may also take treatment measures before, during, and after physiological arousal (such as heart rate) to better assess treatment impact. Although the therapeutic relationship is not the focus of treatment, the behavior therapist believes that good rapport will facilitate a more successful outcome and strives to establish positive but realistic expectations. Also, a positive relationship is necessary to establish patient confidence in the rationale for exposure to the discomfort of unpleasant images.

The therapist will explain the treatment rationale and protocol. Patient understanding and consent are important, since, by intention, he or she will be asked to experience images that arouse unpleasant and uncomfortable physical and psychological associations. The therapist and patient collaborate in creating a list of aversive images uniquely meaningful to the patient that will be applied in the treatment. Standard aversive images include vomiting, snakes, spiders, vermin, and embarrassing social consequences. An aversive image is then selected appropriate to the target problem behavior. Usually, the image with the most powerful aversive response is chosen. The patient is instructed on how to relax—an important precursor to generating intense imagery. The patient is then asked to relax and imagine approaching the situation where the undesirable behavior occurs (for example, purchasing donuts prior to overeating).

If the patient has a difficult time imagining the scene, the image may be presented verbally by the therapist. As the patient imagines getting closer to the situation (donut store), he or she is asked to clearly imagine an unpleasant consequence (such as vomiting) just before indulging in the undesirable behavior (purchasing donuts and overeating). The scene must be imagined with sufficient vividness that a sense of physiological discomfort or high anxiety is actually experienced. Then the patient imagines leaving the situation and experiencing considerable relief. The patient learns to associate unpleasant sensations (nausea and vomiting) with the undesirable behavior, leading to decreased desire and avoidance of the situation in the future. An alternative behavior incompatible with the problem behavior may be recommended (eat fruit when hungry for a donut).

The patient is given the behavioral homework assignment to practice self-administering the treatment. The patient is told to alternate the aversive scenes with scenes of self-controlled restraint in which he or she rejects the undesirable behavior before indulging in it, thus avoiding the aversive stimulus. The procedure is practiced several times with the therapist in the office, and the patient practices the procedure ten to 20 times during each home session between office sessions. The patient is then asked to practice in the actual situation, imagining the aversive consequences and avoiding the situation. With much variation, and depending upon the nature of the behavior targeted for change, the patient may see the therapist anywhere from five to 20 sessions over a period of a few weeks to several months. The treatment goal is to eliminate the undesirable behavior altogether.

Aftercare

Patients completing covert sensitization treatment are likely to be asked by the therapist to return periodically over the following six to twelve months or longer, for booster sessions to prevent **relapse**.

Risks

Covert sensitization is comparatively risk-free. This is in contrast to the medical and ethical concerns raised by some other aversive procedures such as **aversion therapy**, in which potent chemical and pharmacological stimulants may be used as aversants.

Normal results

Depending upon the objectives established at the beginning of treatment, patients successfully completing covert sensitization might expect to stop the undesirable behavior. And, if they practice **relapse prevention** techniques, they can expect to maintain the improvement. Although this treatment may appear to be relatively simple, it has been found to be quite effective for treating many circumscribed problem behaviors.

Resources

BOOKS

Cautela, Joseph, and Albert Kearney. *The Covert Conditioning Handbook*. New York: Springer, 1986.

Kaplan, Harold, and Benjamin Sadock, eds. *Synopsis of Psychiatry*. 8th ed. Baltimore: Williams and Wilkins, 1998.

Plaud, Joseph, and Georg Eifert, eds. *From Behavior Theory to Behavior Therapy*. Boston: Allyn and Bacon, 1998.

ORGANIZATIONS

Association for Advancement of Behavior Therapy. 305 Seventh Ave.—16th Floor, New York, NY 10001-6008. <http://www.aabt.org>.

John Garrison, Ph.D.

Creative therapies

Definition

Creative therapy refers to a group of techniques that are expressive and creative in nature. Creative therapies aim to help clients find a form of expression beyond words or traditional therapy, such as cognitive or **psychotherapy**. Therefore, the scope of creative therapy is as limitless as the imagination in finding appropriate modes of expression. The most commonly used and professionally supported approaches include art therapy, writing, sand play, clay **modeling**, movement therapy, psychodrama, role play, and music therapy.

Purpose

Creative therapy includes techniques that can be used for self-expression and personal growth when clients are unable to participate in traditional "talk therapy," or when that approach has become ineffective. Appropriate clients include children, individuals who are unable to speak due to **stroke** or **dementia**, or people who are dealing with clinical issues that are hidden within the subconscious, beyond the reach of language. The latter often occurs when the focus is on trauma or abuse that may have occurred before the client

A patient makes a silk scarf as part of their creative therapy at St. Michael's Hospice in the United Kingdom. *(Jon Cole/Photo Researchers, Inc)*

was able to speak, or in families where there is a strict code against talking about feelings or "negative" things. Creative therapy is also effective when used to explore fears around medical issues, such as cancer or HIV.

Precautions

Caution is indicated when strong emotions become overwhelming, thus debilitating the client. Possible indications for caution include the presence of flashbacks, panic attacks, recently revealed trauma or abuse, and vivid and realistic nightmares. Other indications for caution include individual characteristics, such as a tendency toward overly emotional responses, difficulty managing change or surprises, and poor coping skills. Therapists should also take care with patients with **psychosis** or **borderline personality disorder**.

Description

Visually expressive forms of creative therapy include drawing, painting, and modeling with clay. The goal is to provide a medium for expression that bypasses words, thus helping individuals connect with emotions about various personal experiences. The scope of the drawings

is limited only by the imagination of the individual and by the creativity of the therapists. This technique can often be continued by clients on their own after beginning the work in session.

Movement and music therapies are often used in conjunction with relaxation approaches. Movement therapy involves dance and the interpretation of feelings or thoughts into movement, and is often set to music. For teens in particular, music and movement are often healthy releases for **stress** and emotions. These therapies can also help people develop appropriate coping skills. Movement and music may be used in nursing homes, gym class, residential treatment centers, a therapist's office, or a home.

The physical and emotional health benefits of journaling techniques have been studied extensively. The application of journaling is broad and can be used in various therapeutic approaches. Journaling can be used on a regular basis for stress relief by writing down whatever comes to mind, or it can be used for specific problem areas, such as focusing attention on goals or on unresolved feelings of **grief** or anger. In journaling, it seems to be more important to focus on emotional aspects, rather than using it to simply record daily events.

Other techniques include sand play, pet therapy, **play therapy**, and horticulture therapy. Sand play is a specialized form of play therapy in which sand is used to form designs or set up stories using play figures. Play therapy is an approach used with children, and is quite extensive in background theory and application. It is a psychological therapy in which children play in a therapist's presence. The therapist then uses a child's fantasies and the symbolic meanings of the play as a medium for understanding and communicating with the child. Pet therapy and horticulture therapy are often used in hospitals and residential treatment centers. Although these therapies are not expressive in the same way as other approaches, they offer a different experience for the individuals participating in them—helping people feel a sense of joy, connection, or accomplishment that may be missing from their lives.

Preparation

Little preparation is needed for the visually expressive forms. Drawing is often used in a first session with young children. When used with adults, drawing or painting is often helpful, especially at a time of impasse when "talk therapy" is not effective, or when focusing on more emotional aspects of the therapeutic work.

Role playing requires the review of specific family roles to determine goals for the work. If the family work is focused on communication, each member may be asked to adopt the role of another family member to clarify perceptions of current roles for themselves and the other family members. The purpose of adopting these roles is to gain insight and understanding about each person's perspective in terms of their thoughts, feelings, and actions. Taking on the role of another helps to build empathy and provide a mechanism for personal growth and change.

A genogram or diagram of family members is sometimes helpful as a guide in identifying specific roles and directing the drama.

Aftercare

For most of the creative therapy techniques, aftercare will largely be maintained by the individual client, unless the individual is participating in a support group or ongoing therapy. One advantage of creative therapy is the ease of implementation. Little special equipment is needed, and many of the techniques easily lend themselves to use in the home. If an individual is participating in a support group or individual

therapy following **hospitalization**, the techniques can be maintained as part of those activities.

Risks

Risks occur when the client is exposed to intense emotional material or memories before the necessary preparatory work has been completed in therapy. Such negative reactions may include a psychotic break, or a need for hospitalization, although this is a rare occurrence.

A more likely risk is that of altering existing family relationships. Working through certain issues surrounding trauma or abuse may alter participants' feelings or thoughts about significant people in their lives. Conflicted feelings about these individuals may arise when clients recognize certain patterns or behaviors. The increased awareness and insight may make it impossible for the clients to continue some relationships. The resulting conflict may be uncomfortable for them.

Normal results

Typical results include increased awareness, the release of suppressed emotions, a general lifting of depressive feelings, increased energy, and the resolution of internal conflict. Ongoing health benefits, such as lowered blood pressure, may result from decreased stress and improved coping skills. Clients often experience a greater sense of self-acceptance and decreased agitation.

Abnormal results

Unusual results include increasingly intense feelings of agitation and stress. For some individuals, the techniques may appear to have no benefits. It is recommended that these individuals seek clinical help.

See also Support groups; Abuse; Grief counseling.

Resources

BOOKS

Bannister, Anne. *Creative Therapies with Traumatized Children.* London: Jessica Kingsley Publishers, 2003.

Carey, Lois, ed. *Expressive and Creative Arts Methods for Trauma Survivors.* London: Jessica Kingsley Publishers, 2006.

Gallo-Lopez, Loretta, and Charles E. Schaefer, eds. *Play Therapy with Adolescents.* Lanham, MD: Jason Aronson, 2005.

Ollier, Kate, and Angela Hobday. *Creative Therapy: Adolescents Overcoming Child Sexual Abuse.* Melbourne: ACER Press, 2004.

ORGANIZATIONS

American Art Therapy Association, Inc. 1202 Allanson Road, Mundelein, IL 60060. Telephone: (888) 290-0878. <www.arttherapy.org>.

OTHER

Arts in Therapy Network. <www.artsintherapy.com>.

Deanna Pledge, PhD
Ruth A. Wienclaw, PhD

Crisis housing

Definition

Crisis housing (or crisis residential services) are supervised short-term residential alternatives to **hospitalization** for adults with serious mental illnesses or children with serious emotional or behavioral disturbances.

Purpose

The course of most serious mental illness (such as **schizophrenia**, **bipolar disorder**, severe **depression**, and **borderline personality disorder**) is cyclical, typically characterized by periods of relative well-being, interrupted by periods of deterioration or **relapse**. When relapse occurs, the individual generally exhibits florid symptoms that require immediate psychiatric attention and treatment. More often than not, relapse is caused by the individual's failure to comply with a prescribed medication regimen (not taking medication regularly, not taking the amount or dose prescribed, or not taking it all). Relapse can also be triggered during periods of great **stress** or can even occur spontaneously, without any marked changes in lifestyle or medication regimen. When these crises recur, the goal of treatment is to stabilize the individual as soon as possible, since research suggests that relapsing patients are also more likely to attempt **suicide**.

Description

Over the past 35 years, crisis housing programs have evolved as short-term, less costly, and less restrictive residential alternatives to hospitalization. Intended to divert individuals from emergency rooms, jails, and hospitals into community-based treatment settings, they offer intensive crisis support to individuals and their families. Services include **diagnosis**, assessment, and treatment (including medication stabilization); rehabilitation; and links to community-based services. These programs are intended to stabilize the individual as rapidly as possible—usually between 8 and 60 days—so they can return to their home or residence in the community.

Some of the earliest crisis housing programs include Soteria House and La Posada, which began in northern California in the 1970s, and the START (short-term acute residential treatment) program that began in San Diego in 1980. While programs vary from location to location, most offer acute services 24 hours a day in a small noninstitutional residential setting. Adequate structure and supervision is provided by an interdisciplinary team of professionals and other trained workers.

Beginning the day they arrive, residents help develop their own plans for recovery and continued care in the community. Patients receive state-of-the art psychopharmacological treatment and other cognitive-behavioral interventions. Residents are encouraged to play an active role in the operation of the household, including meal preparation. The homelike environment is helpful in lessening the **stigma** and sense of failure that often occurs when someone needs to return to an inpatient psychiatric unit.

Similarly, in the case of seriously emotionally disturbed children and adolescents, the goal of crisis housing is to avert visits to the emergency room or hospitalization by stabilizing the individual in as normal a setting as possible. Compared to these services for adults, there is typically greater emphasis placed on involving families and schools in planning for community-based care after discharge.

Evaluations of several of these programs suggest that they may provide high-quality treatment and care at a lower cost than hospitals. Crisis housing is not currently available in all communities, however, although it is becoming more widely available.

See also Bipolar disorder; Borderline personality disorder; Crisis intervention; Schizophrenia.

Resources

BOOKS

Fields, Steven L. "Progress Foundation, San Francisco." Chapter 4 in *Alternatives to the Hospital for Acute Psychiatric Treatment*. R. Warner, ed. Clinical Practice Series No. 32. Washington, D.C.: American Psychiatric Press, 1995.

Torrey, E. Fuller. *Surviving Schizophrenia: A Manual for Families, Consumers and Providers*, 4th ed. New York: HarperCollins, 2001.

U.S. Department of Health and Human Services. *Mental Health: A Report of the Surgeon General*. Rockville, MD: U.S. Department of Health and Human Services, 1999. Available at <http://www.surgeongeneral.gov/library/mentalhealth/home.html>.

PERIODICALS

Burns, Barbara J., Kimberly Hoagwood, and Patricia J. Mrazek. "Effective Treatment for Mental Disorders in Children and Adolescents." *Clinical Child and Family Psychology Review* 2.4 (1999): 223–24.

"Gold Award: A Community-Based Program Providing a Successful Alternative to Acute Psychiatric Hospitalization." *Psychiatric Services* 52, no. 10 (October 2001): 1383–85.

Goodwin, Renee, and John S. Lyons. "An Emergency Housing Program as an Alternative to Inpatient Treatment for Persons with Severe Mental Illness." *Psychiatric Services* 52.1 (Jan. 2001): 92–95.

Hawthorne, W.B., and others. "A Randomized Trial of Short-Term Acute Residential Treatment for Veterans." *Psychiatric Services* 56 (2005): 1379–86.

Irene S. Levine, PhD
Emily Jane Willingham, PhD

Crisis intervention

Definition

Crisis **intervention** refers to methods used to offer immediate, short-term help to individuals who experience an event that produces emotional, mental, phys-

ical, and behavioral distress or problems. A crisis can be any situation in which an individual perceives a sudden loss of ability to use effective problem-solving and coping skills. Any number of events or circumstances can be considered crises, including life-threatening situations such as natural disasters (e.g., earthquakes, tornadoes, hurricanes), sexual assault or other criminal victimization, medical illness, mental illness, thoughts of **suicide** or homicide, or loss or drastic changes in relationships (e.g., death of a loved one or divorce).

Purpose

Crisis intervention has several purposes. It aims to reduce the intensity of an individual's emotional, mental, physical, and behavioral reactions to a crisis. Another purpose is to help individuals return to their level of functioning before the crisis. Functioning may be improved above and beyond this by developing new coping skills and eliminating ineffective ways of coping, such as withdrawal, isolation, and **substance abuse**. In this way, individuals are better equipped to cope with future difficulties. Through talking about what happened, and the feelings about what happened, while developing ways to cope and solve problems, crisis intervention aims to assist individuals in recovering from the crises and to prevent serious long-term problems from developing. Research documents positive outcomes for crisis intervention, such as decreased distress and improved problem solving.

Description

Individuals are more open to receiving help during crises. A person may have experienced the crisis within the last 24 hours or within a few weeks before seeking help. Crisis intervention is conducted in a supportive manner. The length of time for crisis intervention may range from one session to several weeks, with the average being four weeks. Crisis intervention is not sufficient for individuals with long-standing problems. Session length may range from 20 minutes to two or more hours. Crisis intervention is appropriate for children, adolescents, and younger and older adults. It can take place in a range of settings, such as hospital emergency rooms, crisis centers, counseling centers, mental health clinics, schools, correctional facilities, and other social service agencies. Local and national telephone hotlines are available to address crises related to suicide, domestic violence, sexual assault, and other concerns. They are usually available 24 hours a day, seven days a week.

Responses to crisis

A typical crisis intervention progresses through several phases. It begins with an assessment of what happened during the crisis and the individual's responses to it. There are certain common patterns of response to most crises. An individual's reaction to a crisis can include emotional reactions (e.g., fear, anger, guilt, **grief**), mental reactions (e.g., difficulty concentrating, confusion, nightmares), physical reactions (e.g., headaches, dizziness, **fatigue**, stomach problems), and behavioral reactions (e.g., sleep and appetite problems, isolation, restlessness). Assessment of the individual's potential for suicide and/or homicide is also conducted. Also, information about the individual's strengths, coping skills, and social support networks is obtained.

Education

There is an educational component to crisis intervention. It is critical for individuals to be informed about various responses to crises and informed that they are having normal reactions to an abnormal situation. Individuals will also be told that the responses are temporary. Although there is not a specific time that people can expect to recover from crises, individuals can help recovery by engaging in coping and problem-solving skills.

Coping and problem solving

Other elements of crisis intervention include helping individuals understand the crisis and their response to it as well as becoming aware of and expressing feelings, such as anger and guilt. A major focus of crisis intervention is exploring coping strategies. Strategies that the individuals previously used but that have not been used to deal with the current crisis may be enhanced or bolstered. Also, new coping skills may be developed. Coping skills may include relaxation techniques and exercise to reduce body tension and **stress** as well as putting thoughts and feelings on paper through journal writing instead of keeping them inside. In addition, options for social support or spending time with people who provide a feeling of comfort and caring are addressed. Another central focus of crisis intervention is problem solving. This process involves thoroughly understanding the problem and the desired changes, considering alternatives for solving the problem, discussing the pros and cons of alternative solutions, selecting a solution and developing a plan to try it out, and evaluating the outcome. Cognitive therapy, which is based on the notion that thoughts can influence feelings and behavior, can be used in crisis intervention.

In the final phase of crisis intervention, the professional will review changes the individual made in order to point out that it is possible to cope with difficult life events. Continued use of the effective coping strategies that reduced distress will be encouraged. Also, assistance will be provided in making realistic plans for the future, particularly in terms of dealing with potential future crises. Signs that the individual's condition is getting worse or "red flags" will be discussed. Information will be provided about resources for additional help should the need arise. A telephone follow-up may be arranged at some agreed upon time in the future.

Suicide intervention

Purpose

Suicidal behavior is the most frequent mental health emergency. The goal of crisis intervention in this case is to keep the individual alive so that a stable state can be reached and alternatives to suicide can be explored. In other words, the goal is to help the individual reduce distress and survive the crisis.

Assessment

Suicide intervention begins with an assessment of how likely it is that the individual will attempt suicide in the immediate future. This assessment has various components. The professional will evaluate whether or not the individual has a plan for how the act would be attempted, how deadly the method is (shooting, overdosing), if means are available (access to weapons), and if the plan is detailed and specific versus vague. The professional will also assess the individual's emotions, such as **depression**, hopelessness, hostility, and **anxiety**. Past suicide attempts as well as completed suicides among family and friends will be assessed. The nature of any current crisis event or circumstance will be evaluated, such as loss of physical abilities because of illness or accident, unemployment, and loss of an important relationship.

Treatment plan

A written safekeeping contract may be obtained. This is statement signed by such individuals that they will not commit suicide, and that they agree to various actions, such as notifying their clinician, family, friends, or emergency personnel, should thoughts of committing suicide again arise. This contract may also include coping strategies that the individuals agree to engage in to reduce distress. If the individuals state that they are not able to do this, then it may be determined that medical assistance is required and voluntary or involuntary psychiatric **hospitalization** may be implemented. Most individuals with thoughts of suicide do not require hospitalization and respond well to outpatient treatment. Educating family and friends and seeking their support are important aspects of suicide intervention. Individual therapy, **family therapy**, substance **abuse** treatment, and/or psychiatric medication may be recommended.

Critical incident stress debriefing and management

Definition

Critical incident stress debriefing (CISD) uses a structured, small-group format to discuss a distressing crisis event. It is the best-known and most widely used debriefing model. Critical incident stress management (CISM) refers to a system of interventions that includes CISD as well as other interventions, such as one-on-one crisis intervention, **support groups** for family and significant others, stress management education programs, and follow-up programs. It was originally designed to be used with high-risk professional groups, such as emergency services, public safety, disaster response, and military personnel. It can be used with any population, including children. A trained personnel team conducts this intervention. The team usually includes professional support personnel, such as mental health professionals and clergy. In some settings, peer support personnel, such as emergency services workers, will be part of the debriefing team. It is recommended that a debriefing occur after the first 24 hours following a crisis event, but before 72 hours have passed since the incident.

Purpose

This process aims to prevent excessive emotional, mental, physical, and behavioral reactions and **post-traumatic stress disorder** (PTSD) from developing in response to a crisis. Its goal is to help individuals recover as quickly as possible from the stress associated with a crisis.

Phases of CISD

There are seven phases to a formal CISD:

1. introductory remarks: The team sets the tone and rules for the discussion, and encourages participant cooperation.
2. fact phase: Participants describe what happened during the incident.
3. thought phase: Participants state the first or main thoughts while going through the incident.

4. reaction phase: Participants discuss the elements of the situation that were worst.
5. symptom phase: Participants describe the symptoms of distress experienced during or after the incident.
6. teaching phase: The team provides information and suggestions that can be used to reduce the impact of stress.
7. reentry phase: The team answers participants' questions and makes summary comments.

Precautions

Some concern has been expressed in the research literature about the effectiveness of CISD. It has been thought that as long as the provider(s) of CISD have been properly trained, the process should be helpful to individuals in distress. If untrained personnel conduct CISD, then it may result in harm to the participants. CISD is not **psychotherapy** or a substitute for it. It is not designed to solve all problems presented during the meeting. In some cases, a referral for follow-up assessment and/or treatment is recommended to individuals after a debriefing.

Medical crisis counseling

Medical crisis counseling is a brief intervention used to address psychological (anxiety, fear, and depression) and social (family conflicts) problems related to chronic illness in the health care setting. It uses coping techniques and builds social support to help patients manage the stress of being newly diagnosed with a chronic illness or suffering a worsening of a medical condition. It aims to help patients understand their reactions as normal responses to a stressful circumstance and to help them function better.

Preliminary studies of medical crisis counseling indicate that one to four sessions may be needed. Research is also promising in terms of its effectiveness at decreasing patients' levels of distress and improving their functioning.

See also Post-traumatic stress disorder.

Resources

BOOKS

Echterling, Lennis G., Jack Presbury, and J. Edson McKee. *Crisis Intervention: Promoting Resilience and Resolution in Troubled Times.* Upper Saddle River, NJ: Prentice Hall, 2004.

Hendricks, James E., Jerome B. McKean, and Cindy Gillespie Hendricks. *Crisis Intervention: Contemporary Issues for On-Site Interveners.* 3rd ed. Springfield, IL: Charles C. Thomas Publisher, 2003.

Roberts, Albert R. *Crisis Intervention Handbook: Assessment, Treatment, and Research.* New York: Oxford University Press, 2005.

Thyer, Bruce A. "'Tis a Consummation Devoutly to Be Wished." *Foundations of Evidence-Based Social Work Practice,* Albert R. Roberts, and Kenneth R. Yeager, eds. New York: Oxford University Press, 2006.

Wiger, Donald E., and Kathy J. Harowski. *Essentials of Crisis Counseling and Intervention.* New York: John Wiley & Sons, 2003.

PERIODICALS

Allen, Andrea, and others. "An Empirically Informed Intervention for Children Following Exposure to Severe Hurricanes." *The Behavior Therapist* 29.6 (Sept. 2006): 118–24.

Basoglu, Metin, Ebru Salcioglu, and Maria Livanou. "A Randomized Controlled Study of Single-Session Behavioural Treatment of Earthquake-Related Post-Traumatic Stress Disorder Using an Earthquake Simulator." *Psychological Medicine* 37.2 (Feb. 2007): 203–13.

Bruffaerts, Ronny, Marc Sabbe, and Koen Demyttenaere. "Who Visits the Psychiatric Emergency Room for the First Time?" *Social Psychiatry and Psychiatric Epidemiology* 41.7 (July 2006): 580–86.

Everly, George S., Jr., and others. "Introduction to and Overview of Group Psychological First Aid." *Brief Treatment and Crisis Intervention* 6.2 (May 2006): 130–36.

Gard, Betsy A., and Josef I. Ruzek. "Community Mental Health Response to Crisis." *Journal of Clinical Psychology* 62.8 (Aug. 2006): 1029–41.

Roberts, Albert R. "Applying Roberts' Triple ABCD Model in the Aftermath of Crisis-Inducing and Trauma-Inducing Community Disasters." *International Journal of Emergency Mental Health* 8.3 (Summer 2006): 175–82.

Roberts, Albert R. "Juvenile Offender Suicide: Prevalence, Risk Factors, Assessment, and Crisis Intervention Protocols." *International Journal of Emergency Mental Health* 8.4 (Fall 2006): 255–66.

Singer, Jonathan B. "Making Stone Soup: Evidence-Based Practice for a Suicidal Youth With Comorbid Attention Deficit/Hyperactivity Disorder and Major Depressive Disorder." *Brief Treatment and Crisis Intervention* 6.3 (Aug. 2006): 234–47.

Stapleton, Amy B., and others. "Effects of Medical Crisis Intervention on Anxiety, Depression, and Posttraumatic Stress Symptoms: A Meta-Analysis." *Psychiatric Quarterly* 77.3 (Sept. 2006): 231–38.

Vingilis, Evelyn, and others. "Process and Outcome Evaluation of an Emergency Department Intervention for Persons with Mental Health Concerns Using a Population Health Approach." *Administration and Policy in Mental Health and Mental Health Services Research* 34.2 (Mar. 2007): 160–71.

OTHER

National Strategy for Suicide Prevention. <www.mentalhealth.org/suicideprevention>.

Joneis Thomas, PhD
Ruth A. Wienclaw, PhD

Cyclothymic disorder

Definition

Cyclothymic disorder, also known as cyclothymia, is a relatively mild form of bipolar II disorder characterized by mood swings that may appear to be almost within the normal range of emotions. These mood swings range from mild **depression** (dysthymia) to mania of low intensity (**hypomania**).

Description

Cyclothymic disorder, a symptomatically mild form of bipolar II disorder, involves mood swings ranging from mild depression to mild mania. It is possible for cyclothymia to go undiagnosed, and for individuals with the disorder to be unaware that they have a treatable disease. Individuals with cyclothymia may experience episodes of low-level depression, known as dysthymia; or periods of intense energy, creativity, and/or irritability, known as hypomania; or they may alternate between both mood states. Like other bipolar disorders, cyclothymia is a chronic illness characterized by mood swings that can occur as often as every day and last for several days, weeks, or months. Individuals with this disorder are never free of symptoms of either hypomania or mild depression for more than two months at a time.

Persons with cyclothymic disorder differ in the relative proportion of depressive versus hypomanic episodes that they experience. Some individuals have more frequent depressive episodes, whereas others are more likely to feel hypomanic. Most individuals who seek help for the disorder alternate between feelings of mild depression and intense irritability. Those who feel energized and creative when they are hypomanic and find their emotionally low periods tolerable may never seek treatment.

Causes and symptoms

Causes

Controversy exists over whether cyclothymic disorder is truly a mood disorder in either biological or psychological terms, or whether it belongs in the class of disorders known as **personality disorders**. Despite this controversy, most of the evidence from biological and genetic research supports the placement of cyclothymia within the mood disorder category.

Genetic data provide strong support that cyclothymia is indeed a mood disorder. About 30% of all patients with cyclothymia have family histories of bipolar I disorder, which involves full-blown manic episodes alternating with periods of relative emotional stability. Full-blown depressive episodes are frequently, but not always, part of the picture in bipolar I disorder. Reviews of the family histories of bipolar I patients show a tendency toward illnesses that alternate across generations: bipolar I in one generation, followed by cyclothymia in the next, followed again by bipolar I in the third generation. The general prevalence of cyclothymia in families with bipolar I diagnoses is much higher than in families with other mental disorders or in the general population. It has been reported that about one-third of patients with cyclothymic disorder subsequently develop a major mood disorder.

Most psychodynamic theorists believe that the psychosocial origins of cyclothymia lie in early traumas and unmet needs dating back to the earliest stages of childhood development. Hypomania has been described as a deficiency of self-criticism and an absence of inhibitions. The patient is believed to use **denial** to avoid external problems and internal feelings of depression. Hypomania is also believed to be frequently triggered by profound interpersonal loss. The false feeling of euphoria (giddy or intense happiness) that arises in such instances serves as a protection against painful feelings of sadness, and even possibly anger against the lost loved one.

Symptoms

The symptoms of cyclothymic disorder are identical to those of bipolar I disorder except that they are usually less severe. It is possible, however, for the symptoms of cyclothymia to be as intense as those of bipolar I, but of shorter duration. About one-half of all patients with cyclothymic disorder have depression as their major symptom. These persons are most likely to seek help for their symptoms, especially during their depressed episodes. Other patients with cyclothymic disorder experience primarily hypomanic symptoms. They are less likely to seek help than those who suffer primarily from depression. Almost all patients with cyclothymic disorder have periods of mixed symptoms (both depression and hypomania together) during which time they are highly irritable.

Cyclothymic disorder usually causes disruption in all areas of the person's life. Most individuals with this disorder are unable to succeed in their professional or personal lives as a result of their symptoms. However, a few who primarily display hypomanic episodes are high achievers who work long hours and require little sleep. A person's ability to manage the symptoms of the disorder depends upon a number of personal, social, and cultural factors.

The lives of most people diagnosed with cyclothymic disorder are difficult. The cycles of the disorder tend to be much shorter than in bipolar I. In cyclothymic disorder, mood changes are irregular and abrupt, and can occur within hours. While there are occasional periods of normal mood, the unpredictability of the patient's feelings and behavior creates great **stress** not only for the patient but for those who must live or work with him/her. Patients often feel that their moods are out of control. During mixed periods, when they are highly irritable, they may become involved in unprovoked arguments with family, friends, and coworkers, causing stress to all around them.

It is common for cyclothymic disorder patients to **abuse** alcohol and/or other drugs as a means of self-medicating. It is estimated that about 5–10% of all patients with cyclothymic disorder also have substance dependence.

Demographics

Patients with cyclothymic disorder are estimated to constitute 3–10% of all psychiatric outpatients. They may be particularly well represented among those with complaints about marital and interpersonal difficulties. In the general population, the lifetime chance of developing cyclothymic disorder is about 1%. The actual percentage of the general population with cyclothymia is probably somewhat higher, however, as many patients may not be aware that they have a treatable disease or seek treatment if they do.

Cyclothymic disorder frequently coexists with **borderline personality disorder**, which is a severe lifelong illness characterized by emotional instability and relationship problems. An estimated 10% of outpatients and 20% of inpatients with borderline personality disorder have a coexisting **diagnosis** of cyclothymic disorder. The female-to-male ratio in cyclothymic disorder is approximately 3:2. It is estimated that 50–75% of all patients develop the disorder between the ages of 15 and 25.

Diagnosis

Since the symptoms tend to be mild, a diagnosis of cyclothymic disorder is usually not made until a person with the disorder is sufficiently disturbed by the symptoms or their consequences to seek help. While there currently are no laboratory tests or **imaging studies** that can detect the disorder, the patient will usually undergo a general physical examination to rule out general medical conditions that are often associated with depressed mood. The patient will also be given a psychological assessment to evaluate his/her symptoms, mental state, behaviors, and other relevant data. If the patient's history or other aspects of his or her behavior during the assessment suggest the diagnosis of cyclothymic disorder, friends or family members of the patient may be interviewed to gather additional data.

The manual used by mental health professionals to diagnose mental illnesses is called the *Diagnostic and Statistical Manual of Mental Disorders,* fourth edition, text revision, also known as the *DSM-IV-TR.* This manual specifies six criteria that must be met for a diagnosis of cyclothymic disorder. They are:

- Numerous episodes of hypomania and depression that are not severe enough to be considered major depression. These episodes must have occurred for at least two years.

- During the same two-year period (one year for children and adolescents), the individual has not been free from either hypomania or mild depression for more than two months at a time.

- No major depression, mania, or mixed (both depression and mania together) condition has been present during the first two years of the disorder.

- The individual does not have a thought disorder such as schizophrenia or other psychotic condition.

- The symptoms are not due to the direct effects of substance use (such as a drug of abuse or a prescribed medication) or to a medical condition.

- The symptoms cause significant impairment in the patient's social, occupational, family, or other important areas of life functioning.

Treatments

Biological therapy

Medication is an important component of treatment for cyclothymic disorder. A class of drugs known as antimanic medications is usually the first line of treatment for these patients. Drugs such as lithium, **carbamazepine** (Tegretol), and sodium valproate (Depakene), have all been reported to be effective. While antidepressant medications might be prescribed, they should be used with caution, because these patients are highly susceptible to hypomanic or full-blown manic episodes induced by **antidepressants**. It is estimated that 40–50% of all patients with cyclothymic disorder who are treated with antidepressants experience such episodes.

Psychosocial therapy

Psychotherapy with individuals diagnosed with cyclothymic disorder is best directed toward increasing the patients' awareness of their condition and helping them develop effective coping strategies for mood swings. Often, considerable work is needed to improve the patient's relationships with family members and workplace colleagues because of damage done to these relationships during hypomanic episodes. Because cyclothymic disorder is a lifelong condition, psychotherapy is also a long-term commitment. Working with families of cyclothymic patients can help them adjust more effectively to the patients' mood swings as well.

Prognosis

While some patients later diagnosed with cyclothymic disorder were considered sensitive, hyperactive, or moody as children, the onset of cyclothymic disorder usually occurs gradually during the patient's late teens or early twenties. Often school performance becomes a problem along with difficulty establishing peer relationships. Approximately one-third of all patients with cyclothymic disorder develop a major mood disorder during their lifetime, usually bipolar II disorder.

Prevention

Cyclothymic disorder appears to have a strong genetic component. It is far more common among

KEY TERMS

Bipolar I disorder—A major mood disorder characterized by full-blown manic episodes, often interspersed with episodes of major depression.

Bipolar II disorder—Disorder with major depressive episodes and mild manic episodes known as hypomania.

Borderline personality disorder—A severe and usually life-long mental disorder characterized by violent mood swings and severe difficulties in sustaining interpersonal relationships.

Cyclothymia—An alternate name for cyclothymic disorder.

Denial—A psychological defense mechanism that reduces anxiety by excluding recognition of an addiction or similar problem from the conscious mind.

Dysthymia—Depression of low intensity.

Hypomania—A milder form of mania which is characteristic of bipolar II disorder.

Psychodynamic theorists—Therapists who believe that the origins of mental problems lie in a person's internal conflicts and complexes.

Psychosocial—A term that refers to the emotional and social aspects of psychological disorders.

the first-degree biological relatives of persons with bipolar I disorder than among the general population. At this time, there are no known effective preventive measures that can reduce the risk of developing cyclothymic disorder. Genetic counseling, which assists a couple in understanding their risk of producing a child with the disorder, may be of some help.

See also Affect; Amitriptyline; Borderline personality disorder; Bupropion; Depression and depressive disorders overview; Fluoxetine; Mixed episode; Personality disorders.

Resources

BOOKS

American Psychiatric Association. *Diagnostic and Statistical Manual of Mental Disorders,* 4th ed., Text rev. Washington, D.C.: American Psychiatric Association, 2000.

Drevets, Wayne C., and Richard D. Todd. "Depression, Mania, and Related Disorders." *Adult Psychiatry* 2nd ed. Eugene H. Rubin and Charles F. Zorumski, eds. Malden, MA: Blackwell Publishing, 2005, 91–129.

PERIODICALS

Andlin-Sobocki, Patrik, and Hans-Ulrich Wittchen. "Cost of Affective Disorders in Europe." *European Journal of Neurology* 12, s1 (June 2005): 34–38.

ORGANIZATIONS

American Psychiatric Association. 1400 K Street NW, Washington, DC 20002. Telephone: (202) 336-5500.

Mental Illness Foundation. 420 Lexington Avenue, Suite 2104, New York, NY 10170. Telephone: (212) 682-4699.

Barbara S. Sternberg, PhD
Ruth A. Wienclaw, PhD

Cylert *see* **Pemoline**

D

Dalmane *see* **Flurazepam**
Dance therapy *see* **Bodywork therapies**

▌ Deinstitutionalization

Definition

Deinstitutionalization is a long-term trend wherein fewer people reside as patients in mental hospitals and fewer mental health treatments are delivered in public hospitals. This trend is directly due to the process of closing public hospitals and the ensuing transfers of patients to community-based mental health services in the late twentieth century. It represents the dissipation of patients over a wider variety of health care settings and geographic areas. Deinstitutionalization also illustrates evolution in the structure, practice, experiences, and purposes of mental health care in the United States.

History

Hospital care for mental health

In the United States in the nineteenth century, hospitals were built to house and care for people with chronic illness, and mental health care was a local responsibility. As with most chronic illness, **hospitalization** did not always provide a cure. Individual states assumed primary responsibilities for mental hospitals beginning in 1890. In the first part of the twentieth century, while mental health treatments had very limited efficacy, many patients received custodial care in state hospitals. Custodial care refers to care in which the patient is watched and protected, but a cure is not sought.

After the founding of the National Institutes of Mental Health (NIMH), new psychiatric medications were developed and introduced into state mental hospitals beginning in 1955. These new medicines brought new hope, and helped address some of the symptoms of mental disorders.

President John F. Kennedy's 1963 **Community Mental Health** Centers Act accelerated the trend toward deinstitutionalization with the establishment of a network of community mental health centers. In the 1960s, with the introduction of Medicare and Medicaid, the federal government assumed an increasing share of responsibility for the costs of mental health care. That trend continued into the 1970s with the implementation of the Supplemental Security Income program in 1974. State governments helped accelerate deinstitutionalization, especially of elderly people. In the 1960s and 1970s, state and national policies championed the need for comprehensive community mental health care, though this ideal was slowly and only partially realized.

Beginning in the 1980s, **managed care** systems began to review systematically the use of inpatient hospital care for mental health. Both public concerns and private health insurance policies generated financial incentives to admit fewer people to hospitals and discharge inpatients more rapidly, limit the length of patient stays, or to transfer responsibility to less costly forms of care.

Indicators and trends

Many statistical indicators show the amount of inpatient hospital care for persons with mental illness decreased during the latter half of the twentieth century, while the total volume of mental health care increased.

A patient care episode is a specific measure of the volume of care provided by an organization or system. It begins when a person visits a health care facility for treatment and ends when the person leaves the facility. In 1955, 77% of all patient care episodes in mental health organizations took place in 24-hour hospitals.

By 1994, although the numbers of patient care episodes increased by more than 500%, only 26% of mental health treatment episodes were in these hospitals. The timing of this trend varied across different states and regions, but it was consistent across a variety of indicators.

The number of inpatient beds available to each group of 100,000 civilians decreased from over 200 beds in 1970 to less than 50 in 1992. The average number of patients in psychiatric hospitals decreased from over 2,000 in 1958 to about 500 in 1978. While adjusted per-capita spending on mental health rose from $16.53 in 1969 to $19.33 in 1994, the portion of funds spent on state and county mental hospitals fell from $9.11 to $4.56.

Transinstutionalization

Trends toward deinstitutionalization also reflect shifting demographics and boundaries of care. For example, decreases in inpatient mental health care can be complemented by increases in outpatient mental health care. Decreases in inpatient mental health care can also be paired with increases in other forms of care, such as social welfare, criminal justice, or nursing home care. Thus deinstitutionalization is part of a process sometimes called transinstutionalization, the transfer of institutional populations from hospitals to jails, nursing homes, and shelters.

Causes and consequences

Causes

Deinstitutionalization, originally and idealistically portrayed by advocates and consumers as a liberating, humane policy alternative to restrictive care, may also be interpreted as a series of health policy reforms that are associated with the gradual demise of mental health care dependent on large, state-supported hospitals. Deinstitutionalization is often attributed to decreased need for hospital care and to the advent of new psychiatric medicines.

Consequences

Ideally, deinstitutionalization represents more humane and liberal treatment of mental illness in community-based settings. Pragmatically, it represents a change in the scope of mental health care from longer, custodial inpatient care to shorter outpatient care.

The process of deinstitutionalization, combined with the scarcity of community-based care, is also associated with the visible problems of **homelessness**. Between 30-50% of homeless people in the United States

KEY TERMS

Patient care episodes—A specific measure of the volume of care provided by an organization or system. It begins with a treatment visit to a health care facility (a hospital or residential treatment center, for example) and ends when a person leaves the facility, so it may vary by patient and visit. Over time, the volume of patient care episodes indicates the degree to which a population uses certain health care capacities. Other measures that may be used to measure volume of care include number of beds or bed-days, total number of patients served, and also more specific measures like patient-contact hours.

are people with mental illness, and people with mental illness are disproportionate among the homeless.

Experience and adjustment

Deinstitutionalization also describes the adjustment process whereby people with illness are removed from the effects of life within institutions. Since people may become socialized to highly structured institutional environments, they often adapt their social behavior to institutional conditions. Therefore adjusting to life outside of an institution may be difficult.

Defined experientially, deinstitutionalization allows individuals to regain freedom and empower themselves through responsible choices and actions. With the assistance of **social workers** and through psychiatric rehabilitation, former inpatients can adjust to everyday life outside of institutional rules and expectations. This aspect of deinstitutionalization promotes hope and recovery, ongoing debates over the best structure and process of mental health service delivery notwithstanding.

Resources

BOOKS

Dowdall, George. "Mental Hospitals and Deinstitutionalization." *Handbook of the Sociology of Mental Health*, edited by C. Aneshensel and J. Phelan. New York, Kluwer Academic. 1999.

Scheid, Teresa, and Allan Horwitz. "Mental Health Systems and Policy." *Handbook for the Study of Mental Health*. New York, Cambridge University Press. 1999.

Schlesinger, Mark, and Bradford Gray. "Institutional Change and Its Consequences for the Delivery of Mental Health Services." *Handbook of the Sociology of Mental Health*, edited by C. Aneshensel and J. Phelan. New York, Kluwer Academic. 1999.

Scull, Andrew. *Social Order/Mental Disorder*. Berkeley: University of California Press, 1989.

PERIODICALS

Grob, Gerald. "Government and Mental Health Policy: A Structural Analysis." *Milbank Quarterly* 72, no. 3 (1994): 471-500.

Redick, Richard, Michael Witkin, Joanne Atay, and others. "Highlights of Organized Mental Health Services in 1992 and Major National and State Trends." Chapter 13 in *Mental Health, United States, 1996,* edited by Ronald Mandersheid and Mary Anne Sonnenschein. Washington D.C.: US-GPO, US-DHHS, 1996.

Witkin, Michael, Joanne Atay, Ronald Manderscheid, and others. "Highlights of Organized Mental Health Services in 1994 and Major National and State Trends." Chapter 13 in *Mental Health, United States, 1998,* edited by Ronald Mandersheid and Marilyn Henderson. Washington D.C.: US-GPO, US-DHHS Pub. No. (SMA) 99-3285, 1998.

ORGANIZATIONS

American Psychiatric Association. 1400 K Street NW, Washington DC 20005. <http://www.psych.org>.

American Sociological Association. 1307 New York Ave., Washington DC 20005-4701. <http://www.asanet.org >.

National Institute of Mental Health. 6001 Executive Boulevard, Rm. 8184, MSC 9663, Bethesda, MD 20892-9663. (301) 443-4513. <http://www.nimh.nih.gov>.

Substance Abuse and Mental Health Services Administration (SAMHSA). Center for Mental Health Services (CMHS), Department of Health and Human Services, 5600 Fishers Lane, Rockville MD 20857. <http://www.samhsa.org>.

Michael Polgar, Ph.D.

Delirium

Definition

Delirium is a medical condition characterized by a general disorientation accompanied by cognitive impairment, mood shift, self-awareness, and inability to attend (the inability to focus and maintain attention). The change occurs over a short period of time—hours to days—and the disturbance in consciousness fluctuates throughout the day.

Description

The word delirium comes from the Latin *delirare*. In its Latin form, the word means to become crazy or to rave. A phrase often used to describe delirium is "clouding of consciousness," meaning the person has a diminished awareness of their surroundings. In the *Diagnostic and Statistical Manual of Mental Disorders IV, Text Revision*, also known as the *DSM-IV-TR*, delirium is classified according to its assumed causes; for example, "Substance-Induced Delirium" is one classification. These disorders involving delirium are listed in the same section as those involving **dementia**, but the two manifestations of illness differ in several characteristics. Dementia, for example, may exhibit a longer developmental process and is typically accompanied by multiple cognitive deficits.

While the delirium is active, the person tends to fade into and out of lucidity, meaning that he or she will sometimes appear to know what's going on, and at other times, may show disorientation to time, place, person, or situation. It appears that the longer the delirium goes untreated, the more progressive the disorientation becomes. It usually begins with disorientation to time, during which a patient will declare it to be morning, even though it may be late night. Later, the person may state that he or she is in a different place rather than at home or in a hospital bed. Still later, the patient may not recognize loved ones, close friends, or relatives, or may insist that a visitor is someone else altogether. Finally, the patient may not recognize the reason for his/her **hospitalization** and might accuse staff or others of some covert reason for his/her hospitalization. In fact, this waxing and waning of consciousness is often worse at the end of a day, a phenomenon known as "sundowning."

A delirious patient will have a difficult time with most mental operations. Because the patient cannot attend consistently to the environment, disorientation can result. Nevertheless, disorientation and memory loss are not essential to the **diagnosis** of delirium; the inability to focus and maintain attention, however, is essential to rendering a correct diagnosis. Left un-checked, delirium tends to transition from inattention to increased levels of lethargy, leading to torpor, stupor, and coma. In its other form, delirious patients become agitated and almost hypervigilant, with their sleep-wake cycle dramatically altered, fluctuating between great guardedness and **hypersomnia** (excessive drowsiness) during the day and wakefulness during the night. Delirious patients can also experience **hallucinations** of the visual, auditory, or tactile type. In such cases, the patient will see things others cannot see, hear things others cannot hear, and/or feel things that others cannot, such as feeling as though his or her skin is crawling. In short, the extremes of delirium range from the appearance of simple confusion and **apathy** to the anxious, agitated, and hyperactive type, with some patients experiencing both ends of the spectrum during a single episode. It is imperative that a quick evaluation occur if delirium is suspected because the condition can lead to death.

Demographics

Children, possibly because of their immature **brain** development and physiological differences from adults, can be particularly susceptible to delirium. This susceptibility is most common in association with fevers or some kinds of medications (such as anticholinergics, medications used for motor control problems). A child in a state of delirium may exhibit behavior that can be mistaken for willful lack of cooperation.

The elderly are also particularly sensitivity to delirium, also probably because of differences in physiology as we age. Being male and elderly enhances this risk.

Causes and symptoms

Causes

While the symptoms of delirium are numerous and varied, the causes of delirium fall into four basic categories: metabolic, toxic, structural, and infectious. Stated another way, the bases of delirium may be medical, chemical, surgical, or neurological. The *DSM-IV* lists four classifications of delirium: delirium due to a general medical condition; substance-induced delirium, which includes delirium resulting as a side effect of medication; delirium due to multiple etiologies, meaning it has many different causes; and delirium not otherwise specified, a category applied when the symptom does not fit into any of the other groups. Delirium is often associated with factors that result in a disturbance of the normal sleep-wake cycle.

METABOLIC CAUSES. Many metabolic disorders, such as hypothyroidism, hyperthyroidism, hypokalemia, and anoxia can cause delirium. For example, hypothyroidism (the thyroid gland emits reduced levels of thyroid hormones) brings about a change in emotional responsiveness, which can appear similar to depressive symptoms and cause a state of delirium. Other metabolic sources of delirium involve the dysfunction of the pituitary gland, pancreas, adrenal glands, and parathyroid glands. It should be noted that when a metabolic imbalance goes unattended, the brain may suffer irreparable damage.

DELIRIUM AND MEDICATION. One of the most frequent causes of delirium in the elderly is overmedication. The use of medications such as tricyclic **antidepressants** and antiparkinsonian medications can bring about an anticholinergic toxicity and subsequent delirium. In addition to the anticholinergic drugs, other drugs that can be the source of a delirium are:

- anticonvulsants, used to treat epilepsy
- antihypertensives, used to treat high blood pressure
- cardiac glycosides, such as Digoxin, used to treat heart failure

- cimetidine, used to reduce the production of stomach acid
- disulfiram, used in the treatment of alcoholism
- insulin, used to treat diabetes
- opiates, used to treat pain
- phencyclidine (PCP), used originally as an anesthetic, but later removed from the market, now only produced and used illicitly
- salicylates, basically found in aspirin
- steroids, sometimes used to prevent muscle wasting in bedridden or other immobile patients

Additionally, systemic poisoning by chemicals or compounds such as carbon monoxide, lead, mercury, or other industrial chemicals can be the source of delirium.

DELIRIUM AND OTHER SUBSTANCES. Just as the ingestion of certain drugs may cause delirium in some patients, the withdrawal of drugs can also cause it. Alcohol is the most widely used and most well known of these drugs whose withdrawal symptoms may include delirium. Delirium onset from the abstinence of alcohol in a chronic user can begin within three days of cessation of drinking. The term delirium tremens is used to describe this form of delirium. The resulting symptoms of this delirium are similar in nature to other delirious states but may be preceded by clear-headed auditory hallucinations. In other words, the delirium has not begun, but the patient may experience auditory hallucinations. Delirium tremens follow and can have ominous consequences with as many as 15% of those affected dying.

OTHER CAUSES OF DELIRIUM. Some of the structural causes of delirium include vascular blockage, subdural hematoma, and brain tumors. Any of these can damage the brain, through oxygen deprivation or direct insult, and cause delirium. Some patients become delirious following surgery. This can be due to any of several factors, such as effects of anesthesia, infections, or a metabolic imbalance.

Infectious diseases can also cause delirium. Commonly diagnosed diseases such as urinary tract infections, pneumonia, or fever from a viral infection can induce delirium. Additionally, diseases of the liver, kidney, lungs, and cardiovascular system can cause delirium. Finally, an infection, specific to the brain, can cause delirium. Even a deficiency of thiamine (vitamin B_1) can be a trigger for delirium.

Symptoms

Symptoms of delirium are often those associated with the disturbed sleep-wake cycle and include a confused state of mind accompanied by poor attention, impaired recent memory, irritability, inappropriate behavior (e.g., use of vulgar language, despite lack of a history of such behavior), and **anxiety** and fearfulness. In some cases, the person can appear to be psychotic, fostering illusions, **delusions**, hallucinations, and/or **paranoia**. In other cases, the patient may simply appear to be withdrawn and apathetic. In still other cases, the patient may become agitated and restless, unable to remain in bed, and feel a strong need to pace the floor. This restlessness and hyperactivity can alternate with periods of apparent stupor.

A few examples of people affected by delirium follow:

- One man, who had already been in the hospital for three days, when asked if he knew where he was, stated the correct city and hospital. He immediately followed this by saying, "but I started out in Dallas, Texas, this morning." The hospital location was some 1,800 miles from Dallas, Texas, and as previously indicated, he had been in the same hospital for three days.

- In another case, an elderly man was placed in a private room that had a wonderful large mural on one wall. The mural was that of a forest scene—no animals or people, only trees and sunlight. His chief complaint at various points during the day was that evil people were watching him from behind the trees in the forest scene.

- An elderly woman had to be subdued while attempting to flee from the hospital because she was convinced that she had been brought there so surgeons could harvest her organs. Despite the lack of surgical scars or incisions, she insisted that she had been taken to the basement of the hospital the previous night and that a surgeon had removed one of her kidneys.

Diagnosis

The diagnosis of delirium relies on a distinction of its occurrence from dementia. It should be determined not to arise from previously existing dementia. Other features include identifying it as a loss of clarity about the environment (inattention), sudden changes in cognition (e.g., disorientation), and a relatively sudden onset (compared to dementia).

Diagnosis of some cases of delirium may not occur at all; whether or not delirium is diagnosed in a patient depends on how it is manifested. If the person is an elderly, postoperative patient who appears quiet and apathetic, the condition may go undiagnosed. However, if the patient presents with the agitated,

uncooperative type of delirium, it will certainly be noticed. In any case, where there is sudden onset of a confused state accompanied by a behavioral change, delirium should be considered. This is not intended to imply that such a diagnosis will be made easily.

Frequent mental status examinations, at various times throughout the day, may be required to render a diagnosis of delirium. This assessment is generally done using the **Mini-Mental State Examination** (MMSE). This abbreviated form of mental status examination begins by first assessing the patient's ability to attend. If the patient is inattentive or in a stuporous state, further examination of mental status cannot be done. However, assuming the patient can respond to questions asked, the examination can proceed. The Mini-Mental State Exam assesses the areas of orientation, registration, attention and concentration, recall, language, and spatial perception. Another tool for use in diagnosing delirium is the Delirium Rating Scale-Revised-98, although studies regarding its ability to differentiate different types of delirium have not been undertaken. Yet another diagnostic tool is the Memorial Delirium Assessment Scale, or MDAS. One tool that does not require patient participation is the Confusion Assessment Method, or CAM.

At times, the untrained observer may mistake psychotic features of delirium for another primary mental illness such as **schizophrenia** or a **manic episode** such as that associated with **bipolar disorder**. However, it should be noted that there are major differences between these diagnoses and delirium. In people who have schizophrenia, their odd behavior, stereotyped motor activity, or abnormal speech persists in the absence of disorientation like that seen with delirium. The schizophrenic appears alert and although his/her delusions and/or hallucinations persist, he/she could be formally tested. In contrast, the delirious patient appears hapless and disoriented between episodes of lucidity. The delirious patient may not be testable. A manic episode could be misconstrued for agitated delirium, but consistency of elevated mood would contrast sharply to the less consistent mood of the delirious patient. Once again, delirium should always be considered when there is a rapid onset and especially when there is waxing and waning of the ability to attend and the confusion state.

Because delirium can be superimposed into a preexisting dementia, the most often posed question, when diagnosing delirium, is whether the person might have dementia instead. Both cause disturbances of memory, but a person with dementia does not reflect the disturbance of consciousness depicted by someone with delirium. Expert history taking is a must in differentiating dementia from delirium. Dementia is insidious in nature and thus progresses slowly, while delirium begins with a sudden onset and acute symptoms. A person with dementia can appear clearheaded, but can harbor delusions not elicited during an interview. One does not see the typical fluctuation of consciousness in dementia that manifests itself in delirium. It has been stated that, as a general rule, delirium comes and goes, but dementia comes and stays. Delirium rarely lasts more than a month. As a final caution, the clinician must be prepared to rule out **factitious disorder** and **malingering** as possible causes for the delirium.

When a state of delirium is confirmed, the clinician is faced with the task of making the diagnosis in appropriate context to its cause. The delirium may be caused by a general medical condition. In such a case, the clinician must identify the source of the delirium within the diagnosis. For example, if the delirium is caused by liver dysfunction, in which the liver cannot rid the system of toxins and allows them to enter the system and thus the brain, the diagnosis would be delirium due to hepatic encephalopathy. The delirium might also be caused by a substance such as alcohol. To render a diagnosis of alcohol intoxication delirium, the cognitive symptoms should be more exaggerated than those found in intoxication syndrome. The delirium could also be caused by withdrawal from a substance. Continuing the alcohol theme, the diagnosis would be alcohol withdrawal delirium (delirium tremens could be a feature of this diagnosis).

There may be instances in which delirium has multiple causes, such as when a patient has a head trauma and liver failure, or viral encephalitis and alcohol withdrawal. When delirium comes from multiple sources, a diagnosis of delirium precedes each medical condition that contributes.

Treatment

Treating delirium means treating the underlying illness that is its basis. This could include correcting any chemical disparities within the body, such as electrolyte imbalances, treating an infection, reducing a fever, or removing or discontinuing a medication or toxin. A review of anticholinergic effects of medications administered to the patient should take place. It is suggested that **sedatives** and hypnotic-type medications not be used; however, despite the fact that they can sometimes contribute to delirium, in cases of agitated delirium, the use of these may be necessary. Medications that are often used to treat agitated delirium include **haloperidol**, **thioridazine**, and **risperidone**. These can reduce the psychotic features and

curb some of the volatility of the patient, but they are only treating symptoms of the delirium and not the source. **Benzodiazepines** (medications that slow the central nervous system to relax the patient) can also assist in controlling agitated patients, but since they can contribute to delirium, they should be used in the lowest therapeutic doses possible. The reduction and discontinuance of all psychotropic drugs should be the goal of treatment and occur as soon as possible to permit recovery and viable assessment of the patient.

Prognosis

If a quick diagnosis and treatment of delirium occur, the condition is frequently reversible. However, if the condition goes unchecked or is treated too late, there is a high incidence of mortality or permanent brain damage associated with it. The underlying illness may respond quickly to a treatment regimen, but improvement in mental functioning may lag behind, especially in the elderly. Moreover, one study disclosed that one group of elderly survivors of delirium, at three years following hospital discharge, had a 33% higher rate of death than other patients. As a final note, delirium is a medical emergency, requiring prompt attention to avoid the potential for permanent brain damage or even death.

Resources

BOOKS

American Psychiatric Association. *Diagnostic and Statistical Manual of Mental Disorders*. 4th edition, text revised. Washington, DC: American Psychiatric Association, 2000.

Kaplan, Harold and Benjamin Sadock. *Synopsis of Psychiatry*. 8th edition. New York: Lippincott, Williams and Wilkins, 1997.

The Merck Manual. 17th edition. Whitehouse Station, N.J.: Merck Research Laboratories, 1999.

PERIODICALS

Chan, Daniel. "Delirium: Making the Diagnosis, Improving the Prognosis." *Geriatrics* 54 (1999): 28–42.

Curyto, Kim J., Jerry Johnson, Thomas TenHave, Jana Mossey, Kathryn Knott, and Ira R. Katz. "Survival of Hospitalized Elderly Patients With Delirium: A Prospective Study." *American Journal of Geriatric Psychiatry* 9 (2001): 141–147.

de Rooij, S.E., Schuurmans, M.J., van der Mast, R.C., and Levi, M. "Clinical subtypes of delirium and their relevance for daily clinical practice." *International Journal of Geriatric Psychiatry* 20 (2005): 60–615.

Katz, Ira R., Kim J. Curyto, Thomas TenHave, Jana Mossey, Laura Sands, and Michael Kallan. "Validating the Diagnosis of Delirium and Evaluating its Association With Deterioration Over a One-Year Period." *American Journal of Geriatric Psychiatry* 9 (2001): 148–159.

Trzepacz, Paula T. "The Delirium Rating Scale: Its Use in Consultation-Liaison Research." *Psychosomatics* 40 (1999): 193–204.

Trzepacz, Paula T., Dinesh Mittal, Rafael Torres, Kim Kanary, John Norton, and Nita Jimerson. "Validation of The Delirium Rating Scale-Revised-98: Comparison with the delirium rating scale and the cognitive test for delirium." *Journal of Neuropsychiatry and Clinical Neuroscience* 13 (2001): 229–242.

Webster, Robert and Suzanne Holroyd. "Prevalence of Psychotic Symptoms in Delirium." *Psychosomatics* 41 (2000): 519–522.

OTHER

National Guideline Clearinghouse. "Management of alcohol-based delirium tremens." <http://www.guideline.gov/summary/summary.aspx?ss=15&doc_id=6543&nbr=4109> (accessed January 20, 2007).

National Cancer Center. "Cognitive disorders and delirium." <http://www.cancer.gov/cancertopics/pdq/supportivecare/delirium/healthprofessional/allpages> (accessed January 20, 2007).

Jack H. Booth, Psy.D.

Delusional disorder

Definition

Delusional disorder is characterized by the presence of recurrent, persistent non-bizarre **delusions**.

Delusions are irrational beliefs, held with a high level of conviction, that are highly resistant to change even when the delusional person is exposed to forms of proof that contradict the belief. Non-bizarre delusions are considered to be plausible; that is, there is a possibility that what the person believes to be true could actually occur a small proportion of the time. Conversely, bizarre delusions focus on matters that would be impossible in reality. For example, a non-bizarre delusion might be the belief that one's activities are constantly under observation by federal law enforcement or intelligence agencies, which actually does occur for a small number of people. By contrast, a man who believes he is pregnant with German Shepherd puppies holds a belief that could never come to pass in reality. Also, for beliefs to be considered delusional, the content or themes of the beliefs must be uncommon in the person's culture or religion. Generally, in delusional disorder, these mistaken beliefs are organized into a consistent world-view that is logical other than being based on an improbable foundation.

In addition to giving evidence of a cluster of inter-related non-bizarre delusions, persons with delusional disorder experience **hallucinations** far less frequently than do individuals with **schizophrenia** or **schizoaffective disorder**.

Description

Unlike most other psychotic disorders, the person with delusional disorder typically does not appear obviously odd, strange or peculiar during periods of active illness. Yet the person might make unusual choices in day-to-day life because of the delusional beliefs. Expanding on the previous example, people who believe they are under government observation might seem typical in most ways but could refuse to have a telephone or use credit cards in order to make it harder for "those Federal agents" to monitor purchases and conversations. Most mental health professionals would concur that until the person with delusional disorder discusses the areas of life affected by the delusions, they would experience difficulty in distinguishing the patient from members of the general public who are not psychiatrically disturbed. Another distinction of delusional disorder compared with other psychotic disorders is that hallucinations are either absent or occur infrequently.

The person with delusional disorder may or may not come to the attention of mental health providers. Typically, while people with delusional disorder may be distressed about the delusional "reality," they may not have the insight to see that anything is wrong with the way they are thinking or functioning. Regarding the earlier example, those experiencing delusion might state that the only thing wrong or upsetting in their lives is that the government is spying, and if the surveillance would cease, so would the problems. Similarly, people with the disorder attribute any obstacles or problems in functioning to the delusional reality, separating it from their internal control. Furthermore, whether unable to get a good job or maintain a romantic relationship, the difficulties would be blamed on "government interference" rather than on their own failures or omissions. Unless the form of the delusions causes illegal behavior, somehow affects an ability to work, or otherwise deal with daily activities, the person with delusional disorder may adapt well enough to navigate life without coming to clinical attention. When people with delusional disorder decide to seek mental health care, the motivation for getting treatment is usually to decrease the negative emotions of **depression**, fearfulness, rage, or constant worry caused by living under the cloud of delusional beliefs, not to change the unusual thoughts themselves.

Forms of delusional disorder

An important aspect of delusional disorder is the identification of which form of delusion characterizes the individual. The most common form of delusional disorder is the persecutory or paranoid subtype, in which the patients are certain that others are striving to harm them.

In the erotomanic form of delusional disorder, the primary delusional belief is that some important person is secretly in love with the individual. The erotomanic type is more common in women than men. Erotomanic delusions may prompt stalking the love object and even violence against the beloved or those viewed as potential romantic rivals.

The grandiose subtype of delusional disorder involves the conviction of one's importance and uniqueness, and takes a variety of forms: believing that one has a distinguished role, has some remarkable connections with important persons, or enjoys some extraordinary powers or abilities.

In the somatic subtype, there is excessive concern and irrational ideas about bodily functioning, which may include worries regarding infestation with parasites or insects, imagined physical deformity, or a conviction that one is emitting a foul stench when there is no problematic odor.

The form of disorder most associated with violent behavior, usually between romantic partners, is the jealous subtype of delusional disorder. Patients are firmly convinced of the infidelity of a spouse or partner, despite contrary evidence and based on minimal data (like a messy bedspread or more cigarettes than usual in an ashtray, for instance). People with delusional jealousy may gather scraps of conjectured "evidence," and may try to constrict their partners' activities or confine them to home. Delusional disorder cases involving aggression and injury toward others have been most associated with this subtype.

Delusion and other disorders

Even though the main characteristic of delusional disorder is a noticeable system of delusional beliefs, delusions may occur in the course of a large number of other psychiatric disorders. Delusions are often observed in persons with other psychotic disorders such as schizophrenia and schizoaffective disorder. In addition to occurring in the psychotic disorders, delusions also may be evident as part of a response to physical, medical conditions (such as **brain** injury or brain tumors), or reactions to ingestion of a drug.

Delusions also occur in the dementias, which are syndromes wherein psychiatric symptoms and memory loss result from deterioration of brain tissue. Because delusions can be shown as part of many illnesses, the **diagnosis** of delusional disorder is partially conducted by process of elimination. If the delusions are not accompanied by persistent, recurring hallucinations, then schizophrenia and schizoaffective disorder are not appropriate diagnoses. If the delusions are not accompanied by memory loss, then **dementia** is ruled out. If there is no physical illness or injury or other active biological cause (such as drug ingestion or drug withdrawal), then the delusions cannot be attributed to a general medical problem or drug-related causes. If delusions are the most obvious and pervasive symptom, without hallucinations, medical causation, drug influences or memory loss, then delusional disorder is the most appropriate categorization.

Because delusions occur in many different disorders, some clinician-researchers have argued that there is little usefulness in focusing on what diagnosis the person has been given. Those who ascribe to this view believe it is more important to focus on the symptom of delusional thinking, and find ways to have an effect on delusions, whether they occur in delusional disorder or schizophrenia or schizoaffective disorder. The majority of **psychotherapy** techniques used in delusional disorder come from symptom-focused (as opposed to diagnosis-focused) researcher-practitioners.

Causes and symptoms

Causes

Because clear identification of delusional disorder has traditionally been challenging, scientists have conducted far less research relating to the disorder than studies for schizophrenia or mood disorders. Still, some theories of causation have developed, which fall into several categories.

GENETIC OR BIOLOGICAL. Close relatives of persons with delusional disorder have increased rates of delusional disorder and paranoid personality traits. They do not have higher rates of schizophrenia, schizoaffective disorder or mood disorder compared to relatives of non-delusional persons. Increased incidence of these psychiatric disorders in individuals closely genetically related to persons with delusional disorder suggest that there is a genetic component to the disorder. Furthermore, a number of studies comparing activity of different regions of the brain in delusional and non-delusional research participants yielded data about differences in the functioning of the brains between members of the two groups. These differences in brain activity suggest that, persons neurologically with delusions tend to react as if threatening conditions are consistently present. Non-delusional persons only show such patterns under certain kinds of conditions where the interpretation of being threatened is more accurate. With both brain activity evidence and family heritability evidence, a strong chance exists that there is a biological aspect to delusional disorder.

DYSFUNCTIONAL COGNITIVE PROCESSING. An elaborate term for thinking is "cognitive processing." Delusions may arise from distorted ways people have of explaining life to themselves. The most prominent cognitive problems involve the manner in which peo-

ple with delusion develop conclusions both about other people, and about causation of unusual perceptions or negative events. Studies examining how people with delusions develop theories about reality show that the subjects have ideas which they tend to reach an inference based on less information than most people use. This "jumping to conclusions" bias can lead to delusional interpretations of ordinary events. For example, developing flu-like symptoms coinciding with the week new neighbors move in might lead to the conclusion, "the new neighbors are poisoning me." The conclusion is drawn without considering alternative explanations—catching an illness from a relative with the flu, that a virus seems to be going around at work, or that the tuna salad from lunch at the deli may have been spoiled. Additional research shows that persons prone to delusions "read" people differently than non-delusional individuals do. Whether they do so more accurately or particularly poorly is a matter of controversy. Delusional persons develop interpretations about how others view them that are distorted. They tend to view life as a continuing series of threatening events. When these two aspects of thought co-occur, a tendency to develop delusions about others wishing to do them harm is likely.

MOTIVATED OR DEFENSIVE DELUSIONS. Some predisposed persons might experience the onset of an ongoing delusional disorder when coping with life and maintaining high self-esteem becomes a significant challenge. In order to preserve a positive view of oneself, a person views others as the cause of personal difficulties that may occur. This can then become an ingrained pattern of thought.

Symptoms

The criteria that define delusional disorder are furnished in the *Diagnostic and Statistical Manual of Mental Disorders*, Fourth Edition Text Revision, or *DSM-IV-TR*, published by the American Psychiatric Association. The criteria for delusional disorder are as follows:

- non-bizarre delusions that have been present for at least one month

- absence of obviously odd or bizarre behavior

- absence of hallucinations, or hallucinations that only occur infrequently in comparison to other psychotic disorders

- no memory loss, medical illness or drug or alcohol-related effects are associated with the development of delusions

Demographics

The base rate of delusional disorder in adults is unclear. The prevalence is estimated at 0.025-0.03%, lower than the rates for schizophrenia (1%). Delusional disorder may account for 1–2% of admissions to inpatient psychiatric hospitals. Age at onset ranges from 18–90 years, with a mean age of 40 years. More females than males (overall) develop delusional disorder, especially the late onset form that is observed in the elderly.

Diagnosis

Client interviews focused on obtaining information about the individual's life situation and past history aid in identification of delusional disorder. With the client's permission, the clinician obtains details from earlier medical records, and engages in thorough discussion with the client's immediate family—helpful measures in determining whether delusions are present. The clinician may use a semi-structured interview called a mental status examination to assess the patient's concentration, memory, understanding the individual's situation and logical thinking. The mental status examination is intended to reveal peculiar thought processes in the patient. The Peters Delusion Inventory (PDI) is a psychological test that focuses on identifying and understanding delusional thinking; but its use is more common in research than in clinical practice.

Even using the *DSM-IV-TR* criteria, classification of delusional disorder is relatively subjective. The criteria "non-bizarre" and "resistant to change" and "not culturally accepted" are all subject to very individual interpretations. They create variability in how professionals diagnose the illness. The utility of diagnosing the syndrome rather than focusing on successful treatment of delusion in any form of illness is debated in the medical community. Some researchers further contend that delusional disorder, currently classified as a psychotic disorder, is actually a variation of depression and might respond better to **antidepressants** or therapy more similar to that utilized for depression. Also, the meaning and implications of "culturally accepted" can create problems. The cultural relativity of "delusions"—most evident where the beliefs shown are typical of the person's subculture or religion yet would be viewed as strange or delusional by the dominant culture—can force complex choices to be made in diagnosis and treatment. An example could be that of a Haitian immigrant to the United States who believed in voodoo. If that person became aggressive toward neighbors issuing curses or hexes, believing that death is imminent at the hands of those neighbors, a question arises. The belief is typical of the individual's subculture, so the issue is whether it should be diagnosed or treated. If it were to be treated, whether the remedy should come through Western medicine, or be conducted through voodoo shamanistic treatment is the problem to be solved.

Treatments

Delusional disorder treatment often involves atypical (also called novel or newer-generation) antipsychotic medications, which can be effective in some patients. **Risperidone** (Risperdal), **quetiapine** (Seroquel), and **olanzapine** (Zyprexa) are all examples of atypical or novel antipsychotic medications. If agitation occurs, a number of different antipsychotics can be used to conclude the outbreak of acute agitation. Agitation, a state of frantic activity experienced concurrently with anger or exaggerated fearfulness, increases the risk that the client will endanger self or others. To decrease **anxiety** and slow behavior in emergency situations where agitation is a factor, an injection of **haloperidol** (Haldol) is often given usually in combination with other medications (often **lorazepam**, also known as Ativan). Agitation in delusional disorder is a typical response to severe or harsh confrontation when dealing with the existence of the delusions. It can also be a result of blocking the individual from performing inappropriate actions the client views as urgent in light of the delusional reality. A novel antipsychotic is generally given orally on a daily basis for ongoing treatment meant for long term effect on the symptoms. Response to antipsychotics in delusional disorder seems to follow the "rule of thirds," in which about one-third of patients respond somewhat positively, one-third show little change, and one-third worsen or are unable to comply.

Cognitive therapy has shown promise as an emerging treatment for delusions. The cognitive therapist tries to capitalize on any doubt the individual has about the delusions; then attempts to develop a joint effort with the patient to generate alternative explanations, assisting the client in checking the evidence. This examination proceeds in favor of the various explanations. Much of the work is done by use of empathy, asking hypothetical questions in a form of therapeutic Socratic dialogue—a process that follows a basic question and answer format, figuring out what is known and unknown before reaching a logical conclusion. Combining pharmacotherapy with cognitive therapy integrates both treating the possible underlying biological problems and decreasing the symptoms with psychotherapy.

KEY TERMS

Hallucinations—False sensory perceptions. A person experiencing a hallucination may "hear" sounds or "see" people or objects that are not really present. Hallucinations can also affect the senses of smell, touch, and taste.

Psychosis or psychotic symptoms—Disruptions in perceiving reality, thinking logically, and speaking or behaving in normal fashion. Hallucinations, delusions, catatonic behavior and peculiar speech are all symptoms of psychosis. In *DSM-IV-TR*, psychosis is usually one feature of an over-arching disorder, not a disorder in itself (with the exception of the diagnosis psychosis not otherwise specified.

Prognosis

Evidence collected to date indicates about 10% of cases will show some improvement of delusional symptoms though irrational beliefs may remain; 33–50% may show complete remission; and, in 30–40% of cases there will be persistent non-improving symptoms. The prognosis for clients with delusional disorder is largely related to the level of conviction regarding the delusions and the openness the person has for allowing information that contradicts the delusion.

Prevention

Little work has been done thus far regarding prevention of the disorder. Effective means of prevention have not been identified.

See also Dementia; Depression (with psychotic features); Paranoia; Paranoid personality disorder; Schizoaffective disorder; Schizophrenia.

Resources

BOOKS

American Psychiatric Association. *Diagnostic and Statistical Manual of Mental Disorders.* 4th edition, text revised. Washington, DC: American Psychiatric Association, 2000.

Chadwick, Paul, Max Birchwood, and Peter Trower. *Cognitive Therapy for Delusions, Voices and Paranoia.* Chichester, United Kingdom: Wiley and Sons, 1996.

Fuller, Matthew, and M. Sajatovic. *Drug Information for Mental Health* Hudson, Ohio: Lexi-comp, 2000.

PERIODICALS

Bentall, Richard P., Rhiannon Corcoran, Robert Howard, Nigel Blackwood, and Peter Kinderman. "Persecutory delusions: A review and theoretical integration." *Clinical Psychology Review* 21, no. 8 (2001): 1143–1193.

Garety, Philippa A. and Daniel Freeman. "Cognitive approaches to delusions: A critical review of theories and evidence." *British Journal of Clinical Psychology* 38 (1999): 113–154.

Haddock, Gillian, Nicholas Tarrier, William Spaulding, Lawrence Yusupoff, Caroline Kinney and Eilis McCarthy. "Individual cognitive therapy in the treatment of hallucinations and delusions: A review." *Clinical Psychology Review* 18, no. 7 (1998): 821–838.

ORGANIZATIONS

National Alliance for the Mentally Ill. Colonial Place Three, 2107 Wilson Blvd., Suite 300, Arlington, VA 22201. Telephone: (703) 524-7600. NAMI HelpLine: 1-800-950-NAMI (6264). <http://www.nami.org>.

Deborah Rosch Eifert, Ph.D.

Delusions

Description

A delusion is a belief that is clearly false and that indicates an abnormality in the affected person's content of thought. The false belief is not accounted for by the person's cultural or religious background or his or her level of intelligence. The key feature of a delusion is the degree to which the person is convinced that the belief is true. A person with a delusion will hold firmly to the belief regardless of evidence to the contrary. Delusions can be difficult to distinguish from overvalued ideas, which are unreasonable ideas that a person holds, but the affected person has at least some level of doubt as to its truthfulness. A person with a delusion is absolutely convinced that the delusion is real.

Delusions are a symptom of either a medical, neurological, or mental disorder. Delusions may be present in any of the following mental disorders:

- psychotic disorders, or disorders in which the affected person has a diminished or distorted sense of reality and cannot distinguish the real from the unreal, including **schizophrenia, schizoaffective disorder, delusional disorder,** schizophreniform disorder, shared psychotic disorder, brief psychotic disorder, and substance-induced psychotic disorder
- bipolar disorder
- major depressive disorder with psychotic features
- delirium
- **dementia**

Overvalued ideas may be present in **anorexia nervosa**, **obsessive-compulsive disorder**, **body dysmorphic disorder**, and **hypochondriasis**.

Types

Delusions are categorized as either bizarre or non-bizarre and as either mood-congruent or mood-incongruent. A bizarre delusion is a delusion that is very strange and completely implausible for the person's culture; an example of a bizarre delusion would be that aliens have removed the affected person's **brain**. A non-bizarre delusion is one whose content is definitely mistaken, but is at least possible; an example may be that the affected person mistakenly believes that he or she is under constant police surveillance. A mood-congruent delusion is any delusion whose content is consistent with either a depressive or manic state; for example, a depressed person may believe that the world is ending, or a person in a manic state (a state in which the person feels compelled to take on new projects, has a lot of energy, and needs little sleep) believes that he or she has special talents or abilities, or is a famous person. A mood-incongruent delusion is any delusion whose content is not consistent with either a depressed or manic state or is mood-neutral. An example is a depressed person who believes that thoughts are being inserted into his or her mind from some outside force, person, or group of people, and these thoughts are not recognized as the person's own thoughts (called "thought insertion").

In addition to these categories, delusions are often categorized according to theme. Although delusions can have any theme, certain themes are more common. Some of the more common delusion themes are:

- delusion of control. This is a false belief that another person, group of people, or external force controls one's thoughts, feelings, impulses, or behavior. A person may describe, for instance, the experience that aliens actually make him or her move in certain ways and that the person affected has no control over the bodily movements. Thought broadcasting (the false belief that the affected person's thoughts are heard aloud), thought insertion, and thought withdrawal (the belief that an outside force, person, or group of people is removing or extracting a person's thoughts) are also examples of delusions of control.

- nihilistic delusion. A delusion whose theme centers on the nonexistence of self or parts of self, others, or the world. A person with this type of delusion may have the false belief that the world is ending.

- delusional jealousy (or delusion of infidelity): A person with this delusion falsely believes that his or her spouse or lover is having an affair. This delusion stems from pathological jealousy and the person often gathers "evidence" and confronts the spouse about the nonexistent affair.

- delusion of guilt or sin (or delusion of self-accusation): This is a false feeling of remorse or guilt of delusional intensity. A person may, for example, believe that he or she has committed some horrible crime and should be punished severely. Another example is a person who is convinced that he or she is responsible for some disaster (such as fire, flood, or earthquake) with which there can be no possible connection.

- delusion of mind being read: The false belief that other people can know one's thoughts. This is different from thought broadcasting in that the person does not believe that his or her thoughts are heard aloud.

- delusion of reference: The person falsely believes that insignificant remarks, events, or objects in one's environment have personal meaning or significance. For instance, a person may believe that he or she is receiving special messages from the news anchorperson on television. Usually the meaning assigned to these events is negative, but the "messages" can also have a grandiose quality.

- erotomania: A delusion in which one believes that another person, usually someone of higher status, is in love with him or her. It is common for individuals with this type of delusion to attempt to contact the other person (through phone calls, letters, gifts, and sometimes stalking).

- grandiose delusion: An individual exaggerates his or her sense of self-importance and is convinced that he or she has special powers, talents, or abilities. Sometimes, the individual may actually believe that he or she is a famous person (for example, a rock star or Christ). More commonly, a person with this delusion believes he or she has accomplished some great achievement for which he or she has not received sufficient recognition.

- persecutory delusions: These are the most common type of delusions and involve the theme of being followed, harassed, cheated, poisoned or drugged, conspired against, spied on, attacked, or obstructed in the pursuit of goals. Sometimes the delusion is isolated and fragmented (e.g., the false belief that co-workers are harassing), but sometimes are well-organized belief systems involving a complex set of delusions ("systematized delusions"). A person with a set of persecutory delusions may be believe, for example, that he or she is being followed by government organizations because the "persecuted" person has been falsely identified as a spy. These systems of

KEY TERMS

Delusion—A false belief that is resistant to reason or contrary to actual fact.

Overvalued idea—An unreasonable, sustained belief that is held with less than delusional intensity (i.e., the person can acknowledge, to some degree, that the belief may be false). The belief is not accounted for by the individual's cultural or religious background.

beliefs can be so broad and complex that they can explain everything that happens to the person.

- religious delusion: Any delusion with a religious or spiritual content. These may be combined with other delusions, such as grandiose delusions (the belief that the affected person was chosen by God, for example), delusions of control, or delusions of guilt. Beliefs that would be considered normal for an individual's religious or cultural background are not delusions.

- somatic delusion: A delusion whose content pertains to bodily functioning, bodily sensations, or physical appearance. Usually the false belief is that the body is somehow diseased, abnormal, or changed. An example of a somatic delusion would be a person who believes that his or her body is infested with parasites.

Delusions of control, nihilistic delusions, and thought broadcasting, thought insertion, and thought withdrawal are usually considered bizarre delusions. Most persecutory, somatic, grandiose, and religious delusions, as well as most delusions of jealousy, delusions of mind being read, and delusions of guilt would be considered non-bizarre.

See also Hallucinations.

Resources

BOOKS

American Psychiatric Association. *Diagnostic and Statistical Manual of Mental Disorders.* 4th ed., text rev. Washington, D.C.: American Psychiatric Association, 2000.

Kaplan, Harold I., MD, and Benjamin J. Sadock, MD. *Kaplan and Sadock's Synopsis of Psychiatry: Behavioral Sciences, Clinical Psychiatry.* 8th ed. Baltimore: Williams and Wilkins, 2002.

PERIODICALS

Leeser, Jaimie, and William O'Donohue. "What is a Delusion? Epistemological Dimensions." *Journal of Abnormal Psychology* 108 (1999): 687–94.

Jennifer Hahn, Ph.D.
Margaret Brantley

Dementia

Definition

Dementia is not a specific disorder or disease. It is a syndrome (group of symptoms) associated with a progressive loss of memory and other intellectual functions that is serious enough to interfere with performing the tasks of daily life. Dementia can occur to anyone at any age from an injury or from oxygen deprivation, although it is most commonly associated with aging. It is the leading cause of institutionalization of older adults.

Description

The definition of dementia has become more inclusive over the past several decades. Whereas earlier descriptions of dementia emphasized memory loss, the last three editions of the professional's diagnostic handbook, ***Diagnostic and Statistical Manual of Mental Disorders*** (also known as the *DSM*) define dementia as an overall decline in intellectual function, including difficulties with language, simple calculations, planning and judgment, and motor (muscular movement) skills, as well as loss of memory. Although dementia is not caused by aging itself—most researchers regard it as resulting from injuries, infections, **brain** diseases, tumors, or other disorders—it is quite common in older people. The prevalence of dementia increases rapidly with age; it doubles every five years after age 60. Dementia affects only 1% of people aged 60–64 but 30%–50% of those older than 85. About four to five million persons in the United States are affected by dementia as of 2006. Surveys have indicated that dementia is the condition most feared by older adults in the United States.

Causes and symptoms

Causes

Dementia can be caused by almost 40 different diseases and conditions, ranging from dietary deficiencies and metabolic disorders to head injuries and inherited diseases. The possible causes of dementia can be categorized as follows:

- Primary dementia. These dementias are characterized by damage to or wasting away of the brain tissue itself. They include Alzheimer's disease (AD), frontal lobe dementia (FLD), and Pick's disease. FLD is dementia caused by a disorder (usually genetic) that affects the front portion of the brain, and Pick's disease is a rare type of primary dementia that is characterized by a progressive loss of social skills,

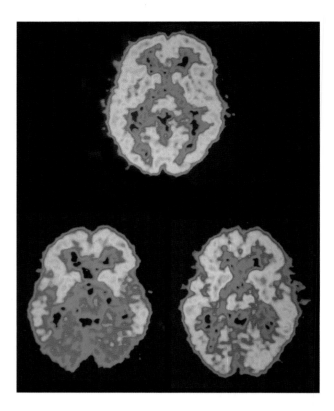

Three PET scans: top scan is a normal brain; bottom left scan is of a patient with HIV-induced dementia; bottom right is the same patient following treatment with AZT (azidothymidine). *(Medical-on-Line/Alamy)*

language, and memory, leading to personality changes and sometimes loss of moral judgment.

- Multi-infarct dementia (MID). Sometimes called vascular dementia, this type is caused by blood clots in the small blood vessels of the brain. When the clots cut off the blood supply to the brain tissue, the brain cells are damaged and may die. (An infarct is an area of dead tissue caused by obstruction of the circulation.)

- Lewy body dementia. Lewy bodies are areas of injury found on damaged nerve cells in certain parts of the brain. They are associated with AD and Parkinson's disease, but researchers do not yet know whether dementia with Lewy bodies is a distinct type of dementia or a variation of AD or Parkinson's disease.

- Dementia related to alcoholism or exposure to heavy metals (arsenic, antimony, bismuth).

- Dementia related to infectious diseases. These infections may be caused by viruses (HIV, viral encephalitis); spirochetes (Lyme disease, syphilis); or prions (Creutzfeldt-Jakob disease). Spirochetes are certain kinds of bacteria, and prions are protein particles that lack nucleic acid.

- Dementia related to abnormalities in the structure of the brain. These may include a buildup of spinal fluid in the brain (hydrocephalus); tumors; or blood collecting beneath the membrane that covers the brain (subdural hematoma).

Dementia may also be associated with **depression**, low levels of thyroid hormone, or niacin or vitamin B_{12} deficiency. Dementia related to these conditions is often reversible.

Genetic factors in dementia

Genetic factors play a role in several types of dementia, but the importance of these factors in the development of the dementia varies considerably. AD is known, for example, to have an autosomal (non-sex-related) dominant pattern in most early-onset cases as well as in some late-onset cases, and to show different degrees of penetrance (frequency of expression) in late-life cases. Recently, two forms of a gene responsible for recycling the proteins thought to be involved in forming the neuron-destroying amyloid plaques of AD were identified and associated with late-onset disease. Researchers have not yet discovered how the genes associated with dementia interact with other risk factors to produce or trigger the dementia. One non-genetic risk factor presently being investigated is toxic substances in the environment.

EARLY-ONSET ALZHEIMER'S DISEASE. In early-onset AD, which accounts for 2%–7% of cases of AD, the symptoms develop before age 60. It is usually caused by an inherited genetic mutation. Early-onset AD is also associated with Down syndrome (trisomy 21), in that persons with trisomy 21 (three forms of human chromosome 21 instead of a pair) often develop early-onset AD. Development of AD in persons with Down syndrome has been traced to the presence of BACE1, which increases under low oxygen conditions in mice. The researchers had investigated the effects of low oxygen because of the relationship between a history of **stroke**, which cuts off oxygen to the brain, and AD.

LATE-ONSET ALZHEIMER'S DISEASE. Recent research indicates that late-onset AD is a polygenic disorder; that is, its development is influenced by more than one gene. It has been known since 1993 that a specific form of a gene (the APOE gene) on human chromosome 19 is a genetic risk factor for late-onset AD. In 1998 researchers at the University of Pittsburgh reported on another gene that controls the production of bleomycin hydrolase (BH) as a second genetic risk factor that acts independently of the APOE gene. In December 2000, three separate research studies reported that a gene on chromosome 10 that may affect the processing of a protein (called amyloid-beta protein) is also involved in the development of late-onset AD. When this protein is not properly broken down, a starchy substance builds up in the brains of people with AD to form the plaques that are characteristic of the disease. The most recent development is the confirmation of the involvement of variant forms of a gene called SORL1. The proteins controlled by this gene are related to the production of amyloid-beta protein. Low levels of the SORL1 protein cause amyloid-beta levels near cells to rise.

MULTI-INFARCT DEMENTIA (MID). While the chief risk factors for MID are high blood pressure, advanced age, and male sex, there is an inherited form of MID called CADASIL, which stands for cerebral autosomal dominant arteriopathy with subcortical infarcts and leukoencephalopathy. CADASIL can cause psychiatric disturbances and severe headaches as well as dementia.

FRONTAL LOBE DEMENTIAS. Researchers think that between 25% and 50% of cases of frontal lobe dementia involve genetic factors. Pick's dementia appears to have a much smaller genetic component than FLD. It is not yet known what other risk factors combine with inherited traits to influence the development of frontal lobe dementias.

FAMILIAL BRITISH DEMENTIA (FBD). FBD is a rare autosomal dominant disorder that was first reported in the 1940s in a large British family extending over nine generations. FBD resembles AD in that the patient develops a progressive dementia related to amyloid deposits in the brain. In 1999, a mutated gene that produces the amyloid responsible for FBD was discovered on human chromosome 13. Studies of this mutation may yield further clues to the development of AD as well as FBD itself.

CREUTZFELDT-JAKOB DISEASE. Although Creutzfeldt-Jakob disease is caused by a prion (a proteinaceous infectious particle consisting only of protein, as opposed to a virus, which consists of protein and nucleic acid, or a virion, which consists of nucleic acid), researchers think that 5%–15% of cases may have a genetic component.

Symptoms

DSM-IV-TR identifies certain symptoms as criteria that must be met for a patient to be diagnosed with dementia. One criterion is significant weakening of the patient's memory with regard to learning new infor-

mation as well as recalling previously learned information. In addition, the patient must be found to have one or more of the following disturbances:

- aphasia. Aphasia refers to loss of language function. A person with dementia may use vague words like "it" or "thing" often because he or she cannot recall the exact name of an object; the affected person may echo what other people say, or repeat a word or phrase over and over. People in the later stages of dementia may stop speaking at all.
- apraxia. Apraxia refers to loss of the ability to perform intentional movements even though the person is not paralyzed, has not lost the sense of touch, and knows what he or she is trying to do. For example, a patient with apraxia may stop brushing his teeth, or have trouble tying his shoelaces.
- agnosia. Agnosia refers to loss of the ability to recognize objects even though the person's sight and sense of touch are normal. People with severe agnosia may fail to recognize family members or even their own face reflected in a mirror.
- problems with abstract thinking and complex behavior. This criterion refers to the loss of the ability to make plans, carry out the steps of a task in the proper order, make appropriate decisions, evaluate situations, show good judgment, etc. For example, a patient might light a stove burner under a saucepan before putting food or water in the pan, or be unable to record checks and balance a checkbook.

DSM-IV-TR also specifies that these disturbances must be severe enough to cause problems in the person's daily life, and that they must represent a decline from a previously higher level of functioning.

In addition to the changes in cognitive functioning, the symptoms of dementia may also include personality changes and emotional instability. Patients with dementia sometimes become mildly paranoid because their loss of short-term memory leads them to think that mislaid items have been stolen. About 25% of patients with dementia develop a significant degree of **paranoia**, that is, generalized suspiciousness or specific **delusions** of persecution. Mood swings, **anxiety**, and irritability or anger are also frequent occurrences, particularly when patients with dementia are in situations that force them to recognize the extent of their impairment.

The following signs and symptoms are used to differentiate among the various types of dementia during a diagnostic evaluation.

ALZHEIMER'S DISEASE. Dementia related to AD often progresses slowly; it may be accompanied by irritability, wide mood swings, and personality changes in the early stage. Many patients, however, retain their normal degree of sociability in the early stages of AD. In second-stage AD, the patient typically gets lost easily, is completely disoriented with regard to time and space, and may become angry, uncooperative, or aggressive. Patients in second-stage AD are at high risk for falls and other accidents. In final-stage AD, the patient is completely bedridden, has lost control over bowel and bladder functions, and may be unable to swallow or eat. The risk of **seizures** increases as the patient progresses from early to end-stage AD. Death usually results from an infection or from malnutrition.

MULTI-INFARCT DEMENTIA. In MID, the symptoms are more likely to occur after age 70. In the early stages, the patient retains his or her personality more fully than a patient with AD. Another distinctive feature of this type of dementia is that it often progresses in a stepwise fashion; that is, the patient shows rapid changes in functioning, then remains at a plateau for a while rather than showing a continuous decline. The symptoms of MID may also have a "patchy" quality; that is, some of the patient's mental functions may be severely affected while others are relatively undamaged. Other symptoms of MID include exaggerated reflexes, an abnormal gait (manner of walking), loss of bladder or bowel control, and inappropriate laughing or crying.

DEMENTIA WITH LEWY BODIES. This type of dementia may combine some features of AD, such as severe memory loss and confusion, with certain symptoms associated with Parkinson's disease, including stiff muscles, a shuffling gait, and trembling or shaking of the hands. Visual **hallucinations** may be one of the first symptoms of dementia with Lewy bodies.

FRONTAL LOBE DEMENTIAS. The frontal lobe dementias are gradual in onset. Pick's dementia is most likely to develop in persons between 40 and 60, while FLD typically begins before the age of 65. The first symptoms of the frontal lobe dementias often include socially inappropriate behavior (rude remarks, sexual acting-out, disregard of personal hygiene, etc.). Patients are also often obsessed with eating and may put non-food items in their mouths or making frequent sucking or smacking noises. In the later stages of frontal lobe dementia or Pick's disease, the patient may develop muscle weakness, twitching, and delusions or hallucinations.

CREUTZFELDT-JAKOB DISEASE. The dementia associated with Creutzfeldt-Jakob disease occurs most often in persons between 40 and 60. It is typically preceded by a period of several weeks in which the patient complains of unusual fatigue, anxiety, loss of

appetite, or difficulty concentrating. This type of dementia also usually progresses much more rapidly than other dementias, resulting in the death of the affected person within a few months to one year.

Demographics

The demographic distribution of dementia varies somewhat according to its cause. Moreover, recent research indicates that dementia in many patients has overlapping causes, so that it is not always easy to assess the true rates of occurrence of the different types. For example, AD and MID are found together in about 15%–20% of cases.

Alzheimer's disease

AD is by far the most common cause of dementia in the elderly, accounting for 60%–80% of cases. It is estimated that four million adults in the United States have AD. The disease strikes women more often than men, but researchers do not know yet whether the sex ratio simply reflects the fact that women in developed countries tend to live longer than men, or whether female sex is itself a risk factor for AD. One well-known long-term study of Alzheimer's in women is the Nun Study, begun in 1986 and presently conducted at the University of Kentucky. The researchers have identified numerous relationships between factors from early, mid-, and late life and the risk of AD.

Multi-infarct dementia

MID is responsible for between 15% and 20% of cases of dementia (not counting cases in which it coexists with AD). Unlike AD, MID is more common in men than in women. Diabetes, high blood pressure, a history of smoking, and heart disease are all risk factors for MID. Researchers in Sweden have suggested that MID is underdiagnosed, and may coexist with other dementias more frequently than is presently recognized.

Dementia with Lewy bodies

Dementia with Lewy bodies is now thought to be the second most common form of dementia after AD. But because researchers do not completely understand the relationship between Lewy bodies, AD, and Parkinson's disease, the demographic distribution of this type of dementia is also unclear.

Other dementias

FLD, Pick's disease, Huntington's disease, Parkinson's disease, HIV infection, alcoholism, head trauma, etc. account for about 10% of all cases of dementia. In FLD and Pick's dementia, women appear to be affected slightly more often than men.

Diagnosis

In some cases, a patient's primary physician may be able to diagnose the dementia; in many instances, however, the patient will be referred to a neurologist or a gerontologist (specialist in medical care of the elderly). Distinguishing one disorder from other similar disorders is a process called differential **diagnosis**. The differential diagnosis of dementia is complicated because of the number of possible causes; because more than one cause may be present at the same time; and because dementia can coexist with such other conditions as depression and **delirium**. Delirium is a temporary disturbance of consciousness marked by confusion, restlessness, inability to focus one's attention, hallucinations, or delusions. In elderly people, delirium is frequently a side effect of surgery, medications, infectious illnesses, or dehydration. Delirium can be distinguished from dementia by the fact that delirium usually comes on fairly suddenly (in a few hours or days) and may vary in severity—it is often worse at night. Dementia develops much more slowly, over a period of months or years, and the patient's symptoms are relatively stable. It is possible for a person to have delirium and dementia at the same time.

Another significant diagnostic distinction in elderly patients is the distinction between dementia and age-associated memory impairment (AAMI), which is sometimes called benign senescent forgetfulness. Older people with AAMI have a mild degree of memory loss; they do not learn new information as quickly as younger people, and they may take longer to recall a certain fact or to balance their checkbook. But they do not experience the degree of memory impairment that characterizes dementia, and they do not get progressively worse.

Clinical interview

In making a diagnosis, the doctor will begin by taking a full history, including the patient's occupation and educational level as well as medical history. The occupational and educational history allows the examiner to make a more accurate assessment of the extent of the patient's memory loss and intellectual decline. In some cases, the occupational history may indicate exposure to heavy metals or other toxins. A complete medical history allows the doctor to assess such possibilities as delirium, depression, alcohol-related dementia, dementia related to head injury, or dementia caused by infection. It is particularly important for the doctor to have a list of all the patient's medications, including over-the-counter and alternative herbal preparations, because of the possibility that the patient's symptoms are related to side effects of these substances.

Whenever possible, the examiner will consult the patient's family members or close friends as part of the history-taking process. In many cases, friends and relatives can provide more detailed information about the patient's memory problems and loss of function.

Mental status examination

A mental status examination (MSE) evaluates the patient's ability to communicate, follow instructions, recall information, perform simple tasks involving movement and coordination. The MSE also gives information about the patient's emotional state and general sense of space and time. The MSE includes the doctor's informal evaluation of the patient's appearance, vocal tone, facial expressions, posture, and gait as well as formal questions or instructions. A common form that has been used since 1975 is the so-called Folstein Mini-Mental Status Examination, or MMSE. Questions that are relevant to diagnosing dementia include asking the patient: to count backward from 100 by 7s, to make change, to name the current President of the United States, to repeat a short phrase after the examiner (e.g., "no ifs, ands, or buts"); to draw a clock face or geometric figure, and to follow a set of instructions involving movement (e.g., "Show me how to throw a ball" or "Fold this piece of paper and place it under the lamp on the bookshelf.") The examiner may test the patient's abstract reasoning ability by asking him or her to explain a familiar proverb (e.g., "People who live in glass houses shouldn't throw stones") or test the patient's judgment by asking about a problem with a common-sense solution, such as what one does when a prescription runs out.

Neurological examination

A neurological examination includes an evaluation of the patient's cranial nerves and reflexes. The cranial nerves govern the ability to speak as well as sight, hearing, taste, and smell. The patient will be asked to stick out her tongue, follow the examiner's finger with her eyes, raise her eyebrows, etc. The patient is also asked to perform certain actions (e.g., touching the nose with the eyes closed) that test coordination and spatial orientation. The doctor will usually touch or tap certain areas of the body, such as the knee or the sole of the foot, to test the patient's reflexes. Failure to respond to the touch or tap may indicate damage to certain parts of the brain.

Laboratory tests

Blood and urine samples may be collected in order to rule out such conditions as thyroid deficiency, niacin or vitamin B_{12} deficiency, heavy metal poisoning, liver disease, HIV infection, syphilis, anemia, medication reactions, or kidney failure. A lumbar puncture (spinal tap) may be done to rule out neurosyphilis.

Diagnostic imaging

The patient may be given a **computed tomography** (CT) scan or **magnetic resonance imaging** (MRI) to detect evidence of strokes, disintegration of the brain tissue in certain areas, blood clots or tumors, a buildup of spinal fluid, or bleeding into the brain tissue. Positron-emission tomography (PET) or single-emission computed tomography (SPECT) imaging is not used routinely to diagnose dementia, but may be used to rule out AD or frontal lobe degeneration if a patient's CT scan or MRI is unrevealing.

Treatments

Reversible and responsive dementias

Some types of dementia are reversible, and a few types respond to specific treatments related to their causes. Dementia related to dietary deficiencies or metabolic disorders is treated with the appropriate vitamins or thyroid medication. Dementia related to HIV infection often responds well to zidovudine (Retrovir), a drug given to prevent the AIDS virus from replicating. Multi-infarct dementia is usually treated by controlling the patient's blood pressure and/or diabetes; while treatments for these disorders cannot undo damage already caused to brain tissue, they can slow the progress of the dementia. Patients with alcohol-related dementia often improve over the long term if they are able to stop drinking. Dementias related to head injuries, hydrocephalus, and tumors are treated by surgery.

It is important to evaluate and treat elderly patients for depression, because the symptoms of depression in older people often mimic dementia. This condition is sometimes called pseudodementia. In addition, patients who have both depression and dementia often show some improvement in intellectual functioning when the depression is treated. The medications most often used for depression related to dementia are the **selective serotonin reuptake inhibitors (SSRIs) paroxetine** and **sertraline**. The mental status examination should be repeated after 6–12 weeks of antidepressant medication.

Irreversible dementias

As of 2006, there were no medications or surgical techniques that can cure AD, the frontal lobe dementias, MID, or dementia with Lewy bodies. There are also no "magic bullets" that can slow or stop the progression of these dementias. There are, however, several medications that are used to slow cognitive deterioration in AD. Four of these medications are cholinesterase inhibitors, which increase levels of acetylcholine in the brain, and these medications are effective in some people who have mild or moderate AD. Acetylcholine is a neurotransmitter (nerve signaling molecule) that facilitates communication among neurons. Another type of drug is the NMDA receptor antagonist **memantine** (available in the U.S. under the trade name Namenda), which may help stabilize memory in people with moderate to severe AD.

In April 2005, the U.S. Food and Drug Administration (FDA) issued a public health advisory regarding unapproved, "off-label" use of certain antipsychotic drugs that were approved for treatment of **schizophrenia** and mania. Clinical studies showed that use of these atypical antipsychotic medications in elderly patients with dementia to treat behavioral disorders is associated with increased mortality.

Patients may be given medications to ease the depression, anxiety, sleep disturbances, and other behavioral symptoms that accompany dementia, but most physicians prescribe relatively mild dosages in order to minimize the troublesome side effects of these drugs. Dementia with Lewy bodies appears to respond better to treatment with the newer antipsychotic medications than to treatment with such older drugs as **haloperidol** (Haldol).

Patients in the early stages of dementia can often remain at home with some help from family members or other caregivers, especially if the house or apartment can be fitted with safety features (handrails, good lighting, locks for cabinets containing potentially dangerous products, nonslip treads on stairs, etc.). Patients in the later stages of dementia, however, usually require skilled care in a nursing home or hospital.

Prognosis

The prognosis for reversible dementia related to nutritional or thyroid problems is usually good once the cause has been identified and treated. The prognoses for dementias related to alcoholism or HIV infection depend on the patient's age and the severity of the underlying disorder.

The prognosis for the irreversible dementias is gradual deterioration of the patient's functioning

KEY TERMS

Age-associated memory impairment (AAMI)— A condition in which an older person has some memory loss and takes longer to learn new information. AAMI is distinguished from dementia in that it is not progressive and does not represent a serious decline from the person's previous level of functioning. Benign senescent forgetfulness is another term for AAMI.

Agnosia—Loss of the ability to recognize familiar people, places, and objects.

Amyloid—A waxy translucent substance composed mostly of protein, that forms plaques (abnormal deposits) in the brain during the progression of Alzheimer's disease.

Aphasia—Loss of previously acquired ability to understand or use written or spoken language, due to brain damage or deterioration.

Apraxia—Inability to perform purposeful movements that is not caused by paralysis or loss of feeling.

Creutzfeldt-Jakob disease—A degenerative disease of the central nervous system caused by a prion, or "slow virus."

Delirium—A disturbance of consciousness marked by confusion, difficulty paying attention, delusions, hallucinations, or restlessness. It can be distinguished from dementia by its relatively sudden onset and variation in the severity of the symptoms.

Diagnostic and Statistical Manual of Mental Disorders—A handbook for mental health professionals that includes lists of symptoms that indicate different mental disorders.

Frontal lobe dementia—Dementia caused by a disorder, usually genetic, that affects the front portion of the brain.

Hematoma—An accumulation of blood, often clotted, in a body tissue or organ, usually caused by a break or tear in a blood vessel.

Huntington's disease—A hereditary disorder that appears in middle age and is characterized by gradual brain deterioration, progressive dementia, and loss of voluntary movement. It is sometimes called Huntington's chorea.

Hydrocephalus—The accumulation of cerebrospinal fluid (CSF) in the ventricles of the brain.

Lewy bodies—Areas of injury found on damaged nerve cells in certain parts of the brain associated with dementia.

Multi-infarct dementia—Dementia caused by damage to brain tissue resulting from a series of blood clots or clogs in the blood vessels. It is also called vascular dementia.

Parkinson's disease—A disease of the nervous system most common in people over 60, characterized by a shuffling gait, trembling of the fingers and hands, and muscle stiffness. It may be related in some way to Lewy body dementia.

Pick's disease—A rare type of primary dementia that affects the frontal lobes of the brain. It is characterized by a progressive loss of social skills, language, and memory, leading to personality changes and sometimes loss of moral judgment.

Prion—A protein particle that lacks nucleic acid.

Pseudodementia—A term for a depression with symptoms resembling those of dementia. The term "dementia of depression" is now preferred.

ending in death. The length of time varies somewhat. Patients with AD may live 2–20 years with the disease, with an average of seven years. Patients with frontal lobe dementia or Pick's disease live on average 5–10 years after diagnosis. The course of Creutzfeldt-Jakob disease is much more rapid, with patients living 5–12 months after diagnosis.

Prevention

The reversible dementias related to thyroid and nutritional disorders can be prevented in many cases by regular physical checkups and proper attention to diet. Dementias related to toxic substances in the

workplace may be prevented by careful monitoring of the work environment and by substituting less hazardous materials or substances in manufacturing processes. Dementias caused by infectious diseases are theoretically preventable by avoiding exposure to the prion, spirochete, or other disease agent. Multi-infarct dementia may be preventable in some patients by attention to diet and monitoring of blood pressure. Dementias caused by abnormalities in the structure of the brain are not preventable as of 2006.

With regard to genetic factors, tests are now available for the APOE gene implicated in late-onset AD, but these tests are used primarily in research instead of

Denial

clinical practice. One reason is that the test results are not conclusive; about 20% of people who eventually develop AD do not carry this gene. Another important reason is the ethical implications of testing for a disease that presently has no cure. These considerations may change, however, if researchers discover better treatments for primary dementia, more effective preventive methods, or more reliable genetic markers.

See also Respite care.

Resources

BOOKS

American Psychiatric Association. *Diagnostic and Statistical Manual of Mental Disorders.* 4th edition, text revised. Washington, DC: American Psychiatric Association, 2000.

"Dementia." *The Merck Manual of Diagnosis and Therapy*, edited by Mark H. Beers, M.D., and Robert Berkow, M.D. Whitehouse Station, NJ: Merck Research Laboratories, 1999.

Lyon, Jeff, and Peter Gorner. *Altered Fates: Gene Therapy and the Retooling of Human Life.* New York and London: W. W. Norton & Co., Inc., 1996.

Marcantonio, Edward, M.D. "Dementia." Chapter 40 in *The Merck Manual of Geriatrics*, edited by Mark H. Beers, M.D., and Robert Berkow, M.D. Whitehouse Station, NJ: Merck Research Laboratories, 2000.

Morris, Virginia. *How to Care for Aging Parents.* New York: Workman Publishing, 1996.

PERIODICALS

"Alzheimer's Disease: Recent Progress and Prospects." *Harvard Mental Health Letter (Parts 1, 2, and 3)* 18 (October–December 2001).

Rogaeva, Ekaterina, et al. "The neuronal sortilin-related receptor SORL1 is genetically associated with Alzheimer disease." *Nature Genetics* Advance online publication; doi:10.1038/ng1943.

Sun, Xiulian, Guiqiong He, Hong Qing, Zhou Wiehui, Frederick Dobie, Cai Fang, Matthias Staufenbiel, L. Eric Huang, and Weihong Song. "Hypoxia facilitates Alzheimer's disease pathogenesis by up-regulating BACE1 gene expression." *Proceedings of the National Academy of Science* 103 (2006): 18727-18732.

ORGANIZATIONS

Alzheimer's Association. 919 North Michigan Avenue, Suite 1000, Chicago, IL 60611. Toll Free: (800) 272-3900.

Alzheimer's Disease International. 45/46 Lower Marsh, London SE1 7RG, United Kingdom. Telephone: (+44 20) 7620 3011. E-mail: adi@alz.co.uk. <www.alz.co.uk>.

National Family Caregivers Association. 10400 Connecticut Avenue, Suite 500, Kensington, MD, 20895-3944. Toll Free: (800) 896-3650. Telephone: (301)942-6430. Fax: (301) 942-2302. Website: < http://www.nfcacares.org/>.

National Institute of Mental Health. 6001 Executive Boulevard, Room 8184, MSC 9663, Bethesda, MD 20892-9663. Telephone: (301) 443-4513. <www.nimh.nih.gov>.

National Institute of Neurological Disorders and Stroke (NINDS). Building 31, Room 8A06, 9000 Rockville Pike, Bethesda, MD 20892. Telephone: (301) 496-5751. <www.ninds.nih.gov>.

National Institute on Aging Information Center. P.O. Box 8057, Gaithersburg, MD 20898. Telephone: (800) 222-2225 or (301) 496-1752.

National Organization for Rare Disorders (NORD). P. O. Box 8923, New Fairfield, CT 06812. Telephone: (800) 447-6673 or (203) 746-6518.

OTHER

Alzheimer's Disease Education and Referral (ADEAR). <www.alzheimers.org>.

The Nun Study. <www.coa.uky.edu/nunnet>.

National Library of Medicine. "Dementia." <http://www.nlm.nih.gov/medlineplus/dementia.html> (accessed January 16, 2007).

National Guideline Clearinghouse. <http://www.guideline.gov/> (accessed January 16, 2007).

Rebecca Frey, Ph.D.
Emily Jane Willingham, Ph.D.

Dementia of the Alzheimer's type *see* Alzheimer's disease

Denial

Definition

Denial is refusal to acknowledge the existence or severity of unpleasant external realities or internal thoughts and feelings.

Theory of denial

In psychology, denial is a concept originating with the psycho dynamic theories of Sigmund Freud. According to Freud, three mental dynamics, or motivating forces, influence human behavior: the id, ego, and superego. The id consists of basic survival instincts and what Freud believed to be the two dominant human drives: sex and aggression. If the id were the only influence on behavior, humans would exclusively seek to increase pleasure, decrease pain, and achieve immediate gratification of desires. The ego consists of logical and rational thinking. It enables humans to analyze the realistic risks and benefits of a situation, to tolerate some pain for future profit, and to consider alternatives to the impulse-driven behavior of the id. The superego consists of moralistic standards and forms the basis of the conscience. Although the superego is essential to a sense of right and wrong, it can also include extreme, unrealistic ideas about what one should and should not do.

These three forces all have different goals (id, pleasure; ego, reality; superego, morality) and continually strive for dominance, resulting in internal conflict. This conflict produces **anxiety**. The ego, which functions as a mediator between the two extremes of the id and the superego, attempts to reduce this anxiety by using defense mechanisms. Defense mechanisms are indirect ways of dealing or coping with anxiety, such as explaining problems away or blaming others for problems. Denial is one of many defense mechanisms. It entails ignoring or refusing to believe an unpleasant reality. Defense mechanisms protect one's psychological well-being in traumatic situations, or in any situation that produces anxiety or conflict. However, they do not resolve the anxiety-producing situation and, if overused, can lead to psychological disorders. Although Freud's model of the id, ego, and superego is not emphasized by most psychologists today, defense mechanisms are still regarded as potentially maladaptive behavioral patterns that may lead to psychological disorders.

Examples of denial

Death is a common occasion for denial. When someone learns of the sudden, unexpected death of a loved one, at first he or she may not be able to accept the reality of this loss. The initial denial protects that person from the emotional shock and intense **grief** that often accompanies news of death. Chronic or terminal illnesses also encourage denial. People with such illnesses may think, "It's not so bad; I'll get over it," and refuse to make any lifestyle changes.

Denial can also apply to internal thoughts and feelings. For instance, some children are taught that anger is wrong in any situation. As adults, if these individuals experience feelings of anger, they are likely to deny their feelings to others. Cultural standards and expectations can encourage denial of subjective experience. Men who belong to cultures with extreme notions of masculinity may view fear as a sign of weakness and deny internal feelings of fear. The Chinese culture is thought to discourage the acknowledgment of mental illness, resulting in individuals denying their psychological symptoms and often developing physical symptoms instead.

Certain **personality disorders** tend to be characterized by denial more than others. For example, those with **narcissistic personality disorder** deny information that suggests they are not perfect. Antisocial behavior is characterized by denial of the harm done to others (such as with sexual offenders or substance abusers).

Denial can also be exhibited on a large scale—among groups, cultures, or even nations. Lucy Bregman gives an example of national denial of imminent mortality in the 1950s: school children participated in drills where they hid under desks in preparation for atomic attacks. Another example of large-scale denial is the recent assertion by some that the World War II Holocaust never occurred.

Treatment of denial

Denial is treated differently in different types of therapy. In psychoanalytic therapy, denial is regarded as an obstacle to progress that must eventually be confronted and interpreted. Timing is important, however. Psychoanalytic therapists wait until clients appear emotionally ready or have some degree of insight into their problems before confronting them. In the humanistic and existential therapies, denial is considered the framework by which clients understand their world. Not directly confronting denial, therapists assist clients in exploring their world view and considering alternative ways of being. In cognitive-behavioral therapies, denial is not regarded as an important phenomenon. Rather, denial would suggest that an individual has not learned the appropriate behaviors to cope with a stressful situation. Therapists assist individuals in examining their current thoughts and behaviors and devising strategic ways to make changes.

Traditional treatment programs for **substance abuse** and other addictions view denial as a central theme. Such programs teach that in order to overcome **addiction**, one must admit to being an alcoholic or addict. Those who are unable to accept such labels are informed they are in denial. Even when the labels are accepted, individuals are still considered to be in denial if they do not acknowledge the severity of their addictions. From this perspective, progress cannot be made until individuals recognize the extent of their denial and work toward acceptance. However, there is much controversy in the field of addictions regarding the role of denial and how it should be addressed. Traditional programs such as these stress direct confrontation. Other professionals do not insist on the acceptance of labels. They believe that denial should be worked through more subtly, empathically focusing on the personal reasons surrounding denial and seeking to strengthen

KEY TERMS

Antisocial behavior—Behavior characterized by high levels of anger, aggression, manipulation, or violence.

Cognitive-behavioral therapies—An approach to psychotherapy that emphasizes the correction of distorted thinking patterns and changing one's behaviors accordingly.

Defense mechanisms—Indirect strategies used to reduce anxiety rather than directly facing the issues causing the anxiety.

Dependent personality disorder—Personality disorder characterized by a constant, unhealthy need to be liked and appreciated by others at all costs.

Ego—In Freudian psychology, the conscious, rational part of the mind that experiences and reacts to the outside world.

Humanistic and existential therapies—Therapies that focus on achieving one's full potential, guided by subjective experience.

Id—A construct in Freudian psycho dynamic theory that represents the irrational, self-centered aspects of human thought.

Motivational enhancement therapy—Therapy that focuses on increasing motivation for change by empathically comparing and contrasting the consequences and benefits of changing or not changing.

Narcissistic personality disorder—Personality characterized by continually exaggerating one's own positive qualities and refusing to recognize personal defects or flaws.

Psychoanalytic therapy—Therapy based on the psycho dynamic theory of Sigmund Freud.

Psychodynamic—Referring to the motivational forces, unconscious as well as conscious, that form human attitudes and behavior.

Superego—According to Freud, the part of the mind that represents traditional parental and societal values. The superego is the source of guilt feelings.

the desire to change. This subtle form of addressing denial is known as motivational enhancement therapy, and can be used with other types of disorders as well.

See also Grief; Psychoanalysis; Psychodynamic psychotherapy; Substance abuse and related disorders.

Resources

BOOKS

Bregman, Lucy. *Beyond Silence and Denial: Death and Dying Reconsidered.* Louisville, Kentucky: Westminster John Knox Press, 1999.

Millon, Theodore, and Roger Davis. *Personality Disorders in Modern Life.* New York: John Wiley and Sons, 2000.

PERIODICALS

Cramer, Phebe, and Melissa A. Brilliant. "Defense Use and Defense Understanding in Children." *Journal of Personality* 69, no. 2 (2001): 297–322.

Parker, Gordon, Gemma Gladstone, and Kuan Tsee Chee. "Depression in the Planet's Largest Ethnic Group: The Chinese." *American Journal Of Psychiatry* 158, no. 6 (2001): 857–864.

Schneider, Sandra L., and Robert C. Wright. "The FoSOD: A Measurement Tool for Reconceptualizing the Role of Denial in Child Molesters." *Journal of Interpersonal Violence* 16, no. 6 (2001): 545–564.

ORGANIZATIONS

The American Psychoanalytic Association. 309 East 49th Street, New York, New York 10017. Telephone: (212) 752-0450. <http://www.aapsa.org>.

Sandra L. Friedrich, M.A.

Depakene *see* **Valproic acid**
Depakote *see* **Divalproex sodium**

Dependent personality disorder

Definition

Dependent personality disorder is characterized by an excessive need to be taken care of or to depend upon others. Persons with this disorder are typically submissive and display clinging behavior toward those they from whom they fear separation.

Dependent personality disorder is one of several **personality disorders** listed in the newest edition of the standard reference guide: the *Diagnostic and Statistical Manual of Mental Disorders,* the fourth edition, text revision, also known as the *DSM-IV-TR.*

Description

Persons with dependent personality disorder are docile, passive, and nonassertive. They exert a great deal of energy to please others, are self-sacrificing, and constantly attempt to elicit the approval of others. They are reluctant to express disagreement with others and are often willing to go to abnormal lengths to win the approval of those on whom they rely. They are readily influenced and can be taken advantage of easily. This **compliance** and reliance upon others leads to a subtle message that someone should assume responsibility for significant areas of the patient's life. This is often displayed as helplessness, even for completion of seemingly simple tasks.

Patients with dependent personality disorder have a low level of confidence in their own intelligence and abilities. They often have difficulty making decisions and undertaking projects on their own. They are prone to be pessimistic and self-doubting, and to belittle their own accomplishments. They shy away from responsibility in occupational settings.

Affected individuals are uneasy being alone and are preoccupied with the fear of being abandoned or rejected by others. Their moods are characterized by frequent bouts of **anxiety** or fearfulness; generally, their demeanor is sad. Their style of thinking is naïve, uncritical, and lacks discretion.

Causes and symptoms

Causes

It is commonly thought that the development of dependency in these individuals is a result of overinvolvement and intrusive behavior by their primary caretakers. Caretakers may foster dependence in the child to meet their own dependency needs and may reward extreme loyalty but reject attempts the child makes towards independence. Families of those with dependent personality disorder often do not express their emotions and controlling; they demonstrate poorly defined relational roles within the family unit.

Individuals with dependent personality disorder often have been socially humiliated by others in their developmental years. They may carry significant doubts about their abilities to perform tasks, to take on new responsibilities, and generally to function independently of others. This reinforces their suspicions that they are incapable of living autonomously. In response to these feelings, they portray helplessness in order to elicit caregiving behavior from some people in their lives.

Symptoms

The *DSM-IV-TR* specifies eight diagnostic criteria for dependent personality disorder. Individuals with this disorder:

- have difficulty making common decisions. These individuals typically need an excessive amount of advice and reassurance before they can make even simple decisions, such as the clothing to wear on a given day.

- need others to assume responsibility for them. Because they view themselves as incapable of being autonomous, they withdraw from adult responsibilities by acting passive and helpless. They allow others to take the initiative for many areas of their life. Adults with this disorder typically depend on a parent or spouse to make major decisions for them, such as where to work or live, or with whom to be friends.

- have difficulty expressing disagreement with others. Disagreeing with others is often viewed as too risky. It might sever the support or approval of those they upon whom they depend. They are often overly agreeable because they fear alienating other people.

- have difficulty initiating or doing things on their own. They lack self-confidence and believe they need help to begin or sustain tasks. They often present themselves as inept and unable to understand or accomplish the task at hand.

- go to excessive lengths to obtain support or nurturing from others. They may even volunteer to do unpleasant tasks if they believe that doing so will evoke a positive response from others. They may subject themselves to great personal sacrifice or tolerate physical, verbal, or sexual abuse in their quest to get what they believe they need from others.

- feel helpless when alone. Because they feel incapable of caring for themselves, they experience significant anxiety when alone. To avoid being alone, they may be with people in whom they have little interest.

- quickly seek a new relationship when a previous one ends. When a marriage, dating, or other close relationship ends, there is typically an urgency to find a new relationship that will provide the support of the former relationship.

- are preoccupied with fears of being left to take care of themselves. Their greatest fear is to be left alone and to be responsible for themselves. Even as adults, their dependence upon others may appear childlike.

Demographics

Dependent personality disorder should rarely, if ever, be diagnosed in children or adolescents because of their inherent dependence on others resulting from their age and developmental limitations.

Diagnosis

Age and cultural factors should be considered in diagnosing dependent personality disorder. Certain cultural norms suggest a submissive, polite, or dependent posture in relating to the opposite sex or authority figures. Dependent personality disorder should only be diagnosed when it meets the above criteria and is clearly outside one's cultural norms.

The **diagnosis** of dependent personality disorder is based on a clinical interview to assess symptomatic behavior. Other assessment tools helpful in confirming the diagnosis of dependent personality disorder include:

- The Dependent Personality Questionnaire
- Minnesota Multiphasic Personality Inventory (MMPI-2)
- Millon Clinical Multi-axial Inventory (MCMI-II)
- Rorschach Psychodiagnostic Test
- Thematic Appreception Test (TAT)

For a person to be diagnosed with dependent personality disorder, at least five of the eight symptoms described must be the present, and these symptoms must begin by early adulthood and be evident in a variety of contexts.

The diagnosis of dependent personality disorder must be distinguished from **borderline personality disorder**, since there are common characteristics. Borderline personality disorder is characterized by fear of abandonment, as well, but with feelings of emptiness and rage. In contrast, the dependent personality responds to this fear of abandonment with submissiveness and searches for a replacement relationship to maintain dependency.

Likewise, persons with histrionic personality disorder have a strong need for reassurance and approval and may appear childlike in their clinging behavior. Histrionics are characterized by a gregarious demeanor and make active demands for attention, while dependents respond with docile and self-deprecating behavior.

The **avoidant personality disorder** can also be confused with dependent personality disorder. Both are characterized by feelings of inadequacy, oversensitivity to criticism, and a frequent need for assurance. However, these patients typically have such an intense fear of rejection that they will instinctively withdraw until they are certain of acceptance. Dependents, in contrast, actually seek out contact with others because they need the approval of others.

Treatments

The general goal of treatment of dependent personality disorder is to increase the individual's sense of autonomy and ability to function independently.

Psychodynamically oriented therapies

A long-term approach to psychodynamic treatment can be successful, but may lead to heightened dependencies and difficult separation in the therapeutic relationship over time. The preferred approach is a time-limited treatment plan consisting of a predetermined number of sessions. This has been proved to facilitate the exploration process of dependency issues more effectively than long-term therapy in most patients.

Cognitive-behavioral therapy

Cognitive-behavioral approaches attempt to increase the affected person's ability to act independently of others, improve their self-esteem, and enhance the quality of their interpersonal relationships. Often, patients will play an active role in setting goals. Methods often used in **cognitive-behavioral therapy** (CBT) include assertiveness and **social skills training** to help reduce reliance on others, including the therapist.

Interpersonal therapy

Treatment using an interpersonal approach can be useful because the individual is usually receptive to treatment and seeks help with interpersonal relationships. The therapist would help the patient explore their long-standing patterns of interacting with others, and understand how these have contributed to dependency issues. The goal is to show the patient the high price they pay for this dependency, and to help them develop healthier alternatives. **Assertiveness training** and learning to identify feelings is often used to heighten improve interpersonal behavior.

Group therapy

When a person is highly motivated to see growth, a more interactive therapeutic group can be successful in helping the him/her to explore passive-dependent behavior. If the individual is socially reluctant or impaired in his/her assertiveness, decision making, or negotiation, a supportive decision-making group would be more appropriate. Time-limited assertiveness-training groups with clearly defined goals have been proven to be effective.

Family and marital therapy

Individuals with dependent personality disorder are usually brought to therapy by their parents. They are often young adults who are struggling with neurotic or psychotic symptoms. The goal of **family therapy** is often to untangle the enmeshed family relationships, which usually elicits considerable resistance by most family members unless all are in therapy.

KEY TERMS

Millon Clinical Multiaxial Inventory (MCMI-II)—
A self-report instrument designed to help the clinician assess *DSM-IV*-related personality disorders and clinical syndromes. It provides insight into 14 personality disorders and 10 clinical syndromes.

Minnesota Multiphasic Personality Inventory (MMPI-2)—A comprehensive assessment tool widely used to diagnosed personality disorders.

Rorschach Psychodiagnostic Test—This series of 10 "ink blot" images allows the patient to project their interpretations which can be used to diagnosed particular disorders.

Thematic Apperception Test (TAT)—A projective test using stories and descriptions of pictures to reveal some of the dominant drives, emotions, sentiments, conflicts, and complexes of a personality.

Marital therapy can be productive in helping couples reduce the anxiety of both partners, who seek and meet dependency needs that arise in the relationship.

Medications

Individuals with dependent personality disorder can experience anxiety and **depressive disorders** as well. In these cases, it may occasionally prove useful to use **antidepressants** or antianxiety agents. Unless the anxiety or **depression** is considered worthy of a primary diagnosis, medications are generally not recommended for treatment of the dependency issues or the anxiety or depressive responses. Persons with dependent personality disorder may become overly dependent on any medication used.

Prognosis

The general prognosis for individuals with dependent personality disorder is good. Most dependents have had a supportive relationship with at least one parent. This enables them to engage in treatment to varying degrees and to explore the source of their dependent behavior. If persons who enter treatment can learn to become more autonomous, improved functioning can be expected.

Prevention

Because dependent personality disorder originates in the patient's family, the only known preventive

measure is a nurturing, emotionally stimulating, and expressive caregiving environment.

Resources

BOOKS

American Psychiatric Association. *Diagnostic and Statistical Manual of Mental Disorders*, 4th ed., Text rev. Washington, D.C.: American Psychiatric Association, 2000.

Beers, Mark H., MD, and Robert Berkow, MD, eds. *The Merck Manual of Diagnosis and Therapy*. 17th ed. Whitehouse Station, NJ: Merck Research Laboratories, 1999. Also available updated (2005) online at: <http://www.merck.com/mmpe/index.html>

Millon, Theodore, PhD, D.Sc. *Disorders of Personality: DSM IV and Beyond*. New York: John Wiley and Sons, 1996.

Sperry, Len, MD, PhD. *Handbook of Diagnosis and Treatment of DSM-IV Personality Disorders*. New York: Brunner/Mazel, 1995.

PERIODICALS

Tyrer, P., J. Morgan, and D. Cicchetti. "The Dependent Personalilty Questionnaire (DPQ): A Screening Instrument for Dependent Personality." *International Journal of Social Psychiatry* 50 (2004): 10–17.

ORGANIZATIONS

American Psychiatric Association. 1400 K Street NW, Washington, D.C. 20005. <http://www.psych.org >.

International Society for the Study of Personality Disorders. *Journal of Personality Disorders* Guilford Publications, 72 Spring Street, New York, NY 10012. Telephone: (800) 365-7006. <http://www.guilford.com>.

OTHER

National Library of Medicine, National Institutes of Health. "Dependent Personality Disorder." (2005) Web site: <http://medlineplus.nlm.nih.gov/medlineplus/ency/article/000941.htm>.

Gary Gilles, MA
Emily Jane Willingham, PhD

Depersonalization

Definition

Depersonalization is a mental state in which people feel detached or disconnected from their personal identities or selves. This may include the sense that one is "outside" oneself, or is observing one's own actions, thoughts, or body.

Description

People experiencing depersonalization may feel so detached that they feel more like robots than human beings. However, such people always are aware that this is just a feeling; there is no delusion that one is a lifeless robot or that one has no personal identity. The sense of detachment that characterizes the state may result in mood shifts, difficulty thinking, and loss of some sensations—a state that can be described as numbness or sensory anesthesia.

Depersonalization can also occur transiently in people in many different stress-inducing situations, including sleep deprivation, test taking, or being in a traffic accident. The feeling of detachment also can arise as a result of anesthesia or from using nitrous oxide. In addition, people experience depersonalization in different ways. People may feel like they are floating on the ceiling, watching themselves, or as though they are in a dream. Individuals with depersonalization may feel that events and the environment are unreal or strange, a state called derealization. Derealization, a **dissociation** symptom, differs from depersonalization in that it is the environment that seems unreal or dreamlike.

Episodes of depersonalization can last from a few seconds to years. The frequency may increase after traumatic events such as exposure to combat, accidents, or other forms of violence or **stress**. Treatment depends on the context of the depersonalization episode or episodes.

Depersonalization can be a symptom of other disorders, including **panic disorder**, **borderline personality disorder**, **post-traumatic stress disorder** (PTSD), **acute stress disorder**, or one of several **dissociative disorders**, including depersonalization disorders. A person will not be diagnosed with **depersonalization disorder** as the primary problem if the episodes of depersonalization occur only during panic attacks or following a traumatic stressor.

Depersonalization is a common experience in the general adult population, although twice as many women as men receive treatment for it. However, when a patient's symptoms are severe enough to cause significant emotional distress or to interfere with normal functioning, they may meet the criteria of the *Diagnostic and Statistical Manual of Mental Disorders*, fourth edition, text revision (the *DSM-IV-TR*) for "depersonalization disorder."

See also Acute stress disorder; Dissociation and dissociative disorders; Post-traumatic stress disorder; Schizophrenia.

Resources

BOOKS

American Psychiatric Association. *Diagnostic and Statistical Manual of Mental Disorders*. 4th ed., Text rev. Washington, D.C.: American Psychiatric Association, 2000.

"Depersonalization Disorder." *The Merck Manual of Diagnosis and Therapy,* eds. Mark H. Beers, MD, and Robert Berkow, MD. Sec. 15, Chap. 188. Whitehouse Station, NJ: Merck Research Laboratories, 2001.

Medical Economics staff. *Physicians' Desk Reference*. 56th ed. Montvale, NJ: Medical Economics Company, 2002.

ORGANIZATIONS

International Society for the Study of Dissociation (ISSD). 8201 Greensboro Drive, Suite 300. McLean, VA 22102. Telephone: (703) 610-9037. Web site: <http://www.issd.org/index_actual.html>.

National Institute of Mental Health. 6001 Executive Boulevard, Room 8184, MSC 9663, Bethesda, MD 20892-9663. Telephone: (301) 443-4513. Web site: <www.nimh.nih.gov>.

National Organization for Rare Disorders. P. O. Box 8923, New Fairfield, CT 06812-8923. Telephone: (203) 746-6518. Web site: <www.rarediseases.org>.

Society for Traumatic Stress Studies. 60 Revere Drive, Suite 500, Northbrook, IL 60062. Telephone: (708) 480-9080.

OTHER

The Mayo Clinic. "Dissociative Disorders." <http://www.mayoclinic.com/health/dissociative-disorders/DS00574/DSECTION=5>.

Dean A. Haycock, PhD
Emily Jane Willingham, PhD

Depersonalization disorder

Definition

Depersonalization is a state in which the individual ceases to perceive the reality of the self or the environment. The patient feels that his or her body is unreal, is changing, or is dissolving; or that he or she is outside of the body.

Depersonalization disorder is classified by the *Diagnostic and Statistical Manual of Mental Disorders*, fourth edition, text revision, also known as the *DSM-IV-TR* as one of the **dissociative disorders**. These are mental disorders in which the normally well-integrated functions of memory, identity, perception, and consciousness are separated (dissociated). The dissociative disorders are usually connected to trauma in the recent or distant past, or with an intense internal conflict that forces the mind to separate incompatible or unacceptable knowledge, information, or feelings. In depersonalization disorder, the patient's self-perception is disrupted. Patients feel as if they are external observers of their own lives, or that they are detached from their own bodies. Depersonalization disorder is sometimes called "depersonalization neurosis."

Depersonalization as a symptom may occur in **panic disorder**, **borderline personality disorder**, **post-traumatic stress disorder** (PTSD), **acute stress disorder**, or another dissociative disorder. The patient is not given the **diagnosis** of depersonalization disorder if the episodes of depersonalization occur only during panic attacks or following a traumatic stressor.

The symptom of depersonalization can also occur in normal individuals under such circumstances as sleep deprivation, the use of certain anesthetics, experimental conditions in a laboratory (experiments involving weightlessness, for example), and emotionally stressful situations (such as taking an important academic examination or being in a traffic accident). One such example involves some of the rescue personnel from the September 11, 2001, terrorist attacks on the World Trade Center and the Pentagon. These individuals experienced episodes of depersonalization after a day and a half without sleep. A more commonplace example is the use of nitrous oxide, or "laughing gas," as an anesthetic during oral surgery. Many dental patients report a sense of unreality or feeling of being outside their bodies during nitrous oxide administration.

To further complicate the matter, depersonalization may be experienced in different ways by different individuals. Common descriptions include a feeling of being outside one's body; "floating on the ceiling looking down at myself;" feeling as if one's body is dissolving or changing; feeling as if one is a machine or robot; an "unreal" feeling that one is in a dream or that one "is on automatic pilot." Most patients report a sense of emotional detachment or uninvolvement, or a sense of emotional numbing. Depersonalization is distinct from a dissociative symptom called derealization, in which people perceive the external world as unreal, dreamlike, or changing. The various ways that people experience depersonalization are related to their bodies or their sense of self.

Depersonalization is a common experience in the general adult population. However, when a patient's symptoms of depersonalization are severe enough to cause significant emotional distress, or interfere with normal functioning, the criteria of the *DSM-IV-TR* for depersonalization disorder are met.

Description

A person with depersonalization disorder experiences subjective symptoms of unreality that make him or her uneasy and anxious. "Subjective" is a word that refers to the thoughts and perceptions inside an individual's mind, as distinct from the objects of those thoughts and perceptions outside the mind. Because depersonalization is a subjective experience, many people who have chronic or recurrent episodes of depersonalization are afraid others will not understand if they try to describe what they are feeling, or will think they are "crazy." As a result, depersonalization disorder may be underdiagnosed because the symptom of depersonalization is underreported.

Causes and symptoms

Causes

Depersonalization disorder, like the dissociative disorders in general, has been regarded as the result of severe abuse in childhood. This can be of a physical, emotional, and/or sexual nature.

Trauma and emotional abuse in particular are strong predictors of depersonalization disorder in adult life, as well as of depersonalization as a symptom in other mental disorders. Analysis of one study of 49 patients diagnosed with depersonalization disorder indicated much higher scores than the control subjects for the total amount of emotional abuse endured and for the maximum severity of this type of abuse. The researchers concluded that emotional abuse has been relatively neglected by psychiatrists compared to other forms of childhood trauma.

It is thought that abuse in childhood or trauma in adult life may account for the distinctive cognitive (knowledge-related) profile of patients with depersonalization disorder. These patients have significant difficulties in focusing their attention, with spatial reasoning, and with short-term visual and verbal memory. However, they have intact reality testing. (Reality testing refers to a person's ability to distinguish between their internal experiences and the objective reality of persons and objects in the outside world.) Otherwise stated, a patient with depersonalization disorder may experience his/her body as unreal, but knows that "feelings aren't facts." The *DSM-IV-TR* specifies intact reality testing as a diagnostic criterion for depersonalization disorder.

The causes of depersonalization disorder are not completely understood. Recent advances in **brain** imaging and other forms of neurological testing, however, have confirmed that depersonalization disorder is a distinct diagnostic entity and should not be considered a subtype of PTSD. A recent study using brain-imaging techniques found that patients with depersonalization disorder do not process emotional information in the same way as healthy controls, and their differences on brain imaging reflect their reported reduced or absent emotional response to verbal material that normally would elicit strong emotion, such as "There is a bomb inside the parcel."

NEUROBIOLOGICAL. In the past few years, several features of depersonalization disorder have been traced to differences in brain functioning. A group of British researchers found that the emotional detachment that characterizes depersonalization is associated with a lower level of nerve-cell responses in regions of the brain that are responsible for emotional feeling; an increased level of nerve-cell responses was found in regions of the brain related to emotional regulation.

A group of American researchers concluded that patients with depersonalization disorder had different patterns of response to tests of the hypothalamic-pituitary-adrenal axis (HPA; the part of the brain involved in the "fight-or-flight" reaction to **stress**) than did patients with PTSD. Other tests by the same research team showed that patients with depersonalization disorder can be clearly distinguished from patients with major **depression** by tests of the functioning of the HPA axis.

Other neurobiological studies involving **positron emission tomography** (PET) measurements of glucose (sugar) metabolism in different areas of the brain found that patients with depersonalization disorder appear to have abnormal functioning of the sensory cortex. The sensory cortex is the part of the brain that governs the senses of sight, hearing, and perceptions of the location of one's body in space. These studies indicate that depersonalization is symptom that involves differences in sensory perception and subjective experiences. In the study of patients and their processing of emotional information, the authors found that in patients showed a similar response in the visual cortex to emotional and neutral verbal information. They did not appear to distinguish these two classes of material, which could either be because they have an overall reduced emotional response or because their response to neutral material is enhanced.

HISTORICAL. Depersonalization disorder may be a reflection of changes in people's sense of self or personal identity within Western cultures since the eighteenth century. Historians of psychiatry have noted that whereas some mental disorders, such as depression, have been reported since the beginnings of Western medicine, no instances of the dissociative disorders were recorded before the 1780s. It seems that changes in social institutions and the structure of the family since the mid-eighteenth century may have produced a psychological structure in Westerners that makes individuals increasingly vulnerable to self disorders—as they are now called. Experiences of the unreality of one's body or one's self, such as those that characterize depersonalization disorder, presuppose a certain notion of how the self is presumed to feel. The emphasis on individualism and detachment from one's family is a mark of adult maturity in contemporary Western societies that appears to be a contributing factor to the frequency of dissociative symptoms and disorders.

Symptoms

Although the *DSM-IV-TR* does not specify a list of primary symptoms of depersonalization, clinicians generally consider the triad of emotional numbing, changes in visual perception, and altered experience of one's body to be important core symptoms of depersonalization disorder.

The *DSM-IV-TR* notes that patients with depersonalization disorder frequently score high on measurements of hypnotizability.

Demographics

The lifetime prevalence of depersonalization disorder in the general population is unknown, possibly because many people are made anxious by episodes of depersonalization and afraid to discuss them with a primary care physician. One survey done by the National Institutes of Mental Health (NIMH) indicates that about half of the adults in the United States have had one or two brief episodes of depersonalization in their lifetimes, usually resulting from severe stress. About a third of people exposed to life-threatening dangers develop brief periods of depersonalization, as do 40% of psychiatric inpatients. Estimates of the prevalence of depersonalization disorder in the general population range from 2.4% to 20%.

Depersonalization disorder is diagnosed about twice as often in women as in men. It is not known, however, whether this sex ratio indicates that women are at greater risk for the disorder or if they are more likely to seek help for its symptoms, or both. Little information is available about the incidence of the disorder in different racial or ethnic groups.

KEY TERMS

Abuse—Physical, emotional, or sexual harm.

Depersonalization—A dissociative symptom in which the patient feels that his or her body is unreal, is changing, or is dissolving; or that he or she is outside the body.

Depersonalization neurosis—Another name for depersonalization disorder.

Derealization—A dissociative symptom in which the external environment is perceived as unreal or dreamlike.

Dissociation—A reaction to trauma in which the mind splits off certain aspects of the traumatic event from conscious awareness. Dissociation can affect the patient's memory, sense of reality, and sense of identity.

Dissociative disorders—A group of disorders marked by the separation (dissociation) of perception, memory, personal identity, and consciousness. Depersonalization disorder is one of five dissociative disorders defined by *DSM-IV-TR*.

Hypothalamic-pituitary-adrenal (HPA) system—A part of the brain involved in the human stress response. The HPA system releases cortisol, the primary human stress hormone, and neurotransmitters that activate other brain structures associated with the fight-or-flight reaction. The HPA system appears to function in abnormal ways in patients diagnosed with depersonalization disorder. It is sometimes called the HPA axis.

Reality testing—A phrase that refers to a person's ability to distinguish between subjective feelings and objective reality. A person who knows that their body is real even though they may be experiencing it as unreal, for example, is said to have intact reality testing. Intact reality testing is a *DSM-IV-TR* criterion for depersonalization disorder.

Selective serotonin reuptake inhibitors—Commonly prescribed drugs for treating depression. SSRIs affect the chemicals that nerves in the brain use to send messages to one another.

Serotonin—A widely distributed neurotransmitter that is found in blood platelets, the lining of the digestive tract, and in the brain where it works in combination with norepinephrine. It causes very powerful contractions of smooth muscle, and is associated with mood, attention, emotions, and sleep. Low levels of serotonin are associated with depression.

Stress—A physical and psychological response that results from being exposed to a demand or pressure.

Stressor—A stimulus or event that provokes a stress response in an organism. Stressors can be categorized as acute or chronic, and as external or internal to the organism.

Subjective—Referring to a person's unique internal thoughts and feelings, as distinct from the objects of those thoughts and feelings in the eternal world.

Tricyclic antidepressants (TCAs)—Antidepressant medications that have the common characteristic of a three-ring nucleus in their chemical structure. Imipramine and amitriptyline are examples of tricyclic antidepressants.

Diagnosis

The diagnosis of depersonalization disorder is usually a diagnosis of exclusion. The doctor will take a detailed medical history, give the patient a physical examination, and order blood and urine tests in order to rule out depersonalization resulting from epilepsy, **substance abuse**, medication side effects, or recent periods of sleep deprivation.

There are several standard diagnostic questionnaires that may be given to evaluate the presence of a dissociative disorder. The Dissociative Experiences Scale (DES) is a frequently administered self-report screener for **dissociation**. The **Structured Clinical Interview for DSM-IV** Dissociative Disorders, or SCID-D, can be used to make the diagnosis of depersonalization disorder distinct from the other dissociative disorders defined by *DSM-IV*. The SCID-D is a semistructured interview, which means that the examiner's questions are open-ended and allow the patient to describe experiences of depersonalization in some detail—distinct from simple yes-or-no answers.

In addition to these instruments, a six-item Depersonalization Severity Scale, or DSS, has been developed to discriminate between depersonalization disorder and other dissociative or post-traumatic disorders, and to measure the effects of treatment in patients.

Treatments

Depersonalization disorder sometimes resolves on its own without treatment. Specialized treatment is recommended only if the symptoms are persistent, recurrent, or upsetting to the patient. Insight-oriented **psychodynamic psychotherapy**, cognitive-behavior therapy, and hypnosis have been demonstrated to be effective with some patients. There is, however, no single form of **psychotherapy** that is effective in treating all patients diagnosed with depersonalization disorder.

Medications that have been helpful to patients with depersonalization disorder include the benzodiazepine tranquilizers, such as **lorazepam** (Ativan), **clorazepate** (Tranxene), and **alprazolam** (Xanax), and the tricyclic **antidepressants**, such as **amitriptyline** (Elavil), **doxepin** (Sinequan), and **desipramine** (Norpramin). **Selective serotonin reuptake inhibitors (SSRIs)**, which include **fluoxetine** (Prozac), **sertraline** (Zoloft), and **paroxetine** (**Paxil**), may also be effective. **SSRIs** affect levels of the brain chemicals that nerve cells use to send messages to each another. These chemical messengers, called (**neurotransmitters**), are released by one nerve cell and taken up by others. If the receiving cell does not take up the chemical, the sending cell will take it up, a process called "reuptake." SSRIs work by preventing the reuptake of serotonin, leaving more serotonin for nerve signaling. Serotonin signaling is associated with feelings of well-being.

Unfortunately, there have been very few well-designed studies comparing different medications for depersonalization disorder. Because depersonalization disorder is frequently associated with trauma, effective treatment must include other stress-related symptoms, as well.

Relaxation techniques have been reported to be a beneficial adjunctive treatment for persons diagnosed with depersonalization disorder, particularly for those who are worried about their sanity.

Prognosis

The prognosis for recovery from depersonalization disorder is good. Most patients recover completely, particularly those who developed the disorder in connection with traumas that can be explored and resolved in treatment. A few patients develop a chronic form of the disorder; this is characterized by periodic episodes of depersonalization in connection with stressful events in their lives.

Prevention

Some clinicians think that depersonalization disorder has an undetected onset in childhood, even though most patients first appear for treatment as adolescents or young adults. Preventive strategies could include the development of screening techniques for identifying children at risk, as well as further research into the effects of emotional abuse on children.

Further neurobiological research may lead to the development of medications or other treatment modalities for preventing, as well as treating, depersonalization.

Resources

BOOKS

American Psychiatric Association. *Diagnostic and Statistical Manual of Mental Disorders,* 4th ed., Text rev. Washington, D.C.: American Psychiatric Association, 2000.

"Depersonalization Disorder." *The Merck Manual of Diagnosis and Therapy.*, Mark H. Beers, MD, and Robert Berkow, MD, eds. Whitehouse Station, NJ: Merck Research Laboratories, 2001.

Ellenberger, Henri. *The Discovery of the Unconscious.* New York: Basic Books, 1970.

Herman, Judith, MD. *Trauma and Recovery,* 2nd ed., revised. New York: Basic Books, 1997.

Medical Economics Staff. *Physicians' Desk Reference,* 56th ed. Montvale, NJ: Medical Economics Company, 2002.

Stout, Martha, PhD. *The Myth of Sanity: Tales of Multiple Personality in Everyday Life.* New York: Penguin Books, 2001.

PERIODICALS

Berrios, G. E., and M. Sierra. "Depersonalization: A Conceptual History." *Historical Psychiatry* 8 (June 1997): 213–29.

Guralnik, O., J. Schmeidler, and D. Simeon. "Feeling Unreal: Cognitive Processes in Depersonalization." *American Journal of Psychiatry* 157 (Jan. 2000): 103–109.

Lambert, M. V., C. Senior, M. L. Phillips, and others. "Visual Imagery and Depersonalisation." *Psychopathology* 34 (Sept.–Oct. 2001): 259–64.

Medford, Nicholas, et al. "Emotional Memory in Depersonalization Fisorder: A Functional MRI Study." *Psychiatry Research* 148 (2006): 93–102.

Phillips, M. L., N. Medford, C. Senior, and others. "Depersonalization Disorder: Thinking Without Feeling." *Psychiatry Research* 108 (Dec. 30, 2001): 145–60.

Sierra, M., and others. "Lamotrigine in the Treatment of Depersonalization Disorder." *Journal of Clinical Psychiatry* 62 (Oct. 2001): 826–27.

Sierra, M., and G. E. Berrios. "The Phenomenological Stability of Depersonalization: Comparing the Old with the New." *Journal of Nervous and Mental Disorders* 189 (Sept. 2001): 629–36.

Simeon, D., and others. "Personality Factors Associated with Dissociation: Temperament, Defenses, and Cognitive Schemata." *American Journal of Psychiatry* 159 (Mar. 2002): 489–91.

Simeon, D., O. Guralnik, E. A. Hazlett, and others. "Feeling Unreal: A PET Study of Depersonalization Disorder." *American Journal of Psychiatry* 157 (Nov. 2000): 1782–88.

Simeon, D., O. Guralnik, M. Knutelska, and others. "Hypothalamic-Pituitary-Adrenal Axis Dysregulation in Depersonalization Disorder." *Neuropsychopharmacology* 25 (Nov. 2001): 793–95.

Simeon, D., O. Guralnik, and J. Schmeidler. "Development of a Depersonalization Severity Scale." *Journal of Traumatic Stress* 14 (April 2001): 341–49.

Simeon, D., O. Guralnik, J. Schmeidler, and others. "The Role of Childhood Interpersonal Trauma in Depersonalization Disorder." *American Journal of Psychiatry* 158 (July 2001): 1027–33.

Simeon, D., D. J. Stein, and E. Hollander. "Treatment of Depersonalization Disorder with Clomipramine." *Biological Psychiatry* 44 (Aug. 15, 1998): 302–303.

Spitzer, Carsten, Sven Barnow, Harald J. Freyberger, and Hans Joergen Grabe. "Recent Developments in the Theory of Dissociation." *World Psychiatry* 5 (2006): 82–86.

Stanton, B. R., A. S. David, A. J. Cleare, and others. "Basal Activity of the Hypothalamic-Pituitary-Adrenal Axis in Patients with Depersonalization Disorder." *Psychiatry Research* 104 (Oct. 2001): 85–89.

Zanarini, M. C., and others. "The Dissociative Experiences of Borderline Patients." *Comparative Psychiatry* 41 (May–June 2000): 223–27.

ORGANIZATIONS

International Society for the Study of Dissociation (ISSD). 8201 Greensboro Drive, Suite 300. McLean, VA 22102. Telephone: (703) 610-9037. Fax: (703) 610-9005. <http://www.issd.org/index_actual.html>.

National Institute of Mental Health. 6001 Executive Boulevard, Room 8184, MSC 9663, Bethesda, MD 20892-9663. Telephone: (301) 443-4513. <www.nimh.nih.gov>.

National Organization for Rare Disorders. P. O. Box 8923, New Fairfield, CT 06812-8923. Telephone: (203) 746-6518. <www.rarediseases.org>.

Society for Traumatic Stress Studies. 60 Revere Drive, Suite 500, Northbrook, IL 60062. Telephone: (708) 480-9080.

OTHER

The Mayo Clinic. "Dissociative Disorders." <http://www.mayoclinic.com/health/dissociative-disorders/DS00574/DSECTION=5>.

Rebecca J. Frey, PhD
Emily Jane Willingham, PhD

Depression and depressive disorders

Definition

Depression or depressive disorders (unipolar depression) are mental illnesses characterized by a profound and persistent feeling of sadness or despair

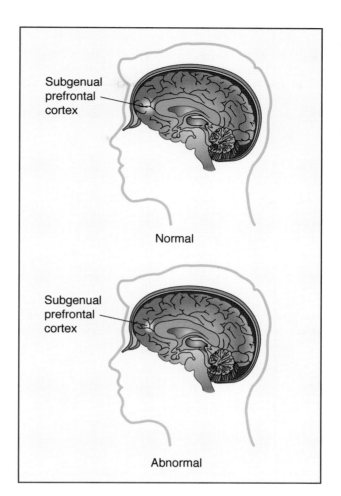

A normal brain, and one with an abnormal subgenual prefrontal cortex. *(Electronic Illustrators Group)*

and/or a loss of interest in things that were once pleasurable. Disturbance in sleep, appetite, and mental processes are a common accompaniment.

Description

Everyone experiences feelings of unhappiness and sadness occasionally. But when these depressed feelings start to dominate everyday life and cause physical and mental deterioration, they become what are known as depressive disorders. Each year in the United States, depressive disorders affect an estimated 18.8 million people, or about 9.5% of the adult population, at an approximate annual direct and indirect cost of more than $51 billion. One in four women is likely to experience an episode of severe depression in her lifetime, with a 10–20% lifetime prevalence, compared to 5–10% for men. The average age a first depressive episode occurs is in the mid-20s, although the disorder strikes all age groups indiscriminately,

ANTIDEPRESSANT DRUGS	
Brand Name (Generic Name)	*Possible Common Side Effects Include:*
Desyrel (trazodone hydrochloride)	Allergic skin reactions, blurred vision, decreased appetite, fluid retention, headache
Effexor (venlafaxine hydrochloride)	Diarrhea, dizziness, gas, headache, insommia, rash, vomiting
Elavil (amitriptyline hydrochloride)	Constipation, dizziness, high blood pressure, fever, nausea, rash, weight gain or loss
Nardil (phenelzine sulfate)	Dry mouth, fatigue, headache, muscle spasms, tremors
Norpramin (desipramine hydrochloride)	Blurred vision, cramps, hallucinations, hair loss, vomiting
Pamelor (nortriptyline hydrochloride)	Diarrhea, fatigue, headache, decreased coordination
Paxil (paroxetine hydrochloride)	Cold symptoms, drowsiness, nervousness, stomach pain
Prozac (fluoxetine hydrochloride)	Bronchitis, drowsiness, fatigue, nausea, tremors
Sinequan (doxepin hydrochloride)	Bruising, constipation, fluid retention, itching, increased heartbeat
Surmontil (trimipramine maleate)	Disorientation, flushing, headache, nausea, vomiting
Tofranil (imipramine hydrochloride)	Bleeding sores, fever, hives, decreased coordination
Travil	Asthma, diarrhea, dizziness, fatigue, seizures
Wellbutrin (bupropion hydrochloride)	Agitation, dry mouth, headache, nausea, rash
Zoloft (sertraline)	Diarrhea, fainting, gas, headache, nervousness

Several types of antidepressants and their possible side effects. *(Stanley Publishing)*

from children to the elderly. In fact, the rate of increase in depression among children in 23%.

There are two main categories of depressive disorders: **major depressive disorder** and **dysthymic disorder**. Major depressive disorder is a moderate to severe episode of depression lasting two or more weeks. Individuals experiencing this major depressive episode may have trouble sleeping, lose interest in activities they once took pleasure in, experience a change in weight, have difficulty concentrating, feel worthless and hopeless, or have a preoccupation with death or **suicide**. In children, the major depression may appear as irritability.

While major depressive episodes may be acute (intense but short-lived), dysthymic disorder is an ongoing, chronic depression that lasts two or more

years (one or more years in children) and has an average duration of 16 years. The mild to moderate depression of dysthymic disorder may rise and fall in intensity, and those afflicted with the disorder may experience some periods of normal, non-depressed mood of up to two months in length. Its onset is gradual, and dysthymic patients may not be able to pinpoint exactly when they started feeling depressed. Individuals with dysthymic disorder may experience a change in sleeping and eating patterns, low self-esteem, **fatigue**, trouble concentrating, and feelings of hopelessness.

Depression can also occur in **bipolar disorder**, a mood disorder that causes radical emotional changes and mood swings, from manic highs to depressive lows. The majority of bipolar individuals experience alternating episodes of mania and depression.

Demographics

Major depressive disorder occurs twice as frequently in adolescent and adult females as in the corresponding male populations. Both genders of preadolescent children are affected equally.

Causes and Symptoms

The causes behind depression are complex and not yet fully understood. While an imbalance of certain neurotransmitters—the chemicals in the **brain** that transmit messages between nerve cells—are thought to be key to depression, external factors such as upbringing (more so in dysthymia than major depression) may be as important. For example, it is speculated that, if an individual is abused and neglected throughout childhood and adolescence, a pattern of low self-esteem and negative thinking may emerge. From that, a lifelong pattern of depression may follow.

Depression is also associated with an imbalance of cortisol, the main hormone secreted by the adrenal glands. Other physiological factors sometimes associated with depression include viral infections, low thyroid hormone levels, and biological rhythms, including women's menstrual cycles—depression is a prominent symptom of **premenstrual syndrome** (PMS).

Heredity seems to play a role in the development of depressive disorders. Individuals with major depression in their immediate family are up to three times more likely to have the disorder themselves. It would seem that biological and genetic factors may make certain individuals predisposed or prone to depressive disorders, but environmental circumstances may often trigger the disorder.

External stressors and significant life changes, such as chronic medical problems, death of a loved one, divorce or estrangement, miscarriage, or loss of a job, can also result in a form of depression known as adjustment disorder. Although periods of adjustment disorder usually resolve themselves, occasionally they may evolve into a major depressive disorder.

In addition, chemical imbalance in the brain, certain medical conditions, diet, and alcohol or drug use may lead to depression.

The primary symptoms of major depressive disorder are depressed mood or anhedonia (the inability to enjoy experiences or activities normally considered to be pleasant) over a period of at least two weeks. Other symptoms that may be symptomatic of major depression include:

- change in appetite with marked weight gain or loss

KEY TERMS

Psychotropic drug—A drug that acts on or influences the activity of the mind.

- decreased pleasure or interest in daily activities
- difficulty concentrating
- disturbed sleep patterns (e.g., insomnia or excessive sleep)
- fatigue or loss of energy
- feelings of abandonment
- feelings of guilt
- feelings of overwhelming sadness or fear
- intense feelings of helplessness, hopelessness, worthlessness, anxiety
- recurrent thoughts of death

Treatments

Depression is typically treated with a combination of psychotropic drugs and **psychotherapy**. Antidepressant medications include monoamine oxidase inhibitors (MAOIs), tricyclic **antidepressants**, **selective serotonin reuptake inhibitors** (**SSRIs**), norepinephrine reuptake inhibitors (NRIs), norepinephrine-dopamine reuptake inhibitors, serotonin-norepinephrine reuptake inhibitors (SNRIs), and noradrenergic and specific serotonergic antidepressants (NASSAs). Severe cases of depression that are not responsive to these treatments have historically been treated with **electroconvulsive therapy** (ECT). ECT is a controversial treatment in which controlled, low-dose electrical currents are used to cause a seizure. Although rarely used today, ECT is still sometimes used in the treatment of severe depression. The benefits of ECT in the treatment of depression are temporary. Currently, research is underway investigating the effectiveness of **transcranial magnetic stimulation** (TMS). TMS is a non-invasive experimental procedure that gently stimulates the brain using short bursts of electromagnetic energy received through focused powerful magnets placed on the patient's scalp.

Resources

BOOKS

American Psychiatric Association. *Diagnostic and Statistical Manual of Mental Disorders*. 4th edition, text revised. Washington, DC: American Psychiatric Association, 2000.

DePaulo, J. Raymond, Jr., and Leslie Alan Horvitz. *Understanding Depression: What We Know and What You Can Do About It*. New York: John Wiley and Sons, 2002.

Freeman, Arthur; James Pretzer; Barbara Fleming; and Karen M. Simon, *Clinical Applications of Cognicitive Therapy,* 2nd ed. New York: Kluwer Academic/Plenum Publishers, 2004.

Kasper, Siegfried; Johan A. den Boer; and J. M. Sitsen, Ad, Eds. *Handbook of Depression and Anxiety,* 2nd ed. New York: Marcel Dekker, 2003.

VandenBos, Gary R., Ed. *APA Dictionary of Psychology.* Washington, DC: American Psychological Association, 2007.

PERIODICALS

Jarema, Marek, III. "Atypical Antipsychotics in the Treatment of Mood Disorders." *Current Opinion in Psychiatry* 20(1) (Jan 2007): 23–29.

Nemeroff, Charles B. "The Burden of Severe Depression: A Review of Diagnostic Challenges and Treatment Alternatives." *Journal of Psychiatric Research* 41(3–4) (Apr–Jun 2007): 89–206.

Rihmer, Zoltán. "Suicide Risk in Mood Disorders." *Current Opinion in Psychiatry* 20(1) (Jan 2007): 17-22.

Paula Anne Ford-Martin, M.A.
Ruth A. Wienclaw, Ph.D.

Dermatotillomania

Definition

Dermatotillomania, also called psychogenic excoriation (skin removal), neurotic excoriation, acne excoriée, and pathological or compulsive skin picking, is characterized by excessive picking, scratching, or squeezing of skin. This syndrome is not formally included in *Diagnostic and Statistical Manual of Mental Disorders*, Fourth Edition, Text Revision (*DSM-IV-TR*), although dermatotillomania is hypothesized to be an impulse control disorder related to **obsessive-compulsive disorder** (OCD) and/or to **depression**. Dermatotillomania can therefore be distinguished from other dermatological diseases that are influenced by psychological factors (e.g., psoriasis or alopecia) because it is a dermatological manifestation of a psychiatric syndrome.

Description

Behaviors associated with dermatotillomania include excessive excoriation of skin at multiple sites that are easily reachable. Excoriation may occur at sites of skin lesions (e.g., acne, scabs, insect bites) or in response to skin sensations such as dryness, tingling, or pain. The face is the most common site of excoriation that is usually performed with the fingers or fingernails but may involve the teeth or other instruments. Excor-

iation may occur in brief bouts or for extended periods and is usually worse in the evening.

Impulse control disorders are characterized by irresistible impulses to commit acts that may be harmful to one's self or others. Feelings of tension or **anxiety** may precede these acts that may then be followed by pleasure or gratification following the performance of the act. Guilt or regret may, or may not, be felt subsequent to the act. A person experiencing dermatotillomania is likely to be under substantial distress and may feel embarrassed about the excoriating behavior. Social functioning may be decreased, especially those functions in which skin lesions will be exposed. Excoriation may result in varied medical complications including bleeding, ulcers, infections, and temporary or permanent disfigurement.

Causes and symptoms

Causes

Co-occurring psychiatric conditions, especially mood and **anxiety disorders**, are common in patients with dermatotillomania. Mood disorders such as major depression and obsessive-compulsive disorder, as well as anxiety disorders including **panic disorder**, social and simple phobias, **post-traumatic stress disorder**, and **generalized anxiety disorder** are frequently seen in individuals with dermatotillomania. **Depressive disorders** are the most common co-occuring psychiatric diagnoses in people with dermatotillomania, suggesting that the underlying pathophysiology in people with dermatotillomania may be major depression.

Symptoms

The most prominent symptoms are excessive picking, scratching, or squeezing of skin. The duration of each episode and the total daily duration are variable. Episodes may be more frequent during the evening hours. Skin excoriation is performed throughout the duration of the disorder.

Demographics

The mean age of onset for dermatotillomania is between 15 and 40 years. The mean duration of symptoms is between five and 21 years. This syndrome is thought to have an incidence of 2% of patients seen in dermatological clinics, with women affected more often than men.

Diagnosis

The **diagnosis** of dermatotillomania is made by history and interview in the absence of formal inclusion in *DSM-IV-TR*. The behaviors associated with dermatotillomania are heterogeneous. Co-occuring impulse control and/or depression symptoms coupled with the prominent dermatological features allow for diagnosis. Several related disorders have features of dermatotillomania, including **trichotillomania** (compulsive hair pulling) and **body dysmorphic disorder** (concerns about appearance, especially related to the skin or hair in which obsessions are related to any aspect of the skin, such as color, marks, veins, pores, wrinkles, stretch marks, or sagging). It is possible that an underlying dermatological condition produces the observed symptoms although the lack of obsessive or compulsive-impulsive behavior would rule out dermatotillomania in these cases.

Treatments

Medications

Case reports and small trials have examined the efficacy of various types of drugs for dermatotillomania: **antidepressants**, including **selective serotonin reuptake inhibitors** (**SSRIs**, such as **fluvoxamine**) and tricyclics (e.g., **doxepin** and **clomipramine**), opiate antagonists (**naltrexone**), typical antipsychotics (**pimozide**), and atypical antipsychotics (**olanzapine, aripiprazole**). In some cases (for example, the SSRI **fluoxetine**), there appeared to be a separation in the efficacy of the drug on skin excoriation and a comorbid symptom (depression or anxiety), suggesting that the drug may have a primary effect on skin excoriation.

Alternative therapies

Behavioral treatments, including **psychotherapy** and hypnosis, have been examined for effectiveness in dermatotillomania. Small-scale studies or case reports have suggested that habit-reversal therapy, in which a program of self-monitoring is paired with competing response practice, and psychotherapy, in which behavioral and emotional as well as topical therapies are practiced, can be effective.

Prognosis

Large-scale outcome studies are lacking, although it has been suggested that presentation to a dermatologist prior to experiencing symptoms for one year results in a better prognosis. Complications from lesion infection are possible and chronic rebuilding of lesioned tissues has been suggested to be a potential causative factor for skin cancer.

Prevention

Obsessive-compulsive disorders and depression are major psychiatric disorders whose underlying pathophysiology involves alterations in neurotransmission. Since dermatotillomania is a dermatologic manifestation of one, or both, of these disorders, its elimination is dependent on curing the underlying illness.

Resources

BOOKS

American Psychiatric Association. *Diagnostic and Statistical Manual of Mental Disorders* 4th ed., Text rev. Washington, D.C.: American Psychiatric Association, 2000.

PERIODICALS

Arnold, L. M., M. B. Auchenbach, and S. L. McElroy. "Psychogenic Excoriation. Clinical Features, Proposed Diagnostic Criteria, Epidemiology and Approaches to Treatment." *CNS Drugs* 15.5 (2001): 351–59.

Arnold, L. M., and others. "An Open Clinical Trial of Fluvoxamine Treatment of Psychogenic Excoriation." *Journal of Clinical Psychopharmacology* 19.1 (February 1999): 15–18.

Blanch, J., F. Grimalt, G. Massana, and V. Navarro. "Efficacy of Olanzapine in the Treatment of Psychogenic Excoriation." *British Journal of Dermatology* 151.3 (September 2004): 714–16.

Calikusu, C., B. Yucel, A. Polat, and C. Baykal. "The Relation of Psychogenic Excoriation with Psychiatric Disorders: A Comparative Study." *Comprehensive Psychiatry* 44.3 (May–June 2003): 256–61,

Carter, W.G., III, and S. D. Shillcutt. "Aripiprazole Augmentation of Venlafaxine in the Treatment of Psychogenic Excoriation." *Journal of Clinical Psychiatry* 67.8 (August 2006): 1311.

Osaba, O., and G. Mahr. "Psychogenic Excoriation and Cancer." *Psychosomatics* 43.3 (May–June 2002): 251–52.

Andrew J. Bean, PhD

Desensitization *see* **Systematic desensitization**

Desipramine

Definition

Desipramine is an antidepressant drug used to elevate mood and promote recovery of a normal range of emotions in patients with **depressive disorders**. In addition, desipramine has uses in a number of other psychiatric and medical conditions. In the United States, the drug is also known by its brand name, Norpramin.

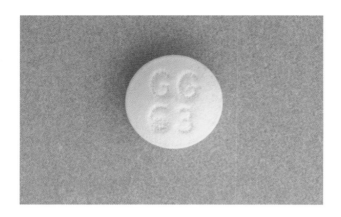

A desipramine tablet. *(Custom Medical Stock Photo, Inc. Reproduced by Permission.)*

Purpose

Desipramine is known principally as an antidepressant drug used to promote recovery of depressed patients. It also has therapeutic uses in **panic disorder**, pain management, **attention deficit/hyperactivity disorder** (ADHD), sleep attacks (**narcolepsy** and cataplexy), **binge eating** (bulimia), and for **cocaine** craving in the treatment of **addiction**.

Description

Desipramine is one of the tricyclic **antidepressants**, so-called because of the three-ring chemical structure common to these drugs. Until the late 1980s, desipramine and other tricyclic antidepressants, such as **imipramine**, formed the mainstay of the pharmacological treatment of depressive disorders.

The therapeutic action of antidepressants is not completely understood. It is known that these drugs boost the levels of certain messenger chemicals, called **neurotransmitters**, which are involved in transmitting signals between nerve cells in the **brain**. This action may help to restore normal emotional feelings by counteracting abnormalities of nerve signal transmission that occur in depressive disorders.

Desipramine is one of a large number of tricyclic antidepressant compounds. Each was developed for somewhat differing pharmacological effects and side-effect profiles. The effects of desipramine are very similar to those of other tricyclics, although some individual patients may find one drug of this group more effective or more tolerable than another. It is available as Norpramin in 10-, 25-, 50-, 75-, 100-, and 150-mg tablets; although generic manufacturers may supply a somewhat different set of dosages.

Recommended dosage

For adults, desipramine is usually administered in dosages of 100–200 mg per day. Doses ranging from 75 mg to 300 mg per day are sometimes prescribed. The initial daily dose is usually low to avoid side effects, and it is usually increased, as necessary, until a therapeutic effect is achieved. Desipramine may be administered in divided doses or a single daily dose.

Geriatric patients, children, and adolescents are more sensitive to the side effects and toxicities of tricyclic antidepressants than other people. For geriatric patients, the dose may range from 25 mg to 100 mg per day. For children six to 12 years old, the recommended dose ranges from 10 mg to 30 mg per day in divided doses. For adolescents, daily dosages range from 25 mg to 50 mg but may be increased up to 100 mg, if needed.

Precautions

Desipramine and other tricyclic antidepressants may cause drowsiness. Activities requiring alertness, such as driving, may be impaired. Dizziness or lightheadedness may occur on arising due to sudden decreases in blood pressure. Fainting may also occur. Some patients may experience difficulty urinating, especially men with prostate enlargement. Glaucoma may be aggravated. Sensitivity to ultraviolet light may be increased, and sunburns may occur more easily. Sweating may be reduced, causing sensitivity to heat and hot weather. Among patients with epilepsy, **seizures** may become more frequent.

Tricyclic antidepressants, including desipramine, should be used with caution in patients with heart disease because of the possibility of adverse effects on heart rhythm. Adverse effects on the heart occur frequently when tricyclics are taken in overdose. Only small quantities of these drugs should be given to patients who may be suicidal.

Tricyclic antidepressants may cause dry mouth due to decreased saliva, possibly contributing to the development of tooth decay, gum disease, and mouth infections. Patients should avoid sweets, sugary beverages, and chewing gum containing sugar.

It has not been determined whether desipramine is safe to take during pregnancy, and the patient's need for this medicine should be balanced against the possibility of harm to the fetus. Tricyclic antidepressants may be secreted in breast milk and may cause sedation and depressed breathing in a nursing infant.

Side effects

Desipramine may cause many side effects. Initially, the side effects of tricyclic drugs may be more

KEY TERMS

Autonomic—The part of the nervous system that governs the heart, involuntary muscles, and glands.

Cataplexy—A symptom of narcolepsy marked by a sudden episode of muscle weakness triggered by strong emotions. The muscle weakness may cause the person's knees to buckle, or the head to drop. In severe cases, the patient may become paralyzed for a few seconds or minutes.

Epilepsy—A neurological disorder characterized by the onset of seizures. Seizures are caused by a disturbance in the electrical activity in the brain and can cause loss of consciousness, muscle spasms, rhythmic movements, abnormal sensory experiences, or altered mental states.

Glaucoma—A group of eye diseases characterized by increased pressure within the eye significant enough to damage eye tissue and structures. If untreated, glaucoma results in blindness.

Neurotransmitter—A chemical in the brain that transmits messages between neurons, or nerve cells.

pronounced, but sensitivity may decrease with continued treatment. The following more common side effects are grouped by the body system affected:

- cardiovascular: decreases of blood pressure on rising from a sitting or lying position, which may cause dizziness or fainting; increases of blood pressure, rapid heart rate, pounding heart, altered heart rhythm.
- nervous system: sedation, confusion, nervousness, restlessness, sleep difficulties, numbness, tingling sensations, tremors, increased seizure tendency.
- autonomic: blurred vision, dry mouth, decreased sweating, difficulty urinating, constipation.
- skin: rashes, sensitivity to sunlight.
- body as a whole: weight gain.

Less commonly, tricyclic drugs may cause adverse effects on almost any organ or system of the body, particularly the blood, hormones, kidney, and liver. Patients should consult their physicians if symptoms develop or bodily changes occur.

Interactions

Tricyclic antidepressants such as desipramine may interact with many other drugs. Patients should inform their physicians about all other drugs they are taking. Tricyclic drugs may intensify the effects of drugs caus-

ing sedation, including alcohol, **barbiturates**, narcotic pain medications, minor tranquilizers, and antihistamines. Tricyclics may cause excessive drops in blood pressure in patients taking blood-pressure medicine, especially upon sitting up or standing. Conversely, these drugs may interfere with the pressure-reducing effects of certain other blood pressure medicines. Tricyclics may interact with thyroid medications to produce heart rhythm abnormalities. Also, they may increase seizure tendency in patients with epilepsy, requiring adjustment of anti-epileptic medication. Concurrent use of tricyclic antidepressants with other antidepressants or other psychiatric medicines may result in intensification of certain side effects.

Certain drugs may interfere with the elimination of tricyclic antidepressants from the body causing higher blood levels and increased side effects. This effect may occur with cimetidine (Tagamet), other antidepressants, **methylphenidate** (Ritalin, Concerta), and some antipsychotic medications.

See also Addiction; Cocaine and related disorders; Depression and depressive disorders; Panic attack; Psychosis.

Resources

BOOKS

Preston, John D., John H. O'Neal, and Mary C. Talaga. *Handbook of Clinical Psychopharmacology for Therapists,* 4th ed. Oakland, CA: New Harbinger Publications, 2004.

PERIODICALS

Amitai, Yona, and Henri Frischer. "Excess Fatality from Desipramine in Children and Adolescents." *Journal of the American Academy of Child and Adolescent Psychiatry* 45.1 (Jan 2006): 54–60.

DeRubeis, Robert J., Steven D. Hollon, Jay D. Amsterdam, and others. "Cognitive Therapy vs Medications in the Treatment of Moderate to Severe Depression." *Archives of General Psychiatry* 62.4 (Apr. 2005): 409–16.

Mayers, Andrew G., and David S. Baldwin. "Antidepressants and Their Effect on Sleep." *Human Psychopharmacology: Clinical and Experimental* 20.8 (December 2005): 533–59.

McDowell, David, Edward V. Nunes, Angela M. Seracini, and others. "Desipramine Treatment of Cocaine-Dependent Patients with Depression: A Placebo-Controlled Trial." *Drug and Alcohol Dependence* 80.2 (November 2005): 209–21.

Musselman, Dominique L., Wendy I. Somerset, Ying Guo, and others. "Double-Blind, Multicenter, Parallel-Group Study of Paroxetine, Desipramine, or Placebo in Breast Cancer Patients (stages I, II, III, and IV) with Major Depression." *Journal of Clinical Psychiatry* 67.2 (February 2006): 288–96.

Rains, Adrienne and Lawrence. "Nonstimulant Medications for the Treatment of ADHD." *Journal of Child and Adolescent Psychiatric Nursing* 19.1 (February 2006): 44–47.

Walsh, B. Timothy, Robyn Sysko, and Michael K. Parides. "Early Response to Desipramine Among Women with Bulimia Nervosa." *International Journal of Eating Disorders* 39.1 (Jan. 2006): 72–75.

Wilens, Timothy E., Paul G. Hammerness, Joseph Biederman, and others. "Blood Pressure Changes Associated with Medication Treatment of Adults with Attention-Deficit/Hyperactivity Disorder." *Journal of Clinical Psychiatry* 66.2 (February 2005): 253–59.

Richard Kapit, MD
Ruth A. Wienclaw, PhD

Desoxyn *see* **Amphetamines**
Desyrel *see* **Trazodone**

Detoxification

Definition

Detoxification is a process in which the body is allowed to free itself of a drug. During this period, the symptoms of withdrawal are also treated. Detoxification is the primary step in any drug treatment program and is used as the initial phase in treating alcohol, heroin, inhalant, sedative, and hypnotic addictions.

Purpose

The goal of detoxification is to clear the toxins out of the body so that the body can adjust and heal itself after being dependent on a substance. For the recovering person to stay abstinent on a long-term basis, detoxification needs to lead into long-term community residential program treatment or outpatient drug treatment lasting three to six months.

Precautions

When individuals are physically dependent on a substance, they experience withdrawal symptoms when they abstain from the drug. Withdrawal symptoms vary with each drug of **abuse**, but can be severe, and even dangerous. Patients who want to overcome their dependence need help managing the withdrawal symptoms. The patient's medical team strives to get the patient off a substance on which he or she is physically dependent, while treating the withdrawal symptoms.

Pregnant women cannot be detoxified from opiates (also called narcotics, including morphine, heroin, and similar drugs) because strict detoxification can increase the risk of spontaneous abortion or premature birth. These women can be treated with **methadone** as an alternative. Methadone acts as a replacement for the heroin in the woman's body, but the methadone does not provide the "high" that the heroin provides. In addition, methadone is safer for the fetus than heroin.

To be an effective first step of treatment, detoxification must be an individualized process because patients have varying needs.

Description

The body, when allowed to be free from drugs, detoxifies itself through its normal metabolic processes. The withdrawal symptoms are treated during this process so that the patient will be comfortable while the body detoxifies itself.

The process of substance addiction

Before discussing detoxification, it may be useful to understand how the body becomes addicted and why withdrawal symptoms are experienced. In physical **addiction** or dependence, as a person uses a substance or chemical over a long period of time, his or her body chemistry changes. Once a substance enters the body through drinking, smoking, injecting, or inhaling, it travels through the bloodstream to the **brain**. The brain has a complex reward system built in; when people engage in activities that are important for survival (such as eating), special nerve cells in the brain release chemicals (**neurotransmitters**, including **dopamine**) that induce feelings of pleasure. Because of this reward system in the brain, humans are programmed to want to repeat actions that elicit those pleasant sensations. In other words, feelings of pleasure reinforce certain activities or behaviors. Addictive substances interfere with this reward system. Some drugs mimic the effects of a natural chemical, some block the communication between nerve cells, and some substances trigger a larger-than-normal release of neurotransmitters like dopamine. The result of this interference is that dependent drug users physically need the drug to feel pleasure. As they become more dependent, their bodies becomes less responsive to the substance, and need more of it to get the desired response—a phenomenon called tolerance. Also as a result of the interference with the brain's system, when the dependent user does not have the drug in his or her system, feelings of **depression** or unpleasant withdrawal symptoms may be experienced. These consequences also reinforce the substance use. People dependent on substances resort to using more drugs to avoid the depression or the withdrawal symptoms.

Withdrawal symptoms

The symptoms and severity of these symptoms vary from one substance to another.

ALCOHOL. After a person who has used alcohol heavily for a long time stops drinking, he or she may experience increased heart rate, shaking, difficulty sleeping, nausea, restlessness, **anxiety**, and even **seizures**. The affected person may also experience **hallucinations** (seeing, hearing, or feeling something that isn't really present). In some cases, **delirium** tremens (DTs) may occur as part of the withdrawal. Delirium tremens is a violent delirium (fading in and out of consciousness) with tremors, increased motor activity, visual hallucinations, disorientation, confusion, and fever that happens 48-96 hours after the alcohol-dependent person has had his or her last drink. These symptoms can last anywhere from three to 10 days. This state is a medical emergency because it could be fatal.

HEROIN AND OTHER OPIATES. Heroin is part of a family of drugs called opiates or **opioids**, which are made up of drugs that come from the seeds of the Asian poppy (heroin, opium and morphine, for example) and also manufactured drugs that act like the natural drugs (meperidine or Demerol). Symptoms of opiate withdrawal include restlessness, **insomnia**, anxiety, irritability, loss of appetite, diarrhea, abdominal cramps, nausea, sweating, chills, and runny eyes and nose.

SEDATIVES AND HYPNOTICS. Sedatives and hypnotics are drug families that are often considered in one group called the sedative-hypnotics. These drugs depress or slow down the body's functions, and can be used to calm anxiety or to induce sleep. When taken in high doses or when abused, these drugs can cause unconsciousness or death. These drugs include **barbiturates** and **benzodiazepines**. Some barbiturates are amobarbital (Amytal), pentobarbital (Nembutal), and secobarbital (Seconal). Some benzodiazepines include **diazepam** (Valium), **chlordiazepoxide** (Librium), and **lorazepam** (Ativan). When a person dependent on these drugs stops taking them suddenly, he or she might experience restlessness, muscle cramps, anxiety, insomnia, irritability, paranoid behavior, and even seizures or death.

Alcohol detoxification

Patients being detoxified from alcohol can safely be treated with rest, nutrition, vitamins, and thiamin (a B vitamin whose absorption is affected by alcohol abuse). Detoxification can be completed in an inpatient setting, or patients may participate in intensive outpatient (day hospital) treatment. People with mild or moderate withdrawal symptoms undergo detoxification over a five-day period and receive a benzodiazepine or phenobarbital to help ease the withdrawal symptoms. Delirium tremens can be treated with very high-dose benzodiazepines (such as chlordiazepoxide or diazepam) or with antipsychotic medications such as Haldol (**haloperidol**). The patient usually receives medication at doses high enough to give 60 mg or more of the medication over a 24- to 36-hour period, and the doses of these medications are gradually decreased by 20% each day. Patients who have liver disease, **dementia**, or patients who are over the age of 65 or with significant medical problems may receive lorazepam for the withdrawal symptoms.

Heroin detoxification

Patients with heroin dependence may receive help with their detoxification in one of two forms. Opioid agonists are drugs that act like heroin in the patient's body but do not provide the same "high," and are given in gradually decreasing doses. Because these medications "act" like heroin, the person does not experience withdrawal symptoms. Some examples of this kind of medication are methadone and levo-alpha-acetylmethadol (LAAM); buprenorphine is a partial opioid agonist, which means that it acts like heroin or methadone, but it limits the effects of opioids so that higher doses produce no greater effects. It is available as a monotherapy (meaning it is the only drug taken) or in combination with another drug, naloxone, as therapy for heroin detoxification. Some studies have found that buprenoporphine shows promise in treating pregnant women for opiate addiction; however, the current standard of care remains methadone replacement for pregnant women. The second form of help for patients undergoing heroin detoxification is the use of a drug, such as **clonidine** (Catapres), that blocks some of the withdrawal symptoms. There is also a controversial method of heroin detoxification called ultra-rapid opioid detoxification under anesthesia/sedation, and there is an experimental method using a medication called lofexidine.

METHADONE SUBSTITUTION. Methadone substitution can occur in outpatient or inpatient settings, and is a method of detoxification that involves helping patients off substances such as heroin by substituting these substances with methadone to ease the withdrawal symptoms, and gradually decreasing the dose until no methadone is needed for the symptoms. Patients may begin with a dose of methadone that is between 20 mg and 40 mg per day. The initial dose may be adjusted so that the most beneficial dose can be discovered, based on the patient's withdrawal symptoms. The dose is then gradually decreased over the next several days. The decrease in methadone dosage is called tapering. If the detoxification is being completed in an inpatient setting, the methadone dose can be tapered more quickly, because medical staff can closely monitor patients for withdrawal, and detoxification can be achieved in about five to 10 days. However, in the case of outpatient detoxification, the taper has to be done much more slowly to assure that the patient does not have an adverse reaction or **relapse** (use the drug of abuse again) to treat their withdrawal symptoms. The dose may be decreased about 10% per week initially until a dose of 20 mg is reached. Then the dose can be decreased by 3% per week for the rest of the time that the patient needs to be detoxified. Patients are usually comfortable with the slow decrease of the medication until the dose gets below 20 mg/day. At that point, patients tend to become fearful of being off opioids and having symptoms of withdrawal.

Clonidine is used much more frequently than methadone in detoxification. Methadone is used frequently as long-term maintenance treatment for heroin addiction.

BUPRENORPHINE. Buprenorphine is another medication that is used during opioid detoxification. Because it also acts like heroin in the body, the patient does not experience the withdrawal symptoms as the heroin is being eliminated from the body. It is given as an intramuscular injection or intravenously. It begins to work within 15 minutes and its effects last six hours. It is given as part of three phases of detoxification: induction, stabilization, and maintenance. Induction is the initiation of buprenoporphine therapy, which is administered once the patient has not used opiates for 12 to 24 hours. During stabilization, the dose may be adjusted as the patient stops having cravings or experiences fewer side effects. The length of the maintenance phase varies depending on the needs of the individual, and ends with medically supervised withdrawal. This drug has shown greater effectiveness than other replacement therapies in treating opiate withdrawal.

CLONIDINE. Clonidine is a medication that decreases many of the symptoms of opioid withdrawal. Patients may require nonsteroidal anti-inflammatory drugs (NSAIDS, such as ibuprofen) for the treatment of muscle aches. Clonidine's major side effects include sedation and hypotension (low blood pressure) because it is used to treat high blood pressure. Patients undergoing detoxification using clonidine will have their blood pressure and pulse checked regularly. The starting dose of clonidine is 0.1–0.3 mg every four to six hours—the maximum amount that can be given in one day is 1 mg. During days two through four of the detoxification, the dose of clonidine is adjusted to control the withdrawal symptoms. Again, however, the dose cannot exceed the maximum dose. On the fifth day of detoxification, the dose may be slowly tapered.

The clonidine patch is a transdermal patch, allowing the drug to be delivered through the skin and exposing the patient to a constant amount of the drug over a seven-day period. It also allows the person to experience a more comfortable heroin detoxification. It comes in three doses: 0.1-mg, 0.2-mg, and 0.3-mg. Patients who will use the clonidine patch need to have both the patch on and take oral clonidine during the first two days of the detoxification, because it takes the patch two days to reach a steady state and be effective. The patient takes oral clonidine 0.2 mg three times a day, and the weight of the patient determines the dose of the patch. On day two, the amount of clonidine that the patient takes by mouth is reduced by half and then it is completely stopped after day three. After seven days, the patch is removed and replaced with a patch that is half the amount of the original dose. The patch is continued for as long as the patient continues to have symptoms of withdrawal. Blood pressure is monitored for the patient using the patch, as well. The detoxification process in general takes about seven days using clonidine.

CLONIDINE-NALTREXONE ULTRA-RAPID DETOXIFICATION. Clonidine-naltrexone ultra-rapid detoxification has been attempted as a faster means of detoxification than using clonidine alone, and a similar "ultra-fast" method in combination with anesthesia has also been tested. These approaches remain quite controversial, and published clinical data supporting their efficacy are lacking, as are controlled trials.

LOFEXIDINE. Lofexidine is used experimentally in the United Kingdom for opioid detoxification. It appears to cause less sedation and fewer cases of low blood pressure than clonidine. In the United States, the National Institute of Drug Abuse (NIDA) is conducting studies on treatments using this drug in combination with **naltrexone**.

Mixed substance abuse

Mixed **substance abuse** (also called polysubstance abuse) occurs when individuals abuse more than one substance. Many doctors prefer to use phenobarbital to detoxify patients with polysubstance abuse problems. Patients receiving phenobarbital may receive a test dose, and then based on his or her tolerance and symptoms, the dose will be adjusted. Patients cannot receive more than 600 mg of phenobarbital a day. After two to three days, once the patient is doing well, the dose can be reduced by 30–60 mg. Whether detoxification for polysubstance abusers will be completed on an inpatient or outpatient status depends on the drugs the patient abuses.

Benzodiazepines

These medications are often used to help patients during detoxification, but these substances themselves can be abused and addictive. Patients who have taken a prescribed benzodiazepine for two weeks, even in a therapeutic dose, need to be safely detoxified with a slow taper. The amount of drug the person takes is dropped by 10–25% every week if the patient has minimal withdrawal symptoms. If the patient has taken very high doses for long periods of time, he or she is at increased risk for addiction. If the person has been taking a benzodiazepine medication for years, it can take months before he or she can get off the drug. Anticonvulsant medications like **carbamazepine** (Tegretol) and **divalproex sodium** (Depakote) can be used to make the detoxification process faster and more comfortable for the patient.

Preparation

The first step in any detoxification, regardless of the substance, is a physical exam and history taken by a physician. This information gathering and examination will help the treatment team assess the patient's overall health. In general, the healthier the patient is, the better the chances are that the patient will experience a detoxification without serious or life-threatening complications. Patients also need to give urine and blood samples to test for drugs and alcohol.

Aftercare

After the patient has completed detoxification, he or she needs further treatment either at an outpatient, inpatient, residential, or day hospital program in order to remain drug-free for the long term. Patients are treated by trained health care professionals, and some patients are also counseled by people who are recovering from addiction themselves. Many patients also benefit from 12-step programs or **self-help groups**, such as Alcoholics Anonymous (AA) or Narcotics Anonymous (NA).

Most opioid users are treated with ambulatory or outpatient detoxification or residential treatment followed by outpatient counseling. Some people who have abused opioids and have undergone detoxification and counseling are able to remain drug-free. Many, however, relapse, even after receiving **psychotherapy**. People recovering from opioid addiction can receive methadone or LAAM as maintenance therapy to prevent relapse. Similar to the aid these medications can give patients during detoxification, when taken daily as a therapy they continue to "act" as heroin, keeping the withdrawal symptoms from appearing. Methadone maintenance therapy can be provided through either residential or therapeutic communities and outpatient drug-free programs. Methadone maintenance treatment therapy is controversial, however, because it does not cure the person's addiction—it replaces it with another substance. Proponents of methadone maintenance therapy argue that people receiving methadone are able to function much better in society than people addicted to heroin. Because their drug-seeking behavior is reduced, these patients can become productive at work and their interpersonal relations improve.

People recovering from alcoholism can also benefit from counseling and support after detoxification, and a maintenance therapy is available to them, as well. **Disulfiram** (Antabuse) is a medication that interferes with the body's breakdown and processing of alcohol. When alcohol is consumed while a patient is taking disulfiram, the medication makes the effects of the alcohol much worse than the patient would normally experience; facial flushing, headache, nausea, and vomiting occurs, even if alcohol is consumed in a small amount. In order for disulfiram to be effective, the patient must want this kind of **reinforcement** to maintain abstinence and must be committed to it. Patients also must note that any form of alcohol can trigger the undesired effects, including cooking wine or mouthwash with alcohol. This drug, when used in combination with buprenorphine, also appears to be effective in treating **cocaine** addiction in people who also are addicted to heroin.

Risks

When benzodiazepines are the drug of addiction, they must be discontinued and cannot be given on an outpatient basis because of their potential for abuse. For all patients undergoing detoxification, benzodiazepine use must be monitored carefully because of the potential for new addiction. Elderly patients undergoing detoxification and receiving benzodiazepines must be monitored closely because they are more sensitive to the sedating effects of these drugs and are also more prone to falls while receiving these drugs. If benzodiazepines are not discontinued gradually, patients can have withdrawal symptoms such as irritability, poor sleep, agitation and seizures. Ultrarapid opioid detoxification under anesthesia/sedation is a serious procedure. Patients have died undergoing this procedure, and it remains controversial.

It should also be noted that many substances used in detoxification can themselves cause addiction. An example of this risk has already been given with benzodiazepines—these medications ease withdrawal symptoms during detoxification, but patients can become addicted to these medications, as well.

Normal results

Normal results for a well-managed detoxification would include freedom from the drug of addiction and ability to enter long-term treatment.

Success rates vary among people recovering from substance abuse. As might be expected, patients who successfully complete a full treatment program after detoxification (that includes counseling, psychotherapy, **family therapy**, and/or **group therapy** or some combination of those therapy types) achieve higher rates of success at remaining drug-free. Patients who were addicted for shorter periods of time and patients who spend longer periods in treatment are generally more successful at remaining abstinent from drugs over the long term.

Studies indicate that people who abuse alcohol and who want to stop have a higher chance of success if they undergo inpatient detoxification versus outpatient detoxification.

Abnormal results

One abnormal result that may occur is that patients who received nasogastric or tracheal tubes for opioid detoxification under anesthesia may experience adverse effects or complications. These patients are at risk for: trauma to their lips, vocal cords, larynx, and teeth; nosebleeds; high blood pressure; elevated heart rate; irregular heartbeat; and vomiting, which can lead to aspiration pneumonia.

An additional abnormal result would be a new addiction as a consequence of the detoxification.

KEY TERMS

Agonist—A chemical that reproduces the mechanism of action of a neurotransmitter.

Antagonist—A substance whose actions counteract the effects of or work in the opposite way from another chemical or drug.

Buprenorphine—A medication that blocks some of the withdrawal effects during heroin detoxification.

Detoxification—A process in which the body is allowed to free itself of a drug while the symptoms of withdrawal are treated. It is the primary step in any treatment program for drug or alcohol abuse.

Disulfiram—A medication that helps reinforce abstinence in people who are recovering from alcohol abuse. If a person taking disulfiram drinks even a small amount of alcohol, he or she experiences facial flushing, headache, nausea, and vomiting.

Lofexidine—A medication approved for use in Great Britain to aid the opioid detoxification process.

Methadone—A drug often prescribed legally as a replacement for heroin. It induces a slight high but blocks heroin from producing a more powerful euphoric effect. It may be used in heroin detoxification to ease the process, or it may be used daily after detoxification as maintenance therapy. Methadone maintenance therapy is controversial.

Withdrawal—Symptoms experienced by a person who has become physically dependent on a drug, experienced when the drug use is discontinued.

After the detoxification is completed, a patient may relapse. Support is critical for the patient to continue long-term therapy and successfully overcome addiction.

See also Addiction; Disease concept of chemical dependency.

Resources

BOOKS

Beers, Mark H., MD, and Robert Berkow, MD, eds. "Alcoholism." *The Merck Manual of Diagnosis and Therapy,* 17th ed. Whitehouse Station, NJ: Merck Research Laboratories, 1999.

Jaffe, Jerome H., MD, and others. "Substance-Related Disorders." *Comprehensive Textbook of Psychiatry,* 7th ed. Benjamin J. Sadock, MD, and Virginia A. Sadock, MD, eds. Philadelphia: Lippincott Williams and Wilkins, 2000.

Matthews, John. "Substance-Related Disorders: Cocaine and Narcotics." *Psychiatry Update and Board Preparation* Thomas A. Stern, MD, and John B. Herman, MD, eds. New York: McGraw Hill, 2000.

PERIODICALS

Fuller, Richard K., MD, and Susanne Hiller-Sturmhofel, PhD. "Alcoholism Treatment in the United States: An Overview." *Alcohol Research and Health* 23 (1999): 69–77.

Khantzian, Edward J., MD. "Methadone Treatment for Opioid Dependence." *American Journal of Psychiatry* (Nov. 2000): 1895–96.

Leshner, Alan, PhD. "Heroin Abuse and Addiction." *National Institute on Drug Abuse Research Report Series.* NIH Publication Number 00-4165, Washington, D.C. 2000.

Shreeram, S. S., MD, and others. "Psychosis After Ultra-rapid Opiate Detoxification." *American Journal of Psychiatry* (June 2001): 970.

ORGANIZATIONS

The College on Problems of Drug Dependency (CPDD). CPDD Executive Offices, Department of Pharmacology, 3420 N. Broad Street, Philadelphia, PA19140. Telephone: (215) 707-3242. <http://views.vcu.edu/cpdd>.

Institute for Comprehensive Detoxification and Rehabilitation. Telephone: (877) 704-ICDR (4237). <http://www.views.vcu.edu/cpdd/>.

National Institute on Alcohol Abuse and Alcoholism (NIAAA). 6000 Executive Boulevard, Willco Building, Bethesda, MD 20892-7003. <http://www.niaaa.nih.gov>.

National Institute on Drug Abuse (NIDA). 6001 Executive Boulevard, Room 5213, Bethesda, MD 20892-9561. Telephone: (301) 443-1124. <http://www.nida.nih.gov>.

OTHER

Brady, Kathleen T., MD, PhD. "Issues of Substance Abuse in Women." American Psychiatric Association 2004 Annual Meeting. <http://www.medscape.com/viewarticle/480925>

Center for Substance Abuse Treatment. "Detoxification and Substance Abuse Treatment." Treatment Improvement Protocol (TIP) Series 45. DHHS Publication No. (SMA) 06-4131. Rockville, MD: Substance Abuse and Mental Health Services Administration. (2006) <http://download.ncadi.samhsa.gov/prevline/pdfs/DTXTIP45(3-30-06).PDF>.

Mathias, Robert. National Institute on Drug Abuse. "Alcohol-treatment Medication May Reduce Cocaine Abuse Among Heroin Treatment Patients." NIDA Notes (16) (2005) <http://www.nida.nih.gov/NIDA_notes/NNVol16N1/Alcohol.html>.

National Institute of Drug Abuse. "Effectiveness of Lofexidine to Prevent Stress-Related Opiate Relapse During Naltrexone Treatment." <http://clinicaltrials.gov/ct/gui/show/NCT00142909;jsessionid = 0B14CF2553B3CC2A2D16FE2652613D76?order = 48>.

National Library of Medicine. National Institutes of Health. "Opiate Withdrawal." (2006) <http://www.nlm.nih.gov/medlineplus/ency/article/000949.htm>.

Trachtenberg, Alan I., and Michael F. Fleming. National Institute on Drug Abuse. "Diagnosis and Treatment of Drug Abuse in Family Practice." NIDA Research Monograph. (2005) <http://www.nida.nih.gov/Diagnosis-Treatment/diagnosis.html>.

U.S. Department of Health and Human Services. Substance Abuse and Mental Health Services Administration. Center for Substance Abuse Treatment. "Buprenorphine." <http://buprenorphine.samhsa.gov/about.html>.

Susan Hobbs, MD
Emily Jane Willingham, PhD

Developmental coordination disorder

Definition

Developmental coordination disorder is diagnosed when children do not develop normal motor coordination (coordination of movements involving the voluntary muscles).

Description

Developmental coordination disorder has been known by many other names, some of which are still used today. It has been called clumsy child syndrome, clumsiness, developmental disorder of motor function, and congenital maladroitness. Developmental coordination disorder is usually first recognized when a child fails to reach such normal developmental milestones as walking or beginning to dress him- or herself.

Children with developmental coordination disorder often have difficulty performing tasks that involve both large and small muscles, including forming letters when they write, throwing or catching balls, and buttoning buttons. Children who have developmental coordination disorder generally have developed normally in all other ways. The disorder can, however, lead to social or academic problems for children. Because of their underdeveloped coordination, they may choose not to participate in activities on the playground. This avoidance can lead to conflicts with or rejection by their peers. Also, children who have problems forming letters when they write by hand, or drawing pictures, may become discouraged and give up academic or artistic pursuits even though they have normal intelligence.

Causes and symptoms

The symptoms of developmental coordination disorder vary greatly from child to child. The general characteristic is that the child has abnormal development of one or more types of motor skills when the child's age and intelligence quotient (IQ) are taken into account. In some children these coordination deficiencies manifest as an inability to tie shoes or catch a ball, while in other children they appear as an inability to draw objects or properly form printed letters.

Some investigators believe that there are different subtypes of developmental coordination disorder. While there is disagreement over how to define these different subtypes, they can provide a useful framework for the categorization of symptoms. There are six general groups of symptoms. These include:

- general unsteadiness and slight shaking
- an at-rest muscle tone that is below normal
- muscle tone that is consistently above normal
- inability to move smoothly because of problems putting together the subunits of the whole movement
- inability to produce written symbols
- visual perception problems related to development of the eye muscles

Children can have one or more of these types of motor difficulties.

Developmental coordination disorder usually becomes apparent when children fail to meet normal developmental milestones. Some children with developmental coordination disorder do not learn large motor skills such as walking, running, and climbing until a much later point in time than their peers. Others have problems with such small muscle skills as learning to fasten buttons, close or open zippers, or tie shoes. Some children have problems learning how to handle silverware properly. In others the disorder does not appear until they are expected to learn how to write in school. Some children just look clumsy and often walk into objects or drop things.

There are no known causes of developmental coordination disorder. There are, however, various theories about its possible causes. Some theories attribute the disorder to biological causes. Some of the possible biological causes include such prenatal complications as fetal malnutrition. Low birth weight or prematurity are thought to be possible causes, but there is no hard evidence supporting these claims.

Demographics

It is estimated that as many as 6% of children between the ages of five and 11 have developmental coordination disorder. Males and females are thought to be equally likely to have this disorder, although males may be more likely to be diagnosed. Developmental coordination disorder and speech-language disorders seem to be closely linked, although it is not clear why this is the case. Children with one disorder are more likely to have the other as well.

Diagnosis

The **diagnosis** of developmental coordination disorder is most commonly made when a child's parents or teachers notice that he or she is lagging behind peers in learning motor skills, is having learning problems in school, or has frequent injuries from falls and other accidents resulting from clumsiness. In most cases, the child's pediatrician will perform a physical examination in order to rule out problems with eyesight or hearing that interfere with muscular coordination, and to rule out disorders of the nervous system. In addition to a medical examination, a learning specialist or child **psychiatrist** may be consulted to rule out other types of learning disabilities.

The types of motor impairment that lead to a diagnosis of developmental coordination disorder are somewhat vague, as the disorder has different symptoms in different children. There are many ways in which this kind of motor coordination problem can manifest itself, all of which may serve as criteria for a diagnosis of developmental coordination disorder. The core of the diagnosis rests on the child's being abnormally clumsy. To make this determination, the child's motor coordination must be compared to that of other children of a similar age and intelligence level.

The difference between a child who has developmental coordination disorder and one who is simply clumsy and awkward can be hard to determine. For a child to be diagnosed with developmental coordination disorder there must be significant negative consequences for the child's clumsiness. The negative effects may be seen in the child's performance in school, activities at play, or other activities that are necessary on a day-to-day basis. Also, for developmental coordination disorder to be diagnosed, the child's problems with motor coordination cannot result from such general medical conditions as muscular dystrophy, and cannot result directly from **mental retardation**. Some criteria require that the child have an IQ of at least 70 to be diagnosed with developmental coordination disorder.

Treatments

No treatments are known to work for all cases of developmental coordination disorder. Experts recommend that a specialized course of treatment, possibly involving work with an occupational therapist, be drawn up to address the needs of each child. Many children can be effectively helped in special education settings to work more intensively on such academic problems as letter formation. For other children, physical education classes designed to improve general motor coordination, with emphasis on skills the child can use in playing with peers, can be very successful. Any kind of physical training that allows the child to safely practice motor skills and motor control may be helpful.

It is important for children who have developmental coordination disorder to receive individualized therapy, because for many children the secondary problems that result from extreme clumsiness can be very distressing. Children who have developmental coordination disorder often have problems playing with their peers because of an inability to perform the physical movements involved in many games and sports. Unpopularity with peers or exclusion from their activities can lead to low self-esteem and poor self-image. Children may go to great lengths to avoid physical education classes and similar situations in which their motor coordination deficiencies might be noticeable. Treatments that focus on skills that are useful on the playground or in the gymnasium can help to alleviate or prevent these problems.

Children with developmental coordination disorder also frequently have problems writing letters and doing sums, or performing other motor activities required in the classroom—including coloring pictures, tracing designs, or making figures from **modeling** clay. These children may become frustrated by their inability to master tasks that their classmates find easy, and therefore may stop trying or become disruptive. Individualized programs designed to help children master writing or skills related to arts and crafts may help them regain confidence and interest in classroom activities.

Prognosis

For many people, developmental coordination disorder lasts into adulthood. Through specialized attention and teaching techniques it is possible over time for many children to develop the motor skills that they lack. Some children, however, never fully develop

---

> **KEY TERMS**
>
> **Maladroitness**—Another word for awkwardness or clumsiness.
>
> **Motor skills**—Skills pertaining to or involving muscular movement.

the skills they need. Although many children improve their motor skills significantly, in most cases their motor skills will never match those of their peers at any given age.

Prevention

There is no known way to prevent developmental coordination disorder, although a healthy diet throughout pregnancy and regular prenatal care may help, as they help to prevent many childhood problems.

See also Disorder of written expression.

Resources

BOOKS

American Psychiatric Association. *Diagnostic and Statistical Manual of Mental Disorders*, 4th ed., Text rev. Washington, D.C.: American Psychiatric Association, 2000.

Sadock, Benjamin J., and Virginia A. Sadock, eds. *Comprehensive Textbook of Psychiatry*, 7th ed. Vol. 2. Philadelphia: Lippincott Williams and Wilkins, 2000.

PERIODICALS

Kadesjo, Bjorn, and Christopher Gillberg. "Developmental Coordination Disorder in Swedish 7-Year-Old Children." *Journal of the American Academy of Child and Adolescent Psychiatry* 38 (July 1999): 820–29.

Rasmussen, Peder, and Christopher Gillberg. "Natural Outcome of ADHD with Developmental Coordination Disorder at Age 22 Years: A Controlled, Longitudinal, Community-Based Study." *Journal of the American Academy of Child and Adolescent Psychiatry* 39 (Nov. 2000): 1424.

Smyth, Mary M., Heather I. Anderson, and A. Church. "Visual Information and the Control of Reaching in Children: A Comparison Between Children With and Without Developmental Coordination Disorder." *Journal of Motor Behavior* 33 (Sept. 2001): 306.

ORGANIZATIONS

American Academy of Pediatrics. 141 Northwest Point Boulevard, Elk Grove Village, IL 60007-1098. Telephone: (847) 434-4000. <www.aap.org>.

OTHER

National Library of Medicine. National Institutes of Health. "Developmental Coordination Disorder." <http://www.nlm.nih.gov/medlineplus/ency/article/001533.htm>.

Tish Davidson, A.M.
Emily Jane Willingham, PhD

Developmental disorders *see* **Pervasive developmental disorders**

Developmental reading disorder *see* **Reading disorder**

Deviance *see* **Paraphilias**

Dexedrine *see* **Amphetamines**

Dextroamphetamine *see* **Amphetamines**

Diagnosis

Definition

Diagnosis can be defined as the identification and labeling of a disease based on its signs and symptoms. Mental health clinicians (psychiatrists, psychologists, and psychiatric nurse practitioners) diagnose mental disorders using the criteria listed in the *Diagnostic and Statistical Manual of Mental Disorders*, also known as the *DSM*, published by the American Psychiatric Association (APA).

Description

According to the *DSM*, fourth edition, text revised (the *DSM-IV-TR*), the term *mental disorder* is unfortunate because it implies that a mental disorder is separate from a physical illness, when actually, according to the APA, researchers and scientists now know that that distinction is not a clear one to make. The APA argues that "there is much 'physical' in 'mental disorders' and much 'mental' in 'physical disorders,'" and continues to use the term "mental disorders" because a better term has not yet been found. The APA defines a mental disorder as "a clinically significant behavioral or psychological syndrome or pattern that occurs in an individual and that is associated with present distress or disability or with a significantly increased risk of suffering death, pain, disability, or an important loss of freedom." Many people fear that when a mental disorder is classified, *people* are actually classified, and the *DSM-IV-TR* strives to contradict this notion. The APA believes their manual to be strictly a manual classifying mental disorders themselves, and does not advocate the use of the diagnoses to discriminate.

The manual lists various criteria for each mental disorder included in the book. When an individual seeks the help of a mental health clinician, the clinician interviews the client (along with family members when appropriate), gathers a medical history, and may administer psychological evaluations (various checklists or tests that the patient may complete) in order to establish a diagnosis. Once the clinician has gathered the necessary information, a diagnosis based on the symptoms may be assigned from the *DSM*.

One of the main purposes of diagnosis is to guide treatment planning. If doctors know that a particular disorder has shown to be treated effectively with a drug or with a specific therapy, then the best practice can be applied to a new case of that disorder. The diagnosis also helps to establish a prognosis for the patient and his or her family, and it helps to enable communication among the professionals (including insurers) involved in a patient's care. Additionally, a formal diagnosis as recognized by the *DSM* may be necessary in order for insurers to pay for medical services. The act of labeling a mental disorder may have unintended effects for the person with the disorder, however. Although the *DSM* states that its diagnoses do not label people, in reality, many people who have received diagnoses of mental disorders may feel affected by the label their disorder has been given. People diagnosed with mental disorders may feel stigmatized, and that others' perceptions of them—as well as their self-perceptions—have changed as a result of their diagnosis.

See also Assessment and diagnosis; Stigma.

Resources

BOOKS

Allen, John J. B. "DSM-IV." In *Encyclopedia of Mental Health,* edited by Howard S. Friedman. San Diego, CA: Academic Press, 1998.

American Psychiatric Association. *Diagnostic and Statistical Manual of Mental Disorders.* Fourth edition, text revised. Washington DC: American Psychiatric Association, 2000.

Diagnostic and Statistical Manual of Mental Disorders

Nature and purposes

The *Diagnostic and Statistical Manual of Mental Disorders* is a reference work consulted by psychiatrists, psychologists, physicians in clinical practice, **social workers**, medical and nursing students, pastoral counselors, and other professionals in health care and social service fields. The book's title is often shortened to *DSM*, or an abbreviation that also indicates edition, such as *DSM-IV-TR,* which indicates fourth edition, text revision of the manual, published in 2000. The *DSM-IV-TR* provides a classification of mental disorders, criteria sets to guide the process of differential **diagnosis**, and numerical codes for each disorder to facilitate medical record-keeping. The stated purpose of the *DSM* is threefold: to provide "a helpful guide to clinical practice"; "to facilitate research and improve communication among clinicians and researchers"; and to serve as "an educational tool for teaching psychopathology."

The multi-axial system

The third edition of *DSM*, or *DSM-III*, which was published in 1980, introduced a system of five axes or dimensions for assessing all aspects of a patient's mental and emotional health. The multi-axial system is designed to provide a more comprehensive picture of complex or concurrent mental disorders. According to the *DSM-IV-TR*, the system is also intended to "promote the application of the biopsychosocial model in clinical, educational and research settings." The reference to the biopsychosocial model is significant, because it indicates that the *DSM-IV-TR* does not reflect the view of any specific "school" or tradition within psychiatry regarding the cause or origin (also known as "etiology") of mental disorders. In other words, the *DSM-IV-TR* is atheoretical in its approach to diagnosis and classification—the axes and categories do not represent any overarching theory about the sources or fundamental nature of mental disorders.

The biopsychosocial approach was originally proposed by a **psychiatrist** named George Engel in 1977 as a way around the disputes between psychoanalytically and biologically oriented psychiatrists that were splitting the field in the 1970s. The introduction to *DSM-IV-TR* is quite explicit about the manual's intention to be "applicable in a wide variety of contexts" and "used by clinicians and researchers of many different orientations (e.g., biological, psychodynamic, cognitive, behavioral, interpersonal, family/ systems)."

The atheoretical stance of *DSM-IV-TR* is also significant in that it underlies the manual's approach to the legal implications of mental illness. *DSM* notes the existence of an "imperfect fit between questions of ultimate concern to the law and the information contained in a clinical diagnosis." What is meant here is that the *DSM-IV-TR* diagnostic categories do not meet forensic standards for defining a "mental defect," "mental disability," or similar terms. Because *DSM-IV-TR* states that "inclusion of a disorder in the classification . . . does not require that there be knowledge about its etiology," it advises legal professionals against basing decisions about a person's criminal responsibility, competence, or degree of behavioral control on *DSM* diagnostic categories.

The five diagnostic axes specified by *DSM-IV-TR* are:

- Axis I: Clinical disorders, including anxiety disorders, mood disorders, schizophrenia and other psychotic disorders.

- Axis II: Personality disorders and mental retardation. This axis includes notations about problematic aspects of the patient's personality that fall short of the criteria for a personality disorder.

- Axis III: General medical conditions. These include diseases or disorders that may be related physiologically to the mental disorder; that are sufficiently severe to affect the patient's mood or functioning; or that influence the choice of medications for treating the mental disorder.

- Axis IV: Psychosocial and environmental problems. These include conditions or situations that influence the diagnosis, treatment, or prognosis of the patient's mental disorder. *DSM-IV-TR* lists the following categories of problems: family problems; social environment problems; educational problems; occupational problems; housing problems; economic problems; problems with access to health care; problems with the legal system; and other problems (war, disasters, etc.).

- Axis V: Global assessment of functioning. Rating the patient's general level of functioning is intended to help the doctor draw up a treatment plan and evaluate treatment progress. The primary scale for Axis V is the Global Assessment of Functioning (GAF) Scale, which measures level of functioning on a scale of 1–100. *DSM-IV-TR* includes three specialized global scales in its appendices: the Social and Occupational Functioning Assessment Scale (SOFAS); the Defensive Functioning Scale; and the Global Assessment of Relational Functioning (GARF) Scale. The GARF is a measurement of the maturity and stability of the relationships within a family or between a couple.

Diagnostic categories

The Axis I clinical disorders are divided among 15 categories: disorders usually first diagnosed in infancy, childhood, or adolescence; **delirium, dementia**, amnestic, and other cognitive disorders; medical disorders due to a general medical condition; substance-related disorders; schizophrenia and other psychotic disorders; mood disorders; **anxiety** disorders; somatoform disorders; factitious disorders; **dissociative disorders**; sexual and gender identity disorders; eating disorders; **sleep disorders**; impulse control disorders not elsewhere classified; and **adjustment disorders**.

The diagnostic categories of *DSM-IV-TR* are essentially symptom-based, or, as the manual puts it, based "on criteria sets with defining features." Another term that is sometimes used to describe this method of classification is phenomenological. A phenomenological approach to classification is one that emphasizes externally observable phenomena rather than their underlying nature or origin.

Another important characteristic of *DSM-IV-TR's* classification system is its dependence on the medical model of mental disorders. Such terms as "psychopathology," "mental illness," "differential diagnosis," and "prognosis" are all borrowed from medical practice. One should note, however, that the medical model is not the only possible conceptual framework for understanding mental disorders. Historians of Western science have observed that the medical model for psychiatric problems was preceded by what they term the supernatural model (mental disorders understood as acts of God or the result of demon possession), which dominated the field until the late seventeenth century. The supernatural model was followed by the moral model, which was based on the values of the Enlightenment and regarded mental disorders as bad behaviors deliberately chosen by perverse or ignorant individuals.

The medical model as it came to dominate psychiatry can be traced back to the work of Emil Kraepelin, an eminent German psychiatrist whose *Handbuch der Psychiatrie* was the first basic textbook in the field and introduced the first nosology, or systematic classification, of mental disorders. By the early 1890s Kraepelin's handbook was used in medical schools across Europe. He updated and revised it periodically to accommodate new findings, including a disease that he named after one of his clinical assistants, Alois Alzheimer. The classification in the 1907 edition of Kraepelin's handbook includes 15 categories, most of which are still used nearly a century later. Kraepelin is also important in the history of diagnostic classification because he represented a biologically based view of mental disorders in opposition to the psychoanalytical approach of Sigmund Freud. Kraepelin thought that mental disorders could ultimately be traced to organic diseases of the **brain** rather than disordered emotions or psychological processes. This controversy between the two perspectives dominated

psychiatric research and practice until well after World War II.

Background of *DSM*

The American *Diagnostic and Statistical Manual of Mental Disorders* goes back to the 1840s, when the United States Bureau of the Census attempted for the first time to count the numbers of patients confined in mental hospitals. Isaac Ray, superintendent of the Butler Hospital in Rhode Island, presented a paper at the 1849 meeting of the Association of Medical Superintendents of American Institutions for the Insane (the forerunner of the present American Psychiatric Association) in which he called for a uniform system of naming, classifying and recording cases of mental illness. The same plea was made in 1913 by Dr. James May of New York to the same organization, which by then had renamed itself the American Medico-Psychological Association. In 1933, the New York Academy of Medicine and the Medico-Psychological Association compiled the first edition of the *Statistical Manual for Mental Diseases*, which was also adopted by the American Neurological Association. The *Statistical Manual* went through several editions between 1933 and 1952, when the first edition of the *Diagnostic and Statistical Manual of Mental Disorders* appeared. The task of compiling mental hospital statistics was turned over to the newly formed National Institute of Mental Health in 1949.

DSM-I and *DSM-II*

DSM-I, which appeared in 1952, maintained the coding system of earlier American manuals. Many of the disorders in this edition were termed "reactions," a term borrowed from a German psychiatrist named Adolf Meyer. Meyer viewed mental disorders as reactions of an individual's personality to a combination of psychological, social, and biological factors. *DSM-I* also incorporated the nomenclature for disorders developed by the United States Army and modified by the Veterans Administration (VA) to treat the postwar mental health problems of service personnel and veterans. The VA classification system grouped mental problems into three large categories: psychophysiological, personality, and acute disorders.

DSM-II, which was published in 1968, represented the first attempt to coordinate the American *Diagnostic and Statistical Manual of Mental Disorders* with the World Health Organization's (WHO) *International Classification of Diseases*, or *ICD*. *DSM-II* appeared before the ninth edition of the *ICD*, or *ICD-9*, which was published in 1975. *DSM-II* continued *DSM-I's* psychoanalytical approach to the etiology of the nonorganic mental disorders and personality disorders.

DSM-III, *DSM-III-R* and *DSM-IV*

DSM-III, which was published in 1980 after six years of preparatory work, represented a major break with the first two editions of *DSM*. *DSM-III* introduced the present descriptive symptom-based or phenomenological approach to mental disorders, added lists of explicit diagnostic criteria, removed references to the etiology of disorders, did away with the term "neurosis," and established the present multi-axial system of symptom evaluation. This sweeping change originated in an effort begun in the early 1970s by a group of psychiatrists at the medical school of Washington University in St. Louis to improve the state of research in American psychiatry. The St. Louis group began by drawing up a list of "research diagnostic criteria" for schizophrenia, a disorder that can manifest itself in a variety of ways. The group was concerned primarily with the identification of markers for schizophrenia that would allow the disease to be studied at other research sites without errors introduced by using different types of patients in different centers. What happened with *DSM-III*, *DSM-III-R*, and *DSM-IV*, however, was that a tool for scholarly investigation of a few mental disorders was transformed into a diagnostic method applied to all mental disorders without further distinction. The leaders of this transformation were biological psychiatrists who wanted to empty the diagnostic manual of terms and theories associated with hypothetical or explanatory concepts. The transition from an explanatory approach to mental disorders to a descriptive or phenomenological one in the period between *DSM-II* and *DSM-III* is sometimes called the "neo-Kraepelinian revolution" in the secondary literature. Another term that has been applied to the orientation represented in *DSM-III* and its successors is *empirical*, which denotes reliance on experience or experiment alone, without recourse to theories or hypotheses. The word occurs repeatedly in the description of "The DSM-IV Revision Process" in the Introduction to *DSM-IV-TR*.

DSM-IV built upon the research generated by the empirical orientation of *DSM-III*. By the early 1990s, most psychiatric diagnoses had an accumulated body of published studies or data sets. Publications up through 1992 were reviewed for *DSM-IV*, which was published in 1994. Conflicting reports or lack of evidence were handled by data reanalyses and field trials. The National Institute of Mental Health sponsored 12 *DSM-IV* field trials together with the National Institute on Drug **Abuse** (NIDA) and the National Insti-

tute on Alcohol Abuse and Alcoholism (NIAAA). The field trials compared the diagnostic criteria sets of *DSM-III*, *DSM-III-R*, *ICD-10* (which had been published in 1992), and the proposed criteria sets for *DSM-IV*. The field trials recruited subjects from a variety of ethnic and cultural backgrounds, in keeping with a new concern for cross-cultural applicability of diagnostic standards. In addition to its inclusion of culture-specific syndromes and disorders, *DSM-IV* represented much closer cooperation and coordination with the experts from WHO who had worked on *ICD-10*. A modification of *ICD-10* for clinical practitioners, the *ICD-10-CM*, was introduced in the United States in 2004.

Textual revisions in DSM-IV-TR

DSM-IV-TR does not represent either a fundamental change in the basic classification structure of *DSM-IV* or the addition of new diagnostic entities. The textual revisions that were made to the 1994 edition of *DSM-IV* fall under the following categories:

- correction of factual errors in the text of *DSM-IV*
- review of currency of information in *DSM-IV*
- changes reflecting research published after 1992, which was the last year included in the literature review prior to the publication of *DSM-IV*
- improvements to enhance the educational value of *DSM-IV*
- updating of *ICD* diagnostic codes, some of which were changed in 1996

Critiques of *DSM-IV* and *DSM-IV-TR*

A number of criticisms of *DSM-IV* have arisen since its publication in 1994. They include the following observations and complaints:

- The medical model underlying the empirical orientation of *DSM-IV* reduces human beings to one-dimensional sources of data; it does not encourage practitioners to treat the whole person.
- The medical model perpetuates the social stigma attached to mental disorders.
- The symptom-based criteria sets of *DSM-IV* have led to an endless multiplication of mental conditions and disorders. The unwieldy size of *DSM-IV* is a common complaint of doctors in clinical practice—a volume that was only 119 pages long in its second (1968) edition has swelled to 886 pages in less than thirty years.
- The symptom-based approach has also made it easier to politicize the process of defining new disorders for inclusion in *DSM* or dropping older ones. The

inclusion of post-traumatic stress disorder (PTSD) and the deletion of homosexuality as a disorder are often cited as examples of this concern for political correctness.

- The criteria sets of *DSM-IV* incorporate implicit (implied but not expressly stated) notions of human psychological well-being that do not allow for ordinary diversity among people. Some of the diagnostic categories of *DSM-IV* come close to defining various temperamental and personality differences as mental disorders.
- The *DSM-IV* criteria do not distinguish adequately between poor adaptation to ordinary problems of living and true psychopathology. One by-product of this inadequacy is the suspiciously high rates of prevalence reported for some mental disorders. One observer remarked that " … it is doubtful that 28% or 29% of the population would be judged [by managed care plans] to need mental health treatment in a year."
- The 16 major diagnostic classes defined by *DSM-IV* hinder efforts to recognize disorders that run across classes. For example, PTSD has more in common with respect to etiology and treatment with the dissociative disorders than it does with the anxiety disorders with which it is presently grouped. Another example is body dysmorphic disorder, which resembles the obsessive-compulsive disorders more than it does the somatoform disorders.
- The current classification is deficient in acknowledging disorders of uncontrolled anger, hostility, and aggression. Even though inappropriate expressions of anger and aggression lie at the roots of major social problems, only one *DSM-IV* disorder (intermittent explosive disorder) is explicitly concerned with them. In contrast, entire classes of disorders are devoted to depression and anxiety.
- The emphasis of *DSM-IV* on biological psychiatry has contributed to the widespread popular notion that most problems of human life can be solved by taking pills.

Alternative nosologies

A number of different nosologies or schemes of classification have been proposed to replace the current descriptive model of mental disorders.

The dimensional model

Dimensional alternatives to *DSM-IV* would replace the categorical classification now in use with a recognition that mental disorders lie on a continuum with mildly disturbed and normal behavior, rather than being qualitatively distinct. For example, the personality disorders of Axis II are increasingly regarded as extreme variants of common personality characteristics. In the dimensional model, a patient would be identified in terms of his or her position on a specific dimension of cognitive or affective capacity rather than placed in a categorical "box."

The holistic model

The holistic approach to mental disorders places equal emphasis on social and spiritual as well as pharmacological treatments. A biochemist who was diagnosed with schizophrenia and eventually recovered compared the reductionism of the biological model of his disorder with the empowering qualities of holistic approaches. He stressed the healing potential in treating patients as whole persons rather than as isolated collections of nervous tissue with chemical imbalances: "The major task in recovering from mental illness is to regain social roles and identities. This entails focusing on the individual and building a sense of responsibility and self-determination."

The essential or perspectival model

The third and most complex alternative model is associated with the medical school of Johns Hopkins University, where it is taught as part of the medical curriculum. This model identifies four broad "essences" or perspectives that can be used to identify the distinctive characteristics of mental disorders, which are often obscured by the present categorical classifications.

The four perspectives are:

- Disease. This perspective works with categories and accounts for physical diseases or damage to the brain that produces psychiatric symptoms. It accounts for such disorders as Alzheimer's disease or schizophrenia.
- Dimensions. This perspective addresses disorders that arise from the combination of a cognitive or emotional weakness in the patient's constitution and a life experience that challenges their vulnerability.
- Behaviors. This perspective is concerned with disorders associated with something that the patient is doing (alcoholism, drug addiction, eating disorders, etc.) that has become a dysfunctional way of life.
- Life story. This perspective focuses on disorders related to what the patient has encountered in life, such as events that have injured his or her hopes and aspirations.

In the Johns Hopkins model, each perspective has its own approach to treatment: the disease perspective seeks to cure or prevent disorders rooted in biological disease processes; the dimensional perspective attempts to strengthen constitutional weaknesses; the behavioral

KEY TERMS

Atheoretical—Unrelated to any specific theoretical approach or conceptual framework. The classification system of *DSM-IV-TR* is atheoretical.

Differential diagnosis—The process of distinguishing one disorder from other, similar disorders.

Empirical—Verified by actual experience or by scientific experimentation.

Etiology—The cause or origin of a disease or disorder. The word is also used to refer to the study of the causes of disease.

Forensic—Pertaining to courtroom procedure or evidence used in courts of law.

Holistic—An approach to health care that emphasizes the totality of an individual's well-being, spiritual and psychological as well as physical; and that situates a disease or disorder within that totality.

Implicit—Implied or suggested without being clearly stated. Some critics of *DSM-IV-TR* maintain that its contributors based the criteria sets for certain disorders on an implicit notion of a mentally healthy human being.

Medical model—The basic conceptual framework in the West since the nineteenth century for understanding, researching, and classifying mental disorders.

Nosology—The branch of medicine that deals with the systematic classification of diseases and disorders.

perspective seeks to interrupt the problematic behaviors and assist patients in overcoming their appeal; and the life story perspective offers help in "rescripting" a person's life narrative, usually through cognitive behavioral treatment.

Resources

BOOKS

American Psychiatric Association. *Diagnostic and Statistical Manual of Mental Disorders*. 4th edition, text revised. Washington, DC: American Psychiatric Association, 2000.

Freeman, Hugh, ed. *A Century of Psychiatry*. St. Louis, MO: Mosby, 1999.

Kihlstrom, John F. "To Honor Kraepelin ...: From Symptoms to Pathology in the Diagnosis of Mental Illness." In *Alternatives to the DSM*, edited by L. E. Beutler and M. L. Malik. Washington, DC: American Psychological Association, 2000.

World Health Organization (WHO). *The ICD-10 Classification of Mental and Behavioural Disorders*. Geneva: WHO, 1992.

PERIODICALS

Collins, Geneva. "Radical Makeover Proposed for DSM." *Clinical Psychiatry News* 29 (August 2001): 1.

Diamond, Ellen A. "A Conceptual Structure for Diagnoses." *Psychiatric Times* 18 (November 2001): 4-5.

Fisher, Daniel B. "Recovering from Schizophrenia." *Clinical Psychiatry News* 29 (November 2001): 30.

Kutchins, H., and S. A. Kirk. "DSM-III-R: The Conflict Over New Psychiatric Diagnoses." *Health and Social Work* 14 (May 1989): 91-101.

McHugh, Paul R. "How Psychiatry Lost Its Way." *Commentary* 108 (December 1999): 67-72.

McHugh, Paul R. "A Structure for Psychiatry at the Century's Turn: The View from Johns Hopkins." *Journal of the Royal Society of Medicine* 85 (1992): 483-487.

Ozarin, Lucy D., MD. "DSM: A Brief Historical Note." *Psychatric News* (April 3, 1998).

"Psychiatrists Call for Overhaul of Unwieldy DSM." *Clinical Psychiatry News* 29 (October 2001): 20.

Widiger, T. A. "Adult Psychopathology: Issues and Controversies." *Annual Review of Psychology* (2000).

ORGANIZATIONS

American Psychiatric Association. 1400 K Street, NW, Washington, DC 20005. <www.psych.org>.

National Institute of Mental Health. 6001 Executive Boulevard, Room 8184, MSC 9663, Bethesda, MD 20892-9663. Telephone: (301) 443-4513. <www.nimh.nih.gov>

OTHER

Young, Robert M. "Between Nosology and Narrative: Where Should We Be?" Lecture delivered to the Toronto Psychoanalytic Society, Toronto, Canada. January 8, 1999.

Rebecca J. Frey, Ph.D.

Diazepam

Definition

Diazepam is a mild tranquilizer in the class of drugs known as **benzodiazepines**. It is most commonly sold in the United States under the brand name Valium®. The generic form of this drug is also available.

Purpose

Diazepam is used on a short-term basis to treat patients with mild to moderate **anxiety**. It is also used to treat some types of **seizures** (epilepsy), muscle spasms, nervous tension, and symptoms relating to alcohol withdrawal.

Description

Diazepam is one of many chemically related tranquilizers in the class of drugs called benzodiazepines. Benzodiazepines are sedative-hypnotic drugs that help to relieve nervousness, tension, and other anxiety symptoms by slowing the central nervous system. To do this, they block the effects of a specific chemical involved in the transmission of nerve impulses in the **brain**, decreasing the excitement level of the nerve cells. All benzodiazepines, including diazepam, cause sedation, drowsiness, and reduced mental and physical alertness.

Recommended dosage

The typical dose of diazepam used to treat anxiety or seizures in healthy adults ranges from a total of 6 milligrams (mg) to 40 mg per day given in three or four doses. Elderly people (over age 60) are usually given lower doses in the range of 4–10 mg per day to treat anxiety or nervous tension. For acute treatment of seizures, a higher dose of diazepam is given intravenously (directly into the vein) only in a controlled medical setting such as a hospital or emergency room. For alcohol withdrawal, the typical dose is a total of 30–40 mg per day given in three or four doses.

The typical dose for a child over age six months with anxiety or seizures is a total of 3–10 mg per divided into several doses. In general, children receive lower doses of diazepam even when they have a body weight equivalent to a small adult. Diazepam is usually taken as a pill, but an injectable form is sometimes used when a serious seizure is in progress or when muscle spasms are severe. There is a liquid oral form of the drug available, and diazepam is also available as a rectal gel, marketed as Diastat AcuDial®.

Precautions

The elderly, children, and those with significant health problems need to be carefully evaluated before receiving diazepam. Children under the age of six months should not take diazepam. In addition, people with a history of liver disease, kidney disease, or those with low levels of a protein in the blood called albumin need to be carefully assessed before starting this drug.

People taking diazepam should not drive, operate dangerous machinery, or engage in hazardous activities that require mental alertness, because diazepam can cause drowsiness. Alcohol and any drugs that treat mental illness should not be used when taking this medication. People who have previously had an allergic reaction to any dosage level of diazepam or any other benzodiazepine drug should not take diazepam. People with acute narrow-angle glaucoma should not take diazepam.

The prescribing physician should be consulted regularly if diazepam is taken consistently for more than two weeks. Diazepam and other drugs in this class can be habit-forming. Diazepam can become a drug of **abuse** and should be used with caution in patients with history of **substance abuse**. People taking diazepam should not stop taking the drug abruptly. This can lead to withdrawal effects such as shaking, stomach cramps, nervousness, and irritability.

Side effects

Anxiety, irregular heartbeat, forgetfulness, mental **depression**, and confusion are side effects that could require prompt medical attention. However, these side effects are not common when taking diazepam. Even more unusual but serious events are behavior changes, low blood pressure, muscle weakness, and the yellowing of the eyes or skin (jaundice). More common but less serious side effects include drowsiness, clumsiness, slurred speech, and dizziness. Rare among these less serious side effects are stomach cramps, headache, muscle spasm, nausea, vomiting, and dry mouth.

Once a person stops taking diazepam, the following side effects could occur from withdrawal: sleeping difficulties, nervousness, and irritability. Less common side effects from withdrawal include confusion, abdominal cramps, mental depression, sensitivity to light, nausea, shaking, and increased sweating. Rarely seen side effects include seizures, **hallucinations**, and feelings of distrust in the patient.

Interactions

Diazepam interacts with a long list of other medications. Anyone starting this drug should review the other medications they are taking with their physician and pharmacist for possible interactions. Patients should always inform all their health-care providers, including dentists, that they are taking diazepam. Diazepam can add to the depressive effects of other central nervous system depressant drugs (for example, alcohol, other tranquilizers, or sleeping pills) when taken together. In severe cases, this can result in death.

Several drugs reduce the ability of diazepam to be broken down and cleared from the body. This results in higher levels of the drug in the blood and increases the probability that side effects will occur. These drugs include several antibiotics, such as erythromycin, anti–stomach acid drugs, such as cimetidine (Tagamet®), and

KEY TERMS

Albumin—A simple protein that is widely distributed in human blood.

Anxiety—A feeling of apprehension and fear characterized by physical symptoms (heart palpitations, sweating, and feelings of stress, for example).

Benzodiazepines—A group of central nervous system depressants used to relieve anxiety or to induce sleep.

Glaucoma—A group of eye diseases characterized by increased pressure within the eye significant enough to damage eye tissue and structures. If untreated, glaucoma results in blindness.

Tranquilizer—A medication that induces a feeling of calm and relaxation.

antifungal drugs, such as fluconazole. Alcohol should not be used when taking diazepam and other benzodiazepine drugs. There may also be an interaction between this drug and grapefruit juice. Other drugs that are used to treat mental disorders should not be combined with diazepam unless the patient is under the careful supervision and monitoring of a doctor.

Those who rely on urine tests to monitor blood sugar should know that this drug can produce false results with tests using Clinistix and Diastix, and that they should instead use TesTape for urine testing of sugar.

Resources

BOOKS

Consumer Reports Staff. *Consumer Reports Complete Drug Reference*, 2002 ed. Denver: Micromedex Thomson Healthcare, 2001.

Ellsworth, Allan J. *Mosby's Medical Drug Reference*, 2001–2002 ed. St. Louis: Mosby, 2001.

Hardman, Joel G., Lee E. Limbird, eds. *Goodman & Gilman's The Pharmacological Basis of Therapeutics*, 10th ed. New York: McGraw-Hill, 2001.

Mosby's GenRx Staff. *Mosby's GenRx*, 9th ed. St. Louis: Mosby, 1999.

Venes, Donald, and others. *Taber's Cyclopedic Medical Dictionary*, 19th ed. Philadelphia: F. A. Davis, 2001.

OTHER

National Library of Medicine. National Institutes of Health. "Diazepam." <http://www.nlm.nih.gov/medlineplus/druginfo/medmaster/a682047.html>.

U.S. Food and Drug Administration. "Diazepam Rectal Gel, Patient Information." <http://www.fda.gov/CDER/DRUG/InfoSheets/patient/diazepam_RGPIS.pdf>.

U.S. Food and Drug Administration. "Diazepam Rectal Gel Drug Information Sheet." <http://www.fda.gov/cder/foi/label/2005/020648s008lbl.pdf>.

Mark Mitchell, MD
Emily Jane Willingham, PhD

Diets

Definition

Special diets are designed to help individuals make changes in their usual eating habits or food selection. Some special diets involve changes in the overall diet, such as diets for people needing to gain or lose weight or eat more healthfully. Other special diets are designed to help a person limit or avoid certain foods or dietary components that could interfere with the activity of a medication. Still other special diets are designed to counter nutritional effects of certain medications.

Purpose

Special diets are used in the treatment of people with certain mental disorders to:

• identify and correct disordered eating patterns.
• prevent or correct nutritional deficiencies or excesses.
• prevent interactions between foods or nutrients and medications.

Special types of diets or changes in eating habits have been suggested for people with certain mental disorders. In some disorders, such as eating disorders or **substance abuse**, dietary changes are an integral part of therapy. In other disorders, such as **attention deficit/hyperactivity disorder**, various proposed diets have questionable therapeutic value.

Many medications for mental disorders can affect a person's appetite or nutrition-related functions such as saliva production, ability to swallow, bowel function, and activity level. Changes in diet or food choices may be required to help prevent negative effects of medications.

Finally, interactions can occur between some medications used to treat people with mental disorders and certain foods or nutritional components of the diet. For example, grapefruit and apple juice can interact with some specific psychotropic drugs (medications taken for psychiatric conditions) and should be avoided by individuals taking those medicines.

Tyramine, a natural substance found in aged or fermented foods, can interfere with the functioning of monoamine oxidase inhibitors (MAOIs) and must be restricted in individuals using these types of medications. A person's preexisting medical condition and nutritional needs should be taken into account when designing any special diet.

Special diets for specific disorders

Eating disorders

The two main types of eating disorders are **anorexia nervosa** and **bulimia nervosa**. Individuals with anorexia nervosa starve themselves, whereas individuals with bulimia nervosa usually have normal or slightly above normal body weight but engage in **binge eating** followed by purging with laxatives, vomiting, or exercise.

Special diets for individuals with eating disorders focus on restoration of normal body weight and control of bingeing and purging. These diets are usually carried out under the supervision of a multidisciplinary team, including a physician, **psychologist**, and dietitian.

The overall dietary goal for individuals with anorexia nervosa is to restore a healthy body weight. An initial goal might be to stop weight loss and improve food choices. Energy intake is then increased gradually until normal weight is restored. Because individuals with anorexia nervosa have an intense fear of gaining weight and becoming fat, quantities of foods eaten are increased very slowly so that the patient will continue treatments and therapy.

The overall dietary goal for individuals with bulimia nervosa is to gain control over eating behavior and to achieve a healthy body weight. An initial goal is to stabilize weight and eating patterns to help individuals gain control over the binge-purge cycle. Meals and snacks are eaten at regular intervals to lessen the possibility that hunger and fasting will trigger a binge. Once eating behaviors have been stabilized, energy intake can be gradually adjusted to allow individuals to reach normal body weights healthfully.

For individuals with either anorexia nervosa or bulimia, continued follow-up and support are required even after normal weight and eating behaviors are restored, particularly since the rate of **relapse** is quite high. In addition to dietary changes, **psychotherapy** is an essential part of the treatment of eating disorders and helps individuals deal with fears and misconceptions about body weight and eating behavior.

Attention-deficit/hyperactivity disorder

Attention-deficit/hyperactivity disorder (ADHD) accounts for a substantial portion of referrals to child mental health services. Children with ADHD are inappropriately active, easily frustrated or distracted, impulsive, and have difficulty sustaining concentration. Usual treatment of ADHD involves medication, behavioral management, and education.

Many dietary factors have been proposed as causes of ADHD, including sugar, food additives, and food allergies. In the 1970s the Feingold diet became popular for treatment of ADHD. The Feingold diet excludes artificial colorings and flavorings, natural sources of chemicals called salicylates (found in fruits), and preservatives called BHT and BHA. Although scientific evidence does not support the effectiveness of the Feingold diet, a modified Feingold diet including fruits has been shown to be nutritionally balanced and should not be harmful as long as the child continues to receive conventional ADHD treatment also.

A high intake of sugar and sugary foods has also been implicated as a cause of ADHD. Although carefully controlled studies have shown no association between sugar and ADHD, diets high in sugar should be discouraged because they are often low in other nutrients and can contribute to dental problems.

Food allergies have also been implicated as a cause of ADHD, and some groups have suggested using elimination diets to treat ADHD. Elimination diets omit foods that most commonly cause allergies in children, such as eggs, milk, peanuts, or shellfish. Although research does not support the value of elimination diets for all children with ADHD, children with specific food allergies can become irritable and restless. Children with a suspected food allergy should be evaluated by an allergist.

Stimulant medications used to treat ADHD, such as **methylphenidate** (Ritalin), can cause appetite loss (anorexia) and retard growth, although recent research suggests that a child's ultimate height appears not to be affected by stimulant medications. As a precaution, children on such medicines should receive close monitoring of growth patterns, and parents should carefully observe their child's appetite and interest in meals and snacks. Providing regular meals and snacks, even when the child is not hungry, can help to assure adequate growth.

Mood disorders

Mood disorders include both **depression** (unipolar disorder) and episodes of mania followed by depression (**bipolar disorder**). Both types of disorders can affect appetite and eating behavior.

Although some individuals with depression eat more than usual and gain weight, depression more often causes loss of appetite and weight loss. As individuals with depression lose interest in eating and social relationships, they often skip meals and ignore feelings of hunger. Unintentional weight losses of up to 15% of body mass can occur.

Treatment with antidepressant medications often reverses weight loss and restores appetite and interest in eating. If individuals have lost a significant amount of weight, they may need to follow a high-calorie diet to restore weight to normal levels and replaced nutritional deficiencies. High-calorie diets usually include three balanced meals from all the food groups and several smaller snacks throughout the day. A protein/calorie supplement may also be necessary for some individuals.

Depression is sometimes treated with (MAOIs). Individuals on these medications will need to follow a tyramine-restricted diet.

Individuals with mania are often treated with lithium. Sodium and caffeine intake can affect lithium levels in the blood, and intake of these should not suddenly be increased or decreased. Weight gain can occur in response to some antidepressant medications and lithium.

Schizophrenia

Individuals with **schizophrenia** can have **hallucinations**, delusional thinking, and bizarre behavior. These distorted behaviors and thought processes can also be extended to **delusions** and hallucinations about food and diet, making people with schizophrenia at risk for poor nutrition.

Individuals with schizophrenia may believe that certain foods are poisonous or have special properties. They may think they hear voices telling them not to eat. Some may eat huge quantities of food thinking that it gives them special powers. Individuals with untreated schizophrenia may lose a significant amount of weight. Delusional beliefs and thinking about food and eating usually improve once individuals are started on medication to treat schizophrenia.

Substance abuse

Substance **abuse** can include abuse of alcohol, cigarettes, marijuana, **cocaine**, or other drugs. Individuals abusing any of these substances are at risk for nutritional problems. Many of these substances can reduce appetite, decrease absorption of nutrients into the body, and cause individuals to make poor food choices.

Special diets used for withdrawal from substance abuse are designed to correct any nutritional deficiencies that have developed, aid in the withdrawal of the substance, and prevent the individual from making unhealthful food substitutions as the addictive substance is withdrawn. For example, some individuals may compulsively overeat when they stop smoking, leading to weight gain. Others may substitute caffeine-containing beverages such as soda or coffee for an addictive drug. Such harmful substitutions should be discouraged, emphasizing well-balanced eating combined with adequate rest, **stress** management, and regular exercise. Small, frequent meals and snacks that are rich in vitamins and minerals from healthful foods should be provided. Fluid intake should be generous, but caffeine-containing beverages should be limited.

Individuals withdrawing from alcohol may need extra thiamin supplementation, either intravenously or through a multivitamin supplement because alcohol metabolism in the body requires extra thiamin. Individuals taking drugs to help them avoid alcohol will need to avoid foods with even small amounts of alcohol.

Common withdrawal symptoms and dietary suggestions for coping with these symptoms include:

- appetite loss: Eat small, frequent meals and snacks; limit caffeine; and use nutritional supplements if necessary.
- appetite increase: Eat regular meals; eat a variety of foods; and limit sweets and caffeine.
- diarrhea: Eat moderate amounts of fresh fruits, vegetables, concentrated sugars, juices, and milk; and increase intake of cereal fiber.
- constipation: Drink plenty of fluids; increase fiber in the diet; and increase physical activity.
- fatigue: Eat regular meals; limit sweets and caffeine; and drink plenty of fluid.

Dietary considerations and medications

Medications that affect body weight

Many medications used to treat mental disorders promote weight gain, including:

- anticonvulsants (divalproex)
- certain types of antidepressants (amitriptyline)
- antipsychotic medications (clozapine, olanzapine, quetiapine, and risperidone)

Dietary treatments for individuals taking these medications should focus on a balanced, low-fat diet coupled with an increase in physical activity to counter the side effects of these medications. Nutrient-rich foods such as fruits, vegetables, and whole grain products should be emphasized in the diet, whereas sweets, fats, and other foods high in energy but low in nutrients should be limited. Regular physical activity can help limit weight gain caused by these medications.

Some medications can cause loss of appetite, restlessness, and weight loss. Individuals on such medications should eat three balanced meals and several smaller snacks of protein and calorie-rich foods throughout the day. Eating on a regular schedule rather than depending on appetite can help prevent weight loss associated with loss of appetite.

Medications that affect gastrointestinal function

Many psychiatric medications can affect gastrointestinal functioning. Some drugs can cause dry mouth, difficulty swallowing, constipation, altered taste, heartburn, diarrhea, or nausea. Consuming frequent smaller meals, drinking adequate fluids, modifying texture of foods if necessary, and increasing fiber content of foods can help counter gastrointestinal effects of medications.

Monoamine oxidase inhibitors

Individuals being treated with MAOIs such as **tranylcypromine**, **phenelzine**, and isocarboxazid, must carefully follow a tyramine-restricted diet. Tyramine, a nitrogen-containing substance normally present in certain foods, is usually broken down in the body by oxidase. However, in individuals taking MAOIs, tyramine is not adequately broken down and builds up in the blood, causing the blood vessels to constrict and increasing blood pressure.

Tyramine is normally found in many foods, especially protein-rich foods that have been aged or fermented, pickled, or bacterially contaminated. Cheese is especially high in tyramine. A tyramine intake of less than 5 mg daily is recommended. A diet that includes even just 6 mg of tyramine can increase blood pressure; a diet that provides 25 mg of tyramine can cause life-threatening increases in blood pressure.

TYRAMINE-RESTRICTED DIET. Tyramine is found in aged, fermented, and spoiled food products. The tyramine content of a specific food can vary greatly depending on storage conditions, ripeness, or contamination. Reaction to tyramine-containing foods in individuals taking MAOIs can also vary greatly depending on what other foods are eaten with the tyramine-containing food, the length of time between MAOI dose and eating the food, and individual characteristics such as weight, age, etc.

Foods to avoid on a tyramine-controlled diet include:

- all aged and mature cheeses or cheese spreads, including foods made with these cheeses, such as salad dressings, casseroles, or certain breads
- any outdated or nonpasteurized dairy products
- dry fermented sausages such as summer sausage, pepperoni, salami, or pastrami
- smoked or pickled fish
- nonfresh meat or poultry
- leftover foods containing meat or poultry
- tofu and soy products
- overripe, spoiled, or fermented fruits or vegetables
- sauerkraut
- fava or broad beans
- soups containing meat extracts or cheese
- gravies containing meat extracts or nonfresh meats
- tap beer
- nonalcoholic beer
- yeast extracts
- soy sauce
- liquid powdered protein supplements

Perishable refrigerated items such as milk, meat, or fruit should be eaten within 48 hours of purchase. Any spoiled food and food stored in questionable conditions should not be eaten.

Lithium

Lithium is often used to treat individuals with mania. Lithium can cause nausea, vomiting, anorexia, diarrhea, and weight gain. Almost one-half of individuals taking lithium gain weight.

Individuals taking lithium should maintain a fairly constant intake of sodium (found in table salt and other food additives) and caffeine in their diet. If an individual restricts sodium intake, less lithium is excreted in the urine and blood lithium levels rise. If an individual increases caffeine intake, more lithium is excreted in the urine and blood levels of lithium fall.

Anticonvulsant medications

Sodium caseinate and calcium caseinate can interfere with the action and effectiveness of some anticonvulsants. Individuals taking these drugs should read labels carefully to avoid foods containing these additives.

Psychotropic medications

Some psychotropic medications, such as amitriptyline, can decrease absorption of the vitamin riboflavin from food. Good food sources of riboflavin include milk and milk products, liver, red meat, poultry, fish, whole grain, and enriched breads and cereals. Riboflavin supplements may also be needed.

Other psychotropic drugs, such as **fluvoxamine**, **sertraline**, fesasodone, **alprazolam**, **triazolam**, midazolam, **carbamazepine**, and **clonazepam**, interact with grapefruit juice, so individuals taking these drugs must take care to avoid grapefruit juice. In some cases, apple juice must be avoided as well. Patients should discuss potential drug interactions with their doctors or pharmacists.

Caffeine-restricted diet

Caffeine is a stimulant and can interfere with the actions of certain medications. As stated, people taking lithium and people recovering from addictions may be asked by their treatment team to monitor (and, in the case of addictions, restrict) their caffeine intake. Foods and beverages high in caffeine include:

- chocolate
- cocoa mix and powder
- chocolate ice cream, milk, and pudding
- coffee
- cola beverages
- tea

Alcohol-restricted diet

Alcohol interacts with some medications used to treat mental disorders. In the case of alcoholism recovery, the negative interaction resulting from the combination of one medication (**disulfiram** or Antabuse) and alcohol consumption is actually part of treatment for some people. (The medication causes an extremely unpleasant reaction when any alcohol is consumed, reinforcing or rewarding the avoidance of alcohol.)

When individuals are taking medication that requires that they avoid alcohol, foods containing alcohol must be avoided as well as beverage alcohol. The following foods contain small amounts of alcohol:

- flavor extracts, such as vanilla, almond, or rum flavorings
- cooking wines
- candies or cakes prepared or filled with liqueur

KEY TERMS

Anorexia—Loss of appetite or unwillingness to eat. Can be caused by medications, depression, or many other factors.

Anorexia nervosa—An eating disorder characterized by an intense fear of weight gain accompanied by a distorted perception of one's own underweight body.

Binge—An excessive amount of food consumed in a short period of time. Usually, while people binge eat, they feel disconnected from reality, and feel unable to stop. The bingeing may temporarily relieve depression or anxiety, but after the binge, they usually feel guilty and depressed.

Bulimia nervosa—An eating disorder characterized by binges in which large amounts of food are consumed, followed by forced vomiting.

Psychotropic drug—Medication that has an effect on the mind, brain, behavior, perceptions, or emotions. Psychotropic medications are used to treat mental illnesses because they affect a patient's moods and perceptions.

Purge—When a person rids extra food consumed by inducing vomiting, laxative abuse, or excessive exercise.

Relapse—People experience relapses when they reengage in behaviors that are harmful and that they were trying to change or eliminate. Relapse is a common occurrence after treatment for many disorders, including addictions and eating disorders.

Thiamin—A B-vitamin that is essential to normal metabolism and nerve function, and whose absorption is affected by alcoholism.

Tyramine—An intermediate product between the chemicals tyrosine and epinephrine in the body and a substance normally found in many foods. It is found especially in protein-rich foods that have been aged or fermented, pickled, or bacterially contaminated, such as cheese, beer, yeast, wine, and chicken liver.

- apple cider
- cider and wine vinegar
- commercial eggnog
- bernaise or bordelaise sauces
- desserts such as crepes suzette or cherries jubilee
- teriyaki sauce
- fondues

See also Nutrition counseling; Nutrition and mental health.

Resources

BOOKS

Logue, Alexandra. *The Psychology of Eating and Drinking.* 3rd ed. New York: Routledge, 2004.

Bronner, Felix. *Nutritional Aspects and Clinical Management of Chronic Disorders and Diseases.* Boca Raton, FL: CRC, 2002.

PERIODICALS

Daubenmier, Jennifer J., and others. "The Contribution of Changes in Diet, Exercise, and Stress Management to Changes in Coronary Risk in Women and Men in the Multisite Cardiac Lifestyle Intervention Program." *Annals of Behavioral Medicine* 33.1 (Feb. 2007): 57–68.

Groesz, Lisa M., and Eric Stice. "An Experimental Test of the Effects of Dieting on Bulimic Symptoms: The Impact of Eating Episode Frequency." *Behaviour Research and Therapy* 45.1 (Jan. 2007): 49–62.

Hagler, Athena S., and others. "Psychosocial Correlates of Dietary Intake Among Overweight and Obese Men." *American Journal of Health Behavior* 31.1 (Jan.–Feb. 2007): 3–12.

Jabs, Jennifer, and Carol M. Devine. "Time Scarcity and Food Choices: An Overview." *Appetite* 47.2 (Sept. 2006): 196–204.

Leung, Newman, and Emma Price. "Core Beliefs in Dieters and Eating Disordered Women." *Eating Behaviors* 8.1 (Jan. 2007): 65–72.

Mobbs, Charles V., and others. "Low-Carbohydrate Diets Cause Obesity, Low-Carbohydrate Diets Reverse Obesity: A Metabolic Mechanism Resolving the Paradox." *Appetite* 48.2 (Mar. 2007): 135–38.

Payne, Martha E., and others. "Vascular Nutritional Correlates of Late-Life Depression." *American Journal of Geriatric Psychiatry* 14.9 (Sept. 2006): 787–95.

ORGANIZATIONS

American Dietetic Association. 216 West Jackson Boulevard, Chicago, IL, 60606-6995. Web site: <http://www.eatright.org>.

Nancy Gustafson, MS, RD, F.A.D.A., E.L.S.
Ruth A. Wienclaw, PhD

Diphenhydramine

Definition

Diphenhydramine is an antihistamine used in psychiatric medicine to treat phenothiazine drug-induced abnormal muscle movement. It is also used in general medicine to treat allergies, allergic reactions, motion

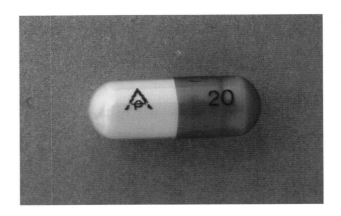

Diphenhyramine capsule. *(Custom Medical Stock Photo, Inc. Reproduced by permission.)*

sickness, **insomnia**, cough, and nausea. When diphenhydramine is used for allergy-related symptoms, it is sold in the United States as an over-the-counter medication Benadryl. For use in the treatment of the tremors caused by phenothiazines, diphenhydramine is prescribed in the generic form.

Purpose

Some drugs called phenothiazines are used to treat psychotic disorder such as **schizophrenia**. As a side effect, these drugs may cause tremors and abnormal involuntary movements of the muscles, referred to as extrapyramidal neurologic **movement disorders**. Diphenhydramine is used to control these symptoms. Other uses of the drug include the treatment of nausea, vomiting, and itching. Diphenhydramine is used to help limit allergic reactions to transfused blood products. It can induce sleep. It is sometimes used to treat the stiffness and tremor of Parkinson's disease. In liquid form, it may relieve minor throat irritation.

Description

Diphenhydramine is an antihistamine that is readily distributed throughout the body. It is easily absorbed when taken by mouth. Maximal action occurs approximately one hour after swallowing the drug. The effects continue for four to six hours. Diphenhydramine acts on cells in the **brain**. It seems to compete with the chemical histamine for specific receptor sites on cells in the brain and central nervous system. This means that it achieves its therapeutic effect by taking the place of the neurotransmitter histamine on these cells. Diphenhydramine is a useful medication for individuals with mild parkinsonism when it is used in combination with centrally acting anticholinergic drugs.

Recommended dosage

The dosage of diphenhydramine must be adjusted according to the needs of individuals and their responses. Adults are generally given 25–50 mg orally, three to four times daily. Diphenhydramine may be administered through a vein or injected deep within a muscle. The usual dosage is 10–50 mg per injection, although some people may require 100 mg. The total daily dosage should not exceed 400 mg. People who forget to take a dose of this drug should skip the dose and take the next one at the regularly scheduled time. They should not double up subsequent doses if one is missed.

People should not take diphenhydramine if they are taking other preparations that contain antihistamines unless specifically directed to do so by a physician.

Precautions

People with peptic ulcer disease, bowel obstructions, an enlarged prostate, angle closure glaucoma, or difficulty urinating due to a blockage in the bladder should not use diphenhydramine without close physician supervision and monitoring. People with asthma, heart disease, high blood pressure, or an overactive thyroid should use this drug with caution. Before taking diphenhydramine, people with these conditions should discuss the risks and benefits of this drug with their doctor. Individuals should not take diphenhydramine for several days before an allergy test, as it will interfere with the results.

Elderly people are more sensitive to the sedating effects of diphenhydramine. The drug may also lower blood pressure and cause dizziness. Older people should slowly change position from sitting or lying to standing while taking this medication to prevent dizziness and fainting.

Side effects

Drowsiness commonly occurs after taking diphenhydramine. This effect may be more pronounced if alcohol or any other central nervous system depressant, such as a tranquilizer or a particular medication for pain, is also taken. People taking the drug should not drive, operate machinery, or perform hazardous tasks requiring mental alertness until the effects of the medication have worn off. In some people, diphenhydramine also may cause dizziness, difficulties with coordination, confusion, restlessness, nervousness, difficulty sleeping, blurry or double vision, ringing in the ears, headache, or convulsions.

KEY TERMS

Anticholinergic—Related to the ability of a drug to block the nervous system chemical acetylcholine. When acetylcholine is blocked, patients often experience dry mouth and skin, increased heart rate, blurred vision, and difficulty in urinating. In severe cases, blocking acetylcholine may cloud thinking and cause delirium.

Antihistamine—A medication used to alleviate allergy or cold symptoms such as runny nose, itching, hives, watering eyes, or sneezing.

Extrapyramidal movement disorders—Involuntary movements that occur as a side effect of some psychiatric medications.

Histamine—Substance released during allergic reactions.

Hypokinesia—A condition of abnormally diminished motor activity.

Parkinson's disease—A disease of the nervous system most common in people over 60, characterized by a shuffling gait, trembling of the fingers and hands, and muscle stiffness.

Parkinsonism—A condition caused by the destruction of the brain cells that produce dopamine (a neurotransmitter); characterized by tremors of the fingers and hands, a shuffling gait, and muscular rigidity.

Phenothiazine—A class of drugs widely used in the treatment of psychosis.

Stomach distress is a relatively common side effect of diphenhydramine. Some people may develop poor appetites, nausea, vomiting, diarrhea, or constipation. Individuals also may experience low blood pressure, palpitations, rapid or irregular heartbeats, frequent urination, or difficulty urinating. Urine may be retained in the bladder. Other side effects of diphenhydramine are associated with persons in age groups that are unlikely to use the drug.

Diphenhydramine may also cause hives, a rash, sensitivity to the sun, and a dry mouth and nose. Thickened lung secretions are common among older persons.

Interactions

Alcohol, pain medications, sleeping pills, tranquilizers, and **antidepressants** may make the drowsiness associated with diphenhydramine more severe.

Diphenhydramine

Diphenhydramine should not be used by persons taking hay-fever medicines, **sedatives**, narcotics, anesthetics, **barbiturates**, or muscle relaxants.

Resources

BOOKS

Foreman, John C. and Torben Johansen. *Textbook of Receptor Pharmacology,* 2nd ed. Boca Raton, FL: CRC Press, 2002.

Page, Clive P., and Michael Murphy. *Integrated Pharmacology*. St. Louis: Mosby-Year Book, 2002.

Preston, John D., John H. O'Neal, and Mary C. Talaga. *Handbook of Clinical Psychopharmacology for Therapists,* 4th ed. Oakland, CA: New Harbinger Publications, 2004.

PERIODICALS

Grillon, Christian, and others. "The Benzodiazepine Alprazolam Dissociates Contextual Fear from Cued Fear in Humans as Assessed by Fear-Potentiated Startle." *Biological Psychiatry* 60.7 (Oct. 2006): 760–66.

Khoromi, Suzan, and others. "Topiramate in Chronic Lumbar Radicular Pain." *Journal of Pain* 6.12 (Dec. 2005): 829–36.

Scaife, J. C., and others. "Sensitivity of Late-Latency Auditory and Somatosensory Evoked Potentials to Threat of Electric Shock and the Sedative Drugs Diazepam and Diphenhydramine in Human Volunteers." *Journal of Psychopharmacology* 20.4 (July 2006): 485–95.

Turner, Claire, Alison D. F. Handford, and Anthony N. Nicholson. "Sedation and Memory: Studies with a Histamine H-1 Receptor Antagonist." *Journal of Psychopharmacology* 20.4 (July 2006): 506–17.

ORGANIZATIONS

American Academy of Family Physicians. 11400 Tomahawk Creek Parkway, Leawood, KS 66211-2672. Telephone: (913) 906-6000. Web site: <http://www.aafp.org>.

American College of Physicians. 190 N Independence Mall West, Philadelphia, PA 19106-1572. Telephone: (800) 523-1546, ext. 2600 or (215) 351-2600. Web site: <http://www.acponline.org>.

American Medical Association. 515 N. State Street, Chicago, IL 60610. Telephone: (312) 464-5000. Web site: <http://www.ama-assn.org>.

American Parkinson Disease Association. Inc. 1250 Hylan Boulevard Suite 4B, Staten Island, NY 10305-1946. Telephone: (800) 223-2732 or (718) 981-8001. Fax: (718) 981-4399. Web site: <http://www.apdaparkinson.com>.

American Psychiatric Association. 1400 K Street NW, Washington, DC 20005. Telephone: (888) 357-7924. Fax (202) 682-6850.

American Society for Clinical Pharmacology and Therapeutics. 528 North Washington Street, Alexandria, VA 22314. Telephone: (703) 836-6981. Fax: 703-836-5223.

American Society for Pharmacology and Experimental Therapeutics. 9650 Rockville Pike, Bethesda, MD 20814-3995. Telephone: (301) 530-7060.

Parkinson's Disease Foundation. 710 West 168th Street, New York, NY 10032-9982. Telephone: (800) 457-6676 or (212) 923-4700. Fax: (212) 923-4778. Web site: <http://www.pdf.org>.

L. Fleming Fallon, Jr, MD, Dr.P.H.
Ruth A. Wienclaw, PhD

Disease concept of chemical dependency

Definition

Disease concept of chemical dependency is the concept that a disorder (such as chemical dependency) is like a disease and has a characteristic set of signs, symptoms, and natural history (clinical course, or outcome).

Description

The disease concept has long been accepted by the medical community. The concept proposes that a disease is characterized by a specific set of signs and symptoms and that the disease, if left untreated, will progress to some endpoint or outcome (clinical course). However, controversy arises when the medical community is faced with new abnormal conditions, owing mostly to the new technologies in genetic engineering. This controversy becomes especially apparent when examining psychological disorders.

In the past, psychological disorders were thought in general to be due to both psychological and social abnormalities. Although these psychosocial problems are still of utmost importance, researchers have since discovered that many psychological disorders, such as alcoholism, also have genetic causes. Recent studies have identified a genetic area (locus) where a gene is located that can transmit alcoholism from affected father to son. Mental health professionals also know from clinical experience that alcoholics demonstrate a characteristic set of specific signs and symptoms. Additionally, it is well established that the ultimate clinical course for untreated alcoholism is death. Therefore alcoholism, once thought to be a disorder of those with a weak will, or "party people" can now be characterized as a disease.

Can it be inferred that other chemical dependencies may also have biological causes? There is compelling evidence that this theory may be correct. It is interesting to note that all psychoactive mood-altering drugs (alcohol, **cocaine**, marijuana, heroin, etc.) act in specific sites in the **brain** and on a specific neurotransmitter (a chemical that delivers impulses from one nerve cell to another) called **dopamine**. These mood-altering substances cause dopamine depletion, inducing an abnormality in nerve cells that "hijacks" the cells into chemical dependence. In other words, the substance introduced in the body affects the dopamine in a way that makes the affected individual unable to experience everyday pleasures—the individual instead needs that substance to experience pleasure. Thus the individual's driving force is any drug that can provide some kind of transient happiness (euphoria). In fact, the gene for alcoholism is located in the dopamine molecule. This can further suggest that chemical dependencies may have a medical (biological) cause.

The disease concept of chemical dependency is gaining worldwide acceptance, but does have some critics who argue instead that **addiction** must be understood as a general pattern of behavior, not as a medical problem. Advocates of the disease concept of chemical dependency model maintain that the identification of biological causes or correlations is crucially important for treatment. They argue that if clinicians can understand the intricate details concerning the mechanisms associated with drug effects, then measures to interrupt the effects can be devised. These interventions can be both medical (developing new drugs to chemical block effects of illicit drugs) and psychological.

According to the disease concept model, psychological **intervention** includes a vital educational component that teaches people with chemical dependency the concept of understanding addiction as disease. As a result of this understanding, affected people then view their dependency as a disease, similar to other diseases with a biological cause (heart disease, cancer, high blood pressure), and with a specific set of signs and symptoms and an outcome in the future (clinical course). Proponents of this approach believe that this understanding can help affected people to follow treatment recommendations, and can reduce shame and guilt commonly associated with chemical dependence. Alcoholics Anonymous is a prominent example of an organization that embodies the disease concept of chemical dependency.

Resources

PERIODICALS

Cadet, J., K. Bolla. "Chronic cocaine use as a neuropsychiatric syndrome: a model for debate." *Synapse* 22 (1996).

Johnson, J., M. K. Leff. "Children of substance abusers: overview of research findings." *Pediatrics* 103, no. 5 (May 1999).

Laith Farid Gulli, M.D.

Disorder of written expression

Definition

Disorder of written expression, formerly called developmental expressive writing disorder, is a learning disability in which a person's ability to communicate in writing is substantially below the level normally expected based on the individual's age, intelligence, life experiences, educational background, or physical impairments. This disability affects both the physical reproduction of letters and words and the organization of thoughts and ideas in written compositions.

Description

Disorder of written expression is one of the more poorly understood learning disabilities. Learning disabilities that manifest themselves only in written work were first described in the late 1960s. These early studies described three main types of written disorders:

- inability to form letters and numbers correctly, also called dysgraphia
- inability to write words spontaneously or from dictation
- inability to organize words into meaningful thoughts

There are several difficulties in studying disorder of written expression and in implementing a remedial program. Disorder of written expression usually appears in conjunction with other reading or language disabilities, making it hard to separate manifestations of the disability related only to written expression. Delays in attention, visual-motor integration, visual processing, and expressive language may also contribute to writing disorders. Also, there are no standard tests specifically designed to evaluate disorder of written expression.

Causes and symptoms

Causes

The causes of disorder of written expression are unknown. Different manifestations of the disorder may have different causes. For example, people who cannot form letters correctly on the page (dysgraphia) may have delays in hand-eye coordination and difficulties concentrating. People who are unable to write words from memory or dictation appear to have deficits in their visual memory. They cannot remember what the words look like. People who produce legible script but cannot organize their thoughts on paper may have cognitive processing problems. Because disorder of written expression is a little-studied disorder, specific causes have not yet been determined.

Symptoms

Symptoms that suggest disorder of written expression include:

- poor or illegible handwriting
- poorly formed letters or numbers
- excessive spelling errors
- excessive punctuation errors
- excessive grammar errors
- sentences that lack logical cohesion
- paragraphs and stories that are missing elements and that do not make sense or lack logical transitions
- deficient writing skills that significantly impact academic achievement or daily life

These symptoms must be evaluated in light of the person's age, intelligence, educational experience, and cultural or life experience. Written expression must be substantially below the level of samples produced by others of the same age, intelligence, and background. Normally, several of the symptoms are present simultaneously.

Demographics

Several studies have estimated that between 3% and 5% of students have disorder of written expression. However, it is difficult to separate this disorder from other **learning disorders**. Deficits in written work may be attributed to reading, language, or attention disorders, limited educational background, or lack of fluency in the language of instruction. Disorder of written expression unassociated with any other learning disability is rare. It commonly occurs in conjunction with **reading disorder** or **mathematics disorder**.

Diagnosis

There are no specific tests to diagnose disorder of written expression. This disorder is not normally diagnosed before age eight because of the variability with which children acquire writing skills. It is most commonly diagnosed in the fourth or fifth grade, although it can be noted and diagnosed as soon as the first grade. Requests for testing usually originate with a teacher or parent who notes multiple symptoms of the disorder in a child's writing.

Several standardized tests accurately reflect spelling abilities, but do not assess other writing skills with the same reliability. Tests that might be helpful in diagnosing disorder of written expression include the Diagnostic Evaluation of Writing Skills (DEWS), the Test of Early Written Language (TEWL), and the Test of Adolescent Language. However, assessment using standardized tests is not enough to make a **diagnosis** of disorder of written expression. In addition, a qualified evaluator should compare multiple samples of the student's written work with the written work normally expected from students of comparable backgrounds. The person being evaluated may also be asked to perform tasks such as writing from dictation or copying written material as part of diagnostic testing.

Treatments

Little is known about how to treat disorder of written expression. Intense writing remediation may help, but no specific method or approach to remediation has proved particularly successful. Since disorder of written expression usually occurs in conjunction with other learning disabilities, treatment is often directed at those better-understood learning problems.

Prognosis

Little is known about the long-term outcome for people with disorder of written expression. However, it appears that those who have this disorder may develop low self-esteem and social problems related to their lack of academic achievement. Later in life they may be more likely to drop out of school and may find employment opportunities which require writing skills to be closed to them.

Prevention

There are no known ways to prevent disorder of written expression.

See also Reading disorder; Mathematics disorder.

Resources

BOOKS

American Psychiatric Association *Diagnostic and Statistical Manual of Mental Disorders.* 4th ed, Text revised. Washington D.C.: American Psychiatric Association, 2000.

Sadock, Benjamin J., and Virginia A. Sadock, eds. *Comprehensive Textbook of Psychiatry,* 7th ed. Vol. 2. Philadelphia: Lippincott Williams and Wilkins, 2000.

ORGANIZATIONS

American Academy of Child and Adolescent Psychiatry. P. O. Box 96106, Washington, DC 20090. Telephone: (800) 333-7636. <www.aacap.org>.

Learning Disabilities Association of America. 4156 Library Road, Pittsburgh, PA 15234-1349. Telephone: (412) 341-1515. Web site: <www.ldanatl.org>.

National Center for Learning Disabilities. 381 Park Avenue South Suite 1401, New York, NY 10016. Telephone: (888) 575-7373 (toll free) or (212) 545-7510. <www.ncld.org>.

OTHER

International Dyslexia Association. "Just The Facts: Dysgraphia." Fact Sheet #982. <http://www.knowledge network.ca/literacy/resources/literature/dysgraphia.pdf>.

National Institute for Neurological Disorders and Stroke. Dysgraphia Information Page. <http://www.ninds.nih.gov/disorders/dysgraphia/dysgraphia.htm>.

National Library of Medicine. National Institutes of Health. "Disorders of Written Expression." <http://www.nlm.nih.gov/medlineplus/ency/article/001543.htm>.

Tish Davidson, A.M.
Emily Jane Willingham, PhD

Dissociation and dissociative disorders

Definition

The dissociative disorders are a group of mental disorders that affect consciousness and are defined as causing significant interference with the patient's general functioning, including social relationships and employment.

Description

Dissociation is a mechanism that allows the mind to separate or compartmentalize certain memories or thoughts from normal consciousness. These split-off mental contents are not erased. They may resurface spontaneously or be triggered by objects or events in the person's environment.

Until recently, dissociation was widely considered to be a process that occurs along a spectrum of severity. It was considered a spectrum because people experiencing dissociation do not necessarily always have a dissociative disorder or other mental illness. A mild degree of dissociation occurs with some physical stressors; people who have gone without sleep for a long period of time, have had "laughing gas" for dental surgery, or have been in a minor accident often have brief dissociative experiences. As well, in another commonplace example of dissociation, people completely involved in a book or movie may not notice their surroundings or the passage of time. Yet another example might be driving on the highway and passing several exits without noticing or remembering. Dissociation is related to hypnosis in that hypnotic trance also involves a temporarily altered state of consciousness. Most patients with dissociative disorders are highly hypnotizable.

People in other cultures sometimes have dissociative experiences in the course of religious or other group activities (in certain trance states). These occurrences should not be judged in terms of what is considered "normal" in the United States.

Rather than the pathological forms of the disorder being considered a continuum, they now have been dichotomized into the categories of detachment and compartmentalization. Specific characteristics distinguish each of these, although there can be overlap. For example, compartmentalization might be characteristic of a form of dissociative disorder called **dissociative amnesia**. Patients who have the compartmentalized type of dissociation do not engage in conscious integration of mental systems and do not or cannot consciously access certain areas of memory or information that normally would be available. This type of dissociation also can occur in **conversion disorder**.

A person exhibiting the detachment form of a dissociation disorder experiences the altered state of consciousness that is more commonly associated with the concept of dissociation. In such cases, derealization or **depersonalization** are not merely transient, brief manifestations caused by lack of sleep. Instead, people with dissociation disorder may exhibit a flat affect (outward presentation of mood or emotion) and have a sense of being out of their own bodies. These detachment forms of dissociation may be associated with trauma and **post-traumatic stress disorder**, although post-traumatic **stress** disorder may also elicit crossover symptoms of compartmentalization. Recent studies of trauma indicate that the human **brain** stores traumatic memories in a different way than normal memories. Traumatic memories are not processed or integrated into a person's ongoing life in the same fashion as normal memories. Instead they are dissociated, or "split off," and may erupt into consciousness from time to time without warning. Affected people cannot control or "edit" these memories. Over a period of time, these two sets of memories, the normal and the traumatic, may coexist as parallel sets without being combined or blended. It has been suggested that the detachment may interfere with this process of consolidation. In extreme cases, different sets of dissociated memories may cause people to develop separate personalities for these memories—a disorder known as **dissociative identity disorder** (formerly called multiple personality disorder).

Demographics

Studies suggest a frequency of pathological dissociation in the general North American population of between 2% and 3.3%. In Europe, reported rates are lower, at 0.3% in the nonclinical population and between 1.8% and 2.9% in student populations. Among psychiatric patients, frequency is much higher, between 5.4% and 12.7%, and it also is higher in groups with specific psychiatric diagnoses; for example, its frequency among women with eating disorders can be as high as 48.6%.

Types of dissociative disorders

Dissociative amnesia

Dissociative **amnesia** is a disorder in which the distinctive feature is the patient's inability to remember important personal information to a degree that cannot be explained by normal forgetfulness. In many cases, it is a reaction to a traumatic accident or witnessing a violent crime. Patients with dissociative amnesia may develop depersonalization or trance states as part of the disorder, but they do not experience a change in identity.

Dissociative fugue

Dissociative fugue is a disorder in which those affected temporarily lose their sense of personal identity and travel to other locations where they may assume a new identity. Again, this condition usually follows a major stressor or trauma. Apart from inability to recall their past or personal information, patients with dissociative fugue do not behave strangely or appear disturbed to others. Cases of dissociative fugue are more common in wartime or in communities disrupted by a natural disaster.

Depersonalization disorder

Depersonalization disorder is a disturbance in which the patient's primary symptom is a sense of detachment from the self. Depersonalization as a symptom (not as a disorder) is quite common in college-age populations. It is often associated with sleep deprivation or "recreational" drug use. It may be accompanied by "derealization" (where objects in an environment appear altered). Patients sometimes describe depersonalization as feeling like a robot or watching themselves from the outside. Depersonalization disorder may also involve feelings of numbness or loss of emotional "aliveness."

Dissociative identity disorder (DID)

Dissociative identity disorder (DID) is considered the most severe dissociative disorder and involves all of the major dissociative symptoms. People with this disorder have more than one personality state, and the personality state controlling the person's behavior

---

changes from time to time. Often, a stressor will cause the change in personality state. The various personality states have separate names, temperaments, gestures, and vocabularies. This disorder is often associated with severe physical or sexual abuse, especially abuse during childhood. Women are diagnosed with this disorder more often than men.

Dissociative disorder not otherwise specified (DDNOS)

DDNOS is a diagnostic category ascribed to patients with dissociative symptoms that do not meet the full criteria for a specific dissociative disorder.

Treatments

Studies now suggest that treatment of a specific dissociation disorder should be based on whether or not the manifestations are considered as the compartmentalized type or the detachment type. Treatment recommendations for the compartmentalized types of disorders include focusing on reactivating and integrating the isolated mental compartments, possibly through hypnosis. To address detachment-based dissociation, therapies may include identifying triggers for the detached state, and determining how to stop the triggers and/or stop the detached condition when it is triggered. Standard approaches for these tactics may include **cognitive-behavioral therapy**.

Resources

BOOKS

American Psychiatric Association. *Diagnostic and Statistical Manual of Mental Disorders*. 4th ed., Text rev. Washington, D.C.: American Psychiatric Association, 2000.

PERIODICALS

Spitzer, Carsten, and others. "Recent Developments in the Theory of Dissociation." *World Psychiatry* 5 (2006): 82–86.

ORGANIZATIONS

American Psychiatric Association. 1400 K Street NW, Washington, DC 20005. Telephone: (888) 357-7924. Fax: (202) 682-6850.

The International Society for the Study of Dissociation. 8201 Greensboro Drive, Suite 300, McLean, VA 22102. Telephone: (703) 610-9037, Fax: (703) 610-9005. <http://www.issd.org/index_actual.html>.

OTHER

The Mayo Clinic. "Dissociative Disorders." <http://www.mayoclinic.com/health/dissociative-disorders/DS00574/DSECTION = 5>.

New York Online Access to Health (NOAH). "Dissociative Disorders." 2006. <http://www.noah-health.org/en/mental/disorders/dissociative .html>.

U.S. Department of Health and Human Services. "Dissociation." <http://www.womenshealth.gov/wwd/conditions/dissociative.cfm?style = module>.

Rebecca J. Frey, PhD
Emily Jane Willingham, PhD

Dissociative amnesia

Definition

Dissociative **amnesia** is classified by the ***Diagnostic and Statistical Manual of Mental Disorders***, fourth edition, text revision (also known as the *DSM-IV-TR*), as one of the **dissociative disorders**, which are mental disorders in which the normally well-integrated functions of memory, identity, perception, or consciousness are separated (dissociated). The dissociative disorders are usually associated with trauma in the recent or distant past, or with an intense internal conflict that forces the mind to separate incompatible or unacceptable knowledge, information, or feelings. In dissociative amnesia, the continuity of the patient's memory is disrupted. Patients with dissociative amnesia have recurrent episodes in which they forget important personal information or events, usually connected with trauma or severe **stress**. The information that is lost to the patient's memory is usually too extensive to be attributed to ordinary absentmindedness or forgetfulness related to aging. Dissociative amnesia was formerly called "psychogenic amnesia."

Amnesia is a symptom of other medical and mental disorders; however, the patterns of amnesia differ depending on the cause of the disorder. Amnesia associated with head trauma is typically both retrograde (the patient has no memory of events shortly before the head injury) and anterograde (the patient has no memory of events after the injury). The amnesia that is associated with seizure disorders is sudden onset. Amnesia in patients with **delirium** or **dementia** occurs in the context of extensive disturbances of the patient's cognition (knowing), speech, perceptions, emotions, and behaviors. Amnesia associated with **substance abuse**, which is sometimes called a "blackout," typically affects only short-term memory and is irreversible. In dissociative amnesia, in contrast to these other conditions, the patient's memory loss is almost always anterograde, which means that it is limited to the period following the traumatic event(s). In addition, patients with dissociative amnesia do not have problems learning new information.

Dissociative amnesia as a symptom occurs in patients diagnosed with **dissociative fugue** and **dissociative identity disorder**. If the patient's episodes of dissociative amnesia occur only in the context of these disorders, a separate **diagnosis** of dissociative amnesia is not made.

Description

Patients with dissociative amnesia usually report a gap or series of gaps in their recollection of their life history. The gaps are usually related to episodes of **abuse** or equally severe trauma, although some persons with dissociative amnesia also lose recall of their own **suicide** attempts, episodes of self-mutilation, or violent behavior.

Five different patterns of memory loss have been reported in patients with dissociative amnesia:

- localized. The patient cannot recall events that took place within a limited period of time (usually several hours or one to two days) following a traumatic event. For example, some survivors of the World Trade Center attacks do not remember how they got out of the damaged buildings or what streets they took to get away from the area.

- selective. The patient can remember some, but not all, of the events that took place during a limited period of time. For example, a veteran of D-Day (June 6, 1944) may recall some details, such as eating a meal on the run or taking prisoners, but not others (seeing a close friend hit or losing a commanding officer).
- generalized. The person cannot recall anything in his/her entire life. Persons with generalized amnesia are usually found by the police or taken by others to a hospital emergency room.
- continuous. The amnesia covers the entire period without interruption from a traumatic event in the past to the present.
- systematized. The amnesia covers only certain categories of information, such as all memories related to a certain location or to a particular person.

Most patients diagnosed with dissociative amnesia have either localized or selective amnesia. Generalized amnesia is extremely rare. Patients with generalized, continuous, or systematized amnesia are usually eventually diagnosed as having a more complex dissociative disorder, such as dissociative identity disorder.

Causes and symptoms

Causes

The primary cause of dissociative amnesia is stress associated with traumatic experiences that the patient has either survived or witnessed. These may include such major life stressors as serious financial problems, the death of a parent or spouse, extreme internal conflict, and guilt related to serious crimes or turmoil caused by difficulties with another person.

Susceptibility to hypnosis appears to be a predisposing factor in dissociative amnesia. Thus far, no specific genes have been associated with vulnerability to dissociative amnesia.

Some personality types and character traits seem to be risk factors for dissociative disorders. A group of researchers in the United States has found that persons diagnosed with dissociative disorders have much higher scores for immature psychological defenses than normal subjects.

Symptoms

The central symptom of dissociative amnesia is loss of memory for a period or periods of time in the patient's life. The memory loss may take a variety of different patterns, as described earlier.

Other symptoms that have been reported in patients diagnosed with dissociative amnesia include the following:

- confusion.
- emotional distress related to the amnesia. However, not all patients with dissociative amnesia are distressed. The degree of emotional upset is usually in direct proportion to the importance of what has been forgotten, or the consequences of forgetting.
- mild depression.

Some patients diagnosed with dissociative amnesia have problems or behaviors that include disturbed interpersonal relationships, sexual dysfunction, employment problems, aggressive behaviors, self-mutilation, or suicide attempts.

Demographics

Dissociative amnesia can appear in patients of any age past infancy. Its true prevalence is unknown. In recent years, there has been an intense controversy among therapists regarding the increase in case reports of dissociative amnesia and the accuracy of the memories recovered. Some maintain that the greater awareness of dissociative symptoms and disorders among psychiatrists has led to the identification of cases that were previously misdiagnosed. Other therapists maintain that dissociative disorders are overdiagnosed in people who are extremely vulnerable to suggestion.

It should be noted that psychiatrists in the United States and Canada have significantly different opinions of dissociative disorder diagnoses. On the whole, Canadian psychiatrists, both French- and English-speaking, have serious reservations about the scientific validity and diagnostic status of dissociative amnesia and dissociative identity disorder. Only 30% of Canadian psychiatrists think that these two dissociative disorders should be included in the *DSM-IV-TR* without reservation; and only 13% think that here is strong scientific support for the validity of these diagnoses.

Diagnosis

The diagnosis of dissociative amnesia is usually a diagnosis of exclusion. The doctor will take a detailed medical history, give the patient a physical examination, and order blood and urine tests, as well as an electroencephalogram (EEG) or head x ray to rule out memory loss resulting from seizure disorders, substance abuse (including abuse of inhalants), head injuries, or medical conditions, such as **Alzheimer's disease** or delirium associated with fever.

Some conditions, such as age-related memory impairment (AAMI), may be ruled out on the basis of the patient's age. **Malingering** can usually be detected in patients who are faking amnesia because they typically exaggerate and dramatize their symptoms; they have obvious financial, legal, or personal reasons (for example, draft evasion) for pretending loss of memory. In addition, patients with genuine dissociative amnesia usually score high on tests of hypnotizability. The examiner may administer the Hypnotic Induction Profile (HIP) or a similar measure that evaluates whether the patient is easily hypnotized. This enables the examiner to rule out malingering or **factitious disorder**.

There are several standard diagnostic questionnaires that may be given to evaluate the presence of a dissociative disorder. The Dissociative Experiences Scale (DES) is a frequently administered self-report screener for all forms of **dissociation**. The Structured Clinical Interview for the *DSM-IV-TR* Dissociative Disorders (SCID-D) can be used to make the diagnosis of dissociative amnesia distinct from the other dissociative disorders defined by the *DSM-IV-TR*. The SCID-D is a semi-structured interview, which means that the examiner's questions are open-ended and allow the patient to describe experiences of amnesia in some detail, as distinct from simple "yes" or "no" answers.

Diagnosis of dissociative amnesia in children before the age of puberty is complicated by the fact that inability to recall the first four to five years of one's life is a normal feature of human development. As part of the differential diagnosis, a physician who is evaluating a child in this age group will rule out inattention, **learning disorders**, oppositional behavior, **psychosis**, and seizure disorders or head trauma. To make an accurate diagnosis, several different people (such as teachers, therapists, **social workers**, or the child's primary care physician) may be asked to observe or evaluate the child.

Treatments

Treatment of dissociative amnesia usually requires two distinct periods or phases of **psychotherapy**.

Psychotherapy

Psychotherapy for dissociative amnesia is supportive in its initial phase. It begins with creating an atmosphere of safety in the treatment room. Very often, patients gradually regain their memories when they

feel safe with and supported by the therapist. This rapport does not mean that they necessarily recover their memories during therapy sessions; one study of 90 patients with dissociative amnesia found that most of them had their memories return while they were at home alone or with family or close friends. The patients denied that their memories were derived from a therapist's suggestions, and a majority of them were able to find independent evidence or corroboration of their childhood abuse.

If the memories do not return spontaneously, hypnosis or sodium amytal (a drug that induces a semi-hypnotic state) may be used to help recover them.

After the patient has recalled enough of the missing past to acquire a stronger sense of self and continuity in their life history, the second phase of psychotherapy commences. During this phase, the patient deals more directly with the traumatic episode(s), and recovery from its aftereffects. Studies of the treatments for dissociative amnesia in combat veterans of World War I (1914–1918) found that recovery and cognitive integration of dissociated traumatic memories within the patient's overall personality were more effective than treatment methods that focused solely on releasing feelings.

Medications

At present, there are no therapeutic agents that prevent amnestic episodes or that cure dissociative amnesia itself. Patients may, however, be given **antidepressants** or other appropriate medications for treatment of the depression, **anxiety**, **insomnia**, or other symptoms that may accompany dissociative amnesia.

Legal implications

Dissociative amnesia poses a number of complex issues for the legal profession. The disorder has been cited by plaintiffs in cases of recovered memories of abuse leading to lawsuits against the perpetrators of the abuse. Dissociative amnesia has also been cited as a defense in cases of murder of adults as well as in cases of neonatricide (murder of an infant shortly after birth). Part of the problem is the adversarial nature of courtroom procedure in the United States, but it is generally agreed that judges and attorneys need better guidelines regarding dissociative amnesia in defendants and plaintiffs.

Prognosis

The prognosis for recovery from dissociative amnesia is generally good. The majority of patients eventually recover the missing parts of their past,

Age-associated memory impairment (AAMI)—A condition in which an older person suffers some memory loss and takes longer to learn new information. AAMI is distinguished from dementia because it is not progressive and does not represent a serious decline from the person's previous level of functioning. Benign senescent forgetfulness is another term for AAMI.

Anterograde amnesia—Amnesia for events that occurred after a physical injury or emotional trauma but before the present moment. The type of amnesia that typically occurs in dissociative amnesia is anterograde.

Defense—An unconscious mental process that protects the conscious mind from unacceptable or painful thoughts, impulses, or desires. Examples of defenses include denial, rationalization, projection, and repression.

Delirium—A disturbance of consciousness marked by confusion, difficulty paying attention, delusions, hallucinations, or restlessness. It can be distinguished from dissociative amnesia by its relatively sudden onset and variation in the severity of the symptoms.

Dementia—A group of symptoms (syndrome) associated with a progressive loss of memory and other intellectual functions that is serious enough to interfere with a person's ability to perform the tasks of daily life. Dementia impairs memory, alters personality, leads to deterioration in personal grooming, impairs reasoning ability, and causes disorientation.

Depersonalization—A dissociative symptom in which the patient feels that his or her body is unreal, is changing, or is dissolving.

Derealization—A dissociative symptom in which the external environment is perceived as unreal or dreamlike.

Dissociation—A reaction to trauma in which the mind splits off certain aspects of the traumatic event from conscious awareness. Dissociation can affect the patient's memory, sense of reality, and sense of identity.

Dissociative amnesia—A dissociative disorder characterized by loss of memory for a period or periods of time in the patient's life. May occur as a result of a traumatic event.

Factitious disorder—A type of mental disturbance in which patients intentionally act physically or mentally ill without obvious benefits. It is distinguished from malingering by the absence of an obvious motive, and from conversion disorder by intentional production of symptoms.

Malingering—Knowingly pretending to be physically or mentally ill to avoid some unpleasant duty or responsibility, or for economic benefit.

Retrograde amnesia—Amnesia for events that occurred before a traumatic injury. Retrograde amnesia is not usually found in patients with dissociative amnesia.

Supportive—An approach to psychotherapy that seeks to encourage the patient or offer emotional support to him or her, as distinct from insight-oriented or educational approaches to treatment.

either by spontaneous re-emergence of the memories or through hypnosis and similar techniques. A minority of patients, however, are never able to reconstruct their past; they develop a chronic form of dissociative amnesia. The prognosis for a specific patient depends on a combination of his or her present life circumstances; the presence of other mental disorders; and the severity of stresses or conflicts associated with the amnesia.

Prevention

Strategies for the prevention of child abuse might lower the incidence of dissociative amnesia in the general population. There are no effective preventive strategies for dissociative amnesia caused by traumatic experiences in adult life in patients without a history of childhood abuse.

See also Abuse.

Resources

BOOKS

American Psychiatric Association. *Diagnostic and Statistical Manual of Mental Disorders*. 4th ed., Text rev. Washington, D.C.: American Psychiatric Association, 2000.

Beers, Mark H., MD, and Robert Berkow, MD, eds. "Dissociative Amnesia." *The Merck Manual of Diagnosis and Therapy*, Whitehouse Station, NJ: Merck Research Laboratories, 2001.

Ellenberger, Henri. *The Discovery of the Unconscious.* New York: Basic Books, 1970.

Herman, Judith, MD. *Trauma and Recovery.* 2nd ed., rev. New York: Basic Books, 1997.

Stout, Martha, PhD. *The Myth of Sanity: Tales of Multiple Personality in Everyday Life.* New York: Penguin Books, 2001.

PERIODICALS

Bremner, J. Douglas, and others. "Neural Mechanisms in Dissociative Amnesia for Childhood Abuse: Relevance to the Current Controversy Surrounding the 'False Memory Syndrome.'" *American Journal of Psychiatry* 153 (1996): S71–82.

Brown, P., O. Van der Hart, and M. Graafland. "Trauma-Induced Dissociative Amnesia in World War I Combat Soldiers. II. Treatment Dimensions." *Australia and New Zealand Journal of Psychiatry* 33 (1999): 392–98.

Carrion, V. G., and H. Steiner. "Trauma and Dissociation in Delinquent Adolescents." *Journal of the American Academy of Child and Adolescent Psychiatry* 39 (2000): 353–59.

Chu, J. A., and others. "Memories of Childhood Abuse: Dissociation, Amnesia, and Corroboration." *American Journal of Psychiatry* 156 (1999): 749–55.

Durst, R., A. Teitelbaum, and R. Aronzon. "Amnestic State in a Holocaust Survivor Patient: Psychogenic Versus Neurological Basis." *Israeli Journal of Psychiatry and Related Sciences* 36 (1999): 47–54.

Lalonde, J. K., and others. "Canadian and American Psychiatrists' Attitudes Toward Dissociative Disorders Diagnoses." *Canadian Journal of Psychiatry* 46 (2001): 407–12.

Miller, P. W., and others. "An Unusual Presentation of Inhalant Abuse with Dissociative Amnesia." *Veterinary and Human Toxicology* 44 (2002): 17–19.

Pope, Harrison G., Jr. "Recovered Memories of Childhood Abuse: The Royal College of Psychiatrists Issues Important Precautions." *British Medical Journal* 316 (February 14, 1998): 713.

Porter, S., and others. "Memory for Murder. A Psychological Perspective on Dissociative Amnesia in Legal Contexts." *International Journal of Law and Psychiatry* 24 (2001): 23–42.

Simeon, D., and others. "Personality Factors Associated with Dissociation: Temperament, Defenses, and Cognitive Schemata." *American Journal of Psychiatry* 159 (2002): 489–91.

Spinelli, M. G. "A Systematic Investigation of 16 Cases of Neonaticide." *American Journal of Psychiatry* 158 (2001): 811–13.

Zanarini, M. C., and others. "The Dissociative Experiences of Borderline Patients." *Comparative Psychiatry* 41 (2000): 223–27.

ORGANIZATIONS

International Society for the Study of Dissociation (ISSD). 8201 Greensboro Drive, Suite 300, McLean, VA 22102. Telephone: (703) 610-9037. <http://www.issd.org>.

International Society for Traumatic Stress Studies (ISTSS). 60 Revere Dr., Suite 500, Northbrook, IL 60062. Telephone: (847) 480-9028. <http://www.istss.org>.

National Institute of Mental Health. 6001 Executive Boulevard, Room 8184, MSC 9663, Bethesda, MD 20892-9663. Telephone: (301) 443-4513. <http://www.nimh.nih.gov>.

National Organization for Rare Disorders (NORD). 55 Kenosia Avenue, P.O. Box 1968, Danbury, CT 06813-1968. Telephone: (203) 744-0100. <http://www.rarediseases.org>.

OTHER

National Alliance on Mental Illness, "Dissociative Disorders." <http://www.nami.org/Content/Content Groups/Helpline1/Dissociative _Disorders.htm>.

"Symposium: Science and Politics of Recovered Memories." Special issue of *Ethics and Behavior* 8 (1998). The issue is based on a program chaired by Gerald Koocher of Harvard Medical School at the 1998 convention of the American Psychiatric Association.

Rebecca Frey, PhD
Emily Jane Willingham, PhD

Dissociative fugue

Definition

Dissociative fugue is a rare condition in which a person suddenly, without planning or warning, travels far from home or work and leaves behind a past life. Patients show signs of **amnesia** and have no conscious understanding or knowledge of the reason for the flight. The condition is usually associated with severe **stress** or trauma. Because people cannot remember all or part of their past, at some point they become confused about their identity and the situations in which they find themselves. In rare cases, they may take on new identities. The American Psychiatric Association (APA) classifies dissociative fugue as one of four **dissociative disorders**, along with **dissociative amnesia**, **dissociative identity disorder**, and **depersonalization disorder**.

Description

The key feature of dissociative fugue is "sudden, unexpected travel away from home or one's customary place of daily activities, with inability to recall some or all of one's past," according to the APA. The travels associated with the condition can last for a few hours or as long as several months. Some individuals have traveled thousands of miles from home while in a state of dissociative fugue. (The word *fugue* stems from the Latin word for flight—*fugere*.) At first, people experiencing the condition may appear completely normal. With time, however, confusion appears. This confusion may result from the realization that they cannot remember the past. Those affected may suddenly realize that they do not belong where they find themselves.

During an episode of dissociative fugue, those affected may take on new identities, complete with a new name. They may even establish new homes and ties to their communities. More often, however, those affected realize something is wrong not long after fleeing—in a matter of hours or days. In such cases, they may phone home for help, or come to the attention of police after becoming distressed at finding themselves unexplainably in unfamiliar surroundings.

Dissociative fugue is distinct from dissociative identity disorder (DID). In cases of DID, which previously was called multiple personality disorder, those affected lose memory of events that take place when one of several distinct identities takes control of them. If the person with dissociative fugue assumes a new identity, it does not coexist with other identities, as is typical of DID. Repeated instances of apparent dissociative fugue are more likely a symptom of DID, not true dissociative fugue.

Causes and symptoms

Causes

Episodes of dissociative fugue are often associated with very stressful events. Traumatic experiences, such as war or natural disasters, seem to increase the incidence of the disorder. Other, more personal types of stress might also lead to the unplanned travel and amnesia characteristic of dissociative fugue. The shocking death of a loved one or seemingly unbearable pressures at work or home, for example, might cause some people to run away for brief periods and blank out their pasts.

Symptoms

People in the midst of dissociative fugue episodes may appear to have no psychiatric symptoms at all or to be only slightly confused. Therefore, for a time, it may be very difficult to spot someone experiencing a fugue. After a while, however, patients show significant signs of confusion or distress because they cannot remember recent events, or they realize a complete sense of identity is missing. This amnesia is a characteristic symptom of the disorder.

Demographics

Dissociative fugue is a rare disorder estimated to affect just 0.2% of the population, nearly all of them adults. More people may experience dissociative fugue, however, during or in the aftermath of serious accidents, wars, natural disasters, or other highly traumatic or stressful events.

Diagnosis

The *Diagnostic and Statistical Manual of Mental Disorders*, 4th edition, text revision, also known as the *DSM-IV-TR*, lists four criteria for diagnosing dissociative fugue:

- unexplained and unexpected travel from a person's usual place of living and working along with partial or complete amnesia
- uncertainty and confusion about one's identity, or in rare instances, the adoption of a new identity
- the flight and amnesia that characterize the fugue are not related exclusively to DID, nor is it the result of substance abuse or a physical illness
- an episode must result in distress or impairment severe enough to interfere with the ability of the patient to function in social, work, or home settings

Accurate **diagnosis** typically must wait until the fugue is over and the person has sought help or has been brought to the attention of mental health care providers. The diagnosis can then be made using the patient's history and reconstruction of events that occurred before, during, and after the patient's excursion.

Treatments

Psychotherapy, sometimes involving hypnosis, is often effective in the treatment of dissociative fugue. With support from therapists, patients are encouraged to remember past events by learning to face and cope with the stressful experiences that precipitated the fugue. Because the cause of the fugue is usually a traumatic event, it is often necessary to treat disturbing feelings and emotions that emerge when the patient finally faces the trauma. The troubling events that drove them to run and forget about their past may, when remembered, result in **grief**, **depression**, fear, anger, remorse, and other psychological states that require therapy.

Prognosis

The prognosis for dissociative fugue is often good. Not many cases last longer than a few months and many people make quick recoveries. In more serious cases, patients may take longer to recover memories of the past.

See also Dissociative identity disorder.

Resources

BOOKS

Allen, Thomas E., and others. *A Primer on Mental Disorders: A Guide for Educators, Families, and Students.* Lantham, MD: Scarecrow Press, 2001.

American Psychiatric Association. *Diagnostic and Statistical Manual of Mental Disorders.* 4th ed., Text rev. Washington, D.C.: American Psychiatric Association, 2000.

Beers, Mark H., and Robert Berkow, eds. "Dissociative Fugue." *The Merck Manual of Diagnosis and Therapy.* 17th ed. Whitehouse Station, NJ: Merck Research Laboratories, 1999.

ORGANIZATIONS

American Psychiatric Association. 1400 K Street NW, Washington, DC 20005. Telephone: (888) 357-7924. Fax: (202) 682-6850.

International Society for the Study of Dissociation. 60 Revere Drive, Suite 500, Northbrook, IL 60062. <http://www.issd.org/>.

National Alliance for the Mentally Ill. Colonial Place Three, 2107 Wilson Boulevard, Suite 300, Arlington, VA 22021. <http://www.nami.org/index.html>.

New York Online Access to Health (NOAH). "Dissociative Disorders." 2006. List of online resources at: <http://www.noah-health.org/en/mental/disorders/dissociative.html>.

Dean A. Haycock, PhD
Emily Jane Willingham, PhD

Dissociative identity disorder

Definition

Previously known as multiple personality disorder, dissociative identity disorder (DID) is a condition in which those affected have more than one distinct iden-

Chris Costner Sizemore, famous for her dissociative identity disorder, in a 1984 photo. The book *Three Faces of Eve* described her case. *(Ap Images)*

tity or personality state. At least two of these personalities repeatedly assert themselves to control the behavior of the affected people. Each personality state has a distinct name, past, identity, and self-image.

Psychiatrists and psychologists use a handbook called the ***Diagnostic and Statistical Manual of Mental Disorders***, fourth edition, text revision, or *DSM-IV-TR,* to diagnose mental disorders. In this handbook, DID is classified as a dissociative disorder. Other mental disorders in this category include **depersonalization disorder**, **dissociative fugue**, and **dissociative amnesia**. It should be noted, however, that the nature of DID and even its existence is debated by psychiatrists and psychologists.

Description

"Dissociation" describes a state in which the integrated functioning of a person's identity, including consciousness, memory, and awareness of surroundings, is disrupted or eliminated. **Dissociation** is a mechanism that allows the mind to separate or compartmentalize certain memories or thoughts from normal consciousness. These memories are not erased, but are buried and may resurface at a later time. Dissociation is related to hypnosis in that hypnotic trance also involves a temporarily altered state of consciousness. In severe, impairing dissociation, individuals experience a lack of awareness of important aspects of their identities.

The phrase "dissociative identity disorder" replaced "multiple personality disorder" because the new name emphasizes the disruption of a person's identity that characterizes the disorder. People with the illness are consciously aware of one aspect of their personality or self while being totally unaware of, or dissociated from, other aspects of it. This is a key feature of the disorder. It requires only two distinct identities or personality states to qualify as DID, but there have been cases in which 100 distinct alternate personalities, or alters, were reported. Fifty percent of patients with DID harbor fewer than 11 identities.

Because the alters alternate in controlling the consciousness and behavior of those affected, patients experience long gaps in memory—gaps that far exceed typical episodes of forgetting that occur in those unaffected by DID.

Despite the presence of distinct personalities, one primary identity exists in many cases. The primary identity uses the name the patient was born with and tends to be quiet, dependent, depressed, and guilt-ridden. The alters have their own names and unique traits. They are distinguished by different temperaments, likes, dislikes, manners of expression, and even physical characteristics such as posture and body language. It is not unusual for patients with DID to have alters of different genders, sexual orientations, ages, or nationalities. It typically takes just seconds for one personality to replace another but the shift can be gradual in rarer instances. In either case, the emergence of one personality, and the retreat of another, is often triggered by a stressful event.

People with DID tend to have other severe disorders as well, such as **depression, substance abuse, borderline personality disorder**, and eating disorders, among others. The degree of impairment ranges from mild to severe, and complications may include **suicide** attempts, self-mutilation, violence, or drug **abuse**.

Left untreated, DID can last a lifetime. Treatment for the disorder consists primarily of individual **psychotherapy**.

Causes and symptoms

Causes

The severe dissociation that characterizes patients with DID is currently understood to result from a set of causes:

- an innate ability to dissociate easily
- repeated episodes of severe physical or sexual abuse in childhood
- lack of supportive or comforting people to counteract abusive relative(s)
- influence of other relatives with dissociative symptoms or disorders

The primary cause of DID appears to be severe and prolonged trauma experienced during childhood. This trauma can be associated with emotional, physical, or sexual abuse, or some combination. One theory is that young children, faced with a routine of torture, sexual abuse, or **neglect**, dissociate themselves from their trauma by creating separate identities or personality states. Manufactured alters may suffer while primary identities "escape" the unbearable experiences. Dissociation, which is easy for young children to achieve, thus becomes a useful defense. This strategy displaces the suffering onto another identity. Over time, children, who on average are around six years old at the time of the appearance of the first alter, may create many more.

As stated, there is considerable controversy about the nature, and even the existence, of dissociative identity disorder. The causes are disputed, with some experts identifying extensive trauma in childhood as causative, while others maintain that the cause of the disorder is iatrogenic, or introduced by the news media or therapist. In this latter form, mass media or therapists plant the seeds that patients suppressed memories and dissociation severe enough to have created separate personalities. One cause for the skepticism is the alarming increase in reports of the disorder since the 1980s; more cases of DID were reported between 1981 and 1986 than in the previous 200 years combined. In some cases, people reporting DID and recovered memory became involved in lawsuits related to the recovered memories, only to find that the memories were not, in fact, real. Another disorder, false memory syndrome, then becomes the explanation. Thus, an area of contention is the notion of suppressed memories, a crucial component in DID. Many experts in memory research say that it is almost impossible for anyone to remember things that happened before the age of three, the age when some patients with DID supposedly experience abuse, but the brain's storage, retrieval, and interpretation of childhood memories are still not fully understood. The relationship of **dissociative disorders** to childhood abuse has led to intense controversy and lawsuits concerning the accuracy of childhood memories. Because childhood trauma is a factor in the development of DID, some doctors think it may be a variation of **post-traumatic** stress disorder (PTSD). In both DID and PTSD, dissociation is a prominent mechanism.

Symptoms

The major dissociative symptoms experienced by patients with DID are **amnesia**, **depersonalization**, derealization, and identity disturbances.

AMNESIA. Amnesia in patients with DID is marked by gaps in their memory for long periods of their past, and, in some cases, their entire childhood. Most patients with DID have amnesia, or "lose time," for periods when another personality is "out." They may report finding items in their house that they cannot remember having purchased, finding notes written in different handwriting, or other evidence of unexplained activity.

DEPERSONALIZATION. Depersonalization is a dissociative symptom in which patients feel that their bodies are unreal, are changing, or are dissolving. Some patients with DID experience depersonalization as feeling outside of their bodies, or as watching a movie of themselves.

DEREALIZATION. Derealization is a dissociative symptom in which patients perceive the external environment as unreal. Patients may see walls, buildings, or other objects as changing in shape, size, or color. Patients with DID may fail to recognize relatives or close friends.

IDENTITY DISTURBANCES. People with DID usually have a main personality that psychiatrists refer to as the "host." This is generally not the person's original personality but is rather one developed in response to childhood trauma. It is usually this personality that seeks psychiatric help. Patients with DID are often frightened by their dissociative experiences, which can include losing awareness of hours or even days, meeting people who claim to know them by another name, or feeling "out of body."

Psychiatrists refer to the phase of transition between alters as the "switch." After a switch, people with DID assume whole new physical postures, voices, and vocabularies. Specific circumstances or stressful situations may bring out particular identities. Some patients have histories of erratic performance in school or in their jobs caused by the emergence of alternate personalities during examinations or other stressful situations. Each alternate identity takes control one at a time, denying control to the others. Patients vary with regard to their alters' awareness of one another. One alter may not acknowledge the existence of others or it may criticize other alters. At times during therapy, one alter may allow another to take control.

Demographics

Studies in North America and Europe indicate that as many as 5% of patients in psychiatric wards have undiagnosed DID. Partially hospitalized patients and outpatients may have an even higher incidence. For every man diagnosed with DID, eight or nine women are diagnosed. Among children, boys and girls diagnosed with DID are pretty closely matched 1:1. No one is sure why this discrepancy between diagnosed adults and children exists.

Diagnosis

The *DSM-IV-TR* lists four diagnostic criteria for identifying DID and differentiating it from similar disorders:

- Traumatic stressor: Patients have been exposed to catastrophic events involving actual or threatened death or injury, or a serious physical threat to themselves or others. During exposure to the trauma, their emotional response was marked by intense fear, feelings of helplessness, or horror. In general, stressors caused intentionally by human beings (genocide, rape, torture, abuse, etc.) are experienced as more traumatic than accidents, natural disasters, or "acts of God."
- The demonstration of two or more distinct identities or personality states in an individual. Each separate identity must have its own way of thinking about, perceiving, relating to, and interacting with the environment and self.
- Two of the identities assume control of the patient's behavior, one at a time and repeatedly.
- Extended periods of forgetfulness lasting too long to be considered ordinary forgetfulness.
- Determination that the above symptoms are not due to drugs, alcohol, or other substances and that they cannot be attributed to any other general medical condition. It is also necessary to rule out fantasy play or imaginary friends when considering a diagnosis of DID in children.

Proper diagnosis of DID is complicated because some of the symptoms of DID overlap with symptoms of other mental disorders. Misdiagnoses are common and include depression, **schizophrenia**, borderline personality disorder, **somatization disorder**, and **panic disorder**.

Because the extreme dissociative experiences related to this disorder can be frightening, people with the disorder may go to emergency rooms or clinics because they fear they are going insane.

When a doctor is evaluating a patient for DID, the first step is to rule out physical conditions that

KEY TERMS

Alter—An alternate or secondary personality in a person with dissociative identity disorder. Each alter has a unique way of looking at and interacting with the world.

Amnesia—A general medical term for loss of memory that is not due to ordinary forgetfulness. Amnesia can be caused by head injuries, brain disease, or epilepsy, as well as by dissociation.

Borderline personality disorder—A severe and usually lifelong mental disorder characterized by violent mood swings and severe difficulties in sustaining interpersonal relationships.

Depersonalization—A dissociative symptom in which patients feel that their bodies are unreal, are changing, or are dissolving.

Derealization—A dissociative symptom in which the external environment is perceived as unreal.

Dissociation—A reaction to trauma in which the mind splits off certain aspects of the traumatic event from conscious awareness. Dissociation can affect a patient's memory, sense of reality, and sense of identity.

Dissociative identity disorder (DID)—Term that replaced multiple personality disorder. A condition in which two or more distinctive identities or personality states alternate in controlling a person's consciousness and behavior.

Host—The dominant or main alter in a person with DID.

Hypnosis—The means by which a state of extreme relaxation and suggestibility is induced. Hypnosis is used to treat amnesia and identity disturbances that occur in people with dissociative disorders.

Malingering—Knowingly pretending to be physically or mentally ill to avoid some unpleasant duty or responsibility, or for economic benefit.

Multiple personality disorder (MPD)—An older term for dissociative identity disorder (DID).

Panic disorder—An anxiety disorder in which an individual experiences sudden, debilitating attacks of intense fear.

Post-traumatic stress disorder (PTSD)—A disorder caused by an extremely stressful or traumatic event (such as rape, act of war, or natural disaster), in which the trauma victim is haunted by flashbacks. In the flashbacks, the event is reexperienced in the present. Other symptoms include nightmares and feelings of anxiety.

Primary personality—The core personality of a patient with DID. In women, the primary personality is often timid and passive, and may be diagnosed as depressed.

Schizophrenia—A severe mental illness in which a person has difficulty distinguishing what is real from what is not real. It is often characterized by hallucinations, delusions, language and communication disturbances, and withdrawal from people and social activities.

Shift—The transition of control from one alter to another in a person with DID. Usually shifts occur rapidly, within seconds, but in some cases a more gradual changeover is observed. Also referred to as a switch.

Somatization disorder—A type of mental disorder in which the patient has physical complaints that serve as coping strategies for emotional distress.

Trauma—A disastrous or life-threatening event that can cause severe emotional distress. DID is associated with trauma in a person's early life or adult experience.

---

sometimes produce amnesia, depersonalization, or derealization. These conditions include head injuries, **brain** disease (especially seizure disorders), side effects from medications, substance abuse or intoxication, AIDS **dementia** complex, or recent periods of extreme physical **stress** and sleeplessness. In some cases, the doctor may give the patient an electroencephalograph (EEG) to exclude epilepsy or other seizure disorders. The physician also must consider whether the patient is **malingering** and/or offering fictitious complaints.

If the patient appears to be physically healthy, the doctor will next rule out psychotic disturbances, including schizophrenia. Many patients with DID are misdiagnosed as having schizophrenia because they may "hear" their alters "talking" inside their heads. Doctors who suspect DID can use a screening test called the Dissociative Experiences Scale (DES). Patients with high scores on this test can be evaluated further with the Dissociative Disorders Interview Schedule (DDIS) or the Structured Clinical Interview for Dissociative Disorders (SCID-D).

Treatments

Treatment of DID may last for five to seven years in adults and usually requires several different treatment methods.

Psychotherapy

Ideally, patients with DID should be treated by a therapist with specialized training in dissociation. This specialized training is important because the patient's personality switches can be confusing or startling. In addition, many patients with DID have hostile or suicidal alter personalities. Most therapists who treat patients with DID have rules or contracts for treatment that include such issues as responsibility for the patient's safety. Psychotherapy for patients with DID typically has several stages: an initial phase for uncovering and "mapping" the patient's alters; a phase of treating the traumatic memories and "fusing" the alters; and a phase of consolidating the patient's newly integrated personality.

Most therapists who treat multiples, or patients with DID, recommend further treatment after personality integration, on the grounds that the patients have not learned the social skills that most people acquire in adolescence and early adult life. In addition, **family therapy** is often recommended to help families understand DID and the changes that occur during personality reintegration.

Many patients with DID are helped by **group therapy** as well as individual treatment, provided that the group is limited to people with dissociative disorders. Patients with DID sometimes have setbacks in mixed therapy groups because other patients are bothered or frightened by their personality switches.

Medications

Some doctors will prescribe tranquilizers or **antidepressants** for patients with DID because their alter personalities may have **anxiety** or mood disorders. However, other therapists who treat patients with DID prefer to keep medications to a minimum because these patients can easily become psychologically dependent on drugs. In addition, many patients with DID have at least one alter who abuses drugs or alcohol, substances that are dangerous in combination with most tranquilizers.

Hypnosis

Although not always necessary, hypnosis (or **hypnotherapy**) is a standard method of treatment for patients with DID. Hypnosis may help patients recover repressed ideas and memories. Further, hypnosis can also be used to control problematic behaviors that many patients with DID exhibit, such as self-mutilation, or eating disorders like **bulimia nervosa**. In the later stages of treatment, the therapist may use hypnosis to "fuse" the alters as part of the patient's personality integration process.

Prognosis

Unfortunately, no systematic studies of the long-term outcome of DID currently exist. Some therapists believe that the prognosis for recovery is excellent for children and good for most adults. Although treatment takes several years, it is often ultimately effective. As a general rule, the earlier the patient is diagnosed and properly treated, the better the prognosis. Patients may find they are bothered less by symptoms as they advance into middle age, with some relief beginning to appear in the late 40s. Stress or substance abuse, however, can cause a **relapse** of symptoms at any time.

Prevention

Prevention of DID requires **intervention** in abusive families and treating children with dissociative symptoms as early as possible.

See also Dissociation and dissociative disorders.

Resources

BOOKS

Acocella, Joan. *Creating Hysteria: Women and Multiple Personality Disorder.* San Francisco, CA: Jossey-Bass Publishers, 1999.

Alderman, Tracy, and Karen Marshall. *Amongst Ourselves, A Self-Help Guide to Living with Dissociative Identity Disorder.* Oakland, CA: New Harbinger Publications, 1998.

American Psychiatric Association. *Diagnostic and Statistical Manual of Mental Disorders.* 4th ed., Text rev. Washington, D.C.: American Psychiatric Association, 2000.

Saks, Elyn R., and Stephen H. Behnke. *Jekyll on Trial, Multipersonality Disorder and Criminal Law.* New York: New York University Press, 1997.

PERIODICALS

Gleaves, D. H., M. C. May, and E. Cardena. "An Examination of the Diagnostic Validity of Dissociative Identity Disorder." *Clinical Psychology Review* 21.4 (June 2001): 577–608.

Lalonde, J. K., and others. "Canadian and American Psychiatrists' Attitudes Toward Dissociative Disorders Diagnoses." *Canadian Journal of Psychiatry* 46.5 (June 2001): 407–12.

Spitzer, Carsten, and others. "Recent Developments in the Theory of Dissociation." *World Psychiatry* 5 (2006): 82–86.

Stickley, T., and R. Nickeas. "Becoming One Person: Living with Dissociative Identity Disorder." *Journal of Psychiatric and Mental Health Nursing* 13 (2006): 180–87.

ORGANIZATIONS

American Psychiatric Association. 1400 K Street NW, Washington, DC 20005. Telephone: (888) 357-7924. Fax: (202) 682-6850.

International Society for the Study of Dissociation. 60 Revere Drive, Suite 500, Northbrook, IL 60062. <http://www.issd.org/>.

National Alliance for the Mentally Ill. Colonial Place Three, 2107 Wilson Boulevard, Suite 300, Arlington, VA 22021. <http://www.nami.org/helpline/did.html>.

OTHER

The Mayo Clinic. "Dissociative Disorders." <http://www.mayoclinic.com/health/dissociative-disorders/DS00574/DSECTION=5>.

Merck Manual for Healthcare Professionals. The Merck Manuals Online Medical Library. "Dissociative Identity Disorder." 2005.

Rebecca J. Frey, PhD
Dean A. Haycock, PhD
Emily Jane Willingham, PhD

Disulfiram

Definition

Disulfiram is an aldehyde dehydrogenase inhibitor. It prohibits the activity of aldehyde dehydrogenase, an enzyme found in the liver. In the United States, disulfiram is sold under brand name Antabuse.

Purpose

Disulfiram is used as a conditioning treatment for alcohol dependence. When taken with alcohol, disulfiram causes many unwanted and unpleasant effects, and the fear of these is meant to condition the patient to avoid alcohol.

Description

Two Danish physicians who were investigating disulfiram for its potential benefits to destroy parasitic worms took disulfiram and became sick at a cocktail party. After a series of pharmacological and clinical studies, it was determined that disulfiram interacts with alcohol.

Disulfiram by itself is not toxic. If taken with alcohol, however, it alters certain steps in the breakdown of alcohol. When alcohol is ingested, it is converted first to a chemical called acetaldehyde. Acetaldehyde is further broken down into acetate. In order for acetaldehyde to be broken down into acetate, aldehyde dehydrogenase needs to be active. Disulfiram is an aldehyde dehydrogenase inhibitor. Since disulfiram blocks the activity of aldehyde dehydrogenase, acetaldehyde cannot be broken down and the levels of acetaldehyde become five to ten times higher than the normal levels. This causes uncomfortable effects that encourage the person to avoid alcohol.

Disulfiram comes in a 250- and 500-mg tablet.

Recommended dosage

Disulfiram therapy should be started only after the patient has abstained from alcohol for at least 12 hours. The initial dose may be as high as 500 mg taken once daily. If the medication is sedating, the dose can be administered in the evening. Ideally, though, the daily dose should be taken in the morning—the time the resolve not to drink may be strongest. The initial dosing period can last for one to two weeks.

A maintenance dose can range anywhere from 125–500 mg daily with the average dose being 250 mg daily. Disulfiram therapy should continue until full recovery. This may take months to years, depending upon the patient's response and motivation to stop using alcohol. The duration of disulfiram's activity is 14 days after discontinuation, and patients need to avoid alcohol for this period of time.

Precautions

Before beginning therapy, patients should be carefully evaluated for their intellectual capacity to understand the goal of therapy, which can be described as behavioral modification with negative **reinforcement**. Patients with history of **psychosis**, severe myocardial disease, and coronary occlusion should not take disulfiram. People with diabetes taking disulfiram are at an increased risk for complications. Severe liver failure has been associated with the use of disulfiram in patients with or without a prior history of liver problems. People with advanced or severe liver disease should not take disulfiram. Disulfiram should never be given to patients who are in a state of alcohol intoxication or without the patient's knowledge. Those patients with history of **seizures**, hypothyroidism, or nephritis need to use disulfiram with caution and close monitoring.

Besides avoiding alcohol, patients should also avoid any products containing alcohol. This includes many cold syrups, tonics, and mouthwashes. Patients

KEY TERMS

Coronary occlusion—Blockage of the arteries supplying the blood to the heart.

Hypothyroidism—Thyroid gland that is abnormally low-functioning. A lowered metabolic rate results.

Jaundice—A yellowing of the skin caused by excess bilirubin in the blood; a liver disorder.

MAO inhibitors—A group of antidepressant drugs that decrease the activity of monoamine oxidase, a neurotransmitter found in the brain that affects mood.

Myocardial disease—Disease of the muscular layer of the heart wall.

Nephritis—Inflammation of the kidney.

Psychosis—Severe state that is characterized by loss of contact with reality and deterioration in normal social functioning; examples are schizophrenia and paranoia. Psychosis is usually one feature of an overarching disorder, not a disorder in itself. (Plural: psychoses)

should not even use topical preparations that contain alcohol such as perfume and aftershave lotion.

Side effects

The most common side effect of disulfiram includes drowsiness and **fatigue**. Many patients experience metallic or garlic-like aftertaste, but most patients develop tolerance to this effect.

In addition, disulfiram is also associated with impotence. This is most common in doses of 500 mg daily. Disulfiram can also cause blurred vision, skin discoloration, inflammation of the skin, increased heart rate, and mental changes.

During the first three months of therapy, patients should have their liver function evaluated. Patients need to be monitored for the signs of jaundice, nausea, vomiting, abdominal pain, light stools, and dark urine as these may be the signs of liver damage due to disulfiram. The signs of alcohol ingestion include flushing, headache, nausea, vomiting and abdominal pain.

Interactions

Disulfiram can make cisapride, **benzodiazepines**, astemizole, cyclosporine, erythromycin, and cholesterol-lowering drugs called statins more toxic. Disul-

firam in combination with isoniazid, monoamine oxidase inhibitors (MAOIs) (such as phenelzide and **tranylcypromine**), metronidazole, omeprazole and tricyclic **antidepressants** may cause adverse central nervous system effects.

In addition, disulfiram may raise the concentrations of the medications theophylline and phenytoin in the body. Disulfiram may put patients on warfarin (a blood-thinning drug) at an increased risk of bleeding. Disulfiram should never be used with tranylcypromine and amprenavir oral solution.

Disulfiram may react even with small amounts of alcohol found in over-the-counter cough and cold preparations and any medication that comes in an elixir form.

Resources

BOOKS

Lacy, Charles. *Drug Information Handbook*. Hudson, OH: Lexi-Comp, 2002.

Taylor, David, Robert Kerwin, and Carol Paton. *The Maudsley 2005–2006 Prescribing Guidelines*. New York: Taylor and Francis, 2005.

PERIODICALS

Berglund, Mats. "A Better Widget? Three Lessons for Improving Addiction Treatment from a Meta-Analytical Study." *Addiction* 100.6 (June 2005): 742–50.

Boothby, Lisa, A., and Paul L. Doering. "Acamprosate for the Treatment of Alcohol Dependence." *Clinical Therapeutics: The International Peer-Reviewed Journal of Drug Therapy* 27.6 (June 2005): 695–714.

Buonopane, Alessandra, and Ismene L. Petrakis. "Pharmacotherapy of Alcohol Use Disorders." *Substance Use and Misuse* 40.13–14 (2005): 2001–20.

Krampe, Henning, and others. "Follow-Up of 180 Alcoholic Patients for Up to 7 Years After Outpatient Treatment: Impact of Alcohol Deterrents on Outcome." *Alcoholism: Clinical and Experimental Research* 30 (1) (Jan. 2006): 86–95.

Kulig, Clark C., and Thomas P. Beresford. "Hepatitis C in Alcohol Dependence: Drinking Versus Disulfiram." *Journal of Addictive Diseases* 24.2 (2005): 77–89.

Nava, Felice, Stefania Premi, Ezio Manzato, and Alfio Lucchini. "Comparing Treatments of Alcoholism on Craving and Biochemical Measures of Alcohol Consumptions." *Journal of Psychoactive Drugs* 38.3 (Sept. 2006): 211–17.

Petrakis, Ismene L., and others. "Naltrexone and Disulfiram in Patients with Alcohol Dependence and Comorbid Psychiatric Disorders." *Biological Psychiatry* 57.10 (May 2005): 1128–37.

Sofuoglu, Mehmet, and Thomas R. Kosten. "Novel Approaches to the Treatment of Cocaine Addiction." *CNS Drugs* 19.1 (2005): 13–25.

Suh, Jesse J., Helen M. Pettinati, Kyle M. Kampman, and Charles P. O'Brien. "The Status of Disulfiram: A Half of a Century Later." *Journal of Clinical Psychopharmacology* 26.3 (June 2006): 290–302.

OTHER

Wyeth-Ayerst Laboratories Staff. "Product Information: Antabuse, Disulfiram Tablets." Philadelphia: Wyeth-Ayerst Laboratories, 2000.

Ajna Hamidovic, Pharm.D.
Ruth A. Wienclaw, PhD

Divalproex sodium

Definition

Divalproex sodium is an anticonvulsant (anti-seizure) drug. It is also used to treat mania and to help prevent migraine headaches. It is sold under multiple brand names in the United States, including Depacon, Depakene, Depakote, and Depakote sprinkle.

Purpose

Divalproex sodium is effective in the treatment of epilepsy, particularly for preventing simple, complex (petit mal), absence, mixed, and tonic-clonic (grand mal) **seizures**. Divalproex sodium is also used to treat the manic phase of **bipolar disorder** (also called manic-depressive disorder) in adults, and to prevent migraine headache in adults.

Description

Divalproex sodium is chemically compounded from sodium valproate and **valproic acid** in a 1:1 ratio.

Divalproex sodium is thought to work by increasing the levels of a **brain** neurotransmitter called gamma-aminobutyric acid (GABA). GABA is an inhibitory neurotransmitter, which means that its presence makes it harder for nerve cells (neurons) in the brain to become activated (fire). It is believed that increasing GABA's inhibitory action on brain neurons accounts for the ability of divalproex sodium to decrease seizures, curb manic behaviors, and decrease the frequency of migraine headaches.

Divalproex sodium was discovered to decrease the likelihood of seizure in 1963. In 1978, the United States Food and Drug Administration approved it for this use. Other uses for divalproex sodium were researched and approved subsequently, including use against mania (1995) and use to decrease migraine headache frequency. Divalproex sodium's 1995 approval as an anti-mania medication was considered

an exciting advance, since it represented the first new drug introduced for this use in 25 years.

Recommended dosage

Divalproex sodium is available in tablets of 125 mg, 250 mg, and 500 mg. Divalproex sodium is also available in 125-mg capsules, and in a 500-mg extended release tablet. A syrup is also available, containing 250 mg active drug per 5 mL.

Divalproex sodium therapy is usually started at 10–15 mg per kg of body weight per day. Dosages are then increased until seizures seem to be well controlled. This is usually achieved at averages under 60 mg per kg per day.

To treat mania, divalproex sodium is usually started at a daily dose of about 750 mg.

For migraine prevention, divalproex sodium is started at 250 mg, twice per day. In some patients, this dose will have to be raised to a total of 1,000 mg per day.

Precautions

A greater risk of liver damage exists in patients with kidney disease, known liver disease, Addison's disease, blood diseases, children under the age of two, patients with organic brain diseases (such as Alzheimer's, Parkinson's, slow virus infections, Huntington's chorea, multiple sclerosis, etc.), patients with metabolic disorders present at birth, patients with severe seizure disorders and accompanying **mental retardation**, and patients who are taking several other anticonvulsant drugs.

Because divalproex sodium can affect a patient's blood by dropping the platelet (a type of blood cell that affects clotting) count and interfering with coagulation (clotting) capability, both platelet count and coagulation parameters should be verified before starting the medication and at intervals throughout its use.

Divalproex sodium is known to cause an increased risk of birth defects when taken during pregnancy. An individual and her health care provider must weight the potential risks and benefits of using this medication during pregnancy. Women who take this medicine should not breast-feed, since a small amount will pass into the breast milk

Divalproex sodium causes drowsiness and impairs alertness in some individuals. Patients just beginning to use the medication should avoid driving and using dangerous machinery until they determine how the drug affects them. The sedative effects are increased in the presence of alcohol, so patients should avoid drinking while taking medicines containing divalproex sodium.

KEY TERMS

Absence seizure—An epileptic seizure characterized by a sudden, momentary loss of consciousness, occasionally accompanied by some minor, jerky movements in the neck or upper arms, a twitching of the face, or a loss of muscle tone.

Addison's disease—Disease caused by malfunctioning adrenal glands that can be treated with cortisol replacement therapy. Symptoms include anemia, low blood pressure, digestive complaints, and diarrhea.

Alzheimer's disease—An incurable dementia marked by the loss of cognitive ability and memory over a period of 10–15 years. Usually affects elderly people.

Complex seizure—In complex seizures, the person experiences impaired consciousness.

Huntington's disease—A hereditary disorder that appears in middle age and is characterized by gradual brain deterioration, progressive dementia, and loss of voluntary movement. It is sometimes called Huntington's chorea.

Multiple sclerosis—A disease characterized by patches of hardened tissue in the brain or spinal cord, paralysis, and/or muscle tremors.

Neurons—Nerve cells in the brain that produce nerve impulses.

Neurotransmitter—A chemical in the brain that transmits messages between neurons, or nerve cells.

Parkinson's disease—A disease of the nervous system most common in people over 60, characterized by a shuffling gait, trembling of the fingers and hands, and muscle stiffness.

Simple seizure—Simple partial seizures occur in patients who are conscious.

Tonic-clonic (grand mal) seizure—This is the most common type of seizure and is categorized into several phases beginning with vague symptoms hours or days before an attack. During the seizure, there is abnormal muscle contraction and relaxation and the individual may lose consciousness.

Side effects

Some of the more common side effects of divalproex sodium include mild stomach cramps, change in menstrual cycle, diarrhea, loss of hair, indigestion, decreased appetite, nausea and vomiting, trembling in the hands and arms, and weight loss or weight gain. These side effects usually go away as the patient's body becomes accustomed to the medication.

Less common side effects include severe stomach cramps or continued nausea and vomiting, changes in mood, behavior, or thinking, double vision or seeing spots, severe **fatigue**, easy bruising or unusual bleeding, yellow cast to the skin or the whites of the eyes (jaundice), odd eye movements, and increased seizures. Patients who notice these symptoms should check with their doctor to see if their dosage or medication needs to be adjusted.

Rare side effects that should be checked out by a doctor include clumsiness, difficulty with balance, constipation, dizziness, drowsiness, headache, skin rash, agitation, restlessness, or irritability.

Interactions

Divalproex sodium is broken down (metabolized) in the liver. Other drugs that are metabolized in the liver can have too low or too high concentrations in the body when taken with divalproex sodium. Levels of divalproex sodium may be increased when taken with felbamate, isoniazid, salicylates (aspirin-containing medications), clarithromycin, erythromycin, and troleandomycin. Divalproex sodium may increase levels of **carbamazepine**, phenytoin, **lamotrigine**, nimodipine, phenobarbital, and zidovudine. Use with **clonazepam** may cause absence seizures. Cholestyramine and colestipol may reduce the absorption and the blood levels of divalproex sodium.

Resources

BOOKS

Mosby's Drug Consult. St. Louis: Mosby, Inc., 2002.
Ellsworth, Allan J., and others. *Mosby's Medical Drug Reference.* St. Louis: Mosby, Inc., 1999.

Rosalyn Carson-DeWitt, M.D.

Dolophine *see* **Methadone**

Domestic abuse *see* **Abuse**

Domestic violence *see* **Abuse**

Donepezil

Definition

Donepezil is a drug used to treat mild to moderate **dementia**. In the United States, donepezil is sold under the trade name Aricept.

Purpose

Donepezil is used to help treat symptoms in individuals with mild to moderate **Alzheimer's disease**. The drug may cause small improvements in dementia for a short period of time, but donepezil does not stop the progression of Alzheimer's disease.

Description

The U.S. Food and Drug Administration (FDA) has approved donepezil for treatment of the symptoms of Alzheimer's disease. In Alzheimer's disease, some cells in specific regions of the **brain** die. Because of this cell death, these brain cells lose their ability to transmit nerve impulses. Brain cells normally transmit nerve impulses by secreting various chemicals known as **neurotransmitters**.

Brain cells that make and secrete a neurotransmitter called acetylcholine are affected early in the course of Alzheimer's disease. Donepezil helps prevent the breakdown of acetylcholine in the brain, thus temporarily increasing its concentration. In doing so, donepezil may improve the thinking process by facilitating nerve impulse transmission within the brain.

Donepezil is available as tablets in two different strengths. It is broken down by the liver.

Recommended dosage

The initial dosage of donepezil is 5 mg taken at bedtime. This dose should be continued for four to six weeks. The dosage may then be increased to 10 mg at bedtime, but there is no clear evidence that the higher dosage is more beneficial. However, the higher dosage is likely to cause more side effects.

Precautions

Donepezil may slow heart rate, increase acid in the stomach, make urination difficult, cause breathing difficulties, and may make it more likely for people to have **seizures**. Therefore, people with certain heart conditions, those who are prone to stomach ulcers, people with bladder obstruction, individuals with asthma or chronic obstructive pulmonary disease, and people with a history of seizure disorders should use donepezil carefully under close physician supervision.

People taking donepezil should be reassessed periodically to determine whether the drug is providing any benefits. When caregivers feel the drug is no longer beneficial, it may be stopped.

Side effects

More than 5% of people taking donepezil experience difficulty sleeping, dizziness, nausea, diarrhea, muscle cramps, headache, or other pains.

Diarrhea, nausea, and vomiting occur more often with the 10-mg dose than the 5-mg dosage. These adverse effects are usually mild, short-lived, and typically subside when the drug is stopped. Other less common side effects are abnormal dreams, **depression**, drowsiness, fainting, loss of appetite, weight loss, frequent urination, arthritis, and easy bruising.

Interactions

Recent research has found that the effects of donepezil on Alzheimer's disease may be enhanced through combination therapy with **memantine** (Namenda). According to a study in the *Journal of the American Medical Association* in 2004, studies have shown that the use of memantine in combination therapy with donepezil is frequently more effective than the use of donepezil alone in the treatment of moderate to severe Alzheimer's disease. Using memantine and donepezil in combination therapy does not affect the pharmacokinetics of either drug. **Clinical trials** have shown such combination therapy to be both safe and effective, although the safety precautions for both drugs must be considered before combination therapy is undertaken.

Many drugs may alter the effects of donepezil; likewise, donepezil may alter the action of other drugs. Drugs such as dicyclomine, phenytoin, **carbamazepine**, dexamethasone, rifampin, or phenobarbital may lessen the effects of donepezil. Other drugs such as bethanechol, ketoconazole, or quinidine may increase some of the side effects associated with donepezil. When donepezil and nonsteroidal anti-inflammatory drugs such as ibuprofen (Advil) or naproxen (Aleve) are used together, there may be an increased tendency to develop stomach ulcers. Donepezil may increase the side effects associated with use of **fluvoxamine**, an antidepressant. If succinylcholine, a drug commonly used during anesthesia, is used with donepezil, prolonged muscle paralysis may result.

Resources

BOOKS

Facts and Comparisons Staff. *Drug Facts and Comparisons.* 6th ed. St. Louis: Facts and Comparisons, 2002.

Mosby Staff. *Mosby's Medical Drug Reference.* St. Louis, MO: Mosby, 1999.

VandenBos, Gary R., ed. *APA Dictionary of Psychology.* Washington, D.C.: American Psychological Association, 2007.

PERIODICALS

Asp, Elissa, and others. "Verbal Repetition in Patients with Alzheimer's Disease Who Receive Donepezil." *International Journal of Geriatric Psychiatry* 21.5 (May 2006): 426–31.

Chen, Xiying, and others. "Donepezil Effects on Cerebral Blood Flow in Older Adults with Mild Cognitive Deficits." *Journal of Neuropsychiatry & Clinical Neurosciences* 18.2 (Sept. 2006): 178–85.

Cholongitas, Evangelos, Chrysoula Pipili, and Maria Dasenaki. "Recurrence of Upper Gastrointestinal Bleeding After Donepezil Administration." *Alzheimer Disease and Associated Disorders* 20.4 (Oct.–Dec. 2006): 326.

Cummings, Jeffrey L., Thomas McRae, and Richard Zhang. "Effects of Donepezil on Neuropsychiatric Symptoms in Patients with Dementia and Severe Behavioral Disorders." *American Journal of Geriatric Psychiatry* 14.7 (July 2006): 605–12.

Feldman, Howard H., Frederick A. Schmitt, and Jason T. Olin. "Activities of Daily Living in Moderate-to-Severe Alzheimer Disease: An Analysis of the Treatment Effects of Memantine in Patients Receiving Stable Donepezil Treatment." *Alzheimer Disease and Associated Disorders* 20.4 (Oct.–Dec. 2006): 263–68.

Hogan, David B. "Donepezil for Severe Alzheimer's Disease." *Lancet* 367.9516 (Apr. 2006): 1031–32.

Kitabayashi, Yurinosuke, and others. "Donepezil-Induced Nightmares in Mild Cognitive Impairment." *Psychiatry and Clinical Neurosciences* 60.1 (Feb. 2006): 123–24.

Maruyama, Masahiro, and others. "Benefits of Combining Donepezil Plus Traditional Japanese Herbal Medicine on Cognition and Brain Perfusion in Alzheimer's Disease: A 12-Week Observer-Blind, Donepezil Monotherapy Controlled Trial." *Journal of the American Geriatrics Society* 54.5 (May 2006): 867–71.

Mazeh, D., and others. "Donepezil for Negative Signs in Elderly Patients with Schizophrenia: An Add-On, Double-Blind, Crossover, Placebo-Controlled Study." *International Psychogeriatrics* 18.3 (Sept. 2006): 429–36.

Ringman, John M., and Jeffrey L. Cummings. "Current and Emerging Pharmacological Treatment Options For Dementia." *Behavioural Neurology* 17.1 (2006): 5–16.

Schredl, M., and others. "The Effect of Donepezil on Sleep in Elderly, Healthy Persons: A Double-Blind Placebo-Controlled Study." *Pharmacopsychiatry* 39.6 (Nov. 2006): 205–208.

Stiles, Melissa M., and Sandra Martin. "Does Treatment with Donepezil Improve Memory for Patients With Mild Cognitive Impairment?" *Journal of Family Practice* 55.5 (May 2006): 435–36.

Tariot, Pierre N., and others. "Memantine Treatment in Patients with Moderate to Severe Alzheimer Disease Already Receiving Donepezil: A Randomized Controlled Trial." *Journal of the American Medical Association* 291 (2004): 317–24.

Winblad, Bengt, and others. "Donepezil in Patients with Severe Alzheimer's Disease: Double-Blind, Parallel-Group, Placebo-Controlled Study." *Lancet* 367.9516 (Apr. 2006): 1057–65.

Wong, Shelley. "The Safety of Donepezil in Treating Vascular Dementia." *CNS Spectrums* 11.9 (Sept. 2006): 658–61.

OTHER

Eisai Co., Ltd. *Aricept Prescribing Information.* <http://www.aricept.com/content/pi.pdf>.

Kelly Karpa, R.Ph., PhD
Ruth A. Wienclaw, PhD

Dopamine

Definition

Dopamine, identified as a central nervous system agent in 1959, is a neurotransmitter (nerve-signaling molecule) the body makes from the amino acid tyrosine. Dopamine in turn serves as the molecule the body uses to make **adrenaline** and noradrenaline. In addition to operating in nervous system signaling, it also acts as a hormone in an area of the **brain** called the hypothalamus, regulating release of the hormone prolactin, which is involved in parenting behavior and milk production. The body regulates dopamine' activity in the brain in part by using proteins called dopamine transporters, which can take up dopamine and dump it back into a cell, preventing the signaling molecule from exerting its activity. The body also has five types of proteins, called dopamine receptors, responsible for recognizing the dopamine molecule, binding to it, and transmitting its signal to the cell. Dopamine is at the center of the development of a number of psychiatric disorders, including **addiction** and **schizophrenia**, and it also plays a prominent role in the manifestations of Parkinson's disease.

Description

The brain produces dopamine in three primary areas: the substantia nigra, the ventral tegmental area, and the arcuate nucleus. The first two are of particular interest in terms of psychiatric disorders; the arcuate nucleus is associated with dopamine's role as a neurohormone in prolactin regulation.

Disorders associated with dopamine signaling have a biological basis in the brain that appears to be site-specific. The brain has four major dopamine-signaling pathways.

- The mesocortical pathway connects the ventral tegmental area to the cortex, the part of the brain involved in cognition and that may play a role in motivation. This pathway features in hypotheses of dopamine's association with schizophrenia.

- The mesolimbic pathway also begins in the ventral tegmental area, which is linked to the nucleus accumbens, the largest component of the ventral striatum. Much research has associated the nucleus accumbens and the mesolimbic pathway with brain reward processes and addiction and also with different aspects of schizophrenia.

- The nigrostriatal pathway connects the dopamine-producing nigrostriatal area with the striatum and plays a high-profile role in the development of Parksinon's symptoms.

- The tuberoinfundibular pathway involves the hypothalamus and dopamine as a neurohormone.

In terms of neuropsychiatric disorders, dopamine is probably best known as the neurotransmitter underlying the development and persistence of addiction as part of the mesolimbic reward pathway. In brief, experiences we find rewarding, such as food or sex, can become associated with increased dopamine, as can some pathological behaviors, such as compulsive gambling. Some drugs also directly elicit an increase in dopamine, setting off the reward pathway and leading more use of the drug. Ultimately, some people become addicted to substances or behaviors because of the dopamine release they trigger and the feelings of euphoria or tension relief that can follow the release.

Anatomically, these distinct dopamine-signaling pathways, variously involved in specific pathologies, may overlap with one another. For example, there is some comorbidity among schizophrenia, **depression**, and drug dependence and some anatomical overlap in the dopamine-signaling areas of the brain underlies this.

Dopamine receptors

The dopamine receptors, the five proteins responsible for receiving the dopamine signal for a cell, are divided into two general classes: those that are D1-like, and those that are D2-like. Of the five, the D1A through D1D and D5 receptors are all D1-like, and the D2, D3, and D4 receptors fall into the D2-like category. The distribution of these receptors differs in different dopamine-related areas of the brain. For example, the ventral striatum and limbic cortex of the mesolimbic pathway have more D2-like receptors, and D2 and D4 receptors are more closely associated with people with **substance abuse** problems. The dorsal striatum, involved in dopamine-related disorders such as Parkinson's, has more also D2- than D1-like receptors. But in the prefrontal cortex, where dopamine-signaling dysfunction is associated with schizophrenia, the ratio of D1-like receptors to D2-like receptors is higher. The two general classes of receptors have opposite effects at the molecular level, but they act together in complex ways.

Dopamine and schizophrenia

A much-discussed proposed explanation for the manifestations of schizophrenia is the "dopamine hypothesis of schizophrenia." This hypothesis implicates dopamine-signaling dysfunction along different dopamine pathways in the symptoms associated with schizophrenia. The hypothesis finds its origins in the fact that antipsychotic medications (also called "neuroleptics") exert their effects by blocking or inhibiting D2 receptors. The mesolimbic pathway may be involved, a conclusion based on studies showing a link between dysfunction of this system and the **delusions** and **hallucinations** of schizophrenia, with an increase in striatal dopamine in association with these occurrences. On the other hand, the mesocortical pathway is also probably involved because of its role in working memory, memorization, and manipulation of spatial information, all of which are affected in schizophrenia. A decrease in dopamine in the prefrontal area, which is linked to the ventral tegmental area in the mesocortical pathway, appears to lead to the cognitive deficits of schizophrenia. In addition, the nigrostriatal pathway may be involved: there is an increase in dopamine transmission from the substantia nigra to the striatum in people with schizophrenia.

Dopamine, the brain reward system, and addiction

The nucleus accumbens (in the ventral striatum and part of the mesolimbic pathway) is the focal point of dopamine's involvement in the brain's reward pathway and addiction. There is an increase in dopamine release in the nucleus accumbens in addiction, and activity in this area is a target of models exploring the mechanisms of behavioral or substance addictions. Human **imaging studies**, which have become quite revelatory in terms of the biological underpinnings of psychiatric disorders, show that endogenous release of dopamine in the striatum is correlated with drug-induced feelings of pleasure. For example, a dose of amphetamine or of alcohol will promote dopamine release in the ventral striatum. Dopamine also is associated with the cravings of addiction and may play a role in the significance an addicted person may assign to cues that others perceive as neutral (known as salience). This system has also been implicated in process or behavioral addiction.

Dopamine and movement and repetitive disorders

Dopamine's role in the extrapyramidal (movement and coordination) symptoms of Parkinson's is seated in a shortage of the neurotransmitter in the nigrostriatal pathway, specifically involving the putamen and caudate nucleus. Tourette's, a syndrome characterized by onset in childhood, involuntary tics, stereotypic behaviors, and repetitive thoughts and rituals, is also seated in the dorsal striatum. This syndrome can occur as a comorbidity with **obsessive-compulsive disorder** and/or **attention deficit/hyperactivity disorder** (ADHD), which some studies also have associated with dopamine-signaling dysfunction.

Dopamine and mood disorders

Changes in dopamine signaling may contribute to symptoms of depression, such as an inability to expe-

---

KEY TERMS

D1, D2, etc.—Dopamine receptor proteins.

Dopamine—A neurotransmitter and neurohormone.

Mesolimbic pathway—The "reward pathway" of the brain.

Nucleus accumbens—A part of the brain involved in the mesolimbic reward pathway, which receives dopamine signaling from the ventral tegmental area.

Ventral tegmental area—Produces dopamine and signals to the nucleus accumbens the rest of the striatum.

---

rience pleasure or loss of motivation. Although low levels of dopamine binding to the D2 receptor are associated with social **anxiety**, an increase in dopamine can be associated with the hypersocial behavior of someone experiencing the manic aspects of **bipolar disorder**.

Drugs related to dopamine/dopamine receptor regulation

Drugs may act at any point along a dopamine-signaling pathway. L-dopa, used in treating Parkinson's, is a dopamine precursor that is synthesized into dopamine in the brain and ameliorates the effects of low dopamine levels in the dorsal striatum. Monoamine oxidase inhibitors (MAOIs) block the activity of the enzyme that breaks down dopamine; these may be used as **antidepressants** and can affect dopamine-related pathways. Antipsychotics are divided into two classes, the typical and atypical antipsychotics, and can target different types of dopamine receptors. Atypical antipsychotics, including **clozapine**, may target the D4 receptor more strongly than the D2. Bromocriptine targets D2 and is a partial inhibitor of D1. The recently approved aripirprazole is a partial dopamine agonist (mimic), and **amantadine** is also a dopamine agonist.

Resources

BOOKS

American Psychiatric Association. *Diagnostic and Statistical Manual of Mental Disorders*, 4th edition, Text revision. Washington, D.C.: American Psychiatric Association, 2000.

PERIODICALS

Franken, Ingmar H.A., Jan Booij, and Wim van den Brink. "The Role of Dopamine in Human Addiction: From

---

Reward to Motivated Attention." *European Journal of Pharmacology* 526 (2005): 199–206.

Grant, Jon E., J.D., M.D., M.P.H., Judson A. Brewer, M.D., Ph.D., and Marc N. Potenza, M.D., Ph.D. "The Neurobiology of Substance and Behavioral Addictions." *CNS Spectrum* 11 (2006): 924–930.

Greene, James G. "Gene Expression Profiles of Brain Dopamine Neurons and Relevance to Neuropsychiatric Disease." *Journal of Physiology* 575 (2006): 411–416.

Kienast, T., and A. Heinz. "Dopamine and the Diseased Brain." *CNS and Neurological Disorders-Drug Targets* 5 (2006): 109–131.

Totterdell, Susan. "The Anatomy of Comorbid Neuropsychiatric Disorders Based on Cortico-limbic Synaptic Interactions." *Neurotoxicity Research* 10 (2006): 65–86.

OTHER

"Schizophrenia." National Institutes of Mental Health. (Janaury 15 2007) <http://www.nimh.nih.gov/health informa tion/schizophreniamenu.cfm>.

"Schizophrenia." National Library of Medicine. (Janaury 15 2007) <http://www.nlm.nih.gov/medlineplus/schizophrenia.html>.

Emily Jane Willingham, Ph.D.

Doral *see* **Quazepam**

Doxepin

Definition

Doxepin is an oral antidepressant. It is sold in the United States under the brand name Sinequan and is also available under its generic name.

Purpose

Doxepin is used primarily to treat **depression** and to treat the combination of symptoms of **anxiety** and depression. Like most **antidepressants**, doxepin has also been used to treat **panic disorder**, **obsessive-compulsive disorder**, attention-deficit/hyperactivity disorder, **enuresis** (bed-wetting), eating disorders such as **bulimia nervosa**, **cocaine** dependency, and the depressive phase of bipolar (manic-depressive) disorder. It has also been used to support **smoking cessation** programs.

Description

Doxepin acts to change the balance of naturally occurring chemicals in the **brain** that regulate the transmission of nerve impulses between cells. Its action primarily increases the concentration of nore-

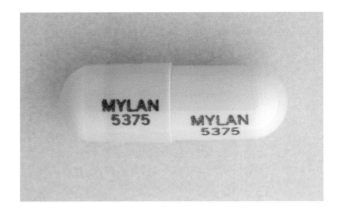

A doxepin tablet. *(Custom Medical Stock Photo, Inc. Reproduced by permission.)*

pinephrine and serotonin (both chemicals that stimulate nerve cells) and, to a lesser extent, blocks the action of another brain chemical, acetylcholine. Although not technically a tricyclic antidepressant, doxepin shares most of the properties of these drugs, which include **amitriptyline**, **clomipramine**, **desipramine**, **imipramine**, **nortriptyline**, **protriptyline**, and **trimipramine**. Studies comparing doxepin with these other drugs have shown that doxepin is no more or less effective than other antidepressants of its type. Its choice for treatment is as much a function of physician preference as any other factor.

The therapeutic effects of doxepin, like other antidepressants, appear slowly. Maximum benefit is often not evident for at least two weeks after starting the drug. People taking doxepin should be aware of this and continue taking the drug as directed even if they do not see immediate improvement.

Recommended dosage

As with any antidepressant, doxepin must be carefully adjusted by the physician to produce the desired therapeutic effect. Doxepin is available as 10-mg, 25-mg, 50-mg, 75-mg, 100-mg, and 150-mg oral capsules as well as an oral concentrate solution containing 10 mg of drug in each milliliter of solution.

Therapy is usually started at 30–150 mg per day and gradually increased to 300 mg daily if needed. There is little evidence that doses above 300 mg daily provide any additional benefits. Amounts up to 150 mg may be taken as a single dose at bedtime to decrease daytime sleepiness. Doses of more than 150 mg per day should be divided into two or three doses and taken throughout the day.

In patients over age 60, therapy should be maintained at the low end of the dosing range and increased cautiously and with physician supervision. Patients with organic brain syndrome (psychiatric symptoms of **dementia** often seen in elderly patients) generally require daily doses of only 25–50 mg.

If the oral concentrate of doxepin is used, each dose should be diluted in at least 4 oz (120 mL) of milk, orange, prune, tomato, pineapple, or grapefruit juice just before administration. Doxepin is not compatible with many carbonated beverages and should not be diluted in them.

Precautions

As with tricyclic antidepressants, doxepin should be used cautiously and with close physician supervision in people, especially the elderly, who have benign prostatic hypertrophy, urinary retention, and glaucoma, especially angle-closure glaucoma (the most severe form). Before starting treatment, people with these conditions should discuss the relative risks and benefits of treatment with their doctors to help determine if doxepin is the right antidepressant for them.

A common problem with antidepressants is sedation (drowsiness, lack of physical and mental alertness). This side effect is especially noticeable early in therapy. In most patients, sedation decreases or disappears entirely with time, but until then patients taking doxepin should not perform hazardous activities requiring mental alertness or coordination. The sedative effect is increased when doxepin is taken with other central nervous system depressants, such as alcoholic beverages, sleeping medications, other **sedatives**, or antihistamines. It may be dangerous to take doxepin in combination with these substances. Doxepin may increase the possibility of having **seizures**. Patients should tell their physician if they have a history of seizures, including seizures brought on by the **abuse** of drugs or alcohol. These people should use doxepin only with caution and be closely monitored by their physician.

Doxepin may increase heart rate and **stress** on the heart. It may be dangerous for people with cardiovascular disease, especially those who have recently had a heart attack, to take this drug or other antidepressants in the same pharmacological class. In rare cases where patients with cardiovascular disease must receive doxepin, they should be monitored closely for cardiac rhythm disturbances and signs of cardiac stress or damage.

Doxepin should not be taken by nursing mothers because it is secreted into breast milk and may cause side effects in the nursing infant.

Side effects

Doxepin shares the side effects of tricyclic antidepressants. The most frequent of these are dry mouth, constipation, urinary retention, increased heart rate, sedation, irritability, dizziness, and decreased coordination. As with most side effects associated with tricyclic antidepressants, the intensity is highest at the beginning of therapy and tends to decrease with continued use.

Dry mouth, if severe to the point of causing difficulty speaking or swallowing, may be managed by dosage reduction or temporary discontinuation of the drug. Patients may also chew sugarless gum or suck on sugarless candy in order to increase the flow of saliva. Some artificial saliva products may give temporary relief.

Men with prostate enlargement who take doxepin may be especially likely to have problems with urinary retention. Symptoms include having difficulty starting a urine flow and more difficulty than usual passing urine. In most cases, urinary retention is managed with dose reduction or by switching to another type of antidepressant. In extreme cases, patients may require treatment with bethanechol, a drug that reverses this particular side effect. People who think they may be experiencing any side effects from this or any other medication should tell their physicians.

Interactions

Dangerously high blood pressure has resulted from the combination of antidepressants such as doxepin and members of another class of antidepressants known as monoamine oxidase inhibitors (MAOIs). Because of this, doxepin should never be taken in combination with MAOIs. Patient's taking any MAOIs, for example Nardil (**phenelzine** sulfate) or Parmate (**tranylcypromine** sulfate), should stop the MAOI then wait at least 14 days before starting doxepin or any tricyclic antidepressant. The same holds true when discontinuing doxepin and starting an MAOI.

Doxepin may decrease the blood pressure-lowering effects of **clonidine**. Patients who take both drugs should be monitored for loss of blood-pressure control and the dose of clonidine increased as needed.

The sedative effects of doxepin are increased by other central nervous system depressants such as alcohol, sedatives, sleeping medications, or medications used for other mental disorders such as **schizophrenia**. The anticholinergic effects of doxepin are additive

Psychoactive Drug Therapy. Baltimore: Williams and Wilkins, 1990.

Jack Raber, Pharm.D.

Draw-a-person test *see* **Figure drawings**

DSM *see* **Diagnostic and Statistical Manual of Mental Disorders**

Dual diagnosis

Definition

Dual **diagnosis** is a term that refers to patients who have both a mental health disorder and substance use disorder. It may be used interchangeably with "co-occurring disorders" or "comorbidity." According to the U.S. **Substance Abuse** and Mental Health Services Administration (SAMHSA), an estimated 10 million people in the United States will have a combination of at least one mental health and one substance **abuse** disorder in any twelve-month period. Substance abuse is the most common and significant co-occurring disorder among adults with such severe mental illnesses as **schizophrenia** or **bipolar disorder**. It may also be observed in individuals with mental health diagnoses that include **depression**, **anxiety**, post traumatic **stress** disorder, or eating disorders. The term "substance abuse" refers to substance use disorders that range along a continuum from abuse to dependence or **addiction**.

The term "dual diagnosis" is considered to be misleading by some professionals because most people with this diagnosis actually have many problems rather than just two discrete illnesses. Occasionally, the term is used to describe a person with developmental disabilities and/or a mental health disorder or substance abuse disorder. More commonly, dual diagnosis refers to those with severe mental illness and a drug or alcohol abuse disorder, and who receive therapy in the public treatment systems.

Description

The prevalence of people with dual diagnoses became fully apparent to clinicians in the early 1980s. Initially, dual diagnoses were thought to be most likely in young adults with schizophrenia or bipolar disorder who also had extensive histories of drug or alcohol abuse. There was a widespread belief, often shared by family members of affected patients, that a young person's initiation into illegal drug use actually caused a subsequent mental illness. It is now more commonly

---

with other anticholinergic drugs such as **benztropine**, **biperiden**, **trihexyphenidyl**, and antihistamines.

See also Neurotransmitters.

Resources

BOOKS

American Society of Health-System Pharmacists. *AHFS Drug Information 2002*. Bethesda: American Society of Health-System Pharmacists, 2002.

DeVane, C. Lindsay, Pharm.D. "Drug Therapy for Mood Disorders." In *Fundamentals of Monitoring*

thought that symptoms of the mental disorder generally appear first, and that the abuse of drugs or alcohol may represent the patient's attempt to self-medicate and alleviate the troublesome symptoms that accompany mental health disorders.

Today it is clear that the co-occurrence of mental illness and substance abuse is common: about 50% of individuals with severe mental illnesses are affected by substance abuse. A dual diagnosis is also associated with a host of negative outcomes that may include higher rates of **relapse**, **hospitalization**, incarceration, violence, **homelessness**, and exposure to such serious infections as HIV and hepatitis.

Despite almost 20 years of evidence regarding the prevalence and serious illnesses of people with dual diagnoses, the United States mental health and substance abuse systems continue to operate on parallel tracks, causing additional confusion to those with concurrent disorders. Refusal to combine services to provide better coordinated treatment has meant unnecessary suffering and expense for thousands of patients and their families.

For many people with dual diagnoses, the criminal justice system—juvenile as well as adult—becomes their *de facto* treatment system. Nearly two-thirds of incarcerated youth with substance abuse disorders have at least one other mental health disorder. The common association between **conduct disorder** or **attention deficit/hyperactivity disorder** and substance abuse is one example of a combination of serious and disabling disorders. A person in need of treatment for dual diagnoses who is in the current criminal justice system may not be evaluated or assessed, let alone provided with appropriate treatment.

Demographics

Children of alcohol or other drug-addicted parents are at increased risk for developing substance abuse and mental health problems. Disruptive behavior disorders coexist with adolescent substance abuse problems more often than not. Other special groups that may be affected include older adults with mood or **anxiety disorders**, especially those who are grieving numerous losses. They may drink or misuse or abuse prescription drugs to cope with their lowered quality of life. These factors can often complicate treatment of hypertension, diabetes, arthritis, and other health-related problems that affect the elderly as well.

Abuse of alcohol or other drugs may occur in persons with eating disorders in an effort to deal with guilt, shame, anxiety, or feelings of self-loathing as a result of bingeing and purging food. Many military veterans develop anxiety, depression or **post-traumatic stress disorder** and have histories of substance abuse. Services for veterans are woefully inadequate, adding to the chronic nature of dual diagnosis among them.

Treatment

One of the difficulties in treating patients with dual diagnoses is that most treatments for mental illness are usually developed for and validated by studies of patients with single diagnoses; therefore, many cases of comorbidity may not be well treated by these approaches. Recent research on services provided to people with dual diagnoses, however, indicates that treatment can be successful, provided certain specific components are included in the treatment process. The critical elements identified as part of treatment programs with the most successful outcomes are:

- staged interventions that begin with engaging the client; persuading him or her to become involved in recovery-focused activities; acquiring skills and support to control the illnesses; and then helping the patient with relapse prevention.
- assertive outreach that may involve intensive case management and meetings in the person's home.
- motivational interventions to help the client become committed to self-management of their illnesses.
- counseling that includes cognitive and behavioral skills.
- social network support and/or family interventions.
- an understanding of the long-term nature of recovery.
- comprehensive scope to treatment that includes personal habits, stress management, friendship networks, housing, and many other aspects of a person's life.
- cultural sensitivity and competence.

The success of 12-step programs in the treatment of substance abuse is well established. Nevertheless, the level of confrontation sometimes found in a traditional 12-step group may feel overwhelming to people with mental illnesses. In addition, the use of psychotropic (mood- or behavior-altering) medications is controversial in some areas of the substance abuse recovery community. As a result, other models of consumer-led **support groups** specifically for people with concurrent disorders, such as Dual Recovery Anonymous and Double Trouble, are being developed.

Resources

BOOKS

Kranzler, H. R., and B. J. Rounsaville, eds. *Dual Diagnosis and Treatment: Substance Abuse and Comorbid Medical and Psychiatric Disorders*. New York: Marcel Dekker, Inc., 1998.

Pepper, Bert, and E. L. Hendrickson. *Developing a Cross Training Project for Substance Abuse, Mental Health and Criminal Justice Professionals Working with Offenders with Co-Existing Disorders (Substance Abuse/Mental Illness)*. New York City: The Information Exchange, 1998.

PERIODICALS

Drake, Robert E., M.D., PhD., Susan M. Essock, PhD., and others. "Implementing Dual Diagnosis Services for Clients with Severe Mental Illness." *Psychiatric Services* 52: (April 2001): 469-476.

Rach Beisel, Jill, M.D., Jack Scott, Sc.D. and Lisa Dixon, M.D., M.P.H. "Co-occuring Severe Mental Illness and Substance Use Disorders: A Review of Recent Research." *Psychiatric Services* 50: (November 1999) 1427-1434.

ORGANIZATIONS

National Alliance for the Mentally Ill (NAMI). 2107 Wilson Blvd., Suite 300, Arlington, VA 22201. <http://www.nami.org>.

National Mental Health Association. 1021 Prince St., Alexandria, VA 22314 <http://www.nmha.org>.

National Mental Health Consumers' Self-Help Clearinghouse. 1211 Chestnut St, Suite 1207, Philadelphia, PA 19107. <http://www.mhselfhelp.org>.

Judy Leaver, M.A.

Dyslexia *see* **Reading disorder**

Dyspareunia

Definition

Dyspareunia is painful sexual intercourse. The same term is used whether the pain results from a medical or a psychosocial problem. Dyspareunia may be diagnosed in men and women, although the **diagnosis** is rare in men; when it does occur in men, it is almost always caused by a physical problem.

Because of the prevalence of this problem among women in the context of psychosocial associations, only women's experiences are emphasized in this entry.

The professional's handbook, the ***Diagnostic and Statistical Manual of Mental Disorders***, fourth edition, text revised (known as the *DSM-IV-TR*), classifies this condition as a sexual dysfunction. There is considerably controversy about whether or not dyspareunia should continue to be classified as it has been in the *DSM-IV*, with some practitioners arguing for its reclassification in the *DSM-V* as a **pain disorder**.

Description

Dyspareunia is any pain experienced any time before, during, or following sexual intercourse. The pain may be located in the genitals or within the pelvis. It is not unusual for women to occasionally have pain during intercourse. This is not true dyspareunia.

A woman who has dyspareunia often also has **vaginismus**. Vaginismus is an involuntary tightening of the vaginal muscles in response to penetration. It can make intercourse painful or impossible.

Causes and symptoms

Causes

Psychosocial causes of dyspareunia include:

- prior sexual trauma. Many women who have been raped or sexually abused as children may have dyspareunia. Even when a woman wishes to have sex with someone later, the act of intercourse may trigger memories of the trauma and interfere with her enjoyment of the act. Vaginismus often occurs in such situations.

- guilt, anxiety, or tension about sex. Any of these can cause tense vaginal muscles and also prevent arousal from occurring. People who were raised with the idea that sex is bad may be more prone to have this problem. Fear of pregnancy may make arousal difficult.

- prior physical trauma to the vaginal area. Women who have had an accidental injury or surgery in the vaginal area may become sensitive to penetration. Vaginismus is common in these cases.

- depression or anxiety in general. Either of these can lead to loss of interest in sex. This can be experienced by either sex.

- problems in a relationship. Dyspareunia may occur when a woman feels her sexual partner is abusive or emotionally distant, she is no longer attracted to her partner, or she fears her partner is no longer attracted to her. Men, too, can lose interest in sex because of prior emotional trauma in a relationship; however, the result is usually impotence, rather than dyspareunia.

- vasocongestion, which can occur when either partner frequently becomes aroused but does not reach orgasm. Vasocongestion is a pooling of blood in dilated blood vessels. Normally, the pelvic area becomes congested with blood when a person becomes sexually aroused. This congestion goes away quickly after orgasm. If there is no orgasm, the congestion takes much longer to resolve.

Any of these factors may cause painful sex. The affected person may then associate pain with sex and find it even harder to relax and become aroused in the future.

Symptoms

The *DSM-IV* diagnostic criteria for dyspareunia are as follows:

- recurrent or persistent genital pain associated with sexual intercourse in either a male or a female.
- the disturbance causes marked distress or interpersonal difficulty.
- the disturbance is not caused exclusively by vaginismus or lack of lubrication, is not better accounted for by another Axis I disorder (except another sexual dysfunction), and is not due exclusively to the direct physiological effects of a substance (such as a drug of abuse or a medication) or a general medical condition.

The most common symptom of dyspareunia from psychosocial causes is pain at the vaginal opening as the penis enters the vagina. Entry may be difficult, and the pain may be burning or sharp. The woman may have a sense of being "dry." Pain may continue or ease as thrusting continues.

Vasocongestion can cause an aching pain in the pelvic area that persists for hours after intercourse. Pain with orgasm, or pain deep in the pelvis with thrusting, is more likely to be a sign of a medical problem but can result from lack of arousal and tension.

A person who experiences pain during sex may feel embarrassed or ashamed. Dyspareunia can cause problems in relationships or lead to the affected person's avoiding relationships altogether.

Demographics

About 15% of women may have pain with intercourse at some point in their lives. About 1–2% have true dyspareunia. The incidence is much higher in women who have been raped or otherwise sexually abused. As stated, dyspareunia in men is rare.

Diagnosis

About 30% to 40% of all women who seek help from a sexual counselor for dyspareunia will have a clear physical cause identified as the reason for their pain. Examples of possible physical causes are infections, sexually transmitted diseases (STDs), estrogen deficiencies, and vulvar vestibulitis (severe pain during vaginal penetration).

A full family and sexual history can help pinpoint possible psychosocial causes. A psychological evaluation can determine the cause of the problem. Women who have been raped or abused may also have **post-traumatic stress disorder** (PTSD) or **generalized anxiety disorder**.

There are two types of dyspareunia. Lifelong or primary dyspareunia means that the condition has been present for the entire sexual life of the affected person. This type is usually associated with sexual abuse, being raised to believe that sex is bad, fear of sex, or a painful first sexual experience. Acquired or secondary dyspareunia begins after a period of normal sexual function. It often has a medical cause, but it may be a result of some sort of trauma, such as rape.

Treatments

Some studies have found that treatments that approach dyspareunia that results from vulvar vestibulitis syndrome as a pain disorder, rather than as a sexual dysfunction, are quite effective in reducing the symptoms of pain.

Counseling is often helpful to identify and reframe negative feelings about sex. **Couples therapy** can help improve communication between partners and resolve problems that may be a factor in the sexual relationship. Women who have been abused or raped may benefit from counseling techniques designed to help overcome fears and issues caused by traumatic experiences.

Sex therapy may be offered to provide information about the physical aspects of arousal and orgasm. A sex therapist will also offer suggestions for how to improve sexual technique. For example, increasing time for foreplay and allowing the woman to control when and how penetration occurs can help her to relax and become aroused more easily.

Women who also have vaginismus may be given a set of devices they can use at home to dilate the opening of the vagina. Affected women start with a very small device and gradually work up to a penis-sized device, proceeding to a larger size only when they can use the smaller one without pain or fear. This retrains the vaginal muscles and helps the involuntary muscle tightening of vaginismus.

Use of a vaginal lubricant, at least temporarily, may be helpful in some women to reduce anxiety about possible pain.

There are no specific medications that treat dyspareunia. Medications that increase blood flow or relax muscles may be helpful in some cases.

KEY TERMS

Dyspareunia—Painful sexual intercourse.

Vaginismus—An involuntary tightening of the vaginal muscles that makes sexual intercourse painful, difficult, or impossible.

Vasocongestion—A pooling of blood in dilated blood vessels.

Vulvar vestibulitis syndrome (VVS)—Vulvar vestibulitis syndrome is thought to be the most frequent cause of dyspareunia in premenopausal women. A chronic, persistent clinical syndrome, vulvar vestibulitis is characterized by severe pain on vestibular touch or attempted vaginal entry.

Prognosis

With treatment, the chance of overcoming dyspareunia and having an enjoyable sexual life is good. Treatment can take several months, particularly in the case of survivors of a violent trauma such as rape.

See also Erectile dysfunction; Post-traumatic stress disorder.

Resources

BOOKS

Hales Robert E., Stuart C. Yudofsky, and John A. Talbott, eds. *The American Psychiatric Press Textbook of Psychiatry*. 3rd ed. Washington, D.C.: American Psychiatric Press, 1999.

Sadock, Benjamin J., and Virginia A. Sadock, eds. *Kaplan & Sadock's Comprehensive Textbook of Psychiatry*. 7th ed. Philadelphia: Lippincott Williams and Wilkins, 2000.

PERIODICALS

Binik, Yitzchak M., MD. "Should Dyspareunia be Retained as a Sexual Dysfunction in DSM-V. A Painful Classification Decision." *Archives of Sexual Behavior* 34 (2005): 11–21.

Heim, Lori J. "Evaluation and Differential Diagnosis of Dyspareunia." *American Family Physician* 63 (2001): 1535–44. Available online at: < http://www .aafp.org/afp/20010415/1535.html>.

OTHER

American Academy of Family Physicians. "Dyspareunia: Painful Sex for Women." *Familydoctor.org*. Aug. 2004. <http://familydoctor.org/669.xml >.

Carson-DeWitt, Rosalind, MD. "Dyspareunia: Painful Sexual Intercourse." *Healthfinder.gov*. Nov. 2006. U.S. Department of Health and Human Services. <http://www.healthfinder.gov/hg/files/?id = 11893>.

National Library of Medicine. "Female Sexual Dysfunction." *Medline Plus*. Mar. 5, 2007. National Institutes of Health. <http://www.nlm.nih.gov/medlineplus/femalesexualdysfunction.html>.

Jody Bower, MSW
Emily Jane Willingham, PhD

Dysthymic disorder

Definition

Dysthymic disorder is defined as a mood disorder with chronic (long-term) depressive symptoms that are present most of the day, more days than not, for a period of at least two years.

Description

Everyone experiences feelings of unhappiness and sadness occasionally. When these depressed feelings start to dominate everyday life and cause physical and mental deterioration, the feelings become known as **depressive disorders**. Depressive disorders can be categorized as **major depressive disorder** or dysthymic disorder. Individuals who have dysthymic disorder have had their depressive symptoms for years—they often cannot pinpoint exactly when they started to feel depressed. People with dysthymic disorder may describe to their doctor feelings of hopelessness, lowered self-esteem, poor concentration, indecisiveness, decreased motivation, sleeping too much or too little, or eating too much or too little. Symptoms are present often and for the whole day and are typically present for at least two years.

Causes and symptoms

Causes

The causes of **depression** are complex and not yet completely understood. Sleep abnormalities, hormones, **neurotransmitters** (chemicals that communicate impulses from one nerve cell to another), upbringing, heredity, and stressors (significant life changes or events that cause **stress**) all have been implicated as causes of depression.

Dysthymic disorder occurs in approximately 25% to 50% of persons who have sleep abnormalities that include reduced rapid eye movement (REM) sleep and impaired sleep continuity. Rapid eye movement sleep is an essential component of the sleep cycle and quality of sleep.

There is some evidence that suggests a correlation with hormonal imbalances of cortisol or thyroid hormones. In many adults, levels of cortisol (a stress hormone) are elevated during acute depressive periods and return to normal when the person is no longer depressed. In children and adolescents, experimental results have been quite inconsistent, although there is some evidence that hypersecretion of cortisol is associated with more severe depressive symptoms and with a higher likelihood of recurrence of depression. A lack of thyroid hormone mimics depression quite well, and thyroid hormone levels are routinely checked in patients with recent-onset depression.

In depression, there appears to be abnormal excess or inhibition of signals that control mood, thoughts, pain, and other sensations. Some studies suggest an imbalance of the neurotransmitter called serotonin. It is assumed that the reason **antidepressants** are effective is that they correct these chemical imbalances. For example, the **selective serotonin reuptake inhibitors** (**SSRIs**), one class of antidepressant medications that includes **fluoxetine** (Prozac), appears to establish a normal level of serotonin. As the name implies, the drug inhibits the reuptake of the serotonin neurotransmitter from the gaps between nerve cells, thus increasing neurotransmitter action, alleviating depressive symptoms.

A child's upbringing may also be key in the development of dysthymic disorder. For example, it is speculated that if a person is abused and neglected throughout childhood and adolescence, a pattern of low self-esteem and negative thinking may emerge, and, from that, a lifelong pattern of depression may follow.

Heredity seems to play a role in the development of depressive disorders. People with major depression in their immediate family are up to three times more likely to have the disorder themselves. It would seem that biological and genetic factors may make certain individuals more prone to depressive disorders, but that environmental circumstances, or stressors, may then trigger the disorder.

Symptoms

The mental health professional's handbook to aid in patient **diagnosis** is the *Diagnostic and Statistical Manual of Mental Disorders*, also called the *DSM*. The 2000 edition of this manual is known as the *DSM-IV-TR* (fourth edition, text revision). The *DSM-IV-TR* has established a list of criteria that can indicate a diagnosis. These criteria include:

- depressed mood for most of the day, more days than not.
- when depressed, two (or more) of the following are also present: decreased appetite or overeating, too much or too little sleep, low energy level, low self-esteem, decreased ability to concentrate, difficulty making decisions, and/or feelings of hopelessness.
- during the two years of the disorder, the patient has never been without symptoms listed for more than two months at a time.
- no major depressive episode (a more severe form of depression) has been present during the first two years of the disorder.
- there has never been a manic disorder, and criteria for a less severe depression called cyclothymic disorder has never been established.
- the disorder does not exclusively occur with psychosis, schizophrenia, or delusional illnesses.
- the symptoms of depression cause clinically significant impairment and distress in occupational, social, and general functioning. Dysthymic disorder can be described as "early onset" (onset before age 21 years), "late onset" (onset is age 21 years or older), and "with atypical features" (features that are not commonly observed).

Demographics

The lifetime prevalence has been estimated to be 4.1% for women and 2.2% for men, with an overall rate of 1.5% of people over age 18 in the U.S. population affected in a given year. This percentage, in actual numbers, is about 3.3 million adults. In adults, dysthymic disorder is more common in women than in men and research suggests that the prevalence in the age group 25 to 64 years is 6% for women. In children, dysthymic disorder can occur equally among both genders. The median age of onset is 31 years.

Diagnosis

To diagnose a patient with this disorder, the *DSM-IV-TR* criteria must be met, and evaluation of this is accomplished through an extensive psychological interview and evaluation. The affected person seeking the clinician's help usually exhibits symptoms of irritability, feelings of worthlessness and hopelessness, crying spells, decreased sex drive, agitation, and thoughts of death. The clinician must rule out any possible medical conditions that can cause depressed affect. (Affect can be defined as the expression of emotion displayed to others through facial expressions, hand gestures, tone of voice, etc.) The diagnosis cannot be made if depression occurs during an active course of psychosis, **delusions**, schizophrenia, or **schizoaffective disorder**. If **substance abuse** is determined as the cause of depression, then a diagnosis of substance-induced mood disorder can be established.

Further psychological tests that can be administered to help in the diagnostic process include the **Beck Depression Inventory** and the **Hamilton Depression Scale**.

Treatments

The goals of treatment include remission of symptoms and psychological and social recovery.

Medications

Studies suggest some treatment success with medications such as tricyclic antidepressants (TCAs) or monoaminoxidase inhibitors (MAOIs). Medications can be effective in patients who have depression due to sleep abnormalities. Some tricyclic antidepressants include **amitriptyline** (Elavil), **imipramine** (Tofranil), and **nortriptyline** (Aventyl, Pamelor), and some MAOIs include **tranylcypromine** (Parnate) and **phenelzine** (Nardil), although these are not considered first-line use antidepressants. **Selective serotonin reuptake inhibitors (SSRIs)** are recommended during initial treatment planning after a definitive diagnosis is well established. The most commonly prescribed SSRIs are fluoxetine (Prozac), **sertraline** (Zoloft), **paroxetine (Paxil)**, **fluvoxamine** (Luvox), and **citalopram** (Celexa). Trials are currently ongoing to assess the effects of several other drugs on the symptoms of dysthymic disorder.

Psychological therapies

Clinical reports suggest that **cognitive-behavioral therapy**, interpersonal **psychotherapy**, or **family therapy** can be effective with concurrent antidepressant medication to treat the symptoms of depression. In these therapies, the goal is to help the patient develop healthy problem-solving and coping skills.

Prognosis

Dysthymic disorder often begins in late childhood or adolescence. The disorder follows a chronic (long-term) course. The development of a more major form of clinical depression called major depressive disorder among children with dysthymic disorder is significant. In other words, childhood onset of dysthymic disorder is considered an early indicator for recurrent mood disorder that may even have more severe clinical symptoms in the patient's future.

Patients with this disorder usually have impaired emotional, social, and physical functioning.

KEY TERMS

Affect—The expression of emotion displayed to others through facial expressions, hand gestures, tone of voice, etc. Types of affect include: flat (inanimate, no expression), blunted (minimally responsive), inappropriate (incongruous expressions of emotion relative to the content of a conversation), and labile (sudden and abrupt changes in type and intensity of emotion).

Cortisol—A steroid hormone released by the cortex (outer portion) of the adrenal gland when a person is under stress.

Neurotransmitter—A chemical in the brain that transmits messages between neurons, or nerve cells.

Serotonin—A widely distributed neurotransmitter that is found in blood platelets, the lining of the digestive tract, and the brain, and that works in combination with norepinephrine. It causes very powerful contractions of smooth muscle, and is associated with mood, attention, emotions, and sleep. Low levels of serotonin are associated with depression.

Thyroid hormone—A complex hormone that regulates metabolic rate of all cells.

In general, the clinical course of dysthymic disorder is not promising. Causes of a poorer outcome include not completing treatment, noncompliance with medication intake, and lack of willingness to change behaviors that promote a depressed state. However, patients can do very well with a short course of medications if they have a desire to follow psychotherapy treatment recommendations.

If left untreated, dysthymic disorder can result in significant financial and occupational losses. People with this disorder tend to isolate themselves by restricting daily activities and spending days in bed. Patients often complain of poor health and incur more disability days when compared to the general population. Higher rates of successful outcome occur in people who undergo psychotherapy and treatment with appropriate medications.

Prevention

There is no known prevention for dysthymic disorder. Early **intervention** for children with depression may be effective in arresting the development of more severe problems.

See also Neurotransmitters; Origin of mental illness.

Resources

BOOKS

Goldman, Lee, and J. Claude Bennett, eds. *Cecil's Textbook of Medicine,* 21st ed. Philadelphia: W. B. Saunders Company, 2000.

Tasman, Allan, and others. *Psychiatry,* 1st ed. Philadelphia: W. B. Saunders Company, 1997.

PERIODICALS

Brown, C. S. "Depression and Anxiety Disorders." *Obstetrics and Gynecology Clinics* 28.2 (June 2001): 241–68.

Youdim, Moussa B. H., Dale Edmondson, and Keith F. Tipton. "The Therapeutic Potential of Monoamine Oxidase Inhibitors." *Nature Reviews Neuroscience* 7 (2006): 295–309.

OTHER

National Institute of Mental Health. NIH Publication 01-4591. "The Invisible Disease: Depression." (updated 2006). <http://www.nimh.nih.gov/publicat/invisible.cfm>.

National Institute of Mental Health. NIH Publication 06-4584. "The Numbers Count: Mental Disorders in America." (updated 2006). <http://www.nimh.nih.gov/publicat/numbers.cfm>.

Laith Farid Gulli, MD
Linda Hesson, MA, LLP, CAC
Emily Jane Willingham, PhD

E

Eating disorders *see* **Anorexia nervosa and Bulimia nervosa**

Ecstasy

Definition

Ecstasy is the popular name for the synthetic, psychoactive drug 3,4-methylenedioxymethamphetamine, or MDMA. It is chemically similar to **methamphetamine** and the hallucinogen mescaline. MDMA acts both as a stimulant and psychedelic, producing an energizing effect, as well as distortions in time and perception and enhanced enjoyment from tactile experiences. MDMA exerts its primary effects in the **brain** on neurons that use the chemical serotonin to communicate with other neurons. The serotonin system plays an important role in regulating mood, aggression, sexual activity, sleep, and sensitivity to pain. Ecstasy has a large number of other street names. These include Adam, B-bombs, bean, Blue Nile, clarity, crystal, decadence, disco biscuit, E, essence, Eve, go, hug drug, Iboga, love drug, morning shot, pollutants, Rolls Royce, Snackies, speed for lovers, sweeties, wheels, X, and XTC.

Description

MDMA was first synthesized in 1912 by the German pharmaceutical company Merck. Merck patented the drug in 1914. The U.S. military conducted some studies of MDMA in the 1950s, but the public knew virtually nothing about the drug until the 1970s. In the early 1970s, a few psychotherapists and psychiatrists began to explore the therapeutic uses of MDMA. They believed that they could help people benefit more from treatment if they combined doses of MDMA with **psychotherapy**. The number of clinicians who used

MDMA as an adjunct to psychotherapy grew in the next few years.

The name "ecstasy" was coined in the early 1980s, when distributors began to envision a larger market for the drug. Ecstasy became popular as a "club drug" and was often sold in nightclubs and bars. Because of reports of increases in the recreational use of ecstasy and scientific reports suggesting that the related drug MDA could cause brain damage, the U.S. Drug Enforcement Administration (DEA) banned both ecstasy and 3,4-methylenedioxyamphetamine (MDA) in the mid-1980s. Following the ban on ecstasy, a lawsuit was filed against the DEA by a group of physicians who believed that ecstasy had therapeutic value. Despite the lawsuit, the DEA's ban on ecstasy became permanent. The DEA currently classifies ecstasy as a Schedule I drug. Schedule I drugs are considered to have high potential for **abuse** and no currently accepted medical value. They are not considered safe for use even under medical supervision. It is illegal to use, sell, or manufacture ecstasy in the United States. Ecstasy that is seized by the DEA is manufactured mainly in the Netherlands, Belgium, and Canada, although some is also illegally made in laboratories in the United States.

The recreational use of ecstasy continued to increase despite the DEA ban. Through the late 1980s and 1990s, ecstasy began to be used widely at raves, which are clandestine all-night dance parties often held in warehouses and attended by large numbers of young people.

Ecstasy is sometimes described as an "entactogen," because it gives users feelings of peacefulness, acceptance, empathy, euphoria, and closeness to others. Ecstasy is typically synthesized from precursor chemicals such as piperonyl methylketone, piperonal, isosafrole, or safrole. Safrole is an essential oil that is found in the tree *Sassafras albidum*, which grows in the eastern United States, and in the tree *Ocotea pretiosa*, which grows in South America. Safrole is also found in

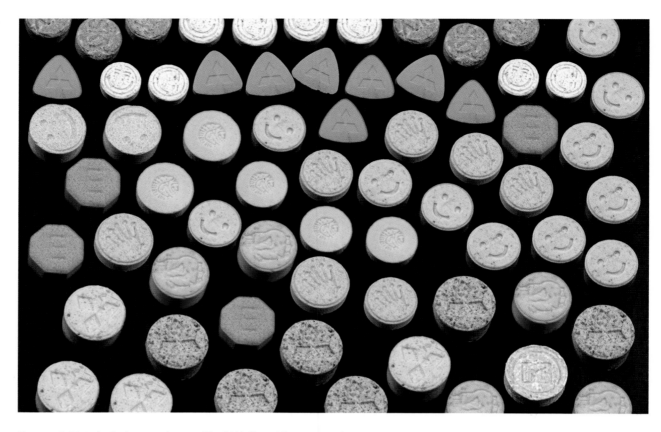

Ecstacy tablets in their many forms. *(David Hoffman Photo Library/Alamy)*

nutmeg, dill, parsley seed, crocus, saffron, vanilla beans, and calamus.

Some people use a product called herbal ecstasy. The main constituents of herbal ecstasy are a combination of legal herbs that are stimulants such as ephedra, guarana, and caffeine. Other herbs and vitamins may also be included. Herbal ecstasy is sold in tablet form as Cloud 9, Herbal Bliss, Ritual Spirit, Herbal X, GWM, Rave Energy, Ultimate Xphoria, and X. The quantities of ephedrine and caffeine in the tablets can vary widely. Although people who take herbal ecstasy believe it to be a legal, safe alternative to ecstasy, there are reports of numerous adverse effects, including severe reactions such as high blood pressure, **seizures**, heart attacks, strokes, and death.

Method of administration

Most users take ecstasy orally. Users also sometimes inhale or inject it. Although ecstasy is available as a capsule or a powder, it is usually sold in tablet form. The tablets are available in different colors, shapes, and sizes, and are often imprinted with logos such as smiley faces, clover leaves, cartoon characters, or the logos of

popular commercial brands, such as those for clothing or automobiles. On average, an ecstasy tablet has about 100 mg of MDMA. However, the MDMA content in tablets can vary a great deal. Pure MDMA salt, which is a white, bitter-tasting substance, is usually not the only ingredient in ecstasy tablets. The MDMA in ecstasy tablets is often contaminated with other drugs such as caffeine, aspirin, dextromethorphan, ephedrine, methamphetamine, and MDA.

Use statistics

The use of ecstasy occurs in dance clubs, at raves, on college and high school campuses, and in private homes. Use is more common in urban areas. Most users of ecstasy are teenagers and young adults, from middle- and upper-class households. The U.S. Office of National Drug Control Policy reports that, according to the National Survey on Drug Use and Health (NSDUH), an estimated 11.5 million Americans aged 12 or older reported in 2005 that they had used MDMA at least once in their lifetimes. This figure represented 4.7% of the U.S. population in that age group. In 2005, the number of people who used MDMA in the past year was approximately 1.9 million, a figure that represented 0.8% of the population aged 12 or older. Although the use of ecstasy by teenagers and young adults rose between 1996 and 2002, use appears to have been decreasing over the past few years. *Monitoring the Future* is a study conducted every year by the University of Michigan and funded by the National Institute on Drug Abuse. In 2006, this study surveyed a total of 48,460 students in 410 secondary schools nationwide. It showed that 1.4% of eighth graders, 2.8% of tenth graders, and 4.1% of twelfth graders surveyed reported that they had used ecstasy in the past year. In 2006, 2.5% of eighth graders, 4.5% of tenth graders, and 6.5% of twelfth graders surveyed reported that they had used ecstasy in their lifetime. In contrast, in 2002, 4.3% of eighth graders, 6.6% of tenth graders, and 10.5% of twelfth graders surveyed reported using ecstasy in their lifetime.

Effects of use

Ecstasy is absorbed quickly after it is taken orally, and it can be detected in the blood within about 30 minutes. It typically has its effect within 20 to 60 minutes after it is ingested. The average time for onset of effects is 30 minutes. It has its peak effects about 60 to 90 minutes after it is ingested. The main effects of ecstasy last about three to five hours. Women are more sensitive to ecstasy than men. Therefore, they are likely to experience an optimal effect of the drug at a lower dose, in proportion to body weight, than men.

Ecstasy mimics the effects of the neurotransmitter serotonin, activating cell receptors in the brain that normally respond to serotonin. Serotonin is involved in many processes in the body, including the regulation of mood, aggression, sexual activity, sleep, sensitivity to pain, and eating. MDMA also causes the release of serotonin, as well as the **neurotransmitters** norepinephrine and **dopamine**. The levels of hormones such as cortisol, prolactin, and testosterone increase when ecstasy is used. The level of vasopressin, a hormone that is involved in elevating blood pressure and retaining water in the body, also increases.

Ecstasy users report intensely pleasurable experiences after taking ecstasy. They feel euphoric and are more aware of sensory stimuli. Users often wear fluorescent jewelry or accessories and use mentholated ointments or sprays to enhance the sensory effects they experience. Users of ecstasy usually feel socially uninhibited and close to other people. They find that they have an increased sense of empathy. They also become emotionally open and have exceptionally clear insight into themselves. Time perception may become distorted. Because ecstasy has a stimulant effect, users

also often feel energetic and can remain awake for long periods of time. Ecstasy increases sensuality, but it does not directly increase sexual drive or appetite. However, because it decreases inhibitions and makes users more open to others, users sometime engage in sexual activity after taking ecstasy. Men sometimes experience delayed orgasms, although orgasms may be more intense than usual.

Ecstasy users also sometimes have undesirable experiences. In one research study, about 25% of users reported having gone through at least one occasion when ecstasy use resulted in unpleasant experiences and body sensations. Short-term adverse reactions that have been reported include dilated pupils, unusual sensitivity to bright light, headache, sweating, increased heart rate, bruxism, trismus, loss of appetite, nausea, muscle aches, **fatigue**, dizziness, vertigo, thirst, numbness, tingling skin, retention of urine, ataxia, unsteadiness, tics, tremors, restlessness, agitation, **paranoia**, and nystagmus. Research has shown that driving a car under the influence of ecstasy is unsafe.

The scientific literature on the effects of ecstasy is somewhat inconsistent. This is partly because well-controlled studies cannot be carried out on ecstasy use. However, most of the scientific community agrees that brain levels of serotonin increase when ecstasy is ingested, and that they decrease after an episode of ecstasy use. The depletion of serotonin is thought to cause midweek blues. This term refers to the lethargy, concentration and memory problems, and depressed mood that many ecstasy users experience for a few days after taking the drug. Other changes that occur for a few days after ecstasy use are increased feelings of aggressiveness, unsociability, irritability, decreased appetite, and poor sleep. Some researchers have reported that chronic, heavy ecstasy use is associated with **sleep disorders**, **depression**, high levels of **anxiety**, impulsiveness and hostility, and problems with memory and attention. Memory and attention deficits may continue for up to six months after drug use is stopped, but symptoms are reported to remit after six to twelve months. The extent of cognitive deficits may depend on the number of tablets taken per occasion of use.

Ecstasy causes body temperature to increase. Abnormal increases in body temperature are more likely when the user is in a hot environment, such as on a crowded dance floor. A number of ecstasy-related deaths have been reported that are attributable to drug-induced increases in body temperature. Several users who later died were admitted to hospitals with abnormally high temperatures, ranging from 104°F

(40°C) to 109°F (43°C). The immediate cause of death in these users was damage to organs such as the liver and heart. Other deaths have occurred because of water intoxication, which can develop when ecstasy users drink too much water to combat hyperthermia. The increase in vasopressin that accompanies the use of ecstasy makes excessive water intake particularly dangerous. Water intoxication results in decreased levels of sodium in the blood, which can be fatal.

Ecstasy users appear to develop tolerance to the drug with repeated use, needing more and more of it to achieve the effect they desire. Novice users tend to take one or two tablets per session, whereas highly experienced users may take more than three tablets per session. The use of increased doses may exacerbate the amphetamine-like effects of the drug. Heavy users sometimes binge-use, either by taking several tablets simultaneously, or by repeatedly taking tablets during a single session that may last up to 48 hours. In such binging sessions, users may go without sleep or food, and sometimes consume up to 20 tablets. In some cases, binge users snort powdered ecstasy or inject it. Binging on ecstasy can result in consequences such as loss of appetite, weight loss, days off from work, and depression.

There are scientific and political debates about whether ecstasy causes long-term damage to the human brain. Some researchers and drug enforcement agencies claim that ecstasy is a dangerous drug capable of causing irreversible brain damage, and other researchers suggest that claims of irreversible neurotoxicity in humans are exaggerated and unproven. Because of ethical considerations, ecstasy cannot be given to people who do not use it to study its effects on the brain. However, studies of brain function are sometimes carried out in people who already take ecstasy, using brain-imaging technology. These types of studies are methodologically complex and results are interpretable in various ways. Therefore, there is still controversy about the potential long-term effects of ecstasy on the human brain. Studies conducted on rats and monkeys have shown that high doses of ecstasy can have long-term negative effects on neurons that contain serotonin. Serotonin levels become depleted in these animals, and serotonin containing nerves become damaged. The degeneration of neurons is exacerbated when the animals are placed in high-temperature environments. In these types of studies, animals are usually given very high doses of ecstasy, and the drug is usually injected. Some researchers have argued that the results of these animal studies cannot

be extrapolated to human users, who use much lower doses and typically ingest the drug orally.

Methodological and ethical problems in ecstasy research

Scientific research on ecstasy use has some limitations. Because ecstasy is classified as a Schedule I drug, researchers cannot easily conduct controlled experimental studies by administering MDMA to people in laboratories. Additionally, people who use ecstasy often use other drugs, such as heroin, **cocaine**, and ketamine, either deliberately or as a result of using contaminated ecstasy. Therefore, it is difficult to determine whether effects observed in users are due to the current or previous use of these other drugs, the use of ecstasy, or the combination of ecstasy with other drugs. Scientists also cannot easily determine whether effects noted in ecstasy users are due to drug use or the personal characteristics of people who choose to use ecstasy recreationally.

Therapeutic use of ecstasy

Some psychiatrists and psychotherapists still advocate for the therapeutic use of ecstasy. While most of these professionals believe that recreational use of ecstasy is likely to be unsafe, they argue that small doses of unadulterated MDMA can be used effectively as an adjunct to psychotherapy, when used once or twice in a controlled therapeutic setting. They believe that MDMA is beneficial because it can help patients put aside their anxiety and fear and explore psychological issues that would normally be too painful to confront. Although ecstasy-assisted psychotherapy may also be indicated in other situations, it is thought to be particularly helpful in the treatment of **post-traumatic stress disorder** (PTSD), and to help people with terminal illness deal with the fear of dying.

Although psychiatrists and psychotherapists used ecstasy in the 1970s as an adjunct to psychotherapy, no controlled **clinical trials** were conducted at the time that could provide evidence for its therapeutic efficacy. After ecstasy became classified as a Schedule I drug, it became difficult for researchers to study its psychotherapeutic uses, because institutional review boards typically do not approve research studies that have the potential for causing harm to humans who participate in them. After much controversy about the ethics of conducting such studies, in 2004 the DEA approved a clinical trial of ecstasy in the treatment of PTSD. The trial is sponsored by the Multidisciplinary Association for Psychedelic Studies, a nonprofit research and educational organization that seeks to develop MDMA as an FDA-approved prescription medicine. The study is ongoing.

KEY TERMS

Ataxia—A loss of muscle coordination.

Brain imaging—Methods that provide a visual representation of the structure and function of the brain.

Bruxism—Grinding of teeth.

Dextromethorphan—A non-prescription cough suppressant.

Ephedrine—A stimulant that is sold as a diet drug.

Hyperthermia—An abnormal increase in body temperature.

Institutional review board—A committee made up of scientists and lay people, which evaluates proposals for research studies, to determine whether they are designed ethically. All institutions that conduct research are required by law to have such a committee.

Ketamine—An anesthetic drug that is often used by veterinarians for treating animals.

Monitoring the Future—An ongoing study of the behaviors, attitudes, and values of secondary school students, college students, and young adults in the United States. It is carried out by the University of Michigan and is funded by the National Institute of Drug Abuse, a component of the U.S. National Institutes of Health.

National Survey on Drug Use and Health—A study that is carried out annually to estimate alcohol, tobacco, illicit drug, and nonmedical prescription drug use in the United States. It is sponsored the Substance Abuse and Mental Health Services Administration, a component of the U.S. Department of Health and Human Services.

Neurotoxicity—Damage to brain structure or function.

Neurotransmitter—A chemical that is involved in sending signals from one nerve cell to another.

Nystagmus—Repeated, involuntary movements of the eyes.

Post-traumatic stress disorder (PTSD)—An anxiety disorder that can develop after a person experiences a traumatic event.

Receptors—Protein molecules in nerve cells, to which neurotransmitters bind.

Tolerance—A process in which a person develops resistance to the drug, so that increasingly larger doses are need to achieve the same effect.

Trismus—Soreness or tightening of the muscles in the jaw.

Vertigo—A sensation that the environment is spinning.

Resources

BOOKS

Espejo, Roman, ed. *Drug Abuse*. San Diego, CA: Greenhaven Press, 2002.

Iversen, Leslie. *Speed, Ecstasy, Ritalin: The Science of Amphetamines*. Oxford: Oxford University Press, 2006.

Wilson, Hugh T., ed. *Drugs, Society and Behavior, 03/04*. 18th ed. Guilford, CT: McGraw-Hill/Dushkin, 2003.

PERIODICALS

Dumont, G. J. H., and R. J. Verkes. "A Review of Acute Effects of 3,4-Methylenedioxymethamphetamine in Healthy Volunteers." *Journal of Psychopharmacology* 20.2 (2006): 176.

Gahlinger, Paul M. "Club Drugs: MDMA, Gamma-hydroxybutyrate (GHB), Rohypnol, and Ketamine." *American Family Physician* 69.11 (2004): 2619.

McCook, Alison. "Renewed Faith in Ecstasy." *The Scientist* 19.4 (2005): 13–14.

Nutt, David. "A Tale of Two Es (Ethanol and Ecstasy)." *Journal of Psychopharmacology* 20.3 (2006). 315–17.

Parrott, A. C. "Editorial: Ecstasy versus Alcohol: Tolstoy and the Variations of Unhappiness." *Journal of Psychopharmacology* 21.1 (2007): 3–7.

Parrott, Andy C., and Charles A. Marsden. "Editorial: MDMA (3,4-Methylenedioxymethamphetamine) or Ecstasy: the Contemporary Human and Animal Research Perspective." *Journal of Psychopharmacology* 20.2 (2006): 143.

Watkins, Katherine E., Phyllis L. Ellickson, Mary E. Vaiana, and Scott Hiromoto. "An Update on Adolescent Drug Use: What School Counselors Need to Know." *Professional School Counseling* 10.2 (2006): 131–39.

Wish, Eric D., Dawn Bonanno Fitzelle, Kevin E. O'Grady, Margaret H. Hsu, and Amelia M. Arria. "Evidence for Significant Polydrug Use Among Ecstasy-Using College Students." *Journal of American College Health* 55.2 (2006): 99–104.

ORGANIZATIONS

Heffter Research Institute. 369 Montezuma Avenue, #153, Santa Fe, NM 87501-2626. Web site: <http://www.heffter.org>.

Monitoring the Future Survey Research Center. Institute for Social Research. University of Michigan. P.O. Box 1248

426 Thompson Street, Ann Arbor, MI 48106-1248. Telephone: (734) 764-8354. Web site: <http://monitoringthefuture.org>.

Multidisciplinary Association for Psychedelic Studies. 10424 Love Creek Road, Ben Lomond, CA 95005. Telephone: (831) 336-HEAL (4325). Web site: <http://www.map.org>.

National Drug Intelligence Center. 319 Washington Street, 5th Floor, Johnstown, PA 15901-1622. Telephone: (814) 532-4601. Web site: <http://www.usdoj.gov/ndic>.

OTHER

"Drug Facts: Club Drugs." *Office of National Drug Control Policy*. January 2007. <http://www.whitehousedrugpolicy.gov/drugfact/club/index.html>.

"MDMA (Ecstasy)." *U.S. Drug Enforcement Administration*. August 2006. <http://www.dea.gov/concern/mdma.html>.

Monitoring the Future, a Continuing Study of American Youth. University of Michigan, Ann Arbor. 2006. <http://monitoringthefuture.org>.

National Survey On Drug Use and Health (NSDUH). SAMHSA. January 2007. <https://nsduhweb.rti.org>.

"NIDA InfoFacts: MDMA (Ecstasy)." *National Institute on Drug Abuse*. April 2006.<http://www.nida.nih.gov/Infofacts/ecstasy.html>.

Ruvanee Pietersz Vilhauer, PhD

EEG *see* **Electroencephalography**

Effexor *see* **Venlafaxine**

Elavil *see* **Amitriptyline**

Electroconvulsive therapy

Definition

Electroconvulsive therapy (ECT) is a controversial procedure in which a patient is treated by using controlled, low-dose electric currents to induce a seizure. The electric current produces a convulsion that may relieve symptoms associated with such mental illnesses as **major depressive disorder**, **bipolar disorder**, acute **psychosis**, and **catatonia**. Symptom relief, however, is often temporary.

Purpose

Also known as electroconvulsive shock therapy or electroshock therapy, ECT uses low-dose electric currents together with anesthesia, muscle relaxants, and oxygen to produce a mild generalized seizure or convulsion. With repeated administration, usually over a period of weeks, ECT may be effective in relieving symptoms of several mental illnesses.

The American Psychiatric Association's *Practice Guidelines for the Treatment of Psychiatric Disorders* discusses the use of ECT in the treatment of major depressive disorder, bipolar disorder, and **schizophrenia**. It is most closely associated with the treatment of severe **depression**. Historically, ECT was the treatment of choice for depression if a patient with severe depression or psychotic symptoms was at increased risk of committing **suicide** and had not responded to other treatments. In addition, patients with catatonia, neuroleptic malignant syndrome, and parkinsonism may also benefit from the procedure.

Although antidepressant medications are effective in many cases, they may take two to six weeks to begin to work. In addition, some patients with mania and schizophrenia may not be able to tolerate the side effects of the antipsychotic medications used to treat these disorders. For these individuals, ECT is an option. ECT is also indicated when patients need a treatment that brings about rapid improvement because they are refusing to eat or drink, or presenting some other danger to themselves.

ECT is also recommended for certain subgroups of patients diagnosed with depression. Many elderly patients, for example, respond better to ECT than to antidepressant medications. Pregnant women are another subgroup that may benefit from ECT. Because ECT does not harm a fetus as some medications might, pregnant women with severe depression can choose ECT for relief of their depressive symptoms.

Today, however, other treatments such as **transcranial magnetic stimulation** (TMS) are becoming available and replacing ECT in such cases. TMS has also been found to be more effective than ECT in many of the more difficult cases. The literature to date on TMS reports few side effects such as those resulting from ECT.

Precautions

Candidates for ECT must be carefully screened. Prior to receiving this treatment, patients receive a thorough evaluation to identify any medical conditions they may have that might complicate their responses to the procedure. This evaluation includes a complete medical history, a physical examination, and routine laboratory tests. In addition to standard blood tests, the patient should receive an electrocardiogram (EKG) to test for heart abnormalities. Evidence of a recent heart attack would disqualify a patient from receiving ECT. Spinal and chest x rays can identify other physical conditions that might complicate a patient's response. Finally, a **computed tomography** (CT) scan

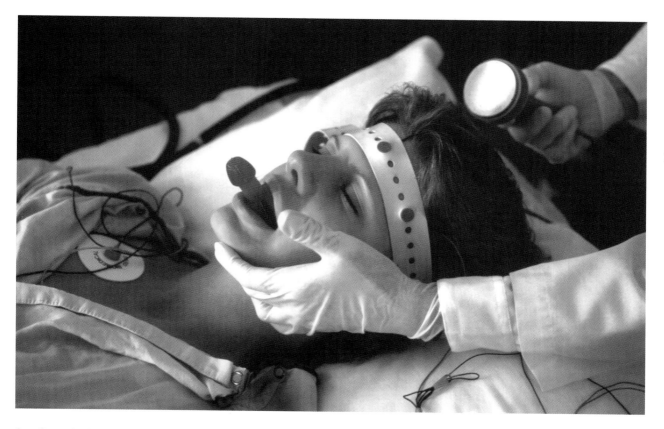

A patient who has been prepped to receive electroconvulsive therapy, a treatment for depression. The rubber mouthpiece will keep her from biting down on teeth or her tongue during the seizure. *(Photo Researchers)*

should be performed to rule out any structural abnormalities in the **brain** that might be made worse by the electrical stimulation and resulting convulsions associated with ECT. Signs of a recent **stroke** or a tumor in the brain, for instance, would disqualify a patient as a candidate for ECT therapy.

The doctors who are administering the procedure must receive the signed **informed consent** of the patient a day before the first treatment is given. In addition, at least two psychiatrists should confirm that ECT is the proper treatment for a specific patient. One of these physicians should serve as the source of a "second opinion" and not be actively involved in treating the patient on a daily basis. This second, or outside, medical consultant should independently determine that ECT is appropriate for a particular patient after conducting a physical examination. The second physician should also confirm that the patient is mentally sound enough to give informed consent to the procedure.

Patients in any age group are eligible for treatment with ECT. However, informed consent for patients under 18 must be given by a parent or legal guardian.

Description

Early history of ECT

Ugo Cerletti and Lucio Bini, who were two Italian physicians working in the 1930s, were the first to use ECT to treat patients with severe mental illnesses. Their first patient was a 39-year-old unidentifiable homeless man who had been found wandering through the railroad station in Rome, mumbling incoherently. The doctors were inspired to try the new method by a notion that intrigued psychiatrists in this period, who were desperate for useful therapies—namely, that epilepsy and schizophrenia never appeared in the same person at the same time. (It was later shown, however, that it is possible for the same individual to have both disorders at the same time.) Because epilepsy causes **seizures**, psychiatrists in the 1930s reasoned that artificially induced seizures might cure schizophrenia. Some in the medical community were receptive to this approach because physicians were already using a variety of chemicals to produce seizures in patients. Unfortunately, many of their patients died or suffered severe injuries because the strength of the convulsions could not be well controlled.

As ECT became more widely used, many members of the general public and some in the psychiatric profession were opposed to its use. To them it seemed barbaric and crude. ECT joined psychosurgery as one of the most intensely distrusted psychiatric and neurological practices. Many people were frightened simply because ECT was called "shock treatment." Many assumed the procedure would be painful; others thought it was a form of electrocution; and still others believed it would cause brain damage. Unfavorable publicity in newspapers, magazines, and movies added to these fears. Indeed, from the 1930s up through the 1960s, doctors and nurses did not explain either ECT or other forms of psychiatric treatment to patients and their families very often. Moreover, many critics had good reasons for opposing the procedure before it was refined. Neither anesthesia nor muscle relaxants were used in the early days of ECT. As a result, patients had violent seizures, and even though they did not remember them, the thought of the procedure itself seemed frightening. Even more unfortunately, this crude, early version of ECT was applied sometimes to patients who could never have benefited from ECT under any conditions.

As the procedures used with ECT became more refined, psychiatrists found that ECT could be an effective treatment for schizophrenia, depression, and bipolar disorder. The use of ECT, however, was phased out when antipsychotic and antidepressant drugs were introduced during the 1950s and 1960s. The psychiatric community reintroduced ECT several years later when patients who did not respond to the new drugs stimulated a search by mental health professionals for effective, and if necessary, non-drug treatments. While the new psychotropic medications provided relief for untold thousands of patients who suffered greatly from their illnesses and would otherwise have been condemned to mental hospitals, the drugs unfortunately produced a number of side effects, some irreversible. Another drawback is that some medications do not have a noticeable effect on the patient's mood for two to six weeks. During this time, the patient may be at risk for suicide. In addition, there are patients who do not respond to any medications or who have severe allergic reactions to them.

ECT in contemporary practice

ECT is performed in both inpatient and outpatient facilities in specially equipped rooms with oxygen, suction, and cardiopulmonary resuscitation equipment readily available to deal with the rare emergency. A team of health care professionals, including a **psychiatrist**, an anesthesiologist, a respiratory therapist, and other assistants, is present throughout the entire procedure.

As of 2000, the American Psychiatric Association has renewed its set of guidelines, first published in 1990, for determining the appropriate use of ECT in patients with depression. They state that patients qualify for ECT if they meet these conditions

• cannot tolerate, or receive no significant benefit from, antidepressant medications

• have responded well to ECT treatments during past depressive episodes

• face a greater risk from taking antidepressant drugs than from undergoing ECT

• need treatment without delay to avoid suicide or other self-destructive acts

Administration of ECT

ECT is performed while the patient is unconscious. Unconsciousness is induced by a short-acting barbiturate such as methohexital (Brevital Sodium), or another appropriate anesthetic drug. The drug is given intravenously. To prevent the patient from harming themselves during the convulsions or seizures induced by ECT, he or she is given succinylcholine (Anectine) or a similar drug that temporarily paralyzes the muscles. Because the patient's muscles are relaxed, the seizures will not produce any violent contractions of the limbs and torso. Instead, the patient lies quietly on the operating table. One of the patient's hands or feet, however, is tied off with a tourniquet before the muscle relaxant is given. The tourniquet prevents the muscles in this limb from being paralyzed like the muscles in other parts of the patient's body. The hand or foot is used to monitor muscle movement induced by the electrical current applied to the brain.

A breathing tube is then inserted into the unconscious patient's airway and a rubber mouthpiece is inserted into the mouth to prevent him or her from biting down on teeth or tongue during the electrically induced convulsion. As the current is applied, brain activity is monitored using **electroencephalography**. These brain wave tracings tell the medical team exactly how long the seizure lasts. The contraction of muscles in the arm or leg not affected by the muscle relaxant also provides an indication of the seizure's duration.

The electrodes for ECT may be placed on both sides of the head (bilateral) or one side (unilateral). Physicians often use bilateral electrode placement during the first week or so of treatments. An electric current is passed through the brain by means of a machine specifically designed for this purpose. The usual dose of electricity is 70–150 volts for 0.1–0.5 seconds. In the first stage of the seizure (tonic phase), the muscles in the body that have not been paralyzed by medication contract for a period of 5–15 seconds. This is followed by the second stage of the seizure (clonic phase) that is characterized by twitching movements, usually visible only in the toes or in a non-paralyzed arm or leg. These are caused by alternating contraction and relaxation of these same muscles. This stage lasts approximately 10–60 seconds. The physician in charge will try to induce a seizure that lasts between one half minute and two minutes. If the first application of electricity fails to produce a seizure lasting at least 25 seconds, another attempt is made 60 seconds later. The session is stopped if the patient has no seizures after three attempts. The entire procedure, from beginning to end, lasts about 30 minutes.

The absence of seizures is most commonly caused either by the patient's physical condition at the time of treatment or by the individual nature of human responses to drugs and other treatment procedures. Just as there are some patients who do not respond to one type of antidepressant medication but do respond to others, some patients do not respond to ECT.

The total number of ECT treatments that will be given depends on such factors as the patient's age, **diagnosis**, the history of illness, family support, and response to therapy. Treatments are normally given every other day at a rate of two to three per week. The ECT treatments are stopped when the patient's psychiatric symptoms show significant signs of improvement. Depending on the patient's condition, this improvement may happen in a few weeks or, rarely, over a six-month period. In most cases, patients with depression require between six and twelve ECT sessions.

Only rarely is ECT treatment extended beyond six months. In such infrequent cases, treatments are decreased from two to four per week after the first month to one treatment every month or so.

No one knows for certain why ECT is effective. Because the treatment involves passing an electric current through the brain, which is electrically excitable tissue, it is not surprising that ECT has been shown to affect many neurotransmitter systems. **Neurotransmitters** are chemical messengers in the nervous system that carry signals from nerve cell to nerve cell. The neurotransmitters affected by ECT include **dopamine**, norepinephrine, serotonin, and gamma-aminobutyric acid (GABA).

Preparation

Patients and their relatives are typically prepared for ECT by viewing a videotape that explains both the procedure and the risks involved. The physician then answers any questions these individuals might have, and the patient is asked to sign an informed consent form. This form gives the doctor and the hospital legal permission to administer the treatment.

After the form has been signed, the doctor performs a complete physical examination and orders a number of tests that can help identify any potential problem. These tests may include a chest x ray, electrocardiogram (EKG), CT scan, urinalysis, spinal x ray, electroencephalogram (EEG), and complete blood count (CBC).

Some medications, such as lithium and a class of **antidepressants** known as monoamine oxidase inhibitors (MAOIs), should be discontinued for some time before ECT administration. Patients are instructed not to eat or drink for at least eight hours prior to the procedure to reduce the possibility of vomiting and choking. During the procedure itself, the members of the health care team closely monitor the patient's vital signs, including blood pressure, heart rate, and oxygen content.

Aftercare

The patient is moved to a recovery area after an ECT treatment. Vital signs are recorded every five minutes until the patient is fully awake, which may take 15–30 minutes. The patient may experience some initial confusion, but this feeling usually disappears in a matter of minutes. The patient may complain of headache, muscle pain, or back pain, which can be relieved by aspirin or another mild medication.

Following successful ECT treatments, patients with bipolar disorder may be given maintenance doses of lithium. Similarly, patients with depression may be given antidepressant drugs. These medications are intended to reduce the chance of **relapse** or the recurrence of symptoms. Some studies have estimated that approximately one-third to one-half of patients treated with ECT relapse within 12 months of treatment. After three years, this figure may increase to two-thirds. Follow-up care with medications for bipolar disorder or depression can reduce the relapse rate in the year following ECT treatment from 50% to 20%. Some patients might relapse because they do not respond well to the medications they take after their ECT sessions are completed. In some cases, patients who relapse may have severe forms of depression that are especially difficult to treat by any method.

KEY TERMS

Acute psychosis—A severe mental disorder marked by delusions, hallucinations, and other symptoms that indicate that the patient is not in contact with reality.

Catatonia—Disturbance of motor behavior with either extreme stupor or random, purposeless activity.

Electroencephalography—The measurement and recording of the brain's electrical activity.

Informed consent—A person's agreement to undergo a medical or surgical procedure, or to participate in a clinical study, after being properly advised of the medical facts related to the procedure or study and the risks involved.

Mania—An elevated or euphoric mood or irritable state that is characteristic of bipolar I disorder. This state is characterized by mental and physical hyperactivity, disorganization of behavior, and inappropriate elevation of mood.

Neuroleptic—Another name for the older antipsychotic medications, such as haloperidol (Haldol) and chlorpromazine (Thorazine).

Neuroleptic malignant syndrome (NMS)—An unusual but potentially serious complication that develops in some patients who have been treated with antipsychotic medications. NMS is characterized by changes in blood pressure, altered states of consciousness, rigid muscles, and fever. Untreated NMS can result in coma and death.

Parkinsonism—A condition caused by the destruction of the brain cells that produce dopamine (a neurotransmitter), and characterized by tremors of the fingers and hands, a shuffling gait, and muscular rigidity.

Psychomotor—Referring to a response or reaction that involves both the brain and muscular movements.

Psychotropic—Having an effect on the mind, brain, behavior, perceptions, or emotions. Psychotropic medications are used to treat mental illnesses because they affect a patient's moods and perceptions.

Relapse—A person experiences a relapse when he or she re-engages in a behavior that is harmful and that he or she was trying to change or eliminate. Relapse is a common occurrence after treatment for many disorders, including addictions and eating disorders.

Schizophrenia—A severe mental illness in which a person has difficulty distinguishing what is real from what is not real. It is often characterized by hallucinations, delusions, language and communication disturbances, and withdrawal from people and social activities.

Tourniquet—A rubber tube or length of cloth that is used to compress a blood vessel in order to stop bleeding or to shut off circulation in a part of the body. The tourniquet is wrapped around the arm (or other limb) and tightened by twisting.

Risks

Recent advances in medical technology have substantially reduced the complications associated with ECT. These include memory loss and confusion. Persons at high risk of having complications following ECT include those with a recent heart attack, uncontrolled high blood pressure, brain tumors, and previous spinal injuries.

One of the most common side effects of electroconvulsive therapy is memory loss. Patients may be unable to recall events that occurred before and after treatment. Elderly patients, for example, may become increasingly confused and forgetful as the treatments continue. In a minority of individuals, memory loss may last for months. For the majority of patients, however, recent memories return in a few days or weeks.

Elderly patients receiving ECT may experience disturbances in heart rhythm, slow heartbeat (bradycardia) or rapid heartbeat (tachycardia), and an increased number of falls. As many as one-third of elderly patients may experience such complications following the procedure.

Normal results

Post-treatment confusion and forgetfulness are common, though disturbing, symptoms associated with ECT. Doctors and nurses must be patient and supportive by providing patients and their families with factual information about the nature and timeframe of the patient's recovery.

A few patients are placed on maintenance ECT. This term means that they must return to the hospital every one to two months as needed for an additional treatment. These persons are thus able to keep their illness under control and lead normal and productive lives.

Abnormal results

If an ECT-induced seizure lasts too long (more than two minutes) during the procedure, physicians will control it with an intravenous infusion of an anticonvulsant drug, usually **diazepam** (Valium).

Overall, ECT is a very safe procedure. There is no convincing evidence of long-term harmful effects from ECT. Researchers are continuing to explore its potential in treating other disorders as well as other methods to replace ECT.

See also Catatonic disorder; Neurotransmitters.

Resources

BOOKS

American Psychiatric Association. *Practice Guidelines for the Treatment of Psychiatric Disorders.* 4th ed., Text rev. Washington, D.C.: American Psychiatric Association, 2000.

Fink, Max. *Electroshock.* New York: Oxford University Press, 2005.

VandenBos, Gary R., ed. *APA Dictionary of Psychology.* Washington, D.C.: American Psychological Association, 2007.

PERIODICALS

Loo, Colleen K., Isaac Schweitzer, and Chris Pratt. "Recent Advances in Optimizing Electroconvulsive Therapy." *Australian and New Zealand Journal of Psychiatry* 40.8 (2006): 632–38.

Munk-Olsen, T., and others. "Electroconvulsive Therapy: Predictors and Trends in Utilization from 1976 to 2000." *Journal of ECT* 22.2 (2006): 127–32.

Stein, Daniel, Abraham Weizman, and Yuval Bloch. "Electroconvulsive Therapy and Transcranial Magnetic Stimulation: Can They Be Considered Valid Modalities in the Treatment of Pediatric Mood Disorders?" *Child and Adolescent Psychiatric Clinics of North America* 15.4 (2006): 1035–56.

ORGANIZATIONS

American Psychiatric Association. 1400 K Street NW, Washington, DC 20005. <http://www.psych.org>.

National Alliance for the Mentally Ill (NAMI). Colonial Place Three, 2107 Wilson Boulevard, Suite 300, Arlington, VA 22021. <http://www.nami.org/index.html>.

Dean A. Haycock, PhD
Ruth A. Wienclaw, PhD

Electroencephalography

Definition

Electroencephalography (EEG) is a neurological diagnostic procedure that records the changes in electrical potentials (**brain** waves) in various parts of the brain.

Purpose

The EEG is an important aid in the **diagnosis** and management of epilepsy and other seizure disorders, as well as in the diagnosis of brain damage related to trauma and diseases, including strokes, tumors, encephalitis, and drug and alcohol intoxication. The EEG is also useful in monitoring brain wave activity and in the determination of brain death. Research is active in determining the role of EEG in the diagnosis and management of **mental retardation**, **sleep disorders**, degenerative diseases such as **Alzheimer's disease** and Parkinson's disease, and in certain mental disorders such as **autism** and **schizophrenia**.

Precautions

The EEG should be administered, monitored, and interpreted only by a specially trained health professional. It is important to recognize that diagnosis should not be based on the EEG alone—the EEG represents an adjunct to the neurological history, examination, and other specialized studies. The EEG is an extremely sensitive instrument, and tracings can be greatly influenced by the actions and the physiologic status of the patient. It is important that the patient be properly prepared physically and psychologically in order to obtain an accurate and reliable record. Patients scheduled for an EEG should withhold from medications such as anticonvulsants, tranquilizers, stimulants—including coffee, tea, and cola drinks—and alcohol for at least 24–48 hours prior to the test. Since as hypoglycemia affects brain wave patterns, the patient should not withhold any meals prior to the EEG.

Description

Brain function is associated with electrical activity, which is always accompanied by an electrical field. This field consists of two parts, the electrical field and the magnetic field, and is called an electromagnetic field. The electrical field is measured by surface electrodes and is recorded by the electroencephalogram. Prior to the recording session, approximately 16–20 electrodes are attached to the patient's scalp with a

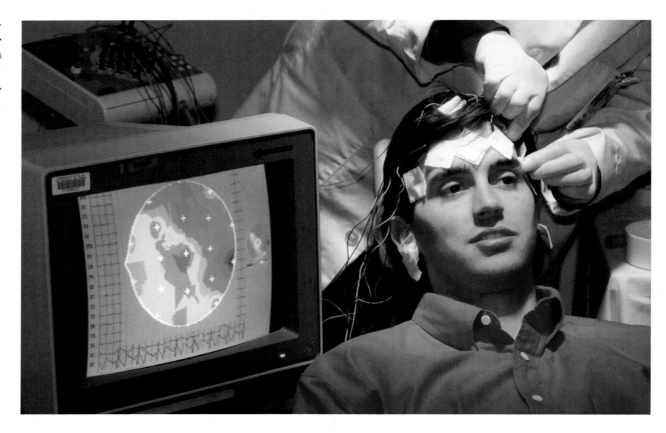

An EEG lab measures the brain waves of a subject. *(Richard T. Nowitz/Photo Researchers, Inc)*

conductive washable paste, or collodion. Depending on the purpose of the EEG, implantable needle electrodes may be utilized, in which case the patient should be informed that there will be mild discomfort.

Patients lie on a bed, padded table, or comfortable reclining chair and are asked to remain quiet and relaxed during the approximate one hour that is usually required for the EEG. If the diagnosis is a seizure disorder, a sleep recording up to three hours in duration is usually obtained. Under certain conditions, various stimuli such as flashing lights or deep breathing may be utilized. In an ambulatory EEG recording, the patient is attached to a portable cassette recorder and goes about regular activities, usually for up to 24 hours.

Magnetoencephalography

Magnetoencephalography, a supplement to EEG, also uses an electroencephalogram to measure the patient's electrical field. Every electrical current generates a magnetic field. The magnetic field is detected by an instrument called a biomagnetometer and recorded as a magnetoencephalograph (MEG). The information provided by the MEG is entirely different

from that provided by **computed tomography** (CT), topographic encephalography, or **magnetic resonance imaging** (MRI)—imaging instruments that provide still, structural, and anatomical information. The information recorded by the MEG provides important supplemental information to that recorded by the encephalogram and, used together and conjointly, they both provide a much more complete and comprehensive idea of cerebral events. Using MEG, the brain can be observed "in action," rather than just being viewed as a still image.

Magnetoencephalography has been used to map the sensory and motor cortices of the brain, to determine the organization of the auditory center of the brain, and to study cognitive functions such as speech, memory, attention, and consciousness. This information is critical for neurosurgical planning such as the removal of brain lesions. Thus, preoperative MEG is valuable in planning the surgical treatment of tumors and malformations. MEG can provide surgeons with real-time computer-generated images of deep-seated lesions that are essential before surgery. The quantitative EEG is also known by the acronym BEAM (brain electrical activity mapping).

Preparation

Prior to the EEG, the patient is given full instructions about how to prepare for the procedure, particularly by avoiding certain medications and food. In cases where a sleep EEG is anticipated, the patient may be requested to minimize sleep or stay awake the night before the procedure. **Sedatives** to induce sleep should be avoided, if possible.

Aftercare

No specific aftercare is required following an EEG. Patients are advised to resume their usual activities, especially the resumption of medications that had been temporarily discontinued.

Risks

The primary risk of EEG is the production of a seizure in a patient with epilepsy. This may result from the temporary discontinuation of anticonvulsant medication or from the provocation of a seizure by an epileptogenic stimulus such as flashing lights or deep breathing. Although the provocation of a seizure may serve to substantiate the diagnosis, all patients with the potential for **seizures** should be carefully monitored to avoid injury in case a seizure does result.

Normal results

The rate, height, and length of brain waves vary depending on the part of the brain being studied, and every individual has a unique and characteristic brain-wave pattern. Age and state of consciousness also cause changes in wave patterns. Several wave patterns have been identified:

- alpha waves: Most of the recorded waves in a normal adult's EEG are the occipital alpha waves, which are best obtained from the back of the head when the subject is resting quietly, awake with eyes closed. These waves, occurring typically in a pattern of 8–13 cycles per second, are blocked by excitement or by opening the eyes.
- beta waves: These waves, obtained from the central and frontal parts of the brain, are closely related to the sensory-motor parts of the brain and are also blocked by opening the eyes. Their frequency is in the range of 8–30 hertz (cycles per second).
- delta waves: These are irregular, slow waves of 2–3 hertz and are normally found in deep sleep and in infants and young children. They indicate an abnormality in an awake adult.
- theta waves: These are characterized by rhythmic, slow waves of 4–7 hertz.

KEY TERMS

Encephalitis—Inflammation of the brain.

Occipital bone—The occipital bone forms the back part of the skull.

Abnormal results

EEG readings of patients with epilepsy or other seizure disorders display bursts, or spikes, of electrical activity. In focal epilepsy, spikes are restricted to one hemisphere of the brain. If spikes are generalized to both hemispheres, multifocal epilepsy may be indicated.

Diagnostic brain-wave patterns of other disorders vary widely. The appearance of excess theta waves (four to eight cycles per second) may indicate brain injury. Brain-wave patterns in patients with brain disease, mental retardation, and brain injury show overall slowing. A trained medical specialist should interpret EEG results in the context of the patient's medical history and other pertinent medical test results.

See also Alcohol and related disorders; Sleep terror disorder; Sleepwalking disorder; Substance abuse and related disorders.

Resources

BOOKS

Ebersole, John S., and Timothy A. Pedley. *Current Practice of Clinical Electroencephalography.* 3rd ed. Hagerstown, MD: Lippincott Williams & Wilkins, 2003.

Niedermeyer, Ernst, and Fernando Lopes da Silva. *Electroencephalography: Basic Principles, Clinical Applications, and Related Fields.* 5th ed. Hagerstown, MD: Lippincott Williams & Wilkins, 2004.

Rowan, A. James, and Eugene Tolunsky. *Primer of EEG: With a Mini-Atlas.* Burlington, MA: Butterworth-Heinemann, 2003.

PERIODICALS

Coburn, Kerry L., and others. "The Value of Quantitative Electroencephalography in Clinical Psychiatry: A Report by the Committee on Research of the American Neuropsychiatric Association." *Journal of Neuropsychiatry & Clinical Neurosciences* 18.4 (Fall 2006): 460–500.

Frith, Chris D. "The Value of Brain Imaging in the Study of Development and Its Disorders." *Journal of Child Psychology and Psychiatry* 47.10 (Nov. 2006): 979–82.

Hurley, Robin A., Ronald Fisher, and Katherine H. Taber. "Windows to the Brain." *Journal of Neuropsychiatry & Clinical Neurosciences* 18.4 (Fall 2006): 436–43.

Knowlton, Robert C., and others. "Magnetic Source Imaging Versus Intracranial Electroencephalogram in Epilepsy

Surgery: A Prospective Study." *Annals of Neurology* 59.5 (May 2006): 835–42.

O'Sullivan, S. S., and others. "The Role of the Standard EEG in Clinical Psychiatry." *Human Psychopharmacology: Clinical and Experimental* 21.4 (June 2006): 265–71.

PaulaAnne Ford-Martin, MA
Ralph Myerson, MD
Ruth A. Wienclaw, PhD

Elimination disorders

Definition

Elimination disorders are disorders that concern the elimination of feces or urine from the body. The causes of these disorders may be medical or psychiatric.

Description

The American Psychiatric Association recognizes two elimination disorders, **encopresis** and **enuresis**. Encopresis is an elimination disorder that involves repeatedly having bowel movements in inappropriate places after the age when bowel control is normally expected. Encopresis is also called fecal incontinence. Enuresis, more commonly called bed-wetting, is an elimination disorder that involves release of urine into bedding, clothing, or other inappropriate places. Both of these disorders can occur during the day (diurnal) or at night (nocturnal). They may be voluntary or involuntary. Encopresis and enuresis may occur together, although most often they occur separately.

Elimination disorders may be caused by a physical condition, a side effect of a drug, or a psychiatric disorder. It is much more common for elimination disorders to be caused by medical conditions than psychiatric ones. In most cases in which the cause is medical, the soiling is unintentional. When the causes are psychiatric, the soiling may be intentional, but it is not always so.

Encopresis

Medical causes of encopresis are usually related to chronic constipation. As hard feces build up in the large intestine, the bowel is stretched out of shape. This allows liquid feces behind the hard stool to involuntarily leak out and stain clothing. Other medical causes of encopresis include malformations of the bowel and side effects of medication. Laxatives (medications that relieve constipation), drugs that kill some of the good bacteria in the intestines, and drugs that increase contractions in the intestines can all cause involuntary encopresis. Pediatricians or family physicians treat almost all cases of encopresis having medical causes. In cases of prolonged involuntary soiling, children may develop feelings of shame and embarrassment, leading to low self-esteem.

Psychiatric causes of encopresis are not as clear. A few children may experience encopresis because of fear of the toilet or because their toilet training was either overly pressured or irregular and incomplete. Older children may soil intentionally, sometimes smearing the feces on wall or clothing or hiding feces around the house. Children who show this pattern of soiling behavior often have clinical behavior problems such as **conduct disorder** or **oppositional defiant disorder**. About one-quarter of children who soil intentionally also have enuresis.

Enuresis

Enuresis also has both medical and psychiatric causes. Primary enuresis occurs when a child has never established bladder control. Medical causes of primary enuresis are often related to malformations of the urinary system, developmental delays, and hormonal imbalances that affect the ability to concentrate urine. There appears to be a genetic component to primary enuresis, since the condition tends to run in families. Primary enuresis may also be caused by psychological stressors such as family instability or erratic toilet training.

Secondary enuresis occurs when a child has established good bladder control for a substantial period, then begins wetting again. Involuntary secondary enuresis is thought to be brought on by life stresses. For example, it is common for young children to begin wetting the bed after moving to a new house or having a new sibling enter the family. Voluntary enuresis is not common. Like voluntary encopresis, it is associated with psychiatric conditions such as conduct disorder and oppositional defiant disorder.

Treatment and prognosis

Most children outgrow their elimination disorders successfully by the time they are teens, with the exception of those children whose elimination disorders are symptoms of other psychiatric disturbances.

Encopresis is treated with stool softeners or laxatives and by instituting regular bowel evacuation patterns. Enuresis is treated by **behavior modification**, including changing nighttime toileting habits. The least expensive and most effective method is by having the child sleep on a special pad that sets off an

KEY TERMS

Constipation—Difficult bowel movements caused by the infrequent production of hard stools.

Feces—Waste products eliminated from the large intestine; excrement.

Incontinence—The inability to control the release of urine or feces.

Laxative—Substance or medication that encourages a bowel movement.

Stools—Feces, bowel movements.

alarm when the pad becomes wet. This wakes the child and allows him to finish relieving in the toilet. Eventually he awakes without assistance before wetting. Drugs can also help in the treatment of enuresis, although **relapse** is common after they are stopped. Secondary enuresis caused by **stress** is treated by resolving the stress. **Psychotherapy** is usually not needed, although it may be helpful to children who develop feelings of shame associated with their elimination disorders. Adults can help children avoid shame and embarrassment by treating elimination accidents in a kind, matter-of-fact way.

Children with voluntary elimination disorders are treated for the diagnosed psychiatric problem associated with the elimination disorder using behavior modification, drugs, and other psychiatric interventions.

Resources

BOOKS

American Psychiatric Association. *Diagnostic and Statistical Manual of Mental Disorders,* 4th ed., Text rev. Washington, D.C.: American Psychiatric Association, 2000.

Hales, Robert E., Stuart C. Yudofsky, and John A. Talbot. *The American Psychiatric Press Textbook of Psychiatry,* 3rd ed. Washington, D.C.: American Psychiatric Press, 2000.

Sadock, Benjamin J. and Virginia A. Sadock, eds. *Comprehensive Textbook of Psychiatry,* 7th ed. Vol. 2. Philadelphia: Lippincott Williams and Wilkins, 2000.

PERIODICALS

Kuhn, Bret R., Bethany A. Marcus, and Sheryl L. Pitner. "Treatment Guidelines for Primary Nonretentive Encopresis and Stool Toileting Refusal." *American Family Physician* 58 (April 15, 1999): 8–18.

Mikkelsen, Edwin J. "Enuresis and Encopresis: Ten Years of Progress." *Journal of the American Academy of Child and Adolescent Psychiatry* 40 (October 2001): 1146–59.

ORGANIZATIONS

American Academy of Child and Adolescent Psychiatry. P. O. Box 96106, Washington, DC 20090. Telephone: (800) 333-7636. <www.aacap.org>.

National Association for Continence. P.O. Box 1019, Charleston, SC 29402-1019. Telephone: (800) 252-3337. <http://www.nafc.org>.

OTHER

National Guideline Clearinghouse. "Practice Parameter for the Assessment and Treatment of Children and Adolescents with Enuresis." (2005) <http://www.guideline.gov/summary/summary.aspx?doc_id=6510&nbr=004079&string=enuresis>.

National Kidney and Urologic Diseases Information Clearinghouse. National Institute of Diabetes and Digestive and Kidney Diseases. "Urinary Incontinence in Children." (2006) <http://kidney.niddk.nih.gov/kudiseases/pubs/uichildren/index.htm>.

National Library of Medicine. National Institutes of Health. "Enuresis." (2005) <http://www.nlm.nih.gov/medlineplus/ency/article/001556.htm>.

Tish Davidson, A.M.
Emily Jane Willingham, PhD

Enabling behaviors *see* **Addiction**

Encopresis

Definition

Encopresis is an elimination disorder that involves repeatedly having bowel movements in inappropriate places after the age when bowel control is normally expected. Encopresis is also called "soiling" or "fecal incontinence."

Description

By four years of age, most children are toilet trained for bowel movements. After that age, if inappropriate bowel movements occur regularly over a period of several months a child may be diagnosed with encopresis. Encopresis can be intentional or unintentional. Intentional soiling is associated with several psychiatric disorders. Involuntary or unintentional soiling is often the result of constipation.

Causes and symptoms

The only symptom of encopresis is that a person has bowel movements in inappropriate places, such as in clothing or on the floor. This soiling is not caused by taking laxatives or other medications and is not due to a disability or physical defect in the bowel. There are two main types of encopresis, and they have different causes.

Involuntary encopresis

With involuntary encopresis, a person has no control over elimination of feces from the bowel. The feces is semi-soft to almost liquid, and it leaks into clothing without the person making any effort to expel it. Leakage usually occurs during the day when the person is active and ranges from infrequent to almost continuous.

Involuntary soiling usually results from constipation. A hard mass of feces develops in the large intestine and is not completely expelled during a regular bowel movement in the toilet. This mass then stretches the large intestine out of shape, allowing liquid feces behind it to leak out. Up to 95% of encopresis is involuntary.

Although involuntary encopresis, called by the American Psychiatric Association (APA) encopresis with constipation and overflow incontinence, is caused by constipation, the constipation may be the result of psychological factors. Experiencing a stressful life event, harsh toilet training, toilet fear, or emotionally disturbing events can cause a child to withhold bowel movements or become constipated. Historically, children separated from their parents during World War II are reported to have shown a high incidence of encopresis, indicating that psychological factors play a role in this disorder.

Voluntary encopresis

A person with voluntary encopresis has control over when and where bowel movements occur and chooses to have them in inappropriate places. Constipation is not a factor, and the feces is usually a normal consistency. Often feces is smeared in an obvious place, although sometimes it is hidden around the house. The APA classifies voluntary encopresis as encopresis without constipation and overflow incontinence.

In young children, voluntary encopresis may represent a power struggle between the child and the caregiver doing the toilet training. In older children, voluntary encopresis is often associated with **oppositional defiant disorder** (ODD), **conduct disorder**, sexual **abuse**, or high levels of psychological stressors.

Demographics

Encopresis occurs in 1–3% of children from ages four to seven years and is seen more often in boys than in girls. The frequency of encopresis appears to be independent of social class, and there is no evidence that it runs in families.

Diagnosis

To receive an APA **diagnosis** of encopresis, a child must have a bowel movement, either intentional or accidental, in an inappropriate place at least once a month for a minimum of three months. In addition, the child must be chronologically or developmentally at least four years old, and the soiling cannot be caused by illness, medical conditions (e.g., chronic diarrhea, spina bifida, or anal stenosis), medications, or disabilities. However, it may be caused by constipation.

Treatments

Involuntary encopresis is treated by addressing the cause of the constipation and establishing soft, pain-free stools. This can include:

- increasing the amount of liquids a child drinks
- adding high-fiber foods to the diet
- short-term use of laxatives or stool softeners
- emptying the large intestine by using an enema
- establishing regular bowel habits

Once the constipation is resolved, involuntary encopresis normally stops.

Treatment of voluntary encopresis depends on the cause. When voluntary encopresis results from a power struggle between child and adult, it is treated with **behavior modification**. In addition to taking the steps listed above to ensure a soft, pain-free stool, the adult should make toileting a pleasant, pressure-free activity. Some experts suggest transferring the initiative for toileting to the child instead of constantly asking him/her to use the toilet. Others recommend toileting at scheduled times, but without pressure to perform. In either case, success should be praised and failure treated in a matter-of-fact manner. If opposition to using the toilet continues, the family may be referred to a child **psychiatrist** or a pediatric **psychologist**.

With older children who smear or hide feces, voluntary encopresis is usually a symptom of another more serious disorder. When children are successfully treated for the underlying disorder with psychiatric interventions, behavior modification, and education, the encopresis is often resolved.

Prognosis

Because 80–95% of encopresis is related to constipation, the success rate in resolving involuntary encopresis is high, although it may take time to

KEY TERMS

Feces—Waste products eliminated from the large intestine; excrement.

Incontinence—The inability to control the release of urine or feces.

Laxative—Substance or medication that encourages a bowel movement.

Stools—Feces; bowel movements.

establish good bowel habits and eliminate a reoccurrence of constipation. The success rate is also good for younger children in a power struggle with adults over toileting, although the results may be slow. The prognosis for older children with associated behavioral disorders is less promising and depends more on the success of resolving those problems than on direct treatment of the symptoms of encopresis.

Prevention

Power struggles during toilet training that lead to encopresis can be reduced by waiting until the child is developmentally ready and interested in using the toilet. Toilet training undertaken kindly, calmly, and with realistic expectations is most likely to lead to success. Successes should be rewarded and failures accepted. Once toilet training has been established, encopresis can be reduced by developing regular bowel habits and encouraging a healthy, high-fiber diet.

Resources

BOOKS

American Psychiatric Association. *Diagnostic and Statistical Manual of Mental Disorders,* 4th ed., Text rev. Washington, D.C.: American Psychiatric Association, 2000.

Sadock, Benjamin J., and Virginia A. Sadock, eds. *Comprehensive Textbook of Psychiatry,* 7th ed. Vol. 2. Philadelphia: Lippincott Williams and Wilkins, 2000.

PERIODICALS

Catto-Smith, Anthony G. "Constipation and Toileting Issues in Children." *Medical Journal of Australia* 182 (2005): 242–46.

Kuhn, Bret R., Bethany A. Marcus, and Sheryl L. Pitner. "Treatment Guidelines for Primary Nonretentive Encopresis and Stool Toileting Refusal." *American Family Physician* 58 (April 15, 1999): 8–18.

ORGANIZATIONS

American Academy of Child and Adolescent Psychiatry. P. O. Box 96106, Washington, DC 20090. Telephone: (800) 333-7636. <www.aacap.org>.

OTHER

American Academy of Family Physicians. "Stool Soiling and Constipation in Children." (2007) <http://familydoctor.org/166.xml>.

Tish Davidson, A.M.
Emily Jane Willingham, PhD

Endep *see* **Amitriptyline**

Energy therapies

Definition

Energy therapies is a collective term used to refer to a variety of alternative and complementary treatments based on the use, modification, or manipulation of energy fields. Most energy therapies presuppose or accept the theory that matter and energy are not exclusive opposites, but that matter is simply a denser form of energy that is more easily perceived by the senses. Some energy therapies are associated with systems of traditional Indian or Chinese medicine that are thousands of years old; others draw upon contemporary scientific theories. Energy therapies can be divided for purposes of discussion into two groups—those that utilize energy fields located in, affecting, or emanating from the human body (biofield therapies); and those that use electromagnetic fields in unconventional ways. In addition, there are energy therapies that combine biofield therapy with some aspects of bodywork—Breema, polarity therapy, and qigong are examples of this combined approach.

Energy therapies vary widely in their understanding of qualifications to be a healer. Some have credentialing or training programs; others do not. Some practitioners of energy therapy believe that all or most people have the capacity to be healers; others regard the ability to use or direct healing energies as a gift or charism that is given only to people who are "chosen" or unusually spiritual.

Although energy therapies are often associated with either Eastern or so-called "New Age" belief systems, most do not expect people in need of healing to give up mainstream Western religious practice or allopathic medical/psychiatric treatments.

Purpose

The purpose of energy therapies can be broadly defined as the healing of mental or physical disorders by rebalancing the energy fields in the human body or by drawing upon spiritual energies or forces for such healing. Some energy therapies include internal **detoxification** or release of trauma-related memories as additional purposes.

Precautions

In general, persons who are interested in Breema, qigong, or any form of energy therapy that involves vigorous physical exercise or bodywork should seek the advice of a qualified medical practitioner before starting such a program. This precaution is particularly important for persons with chronic heart or lung disease, persons recovering from surgery or acute illness, or persons with arthritis or other disorders that affect the muscles and joints.

Some forms of energy therapy may produce unexpected or startling psychological reactions. For example, a type of psychospiritual energy referred to as Kundalini in Indian **yoga** sometimes produces experiences of spiritual crisis that may be interpreted by mainstream psychiatrists as symptoms of **schizophrenia** or another psychotic disorder. Practitioners of Reiki healing have reported instances of patients feeling tingling sensations, "spaciness," an "out of body" sensation, sudden warmth, or similar experiences. As a rule, people in treatment for any mental condition or disorder should consult their therapist before beginning any form of energy treatment. This precaution is particularly important for patients diagnosed with PTSD or a dissociative disorder, and for those who are easily hypnotized. It is also a good idea to find out as much as possible about the background and basic beliefs associated with a specific energy therapy, including the training or credentialing of its practitioners.

Description

Brief descriptions of some of the better known energy therapies follow.

Therapeutic touch

Therapeutic touch, or TT, is a form of energy therapy that developed in the United States. It is a noninvasive method of healing derived from an ancient laying-on of hands technique. In TT, practitioners alter the patient's energy field through a transfer of energy from their hands to the patient. Therapeutic touch was developed in 1972 by Dora Kunz, a psychic healer, and Dolores Krieger, a professor of nursing at New York University. The principle behind TT is restoration of balance or harmony to the human energy field, or aura, that is thought to extend several inches to several feet from the body. When illness occurs, it creates a dis-

turbance or blockage in the vital energy field. The TT practitioner uses her/his hands to discern the blockage or disturbance. Although the technique is called "therapeutic touch," there is generally no touching of the client's physical body, only his or her energetic body or field. TT is usually performed on fully clothed patients who are either lying down on a flat surface or sitting up in a chair.

A therapeutic touch session consists of five steps or phases. The first step is a period of **meditation** on the practitioner's part, to become spiritually centered and energized for the task of healing. The second step is assessment or discernment of the energy imbalances in the patient's aura. In this step, the TT practitioner holds his or her hands about 2–3 inches above the patient's body and moves them in long, sweeping strokes from the patient's head downward to the feet. The practitioner may feel a sense of warmth, heaviness, tingling, or similar cues, as they are known in TT. The cues are thought to reveal the location of the energy disturbances or imbalances. In the third step, known as the unruffling process, the practitioner removes the energy disturbances with downward sweeping movements. In the fourth step, the practitioner serves as a channel for the transfer of universal energy to the patient. The fifth step consists of smoothing the patient's energy field and restoring a symmetrical pattern of energy flow. After the treatment, the patient rests for 10–15 minutes.

Although therapeutic touch has become a popular alternative or complementary approach in some schools of nursing in the United States and Canada, acceptance by the mainstream medical community varies. Many hospitals permit nurses and staff to perform TT on patients at no extra charge. On the other hand, however, therapeutic touch became national news in April 1998 when an elementary-school student carried out research for a science project that questioned its claims. Twenty-one TT practitioners with experience ranging from one to 27 years were blindfolded and asked to identify whether the investigator's hand was closer to their right hand or their left. Placement of the investigator's hand was determined by flipping a coin. The TT practitioners were able to identify the correct hand in only 123 (44%) of 280 trials, a figure that could result from random chance alone. Debate about the merits of TT filled the editorial pages of the *Journal of the American Medical Association* for nearly a year after the news reports, and continues to this day.

Qigong

Qigong is a form of Chinese energy therapy that is usually considered a martial art by most Westerners. It is better understood, however, as an ancient

Chinese system of postures, exercises, breathing techniques and meditations. Its techniques are designed to improve and enhance the body's *qi*. According to traditional Chinese philosophy and medicine, qi is the fundamental life energy responsible for human health and vitality. Qi travels through the body along channels called meridians. There are twelve main meridians in humans. Each major body organ has qi associated with it, and each organ interacts with particular emotions on the mental level. Qigong techniques are designed to improve the balance and flow of energy throughout the meridians, and to increase the overall quantity and volume of a person's qi.

In the context of energy therapy, qigong is sometimes divided into internal and external qigong. Internal qigong refers to a person's practice of qigong exercises to maintain his or her own health and vitality. Some qigong master teachers are renowned for their skills in external qigong, in which the energy from one person is passed on to another for healing. Chinese hospitals use medical qigong along with herbs, **acupuncture** and other techniques of traditional Chinese medicine. In these hospitals, qigong healers use external qigong and also design specific internal qigong exercises for the patients' health problems.

Reiki

Reiki is a holistic alternative therapy based on Eastern concepts of energy flow and the seven chakras (energy centers) in the human body. Reiki was formulated by a Japanese teacher, Mikao Usui, around 1890, based on Vajrayana (Tibetan) Buddhism, but incorporates meditation techniques, beliefs, and symbols that are considerably older. It is distinctive among energy therapies in its emphasis on self-healing, its spiritual principles, and its accreditation of healers through a system of initiation. Reiki practitioners participate in the healing of emotional and spiritual as well as physical pain through the transmission of universal life energy, called "rei-ki" in Japanese. It is believed that ki flows throughout the universe, but that Reiki connects humans in a more direct way to the universal source. Reiki is used for the healing of animals as well as people. A research team at the University of Michigan is studying the effectiveness of Reiki in treating **chronic pain** in patients with diabetic neuropathy. Various other studies are also underway in the United States and Canada, some examining the efficacy of the therapy in coping with pain and **anxiety**.

Although Reiki involves human touch, it is not massage therapy. The patient lies on a table fully clothed except for shoes while the practitioner places her or his hands over the parts of the body and the chakras in sequence. The hands are held palms downward with the fingers and thumbs extended. If the person is in pain or cannot turn over, the practitioner may touch only the affected part(s). Silence or music appropriate for meditation is considered essential to the treatment. Reiki healers practice daily self-healing, in which they place their hands in traditional positions on their own bodies They may use touch, or distant/non-touch.

Reiki healers are initiated into three levels of practice through attunements, which are ceremonies in which teachers transmit the hand positions and "sacred" symbols. Reiki I healers learn the basic hand positions and can practice direct physical, emotional or mental healing on themselves and others. Reiki II healers are taught the symbols that empower them to do distance or absentee healing. In Reiki III the healer makes a commitment to become a master teacher and do spiritual healing.

Polarity therapy

Polarity therapy, which is sometimes called polarity balancing, is a biofield therapy that resembles Reiki in its emphasis on energy flow, human touch, and the energy centers (chakras) in the human body. Polarity therapy was developed by Dr. Randolph Stone (1890-1981), an American chiropractor and naturopath. It integrates bodywork with diet, yoga-based exercise, and self-awareness techniques to release energy blockages in the patient's body, mind, or feelings. Polarity theory divides the body into three horizontal and four vertical zones (right, left, front, and back), each having a positive, negative, or neutral charge. Energy currents in the zones are correlated with five energy centers in the body corresponding to the five elements (ether, air, fire, water, and earth) of Ayurvedic medicine.

Polarity therapy can be done one-on-one or with a group of practitioners working on the patient. The therapist as well as the patient removes shoes. The patient lies fully dressed except for shoes on a massage table or bed, or on the floor. The practitioner takes the patient's history, checks reflexes and touches body parts to determine energy blocks. Polarity therapy uses three levels of touch: no touch (hands held above the body, touching only the energy fields); light touch; and a deep, massaging touch. The therapist balances energy currents in the patient's body by placing his or her "plus" hand on "negative" body parts and vice versa. Polarity therapy involves rocking the patient's body and holding the head as well as more usual massage techniques. It takes about four polarity sessions to treat most conditions, with each session lasting about an hour. After a course of treatment, the polarity practitioner usually suggests drinking plenty of liquids for one to two weeks together with other dietary changes as part of a general internal cleansing or detoxification program. Polarity yoga (stretching exercises) is prescribed for the patient's regular workouts at home.

Breema

Breema is a form of body movement energy therapy that combines elements of bodywork, yoga, chiropractic, and New Age philosophy. Breema began in California in 1980. Its founder is Dr. Jon Schreiber, a graduate of Palmer College of Chiropractic. The Breema Health and Wellness Center was opened in Oakland, California, in 1981. The principles of Breema are intended to free people from the conceptual body, defined as "the ideas and images of our body that we carry in our mind." The aim of Breema "is to increase vitality, not to fight sickness, and to create an atmosphere which allows the body to move toward a natural state of balance." A person receiving a Breema treatment works with an instructor or practitioner through a series of individualized exercises on a padded floor. The instructors and practitioners are certified by the Breema Center in Oakland.

Decrystallization is an important part of Breema therapy. According to Breema, decrystallization is a process in which the body is helped to release deeply held, or "crystallized," patterns of chronic discomfort, tension, or emotional pain. As the body releases its crystallizations, its "core energetic patterns" are balanced and realigned. A decrystallization program consists of one or more Breema treatments per week for a year. It includes a set of personalized self-Breema exercises.

Electromagnetic therapies

Electromagnetic therapies cover a variety of treatments that use a source of physical energy outside the body—most often magnets or electromagnetic field stimulation—to treat a range of musculoskeletal disorders. Some forms of magnetic therapy, such as bracelets, gloves, shoe inserts, and similar items containing small magnets meant to be worn near the affected body part, can be self-administered. This form of magnetic therapy has become quite popular among professional athletes and "weekend warriors" to relieve soreness in joints and muscles from over exercise. At present there are two hypothetical explanations of the effectiveness of magnetic therapy. One theory maintains that the magnets stimulate nerve endings in the skin surface to release endorphins, which are pain-relieving chemicals produced by the body in response to **stress** or injury.

According to the second hypothesis, the magnets attract certain ions (electrically charged molecules) in the blood, which serves to increase the blood flow in that area of the body. The increased blood flow then relieves the tissue swelling and other side effects of over exercise that cause pain.

Other forms of electromagnetic therapy require special equipment and cannot be self-administered. These forms of treatment are most commonly used by naturopathic practitioners. One form, called **transcranial magnetic stimulation**, is used in the treatment of **depression**. Another form, called pulsed electromagnetic field stimulation, has been shown to be effective in the treatment of osteoarthritis.

Preparation

Most forms of energy therapy require little preparation on the patient's part except for the wearing of loose and comfortable clothes. Patients are asked to remove jewelry before a polarity balancing treatment and to remove eyeglasses and shoes prior to Reiki treatment. Qigong should not be practiced on either a full or a completely empty stomach.

Aftercare

Aftercare for therapeutic touch and Reiki usually involves a few moments of quiet rest to maximize the benefits of treatment. Aftercare for polarity therapy includes increased fluid intake for one to two weeks and other dietary adjustments that may be recommended by the practitioner.

Risks

There are no known risks associated with therapeutic touch, or polarity balancing. Using Reiki, precautions should be taken clients diagnosed with schizophrenia, **psychosis**, dissociative disorder, manic/depressive (bipolar) or borderline personality. The risk of physical injury from the exercises involved in Breema or qigong are minimal for patients who have consulted their primary physician beforehand and are working with a qualified instructor.

Mild headache has been reported as a side effect of transcranial magnetic stimulation. No side effects have been associated with self-administered magnetic therapy.

Normal results

Normal results for energy therapies include increased physical vitality, lowered blood pressure, a sense of calm or relaxation, improved sleep at night,

Aura—An energy field that is thought to emanate from the human body and to be visible to people with special psychic or spiritual powers.

Ayurvedic medicine—The traditional medical system of India. Ayurvedic treatments include diet, exercises, herbal treatments, meditation, massage, breathing techniques, and exposure to sunlight.

Biofield therapies—A subgroup of energy therapies that make use of energy fields (biofields) thought to exist within or emanate from the human body. Biofield therapies include such approaches as Reiki, therapeutic touch, qigong, and polarity balancing.

Bodywork—Any technique involving hands-on massage or manipulation of the body.

Breema—An alternative therapy that originated in California in the 1980s. Breema combines biofield therapy with certain elements of chiropractic and bodywork.

Chakra—One of the seven major energy centers in the body, according to traditional Indian yoga.

Endorphins—A group of peptide compounds released by the body in response to stress or traumatic injury. Endorphins react with opiate receptors in the brain to reduce or relieve pain.

Kundalini—In Indian yoga, a vital force or energy at the base of the spine that is activated or released by certain yoga postures or breathing techniques. This release is called the "awakening" of the kundalini. Some Westerners have had kundalini experiences that were diagnosed as psychotic episodes or symptoms of schizophrenia.

Meridians—In traditional Chinese medicine, a network of pathways or channels that convey qi, or vital energy, through the body.

Polarity therapy—A form of energy therapy influenced by Ayurvedic medicine that integrates bodywork with diet, home exercises, and self-awareness techniques. It is sometimes called polarity balancing.

Prana—The Sanskrit word for vital energy, roughly equivalent to qi in traditional Chinese medicine.

Qi—The traditional Chinese term for vital energy or the life force. The word is also spelled "ki" or "chi" in English translations of Japanese and Chinese medical books.

Qigong—A traditional form of Chinese energy therapy that includes physical exercises, breathing techniques, postures, and mental discipline. Internal qigong refers to exercises practiced to maintain one's own health and vitality; external qigong refers to the transfer of energy from a qigong master to another person for healing purposes. External qigong is also known as medical qigong.

Reiki—A form of energy therapy that originated in Japan. Reiki practitioners hold their hands on or slightly above specific points on the patient's body in order to convey universal life energy to that area for healing.

Therapeutic touch (TT)—An American form of energy therapy based on the ancient tradition of the laying-on of hands. TT is thought to work by removing energy blockages or disturbances from the patient's aura.

and a strengthened immune system. Some persons report pain relief and speeded-up healing of wounds from magnetic therapy, Reiki, and qigong.

Abnormal results

Abnormal results from energy therapies include physical injury, severe headache, dizziness, depressed mood, or increased anxiety.

See also Bodywork therapies; Light therapy.

Resources

BOOKS

Collinge, William, PhD. *Subtle Energy: Awakening to the Unseen Forces in Our Lives.* New York: Warner Books, Inc., 1998.

Krieger, Dolores, Ph.D., R.N. *Accepting Your Power to Heal: The Personal Practice of Therapeutic Touch.* New York: Bear and Company, 1993.

Mitchell, Karyn, PhD. *Reiki: A Torch in Daylight.* St. Charles, IL: Mind Rivers Publications, 1994.

Pelletier, Kenneth R., MD. "Spirituality and Healing: As Above . . . So Below." Chapter 11 in *The Best Alternative Medicine.* New York: Simon and Schuster, 2002.

Sovatsky, Stuart, PhD. "Kundalini Awakening: Breakdown or Breakthrough?" In *Living Yoga: A Comprehensive Guide for Daily Life,* edited by Georg Feuerstein and Stephan Bodian. New York: Jeremy P. Tarcher/Perigee Books, 1993.

Stein, Diane. *All Women Are Healers: A Comprehensive Guide to Natural Healing.* Freedom, CA: The Crossing Press, 1990.

Stein, Diane. *Essential Reiki: A Complete Guide to an Ancient Healing Art*. Freedom, CA: The Crossing Press, Inc., 1995.

Svoboda, Robert, and Arnie Lade. *Tao and Dharma: Chinese Medicine and Ayurveda*. Twin Lakes, WI: Lotus Press, 1995.

PERIODICALS

Golden, Jane. "Qigong and Tai Chi as Energy Medicine." *Share Guide* (November-December 2001): 37.

Gordon, A., J. H. Merenstein, and others. "The effects of therapeutic touch on clients with osteoarthritis of the knee." *Journal of Family Practice* 47 (1998): 271–277.

Hudson, Tori. "Naturopathic Medicine, Integrative Medicine and Women's Health." *Townsend Letter for Doctors and Patients* (November 2001): 136.

Johnson, Jerry Alan. "Medical Qigong for Breast Disease." *Share Guide* (November-December 2001): 109.

Rosa, Linda, MSN, Emily Rosa, Larry Sarner, and Stephen Barrett, MD. "A Close Look at Therapeutic Touch." *Journal of the American Medical Association* 279 (April 1, 1998): 1005–11.

ORGANIZATIONS

American Association of Naturopathic Physicians. 601 Valley Street, Suite 105, Seattle, WA 98109. Telephone: (206) 298-0126. <www.naturopathic.org>.

American Polarity Therapy Association. 288 Bluff Street #149, Boulder, CO 80301. Telephone: (303) 545-2080. <www.livelinks.com/sumeria/health/polarity.html>.

The Breema Center. 6076 Claremont Avenue. Oakland, CA 94618. Telephone: (510) 428-0937. Fax (510) 428-9235. <www.breema.com>.

International Society for the Study of Subtle Energies and Energy Medicine (ISSSEEM). 356 Goldco Circle, Golden, CO 80401. Telephone: (303) 278-2228. <www.vitalenergy.com/ISSSEEM>.

The Kundalini Clinic. 3040 Richmond Boulevard, Oakland, CA, 94611. Telephone: (510) 465-2986.

National Center for Complementary and Alternative Medicine (NCCAM) Clearinghouse. P.O. Box 7923, Gaithersburg, MD 20898. Telephone: (888) 644-6226. TTY: (866) 464-3615. Fax: (866) 464-3616. <www.nccam.nih.gov>.

The Nurse Healers Professional Associates International (NH-PAI), the Official Organization of Therapeutic Touch. 3760 S. Highland Drive, Salt Lake City, UT 84106. Telephone: (801) 273-3399. nhpai@therapeutic-touch.org. <www.therapeutic-touch.org>.

Qigong Human Life Research Foundation. PO Box 5327. Cleveland, OH 44101. Telephone: (216) 475-4712.

OTHER

National Center for Complementary and Alternative Medicine (NCCAM). Fact Sheets. *Major Domains of Complementary and Alternative Medicine*. <www.nccam.nih.gov/fcp/classify/>.

Rebecca J. Frey, Ph.D.

Enuresis

Definition

Enuresis, more commonly called bed-wetting, is a disorder of elimination that involves the voluntary or involuntary release of urine into bedding, clothing, or other inappropriate places. In adults, loss of bladder control is often referred to as urinary incontinence rather than enuresis; it is frequently found in patients with late-stage **Alzheimer's disease** or other forms of **dementia**.

Description

Enuresis is a condition that has been described since 1500 B.C. People with enuresis wet the bed or release urine at other inappropriate times. Release of urine at night (nocturnal enuresis) is much more common than daytime, or diurnal, wetting. Enuresis commonly affects young children and is involuntary. Many cases of enuresis clear up by themselves as the child matures, although some children need behavioral or physiological treatment in order to remain dry.

There are two main types of enuresis in children. Primary enuresis occurs when a child has never established bladder control. Secondary enuresis occurs when a person has established bladder control for a period of six months, then relapses and begins wetting. To be diagnosed with enuresis, a person must be at least five years old or have reached a developmental age of five years. Below this age, problems with bladder control are considered normal.

Causes and symptoms

Symptoms

The symptoms of enuresis are straightforward—a person urinates in inappropriate places or at inappropriate times. The causes of enuresis are not so clear. A small number of children have abnormalities in the anatomical structure of their kidney or bladder that interfere with bladder control, but normally the cause is not the physical structure of the urinary system. A few children appear to have to have a lower-than-normal ability to concentrate urine, due to low levels of antidiuretic hormone (ADH). This hormone helps to regulate fluid balance in the body. Large amounts of dilute urine cause the bladder to overflow at night. For the majority of bedwetters, there is no single clear physical or psychological explanation for enuresis.

Causes in children

The fourth edition of the *Diagnostic and Statistical Manual of Mental Disorders*, text revision, or (*DSM-IV-TR*), does not distinguish between children who wet the bed involuntarily and those who voluntarily release urine. Increasingly, however, research findings suggest that voluntary and involuntary enuresis have different causes.

Involuntary enuresis is much more common than voluntary enuresis. Involuntary enuresis may be categorized as either primary or secondary. Primary enuresis occurs when young children lack bladder control from infancy. Most of these children have urine control problems only during sleep; they do not consciously, intentionally, or maliciously wet the bed. Research suggests that children who are nighttime-only bedwetters may have a nervous system that is slow to process the feeling of a full bladder. Consequently, these children do not wake up in time to relieve themselves. In other cases, the child's enuresis may be related to a sleep disorder.

Children with diurnal enuresis wet only during the day. There appear to be two types of daytime wetters. One group seems to have difficulty controlling the urge to urinate. The other group consciously delays urinating until they lose control. Some children have both diurnal and nocturnal enuresis.

Secondary enuresis occurs when a child has stayed dry day and night for at least six months, then returns to wetting. Secondary enuresis usually occurs at night. Many studies have been done to determine if there is a psychological component to enuresis. Researchers have found that secondary enuresis is more likely to occur after a child has experienced a stressful life event such as the birth of a sibling, divorce or death of a parent, or moving to a new house.

Several studies have investigated the association of primary enuresis and psychiatric or behavior problems. The results suggest that primary nocturnal enuresis is not caused by psychological disorders. Bed-wetting runs in families, however, and there is strong evidence of a genetic component to involuntary enuresis.

Unlike involuntary enuresis, voluntary enuresis is not common. It is associated with such psychiatric disorders as **oppositional defiant disorder** and is substantially different from ordinary nighttime bed-wetting. Voluntary enuresis is always secondary.

Causes in adults

Enuresis or urinary incontinence in elderly adults may be caused by loss of independent control of body functions resulting from dementia, bladder infections, uncontrolled diabetes, side effects of medications, or weakened bladder muscles. Urinary incontinence in adults is managed by treatment of the underlying medical condition, if one is present; or by the use of adult briefs with disposable liners.

Demographics

Enuresis is a problem of the young and is twice as common in boys as in girls. At age five, about 7% of boys and 3% of girls have enuresis. This number declines steadily in older children; by age 18, only about 1% of adolescents experience enuresis. Studies done in several countries suggest that there is no apparent cultural influence on the incidence of enuresis in children. On the other hand, the disorder does appear to run in families; children with one parent who wet the bed as a child are five to seven times more likely to have enuresis than children whose parents did not have the disorder in childhood.

Diagnosis

Enuresis is most often diagnosed in children because the parents express concern to the child's doctor. The pediatrician or family physician will give the child a physical examination to rule out medical conditions that may be causing the problem, including structural abnormalities in the child's urinary tract. The doctor may also rule out a sleep disorder as a possible cause. In many cases the pediatrician can reassure the child's parents and give them helpful advice.

According to the American Psychiatric Association, making a **diagnosis** of enuresis requires that a child must have reached the chronological or developmental age of five. Inappropriate urination must occur at least twice a week for three months; or the frequency of inappropriate urination must cause significant distress and interfere with the child's school and/or social life. Finally, the behavior cannot be caused exclusively by a medical condition or as a side effect of medication.

Treatments

Treatment for enuresis is not always necessary. About 15% of children who have enuresis outgrow it each year after age six. When treatment is desired, a physician will rule out obvious physical causes of enuresis through a physical examination and medical history. Several different treatment options are then available.

Behavior modification

Behavior modification is often the treatment of choice for enuresis. It is inexpensive and has a success rate of about 75%. The child's bedding includes a special pad with a sensor that rings a bell when the pad becomes wet. The bell wakes the child, who then gets up and goes to the bathroom to finish emptying his bladder. Over time, the child becomes conditioned to waking up when the bladder feels full.

Once this response is learned, some children continue to wake themselves without help from the alarm, while others are able to sleep all night and remain dry. A less expensive behavioral technique involves setting an alarm clock to wake the child every night after a few hours of sleep, until the child learns to wake up spontaneously. In trials, this method was as effective as the pad-and-alarm system. A newer technique involves an ultrasound monitor worn on the child's pajamas. The monitor can sense bladder size, and sets off an alarm once the bladder reaches a predetermined level of fullness. This technique avoids having to change wet bed pads.

Other behavior modifications that can be used alone or with the pad-and-alarm system include:

- restricting liquids starting several hours before bedtime
- waking the child up in the night to use the bathroom
- teaching urinary retention techniques
- giving the child positive reinforcement for dry nights and being sympathetic and understanding about wet nights

Treatment with medications

There are two main drugs for treating enuresis. **Imipramine**, a tricyclic antidepressant, has been used since the early 1960s. It appears to work in up to 60% of cases, although **relapse** occurs in about 50% of successful treatments. Desmopressin acetate (DDAVP), which acts as an antidiuretic, has been widely used to treat enuresis since the 1990s. It is available as a nasal spray or tablet and can effective in up to 65% of cases. Relapse rates with DDAVP can be as high as 80%.

Alternative therapies

Some success in treating bed-wetting has been reported using hypnosis. When hypnosis works, the results are seen within four to six sessions. **Acupuncture** and massage have also been used to treat enuresis, with inconclusive results.

KEY TERMS

Bladder—A muscular sac in the lower abdomen that holds urine until it is discharged from the body.

Elimination—The medical term for expelling waste from the body.

Enuresis—The inability to control urination; bed-wetting.

Primary enuresis—Bed-wetting in a child who has not yet developed bladder control.

Secondary enuresis—Bed-wetting in a child who has established bladder control but has begun to wet the bed again, usually as the result of emotional stress.

Urinary incontinence—A term that is sometimes used for enuresis in adults. Urinary incontinence is often found in patients with late-stage Alzheimer's disease or other adult-onset dementias.

Urinary system—The kidney, urethra, bladder, and associated organs that process urine and eliminate it from the body.

Psychotherapy

Primary enuresis does not require **psychotherapy**. Secondary enuresis, however, is often successfully treated with therapy. The goal of the treatment is to resolve the underlying stressful event that has caused a relapse into bed-wetting. Unlike children with involuntary enuresis, children who intentionally urinate in inappropriate places often have other serious psychiatric disorders. Enuresis is usually a symptom of another disorder. Therapy to treat the underlying disorder is essential to resolving the enuresis.

Prognosis

Enuresis is a disorder that most children outgrow. The short-term success rate with drug treatments is even higher than with behavioral therapy. Drugs do not, however, eliminate the enuresis. Many children who take drugs to control their bed-wetting relapse when the drugs are stopped.

Prevention

Although enuresis cannot be prevented, one side effect of the disorder is the shame and social embarrassment it causes. Children who wet may avoid sleepovers, camp, and other activities where their bed-wetting will become obvious. Loss of these opportunities can cause a loss of self-esteem, social isolation, and adjustment problems. A kind, low-key approach to enuresis helps to prevent these problems.

Resources

BOOKS

American Psychiatric Association. *Diagnostic and Statistical Manual of Mental Disorders,* 4th ed., Text rev. Washington, D.C.: American Psychiatric Association, 2000.

Mace, Nancy L., and Peter V. Rabins. *The 36-Hour Day.* Revised and updated edition. New York: Warner Books, 2001; by arrangement with The Johns Hopkins University Press.

Maizels, Max, Diane Rosenbaum, and Barbara Keating. *Getting Dry: How to Help Your Child Overcome Bedwetting.* Boston: Harvard Common Press, 1999.

Sadock, Benjamin J., and Virginia A. Sadock, eds. *Comprehensive Textbook of Psychiatry,* 7th ed. Vol. 2. Philadelphia: Lippincott Williams and Wilkins, 2000.

PERIODICALS

Mikkelsen, Edwin J. "Enuresis and Encopresis: Ten Years of Progress." *Journal of the American Academy of Child and Adolescent Psychiatry* 40 (October 2001): 1146–59.

ORGANIZATIONS

American Academy of Child and Adolescent Psychiatry. P. O. Box 96106, Washington, DC 20090. Telephone: (800) 333-7636. <www.aacap.org>.

National Association for Continence. P.O. Box 1019, Charleston. SC 29402-1019. Telephone: (800) 252-3337. <http://www.nafc.org>.

National Kidney Foundation. 30 East 33rd Street, Suite 1100, New York, NY 10016. <www.kidney.org>.

OTHER

"Bedwetting." American Academy of Child & Adolescent Psychiatry (AACAP). AACAP Facts For Families Pamphlet, Number 18. Washington, DC: American Academy of Child & Adolescent Psychiatry, 1999.

"Bedwetting." National Kidney Foundation. 2001. <www.kidney.org/general/atoz/content/bedwetting.html>.

"Enuresis." National Library of Medicine. National Institutes of Health. (2005) <http://www.nlm.nih.gov/medlineplus/ency/article/001556.htm>.

National Guideline Clearinghouse. Practice Parameter for the Assessment and Treatment of Children and Adolescents with Enuresis. (2005) <http://www.guideline.gov/summary/summary.aspx?doc_id=6510&nbr=004079&string=enuresis>.

"Urinary Incontinence in Children." National Kidney and Urologic Diseases Information Clearinghouse. National Institute of Diabetes and Digestive and Kidney Diseases. (2006) <http://kidney.niddk.nih.gov/kudiseases/pubs/uichildren/index.htm>.

Tish Davidson, A.M.
Emily Jane Willingham, PhD

Epinephrine *see* **Adrenaline**

Erectile dysfunction

Definition

Erectile dysfunction (ED) may be defined as the consistent inability to achieve or maintain an erection sufficient to permit satisfactory sexual intercourse. The word "consistent" is included in the definition because most men experience transient episodes of ED that are temporary and usually associated with **fatigue**, anger, **depression**, or other stressful emotions. The use of the formerly used term "impotence" has been virtually abandoned because of its inherent **stigma** of weakness and lack of power.

Erectile dysfunction can occur as part of several mental disorders recognized by the mental health professional's manual, the ***Diagnostic and Statistical Manual of Mental Disorders,*** often shortened to the *DSM*. ED is the main symptom in the disorder the manual calls "male erectile disorder." ED can also be a symptom of other disorders, such as sexual dysfunction due to a general medical condition or substance-induced sexual dysfunction. In this entry, however, ED is examined and discussed as its own medical entity, and not within the strict guidelines of the *DSM*.

Description

Penile erection occurs essentially when the penis becomes engorged with blood. The anatomical compartments (two corpora cavernosa and one corpus spongiosum) are capable of being distended with seven times their normal amount of blood. When this occurs in association with relaxation of the penile muscles, erection results.

The sequence of events resulting in penile erection is complex. It is usually initiated by sexual arousal stimuli arising in the **brain** as a result of visual, auditory, or olfactory sensations or erotic thoughts. Tactile (touch) sensations of the penis acting through the spinal cord play a similar role. Sexual arousal results in the release of a chemical (nitric oxide) from specialized cells. Nitric oxide causes the formation of a substance (cyclic glutamine monophosphate [cGMP]), which is responsible for dilating the blood vessels of the penis and relaxing its muscles, thus allowing for an increase in blood flow and resultant penile erection. Compression of the dilated blood vessels against the firm outer lining of the penis prevents the blood from escaping and perpetuates the erection. A specialized substance (phosphodiesterase 5 [PDE-5]), causes the breakdown of cGMP and, with the help of nerves from the sympathetic nervous system, allows the penis to return to its flaccid relaxed state.

Any defect in this complex cascade of events can result in erectile dysfunction.

Different men experience varying patterns of ED. Men with ED may report the inability to experience any erection from the beginning of a sexual experience, while others experience an erection that is not maintained at penetration. Other men may lose the erection during sexual intercourse, and others can only experience erection upon awakening or during self-masturbation.

Impact of ED

It is well recognized that adults of all ages view sex as an important quality-of-life issue, and that the imposition of ED usually results in a reduced quality of life. In spite of this and for a number of reasons—most of them unfounded—the victims often suffer in silence. Included among the reasons for their silence are the following:

- ignorance of the availability of safe and effective therapy for ED
- inadequate information provided by the physician concerning timing of medication, need for preliminary sexual arousal, etc.
- undue concern about the irreversibility of marital discord and lack of partner support
- concerns about administration of invasive therapies, adverse effects of therapy, discomfort, inconvenience, and cost of therapy
- high rates of discontinuation of therapy due to inadequacy of therapeutic response and associated adverse effects

Demographics

Studies indicate that in the United States, between 15 million and 30 million men have some degree of erectile dysfunction (ED). Of these, 10 to 20 million have a severe degree of ED resulting in the complete inability to attain or maintain a penile erection. The number of men with ED in the United States is projected to increase by nearly 10 million by the year 2025. With the advancement of men's median age in western industrial countries and the general population growth in developing nations, the worldwide incidence is projected to increase to greater than 320 million by 2025. ED accounts for more than 500,000 annual visits to health care professionals.

As with other chronic disorders and the conditions that are commonly associated with ED (diabetes, hypertension, cardiovascular disease), the prevalence of ED increases with advancing age, with an estimated occurrence of 26% in men who are in their 50s, 40% in men who are in their 60s, and 77% in men 75 years and older. These figures may actually underestimate the true dimensions of the problem since ED is notoriously under-reported, undiagnosed and under-treated because of the perceived stigma associated with the **diagnosis** of ED. It is reported that 70% of ED remains undiagnosed and in a survey of general medical practice less than 12% of men with ED reported having received treatment for it.

Causes and symptoms

Causes

A precise determination of the cause of any individual case of ED is often difficult and may be impossible because ED is often due to multiple factors. This is a consequence of the complicated nature of the human sexual response and the complex physiology of penile erection and relaxation. Normal erectile function requires the coordination of vascular, neurologic, hormonal, and psychological factors and any condition that interferes with one or more of these processes may result in ED.

Attitudes concerning age and psychological factors, commonly associated with ED in the past, have changed in the last two decades. Although the prevalence of ED increases with advancing age, ED is no longer regarded as an inevitable consequence of aging. Whereas most cases of ED were once considered primarily psychological and/or psychiatric in origin, it is now well recognized that organic, non-psychological causes of ED play a much more significant role in the development of ED. Most researchers agree that pure psychological (emotional) mechanisms are causative in 10–20% of cases with medical causes responsible for at least 80% of ED cases. In a number of cases, the situation is mixed, with significant secondary psychological and social components such as guilt, depression, **anxiety**, tension, or marital discord being present in addition to one or more underlying organic components.

Causes of ED may be grouped into those factors that arise within the individual (endogenous) and those factors arising from sources outside the body (exogenous). Endogenous factors include endocrine imbalances, cardiovascular and other medical conditions, and emotional causes. Included among exogenous factors are medications, surgery, trauma and irradiation, smoking, and alcohol and **substance abuse**. These endogenous and exogenous factors may include:

- diabetes mellitus. This is the single most common cause of ED by virtue of its combined nerve and blood vessel damage. As many as 50% of male diabetics have ED.
- circulation abnormalities. Vascular (circulation-related) causes include diseases of the aorta or the arteries supplying the pelvis and penis. Hardening of the arteries (arteriosclerosis) is the most common vascular cause, but damage to the arteries may result from trauma, surgery, or irradiation. Surgery involving the prostate gland may involve both the arteries and nerves in that region.
- neurological causes, including diseases of the brain (such as Alzheimer's disease) and spinal cord (e.g., multiple sclerosis).
- hormonal or endocrine causes. These are uncommon causes for ED, however. ED may occur in males with deficient testicular function and low circulating levels of the male sex hormone, testosterone. These cases are referred to as hypogonadism and may be due to congenital abnormalities or testicular disease such as that accompanying mumps.
- penile diseases. Organic causes of ED may be related to diseases of the penis. Many factors influence penile circulation. For instance, Peyronie's disease, a condition characterized by fibrous tissue and a downward bowing of the penis, limits the expandability of the penile tissues, thus preventing venous compression and allowing blood to leave the penis. Similarly, arteriosclerotic plaque, injury to blood vessels' inner lining due to trauma, surgery, or irradiation, or even aortic occlusion (blockage in a main artery leading out of the heart) can be the cause of compromised penile blood flow and prevent penile erection.
- medications. A number of classes of medications can cause ED. Not all agents within each drug class produce the same effects. For example, some antidepressants are associated with ED, whereas an antidepressant called trazodone hydrochloride (Desyrel) has been used in institutional studies for the treatment of ED because of its tendency to produce priapism (prolonged penile erection). Some medication classes that can cause ED include (but are not limited to) medications that reduce high blood pressure, medications taken for central nervous system diseases like Parkinson's disease (methyldopa), antidepressants, sedatives or tranquilizers like barbiturates, anti-anxiety medications like diazepam (Valium), non-prescribed drugs such as tobacco and alcohol, and illicit drugs including heroin.
- psychological factors. Psychological factors that can precipitate ED include stress, fatigue, depression, guilt, low self-esteem, and negative feelings for or by

a sexual partner. Depressive symptoms and/or difficulty coping with anger may be particularly influential.
- lifestyle. Obesity, physical inactivity, cigarette smoking, and excessive intake of alcohol are risk factors for the development of ED. These suggest that changes in lifestyle may constitute an important aspect of both the therapy and prevention of ED.

The identification of risk factors for ED has an important impact not only on the treatment, but on the prevention of ED as well. For example, if a doctor is treating a patient for high blood pressure who is also at risk for ED, the doctor may make an informed decision to prescribe an effective medication that is not associated with ED instead of one that is.

ED AS A MARKER FOR OTHER DISEASES. The frequent association between ED and a number of important vascular conditions such as hypertension and coronary artery heart disease has raised the possibility that ED may serve as an important marker for the detection of these vascular disorders. Additionally, an increased incidence of depression has been noted in men with ED that is believed to be distinct from reactive depression that might occur because of ED. This has led to the recognition of a possible syndrome linking depression and ED. Thus, the presence of depression should be investigated in men presenting with ED.

Symptoms

The main symptom is the inability to attain or maintain adequate erection to complete sexual activity.

As a result of this symptom, affected men may also experience depression and distress, and this symptom can cause interpersonal problems.

Diagnosis

Interview

An essential first step in the diagnosis of ED is taking a thorough sexual, medical, and psychosocial (both psychological and social) history. The sexual history should include information such as the frequency of sexual intercourse, its duration, the quality and degree of penile erection, the presence or absence of nocturnal erections, and the success or failure of penetration. Any sexual dysfunction on the part of the partner, such as painful intercourse (**dyspareunia**) or vaginal dryness, should be ascertained. The use of one of several available self-directed patient questionnaires may be a useful adjunct to the sexual history. The sexual history helps in distinguishing ED from other abnormalities in sexual function such as ejaculatory and orgasmic disturbances and loss of sexual desire.

The general medical history may disclose one or more distinct causes of ED including the presence of associated conditions (such as high blood pressure, diabetes, or arteriosclerosis), the use of medications that can cause the disorder, and/or a history of substance **abuse**.

A psychosocial history, preferably with the participation of the patient's sexual partner, should include current sexual practices, the presence or absence of stress and performance anxiety, and any special circumstances under which ED occurs.

Physical examination

For a patient with ED, the physical examination should not differ substantially from that performed routinely by a primary care physician. The doctor looks for evidence of hypogonadism or congenital conditions in which there is defective testicular function. The examination of the genitourinary, circulatory and neurologic systems might be especially emphasized. The patient's genitalia are carefully examined for testicular size and consistency and penile deformities. A rectal examination is needed to evaluate the size and consistency of the prostate gland and for the performance of certain muscular reflexes. Vital signs such as blood pressure and pulse would be recorded. Because the presence of ED may serve as a marker for high blood cholesterol, hypertension, coronary artery heart disease, and depression, the physician may also request blood work and/or may perform other assessments to check for these conditions.

Other diagnostic methods that may be performed

Laboratory tests may be performed to evaluate levels of hormones including testosterone and prolactin.

Nocturnal studies present a true picture of erectile dysfunction due to organic causes. The most complete evaluation of nocturnal erectile function is obtained in a sleep laboratory, where patients are monitored for nocturnal erections during sleep.

Duplex Doppler ultrasonography has been used extensively in the evaluation of erectile function. It provides information about both arterial and venous blood flow.

Pharmacological testing involves intracavernosal injection of a small amount of an active agent (e.g., 10 micrograms of alprostadil [prostaglandin E1]) that would produce a normal or priapic erection in a patient with normal erectile function but a poor response in a patient with erectile dysfunction.

There are several self-administered questionnaires available to assist in the evaluation of sexual function in men with erectile dysfunction. The best known and most widely used is the International Index of Erectile Function (IIEF). The IIEF addresses the five relevant domains of male sexual function: erectile function, orgasmic function, sexual desire, intercourse satisfaction, and overall satisfaction.

Treatment

The first step in the treatment of ED includes the elimination or alteration of modifiable risk factors or causes, such as lifestyle or psychosocial factors including smoking, obesity, substance and alcohol abuse, and the adjustment of prescription and over-the-counter medications if necessary.

Recommended treatment options for ED include the following medications:

- PDE5 inhibitors. This class of drugs, which includes sildenafil (Viagra), vardenafil hydrochloride (Levitra), and tadalafil (Cialis), work by relaxing the muscles in the penis to increase penile blood flow and produce an erection. These drugs should not be used by men who take nitroglycerin for heart problems, because they can cause a sudden drop in blood pressure. Also, PDE5 inhibitors have been associated with an increased risk of a rare condition called nonarteritic ischemic optic neuropathy, which can lead to sudden sight loss.

- Apomorphine. This morphine derivative targets dopamine receptors to facilitate erections.

- Alpha adrenergic blockers. These drugs target adrenergic receptors in smooth muscles, causing the blood vessels to dilate more easily.

If those therapies are unsuccessful, the following treatment options may be recommended:

- vacuum constriction device therapy. Vacuum constriction device therapy involves a mechanical device to increase penile blood flow and erection may also be recommended. Psychosexual therapy is also recommended so that any psychological causes for ED can be detected and therapy can be instituted. Individual psychotherapy or couples therapy may be helpful. These various treatment methods can be used alone or in combination.

- intracavernous therapy (ICIT). This therapy involves injection of the penile structures with the drugs alprostadil (Caverject), papaverine (Pavabid), or phentolamine, which promote blood flow and produce erection.

KEY TERMS

Diabetes mellitus—A chronic disease affecting the metabolism of carbohydrates that is caused by insufficient production of insulin in the body.

Hypertension—High blood pressure, often brought on by smoking, obesity, or other causes; one of the major causes of strokes.

Hypogonadism—Abnormally decreased gonad function with retardation of sexual development.

Priapism—Persistent abnormal erection of the penis, usually without sexual desire, and accompanied by pain and tenderness.

Prostate gland—The gland at the base of a male's urethra that produces a component of semen.

- intraurethral therapy. The medication alprostadil is inserted into the urethra and acts to increase blood flow and muscle relaxation, allowing for erection.
- penile prostheses. These are various devices inserted surgically into the penis to produce the erect state.
- surgery. In rare cases, surgery may be used to correct a defect that interferes with penile erection.

Regardless of the therapy chosen, follow-up at regular intervals and good communication between the patient and the doctor is essential. Patients need to keep their doctors informed about adverse reactions, and patients need to be informed about drug interactions. The doctor may adjust the dosage of medication, or may substitute or add a therapeutic agent into the treatment, as necessary.

The patient and his sexual partner can work with their treatment team so that they are both well informed about various treatment options and can maximize treatment results.

Prognosis

The combination of the increased understanding of ED, an improved approach to the problem and the development of newer and more effective therapies has resulted in a marked improvement in the prognosis of ED. It is estimated that at least 65% of all cases of ED currently have a satisfactory therapeutic outcome. However, several factors affect individual prognostic forecasts. Risk factors that cannot be changed and that have a negative effect on individual prognoses include increasing age, the presence of comorbid (co-occurring) conditions such as diabetes, and pelvic sur-

gery in which the nerves were not spared. In contrast, potentially modifiable risk factors such as physical inactivity, smoking, excessive alcoholic intake, certain medications, and obesity improve prognosis when treated effectively.

Resources

BOOKS

Carson, Culley. *Erectile Dysfunction, An Issue of Urologic Clinics.* New York: Saunders, 2005.

Dorey, Grace. *Pelvic Dysfunction in Men: Diagnosis and Treatment of Male Incontinence and Erectile Dysfunction.* 1st ed. Hoboken, NJ: John Wiley and Sons, 2006.

Lue, Kirby, Roger S. *An Atlas of Erectile Dysfunction.* 2nd ed. New York: Taylor and Francis, 2003.

ORGANIZATIONS

American Urological Association. 1000 Corporate Boulevard, Linthicum, MD 21090. Telephone: (866) 746-4282. <http://www.auanet.org/>.

National Kidney and Urologic Diseases Information Clearinghouse. 3 Information Way, Bethesda, MD 20892-3580. Telephone: (800) 891-5390. <http://kidney.niddk.nih.gov>.

Ralph Myerson, MD
Stephanie Watson

Eskalith *see* **Lithium carbonate**

Estazolam

Definition

Estazolam is a sedative-hypnotic drug belonging to the class of drugs known as **benzodiazepines**. It is sold in the United States under the names ProSom and Sedarest.

Purpose

Estazolam is used as a short-term treatment for **insomnia**. Given at bedtime, estazolam can help patients who have trouble falling asleep, staying asleep, or who have unwanted early morning awakening.

Description

Estazolam belongs to a group of drugs called benzodiazepines. Benzodiazepines are sedative-hypnotic drugs that help to relieve nervousness, tension, and other **anxiety** symptoms by slowing the central nervous system. To do this, they block the effects of a specific chemical involved in the transmission of nerve impulses in the **brain**, decreasing the excitement level of the nerve cells.

Estazolam, like other benzodiazepines, can be habit-forming and can cause tolerance. Tolerance occurs when a given dosage has less and less effect when the drug is taken over a long time. Therefore, estazolam is recommended only for short-term use.

Estazolam is available in 1- and 2-mg tablets, for oral use.

Recommended dosage

Adults are usually prescribed a single 1–2 mg dose of estazolam to be taken at bedtime. The elderly (over age 60) or people with serious health problems require much smaller doses, and are usually started at 0.5 mg at bedtime.

Precautions

Care must be taken when prescribing this medication to anyone with decreased liver or kidney functioning; the elderly; those with a history of **substance abuse**, **depression**, respiratory depression (such as asthma, chronic obstructive pulmonary disease, chronic bronchitis, or other chronic respiratory diseases); narrow-angle glaucoma; or known sleep apnea. People with these health conditions should discuss the risks and benefits of using estazolam with their doctor before starting treatment.

Pregnant women should not use estazolam, because it causes damage to the developing fetus. Because estazolam shows up in breast milk, women who are breast-feeding should not take this drug.

Because estazolam is a nervous system and respiratory depressant, it should not be taken with other such depressants, such as alcohol or other **sedatives**, sleeping pills, or tranquilizers. Furthermore, patients should not drive, operate dangerous machinery, or engage in hazardous activities until the drug's effects have worn off.

Suddenly discontinuing estazolam after several weeks of use may cause uncomfortable symptoms of withdrawal. Patients should discuss with their doctor how to discontinue estazolam use gradually to avoid such symptoms.

Side effects

The most common side effects of estazolam include sleepiness, slowness of movement, dizziness, and difficulty with coordination.

KEY TERMS

Benzodiazapines—A group of central nervous system depressants used to relieve anxiety or to induce sleep.

Delusion—A false belief that is resistant to reason or contrary to actual fact.

Depressant—Something that slows down functioning.

Glaucoma—A group of eye diseases characterized by increased pressure within the eye significant enough to damage eye tissue and structures. If untreated, glaucoma results in blindness.

Hallucinations—False sensory perceptions. A person experiencing a hallucination may "hear" sounds or "see" people or objects that are not really present. Hallucinations can also affect the senses of smell, touch, and taste.

Sleep apnea—Short periods where a person stops breathing during sleep. Breathing restarts spontaneously, however, this condition can lead a lack of oxygen in the body.

Less common side effects include anxiety, confusion, depression, memory loss for events occurring after the drug is taken, increased heart rate, and pounding or irregular heartbeat.

Rare side effects include confused thinking, disorientation, **delusions**, irritability, agitation, **hallucinations**, **seizures**, bizarre and/or aggressive behavior, a drop in blood pressure, weak muscles, skin rash or itching, sores in mouth or throat, fever and chills, difficulty sleeping, odd body and/or eye movements, unusual bruising or easy bleeding, severe **fatigue** or weakness, and yellow eyes or skin (jaundice).

Interactions

Cimetidine (Tagamet), **disulfiram** (Antabuse), and erythromycin (an antibiotic) may increase estazolm's sedative effects.

Rifampin may decrease the effects of estazolam.

Resources

BOOKS

Mosby's Drug Consult. St. Louis: Mosby, 2002.

Preston, John D., John H. O'Neal, and Mary C. Talaga. *Handbook of Clinical Psychopharmacology for Therapists,* 4th ed. Oakland, CA: New Harbinger Publications, 2004.

PERIODICALS

Rosenberg, Russell P. "Sleep Maintenance Insomnia: Strengths and Weaknesses of Current Pharmacologic Therapies." *Annals of Clinical Psychiatry* 18.1 (Jan.–Mar.) 2006: 49–56.

Rosalyn Carson-DeWitt, MD
Ruth A. Wienclaw, PhD

Etiology of mental illness *see* **Origin of mental illnesses**

Evening primrose oil

Definition

Evening primrose oil is a dietary supplement derived from the seeds of the evening primrose plant, *Oenothera biennis*. Its Latin name is derived from the Greek word for wine, reflecting the folk belief that the plant could relieve the symptoms of a hangover. Other names for the plant are tree primrose and sundrop. Native Americans used the leaves and bark of evening primrose as a sedative and astringent; it was given for stomach and liver complaints as well as disorders of the female reproductive system. More recently, the discovery of antioxidant and other properties of the seed oil has focused attention on its usefulness in treating a range of diseases and disorders, including as an anti-inflammatory, and for **premenstrual syndrome** (PMS), rheumatoid arthritis, diabetes, osteoporosis, ulcerative colitis, menopausal problems, and heart disease.

Purpose

Evening primrose oil is given by contemporary naturopaths and other alternative practitioners to relieve the discomfort of symptoms associated with PMS, eczema, sunburn, fibrocystic breast disease, arthritis, and diabetes. It is also given to lower the risk of pre-eclampsia and eclampsia in pregnancy and osteoporosis in older women.

Description

Evening primrose oil is obtained from the seeds of the plant by pressing. The oil can be taken directly as a liquid or in the form of capsules.

Evening primrose oil is considered a useful dietary supplement because it is a good source of essential fatty acids (EFAs), Omega 6 predominately. EFAs are called essential fatty acids because the human body

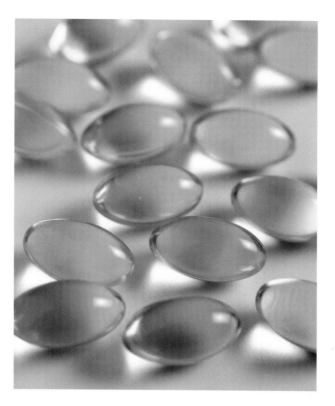

Evening primrose capsule. *(Gusto/Photo Researchers, Inc)*

cannot produce them; they must be obtained from the diet. EFAs maintain the function of cell membranes, regulate pain and inflammation, prevent blood clots, regulate blood pressure and cholesterol levels, and help to produce hormone-like substances known as prostaglandins. Prostaglandins function as inflamation mediators in the short-term regulation of glands and other body organs. It is thought that evening primrose oil relieves the symptoms of PMS by preferentially stimulating anti-inflammatory prostaglandins.

Under normal conditions, the body uses an EFA called linoleic acid to produce a compound called gamma linoleic acid, or GLA. Evening primrose oil contains both linoleic acid (74%) and GLA (9%), making it the most familiar and popular source of GLA. The other compounds contained in evening primrose oil are oleic acid (11%) and palmitic acid (6%).

Recommended dosage

Evening primrose oil can be obtained in health food stores in either liquid or capsule form. Look for that which is organic and cold-pressed, not oxidized by heating. Store it in the refrigerator. Standard dosage varies according to the condition being treated.

KEY TERMS

Antioxidant—Substance that protects the body from damaging reactive oxygen molecules in the body. These reactive oxygen molecules can come from inside the body or from environmental pollution and are thought to play a role in the aging process and the development of degenerative disease.

Astringent—A substance or compound that causes contraction or constriction of soft tissue.

Eczema—An inflammation of the skin characterized by itching and oozing of a clear fluid.

Essential fatty acids (EFAs)—a group of polyunsaturated fats that are essential to life and growth but cannot be produced by the body.

Fibrocystic breast disease—A benign disorder of breast tissue characterized by fibrous saclike growths (cysts) that cause pain and tenderness.

Preeclampsia—A complication of pregnancy characterized by high blood pressure, fluid retention, and protein in the urine. If the patient develops convulsions, the condition is called eclampsia.

Prostaglandins—A group of unsaturated fatty acids involved in the contraction of smooth muscle, control of inflammation, and many other body processes.

Topical—A type of medication or preparation intended for use on the skin or external suface of the body. Evening primrose oil is used in topical preparations to soothe sunburn and relieve the itching of eczema.

The dosage for breast pain from fibrocystic disease is 3 g per day. For sunburn, patients may take up to eight capsules daily until the symptoms subside. Dosages for eczema and rheumatoid arthritis depend on the concentration of GLA in the preparation of evening primrose oil, and should be decided in consultation with a physician, or naturopathic practitioner.

Evening primrose oil can also be used as a topical preparation to treat sunburn and eczema. One recipe for a homemade topical preparation calls for mixing one part of diced plant with four parts of heated petroleum jelly. The mixture is stored in a tightly closed container and refrigerated, as well.

All parts of the evening primrose plant are safe to eat. The roots can be boiled and eaten like parsnips. The seeds were roasted and used as a coffee substitute when food rationing was in effect during World War II.

Precautions

Evening primrose oil should not be given to patients with epilepsy, and only after a consultation with a physician should it be given to children.

Side effects

Evening primrose oil has not been reported as having toxic or severe side effects. Some patients, however, have reported nausea, headache, and softening of the stools.

Reports of side effects from using evening primrose oil in topical preparations for sunburn and other skin problems are the same as with any EFA supplement. Bruising due to damage of the blood platelet function is possible.

Interactions

Experts in pharmacology advise against using evening primrose oil with phenytoin (Dilantin) and other anticonvulsant medications, as the oil may lower the threshold for **seizures**. No other significant drug interactions have been reported.

Resources

BOOKS

Murray, Michael, ND, and Joseph Pizzorno, ND. *Encyclopedia of Natural Medicine*. Rocklin, CA: Prima Publishing, 1991.

Pelletier, Kenneth R., MD. "Naturopathic Medicine." Chapter 7 in *The Best Alternative Medicine*. New York: Simon & Schuster, 2002.

PERIODICALS

Belch, Jill, and Alexander Hill. "Evening Primrose Oil and Borage Oil in Rheumatologic Conditions." *American Journal of Clinical Nutrition* 71 (January 2000): 352S.

Birch, A. E., and others. "Antioxidant Properties of Evening Primrose Seed Extracts." *Journal of Agricultural and Food Chemistry* 49 (September 2001): 4502–4507.

Donohue, Maureen. "Evening Primrose Oil May Ease PMS Symptoms." *OB/GYN News* (April 1, 2000).

Dove, D., and P. Johnson. "Oral Evening Primrose Oil: Its Effect on Length of Pregnancy and Selected Intrapartum Outcomes in Low-Risk Nulliparous Women." *Journal of Nurse-Midwifery* 44 (1999): 320–324.

Horowitz, S. "Combining Supplements and Prescription Drugs: What Your Patients Need to Know." *Alternative Complementary Therapy* 6 (April 2000): 177.

Hudson, Tori. "Evening Primrose Oil." *Townsend Letter for Doctors and Patients* (January 2001): 7.

Miller, Lucinda G. "Herbal Medicinals." *Archives of Internal Medicine* 158 (1998).

Yoon, S., J. Lee, and S. Lee. "The Therapeutic Effect of Evening Primrose Oil in Atopic Dermatitis Patients with Dry Scaly Skin Lesions is Associated with the

Normalization of Serum Gamma-Interferon Levels." *Skin Pharmacology and Applied Skin Physiology* 15 (January-February 2002).

Rebecca J. Frey, Ph.D.

Executive function

Definition

The term executive function describes a set of cognitive abilities that control and regulate other abilities and behaviors. Executive functions are necessary for goal-directed behavior. They include the ability to initiate and stop actions, to monitor and change behavior as needed, and to plan future behavior when faced with novel tasks and situations. Executive functions allow us to anticipate outcomes and adapt to changing situations. The ability to form concepts and think abstractly are often considered components of executive function.

Description

As the name implies, executive functions are high-level abilities that influence more basic abilities like attention, memory and motor skills. For this reason, they can be difficult to assess directly. Many of the tests used to measure other abilities, particularly those that look at more complex aspects of these abilities, can be used to evaluate executive functions. For example, a person with executive function deficits may perform well on tests of basic attention, such as those that simply ask the individual to look at a computer screen and respond when a particular shape appears, but have trouble with tasks that require divided or alternating attention, such as giving a different response depending on the stimulus presented. Verbal fluency tests that ask people to say a number of words in a certain period of time can also reveal problems with executive function. One commonly used test asks individuals to name as many animals or as many words beginning with a particular letter as they can in one minute. A person with executive function deficits may find the animal naming task simple, but struggle to name words beginning with a particular letter, since this task requires people to organize concepts in a novel way. Executive functions also influence memory abilities by allowing people to employ strategies that can help them remember information. Other tests are designed to assess cognitive function more directly. Such tests may present a fairly simple task but without instructions on how to complete it. Executive functions allow most people to figure out the task demand through trial and error and change strategies as needed.

Executive functions are important for successful adaptation and performance in real-life situations. They allow people to initiate and complete tasks and to persevere in the face of challenges. Because the environment can be unpredictable, executive functions are vital to human ability to recognize the significance of unexpected situations and to quickly make alternative plans when unusual events arise and interfere with normal routines. In this way, executive function contributes to success in work and school and allows people to deal effectively with the stresses of daily life. Executive functions also enable people to inhibit inappropriate behaviors. People with poor executive functions often have problems interacting with other people since they may say or do things that are bizarre or offensive to others. Most people experience impulses to do or say things that could get them in trouble, such as making a sexually explicit comment to a stranger, commenting negatively on someone's appearance, or insulting an authority figure like a boss or police officer; but most people have no trouble suppressing these urges. When executive functions are impaired, however, these urges may not be suppressed. Executive functions are thus an important component of our ability to fit in socially.

Executive function deficits are associated with a number of psychiatric and developmental disorders, including **obsessive-compulsive disorder**, Tourette's syndrome, **depression**, **schizophrenia**, **attention deficit hyperactivity disorder**, and **autism**. Executive function deficits also appear to play a role in antisocial behavior. Chronic heavy users of drugs and alcohol show impairments on tests of executive function. Some of these deficits appear to result from heavy substance use, but there is also evidence suggesting that problems with executive functions may contribute to the development of substance use disorders.

Because executive functions govern so many lower-level abilities, there is some controversy about their physiological basis. Nevertheless, most people who study these abilities agree that the frontal lobes of the brain play a major role in executive function. The frontal lobes are the large portions of the brain cortex that lie near the front of the brain. The cortex is the site in the brain where lower level processes like sensation and perception are processed and integrated into thoughts, memories and abilities, and actions are planned and initiated. People with frontal lobe injuries have difficulty with the higher level processing that underlies executive functions. Because of its complexity, the frontal cortex develops more slowly than other parts of the brain, and not surprisingly, many executive

Lichter, David G., and Jeffrey L. Cummings. *Frontal-subcortical Circuits in Psychiatric and Neurological Disorders*. New York: The Guilford Press, 2001.

PERIODICALS

Anderson, Vicki A., Peter Enderson, Elisabeth Northam, Rani Jacobs, and Cathy Catroppa. "Development of executive functions through late childhood and adolescence in an Australian sample." *Developmental Neuropsychology* 20, no. 1 (2001): 385–406.

Bryan, Janet and Mary A. Luszcz. "Measurement of executive function: Considerations for detecting adult age differences." *Journal of Clinical and Experimental Neuropsychology* 22, no. 1 (2000): 40–55.

Morgan, Alex B., and Scott O. Lilienfeld. "A meta-analytic reviw of the relation between antisocial behavior and neuropsychological measures of executive function." *Clinical Psychology Review* 20, no. 1 (2000): 113–136.

Nathan, Joanna, David Wilkinson, Sue Stammers, and J. Lorraine Low. "The role of tests of frontal executive function in the detection of mild dementia." *International Journal of Geriatric Psychiatry* 16 (2001): 18–26.

Ready, Rebecca E., Laura Stierman, and Jane S. Paulsen. "Ecological validity of neuropsychological and personality measures of executive functions." *The Clinical Neuropsychologist* 15, no. 3 (2001): 314–323.

Wecker, Nancy S., Joel H. Kramer, Amy Wisniewski, Dean C. Delis, and Edith Kaplan. "Age effects on executive ability." *Neuropsychology* 14, no. 3 (2000): 409–414.

ORGANIZATIONS

American Psychological Association. Division 40, 750 First Street, N.E., Washington, DC 20002-4242. <http://www.div40.org/>.

International Neuropsychological Society. 700 Ackerman Road, Suite 550, Columbus, OH 43202. <http://www.acs.ohio-state.edu/ins/>.

National Academy of Neuropsychology. 2121 South Oneida Street, Suite 550, Denver, CO 80224-2594. <http://nanonline.org/>.

Danielle Barry, M.S.

Exelon *see* **Rivastigmine**

---

functions do not fully develop until adolescence. Some executive functions also appear to decline in old age, and some executive function deficits may be useful in early detection of mild dementia.

See also Autism; Dementia; Schizophrenia; Tourette syndrome.

Resources

BOOKS

Lezak, Muriel Deutsh. *Neuropsychological Assessment*. 3rd edition. New York: Oxford University Press, 1995.

Exercise/exercise-based treatment

Definition

Exercise is any physical movement that conditions a part or parts of the human body. This includes the central nervous system, especially the **brain** and with it, the mind. Successful exercise used as an adjunct treatment for mental disorders retrains the body and the mind by (1) creating a more positive body image that increases self esteem, (2) increasing certain chemicals produced by the body that create a more positive mental perspective and body health, (3) increasing the metabolism to allow the reduction of prescribed medications and thus, the incidence of negative side effects, and (4) changing how a patient thinks to patterns that include healthier mental processes. Exercise as treatment is well planned, structured, and repetitive in nature for short-term and long-term mental health status. This type of exercise improves and maintains mental fitness and endurance, improves social skills and socialization that lead to better mental well-being, and facilitates mental rehabilitation from several mental illnesses.

Applications

Exercise is a preventative and treatment measure in the management of mental illnesses. Of the disorders listed in the 2000 edition of the *Diagnostic and Statistical Manual (DSM-IV)* of the American Psychiatric Association, exercise is a successful adjunct treatment or preventive measure in the following disorders: alcohol **abuse**, **Alzheimer's disease**, **anxiety**, chronic **pain disorder**, cognitive dysfunction, co-occurring disorders, eating disorders, dementias, **depression**, and **substance abuse**.

Anxiety, depression, substance/alcohol abuse

Exercise increases the overall metabolism and the production of endorphins in the human body. These endorphins are chemicals released in the brain that cause a feeling of well-being. When exercise is used as an adjunct treatment in cases of anxiety, depression, and substance and/or alcohol abuse, the increased levels of endorphins can replace the need or desire for some psychiatric medications, pain medications, and substances or alcohol. In addition, in physical and substance abuse rehabilitation programs from the early 1980s to the present, exercise has enhanced the positive results of most prescribed medications, allowing physicians to reduce or eliminate dosages.

Researchers have also found that because exercise, especially aerobic exercise, increases body metabolism and waste elimination, states of anxiety and depression can reduce in intensity and frequency. These disorders increase the levels of **stress** hormones secreted in the body, while exercise acts against these stress hormones. Exercise helps to eliminate these hormones by (1) reducing their production and (2) speeding their elimination, while raising endorphin levels in their place.

Alzheimer's disease, dementia, cognitive disorders

Aerobic exercise is well known to increase the body's ability to use oxygen efficiently, increasing oxygenation to the central nervous system, most notably the brain. Increased levels of oxygen increase the positive function of the brain's cognitive operations. Increased oxygen use aids in problem solving, memory, logic, general reasoning, and abstract thinking. Increased oxygen levels also reduce the occurrence of dementias and may prohibit the formation of the physical anomalies of plaques and tangles in the brain that are commonly seen in Alzheimer's disease.

Co-occurring disorders and other illnesses

Co-occurring disorders respond best to a holistic retinue of therapies that often include exercise as a treatment. Depression is the most common co-disorder occurring with substance/alcohol type disorders in these dual diagnoses. Exercise can help alleviate depressive symptoms, as well as anxieties that co-occur, as described above. Similarly, exercise may benefit patients with eating disorders by reducing the anxiety and depression that relate to these conditions, unless compulsive exercise is a component of the eating disorder. In that case, the patient can learn to use exercise in a healthier way to reduce anxiety and depression and to build self esteem. Exercise may also benefit other mental disorders by providing a method to increase self-esteem and metabolism and is prescribed on an individual basis.

Supervision

Before beginning exercise treatment, an individual needs to have a complete health evaluation, including physical and mental dimensions. The client's physician and/or treatment team will examine the client to determine whether strenuous exercise will benefit or harm the individual. They will then establish what type of exercise will benefit the mental health issues present. It is important that the type, frequency, and duration of exercises chosen will work well within the overall client treatment plan and not work against other elements of it. Because exercise increases body metabolism, the use of any prescribed medications, over-the-counter remedies, and nutritional supplements must be well monitored during the course of treatment. Exercise treatment must be well planned and consistently supervised by the client's physicians and counselors. If physical or mental symptoms occur during exercise, the client should stop and call the physician to discuss such symptoms before resuming exercise. Symptoms that need to be

KEY TERMS

Adjunct treatment—A treatment that enhances the primary treatment or treatments and is not used alone. It can include exercise, massage, biofeedback, drama therapy, art/music therapy, dance therapy, journaling, creative writing, and others.

Aerobic exercise—Exercise that uses oxygen and provides sufficient cardiovascular overload to increase cardiac output.

Dementia—A mental condition in which there occur hallucinations, delusions, and memory loss, along with disorientation as to person, place, and thing (who, where, and what).

Isokinetics—A form of strength training that uses exercise machines to control the speed of muscle contraction.

Isometrics—Exercises used in strength training that contract the muscles without moving the joints.

Isotonics—A form of strength training that uses weight lifting or rubberized exercise bands for resistance training.

Muscle load—The work that is produced by a muscle when it is strained with a movement (exercise).

Range of motion exercise—Exercises that increase movement of specific joints for flexibility and freedom.

Stress hormones—Chemicals secreted by the human body to produce energy for action when confronted by the fight-or-flight circumstances. They include corticotropin releasing factor, or CRF, and adrenaline, epinephrine, and cortisol.

reported include dizziness, nausea, blurred vision, disorientation, headache, unusual shortness of breath, panic attacks, **hallucinations**, unusual body pains, or any chest pain.

Types

Strength training slightly strains a muscle further than average, increasing "muscle load" (workload) to stimulate muscle protein growth at the cellular level. This increases muscle mass and strength, bone strength, and metabolism. It helps to achieve good body image and self-esteem. Strength training can be accomplished via isometrics, isotonics, and isokinetics, along with range of motion.

Range of motion exercise increases movement of specific joints for flexibility and freedom. Isometric exercises contract the muscles, but joints do not move during contraction. Isotonics uses weight lifting or rubberized exercise bands for resistance training, and isokinetics uses exercise machines, such as stationary bikes, to control the speed of muscle contraction.

Risks

Neglected or improper warm-up procedures can lead to injuries that will increase anxiety that is counterproductive to therapy. Overworking the body without enough downtime between exercise sessions for physical and mental rest can also lead to injury, unnecessary pain, and/or avoidance of future exercise that will work against recovery. If exercise becomes boring or routine, exercise burnout can cause individuals to stop their exercise programs and lose the benefit of treatment, possibly resulting in depression and **relapse** of other symptoms. In the course of some mental disorders, exercise can become a compulsive set of behaviors. This reinforces the need for consistent professional monitoring of exercise treatment. Overall, the total client treatment plan must be monitored to ensure that exercise and other components are not working together to create unwanted or unexpected physical or mental issues.

Resources

CONFERENCES

Hays, Kate, PhD. "Working It Out: Using Exercise in Psychotherapy." From the Conference *Getting Healthy: Psychology's Response to Life's Stages.* Reported in the New York State Psychology Association's *NYSPA Notebook.* July–Aug. 2003: 16–18.

PERIODICALS

Chow, Atlantis, CM, and Kirby Singh, MF. "An Effective Exercise-Based Intervention for Improving Mental Health and Quality of Life Measures: A Randomized Trial." *Preventive Medicine* 39.2 (2004): 424–34.

George, Steven Z., Joel E. Bialosky, and Julie M. Fritz. "Physical Therapist Management of a Patient with Acute Low Back Pain and Elevated Fear-Avoidance Beliefs." *Physical Therapy* 84.6 (2004): 538–49.

Keller, Joy. "U.S. to Introduce New Physical Activity Guidelines: IDEA Members Share Their Visions for What the Recommendations Should Include." *IDEA Fitness Journal* 4.1 (2007): 16–17.

Kim, Doyeon, and Len Kravitz. "Childhood Obesity: Prevalence, Treatment and Prevention: Become an Advocate for Kids by Taking a Leadership Role in the War on Obesity." *IDEA Fitness Journal* 4.1 (2007): 22–24.

Read, Jennifer, and Richard Brown. "The Role of Physical Exercise in Alcoholism Treatment and Recovery."

Professional Psychology: Research and Practice 34.1 (2003): 49–56.

Read, Jennifer, PhD, Richard Brown, PhD, Bess Marcus, PhD, Christopher Kahler, PhD, Susan Ramsey, PhD, Mary Ellen Dubreuil, PhD, Jon Jakicic, PhD, and Caren Francione, BA. "Exercise Attitudes and Behaviors among Personas in Treatment for Alcohol Use Disorders." *Journal of Substance Abuse Treatment* 21.4 (2001): 199–206.

Sander, Ruth. "Exercise is Associated with a Delayed Onset of Dementia." *Nursing Older People* 18.12 (2007): 39–40.

Yu, Fang, Ann M. Kolanowski, Neville E. Strumpf, and Paul J. Eslinger. "Improving Cognition and Function Through Exercise Intervention in Alzheimer's Disease." *Journal of Nursing Scholarship* 38.4 (2006): 358–65.

ORGANIZATIONS

Mayo Clinic, Rochester, MN. <http://www.mayoclinic.com/health/depression-and-exercise/MH00043>.

The President's Council on Physical Fitness and Sports. Department W., 200 Independence Avenue SW, Room 738-H, Washington, DC 20201. Telephone: (202) 690-9000. < http://www.fitness.gov>.

YMCA of the USA. 101 North Wacker Drive, Chicago, IL 60606. Telephone: (800) 872-9622. <http://www.ymca.net>.

YWCA USA. 1015 18th Street NW, Suite 1100, Washington, DC 20036. Telephone: (202) 467-0801. <http://www.ywca.org>.

Patty Inglish, MS

Exhibitionism

Definition

Exhibitionism is a mental disorder characterized by a **compulsion** to display one's genitals to an unsuspecting stranger. The ***Diagnostic and Statistical Manual of Mental Disorders***, also known as the *DSM-IV-TR*, classifies exhibitionism under the heading of the "paraphilias," a subcategory of sexual and gender identity disorders. The **paraphilias** are a group of mental disorders marked by **obsession** with unusual sexual practices or with sexual activity involving nonconsenting or inappropriate partners (e.g., children or animals). The term *paraphilia* is derived from two Greek words meaning "outside of" and "friendship-love."

In the United States and Canada, the slang term "flasher" is often used for exhibitionists.

Description

Exhibitionism is described in the *DSM-IV-TR* as the exposure of one's genitals to a stranger, usually with no intention of further sexual activity with the other person. For this reason, the term exhibitionism is sometimes grouped together with "voyeurism," ("peeping," or watching an unsuspecting person or people, usually strangers, undressing or engaging in sexual activity) as a "hands-off" paraphilia. This contrasts with the "hands-on disorders" which involve physical contact with other persons.

In some cases, the exhibitionist masturbates while exposing himself (or while fantasizing that he is exposing himself) to the other person. Some exhibitionists are aware of a conscious desire to shock or upset their target; while others fantasize that the target will become sexually aroused by their display.

Causes and symptoms

Causes

Several theories have been proposed regarding the origins of exhibitionism, although none are considered conclusive. They include:

- biological theories. These generally hold that testosterone, the hormone that influences the sexual drive in both men and women, increases the susceptibility of males to develop deviant sexual behaviors. Some medications used to treat exhibitionists are given to lower the patients' testosterone levels.

- learning theories. Several studies have shown that emotional abuse in childhood and family dysfunction are both significant risk factors in the development of exhibitionism. A Swedish survey (Sweden is globally recognized for its excellent health data survey system) found that exhibitionism is associated with psychological problems, although whether the problems precipitate the behavior or vice versa was not identified. This same study found no association between exhibitionistic behavior and a history of sexual abuse.

- psychoanalytical theories. These are based on an unsubstantiated assumption that male gender identity requires the male child's separation from his mother psychologically so that he does not identify with her as a member of the same sex, the way a girl does. It is thought that exhibitionists regard their mothers as rejecting them on the basis of their different genitals. Therefore, they grow up with the desire to force women to accept them by making women look at their genitals.

- head trauma. There are a small number of documented cases of men becoming exhibitionists following traumatic brain injury (TBI) without previous histories of alcohol abuse or sexual offenses.

- a childhood history of **attention deficit/hyperactivity disorder** (ADHD). The reason for the connection is not yet known, but researchers at Harvard have discovered that patients with multiple paraphilias have a much greater likelihood of having had ADHD as children than men with only one paraphilia.

Some psychiatrists disagree about whether exhibitionism should be considered a disorder of impulse control or whether it falls within the spectrum of obsessive-compulsive disorders (OCDs). Recent studies suggest that there is an obsessive-compulsive element to these behaviors, and some papers now describe these behaviors in a category of compulsive-impulsive sexual behaviors. Single case studies have suggested some effectiveness of drugs used to treat **bipolar disorder** in treating exhibitionistic behaviors, implying a potential link also to bipolar disorders. People who exhibit **pedophilia**, which is also characterized as a paraphilia, have abnormalities in brain **imaging studies** that are similar to those observed in imaging studies of people with **obsessive-compulsive disorder**. Disruption of **dopamine** and serotonin (both nerve signaling molecules) pathways is implicated in many of these disorders.

Symptoms

One expert in the field of treating paraphilias has suggested classifying the symptoms of exhibitionism according to level of severity, based on criteria from the *DSM-III-R* (1987):

- Mild. The person has recurrent fantasies of exposing himself, but has rarely or never acted on them.

- Moderate. The person has occasionally exposed himself (three targets or fewer) and has difficulty controlling urges to do so.

- Severe. The person has exposed himself to more than three people and has serious problems with control.

- A fourth level of severity, catastrophic, would not be found in exhibitionists without other paraphilias. This level denotes the presence of sadistic fantasies which, if acted upon, would result in severe injury or death to the victim.

Because exhibitionism is a hands-off paraphilia, it rarely rises above the level of moderate severity in the absence of other paraphilias.

Demographics

The incidence of exhibitionism in the general population is difficult to estimate because persons with this disorder do not usually seek counseling by their own free will. Exhibitionism is one of the three most common sexual offenses in police records (the other two are **voyeurism** and pedophilia). It is rarely diagnosed in general mental health clinics, but most professionals believe that it is probably underdiagnosed and underreported.

In terms of the technical definition of exhibitionism, almost all reported cases involve males. A number of mental health professionals, however, have noted that gender bias may be built into the standard definition. Some women engage in a form of exhibitionism by undressing in front of windows as if they are encouraging someone to watch them. In addition, wearing the low-cut gowns favored by some models and actresses have been described as socially sanctioned exhibitionism. One textbook description of exhibitionism says "women exhibit everything but the genitals; men, nothing but."

Although the stereotype of an exhibitionist is a "dirty old man in a raincoat," most males arrested for exhibitionism are in their late teens or early twenties. The disorder appears to have its onset before age 18. Like most paraphilias, exhibitionism is rarely found in men over 50 years of age.

In the United States most exhibitionists are Caucasian males. About half of exhibitionists are married.

Diagnosis

Diagnosis of exhibitionism is complicated by several factors. For example, most persons with the disorder come to therapy because of court orders. Some are motivated by fear of discovery by employers or family members, and a minority of exhibitionists enter therapy because their wife or girlfriend is distressed by the disorder. Emotional attitudes toward the disorder vary; some men maintain that the only problem they have with exhibitionism is society's disapproval of it; others, however, feel intensely guilty and anxious.

A second complication of diagnosing exhibitionism is the high rate of comorbidity among the paraphilias as a group and between the paraphilias as a group and other mental disorders. In other words, a patient in treatment for exhibitionism is highly likely to engage in other forms of deviant sexual behavior and to have **depression** (an **anxiety** or substance-abuse disorder). In addition, many patients with paraphilias do not cooperate with physicians, who may have considerable difficulty making an accurate diagnosis of other disorders that may also exist.

A diagnosis of exhibitionism follows a somewhat different pattern from the standard procedures for diagnosing most mental disorders. A thorough workup in a clinic for specialized treatment of sexual disorders includes the following components:

- a psychiatric evaluation and mental status examination to diagnose concurrent psychiatric and medical conditions, and to rule out schizophrenia, post-traumatic stress disorder (PTSD), mental retardation, and depression.
- a neurologic examination to rule out head trauma, seizures, or other abnormalities of brain structure and function, followed by a computed tomography (CT) scan or magnetic resonance imaging (MRI), if needed.
- blood and urine tests for substance abuse and sexually transmitted diseases, including an HIV screen.
- assessment of sexual behaviors. This includes creation of a sex hormone profile and responses to questionnaires. The questionnaires are intended to measure cognitive distortions regarding rape and other forms of coercion, pedophilia, aggression, and impulsivity.

Treatments

Exhibitionism is usually treated with a combination of **psychotherapy**, medications, and adjunctive treatments.

Psychotherapy

Several different types of psychotherapy have been found helpful in treating exhibitionism:

- cognitive-behavioral therapy (CBT). This approach is generally regarded as the most effective form of psychotherapy for exhibitionism. Patients are encouraged to recognize the irrational justifications that they offer for their behavior, and to alter other distorted thinking patterns.
- orgasmic reconditioning. In this technique, the patient is conditioned to replace fantasies of exposing himself with fantasies of more acceptable sexual behavior while masturbating.
- group therapy. This form of therapy is used to get patients past the denial frequently associated with paraphilias, and as a form of relapse prevention.
- twelve-step groups for sexual addicts. Exhibitionists who feel guilty and anxious about their behavior are often helped by the social support and emphasis on healthy spirituality found in these groups, as well as by the cognitive restructuring that is built into the twelve steps.

- couples therapy or family therapy. This approach is particularly helpful for patients who are married and whose marriages and family ties have been strained by their disorder.

Medications

There are several different classes of drugs used to treat the patient with exhibitionism and the other paraphilias. However, one difficulty in evaluating the comparative efficacy of different medications should be noted: ethical limitation. Double-blind placebo-controlled studies of medication treatment of sexually deviant men raises the ethical question of the possibility of relapse in the subjects who receive the placebo. Withholding a potentially effective drug in circumstances that might lead to physical or psychological injury to a third party is difficult to justify.

Medications are often the only form of treatment for patients with exhibitionism that can suppress deviant behaviors. The categories of drugs used to treat exhibitionism are as follows:

- selective serotonin reuptake inhibitors (SSRIs). The SSRIs show promise in treating the paraphilias, as well as depression and other mood disorders. It has been found that decreased levels of serotonin in the brain result in an increased sex drive. The SSRIs are appropriate for patients with mild- or moderate-level paraphilias; these patients include the majority of exhibitionists.
- hormones, their mimics, and their antagonists. The three classes of medications most often used to treat paraphilias are hormones, particularly the synthetic medroxyprogesterone acetate, or MPA; luteinizing hormone-releasing hormone (LHRH) agonists (mimics), which include such drugs as triptorelin (Trelstar), leuprolide acetate, and goserelin acetate; and antiandrogens, which block the uptake and metabolism of testosterone as well as reducing blood levels of this hormone. In particular, these drugs with antiandrogenic effects (interfering with the action of the body's androgenic hormones) have shown some effectiveness.

Surgery

Surgical castration, which involves removal of the testes, is effective in significantly reducing levels of testosterone in blood plasma. This form of treatment for paraphilias, however, is generally reserved for more serious offenders than exhibitionists (violent rapists and pedophiles with a history of repeated offenses, for example).

KEY TERMS

Aversion therapy—An approach to treatment in which an unpleasant or painful stimulus is linked to an undesirable behavior in order to condition the patient to dislike or avoid the behavior.

Castration—Desexing a person or animal by surgical removal of the testes (in males) or ovaries (in females). Castration is sometimes offered as a treatment option to violent rapists and pedophiles who are repeat offenders.

Comorbidity—Association or presence of two or more mental disorders in the same patient. A disorder that is said to have a high degree of comorbidity is likely to occur in patients diagnosed with other disorders that may share or reinforce some of its symptoms.

Compliance—In medicine or psychiatry, cooperation with a treatment plan or schedule of medications.

Denial—A psychological defense mechanism that reduces anxiety by excluding recognition of an addiction or similar problem from the conscious mind.

Double-blind placebo-controlled study—A study in which patients are divided into two groups—those who will recive a medication, and those who will receive a placebo (a pill that looks like the medica-

tion but has no active ingredients). Neither the patients nor their physicians know which pill any specific patient is receiving.

Paraphilias—A group of mental disorders that is characterized by recurrent intense sexual urges and sexually arousing fantasies generally involving (1) nonhuman objects, (2) the suffering or humiliation of oneself or one's partner (not merely simulated), or (3) children or other nonconsenting persons.

Placebo—An inactive substance or preparation used as a control in experiments with human subjects to test the effectiveness of a medication.

Recidivism—A tendency to return to a previously treated activity, or repeated relapse into criminal or deviant behavior.

Serotonin—A chemical produced by the brain that functions as a neurotransmitter. Low serotonin levels are associated with the paraphilias as well as with mood disorders. Medications known as selective serotonin reuptake inhibitors (SSRIs) can be used to treat exhibitionism and other paraphilias.

Voyeurism—A paraphilia that involves watching unsuspecting people, usually strangers, undress or engage in sexual activity.

Other treatment methods

Another treatment method that is often offered to people with exhibition disorder is **social skills training**. It is thought that some men develop paraphilias partially because they do not know how to form healthy relationships, whether sexual or nonsexual, with other people. Although social skills training is not considered a substitute for medications or psychotherapy, it appears to be a useful adjunctive treatment for exhibitionism disorder.

Legal considerations

People with exhibitionism disorder are at risk for lifetime employment problems if they acquire a police record. An attorney who specializes in employment law has pointed out that the Americans with Disabilities Act (ADA), enacted by Congress in 1990 to protect workers against discrimination on grounds of mental impairment or physical disability, does not protect persons with paraphilias. People with exhibitionism disorder were specifically excluded by Congress from

the provisions of the ADA, along with voyeurs and persons with other sexual behavior disorders.

Prognosis

The prognosis for people with exhibition disorder depends on a number of factors, including the age of onset, the reasons for the patient's referral to psychiatric care, degree of his cooperation with the therapist, and comorbidity with other paraphilias or other mental disorders. For some patients, exhibitionism is a temporary disorder related to sexual experimentation during their adolescence. For others, however, it is a lifelong problem with potentially serious legal, interpersonal, financial, educational, and occupational consequences. People with exhibition disorder have the highest recidivism rate of all the paraphilias; between 20% and 50% of men arrested for exhibitionism are rearrested within two years.

Prevention

One important preventive strategy includes the funding of programs for the treatment of paraphilias in adolescents. According to one expert in the field, males in this age group have not been studied and are undertreated, yet it is known that paraphilias are usually established before age 18. Recognition of paraphilias in adolescents and treatment for those at risk would lower the risk of recidivism. A second important preventive approach is early recognition and appropriate treatment of people who have committed child abuse.

Resources

BOOKS

American Psychiatric Association. *Diagnostic and Statistical Manual of Mental Disorders,* 4th ed., Text rev. Washington, D.C.: American Psychiatric Association, 2000.

Beers, Mark H., MD, and Robert Berkow, MD. "Exhibitionism," In *The Merck Manual of Diagnosis and Therapy.* Whitehouse Station, NJ: Merck Research Laboratories, 1999.

Carnes, Patrick. *Out of the Shadows: Understanding Sexual Addiction.* Minneapolis, MN: CompCare Publications, 1983.

Kasl, Charlotte D. *Women, Sex, and Addiction.* New York: Harper and Row, Publishers, 1990.

PERIODICALS

Abouesh, A., and A. Clayton. "Compulsive Voyeurism and Exhibitionism: A Clinical Response to Paroxetine." *Archives of Sexual Behavior* 28 (February 1999): 23–30.

Bradford, John M. W. "The Treatment of Sexual Deviation Using a Pharmacological Approach." *Journal of Sex Research* 37 (August 2000): 485–92.

Brannon, Guy E., MD. "Paraphilias." *eMedicine Journal* 3 (January 14, 2002).

Carnes, P., and J. P. Schneider. "Recognition and Management of Addictive Sexual Disorders: Guide for the Primary Care Clinician." *Lippincotts Primary Care Practitioner* 4 (May–June 2000): 302–18.

de Silva, W. P. "Sexual Variations." *British Medical Journal* 318 (March 6, 1999): 654.

Greenberg, D. M. "Sexual Recidivism in Sex Offenders." *Canadian Journal of Psychiatry* 43 (June 1998): 459–65.

Kafka, Martin P., and J. Hennen. "Psychostimulant Augmentation During Treatment with Selective Serotonin Reuptake Inhibitors in Men with Paraphilias and Paraphilia-Related Disorders: A Case Series." *Journal of Clinical Psychiatry* 61 (2000): 664–70.

Langstrom, Niklas, and Michael C. Seto. Exhibitionistic and Voyeuristic Behavior in a Swedish National Population Survey. *Archives of Sexual Behavior* 35 (2006): 427–35.

Lee, J. K., and others. "Developmental Risk Factors for Sexual Offending." *Child Abuse and Neglect* 26 (January 2002): 73–92.

Marazziti, Donatella, and Bernardo Dell'Osso. "Topiramate Plus Citalopram in the Treatment of Compulsive-Impulsive Sexual Behaviors." *Clinical Practice in Epidemiology in Mental Health* 2 (2006): 9.

Schiffer, Boris, and others. "Structural Brain Abnormalities in the Frontostriatal System and Cerebellum in Pedophilia." *Journal of Psychiatric Research* (2006).

Schober, Justine M., Peter M. Byrne, and Phyllis J. Kuhn. "Leuprolide Acetate is a Familiar Drug That May Modify Sex-Offender Behavior: the Urologist's Role." *BJU International* 97 (2006): 684–86.

Simpson, G., A. Blaszczynski, and A. Hodgkinson. "Sex Offending as a Psychosocial Sequela of Traumatic Brain Injury." *Journal of Head Trauma and Rehabilitation* 14 (December 1999): 567–80.

Sonnenberg, Stephen P., JD. "Mental Disabilities in the Workplace." *Workforce* 79 (June 2000): 632.

ORGANIZATIONS

Augustine Fellowship, Sex and Love Addicts Anonymous. PO Box 119, New Town Branch, Boston, MA 02258. Telephone: (617) 332-1845.

National Association on Sexual Addiction Problems (NASAP). 22937 Arlington Avenue, Suite 201, Torrance, CA 90501. Telephone: (213) 546-3103.

Rebecca Frey, PhD
Emily Jane Willingham, PhD

Exposure treatment

Definition

Exposure treatment is a technique that is widely used in **cognitive-behavioral therapy** (CBT) to help patients systematically confront a feared stimulus in a live or virtual environment or in the imagination. Through repeated exposure to the stimulus, patients are helped to nullify fears and increase self-efficacy. Exposure treatment is also called exposure therapy.

Purpose

Exposure treatment is used for a variety of **anxiety disorders,** and it has also recently been extended to the treatment of substance-related disorders. Generally speaking, exposure treatment involves presenting patients with anxiety-producing stimulus for a long enough time to decrease the intensity of their emotional reactions. As a result, the feared situation or object no longer makes the patients anxious. Exposure treatment can be carried out in real situations, which is called in vivo exposure, or it can be done through imagination, which is called imaginal exposure. More recently, exposure treatment has been extended to include the use of computer-based virtual environments.

The category of imaginal exposure includes **systematic desensitization,** in which patients imagine certain aspects of the feared object or situation combined with relaxation. Graded or graduated exposure refers to exposing the patients to the feared situation in a gradual manner. Flooding refers to exposing patients to the anxiety-provoking or feared situation all at once and keeping them in it until the **anxiety** and fear subside. There are several variations in the delivery of exposure treatment: patient-directed exposure instructions or self-exposure; therapist-assisted exposure; group exposure; and exposure with response prevention.

The basic purpose of exposure treatment is to decrease a person's anxious and fearful reactions (emotions, thoughts, or physical sensations) through repeated exposures to anxiety-producing material. This reduction of the patient's anxiety response is known as habituation. A related purpose of exposure treatment is to eliminate the anxious or fearful response altogether so that patients can face the feared situation repeatedly without experiencing anxiety or fear. This elimination of the anxiety response is known as extinction.

Precautions

Exposure treatment is generally a safe treatment method; however, some patients may find that the level of anxiety that occurs during treatment sessions is higher than they can handle. Some studies of exposure treatment have reported a high dropout rate, perhaps because the method itself produces anxiety. In addition, exposure treatment is not effective for all patients; after treatment, some continue to experience anxiety symptoms.

Description

Exposure treatment usually begins with making lists or hierarchies of situations that make the patients anxious or fearful. The situations are ranked on a scale of zero (representing the situation producing the least anxiety) to ten (representing the situation of highest anxiety). In addition, patients are usually asked to rate their level of anxiety in each situation on a scale from zero (no anxiety or discomfort) to 100 (extreme anxiety and discomfort). This scale is called the subjective units of distress scale (SUDS). Patients may be asked to provide SUDS ratings at regular intervals (for example every five minutes) during exposure treatment.

Methods of delivering exposure treatment

PATIENT-DIRECTED EXPOSURE. Patient-directed exposure is the simplest variation of exposure treatment. After patients make their hierarchy lists with their

therapist, they are instructed to move through the situations on the hierarchy at their own rates. Patients start with the lowest anxiety situation on the list, and keep a journal of their experiences. They continue the patient-directed exposure on a daily basis until their fears and anxieties have decreased. For example, if patients are afraid of leaving the house, the first item on the hierarchy might be to stand outside the front door for a certain period of time. After they are able to perform this action without feeling anxious, they would move to the next item on the hierarchy, which might be walking to the end of the driveway. Treatment would proceed in this way until the patients have completed all the items on the hierarchy. During therapy sessions, the therapist reviews their journal, gives them positive feedback for any progress that they have made, and discusses any obstacles that they encountered during exposures to the feared situation.

THERAPIST-ASSISTED EXPOSURE. In this form of exposure treatment, therapists go with patients to the feared location or situation and provides on-the-spot coaching to help them manage their anxieties. Therapists may challenge their patients to experience the maximum amount of anxiety. In prolonged in vivo exposure, therapists and patients stay in the situation as long as it takes for the anxiety to decrease. For example, they might remain in a crowded shopping mall for four or more hours. The therapists also explore the thoughts of patients during this exposure to confront any irrational ways of thinking.

GROUP EXPOSURE. In group exposure, self-exposure and practice are combined with group education and discussion of experiences during exposure to feared situations. These sessions may last as long as three hours and include 30 minutes of education, time for individual exposure practice, and 45 minutes of discussion. Group sessions may be scheduled on a daily basis for 10–14 days.

Exposure treatment for specific anxiety disorders

AGORAPHOBIA. Many research studies have shown that graded exposure treatment is effective for **agoraphobia**. Long-term studies have shown that improvement can be maintained for as long as seven years. Exposure treatment for agoraphobia is best conducted in vivo, in the actual feared situation, such as entering a packed subway car. Exposure treatment for agoraphobia is likely to be more effective when the patient's spouse or friend is involved, perhaps because of the support a companion can offer the patient during practice sessions.

PANIC DISORDER. Exposure treatment is the central component of cognitive-behavioral treatment for **panic disorder**. Treatment for this disorder involves identifying patients' specific fears within their experiences of panic, such as fears of being sick, of losing control, and of embarrassment. Once these fears are identified, patients are instructed to expose themselves to situations in which the fearful thoughts arise (such as walking away from a safe person or place). The rationale behind this instruction is that enduring the anxiety associated with the situation will accustom patients to the situation itself, so that over time the anxiety will diminish or disappear. In this way, patients discover that the feared consequences do not happen in real life.

In some patients, physical symptoms of panic lead to fears about the experience of panic itself. Fears related to the physical symptoms associated with panic can be targeted for treatment by inducing the bodily sensations that mimic those experienced during panic attacks. This technique is called interoceptive exposure. Patients are asked to induce the feared sensations in a number of ways. For example, patients may spin in a revolving chair to induce dizziness or run up the stairs to induce increased heart rate and shortness of breath. They are then instructed to notice what the symptoms feel like, and allow them to remain without doing anything to control them. With repeated exposure, patients learn that the bodily sensations do not signal harm or danger, and therefore need not be feared. Patients are taught such strategies as muscle relaxation and slow breathing to control anxiety before, during, and after the exposure.

Interoceptive exposure treatment for panic usually begins with practice sessions in a therapist's office. Patients may be instructed to practice at home and then practice in a less "safe" environment, such as their work setting or a nearby park. The next step is the addition of the physical activities that naturally produce the feared symptoms. Situational or in vivo exposure would then be introduced for patients with agoraphobia combined with panic disorder. Patients would be instructed to go back into situations that they have been avoiding, such as elevators or busy railroad terminals. If patient develop symptoms of anxiety, they are instructed to use the techniques for controlling anxiety that were previously learned.

The effectiveness of exposure treatment for decreasing panic attacks and avoidance has been well demonstrated. In research studies, 50–90% of patients experience relief from symptoms.

SPECIFIC PHOBIA AND SOCIAL PHOBIA. Graded exposure is used most often to treat specific or simple phobias. In graded exposure, patients approach the feared object or situation by degrees. For example, those afraid of swimming in the ocean might begin by looking at photographs of the ocean, then watching movies of people swimming, then going to the beach and walking along the water's edge, and then working up to a full swim in the ocean. Graded exposure can be done through patient-directed instruction or therapist-assisted exposure. Research studies indicate that most patients respond quickly to graded exposure treatment, and that the benefits of treatment are well maintained.

Treatment for **social phobia** usually combines exposure treatment with cognitive restructuring. This combination seems to help prevent a recurrence of symptoms. In general, studies of exposure treatment for social phobia have shown that it leads to a reduction of symptoms. Since cognitive restructuring is usually combined with exposure, it is unclear which component is responsible for patients' improvement, but there is some indication that exposure alone may be sufficient.

Exposure treatment can be more difficult to arrange for treating social phobia, however, because patients have less control over social situations, which are unpredictable by their nature and can unexpectedly become more intense and anxiety-provoking. Furthermore, social exchanges usually last only a short time; therefore, they may not provide the length of exposure that patients need.

OBSESSIVE-COMPULSIVE DISORDER. The most common nonmedication treatment for **obsessive-compulsive disorder** (OCD) is exposure to the feared or anxiety-producing situation plus response prevention (preventing the patient from performing a compulsive behavior, such as hand washing after exposure to something thought to be contaminated). This form of treatment also uses a hierarchy, and begins with the easiest situation and gradually moves to more difficult situations. Research has shown that exposure to contamination situations leads to a decrease in fears of contamination, but does not lead to changes in the compulsive behavior. In a similar fashion, the response prevention component leads to a decrease in compulsive behavior, but does not affect the patient's fears of contamination. Since each form of treatment affects different OCD symptoms, a combination of exposure and response prevention is more effective than either modality by itself. Exposure combined with response prevention also appears to be effective for treating children and adolescents with OCD.

Prolonged continuous exposure is better than short, interrupted periods of exposure in treating people with OCD. On average, exposure treatment of people with OCD requires 90-minute sessions, although the frequency of sessions varies. Some studies have shown good results with 15 daily treatments spread over a period of three weeks. This intensive treatment format may be best suited for cases that are more severe and complex, as in patients with **depression** as well as OCD. Patients who are less severely affected and are highly motivated may benefit from sessions once or twice a week. Treatment may include both therapist-assisted exposure and self-exposure as homework between sessions. Imaginal exposure may be useful for addressing fears that are hard to incorporate into in vivo exposure, such as fears of a loved one's death. Patients usually prefer gradual exposure to the most distressing situations in their hierarchy; however, gradual exposure does not appear to be more effective than flooding or immediate exposure to the situation.

POST-TRAUMATIC STRESS DISORDER. Exposure treatment has been used successfully in the therapy of **post-traumatic stress disorder** (PTSD) resulting from such traumatic experiences as combat, sexual assault, and motor vehicle accidents. Research studies have reported encouraging results for exposure treatment in reducing PTSD or PTSD symptoms in children, adolescents, and adults. Intrusive symptoms of PTSD, such as nightmares and flashbacks, may be reduced by having patients relive the emotional aspects of the trauma in a safe, therapeutic environment. It may take 10–15 exposure sessions to decrease the negative physical sensations associated with PTSD. These sessions may range from one to two hours in length and may occur once or twice a week. Relaxation techniques are usually included before and after exposure. The exposure may be therapist-assisted or patient-directed.

A recent study showed that imaginal exposure and cognitive treatment are equally effective in reducing symptoms associated with chronic or severe PTSD, but that neither brought about complete improvement. In addition, more patients treated with exposure worsened over the course of treatment than patients treated with cognitive approaches. This finding may have been related to the fact that the patients receiving exposure treatment had less frequent sessions with long periods of time between sessions. Some patients diagnosed with PTSD, however, do not seem to benefit from exposure therapy. They may have difficulty tolerating exposure, or have difficulty imagining, visualizing, or describing their traumatic experiences.

The use of cognitive therapy to help the patient focus on thoughts may be a useful adjunctive treatment, or serve as an alternative to exposure treatment.

Many people who have experienced sexual assault or rape meet the criteria for PTSD defined in the ***Diagnostic and Statistical Manual of Mental Disorders***, fourth edition, text revision (*DSM-IV-TR*). They may reexperience the traumatic event, avoid items or places associated with the trauma, and have increased levels of physical arousal. Exposure treatment in these cases involves using either imaginal or in vivo exposure to reduce anxiety and any tendencies to avoid aspects of the situation that produce anxiety (also known as avoidance behavior). Verbal description of the event (imaginal exposure) is critical for recovery, although it usually feels painful and threatening to patients. It is important that the patients' verbal descriptions of the traumatic events, along with their expressions of thoughts and feelings related to it, occur as early in the treatment process as possible, to minimize long-term suffering.

Prolonged exposure is the most effective nonmedical treatment for reducing traumatic memories related to PTSD. It combines flooding with systematic desensitization. The goal is to expose patients using both imaginal and in vivo exposure techniques in order to reduce avoidance behaviors and fears. Prolonged exposure may occur over nine to 12 90-minute sessions. During the imaginal exposure phase of treatment, patients are asked to describe the details of the traumatic experiences repeatedly, in the present tense. Patients use the SUDS scale to monitor levels of fear and anxiety. The in vivo component occurs outside a therapist's office; this component involves having clients expose themselves to cues in the environment that they have been avoiding—for example, the place where the motor vehicle accident or rape occurred. Patients are instructed to stay in the fear-producing situation for at least 45 minutes, or until their anxiety levels have gone down significantly on the SUDS rating scale. Often patients will use a coach or someone who will stay with them at the beginning of in vivo practice. The coach's role gradually decreases over time as the patients experience less anxiety.

Recent innovations in exposure treatment

VIRTUAL REALITY EXPOSURE TREATMENT. Virtual reality is a technique that allows people to participate actively in a computer-generated (or virtual) scenario or environment. The participants have a sense of being present in the virtual environment. Virtual reality uses a device mounted on the participant's head that shows computer graphics and visual displays in real time, and tracks the person's body movements. Some forms of virtual reality also allow participants to hold a second device in their hands that enables them to interact more fully with the virtual environment, such as opening a car door.

Virtual reality has been proposed as a new way of conducting exposure therapy because it can provide a sense of being present in a feared situation. Virtual reality exposure may be useful for treating such phobias as fear of heights, flying, or driving, as well as for treating PTSD. This method appears to have several advantages over standard exposure therapy. First, virtual reality may offer patients a greater sense of control because they can instantly turn the device on and off or change its level of intensity. Second, virtual reality protects patients from harm or social embarrassment during their practice sessions. Third, it can be implemented regardless of the patient's ability to imagine or to remain with prolonged imaginal exposure. These proposed advantages of virtual reality over standard exposure therapy have yet to be tested, however.

Some studies have been conducted using virtual reality in the treatment of patients with fear of heights and fear of flying, and in a sample of Vietnam veterans diagnosed with PTSD. These studies of virtual reality exposure therapy have limitations in terms of study design and small sample size, but their positive results suggest that virtual reality exposure therapy deserves further investigation.

CUE EXPOSURE TREATMENT FOR ALCOHOL DEPENDENCE. Cue exposure is a relatively new approach to treating substance-related disorders. It is designed to re-create real-life situations in safe therapeutic environments that expose patients repeatedly to alcohol-related cues, such as the sight or smell of alcohol. It is thought that this repeated exposure to cues, plus prevention of the usual response (drinking alcohol) will reduce and possibly eliminate urges experienced in reaction to the cues.

People diagnosed with alcohol dependence face a number of alcohol-related cues in their environments, including moods associated with previous drinking patterns; people, places, times, and objects associated with the pleasurable effects of alcohol; and the sight or smell of alcoholic beverages. Exposure to these cues increases the patient's risk of **relapse**, because the cues can interfere with a person's use of coping skills to resist the urge to drink. The purpose of cue exposure is to teach patients coping skills for responding to these urges. It is thought that people who practice coping skills in the presence of cues will find the coping skills

strengthened, along with the conviction that they can respond effectively when confronted by similar cues in real-life situations.

There are various approaches to cue exposure. The choice of cues is usually based on treatment philosophy and goals, which may require abstinence from alcohol or permit moderate drinking. In abstinence-only programs, patients may be exposed to actual alcohol cues and/or imagined high-risk situations. This imaginal exposure is useful for dealing with cues and circumstances that cannot be reproduced in treatment settings, such as fights. Patients learn and practice urge-specific coping skills. While patients may learn to cope successfully with one cue (e.g., the smell of alcohol), the urge to drink may reappear in response to another cue, such as seeing a friend with whom they used to go to bars. Patients would then learn how to manage this particular cue. This program may take six to eight individual or group sessions and may occur on an inpatient or outpatient basis. Often patients remain in the treatment setting for several hours after the exposure to ensure that any lasting urges are safely managed with a therapist's help.

More specifically, cue exposure focuses on the aspect of alcohol consumption that produces the strongest urge. Patients would report each change in their level of urgency, using a scale of zero to 10 that resembles the SUDS scale. The urge to drink usually peaks after one to five minutes. When the desire for a drink arises, patients are instructed to focus on the cue to see what happens to their desire. In most cases the urge subsides within 15 minutes, which is often different from what the patients expected. In later sessions, the patients are instructed when the urge peaks to imagine using the coping skills that they recently learned. Patients may also be instructed to imagine being in high-risk situations and using the coping skills. Some examples of these coping skills include telling oneself that the urge will go away, picturing the negative consequences of drinking alcohol, and thinking of the positive consequences of staying sober.

Although there has been little research on cue exposure, available studies show positive outcomes in terms of decreasing the patients' consumption of alcohol. There have been, however, few outcome studies comparing cue exposure treatment to other treatment approaches. It may be hard to separate the benefits of exposure from the benefits of coping skills training. In any event, cue exposure treatment is a promising approach that deserves further study to determine if either component alone is sufficient or if a combination of the two is more effective.

KEY TERMS

Cognitive restructuring—An approach to psychotherapy that focuses on helping patients examine distorted patterns of perceiving and thinking in order to change their emotional responses to people and situations.

Cue—Any behavior or event in a person's environment that serves to stimulate a particular response. For example, the smell of liquor may be a cue for some people to pour themselves a drink.

Desensitization—The reduction or elimination of an overly intense reaction to a cue by controlled repeated exposures to the cue.

Extinction—The elimination or removal of a person's reaction to a cue as a result of exposure treatment.

Flooding—A type of exposure treatment in which patients are exposed to anxiety-provoking or feared situations all at once and kept in it until the anxiety and fear subside.

Habituation—The reduction of a person's emotional or behavioral reaction to a cue by repeated or prolonged exposure.

Hierarchy—In exposure therapy, a list of feared items or situations, ranked from least fearsome to most fearsome.

In vivo—A Latin phrase that means "in life." In modeling and exposure therapies, it refers to practicing new behaviors in a real setting, as distinct from using imagery or imagined settings.

Interoceptive—Referring to stimuli or sensations that arise inside the body. In interoceptive exposure treatment, patients are asked to exercise or perform other actions that produce feared internal physical sensations.

Modality—The medical term for a method of treatment.

Subjective units of distress (SUDS) scale—A scale used by patients during exposure treatment to rate their levels of fear and anxiety with numbers from zero to 100.

Virtual reality—A realistic simulation of an environment, produced by a computer system using interactive hardware and software.

Normal results

Progress in exposure therapy is often slow in the beginning, and occasional setbacks are to be expected. As patients gain experience with various anxiety-producing situations, their rates of progress may increase. While flooding can produce positive results more quickly than graded exposure, it is rarely used because of the high level of discomfort associated with it.

See also Agoraphobia; Alcohol and related disorders; Anxiety and anxiety disorders; Anxiety-reduction techniques; Cognitive-behavioral therapy; Obsessive-compulsive disorder; Panic disorder; Panic disorder with agoraphobia; Panic disorder without agoraphobia; Phobias; Systematic desensitization.

Resources

BOOKS

American Psychiatric Association. *Practice Guidelines for the Treatment of Psychiatric Disorders: Compendium 2000.* Washington, D.C.: American Psychiatric Association, 2000.

Richard, David C. S., and Dean Lauterbach, eds. *Handbook of Exposure Therapies.* San Diego, CA: Academic Press, 2006.

Rosqvist, Johan. *Exposure Treatments for Anxiety Disorders: A Practioner's Guide to Concepts, Methods, and Evidence-Based Practice.* New York: Routledge, 2005.

VandenBos, Gary R., ed. *APA Dictionary of Psychology.* Washington, D.C.: American Psychological Association, 2006.

PERIODICALS

Bornas, Xavier, Miquel Tortella-Feliu, and Jordi Llabrés. "Do All Treatments Work for Flight Phobia? Computer-Assisted Exposure Versus a Brief Multicomponent Nonexposure Treatment." *Psychotherapy Research* 16.1 (Jan. 2006): 41–50.

Conklin, Cynthia A. "Environments as Cues to Smoke: Implications for Human Extinction-Based Research and Treatment." *Experimental and Clinical Psychopharmacology* 14.1 (Feb. 2006): 12–9.

Cottraux, Jean. "Recent Developments in Research and Treatment for Social Phobia (Social Anxiety Disorder)." *Current Opinion in Psychiatry* 18.1 (Jan. 2005): 51–54.

Massad, Phillip M., and Timothy L. Hulsey. "Exposure Therapy Renewed." *Journal of Psychotherapy Integration* 16.4 (Dec. 2006): 417–28.

Thewissen, Roy, and others. "Renewal of Cue-Elicited Urge to Smoke: Implications for Cue Exposure Treatment." *Behaviour Research and Therapy* 44.10 (Oct. 2006): 1441–49.

Vansteenwegen, Debora, and others. "Verbal, Behavioural and Physiological Assessment of the Generalization of Exposure-Based Fear Reduction in a Spider-Anxious Population." *Behaviour Research and Therapy* 45.2 Feb. 2007): 291–300.

Wilhelm, Frank H., and others. "Mechanisms of Virtual Reality Exposure Therapy: The Role of the Behavioral Activation and Behavioral Inhibition Systems." *Applied Psychophysiology and Biofeedback* 30.3 (Sept. 2005): 271–84.

Joneis Thomas, PhD
Ruth A. Wienclaw, PhD

Expressive language disorder

Definition

Expressive language disorder occurs when an individual has problems expressing him- or herself using spoken language.

Description

Expressive language disorder is generally a childhood disorder. There are two types of expressive language disorder: the developmental type and the acquired type. Developmental expressive language disorder does not have a known cause and generally appears at the time a child is learning to talk. Acquired expressive language disorder is caused by damage to the **brain**. It occurs suddenly after events such as **stroke** or traumatic head injury. The acquired type can occur at any age.

Causes and symptoms

Causes

There is no clearly identified cause of developmental expressive language disorder. Research is ongoing to determine which biological or environmental factors may be the cause. Acquired expressive language disorder is caused by damage to the brain. Damage can be sustained during a stroke, or as the result of traumatic head injury, **seizures**, or other medical conditions. The way in which acquired expressive language disorder manifests itself in a specific person depends on which parts of the brain are injured and how badly they are damaged.

Symptoms

Expressive language disorder is characterized by a child having difficulty with self-expression using speech. The signs and symptoms vary drastically from child to child. The child does not have problems with the pronunciation of words, as occurs in **phonological disorder**. The child does have problems putting sentences together coherently, using proper grammar, recalling the appropriate word to use, or other similar problems. A child with expressive language disorder cannot communicate thoughts, needs, or wants at the same level or with the same complexity as peers and often has a smaller vocabulary compared to peers.

Children with expressive language disorder have the same ability to understand speech as their peers and have the same level of intelligence. Therefore, a child with this disorder may understand words but be unable to use the same words in sentences. The child may understand complex spoken sentences and be able to carry out intricate instructions, although unable to form complex sentences.

There are many different ways in which expressive language disorder can manifest itself. Some children do not properly use pronouns, or leave out functional words such as "is" or "the." Other children cannot recall words that they want to use in the sentence and substitute general words such as "thing" or "stuff." Some children cannot organize their sentences so that the sentences are easy to understand. These children do comprehend the material they are trying to express—they just cannot create the appropriate sentences with which to express their thoughts.

Demographics

Expressive language disorder is a relatively common childhood disorder. Language delays occur in 10–15% of children under age three, and in 3–7% of school-age children. Expressive language disorder is more common in boys than in girls: studies suggest that developmental expressive language disorder occurs two to five times more often in boys. The developmental form of the disorder is far more common than the acquired type.

Diagnosis

To diagnose expressive language disorder, children must be performing below their peers at tasks that require communication in the form of speech. This can be hard to determine because it must be shown that an individual understands the material but cannot express that comprehension. Therefore, nonverbal tests must be used in addition to tests that require spoken answers. Hearing should also be evaluated because children who do not hear well may have problems putting together sentences, in a way that is similar to children with expressive language disorder. In children who are mildly hearing-impaired, the problem can often be resolved by using hearing aids to enhance the child's hearing. Also, children who speak a language other than the dominant language of their society (e.g., English in the United States) in the home should be tested in that language if possible. The child's ability to communicate in English may be the problem, not the child's ability to communicate in general.

The **Diagnostic and Statistical Manual of Mental Disorders**, fourth edition, text revision (known as the *DSM-IV-TR*), states that there are four general criteria for diagnosing expressive language disorder. The first is that the child communicates using speech at a level that is less developed than expected for his or her intelligence and ability to understand spoken language. This problem with communication using speech must create difficulties for the child in everyday life or in achieving goals. The child must understand what is being said at a level that is age-appropriate, or at a developmental level consistent with the child's. Otherwise the diagnoses should be **mixed receptive-expressive language disorder**. If the child has **mental retardation**, poor hearing, or other problems, the difficulties with speech must be greater than is generally associated with the handicaps of the child.

Treatment

There are two types of treatment used for expressive language disorder. The first involves the child working one-on-one with a speech therapist on a regular schedule and practicing speech and **communication skills**. The second type of treatment involves the child's parents and teachers working together to incorporate spoken language that the child needs into everyday activities and play. Both of these kinds of treatment can be effective and are often used together.

Prognosis

The developmental form of expressive language disorder generally has a good prognosis. Most children develop normal or nearly normal language skills by high school. In some cases, minor problems with expressive language may never resolve. The acquired type of expressive language disorder has a prognosis that depends on the nature and location of the brain injury. Some people get their language skills back over days or

months. For others it takes years, and some people never fully recover expressive language function.

Prevention

There is no known way to prevent developmental expressive language disorder. Because acquired language disorder is caused by damage to the brain, anything that would help to prevent brain damage may help to prevent that type of the disorder. This can include such things ranging from lowering cholesterol to preventing stroke to wearing a bicycle helmet to prevent traumatic brain injury.

Resources

BOOKS

American Psychiatric Association. *Diagnostic and Statistical Manual of Mental Disorders,* 4th ed., Text rev. Washington, D.C.: American Psychiatric Association, 2000.

Sadock, Benjamin J., and Virginia A. Sadock, eds. *Comprehensive Textbook of Psychiatry,* 7th ed. Philadelphia: Lippincott Williams and Wilkins, 2000.

PERIODICALS

Roberts, Joanne E., Richard M. Rosenfeld, and Susan A. Zeisel. "Otitis Media and Speech and Language: A Meta-Analysis of Prospective Studies." *Pediatrics* 113 (2004): 238–48.

Stein, Martin T., Steven Parker, James Coplan, and Heidi Feldman. "Expressive Language Delay in a Toddler." *Journal of Developmental & Behavioral Pediatrics* 22.2 (April 2001): 99.

ORGANIZATIONS

The American Academy of Pediatrics. 141 Northwest Point Boulevard, Elk Grove Village, IL 60007-1098. Telephone: (847) 434-4000. <www.aap.org>.

American Psychological Association. 750 First Street NE, Washington, DC 20002-4242. Telephone: (800) 374-2721. <www.apa.org>.

American Speech-Language-Hearing Association. 10801 Rockville Pike, Rockville, MD 20852. Telephone: (800) 638-8355. <http://www.asha.org>.

OTHER

"Expressive Language Disorder, Developmental." National Library of Medicine. National Institutes of Health. (2006) <http://www.nlm.nih.gov/medlineplus/ency/article/001544.htm>.

Simms, Mark D., MD, M.PH. "The Late-Talking Child: What Should the Pediatrician Do?" (2006) <http://www.chw.org/display/PPF/DocID/35351/router.asp>.

Tish Davidson, A.M.
Emily Jane Willingham, PhD

Factitious disorder

Definition

Factitious disorder (FD) is an umbrella category that covers a group of mental disturbances in which patients intentionally act physically or mentally ill without obvious benefits. According to one estimate, the unnecessary tests and waste of other medical resources caused by FD cost the United States $40 million per year. The name *factitious* comes from a Latin word that means "artificial" or "contrived."

The ***Diagnostic and Statistical Manual of Mental Disorders,*** fourth edition, text revision (*DSM-IV-TR*) distinguishes FD from **malingering**, which is defined as pretending illness when the individual has a clear motive—usually to benefit economically or to avoid legal trouble.

FD is sometimes referred to as hospital **addiction**, pathomimia, or polysurgical addiction. Variant names for individuals with FD include hospital vagrants, hospital hoboes, peregrinating patients, problem patients, and professional patients.

Description

Cases of FD are referenced in the medical literature as early as the second century A.D. by Galen, a famous Roman physician. The term factitious is derived from a book by an English physician named Gavin, published in 1843, entitled *On Feigned and Factitious Diseases.* The modern study of FD, however, began with a 1951 article in *Lancet* by a British **psychiatrist**, Richard Asher, who also coined the term Munchausen's syndrome to describe a chronic subtype of FD. The name Munchausen comes from an eighteenth-century German baron whose stories of his military exploits were published with substantial embellishments. In 1977, Gellengerg first reported a case of FD with primarily psychological symptoms. FD was recognized as a formal diagnostic category by *DSM-III* in 1980.

DSM-IV-TR defines FD as having three major subtypes: FD with predominantly psychological signs and symptoms; FD with predominantly physical signs and symptoms; and FD with combined psychological and physical signs and symptoms. A fourth syndrome, known as Ganser syndrome, has been classified in the past as a form of FD, although *DSM-IV-TR* groups it with the **dissociative disorders**.

DSM-IV-TR specifies three criteria for FD:

- the patient is intentionally producing or pretending to have physical or psychological symptoms or signs of illness

- the patient's motivation is to assume the role of a sick person

- there are no external motives (as in malingering) that explain the behavior

Psychological FD

FD with predominantly psychological signs and symptoms is listed by *DSM-IV-TR* as the first subcategory of the disorder. It is characterized by the individual feigning psychological symptoms.

Some researchers have suggested adding the following criteria for this subtype of FD:

- the symptoms are inconsistent, changing markedly from day to day and from one hospitalization to the next

- the changes are influenced by the environment (as when the patient feels observed by others) rather than by the treatment

- the patient's symptoms are unusual or unbelievable.

- the patient has a large number of symptoms that belong to several different psychiatric disorders

Jennifer Bush relaxes with mother Kathy in 1996 photo; Kathy Bush was jailed for a rare form of child abuse called Munchausen Syndrome by Proxy. The disease is also known as factitious disorder. *(AP Images)*

Physical FD

FD with predominantly physical signs and symptoms is the most familiar to medical personnel. Chronic FD of this type is often referred to as Munchausen's syndrome. The most common ways of pretending illness are: presenting a factitious history (claiming to have had a seizure that never happened); combining a factitious history with external agents that mimic the symptoms of disease (adding blood from a finger prick to a urine sample); or combining a factitious history with maneuvers that produce a genuine medical condition (taking a psychoactive drug to produce psychiatric symptoms). In most cases, these patients sign out of the hospital when they are confronted by staff with proof of their pretending, usually in the form of a laboratory report. Many individuals with Munchausen's syndrome move from hospital to hospital, seeking treatment, and thus are known commonly as "hospital hoboes."

FD with mixed symptoms

FD in this category is characterized by a mix of psychological and physical signs and symptoms.

FD not otherwise specified

FD not otherwise specified is a category that *DSM-IV-TR* included to cover a bizarre subtype in which one person fabricates misleading information about another's health or induces actual symptoms of illness in the other person. First described in 1977 by an American pediatrician, this syndrome is known as Munchausen syndrome by proxy (MSBP) and almost always involves a parent (usually the mother) and child. MSBP is now understood as a form of child abuse involving premeditation rather than impulsive acting out. Many pediatricians in the United States believe that MSBP is underdiagnosed.

Ganser syndrome

Ganser syndrome is a rare disorder (with about a 100 documented cases worldwide) that has been variously categorized as a FD or a dissociative disorder. It is named for a German psychiatrist named Sigbert Ganser, who first described it in 1898 from an examination of male prisoners who were thought to be psychotic. Ganser syndrome is used to describe dissociative symptoms and the pretending of **psychosis** that occur in forensic settings.

There are four symptoms regarded as diagnostic of Ganser syndrome:

- *Vorbeireden*: A German word that means "talking beside the point," it refers to a type of approximate answer to an examiner's questions that may appear silly but usually indicates that the patient understands the question. If the examiner asks how many legs a dog has, the patient may answer, "five."
- clouding of consciousness: The patient is drowsy or inattentive.
- conversion symptoms: These are physical symptoms produced by unconscious psychological issues rather than diagnosable medical causes. A common conversion symptom is temporary paralysis of an arm or leg.
- hallucinations.

Virtual FD

Although virtual FD does not appear as a heading in any present diagnostic manual, it is a phenomenon that has appeared with increasing frequency with the rise of Internet usage. The growing use of the personal computer has affected presentations of FD in two important ways. First, computers allow people with sufficient technical skills to access medical records from hospital databases and to cut and paste changes into their own records to falsify their medical histories.

Second, computers allow people to enter Internet chat rooms for people with serious illnesses and pretend to be patients with that illness to obtain attention and sympathy. "Munchausen by Internet" can have devastating effects on chat groups, destroying trust when the hoax is exposed.

Causes and symptoms

Causes

The causes of FD, whether physical or psychiatric, are difficult to determine because these patients are often lost to follow-up when they sign out of the hospital. **Magnetic resonance imaging** (MRI) has detected abnormalities in the **brain** structure of some patients with chronic FD, suggesting that there may be biological or genetic factors associated with the disorder. Positron-emission tomography (PET) scans of patients diagnosed with Ganser syndrome have also revealed brain abnormalities. The results of EEG (**electroencephalography**) studies of these patients are nonspecific.

Several different psychodynamic explanations have been proposed for FD. These include:

- patients with FD are trying to reenact unresolved childhood issues with parents.
- they have underlying problems with masochism.
- they need to be the center of attention and feel important.
- they need to receive care and nurturance.
- they are bothered by feelings of vulnerability.
- deceiving a physician allows them to feel superior to an authority figure.

There are several known risk factors for FD, including:

- the presence of other mental or physical disorders in childhood that resulted in considerable medical attention.
- a history of significant past relationships with doctors, or of grudges against them.
- present diagnosis of borderline, narcissistic, or antisocial personality disorder.

Symptoms

SYMPTOMS OF FACTITIOUS DISORDER IN ADULTS OR ADOLESCENTS. Reasons for suspecting FD include:

- the individual's history is vague and inconsistent, or the individual has a long medical record with many admissions at different hospitals in different cities.

- the patient has an unusual knowledge of medical terminology or describes the illness as if reciting a textbook description of it.
- the patient is employed in a medical or hospital-related occupation.
- *pseudologia fantastica,* a Latin phrase for "uncontrollable lying," is a condition in which the individual provides fantastic descriptions of events that never took place.
- the patient visits emergency rooms at times such as holidays or late Friday afternoons when experienced staff are not usually present and obtaining old medical records is difficult.
- the patient has few visitors even though claiming to be an important person.
- the patient is unusually accepting of surgery or uncomfortable diagnostic procedures.
- the patient's behavior is controlling, attention-seeking, hostile, or disruptive.
- symptoms are present only when the patient is being watched.
- the patient is abusing substances, particularly prescription painkillers or tranquilizers.
- the course of the "illness" fluctuates, or complications develop with unusual speed.
- the patient has multiple surgical scars, a so-called "gridiron abdomen," or evidence of self-inflicted wounds or injuries.

SYMPTOMS OF MUNCHAUSEN SYNDROME BY PROXY. Factors that suggest a diagnosis of MSBP include:

- the patient is a young child; the average age of patients with MSBP is 40 months.
- there is a history of long hospitalizations and frequent emergency room visits.
- siblings have histories of MSBP, failure to thrive, or death in early childhood from an unexplained illness.
- the mother is employed in a health care profession.
- the mother has been diagnosed with depression or histrionic or borderline personality disorder.
- there is significant dysfunction in the family.

Demographics

The demographics of FD vary considerably across the different subtypes. Most individuals with the predominantly psychological subtype of FD are males with a history of hospitalizations beginning in late adolescence; few of these people, however, are older than 45. For non-chronic FD with predominantly physical symptoms, women outnumber men by a 3:1 ratio. Most of these women are between 20 and 40 years of age. Individuals with Munchausen syndrome are mostly middle-aged males who are unmarried and estranged from their families. Mothers involved in MSBP are usually married, educated, middle-class women in their early 20s.

Little is known about the rates of various subcategories of FD in different racial or ethnic groups.

The prevalence of FD worldwide is not known. In the United States, some experts think that FD is underdiagnosed because hospital personnel often fail to spot the deceptions that are symptomatic of the disorder. In addition, people with this disorder tend to migrate from one medical facility to another, making tracking difficult. It is also not clear which subtypes of FD are most common. Most observers in developed countries agree, however, that the prevalence of factitious physical symptoms is much higher than the prevalence of factitious psychological symptoms. A large teaching hospital in Toronto reported that 10 of 1,288 patients referred to a consultation service had FD (0.8%). The National Institute for Allergy and Infectious Disease reported that 9.3% of patients referred for fevers of unknown origin had FD. A clinic in Australia found that 1.5% of infants brought in for serious illness by parents were cases of Munchausen syndrome by proxy.

Diagnosis

Diagnosis of FD is usually based on a combination of laboratory findings and the gradual exclusion of other possible diagnoses. In the case of MSBP, the abuse is often discovered through covert video surveillance.

The most important differential diagnoses, when FD is suspected, are malingering, **conversion disorder**, or another genuine psychiatric disorder.

Treatments

Medications

Medications have not proved helpful in treating FD by itself, although they may be prescribed for symptoms of **anxiety** or depression if the individual also meets criteria for an anxiety or mood disorder.

Psychotherapy

Knowledge of the comparative effectiveness of different psychotherapeutic approaches is limited by the fact that few people diagnosed with FD remain in long-term treatment. In many cases, however, the factitious disorder improves or resolves if the individual receives appropriate therapy for a comorbid psychiat-

ric disorder. Ganser syndrome usually resolves completely with supportive **psychotherapy**.

One approach that has proven helpful in confronting patients with an examiner's suspicions is a supportive manner that focuses on the individual's emotional distress as the source of the illness rather than on the anger or righteous indignation of hospital staff. Although most individuals with FD refuse psychiatric treatment when it is offered, those who accept it appear to benefit most from supportive rather than insight-oriented therapy.

Family therapy is often beneficial in helping family members understand the individual's behavior and need for attention.

Legal considerations

In dealing with cases of Munchausen syndrome by proxy, physicians and hospital staff should seek appropriate legal advice. Although covert video surveillance of parents suspected of MSBP is highly effective (between 56% and 92%) in exposing the fraud, it may also be considered grounds for a lawsuit by the parents on argument of entrapment. Hospitals can usually satisfy legal concerns by posting signs stating that they use hidden video monitoring.

All 50 states presently require hospital staff and physicians to notify law enforcement authorities when MSBP is suspected, and to take steps to protect the child. Protection usually includes removing the child from the home, but it should also include an evaluation of the child's sibling(s) and long-term monitoring of the family. Criminal prosecution of one or both parents may also be necessary.

Prognosis

The prognosis of FD varies by subcategory. Males diagnosed with the psychological subtype of FD are generally considered to have the worst prognosis. Self-mutilation and **suicide** attempts are common in these individuals. The prognosis for Munchausen's syndrome is also poor; the statistics for recurrent episodes and successful suicides range between 30% and 70%. These individuals do not usually respond to psychotherapy. The prognosis for non-chronic FD in women is variable; some of these patients accept treatment and do quite well. This subcategory of FD, however, often resolves itself after the patient turns 40. MSBP involves considerable risks for the child; 9–10% of these cases end in the child's death.

Ganser syndrome is the one subtype of FD with a good prognosis. Almost all patients recover within days of the diagnosis, especially if the **stress** that precipitated the syndrome is resolved.

KEY TERMS

Conversion disorder—A type of somatoform disorder in which unconscious psychological conflicts or other factors take the form of physical symptoms that are produced unintentionally. Conversion disorder is part of the differential diagnosis of factitious disorder.

Forensic—Pertaining to courtroom procedure or evidence used in courts of law.

Ganser syndrome—A rare subtype of factitious disorder accompanied by dissociative symptoms. It is most often seen in male patients under severe stress in prison or courtroom settings.

Gridiron abdomen—An abdomen with a network of parallel scars from repeated surgical operations.

Malingering—Knowingly pretending to be physically or mentally ill to avoid some unpleasant duty or responsibility, or for economic benefit.

Masochism—A mental disorder in which people obtain sexual satisfaction through pain or humiliation inflicted by themselves or by another person. The term is sometimes used more generally to refer to a tendency to find pleasure in submissiveness or self-denial.

Prevention

FD is not sufficiently well understood to allow for effective preventive strategies—apart from protection of child patients and their siblings in cases of MSBP.

Resources

BOOKS

American Psychiatric Association. *Diagnostic and Statistical Manual of Mental Disorders.* 4th ed., Text rev. Washington, D.C.: American Psychiatric Association, 2000.

Eisendrath, Stuart J., MD. "Psychiatric Disorders." *Current Medical Diagnosis & Treatment 2000,* edited by Lawrence M. Tierney, Jr., MD, and others. Stamford, CT: Appleton and Lange, 2000.

"Psychiatry in Medicine," Section 15, Chapter 185. *The Merck Manual of Diagnosis and Therapy,* edited by Mark H. Beers, MD, and Robert Berkow, MD. Whitehouse Station, NJ: Merck Research Laboratories, 2000.

PERIODICALS

Andersen, H. S., D. Sestoft, and T. Lillebaek. "Ganser Syndrome After Solitary Confinement in Prison: A Short Review and a Case Report." *Norwegian Journal of Psychiatry* 55 (2001): 199–201.

Daly, Robert C., MPH, and Can M. Savasman, MD. "Ganser Syndrome." *eMedicine Journal* 3.1 (January 14, 2002).

Elwyn, Todd S., MD, and Iqbal Ahmed, MD. "Factitious Disorder." *eMedicine Journal* 2.11 (November 5, 2001).

Feldman, Marc D., and Charles V. Ford. "Liejacking." *Journal of the American Medical Association* 271 (May 25, 1994): 574.

Gordon, Leo A. "Munchausen Patients Have Found the Computer." *Medical Economics* 74 (September 8, 1997): 118–22.

Libow, Judith A., MD. "Child and Adolescent Illness Falsification." *Pediatrics* 105 (February 2000): 58–64.

McEwen, Donna R., BSN. "Recognizing Munchausen's Syndrome." *AORN Journal* 67 (February 1998): 206–11.

Paulk, David. "Munchausen Syndrome by Proxy." *Clinician Reviews* 11 (August 2001): 783–91.

Snyder, S. L., M. S. Buchsbaum, and R. C. Krishna. "Unusual Visual Symptoms and Ganser-Like State Due to Cerebral Injury: A Case Study Using (18) F-Deoxyglucose Positron Emission Tomography." *Behavioral Neurology* 11 (1998): 51–54.

Stephenson, Joan. "Patient Pretenders Weave Tangled 'Web' of Deceit." *Journal of the American Medical Association* 280 (October 21, 1998): 1297.

Stern, Theodore A. "How to Spot the Patient Who's Faking It." *Medical Economics Journal* 76 (May 24, 1999): 54–56.

Szoke, Andrei, MD, and Didier Boillet, MD. "Factitious Disorder with Psychological Signs and Symptoms: Case Reports and Proposals for Improving Diagnosis." *Psychiatry On-Line,* 1999.

ORGANIZATIONS

American Academy of Child and Adolescent Psychiatry. 3615 Wisconsin Avenue, NW, Washington, DC 20016-3007. Telephone: (202) 966-7300. Fax: (202) 966-2891. <www.aacap.org>.

Munchausen by Proxy Survivors Network. P.O. Box 806177, Saint Clair Shores, MI 48080. <www.mbpsnetwork.com>.

OTHER

The Cleveland Clinic. "An Overview of Factitious Disorders." 2007. <http://www.clevelandclinic.org/health/health-info/docs/2800/2820.asp?index=9832>.

Elwyn, Todd S., and Iqbal Ahmed. "Factitious Disorder." 2006. <http://www.emedicine.com/med/topic3125.htm>.

Feldman, Marc, MD. "Dr. Marc Feldman's Munchausen Syndrome, Malingering, Factitious Disorder, and Munchausen by Proxy Page." <http:www.munchausen.com>.

Rebecca Frey, PhD
Emily Jane Willingham, PhD

False belief of pregnancy *see* **Pseudocyesis**

Family education

Definition

Family education or "psychoeducation" is the ongoing process of educating family members about a serious mental illness in order to improve their coping skills and their ability to help a relative affected by the illness.

Purpose

When someone is diagnosed with a chronic illness, such as diabetes or heart disease, efforts are typically made by his or her doctor not only to educate the individual directly affected by the illness, but to educate and involve his/her family in treatment and care. Historically, this has not been the case with severe mental illnesses such as **schizophrenia**, major **depression**, **bipolar disorder**, or **schizoaffective disorder**.

Historically, most mental health professionals did not educate families about what to expect or how to care for their loved one. In fact, for much of the twentieth century it was believed that mental illness was caused by overly strict or overly permissive parenting styles, and families were unfairly blamed for causing these disorders. Mothers were labeled "schizophrenogenic" and even well-meaning clinicians tried to keep them and other family members at a distance. Bateson's "double-bind" theory of the time suggested that contradictory messages and communications by parents were the root cause of the problem. Because of these ideas and the **stigma** associated with mental illness, families felt isolated and alone, with few resources to assist them. After **diagnosis**, the only recourse for most families was to go to public libraries to read and learn as much as they could on their own.

Over the last 20 years, however, advances in genetics, neuroscience, and imaging techniques have provided new evidence that severe mental illnesses are neurobiological in origin. With this scientific knowledge has come greater awareness and understanding that these are "no-fault" **brain** illnesses, and that neither families nor patients should be blamed. Rather, they both should receive the necessary information and support to help them better cope with these complex disorders.

Description

In the United States and elsewhere, the large majority of individuals with severe mental illness live with their families and depend on them for housing, financial assistance, advocacy, and support. For this reason families require knowledge and skills to actively help their relative benefit from treatment, avoid **relapse**, and achieve recovery. Specifically, family caregivers require information about the illness and its symptoms, how to better communicate with their family member and professionals, the pros and cons of different treatment options, medications and their therapeutic uses and their adverse side effects, signs of relapse, availability of community services and supports, how to access benefits and entitlements, and how to handle crises or bizarre and troubling behaviors. Because living with an individual with a serious mental disorder can be very stressful, family education must also focus on teaching families about the importance of taking care of themselves.

The National Alliance for the Mentally Ill (NAMI) is an umbrella organization of more than 1,100 local support and advocacy groups in 50 states. The organization comprises families and individuals affected by serious mental illness who come together for family education, mutual support, and advocacy. Through conferences, **support groups**, and newsletters, family members have opportunities to educate one another and exchange experiences. NAMI has also made great inroads in teaching mental health professionals about the importance of educating family members and involving them in plans for the patient's treatment and rehabilitation. On a more formal level, NAMI has sponsored Family to Family, a 12-week education course that has been attended by 50,000 family members in more than 42 states. Taught by family volunteers, this is the first peer program in family education in the United States.

Family education is slowly becoming an integral part of treatment, as the practice guidelines for professionals have begun to recommend its use. Families are also utilizing a new generation of books about mental illness—some written by professionals, and others written by, and for, family members. Families are also increasingly using the Internet to learn more about mental disorders.

Family education for parents of children and adolescents

Because major mental illnesses tend to occur in adolescence or early adulthood, most family interventions focus on parents of adult children. However, any parent of a younger child with an emotional or behavioral disturbance can testify to the extraordinary challenges involved in coordinating care. For this reason, more public and private agencies are beginning to provide training, information, education, and financial assistance to family members of children and adolescents with emotional disturbances. The results of research about family education interventions for parents of children with serious emotional disturbances are just beginning to emerge. Some research suggests that family participation improves service delivery and patient outcomes for this group. In a randomized controlled trial of the training of 200 parents who did or did not receive training, while there were no significant effects on child mental health status, those family members who were trained showed significant knowledge enhancement and increased effectiveness.

Results

Recent research has provided evidence that family education and support leads to improved patient outcomes. For example, **family psychoeducation** provided by mental health professionals has such a compelling research base that it is considered a practice based on the findings of real-life studies of family education and support.

Another type of therapy discussed in the scientific literature has been used in China and India. The "family consultation" model uses individualized, private consultations between the family and a trained consultant to assist the family on an as-needed basis.

Resources

BOOKS

Torrey, E. Fuller. *Surviving Schizophrenia: A Manual for Families, Consumers and Providers,* 4th ed. New York: HarperCollins, 2001.

PERIODICALS

Archie, Suzanne, Jane Hamilton Wilson, Kevin Woodward, Heather Hobbs, Shelley Osborne, and Jean McNiven. "Psychotic Disorders Clinic and First-Episode Psychosis: A Program Evaluation." *Canadian Journal of Psychiatry* 50.1 (Jan. 2005): 46–51.

Dunbar, Sandra B., Patricia C. Clark, Christi Deaton, Andrew L. Smith, Anindya K. De, and Marian C. O'Brien. "Family Education and Support Interventions in Heart Failure. A Pilot Study." *Nursing Research* 54.3 (May–June 2005): 158–66.

Edelman, Perry, Daniel Kuhn, Bradley R. Fulton, and Gregory A. Kyrouac. "Information and Service Needs of Persons With Alzheimer's Disease and Their Family Caregivers Living in Rural Communities." *American Journal of Alzheimer's Disease and Other Dementias* 21.4 (Aug.–Sept. 2006): 226–33.

Murray-Swank, Aaron B., Alicia Lucksted, Deborah R. Medoff, Ye Yang, Karen Wohlheiter, and Lisa B. Dixon. "Religiosity, Psychosocial Adjustment, and Subjective Burden of Persons Who Care for Those With

Mental Illness." *Psychiatric Services* 57.3 (Mar. 2006): 361–65.

ORGANIZATIONS

National Alliance for the Mentally Ill (NAMI). Colonial Place Three, 2107 Wilson Blvd., Suite 300 Arlington, VA 22201-3042. Telephone: (800) 950-NAMI (6264) or (703) 524-7600. Web site: <http://www.nami.org>.

National Family Caregivers Association. 10400 Connecticut Avenue, #500, Kensington, MD 20895-3944. Telephone: (800) 896-3650 Fax: (301) 942-2302. Web site: <http://www.nfcacares.org/>.

National Mental Health Association (NMHA). 1021 Prince Street Alexandria, VA 22314-2971. Telephone: (800) 969-6642 or (703) 684-7722. Web site: <http://www.nmha.org>.

OTHER

National Institute of Mental Health. "Schizophrenia." <http://www.nimh.nih.gov/publicat/schizoph.htm>.

U.S. Department of Health and Human Services. *Mental Health: A Report of the Surgeon General.* Rockville, MD: U.S. Department of Health and Human Services, 1999. Available at: <http://www.surgeongeneral.gov/library/mentalhealth/home.html>.

Irene S. Levine, PhD
Ruth A. Wienclaw, PhD

Family psychoeducation

Definition

Family psychoeducation is a method for training families to work together with mental health professionals as part of a team to help family members with psychiatric disorders recover and maintain psychological health. Family psychoeducation has been shown to improve patient outcomes for people with **schizophrenia**, bipolar disorders, **depression**, and other major mental illnesses.

Purpose

The goal of family psychoeducation is to prevent patients with severe mental illnesses from relapsing, and to promote their reentry into their home communities, with particular regard for their social and occupational functioning. To achieve this goal, family psychoeducation programs seek to provide families with the information they need about mental illness and give them the coping skills to deal with their family members' psychiatric disorders.

An associated goal of family psychoeducation is to provide support for the patients' families. Families experience many burdens (financial, social, and psychological) in serving as long-term caregivers for their loved ones. Although the primary focus of family psychoeducation groups is improved patient outcomes, an essential intermediate goal is to promote the well-being of the family.

Description

There are several different models of family psychoeducation. Although they include many common elements, these different models are: single- and multiple-family groups; mixed groups that include family members and consumers (patients); groups of varying duration ranging from nine months to more than five years; and groups that focus on patients and families at different phases in the illness. Family psychoeducation programs have been studied extensively and refined by a number of researchers, including Drs. Ian Falloon, Gerald Hogarty, William McFarlane, and Lisa Dixon.

The evidence suggests that multifamily groups, which bring together several patients and their families, lead to better outcomes than single-family psychoeducation groups. The origins of multiple-family **group therapy** go back as far as 1960, when these groups were first assembled to solve ward-management problems in a psychiatric hospital. Lasting a minimum of nine months, the programs provided their participants with information about mental illness, its symptoms and treatment; medication and its side effects; how to communicate with a person with mental illness; and techniques for **crisis intervention** and mutual problem solving.

Dr. Dixon recently outlined the characteristics of successful family psychoeducation programs. They include:

- the programs consider schizophrenia an illness like any other.
- they are led by mental health professionals.
- they are part of a total treatment plan that includes medication.
- families are treated as partners rather than patients.
- the programs focus primarily on patient outcomes, and secondarily on family outcomes.
- the programs differ from traditional family therapy in that they do not treat families as part of the problem; they see them as part of the solution.

It is also important that **family education** programs take into account the phase of the patient's illness, the life cycle of both the patient and the family, and the family's cultural context.

KEY TERMS

Burden—First described by M. B. Treudley in 1946, this term generally refers to the consequences for the family of close contact with people who have severe mentally illnesses.

Meta-analysis—The statistical analysis of a large collection of analyses from individual studies for the purpose of integrating the findings.

Results

A large body of evidence supports the use of family psychoeducation as a "best practice" for young adults with schizophrenia and their families. Because of this compelling evidence, researchers at the University of Maryland, as part of the Schizophrenia Patient Outcomes Research Team (PORT), identified family psychoeducation as an evidence-based practice that should be offered to all families. This and other research studies have shown reduced rates of **relapse** and lower rates of **hospitalization** among patients and families involved in these programs. Other outcomes included increased rates of patient participation in **vocational rehabilitation** programs and employment, decreased costs of care, and improved well-being of family members.

A meta-analysis of 16 individual studies found that family interventions of fewer than 10 sessions have no effect on the reduction of family burden. There are also several controlled studies that support the effectiveness of single- and multiple-family interventions for **bipolar disorder**, major depression, **obsessive-compulsive disorder**, **anorexia nervosa**, and **borderline personality disorder**. Studies of family psychoeducation have been conducted with a Hispanic population in Los Angeles, California, and outside the United States in China, Norway, and the Netherlands.

Unfortunately, putting family psychoeducation into effect in clinical settings has not kept pace with research. The PORT study found that only 31% of patients studied reported that their families received information about their illness. One recent strategy to expand these programs includes integrating family psychoeducation into assertive community treatment (ACT) programs.

See also Case management.

Resources

BOOKS

Corcoran, Jacqueline. *Clinical Applications of Evidence-Based Family Interventions.* New York: Oxford University Press, 2003.

Lefley, Harriet P., and Dale L. Johnson, eds. *Family Interventions in Mental Illness: International Perspectives.* Westport, CT: Praeger Publishers, 2002.

PERIODICALS

Klaus, Nicole, and Mary A. Fristad. "Family Psychoeducation as a Valuable Adjunctive Intervention for Children With Bipolar Disorder." *Directions in Psychiatry* 25.3 (2005): 217–30.

Lopez, Molly A, and others. "A Psychoeducational Program for Children with ADHD or Depression and their Families: Results from the CMAP Feasibility Study." *Community Mental Health Journal* 41.1 (Feb. 2005): 51–66.

Mino, Yoshio, and others. "Medical Cost Analysis of Family Psychoeducation for Schizophrenia." *Psychiatry and Clinical Neurosciences* 61.1 (Feb. 2007): 20–24.

Motlova, Lucie, and others. "Relapse Prevention in Schizophrenia: Does Group Family Psychoeducation Matter? One-Year Prospective Follow-Up Field Study." *International Journal of Psychiatry in Clinical Practice* 10.1 (Mar. 2006): 38–44.

Sanford, Mark, and others. "A Pilot Study of Adjunctive Family Psychoeducation in Adolescent Major Depression: Feasibility and Treatment Effect." *Journal of the American Academy of Child & Adolescent Psychiatry* 45.4 (Apr. 2006): 386–95.

ORGANIZATIONS

National Alliance for the Mentally Ill (NAMI). Colonial Place Three, 2107 Wilson Boulevard, Suite 300, Arlington, VA 22201-3042. Telephone: (800) 950-NAMI (6264) or (703) 524-7600. <http://www.nami.org>.

National Mental Health Association (NMHA). 1021 Prince Street, Alexandria, VA 22314-2971. Telephone: (800) 969-6642 or (703) 684-7722. <http://www.nmha.org>.

OTHER

National Institute of Mental Health. "Schizophrenia". <http://www.nimh.nih.gov/publicat/schizoph.htm>.

Irene S. Levine, PhD
Ruth A. Wienclaw, PhD

Family therapy

Definition

Family therapy is a form of **psychotherapy** that involves all the members of a nuclear or extended family. The purpose of family therapy is to improve relationships between family members and improve behavior patterns of the family as a whole or subgroups within the family. Family therapy may be conducted by a pair of therapists—often a man and a woman—to treat gender-related issues or serve as

role models for family members. Although some types of family therapy are based on behavioral or psychodynamic principles, the most widespread form is based on family systems theory, an approach that regards the entire family as the unit of treatment, and emphasizes such factors as relationships and communication patterns rather than traits or symptoms in individual members.

History

Family therapy is a relatively recent development in psychotherapy. It began shortly after World War II, when doctors who were treating patients with **schizophrenia** noticed that the patients' families communicated in disturbed ways. The doctors also found that patients' symptoms rose or fell according to the level of tension between their parents. These observations led to considering a family as an organism (or system) with its own internal rules, patterns of functioning, and tendency to resist change. When the therapists began to treat the families as whole units instead of focusing solely on the hospitalized member, they found that in many cases the family member with schizophrenia improved. (This does not mean that schizophrenia is caused by family problems, although they may aggravate its symptoms.) This approach was then applied to families with problems other than schizophrenia. Family therapy is becoming an increasingly common form of treatment as changes in American society are reflected in family structures; it is also helpful when a child or other family member develops a serious physical illness.

Purpose

Family therapy is often recommended when:

- a family member has schizophrenia or another severe psychosis; the goal in these cases is to help other family members understand the disorder and adjust to the psychological changes that may be occurring in the patient.
- problems cross generational boundaries, such as when parents share a home with grandparents, or children are being raised by grandparents.
- families deviate from social norms (unmarried parents, gay couples rearing children, etc.). These families may or may not have internal problems, but could be troubled by societal attitudes.
- members come from mixed racial, cultural, or religious backgrounds.
- one member is being scapegoated, or their treatment in individual therapy is being undermined.

VIRGINIA SATIR (1916–1988)

For the techniques she created to treat troubled families, Virginia Satir was known worldwide as a pioneer in the development of family therapy. After earning a bachelor's degree from Wisconsin State University in 1936, Satir taught for six years at schools in Wisconsin, Michigan, and Louisiana. She became interested in the relationship between dysfunctional individuals and their families, and, deciding to specialize in family analysis, went back to school to earn a master's degree in 1948 at the University of Chicago. Satir subsequently worked as a therapist and social worker at mental hospitals and public welfare programs and conducted more than four hundred workshops for the government, hospitals, and universities throughout the United States. In addition, Satir helped found the Mental Research Institute in 1959 and, twenty years later, established the International Human Learning Resource Network. A leader in developing the concept of self-worth, Satir conveyed her psychological philosophies in such books as *Conjoint Family Therapy: A Guide to Theory and Technique, Peoplemaking, Self Esteem, Helping Families to Change,* and *Making Contact.*

- the identified patient's problems seem inextricably tied to problems with other family members.
- a blended (i.e. step-) family is having adjustment difficulties.

Precautions

Families not considered suitable candidates for family therapy include those in which:

- one or both parents is psychotic or has been diagnosed with antisocial or paranoid personality disorder.
- cultural or religious values are opposed to, or suspicious of, psychotherapy.
- family members cannot participate in treatment sessions because of illness or other physical limitations.
- individuals have very rigid personality structures and might be at risk for an emotional or psychological crisis.
- members cannot or will not be able to meet regularly for treatment.
- the family is unstable or on the verge of breakup.

Intensive family therapy may be difficult for family members with psychoses.

Description

Family therapy tends to be short-term, usually several months in length, and is aimed at resolving specific problems such as eating disorders, difficulties with school, or adjustments to bereavement or geographical relocation. It is not normally used for long-term or intensive restructuring of families with severe dysfunctions.

In therapy sessions, all members of the family and both therapists (if there is more than one) are present. The therapists try to analyze communication and interaction between all members of the family; they do not side with specific members, although they may make occasional comments to help members become more conscious of patterns previously taken for granted. Therapists who work as a team also model new behaviors through their interactions with each other.

Family therapy is based on systems theory, which maintains that the family is a living organism that is more than the sum of its individual members and evaluates family members in terms of their position or role within the system. Problems are treated by changing the way the system works rather than trying to "fix" a specific member.

Family systems theory is based on several major concepts:

- the identified patient: The identified patient (IP) is the family member with the symptom that has brought the family into treatment. The concept of the IP is used to keep the family from scapegoating the IPs or using them as a way of avoiding problems in the rest of the system.
- homeostasis: This concept presumes that the family system tends to resist change and seeks to maintain its customary organization and functioning over time. The family therapist can use homeostasis to explain why a certain family symptom has surfaced at a given time, why a specific member has become the IP, and what is likely to happen when the family begins to change.
- the extended family field: The extended family field is the nuclear family plus the network of grandparents and other members of the extended family. This concept is used to explain the intergenerational transmission of attitudes, problems, behaviors, and other issues.
- differentiation: Differentiation refers to each family member's ability to maintain a sense of self while remaining emotionally connected to the family; this is the mark of a healthy family.
- triangular relationship: Family systems theory maintains that emotional difficulties in families are usually triangular—whenever any two people have problems with each other, they will "triangle in" a third member to stabilize their own relationship.

These triangles usually interlock in a way that maintains homeostasis. Common family triangles include a child and the parents; two children and one parent; a parent, a child, and a grandparent; three siblings; or, husband, wife, and an in-law.

Preparation

Families are often referred to a specialist in family therapy by a pediatrician or other primary care provider. (Some estimates suggest that as many as 50% of pediatric office visits concern developmental problems in children that are affecting their families.) Physicians may use symptom checklists or psychological screeners to assess a family's need for therapy.

Family therapists can be psychiatrists, clinical psychologists, or other professionals certified by a specialty board in marriage and family therapy. They will usually evaluate a family for treatment by scheduling a series of interviews with members of the immediate family, including young children, as well as significant or symptomatic members of the extended family. This allows the therapists to learn how each family member sees the problem and provides a first impression of the family's functioning. Therapists typically evaluate the level and types of emotions expressed, patterns of dominance and submission, roles played by family members, communication styles, and the existence of emotional triangles. They also note whether these patterns are rigid or relatively flexible.

Preparation also usually includes creating a genogram, a diagram that depicts significant people and events in the family's history. Genograms include annotations about the medical history and major personality traits of each member and help uncover intergenerational patterns of behavior, marriage choices, family alliances and conflicts, the existence of family secrets, and other information that sheds light on the family's present situation.

Risks

There are no major risks involved in receiving family therapy, especially if family members seek therapy with honesty, openness, and a willingness to change. Changes that result from the therapy may be seen as "risks"—the possible unsettling of rigid personality defenses in individuals, or the unsettling of couple relationships that had been fragile before the beginning of therapy, for example.

Normal results

The goal of therapy is the identification and resolution of the problem that is causing the family's unhealthy interactions. Results vary, but in good circumstances they include greater insight, increased differentiation of individual family members, improved communication within the family, and loosening of previously automatic behavior patterns.

KEY TERMS

Blended family—A family formed by the remarriage of a divorced or widowed parent. It includes a new husband and wife, plus some or all of their children from previous marriages.

Differentiation—The ability to retain one's identity within a family system while maintaining emotional connections with the other members.

Extended family field—A person's family of origin plus grandparents, in-laws, and other relatives.

Family systems theory—An approach to treatment that emphasizes the interdependency of family members rather than focusing on individuals in isolation from the family. This theory underlies the most influential forms of contemporary family therapy.

Genogram—A family tree diagram that represents the names, birth order, sex, and relationships of the members of a family. Therapists use genograms to detect recurrent patterns in the family history and to help the members understand their problems.

Homeostasis—The tendency of a family system to maintain internal stability and resist change.

Identified patient (IP)—The family member whose symptom has emerged or is most obvious.

Nuclear family—The basic family unit, consisting of father, mother, and their biological children.

Scapegoating—The emergence of behavioral problems in one family member, usually the identified patient, who is often punished for problems within the entire family.

Triangling—A process in which two family members diminish the tension between them by drawing in a third member.

Resources

BOOKS

Gladding, Samuel T. *Family Therapy: History, Theory, and Practice.* 4th ed. Upper Saddle River, NJ: Prentice Hall, 2006.

Goldenberg, Herbert, and Irene Goldenberg. *Family Therapy: An Overview.* Belmont, CA: Brooks/Cole, 2007.

McGoldrick, Monica, Joe Giordano, and Nydia Garcia-Preto, eds. *Ethnicity and Family Therapy.* 3rd ed. New York: The Guilford Press, 2005.

Minuchin, Salvador, and H. Charles Fishman. *Family Therapy Techniques*. Cambridge, MA: Harvard University Press, 2004.

Nichols, Michael P., and Richard C. Schwartz. *Family Therapy: Concepts and Methods*. 7th ed. Boston: Allyn & Bacon, 2005.

Nichols, Michael P., and Richard C. Schwartz *Essentials of Family Therapy*. 3rd ed. Boston: Allyn & Bacon, 2006.

VandenBos, Gary R., ed. *APA Dictionary of Psychology*. Washington, D.C.: American Psychological Association, 2006.

PERIODICALS

Betz, Gabrielle, and Jill M. Thorngren. "Ambiguous Loss and the Family Grieving Process." *Family Journal: Counseling and Therapy for Couples and Families* 14.4 (Oct. 2006): 359–65.

Hogue, Aaron, and others. "Treatment Techniques and Outcomes in Multidimensional Family Therapy for Adolescent Behavior Problems." *Journal of Family Psychology* 20.4 (Dec. 2006): 535–43.

Hunter, Sally V. "Understanding the Complexity of Child Sexual Abuse: A Review of the Literature with Implications for Family Counseling." *Family Journal: Counseling and Therapy for Couples and Families* 14.4 (Oct. 2006): 349–58.

Lemmens, Gilbert, and others. "Family Discussion Group Therapy for Major Depression: A Brief Systemic Multi-Family Group Intervention for Hospitalized Patients and Their Family Members." *Journal of Family Therapy* 29.1 (Feb. 2007): 49–68.

Lock, James, and others. "Is Family Therapy Useful for Treating Children With Anorexia Nervosa? Results of a Case Series." *Journal of the American Academy of Child & Adolescent Psychiatry* 45.11 (Nov. 2006): 1323–28.

Miklowitz, David J., and Dawn O. Taylor. "Family-Focused Treatment of the Suicidal Bipolar Patient." *Bipolar Disorders* 8.5 part 2 (Oct. 2006): 640–51.

St. George, Sally, and Dan Wulff. "A Postmodern Approach to Teaching Family Therapy as Community Practice." *Journal of Systemic Therapies* 25.4 (Winter 2006): 73–83.

Schweitzer, Jochen, and others. "Training Psychiatric Teams to Do Family Systems Acute Psychiatry." *Journal of Family Therapy* 29.1 (Feb. 2007): 3–20.

Trepal, Heather C., and Kelly L. Wester. "Self-Injury and Postvention: Responding to the Family in Crisis." *Family Journal: Counseling and Therapy for Couples and Families* 14.4 (Oct. 2006): 342–48.

Rebecca J. Frey, PhD
Ruth A. Wienclaw, PhD

Fatigue

Introduction

Fatigue may be defined as a subjective state in which one feels tired or exhausted, and in which the capacity for normal work or activity is reduced. There is, however, no commonly accepted definition of fatigue when it is considered in the context of health and illness. This lack of definition results from the fact that a person's experience of fatigue depends on a variety of factors. These factors include culture, personality, the physical environment (light, noise, vibration), availability of social support through networks of family members and friends, the nature of a particular fatiguing disease or disorder, and the type and duration of work or exercise. For example, the experience of fatigue associated with disease will be different for someone who is clinically depressed, socially isolated, and out of shape compared to another person who is not depressed, has many friends, and is aerobically fit.

Fatigue is sometimes characterized as normal or abnormal. For example, the feeling of tiredness or even exhaustion after exercising is a normal response and is relieved by resting; many people report that the experience of ordinary tiredness after exercise is pleasant. Moreover, this type of fatigue is called "acute" because the onset is sudden and the desired activity level returns after resting. On the other hand, there is a kind of fatigue that is not perceived as ordinary and that may develop insidiously over time. This type of fatigue is unpleasant or seriously distressing and is not resolved by rest. Fatigue of this nature is abnormal and referred to as "chronic."

Some researchers regard fatigue as a defense mechanism that promotes the effective regulation of energy expenditures. According to this theory, when people feel tired, they take steps to avoid further **stress** (physical or emotional) by resting or by avoiding the stressor. They are then conserving energy. Because chronic fatigue is not normal, however, it is an important symptom of some mental disorders, a variety of physical diseases with known etiologies (causes), and some medical conditions that have no biological markers although they are recognizable syndromes (patterns of symptoms and signs).

Fatigue is sometimes described as being primary or secondary. Primary fatigue is a symptom of a disease or mental disorder and may be part of a cluster of such symptoms as pain, fever, or nausea. As the disease or disorder progresses, however, the fatigue may be intensified by the patient's worsening condition, other disease symptoms, or surgical or medical treatment. This subsequent fatigue is called secondary.

Risk factors

Fatigue is a common experience. It is one of the top ten symptoms that people mention when they visit the doctor. Some people, however, are at higher risk for developing fatigue. For example, the risk for women is about 1.5 times the risk for men, and the risk for people who do not exercise is twice that of active people. Some researchers question whether women really are at higher risk: they are more likely than men to go to the doctor with health problems, and men are less likely to admit feeling fatigued. Other risk factors include **obesity**, smoking, use of alcohol, high stress levels, **depression**, **anxiety**, and low blood pressure. Having low blood pressure is usually considered desirable in the United States but is regarded as a treatable condition in other countries. Low blood pressure or postural hypotension (sudden lowering of blood pressure caused by standing up) may cause fatigue, dizziness, or fainting.

Major sources of chronic fatigue

Disease

There are many diseases and disorders in which fatigue is a major symptom. These include cancer, cardiovascular disease, emphysema, multiple sclerosis, rheumatic arthritis, systemic lupus erythematosus, HIV/AIDS, infectious mononucleosis, chronic fatigue syndrome, and fibromyalgia. The reasons for the fatigue, however, vary according to the organ system or body function affected by the disease. Physical reasons for fatigue include:

- circulatory and respiratory impairment. When the patient's breathing and blood circulation are impaired or when the patient has anemia (low levels of red blood cells), body tissues do not receive as much oxygen and energy. Hence, the patient experiences a general sense of fatigue. Fatigue is also an important warning sign of heart trouble because it precedes 30–55% of myocardial infarctions (heart attacks) and sudden cardiac deaths.

- infection. Microorganisms that disturb body metabolism and produce toxic wastes cause disease and lead to fatigue. Fatigue is an early primary symptom of chronic, nonlocalized infections found in such diseases as AIDS, Lyme disease, and tuberculosis.

- nutritional disorders or imbalances. Malnutrition is a disorder that promotes disease. It is caused by insufficient intake of important nutrients, vitamins, and minerals; by problems with absorption of food through the digestive system; or by inadequate calorie consumption. Protein-energy malnutrition (PEM) occurs when people do not consume enough protein or calories; this condition leads to wasting of muscles and commonly occurs in developing countries. In particular, young children who are starving are at risk of PEM, as are people recovering from major illness. In general, malnutrition damages the body's

immune function and encourages disease and fatigue. Taking in too many calories for the body's needs, on the other hand, results in obesity, which is a predictor of many diseases related to fatigue.

- dehydration. Dehydration results from water and sodium imbalances in body tissues. The loss of total body water and sodium may be caused by diarrhea, vomiting, bed rest, exposure to heat, or exercise. Dehydration contributes to muscle weakness and mental confusion; it is a common and overlooked source of fatigue. Once fatigued, people are less likely to consume enough fluids and nutrients, worsening the fatigue and confusion.

- deconditioning. This term refers to generalized organ system deterioration resulting from bed rest and lack of exercise. In the 1950s and 1970s, the National Aeronautics and Space Administration (NASA) studied the effects of bed rest on healthy athletes. The researchers found that deconditioning set in quite rapidly (within 24 hours) and led to depression and weakness. Even mild exercise can counteract deconditioning and has become an important means of minimizing depression and fatigue resulting from disease and hospitalization.

- pain. When pain is severe enough, it may disrupt sleep and lead to the development of sleep disorders such as insomnia or hypersomnia. Insomnia is the term for having difficulty falling and/or staying asleep. Hypersomnia refers to excessive sleeping. In general, disrupted sleep is not restorative; people wake up feeling tired, and as a result their pain is worsened and they may become depressed. Furthermore, pain may interfere with movement or lead to too much bed rest, which results in deconditioning. Sometimes pain leads to social isolation because the person cannot cope with the physical effort involved in maintaining social relationships, or because family members are unsympathetic or resentful of the ill or injured person's reduced capacity for work or participation in family life. All of these factors worsen pain, contributing to further sleep disruption, fatigue, and depression.

- stress. When someone experiences ongoing pain and stress, organ systems and functional processes eventually break down. These include cardiovascular, digestive, and respiratory systems, as well as the efficient elimination of body wastes. According to the American Psychiatric Association, various chronic diseases are related to stress, including rheumatoid arthritis, cardiac angina, and secondary dysmenorrhea (painful menstruation).

- sleep disorders. There are a variety of sleep disorders that cause fatigue, including insomnia, hypersomnia, sleep apnea, and restless legs syndrome. For example, hypersomnia may be the result of brain abnormalities caused by viral infections. Researchers studying the aftermath of infectious mononucleosis proposed that exposure to viral infections might change brain function with the effect of minimizing restorative sleep; hence, some people developed hypersomnia. Another common disorder is sleep apnea, in which the patient's breathing stops for at least ten seconds, usually more than 20 times per hour. Snoring is common. People may experience choking and then wake up gasping for air; they may develop daytime hypersomnia to compensate. Sleep apnea is associated with aging, weight gain, and depression. It is also a risk factor for stroke and myocardial infarctions. Restless legs syndrome is a condition in which very uncomfortable sensations in the patient's legs cause them to move and wake up from sleep, or keep them from falling asleep. All of these disorders reduce the quality of a person's sleep and are associated with fatigue.

Fibromyalgia and chronic fatigue syndrome

Fibromyalgia (also known as myofascial syndrome or fibrositis) is a syndrome characterized by pain and achiness in muscles, tendons, and ligaments. There are 18 locations on the body where patients typically feel sore. These locations include areas on the lower back and along the spine, neck, and thighs. A diagnostic criterion for fibromyalgia (FM) is that at least 11 of the 18 sites are painful. In addition to pain, people with FM may experience sleep disorders, fatigue, anxiety, and irritable bowel syndrome. Experts have suggested that FM and chronic fatigue syndrome (CFS) are manifestations of the same pain and fatigue syndrome. The care that patients receive for FM or CFS depends in large measure on whether they were referred to a rheumatologist (a doctor who specializes in treating diseases of the joints and muscles), neurologist, or **psychiatrist**.

A few doctors may still not accept CFS (also known as myalgic encephalomyelitis in Great Britain) as a legitimate medical problem. This refusal is stigmatizing and distressing to the person who must cope with disabling pain and fatigue. It is not uncommon for people with CFS to see a number of different physicians before finding one who is willing to diagnose CFS. Nevertheless, major health agencies, such as the Centers for Disease Control (CDC) in the United States, have studied the syndrome. As a result, the CDC has developed a case definition for CFS that lists major and minor criteria for **diagnosis**. The major criteria of CFS include the presence of chronic and persistent fatigue for at least six months; fatigue that does not improve with rest; and fatigue that causes significant interference with the patient's daily activities. There are also eight other characteristic symptoms that include fever, sore throat, swollen lymph nodes, myalgia (muscle pain), difficulty with a level of physical exercise that the patient had performed easily before the illness, sleep disturbances, and headaches. Additionally, people often have difficulty concentrating and remembering information, and they experience extreme frustration and depression as a result of the limitations imposed by CFS. Full recovery from CFS is rare, occurring in only 5% to 10% of cases, although a 2005 report found that 8% to 63% of patients may experience improvement.

Psychological disorders

While fatigue may be caused by many organic diseases and medical conditions, it is a chief complaint for several mental disorders, including **generalized anxiety disorder** and clinical depression. Moreover, mental disorders may coexist with physical disease. When there is considerable symptom overlap, the differential diagnosis of fatigue is especially difficult.

GENERALIZED ANXIETY DISORDER. People are diagnosed as having generalized anxiety disorder (GAD) if they experience overwhelming worry or apprehension that persists, usually daily, for at least six months, and if they also experience some of the following symptoms: unusual tiredness, restlessness and irritability, problems with concentration, muscle tension, and disrupted sleep. Stressful life events such as divorce, unemployment, illness, or being the victim of a violent crime are associated with GAD, as is a history of psychiatric problems. Some evidence suggests that women who have been exposed to danger are at risk of developing GAD; women who suffer loss are at risk of developing depression; and women who experience danger and loss are at risk of developing a mix of both GAD and depression.

While the symptoms of CFS and GAD overlap, the disorders have different primary complaints. Patients with CFS complain primarily of tiredness, whereas people with GAD describe being excessively worried. In general, some researchers believe that anxiety contributes to fatigue by disrupting rest and restorative sleep.

DEPRESSION. In the fourth edition of the *Diagnostic and Statistical Manual of Mental Disorders* (*DSM-IV*), the presence of depressed mood or sadness, or loss of pleasure in life, is an important diagnostic criterion for depression. Daily fatigue, lack of energy, insomnia, and hypersomnia are indicators of a depressed mood. The symptoms of depression overlap with those of CFS; for example, some researchers report that 89% of people with depression are fatigued, as compared to 86–100%

of people with CFS. The experience of fatigue, however, seems to be more disabling with CFS than with depression. Another difference between CFS and depression concerns the onset of the disorder. Most patients with CFS experience a sudden or acute onset, whereas depression may develop over a period of weeks or months. Also, while both types of patients experience sleep disorders, CFS patients tend to have difficulty falling asleep, whereas depressed patients tend to wake early in the morning. It is possible for CFS and depression to be comorbidities.

Some researchers believe that there is a link between depression, fatigue, and exposure to too much REM sleep. There are five distinct phases in human sleep. The first two are characterized by light sleep; the second two by a deep restorative sleep called slow-wave sleep; and the last by rapid eye movement or REM sleep. Most dreams occur during REM sleep. Throughout the night, the intervals of REM sleep increase and usually peak around 8:30 A.M. A sleep deprivation treatment for depression involves reducing the patient's amount of REM sleep by waking him or her around 6:00 A.M. Researchers think that some fatigue associated with disease may be a form of mild depression and that reducing the amount of REM sleep will reduce fatigue by moderating depression.

Managing fatigue

The management of fatigue depends in large measure on its causes and the person's experience of it. For example, if fatigue is acute and normal, the person will recover from feeling tired after exertion by resting. In cases of fatigue associated with influenza or other infectious illnesses, the person will feel energy return as they recover from the illness. When fatigue is chronic and abnormal, however, the doctor will tailor a treatment program to the patient's needs. There are a variety of approaches that include:

- aerobic exercise. Physical activity increases fitness and counteracts depression.

- hydration (adding water). Water improves muscle turgor or tension and helps to carry electrolytes.

- improving sleep patterns. The patient's sleep may be more restful when its timing and duration are controlled.

- pharmacotherapy (treatment with medications). The patient may be given various medications to treat physical diseases or mental disorders, to control pain, or to manage sleeping patterns.

- psychotherapy. There are several different treatment approaches that help patients manage stress, understand the motives that govern their behavior, or

---

KEY TERMS

Biological marker—An indicator or characteristic trait of a disease that facilitates differential diagnosis (the process of distinguishing one disorder from other, similar disorders).

Deconditioning—Loss of physical strength or stamina resulting from bed rest or lack of exercise.

Electrolytes—Substances or elements that dissociate into electrically charged particles (ions) when dissolved in the blood. The electrolytes in human blood include potassium, magnesium, and chloride.

Metabolism—The group of biochemical processes within the body that release energy in support of life.

Stress—A physical and psychological response that results from being exposed to a demand or pressure.

Syndrome—A group of symptoms that together characterize a disease or disorder.

---

change maladaptive ideas and negative thinking patterns.

- physical therapy. This form of treatment helps patients improve or manage functional impairments or disabilities.

In addition to seeking professional help, people can understand and manage fatigue by joining appropriate **self-help groups**, reading informative books, seeking information from clearinghouses on the Internet, and visiting Web sites maintained by national organizations for various diseases.

See also Brain; Breathing-related sleep disorder; Caffeine and related sleep disorders; Circadian rhythm sleep disorder; Pain disorder; Self-help groups; Somatization and somatoform disorders.

Resources

BOOKS

Beers, Mark H., and Robert Berkow, eds. *The Merck Manual of Diagnosis and Therapy,* 17th ed. Whitehouse Station, NJ: Merck Research Laboratories, 1999.

Glaus, A. *Fatigue in Patients with Cancer: Analysis and Assessment.* Recent Results in Cancer Research, No. 145. Berlin, Germany: Springer-Verlag, 1998.

Hubbard, John R., and Edward A. Workman, eds. *Handbook of Stress Medicine: An Organ System Approach.* Boca Raton, FL: CRC Press, 1998.

Natelson, Benjamin H. *Facing and Fighting Fatigue: A Practical Approach.* New Haven, CT: Yale University Press, 1998.

Winningham, Maryl L., and Margaret Barton-Burke, eds. *Fatigue in Cancer: A Multidimensional Approach.* Sudbury, MA: Jones and Bartlett Publishers, 2000.

PERIODICALS

Natelson, Benjamin H. "Chronic Fatigue Syndrome." *JAMA: Journal of the American Medical Association* 285.20 (May 23–30 2001): 2557–59.

ORGANIZATIONS

MEDLINE plus Health Information, U.S. National Library of Medicine. 8600 Rockville Pike, Bethesda, MD 20894. Telephone: (888) 346-3656. <http://www.medlineplus.gov>.

National Chronic Fatigue Syndrome and Fibromyalgia Association. P.O. Box 18426, Kansas City, MO 64133. Telephone: (816) 313-2000. <http://www.4woman.gov/nwhic/references/mdreferrals/ncfsfa.htm>.

WEB SITES

Centers for Disease Control. "Chronic Fatigue Syndrome". (2006) <http://www.cdc.gov/cfs/cfsbasicfacts.htm>

Davis, Caralyn. "What's In a Name: Fibro vs. CFS." Arthritis Foundation. <http://www.arthritis.org/resources/news/news_fibro_cfs.asp>

Tanja Bekhuis, PhD
Emily Jane Willingham, PhD

Feeding disorder of infancy or early childhood

Definition

Feeding disorder of infancy or early childhood is characterized by the failure of an infant or child under six years of age to eat enough food to gain weight and grow normally over a period of one month or more. The disorder can also be characterized by the loss of a significant amount of weight over one month. Feeding disorder is similar to failure to thrive, except that no medical or physiological condition can explain the low food intake or lack of growth.

Description

Infants and children with a feeding disorder fail to grow adequately, or even lose weight with no underlying medical explanation. They do not eat enough energy or nutrients to support growth and may be irritable or apathetic. Factors that contribute to development of a feeding disorder include lack of nurturing, failure to accurately read the child's hunger and satiety cues, poverty, or parental mental illness. Successful treatment involves dietary, behavioral, social, and

psychological **intervention** by a multidisciplinary team of health professionals.

Causes and symptoms

Causes

Feeding disorder of infancy or early childhood can occur with inappropriate parent-child interactions, such as failure to read the child's hunger cues or forcing food when the child is not hungry. Lack of nurturing and/or parental aggression, anger, or **apathy** can make eating a negative experience for the child, increasing the risk of feeding disorders.

Feeding disorders are more common in infants and children who are born prematurely, had a low birth weight, or who are developmentally delayed. Many medical (or physiological) causes can contribute to eating difficulties, eating aversions, or failure to thrive, including:

- diseases of the central nervous system
- metabolic diseases
- sensory defects
- anatomical abnormalities, such as cleft palate
- muscular disorders, such as cerebral palsy
- heart disease
- gastrointestinal diseases, such as Crohn's disease

To meet criteria for a true feeding disorder of infancy or childhood, these medical conditions must be ruled out.

Symptoms

Because the child or infant with a feeding disorder is not consuming enough energy, vitamins, or minerals to support normal growth, symptoms resemble those seen in malnourished or starving children. The infant or child may be irritable, difficult to console, apathetic, withdrawn, and unresponsive.

Delays in development, as well as growth, can occur. In general, the younger the child, the greater the risk of developmental delays associated with the feeding disorder.

Laboratory abnormalities may also be associated with the disorder. Blood tests may reveal a low level of protein or hemoglobin in the blood. Hemoglobin is an iron-containing substance in blood that carries oxygen to body cells.

Demographics

Although minor feeding problems are common in infancy and childhood, true feeding disorder of infancy or early childhood is estimated to occur in

1% to 3% of infants and children. Children separated from their families or living in conditions of poverty or **stress** are at greater risk. Mental illness in a parent, or child abuse or **neglect**, may also increase the risk of the child developing a feeding disorder.

Diagnosis

Between 25% and 35% of normal children experience minor feeding problems. In infants born prematurely, 40% to 70% experience some type of feeding problem. For a child to be diagnosed with feeding disorder of infancy or early childhood, the disorder must be severe enough to affect growth for a significant period of time. Generally, growth failure is considered to be below the fifth percentile of weight and height.

Feeding disorder of infancy of early childhood is diagnosed if all four of the following criteria are present:

- failure to eat adequately over one month or more, with resultant weight loss or failure to gain weight.
- inadequate eating and lack of growth not be explained by any general medical or physiological condition, such as gastrointestinal problems, nervous system abnormalities, or anatomical deformations.
- the feeding disorder cannot be better explained by lack of food or by another mental disorder, such as rumination disorder.
- the inadequate eating and weight loss or failure to gain weight occurs before the age of six years. If feeding behavior or weight gain improves when another person feeds and cares for the child, the existence of a true feeding disorder, rather than some underlying medical condition, is more likely.

Treatments

Successful treatment of feeding disorders requires a multidisciplinary team approach to assess the child's needs and to provide recommendations and education to improve feeding skills, behavior, and nutrient intake. The multidisciplinary team for treatment of feeding disorders in childhood usually includes physicians specializing in problems of the gastrointestinal tract or of the ear, nose, and throat; a dietitian, a **psychologist**, a speech pathologist, and an occupational therapist. Support from **social workers** and physicians in related areas of medicine is also helpful.

An initial evaluation should focus on feeding history, including detailed information on type and timing of food intake, feeding position, meal duration, energy and nutrient intake, and behavioral and parental factors that influence the feeding experience. Actual observation of a feeding session can give valuable insight into the cause of the feeding disorder and appropriate treatments. A medical examination should also be conducted to rule out any potential medical problems or physical causes of the feeding disorder.

After a thorough history is taken and assessment completed, dietary and behavioral therapy is started. The goal of diet therapy is to gradually increase energy and nutrient intake as tolerated by the child to allow for catch up growth. Depending on the diet history, energy and nutrient content of the diet may be kept lower initially to avoid vomiting and diarrhea. As the infant or child is able to tolerate more food, energy and nutrient intake is gradually increased over a period of one to two weeks, or more. Eventually, the diet should provide about 50% more than normal nutritional needs of infants or children of similar age and size.

Behavioral therapy can help the parent and child overcome conditioned feeding problems and food aversions. Parents must be educated to accurately recognize their child's hunger and satiety cues and to promote a pleasant, positive feeding environment. Changing the texture of foods, the pace and timing of feedings, the position of the body, and even feeding utensils can help the child overcome aversions to eating. If poverty, abuse, or parental mental illness contribute to the feeding disorder, these issues must also be addressed.

Prognosis

If left untreated, infants and children with feeding disorders can have permanent physical, mental, and behavioral damage. However, most children with feeding disorders show significant improvements after treatment, particularly if the child and parent receive intensive nutritional, psychological, and social intervention.

Prevention

Providing balanced, age-appropriate foods at regular intervals—for example, three meals and two or three snacks daily for toddlers—can help to establish healthy eating patterns. If a child is allowed to fill up on soft drinks, juice, chips, or other snack prior to meals, appetite for other, more nutritious foods will decrease.

Positive infant and childhood feeding experiences require the child to effectively communicate hunger and satiety and the parent or caregiver to accurately interpret these signals. This set of events requires a nurturing environment and an attentive, caring adult. Efforts should be made to establish feeding as a positive, pleasant experience. Further, forcing a child to eat or punishing a child for not eating should be avoided.

Resources

BOOKS

American Psychiatric Association. *Diagnostic and Statistical manual of Mental Disorders.* 4th edition, text revised. Washington, DC: American Psychiatric Association, 2000.

Queen, Patricia M., M.M.Sc., R.D. and Carol E. Lang, M.S., R.D. *Handbook of Pediatric Nutrition.* Gaithersburg, Maryland: Aspen Publishers, Inc., 1993.

PERIODICALS

Rudolph, Colin D., and Dana Thompson Link. "Feeding Disorders in Infants and Children." *Pediatric Clinics of North America* 49 (2002): 97-112.

Nancy Gustafson, M.S., R.D., F.A.D.A., E.L.S.

Female orgasmic disorder

Definition

Female orgasmic disorder (FOD) is the persistent or recurrent inability of a woman to have an orgasm (climax or sexual release) after adequate sexual arousal and sexual stimulation. According to the handbook used by mental health professionals to diagnose mental disorders, the **Diagnostic and Statistical Manual of Mental Disorders**, fourth edition, text revision (also known as the *DSM-IV-TR*), this lack of response can be primary (a woman has never had an orgasm) or secondary (acquired after trauma), and can be either general or situation-specific. There are both physiological and psychological causes for a woman's inability to have an orgasm. To receive the **diagnosis** of FOD, the inability to have an orgasm must not be caused only by physiological problems or be a symptom of another major mental health problem. FOD may be diagnosed when the disorder is caused by a combination of physiological and psychological difficulties. To be considered FOD, the condition must cause personal distress or problems in a relationship. In earlier versions of the *DSM*. FOD was called "inhibited sexual orgasm."

Description

FOD is the persistent or recurrent inability of a woman to achieve orgasm. This lack of response affects the quality of the woman's sexual experiences.

To understand FOD, it is first necessary to understand the physiological changes that normally take place in a woman's body during sexual arousal and orgasm.

Normally, when a woman is sexually excited, the blood vessels in the pelvic area expand, allowing more blood to flow to the genitals, as also occurs in men. This effusion is followed by the seepage of fluid out of blood vessels and into the vagina to provide lubrication before and during intercourse. These events are called the "lubrication-swelling response."

Body tension and blood flow to the pelvic area continue to build as a woman receives more sexual stimulation; this occurs either by direct pressure on the clitoris or as pressure on the walls of the vagina and cervix. This tension builds as blood flow increases. When tension is released, pleasurable rhythmic contractions of the uterus and vagina occur; this release is called an orgasm. The contractions carry blood away from the genital area and back into general circulation.

It is normal for orgasms to vary in intensity, length, and number of contractions from woman to woman, as well as in a single individual from experience to experience. Unlike men, woman can have multiple orgasms in a short period of time. Mature women, who may be more sexually experienced than younger women, may find it easier to have orgasms than adolescents or the sexually inexperienced.

In a woman with FOD, sexual arousal and lubrication occur. Body tension builds, but the woman is unable or has extreme difficulty reaching climax and releasing the tension. This inability can lead to frustration and unfulfilling sexual experiences for both partners. FOD often occurs in conjunction with other **sexual dysfunctions**. Also, lack of orgasm can cause anger, frustration, and other problems in the relationship.

Causes and symptoms

With FOD, a woman either does not have an orgasm or has extreme difficulty regularly reaching climax. It is normal for women to lack this response occasionally, or to have an orgasm only with specific types of stimulation. The occasional failure to reach orgasm or dependence on a particular type of stimulation is not the same as FOD.

The causes of FOD can be both physical and psychological. FOD is most often a primary or lifelong disorder, meaning that a woman has never achieved orgasm under any type of stimulation, including self-stimulation (masturbation), direct stimulation of the clitoris by a partner, or vaginal intercourse. Some women experience secondary or acquired FOD. These women have had orgasms, but lose the ability after illness, emotional trauma, or as a side effect of surgery or medication. Acquired FOD is often temporary.

FOD can be generalized or situation-specific. In generalized FOD, the failure to have an orgasm occurs with different partners and in many different settings. In situational FOD, inability to reach climax occurs only with specific partners or under particular circumstances. FOD may be due either to psychological factors or a combination of physiological and psychological factors, but not due to physiological factors alone.

Physiological causes of FOD include:

- damage to the blood vessels of the pelvic region
- spinal cord lesions or damage to the nerves in the pelvic area
- side effects of medications (i.e., antipsychotics, antidepressants, narcotics) or illicit substance abuse
- removal of the clitoris (also called female genital mutilation, a cultural practice in parts of Africa, the Middle East, and Asia)

Psychological causes of FOD include:

- past sexual abuse, rape, incest, or other traumatic sexual experiences
- emotional abuse
- fear of becoming pregnant
- fear of rejection by partner
- fear of loss of control during orgasm
- self-image problems
- relationship problems with partner
- life stresses, such as financial worries, job loss, or divorce
- guilt about sex or sexual pleasure
- religious or cultural beliefs about sex
- other mental health disorders such as major depression

Recent studies of twins suggest that genes play a large role in the development of orgasmic dysfunction in women. Researchers have found a level of genetic involvement in this disorder that is similar to that for age of onset of menses or menopause, or presence of depression or **anxiety**.

Demographics

Inability to have an orgasm, discontent with the quality of orgasms, and the ability to have orgasms only with one type of stimulation are common sexual complaints among women. Some studies have found that about half of all women experience some orgasmic difficulties, but not all of these difficulties are considered FOD. About 50% of women experience orgasm through direct clitoral stimulation but not during intercourse, thus not meeting the criteria for a diagnosis of FOD. About 10% of women never experience an orgasm, regardless of the situation or stimulation. These women are more likely to be unmarried, young, and sexually inexperienced.

Diagnosis

FOD is diagnosed through a medical and psychological history, and history of the conditions under which orgasm fails to occur. It is especially helpful for the clinician or sex therapist to understand how long the problem has persisted, and whether it is general or situational. FOD is sometimes found in conjunction with **sexual aversion disorder** and **female sexual arousal disorder**, making the diagnosis complex. To be diagnosed with FOD, the lack of orgasmic response must occur regularly over an extended period of time; based on the clinician's judgment, it must be less than would be reasonable based on age, sexual experience, and the adequacy of sexual stimulation. The lack of orgasm must cause emotional distress or relationship difficulties for the woman and be caused either only by psychological factors alone or by a combination of psychological and physical factors. According to the American Psychiatric Association (APA), a diagnosis of FOD is not appropriate if failure to climax is due only to physiological factors. FOD is also not diagnosed if it is a symptom of another major psychological disorder, such as depression.

Treatments

When failure to reach orgasm is caused by a physical problem, the root problem is treated. In other cases, a combination of education, counseling, **psychotherapy**, and sex therapy are used—often along with directed exercises to increase stimulation and decrease inhibitions.

Sex therapists have special training to help individuals and couples focus on overcoming specific sexual dysfunctions. In couples' therapy, therapists often assign "homework" that focuses on relaxation techniques, sexual exploration, improving sexual communication, decreasing inhibitions, and increasing direct clitoral stimulation. Individually, a woman might be encouraged to masturbate either through self-stimulation or with a vibrator. In addition, Kegel exercises, which improve the strength and tone of the muscles in the genital area, may be recommended.

Traditional psychotherapy, or **talk therapy**, alone or in conjunction with sex therapy, can be effective in resolving psychological causes of FOD, especially when those causes are rooted in past sexual or emotional exploitation or cultural taboos. Psychotherapy is also helpful in resolving relationship tensions that develop as a result of frustration from FOD.

Experts Jennifer and Laura Berman found that a patient who took a synthetic form of testosterone found some improvement with her condition. These same experts also recommend that women do Kegel exercises—contraction and release of the muscles of the pelvic floor, the same ones women use to stop a urine stream—to improve their orgasmic experiences.

Prognosis

Many women with FOD can be helped to achieve orgasm through a combination of psychotherapy and guided sexual exercises. However, this does not mean that they will be able to achieve orgasm all the time or in every situation, or that they will always be satisfied with the strength and quality of their climax. Couples often need to work through relationship issues that have either caused or resulted from FOD before they see improvement. This process takes time and requires a joint commitment to problem solving.

Prevention

There are no sure ways to prevent FOD. However, reducing life factors that cause **stress** can be effective. Seeking counseling or psychotherapy for past trauma, or when problems begin to appear in a relationship, can help minimize sexual dysfunction problems.

Resources

BOOKS

American Psychiatric Association. *Diagnostic and Statistical Manual of Mental Disorders*. 4th ed., Text rev. Washington D.C.: American Psychiatric Association, 2000.

Berman, Jennifer, MD, and Laura Berman, PhD. *For Women Only: A Revolutionary Guide to Overcoming Sexual Dysfunction and Reclaiming Your Sex Life*. New York: Henry Holt, 2001.

Sadock, Benjamin J., and Virginia A. Sadock, eds. *Comprehensive Textbook of Psychiatry*. 7th ed. Vol. 2. Philadelphia: Lippincott Williams and Wilkins, 2000.

PERIODICALS

Dunn, Kate M., Lynn F. Cherkas, and Tim D. Spector. "Genetic Influences on Variation in Female Orgasmic Function: A Twin Study." *Biology Letters* 1 (2005): 260–63.

Everaerd, Walter, and Ellen Laan. "Drug Treatments for Women's Sexual Disorders." *Journal of Sex Research* 37 (Aug. 2000): 195–213.

Phillips, Nancy. "Female Sexual Dysfunction: Evaluation and Treatment." *American Family Physician* (July 1, 2000).

ORGANIZATIONS

American Association of Sex Educators, Counselors, and Therapists (AASECT). P.O. Box 238, Mount Vernon, IA 53214-0238. Telephone: (319) 895-8407. <www.aasect.org>.

Sexual Information and Education Council of the United States (SIECUS). West 42nd Street, Suite 350, New York, NY 10036-7802. <www.siecus.org>.

WEB SITE

Berney, Karen. "Female Orgasmic Disorder: 'I'm not able to climax'." Discovery Health. <http://health.discovery.com/centers/sex/articles/orgasmic.html>.

Tish Davidson, A.M.
Emily Jane Willingham, PhD

Female sexual arousal disorder

Definition

Female sexual arousal disorder (FSAD) refers to the persistent or recurrent inability of a woman to achieve or maintain an adequate lubrication-swelling response during sexual activity. This lack of physical response may be either lifelong or acquired, and either generalized or situation-specific. FSAD has both physiological and psychological causes. The results of FSAD are often sexual avoidance, painful intercourse, and sexual tension in relationships.

Description

FSAD results from the body's inability to undergo specific physiological changes, called the lubrication-swelling response, in response to sexual desire and stimulation. This lack of response then affects the woman's desire for and satisfaction obtained from intercourse. To understand FSAD, it is helpful to have an outline of the physiological changes that normally take place in a woman's body during sexual arousal.

William Masters and Virginia Johnson were the first researchers to examine extensively the physical components of human sexual arousal. They recorded four stages of sexual response: excitement, plateau, climax (or orgasm), and resolution. Since then, other models have been suggested that include the emotional aspects of arousal. One model suggests three stages: desire, arousal, and orgasm. FSAD affects the excitement or arousal stage of sexual activity.

Normally, when a woman is aroused or sexually excited, the first physiological change that she experiences is expansion of the blood vessels in the pelvic region, allowing more blood to flow to her lower abdomen and genitals. Some women notice this as a feeling of fullness in the pelvis and either consciously or involuntarily contract the muscles in the genital area.

The increased blood flow also causes a phenomenon called transudation, which refers to the seepage of fluid through the walls of the blood vessels. In this case, the fluid seeps into the vagina to provide lubrication before and during intercourse. Often this moisture is noticeable to the woman and her partner. Lubrication of the vagina can happen very rapidly, within a minute.

The increase in blood flow produces other changes in the tissues of the female genitals. The upper part of the vagina, the uterus, the cervix, and the clitoris all expand. At the same time, the lower third of the vagina and the outer labia swell, so that the opening to the vagina becomes smaller. The inner labia also swell, and push apart the opening to the vagina. These changes taken together make up the lubrication-swelling response and are designed to facilitate the entry of the penis into the vagina.

A woman with FSAD either does not have these physical responses or does not maintain them through completion of sexual activity. The lack of arousal and lubrication may result in painful intercourse (**dyspareunia**), emotional distress, or relationship problems.

Causes and symptoms

The symptoms of FSAD include lack of or insufficient transudation. A woman diagnosed with FSAD does not produce enough fluid to lubricate the vagina. As a result, intercourse is often painful and unsatisfactory. The woman may then avoid sexual activity and intimacy, creating relationship difficulties.

The causes of FSAD are quite complex. For some women, FSAD is a lifelong disorder; they have never experienced a normal lubrication-swelling response. For

other women, FSAD develops after illness or emotional trauma, through physiological changes, or as a side effect of surgery, radiation therapy for cancer, or medication. FSAD can be generalized, occurring with different partners and in many different settings, or it can be situation-specific, occurring only with certain partners or under particular circumstances. In addition, FSAD may be due either to psychological factors or to a combination of physiological and psychological factors.

Physiological causes of FSAD include:

- damage to the blood vessels of the pelvic region resulting in reduced blood flow
- damage to the nerves in the pelvic area resulting in diminished arousal
- general medical conditions that damage blood vessels (coronary artery disease, high blood pressure, diabetes mellitus)
- nursing a baby (lactation)
- general medical conditions that cause changes in hormone levels (thyroid disorders, adrenal gland disorders, removal of the ovaries)
- lower levels of sex hormones due to aging (menopause)
- side effects of medications (i.e., antidepressants, antipsychotic drugs, drugs to lower blood pressure, sedatives, birth control pills, or other hormone-containing pills)

Psychological causes of FSAD include:

- chronic mild depression (dysthymia)
- emotional stress
- past sexual abuse
- emotional abuse
- bereavement
- self-image problems
- relationship problems with partner
- other mental health disorders (major depression, post-traumatic stress disorder, or obsessive-compulsive disorder)

The physical and psychological factors leading to FSAD often appear together. For example, a woman who does not experience arousal because of illness or the side effects of medication may then develop self-image and relationship problems that reinforce her difficulty in reaching arousal.

Demographics

It is difficult to determine the incidence of FSAD, because many women are reluctant to seek help for this problem. FSAD may also be present concurrently with other female **sexual dysfunctions** and be difficult to distinguish from them. In addition, there is some

ALFRED KINSEY (1894–1956)

Alfred Kinsey became a household name in the 1950s for his research on the sexual mores of American women and men. His two major texts, *Sexual Behavior in the Human Male* (1948) and *Sexual Behavior in the Human Female* (1953), broke new ground in the field of sex research and led to more open and honest investigations of sexual practices.

During the 1940s, Kinsey embarked on a large-scale study of the sexual habits of men and women. Initially, his resources were limited, and he used his own money to hire staff and pay expenses. In 1943, he received a $23,000 grant from the Rockefeller Foundation, which enabled him to hire more staff and expand his efforts. Chief among his staff were colleagues W. B. Pomeroy, who also conducted thousands of sex interviews, Paul Gebhard, and Clyde Martin. The funding briefly legitimized his undertaking, which became known as the Institute for Sex Research of Indiana University, where Kinsey taught.

By 1948 Kinsey and his colleagues were ready to release their initial findings. He chose a well-established medical publications firm, W. B. Saunders of Philadelphia, to publish the book, attempting to stress the scientific nature of the text rather than its potentially more lurid aspects. To avoid possible financial retribution against Indiana University, the book was published while the Indiana legislature was in recess in December 1948. The 804 page book, *Sexual Behavior in the Human Male*, sold 185,000 copies in its first year in print and made the New York Times bestseller list. The book employed frank descriptions of biological functions and was nonjudgmental of its subject's activities.

Early polls indicated that most Americans agreed with Kinsey's findings. The most vehement criticism came later from the expected sources: conservative and religious organizations. Most of these attacks were emotionally rather than scientifically based, but few of Kinsey's colleagues came to his defense. Kinsey's second sex book, as he expected, caused an even greater uproar than the first. Some of *Sexual Behavior in the Human Female*'s more controversial findings concerned the low rate of frigidity, high rates of premarital and extramarital sex, the rapidness of erotic response, and a detailed discussion of clitoral versus vaginal orgasm. The book soared up the best-seller charts, eventually reaching sales of 250,000 in the U.S. alone. Criticism was harsh, and Kinsey's methods and motives were once again questioned. Evangelist Billy Graham was quoted as stating: "It is impossible to estimate the damage this book will do to the already deteriorating morals of America."

The notoriety of the books caused Kinsey's funding to be revoked, which caused Kinsey to struggle for the remainder of his life to gain adequate support for his work. On August 25, 1956, at the age of 62, Kinsey died of pneumonia and heart complications.

---

disagreement in the medical community on the exact descriptions of different female sexual dysfunctions. One published review of the medical literature, however, found that 22–43% of women experience some form of sexual dysfunction. A study that looked specifically at lubrication found that about 20% of women reported problems in this area. Both of these estimates include women whose dysfunction arises from physiological and psychological causes.

Diagnosis

FSAD is usually diagnosed when a woman reports her concerns to her doctor, usually a gynecologist (a doctor who specializes in women's health issues), or a family doctor or psychotherapist. The doctor will take a complete medical and psychological history, including a list of the medications that the patient is currently taking. The doctor will then give the patient a physical examination to evaluate medical aspects of the disorder; if necessary, blood and urine samples may be taken for laboratory testing to rule out previously undiagnosed diabetes or other medical conditions. In order to be diagnosed with FSAD, the lack of lubrication-swelling response must happen persistently or intermittently over an extended period. It is normal for women to have occasional problems with arousal, and these occasional difficulties are not the same as FSAD. The lack of sexual response must cause emotional distress or relationship difficulties for the woman and be caused either only by psychological factors or by a combination of psychological and physical factors to meet the criteria for a **diagnosis** of FSAD.

According to the mental health professional's handbook, the ***Diagnostic and Statistical Manual of Mental Disorders***, fourth edition, text revision, which is also called *DSM-IV-TR*, a diagnosis of FSAD is not appropriate if problems with arousal are caused only by physiological factors. These factors may include injuries to the genital area, illness, or menopause. When the causes are only physiological, a diagnosis of sexual dysfunction due to a general medical condition is appropriate. If lack of arousal is caused by the side effects of medication or **substance abuse**, a diagnosis of substance-induced sexual dysfunction would be made. FSAD is also not diagnosed if it is a symptom of another major psychological disorder. If a woman receives inadequate sexual stimulation from a partner, that also is not considered a cause of FSAD.

Treatments

Treatment varies depending on the cause of FSAD. When there are physical causes, the root problem or disease is treated. Many women who have difficulties with lubrication due to naturally decreasing hormone levels associated with aging are helped by some forms of hormone replacement therapy (HRT), such as estrogen or testosterone. Some new drug targets are the mechanisms that result in increased blood flow to the genitals, which in turn causes increased lubrication. Among these are drugs aimed at increasing nitric oxide levels, as the drug sildenafil (Viagra®) does for men. There are also nonprescription preparations available in pharmacies for supplementing the woman's natural lubricant. Many women find these preparations quite satisfactory, particularly if they have only occasional problems with arousal.

The U.S. Food and Drug Administration (FDA) has approved one medical device for treating FSAD. The Eros-Clinical Therapy Device (Eros-CTD) is a small vacuum pump that fits over the clitoral area. The pump produces a gentle sucking action that stimulates blood flow in the area. In **clinical trials** the device proved safe and effective in increasing blood flow, sensation, and vaginal lubrication.

Psychotherapy, or **talk therapy**, is most commonly used to treat the psychosocial aspects of FSAD. Sex therapy focuses primarily on the sexual dysfunction. Sex therapists have special training to help individuals and couples overcome their sexual difficulties. Traditional psychotherapy focuses on problems in relationships, seeking to clarify problems, identify emotions, improve communication, and promote problem-solving strategies. Therapy can involve either the woman alone or the woman and her partner (**couples therapy**). Many couples experiencing sexual dysfunction develop relationship problems related to sexual expectations, and benefit from traditional psychotherapy even when difficulties with sexual arousal are resolved.

Prognosis

Because FSAD has multiple causes, individual response to treatment varies widely. Difficulties with lubrication related to menopause generally have a good prognosis. Stress-related difficulties with arousal typically resolve when the stressor is no longer present. Couples often need to work through relationship issues that have either caused or resulted from sexual dysfunction before

> ## KEY TERMS
>
> **Adrenal gland**—A small organ located above each kidney that produces hormones related to the sex drive.
>
> **Cervix**—The neck or narrow lower end of a woman's uterus.
>
> **Clitoris**—The most sensitive area of the external genitals. Stimulation of the clitoris causes most women to reach orgasm.
>
> **Labia**—The outside folds of tissue that surround the clitoris and the opening of the urethra in women.
>
> **Menopause**—A period of decreasing hormonal activity in women, when ovulation stops and conception is no longer possible.
>
> **Pelvis**—The basin-like cavity in the human body below the abdomen, enclosed by a framework of four bones.
>
> **Penis**—The external male sex organ.
>
> **Thyroid**—A gland in the neck that produces the hormone thyroxine, which is responsible for regulating metabolic activity in the body. Supplemental synthetic thyroid hormone is available as pills taken daily when the thyroid fails to produce enough hormone.
>
> **Uterus**—The hollow muscular sac in which a fetus develops; sometimes called the womb.
>
> **Vagina**—The part of the female reproductive system that opens to the exterior of the body and into which the penis is inserted during sexual intercourse.

they see an improvement in sexual arousal. This process takes time and a joint commitment to problem solving.

Prevention

There are no sure ways to prevent FSAD. Eating a healthy, well-balanced diet, getting enough rest, having regular gynecological checkups, and seeking counseling or psychotherapy when problems begin to appear in a relationship can help minimize sexual arousal problems.

See also Female orgasmic disorder; Sexual aversion disorder.

Resources

BOOKS

American Psychiatric Association. *Diagnostic and Statistical Manual of Mental Disorders.* 4th ed., Text rev. Washington D.C.: American Psychiatric Association, 2000.

Berman, Jennifer, MD, and Laura Berman, PhD. *For Women Only: A Revolutionary Guide to Overcoming Sexual Dysfunction and Reclaiming Your Sex Life.* New York: Henry Holt, 2001.

Greenwood, Sadja, MD. *Menopause Naturally: Preparing for the Second Half of Life.* 3rd ed. Volcano, CA: Volcano Press, 1992.

Sadock, Benjamin J., and Virginia A. Sadock, eds. *Comprehensive Textbook of Psychiatry.* 7th ed. Vol. 2. Philadelphia: Lippincott Williams and Wilkins, 2000.

PERIODICALS

Everaerd, Walter, and Ellen Laan. "Drug Treatments for Women's Sexual Disorders." *Journal of Sex Research* 37 (Aug. 2000): 195–213.

Goldstein, I. "Female Sexual Arousal Disorder: New Insights." *International Journal of Impotence Research* 4 (Oct. 12, 2000): S152–57.

Mayor, Susan. "Pfizer Will Not Apply for a License for Sildenafil for Women." *British Medical Journal* 328 (2004): 542.

Uckert, Stefan, and others. "Potential Future Options in the Pharmacotherapy of Female Sexual Dysfunction." *World Journal of Urology* 24 (2006): 630–38.

ORGANIZATIONS

American Association of Sex Educators, Counselors, and Therapists (AASECT). P.O. Box 238, Mount Vernon, IA 53214-0238. Telephone: (319) 895-8407. <www.aasect.org>.

Sexual Information and Education Council of the United States (SIECUS). West 42nd Street, Suite 350, New York, NY 10036-7802. <www.siecus.org>.

Tish Davidson, A.M.
Emily Jane Willingham, PhD

Fetal alcohol syndrome

Definition

Fetal alcohol syndrome (FAS) is a birth defect caused by prenatal exposure to alcohol and is one of the leading known preventable causes of **mental retardation** and birth defects. Rather than a single defect, the word "syndrome" refers to a constellation of abnormalities in children whose mothers drank alcohol while pregnant. FAS is a lifelong condition that causes physical and mental disabilities, and it is characterized by abnormal facial features, growth deficiencies, central nervous system (CNS) problems, and behavioral difficulties. It affects every aspect of an individual's life and the lives of his or her family. Some cases are mild, with only subtle dysfunction and deformity, and other cases are severe, leaving the afflicted seriously disabled and unable to lead independent lives.

A related disorder known as fetal alcohol spectrum disorder (FASD) may include any of the physical and mental symptoms of fetal alcohol syndrome but typically falls short in one diagnostic area. Abnormalities present may still be quite severe; FASD does not imply mildness of disease. For example, a child with FASD may have severe mental retardation but lack the facial abnormalities that are characteristic of fetal alcohol syndrome.

Description

FAS is caused by exposure to alcohol during fetal development in the mother's uterus. When a mother drinks, alcohol crosses the placenta rapidly and enters the fetus. Once there, alcohol acts on virtually every organ system of the developing baby, affecting cellular processes such as growth, differentiation, maturation, and nutrient metabolism. In short, alcohol is a teratogen, which means it causes birth defects.

Alcohol use during pregnancy puts the fetus at risk for delayed and stunted growth and physical deformities, and it puts the child at risk for developing learning disabilities, deficits in attention and impulse control, and other mental health problems. In addition, there are risks to the pregnancy itself, including spontaneous abortion, premature birth, and stillbirth.

Demographics

The primary risk for developing FAS is the consumption of alcohol by women who are pregnant. There is no known amount of alcohol use that is safe during pregnancy, nor is there a particular stage of pregnancy during which alcohol use is safe.

In the United States, the incidence of FAS has been estimated to be 1–3 cases per 1,000 live births, with reported rates of FAS varying widely. The frequency of FASD is much harder to study because the syndrome is less narrowly defined. Nonetheless, estimates have been approximated to occur three times as frequently as FAS. Some studies have tried to estimate the rate of FAS occurrence in women who are heavy drinkers. Whereas such studies are confounded by the unreliability of self-report for such behavior, varying definitions of heavy drinking, and inconsistent **diagnosis**, incidence rates in this group are reported to range from 4% to 44%.

FAS occurs without regard to race or ethnicity; the primary cause is drinking alcohol. Rates of FAS are higher in low socioeconomic women, although the reason

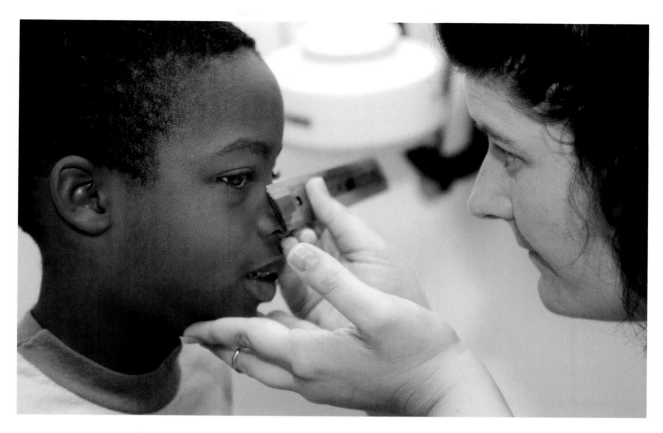

A nurse checks the eyes of a child with Fetal Alcohol Syndrome. *(AP Images)*

for this is unknown. Some have hypothesized that factors such as poor health and nutrition may be related to the increased risk. There also is higher risk associated with alcoholism and with bearing previous children with FAS.

Causes

The primary and only necessary cause of FAS is maternal alcohol consumption. In the fetus, alcohol primarily affects **brain** development and because major developmental events take place in the brain throughout pregnancy, drinking during any one of the three trimesters poses a risk.

The quantity and pattern of maternal drinking are important factors in conferring risk. But while heavy drinking during pregnancy has been strongly linked to FAS in children, lighter consumption of alcohol has not been studied well enough to suggest that any level of intake is safe. Because of this, the U.S. Surgeon General advises all women to abstain from drinking alcohol while pregnant.

Studies on women who report heavy drinking show a dose-effect response, so that the more a woman drinks, the greater the risk she has for bearing a child with FAS.

Moreover, **binge drinking** during pregnancy appears to be the riskiest pattern of consumption. Women who regularly use alcohol are also more likely to drink in the early weeks of an unrecognized pregnancy.

Maternal age greater than 30 years, a history of alcohol **abuse**, poor nutritional status, and previous pregnancies resulting in children with FAS are all factors that increase the risk of FAS. One factor that may reduce the risk of FAS is a genetic trait of rapid alcohol metabolism, which may be protective to the developing fetus.

Symptoms

FAS is not a single birth defect but rather a cluster of related problems. Symptoms of fetal alcohol syndrome are recognized in three general areas: physical characteristics, particularly facial anomalies; retarded growth in the fetus and/or infant; and evidence of neurobehavioral abnormalities. The severity of these symptoms can greatly vary among those afflicted.

Specific facial characteristics include a thin upper lip, smoothness between the upper lip and the nose (where a vertical indentation is the norm), a flatness across the bridge of the nose, an unnatural smallness of the eyes, and a slightly concave look to the face, because the center of the face as a whole is underdeveloped. Those afflicted often are nearsighted but also may have a wandering eye, a chronic squint, and/or drooping eyelids. Elsewhere in the body, small head size and skeletal defects in the extremities, such as the arm bones being abnormally fused and fingers permanently flexed, are sometimes present. Spinal defects include fusion of the neck vertebrae, abnormally shaped vertebrae, and curvature of the spine. Other major defects can occur in the kidneys, the heart, and specific endocrine glands.

Growth deficiencies are manifested as low birth weight, infants small for their gestational age, and postnatal growth deficits.

Neurodevelopmental problems seen in FAS include mild-to-moderate mental retardation, cognitive impairment, developmental delays, learning disabilities, irritability, hyperactivity, poor impulse control, and seizure disorders. Specific CNS abnormalities include delayed or deficient myelination of the nerves and incomplete development of the corpus callosum, the structure that connects the two sides of the brain.

Diagnosis

Diagnosis is difficult because a cluster of symptoms must be recognized in connection with knowledge of the prenatal exposure of a child to alcohol. Further, many of the signs and symptoms of FAS are similar to other birth defects, learning disabilities, and mental health disorders. Individual features of the disease can be subtle enough so that individuals can pass through life undiagnosed.

Clearly, diagnosis is aided when valid maternal reports of alcohol use are available. However, FAS can be diagnosed in the absence of such information. Evidence must be clear in each of three broad areas: characteristic facial anomalies, prenatal or postnatal growth retardation, and CNS neurodevelopmental abnormalities.

Prognosis

The prognosis for individuals with FAS or FASD is wide ranging. Some data suggest that having a confirmed diagnosis improves patient outcomes, presumably because of early **intervention** or improved access to healthcare services. Such patients may have a long list of mental health problems and associated social dilemmas: alcohol and drug problems, inappropriate sexual behavior, problems with employment, trouble with the law, inability to live independently, and, far too often, confinement in prison, drug or alcohol treatment centers, or psychiatric institutions.

KEY TERMS

Alcohol—An organic chemical and the active agent in beer, wine, and liquor; chemically known as ethanol.

Alcoholism—Chronic and compulsive use of alcohol that interferes with everyday life.

Binge drinking—The practice of drinking alcoholic beverages to the point of intoxication.

Fetus—The stage of development between embryo and newborn.

Mental retardation—Characterized by persistently slow learning and below normal intelligence.

Prenatal exposure—Coming in contact with a fetus during pregnancy.

Teratogen—An agent or chemical that causes a birth defect.

Treatment

No cure exists for FAS. The physical and mental symptoms of the disease persist throughout life. A supportive environment with responsive caregivers can be protective in terms of poor outcomes related to learning disabilities and behavioral problems. Treatments for many of the symptoms of FAS do, however, exist, including surgery for heart defects, special education services for learning disabilities, and psychiatric care and medicines for behavioral disorders.

For parents and caregivers of children with FAS, providing structure to a child's daily activities are key elements in maximizing functionality. Such things as implementing regular daily routines, creating simple rules and limits, rewarding desirable behavior, and helping the child find solutions to everyday problems are beneficial.

Prevention

The U.S. Institute of Medicine has outlined a public health model of prevention, starting by educating women about the risks of alcohol for the developing fetus and about the importance of avoiding alcohol consumption during pregnancy. In the highest risk women, those who are drinking large amounts of alcohol and who are likely to become pregnant, and particularly women who have previously delivered an affected child and who continue to drink, intervention might be treating such women for alcohol dependence and with **case management**.

Resources

BOOKS

Beers, Mark H., ed. "Prenatal Drug Exposure." *The Merck Manual of Diagnosis and Therapy, Professional Edition.* 18th ed. Whitehouse Station, NJ: Merck & Co., 2005.

Streissguth, Ann. *Fetal Alcohol Syndrome: A Guide for Families and Communities.* Baltimore: Paul H. Brooks, 1997.

OTHER

"Fetal Alcohol Syndrome." *Mayoclinic.com* May 25, 2005. <http://mayoclinic.com/health/fetal-alcohol-syndrome/DS00184>.

Jill U. Adams

Fetishism

Definition

Fetishism is a form of paraphilia, a disorder characterized by recurrent intense sexual urges and sexually arousing fantasies generally involving nonhuman objects, the suffering or humiliation of oneself or one's partner (not merely simulated), or children or other nonconsenting persons. The essential feature of fetishism is recurrent intense sexual urges and sexually arousing fantasies involving specific objects. While any object may become a fetish in the psychological sense, the distinguishing feature is its connection with sex or sexual gratification. A **diagnosis** of fetishism is made only if an individual has acted on these urges, is markedly distressed by them, or if the fetish object is required for gratification.

For some people with a paraphilia such as fetishism, paraphilic fantasies or stimuli may be necessary for erotic arousal and are always included in sexual activity, or the presence of the fetish object may occur only episodically. For example, the fetish object may only be necessary for arousal during periods of **stress**, and at other times the person can function sexually without the fetish or stimuli related to the fetish.

Description

As stated, a fetish is a form of paraphilia, and in fetishism, the affected person has created a strong association between an object and sexual pleasure or gratification. A fetish is not simply a pleasant memory—it is a dominant component of most sexual situations. Most fetishes are objects or body parts. Common fetishes involve items of clothing, stuffed animals, or other nonsexual objects. Body fetishes may involve breasts, legs, buttocks, or genitals.

A person with a fetish often spends significant amounts of time thinking about the object of the fetish. Further, the object is intimately related to sexual pleasure or gratification. In the extreme, the presence of the fetish object is required for sexual release and gratification.

Causes and symptoms

Causes

The cause of the association between an object and sexual arousal may be adolescent curiosity or a random association between the object and feelings of sexual pleasure. A random association may be innocent or unappreciated for its sexual content when it initially occurs. For example, a male may enjoy the texture or tactile sensation of female undergarments or stockings. At first, the pleasurable sensation occurs randomly, and then, in time and with experience, the behavior of using female undergarments or stockings as part of sexual activity is reinforced, and the association between the garments and the sexual arousal is made. A person with a fetish may not be able to pinpoint exactly when his or her fetish began. A fetish may be related to activities associated with sexual abuse.

Symptoms

Early symptoms for a fetish involve touching the object of desire. The amount of time spent thinking about the fetish object may increase. Over time, the importance of the fetish object expands. In the extreme, it becomes a requirement for achieving sexual pleasure and gratification.

Demographics

How many people have a fetish and the extent to which the fetish influences their lives and sexual activities are not accurately known. In some rare instances, people with fetishes may enter the legal system as a result of their fetishes, and those cases may be counted or tracked.

Paraphilias such as fetishism are uncommon among females, but some cases have been reported. Females may attach erotic thoughts to specific objects such as items of clothing or pets, but these are uncommon elements in sexual activity. Virtually no information is available on family patterns.

A pair of stillettos with seven-inch heels. Shoe fetishism is just one of many documented fetishes. *(AP Images)*

Diagnosis

A diagnosis of a paraphilia involving a fetish is most commonly made by taking a detailed history or by direct observation. According to the ***Diagnostic and Statistical Manual of Mental Disorders*** (the fourth edition, text revision, or *DSM-IV-TR*), the person must have experienced the fantasies or urges centered on a nonliving object or objects for at least six months. In addition, these fantasies, urges, or behaviors must meet the criterion of causing significant distress or impairment in the person's ability to function socially or at work, or in other important environments. Last, the fetish cannot be solely focused on female clothing used in cross-dressing (which falls into the classification of Tranvestic Fetishism) or on sex-aid devices that promote tactile genital stimulation, such as vibrators.

Treatments

In the earliest stages of behavior therapy, fetishes were narrowly viewed as attractions to inappropriate objects. Aversive stimuli such as shocks were administered to persons undergoing therapy. This approach was not successful. People with fetishes have also been behaviorally treated by orgasmic reorientation, which attempts to help them develop sexual responses to culturally appropriate stimuli that have been otherwise neutral. This therapy has had only limited success.

Most persons who have a fetish never seek treatment from professionals. Many can achieve sexual gratification in culturally appropriate situations. In recent years, American society has developed more tolerance for persons with fetishes than in the past,

KEY TERMS

Paraphilia—A disorder that is characterized by recurrent intense sexual urges and sexually arousing fantasies generally involving (1) nonhuman objects, (2) the suffering or humiliation of oneself or one's partner (not merely simulated), or (3) children or other nonconsenting persons.

thus further reducing the already minimal demand for professional treatment.

Prognosis

The prognosis for eliminating a fetish is poor because fetishism is generally chronic. Most cases in which treatment has been demanded as a condition of continuing a marriage have not been successful. Most fetishes are relatively harmless in that they usually do not involve other persons or endanger the person with the fetish. Persons with a fetish rarely involve nonconsenting partners.

The personal prognosis for a person with a fetish is good if the fetish and related activities do not impact others or place the person with the fetish in physical danger.

Prevention

Most experts agree that providing gender-appropriate guidance in a culturally appropriate situation will prevent the formation of a fetish. The origin of some fetishes may be random associations between a particular object or situation and sexual gratification. There is no way to predict such an association.

Resources

BOOKS

American Psychiatric Association. *Diagnostic and Statistical Manual of Mental Disorders*, 4th ed., Text rev. Washington, D.C.: American Psychiatric Association, 2000.

Gelder, Michael, Richard Mayou, and Philip Cowen. *Shorter Oxford Textbook of Psychiatry*, 4th ed. New York: Oxford University Press, 2001.

Wilson, Josephine F. *Biological Foundations of Human Behavior*. New York: Harcourt, 2002.

PERIODICALS

Chalkley, A. J., and G. E. Powell. "The Clinical Description of Forty-Eight Cases of Sexual Fetishism." *British Journal of Psychiatry* 142 (1983): 292–95.

FitzGerald, W. A. "Explaining the Variety of Human Sexuality." *Medical Hypotheses* 55.5 (2000): 435–39.

Nersessian E. "A Cat as Fetish: a Contribution to the Theory of Fetishism." *International Journal of Psychoanalysis* 79.4 (1998): 713–25.

Reed, G. S. "The Analyst's Interpretation as Fetish." *Journal of the American Psychoanalytical Association* 45.4 (1998): 1153–81.

Weiss, J. "Bondage Fantasies and Beating Fantasies." *Psychoanalytic Quarterly* 67.4 (1998): 626–44.

Wise, T. N. and R. C. Kalyanam. "Amputee Fetishism and Genital Mutilation: Case Report and Literature Review." *Journal of Sexual and Marital Therapy* 26.4 (2000): 339–44.

ORGANIZATIONS

American Psychiatric Association. 1400 K Street NW, Washington, DC 20005. Web site: <http://www.psych.org>.

American Psychological Association. 750 First Street, NE, Washington, DC 20002-4242. Telephone: (202) 336-5500. Web site: <http://www.apa.org>.

L. Fleming Fallon, Jr., MD, Dr.P.H.
Emily Jane Willingham, PhD

Figure drawings

Definition

Figure drawings are projective diagnostic techniques in which an individual is instructed to draw a person, an object, or a situation so that cognitive, interpersonal, or psychological functioning can be assessed.

Purpose

A projective test is one in which a test taker responds to or provides ambiguous, abstract, or unstructured stimuli, often in the form of pictures or drawings. While other projective tests, such as the **Rorschach Technique** and **Thematic Apperception Test**, ask the test taker to interpret existing pictures, figure drawing tests require the test taker to create the pictures themselves. In most cases, figure drawing tests are given to children. This is because it is a simple, manageable task that children can relate to and enjoy.

Some figure drawing tests are primarily measures of cognitive abilities or cognitive development. In these tests, there is a consideration of how well a child draws and the content of a child's drawing. In some tests, the child's self-image is considered through the use of the drawings. In other figure drawing tests, interpersonal relationships are assessed by having the child draw a family or some other situation in which more than one person is present. Some tests are used for the evaluation of child abuse. Other tests involve personality interpretation through drawings of objects, such as a tree or a house, as well as people. Finally, some figure drawing tests are used as part of the diagnostic procedure for specific types of psychological or neuropsychological impairment, such as central nervous system dysfunction or **mental retardation**.

Precautions

Despite the flexibility in administration and interpretation of figure drawings, these tests require skilled and trained administrators familiar with both the theory behind the tests and the structure of the tests themselves. Interpretations should be made with caution and the limitations of projective tests should be considered. It is generally a good idea to use projective tests as part of an overall test battery. There is little professional support for the use of figure drawing, so the examples that follow should be interpreted with caution.

Description

The Draw-A-Man Test, developed by Goodenough in 1926 was the first formal figure drawing test. It was used to estimate a child's cognitive and intellectual abilities reflected in the drawing's quality. The test was later revised by Harris in 1963 as the Goodenough Harris Drawing Test (GHDT), which included a detailed scoring system and allowed for drawings of men, women, and the self. The scoring system primarily reflected the way in which the child is maturing cognitively. The GHTD is appropriate for children between the ages of three and 17, although it has been found to be most useful for children between three and 10.

The Draw-A-Person test (DAP) was developed by Machover in 1948 and used figure drawings in a more projective way, focusing on how the drawings reflected the anxieties, impulses, self-esteem, and personality of the test taker. In this test, children are first asked to draw a picture of a person. Then, they are asked to draw a picture of a person of the sex opposite of the first drawing. Sometimes, children are also asked to draw a picture of the self and/or family members. Then, they are asked a series of questions about themselves and the drawings. These questions can be about the mood, the ambitions, and the good and bad qualities of the people in the drawings. The pictures and the questions on the DAP are meant to elicit information about the child's anxieties, impulses, and overall personality. The DAP is the most frequently used figure drawing test today. A scoring system appropriate for

adults was developed in 1993 by Mitchel, Trent, and McArthur.

In 1992, Naglieri and his colleagues created a more specific scoring system for figure drawing tests called the Draw-A-Person: Screening Procedure of Emotional Disturbance (DAP:SPED), based on a large standardization sample. This scoring method includes 55 items rated by the test administrator and based on the child's drawings and responses to questions. The DAP:SPED is appropriate for children aged six to 17. It is often used as a screening method for children who may be having difficulties with regard to social adjustment and require further evaluation.

The House-Tree-Person (HTP) test, created by Buck in 1948, provides a measure of a self-perception and attitudes by requiring the test taker to draw a house, a tree, and a person. The picture of the house is supposed to conjure the child's feelings toward his or her family. The picture of the tree is supposed to elicit feelings of strength or weakness. The picture of the person, as with other figure drawing tests, elicits information regarding the child's self-concept. The HTP, though mostly given to children and adolescents, is appropriate for anyone over the age of three.

The Kinetic Family Drawing technique (KFD), developed in 1970 by Burns and Kaufman, requires the test taker to draw a picture of his or her entire family. Children are asked to draw a picture of their family, including themselves, "doing something." This picture is meant to elicit the child's attitudes toward his or her family and the overall family dynamics. The KFD is sometimes interpreted as part of an evaluation of child abuse.

The Kinetic School Drawing technique (KSD), developed in 1974 by Prout and Phillips, requires the child to draw a picture of himself or herself, a teacher, and one or more classmates. This picture is meant to elicit the child's attitudes toward people at school and his or her functioning in the school environment.

Results

As with all projective measures, scoring on figure drawing tests is more subjective. Specific scoring systems, such as the DAP:SPED can be used to provide more objective information. Most figure drawing tests have some sort of objective scoring system; however, the instructions given to the child, the questions asked by the test administrator, and the interpretations the administrator makes of the drawings are flexible and this makes it difficult to compare results between children, even on the same measure. Also, many clinicians choose not to rely on the scoring systems and rely entirely on their own intuitive judgments regarding their interpretation of picture content.

Figure drawings are often interpreted with regard to appropriate cognitive development. Naglieri's DAP:SPED scoring system includes a consideration of what features in a drawing are appropriate for children of various ages. For example, five-year old children are expected to make fairly basic drawings of people, consisting of a head, eyes, nose, mouth, body, arms, and legs. An 11-year-old, on the other hand is expected to have more details in the picture, such as a more defined neck, clothes, and arms in a particular direction.

Sometimes, figure drawings are assessed with regard to self image. Children often projective themselves in the drawings. For example, females with body image concerns may reflect these concerns in their drawings. Victims of sexual abuse may stress sexual characteristics in their drawings.

Psychological, neuropsychological, or emotional dysfunction can also be considered in figure drawing interpretation. This type of interpretation is often done with figure drawings made by adults. For example, a person who omits or distorts body parts may have emotional impairment. Excessive detail with regard to the sexual nature of the drawing may indicate sexual maladjustment.

Family dynamics are also interpreted through figure drawings. For example, in the Kinetic Family Drawing test, a picture where family members are in separate rooms may indicate isolation or a lack of interaction between family members.

Figure drawings are also interpreted with regard to child abuse. In 1994, Von Hutton developed a scoring system for both the HTP and DAP focusing on indicators of child abuse that may be present in drawings. The drawing of the family in the KFD test may also provide indicators of abuse.

There has been much debate over the overall reliability and validity of figure drawing tests (and projective tests in general). For example, when structured scoring systems are used, the DAP has been found to be a reliable measure, especially for cognitive development in children. However, with regard to specific personality characteristics, self-image issues, or personality dysfunctions, there has been relatively little support for the use of figure drawings.

KEY TERMS

Projective test—A psychological test in which the test taker responds to or provides ambiguous, abstract, or unstructured stimuli, often in the form of pictures or drawings.

Reliability—The ability of a test to yield consistent, repeatable results.

Standardization—The administration of a test to a sample group of people for the purpose of establishing scoring norms. The DAP:SPED structured scoring system was standardized using a sample of over 2,300 children and adolescents.

Validity—The ability of a test to measure accurately what it claims to measure.

Resources

BOOKS

Groth-Marnat, Gary. *Handbook of Psychological Assessment* 3rd edition. New York: John Wiley and Sons, 1997.

Kline, Paul. *The Handbook of Psychological Testing*. New York: Routledge, 1999.

Reynolds, Cecil R. *Comprehensive Clinical Psychology, Volume 4: Assessment*. Amsterdam: Elsevier, 1998.

Ali Fahmy, Ph.D.

Flooding *see* **Exposure treatment**

Fluoxetine

Definition

Fluoxetine is an antidepressant of the type known as **selective serotonin reuptake inhibitors** (SSRI). It is sold in the United States under the brand names Prozac and Sarafem.

Purpose

Fluoxetine is used to treat **depression, premenstrual syndrome**, bulimia, and **obsessive-compulsive disorder**.

Description

Serotonin is a neurotransmitter—a **brain** chemical that carries nerve impulses from one nerve cell to another. Researchers think that depression and certain other

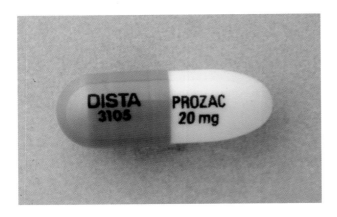

Prozac (fluoxetine hydrochloride) capsule *(Custom Medical Stock Photo, Inc. Reproduced by permission.)*

mental disorders may be caused, in part, because there is not enough serotonin being released and transmitted in the brain. Like the other SSRI **antidepressants**, **fluvoxamine** (Luvox), **sertraline** (Zoloft), and **paroxetine** (**Paxil**), fluoxetine increases the level of brain serotonin (also known as 5-HT). Increased serotonin levels in the brain may be beneficial in patients with obsessive-compulsive disorder, alcoholism, certain types of headaches, **post-traumatic stress disorder** (PTSD), premenstrual tension and mood swings, and **panic disorder**.

Fluoxetine was the first of the class of antidepressants called **SSRIs** to be approved for use in the United States. In 2000, fluoxetine was approved by the Food and Drug Administration (FDA) for use in treating premenstrual dysphoric disorder.

The benefits of fluoxetine develop slowly over a period of several weeks. Patients should be aware of this and continue to take the drug as directed, even if they feel no immediate improvement.

Fluoxetine (marketed as Prozac) is available in 10-, 20-, and 40-mg capsules, 10-mg tablets, and in a liquid solution with 20 mg of active drug per 5 ml. Prozac Weekly capsules are a time-release formula containing 90 mg of active drug. Sarafem is available in 10- and 20-mg capsules.

Recommended dosage

Fluoxetine therapy in adults is started as a single 20-mg dose, initially taken in the morning. Depending on the patient's response after four to six weeks of therapy, this dose can be increased up to a total of 80 mg per day. Doses over 20 mg per day can be given as equally divided morning and afternoon doses.

Precautions

Patients taking fluoxetine should be monitored closely for **insomnia**, **anxiety**, mania, significant weight loss, **seizures**, and thoughts of **suicide**.

Caution should also be exercised when prescribing fluoxetine to patients with impaired liver or kidney function, the elderly (over age 60) children, individuals with known manic-depressive disorder or a history of seizures, people with diabetes, and individuals expressing ideas of committing suicide.

Individuals should not take monoamine oxidase inhibitors (MAOIs) during fluoxetine therapy, for two weeks prior to beginning fluoxetine therapy, and for five weeks after stopping fluoxetine therapy.

Care should be taken to weigh the risks and benefits of this drug in women who are, or wish to become, pregnant, as well as in breast-feeding mothers.

People with diabetes should monitor their blood or urine sugar more carefully, since fluoxetine can affect blood sugar.

Until an individual understands the effects that fluoxetine may have, he or she should avoid driving, operating dangerous machinery, or participating in hazardous activities. Alcohol should not be used while taking fluoxetine.

Side effects

More common side effects include decreased sexual drive, restlessness, difficulty sitting still, skin rash, hives, and itching.

Less common side effects include fever and/or chills, and pain in joints or muscles.

Rare side effects include pain or enlargement of breasts and/or abnormal milk production in women, seizures, fast heart rate, irregular heartbeats, red or purple spots on the skin, low blood sugar and its symptoms (anxiety, chills, cold sweats, confusion, difficulty concentrating, drowsiness, excess hunger, rapid heart rate, headache, shakiness or unsteadiness, severe **fatigue**), low blood sodium and its symptoms (including confusion, seizures, drowsiness, dry mouth, severe thirst, decreased energy), serotonin syndrome (usually at least three of the following: diarrhea, fever, sweatiness, mood or behavior changes, overactive reflexes, fast heart rate, restlessness, shivering or shaking), excitability, agitation, irritability, pressured talking, difficulty breathing, and odd body or facial movements.

KEY TERMS

Bulimia—An eating disorder characterized by binges in which large amounts of food are consumed, followed by forced vomiting.

Obsessive-compulsive disorder—Disorder in which the affected individual has an obsession (such as a fear of contamination, or thoughts he or she does not like to have and cannot control) and feels compelled to perform a certain act to neutralize the obsession (such as repeated hand washing).

Premenstrual syndrome—A severe change in mood that occurs in women immediately prior to, and during, their menstrual period.

Interactions

Fluoxetine interacts with a long list of other medications. People starting this drug should review the other medications they are taking with their physician and pharmacist for possible interactions. Patients should always inform all of their health-care providers, including dentists, that they are taking fluoxetine.

When taken with fluoxetine, blood levels of the following drugs may increase: **benzodiazepines**, **beta blockers**, **carbamazepine**, dextromethorphan, **haloperidol**, atorvastatin, lovastatin, simvastatin, phenytoin, and tricyclic antidepressants.

The following drugs may increase the risk of serotonin syndrome: dexfenfluramine, fenfluramine, and tryptophan.

When **buspirone** is taken with fluoxetine, the therapeutic effect of buspirone may be impaired.

Low blood sodium may occur when fluoxetine is taken along with diuretics.

Increased risk of mania and high blood pressure occurs when selegiline is taken along with fluoxetine.

Severe, fatal reactions have occurred when fluoxetine is given along with MAOIs.

Resources

BOOKS

Preston, John D., John H. O'Neal, and Mary C. Talaga. *Handbook of Clinical Psychopharmacology for Therapists*, 4th ed. Oakland, CA: New Harbinger Publications, 2004.

PERIODICALS

Anderson, Shawanda W., and Marvin B. Booker. "Cognitive Behavioral Therapy Versus Psychosurgery for Refractory Obsessive-Compulsive Disorder." *Journal of Neuropsychiatry and Clinical Neurosciences* 18.1 (Winter 2006): 129.

Denninger, John W., and others. "Somatic Symptoms in Outpatients With Major Depressive Disorder Treated With Fluoxetine." *Psychosomatics: Journal of Consultation Liaison Psychiatry* 47.4 (Jul.–Aug.) 2006: 348–52.

Fava, Maurizio, and others. "Eszopiclone Co-Administered with Fluoxetine in Patients with Insomnia Coexisting with Major Depressive Disorder." *Biological Psychiatry* 59.11 (June 2006): 1052–60.

Hammad, Tarek A., Thomas Laughren, and Judith Racoosin. "Suicidality in Pediatric Patients Treated with Antidepressant Drugs." *Archives of General Psychiatry* 63.3 (Mar. 2006): 332–39.

Kratochvil, Christopher J., and others. "Selecting an Antidepressant for the Treatment of Pediatric Depression." *Journal of the American Academy of Child and Adolescent Psychiatry* 45.3 (Mar. 2006): 371–73.

Lam, Raymond W., and others. "The Can-SAD Study: A Randomized Controlled Trial of the Effectiveness of Light Therapy and Fluoxetine in Patients With Winter Seasonal Affective Disorder." *American Journal of Psychiatry* 163.5 (May 2006): 805–12.

Martenyi, Ferenc, and Victoria Soldatenkova. "Fluoxetine in the Acute Treatment and Relapse Prevention of Combat-Related Post-Traumatic Stress Disorder: Analysis of the Veteran Group of a Placebo-Controlled, Randomized Clinical Trial." *European Neuropsychopharmacology* 16.5 (July 2006): 340–49.

McGrath, Patrick J., and others. "Predictors of Relapse in a Prospective Study of Fluoxetine Treatment of Major Depression." *American Journal of Psychiatry* 163.9 (Sept. 2006): 1542–48.

Moreno, Carmen, Ansley M. Roche, and Laurence L. Greenhill. "Pharmacotherapy of Child and Adolescent Depression." *Child and Adolescent Psychiatric Clinics of North America* 15.4 (Oct. 2006): 977–98.

Mowla, Arash, Ahmad Ghanizadeh, and Azadeh Pani. "A Comparison of the Effects of Fluoxetine and Nortriptyline on the Symptoms of Major Depressive Disorder." *Journal of Clinical Psychopharmacology* 26.2 (Apr. 2006): 209–11.

Mulder, Roger T., and others. "Six Months of Treatment for Depression: Outcome and Predictors of the Course of Illness." *American Journal of Psychiatry* 163.1 (Jan. 2006): 95–100.

Nemeroff, Charles B., and Michael E. Thase. "A Double-Blind, Placebo-Controlled Comparison of Venlafaxine and Fluoxetine Treatment in Depressed Outpatients." *Journal of Psychiatric Research* 41.3–4 (Apr.–June 2007): 351–59.

Pinto-Meza, Alejandra, and others. "Gender Differences in Response to Antidepressant Treatment Prescribed in Primary Care. Does Menopause Make a Difference?" *Journal of Affective Disorders* 93.1–3 (July 2006): 53–60.

Pollack, Mark H., and others. "Olanzapine Augmentation of Fluoxetine for Refractory Generalized Anxiety

Disorder: A Placebo Controlled Study." *Biological Psychiatry* 59.3 (Feb. 2006): 211–15.

Schreiber, Shaul, and Chaim G. Pick. "From Selective to Highly Selective SSRIs: A Comparison of the Antinociceptive Properties of Fluoxetine, Fluvoxamine, Citalopram and Escitalopram." *European Neuropsychopharmacology* 16.6 (Aug. 2006): 464–68.

Serrano-Blanco, A., and others. "Effectiveness and Cost-Effectiveness of Antidepressant Treatment in Primary Health Care: A Six-Month Randomised Study Comparing Fluoxetine to Imipramine." *Journal of Affective Disorders* 91.2–3 (Apr. 2006): 153–63.

Taravosh-Lahn, Kereshmeh Christel Bastida, and Yvon Delville. "Differential Responsiveness to Fluoxetine During Puberty." *Behavioral Neuroscience* 120.5 (Oct. 2006): 1084–92.

Taylor, Bonnie P., and others. "Psychomotor Slowing as a Predictor of Fluoxetine Nonresponse in Depressed Outpatients." *American Journal of Psychiatry* 163.1 (Jan. 2006): 73–78.

Tiihonen, Jari, and others. "Antidepressants and the Risk of Suicide, Attempted Suicide, and Overall Mortality in a Nationwide Cohort." *Archives of General Psychiatry* 63.12 (Dec. 2006): 1358–67.

Vasa, Roma A., Anthony R. Carlino, and Daniel S. Pine. "Pharmacotherapy of Depressed Children and Adolescents: Current Issues and Potential Directions." *Biological Psychiatry* 59.11 (June 2006): 1021–28.

Rosalyn Carson-DeWitt, MD
Ruth A. Wienclaw, PhD

Fluphenazine

Definition

Fluphenazine is a phenothiazine antipsychotic sold under the brand names Permitil and Prolixin in the United States. It is also available under its generic name.

Purpose

Fluphenazine is a drug used to treat psychotic disorders, agitation, and **dementia**.

Description

Fluphenazine is one of many drugs in the group called the phenothiazines. Phenothiazines work by inhibiting the actions of the **brain** chemicals, **dopamine** and norepinephrine, which are overproduced in individuals with **psychosis**.

Fluphenazine is available in 1-mg, 2.5-mg, 5-mg, and 10-mg tablets, a liquid concentrate containing 5 mg/mL, a rapid-onset injectable form containing 2.5 mg/mL, and a long-acting injectable form containing 25 mg/mL.

Recommended dosage

In children over age 16 and in adults, fluphenazine is usually given in oral dosages ranging from 0.5–10 mg daily. The total dosage is usually divided and taken two to four times throughout the day. The dosage is typically reduced at a gradual pace over time to a range between 1 mg and 5 mg. Older adults usually receive lower doses that begin in the range of 1.0–2.5 mg per day. In children under age 16, the usual range is 0.25–3.5 mg per day divided into several doses. Maximum dosage is normally 10 mg per day for this age group.

This drug is also available by injection. In adults, injections into the muscle range from 1.25–10 mg per day divided into several doses. A long-acting injectable form can also be administered to patients who have been stabilized on the drug. The dose for the long-acting preparation ranges from 12.5–25 mg given every one to four weeks in adults. The dosage for children is lower in all cases.

Precautions

People with a history of **depression**, lung problems, heart disease, glaucoma, **seizures**, and kidney disease should take fluphenazine only after careful evaluation by their physician. In addition, those undergoing alcohol withdrawal and those who have received **electroconvulsive therapy** should take this drug with great caution and close physician supervision after discussing the risks and benefits with their doctor. Those over age 60 and children under age 12 should take fluphenazine only after a thorough assessment from their physician. Pregnant women should use fluphenazine with great caution.

Fluphenazine may cause drowsiness. People who take this drug should not drive, operate heavy machinery, or perform other hazardous tasks requiring mental alertness until they see how the drug affects them. People taking fluphenazine should avoid significant exposure to sunlight, as the drug may cause people to sunburn more easily. This drug can sometimes change the color of urine to a pinkish or reddish-brown color. Fluphenazine use can make people more susceptible to heat and increase the risk of heatstroke. People taking fluphenazine should get up slowly after being in a reclining position because of potential dizziness.

Side effects

Relatively common side effects that accompany fluphenazine include drowsiness, dizziness, rash, dry mouth, **insomnia**, **fatigue**, muscular weakness, anorexia, blurred vision, some loss of muscular control, and amenorrhea (lack of menstruation) in women.

Dystonia (difficulty walking or moving) may occur with fluphenazine use. This condition may subside in 24 to 48 hours even when the person continues taking the drug and usually disappears when fluphenazine is discontinued.

Fluphenazine use may lead to the development of symptoms that resemble Parkinson's disease. These symptoms may include a tight or mask-like expression on the face, drooling, tremors, "pill-rolling" motions in the fingers, cogwheel rigidity (abnormal rigidity in muscles characterized by jerky movements when the muscle is passively stretched), and a shuffling gait. Taking anti-Parkinson drugs **benztropine** mesylate or **trihexyphenidyl** hydrochloride along with the fluphenazine usually controls these symptoms.

Fluphenazine has the potential to produce a serious side effect called **tardive dyskinesia**. This syndrome consists of involuntary, uncoordinated movements that may appear late in therapy and may not disappear even after the drug is stopped. Tardive dyskinesia involves involuntary movements of the tongue, jaw, mouth or face or other groups of skeletal muscles. The incidence of tardive dyskinesia increases with increasing age and with increasing dosage of fluphenazine. Women are at greater risk than men for developing tardive dyskinesia. There is no known effective treatment for tardive dyskinesia, although gradual (but rarely complete) improvement may occur over a long period.

An occasionally reported side effect of fluphenazine is neuroleptic malignant syndrome. This is a complicated and potentially fatal condition characterized by muscle rigidity; high fever; alterations in mental status; and cardiac symptoms such as irregular pulse or blood pressure, sweating, tachycardia (fast heartbeat), and arrhythmias (irregular heartbeat). People who think they may be experiencing any side effects from this or any other medication should tell their physician immediately.

Interactions

Barbiturates and the blood pressure drugs known as **beta blockers** can decrease the level of fluphenazine in the blood. Bromocriptine, a drug used for Parkinson's disease, also lowers the level of fluphenazine in

---

KEY TERMS

Agitation—Excessive restlessness or emotional disturbance that is often associated with anxiety or psychosis.

Anticholinergic—Related to the ability of a drug to block the nervous system chemical acetylcholine. When acetylcholine is blocked, patients often experience dry mouth and skin, increased heart rate, blurred vision, and difficulty in urinating. In severe cases, blocking acetylcholine may cloud thinking and cause delirium.

Dementia—A group of symptoms (a syndrome) associated with a progressive loss of memory and other intellectual functions that is serious enough to interfere with a person's ability to perform the tasks of daily life. Dementia impairs memory, alters personality, leads to deterioration in personal grooming, impairs reasoning ability, and causes disorientation.

Psychosis—Severe state that is characterized by loss of contact with reality and deterioration in normal social functioning; examples are schizophrenia and paranoia. Psychosis is usually one feature of an overarching disorder, not a disorder in itself. (Plural: psychoses).

---

the blood. Conversely, antimalarial drugs can increase the level of fluphenazine in the blood.

The combination of fluphenazine with the drugs known as cyclic **antidepressants** lowers the concentrations of both drugs in the blood. Fluphenazine inhibits the blood pressure–lowering effects of the drug called guanadrel. Levodopa, a drug given to patients with Parkinson's disease, is less effective when combined with fluphenazine. The combination of fluphenazine with meperidine can cause very low blood pressure and significant depression of the central nervous system. The use of the muscle relaxant, orphenadrine, can lower the effective levels of fluphenazine in the blood.

Resources

BOOKS

Ananth, Jambur. "Mode of Action of Antipsychotic Agents." *Trends in Schizophrenia Research.* Hauppauge, NY: Nova Biomedical Books, 2005.

Consumer Reports Staff. *Consumer Reports Complete Drug Reference,* 2002 ed. Denver: Micromedex Thomson Healthcare, 2001.

Ellsworth, Allan J., and others. *Mosby's Medical Drug Reference,* 2001–2002 ed. St. Louis: Mosby, 2001.

Hardman, Joel G., Lee E. Limbird, eds. *Goodman & Gilman's The Pharmacological Basis of Therapeutics,* 10th ed. New York: McGraw-Hill, 2001.

Preston, John D., John H. O'Neal, and Mary C. Talaga. *Handbook of Clinical Psychopharmacology for Therapists,* 4th ed. Oakland, CA: New Harbinger Publications, 2004.

PERIODICALS

Bhagar, Harpriya A., and Alan D. Schmetzer. "The Conventional Long-Acting Antipsychotics." *Annals of the American Psychotherapy Association* 9.1 (Spring 2006): 26–27.

Conley, Robert R., and others. "Risperidone, Quetiapine, and Fluphenazine in the Treatment of Patients with Therapy-Refractory Schizophrenia." *Clinical Neuropharmacology* 28.4 (July–Aug. 2005): 163–68.

Kelly, Deanna L., and Robert R. Conley. "Thyroid Function in Treatment-Resistant Schizophrenia Patients Treated With Quetiapine, Risperidone, or Fluphenazine." *Journal of Clinical Psychiatry* 66.1 (Jan. 2005): 80–84.

Kelly, Deanna L., and Robert R. Conley. "A Randomized Double-Blind 12-Week Study of Quetiapine, Risperidone or Fluphenazine on Sexual Functioning in People with Schizophrenia." *Psychoneuroendocrinology* 31.3 (Apr. 2006): 340–46.

Stöllberger, Claudia, Johannes O. Huber, and Josef Finsterer. "Antipsychotic Drugs and QT Prolongation." *International Clinical Psychopharmacology* 20.5 (Sept. 2005): 243–51.

Mark Mitchell, MD
Ruth A. Wienclaw, PhD

Flurazepam

Definition

Flurazepam is a benzodiazepine hypnotic (sleeping medication) that is given by mouth. It is sold in the United States under the brand name of Dalmane, but is also manufactured and sold by several companies under its generic name.

Purpose

Flurazepam is used for the short-term treatment of **insomnia**, which is a sleep disorder characterized by difficulty in falling or staying asleep.

Description

Flurazepam is a benzodiazepine, which means that it belongs to a class of drugs whose primary actions are to reduce the patient's **anxiety**, relax the skeletal muscles, and bring on sleep. Flurazepam is chemically and pharmacologically related to such other benzodiazepine hypnotics as **temazepam** (Restoril), **triazolam** (Halcion), **quazepam** (Doral), and **estazolam**. All the **benzodiazepines** work by enhancing the effects of a naturally occurring chemical in the body called gamma-aminobutyric acid (GABA). GABA is a neurotransmitter, or chemical that helps to conduct nerve impulses across the tiny gaps between nerve cells. GABA acts to lower the level of activity in the central nervous system; it is involved in muscle relaxation, sedation, and sleep, and plays a role in preventing seizure activity.

Flurazepam decreases the time it takes the patient to fall asleep, thus reducing the number of nighttime awakenings and increasing the length of total sleep time. The difference between a benzodiazepine like flurazepam that is used to help patients fall asleep and those that are used as tranquilizers is the way that each type acts in the **brain**. The sleep-inducing benzodiazepines are faster in getting to the part of the brain that controls sleep. They also reach higher levels of concentration there than the benzodiazepines that are used as tranquilizers.

Flurazepam is available in 15- and 30-mg capsules.

Recommended dosage

The usual dose of flurazepam is 15–30 mg taken by mouth at bedtime. Older or physically weakened patients are usually given the lower dose. Children younger than 15 and women who are pregnant or nursing a baby should not be given flurazepam. In addition, the drug should not be used for longer than four weeks.

Precautions

Some of the flurazepam is metabolized (broken down) in the body to form another compound called desalkylflurazepam, which can also cause drowsiness the next day because it remains in the body for hours. This "hangover" effect is most common in people who are taking flurazepam on a daily basis. People who are taking flurazepam may not be able to safely operate machinery or drive a car the next day.

Patients who take flurazepam for several days or weeks may experience a reaction called rebound insomnia when they stop taking it. When a person takes a medication for sleep on a regular basis, the body adjusts to the presence of the drug. It tries to counteract the effects of the medication. As a result, when the person stops taking the sleeping medication, the body will take a few nights to return to its normal condition.

KEY TERMS

Benzodiazepines—A group of central nervous system depressants used to relieve anxiety or to induce sleep.

Central nervous system depressant—Any drug that lowers the level of stimulation or excitement in the central nervous system.

Central nervous system stimulant—Any drug that raises the level of activity in the central nervous system.

Gamma-aminobutyric acid (GABA)—A neurotransmitter that helps to lower or reduce the level of excitement in the nerves, leading to muscle relaxation, calmness, sleep, and the prevention of seizures.

Hypnotic—A type of medication that induces sleep.

Metabolism—The group of biochemical processes within the body that release energy in support of life.

Neurotransmitter—A chemical in the brain that transmits messages between neurons, or nerve cells.

Rebound effect—A physical reaction to stopping a medication characterized by the reappearance of the symptom that the medication was given to suppress. For example, people who stop taking flurazepam may experience rebound insomnia.

During this period of readjustment, the person may experience a few sleepless hours each night.

The sleepiness that flurazepam brings about may be intensified if the patient drinks alcoholic beverages or takes other medications that contain central nervous system depressants. Common types of medications that may cause problems when combined with flurazepam include tranquilizers and antihistamines (allergy medications).

Elderly patients who are taking flurazepam should be monitored for signs of dizziness or loss of coordination. They are at increased risk of falling if they wake up and get out of bed during the night to get a drink of water or use the bathroom.

Side effects

Some people experience dizziness, daytime drowsiness, and loss of coordination while they are taking flurazepam. Elderly patients may lose their balance and fall. Less common side effects include blurred vision, nausea and vomiting, diarrhea or constipation, nightmares, and a feeling of **depression**.

Interactions

The effects of flurazepam are increased by other central nervous system depressants. These types of chemicals include alcohol, **sedatives**, and antihistamines. In addition, flurazepam may interact with antiseizure medications.

See also Sedatives and related drugs; Sleep disorders.

Resources

BOOKS

American Society of Health-System Pharmacists. *AHFS Drug Information 2002*. Bethesda, MD: American Society of Health-System Pharmacists, 2002.

Preston, John D., John H. O'Neal, and Mary C. Talaga. *Handbook of Clinical Psychopharmacology for Therapists*, 4th ed. Oakland, CA: New Harbinger Publications, 2004.

PERIODICALS

Blin, Olivier, and others. "A Double-Blind, Placebo- and Flurazepam-Controlled Investigation of the Residual Psychomotor and Cognitive Effects of Modified Release Zolpidem in Young Healthy Volunteers." *Journal of Clinical Psychopharmacology* 26.3 (June 2006): 284–89.

Rosenberg, Russell P. "Sleep Maintenance Insomnia: Strengths and Weaknesses of Current Pharmacologic Therapies." *Annals of Clinical Psychiatry* 18.1 (Jan.–Mar. 2006): 49–56.

Rowlett, James K., and others. "Anti-Conflict Effects of Benzodiazepines in Rhesus Monkeys: Relationship with Therapeutic Doses in Humans and Role of GABA-Sub (A) Receptors." *Psychopharmacology* 184.2 (Jan. 2006): 201–11.

Tamblyn, Robyn, and others. "A 5-Year Prospective Assessment of the Risk Associated with Individual Benzodiazepines and Doses in New Elderly Users." *Journal of the American Geriatrics Society* 53.2 (Feb. 2005): 233–41.

Thomas, Sandra P. "From the Editor—Caution Urged in Prescribing Psychotropic Drugs for Older Patients." *Issues in Mental Health Nursing* 26.4 (May 2005): 357–58.

Jack Raber, Pharm.D.
Ruth A. Wienclaw, PhD

Fluvoxamine

Definition

Fluvoxamine is an antidepressant of the type known as **selective serotonin reuptake inhibitors** (SSRI). It is marketed in the United States under the brand name Luvox.

Purpose

Fluvoxamine is used to treat **depression**. It is also the first SSRI to be approved by the U.S. Food and Drug Administration (FDA) for use in **obsessive-compulsive disorder** in children, adolescents, and adults.

Description

Serotonin is a **brain** chemical that carries nerve impulses from one nerve cell to another. Researchers think that depression and certain other mental disorders may be caused, in part, because there is not enough serotonin being released and transmitted in the brain. Like the other SSRI **antidepressants**, **fluoxetine** (Prozac), **sertraline** (Zoloft), and **paroxetine** (**Paxil**), fluvoxamine increases the level of brain serotonin (also known as 5-HT). Increased serotonin levels in the brain may be beneficial in patients with obsessive-compulsive disorder, alcoholism, certain types of headaches, **post-traumatic stress disorder** (PTSD), premenstrual tension and mood swings, and **panic disorder**.

Fluvoxamine was approved for use in adults in 1993. In 1997, the FDA approved this medication for the treatment of obsessive-compulsive disorder in children and adolescents.

Fluvoxamine is available in 25-, 50- and 100-mg tablets.

Recommended dosage

Fluvoxamine therapy in adults is started as a single 50-mg dose taken at bedtime. Based on the patient's response to the medication, the dosage can be increased by 50 mg every four to seven days, until maximum benefit is achieved. Maximum dosage is 300 mg per day. Dosage over 100 mg per day should be given as equally divided morning and afternoon doses.

Fluvoxamine therapy in children is started as a single 25-mg dose, initially taken at bedtime. Based on the patient's response to the medication, the dosage can be increased by 25 mg every four to seven days, until maximum benefit is achieved. Maximum dosage in children is 200 mg per day. Dosage over 100 mg per day should be given as equally divided morning and afternoon doses.

Precautions

Patients taking fluvoxamine should be monitored closely for the onset of mania, **seizures**, thoughts of **suicide**, and skin problems (including itching, hives, and rashes).

People with impaired liver function, **bipolar disorder** (manic depression), a history of seizures, or individuals contemplating suicide should take fluvoxamine only under close physician supervision.

A group of serious side effects, called serotonin syndrome, has resulted from the combination of SSRI drugs such as fluvoxamine and members of another class of antidepressants known as monoamine oxidase inhibitors (MAOIs). Serotonin syndrome usually consists of at least three of the following symptoms: diarrhea, fever, extreme perspiration, mood or behavior changes, overactive reflexes, fast heart rate, restlessness, shivering or shaking. Because of this, fluvoxamine should never be taken in combination with MAOIs. People taking any MAOIs, for example Nardil (**phenelzine** sulfate) or Parmate (**tranylcypromine** sulfate), should stop the MAOI inhibitor and wait at least 14 days before starting fluvoxamine or any other antidepressant. The same holds true when discontinuing fluvoxamine and starting an MAOI.

Physicians and their patients should weigh the risks and benefits of this drug for women who are or wish to become pregnant, as well as in breast-feeding mothers.

Until an individual understands the effects that fluvoxamine may have on them, he or she should avoid driving, operating dangerous machinery, or participating in hazardous activities.

People should not use alcohol while taking fluvoxamine.

Side effects

Common side effects of fluvoxamine therapy include decreased sex drive and diminished sexual performance.

Less common side effects of fluvoxamine therapy include changes in mood, behavior, or thinking; difficulty breathing; difficulty urinating; and twitches or uncontrollable movements of the face or body.

Rare side effects include difficulty moving, blurred vision, clumsiness, or problems with balance; seizures; difficulty moving the eyes; increased uncontrollable movements of the body or face; changes in the menstrual period; redness or irritation of the eyes or skin; peeling, itching, or burning sensation of the skin; sore throat, fever, and/or chills; easy bruising; nosebleeds; and, in women, abnormal milk production. People may also experience symptoms of serotonin syndrome, which usually consists of at least three of the following: restlessness, overexcitement, irritability, confusion, diarrhea, fever,

KEY TERMS

Serotonin syndrome—A condition characterized by at least three of the following symptoms: diarrhea, fever, extreme perspiration, mood or behavior changes, overactive reflexes, fast heart rate, restlessness, shivering or shaking. It is a result of too much serotonin in the body.

overactive reflexes, difficulty with coordination, uncontrollable shivering or shaking, and trembling or twitching.

Interactions

Fluvoxamine interacts with a long list of other medications. Anyone starting this drug should review the other medications they are taking with their physician and pharmacist for possible interactions. Patients should always inform all their health-care providers, including dentists, that they are taking fluvoxamine.

When taken together with fluvoxamine, the effect of the following drugs may be enhanced: **benzodiazepines**, **beta blockers**, **clozapine**, anti-seizure drugs phenytoin and **carbamazepine**, tricyclic antidepressants, **pimozide**, and cholesterol-lowering drugs such as atorvastatin, lovastatin, and simvastatin.

The diet pills dexfenfluramine and fenfluramine may increase the incidence of serotonin syndrome when taken with fluvoxamine.

When **buspirone** is given with fluvoxamine, the therapeutic effect of buspirone may be decreased and the risk of seizures increased.

Increased risk of mania and high blood pressure occurs with selegiline.

Severe, fatal reactions mentioned above have occurred when fluvoxamine is given along with MAOIs.

Fluvoxamine given with warfarin (a blood thinner) may increase the possibility of bleeding.

Resources

BOOKS

Preston, John D., John H. O'Neal, and Mary C. Talaga. *Handbook of Clinical Psychopharmacology for Therapists*, 4th ed. Oakland, CA: New Harbinger Publications, 2004.

PERIODICALS

Albers, Lawrence J., and others. "Low-Dose Fluvoxamine as an Adjunct to Reduce Olanzapine Therapeutic Dose Requirements: A Prospective Dose-Adjusted Drug Interaction Strategy." *Journal of Clinical Psychopharmacology* 25.2 (Apr. 2005): 170–74.

Erzegovesi, Stefano, and others. "Low-Dose Risperidone Augmentation of Fluvoxamine Treatment in Obsessive-Compulsive Disorder: A Double-Blind, Placebo-Controlled Study." *European Neuropsychopharmacology* 15.1 (Jan. 2005): 69–74.

Ginsburg, Golda S., Mark A. Riddle, and Mark Davies. "Somatic Symptoms in Children and Adolescents With Anxiety Disorders." *Journal of the American Academy of Child and Adolescent Psychiatry* 45.10 (Oct. 2006): 1179–87.

Husted, David S., and others. "Effect of Comorbid Tics on a Clinically Meaningful Response to 8-Week Open-Label Trial of Fluoxetine in Obsessive Compulsive Disorder." *Journal of Psychiatric Research* 41.3–4 (Apr.–June 2007): 332–37.

Irons, Jane. "Fluvoxamine in the Treatment of Anxiety Disorders." *Neuropsychiatric Disease And Treatment* 1.4 (2005): 289–99.

Mandelli, Laura, and others. "Improvement of Cognitive Functioning in Mood Disorder Patients with Depressive Symptomatic Recovery During Treatment: An Exploratory Analysis." *Psychiatry and Clinical Neurosciences* 60.5 (Oct. 2006): 598–604.

Morishita, Shigeru, and Seizabur Arita. "Clinical Characteristics as Predictors of Response to Fluvoxamine, Paroxetine and Milnacipran in Patients with Depression." *Current Psychiatry Reviews* 1.3 (Nov. 2005): 319–24.

Morishita, Shigeru, and Seizaburo Arita. "Treatment of Bipolar II Depression with Milnacipran, Fluvoxamine, Paroxetine, or Maprotiline." *International Medical Journal* 12.4 (Dec. 2005): 283–85.

O'Connor, K. P., and others. "Cognitive Behaviour Therapy and Medication in the Treatment of Obsessive-Compulsive Disorder." *Acta Psychiatrica Scandinavica* 113.5 (May 2006): 408–19.

Preskorn, Sheldon H., and others. "The Potential for Clinically Significant Drug-Drug Interactions Involving the CYP 2D6 System: Effects with Fluoxetine and Paroxetine Versus Sertraline." *Journal of Psychiatric Practice* 13.1 (Jan. 2007): 5–12.

Schreiber, Shaul, and Chaim G. Pick. "From Selective to Highly Selective SSRIs: A Comparison of the Antinociceptive Properties of Fluoxetine, Fluvoxamine, Citalopram and Escitalopram." *European Neuropsychopharmacology* 16.6 (Aug. 2006): 464–68.

van Oppen, Patricia, and others. "Cognitive Therapy and Exposure in Vivo Alone and in Combination With Fluvoxamine in Obsessive-Compulsive Disorder: A 5-Year Follow-Up." *Journal of Clinical Psychiatry* 66.11 (Nov 2005): 1415–22.

Yoshimura, Reiji, and others. "Successful Treatment for Obsessive-Compulsive Disorder with Addition of

Low-Dose Risperidone to Fluvoxamine: Implications for Plasma Levels of Catecholamine Metabolites and Serum Brain-Derived Neurotrophic Factor Levels." *Psychiatry and Clinical Neurosciences* 60.3 (June 2006): 389–93.

Rosalyn Carson-DeWitt, MD
Ruth A. Wienclaw, PhD

Folie á deux *see* **Shared psychotic disorder**

Frotteurism

Definition

Frotteurism is a disorder in which a person derives sexual pleasure or gratification from rubbing, especially the genitals, against another person, usually in a crowd. The person being rubbed is a victim. Frotteurism is a paraphilia, a disorder that is characterized by recurrent intense sexual urges and sexually arousing fantasies generally involving objects, the suffering or humiliation of oneself or one's partner (not merely simulated), or children or other nonconsenting people.

Description

The primary focus of frotteurism is touching or rubbing one's genitals against the clothing or body of a nonconsenting person. This behavior most often occurs in situations that allow rapid escape. The frottage (the act of rubbing against the other person) is most commonly practiced in crowded places such as malls, elevators, on busy sidewalks, and on public transportation vehicles.

The most commonly practiced form of frotteurism is rubbing one's genitals against the victim's thighs or buttocks. A common alternative is to rub one's hands over the victim's genitals or breasts.

Most people who engage in frotteurism (sometimes called frotteurs) usually fantasize that they have an exclusive and caring relationship with their victims during the moment of contact. However, once contact is made and broken, the person committing the act realizes that escape is important to avoid prosecution.

Causes and symptoms

Causes

There is no scientific consensus concerning the cause of frotteurism. Most experts attribute the behavior to an initially random or accidental touching of another's genitals that the person finds sexually exciting. Successive repetitions of the act tend to reinforce and perpetuate the behavior.

Symptoms

For the disorder to be clinically diagnosed, the symptoms must meet the diagnostic criteria as listed in the professional's handbook, the *Diagnostic and Statistical Manual of Mental Disorders.* These symptoms include:

- experiencing recurrent, intense, or sexually arousing fantasies, sexual urges, or behaviors that involve touching and rubbing against a nonconsenting person
- acting on these sexual urges, or the fantasies or urges cause significant distress to the individual or are disruptive to his everyday functioning

Demographics

Males are much more likely to engage in frotteurism than females. Females are the most common victims of frotteurism. Most acts of frotteurism are performed by people between 15 to 25 years of age. After the age of 25, the acts decline.

Diagnosis

Most people with frotteurism never seek professional help, but people with the disorder may come into the mental health system as a result of a court order. The **diagnosis** is established in an interview between the person accused of frotteurism and the mental health professional (a **psychiatrist** or a **psychologist**, for example). In the interview, the individual acknowledges that touching others is a preferred or exclusive means of sexual gratification. Because this acknowledgment can bring criminal charges, the disorder is underdiagnosed and its prevalence is largely unknown. In some cases, other people besides the accused may be interviewed, including observers or the victim.

Treatments

For treatment to be successful, the patient must want to modify existing patterns of behavior. This initial step is difficult for most people with this disorder to take.

Behavior therapy is commonly used to try to treat frotteurism. The patient must learn to control the impulse to touch nonconsenting victims. One pharmacological therapy that has been tried with some success

KEY TERMS

Frottage—The act of touching or rubbing against the body or genitals of a nonconsenting individual.

Paraphilia—A disorder that is characterized by recurrent intense sexual urges and sexually arousing fantasies generally involving (1) nonhuman objects, (2) the suffering or humiliation of oneself or one's partner (not merely simulated), or (3) children or other nonconsenting people.

in people who engage in frotteurism and other **paraphilias** is leuprolide. The action of this drug ultimately results in suppression of testosterone production, with the effect of reducing sexual urges.

Frotteurism is a criminal act in many jurisdictions. It is usually classified as a misdemeanor. As a result, legal penalties are often minor. It is also not easy to prosecute people who are charged with frotteurism because intent to touch is difficult to prove. In their defense statements, the accused often claim that the contact was accidental.

Prognosis

The prognosis for eliminating frotteurism is poor as most people who engage in the behavior have no desire to change it. Because frotteurism involves nonconsenting partners and is against the law in many jurisdictions, the possibility of embarrassment may deter some individuals.

Prevention

Most experts agree that providing guidance as to behavior that is culturally acceptable will prevent the development of a paraphilia such as frotteurism. The origin of some instances of frotteurism may be a truly accidental contact that becomes associated with sexual gratification. There is no way to predict when such an association will occur.

Resources

BOOKS

American Psychiatric Association. *Diagnostic and Statistical Manual of Mental Disorders*. 4th ed., Text rev. Washington D.C.: American Psychiatric Association, 2000.

Gelder, Michael, Richard Mayou, and Philip Cowen. *Shorter Oxford Textbook of Psychiatry*. 4th ed. New York: Oxford University Press, 2001.

Kohut, John J., and Roland Sweet. *Real Sex: Titillating but True Tales of Bizarre Fetishes, Strange Compulsions, and Just Plain Weird Stuff*. New York: Plume, 2000.

Wilson, Josephine F. *Biological Foundations of Human Behavior*. New York: Harcourt, 2002.

PERIODICALS

Eiguer, A. "Cynicism: Its Function in the Perversions." *International Journal of Psychoanalysis* 80.4 (1999): 671–84.

Rosler, A., and E. Witztum. "Pharmacotherapy of Paraphilias in the Next Millennium." *Behavioral Science Law* 18.1 (2000): 43–56.

Schober, Justine M., Peter M. Byrne, and Phyllis J. Kuhn. "Leuprolide Acetate is a Familiar Drug that May Modify Sex-Offender Behavior: The Urologist's Role." *BJU International* 97 (2006):684–86.

Seelig, B. J., and L. S. Rosof. "Normal and Pathological Altruism." *Journal of the American Psychoanalytic Association* 49.3 (2001): 933–59.

ORGANIZATIONS

American Medical Association. 515 N. State Street, Chicago, IL 60610. Telephone: (312) 464-5000. Web site: <http://www.ama-assn.org/>.

American Psychiatric Association. 1400 K Street NW, Washington, DC 20005. Telephone: (888) 357-7924. Fax: (202) 682-6850. Web site: <http://www.psych.org/>.

American Psychological Association. 750 First Street NW, Washington, DC, 20002-4242, Telephone: (800) 374-2721 or (202) 336-5500. Web site: <http://www.apa.org/>.

L.Fleming Fallon, Jr., MD, Dr.P.H.
Emily Jane Willingham, PhD

Fugue *see* **Dissociative fugue**

G

Gabapentin

Definition

Gabapentin is an antiseizure medication. It is sold in the United States under the trade name Neurontin.

Purpose

Gabapentin is used in combination with other antiseizure (anticonvulsant) drugs to manage partial **seizures** with or without generalization in individuals over the age of 12. Gabapentin can also be used to treat partial seizures in children between the ages of three and 12. Off-label uses (legal uses not specifically approved by the U.S. Food and Drug Administration [FDA]) include treatment of severe, **chronic pain** caused by nerve damage, such as occurs in shingles, diabetic neuropathy, multiple sclerosis, or post-herpetic neuralgia. Studies are also looking at using gabapentin to treat **bipolar disorder** (also known as manic-depressive disorder), with the most recent work focusing on using the drug as a prophylaxis. It has not shown good effectiveness as an acute treatment for bipolar disorder.

Description

Brain cells normally transmit nerve impulses from one cell to another by secreting chemicals known as **neurotransmitters**. Gabapentin is chemically related to a naturally occurring neurotransmitter called GABA (gamma-amino butyric acid). The actual mechanism of action by which gabapentin acts in the brain to control seizures and treat pain is not known, although it appears to alter the action of nerve cells.

Gabapentin was approved for use in the United States in 1993. A liquid formulation was approved for use in 2000. Use in children ages three to 12 was also approved by the FDA in 2000.

Gabapentin is available in 100-, 300-, and 400-mg capsules; in 600- and 800- mg tablets; and in a liquid solution containing 250 mg per 5 ml.

Recommended dosage

For epilepsy

People over the age of 12 can begin with an initial does of 300 mg three times a day, which can be gradually increased as necessary, usually to no more than 1,800 mg daily. For children ages three to 12, the dose is based on body weight, initially 10–15 mg per kilogram per day in three separate doses. The physician may choose to increase this dose as necessary. For a child under the age of three, the decision about use and dosage will be made by the doctor. For older adults, the maximum daily dose does not usually exceed 600 mg three times a day.

For pain

This dosing involves a gradual increase, with an initial does of 300 mg on the first day, followed by 300 mg twice on the second day, and 300 mg three times on day three. A physician may increase this dose to a maximum daily dose of 1,800 mg.

Precautions

Women who are breast-feeding and people who have decreased kidney functioning should discuss the risks and benefits of this drug with their physician. Women who are or wish to become pregnant will also require a careful assessment of the risks and benefits of gabapentin.

Patients should not suddenly discontinue gabapentin, which can result in an increased risk of seizures. If the medication needs to be discontinued, the dosage should be reduced gradually over a week.

Until an individual understands the effects that gabapentin may have, he or she should avoid driving,

KEY TERMS

Diabetic neuropathy—A condition in which the nerve endings, particularly in the legs and feet, become less sensitive. Minor injuries, such as blisters or callouses, are not felt and can thus become infected and become more serious problems.

Multiple sclerosis—A disease characterized by patches of hardened tissue in the brain or spinal cord, paralysis, and/or muscle tremors.

Neuralgia—Pain that extends along the course of a nerve.

Neurotransmitter—A chemical in the brain that transmits messages between neurons, or nerve cells.

operating dangerous machinery, or participating in hazardous activities. Alcohol should be avoided while taking gabapentin.

Side effects

Patients who experience the following side effects of gabapentin should check with their doctor immediately. More common side effects are unsteadiness, clumsiness, and uncontrollable back-and-forth eye movements or eye rolling. Less common side effects include **depression**, irritability, other mood changes or changes in thinking, and decreased memory. Rare side effects include pain in the lower back or side, difficulty urinating, fever and/or chills, cough, or hoarseness.

Children under age 12 who have the following more common side effects should see a doctor immediately: aggressive behavior, irritability, **anxiety**, difficulty concentrating and paying attention, crying, depression, mood swings, increased emotionality, hyperactivity, and suspiciousness or distrust.

Multiple side effects often occur when a patient starts taking gabapentin. While these side effects usually go away on their own, if they last or are particularly troublesome, the patient should consult a doctor. More common side effects that occur when first starting to take gabapentin include blurred or double vision; muscle weakness or pain; swollen hands, feet, or legs; trembling or shaking; and increased **fatigue** or weakness. Less common side effects that occur when initiating gabapentin treatment include back pain, constipation, decreased sexual drive, diarrhea, dry mouth and eyes, frequent urination, headache, indigestion, low blood pressure, nausea, ringing in the ears, runny nose, slurred speech,

difficulty thinking and sleeping, weight gain, twitching, nausea and/or vomiting, weakness.

Interactions

Antacids can decrease gabapentin levels in the blood. They should be taken at least two hours before taking gabapentin.

Resources

BOOKS

Ellsworth, Allan J. *Mosby's Medical Drug Reference*. St. Louis: Mosby, Incorporated, 1999.

Mosby's Drug Consult. St. Louis: Mosby, Incorporated, 2002.

PERIODICALS

Vieta, Eduard, et al. "A Double-Blind, Randomized Placebo-Controlled, Prophylaxis Study of Adjunctive Gabapentin for Bipolar Disorder." *Journal of Clinical Psychiatry* 67 (2006): 473–77.

OTHER

National Library of Medicine. National Institutes of Health. "Gabapentin." <http://www.nlm.nih.gov/medlineplus/druginfo/uspdi/202732.html>.

Rosalyn Carson-DeWitt, MD
Emily Jane Willingham, PhD

Galantamine

Definition

Galantamine belongs to a class of drugs called acetylcholinesterase inhibitors. In the United States, galantamine is sold under the brand name Razadyne (formerly Reminyl).

Purpose

Galantamine is used to treat the symptoms of **Alzheimer's disease**. Galantamine is also being evaluated for the treatment of respiratory **depression**, mania, **vascular dementia** due to **stroke** or cardiac arrest that causes **brain** lesions, and reversal of side effects (e.g., blurred vision and mental changes) caused by medications such as scopolamine, as well as for other mental disorders.

Description

Alzheimer's disease develops when brain cells, called neurons, undergo an early and selective death. It is believed that the premature death of these neurons may be prevented if stimulated by a brain chemical called acetylcholine. Acetylcholine is recycled by an enzyme called acetylcholinesterase. Galantamine works by inhibiting this enzyme. The inhibition of acetylcholinesterase increases the concentration of available acetylcholine.

Galantamine has only been studied, and is only used, in patients with mild-to-moderate Alzheimer's disease according to the Alzheimer's Disease Assessment Scale.

Galantamine is available in 4-mg, 8-mg, and 12-mg tablets.

Recommended dosage

The recommended initial dose of galantamine in adults is 4 mg twice daily. After a minimum of four weeks of treatment with galantamine, the dosage may be increased to 8 mg twice daily. Further increases to 12 mg twice daily should be initiated only after a minimum of four weeks at the previous dose.

Increased side effects associated with higher doses may prevent the increase in dose in some patients. Patients with moderate liver or kidney problems should not exceed 16 mg of galantamine daily.

Precautions

Galantamine should not be used in patients with severe liver or kidney problems. Since there are no well-controlled studies for the use of galantamine in pregnancy, galantamine should only be used if the potential benefits justify the potential risks to the fetus.

Patients who are undergoing anesthesia or bladder or gastrointestinal surgery should take galantamine only after a discussion with their physician. Patients with gastrointestinal problems should be closely monitored if it is decided that they should take galantamine. Galantamine should be used under close physician supervision in patients who have Parkinson's disease, severe asthma, or obstructive pulmonary disease. Because galantamine may slow down the heart, patients with any heart conditions, and especially patients taking other medications that slow down the heart, should be evaluated before starting galantamine.

Side effects

The most common side effects reported with the use of galantamine are nausea, vomiting, diarrhea, anorexia, and abdominal pain. These occur most often at dosage-escalation periods. The average duration of nausea is five to seven days. These side effects tend to be less frequent if the patient is taking a total

---

KEY TERMS

Acetylcholine—A naturally occurring chemical in the body that transmits nerve impulses from cell to cell. Generally, acetylcholine has opposite effects from dopamine and norepinephrine; it causes blood vessels to dilate, lowers blood pressure, and slows the heartbeat. Central nervous system well-being is dependent on a balance among acetylcholine, dopamine, serotonin, and norepinephrine.

Acetylcholinesterase—The chemical responsible for the breakdown of acetylcholine.

Parkinson's disease—A disease of the nervous system most common in people over age 60, characterized by a shuffling gait, trembling of the fingers and hands, and muscle stiffness.

---

daily dosage of 16 mg. Eleven percent of patients receiving 24 mg daily lose weight, while 6% of patients receiving 16 mg daily experience weight loss.

Other common side effects include dizziness, headache, tremors, **fatigue**, depression, agitation, irritation, and **insomnia**. These side effects have a higher incidence and severity if higher doses are used. If side effects become severe, the dosage should be adjusted downward under physician supervision.

Interactions

There is currently little data regarding potential drug interactions with galantamine. Medications that are known to increase levels of galantamine in the body include cimetidine, erythromycin, ketoconazole, and **paroxetine**.

Resources

PERIODICALS

Ancoli-Israel, Sonia, and others. "Effects of Galantamine Versus Donepezil on Sleep in Patients with Mild to Moderate Alzheimer Disease and Their Caregivers: A Double-Blind, Head-To-Head, Randomized Pilot Study." *Alzheimer Disease & Associated Disorders* 19.4 (October–December 2005): 240–45.

Biederman, Joseph, and others. "A Double-Blind Comparison of Galantamine Hydrogen Bromide and Placebo in Adults with Attention-Deficit/Hyperactivity Disorder: A Pilot Study." *Journal of Clinical Psychopharmacology* 26.2 (April 2006): 163–66.

Brodaty, Henry, and others. "Galantamine Prolonged-Release Formulation in the Treatment of Mild to Moderate Alzheimer's Disease." *Dementia and Geriatric Cognitive Disorders* 20.2–3 (August 2005): 120–32.

Harry, Robin D. J., and Konstantine K. Zakzanis. "A Comparison of Donepezil and Galantamine in the treatment of Cognitive Symptoms of Alzheimer's Disease: A Meta-Analysis." *Human Psychopharmacology: Clinical and Experimental* 20.3 (April 2005): 183–87.

Koontz, Jennifer, and Andrius Baskys. "Effects of Galantamine on Working Memory and Global Functioning in Patients with Mild Cognitive Impairment: A Double-Blind Placebo-Controlled Study." *American Journal of Alzheimer's Disease and Other Dementias* 20.5 (September–October 2005): 295–302.

López-Pousa, S., and others. "Differential Efficacy of Treatment with Acetylcholinesterase Inhibitors in Patients with Mild and Moderate Alzheimer's Disease Over a 6-Month Period." *Dementia and Geriatric Cognitive Disorders* 19.4 (March 2005): 189–95.

Ochoa, Enrique L. M. "Galantamine May Improve Attention and Speech in Schizophrenia." *Human Psychopharmacology: Clinical and Experimental* 21.2 (March 2006): 127–28.

Robinson, Dean M., and Greg L. Plosker. "Galantamine Extended Release in Alzheimer's Disease: Profile Report." *Drugs and Aging* 23.10 (2006): 839–42.

Rockwood, Kenneth, and others. "Attainment of Treatment Goals by People with Alzheimer's Disease Receiving Galantamine: A Randomized Controlled Trial." *Canadian Medical Association Journal* 174.8 (April 2006): 1099–1105.

Schubert, Max H., Keith A. Young, and Paul B. Hicks. "Galantamine Improves Cognition in Schizophrenic Patients Stabilized on Risperidone." *Biological Psychiatry* 60.6 (September 2006): 530–33.

Takeda, A., and others. "A Systematic Review of the Clinical Effectiveness of Donepezil, Rivastigmine and Galantamine on Cognition, Quality of Life and Adverse Events in Alzheimer's Disease." *International Journal of Geriatric Psychiatry* 21.1 (January 2006): 17–28.

OTHER

Ortho-McNeil Neurologics, Inc. "Full U.S. Prescribing Information for Razadyne." Available online at <http://www.razadyneer.com/active/janus/en_US/assets/common/company/pi/razadyne.pdf>. Revised May 2006.

Ajna Hamidovic, Pharm.D.
Ruth A. Wienclaw, PhD

Gambling *see* **Pathological gambling disorder**

Ganser's syndrome

Definition

Ganser's syndrome is a rare disorder in which the individual simulates a psychotic illness or dissociated state. The individual's actions are presumed to be the result of unconscious efforts to escape from an intolerable situation, most typically in psychiatric institutions or prisons. The most common feature of Ganser's syndrome is the giving of approximate answers to questions (e.g., $5 + 3 = 7$).

Description

Although this disorder was previously classified as a **factitious disorder**, the American Psychiatric Association has redefined Ganser's syndrome and placed it in the category called "Dissociative Disorder Not Otherwise Specified." Sometimes called "the syndrome of approximate answers," Ganser's syndrome is most often seen in male prisoners. In the past, this was so much the case that early clinicians called the syndrome prison **psychosis**, despite the fact that it is not a true psychosis. (Psychosis is characterized by a radical change in personality and a distorted sense of reality.) The disorder has also been referred to as hysterical pseudodementia, due to the resemblance of responses to those of demented patients. However, data on the prevalence of the syndrome and on links within families have not been gathered and analyzed.

Ganser's syndrome is usually sudden in onset and, like **malingering**, seems to arise in response to an opportunity for personal gain or the avoidance of some responsibility. The patient will offer nearly correct replies when asked questions about facts of common knowledge, such as the number of days in a year, the number of months in a year, subtracting 7 from 100, the product of 4 times 5, etc. To such questions, the patient may respond by stating that there are 360 days in a year, 11 months in a year, 94 for the result of subtracting 7 from 100, and that 21 is the product of 4 times 5. These persons appear to have no difficulty in understanding questions asked, but appear to provide incorrect answers deliberately.

This syndrome is seen in conjunction with a preexisting severe personality disorder. However, unless the patient is willing to admit to the manufactured nature of the symptoms, or unless there is conclusive objective evidence contradicting the syndrome, determining whether the patient has a true disorder may be impossible. As with its sudden onset, disappearance of the symptoms can be just as fast. However, symptoms can also appear to worsen if the patient believes someone is watching. When reviewing a case of Ganser's syndrome, the clinician must consider factitious disorder and malingering as alternative diagnoses.

KEY TERMS

Factitious disorder—A type of mental disturbance in which patients intentionally act physically or mentally ill without obvious benefits. It is distinguished from malingering by the absence of an obvious motive, and from conversion disorder by intentional production of symptoms.

Malingering—Knowingly pretending to be physically or mentally ill to avoid some unpleasant duty or responsibility, or for economic benefit.

Resources

BOOKS

American Psychiatric Association. *Diagnostic and Statistical Manual of Mental Disorders,* 4th ed., Text rev. Washington, D.C.: American Psychiatric Association, 2000.

Enoch, M. David, and Hadrian N. Ball. *Uncommon Psychiatric Syndromes.* New York: Oxford University Press, 2001.

VandenBos, Gary R., ed. *APA Dictionary of Psychology.* Washington, D.C.: American Psychological Association, 2006.

PERIODICALS

Levenson, James L. "Somatoform Disorders: A Medicolegal Guide." *Journal of Psychosomatic Research* 59.5 (November 2005): 349.

Merckelbach, Harald, Maarten Peters, Marko Jelicic, Ineke Brands, and Tom Smeets. "Detecting Malingering of Ganser-Like Symptoms with Tests: A Case Study." *Psychiatry and Clinical Neurosciences* 60.5 (October 2006): 636–38.

Jack H. Booth, PsyD
Ruth A. Wienclaw, PhD

Gender dysphoria *see* **Gender identity disorder**

Gender identity disorder

Definition

Gender identity disorder is a condition characterized by a persistent feeling of discomfort or inappropriateness concerning one's anatomic sex. The disorder typically begins in childhood with gender identity disconnects and is manifested in adolescence or adulthood by a person dressing in clothing associated with the desired gender, as opposed to one's birth gender and exhibiting other behaviors associated with the self-perceived sex identity. In extreme cases, persons with gender identity disorder may seek gender reassignment surgery, also known as a sex-change operation.

Description

Gender identity disorder is distressing to those who have it. It is especially difficult to cope with because it remains unresolved until gender reassignment surgery has been performed. Most people with this disorder grow up feeling rejected and out of place. **Suicide** attempts and **substance abuse** are common. Most adolescents and adults with the disorder eventually attempt to pass or live as members of the opposite sex.

Gender identity disorder may be as old as humanity. Cultural anthropologists and other scientists have observed a number of cross-gender behaviors in classical and Hindu mythology, Western and Asian classical history, and in many late nineteenth- and early twentieth-century pre-literate cultures. This consistent record across cultures and time lends support to the notion that the disorder may be, at least in part, biological in origin. Not all behavioral scientists share this conclusion, however.

Behavioral experimentation, particularly when a child is young, is considered normal. As they grow, children will often experiment with a variety of gender role behaviors as they learn to make the fine distinctions between masculine and feminine role expectations of the society in which they live. Some young boys occasionally exhibit behaviors that Western culture has traditionally labeled "feminine." Examples of these behaviors include wearing a dress, using cosmetics, or playing with dolls.

In a similar manner, some young girls will occasionally assume masculine roles during play. An example of this behavior includes pretending to be the father when playing house. Some girls temporarily adopt a cluster of masculine behaviors. These youngsters are often designated as tomboys. Most experts agree that such temporary or episodic adopting of behaviors opposite to one's gender is normal and usually constitute learning experiences in the acquisition of normal sex role socialization.

In cases that are considered pathological, however, children deviate from the typical model of exploring masculine and feminine behaviors. Such children develop inflexible, compulsive, persistent, and rigidly stereotyped patterns. On one extreme are boys who become excessively masculine. The opposite extreme is seen in effeminate boys who reject their masculinity and rigidly insist that they are really girls or that they want to become mothers and bear children.

Boys with these traits frequently avoid playing with other boys, dress in girls' clothing, play predominantly with girls, try out cosmetics and wigs, and display stereotypically feminine gait, arm movements, and body gestures. Although much less common, some girls may similarly reject traditionally feminine roles and mannerisms in favor of masculine characteristics, including a refusal to urinate sitting down. Professional **intervention** is required for both extremes of gender behavior.

This disorder is different from transvestitism or **transvestic fetishism**, in which cross-dressing occurs for sexual pleasure. Furthermore, the transvestite does not identify with the other sex.

Adults with gender identity disorder sometimes live their lives as members of the opposite sex. They often cross-dress and prefer to be seen in public as a member of the other sex. Some people with the disorder seek sex reassignment surgery.

Persons with gender identity disorder frequently state that they were born the wrong sex. They may describe their sexual organs as being ugly and may refrain from touching their genitalia. People with gender identity disorder may also try to hide their secondary sex characteristics. For instance, males may try to shave off or pluck their body hair. Many men elect to take estrogens in an effort to enlarge their breasts. Females may try to hide their breasts by binding them. There is a growing movement among people who consider themselves transgendered to demand that the condition not be viewed or classified as a disorder but as part of a spectrum of sexual development.

Causes and symptoms

Causes

There is no clearly understood or universally agreed-upon cause for gender identity disorder. However, most experts agree that there may be a strong biological basis for the disorder.

The sex of a human baby is determined by chromosomes. Males have a Y chromosome and one X chromosome, while females have two X chromosomes. The Y chromosome carries a gene known as the testis-determining factor. This gene sets off a developmental pathway that is typically "male," resulting in testes development and development of secondary sexual structures that are male, including a penis and scrotum

and differentiation in the fetal **brain**. Embryos lacking testis-determining factor usually develop as females. The newly formed testes are responsible for releasing the hormones that continue the fetus on a male developmental pathway.

These prenatal events provide the biological basis for gender identity disorder. Hormone levels must be appropriate for male development during the appropriate developmental windows for typical male development to occur. In addition, the cellular pathways that recognize the signals the hormones send must also be in place. Changes in hormone levels from the norm or exposure to environmental compounds that behave like hormones in the fetus can alter male development, resulting in a feminized fetus if this alteration ends in inhibition of typical male development.

Disruptions of hormone signaling may arise from a variety of sources, including a disorder in the mother's endocrine system, maternal **stress**, maternal medications, and some environmental, endocrine-active substances.

Post-mortem studies conducted on male-to-female transsexuals, non-transsexual men, and non-transsexual women show a significant difference in sex-specific brain structures. Studies have shown that in male-to-female transsexuals, for example, brain structures look like those of nontransgendered women. These studies indicate that one's sense of gender resides in the brain and that it may be biochemically determined. A hypothesis underlying the link between gonadal sex and the sex of the brain is the organization-activation hypothesis. According to this hypothesis, the hormones that organize the body as masculine, e.g, result in the formation of a penis rather than a clitoris, also organize the brain as masculine. At puberty, hormones activate the brain for gender-specific sex behavior. In some cases, there may be a disconnect between gonadal development and brain sexual development.

In addition to biological factors, environmental conditions, such as socialization, are thought by some to contribute to gender identity disorder. Social learning theory, for example, proposes that a combination of observational learning and different levels and forms of **reinforcement** by parents, family, and friends determine a child's sense of gender, which, in turn, leads to what society considers sex-appropriate or inappropriate behavior. Recent research, however, suggests that even when people who are transgendered or born with ambiguous genitalia are reared based on their "assigned" sex, they still retain their perceived sexual identity.

Symptoms

The onset of puberty increases the difficulties for people with gender identity disorder. The subsequent development of unwanted secondary sex characteristics, especially in males, increases a person's **anxiety** and frustrations. In an effort to cope with their feelings, some men with gender identity disorder may engage in stereotypical, or even super-masculine, activities. For example, a man struggling with the disorder may engage in such "macho" sports as wrestling and football in order to feel more "male." Unfortunately, the result is usually an increase in anxiety.

This anxious state is characterized by feelings of confusion, shame, guilt, and fear. These individuals are confused over their inability to handle their problem. They feel shame over their inability to control what society considers "perverse" activities. Even though cross-dressing and cross-gender fantasies provide relief, the respite is temporary. These activities often leave individuals with a profound shame over their thoughts and activities.

Closely associated with shame is guilt, particularly about being dishonest with family and friends. Sometimes people with gender identity disorder marry and have children without telling their spouse about their disorder. Typically, their self-identity is kept secret because they have the mistaken conviction that participation in marriage and parenting will eliminate their problems or "cure" them. The fear of being discovered further raises their anxiety. With some justification, people with gender identity disorder fear being labeled "sick" and being rejected and abandoned by people they love.

If an individual's gender identity disorder is profound, a lifestyle adaptation such as occasional cross-dressing may be insufficient. In such a case, gender expression may move from a lifestyle problem to a life-threatening imperative. The result can be extreme **depression** that requires medical treatment. If sufficiently severe, the imperative may result in gender reassignment surgery. If an individual lacks the psychological commitment to undertake surgery, the result may be suicide.

Demographics

Gender identity disorder is more prevalent in males than in females. Reliable estimates of prevalence for either males or females are not available.

Diagnosis

A mental health professional makes a **diagnosis** of gender identity disorder by taking a careful personal history. He or she obtains the age of the patient and determines whether the patient's sexual attraction is to males, females, both, or neither. Laboratory tests are neither available nor required to make a diagnosis of gender identity disorder. However, it is very important not to overlook a physical illness such as a tumor that might mimic or contribute to a psychological disorder. If there is any question that a physical problem might be the underlying cause of an apparent gender identity disorder, a mental health professional should recommend a complete physical examination by a medical doctor. Laboratory tests might be necessary as components of the physical evaluation.

According to the clinician's handbook for diagnosing mental disorders, the **_Diagnostic and Statistical Manual of Mental Disorders_**, fourth edition, text revised _(DSM-IV-TR)_, the following criteria must be met to establish a diagnosis of gender identity disorder.

- a strong and persistent cross-gender identification
- persistent discomfort with his or her sex or having a sense of inappropriateness in the gender role of one's birth sex
- the disturbance is not concurrent with a physical intersex condition, in which a person is born, for example, with the genitalia that exhibit male and female characteristics
- the disturbance causes clinically significant distress or impairment in social, occupational, or other important areas of functioning

A strong and persistent cross-gender identification

In children, the disturbance is manifested by four (or more) of the following:

- repeatedly stating a desire to be, or insistence that he or she is, a member of the other sex
- strong preference for wearing clothes of the opposite gender. In boys, displaying a preference for cross-dressing or simulating female attire; in girls, insistence on wearing only stereotypical masculine clothing
- displaying strong and persistent preferences for cross-sex roles in make-believe play or experiencing persistent fantasies of being a member of the other sex
- having an intense desire to participate in the games and pastimes that are stereotypical of the other sex
- exhibiting a strong preference for playmates of the other sex

Among adolescents and adults, the disturbance is manifested by symptoms such as a stated desire to become a member of the other sex, frequent passing as a person of the other sex, a desire to live or be treated as the other sex, or the conviction that he or she has the typical feelings and reactions of the other sex. These characteristics cannot be merely from a desire for any perceived cultural advantages of being the other sex.

Persistent discomfort with his or her sex or having a sense of inappropriateness in the gender role of one's birth sex

Among children, the disturbance is manifested by any of the following:

- among boys, asserting that his penis or testes are disgusting or will disappear, asserting that it would be better not to have a penis, or having an aversion toward rough-and-tumble play and rejecting male stereotypical toys, games, and activities
- among girls, rejecting the gender-typical practice of urinating in a sitting position, asserting that she has or will grow a penis, or stating that she does not want to grow breasts or menstruate, or having a marked aversion toward normative feminine clothing

Among adolescents and adults, the disturbance is manifested by symptoms such as preoccupation with getting rid of primary and secondary sex characteristics (e.g., request for hormones, surgery, or other procedures to alter sexual characteristics to simulate the other sex) or a belief that he or she was born the wrong sex.

Treatments

One common form of treatment for gender identity disorder is **psychotherapy**. The initial aim of treatment is to help individuals function in their biologic sex roles to the greatest degree possible. The World Professional Association for Transgender Health, which has formulated and published its own *Standards of Care* manual for working with transgendered people, does not support psychotherapy designed to "convert" a transgendered person from their own personal perception of their sex.

Adults who have had severe gender identity disorder for many years sometimes request reassignment of their sex, or sex-change surgery. Before undertaking such surgery, they usually undergo hormone therapy to suppress same-sex characteristics and to accentuate other-sex characteristics. For instance, the female hormone estrogen is given to males to make breasts grow, reduce facial hair, and widen hips. The male hormone testosterone is administered to females to suppress menstruation, deepen the voice, and increase body hair. Following the hormone treatments, pre-operative

KEY TERMS

Cross-dressing—Wearing clothing and other attire typically associated with the opposite sex.

Paraphilia—A disorder that is characterized by recurrent intense sexual urges and sexually arousing fantasies generally involving non-human objects, the suffering or humiliation of oneself or one's partner (not merely simulated), or children or other non-consenting persons.

Transsexual—A person whose gender identity is opposite his or her biologic sex.

Transvestite—A person who derives sexual pleasure or gratification from dressing in clothing of the opposite sex.

candidates are usually required to live in the cross-gender role for at least a year before surgery is performed.

Prognosis

If gender identity disorder persists into adolescence, it tends to be chronic in nature. There may be periods of remission. However, adoption of characteristics and activities typical for one's birth sex is unlikely to occur.

Most individuals with gender identity disorder require and appreciate support from several sources. Families, as well as the person with the disorder, need and appreciate both information and support. Local and national **support groups** and informational services exist, and health care providers and mental health professionals can provide referrals.

Resources

BOOKS

American Psychiatric Association. *Diagnostic and Statistical Manual.* 4th ed., text rev. Washington, D.C.: American Psychiatric Association, 2000.

Gelder, Michael, Richard Mayou, and Philip Cowen. *Shorter Oxford Textbook of Psychiatry.* 4th ed. New York: Oxford University Press, 2001.

Wilson, Josephine F. *Biological Foundations of Human Behavior.* New York: Harcourt, 2002.

PERIODICALS

Green, R. "Family concurrence of 'gender dysphoria': Ten sibling or parent-child pairs." *Archives of Sexual Behavior* 29.5 (2000): 499–507.

Marks, I., R. Green, and D. Mataix-Cols. "Adult Gender Identity Disorder can Remit." *Comprehensive Psychiatry* 41.4 (2000): 273–5.

Reiner, William G. "Gender Identity and Sex-of-rearing in Children With Disorders of Sexual Differentiation." *Journal of Pediatric Endocrinology and Metabolism* 18 (2005): 549–53.

Wylie, Kevan. "ABC of Sexual Health: Gender Related Disorders." *British Medical Journal* 329 (2004): 615–19.

Zucker, K. J., N. Beaulieu, S. J. Bradley, G. M. Grimshaw, and A. Wilcox. "Handedness in boys with gender identity disorder." *Journal of Child Psychology and Psychiatry* 42.6 (2001): 767–76.

ORGANIZATIONS

American Academy of Family Physicians. 11400 Tomahawk Creek Parkway, Leawood, KS 66211-2672. Telephone: (913) 906-6000. Web site: <http://www.aafp.org>.

American Academy of Pediatrics. 141 Northwest Point Boulevard, Elk Grove Village, IL 60007-1098. Telephone: (847) 434-4000. FAX: (847) 434-8000. Web site: <http://www.aap.org/default.htm>.

American Medical Association. 515 N. State Street, Chicago, IL 60610. Telephone: (312) 464-5000. Web site: <http://www.ama-assn.org>.

American Psychiatric Association. 1400 K Street NW, Washington, DC 20005. Telephone: (888) 357-7924. Fax: (202) 682-6850.

American Psychological Association. 750 First Street NW, Washington, DC 20002-4242. Phone: (800) 374-2721 or (202) 336-5500. Web site: <http://www.apa.org>.

World Professional Association for Transgender Health. 1300 South Second Street, Suite 180 Minneapolis, MN 55454. Telephone: (612) 624-9397. Fax: (612) 624-9541. <http://www.wpath.org/IJT.htm>.

L. Fleming Fallon, Jr., MD, Dr.PH
Emily Jane Willingham

Gender issues in mental health

Defining gender

In the social sciences, the concept of gender means much more than biological sex. It refers to socially constructed expectations regarding the ways in which people should think and behave, depending on their sexual classification. These stereotypical expectations are commonly referred to as gender roles. Attitudes toward gender roles are thought to result from complex interactions among societal, cultural, familial, religious, ethnic, and political influences.

Gender affects many aspects of life, including access to resources, methods of coping with **stress**, styles of interacting with others, self-evaluation, spirituality, and expectations of others. These are all factors that can influence mental health either positively or negatively. Psychological gender studies seek to better understand the relationship between gender and mental health in order to reduce risk factors and improve treatment methods.

Traditional gender roles in many Western societies identify masculinity as having power and being in control in emotional situations, in the workplace, and in sexual relationships. Acceptable male behaviors in this traditional construct include competitiveness, independence, assertiveness, ambition, confidence, toughness, anger, and even violence (to varying degrees). Men are expected to avoid characteristics considered feminine, such as emotional expressiveness, vulnerability (weakness, helplessness, insecurity, worry), and intimacy (especially showing affection to other males).

Traditional femininity is defined as being nurturing, supportive, and assigning high priority to one's relationships. Women are expected to be emotionally expressive, dependent, passive, cooperative, warm, and accepting of subordinate status in marriage and employment. Competitiveness, assertiveness, anger, and violence are viewed as unfeminine and are not generally tolerated as acceptable female behavior.

Gender theories

Differences in gender roles have existed throughout history. Evolutionary theorists attribute these differences to the physiological characteristics of men and women that prescribed their best function for survival of the species. In primitive societies, men adopted the roles of hunting and protecting their families because of their physical strength. Women's ability to bear and nurse children led them to adopt the roles of nurturing young, as well as the less physically dependent roles of gathering and preparing food. These gender-dependent labor roles continued into the period of written human history, when people began to live in cities and form the earliest civilized societies.

In the 1800s, the industrial movement marked a prominent division of labor into public and private domains. Men began leaving home to work, whereas women worked within the home. Previously, both men and women frequently engaged in comparably respected, productive activities on their homestead. When men began working in the public domain, they acquired money, which was transferable for goods or services. Women's work, on the other hand, was not transferable. Men's relative economic independence contributed to their power and influence, while women were reduced to an image of frailty and emotionality deemed appropriate only for domestic tasks and child rearing.

Sigmund Freud's psychoanalytic theory of human development, which emerged from Freud's late nineteenth-century European setting and medical training, reflected an attitude of male superiority. Freud asserted that as children, boys recognize they are superior to girls when they discover the difference in their genitals, and that girls, on the other hand, equate their lack of a penis with inferiority. According to Freud, this feeling of inferiority causes girls to idolize and desire their fathers, resulting in passivity, masochistic tendencies, jealousy, and vanity—all seen by Freud as feminine characteristics.

Other developmental theorists rejected Freud's notions. Eric Erikson (in 1950) and Lawrence Kohlberg (in 1969) theorized that all humans begin as dependent on caregivers and gradually mature into independent and autonomous beings. Such theories, however, still favored men because independence has historically been considered a masculine trait. By such a standard, men would consistently achieve greater levels of maturity than females.

Nancy Chodorow's object relations theory (in 1978) favored neither sex. She proposed that children develop according to interactions with their primary caregivers, who tend to be mothers. Mothers, according to her theory, identify with girls to a greater extent, fostering an ability to form rich interpersonal relationships, as well as dependency traits. Mothers push boys toward independence, helping them to adjust to the male-dominated work environment, but rendering them unaccustomed to emotional connection. Chodorow's theory suggests both strengths and weaknesses inherent in male and female development, with neither deemed superior. Around that same time (1974), Sandra Bem advocated for androgyny, or high levels of both masculinity and femininity, as the key to mental health.

In the 1980s, such psychologists as Carol Gilligan sought to build respect for stereotypically feminine traits. They introduced the notion that women function according to an ethic of care and relatedness that is not inferior to men—just different. In 1985, Daniel Stern's developmental theory favored traditional femininity, suggesting that humans start out as unconnected to others and gradually form more complex interpersonal connections as they mature.

The process of learning gender roles is known as socialization. Children learn which behaviors are acceptable or not acceptable for their sex by observing other people. They may also be shamed by caregivers or peers when they violate gender role expectations. As a result, gender roles usually become an internal guide for behavior early in childhood. Current studies focus on the ways in which extreme notions of masculinity or femininity affect mental health, and the social processes that shape one's concept of maleness or femaleness.

Gender role conflict

According to some researchers, the concepts of masculinity and femininity may simply be sets of personality traits that can be exhibited by either sex, and there may be no true gender differences, although this conclusion generates controversy. Individuals vary in degree of adherence to gender roles, resulting in large amounts of behavioral variation within the sexes and potentially less variation between them. However, some scholars maintain that there are specific gender-related traits, including gender bias in mental illness.

Although attitudes toward gender roles are now much more flexible, different cultures retain varying degrees of expectations regarding male and female behavior. Individuals may personally disregard gender expectations, but society may disapprove of their behavior and impose external social consequences. On the other hand, individuals may feel internal shame if they experience emotions or desires characteristic of the opposite sex. In some cultures in which a person's social role is emphasized over individualism, the failure to fulfill that role in ways considered traditionally appropriate can lead to feelings of shame, as well. Gender role conflict, or gender role stress, results when people feel a discrepancy between how they believe theyshould act—based on gender role expectations learned in childhood—and how they actually think, feel, or behave. If these discrepancies are unresolved, gender role conflict contributes to poor mental health.

Women's issues

Typical stressors

Women are often expected to occupy a number of roles at the same time: wife, mother, homemaker, employee, or caregiver to an elderly parent. Meeting the demands of so many roles simultaneously leads to stressful situations in which choices must be prioritized. Women often must choose whether to pursue or further a career versus whether to devote more time to home and family.

Many women prefer to work outside the home because it gives them a greater sense of life satisfaction. For other women, such as those who run single-parent households, employment is not an option—it is a necessity. Compared with men, women frequently have jobs with less autonomy or creativity, which decreases their level of job satisfaction. Women may also have more difficulty being accepted in the workplace because of hierarchical structures preferring men. Documentation repeatedly shows that women's salaries are lower than those of men in comparable positions; women tend to be paid less even when performing the same jobs as men.

When women do choose or are required to work outside the home, they continue to perform the bulk of household duties as well. Sarah Rosenfield reported that, compared to men, women perform 66% more of the domestic work, sleep a half hour less per night, and perform an extra month of work each year. Needless to say, increased workloads and decreased attention to rest and relaxation are stressful and pose obstacles to women's mental health.

Divorce results in more severe consequences for women who choose or are able to stay home in deference to child rearing. Such women depend on marriage for financial security. Such domestic skills as child care and housecleaning are not highly valued by society, and thus are poorly compensated in terms of money. Women who have never been employed and then experience divorce often have few options for securing adequate income.

Although women's ability to form meaningful relationships is a buffer against stress, it can also be a source of stress. Caring about another person can be stressful when that person is not doing well physically or emotionally. Many families take for granted that the female members care for elderly parents who are no longer self-sufficient. As a result, many women in their forties or fifties are caught between the needs of their college-age offspring and the needs of dependent parents or parents-in-law. Interpersonal conflicts resulting from these heavy burdens may cause stress or lower self-esteem. Women may also view unsuccessful relationships as representing failure on their part to fulfill traditional feminine qualities such as nurturance, warmth, and empathy.

Additional sources of stress common to women include victimization, assertiveness, and physical unattractiveness. Victimization is a constant concern due to the power differential between men and women. Assertiveness may be stressful for women who have had little experience in competitive situations. Physical

unattractiveness may cause some women who adhere to unrealistic standards of feminine beauty to experience shame, or place them at risk for developing eating disorders. Women considered unattractive may also experience discrimination in the workplace or in admission to higher education. In addition, the double standard of aging in contemporary society means that all women will eventually have to cope with the **stigma** of the putative unattractiveness associated with aging.

Typical coping strategies

Studies suggest that women typically react to stress by seeking social support, expressing feelings, or using distraction. These strategies might include praying, worrying, venting, getting advice, or engaging in behaviors that are not related to the problem at all (including such antisocial behaviors as drinking alcohol). Seeking social support and distraction are considered avoidant coping strategies because they do not focus on solving or overcoming a problem, only on alleviating the stress associated with the problem. Research is inconclusive regarding whether men or women are more likely to use problem solving, which is considered an active coping strategy.

Typical patterns of psychopathology

Women are more likely than men to experience internalizing disorders. Primary symptoms of internalizing disorders involve negative inner emotions as opposed to outward negative behavior. **Depression** (both mild and severe) and **anxiety** (generalized or "free-floating" anxiety, phobias, and panic attacks) are internalizing disorders common to women. Symptoms include sadness; a sense of loss, helplessness, or hopelessness; doubt about one's ability to handle problems; high levels of worry or nervousness; poor self-esteem; guilt, self-reproach, and self-blame; decreased energy, motivation, interest in life, or concentration; and problems with sleep or appetite. Women also are more likely than men to have eating disorders, and although incidence of **bipolar disorder** is similar between men and women, women manifest rapid cycling more often and have longer depressive episodes.

Men's issues

Typical stressors

Situations that typically produce stress for men are those that challenge their self-identity and cause them to feel inadequate. If their identity closely matches a traditional male role, they will experience stress in situations requiring subordination to women or emotional expressiveness. They will also experience stress if they feel they are not meeting expectations for superior physical strength, intellect, or sexual performance. Research indicates that men who strictly adhere to extreme gender roles are at higher risk for mental disorders.

Certain cultures are thought to adhere more strictly to traditional male gender roles. In a study by Jose Abreu and colleagues, Latin American men were identified as adopting the most exaggerated form of masculinity, followed by European Americans, and then African Americans. The Latino image of masculinity is often referred to as *machismo* and includes such qualities as concern for personal honor, virility, physical strength, heavy drinking, toughness, aggression, risk taking, authoritarianism, and self-centeredness. African American males are also thought to have a unique image of masculinity; however, Abreu's study showed that African Americans are more egalitarian in terms of gender roles than European Americans.

Typical coping strategies

Men may respond to stress by putting on a tough image, keeping their feelings inside, releasing stress through such activities as sports, actively attempting to solve the problem, denying the problem, abusing drugs or alcohol, or otherwise attempting to control the problem. As stated previously, research is inconclusive regarding whether males or females use problem solving strategies more often. This type of coping strategy, however, has more frequently been attributed to males. Problem solving is seen as an active coping strategy, which is more effective than such avoidant strategies as **denial**, **abuse** of drugs or alcohol, or refusal to talk about problems.

Typical patterns of psychopathology

Men are more likely than women to experience externalizing disorders. Externalizing disorders are characterized by symptoms involving negative outward behavior as opposed to internal negative emotions. Such externalizing disorders as **substance abuse** (both drugs and alcohol) and antisocial behavior (such as anger, hostility, aggression, violence, or stealing) are common to men. Substance abuse results in such negative physical and social consequences as **hallucinations**, blackouts, physical dependency, job loss, divorce, arrests, organ and **brain** damage, and financial debt. Antisocial behavior impairs interpersonal relationships and can also result in negative consequences in other areas of life, such as run-ins with the criminal justice system.

Men are not exempt from such internalizing disorders as anxiety and depression. In fact, one study found that high levels of masculinity appear to be related to depression in males. Some researchers feel that men's abuse of substances could be considered the male version of depression. Because male gender roles discourage admitting vulnerability, men may resort to substance abuse as a way of covering their feelings.

Men who adhere to rigid gender roles are also at a disadvantage in interpersonal relationships, especially intimate relationships. They may avoid emotional expressiveness, or may behave in domineering and hostile ways. These behaviors increase their risk of social isolation, disconnection from nurturance, and participation in unhealthy relationships.

Mental health

Research indicates that, overall, neither men nor women are at greater risk for developing mental disorders as such. Being male or female may indicate susceptibility to certain types of disorders, however. Neither masculinity nor femininity is uniformly positive; both gender identifications have strengths and weaknesses. For example, femininity appears to be protective against antisocial behaviors and substance abuse but is associated with high levels of avoidant coping strategies and low levels of achievement. Masculinity appears to be protective against depression but is high in antisocial behavior and substance abuse.

Information about gender roles has implications for treatment. Women may not seek treatment because of lack of such resources as money, transportation, or time away from child care duties. A treatment center sensitive to women's issues should seek to provide these resources in order to facilitate access to treatment. Men, on the other hand, may not seek treatment because it is incongruent with their image of masculinity. Therapists may need to offer men less threatening forms of treatment, such as those that focus on cognitive problem solving rather than on emotions.

The focus of therapy may differ according to one's gender issues. Therapists should recognize the potential for shame and defensiveness when exploring gender norms. Externalizing behaviors may point to underlying hidden shame. For women, the importance placed on various roles in their lives and how closely those roles are tied to their self-identity is relevant. Men may be encouraged to connect to the spiritual aspects of their being and to consider less stringent views of masculinity. Therapists should also consider the associated influences of generation, culture, class,

KEY TERMS

Active coping strategies—Ways of handling stress that affect the problem or situation in some way.

Androgyny—A way of behaving that includes high levels of both masculinity and femininity.

Antisocial behavior—Behavior characterized by high levels of anger, aggression, manipulation, or violence.

Avoidant coping strategies—Ways of coping with stress that do not alter the problem in any way, but instead provide temporary relief or distraction.

Externalizing disorders—Mental disorders with primary symptoms that involve outward behavior as opposed to inner emotions.

Femininity—Prescribed behavior for women, characterized by interpersonal warmth, passivity, and lack of aggression.

Gender role conflict or stress—A negative psychological state resulting from a discrepancy between gender role expectations and how people actually think, feel, or behave.

Gender roles—Stereotypical expectations regarding how one should think, behave, and feel depending on whether one is male or female.

Internalizing disorders—Mental disorders with primary symptoms that involve inner emotions as opposed to outward behavior.

Machismo—The Latin American image of extreme masculinity that includes such qualities as concern for personal honor, virility, physical strength, heavy drinking, toughness, aggression, risk taking, authoritarianism, and self-centeredness.

Masculinity—Prescribed behavior for men, characterized by independence, strength, control, and avoidance of emotional expressiveness.

Masochistic tendencies—Tendencies to direct harm or hatred toward oneself.

Object relations theory—An approach to psychological development that includes Nancy Chodorow's statement that children develop according to interactions with their primary caregivers.

Psychoanalytic theory—A psychological theory proposed by Sigmund Freud involving unconscious conflicts and specific stages of development; central themes include sexuality and male superiority.

Socialization—The process whereby social influences and demands shape one's values, beliefs, or behavior.

occupation, and educational level when exploring gender role issues. Men often are entering therapy under duress, as the result of a court order or a spousal ultimatum, and may begin the therapeutic process from a perspective of defensiveness.

Taking either masculine or feminine qualities to an extreme and to the exclusion of the other appears to be detrimental. A nontraditional gender role orientation would combine the best of both genders: a social focus (reciprocally supportive relationships and a balance between interests of self and others) and active coping strategies.

Flexibility in using coping strategies is also important. Active, problem-focused coping strategies help to change the situation that is causing the problem. Avoidant or emotion-focused coping strategies manage or reduce emotional distress. Avoidant and emotion-focused strategies may be helpful for the immediate crisis, but should be used in combination with more active strategies for complete problem resolution.

See also Stress.

Resources

BOOKS

Gilligan, Carol. *In a Different Voice: Psychological Theory and Women's Development.* Cambridge, MA: Harvard University Press, 1982.

O'Neil, James M. "Assessing Men's Gender Role Conflict." *Problem Solving Strategies and Interventions for Men in Conflict.* Dwight Moore and Fred Leafgrean, eds. Alexandria, VA: American Counseling Association, 1990.

Rosenfield, Sarah. "Gender and Mental Health: Do Women Have More Psychopathology, Men More, or Both the Same (and Why)?" *A Handbook for the Study of Mental Health.* Allan V. Horwitz and Teresa L. Scheid, eds. New York: Cambridge University Press, 1999.

PERIODICALS

Abreu, Jose M., and others. "Ethnic Belonging and Traditional Masculinity Ideology Among African Americans, European Americans, and Latinos." *Psychology of Men and Masculinity* 1.2 (2000): 75–86.

Addis, Michael E., and Geoffrey H. Cohane. "Social Scientific Paradigms of Masculinity and Their Implications for Research and Practice in Men's Mental Health." *Journal of Clinical Psychology* 61 (2005:) 633–47.

Barefoot, John C., and others. "A Longitudinal Study of Gender Differences in Depressive Symptoms From Age 50 to 80." *Psychology and Aging* 16.2 (2001): 342–45.

Bem, Sandra L. "The Measurement of Psychological Androgyny." *Journal of Consulting and Clinical Psychology* 42 (1974): 155–62.

Bruch, Monroe A. "Shyness and Toughness: Unique and Moderated Relations With Men's Emotional Inexpression." *Journal of Counseling Psychology* 49.1 (2002): 28–34.

Efthim, Paul W., Maureen E. Kenny, and James R. Mahalik. "Gender Role Stress in Relation to Shame, Guilt, and Externalization." *Journal of Counseling and Development* 79.4 (2001): 430–38.

Good, Glenn E., Douglas, A. Thomson, and Allyson D. Brathwaite. "Men and Therapy: Critical Concepts, Theoretical Frameworks, and Research Recommendations." *Journal of Clinical Psychology* 61 (2005): 699–711.

Hyde, Jane Shibley. "The Gender Similarities Hypothesis." *American Psychologist* 60 (2005): 581–92.

Kastrup, Marianne C. "Mental Health Consequences of War." *World Psychiatry* 5 (2006): 1.

Lengua, Liliana J., and Elizabeth Stormshak. "Gender, Gender Roles, and Personality: Gender Differences in the Prediction of Coping and Psychological Symptoms." *Sex Roles* 43.11–12 (2000): 787–820.

Lippa, Richard A. "The Gender Reality Hypothesis." *American Psychologist* (Sept. 2006): 639–40.

Mahalik, James R., and Robert J. Cournoyer. "Identifying Gender Role Conflict Messages That Distinguish Mildly Depressed From Nondepressed Men." *Psychology of Men and Masculinity* 1.2 (2000): 109–15.

Mahalik, James R., and Hugh D. Lagan. "Examining Masculine Gender Role Conflict and Stress in Relation to Religious Orientation and Spiritual Well-Being." *Psychology of Men and Masculinity* 2.1 (2001): 24–33.

Mahalik, James R., and others. "Using the Conformity to Masculine Norms Inventory to Work with Men in a Clinical Setting." *Journal of Clinical Psychology* 61 (2005): 661–74.

Marecek, Jeanne. "After the Facts: Psychology and the Study of Gender." *Canadian Psychology* 42.4 (2001): 254–67.

Martire, Lynn M., Mary Ann Parris Stephens, and Aloen L. Townsend. "Centrality of Women's Multiple Roles: Beneficial and Detrimental Consequences for Psychological Well-Being." *Psychology and Aging* 15.1 (2000): 148–56.

ORGANIZATIONS

Society for the Psychological Study of Men and Masculinity. Division 51 Administrative Office. American Psychological Association. 750 First Street, NE, Washington, DC 20002-4242. Telephone: (202) 336-6013. <http://www.apa.org/about/division/div51.html>.

Society for the Psychology of Women. Division 35 Administrative Office. American Psychological Association. 750 First Street, NE, Washington, DC 20002-4242. Telephone: (202) 336-6013. <http://www.apa.org/about/division/div35.html>.

Wellesley Centers for Women (Stone Center for Developmental Services and Studies; Center for Research on Women). Wellesley College, 106 Central Street, Wellesley, MA 02481. Telephone: (781) 283-2500. <http://www.wcwonline.org>.

OTHER

Healthy People 2010, Volume II. "Depression: What Every Woman Should Know." *Healthy People 2010: Objectives for Improving Health, Part B*. 2005. <http://www.nimh.nih.gov/publicat/depwomenknows.cfm#ptdep4>.

Sandra L. Friedrich, MA
Emily Jane Willingham, PhD

Generalized anxiety disorder

Definition

Generalized **anxiety** disorder (GAD) is a disorder characterized by excessive worry and anxiety concerning a number of events and activities. This anxiety is accompanied by such symptoms as restlessness, **fatigue**, inability to concentrate, muscle tension, or disturbed sleep. Individuals with this disorder experience symptoms on most days for a period of at least six months, and find the symptoms difficult to control.

Description

Generalized anxiety disorder is characterized by persistent worry that is excessive and that patients find hard to control. Common worries associated with generalized anxiety disorder include work responsibilities, money, health, safety, car repairs, and household chores. Unlike people with phobias or post-traumatic disorders, people with GAD do not have their worries provoked by specific triggers; they may worry about almost anything having to do with ordinary life. It is not unusual for patients diagnosed with GAD to shift the focus of their anxiety from one issue to another as their daily circumstances change. For example, people with GAD may start worrying about finances when several bills arrive in the mail, and then fret about the state of their health when they notice that one of the bills is for health insurance. Later in the day they may read a newspaper article that moves the focus of the worry to a third concern.

Patients usually recognize that their worry is out of proportion in its duration or intensity to the actual likelihood or impact of the feared situation or event. For example, a husband or wife may worry about an accident happening to a spouse who commutes to work by train, even though the worried partner knows objectively that rail travel is much safer than automobile travel on major highways. The anxiety levels of patients with GAD may rise and fall somewhat over a period of weeks or months but tend to become chronic problems. The disorder typically becomes worse during stressful periods in the patient's life.

The *Diagnostic and Statistical Manual,* fourth edition, text revision (*DSM-IV-TR*) specifies interference with work, family life, social activities, or other areas of functioning as a criterion for generalized anxiety disorder. This may be accompanied by such physical symptoms as **insomnia**, sore muscles, headaches, and digestive upsets. According to the *DSM-IV-TR,* adult patients must experience three symptoms out of a list of six (restlessness, being easily fatigued, having difficulty concentrating, being irritable, high levels of muscle tension, and sleep disturbances) in order to be diagnosed with the disorder.

Patients diagnosed with GAD have a high rate of concurrent mental disorders, particularly major **depression** disorder, other **anxiety disorders**, or a **substance abuse** disorder. They also frequently have or develop such stress-related physical illnesses and conditions as tension headaches, irritable bowel syndrome (IBS), temporomandibular joint dysfunction (TMJ), bruxism (grinding of the teeth during sleep), and hypertension. In addition, GAD often intensifies the discomfort or complications associated with arthritis, diabetes, and other chronic disorders. Patients with GAD are more likely to seek help from a primary care physician than a **psychiatrist**; they are also more likely than patients with other disorders to make frequent medical appointments, to undergo extensive or repeated diagnostic testing, to describe their health as poor, and to smoke tobacco or **abuse** other substances. In addition, patients with anxiety disorders have higher rates of mortality from all causes than people who are less anxious.

In many cases, it is difficult for the patient's doctor to determine whether the anxiety preceded the physical condition or followed it; sometimes people develop generalized anxiety disorder after being diagnosed with a chronic organic health problem. In other instances, the wear and tear on the body caused by persistent and recurrent worrying leads to physical diseases and disorders. There is an overall "vicious circle" quality to the relationship between GAD and other disorders, whether mental or organic.

Children diagnosed with GAD have much the same anxiety symptoms as adults. The mother of a six-year-old boy with the disorder told his pediatrician that her son "acted like a little man" rather than a typical first-grader. He would worry about such matters as arriving on time for school field trips, whether the family had enough money for immediate needs, whether his friends would get hurt climbing on the playground jungle gym, whether there was enough gas in the tank of the family car, and similar concerns. The little boy had these worries in spite of the fact that his family was stable and happy and had no serious financial or other problems.

GAD often has an insidious onset that begins relatively early in life, although it can be precipitated by a sudden crisis at any age above six or seven years. The idea that GAD often begins in the childhood years even though the symptoms may not become clearly noticeable until late adolescence or the early adult years is gaining acceptance. About half of all patients diagnosed with the disorder report that their worrying began in childhood or their teenage years. Many will say that they cannot remember a time in their lives when they were not worried about something. This type of persistent anxiety can be regarded as part of a person's temperament, or inborn disposition; it is sometimes called trait anxiety. It is not unusual, however, for people to develop the disorder in their early adult years or even later in reaction to chronic **stress** or anxiety-producing situations. For example, there are instances of people developing GAD after several years of taking care of a relative with **dementia**, living with domestic violence, or living in close contact with a friend or relative with **borderline personality disorder**.

The specific worries of people with GAD may be influenced by their ethnic background or culture. The *DSM-IV-TR* cited an observation that being punctual is a common concern of patients with GAD that reflects the value that Western countries place on using time as efficiently as possible. One study of worry in college students from different ethnic backgrounds found that Caucasian and African American students tended to worry a variable amount about a wider range of concerns, whereas Asian Americans tended to worry more intensely about a smaller number of issues. Another study found that a community sample of older Puerto Ricans with GAD overlapped with a culture-specific syndrome called *ataque de nervios,* which resembles **panic disorder** but has features of other anxiety disorders as well as dissociative symptoms. (People experience dissociative symptoms when their perception of reality is temporarily altered—they

Generalized anxiety disorder

GALE ENCYCLOPEDIA OF MENTAL HEALTH, SECOND EDITION 507

may feel as if they were in a trance, or that they were observing activity around them instead of participating.) Further research is needed regarding the relationship between people's ethnic backgrounds and their outward expression of anxiety symptoms.

Causes and symptoms

Causes

The causes of generalized anxiety disorder appear to be a mixture of genetic and environmental factors. It has been known for some years that the disorder runs in families. Twin studies as well as the ongoing mapping of the human genome point to a genetic factor in the development of GAD. The role of the family environment (social **modeling**) in an individual's susceptibility to GAD is uncertain. Social modeling, the process of learning behavioral and emotional response patterns from observing one's parents or other adults, appears to be a more important factor for women than for men.

Another factor in the development of GAD is social expectations related to gender roles. Research findings indicate that women have higher levels of emotional distress and lower quality of life than men. The higher incidence of GAD in women has been linked to the diffuse yet comprehensive expectations of women as caregivers. Many women assume responsibility for the well-being and safety of other family members in addition to holding jobs or completing graduate or professional school. The global character of these responsibilities as well as their unrelenting nature has been described as a mirror image of the persistent but nonspecific anxiety associated with GAD.

Socioeconomic status may also contribute to generalized anxiety. One British study found that GAD is more closely associated with an accumulation of minor stressors than with any demographic factors. People of lower socioeconomic status, however, have fewer resources for dealing with minor stressors and so appear to be at greater risk for generalized anxiety.

An additional factor may be the patient's level of muscle tension. Several studies have found that patients diagnosed with GAD tend to respond to physiological stress in a rigid, stereotyped manner. Their autonomic reactions (reactions in the part of the nervous system that governs involuntary bodily functions) are similar to those of people without GAD, but their muscular tension shows a significant increase. It is not yet known, however, whether this level of muscle tension is a cause or an effect of GAD.

Symptoms

The symptomatology of GAD has changed somewhat over time with redefinitions of the disorder in successive editions of the *DSM*. The first edition of the *DSM* and the *DSM-II* did not make a sharp distinction between generalized anxiety disorder and panic disorder. After specific treatments were developed for panic disorder, GAD was introduced in the *DSM-III* as an anxiety disorder without panic attacks or symptoms of major depression. This definition proved to be unreliable. As a result, the *DSM-IV* constructed its definition of GAD around the psychological symptoms of the disorder (excessive worrying) rather than the physical (muscle tension) or autonomic symptoms of anxiety. The *DSM-IV-TR* continued that emphasis.

According to the *DSM-IV-TR*, the symptoms of GAD are:

- excessive anxiety and worry about a number of events or activities occurring more days than not for at least six months.
- worry that cannot be controlled.
- worry that is associated with several symptoms such as restlessness, fatigue, irritability, or muscle tension.
- worry that causes distress or impairment in relationships, at work, or at school.

In addition, to meet the diagnostic criteria for GAD, the content or focus of the worry cannot change the **diagnosis** from GAD to another anxiety disorder such as panic disorder, **social phobia**, or **obsessive-compulsive disorder**, and the anxiety cannot be caused by a substance (a drug or a medication).

One categorization of GAD symptoms that some psychiatrists use in addition to the *DSM* framework consists of three symptom clusters:

- symptoms related to high levels of physiological arousal: muscle tension, irritability, fatigue, restlessness, insomnia.
- symptoms related to distorted thinking processes: poor concentration, unrealistic assessment of problems, recurrent worrying.
- symptoms associated with poor coping strategies: procrastination, avoidance, inadequate problem-solving skills.

Demographics

The National Institute of Mental Health (NIMH) estimates that approximately 6.8 million Americans have GAD. Further it is estimated that twice as many women as men develop GAD. One study that used the *DSM-III-R* criteria concluded that 5% of the

United States population, or one person in every 20, will develop GAD at some point.

Some psychiatrists think that generalized anxiety disorder is overdiagnosed in both adults and children. One reason for this possibility is that diagnostic screening tests used by primary care physicians for mental disorders produce a large number of false positives for GAD. One study of the PRIME-MD, a screening instrument for mental disorders frequently used in primary care practices, found that 7 of 10 patients met the criteria for GAD. In-depth follow-up interviews with the patients, however, revealed that only a third of the GAD diagnoses could be confirmed.

Diagnosis

Diagnosis of GAD, particularly in primary care settings, is complicated by several factors. One is the high level of comorbidity (co-occurrence) between GAD and other mental or physical disorders. Another is the considerable overlap between anxiety disorders in general and depression. Some practitioners believe that depression and GAD may not be separate disorders after all, because studies have repeatedly confirmed the existence and common occurrence of a "mixed" anxiety/depression syndrome.

Evaluating patients for generalized anxiety disorder includes the following steps:

- patient interview. The doctor will ask the patients to describe the anxiety, and will note whether it is acute (lasting hours to weeks) or persistent (lasting from months to years). If the patients describe a recent stressful event, the doctor will evaluate them for "double anxiety," which refers to acute anxiety added to underlying persistent anxiety. The doctor may also give the patients a diagnostic questionnaire to evaluate the presence of anxiety disorders. The Hamilton Anxiety Scale is a commonly used instrument to assess anxiety disorders in general. The Generalized Anxiety Disorder Questionnaire for DSM-IV (GAD-Q-IV) is a more recent diagnostic tool, and is specific to GAD.
- medical evaluation. Nonpsychiatric disorders that are known to cause anxiety (hyperthyroidism, Cushing's disease, mitral valve prolapse, carcinoid syndrome, and pheochromocytoma) must be ruled out, as well as certain medications (steroids, digoxin, thyroxine, theophylline, and selective serotonin reuptake inhibitors) that may also cause anxiety as a side effect. Patients should be asked about their use of herbal preparations as well.
- substance abuse evaluation. Because anxiety is a common symptom of substance abuse and with-

drawal syndrome, doctors will ask about patients' use of caffeine, nicotine, alcohol, and other common substances (including prescription medications) that may be abused.

- evaluation for other psychiatric disorders. This step is necessary because of the frequent overlap between GAD and depression or between GAD and other anxiety disorders.

In some instances the doctor will consult the patient's family for additional information about the onset of the patient's anxiety symptoms, dietary habits, etc.

Treatments

There are several treatment types that have been found effective in treating people with GAD. Most patients with the disorder are treated with a combination of medications and **psychotherapy**.

Medications

Pharmacologic therapy is usually prescribed for patients whose anxiety is severe enough to interfere with daily functioning. Several different groups of medications have been used to treat generalized anxiety disorder.

These medications include the following:

- benzodiazepines. This group of tranquilizers does not decrease worry, but lowers anxiety by decreasing muscle tension and hypervigilance. They are often prescribed for patients with double anxiety because they act very quickly. The benzodiazepines, however, have several disadvantages: they are unsuitable for long-term therapy because they can cause dependence, and GAD is a long-term disorder; they cannot be given to patients who abuse alcohol; and they cause short-term memory loss and difficulty in concentration. One British study found that benzodiazepines significantly increased a patient's risk of involvement in a traffic accident.
- Buspirone (BuSpar). Buspirone appears to be as effective as benzodiazepines and antidepressants in controlling anxiety symptoms. It is slower to take effect (about two–three weeks), but has fewer side effects. In addition, it treats the worry associated with GAD rather than the muscle tension.
- tricyclic antidepressants. Imipramine (Tofranil), nortriptyline (Pamelor), and desipramine (Norpramin) have been given to patients with GAD. They have, however, some problematic side effects: imipramine has been associated with disturbances in heart rhythm, and the other tricyclics often cause drowsiness, dry

Anxiolytic—A preparation or substance given to relieve anxiety; a tranquilizer.

Ataque de nervios—A culture-specific anxiety syndrome found among some Latin American groups in the United States and in Latin America. It resembles panic disorder in some respects but also includes dissociative symptoms, and frequently occurs in response to stressful events.

Autonomic nervous system—The part of the nervous system that governs the heart, involuntary muscles, and glands.

Double anxiety—Acute anxiety from a recent stressful event combined with underlying persistent anxiety associated with generalized anxiety disorder.

Free-floating—A term used in psychiatry to describe anxiety that is unfocused or lacking an apparent cause or object.

Insidious—Proceeding gradually and inconspicuously but with serious effect.

Social modeling—A process of learning behavioral and emotional response patterns from observing one's parents or other adults. Some researchers think that social modeling plays a part in the development of generalized anxiety disorder in women.

Temperament—A person's natural disposition or inborn combination of mental and emotional traits.

Temporomandibular joint dysfunction—A condition resulting in pain in the head, face, and jaw. Muscle tension or abnormalities of the bones in the area of the hinged joint (the temporomandibular joint) between the lower jaw and the temporal bone are usually the cause.

Trait anxiety—A type of persistent anxiety found in some patients with generalized anxiety disorder. Trait anxiety is regarded as a feature (trait) of a person's temperament.

Twin study—Research studies that use pairs of twins to study the effects of heredity and environment on behavior or other characteristic.

mouth, constipation, and confusion. They increase the patient's risk of falls and other accidents.

- selective serotonin reuptake inhibitors (SSRIs). Paroxetine (Paxil), one of the SSRIs, was approved by the U.S. Food and Drug Administration (FDA) in 2001 as a treatment for GAD. Venlafaxine (Effexor) appears to be particularly beneficial to patients with a mixed anxiety/depression syndrome; it is the first drug to be labeled by the FDA as an antidepressant as well as an anxiolytic. Venlafaxine is also effective in treating patients with GAD whose symptoms are primarily somatic (manifesting as physical symptoms or bodily complaints).

Psychotherapy

Some studies have found cognitive therapy to be superior to medications and **psychodynamic psychotherapy** in treating GAD, but other researchers disagree with these findings. As a rule, patients with GAD who have **personality disorders**, who are living with chronic social stress (e.g., caring for a parent with **Alzheimer's disease**), or who do not trust psychotherapeutic approaches require treatment with medications. The greatest benefit of cognitive therapy is its effectiveness in helping patients with the disorder to learn more realistic ways to appraise their problems and to use better problem-solving techniques.

Family therapy is recommended insofar as family members can be helpful in offering patients a different perspective on their problems. They can also help patients practice new approaches to problem solving.

Alternative and complementary therapies

Several alternative and complementary therapies have been found helpful in treating patients with generalized anxiety disorder. These include **hypnotherapy**, music therapy, Ayurvedic medicine, **yoga**, religious practice, and guided imagery **meditation**.

Biofeedback and relaxation techniques are also recommended for patients with GAD in order to lower physiologic arousal. In addition, massage therapy, hydrotherapy, shiatsu, and **acupuncture** have been reported to relieve muscle spasms or soreness associated with GAD.

One herbal remedy that has been used in **clinical trials** for treating GAD is **passionflower** (*Passiflora incarnata*). One team of researchers found that passionflower extract was as effective as **oxazepam** (Serax) in relieving anxiety symptoms in a group of 36 outpatients diagnosed with GAD according to *DSM-IV* criteria. In addition, the passionflower extract did not impair the subjects' job performance as frequently or as severely as the oxazepam.

Prognosis

Generalized anxiety disorder is generally regarded as a long-term condition that may become a lifelong problem. Patients frequently find their symptoms resurfacing or getting worse during stressful periods in their lives. It is rare for patients with GAD to recover spontaneously.

Prevention

The best preventive strategy, given the early onset of GAD, is the modeling of realistic assessment of stressful events by parents, and the teaching of effective coping strategies to their children.

See also Bodywork therapies; Cognitive-behavioral therapy; Cognitive problem-solving skills training; Stress.

Resources

BOOKS

American Psychiatric Association. *Diagnostic and Statistical Manual of Mental Disorders.* 4th ed., Text rev. Washington, D.C.: American Psychiatric Association, 2000.

Dugas, Michel J., and Melisa Robichaud. *Cognitive-Behavioral Treatment for Generalized Anxiety Disorder: From Science to Practice.* New York: Brunner-Routledge, 2006.

Heimberg, Richard G., Cynthia L. Turk, and Douglas S. Mennin, eds. *Generalized Anxiety Disorder: Advances in Research and Practice.* New York: The Guilford Press, 2004.

Nutt, David J., Karl Rickels, and Dan J. Stein. *Generalized Anxiety Disorder: Symptomatology, Pathogenesis and Management.* Oxford: Informa Healthcare, 2002.

Pelletier, Kenneth R., M.D. *The Best Alternative Medicine.* Part II, "CAM Therapies for Specific Conditions: Anxiety." New York: Simon and Schuster, 2002.

Rygh, Jayne L., and William C. Sanderson. *Treating Generalized Anxiety Disorder: Evidence-Based Strategies, Tools, and Techniques.* New York: The Guilford Press, 2004.

VandenBos, Gary R., ed. *APA Dictionary of Psychology.* Washington, D.C.: American Psychological Association, 2006.

PERIODICALS

Allgulander, Christer. "Generalized Anxiety Disorder: What Are We Missing?" *European Neuropsychopharmacology* 16, Suppl. 2 (July 2006): S101–S108.

Allgulander, Christer, Ioana Florea, and Anna K. Trap Huusom. "Prevention of Relapse in Generalized Anxiety Disorder by Escitalopram Treatment." *International Journal of Neuropsychopharmacology* 9.5 (Oct. 2006): 495–505.

Angst, Jules, and others. "Varying Temporal Criteria for Generalized Anxiety Disorder: Prevalence and Clinical Characteristics in a Young Age Cohort." *Psychological Medicine* 36.9 (Sept. 2006): 1283–92.

Baldwin, David S., Anna Karina Trap Huusom, and Eli Maehlum. "Escitalopram and Paroxetine in the Treatment of Generalised Anxiety Disorder: Randomised, Placebo-Controlled, Double-Blind Study." *British Journal of Psychiatry* 189.3 (Sept. 2006): 264–72.

Connor, Kathryn M., Victoria Payne, and Jonathan R. T. Davidson. "Kava in Generalized Anxiety Disorder: Three Placebo-Controlled Trials." *International Clinical Psychopharmacology* 21.5 (Sept. 2006): 249–53.

Goldston, David B., and others. "Reading Problems, Psychiatric Disorders, and Functional Impairment from Mid- to Late Adolescence." *Journal of the American Academy of Child & Adolescent Psychiatry* 46.1 (Jan. 2007): 25–32.

Gosselin, Patrick, and others. "Benzodiazepine Discontinuation Among Adults With GAD: A Randomized Trial of Cognitive-Behavioral Therapy." *Journal of Consulting and Clinical Psychology* 74.5 (Oct. 2006): 908–19.

Hoge, Elizabeth A., and others. "Cross-Cultural Differences in Somatic Presentation in Patients with Generalized Anxiety Disorder." *Journal of Nervous and Mental Disease* 194.12 (Dec. 2006): 962–66.

Kim, Tae-Suk, and others. "Comparison of Venlafaxine Extended Release Versus Paroxetine for Treatment of Patients with Generalized Anxiety Disorder." *Psychiatry and Clinical Neurosciences* 60.3 (June 2006): 347–51.

Kopecek, Miloslav, Pavel Mohr, and Tomas Novak. "Sedative Effects of Low-Dose Risperidone in GAD Patients and Risk of Drug Interactions." *Journal of Clinical Psychiatry* 67.8 (Aug. 2006): 1307–1308.

Labrecque, Joane, and others. "Cognitive-Behavioral Therapy for Comorbid Generalized Anxiety Disorder and Panic Disorder With Agoraphobia." *Behavior Modification* 30.4 (July 2006): 383–410.

Lyddon, William J. "Review of Generalized Anxiety Disorder: Advances in Research and Practice." *Journal of Cognitive Psychotherapy* 20.4 (Winter 2006): 463–64.

Mennin, Douglas S. "Emotion Regulation Therapy: An Integrative Approach to Treatment-Resistant Anxiety Disorders." *Journal of Contemporary Psychotherapy* 36.2 (June 2006): 95–105.

Montgomery, Stuart A., and others. "Efficacy and Safety of Pregabalin in the Treatment of Generalized Anxiety Disorder: A 6-Week, Multicenter, Randomized, Double-Blind, Placebo-Controlled Comparison of Pregabalin and Venlafaxine." *Journal of Clinical Psychiatry* 67.5 (May 2006): 771–82.

Nutt, David, and others. "Generalized Anxiety Disorder: A Comorbid Disease." *European Neuropsychopharmacology* 16, Suppl. 2 (July 2006): S109–S118.

Skopp, Nancy A., and others. "Investigation of Cognitive Behavior Therapy." *American Journal of Geriatric Psychiatry* 14.3 (Mar. 2006): 292.

Weems, Carl F., and others. "Predisaster Trait Anxiety and Negative Affect Predict Posttraumatic Stress in Youths After Hurricane Katrina." *Journal of Consulting and Clinical Psychology* 75.1 (Feb. 2007): 154–59.

ORGANIZATIONS

Anxiety Disorders Association of America. 11900 Parklawn Drive, Suite 100, Rockville, MD 20852-2624. Telephone: (301) 231-9350. <www.adaa.org>.

Anxiety Disorders Education Program, National Institute of Mental Health. 6001 Executive Boulevard, Room 8184, MSC 9663, Bethesda, MD 20892-9663. Telephone: (301) 443-4513. <www.nimh.nih.gov>.

Freedom From Fear. 308 Seaview Avenue, Staten Island, NY 10305. Telephone: (718) 351-1717. <www.freedomfromfear.com>.

National Mental Health Association. 1021 Prince Street, Alexandria, VA 22314-2971. Telephone: (800) 969-6642. <www.nmha.org>.

OTHER

National Institute of Mental Health (NIMH). *Anxiety Disorders.* NIH Publication No. 00-3879 (2000). <www.nimh.nih.gov/anxiety/anxiety.cfm>.

National Institute of Mental Health (NIMH). *Facts About Generalized Anxiety Disorder.* NIH publication OM-99 4153 (2000). <www.nimh.nih.gov/anxiety/gadfacts.cfm>.

Rebecca J. Frey, PhD
Ruth A. Wienclaw, PhD

Genetic factors and mental disorders

Introduction and overview

In recent years, mental health professionals have become increasingly aware of the importance of genetic factors in the etiology (causes) of mental disorders. Since the Human Genome Project began its mapping of the entire sequence of human DNA in 1990, the implications of its findings for psychiatric **diagnosis** and treatment have accumulated rapidly. A new subspecialty known as biological psychiatry (also called physiological psychology or psychiatric genetics) has emerged from the discoveries of the last two decades. Biological psychiatry got its start in the late 1980s, when several research groups identified genes associated with manic **depression** and **schizophrenia** respectively. These studies ran into difficulties fairly quickly, however, because of the complexity of the relationship between genetic factors and mental illness.

One technological development that has contributed to the major advances in biological psychiatry in the last twenty years is high-speed computing. Faster computers have enabled researchers to go beyond rough estimates of the heritability of various disorders to accurate quantification of genetic effects. In some cases the data have led to significant reappraisals of the causes of specific disorders. As recently as the 1960s and 1970s, for example, schizophrenia was generally attributed to "refrigerator mothers" and a chilly emotional climate in the patients' extended families. However, the application of computer models to schizophrenia indicates that the heritability of the disorder may be as high as 80%. Similarly, **autism** was once blamed on faulty parenting. However, it is now known to be over 90% heritable.

The ongoing search for genes related to psychiatric symptoms and disorders is complicated by several factors:

- psychiatric diagnosis relies on a doctor's human judgment and evaluation of a patient's behavior or appearance to a greater degree than diagnosis in other fields of medicine. For example, there is no blood or urine test for schizophrenia or a personality disorder. Diagnostic questionnaires for mental disorders are helpful in trimming the list of possible diagnoses but do not have the same degree of precision or objectivity as laboratory findings.

- mental disorders almost always involve more than one gene. Studies have shown that one mental disorder can be caused by different genes on different chromosomes in different populations. For example, one study in the late 1980s found two genes on two different chromosomes among two populations that caused manic depression. Studies of schizophrenia done in the late 1980s and early 1990s revealed the same finding—different genes on different chromosomes produced schizophrenia in different populations. It now appears that specific mental disorders are related to different sets of genes that vary across family and ethnic groups.

- genes associated with mental disorders do not always show the same degree of penetrance, which is defined as the frequency with which a gene produces its effects in a specific group of people. Penetrance is expressed as a percentage. For example, a gene for manic depression may have 20% penetrance, which means that 20% of the members of the family being studied are at risk of developing the disorder.

- genetic factors in mental disorders interact with a person's family and cultural environment. For example, a person who has a gene associated with susceptibility to alcohol abuse may not develop the disorder if he or she grows up in a family that teaches effective ways to cope with stress and responsible attitudes toward drinking.

Genetic causality in mental disorders

Genes appear to influence the development of mental disorders in three major ways: They may govern the organic causes of such disorders as **Alzheimer's disease** (AD) and schizophrenia; they may be responsible for abnormalities in a person's development before or after birth; and they may influence a person's susceptibility to **anxiety**, depression, **personality disorders**, and **substance abuse** disorders.

Mental disorders with organic causes

The two most important examples of mental disorders caused by organic changes or abnormalities in the **brain** are late-onset AD and schizophrenia. Both disorders are polygenic, which means that their expression is determined by more than one gene. Another disorder that is much less common, Huntington's disease, is significant because it is one of the few mental disorders that is monogenic, or determined by a single gene.

SCHIZOPHRENIA. Researchers have known for many years that first-degree biological relatives of patients with schizophrenia have a greater risk of developing the disorder than the general population. The identical twin of a person with schizophrenia has a 40–50% risk.

Late-onset AD is another polygenic disorder. It has been known since 1993 that a specific form of a gene for apolipoprotein E (apoE4) on human chromosome 19 is a genetic risk factor for late-onset AD. People who have the apoE4 gene from one parent have a 50% chance of developing AD; they have a 90% chance if they inherited the gene from both parents. They are also likely to develop AD earlier in life. One of the remaining puzzles about this particular gene, however, is that it is not a consistent marker for AD. In other words, some people who have the apoE4 gene do not develop AD, and some who do not have the gene do develop the disorder.

There are two other forms of AD, early-onset AD and familial AD (FAD), which have different patterns of genetic transmission. Early-onset AD is caused by a defect in one of three genes known as APP, presenilin-1, and presenilin-2, found on human chromosomes 21, 14, and 1, respectively. Early-onset AD is also associated with Down syndrome, in that persons with trisomy 21 (three forms of human chromosome 21 instead of a pair) often develop this form of AD. The brains of people with Down syndrome age prematurely, so that those who develop early-onset AD are often only in their late 40s or early 50s when the symptoms of the disease

first appear. FAD appears to be related to abnormal genes on human chromosomes 21 and 14.

HUNTINGTON'S DISEASE. Huntington's disease, or Huntington's chorea, is a neurological disorder that kills the cells in the caudate nucleus, the part of the brain that coordinates movement. It also destroys the brain cells that control cognitive functions. In 1983, the gene that causes Huntington's disease was discovered on the short arm of human chromosome 4. Ten years later, the gene was identified as an instance of a triplet or trinucleotide repeat. Nucleotides are the molecular "building blocks" of DNA and RNA. Three consecutive nucleotides form a codon, or triplet, in messenger RNA that codes for a specific amino acid. In 1991, researchers discovered not only that nucleotide triplets repeat themselves, but that these repetitions sometimes expand in number during the process of genetic transmission. This newly discovered type of mutation is known as a dynamic or expansion mutation. Since 1991, more than a dozen diseases have been traced to expansion mutations. Eight of them are caused by repeats of the triplet cytosine-adenine-guanine (CAG), which codes for an amino acid called glutamine. In 1993, Huntington's disease was identified as a CAG expansion mutation disorder. Where the genetic material from a normal chromosome 4 has about 20 repeats of the CAG triplet, the Huntington's gene has a minimum of 45 repeats, sometimes as many as 86. The higher the number of CAG triplet repeats in a Huntington's gene, the earlier the age at which the symptoms will appear. The expansion mutation in Huntington's disease results in the production of a toxic protein that destroys the cells in the patient's brain that control movement and cognition.

Childhood developmental disorders

Developmental disorders of childhood are another large category of mental disorders caused by mutations, deletions, translocations (rearrangements of the arms of chromosomes), and other alterations in genes or chromosomes.

TRIPLET REPEAT DISORDERS. Since 1991, expansion mutations have been identified as the cause of several diseases. Some, such as Huntington's disease, are characterized by long expansion mutations of the trinucleotide sequence CAG, which in effect adds so much glutamine to the protein being synthesized that it becomes toxic to the nervous system. A second category of triplet repeat disorders contains extra triplets that add an amino acid called alanine to the protein. The sequence of nucleotides is cytosine-guanine-N, where N stands for any of the four basic nucleotides. Although the proteins produced by this type of expansion mutation are not toxic, their normal function in the body is disrupted. The developmental disorders related to these CGN triplets are characterized by abnormalities of the skeleton. One of these disorders is synpolydactyly, in which the patient has more than the normal number of fingers or toes. Another is cleidocranial dysplasia, a disorder marked by abnormal development of the skull.

Other developmental disorders are caused by expansion mutations outside the regions of the gene that code for proteins. The segments of DNA that specify the sequence of a portion of a protein are known as exons, while the stretches of DNA that lie between the exons and do not code for proteins are called introns. The CAG and CGN groups of triplet disorders are expansion mutations that occur within exons. A third group of triplet disorders results from expansion mutations in introns. Expansions in this third group are usually much longer than those in the first two categories; some repeat several hundred or even several thousand times. The best-known expansion mutation in this group causes the disorder known as fragile X syndrome. Fragile X syndrome is the most common inherited form of **mental retardation** and should be considered in the differential diagnosis of any child with developmental delays, mental retardation, or learning difficulties. The syndrome is caused by a large expansion of a cytosine-guanine-guanine (CGG) repeat, which interferes with normal protein transcription from a gene called the FMR1 gene on the X chromosome. Males with the mutation lack a second normal copy of the gene and are more severely affected than females who have a normal FMR1 gene on their second X chromosome. In both sexes there is a correlation between the length of the expansion mutation and the severity of the syndrome.

The discovery of expansion mutations was the solution to a long-standing genetic riddle. Clinicians had noticed as early as 1910 that some disorders produce a more severe phenotype or occur at earlier and earlier ages in each successive generation of an affected family. This phenomenon is known as anticipation, but its biological basis was not understood until recently. It is now known that triplet repeats that are long enough to cause disorders are unstable and tend to grow longer from generation to generation. For example, an expansion mutation of the cytosine-thymine-guanine (CTG) triplet causes a potentially life-threatening developmental disorder known as myotonic dystrophy. Repeats of the CTG triplet that are just above the threshold for myotonic dystrophy itself may produce a relatively mild disorder, namely eye cataracts in later life. Within two to three generations, however, the CTG repeats become longer, producing a fatal congenital illness. In addition to developmental disorders of childhood,

expansion mutations may also be involved in other psychiatric disorders. Anticipation has been found in some families affected by **bipolar disorder** and schizophrenia, and some researchers think that it may also be present in some forms of autism.

GENOMIC IMPRINTING. Another recent discovery in the field of biological psychiatry is the phenomenon of genomic imprinting, which distinguishes between chromosomes derived from a person's father and those derived from the mother. Genomic imprinting was discovered in the late 1980s as an exception to Gregor Mendel's laws of biological inheritance. A small subset of human genes are expressed differently depending on the parent who contributes them to a child's genetic makeup. This phenomenon has helped researchers understand the causation of two well-known genetic disorders—Prader-Willi and Angelman syndromes.

In the 1980s, researchers studying Prader-Willi syndrome and Angelman syndrome noticed that both disorders were caused by a deletion on the long arm of chromosome 15 in the very same region, extending from 15q11 to 15q13. This finding was surprising, because the two syndromes have markedly different phenotypes. Children with Prader-Willi syndrome have severe mental retardation, poor muscle tone, small hands and feet, and a voracious appetite (hyperphagia) that begins in childhood. As a result, they are often obese by adolescence. Children with Angelman syndrome, on the other hand, do not speak, are often hyperactive, and have **seizures** and sleep disturbances. In the late 1980s, advances in molecular genetics revealed that the different expressions of the same deletion on the same chromosome were determined by the sex of the parent who contributed that chromosome. Children with Prader-Willi syndrome had inherited their father's copy of chromosome 15, while the children with Angelman syndrome had inherited their mother's. Highly specific diagnostic tests for these two disorders have been developed within the past decade.

BEHAVIORAL PHENOTYPES. Although medical professionals are familiar with the physical phenotypes associated with genetic disorders, the notion of behavioral phenotypes is still controversial. A behavioral phenotype is the characteristic set of behaviors found in patients with a genetic disorder. Behavioral phenotypes include patterns of language usage, cognitive development, and social adjustment as well as behavioral problems in the narrow sense. It is important for psychiatrists who treat children and adolescents to understand behavioral phenotypes, because they are better able to identify problem behaviors as part of a genetic syndrome and refer children to a geneticist for an accurate genetic diagnosis.

Examples of behavioral phenotypes are those associated with Down, Prader-Willi, and Williams syndromes. Children with Down syndrome have an increased risk of developing early-onset Alzheimer's disease. They are usually quiet and good-tempered, but may also be hyperactive and impulsive. Their behavioral phenotype includes delayed language development and moderate to severe mental retardation.

Children with Prader-Willi syndrome are often quiet in childhood but develop stubborn, aggressive, or impulsive patterns of behavior as they grow older. The onset of their hyperphagia is often associated with temper tantrums and other behavioral problems. They are typically obsessed with food, frequently hoarding it, stealing it, or stealing money to buy food. About 50% of children diagnosed with Prader-Willi syndrome meet the criteria for **obsessive-compulsive disorder** (OCD).

Williams syndrome is a genetic disorder that results from a deletion of locus 23 on chromosome 7q11. Children with this syndrome often have an "elf-like" face with short upturned noses and small chins. Their behavioral phenotype includes talkativeness, friendliness, and a willingness to follow strangers. They are also hyperactive and easily distracted from tasks. The personality profile of children with Williams syndrome is so distinctive that many are diagnosed on the basis of the behavioral rather than the physical phenotype.

Psychological/behavioral vulnerability in adults

Although psychiatrists at one time regarded emotional wounds in early childhood as the root cause of anxiety and **depressive disorders** in later life, inherited vulnerability to these disturbances is the subject of intensive study at the present time. In the past two decades, genetic factors have been shown to influence the likelihood of a person's developing mood disorders or post-traumatic syndromes in adult life. A study done in 1990 showed that first-degree relatives of a person diagnosed with major depression were two to four times as likely to develop depression themselves as people in the general population. However, the genetic patterns involved in depression appear to be quite complex; there is some evidence that both genomic imprinting and the phenomenon of anticipation may be present in some families with multigenerational histories of depression. In addition, the evidence indicates that susceptibility to major depression is governed by several different genes on several different chromosomes.

POST-TRAUMATIC SYNDROMES. Researchers have found that some persons are more vulnerable than others to developing dissociative and anxiety-related symptoms following a traumatic experience. Vulnerability to trauma is affected by such inherited factors as temperament as well as by family or cultural influences; shy or introverted persons are at greater risk for developing **post-traumatic stress disorder** (PTSD) than their extroverted or outgoing peers. In addition, twin studies indicate that certain abnormalities in brain hormone levels and brain structure are inherited, and that these increase a person's susceptibility to developing **acute stress disorder** (ASD) or PTSD following exposure to trauma.

ANXIETY DISORDERS. It has been known for some time that **anxiety disorders** run in families. Recent twin studies as well as the ongoing mapping of the human genome point to a genetic factor in the development of **generalized anxiety disorder** (GAD).

Research has also confirmed earlier hypotheses that there is a genetic component to **agoraphobia**, and that it can be separated from susceptibility to **panic disorder** (PD). Panic disorder was found to be associated with two loci, one on human chromosome 1 and the other on chromosome 11q. Researchers have concluded that agoraphobia and PD are common, heritable anxiety disorders that share some but not all of their genetic loci for susceptibility.

BEHAVIORAL TRAITS. There has been considerable controversy in the past decade concerning the mapping of genetic loci associated with specific human behaviors, as distinct from behavioral phenotypes related to developmental disorders. Research into the genetic component of human behavior is currently conducted with one eye, so to speak, on the social and political implications of its potential results. Given contemporary concerns about the misuse of findings related to biological race or sex, investigators are usually careful to acknowledge the importance of environmental as well as genetic factors.

Genetic epidemiology

Genetic epidemiology is the branch of medicine that investigates the incidence and prevalence of genetic disorders in specific populations. Researchers in this field make use of specific types of studies to assess the relative importance of genetic and environmental factors in families with a history of inherited disorders.

Anticipation—In medicine, a phenomenon in which certain diseases manifest at earlier ages or in more severe phenotypes in each successive generation of an affected family.

Apolipoprotein E—A protein that transports cholesterol through the body. One form of this protein, apoE4, is associated with a 60% risk of late-onset Alzheimer's disease (AD).

Behavioral phenotype—The greater likelihood that people with a specific genetic syndrome will have certain behavioral or developmental characteristics compared to people who do not have the syndrome. The concept of a behavioral phenotype is used most often with reference to patterns of behavior found in certain developmental disorders of childhood, such as Down syndrome or Prader-Willi syndrome. However, this does not mean that every person diagnosed with a given genetic syndrome will invariably develop these characteristics.

Codon—A three-member nucleotide sequence in messenger RNA that codes for a specific amino acid in synthesizing protein molecules.

Cytogenetics—The branch of biology that combines the study of genetic inheritance with the study of cell structure.

Dizygotic—Developed from two fertilized ova. Dizygotic twins are sometimes called fraternal twins.

Down syndrome—A genetic disorder characterized by an extra chromosome 21 (trisomy 21), mental retardation, and susceptibility to early-onset Alzheimer's disease.

Epidemiology—The study of the causes, incidence, transmission, and control of diseases.

Etiology—The cause or origin of a disease or disorder. The word is also used to refer to the study of the causes of disease.

Exon—A segment of DNA that is transcribed to RNA and encodes information about the protein sequence.

Expansion mutation—A genetic mutation caused by additional repetitions of a triplet, or trinucleotide sequence, during the process of genetic transmission. In Huntington's disease, the expansion mutation produces more of a toxic gene product.

Genome—The total genetic makeup of a cell or organism. The human genome is the complete genetic constitution of a human being.

Genomic imprinting—The process in which specific genes or DNA segments are modified during the development of sperm or egg cells in a parent-specific fashion. The modification is reversible and appears to include the addition or removal of methyl groups to specific areas within the DNA sequence.

Twin studies

Twin studies are based on the assumption that twins reared in the same family share a common environment. Monozygotic (identical) twins have all their genes in common, whereas dizygotic (fraternal) twins share only half their genes. If a certain disorder appears more frequently in monozygotic twins of affected persons than in dizygotic twins, one may assume that the difference is due to genetic factors rather than the family environment. Some phenotypes show clear differences between identical and fraternal twins, including schizophrenia, childhood autism, **attention deficit/hyperactivity disorder**, unipolar depression, manic depressive disorder, and cognitive abilities as measured by IQ tests.

Twin studies have proved to be particularly important in genetic research into autism. Until the early 1970s, autism was assumed to be caused primarily by parental coldness toward the child. In part, the lack of interest in genetic aspects of the disorder was due to the fact that cytogenetic research (research that studies the links between genetic inheritance and cell structure) was not sufficiently advanced in the late 1960s to have demonstrated any chromosomal abnormalities in people diagnosed with autism. The first small-scale twin study of children with autism was done in 1977; its findings showed, first, that there is a significant difference between monozygotic and dizygotic twin pairs with regard to the appearance of the disorder in siblings. More importantly, the study showed that the similarities within monozygotic pairs of twins included a range of social and cognitive disabilities, not just autism itself. This finding implies that the phenotype of autism is broader than the older diagnostic categories assumed. In the 1970s and 1980s, advances in cytogenetic techniques led to the discovery that autism is associated with several different chromosomal abnormalities, including the defect that produces fragile X syndrome. A much larger British twin study done in 1995 confirmed earlier findings in the United States: A monozygotic twin of a child diagnosed with autism was 12 times more likely to have the disorder than a

Genotype—The genetic makeup of an organism or a set of organisms. A person's genotype is the sum total of the genetic material transmitted from his or her parents.

Huntington's disease—A hereditary disorder that appears in middle age and is characterized by gradual brain deterioration, progressive dementia, and loss of voluntary movement. It is sometimes called Huntington's chorea.

Hyperphagia—An abnormally large appetite for food. Hyperphagia is one of the symptoms of Prader-Willi syndrome.

Intron—A segment of DNA that interrupts an exon and that does not encode any information about the protein sequence.

Monogenic—Determined or controlled by a single gene. Huntington's disease is one of the few psychiatric disorders that is monogenic.

Monozygotic—Developed from a single fertilized ovum. Monozygotic twins are sometimes called identical twins.

Nosology—The branch of medicine that deals with the systematic classification of diseases and disorders.

Nucleotide—One of the molecules that form the building blocks of DNA or RNA. The nucleotides

of DNA include a phosphate group, four chemical bases (adenine, cytosine, guanine, and thymine), and a sugar containing five carbon atoms. In RNA the thymine base is replaced by uracil.

Penetrance—In genetics, the frequency with which a specific gene produces its effects in a group of people or other organisms. Penetrance is expressed as a percentage.

Phenotype—The observable signs, symptoms, and other aspects of the makeup of an organism. A person's phenotype is the observable signs, symptoms, and other aspects of his or her appearance. The term is also used sometimes to refer to the appearance of an organism resulting from the interaction between its genotype and its environment.

Polygenic—A trait or disorder that is determined by a group of genes acting together. Most human characteristics, including height, weight, and general body build, are polygenic. Schizophrenia and late-onset Alzheimer's disease are considered polygenic disorders.

Prader-Willi syndrome—A developmental disorder of childhood characterized by mental retardation; poor muscle tone; delayed growth and sexual maturation; and childhood onset of an abnormally large appetite for food.

dizygotic twin (60% versus 5%). Secondly, the British study confirmed the hypothesis that the genetic risk of autism extends to a broader phenotype; over 90% of the monozygotic twin pairs in the British study shared social and intellectual disabilities similar to those found in patients with autism, but less severe.

Family studies

Family studies are important tools for evaluating environmental effects on children with genetic disorders—and also for evaluating the impact of the disorder on the family environment. Family studies have indicated that families may develop problems in response to a child's illness that may also affect the child's prognosis for recovery.

Family factors fall into three categories: shared genetic material; shared environment; and nonshared environment. These three categories are complicated, however, by the fact that genetic as well as environmental factors affect interactions between parents and

children. For example, a parent's behavior toward a child diagnosed with depression is partly shaped by the parent's genetic vulnerability to depression.

In general, much of the impact of a family's environment on a child with a mental disorder is due to nonshared rather than shared interactions. A clinical research measurement called expressed emotion (EE), originally developed to study young adults with schizophrenia, is now used to study families with younger children with mental disorders. EE measures three primary aspects of family members' attitudes toward the child with the illness: criticism, hostility, and emotional overinvolvement. A growing number of research studies indicate that EE is a good predictor of the outcome of the child's illness; high EE is a marker of a more difficult course of the disorder and a poorer prognosis.

Clinical applications of biological psychiatry

Recent advances in genetics have affected the practice of psychiatry in several ways:

- genetic counseling. Genetic counseling is recommended when a couple has already produced a child with mental retardation, dysmorphic (malformed) features, or developmental delays; when either parent is suspected or known to have a genetic disorder; when the mother is over 35; when there is a family history of a genetic disorder, especially if several members are affected; or if the mother has been exposed during pregnancy to drugs or environmental toxins known to cause birth defects. Genetic counselors do not try to control the couple's decision about a present or future pregnancy; rather, they offer information about the disorder, including treatment options as well as the risk of recurrence. They discuss possible reproductive choices available to the couple and help them adjust to caring for a child who is already affected.

- medication selection and dosage. Preliminary studies of patients with schizophrenia indicate that DNA testing of the gene for a specific serotonin receptor can predict the patient's response to antipsychotic drugs. A similar form of gene testing can predict which children with asthma will respond to an inhaled medication known as albuterol and which will not. In the near future, researchers hope to devise genetic tests that will measure patients' responsiveness to specific antidepressant and antianxiety medications. Such tests would greatly simplify the present process of trial-and-error prescribing of drugs for psychiatric disorders.

- psychiatric nosology. Nosology is the branch of psychiatry that deals with the classification of mental disorders. Some current diagnostic labels, including autism and attention-deficit/hyperactivity disorder, may represent groups of related syndromes rather than a single diagnostic entity. In other instances, genetic studies may lead to eventual reclassification of certain disorders. Some studies, for example, suggest that body dysmorphic disorder is more closely related to obsessive-compulsive disorder than to the somatoform disorders with which it is presently grouped.

- diagnosis of disorders with major psychological consequences. It is possible for people to find out whether they have the gene for Huntington's disease or the BRCA1 or BRCA2 genes for breast cancer. Although some people may choose not to know, others may prefer the possibility of bad news to years of chronic uncertainty and anxiety.

Ethical concerns

As the number of tests available for determining genetic markers for mental disorders continues to increase, ethical issues are being debated. These concerns include:

- regulation of genetic testing. Some companies have started to market tests for the apoE4 Alzheimer's gene even though the present benefits of such testing are not clear. The Department of Health and Human Services has established an advisory committee to study the question of government regulation of genetic testing.

- confidentiality. The fear of losing health insurance is a major barrier to acceptance of genetic testing in the general population. Many people do not trust hospitals or research laboratories to keep test results confidential.

- discrimination. Some people are concerned that genetic findings could be used to deny college or graduate school admission to persons at risk for certain disorders, or to restrict their access to employment opportunities.

- reproductive issues. As more and more human traits are found to have a genetic component, questions inevitably arise regarding the possibility of government control over reproduction. But while few people would want to preserve the gene for Huntington's disease, for example, they are likely to disagree about the desirability of other human traits, such as a tendency toward short stature.

Resources

BOOKS

American Psychiatric Association. *Diagnostic and Statistical Manual of Mental Disorders*. 4th ed., Text rev. Washington, D.C.: American Psychiatric Association, 2000.

Faraone, Stephen V., Ming T. Tsuang, and Debby W. Tsuang. *Genetics of Mental Disorders: What Practitioners and Students Need to Know*. New York: The Guilford Press, 2001.

Gershon, Elliot S., and C. Robert Cloninger, eds. *Genetic Approaches to Mental Disorders*. Arlington, VA: American Psychiatric Publishing, 1994.

PERIODICALS

Boomsma, Dorret I., and others. "Longitudinal Stability of the CBCL-Juvenile Bipolar Disorder Phenotype: A Study in Dutch Twins." *Biological Psychiatry* 60.9 (2006): 912–20.

Douthit, Kathryn Z. "The Convergence of Counseling and Psychiatric Genetics: An Essential Role for Counselors." *Journal of Counseling & Development* 84.1 (2006): 16–28.

Durston, Sarah, and others. "Activation in Ventral Prefrontal Cortex Is Sensitive to Genetic Vulnerability for Attention-Deficit Hyperactivity Disorder." *Biological Psychiatry* 60.10 (2006): 1062–70.

Farmer, Anne, Amanda Elkin, and Peter McGuffin. "The Genetics of Bipolar Affective Disorder." *Current Opinion in Psychiatry* 20.1 (2007): 8–12.

Giménez-Llort, L., and others. "Modeling Behavioral and Neuronal Symptoms of Alzheimer's Disease in Mice: A

Role for Intraneuronal Amyloid." *Neuroscience & Biobehavioral Reviews* 1.1 (2007): 125–47.

Harris, Julie Aitken, Philip A. Vernon, and Kerry L. Jang. "Rated Personality and Measured Intelligence in Young Twin Children." *Personality and Individual Differences* 42.1 (2007): 75–86.

Hurd, Yasmin L. "Perspectives on Current Directions in the Neurobiology of Addiction Disorders Relevant to Genetic Risk Factors." *CNS Spectrums* 11.11 (2006): 855–62.

Nierenberg, Andrew A., and others. "Family History of Mood Disorder and Characteristics of Major Depressive Disorder: A STAR*D (Sequenced Treatment Alternatives to Relieve Depression) Study." *Journal of Psychiatric Research* 41.3–4 (2007): 214–21.

O'Tuathaigh, Colm M. P., and others. "Susceptibility Genes for Schizophrenia: Characterisation of Mutant Mouse Models at the Level of Phenotypic Behaviour." *Neuroscience & Biobehavioral Reviews* 31.1 (2007): 60–78.

Potter, Alexandra S., Paul A. Newhouse, and David J. Bucci. "Central Nicotinic Cholinergic Systems: A Role in the Cognitive Dysfunction in Attention-Deficit/Hyperactivity Disorder?" *Behavioural Brain Research* 175.2 (2006): 201–11.

Taylor, Warren D., David C. Steffens, and K. Ranga Krishnan. "Psychiatric Disease in the Twenty-First Century: The Case for Subcortical Ischemic Depression." *Biological Psychiatry* 60.12 (2006): 1299–1303.

Rebecca Frey, PhD
Ruth Wineclaw, PhD

Geodon *see* **Ziprasidone**

Geriatric Depression Scale

Definition

The Geriatric **Depression** Scale (GDS) is a 30-item self-report assessment designed specifically to identify depression in the elderly. The items may be answered yes or no, which is thought to be simpler than scales that use a five-category response set. It is generally recommended as a routine part of a comprehensive geriatric assessment. One point is assigned to each answer and corresponds to a scoring grid. A score of 10 or 11 or lower is the usual threshold to separate depressed from nondepressed patients. However, a **diagnosis** of clinical depression should not be made on the GDS results alone. Although the test has well-established reliability and validity, responses should be considered in conjunction with other results from a comprehensive diagnostic work-up. A short version of the GDS containing 15 questions has been developed. The GDS is also available in a number of languages other than English.

Purpose

Depression is widespread among elderly persons, affecting one in six patients treated in general medical practice and an even higher percentage of those in hospitals and nursing homes. Older people have the highest **suicide** rate of any group, and many medical problems common to older people may be related to, or intensified by, a depressive disorder. Recognition of the prevalence of depression among older people prompted the development of the geriatric depression scale in 1982-83. Yes/no responses are thought to be more easily used than the graduated responses found on other standard assessment scales such as the **Beck Depression Inventory**, the Hamilton rating scale for depression, or the Zung self-rating depression scale.

While it is not found in the ***Diagnostic and Statistical Manual of Mental Disorders*** (*DSM-IV-TR*) produced by the American Psychiatric Association, the GDS is widely recommended for clinical use and is included as a routine part of a comprehensive geriatric assessment. It is also increasingly being used in research on depression in the elderly.

Precautions

Depression scales are either interviewer-administered or by self-report means. The GDS is a self-report assessment developed in 1982 by J. A. Yesavitch and colleagues. A self-report assessment is easier and quicker to administer, though an interviewer-administered test is generally more sensitive and specific—another reason for using more than one tool to obtain an accurate diagnosis.

There is some controversy over whether the GDS is reliable for depression screening in individuals with mild or moderate **dementia**. Several studies have shown good agreement with observer ratings of depression, whether or not the patient had dementia. However, persons with dementia may deny symptoms of depression. It also appears that less educated people are more likely to score in the depressed range on the GDS 15-item short form. These caveats notwithstanding, the GDS can be usefully applied in general medical settings in combination with other clinical assessments, observation, and interviews with elder patient and their families.

Both symptom pattern and symptom severity must be considered when trying to identify depression. These dimensions are taken into account in the development of symptom scales and, while clinical judgment takes priority, a scale such as the GDS can help in identifying persons with depression, whether they are making satisfactory progress with treatment, or when they may need further assessment or referral.

Description

Yesavitch and his coworkers chose 100 statements that they determined were related to seven common characteristics of depression in later life. These included:

- somatic concern
- lowered affect (affect is the outward expression of emotion)
- cognitive impairment
- feelings of discrimination
- impaired motivation
- lack of future orientation
- lack of self-esteem

The best 30 items were selected after administration of the 100 items to 46 depressed and normal elders. Those items were then administered to 20 elders without depression and 51 who were in treatment for depression. The test was 84% sensitive and 95% specific for a depression diagnosis. Repeated studies have demonstrated the value of GDS.

Examples of the questions in the GDS include:

- Are you basically satisfied with your life?
- Have you dropped many of your activities and interests?
- Are you hopeful about the future?
- Do you often get restless and fidgety?
- Do you frequently get upset over little things?
- Do you enjoy getting up in the morning?

A time frame should be specified for administration of the test, for example, "Answer these questions by thinking of how you've felt the past two weeks."

Results

A scoring grid accompanies the GDS. One point is given for each respondent's answer that matches those on the grid. For example, the grid response to "Are you basically satisfied with your life?" is "no." If the elderly person responds in the negative one point is scored; if the response is "yes," then no point is scored. For the 30-item assessment, a score of 0–9 is considered normal; 10–19 indicates mild depression, and a score over 20 is suggestive of severe depression. The maximum number of points that can be scored is 30.

See also Depression and depressive disorders.

KEY TERMS

Low affect—Severe lack of interest and emotions; emotional numbness.

Somatic concern—Excessive concern about the body, particularly in relation to illness.

Resources

BOOKS

Gallo, Joseph J., M.D., M.P.H., William Reichel, M.D., and Lillian M. Andersen, R.N., Ed.D. *Handbook of Geriatric Assessment.* 2nd edition. Gaithersburg, MD: Aspen Publishers, Inc., 1995.

Sadavoy, Joel, M.D., F.R.C.P.C., Lawrence W. Lazarus, M.D., Lissy F. Jarvik, M.D., Ph.D., and George T. Grossberg, M.D. eds. *Comprehensive Review of Geriatric Psychiatry-II.* Washington, DC: American Psychiatric Press, Inc., 1997.

PERIODICALS

Reynolds, Charles F. III, M.D., and David J. Kupfer, M.D. "Depression and Aging: A Look to the Future." *Psychiatric Services* 50 (September 1999): 1167-1172.

Yesavage J. A., T. L. Brink, T. L. Rose, O. Lum, V. Huang, M. Adey, and V. O. Leirer. "Development and Validation of a Geriatric Depression Screening Scale: A Preliminary Report." *Journal of Psychiatric Research* 17.1 (1982-83): 37-49.

ORGANIZATIONS

American Association for Geriatric Psychiatry. 7910 Woodmont Ave., Suite 1050, Bethesda, MD, 20814. Telephone: (301) 654-7850. <http://www.aagponline.org>.

Judy Leaver, MA

Gestalt therapy

Definition

Gestalt therapy is a form of **psychotherapy** that helps the client focus on the here and now rather than on the past. Gestalt therapy stresses the development of client self-awareness and personal responsibility.

Purpose

The goal of Gestalt therapy is to raise clients' awareness regarding how they function in their environment; with family, at work or school, and with friends. The focus of therapy is more on what is happening (the moment-to-moment process) than what is being discussed (the content). Awareness is being alert to the most important events in one's life and environment with full sensorimotor, emotional, cognitive, and energy support. Support is defined as anything that makes contact with or withdrawal from the environment possible, including energy, body support, breathing, information, concern for others, and language, for example.

In therapy, clients become aware of what they are doing, how they are doing it, and how they can change themselves, and at the same time, they learn to accept and value themselves. According to this approach, individuals define, develop, and learn about themselves in relationship to others, and they are constantly changing.

Gestalt therapy is "unpredictable" in that the therapist and client follow moment-to-moment experience and neither knows exactly where this will take them. Gestalt therapy is complex and intuitive, but it is based on the following principles:

- Holism. Gestalt therapy takes into account the whole person including thoughts, feelings, behavior, body sensations, and dreams. The focus is on integration, that is, how the many parts of the person fit together, and how the client makes contact (interacts) with the environment.
- Field theory. According to this theory, everything is related, in flux, interrelated, and in process. The therapist focuses on how the client makes contact with the environment (family, work, school, friends, authority figures).
- The figure-formation process describes how individuals organize or manipulate their environment from moment to moment.
- Organismic self-regulation is the creative adjustment the organism (person) makes in relation to the environment. The person's equilibrium with his or her environment is "disturbed" by the emergence of a client need, sensation, or interest and is related to the figure-formation process in that the need of the person organizes the field. For example, if an individual wants coffee, this coffee need is what comes out of the diffuse background and becomes "figural" (comes to the forefront of the client's environment or field) and when the individual enters a room, the figural will be related to the coffee need. The therapist is interested in what is figural for a person because it may provide insight into the person's need(s).
- The Now. The concept of the here and now is what is being done, thought, and felt at the moment, and not in the past or the future.
- Unfinished business is defined as the unexpressed feelings that are associated with distinct memories and fantasies. These feelings may be resentment, rage, hatred, pain, anxiety, grief, guilt, and/or abandonment that are not fully experienced in awareness and linger on in the background. The feelings are carried into the present life and cause preoccupations, compulsive behaviors, wariness, and other self-defeating behaviors. Unfinished business will persist until the person faces and deals with these denied or alienated feelings.

The current practice of Gestalt therapy includes treatment of a wide range of problems and has been successfully used to address a wide range of "psychosomatic" disorders including migraine, ulcerative colitis, and spastic neck and back. Therapists work with couples and families, and with individuals who have difficulties coping with authority figures. In addition, Gestalt therapy has been used for brief **crisis intervention**, to help persons with post-traumatic **stress** disorders, alcohol and drug **abuse**, **depression**, or **anxiety disorders**; with adults in a poverty program; with seriously mentally ill individuals with psychotic disorders; and those with borderline **personality disorders**.

Description

The relationship between the therapist and the client is the most important aspect of psychotherapy in Gestalt therapy. In Gestalt therapy, the interaction between therapist and client is an ever-changing dialogue marked by straightforward caring, warmth, acceptance, and self-responsibility. There are four characteristics of dialogue:

- inclusion, in which the therapist puts him- or herself, as much as is possible, into the experience of the client. The therapist does not judge, analyze, or interpret what he or she observes.
- presence refers to the therapist expressing his or her observations, preferences, feelings, personal experience, and thoughts to the client.
- commitment to dialogue allows a feeling of connection, or contact, between the therapist and the client.
- dialogue is active and can be nonverbal as well as verbal. It can be dancing, song, words, or any modality that expresses and moves the energy between the therapist and the client.

Gestalt therapy holds the view that people are endlessly remaking or discovering themselves; therefore, individuals are always in constant transformation. The therapist's approach is to help clients: increase or deepen their awareness of themselves and their relationships with others, by attending and engaging with the client; to explore the client's experience; and to describe what is perceived. All techniques used within the therapeutic relationship help clients to work through and move beyond painful emotional blocks. This allows the client to explore new behavior, first in the context of the therapeutic relationship and then, as appropriate, in the outside world.

The therapeutic process begins at the first contact between client and therapist. Assessment and screening are usually done as part of the ongoing relationship with the client and not as a separate period of diagnostic testing and history taking. Assessment information is obtained by beginning the therapeutic work and includes the client's willingness and support for work in the Gestalt therapy framework, the match between the client and the therapist, diagnostic and personality information, the decision regarding the frequency of sessions, the need for adjunctive treatment (such as day treatment or **biofeedback** training), and the need for medication and medical consultation.

Gestalt therapists now make use of the traditional diagnostic categories to obtain necessary information to help patients with serious mental illnesses (such as psychotic disorders and borderline disorders) and because of administrative and insurance reimbursement procedures. Despite these changes, it is believed that Gestalt therapy assessment techniques will continue to be varied since Gestalt therapists draw on other therapeutic systems.

In therapy, the Gestalt therapist is active and sessions are lively and characterized by warmth, acceptance, caring, and self-responsibility and promote direct experiencing of a situation or event rather than passively talking about the event. Events recalled from the past are explored and felt in the here and now of the therapy session. Clients receive input from the therapists in many ways: they can see and hear the therapists react; the therapists can tell them how they are seen and what is seen; therapists may share their own feelings and reveal personal information about themselves; and therapists can discuss how client awareness is limited by how the client and therapist interact with or engage each other—that is, make contact.

The Gestalt therapist has a wide range of active interventions (cognitive and behavioral) at his or her disposal and may use any techniques or methods as long as they are (a) aimed toward increasing awareness, (b) arise out of the dialogue and the therapist's perception of what is going on with the client (sensing, feeling, thinking) in the immediate therapy session, and (c) within the parameters of ethical practice.

Exercises and experiments

Many therapeutic interventions called exercises and experiments have been developed to enhance awareness and bring about client change. Exercises are defined as ready-made techniques that are sometimes used to evoke certain emotions (such as the expression of anger) in clients. Experiments, on the other hand, grow out of the immediate interaction (dialogue) between client and therapist. They are spontaneous, one-of-a-kind, and relevant to a particular moment and the particular development of an emerging issue such as the client's reports of a need, dream, fantasy, and body awareness. Experiments are done with full participation and collaboration with clients and are designed to expand clients' awareness and to help them to try out new ways of behaving rather than to achieve a particular result. These experiments may take many forms. According to Gerald Corey, some are: "imagining a threatening future event; setting up a dialogue between a client and some significant person in his and her life; dramatizing the memory of a painful event; reliving a particularly profound early experience in the present; assuming the identity of one's mother or father through role-playing; focusing on gestures, posture, and other nonverbal signs of inner expression; carrying on a dialogue between two conflicting aspects within the person."

While participating in experiments, clients actually experience the feelings associated with their conflicts or issues. Experiments are tailored to each individual client and used in a timely manner; they are to be carried out in a context that offers safety and support while encouraging the client to risk trying out new behavior. The Gestalt therapy focus is on the entire person and all parts—verbal and nonverbal behaviors, emotional feelings—all are attended to.

Gestalt therapists are said to rely on spontaneity, inventiveness, "present-centeredness," and a range of possible therapeutic encounters, interactions that lead to exercises, and experiments are potentially infinite but can be categorized as follows.

USING STATEMENTS AND QUESTIONS TO FOCUS AWARENESS. Many interventions have to do with simply asking what the client is aware of experiencing or asking simple and direct questions as, "What are you feeling?" and "What are you thinking?" The client may be instructed to start a sentence with "Now, I am aware . . ." or asked to repeat a behavior, as in, "Please wring your hands together again." A frequent technique is to follow the client's awareness report with the instruction, "Stay with it!" or "Feel it out!"

CLIENT'S VERBAL BEHAVIOR OR LANGUAGE. Awareness can be enhanced and emphasized through the client's verbal behavior or language since client speech patterns are considered to be an expression of their feelings, thoughts, and attitudes. Some aspects of language that might indicate the clients' avoidance of strong emotions or of self-responsibility are the general pronouns such as "it" and "you." Clients are instructed to substitute, when appropriate, the personal pronoun "I" for these pronouns to assume a sense of responsibility for his or her feelings or thoughts (ownership). Sometimes clients may be asked to change their questions into direct statements in order to assume responsibility for what they say. Other examples of helping clients to be more in control using language are to have them omit qualifiers and disclaimers such as "maybe," "perhaps," or "I guess" from their language patterns. This changes ambivalent and weak statements into more clear and direct statements; to substitute "I won't" for "I can't" because often "can't" gives the feeling of being unable to do something. It may be more accurate to say "I won't" meaning "I choose not to do this for any of various reasons," or use the word, "want" instead of "need" which is considered an indication of urgency and anxiety, and is less accurate. Other changes might be to change "should" and "ought" to "I choose to" or "I want to" increasing the clients' power and control of their lives.

NONVERBAL BEHAVIOR. Awareness can also be enhanced by focusing on nonverbal behavior and may include any technique that makes the clients more aware of their body functioning or helps them to be see how they can use their bodies to support excitement, awareness, and contact. The parts of the body that therapists may attend to include the mouth, jaw, eyes, nose, neck, shoulders, arms, hands, torso, legs, and feet, or the entire body. The therapist, for example, may point out to and explore with the client how he or she is smiling while at the same time expressing anger.

SELF-DIALOGUE. Self-dialogue by clients is an **intervention** used by Gestalt therapists that allows clients to get in touch with feelings that they may be unaware of and, therefore, increase the integration of different parts of clients that do not match or conflicts in clients. Examples of some common conflicts include: "the parent inside versus the child inside," "the responsible one versus the impulsive one," "the puritanical side versus the sexual side," "the good side versus the bad side," "the aggressive self versus the passive self," "the autonomous side versus the resentful side," and "the hard worker versus the goof-off." The client is assisted in accepting and learning to live with his or her polarities and not necessarily getting rid of any one part or trait.

The client is engaged in the self-dialogue by using what is called the empty-chair technique. Using two chairs, the client is asked to take one role (the parent inside, for example) in one chair and then play the other role (the child inside) in the second chair. As the client changes roles and the dialogue continues between both sides of the client he or she moves back and forth between the two chairs. Other examples of situations in which dialogues can be used, according to Corey, include "one part of the body versus the other (one hand versus the other), between a client and another person, or between the self and object such as a building or an accomplishment."

ENACTMENT AND DRAMATIZATION. Enactment increases awareness through the dramatizing of some part of the client's existence by asking him or her to put his or her feelings or thoughts into action, such as instructing the client to "Say it to the person" (when in **group therapy**), or to role-play using the empty chair technique. Exaggeration is a form of enactment in which clients are instructed to exaggerate a feeling, thought, or movement in order to provide more intensity of feelings. Enactment can be therapeutic and give rise to creativity.

GUIDED FANTASY. Guided fantasy (visualization) is a technique some clients are able to use more effectively than using enactment to bring an experience into the here and now. Clients are asked to close their eyes and, with the guidance of the therapist, slowly imagine a scene of the past or future event. More and more details are used to describe the event with all senses and thoughts.

DREAM WORK. Dream work is most important in Gestalt therapy. Working with clients' dreams requires developing a list of all the details of the dream, remembering each person, event, and mood in it and then becoming each of these parts through role-playing and inventing dialogue. Each part of the dream is thought to represent the clients' own contradictory and inconsistent sides. Dialogue between these opposing sides leads clients toward gradual insight into the range of their feelings and important themes in their lives.

AWARENESS OF SELF AND OTHERS. An example of how this technique is used by the Gestalt therapist would be asking the client to "become" another person such as asking the client to be his mother and say what his mother would say if the client came in at 2:00 A.M. This provides more insight for the client rather just asking what the client thinks his mother would say if he came home at 2:00 A.M.

AVOIDANCE BEHAVIORS. Awareness of and the reintegration the client's avoidance behaviors are assisted by the interventions used to increase and enhance awareness of feelings, thoughts, and behaviors.

HOMEWORK. Homework assignments between therapy sessions may include asking clients to write dialogues between parts of themselves or between parts of their bodies, gather information, or do other tasks that are related to and fit with what is going on in the therapy process. Homework may become more difficult as the awareness develops.

Therapy sessions are generally scheduled once a week and individual therapy is often combined with group therapy, marital or **family therapy**, movement therapy, **meditation**, or biofeedback training. Sessions can be scheduled anywhere from once every other week to five times a week and depends on how long the client can go between sessions without loss of continuity or relapsing. Meetings less frequent than once a week are thought to diminish the intensity of the therapy unless the client attends a weekly group with the same therapist. More than twice a week is not usually indicated except with clients who have psychotic disorders, and is contraindicated with those who have a **borderline personality disorder**.

Weekly group therapy may vary from one and one-half hours to three hours in length, with the average length being two hours. A typical group is composed of ten members and usually balanced between males and females. Any age is thought to be appropriate for Gestalt therapy. There are groups for children as well.

Gestalt therapy is considered to have a greater range of styles and modalities than any other therapeutic system, and is practiced in individual therapy, groups, workshops, couples, families, with children, and in agencies such as clinics, family service agencies, hospitals, private practice, growth centers. According to Corey, "The therapeutic style of therapists in each modality vary drastically on many dimensions including degree and type of structure; quantity and quality of techniques used; frequency of sessions, abrasiveness and ease of relating, focus on body, cognitions, feelings; interpersonal contact; knowledge of work within psychodynamic themes; and degree of personal encountering."

Risks

Gestalt therapy is considered to have pioneered the development of many useful and creative innovations in psychotherapy theory and practice. However, there is some concern regarding the abuse of power by the therapist, as well as the high-intensity interaction involved. Therapists who use other techniques can become enchanted with using the techniques of Gestalt therapy without having the appropriate training in Gestalt therapy theory. Gestalt therapists are very active and directive within the therapy session and, therefore, care must be taken that they have characteristics that include sensitivity, timing, inventiveness, empathy, and respect for the client. These characteristics, are dependent on the skill, training, experience, ethics, and judgment of the therapist. In addition, the intensity of the therapy might not be suitable for all patients, and even disruptive for some, despite the competence of the therapist.

Normal results

Gestalt therapists expect that as a result of their involvement in the Gestalt process clients will: have increased awareness of themselves; assume ownership of their experience rather than making others responsible for what they are thinking, feeling, or doing; develop skills and acquire values that will allow them to satisfy their needs without violating the rights of others; become aware of all their senses (smelling, tasting, touching, hearing, and seeing); accept responsibility for their actions and the resulting consequences; move from expectations for external support toward internal self-support; to be able to ask for and get help from others and be able to give to others.

Resources

BOOKS

Blom, Rinda. *The Handbook of Gestalt Play Therapy: Practical Guidelines for Child Therapists*. London: Jessica Kingsley Publishers, 2006.

Corey, Gerald. "Gestalt Therapy." *Theory and Practice of Counseling and Psychotherapy*. 7th.ed. Belmont, CA: Thomson/Brooks/Cole, 2005.

O'Leary, Eleanor. "Breathing and Awareness: The Integrating Mechanisms of Cognitive-Behavioural Gestalt Therapy in Working with Cardiac Patients." In *New Approaches to Integration in Psychotherapy*. Ed. Eleanor O'Leary, and Mike Murphy. New York: Routledge/ Taylor and Francis Group, 2006.

VandenBos, Gary R., ed. *APA Dictionary of Psychology*. Washington, D.C.: American Psychological Association, 2006.

Woldt, Ansel L., and Sarah M. Toman. *Gestalt Therapy: History, Theory, and Practice*. Thousand Oaks, CA: Sage, 2005.

PERIODICALS

Bowman, Deborah, and Tricia A. Leakey. "The Power of Gestalt Therapy in Accessing the Transpersonal: Working with Physical Difference and Disability." *Gestalt Review* 10.1 (2006): 42–59.

Kitzler, Richard. "The Ontology of Action: A Place on Which to Stand for Modern Gestalt Therapy Theory." *International Gestalt Journal* 29.1 (Spring 2006): 43–100.

Miller, Michael Vincent. "Presenting the Present." *International Gestalt Journal* 29.1 (Spring 2006): 135–43.

Wheeler, Gordon. "New Directions in Gestalt Theory and Practice: Psychology and Psychotherapy in the Age of Complexity." *International Gestalt Journal* 29.1 (Spring 2006): 9–41.

Williams, Lynn. "Spirituality and Gestalt: A Gestalt-Transpersonal Perspective." *Gestalt Review* 101 (2006): 6–21.

ORGANIZATIONS

American Psychological Association. 750 First Street, N.E., Washington, DC 20002. Telephone: (202) 336-5800. Web site: <http://helping.apa.org>.

The Association for the Advancement of Gestalt Therapy. 7861 Spring Avenue, Elkins Park, PA 19027. Telephone: (215) 782-1484. Web site: <http://www.aagt.org>.

National Institute of Mental Health. 6001 Executive Boulevard, RM 8184, MSC 9663, Bethesda, MD 20892-9663. Telephone: (301) 443-4513. Web site: <http://www.nimh.nih.gov>.

National Mental Health Association. 1021 Prince Street, Alexandria, VA 22314-2971. Telephone: (703) 684-7722. Web site: <http://www.nmha.org>.

Janice Van Buren, PhD
Ruth A. Wienclaw, PhD

Ginkgo biloba

Definition

Ginkgo biloba is an herbal remedy that has been utilized for thousands of years in China and elsewhere. It is obtained from the leaves and seeds of a plant that is commonly known as the maiden hair tree, believed to be the oldest living species of tree.

Purpose

Ginkgo preparations have been used to treat such conditions as asthma, inflammation, dizziness, memory problems, and circulatory problems throughout the **brain** and body. As of 2002, research has been concentrating on the possibility that Ginkgo biloba may be a helpful adjunct therapy for memory deficits occurring in Alzheimer's disease. Ginkgo is also being explored as a possible treatment for impotence and other circulatory disorders.

Description

Recent research into how Ginkgo biloba affects memory suggests that Ginkgo improves blood flow to the brain by preventing blockages in small blood vessels. These blockages can occur when platelets (blood

Gingko biloba tree with leaves and blossoms. *(Adam Jones/ Photo Researchers, Inc)*

components that aid in clotting) clump together. Ginkgo seems to decrease platelet stickiness, thus preventing clumping.

The active ingredients of Ginkgo biloba appear to include flavone glycosides and terpene lactones. Flavone glycosides have antioxidant properties. They prevent damage to the cells in the brain by chemicals called free radicals. Terpene lactones improve memory by improving the uptake of the neurotransmitter component choline in the nerve synapses. Terpene lactones also help guard against blood clots within the brain, and may provide some protection against metabolic injury. Improved bloodflow throughout the brain seems to help preserve/improve memory.

Ginkgo biloba is available in a variety of forms, including extracts, capsules, and tinctures.

Recommended dosage

As with other herbal supplements, standardization issues sometimes make it difficult to verify the actual dose being administered. In general, efficacious preparations appear to contain at least 24% gingko flavone glycosides and 6% terpene lactones. This is the standardized extract that is commonly used in research about this remedy.

Adults may take between 120 mg and 240 mg of Ginkgo biloba daily, divided into two or three doses.

Precautions

Because of Ginkgo's effects on platelets, there has been some concern regarding interactions between Ginkgo biloba and anticoagulant medicines, such as

PERIODICALS

Zink, Therese, and Jody Chaffin. "Herbal 'Health' Products: What Family Physicians Need to Know." *American Family Physician* (October 1, 1998).

Rosalyn Carson-DeWitt, MD

KEY TERMS

Alzheimer's disease—An incurable dementia marked by the loss of cognitive ability and memory over a period of 10–15 years. Usually affects elderly people.

Anticoagulant—A medication (such as warfarin, Coumadin, or Heparin) that decreases the blood's clotting ability preventing the formation of new clots. Although anticoagulants will not dissolve existing clots, they can stop them from getting larger. These drugs are commonly called blood thinners.

Thiazide diuretic—Also called water pill, helps the body get rid of excess fluids. Examples include diuril, hydrodiuril, and microzide.

warfarin (Coumadin) and aspirin. Studies so far have indicated that Ginkgo does decrease platelet function occasionally. For patients taking Ginkgo, their physician can monitor their platelet function. Rare case reports exist of patients experiencing hemmorhage (including cerebral) while taking Ginkgo.

Side effects

Most reports on Ginkgo biloba suggest that side effects are relatively rare. However, some people may experience stomach upset, including nausea and/or diarrhea. Others who have taken Ginkgo biloba report headache, dizziness, and weakness.

Interactions

To avoid the possibility of increased bleeding, Ginkgo biloba preparations should not be used by patients who are also taking blood thinners (anticoagulants), such as aspirin, warfarin (Coumadin), clopidogrel, dipyridamole, heparin, or ticlopidine.

Ginkgo preparations may interfere with the efficacy of anticonvulsants, such as **carbamazepine** and **valproic acid**.

Caution should be used when taking Ginkgo with thiazide diuretics or with the antidepressant, **trazodone**.

Resources

BOOKS

Blumenthal, Mark, and others, eds. *The Complete German Commission E Monographs: Therapeutic Guide to Herbal Medicines.* Austin: American Botanical Council, 1998.

Ginseng

Definition

Ginseng is an herbal preparation derived from the aromatic root of a plant of the genus *Panax*, which is native to East Asia. Ginseng belongs to the Araliaceae family of plants. Siberian ginseng belongs to a different genus, *Eleutherococcus senticosus*. The English name of the plant is a modification of its Chinese name, *ren shen*, which means "man" and "herb." The Chinese name comes from the ginseng root's resemblance to the shape of the human body, hence the plant's traditional use as a tonic for male sexual vigor and potency. The Latin name for the species, *Panax*, is derived from the Greek word *panacea*, which means "cure-all,"or, "all-healer."

There are three species of ginseng in common use in the United States: American ginseng, Korean ginseng, and Siberian ginseng. All are regarded as adaptogens, that normalize immune functions, and are preparations that help the body adapt to change, thus lowering the risk of stress-related illness. American ginseng, whose botanical name is *Panax quinquefolius*, has recently been evaluated as a treatment for high blood sugar in patients with type 2 (adult-onset) diabetes. It is considered to be less stimulating than the Korean or Siberian varieties. Korean ginseng, or *Panax ginseng*, is the species most often studied in Western as well as Asian trials of botanical preparations. Siberian ginseng, or *Eleutherococcus senticosus*, has been used in Russian sports medicine to boost athletic performance and strengthen the immune system.

Ginseng is one of the most expensive herbs in the world, costing as much as $20 per ounce, or more for red ginseng with the root, which is over 10,000 years old. It is one of the top three herbal products sold in the United States.

Purpose

In traditional Chinese medicine (TCM), ginseng is regarded as having a "sweet" and "neutral" nature. It is thought to have a particular affinity for the spleen and lungs. It is used as an aphrodisiac; a tonic for the spleen, kidney and adrenal functions, and lungs; and a

Ginseng root, a part of the Araliaceae family of plants.
(foodfolio/Alamy)

general restorative for the qi or vital energy in the body. TCM also recommends ginseng for asthma, weak pulse, indigestion, lack of appetite, rectal prolapse, hypertension, diabetes, **insomnia**, angina, congestive heart failure, and heart palpitations. It is important to note that ginseng is an exception to the rule that Chinese herbal medicine rarely uses a single herb in the manner of Western herbalism. Ginseng is often listed as one ingredient among several in Chinese medicines; it is, however, one of the few herbs in TCM that is sometimes prescribed by itself.

In the West, ginseng is frequently advertised as an energy booster, a memory aid, a sexual stimulant, a treatment for impotence and gastrointestinal disorders, and a promoter of longevity. Many Western researchers consider these claims inflated; some studies have found no difference between ginseng and a placebo in terms of the energy levels or general well-being reported by test subjects. Most studies nevertheless have shown improved energy, memory function and performance especially when fatigued, though most of the studies have been short-term. Ginseng's association with the male reproductive system is sufficiently strong that Western feminist herbalists frequently advise women against taking ginseng for any reason.

Description

The part of the ginseng plant that is used medicinally is the root. Ginseng roots are not harvested until the plant is four to six years old. The active ingredients in ginseng root are saponin triterpenoid glycosides, or chemicals commonly called ginsenosides. Other compounds found in Asian ginseng include glycans (pan-

axans); polysaccharide fraction DPG-3-2; peptides; maltol; and volatile oil. The active compounds in Siberian ginseng are called eleutherosides. Eleutherosides are somewhat different from the ginsenosides found in the *Panax* varieties of ginseng. There has been some debate among herbalists whether Siberian ginseng should be considered a true ginseng at all, due to this difference in active ingredients. Ginseng root from any of the three varieties is dried and can then be made into powder, capsules, or a liquid tincture. American ginseng is also available in the United States as whole roots.

Recommended dosages

Dosages of Korean ginseng used in traditional Chinese medicine are given as 2–8 g as a tonic and 15–20 g for acute conditions.

Researchers who studied the potenial effectiveness of ginseng as a treatment for diabetes found that 1–3 g of American ginseng taken 40 minutes before a meal was effective in reducing blood sugar levels. Because dried ginseng root is hard and brittle, it must be simmered for about 45 minutes to extract the ginsenosides. Two to three teaspoonsful of dried root are used per cup. Powder made from American ginseng can be made into tea or taken with water or juice. One-half to one teaspoon is recommended per serving. American ginseng is usually taken two to three times per day between meals.

For Siberian ginseng, the recommended dosage for the powdered form is 1–2 g daily, taken in capsules or mixed with water or juice. The dose should be divided and taken two or three times per day between meals. The recommended dosage for liquid extract of Siberian ginseng is 1–2 mL twice daily.

Precautions

Because ginseng is considered a dietary supplement rather than a drug, it is not regulated by the Food and Drug Administration (FDA). Studies done between 1999 and 2001 found that many ginseng products for sale in the United States contain little or no ginseng. There have been no recent reports of contaminated products.

It is important for patients with Type 2 diabetes who are taking oral prescription medications to lower blood sugar levels to tell their physician if they are using any products containing ginseng. One Chinese-American physician reported several incidents of patients developing hypoglycemia (low blood sugar) from taking ginseng preparations alongside their regular prescription drugs.

People who use ginseng should discontinue it prior to abdominal or dermatologic surgery, or dental extraction. It has been associated with bleeding problems following surgery.

The American Herbal Products Association (AHPA) states that ginseng should not be taken by people with hypertension (high blood pressure). Data suggests variable effects on blood pressure. Some patients experience hypertension and some experience hypotension.

Ginseng should not be given to children. In addition, pregnant or lactating women should not use ginseng, as it may lower estrogen production.

Ginseng should not be used uninterruptedly for long periods of time. In Asian medicine, it is customary to take ginseng for two months and then stop for a full month before taking it again, but the basis for this is uncertain.

Side effects

Ginseng can have serious side effects. The AHPA classifies ginseng as a Class 2d herb, which means that its use is subject to restrictions.

Contemporary Chinese practitioners recognize a condition known as ginseng **abuse** syndrome, caused by taking ginseng incorrectly or excessively. In China, ginseng is almost always used for longevity by people over the age of 60; it is not given to younger people unless they are severely debilitated. Chinese medicine also recommends ginseng for use in winter only; it is not taken year round. The symptoms of ginseng abuse syndrome include include heart palpitations, heaviness in the chest, high blood pressure, dizziness, insomnia, agitation, restlessness, nausea, vomiting, abdominal pain and/or bloating, diarrhea, possible upper digestive tract bleeding, edema, and a red skin rash that is most noticeable on the face. Western herbalists recommend that anyone taking ginseng who develops these symptoms should stop taking the herb at once and contact a licensed practitioner of TCM to determine whether ginseng abuse is the cause of the problem.

A number of case studies involving severe side effects from habitual use of ginseng have been reported in American medical journals. These studies include a case of Stevens-Johnson syndrome (a disorder of the skin and mucosa usually caused by reactions to corticosteroids and a few other systemic drugs) in a Chinese student; a case of cerebral arthritis in a 28-year-old woman following a large dose of ginseng extract; a case of metrorrhagia (uterine hemorrhage)

KEY TERMS

Adaptogen—A remedy that helps the body adapt to change, and thus lowers the risk of stress-related illnesses.

Aphrodisiac—A medication or preparation given to stimulate sexual desire.

Douche—A jet or current of water, often with a medication or cleansing agent dissolved in it, applied to a body cavity for medicinal or hygienic purposes.

Ginseng abuse syndrome—A group of symptoms recognized by Chinese physicians as the result of excessive use of ginseng. The symptoms include dizziness, high blood pressure, restlessness, nausea, possible bleeding from the digestive tract, and skin rashes.

Panacea—A medicine or other substance regarded as a cure for all ills. Ginseng should not be considered a panacea.

Qi—The Chinese term for energy, life force, or vital force.

following two months of steady use of ginseng; and a case of hemorrhagic bleeding from the vagina following habitual use of ginseng douches.

Interactions

Ginseng has been reported to interact with caffeine to cause overstimulation and insomnia in some people. It has also been reported to increase the effects of digoxin, a medication used to treat congestive heart failure; and to interact with **phenelzine**, an antidepressant. Its interactions with phenelzine cause symptoms ranging from manic episodes to headaches. It also may alter the effects of the drug Coumadin, and any anticoagulant therapies.

Resources

BOOKS

Medical Economics staff. *PDR for Herbal Medicines*. Montvale, NJ: Medical Economics Company, 1998.

Pelletier, Kenneth R., MD. "Western Herbal Medicine: Nature's Green Pharmacy." Chapter 6 in *The Best Alternative Medicine*. New York: Simon & Schuster, 2002.

Reid, Daniel P. *Chinese Herbal Medicine*. Boston, MA: Shambhala, 1993.

Sander, Pela. "Natural Healing Therapies." In *Women of the 14th Moon: Writings on Menopause*, edited by Dena

Taylor and Amber Coverdale Sumrall. Freedom, CA: The Crossing Press, 1991.

PERIODICALS

Ang-Lee, Michael K., Jonathan Moss, and Chun-Su Yuan. "Herbal Medicines and Perioperative Care." *Journal of the American Medical Association* 286 (July 11, 2001): 208.

Bone, Kerry. "Safety Issues in Herbal Medicine: Adulteration, Adverse Reactions and Organ Toxicities." *Townsend Letter for Doctors and Patients* (October 2001): 142.

Cardinal, Bradley J., and Hermann-Johann Engels. "Ginseng Does Not Enhance Psychological Well-Being in Healthy, Young Adults: Results of a Double-Blind, Placebo-Controlled, Randomized Clinical Trial." *Journal of the American Dietetic Association* 101 (June 2001): 655–660.

Cheng, Tsung O. "Panax (Ginseng) is Not a Panacea." *Archives of Internal Medicine* 160 (November 27, 2000): 3329.

Flaws, Bob. "Using Ginseng Wisely." *Townsend Letter for Doctors and Patients* (October 2001): 28.

Harkey, Martha R., Gary L. Henderson, M. Eric Gershwin, and others. "Variability in Commercial Ginseng Products: An Analysis of 25 Preparations." *American Journal of Clinical Nutrition* 73 (June 2001): 1101.

Hoffman, R. J., and others. "Life-Threatening Vaginal Hemorrhage Caused by Therapeutic Chinese Ginseng Douche." *Journal of Toxicology: Clinical Toxicology* 39 (April 2001): 313.

Miller, Lucinda G., PharmD. "Herbal Medicinals." *Archives of Internal Medicine* 158 (1998): 2200–2211.

Tyler, Varro E. "Drug-Free Hope for Type 2 Diabetes." *Prevention* 53 (October 2001): 107.

Vuksan, Vladimir, John L. Sievenpiper, Julia Wong, and others. "American Ginseng (*Panax quinquefolius* L.) Attenuates Postprandial Glycemia in a Time-Dependent But Not Dose-Dependent Manner in Healthy Individuals." *American Journal of Clinical Nutrition* 73 (April 2001): 753.

"Watch for Use of Three Herbal Gs in Surgical Patients." *Skin & Allergy News* 32 (October 2001): 9.

OTHER

American Association of Oriental Medicine. 433 Front Street, Catasaqua, PA 18032. Telephone: (610) 266-1433. Fax: (610) 264-2768. <www.aaom.org>.

American Botanical Council. PO Box 144345. Austin, TX 78714-4345. <www.herbalgram.org>.

Herb Research Foundation. 1007 Pearl Street. Suite 200. Boulder, CO 80302. <www.herbs.org>.

National Center for Complementary and Alternative Medicine (NCCAM) Clearinghouse. P.O. Box 7923, Gaithersburg, MD 20898. Telephone: (888) 644-6226. TTY: (866) 464-3615. Fax: (866) 464-3616. <www.nccam.nih.gov>.

Rebecca J. Frey, Ph.D

Grief

Definition

Grief, which is also known as bereavement, is a term used to describe the intense and painful emotions experienced when someone or something a person cares about either dies or is lost. The emotional pain from losing a loved one, whether it is a spouse, child, parent, sibling, friend, or pet, can be the most severe suffering a person must endure. At its most intense, grief can dominate every facet of a person's life, making the carrying out of ordinary responsibilities impossible. Loss and subsequent grief, however, are an inevitable part of life and loving other people or companion animals. Painful as it is, grief is a normal response to loss and generally resolves with the passage of time.

Description

Grief is usually characterized by numbness, tearfulness, physical feelings of emptiness in the pit of the stomach, weak knees, shortness of breath, a tendency to sigh deeply, a sense of unreality, and overall emotional distress. **Anxiety** and longing may alternate with **depression** and despair. **Insomnia** and loss of appetite are common. Initially, people often feel numb and unable to accept their loss. Numbness is followed by shock as reality begins to penetrate.

There is generally a disorganization of normal behavior patterns that may make it impossible for a bereaved person to return to work immediately or take social initiatives. Such acute symptoms usually begin to subside after several months, with emotional balance being regained within a year. Studies using instruments developed to measure symptoms of grief and bereavement demonstrate wide individual variations in specific symptoms and their intensity. Long after the immediate period of mourning, bereaved persons may continue to feel upset, empty, or tearful. In addition, further losses, additional stressors, or dates of such important anniversaries as a wedding, birthday, or the date of death can reactivate the acute symptoms of grief.

Dimensions of grief

Grief and mourning are important life experiences in that they permit a bereaved person to accept the reality of loss and begin to find ways of filling the resultant emptiness. Loss is a significant part of the aging process and can contribute to emotional problems in older people. The impact of loss and

ELISABETH KÜBLER-ROSS (1926–2004)

Swiss-born American psychiatrist Elisabeth Kübler-Ross dedicated her career to a topic that had previously been avoided by many physicians and mental-health care professionals–the psychological state of the dying. In her counseling of and research on dying patients, Kübler-Ross determined that individuals go through five distinct mental stages when confronted with death, a discovery that has helped other counselors to provide more appropriate advice and treatment to their clients. Her ideas have been presented to the public in a number of popular texts, including her groundbreaking 1969 work, *On Death and Dying*. She also offered instruction and treatment at the seminars and healing centers she ran for the terminally ill and their caretakers.

resulting grief and mourning is not limited to the death of a loved one. It is also present to a lesser extent in the loss of physical acuity and agility and the loss of social of status as a result of retirement and/or growing older.

Unfortunately, people in the United States do not generally receive cultural support for the losses they experience and the need to mourn those losses. Unlike other cultures with specific rituals for grief and mourning, there is often subtle but insistent pressure on Americans—particularly males—to stop crying and move forward with resumption of regular activities. Onlookers may try to divert the mourner's attention to other topics or discourage crying or talking about the loved one. These responses suggest that grief is not healthy or that it should be minimized or avoided. If the grief is associated with the loss of a pet, the person may be shamed for grieving because "it was just an animal." Women who have had a pregnancy ended by miscarriage also encounter responses that minimize or trivialize the loss of their expected child. Social insensitivity may drive the mourner to grieve in secret or feel guilty because of continued intense feelings of loss.

Stages of grief

Elizabeth Kübler-Ross, the noted researcher on death and dying, identified five stages of acceptance in the process of dying. While her work initially referred to the person who is dying, the five stages are also applied to people who are grieving a loss. The stages

are sometimes collapsed into three, but the general grieving process includes these components:

- Shock/denial. This stage comprises the initial period after receiving news of the loss. The affected person may say, "There must be a mistake," "This can't be true," or similar expressions of disbelief. People often describe feeling numb or cold in this stage.
- Bargaining. This stage represents an attempt to persuade God or a higher power to change the reality of loss in exchange for improved behavior or some sacrifice on the part of the bereaved person. The mourner may offer, for example, to take better care of their relationship with the loved one if God will only bring them back.
- Anger. This emotion may be directed toward the medical establishment, family members, God, or even the person who has died.
- Depression. In this stage, the person's body begins to absorb the reality of the loss. The bereaved person may be unable to eat, sleep, or talk normally with people. They may have episodes of spontaneous crying and such physical symptoms as nausea, headaches, chills or trembling.
- Acceptance. This is the phase in which the mourner comes to terms with the loss and begins to look ahead once more. Energy returns and the bereaved person is able to reconnect with others, engage in enjoyable activities, and make plans for the future.

There is, however, no "normal" pattern for grief; it is a highly variable experience. People pass through the stages outlined by Kübler-Ross at their own rate, depending on the significance of the loss, number of previous losses, individual resiliency, presence of a support system, and permission to grieve from those around them. Grieving is not a linear process. There is movement back and forth between the stages until acceptance is reached. Occasionally, a person may remain "stuck" in one stage, particularly anger or depression, and may benefit from professional help in order to move on. Remaining in one of the stages indefinitely can create emotional and occupational difficulties.

Bereavement and marriage

Studies show that some widowed people have **hallucinations** or **delusions** of contact with the lost spouse that may last for years. These hallucinations are more likely to occur in people who were happily married. The most common hallucination reported is a sense of the dead spouse's presence. Others report seeing, hearing, or being touched by or spoken to by the spouse.

The interplay of grief and marital quality has led to research findings that contradict earlier widespread beliefs. A study by Deborah Carr and her colleagues in 2000 found that anxiety was greater in those who had been highly dependent on their spouses than in those who were less dependent. People who had been in conflicted relationships reported lower levels of yearning for the spouse than those who had enjoyed high levels of marital closeness. Women who had relied on their husbands to do the driving and perform other similar tasks had much higher levels of yearning than men who depended on their wives. This finding contradicts the common belief that grief is more severe if the marriage was conflicted, suggesting a more complex relationship between bereavement and characteristics of the marriage.

Another suggestion of the complex relationship between bereavement and marriage is reflected in studies of sudden and anticipated loss among older widowed people. The sudden death of a spouse was associated with slightly higher levels of yearning among women, but significantly lower yearning among men. Forewarning of the death (extended illness, advancing age) did not affect depression, anger, shock or overall grief six or 18 months after the loss. Prolonged forewarning was associated with increased anxiety at six and 18-month follow-up interviews after the death.

Grief and mourning may also occur when the loss of a partner occurs through divorce or the end of a dating relationship. Some researchers think that moving to the stage of acceptance is more difficult in such cases because the partner can still be contacted, especially if there are children involved. Seeing a former partner involved in a new relationship can cause the partner mourning the loss to re-experience acute symptoms of grief. Some research evidence suggests that grief related to the breakup of an intimate relationship is more intense for the individual who was left behind than for the person who ended the relationship.

Grieving may be particularly prolonged and intense when certain unexpected losses occur that are outside the ordinary progression of life events. The loss of a parent before a child reaches adulthood or a parent's loss of a child inflict deep emotional wounds for an extended period of time. Similarly, the loss of a loved one to murder, terrorism, or other acts of intentional violence is harder to bear than death resulting from natural causes or accidents. Death from **suicide** complicates grief by adding shame to the other painful emotions associated with bereavement. The opportunity to fully grieve such significant losses, however, enables survivors to move forward despite the magnitude of their loss.

See also Adjustment disorder; Bereavement; Suicide.

Resources

BOOKS

Butler, Robert N., Myrna I. Lewis, and Trey Sunderland. *Aging and Mental Health.* 5th edition. Boston: Allyn and Bacon, 1998.

Harris, Maxine, Ph.D. *The Loss That Is Forever: The Lifelong Impact of the Early Death of a Mother or Father.* New York: Dutton, 1995.

Kubler-Ross, Elizabeth, and David Kessler. *Life Lessons.* New York: Simon and Schuster and the Elizabeth Kubler-Ross Family Partnership, Ltd. 2000.

Vaughan, Diane, Ph.D. *Uncoupling: Turning Points in Intimate Relationships.* New York: Oxford University Press, 1986.

PERIODICALS

Carr, Deborah, James S. House, Ronald C. Kessler, Randolph M. Nesse, John Sonnega, and Camille Wortman. "Marital Quality and Psychological Adjustment to Widowhood Among Older Adults." *Journals of Gerontology Series B: Psychological Sciences and Social Sciences* 55 (2000): S197-S207.

Carr, Deborah, James S. House, Camille Wortman, Randolph Nesse, and Ronald C. Kessler. "Psychological Adjustment to Sudden and Anticipated Spousal Loss Among Older Widowed Persons." *Journals of Gerontology Series B: Psychological Sciences and Social Sciences* 56 (2001): S237-S248.

Zisook, S., R. A. Devaul, and M. A. Click Jr. "Measuring Symptoms of Grief and Bereavement." *American Journal of Psychiatry* 139 (1982): 1590-1593.

ORGANIZATIONS

The Compassionate Friends, Inc. P.O. Box 3696, Oak Brook, IL 60522. <http://wwwcompassionatefriends.org>.

GROWW (Grief Recovery Online [founded by] Widows & Widowers). 931 N. State Road 434, Suite 1201-358, Altamonte Springs, FL 32714. <http://www.groww.org>.

Judy Leaver, MA

Grief counseling

Definition

Grief counseling refers to a specific form of therapy, or a focus in general counseling with the goal of helping the individual grieve and address personal loss in a healthy manner. Grief counseling is offered individually by psychologists, clergy, counselors or **social workers**, in groups led by professionals, as well as informal **support groups** offered by churches, community groups, or organizations devoted to helping individuals grieve specific losses.

Specific tasks of grief counseling include emotional expression about the loss (which can include a wide range of feelings), accepting the loss, adjusting to life after the loss, and coping with the changes within oneself and the world after the loss. Typical feelings experienced by individuals, and addressed in grief counseling, include sadness, **anxiety**, anger, loneliness, guilt, relief, isolation, confusion, or numbness. Behavioral changes may also be noticed, such as being disorganized, feeling tired, having trouble concentrating, sleep problems, appetite changes, vivid dreams, or daydreaming about the deceased.

Purpose

The purpose of grief counseling is to help individuals work through the feelings, thoughts, and memories associated with the loss of a loved one. Although grieving can occur for other types of loss as well (such as loss of goals, ideals, and relationships), grief counseling is generally directed toward positive adjustment following loss after the death of a loved one.

Grief counseling helps the individual recognize normal aspects of the grieving or mourning process, cope with the pain associated with the loss, feel supported through the anxiety surrounding life changes that may follow the loss, and develop strategies for seeking support and self-care.

Precautions

Grieving is a normal life process—an adjustment reaction to a loss. Grief counseling is meant to facilitate that normal process. No specific precautions are warranted. However, there are certain circumstances in which complications to the normal grieving process may occur. These circumstances may involve the loss of a child, or the loss of a loved one due to an accident or homicide, for example.

In these cases of complicated grieving, more extreme responses to the loss may be observed, depending on the individual's capacity for coping, personal resiliency, and support system. For example, if the individual feels isolated, he may be at greater risk for severe depressive symptoms or a **suicide** attempt. Alternatively, if the survivors feel rage or anger over the loss, there may be a risk of harm to others.

Description

Grief counseling helps the individual work through the feelings associated with the loss of another, accept that loss, determine how life can go on without that person, and consolidate memories in order to be able to move forward. Grief counseling also provides informa-

tion about the normal grieving process, to help individuals understand that many of the symptoms and changes they are experiencing are a normal, temporary reaction to loss. For some individuals, the primary focus of grief counseling is to help identify ways to express feelings about the loss that the person has been unable to express on his or her own. Individuals who seek grief counseling may be experiencing an emotional numbness, or a residual shock in reaction to the loss, and need assistance to return to a normal life. In those cases, grief counseling will focus on helping the individual get in touch with those feelings and become more active in the daily routine. This often requires accepting the loss as a reality.

For some people, grieving may initially be so extreme that physical and psychological symptoms may be experienced, while other people appear to experience no symptoms whatsoever, similar to the numbness described above. Activities of daily living may feel overwhelming to an individual who has experienced a loss. In these cases, grief counseling may focus on specific coping skills to help the individual resume some normalcy in his or her daily routine. For example, if sleep patterns are disrupted, grief counseling may include consultation with the individual's physician to assist with temporary strategies to increase sleep. If the individual is having trouble getting to work on time, behavioral strategies may be used as an interim measure to help the person return to aspects of normal daily life.

Additional work in grief counseling may involve identifying ways to let go or say good-bye if the individual has not been able to do so successfully. Therapeutic letters may be a helpful mechanism to express thoughts that were not conveyed prior to the death. Dreams are frequently experienced by survivors, and these can be a focus in grief counseling as well. The dreams can often be a way of consolidating the memories about the deceased.

Preparation

No specific preparation is required by the participant; however, a need for grief counseling is indicated by prolonged symptoms (such as crying spells, preoccupation with the deceased, lack of motivation, or suicidal thoughts), and the severity of personal distress over the loss. A patient seeking grief counseling would most likely undergo a clinical evaluation by a therapist, before the grief counseling began, so that the therapist could understand the patient's personal history and goals for treatment.

Aftercare

Aftercare is usually provided through informal support systems, which may include family and friends, as well as support groups.

Risks

A slight risk exists regarding treatment of complicated grief. Such circumstances include chronic, prolonged grieving or unexpected loss (particularly due to a violent accident, suicide, homicide, or the death of a child). These factors complicate the grieving process due to the unexpected, sometimes violent nature of the loss, that feels inconsistent with expectations and desires for loved ones. In these cases, an initial adverse effect may be seen from participation in treatment, due to the increased focus on the loss. This reaction improves over time, as adjustment is facilitated. Two other factors impacting individual adjustment include the type of relationship the individual had with the deceased, and the resiliency of the individual.

Normal results

Normal results from grief counseling include being able to move on with one's life, recognizing and accepting the physical loss of the individual, and being able to bridge that loss with positive memories of the deceased. Successful coping will be characterized by a return to normal routines, although some symptoms may be experienced periodically throughout the year or so following the loss.

Abnormal results

Abnormal results would include an unsuccessful outcome of prolonged grief, exhibited by continued preoccupation with the loss of the individual, crying spells, and depressive symptoms being the most likely complications. Some disruption of the daily routine would persist, and there may be extreme emotional responses, that could include no apparent reaction to difficulty containing feelings. Other complications include "unfinished business," or feelings of unresolved issues with the deceased. Sometimes the feelings of unresolved issues can be as simple as wishing they had communicated their love and affection for the person the last time they saw them, or may be as complicated as unresolved feelings about a history of abuse by the deceased.

See also Creative therapies; Support groups.

> ## KEY TERMS
>
> **Therapeutic letter**—A letter written to the deceased in order to help the survivors express feelings and thoughts they may not have been able to before the loss.

Resources

BOOKS

Coor, C. A., and D. E. Balk, eds. *Handbook of Adolescent Death and Bereavement*. New York, NY: Springer Publishing Co., Inc., 1996.

Volkan, V.D., and E. Zintl. *Life After Loss: The Lessons of Grief*. Charles Scribner's Sons: New York, NY, 1993.

PERIODICALS

Beem, E. E., H. Hooijkaas, M. Cleiren, H. Schut, B. Garssen, M. Croon, L. Jabaaij, K. Goodkin, H. Wind, and M. de Vries. "The immunological and psychological effects of bereavement: Does grief counseling really make a difference?" *Psychiatry Ressearch* 85.1 (Jan. 1999): 81-93.

ORGANIZATIONS

The Compassionate Friends. P. O. Box 3696, Oak Brook, IL 60522. Telephone: (630) 990-0010. <http://www.compassionatefriends.org>.

SHARE Pregnancy and Infant Loss Support. St. Joseph Health Center, 300 First Capital Drive, St. Charles, MO 63301. Telephone: (800) 821-6819.

SIDS Alliance. 1314 Bedford Ave., Suite 230, Baltimore, MD 21208. Telephone: (800) 221-SIDS. <http://www.sidsalliance.org>.

Widowed Persons Service, AARP. 601 E. Street, NW, Washington, DC 20049. Telephone: (202) 434-2260.

Deanna Pledge, PhD

Group homes

Definition

Group homes are small, residential facilities located within a community and designed to serve children or adults with chronic disabilities. These homes usually have six or fewer occupants and are staffed 24 hours a day by trained caregivers.

Description

Most group homes are standard, single-family houses, purchased by group home administrators and adapted to meet the needs of the residents. Except for any adaptive features such as wheelchair ramps, group homes are virtually indistinguishable from other homes in the surrounding neighborhood. Group homes may be located in neighborhoods of any socioeconomic status.

Residents of group homes usually have some type of chronic mental disorder that impairs their ability to live independently. Many residents also have physical disabilities such as impairments of vision communication, or ambulation. These individuals require continual assistance to complete daily living and self-care tasks. Some also require supervision due to behavior that may be dangerous to self or others, such as aggression or a tendency to run away.

Although most group homes provide long-term care, some residents eventually acquire the necessary skills to move to more independent living situations. Group homes for children are usually temporary placements, providing care until a foster family can be secured. Others may return to their natural families. Occasionally, halfway homes for people recently released from prison or discharged from a **substance abuse** program may also be referred to as group homes. These types of group homes are also transitory in nature.

History and mission

The development of group homes occurred in response to the **deinstitutionalization** movement of the 1960s and 1970s. As psychiatric hospitals closed, discharged individuals needed places to live. Group homes were designed to provide care in the least restrictive environment and to integrate individuals with disabilities into the community, reducing **stigma** and improving quality of life. The environment of a group home was intended to simulate typical family life as much as possible.

Since the passage of the **Community Mental Health** Centers Act in 1963, grants have been available to group homes. State and federal funds such as the Medicaid Home and Community-Based Waiver continue to support the majority of group homes. However, some homes operate on donations from private citizens or civic and religious organizations. Most group homes are owned by private rather than governmental organizations, and can be either nonprofit or for-profit organizations. Group homes are considered more cost effective compared to institutional care. Unfortunately, the number of available group homes has not always matched need, resulting in **homelessness** or re-hospitalization for some individuals.

One of the goals of group home living is to increase the independence of residents. Group home staff members teach residents daily living and self-care skills, providing as little assistance as possible. Daily living skills include meal preparation, laundry, housecleaning, home maintenance, money management, and appropriate social interactions. Self-care skills include bathing or showering, dressing, toileting, eating, and taking prescribed medications.

Staff also assure that residents receive necessary services from community service providers, including medical care, physical therapy, occupational therapy, vocational training, education, and mental health services. Most group home residents are assigned a case manager from a community mental health center or other government agency who oversees their care. Case managers review group home documentation regarding skills learned and services received, and make recommendations for adjustments in care.

The NIMBY phenomenon

Unfortunately, group homes have received much opposition from communities. NIMBY (acronym for Not In My Backyard) describes the common reaction of community residents when they discover that a group home is targeted for their neighborhood. Current research suggests that protests frequently involve concerns over personal security, declining property values, or a generalized threat to the neighborhood's quality. Some researchers believe that prejudiced attitudes such as ignorance, fear, and distrust are the true reasons for protest.

Usually, neighborhood opposition is unsuccessful due to provisions of the Fair Housing Act of 1968. However, such opposition can be detrimental to the goal of integrating residents into the community. The NIMBY phenomenon is also a concern because as deinstitutionalization continues, the need for additional group homes increases. Statistics show that between 1987 and 1999, the use of group homes serving individuals with developmental disabilities and containing six residents or less increased by 240%.

Social service workers are constantly looking for ways to address the NIMBY phenomenon. Some research has suggested that community concerns decrease with time as community members become familiar with group home residents. A recent study proposed that opposition can be decreased by providing advanced notice of plans for a group home, as well as adequate information and discussion about expectations.

Factors affecting group home success

Initially, many people were skeptical about the adequacy of group home care compared to psychiatric hospitals or other institutions. Over the past 25 years,

KEY TERMS

Ambulation—Ability to walk.

Case manager—A professional who designs and monitors implementation of comprehensive care plans (i.e., services addressing medical, financial, housing, psychiatric, vocational, social needs) for individuals seeking mental health or social services.

Community mental health centers—Organizations that manage and deliver a comprehensive range of mental health services, education, and outreach to residents of a given community.

Community Mental Health Centers Act of 1963—Federal legislation providing grants for the operation of community mental health centers and related services.

Deinstitutionalization—The process of moving people out of mental hospitals into treatment programs or halfway houses in local communities. With this movement, the responsibility for care shifted from large (often governmental) agencies to families and community organizations.

Fair Housing Act of 1968—Federal legislation regarding access to housing that prohibits discrimination based on race, color, national origin, sex, religion, disability, or familial status.

Least restrictive environment—Refers to care options that involve the least amount of restraint and the greatest degree of independence possible, while still meeting the individual's needs and maintaining safety.

Medicaid Home and Community Based-Waiver—Legislation regarding the use of Medicaid funds for care services; allows certain federal requirements to be bypassed so that states can use the funds more flexibly for accessing home- and community-based services rather than using hospitals or intermediate-care facilities.

NIMBY phenomenon—Acronym for Not In My Backyard, describing the common opposition displayed by citizens toward the placement of group homes or other social service facilities in their neighborhoods.

Non-ambulatory—Unable to walk.

---

many studies have examined the impact of group home care on residents. These studies have consistently shown increases in adaptive behavior, productivity, community integration, and level of independence.

Risks involved in successfully transitioning an individual to a group home include psychological deterioration such as severe cognitive or physical impairments, physical deterioration that includes being non-ambulatory, or mortality issues such as being age 70 or older.

Before considering group home placement—especially for those in the high risk category—extensive planning should be conducted. A complete assessment plan of the individual's needs should specify which agency will be responsible for meeting medical needs, particularly in the event of a crisis. The individual's strengths should be incorporated into the plan whenever possible. For example, if a supportive family is an identified strength, the preferred group home should be close in proximity to facilitate family visits.

Other factors that contribute to group home success are a small staff-to-resident ratio, well-trained staff, and a home-like atmosphere. As with any type of organization, some group homes are better run than

others. A careful investigation into a home's procedures is recommended. Research suggests that individuals with severe cognitive impairments often experience a period of disorientation, and may need additional support or supervision for the first few months while adjusting to their new surroundings. Pre-placement visits and discussion can reduce **anxiety** for the future resident.

See also Case management.

Resources

BOOKS

Robinson, Julia W., and Travis Thompson. "Stigma and Architecture." In *Enabling Environments: Measuring the Impact of Environment on Disability and Rehabilitation,* edited by Edward Steinfeld and G. Scott Danford. New York: Kluwer Academic/Plenum Publishers, 1999.

Udell, Leslie. "Supports in Small Group Home Settings." In *Dementia, Aging, and Intellectual Disabilities: A Handbook,* edited by Matthew P. Janicki and Arthur J. Dalton. Philadelphia: Brunner/Mazel, Inc., 1999.

PERIODICALS

Anderson, George M. "Of Many Things." *America* 185, no. 8 (2001): 2.

Anderson, Lynda, Robert Prouty, and K. Charlie Lakin. "Parallels in Size of Residential Settings and Use of Medicaid-Financed Programs." *Mental Retardation* 38.5 (2000): 468-471.

Ducharme, Joseph M., Larry Williams, Anne Cummings, Pina Murray, and Terry Spencer. "General Case Quasi-Pyramidal Staff Training to Promote Generalization of Teaching Skills in Supervisory and Direct-Care Staff." *Behavior Modification* 25.2 (2001): 233-254.

Kim, Dong Soo. "Another Look at the NIMBY Phenomenon." *Health & Social Work* 25.2 (2000): 146-148.

Piat, Myra. "The NIMBY Phenomenon: Community Residents' Concerns About Housing for Deinstitutionalized People." *Health & Social Work* 25.2 (2000): 127-138.

Rauktis, Mary Elizabeth. "The Impact of Deinstitutionalization on the Seriously and Persistently Mentally Ill Elderly: A One-Year Follow-Up." *Journal of Mental Health and Aging* 7.3 (2001): 335-348.

Spreat, Scott, and James W. Conroy. "Community Placement for Persons with Significant Cognitive Challenges: An Outcome Analysis." *The Journal of the Association for Persons with Severe Handicaps* 26.2 (2001): 106-113.

Whittaker, James K. "The Future of Residential Group Care." *Child Welfare* 79.1 (2000): 59-74.

ORGANIZATIONS

Child Welfare League of America-Headquarters. 440 First Street, NW, Third Floor, Washington, DC 20001-2085. Telephone: (202) 638-2952. < http://cwla.org>.

National Institute of Mental Health. 600 Executive Boulevard, Room 8184, MSC 9663, Bethesda, Maryland 20892-9663. Telephone: (301) 443-4513. <http://www.nimh.nih.gov>.

Office of Fair Housing and Equal Opportunity. Room 5116, Department of Housing and Urban Development, 451 Seventh Street, SW, Washington, DC 20410-2000. Telephone: (202) 708-2878. <http://www.hsh.com>.

The ARC National Headquarters. 1010 Wayne Avenue, Suite 650, Silver Spring, Maryland 20910. Telephone: (301) 565-3842. <http://www.thearc.org>.

Sandra L. Friedrich, MA

Group therapy

Definition

Group therapy is a form of **psychotherapy** in which a small, carefully selected group of individuals meets regularly with a therapist.

Purpose

The purpose of group therapy is to assist each individual in emotional growth and personal problem solving.

Description

Group therapy encompasses many different kinds of groups with varying theoretical orientations that exist for varying purposes. All therapy groups exist to help individuals grow emotionally and solve personal problems. All use the power of the group, as well as the therapist who leads it, in this process.

Unlike the simple two-person relationship between patient and therapist in individual therapy, group therapy offers multiple relationships to assist the individual in growth and problem solving. The noted **psychiatrist** Dr. Irvin D. Yalom in his book *The Theory and Practice of Group Therapy* identified 11 "curative factors" that are the "primary agents of change" in group therapy.

Instillation of hope

All patients come into therapy hoping to decrease their suffering and improve their lives. Because each member in a therapy group is inevitably at a different point on the coping continuum and grows at a different rate, watching others cope with and overcome similar problems successfully instills hope and inspiration. New members or those in despair may be particularly encouraged by others' positive outcomes.

Universality

A common feeling among group therapy members, especially when a group is just starting, is that of being isolated, unique, and apart from others. Many who enter group therapy have great difficulty sustaining interpersonal relationships and feel unlikable and unlovable. Group therapy provides a powerful antidote to these feelings. For many, it may be the first time they feel understood and similar to others. Enormous relief often accompanies the recognition that they are not alone, a special benefit of group therapy.

Information giving

An essential component of many therapy groups is increasing members' knowledge and understanding of a common problem. Explicit instruction about the nature of their shared illness, such as bipolar disorders, **depression**, panic disorders, or bulimia, is often a key part of the therapy. Most patients leave the group far more knowledgeable about their specific condition than when they entered, making them increasingly able to help others with the same or similar problems.

ABRAHAM H. MASLOW (1908–1970)

Abraham H. Maslow, founder of humanistic psychology, was born in Brooklyn, N.Y. Maslow received his M.A. from the University of Wisconsin in 1931, and his Ph.D. in 1934. In his most important work, *Motivation and Personality* (1954), Maslow did not repudiate classical psychology; rather, he attempted to enlarge upon its conception of personality by stressing man's higher nature. In contrast to "the analytic-dissecting-atomistic-Newtonian approach" of behaviorism and Freudian psychoanalysis, it emphasized the holistic character of human nature. It defined and explained "the need hierarchy," "self-actualization," and "peak experiences," phrases that have become part of the vocabulary of psychologists.

In 1967, Maslow was named humanist of the year by the American Humanist Association. That same year he was elected president of the American Psychological Association. He also played a major role in organizing both the Journal of Humanistic Psychology and the Journal of Transpersonal Psychology. At the time of his death he was a resident fellow at the Laughlin Foundation in California.

Like the early humanists, he emphasized the inherent goodness in people. Maslow viewed humans as exercising a high degree of conscious control over their lives and as having a high resistance to pressures from the environment. He viewed personality development as the process of breaking the chains binding an individual to the animal world and building a more human world.

Maslow's theories have had a major impact upon practicing psychologists because of his ideas' direct, personal, and subjective plausibility. Synanon, the drug-addiction rehabilitation center, and the Esalen Institute, one of the best-known centers for practicing group-encounter psychotherapy, make use of Maslow's ideas, but the need hierarchy and other popular conceptions have had little influence on psychological research. Maslow was a global theorist who tested his ideas imprecisely and nonquantitatively. He believed that his theories could never be tested in an animal laboratory or test tube but that they required "a life situation of the total human being in his social environment."

Altruism

Group therapy offers its members a unique opportunity: the chance to help others. Often patients with psychiatric problems believe they have very little to offer others because they have needed so much help themselves, and thus feel inadequate. The process of helping others is a powerful therapeutic tool that greatly enhances self-esteem and feelings of self-worth.

Corrective recapitulation of the primary family

Many people who enter group therapy had troubled family lives during their formative years. The group becomes a substitute family that resembles—and improves upon—the family of origin in significant ways. Like a family, a therapy group consists of a leader (or coleaders), an authority figure who evokes feelings similar to those felt toward parents. Other group members substitute for siblings, vying for attention and affection from the leader/parent, and forming subgroups and coalitions with other members. This recasting of the family of origin gives members a chance to correct dysfunctional interpersonal relationships in a way that can have a powerful therapeutic impact.

Improved social skills

According to Yalom, social learning, or the development of basic social skills, is a therapeutic factor that occurs in all therapy groups. Some groups place considerable emphasis on improving social skills, for example, with adolescents preparing to leave a psychiatric hospital, or among bereaved or divorced members seeking to date again. Group members offer feedback to one another about the appropriateness of the others' behavior. Although this may be painful, the directness and honesty with which it is offered can provide much-needed behavioral correction and thus improve relationships both within and outside the group.

Imitative behavior

Research shows that therapists exert a powerful influence on the communication patterns of group members by **modeling** certain behaviors. For example, therapists model active listening, giving nonjudgmental feedback, and offering support. Over time, members pick up these behaviors and incorporate them. This earns them increasingly positive feedback from others, enhancing their self-esteem and emotional growth.

Interpersonal learning

Humans are social animals, born ready to connect. Our lives are characterized by intense and persistent relationships, and much of our self-esteem is developed via feedback and reflection from important others. Yet we all develop distortions in the way we see others, and these distortions can damage even our most important relationships. Therapy groups provide an opportunity for members to improve their ability to relate to others and live far more satisfying lives because of it.

Group cohesiveness

Belonging, acceptance, and approval are among the most important and universal of human needs. Fitting in with our peers as children and adolescents, pledging a sorority or fraternity as young adults, and joining a church or other social group as adults all fulfill these basic human needs. Many people with emotional problems, however, have not experienced success as group members. For them, group therapy may make them feel truly accepted and valued for the first time. This can be a powerful healing factor as individuals replace their feelings of isolation and separateness with a sense of belonging.

Catharsis

Catharsis is a powerful emotional experience—the release of conscious or unconscious feelings—followed by a feeling of great relief. Catharsis is a factor in most therapies, including group therapy. It is a type of emotional learning, as opposed to intellectual understanding, that can lead to immediate and long-lasting change. Although catharsis cannot be forced, a group environment provides ample opportunity for members to have these powerful experiences.

Existential factors

Existential factors are certain realities of life including death, isolation, freedom, and meaninglessness. Becoming aware of these realities can lead to **anxiety**. The trust and openness that develop among members of a therapy group, however, permits exploration of these fundamental issues and can help members develop an acceptance of difficult realities.

History of group therapy

Group therapy in the United States can be traced back to the late nineteenth and early twentieth centuries, when millions of immigrants moved to American shores. Most of these immigrants settled in large cities, and organizations such as Hull House in Chicago were founded to assist them adjust to life in the United States. Known as settlement houses, these agencies helped immigrant groups lobby for better housing, working conditions, and recreational facilities. These early social work groups valued group participation, the democratic process, and personal growth.

In 1905 a Boston physician named Joseph Pratt formed groups of impoverished patients suffering from a common illness—tuberculosis. Pratt believed that these patients could provide mutual support and assistance. Like settlement houses, his early groups were another forerunner of group therapy.

Some early psychoanalysts, especially Alfred Adler, a student of Sigmund Freud, believed that many individual problems were social in origin. In the 1930s Adler encouraged his patients to meet in groups to provide mutual support. At around the same time social work groups began forming in mental hospitals, child guidance clinics, prisons, and public assistance agencies. A contemporary descendent of these groups is today's support group, in which people with a common problem come together, without a leader or therapist, to help each other solve common problems. Groups such as Alcoholics Anonymous, Narcotics Anonymous, and Survivors of Incest all have their roots in this early social work movement.

Types of therapy groups

PSYCHODYNAMIC THERAPIES. Psychodynamic theory was conceived by Sigmund Freud, the father of **psychoanalysis**. Freud believed that unconscious psychological forces determine thoughts, feelings, and behaviors. By analyzing the interactions among group members, psychodynamic therapies focus on helping individuals become aware of their unconscious needs and motivations as well as the concerns common to all group members. Issues of authority (the relationship to the therapist) and affection (the relationships among group members) provide rich sources of material that the therapist can use to help group members understand their relationships and themselves.

PHENOMENOLOGICAL THERAPIES. Until the 1940s virtually all psychotherapy was based on psychoanalytic principles. Several group therapy approaches were developed by psychoanalytically trained therapists looking to expand their focus beyond the unconscious to the interpretations individuals place on their experiences. Underlying this focus is the belief that human beings are capable of consciously controlling their behavior and taking responsibility for their decisions. Some phenomenological therapies include:

- psychodrama—developed by Jacob Moreno, an Austrian psychiatrist. This technique encourages members to play the parts of significant individuals in their lives to help them solve interpersonal conflicts.

Psychodrama brings the conflict into the present, emphasizing dramatic action as a way of helping group members solve their problems. Catharsis, the therapeutic release of emotions followed by relief, plays a prominent role. This approach is particularly useful for people who find it difficult to express their feelings in words.

- person-centered therapy—a therapeutic approach developed by the psychologist Carl Rogers. Rather than viewing the therapist as expert, Rogers believed that the client's own drive toward growth and development is the most important healing factor. The therapist empathizes with clients' feelings and perceptions, helping them gain insight and plan constructive action. Rogers's person-centered therapy became the basis for the intensive group experience known as the encounter group, in which the leader helps members discuss their feelings about one another and, through the group process, grow as individuals. Rogers emphasized honest feedback and the awareness, expression, and acceptance of feelings. He believed that a trusting and cohesive atmosphere is fundamental to the therapeutic effect of the group.

- Gestalt therapy—In the 1940s Fritz Perls challenged psychoanalytic theory and practice with this approach. Members take turns being in the "hot seat," an empty chair used to represent people with whom the person is experiencing conflicts. The therapist encourages the client to become aware of feelings and impulses previously denied.

BEHAVIOR THERAPIES. Behavior therapies comprise a number of techniques based upon a common theoretical belief: Maladaptive behaviors develop according to the same principles that govern all learning. As a result, they can be unlearned, and new, more adaptive behaviors learned in their place. The emergence of behavior therapies in the 1950s represented a radical departure from psychoanalysis.

Behavior therapies focus on how a problem behavior originated, and on the environmental factors that maintain it. Individuals are encouraged to become self-analytical, looking at events occurring before, during, and after the problem behavior takes place. Strategies are then developed and employed to replace the problem behavior with new, more adaptive behaviors.

An important offshoot of behavior therapy is **cognitive-behavioral therapy**, developed in the 1960s and 1970s, which is the predominant behavioral approach used today. It emphasizes the examination of thoughts with the goal of changing them to more rational and less inflammatory ones. Albert Ellis, a psychologist who believed that we cause our own unhappiness by our interpretations of events, rather than by the events themselves, is a major figure in cognitive-behavior therapy. By changing what we tell ourselves, Ellis believes we can reduce the strength of our emotional reactions, as well.

Who belongs in a therapy group?

Individuals who share a common problem or concern are often placed in therapy groups where they can share their mutual struggles and feelings. Groups for bulimic individuals, victims of sexual abuse, adult children of alcoholics, and recovering drug addicts are some types of common therapy groups.

People who are suicidal, homicidal, psychotic, or in the midst of a major life crisis are not typically placed in group therapy until their behavior and emotional states have stabilized. People with organic **brain** injury and other cognitive impairments may also be poor candidates for group therapy, as are patients with sociopathic traits, who show little ability to empathize with others.

How are therapy groups constructed?

Therapy groups may be homogeneous or heterogeneous. Homogeneous groups, described above, have members with similar diagnostic backgrounds (for example, they may all have depression). Heterogeneous groups contain a mix of individuals with different emotional problems. The number of group members typically ranges from five to 12.

How do therapy groups work?

The number of sessions in group therapy depends upon the group's makeup, goals, and setting. Some are time-limited, with a predetermined number of sessions known to all members at the beginning. Others are indeterminate, and the group and/or therapist determine when the group is ready to disband. Membership may be closed or open to new members. The therapeutic approach used depends on both the focus of the group and the therapist's orientation.

In group therapy sessions, members are encouraged to discuss the issues that brought them into therapy openly and honestly. The therapist works to create an atmosphere of trust and acceptance that encourages members to support one another. Ground rules may be set at the beginning, such as maintaining confidentiality of group discussions, and restricting social contact among members outside the group.

The therapist facilitates the group process, that is, the effective functioning of the group, and guides

KEY TERMS

Altruism—An unselfish willingness to help others.

Behavior therapies—Numerous techniques all having their roots in principles of learning.

Catharsis—A powerful emotional release followed by a feeling of great relief.

Cognitive-behavior therapy—An approach to psychotherapy that emphasizes the correction of distorted thinking patterns and changing one's behaviors accordingly.

Existential factors—Realities of life including death, isolation, freedom, and meaninglessness that must be faced by all individuals.

Gestalt therapy—A therapeutic approach that focuses on increasing awareness of feelings and impulses in the present.

Group cohesiveness—The degree to which a group functions well in its assigned task; the importance the group develops to each of its members.

Group psychotherapy—A form of therapy in which a small, carefully selected group of individuals meets regularly with a therapist to assist each individual in emotional growth and personal problem solving.

Imitative behavior—Behaviors of a therapist or group member that are imitated, consciously or unconsciously, by other group members.

Individual psychotherapy—A relationship between therapist and patient designed to foster the patient's emotional growth and personal problem-solving skills.

Information giving—Imparting of information about a disease or condition as part of the therapeutic process.

Interpersonal learning—Learning that takes place via feedback from others.

Person-centered therapy—A therapeutic approach that believes the client's own drive toward growth and development is the most important factor in healing.

Phenomenological therapy—A therapeutic approach that focuses on the interpretations individuals place on their experiences.

Psychodrama—A form of group therapy that has group members act out parts of important people in the lives of individual group members.

Psychodynamic groups—Psychotherapy groups that utilize the principles of unconscious needs and motivations developed by Sigmund Freud.

Self-help groups—Groups that fall outside the realm of psychotherapy groups, but that offer help to individuals around a particular problem or concern. These groups typically are not professionally led.

Termination—The process of ending a therapy group; an important part of a group therapy.

Universality—The feeling of being isolated, unique, and separate from others, often experienced by therapy group members.

individuals in self-discovery. Depending upon the group's goals and the therapist's orientation, sessions may be either highly structured or fluid and relatively undirected. Typically, the leader steers a middle course, providing direction when the group gets off track, yet letting members set their own agenda. The therapist may guide the group by reinforcing the positive behaviors they engage in. For example, if one member shows empathy and supportive listening to another, the therapist might compliment that member and explain the value of that behavior to the group. In almost all group therapy situations, the therapist will emphasize the commonalities among members to instill a sense of group identity.

Self-help or **support groups** like Alcoholics Anonymous and Weight Watchers fall outside of the psychotherapy realm. These groups offer many of the same benefits, including social support, the opportunity to identify with others, and the sense of belonging that makes group therapy effective for many. **Self-help groups** also meet to share their common concern and help one another cope. These groups, however, are typically leaderless or run by a member who takes on the leader role for one or more meetings. Sometimes self-help groups can be an adjunct to psychotherapy groups.

How are patients referred for group therapy?

Individuals are typically referred for group therapy by a psychologist or psychiatrist. Some may participate in both individual and group therapy. Before people begin in a therapy group, the leader interviews the individuals to ensure a good fit between their needs and the group's. The individuals may be given some preliminary information before sessions begin, such as guidelines and ground rules, and information about the problem on which the group is focused.

How do therapy groups end?

Therapy groups end in a variety of ways. Some, such as those in drug rehabilitation programs and psychiatric hospitals, may be ongoing, with patients coming and going as they leave the facility. Others may have an end date set from the outset. Still others may continue until the group and/or the therapist believe the group goals have been met.

The termination of a long-term therapy group may cause feelings of **grief**, loss, abandonment, anger, or rejection in some members. The therapist attempts to deal with these feelings and foster a sense of closure by encouraging exploration of feelings and use of newly acquired coping techniques for handling them. Working through this termination phase is an important part of the treatment process.

Who drops out of group therapy?

Individuals that are emotionally fragile or unable to tolerate aggressive or hostile comments from other members are at risk of dropping out, as are those who have trouble communicating in a group setting. If the therapist does not support them and help reduce their sense of isolation and aloneness, they may drop out and feel like failures. The group can be injured by the premature departure of any of its members, and it is up to the therapist to minimize the likelihood of this occurrence by careful selection and management of the group process.

Results

Studies have shown that both group and individual psychotherapy benefit about 85% of the patients who participate in them. Ideally, patients leave with a better understanding and acceptance of themselves, and stronger interpersonal and coping skills. Some individuals continue in therapy after the group disbands, either individually or in another group setting.

See also Abuse; Addiction; Alcohol and related disorders; Amphetamines and related disorders; Anxiety and anxiety disorders; Bulimia nervosa; Cannabis and related disorders; Cocaine and related disorders; Cognitive-behavioral therapy; Grief counseling and therapy; Modeling; Nicotine and related disorders; Obesity; Opioids and related disorders; Peer groups; Psychodynamic therapy; Rational emotive therapy; Reinforcement; Self-help groups; Social skills training; Substance abuse and related disorders; Support groups.

Resources

BOOKS

Hales, Dianne, and Robert E. Hales. *Caring for the Mind: A Comprehensive Guide to Mental Health.* New York: Bantam Books, 1995.

Kaplan, Harold I., and Benjamin J. Sadock. *Synopsis of Psychiatry.* 8th ed. Baltimore: Lippincott Williams and Wilkins, 1998.

Panman, Richard, and Sandra Panman. "Group Counseling and Therapy." *The Counseling Sourcebook: A Practical Reference on Contemporary Issues,* eds. Judah L. Ronch, William Van Ornum, and Nicholas C Stilwell. New York: Crossroad, 2001.

Yalom, Irvin D. *The Theory and Practice of Group Psychotherapy.* 4th ed. New York: Basic Books, 1995.

ORGANIZATIONS

American Psychiatric Association. 1400 K Street NW, Washington, DC 20005. Telephone: (888) 357-7924. Web site: <http://www.psych.org.>

American Psychological Association (APA). 750 First Street NE, Washington, DC 20002-4242. Telephone: (202) 336-5700. Web site: <www.apa.org.>

American Society of Group Psychotherapy and Psychodrama. 301 N. Harrison Street, Suite 508, Princeton, NJ 08540. Telephone: (609) 452-1339. Website: <http://www.asgpp.org/html/about_us.html.>

National Institute of Mental Health. 6001 Executive Boulevard, Room 8184, MC 9663, Bethesda, MD 20892-9663. Telephone: (301) 443-4513. Web site: <http://www.nimh.nih.gov.>

OTHER

American Academy of Family Physicians. "Cognitive Therapy." Available online at: <http://familydoctor.-org/882.xml>.

Kleber, Herbert D., and others. *Practice Guideline for Treatment of Patients with Substance Use Disorders.* 2nd ed. 2006. Available online through the American Psychiatric Association at: <http://www.psych.org/psych_pract/treatg/pg/SUD2ePG_04-28-06.pdf>.

National Alliance on Mental Illness. "Cognitive-Behavioral Therapy." Available online at: <http://www.nami.org/Template.cfm?Section=About_Treatments_and_Supports&template=/ContentManagement/ContentDisplay.cfm&ContentID=7952>.

Barbara S. Sternberg, PhD
Emily Jane Willingham, PhD

Guided imagery therapy

Definition

Guided imagery therapy is a cognitive-behavioral technique in which a client is guided in imagining a relaxing scene or series of experiences.

Purpose

Numerous clinical observations suggest that an individual visualizing an imagined scene reacts as though it were actually occurring; therefore, "induced" images can have a profound effect on behavior. The usefulness of guided imagery techniques have been shown to be effective in helping individuals learn or modify behaviors such as:

- learning to relax
- changing or controlling their negative emotions in response to a particular situation, event (loss of a job), or belief
- preparing themselves for changes they are likely to have to deal with in the future (children leaving home, parent moving)
- eliminating or reducing undesirable behaviors (smoking, obesity)
- increasing effective pain management
- coping with difficult situations (a difficult boss)
- learning new and desirable behaviors (assertiveness)
- becoming more motivated (doing homework between therapy sessions) in dealing with their problems
- dealing with how they behaved in an earlier situation (had a temper tantrum) in order to feel less shame or guilt
- experimenting with ways to deal with stressful or anxiety-producing situations (giving a presentation in public) by mentally rehearsing the needed behavior(s)

Guided imagery techniques have been applied to—and found to be effective or show promise with—a variety of populations, including individuals with:

- phobias (including agoraphobia, social phobia, and specific phobias)
- mild to moderate depression
- generalized anxiety disorders
- post-traumatic stress disorder
- obsessive-compulsive disorder
- sexual difficulties
- habit disorders

- chronic fatigue syndrome
- children's behavioral disorders
- stuttering
- acute and chronic pain (and other physical disorders)

Guided imagery has also contributed to the achievement of skills and overcoming anxiety in normal life situations that include learning or improving motor skills, test-taking, and public speaking. In addition, visualization and imagery, along with other behavioral techniques, have been applied to the fields of business, industry, child rearing, education, behavioral medicine, and sports.

Description

Imagery techniques have been combined with a wide range of behavioral and cognitive procedures and treatment methods of some psychotherapeutic approaches, including **behavior modification**, cognitive processing therapy, rational-emotive therapy, multimodal therapy, and **hypnotherapy**. Combinations of treatment methods among these approaches leads to the following general uses of imagery:

- antifuture shock imagery (preparing for a feared future event)
- positive imagery (using pleasant scenes for relaxation training)
- aversive imagery (using an unpleasant image to help eliminate or reduce undesirable behavior)
- associated imagery (using imagery to track unpleasant feelings)
- coping imagery (using images to rehearse to reach a behavioral goal or manage a situation)
- "step-up" technique (exaggerating a feared situation and using imagery to cope with it)

An assessment of the individual's presenting problems is an essential part of treatment, both at the beginning of therapy and throughout the entire process. This is to ensure that the therapist has sufficient understanding of the client's situation and **diagnosis** of the problem(s). The assessment generally covers a variety of areas, such as developmental history (including family, education, employment, and social relationships), past traumatic experiences, medical and psychiatric treatments, and client goals. Often, clients have several problems, and both the therapist and the client work together on prioritizing specific treatment goals.

Following the assessment, the therapist will present a general rationale for the use of imagery.

The therapist might explain that the client will learn techniques in which he or she imagines they or another person are performing a particular behavior. To enhance visualization, it is important to involve all senses in the image. For example, if the client is to be walking down a busy street, he or she is encouraged to imagine hearing sounds from traffic and other people, smell exhaust fumes from buses and aromas from a nearby bakery, and observe body movements and wind in the face. It is stressed to the client that the most critical aspect of imagining is the feeling of actually experiencing the scene—of being in it rather than just seeing oneself in it.

Both the therapist and the client construct a relaxing scene by discussing exactly what the client finds pleasant. It is better if the client chooses all images (positive or negative) and the therapist trains the client to visualize the selected images as vividly as possible.

Once a pleasant scene is decided upon, the client is asked to assume a relaxed position and with closed eyes, if this is comfortable, before being guided in visualization. A common beginning instruction may be: "Imagine you are lying on a warm sandy beach." The therapist continues to guide the relaxation by saying such phrases as: "Notice the texture of the sand and the color of the sky. Focus on the sounds you hear, and the smells . . . " The client is asked to practice the image at home between sessions. A tape of the guided imagery in the familiar voice of the therapist can be helpful to some clients in practicing at home.

During visualization, clients are given permission to take control if they need to by changing the image or stopping the activity completely. To help clients maintain control of the image, the therapist may also say to the client: "Take as long as you need to relax," and "Do whatever you need to do in order to feel safe." This empowers clients in using such techniques.

Length of treatment

Treatments using behavioral techniques tend to be relatively brief. However, many factors determine the length of therapy. Generally, treatment takes longer if target behaviors are more numerous and more difficult to specify. Some types of treatments require more sessions than others. For example, techniques using imagery require more sessions than treatments in which the client is exposed to the actual feared situations in real life.

Other factors that determine the length of treatment are the types of presenting disorders, the client's willingness to do homework, how long the client has had the problem, client financial resources, and whether there are supportive family members and friends. The therapist's style and experience may also affect the length of therapy. Clients may be seen several times (two to five times) a week at the start of therapy and then once weekly for several months, and every other month for follow-up for a few more months.

Normal results

Guided imagery techniques have been taken from behavior therapy and are used by different psychological theories and systems of counseling and **psychotherapy**, including **cognitive-behavioral therapy**. Research has shown these techniques to be effective when applied to specific problems.

Depending on the combination of visualization and imagery techniques used, the therapeutic approach, and client problem(s), it is expected that clients will have positive changes in specifically defined target behaviors; a reduction in biases or distortions in thinking, resulting in more effective functioning that, in turn, leads to more positive feelings, behavior, and thinking; and experience less emotional disturbances, increased effective coping skills, decreased self-defeating behaviors, and less tension.

Abnormal results

Guided imagery is not used in isolation but as a part of a therapeutic formulation and is appropriate for a range of problems and disorders. It is, however, thought that some techniques—such as imagery used in rational-emotive therapy—can trigger high levels of anxiety in some clients. Therefore, caution should be taken when using these techniques if clients have the following conditions:

- asthma attacks triggered by stress or anxiety
- seizures triggered by stress or anxiety
- cardiac condition or related conditions
- depression with suicidal ideation
- hysteria
- pregnancy
- severe psychiatric disorders

In these instances, other strategies and techniques that do not trigger high levels of anxiety, such as relaxation exercises or coping imagery, should be considered. When working with clients with these conditions, the therapist should be in consultation with their medical provider.

See also Aversion therapy; Covert sensitization.

KEY TERMS

Rational emotive therapy—A form of psychotherapy developed by Albert Ellis and other psychotherapists based on the theory that emotional response is based on the subjective interpretation of events, not on the events themselves.

Resources

BOOKS

Corey, Gerald. *Theory and Practice of Counseling and Psychotherapy*. 6th ed. California: Wadsworth and Thomson Learning, 2001.

Dryden, Windy. "Rational Emotive Behaviour Therapy." In *Handbook of Counselling and Psychotherapy*, edited by Colin Feltham and Ian Horton. London: Sage Publications, 2000.

Lovell, Karina. "Behaviour Psychotherapy." In *Handbook of Counseling and Psychotherapy*, edited by Colin Feltman and Ian Horton. London: Sage Publications, 2000.

Mullin, Rian E., PhD. *The New Handbook of Cognitive Therapy Techniques*. New York: W. W. Norton and Company, 2000.

ORGANIZATIONS

National Institute of Mental Health. 6001 Excutive Boulevard, Room 8184, MSC 9663, Bethesda MD 20892-9663. <http://www.nimh.nih.gov/>.

Anxiety Disorders Association of America. 11900 Parklawn Dr., Suite 100, Rockville MD. 20852-2624. <http://www.adaa.org/>.

National Mental Health Association. 1021 Prince Street, Alexander, VA 22314-2071. <http://www.nmha.org>.

Janice Van Buren, PhD

H

Halcion *see* **Triazolam**

Haldol *see* **Haloperidol**

Hallucinations

Description

A hallucination is a false perception occurring without any identifiable external stimulus and indicates an abnormality in perception. The false perceptions can occur in any of the five sensory modalities. Therefore, a hallucination essentially is seeing, hearing, tasting, feeling, or smelling something that is not there. The false perceptions are not accounted for by the person's religious or cultural background, and the person experiencing hallucinations may or may not have insight into them. Therefore, some people experiencing hallucinations may be aware that the perceptions are false, whereas others may truly believe that what they are seeing, hearing, tasting, feeling, or smelling is real. In cases when the person truly believes the hallucination is real, the individual may also have a delusional interpretation of the hallucination.

Hallucinations must be distinguished from illusions, which are misperceptions of actual external stimuli. In other words, an illusion is essentially seeing, hearing, tasting, feeling, or smelling something that is there, but perceiving it or interpreting it incorrectly. An example of an illusion might be hearing one's name called when the radio is playing. There is an external auditory stimulus, but it is misperceived. True hallucinations do not include false perceptions that occur while dreaming, while falling asleep, or while waking up. Unusual perceptual experiences one may have while falling asleep are referred to as hypnagogic experiences. Unusual perceptual experiences one may have while waking up are referred to as hypnopompic experiences. Hallucinations also do not include very vivid experiences one may have while fully awake (e.g., especially vivid daydreaming or imaginative play).

Hallucinations are a symptom of either a medical (e.g., epilepsy), neurological, or mental disorder. Hallucinations may be present in any of the following mental disorders: psychotic disorders (including **schizophrenia**, **schizoaffective disorder**, **schizophreniform disorder**, **shared psychotic disorder**, **brief psychotic disorder**, **substance-induced psychotic disorder**), **bipolar disorder**, major **depression** with psychotic features, **delirium**, or **dementia**. Auditory hallucinations, in particular, are common in psychotic disorders such as schizophrenia.

Use of certain recreational drugs may induce hallucinations. These drugs include **amphetamines** and **cocaine**, hallucinogens (e.g., lysergic acid diethylamide or LSD), **phencyclidine** (PCP), and **cannabis** or marijuana. Visual hallucinations are commonly associated with substance use. Individuals may report false perceptions of little people or animals (sometimes referred to as Lilliputian hallucinations). In addition, withdrawal from some recreational drugs—including alcohol, **sedatives**, hypnotics, or anxiolytics—can produce hallucinations. Withdrawal from alcohol, for instance, commonly causes visual hallucinations, especially at nighttime.

Types

Hallucinations are categorized according to which sensory modality is involved and are categorized as either mood-congruent or mood-incongruent. The types of hallucinations are:

• auditory: The false perception of sound, music, noises, or voices. Hearing voices when there is no auditory stimulus is the most common type of auditory hallucination in mental disorders. The voice may be heard either inside or outside one's head and is generally considered more severe when coming from outside one's head. The voices may be male or female, recognized as the voice of someone familiar or not recognized as familiar, and may be critical or positive. In mental disorders such as schizophrenia, however, the content of what the voices say is usually unpleasant and negative. In schizophrenia, a common symptom is to hear voices conversing and/or commenting. When someone hears voices conversing, they hear two or more voices speaking to each other (usually about the person who is hallucinating). In voices commenting, the person hears a voice making comments about his or her behavior or thoughts, typically in the third person (e.g., "isn't he silly"). Sometimes the voices consist of hearing a "running commentary" on the person's behavior as it occurs ("she is showering"). Other times, the voices may tell the person to do something (commonly referred to as "command hallucinations").

- gustatory: A false perception of taste. Usually, the experience is unpleasant. For instance, an individual may complain of a persistent taste of metal. This type of hallucination is more commonly seen in some medical disorders (e.g., epilepsy) than in mental disorders.

- mood-congruent hallucination: Any hallucination whose content is consistent with either the depressive or manic state the person may be in at the time. Depressive themes include guilt, death, disease, personal inadequacy, and deserved punishment. Manic themes include inflated sense of self-worth, power, knowledge, skills, and identity and may include belief in a special relationship with a famous person or deity. For example, a depressed person may hear voices saying that he or she is a horrible person, whereas a manic person may hear voices saying that he or she is an incredibly important person.

- mood-incongruent hallucination: Any hallucination whose content is not consistent with either the depressed or manic state the person is in at the time, or is mood-neutral. For example, a depressed person may experience hallucinations without any themes of guilt, death, disease, personal inadequacy, or deserved punishment. Similarly, a manic person may experience hallucinations without any themes of inflated self-worth, power, knowledge, skills, or identity or a special relationship to a famous person or deity.

- olfactory hallucination: A false perception of odor or smell. Typically, the experience is very unpleasant. For example, the person may smell decaying fish, dead bodies, or burning rubber. Sometimes, those experiencing olfactory hallucinations believe the odor emanates from them. Olfactory hallucinations are more typical of medical disorders than mental disorders.

- somatic/tactile hallucination: A false perception or sensation of touch or something happening in or on the body. A common tactile hallucination is feeling like something is crawling under or on the skin (also

KEY TERMS

Illusion—A misperception or misinterpretation in the presence of a real external stimulus.

known as formication). Other examples include feeling electricity through one's body and feeling like someone is touching one's body while no one is there. Actual physical sensations stemming from medical disorders (perhaps not yet diagnosed) and hypochondriacal preoccupations with normal physical sensations are not thought of as somatic hallucinations.

- visual hallucination: A false perception of sight. The content of the hallucination may be anything (e.g., shapes, colors, and flashes of light) but are typically people or human-like figures. For example, one may perceive a person standing before them when no one is there. Sometimes an individual may experience the false perception of religious figure (e.g., the devil, or Christ). Perceptions that would be considered normal for an individual's religion or culture are not considered hallucinations.

Treatment

The treatment approach to hallucinations depends on the accompanying mental disorder. For example, in the case of schizophrenia, antipyschotics may be used to address aural hallucinations, although cognitive behavioral therapy also shows some efficacy in reducing aural hallucinations in people with schizophrenia.

See also Alcohol and related disorders; Major depressive disorder; Substance abuse and related disorders; Substance-induced psychotic disorders.

Resources

BOOKS

American Psychiatric Association. *Diagnostic and Statistical Manual of Mental Disorders.* 4th edition, text revised. Washington, DC: American Psychiatric Association, 2000.

Kaplan, Harold I., M.D., and Benjamin J. Sadock, M.D. *Kaplan and Sadock's Synopsis of Psychiatry: Behavioral Sciences, Clinical Psychiatry.* 8th edition. Baltimore: Williams and Wilkins.

PERIODICAL

Arehart-Treichel, Joan. "Hallucinations respond to innovative use of CBT." *Psychiatric News* (2004): 46.

WEBSITES

National Library of Medicine. "Hallucinations." <http://www.nlm.nih.gov/medlineplus/ency/article/003258.htm>.

Jennifer Hahn, PhD

Hallucinogens and related disorders

Definition

Hallucinogens are a chemically diverse group of drugs that cause changes in a person's thought processes, perceptions of the physical world, and sense of time passing. Hallucinogens can be found naturally in some plants and can be synthesized in the laboratory. Most hallucinogens are abused as recreational drugs. Hallucinogens are also called psychedelic drugs.

Description

Use of hallucinogens is at least as old as civilization. Many cultures have recorded eating certain plants specifically to induce visions or alter the perception of reality. Often these **hallucinations** were part of a religious or prophetic experience. Shamans in Siberia were known to eat the hallucinogenic mushroom *Amanita muscaria*. The ancient Greeks and the Vikings also used naturally occurring plant hallucinogens. Peyote, a spineless cactus native to the southwestern United States and Mexico, was used by native peoples, including the Aztecs, to produce visions.

Although several hundred plants are known to contain compounds that cause hallucinations, most hallucinogens are synthesized in illegal laboratories for delivery as street drugs. The best known hallucinogens are lysergic acid diethylamide (LSD), mescaline, psilocybin, and MDMA (**ecstasy**). **Phencyclidine** (PCP, angel dust) can produce hallucinations, as can **amphetamines** and marijuana, but these drugs are considered dissociative drugs, rather than hallucinogens, and act by a different pathway from classic hallucinogens. Dextromorphan, the main ingredient in many cough medicines, has become popular among some populations because of the PCP-like hallucinations it produces. In addition, new designer drugs that are chemical variants of classic hallucinogens are apt to appear on the street at any time. A drug that only recently was added to Schedule I of the 1970 Controlled Substances Act (the classification for many other "hard" drugs with no known therapeutic value) is 5-methoxy-N, N-diisopropyltryptamine (5-MeO-DIPT), a drug derived from the chemical tryptamine that is more commonly known as Foxy or Foxy Methoxy. A related hallucinogen, dimethyltryptamine, occurs naturally in plants in the Amazon but is now synthesized in labs. This drug, more commonly known as DMT, can be a powerful hallucinogen.

Although the various hallucinogens produce similar physical and psychological effects, they are a diverse group of compounds. However, all hallucinogens appear to affect the **brain** in similar ways. While the mechanism of action of hallucinogens is not completely understood, researchers have shown that these drugs bind with one type of serotonin receptor (5-HT_2) in the brain.

Serotonin is a neurotransmitter that facilitates transmission of nerve impulses in the brain and is associated with feelings of well-being, as well as many physiological responses. When a hallucinogenic compound binds with serotonin receptors, serotonin is blocked from those receptor sites, and nerve transmission is altered. There is an increase in free (unbound) serotonin in the brain. The result is a distortion of the senses of sight, sound, and touch, disorientation in time and space, and alterations of mood. In the case of hallucinogen intoxication, however, a person is not normally delirious, unconscious, or dissociated. He or she is aware that these changes in perception are caused by the hallucinogen.

LSD

LSD was first synthesized by Alfred Hoffman for a pharmaceutical company in Germany in 1938 while he was searching for a headache remedy. Hoffman discovered the hallucinogenic properties of LSD accidentally in 1943. The drug became popular with counter-culture "hippies" in the mid-1960s when its sense-altering properties were reputed to offer a window into enhanced creativity and self-awareness. LSD also occurs naturally in morning glory seeds.

Pure LSD is a white, odorless, crystalline powder that dissolves easily in water, although contaminants can cause it to range in color from yellow to dark brown. LSD was listed as a Schedule I drug under the Controlled Substance Act of 1970, meaning that it has no medical or legal uses and has a high potential for **abuse**. LSD is not easy to manufacture in a home laboratory, and some of its ingredients are controlled substances that are difficult to obtain. However, LSD is very potent, and a small amount can produce a large number of doses.

On the street, LSD is sold in several forms. Microdots are tiny pills smaller than a pinhead. Windowpane is liquid LSD applied to thin squares of gelatin. Liquid LSD can also be sprayed on sugar cubes. The most common street form of the drug is liquid LSD sprayed onto blotter paper and dried. The paper, often printed with colorful or psychedelic pictures, is divided into tiny squares, each square being one dose. Liquid LSD can also be sprayed on the back of a postage stamp and licked off. Street names for the drug include acid, yellow sunshine, windowpane, cid, doses, trips, and boomers.

Mescaline

Mescaline is a naturally occurring plant hallucinogen. Its primary source is the cactus *Lophophora williamsii*. This cactus is native to the southwestern United States and Mexico. The light blue-green plant is spineless and has a crown called a peyote button. This button contains mescaline and can be eaten or made into a bitter tea. Mescaline is also the active ingredient of at least ten other cacti of the genus *Trichocereus* that are native to parts of South America.

Mescaline was first isolated in 1897 by the German chemist Arthur Hefftner and first synthesized in the laboratory in 1919. Some experiments were done with the drug to determine if it was medically useful, but no medical uses were found. However, peyote is culturally significant. It has been used for centuries as part of religious celebrations and vision quests of Native Americans. The Native American Church, which fuses elements of Christianity with indigenous practices, has long used peyote as part of its religious practices.

In 1970 mescaline was listed as a Schedule I drug under the Controlled Substances Act. However, that same year the state of Texas legalized peyote for use in Native American religious ceremonies. In 1995, a federal law was passed making peyote legal only for this use in all 50 states.

Psilocybin

Psilocybin is the active ingredient in what are known on the street as magic mushrooms, shrooms, mushies, or Mexican mushrooms. There are several species of mushrooms that contain psilocybin, including *Psilocybe mexicana*, *P. muscorumi*, and *Stropharia cubensis*. These mushrooms grow in most moderate, moist climates.

Psilocybin-containing mushrooms are usually cooked and eaten (they have a bitter taste), or dried and boiled to make a tea. Although psilocybin can be made synthetically in the laboratory, there is no street market for synthetic psilocybin, and virtually all the drug comes from cultivated mushrooms. In the United States, it is legal to possess psilocybin-containing mushrooms, but it is illegal to traffic in them, and psilocybin and psilocyn (another psychoactive drug found in small quantities in these mushrooms) are both Schedule I drugs.

MDMA

MDMA, short for 3,4-methylenedioxymethamphetamine, and better known as ecstasy, XTC, E, X, or Adam, has become an increasingly popular club drug since the 1980s. The hallucinogenically active portion of the drug is chemically similar to mescaline, while its stimulant portion is similar to **methamphetamine**. MDMA was first synthesized in 1912 by a German pharmaceutical company looking for a new compound that would stop bleeding. The company patented the drug, but never did anything with it. A closely related drug, methylenedioxyamphetimine or MDA, was tested by a pharmaceutical company as an appetite suppressant in the 1950s, but its use was discontinued when it was discovered to have hallucinogenic properties. In the 1960s, MDA was a popular drug of abuse in some large cities such as San Francisco.

During the early 1980s therapists experimented with MDMA, which was legal at the time, as a way to help patients open up and become more empathetic. Recreational use soon followed, and it was declared an illegal Schedule I drug in 1985. For about a year between 1987 and 1988, the drug was again legal as the result of court challenges, but it permanently joined other Schedule I hallucinogens in March 1988.

MDMA is a popular club drug often associated with all-night raves or dance parties. The drug, sold in tablets, is attractive because it combines stimulant effects that allow ravers to dance for hours with a feeling of empathy, reduced **anxiety**, and reduced inhibitions, and euphoria. Some authorities consider MDA and MDMA stimulant-hallucinogens and do not group them with classic hallucinogens such as LSD, but research indicates that MDA and MDMA affect the brain in the same way as classic hallucinogens. The American Psychiatric Association considers MDMA as a drug that can cause hallucinogen-related disorders.

Causes and symptoms

A cause of hallucinogen use is that hallucinogens are attractive to recreational drug users for a number of reasons, including:

- they are minimally addictive and there are no physical withdrawal symptoms upon stopping use.
- they produce few serious or debilitating physical side effects.
- they do not usually produce a delusional state, excessive stupor, or excessive stimulation.
- they do not cause memory loss with occasional use.
- they are easily and cheaply available.

- they produce a high that gives the illusion of increasing creativity, empathy, or self-awareness.
- deaths from overdoses are rare.

Despite their perceived harmlessness, strong hallucinogens such as LSD can cause frightening and anxiety-evoking emotional experiences, known as bad trips. Flashbacks, where the sensations experienced while under the influence of a drug recur uncontrollably without drug use, can occur for months after a single drug use. During hallucinogen intoxication, reality may be so altered that a person may endanger himself by believing he is capable of feats such as flying off buildings. Hallucinogens also may induce or cause a worsening of latent psychiatric disorders such as anxiety, **depression**, and **psychosis**. Hallucinogens can also cause **paranoia**, long-term memory loss, personality changes (especially if there is a latent psychiatric disorder), and psychological drug dependence.

Psychological symptoms

Hallucinogens work primarily on the perception of reality. They usually do not create true hallucinations, which are imagined visions or sounds (voices heard in the head, for example) in the absence of any corresponding reality. Instead, classic hallucinogens alter the perception of something that is physically present. A face may appear to "melt" or colors may become brighter, move, and change shape. Sounds may be "seen," rather than heard.

More than with other drugs, the mental state of the hallucinogen user and the environment in which the drug is taken influence the user's experience. LSD, especially, is known for symptoms that range from mellowness and psychedelic visions (good trips) to anxiety and panic attacks (bad trips). Previous good experiences with a drug do not guarantee continued good experiences. People with a history of psychiatric disorders are more likely to experience harmful reactions, as are those who are given the drug without their knowledge.

Normally, mescaline and psilocybin produce uniformly milder symptoms than LSD. During a single drug experience, the user can experience a range of symptoms. Mood can shift from happy to sad or pleasant to frightening and back again several times. Some symptoms occur primarily with MDMA, as indicated. Psychological symptoms of hallucinogen intoxication include:

- distortion of sight, sound, and touch
- confusion of the senses—sounds are "seen" or vision is "heard"
- disorientation in time and space
- delusions of physical invulnerability (especially with LSD)
- paranoia
- unreliable judgment and increased risk taking
- anxiety attacks
- flashbacks after the drug has been cleared from the body
- blissful calm or mellowness
- reduced inhibitions
- increased empathy (MDMA)
- elation or euphoria
- impaired concentration and motivation
- long-term memory loss
- personality changes, especially if there is a latent psychiatric disorder
- psychological drug dependence

Physical symptoms

Although the primary effects of hallucinogens are on perceptions, some physical effects do occur. Physical symptoms include:

- increased blood pressure
- increased heart rate
- nausea and vomiting (especially with psilocybin and mescaline)
- blurred vision which can last after the drug has worn off
- poor coordination
- enlarged pupils
- sweating
- diarrhea (plant hallucinogens)
- restlessness
- muscle cramping (especially clenched jaws with MDMA)
- dehydration (MDMA)
- serious increase in body temperature leading to seizures (MDMA)

Demographics

Hallucinogen use, excluding MDMA, peaked in the United States late 1960s as part of the counterculture movement. Hallucinogen use then gradually declined until the early 1990s, when it again picked up. A recent government survey found that about 33.7 million Americans (13.9%) age 12 or older report having tried a hallucinogen at least once in their lives. About 22.4 million Americans (9.2% of the population) age 12 or older report having used LSD at least once, with 104,000 reporting use within the last month. Among teenagers, use of these drugs has remained fairly stable with some declines in recent years.

A recent U.S. government survey found that about 11.5 million Americans age 12 or older report having tried MDMA at least once. About 0.2% of the population reported having used the drug in the last month. Among adolescents, use of the drug appears to have increased in recent years. A total of 6.5% of twelfth graders reported having tried MDMA in the past month according to a recent survey.

Diagnosis

Although not all experts agree, the *Diagnostic and Statistical Manual of Mental Disorders* (the fourth edition, text revision or *DSM-IV-TR*), which presents guidelines used by the American Psychiatric Association for **diagnosis** of mental disorders, recognizes two hallucinogen-related disorders: hallucinogen dependence and hallucinogen abuse. Hallucinogen dependence is the continued use of hallucinogens even when the substances cause the affected individual significant problems, or when the individual knows of adverse effects (memory impairment while intoxicated, anxiety attacks, flashbacks), but continues to use the substances anyway. "Craving" hallucinogens after not using them for a period of time has been reported. Hallucinogen abuse is repeated use of hallucinogens even after they have caused the user impairment that undermines his or her ability to fulfill obligations at work, school, or home, but the use is usually not as frequent as it is among dependent users. In addition to these two disorders, the American Psychiatric Association recognizes eight hallucinogen-induced disorders. These are:

- hallucinogen intoxication
- hallucinogen persistent perception disorder (flashbacks)
- hallucinogen intoxication delirium
- hallucinogen-induced psychotic disorder with delusions
- hallucinogen-induced psychotic disorder with hallucinations
- hallucinogen-induced mood disorder
- hallucinogen-induced anxiety disorder
- hallucinogen-related disorder not otherwise specified

Hallucinogen dependence and abuse are normally diagnosed from reports by the patient or person accompanying the patient of use of a hallucinogenic drug. Active hallucinations and accompanying physical symptoms can confirm the diagnosis, but do not have to be present. Routine drug screening does not detect LSD in the blood or urine, although specialized laboratory methods can detect the drug. Hallucinogen dependence differs from other drug dependence in that there are no withdrawal symptoms when the drug is stopped, and the extent of tolerance, (needing a higher and higher dose to achieve the same effect) appears minimal.

Hallucinogen intoxication is diagnosed based on psychological changes, perceptual changes, and physical symptoms that are typical of hallucinogen use. These changes must not be caused by a general medical condition, other **substance abuse**, or another mental disorder.

Hallucinogen persisting perception disorder, better known as flashbacks, occur after hallucinogen use followed by a period of lucidity. Flashbacks may occur weeks or months after the drug was used, and may occur after a single use or many uses.

To be diagnosed as a psychiatric disorder, flashbacks must cause significant distress or interfere with daily life activities. They can come on suddenly with no warning, or be triggered by specific environments. Flashbacks may include emotional symptoms, seeing colors, geometric forms, or, most commonly, persistence of trails of light across the visual field. They may last for months. Flashbacks are most strongly associated with LSD.

Hallucinogen intoxication delirium is rare unless the hallucinogen is contaminated by another drug or chemical such as strychnine. In hallucinogen intoxication, the patient is still grounded in reality and recognizes that the experiences of altered perception are due to using a hallucinogen. In hallucinogen intoxication delirium, the patient is no longer grounded in reality. Hallucinogen-induced psychotic disorders are similar in that the patient loses touch with reality. Psychotic states can occur immediately after using the drug, or days or months later.

Hallucinogen-induced mood disorder and hallucinogen-induced anxiety disorder are somewhat controversial, as hallucinogen use may uncover latent or preexisting anxiety or mood disorders rather than being the cause of them. However, it does appear that MDMA use can cause major depression.

Treatments

Acute treatment is aimed at preventing the patient from harming himself or anyone else. Since most people experiencing hallucinogen intoxication remain in touch with reality, "talking down" or offering reassurance and support that emphasizes that the disturbing sensatinos, anxiety, **panic attack**, or paranoia will pass as the drug wears off is often helpful. Patients are kept

KEY TERMS

Dissociated—Feelings of experiencing an altered state of reality, similar to a trance state. During the period of dissociation, the affected person may feel as if he or she is an observer instead of a participant in events, and may feel as if surroundings are unreal or distorted.

Psychosis—Severe state that is characterized by loss of contact with reality and deterioration in normal social functioning; examples are schizophrenia and paranoia. Psychosis is usually one feature of an overarching disorder, not a disorder in itself. (Plural: psychoses)

in a calm, pleasant, but lighted environment, and are encouraged to move around while being helped to remain oriented to reality. Occasionally, drugs such as **lorazepam** are given for anxiety. Complications in treatment occur when the hallucinogen has been contaminated with other street drugs or chemicals. The greatest life-threatening risk is associated with MDMA, in which users may develop dangerously high body temperatures. Reducing the patient's temperature is an essential acute treatment.

Treatment for long-term effects of hallucinogen use involve long-term **psychotherapy** after drug use has stopped. Many people find 12-step programs or group support helpful. In addition, underlying psychiatric disorders must be addressed.

Prognosis

Because hallucinogens are not physically addictive, many people are able to stop using these drugs successfully. However, users may be haunted by chronic problems such as flashbacks or mood and **anxiety disorders** either brought about or worsened by use of hallucinogens. It is difficult to predict who will have long-term complications and who will not.

Prevention

Hallucinogen use is difficult to prevent, because these drugs have a reputation for being nonaddictive and "harmless." Drug education and social outlets that provide people with a sense of self-worth are the best ways to prevent hallucinogen and other substance abuse.

See also Amphetamines and related disorders; Cannabis and related disorders; Phencyclidine and related disorders.

Resources

BOOKS

American Psychiatric Association. *Diagnostic and Statistical Manual of Mental Disorders*, 4th ed., Text rev. Washington, D.C.: American Psychiatric Association, 2000.

Galanter, Marc, and Herbert D. Kleber, eds. *Textbook of Substance Abuse Treatment*, 2nd ed. Washington, D.C.: American Psychiatric Press, Inc., 1999.

Giannini, James. *Drug Abuse: A Family Guide to Detection, Treatment and Education*. Los Angeles: Health Information Press, 1999.

Holland, Julie, ed. *Ecstasy: The Complete Guide*. Rochester, Vermont: Park Street Press, 2001.

Sadock, Benjamin J., and Virginia A. Sadock, eds. *Comprehensive Textbook of Psychiatry*, 7th ed., Vol. 1. Philadelphia: Lippincott Williams and Wilkins, 2000.

ORGANIZATIONS

National Clearinghouse for Alcohol and Drug Information. P. O. Box 2345, Rockville, MD 20852. Telephone: (800) 729-6686. Web site: <http://www.health.org>.

National Institute on Drug Abuse. 5600 Fishers Lane, Room 10 A-39, Rockville, MD 20857. Telephone: (888) 644-6432. Web site: <http://niad.nih.gov>.

Partnership for a Drug-Free America. 405 Lexington Avenue, New York, NY 10174. Telephone: (212) 922-1560. Web site: <http://www.drugfreeamerica.org>.

OTHER

Office of National Drug Control Policy. "Drug Facts: Hallucinogens." (2007) Available online at: <http://www.whitehousedrugpolicy.gov/drugfact/hallucinogens/index.html>.

Office of National Drug Control Policy. "Drug Facts: Club Drugs." (2007). Available online at: <http://www.whitehousedrugpolicy.gov/drugfact/club/index.html>.

Substance Abuse and Mental Health Services Administration. (2006). *Results from the 2005 National Survey on Drug Use and Health: National Findings* (Office of Applied Studies, NSDUH Series H-30, DHHS Publication No. SMA 06-4194). Rockville, MD. Available online at: <http://www.oas.samhsa.gov/NSDUH/2k5NSDUH/2k5results.htm>.

Tish Davidson, AM
Emily Jane Willingham, PhD

Haloperidol

Definition

Haloperidol is a major tranquilizer. It is used to treat psychoses, senile **dementia**, Tourette's syndrome, and certain serious behavioral disorders in children. In the United States it is sold under the brand name Haldol.

Purpose

Haloperidol is used in the management of symptoms in people requiring long-term antipsychotic therapy. It is also used for controlling tics and inappropriate vocalizations associated with Tourette's syndrome in both children and adults.

In children, haloperidol is occasionally used to treat severe behavior problems such as combativeness and extreme outbursts that occur without immediate provocation. Occasionally it is used for short-term treatment of children who display excessive motor activity with accompanying difficulty in attention, aggression, impulse control, mood changes, and coping with frustration. Haloperidol is used only after **psychotherapy** and other medications have been tried and are found to be unsuccessful.

Description

Haloperidol is a major tranquilizer. It is used to control symptoms of psychotic disorders. It can be administered as a pill or by intramuscular injection (a shot).

The precise way in which haloperidol helps control symptoms associated with psychoses or dementia has not yet been clearly established.

Recommended dosage

For adults, the recommended initial dosage of haloperidol is 0.5–5.0 mg taken two or three times each day. The initial dosage depends on the severity of the symptoms in the person being treated. All people taking haloperidol must be carefully monitored to establish an individualized dosage. Physicians have found a great variability in the amount of haloperidol required to control symptoms.

Children require smaller dosages of haloperidol than do adults. The recommended initial dosage of haloperidol for controlling psychotic symptoms in children is 0.5–2.0 mg taken two or three times each day. The recommended dosage for controlling symptoms of Tourette's syndrome and other nonpsychotic disorders is between 0.075 mg and 0.05 mg per kilogram (2.2 pounds) of body weight per day. The total dosage is usually divided into two or three administrations per day. The goal of therapy is to use the smallest amount of haloperidol that will control symptoms. Children under age three should not be given this drug.

Precautions

Haloperidol may cause low blood pressure (hypotension). For this reason people with heart and blood pressure problems should be carefully monitored while taking the drug. Haloperidol also increases the possibility of having **seizures**. People with a history of seizures or who are taking anticonvulsants (medication to control seizures) should take lower dosages of haloperidol and be closely monitored by a physician until a safe dosage is established. Haloperidol also interferes with the action of the anticoagulant (blood thinning) drug phenindione.

Haloperidol may increase the action of central nervous system depressants such as anesthetics, alcohol, and opiates (some pain killers and sleeping pills). It may also decrease the time required to change from mania to **depression** among people with bipolar (manic-depressive) disorder.

Side effects

Haloperidol has the potential to produce a serious side effect called **tardive dyskinesia**. This syndrome consists of involuntary, uncoordinated movements that may not disappear or may only partially improve after the drug is stopped. Tardive dyskinesia involves involuntary movements of the tongue, jaw, mouth, face, or other groups of skeletal muscles. These side effects may appear after people have stopped taking haloperidol. The chance of developing tardive dyskinesia increases with increasing age and dosage of haloperidol. Women are at greater risk than men for developing tardive dyskinesia. There is no known effective treatment for tardive dyskinesia, although gradual (but rarely complete) improvement may occur over a long period.

Haloperidol use may lead to the development of symptoms that resemble Parkinson's disease, but that are not caused by Parkinson's. These symptoms may include a taut or mask-like expression on the face, drooling, tremors, pill-rolling motions in the hands, cogwheel rigidity (abnormal rigidity in muscles characterized by jerky movements when the muscle is passively stretched), and a shuffling gait. Taking the anti-Parkinson's drugs **benztropine** mesylate or **trihexyphenidyl** hydrochloride along with haloperidol help to control these symptoms. Medication to control parkinsonian symptoms may have to be continued after haloperidol is stopped. This is due to different rates of elimination of these drugs from the body.

Other side effects of haloperidol include **anxiety**, restlessness, agitation, **insomnia**, headache, euphoria, drowsiness, depression, confusion, dizziness, and seizures. Unwanted or unexpected effects associated with the use of haloperidol have been reported for virtually

KEY TERMS

Anticoagulant—A medication (such as warfarin, Coumadin, or Heparin) that decreases the blood's clotting ability, preventing the formation of new clots. Although anticoagulants will not dissolve existing clots, they can stop them from getting larger. These drugs are commonly called blood thinners.

Anticonvulsant—A medication used to control abnormal electrical activity in the brain that causes seizures.

Tic—A sudden involuntary behavior that is difficult or impossible for the person to suppress. Tics may be either motor (related to movement) or vocal, and may become more pronounced under stress.

Tourette's syndrome—Neurological disorder characterized by multiple involuntary movements and uncontrollable vocalizations called tics that come and go over years, usually beginning in childhood and becoming chronic. Sometimes the tics include inappropriate language.

Tranquilizer—A medication that induces a feeling of calm and relaxation.

all organ systems in the body. Although numerous, such side effects are relatively uncommon.

Interactions

The simultaneous use of haloperidol and lithium, a common treatment for bipolar (manic-depressive) disorder, has been associated with an encephalopathic syndrome. People with this syndrome have symptoms of weakness, lethargy, fever, confusion, and high levels of white blood cells.

Haloperidol may increase the effect of central nervous system depressants such as anesthetics, opiates, and alcohol.

Resources

BOOKS

Foreman, John C., and Torben Johansen. *Textbook of Receptor Pharmacology*. 2nd ed. Boca Raton, FL: CRC Press, 2002.

Page, Clive P., and Michael Murphy. *Integrated Pharmacology*. St. Louis: Mosby-Year Book, 2002.

Von Boxtel, Chris J., and others. *Handbook of Clinical Psychopharmacology for Therapists*. 4th ed. Oakland, CA: New Harbinger Publications, 2004.

PERIODICALS

Akhondzadeh, Shahin, and others. "Allopurinol as an Adjunct to Lithium and Haloperidol for Treatment of Patients With Acute Mania: A Double-Blind, Randomized, Placebo-Controlled Trial." *Bipolar Disorders* 8.5, part 1 (Oct. 2006): 485–89.

Aziz, Mohamed, and others. "Remission of Positive and Negative Symptoms in Refractory Schizophrenia with a Combination of Haloperidol and Quetiapine: Two Case Studies." *Journal of Psychiatric Practice* 12.5 (Sept. 2006): 332–36.

Dunn, Michael J., and Simon Killcross. "Clozapine but Not Haloperidol Treatment Reverses Sub-Chronic Phencyclidine-Induced Disruption of Conditional Discrimination Performance." *Behavioural Brain Research* 175.2 (Dec. 2006): 271–77.

Emsley, Robin, Jonathan Rabinowitz, and Rossella Medori. "Remission in Early Psychosis: Rates, Predictors, and Clinical and Functional Outcome Correlates." *Schizophrenia Research* 89.1–3 (Jan. 2007): 129–39.

Green, A. I., and others. "Olanzapine and Haloperidol in First Episode Psychosis: Two-Year Data." *Schizophrenia Research* 86.1–3 (Sept. 2006): 234–43.

Morrens, Manuel, and others. "Psychomotor and Memory Effects of Haloperidol, Olanzapine, and Paroxetine in Healthy Subjects After Short-Term Administration." *Journal of Clinical Psychopharmacology* 27.1 (Feb. 2007): 15–21.

Nasrallah, Henry A, Martin Brecher, and Björn Paulsson. "Placebo-Level Incidence of Extrapyramidal Symptoms (EPS) with Quetiapine in Controlled Studies of Patients with Bipolar Mania." *Bipolar Disorders* 8.5, part 1 (Oct. 2006): 467–74.

Woodward, Neil D., and others. "A Meta-Analysis of Cognitive Change with Haloperidol in Clinical Trials of Atypical Antipsychotics: Dose Effects and Comparison to Practice Effects." *Schizophrenia Research* 89.1–3 (Jan. 2007): 211–24.

Zhang, Xiang Yang, and others. "The Effects of Ginkgo Biloba Extract Added to Haloperidol on Peripheral T Cell Subsets in Drug-Free Schizophrenia: A Double-Blind, Placebo-Controlled Trial." *Psychopharmacology* 188.1 (Sep. 2006): 12–17.

ORGANIZATIONS

American Academy of Clinical Toxicology. 777 East Park Drive, P.O. Box 8820, Harrisburg, PA 17105-8820. Telephone: (717) 558-7750. Web site: <http://www.clintox.org/index.html>.

American Academy of Family Physicians. 11400 Tomahawk Creek Parkway, Leawood, KS 66211-2672. Telephone: (913) 906-6000. Web site: <http://www.aafp.org/>.

American Medical Association. 515 N. State Street, Chicago, IL 60610. Telephone: (312) 464-5000. Web site: <http://www.ama-assn.org/>.

American Psychiatric Association. 1400 K Street NW, Washington, DC 20005. Telephone: (888) 357-7924. Web site: <http://www.psych.org/>.

American Society for Clinical Pharmacology and Therapeutics. 528 North Washington Street, Alexandria, VA 22314. Telephone: (703) 836-6981.

American Society for Pharmacology and Experimental Therapeutics. 9650 Rockville Pike, Bethesda, MD 20814-3995. Telephone: (301) 530-7060. Web site: <http://www.aspet.org/>.

L.Fleming Fallon, Jr., MD, DrPH
Ruth A. Wienclaw, PhD

Halstead-Reitan Battery

Definition

The Halstead-Reitan Neuropsychological Test Battery is a fixed set of eight tests used to evaluate **brain** and nervous system functioning in individuals aged 15 years and older. Children's versions are the Halstead Neuropsychological Test Battery for Older Children (ages nine to 14) and the Reitan Indiana Neuropsychological Test Battery (ages five to eight).

Purpose

Neuropsychological functioning refers to the ability of the nervous system and brain to process and interpret information received through the senses. The Halstead-Reitan evaluates a wide range of nervous system and brain functions, including visual, auditory, and tactual input; verbal communication; spatial and sequential perception; the ability to analyze information, form mental concepts, and make judgments; motor output; and attention, concentration, and memory.

The Halstead-Reitan is typically used to evaluate individuals with suspected brain damage. The battery also provides useful information regarding the cause of damage (for example, closed head injury, alcohol **abuse**, **Alzheimer's disease**, **stroke**), which part of the brain is damaged, whether the damage occurred during childhood development, and whether the damage is getting worse, staying the same, or getting better. Information regarding the severity of impairment and areas of personal strengths can be used to develop plans for rehabilitation or care.

Precautions

Because of its complexity, the Halstead-Reitan requires administration by a professional examiner and interpretation by a trained **psychologist**. Test results are affected by the examinee's age, education level, intellectual ability, and—to some extent—gender or ethnicity, which should always be taken into account. Because the Halstead-Reitan is a fixed battery of tests, some unnecessary information may be gathered or some important information may be missed. Overall, the battery requires five to six hours to complete, involving considerable patience, stamina, and cost. The battery has also been criticized for not including specific tests of memory; rather, memory is evaluated within the context of other tests.

Description

Ward Halstead and Ralph Reitan are the developers of the Halstead-Reitan Battery. Based on studies of patients with neurologic impairments at the University of Chicago, Halstead recognized the need for an evaluation of brain functioning that was more extensive than intelligence testing. He began experimenting with psychological tests that might help identify types and severity of brain damage through observation of a person's behavior in various tasks involving neuropsychological abilities. Initially he chose a set of ten tests; all but three are in the current Halstead-Reitan Battery.

Ralph Reitan, one of Halstead's students, contributed to the battery by researching the tests' ability to identify neurological problems. In a remarkable study, Reitan diagnosed 8,000 patients using only their test results—without meeting the patients or knowing anything about their background. This provided strong support for the battery's effectiveness. Reitan adapted the original battery by including additional tests.

The Halstead-Reitan has been researched more than any other neuropsychological test battery. Research continues to support its ability to accurately detect impairment in a large range of neuropsychological functions.

Category Test

A series of 208 pictures consisting of geometric figures are presented, sorted in groups according to some underlying principle, which the test subject is asked to determine. For each picture, individuals are asked to decide which of four principles they believe is represented and to press a key that corresponds to the number of choice. If they chose correctly, a chime sounds. If they chose incorrectly, a buzzer sounds. The pictures are presented in seven subtests.

The key to this test is that one principle, or common characteristic, underlies each subtest. The numbers 1, 2,

3, and 4 represent the possible principles. If individuals are able to recognize the correct principle in one picture, they will respond correctly for the remaining pictures in that subtest. The next subtest may have the same or a different underlying principle, and individuals must again try to determine that principle using the feedback of the chime and buzzer. The last subtest contains two underlying principles. The test takes approximately one hour to complete, but individuals with severe brain damage may take as long as two hours.

The Category Test is considered the battery's most effective test for detecting brain damage, but does not help determine where the problem is occurring in the brain. The test evaluates abstraction ability, or the ability to draw specific conclusions from general information. Related abilities are solving complex and unique problems, and learning from experience. Children's versions consist of 80 items and five subtests for young children, and 168 items and six subtests for older children.

Scoring involves recording the number of errors. Based on traditional scoring using cutoff values (cut-off scores are scores that indicate the borderline between normal and impaired functioning), scores above 41 are considered indicative of brain impairment for ages 15 to 45. For ages 46 and older, scores above 46 indicate impairment. Reitan has suggested a cutoff of 50 or 51 errors. Recommended cutoffs also vary depending on age and education level.

Tactual Performance Test

A form board containing 10 cutout shapes, and 10 wooden blocks matching those shapes are placed in front of a blindfolded individual. Individuals are then instructed to use only their dominant hand to place the blocks in their appropriate space on the form board. The same procedure is repeated using only the non-dominant hand, and then using both hands. Finally, the form board and blocks are removed, followed by the blindfold. From memory, individuals are asked to draw the form board and the shapes in their proper locations. The test usually takes anywhere from 15 to 50 minutes to complete. There is a time limit of 15 minutes for each trial, or each performance segment.

Other names for this test are the Form Board Test and the Seguin-Goddard Formboard. It evaluates sensory ability, memory for shapes and spatial location, motor functions, and the brain's ability to transfer information between its two hemispheres. In addition to simple detection of brain damage, this test also helps determine the side of the brain where damage

may have occurred. For children under the age of 15, only six shapes are used.

Scoring involves recording the time to complete each of the three blindfolded trials and the total time for all trials combined (time score), the number of shapes recalled (memory score), and the number of shapes drawn in their correct locations (localization score). Generally, the trial for the non-dominant hand should be 20–30% faster than the trial for the dominant hand, due to the benefit of practice. If the non-dominant hand is slower than the dominant hand—it should be slower, but is a question of how much slower—or more than 30% faster than the dominant hand, brain damage is possible. However, some people without brain damage do not exhibit this typical improvement rate. Injuries of the arms, shoulders, or hands can also affect performance. Scores should be adjusted depending on education level and may vary depending on age.

Trail Making Test

This test consists of two parts. Part A is a page with 25 numbered circles randomly arranged. Individuals are instructed to draw lines between the circles in increasing sequential order until they reach the circle labeled "End." Part B is a page with circles containing the letters A through L and 13 numbered circles intermixed and randomly arranged. Individuals are instructed to connect the circles by drawing lines alternating between numbers and letters in sequential order, until they reach the circle labeled "End." If individuals make mistakes, the mistakes are quickly brought to their attention, and they continue from the last correct circle. The test takes approximately five to 10 minutes to complete.

This test was originally known as Partingon's Pathways, or the Divided Attention Test, which was part of the Army Individual Test Battery. The test evaluates information-processing speed, visual-scanning ability, integration of visual and motor functions, letter and number recognition and sequencing, and the ability to maintain two different trains of thought. The test can be administered orally if an individual is incapable of writing. The Color Trails Test, designed for children and individuals of different cultures, uses colors instead of numbers and letters.

Scoring is simply the time to complete each part. Errors naturally increase the total time. Some have argued that the time taken to alert individuals of errors may vary depending on the person giving the test. For adults, scores above 40 seconds for Part A and 91 seconds for Part B have traditionally indicated brain impairment. Current research discourages the use of such traditional cutoffs, preferring ranges depending on age, education, and gender. For example, one study reported that for ages 15 to 19, the average time to complete Part A was 25.7 seconds and the time to complete Part B was 49.8 seconds. For ages 80 to 85, however, the average time to complete Part A was 60.7 seconds and the time to complete Part B was 152.2 seconds. This demonstrates the importance of considering other variables when scoring.

Finger Tapping Test

Individuals place their dominant hand palm down, fingers extended, with the index finger resting on a lever that is attached to a counting device. Individuals are instructed to tap their index finger as quickly as possible for ten seconds, keeping the hand and arm stationary. This trial is repeated five to 10 times, until the examiner has collected counts for five consecutive trials that are within five taps of each other. Before starting the test, individuals are given a practice session. They are also given brief rests between each 10-second trial, and one- to two-minute rests after every third trial. This entire procedure is repeated with the nondominant hand. The test takes approximately 10 minutes to complete.

This test is also called the Finger Oscillation Test. The children's version uses an electronic tapper instead of a manual one, which was difficult for children to operate. The test measures motor speed and helps determine particular areas of the brain that may be damaged. Scoring involves using the five accepted trials to calculate an average number of taps per trial for each hand. In general, the dominant hand should perform 10% better than the nondominant hand. Yet this is not always the case, especially with left-handed individuals. Men and younger people tend to perform better than women and older people. Interpretation should also consider education level, intelligence, **fatigue**, general weakness or lack of coordination, **depression**, and injuries to the shoulders, arms, or hands. This test should only be interpreted in combination with other tests in the battery.

Rhythm Test

Thirty pairs of tape-recorded, nonverbal sounds are presented. For each pair, individuals decide if the two sounds are the same or different, marking "S" or "D" respectively on their answer sheets. The pairs are grouped into three subtests. This test is also called the Seashore Rhythm Test, and is based on the Seashore Tests of Musical Ability. It evaluates auditory attention and concentration, and the ability to discriminate

between nonverbal sounds. The test helps detect brain damage, but not the location of damage. Adequate hearing and visual abilities are needed to take this test. Scoring is based on the number of correct items, with higher scores indicating less damage or good recovery. Scores should be interpreted along with information from other tests. Some researchers consider this test unreliable and simplistic. The children's version does not include this test.

Speech Sounds Perception Test

Sixty tape-recorded nonsense syllables containing the sound "ee" (for example, "meer" and "weem") are presented. After each syllable, individuals underline, from a set of four written syllables, the spelling that represents the syllable they heard. This test evaluates auditory attention and concentration and the ability to discriminate between verbal sounds. It provides some information regarding specific areas of brain damage, and may also indicate attention deficits or hearing loss. Scoring and interpretation are similar to that used for the Rhythm Test. The children's version contains fewer syllable choices.

Reitan-Indiana Aphasia Screening Test

Aphasia is the loss of ability to understand or use written or spoken language, due to brain damage or deterioration. In this test, individuals are presented with a variety of questions and tasks that would be easy for someone without impairment. Examples of test items include verbally naming pictures, writing the name of a picture without saying the name aloud, reading printed material of increasing length, repeating words stated by the examiner, simple arithmetic problems, drawing shapes without lifting the pencil, and placing one hand to an area on the opposite side of the body.

This test is a modification of the Halstead-Wepman Aphasia Screening Test. It evaluates language-related difficulties, right/left confusion, and nonverbal tasks. A typical scoring procedure is not used because this is a screening test; its purpose is to detect possible signs of aphasia that may require further evaluation. Subtle language deficits may not be detected.

Reitan-Klove Sensory-Perceptual Examination

This test detects whether individuals are unable to perceive stimulation on one side of the body when both sides are stimulated simultaneously. It has tactile, auditory, and visual components involving the ability to (a) specify whether touch, sound, or visible movement is occurring on the right, left, or both sides of the body; (b) recall numbers assigned to particular fingers (the examiner assigns numbers by touching each finger and stating the number with the individual's eyes closed); (c) identify numbers "written" on fingertips while eyes are closed; and (d) identify the shape of a wooden block placed in one hand by pointing to its shape on a form board with the opposite hand.

Ancillary tests

In addition to the core tests, examiners may choose to administer other tests based on the difficulties that individuals experience. Tests commonly used in combination with the Halstead-Reitan Battery include the Grip Strength Test, the Grooved Pegboard Test, the Reitan-Klove Lateral Dominance Examination, the Wechsler Memory Scale, the California Verbal Learning Test, the Buschke Selective Reminding Test, the Rey Auditory Verbal Memory Test, the Rey Complex Figure Test, the Test of Memory and Learning, the **Wide Range Achievement Test**, the **Minnesota Multiphasic Personality Inventory**, and the **Wechsler Adult Intelligence Scale** or Wechsler Intelligence Scales for Children. Some of these tests expand on these measures of functioning in the latest revision of the battery.

Results

Interpretation of the Halstead-Reitan involves analysis of various factors:

- overall performance on the battery. The Halstead Impairment Index (HII) and the General Neuropsychological Deficit Scale (GNDS) are commonly used to obtain an overall score, although the latest revision now facilitates calculation of a global deficit score that reflects the number and severity of deficits or impairments and incorporates more test measures than were used in previous versions. This summary score weighs deficits more heavily than strengths, which reduces the chance that better performance on a few components of the test will hide impairments. The HII is calculated by counting the total number of tests in the impaired range, and dividing that number by the total tests administered, resulting in a decimal between zero and one (0.0–0.2: normal functioning; 0.3–0.4: mild impairment; 0.5–0.7: moderate impairment; and 0.8–1.0: severe impairment). The GNDS is calculated by assigning a value between zero and four to 42 variables contained in the tests, then summing those values (0–25: normal functioning; 26–40: mild impairment; 41–67: moderate impairment; and 68 and higher: severe impairment).
- performance on individual tests. Each test must be interpreted in relation to other tests in the battery. Significantly poor performance on one test may be

---

KEY TERMS

Abstraction—Ability to think about concepts or ideas separate from specific examples.

Aphasia—Loss of previously acquired ability to understand or use written or spoken language, due to brain damage or deterioration.

Cutoff scores—In psychological testing, scores that indicate the borderline between normal and impaired functioning.

Dominant hand—The hand that one prefers to use when performing various tasks such as writing or throwing an object.

Lateralization—The control of specific neurological functions by one side of the brain or the other; for example, in most right-handed people, language functions are controlled by the left side of the brain and spatial and visual functions are controlled by the right side of the brain.

Localization—The control of specific neurological functions by specific areas in the brain.

Motor—Involving muscle movement.

Neurologic—Pertaining to the nervous system (brain and nerve cells).

Neuropsychological functioning—The ability of the nervous system and brain to process and interpret information received through the senses.

Nondominant hand—The hand that one does not typically use when performing various tasks such as writing or throwing an object.

Tactile/tactual—A pulse rate above 100 beats per minute.

---

due to various factors. However, if a pattern of poor performance occurs on three or more tests, or if significant discrepancies occur on two or more tests, impairment is likely.

- indications of lateralization and localization. This refers to the particular region of the brain that is damaged. Performance on sensory and motor tasks provides the necessary clues.

With the above information, a psychologist can diagnose the type of condition present, predict the course of the impairment (staying the same, getting better, or getting worse), and make recommendations regarding treatment, care, or rehabilitation.

In 2004, a revision in the norms used to make determinations about results on the battery was published.

This revision includes corrections based on ethnicity in addition to age, gender, and education. The results can be adjusted to demographic components, including African American or Caucasian ethnicity. Also updated is the global deficit score, which reflects the severity and number of deficits on more test measures than previously assessed. The sample used to determine the norms for this 2004 revision also was larger, including more than 1,000 adults, ages 20 to 85, for most test endpoints. The revision also has expanded measures of psychological functioning, including Wechsler scores.

See also Assessment and diagnosis; Brain; Dementia; Executive function; Luria-Nebraska Inventory; Mini-Mental State Exam; Neuropsychological Status Exam; Neuropsychological testing.

Resources

BOOKS

Broshek, Donna K., and Jeffrey T. Barth. "The Halstead-Reitan Neuropsychological Test Battery." In *Neuropsychological Assessment in Clinical Practice: A Guide to Test Interpretation and Integration*. Gary Groth-Marnat, ed. New York: John Wiley and Sons, 2000.

Evans, Jovier D., and others. "Cross-cultural Applications of the Halstead-Reitan Batteries." In *Handbook of Cross-cultural Neuropsychology: Critical Issues in Neuropsychology*. Elaine Fletcher-Janzen, Tony L. Strickland, and others, eds. New York: Kluwer Academic/Plenum Publishers, 2000.

Horton, Arthur MacNeill, ed. "The Halstead-Reitan Neuropsychological Test Battery: Problems and Prospects." *The Neuropsychology Handbook*. New York: Springer Publishing Company, 1997.

Otrfied, Spreen, and Esther Strauss. *A Compendium of Neuropsychological Tests: Administration, Norms, and Commentary*. 2nd ed. New York: Oxford University Press, 1998.

Vanderploeg, Rodney D., ed. *Clinician's Guide to Neuropsychological Assessment*. Mahwah, New Jersey: Lawrence Erlbaum Associates, 2000.

PERIODICALS

Burger, Denney C., and R. L. Lee. "The Kaufman Neuropsychological Assessment Procedure and the Halstead-Reitan Neuropsychological Battery: A Comparison Using Participants Referred by Vocational Rehabilitation." *Archives of Clinical Neuropsychology* 15.8 (2000): 696.

Morgan, Joel E., and Elise Caccappolo-van Vliet. "Advanced Years and Low Education: The Case Against the Comprehensive Norms." *Journal of Forensic Neuropsychology* 2.1 (2001): 53–69.

Reitan, Ralph M., and Deborah Wolfson. "The Neuropsychological Similarities of Mild and More Severe Head Injury." *Archives of Clinical Neuropsychology* 15.5 (2000): 433–42.

ORGANIZATIONS

Division of Clinical Neuropsychology. Division 40, American Psychological Association, 750 First Street, NE, Washington, DC 20002-4242. Telephone: (202) 336-6013. Web site: <http://www.div40.org>.

International Neuropsychology Society. 700 Ackerman Road, Suite 550, Columbus, OH 43202. Telephone: (614) 263-4200. Web site: <http://www.osu.edu/ins>.

OTHER

Heaton, R. K., and others. "Revised Comprehensive Norms for an Expanded Halstead-Reitan Battery: Demographically Adjusted Neuropsychological Norms for African American and Caucasian Adults." Lutz, FL: Psychological Assessment Resources, 2004. Available online at: <http://www3.parinc.com/products/product.aspx?Productid = RCNAAC>.

Sandra L. Friedrich, MA
Emily Jane Willingham, PhD

Hamilton Anxiety Scale

Definition

The Hamilton **Anxiety** Scale (HAS or HAMA) is a 14-item test measuring the severity of anxiety symptoms. It is also sometimes called the Hamilton Anxiety Rating Scale (HARS).

Purpose

The HAS is used to assess the severity of anxiety symptoms present in children and adults. It is also used as an outcome measure when assessing the impact of antianxiety medications, therapies, and treatments and is a standard measure of anxiety used in evaluations of psychotropic drugs. The HAS can be administered prior to medication being started and then again during follow-up visits, so that medication dosage can be changed in part based on the patient's test score.

The HAS was developed by Max Hamilton in 1959. It provides measures of overall anxiety, psychic anxiety (mental agitation and psychological distress), and somatic anxiety (physical complaints related to anxiety). Hamilton developed the HAS to be appropriate for adults and children; although it is most often used for younger adults, there has been support for the test's use with older adults as well. Hamilton also developed the widely used **Hamilton Depression Scale** (HDS) to measure symptoms of **depression**.

Hamilton developed the scale by using the statistical technique of factor analysis. With this method, he generated a set of symptoms related to anxiety and further determined which symptoms related to psychic anxiety and which related to somatic anxiety.

Precautions

The test has been criticized on the grounds that it does not always discriminate between people with anxiety symptoms and those with depressive symptoms (people with depression also score fairly high on the HAS).

Because the HAS is administered and rated by the interviewer, there is some subjectivity when it comes to interpretation and scoring. Interviewer bias can affect the results. For this reason, some people prefer self-report measures where scores are completely based on the interviewee's responses.

Description

The HAS is administered by an interviewer who asks a semistructured series of questions related to symptoms of anxiety. The interviewer then rates the individuals on a five-point scale for each of the 14 items. Seven of the items specifically address psychic anxiety, and the remaining seven items address somatic anxiety. For example, the third item specifically addresses fears related to anxiety, the fifth item addresses **insomnia** and sleeping difficulties related to anxiety, and the tenth item addresses respiratory symptoms related to anxiety.

According to Hamilton, examples of psychic symptoms elicited by the HAS interview include a generally anxious mood, heightened fears, feelings of tension, and difficulty concentrating. Examples of somatic symptoms include muscular pain, feelings of weakness, cardiovascular problems, and restlessness.

Results

For the 14 items, the values on the scale range from zero to four: zero means that there is no anxiety, one indicates mild anxiety, two indicates moderate anxiety, three indicates severe anxiety, and four indicates very severe or grossly disabling anxiety. The total anxiety score ranges from zero to 56. The seven psychic anxiety items elicit a psychic anxiety score that ranges from zero to 28. The remaining seven items yield a somatic anxiety score that also ranges from zero to 28.

One reason that the HAS is widely used is that reliability studies have shown that it measures anxiety symptoms in a fairly consistent way. The measure's validity has also been supported by research.

KEY TERMS

Factor analysis—A statistical method for summarizing relationships between variables. For the HAS, factor analysis was utilized to determine the specific sets of symptoms relating to overall anxiety, somatic anxiety, and psychic anxiety.

Psychotropic medication—Medication that has an effect on the mind, brain, behavior, perceptions, or emotions. Psychotropic medications are used to treat mental illnesses because they affect a patient's moods and perceptions.

Reliability—The ability of a test to yield consistent, repeatable results.

Validity—The ability of a test to measure accurately what it claims to measure.

Studies have shown that individuals with **anxiety disorders** score fairly high on the HAS. For example, persons with **generalized anxiety disorder** and **panic disorder** tend to have a total anxiety score above 20 on the HAS. On the other hand, people with no disorder or **diagnosis** score very low on the HAS.

While there is a tendency for depressed people to also score high on the HAS, some researchers have suggested that anxiety and depression are so closely linked that people can easily score high on measures of both types of symptoms.

The paper and pencil version of this test is in the public domain, meaning that it can easily be found on the Internet for people who are interested in reviewing it. There is also a computer-administered version for use in a computerized, telephone-based interview. This version uses voice recognition to take answers to the respondent's questions. The computerized "interviewer" can even interact in a programmed way with the respondent. A study has indicated that some respondents feel more comfortable answering the questions when they are administered in the telephone format compared to the in-person format.

Resources

BOOKS

Edelstein, Barry. *Comprehensive Clinical Psychology, Vol. 7: Clinical Geropsychology.* Amsterdam: Elsevier, 1998.

Maruish, Mark R. *The Use of Psychological Testing for Treatment Planning and Outcomes Assessment.* Mahwah, NJ: Lawrence Erlbaum Associates, 1999.

Ollendick, Thomas. *Comprehensive Clinical Psychology, Vol. 5: Children and Adolescents: Clinical Formulation and Treatment.* Amsterdam: Elsevier, 1998.

Schutte, Nicola S., and John M. Malouff. *Sourcebook of Adult Assessment Strategies*. New York: Plenum Press, 1995.

OTHER

"Healthcare Technology Systems." Producers of the IVR version of the Hamilton Anxiety Scale. Available online at: <http://www.healthtechsys.com/ivr/assess/ivrhama.html>.

Kobak, K.A., J.H. Greist, J.W. Jefferson, J.C. Mundt, and D.J. Katzelnick. "Computerized Assessment of Depression and Anxiety over the Telephone Using Interactive Voice Response." *MD Computing* 16 (1999): 64–68.

Ali Fahmy, PhD
Emily Jane Willingham, PhD

Hamilton Depression Scale

Definition

The Hamilton **Depression** Scale (HDS or HAMD) is a test measuring the severity of depressive symptoms in individuals, often those who have already been diagnosed as having a depressive disorder. It is sometimes known as the Hamilton Rating Scale for Depression (HRSD) or the Hamilton Depression Rating Scale (HDRS).

Purpose

The HDS is used to assess the severity of depressive symptoms present in both children and adults. It is often used as an outcome measure of depression in evaluations of antidepressant psychotropic medications and is a standard measure of depression used in research of the effectiveness of depression therapies and treatments. It can be administered prior to medication being started and then again during follow-up visits, so that medication dosage can be changed in part based on the patient's test score. The HDS is often used as the standard against which other measures of depression are validated. There is a computerized version available intended for administration by telephone using a voice-recognition system and a computerized "interviewer."

The HDS was developed by Max Hamilton in 1960 as a measure of depressive symptoms that could be used in conjunction with clinical interviews with depressed patients. It was later revised in 1967. Hamilton also designed the Hamilton Depression Inventory (HDI), a self-report measure for adults consistent with his theoretical formulation of depression in the

HDS, and the **Hamilton Anxiety Scale** (HAS), an interviewer-rated test measuring the severity of **anxiety** symptoms.

Precautions

Some symptoms related to depression, such as self-esteem and self-deprecation, are not explicitly included in the HDS items. Also, because anxiety is specifically asked about on the HDS, it is not always possible to separate symptoms related to anxiety from symptoms related to depression.

Because the HDS is administered and rated by the interviewer, there is some subjectivity when it comes to interpretation and scoring. Interviewer bias can affect the results. For this reason, some people prefer self-report measures where scores are completely based on the interviewee's responses.

Description

Depending on the version used, an interviewer can provide ratings for a test with 17 or 24 items. In addition to the items on the 17-item scale, the 24-item scale also addresses daytime-only symptoms, helplessness, hopelessness, worthlessness, obsessional symptoms, and paranoid feelings. A 21-item version has also been used for evaluations. Along with the patient interview answers, other information can be used in formulating ratings, such as information gathered from family, friends, and patient records. Hamilton stressed that the interview process be easygoing and informal and that there are no specific questions that must be asked.

Examples of items for which interviewers must give ratings include overall depression, guilt, **suicide**, **insomnia**, problems related to work, psychomotor retardation, agitation, anxiety, gastrointestinal and other physical symptoms, loss of libido, **hypochondriasis**, loss of insight, and loss of weight. For the overall rating of depression, for example, Hamilton believed one should look for feelings of hopelessness and gloominess, pessimism regarding the future, and a tendency to cry. For the rating of suicide, an interviewer should look for suicidal ideas and thoughts, as well as information regarding suicide attempts.

Results

In the 17-item version, which is most commonly used, nine of the items are scored on a five-point scale, ranging from zero to four. A score of zero represents an absence of the depressive symptom being measured, a score of one indicates doubt concerning the presence of the symptom, a score of two indicates mild

KEY TERMS

Hypochondriasis—A mental condition in which the affected person perceives illness or symptoms of illness when none exist.

Psychomotor retardation—Slowdown in motor activity directly proceeding from mental activity.

Psychotropic medication—Medication that has an effect on the mind, brain, behavior, perceptions, or emotions. Psychotropic medications are used to treat mental illnesses because they affect a patient's moods and perceptions.

Reliability—The ability of a test to yield consistent, repeatable results.

Validity—The ability of a test to measure accurately what it claims to measure.

to moderate symptoms, a score of three indicates moderate to severe symptoms, and a score of four represents the presence of extreme symptoms. The remaining eight items are scored on a three-point scale, from zero to two, with zero representing absence of symptom, one indicating that the symptom is present to a mild or moderate degree, and two representing clear presence of symptoms.

For the 17-item version, scores can range from zero to 54. One formulation suggests that scores between zero and six indicate a person who is typical and lacks morbidity with regard to depression; scores between seven and 17 indicate mild depression; scores between 18 and 24 indicate moderate depression; and scores over 24 indicate severe depression.

There has been evidence to support the reliability and validity of the HDS. The scale correlates highly with other clinician-rated and self-report measures of depression.

Resources

BOOKS

Edelstein, Barry. *Comprehensive Clinical Psychology, Vol. 7: Clinical Geropsychology.* Amsterdam: Elsevier, 1998.

Maruish, Mark R. *The Use of Psychological Testing for Treatment Planning and Outcomes Assessment.* Mahwah, NJ: Lawrence Erlbaum Associates, 1999.

Ollendick, Thomas. *Comprehensive Clinical Psychology, Vol. 5: Children and Adolescents: Clinical Formulation and Treatment.* Amsterdam: Elsevier, 1998.

Schutte, Nicola S., and John M. Malouff. *Sourcebook of Adult Assessment Strategies.* New York: Plenum Press, 1995.

OTHER

Because the scale is in the public domain, it is available on numerous Web sites. One example is at <http://healthnet.umassmed.edu/mhealth/HAMD.pdf>. Note that this scale is intended to be administered and interpreted by a trained professional.

U.S. Food and Drug Administration. Description of the Hamilton Depression Rating Scale (HAMD) and the Montgomery-Asberg Depression Rating Scale (MADRS). (2007) Available online at: <http://www.fda.gov/ohrms/dockets/AC/07/briefing/2007-4273b1_04-DescriptionofMADRSHAMDDepressionR(1).pdf>.

Ali Fahmy, PhD
Emily Jane Willingham, PhD

Hare Psychopathy Checklist

Definition

The Hare Psychopathy Checklist-Revised (PCL-R) is a diagnostic tool used to rate a person's psychopathic or antisocial tendencies. Psychopaths are people who prey ruthlessly on others using charm, deceit, violence or other methods that allow them to get with they want. The symptoms of psychopathy include lack of a conscience or sense of guilt; lack of empathy; egocentricity; pathological lying; repeated violations of social norms; disregard for the law; shallow emotions; and a history of victimizing others.

Originally designed to assess people accused or convicted of crimes, the PCL-R consists of a 20-item symptom rating scale that allows qualified examiners to compare a subject's degree of psychopathy with that of a prototypical psychopath. It is accepted by many in the field as the best method for determining the presence and extent of psychopathy in a person.

The Hare checklist is still used to diagnose members of the original population for which it was developed—adult males in prisons, criminal psychiatric hospitals, and awaiting psychiatric evaluations or trial in other correctional and detention facilities. Recent experience suggests that the PCL-R may also be used effectively to diagnose sex offenders as well as female and adolescent offenders.

Purpose

The PCL-R is used for diagnosing psychopathy in individuals for clinical, legal or research purposes. Developed in the early 1990s, the test was originally designed to identify the degree of a person's psychopathic tendencies. Because psychopaths, however, are often repeat offenders who commit sexual assaults or other violent crimes again and again, the PCL-R is now finding use in the courtroom and in institutions as an indicator of the potential risk posed by subjects or prisoners. The results of the examination have been used in forensic settings as a factor in deciding the length and type of prison sentences and the treatment subjects should or should not receive.

Precautions

Diagnosing someone as a psychopath is a very serious step. It has important implications for a person and for his or her associates in family, clinical and forensic settings. Therefore, the test must be administered by professionals who have been specifically trained in its use and who have a wide-ranging and up-to-date familiarity with studies of psychopathy.

Professionals who administer the diagnostic examination should have advanced degrees (MD, PhD, or D.Ed) in a medical, behavioral or social science field; and registered with a reputable organization that oversees psychiatric or psychological testing and diagnostic procedures. Other recommendations include experience working with convicted or accused criminals or several years of some other related on-the-job training. Because the results are used so often in legal cases, those who administer it should be qualified to serve as expert witnesses in the courtroom. It is also a good idea, if possible, for two experts to independently test a subject with the PCL-R. The final rating would then be determined by averaging their scores.

Many studies conducted in North America and Europe attest to the value of the PCL-R for evaluating a person's degree of psychopathic traits and, in many cases, for predicting the likelihood of future violent behavior. Some critics, however, are more skeptical about its value.

Description

The Hare PCL-R contains two parts, a semi-structured interview and a review of the subject's file records and history. During the evaluation, the clinician scores 20 items that measure central elements of the psychopathic character. The items cover the nature of the subject's interpersonal relationships; his or her affective or emotional involvement; responses to other people and to situations; evidence of social deviance; and lifestyle. The material thus covers two key aspects that help define the psychopath: selfish and unfeeling victimization of other people, and an unstable and antisocial lifestyle.

KEY TERMS

Affect—The expression of emotion displayed to others through facial expressions, hand gestures, tone of voice, etc. Types of affect include: flat (inanimate, no expression), blunted (minimally responsive), inappropriate (incongruous expressions of emotion relative to the content of a conversation), and labile (sudden and abrupt changes in type and intensity of emotion).

Egocentricity—Self-centeredness.

Forensic—Pertaining to courtroom procedure or evidence used in courts of law.

Grandiose—Having an exaggerated belief in one's importance or status. In some people, grandiosity may be so extreme as to be delusional.

Psychopath—A person who ruthlessly preys on others, using charm, deceit, violence or other methods that allows him or her to get with they want. Another word that is sometimes used for psychopath is sociopath.

Psychopathy—A psychological syndrome that includes lack of a conscience or sense of guilt, lack of empathy, egocentricity, pathological lying, repeated violations of social norms, disregard of the law, shallow emotions and a history of victimizing others.

The twenty traits assessed by the PCL-R score are:

- glib and superficial charm
- grandiose (exaggeratedly high) estimation of self
- need for stimulation
- pathological lying
- cunning and manipulativeness
- lack of remorse or guilt
- shallow affect (superficial emotional responsiveness)
- callousness and lack of empathy
- parasitic lifestyle
- poor behavioral controls
- sexual promiscuity
- early behavior problems
- lack of realistic long-term goals
- impulsivity
- irresponsibility
- failure to accept responsibility for own actions
- many short-term marital relationships
- juvenile delinquency
- revocation of conditional release
- criminal versatility

The interview portion of the evaluation covers the subject's background, including such items as work and educational history; marital and family status; and criminal background. Because psychopaths lie frequently and easily, the information they provide must be confirmed by a review of the documents in the subject's case history.

Results

When properly completed by a qualified professional, the PCL-R provides a total score that indicates how closely the test subject matches the "perfect" score that a classic or prototypical psychopath would rate. Each of the twenty items is given a score of 0, 1, or 2 based on how well it applies to the subject being tested. A prototypical psychopath would receive a maximum score of 40, while someone with absolutely no psychopathic traits or tendencies would receive a score of zero. A score of 30 or above qualifies a person for a **diagnosis** of psychopathy. People with no criminal backgrounds normally score around 5. Many non-psychopathic criminal offenders score around 22.

See also Antisocial personality disorder; Sexual sadism.

Resources

BOOKS

Black, Donald W., and C. Lindon Larson. *Bad Boys, Bad Men, Confronting Antisocial Personality Disorder*. New York, NY: Oxford University Press, 1999.

Hare, Robert D. *Without Conscience: The Disturbing World of the Psychopaths Among Us*. New York, NY: The Guilford Press, 1993.

PERIODICALS

Freedman, M. David. "False prediction of future dangerousness: Error rates and Psychopathy Checklist-Revised." *Journal of the American Academy of Psychiatry and Law* 29, no. 1 (March, 2001): 89-95.

Grann, M., N. Langström, A. Tengström, and G. Kullgren. "Psychopathy (PCL-R) predicts violent recidivism among criminal offenders with personality disorders in Sweden." *Law and Human Behavior* 23, no. 2 (April, 1999): 205-217.

OTHER

Hare, Robert D. Dr. Robert Hare's Page for the Study of Psychopaths. January 29, 2002 (cited April 5, 2002.) <http://www.hare.org/>.

Dean Haycock, PhD

HCR-20 *see* Historical, Clinical, Risk Management-20

Health maintenance organization *see* Managed care

Historical, Clinical, Risk Management-20

Definition

The Historical, Clinical, Risk Management-20 (HCR-20) is an assessment tool that helps mental health professionals estimate a person's probability of violence.

Purpose

The HCR-20's results help mental health professionals determine best treatment and management strategies for potentially violent, mentally disordered individuals, including parolees, forensic mental health patients, and others. For example, if an individual is standing trial for a violent offense, a judge might order that assessments (such as the HCR-20, as well as others) be performed. The results of the evaluation could be used to determine the person's future potential for violence, how the court should proceed, and which kind of facility the person might require.

Precautions

A professional trained in conducting individual assessments and in the study of violence should administer the HCR-20. The test administrator should have a background in using assessment tests or should consult a mental health professional. The HCR-20 is not intended to be a stand-alone measure, and it does not cover all risk factors. When possible, the test administrator should use supplemental test measures and investigate any unique patterns of violence and its triggers in the person's history. The HCR-20 is not meant to be administered just once; the nature of risk assessment requires ongoing re-assessment as circumstances change. Final interpretation of HCR-20 results should be in the context of several factors, including the reason for the person's test referral, base rates of violence in populations with similar characteristics, and assessment of future risks in the person's environment.

Description

The HCR-20 is an assessment tool. It consists of a list of 20 probing questions about the person being evaluated for violence. The clinician gathers qualitative information about the person being assessed, guided by the HCR-20, and the results are used to make treatment decisions.

The HCR-20 provides significantly improved valid predictions over previous testing methods. Earlier testing methods tended to be more subjective, less well-focused, and based on the loosely supported judgment of test administrators, or on comparing characteristics of the person being tested with base rates of violent behavior in populations with similar characteristics. The HCR-20 extends the methods of earlier tests and supplements them with a review of dynamic variables, such as **stress** and lack of personal support—both factors important to the person's future adjustment. This review adds to the accuracy of the HCR-20, and increases its practicality.

The HCR-20 consists of three main areas: historical, clinical, and risk management. The HCR-20 domains are coded with a rating of 0 (not present), 1 (possible/less serious), or 3 (definite/serious).

Historical area

To rate historical areas, the test administrator must do an exhaustive review of background documents, interview people who know the person being assessed, and complete the **Hare Psychopathy Checklist**, a useful instrument in its own right. The historical area is considered by many to anchor the instrument. It includes 10 domains:

- previous violence
- young age at first violent incident
- relationship instability
- employment problems
- substance use problems
- major mental illness, such as schizophrenia or bipolar disorder
- psychopathy, which can be defined as personality traits that deviate from social norms, such as manipulating and exploiting others for personal gain
- early maladjustment, or exposure to family and social disruptions during childhood that lead to coping problems (could be abuse or divorce, for example)
- personality disorder, such as paranoia
- failure to respond to clinical supervision or treatment in the past—may be related to noncompliance to treatment, such as refusing to take medications or attend therapy sessions

Clinical area

The rating of the clinical area requires a clinical interview between the person being assessed and the mental health professional. The professional will also use his or her judgment, as well. The clinical area consists of five domains:

- lack of insight, or difficulty understanding cause and effect. For example, people with poor insight might

not understand why they do what they do and why their actions matter.
- negative attitudes.
- active symptoms of major mental illness.
- impulsivity.
- unresponsiveness to treatment.

Risk management

The third area, risk management, includes five domains:

- the person's plans lack feasibility
- exposure to destabilizers, which means that family or social supports are missing, or that alcohol and drugs are available
- lack of personal support
- refusal to attend counseling sessions or take medications
- stress

Results

The HCR-20 does not allow for a definite prediction of violence. Predictions based on the HCR-20 are estimates of the likelihood of violence, and should be presented in terms of low, moderate, or high probability of violence. Probability levels should be considered conditional, given short- and long-term time frames, and should be considered in relation to relevant factors the individual may encounter. These factors include situations and states of being that may dispose a person to violence or help insulate them against it. Consideration of such factors can aid in reporting the type and extent of risk presented by a person and in selecting **intervention** strategies intended to reduce the probability that an individual will demonstrate violence. These strategies when taken as a whole are called a risk management plan.

Ultimately, HCR-20 results are intended to provide information for decision-makers, so that criminal and mental health-related decisions can be based on the best available estimates of risk of violence.

Resources

BOOKS

Webster, C., and others. *HCR-20: Assessing Risk for Violence, Version 2.* Burnaby, British Columbia, Canada: Mental Health, Law, and Policy Institute, Simon Fraser University, 1997.

PERIODICALS

Belfrage, H., R. Fransson, and S. Strand. "Prediction of violence using the HCR-20: A prospective study in two maximum security correctional institutions." *Journal of Forensic Psychiatry* 11, no. 1 (2000): 167-175.

Dawes, R., D. Faust, and P. Meehl. "Clinical versus actuarial judgement." *Science* 243 (1989): 1668-1674.

Douglas, K., J. Ogloff, T. Nicholls, and I. Grant. "Assessing risk for violence among psychiatric patients: The HCR-20 violence risk assessment scheme and the Psychopathy Checklist: Screening Version." *Journal of Consulting and Clinical Psychology* 67, no. 6 (1999): 917-930.

Monahan, J. "Violence prediction: The last 20 and the next 20 years." *Criminal Justice and Behavior* 23 (1996): 107-120.

Quinsey, V. "The prediction and explanation of criminal violence." *International Journal of Law and Psychiatry* 18 (1995): 117-127.

Serin, R. "Psychopathy and violence in criminals." *Journal of Interpersonal Violence* 6 (1991): 423-431.

Geoffrey G. Grimm, PhD, LPC

Histrionic personality disorder

Definition

Histrionic personality disorder, often abbreviated as HPD, is a type of personality disorder in which affected individuals display enduring patterns of attention-seeking and excessively dramatic behaviors beginning in early adulthood and present across a broad range of situations. Individuals with HPD are highly emotional, charming, energetic, manipulative, seductive, impulsive, erratic, and demanding.

Mental health professionals use the *Diagnostic and Statistical Manual of Mental Disorders* (the *DSM*) to diagnose mental disorders. The 2000 edition of this manual (the fourth edition, text revision, also called the *DSM-IV-TR*) classifies HPD as a personality disorder. More specifically, HPD is classified as a Cluster B (dramatic, emotional, or erratic) personality disorder. Cluster B includes the histrionic, antisocial, borderline, and narcissistic **personality disorders**.

Description

HPD has a unique position among the personality disorders because it is the only one explicitly connected to a patient's physical appearance. Researchers have found that HPD appears primarily in men and women with above-average physical appearances. Some research has suggested that the connection between HPD and physical appearance holds for women rather than for men. Both women and men with HPD express a strong need to be the center of attention. Individuals with HPD exaggerate, throw temper tantrums, and cry if they are not the center of attention. Patients with HPD are naive and gullible and have a low frustration threshold and strong dependency needs.

Cognitive style can be defined as a way in which individuals work with and solve cognitive tasks such as reasoning, learning, thinking, understanding, making decisions, and using memory. The cognitive style of individuals with HPD is superficial and lacks detail. In their interpersonal relationships, individuals with HPD use dramatization with the goal of impressing others. The enduring pattern of their insincere and stormy relationships leads to impairment in social and occupational areas.

Causes and symptoms

Causes

There is a lack of research on the causes of HPD. Even though the causes for the disorder are not definitively known, it is thought that HPD may be caused by biological, developmental, cognitive, and social factors.

NEUROCHEMICAL/PHYSIOLOGICAL CAUSES. Studies show that patients with HPD have highly responsive noradrenergic systems, the mechanisms surrounding the release of a neurotransmitter called norepinephrine. **Neurotransmitters** are chemicals that communicate impulses from one nerve cell to another in the **brain**, and these impulses dictate behavior. The tendency toward an excessively emotional reaction to rejection, common among patients with HPD, may be attributed to a malfunction in a group of neurotransmitters called catecholamines. Norepinephrine belongs to this group of neurotransmitters.

DEVELOPMENTAL CAUSES. Most psychoanalysts agree that a traumatic childhood can contribute to the development of HPD.

Defense mechanisms are sets of systematic, unconscious methods that people develop to cope with conflict and to reduce **anxiety**. According to Freud, all people use defense mechanisms, but different people use different types of defense mechanisms. Individuals with HPD differ in the severity of the maladaptive defense mechanisms they use. Patients with more severe cases of HPD may use the following defense mechanisms:

- repression. Repression is the most basic defense mechanism. When patients' thoughts produce anxiety or are unacceptable to them, they use repression to bar the unacceptable thoughts or impulses from consciousness.
- denial. Patients who use denial may say that a prior problem no longer exists, suggesting that their competence has increased; however, others may note that there is no change in the patients' behaviors.
- dissociation. When patients with HPD use the defense mechanism of dissociation, they may display two or more personalities. These two or more personalities exist in one individual without integration.

Patients with less severe cases of HPD tend to employ the following defenses:

- displacement. Displacement occurs when patients shift an affect from one idea to another. For example, a man with HPD may feel angry at work because the boss did not consider him to be the center of attention. The patient may displace his anger onto his wife rather than becoming angry with his boss.
- rationalization. Rationalization occurs when individuals explain their behaviors so that they appear to be acceptable to others.

BIOSOCIAL LEARNING CAUSES. A biosocial model in psychology asserts that social and biological factors contribute to the development of personality. Biosocial learning models of HPD suggest that individuals may acquire HPD from inconsistent interpersonal **reinforcement** offered by parents. Proponents of biosocial learning models indicate that individuals with HPD have learned to get what they want from others by drawing attention to themselves.

PERSONAL VARIABLES. Researchers have found some connections between the age of individuals with HPD and the behavior displayed by these individuals. The symptoms of HPD are long-lasting; however, histrionic character traits that are exhibited may change with age. For example, research suggests that young adults employ seductiveness more often than older ones. To impress others, older adults with HPD may shift their strategy from sexual seductiveness to a paternal or maternal seductiveness. Some histrionic

symptoms such as attention-seeking, however, may become more apparent as individuals with HPD age.

Symptoms

The *DSM-IV-TR* lists eight symptoms that form the diagnostic criteria for HPD:

- center of attention: Patients with HPD experience discomfort when they are not the center of attention.
- sexually seductive: Patients with HPD display inappropriate sexually seductive or provocative behaviors toward others.
- shifting emotions: The expression of emotions of patients with HPD tends to be shallow and to shift rapidly.
- physical appearance: Individuals with HPD consistently employ physical appearance to gain attention for themselves.
- speech style: The speech style of patients with HPD lacks detail. Individuals with HPD tend to generalize, and when these individuals speak, they aim to please and impress.
- dramatic behaviors: Patients with HPD display self-dramatization and exaggerate their emotions.
- suggestibility: Other individuals or circumstances can easily influence patients with HPD.
- overestimation of intimacy: Patients with HPD overestimate the level of intimacy in a relationship.

Demographics

General United States population

The prevalence of HPD in the general population is estimated to be approximately 2%-3%.

High-risk populations

Individuals who have experienced pervasive trauma during childhood have been shown to be at a greater risk for developing HPD as well as for developing other personality disorders.

Cross-cultural issues

HPD may be diagnosed more frequently in Hispanic and Latin American cultures and less frequently in Asian cultures. Further research is needed on the effects of culture on the symptoms of HPD.

Gender issues

Clinicians tend to diagnose HPD more frequently in females; however, when structured assessments are used to diagnose HPD, clinicians report approximately equal prevalence rates for men and women. In considering the prevalence of HPD, it is important to recognize that gender role stereotypes may influence the behavioral display of HPD and that women and men may display HPD symptoms differently.

Diagnosis

The **diagnosis** of HPD is complicated because it may seem like many other disorders, and also because it commonly occurs simultaneously with other personality disorders. The 1994 version of the *DSM* introduced the criterion of suggestibility and the criterion of overestimation of intimacy in relationships to further refine the diagnostic criteria set of HPD, so that it could be more easily recognizable. Prior to assigning a diagnosis of HPD, clinicians need to evaluate whether the traits evident of HPD cause significant distress. (The *DSM-IV-TR* requires that the symptoms cause significant distress in order to be considered a disorder.) The diagnosis of HPD is frequently made on the basis of an individual's history and results from unstructured and semistructured interviews.

Time of onset/symptom duration

Some psychoanalysts propose that the determinants of HPD date back to early childhood. The pattern of craving attention and displaying dramatic behavior for individuals with HPD begins by early adulthood. Symptoms can last a lifetime, but may decrease or change their form with age.

Individual variations in HPD

Some classification systems distinguish between different types of individuals with HPD: patients with appeasing HPD and patients with disingenuous HPD. Individuals with appeasing HPD have personalities with histrionic, dependent, and obsessive-compulsive components. Individuals with disingenuous HPD possess personality traits that are classified as histrionic and antisocial. Studies have shown that relationships exist between somatic behaviors and women with HPD and between antisocial behaviors and men with HPD.

Dual diagnoses

HPD has been associated with alcoholism and with higher rates of **somatization disorder**, **conversion disorder**, and **major depressive disorder**. Personality disorders such as borderline, narcissistic, antisocial, and dependent can occur with HPD.

Differential diagnosis

Differential diagnosis is the process of distinguishing one mental disorder from other similar disorders. For example, at times, it is difficult to distinguish between HPD and **borderline personality disorder**. **Suicide** attempts, identity diffusion, and numerous chaotic relationships occur less frequently, however, with people diagnosed with HPD. Another example of overlap can occur between people with HPD and **dependent personality disorder**. Patients with HPD and dependent personality disorder share high dependency needs, but only dependent personality disorder is linked to high levels of self-attributed dependency needs. Whereas patients with HPD tend to be active and seductive, individuals with dependent personality disorder tend to be subservient in their demeanor.

Psychological measures

Self-report inventories and projective tests can also be used to help clinicians diagnose HPD. The Minnesota Multiphasic Personality Inventory-2 (MMPI-2) and the Millon Clinical Multiaxial Inventory-III (MCMI-III) are self-report inventories with extensive empirical support. Results of intelligence examinations for individuals with HPD may indicate a lack of perseverance on arithmetic or on tasks that require concentration.

Treatments

Psychodynamic therapy

HPD, like other personality disorders, may require several years of therapy and may affect individuals throughout their lives. Some professionals believe that psychoanalytic therapy is a treatment of choice for people with HPD because it helps patients become aware of their own feelings. Long-term psychodynamic therapy needs to target the underlying conflicts of individuals with HPD and to assist patients in decreasing their emotional reactivity. Therapists work with thematic material related to intimacy and recall. Individuals with HPD may have difficulty recalling because of their tendency to repress material.

Cognitive-behavioral therapy

Cognitive therapy is a treatment directed at reducing the dysfunctional thoughts of individuals with HPD. Such thoughts include themes about not being able to take care of oneself. Cognitive therapy for people with HPD focuses on a shift from global, suggestible thinking to a more methodical, systematic, and structured focus on problems. Cognitive-behavioral training in relaxation for individuals with HPD emphasizes challenging

KEY TERMS

Behavioral contracts—A behavioral contract is a written agreement that defines the behaviors to be performed and the consequences of the specified behaviors.

Biosocial—A biosocial model in psychology asserts that social and biological factors contribute toward the development of personality.

Catecholamine—A group of neurotransmitters synthesized from the amino acid tyrosine and released by the hypothalamic-pituitary-adrenal system in the brain, in response to acute stress. The catecholamines include dopamine, serotonin, norepinephrine, and epinephrine.

Cognitive style—A way in which individuals work with and perform cognitive tasks such as reasoning, learning, thinking, understanding, making decisions, and using memory.

Differential diagnosis—The process of distinguishing one disorder from other similar disorders.

Disingenuous—Insincere, deceitful, dishonest.

Dissociation—A reaction to trauma in which the mind splits off certain aspects of the traumatic event from conscious awareness. Dissociation can affect the patient's memory, sense of reality, and sense of identity.

Etiology—The cause or origin of a disease or disorder. The word is also used to refer to the study of the causes of disease.

Histrionic—Theatrical.

Identity diffusion—A character formation that is scattered or spread around rather than an identity that becomes solidified or consolidated.

Noradrenergic—Acts similarly to norepinephrine or noradrenaline.

Oral phase—The first of Freud's psychosexual stages of development in which satisfaction is focused on the mouth and lips. During this stage sucking and eating are the primary means of gratification.

Personality disorder—A personality disorder is a maladaptive pattern of behavior, affect, and/or cognitive style displayed in a broad range of settings. The pattern deviates from the accepted norms of the individual's culture and can occur over a lifetime.

Response cost—A behavioral technique that involves removing a stimulus from an individual's environment so that the response that directly precedes the removal is weakened. In a token economy system, response cost is a form of punishment involving loss of tokens due to inappropriate behavior, which consequently results in decreased ability to purchase backup reinforcers.

Somatic—Relating to the body or to the physical.

---

automatic thoughts about inferiority and not being able to handle one's life. **Cognitive-behavioral therapy** teaches individuals with HPD to identify automatic thoughts, to work on impulsive behavior, and to develop better problem-solving skills. Behavioral therapists employ **assertiveness training** to assist individuals with HPD to learn to cope using their own resources. Behavioral therapists use response cost to decrease the excessively dramatic behaviors of these individuals. Response cost is a behavioral technique that involves removing a stimulus from an individual's environment so that the response that directly precedes the removal is weakened. Behavioral therapy for HPD includes techniques such as **modeling** and behavioral rehearsal to teach patients about the effect of their theatrical behavior on others in a work setting.

Group therapy

Group therapy is suggested to assist individuals with HPD to work on interpersonal relationships.

Psychodrama techniques or group role-playing can assist individuals with HPD to practice problems at work and to learn to decrease the display of excessively dramatic behaviors. Using role-playing, individuals with HPD can explore interpersonal relationships and outcomes to understand better the process associated with different scenarios. Group therapists need to monitor the group because individuals with HPD tend to take over and dominate others.

Family therapy

To teach assertion rather than avoidance of conflict, family therapists need to direct individuals with HPD to speak directly to other family members. **Family therapy** can support family members to meet their own needs without supporting the histrionic behavior of the individual with HPD who uses dramatic crises to keep the family closely connected. Family therapists employ behavioral contracts to support assertive behaviors rather than temper tantrums.

Medications

Pharmacotherapy is not a treatment of choice for individuals with HPD unless HPD occurs with another disorder. For example, if HPD occurs with **depression**, **antidepressants** may be prescribed. Medication needs to be monitored for **abuse**.

Alternative therapies

Meditation has been used to assist extroverted patients with HPD to relax and to focus on their own inner feelings. Some therapists employ hypnosis to assist individuals with HPD to relax when they experience a fast heart rate or palpitations during an expression of excessively dramatic, emotional, and excitable behavior.

Prognosis

The personality characteristics of individuals with HPD are long-lasting. Individuals with HPD use medical services frequently, but they usually do not stay in psychotherapeutic treatment long enough to make changes. They tend to set vague goals and to move toward something more exciting. Treatment for HPD can take a minimum of one to three years and tends to take longer than treatment for disorders that are not personality disorders, such as anxiety or mood disorders. Suicidal tendencies are common in people with HPD and should always be taken seriously.

As individuals with HPD age, they display fewer symptoms. Some research suggests that the difference between older and younger individuals may be attributed to the fact that older individuals have less energy.

Research indicates that a relationship exists between poor treatment outcomes and premature termination from treatment for individuals with Cluster B personality disorders. Some researchers suggest that studies that link HPD to continuation in treatment need to consider the connection between overestimates of intimacy and premature termination from therapy.

Prevention

Early diagnosis can assist patients and family members to recognize the pervasive pattern of reactive emotion among individuals with HPD. Educating people, particularly mental health professionals, about the enduring character traits of individuals with HPD may prevent some cases of mild histrionic behavior from developing into full-blown cases of maladaptive HPD. Further research in prevention needs to investigate the relationship between variables such as age, gender, culture, and ethnicity in people with HPD.

See also Minnesota Multiphasic Personality Inventory.

Resources

BOOKS

American Psychiatric Association. *Diagnostic and Statistical Manual of Mental Disorders.* 4th ed., Text rev. Washington, D.C.: American Psychiatric Association, 2000.

Bockian, Neil, PhD, and Arthur E. Jongsma, Jr., PhD. *The Personality Disorders Treatment Planner.* New York: Wiley, 2001.

Bornstein, Robert F. "Dependent and Histrionic Personality Disorders." *Oxford Textbook of Psychopathology.* Theodore Millon, PhD, Paul H. Blaney, and Roger D. Davis, eds. Oxford: Oxford University Press, 1999.

Widiger, Thomas A., PhD, and Robert F. Bornstein, PhD. "Histrionic, Narcissistic, and Dependent Personality Disorders." *Comprehensive Handbook of Psychopathology.* Patricia B. Sutker and Henry E. Adams, eds. 3rd ed. New York: Kluwer Academic/Plenum Publishers, 2001.

PERIODICALS

Bornstein, Robert F. "Histrionic Personality Disorder, Physical Attractiveness, and Social Adjustment." *Journal of Psychopathology and Behavioral Assessment* 21.1 (1999): 79–94.

Bornstein, Robert F. "Implicit and Self-Attributed Dependency Needs in Dependent and Histrionic Personality Disorders." *Journal of Personality Assessment* 71.1 (1998):–14.

Hilsenroth, Mark J., and others. "The Effects of DSM-IV Cluster B Personality Disorder Symptoms on the Termination and Continuation of Psychotherapy." *Psychotherapy* 35.2 (Summer 1998): 163–76.

ORGANIZATIONS

American Psychiatric Association. 1400 K Street NW, Washington, DC 20005. <http://www.psych.org>.

American Psychological Association. 750 First Street, NE, Washington, DC 20002-4242. Telephone: (202) 336-5500. Web site: <http://www.apa.org>.

Judy Koenigsberg, PhD
Emily Jane Willingham, PhD

HMO *see* **Managed care**

Homelessness

Definition

In the United States, definitions of homelessness help determine who is able to receive shelter and assistance from certain health and social service providers.

The Stewart McKinney Homeless Assistance Act of 1987 defines a homeless person as any individual who lacks housing, including an individual whose primary residence during the night is a supervised public or private facility that provides temporary living accommodations or an individual who is a resident in transitional housing. More specifically, this means an individual who lacks fixed, regular, and adequate nighttime residence, and an individual who has a primary nighttime residence that is either (i) a supervised temporary living shelter (including transitional housing for the mentally ill), (ii) an institution that provides temporary residence for individuals intended to be institutionalized, or (iii) a place not designed for or ordinarily used as a regular sleeping accommodation for human beings.

Description

Homelessness is an acute version of residential instability, which can be compared or contrasted with definitions of poverty. Thus the term "homeless" may also be extended to include people who have nowhere to go and are at imminent risk of losing housing through eviction or institutional discharge. Some definitions of homelessness further specify the duration of time without regular and adequate residence, or the types of temporary living shelter or institutions that are not fixed residences. People who live without alternatives in overcrowded or unhealthy housing conditions may be at risk of homelessness. Worldwide, national and cultural groups may have variable and often different definitions of homelessness, different terms for the condition of being without housing, and different definitions of adequate housing. For all of these reasons related both to methods of counting and varying definitions, estimating the size of the homeless population is extremely difficult.

The history of homelessness is intertwined with the history of poverty in the United States. Poverty has always been problematic for humanitarian reasons and because it conflicts with the ideal of prosperity for all. Social welfare, based on individualistic ideas of deserving and undeserving poor, has improved society but not eliminated persistent poverty or homelessness. The 1960s war on poverty was a widely shared value, but in the 1980s concern about homelessness was confounded by moral evaluations of individual behaviors. While many in the United States have been poor or come from poor families, fewer have experienced homelessness. Therefore, the collective understanding of homelessness in the United States is limited in ways that the understanding of poverty is not.

Homeless adults are poor and have high rates of unmet need for health care. This is in part because poverty is associated with higher risk and rates of illness, particularly mental illnesses including **substance abuse**. Homeless people experience disproportionate rates and symptoms of mental health disorders, including substance **abuse** disorders and dual diagnoses. For these reasons, large portions of federally funded homeless services are medical services, and homeless people are often viewed according to their present or past medical classifications.

Studies researching the incidence, distribution, and control of a disease in a population (known as epidemiological studies) find that between one-third and one-half of homeless people have mental health disorders and approximately two-thirds have either a mental health or substance use disorder. People with severe mental illness are likewise more likely to become homeless, particularly when the disorder is co-morbid (co-occurs) with substance abuse. For this reason, changes in rates of homelessness are often associated with changes in mental health care and **hospitalization** policies.

Mental illnesses compound the vulnerability and needs of homeless adults, as reported by the Surgeon General. Psychiatric disorders exacerbate many types of problems, including housing instability, morbidity (disease), and mortality (death). Psychiatric disorders and lack of stable living conditions complicate general health care for homeless adults.

Demographics

Methods for estimating the size of the homeless population are evolving and sometimes contested, and are complicated by varying definitions of homelessness. The U.S. Census, while attempting to identify the number of people who are homeless and who use particular types of homeless services, has complex and service-based definitions of homelessness. It also has recognized its limited abilities to define and enumerate the homeless (it is after all a national household survey). In 2000, the Census Bureau defined the Emergency and Transitional Shelter (E&TS) population by surveying people who use a sample of homeless services. They counted homeless people in emergency shelters for adults, runaway youth shelters, shelters for abused women and their children, soup kitchens, and certain outdoor locations. Technically, however, homeless people may reside in "E&TS," in foster care, in jails and prisons, in **group homes**, in worker dorms, non-sheltered in the outdoors, doubled up with families or friends, or temporarily in Census-recognized households. According to the National Coalition for the Homeless, while counting the number of people who use services such as shelters and soup kitchens can yield important information about services, applying these numbers toward estimating numbers of homeless people can result in underestimates of homelessness.

Further complicating the issue of counting homeless people is the fact that, in many cases, homelessness is a temporary condition. Because of this fact, some researchers advocate a method of counting all the people who are homeless in a given week or, alternatively, over a given period of time. However, the numbers of people who find housing and the number of people who newly find themselves homeless fluctuates over time periods. In contrast, people with mental illness or substance abuse problems tend to be chronically without homes—it is difficult for many of these people to find permanent housing. Thus, while these two time-oriented methods of counting homeless can be useful, they too have statistical problems—they can overestimate the numbers of homeless people.

Census estimates of the size and composition of the homeless population are difficult to create, for reasons described above. The Emergency and Transitional Shelter (ET&S) Population count in the United States in 2000 was 170,706. However, this figure does not include homeless adults not using ET&S services, sampling error, or some groups of homeless people not enumerated in the ET&S count. The ET&S population in 2000 was 61% male and 74% adult. Among the 26% who were youth, 51% were male. For adults, the population was 65% male, 41% were white, 40% were African American, 20% were Latino of any race, 2% were Asian, 2% were Native American, and 9% were one other race alone.

Another estimate of homelessness is a 2007 report by the National Alliance to End Homelessness, which estimated that 744,313 people were homeless in 2005. Forty-four percent of those people were unsheltered, and 56% were sheltered. Forty-one percent of the homeless were families.

The large variation between these estimates illustrates that, as the National Coalition for the Homeless states, "By its very nature, homelessness is impossible to measure with 100% accuracy."

Causes and consequences

Causes

People with mental illness are at higher risk for becoming homeless due to challenges associated with **deinstitutionalization** and transition planning, and both poverty and disability associated with mental illness.

Social research has studied the causes and consequences of homelessness, surveying homeless people, examining entrances into homelessness, exits from homelessness, and effects of homelessness on health and well-being. Promising explanations for increasing rates of homelessness in the 1980s have included mental disability and illness, lack of social support through jobs and marriage, increased use of drugs and alcohol, and the erosion of low-income housing in urban areas. These explanations mirror the processes of deinstitutionalization in mental health policy, unemployment, **addiction** and abuse, and urban decay. In other words, a direct correlation can be demonstrated between policies and trends and the rates of homelessness. As deinstitutionalization occurred, for example, the number of mentally ill people without homes increased.

Consequences

Consequences of homelessness include the exacerbation of problems that may have caused homelessness. Homeless people have reduced access to housing, jobs, health care, and basic needs like food and clothing. Isolation and lack of social support are well-documented aspects of homelessness, particularly for homeless people living with mental health or substance abuse disorders. Homeless women and men have been found to have significantly less family support than never-homeless women and men. Disaffiliation from family often limits opportunities for recovery and prevention.

Homeless service agencies

Services for homeless people can be divided into those providing medical care, those providing housing, and those providing other basic needs. Publicly funded agencies provide the majority of medical care, especially primary and mental health care. Public and private organizations share the responsibilities of providing shelter and housing services, through both large federal programs and smaller need and faith-based programs. Private agencies deliver most other daily needs to homeless people, through food pantries, soup kitchens, and other charities. Limited data exists on vocational services for homeless adults.

Title VI of the McKinney Homeless Assistance Act of 1987 created the Health Care for the Homeless (HCH) program, authorizing federal funds for primary and mental health care to homeless people. Title VI authorizes several programs to provide a HCH program, a **Community Mental Health** Services block grant program, and two demonstration programs providing mental health and alcohol and drug abuse treatment services to homeless people. HCH funds support providers who offer mental health, **case management**, and health education services, as well as substance abuse treatment. In 1987, 109 grants were made for homeless health services with $46 million. In 1992, the Act was amended to include homeless and at-risk children, creating a medical home and source of health insurance for young people. In 2005, Congress appropriated $145 million for health care for the homeless grants. The HCH program is the largest single effort to address the medical needs of the homeless. Each year, the HCH Program serves almost 600,000 clients in the United States To be a HCH service agency requires cultural and linguistic competencies, compassionate community outreach, and providers who reflect the community they serve.

The federal Center for Mental Health Services oversees Projects for Assistance in Transition from Homelessness (PATH) grant program. PATH provides state funds in support services to individuals who are homeless or at risk of becoming homeless and have serious mental illnesses. These funds amounted to more than $52 million allocated to 463 providers in 2005. States contract with local agencies and nonprofit organizations to provide an array of services, including outreach, support services, a limited set of housing services, and mental health treatment.

There are several obstacles or barriers in providing health care to homeless people. First, homeless or persistently poor people may be concerned about their work and sustenance, devaluing their own medical needs. Alienation and **depression** among the homeless can also be an obstacle to providing care. There can be mutual communication problems between providers and patients. Providers may lack cultural understanding that eases work with homeless clients. Finally, lack of preventive maintenance of medical care by the homeless may result in expensive and extensive needs for care, including hospital care, which may stress the capacities of certain service providers.

Homelessness in context

Homelessness is both a form of poverty and an acute condition of residential instability. Homelessness is compounded by behavioral problems, mental health policy changes, disparities in health and health care, racial inequalities, fluctuations in affordable housing, and lack of social support. Overly individualistic views and explanations of homelessness do not reflect its multiple causes and effects. Like all groups, homeless people are diverse, experiencing and exiting homelessness for a myriad of reasons. Services for homeless adults likewise reflect a variety of needs and experiences. Nonetheless, homelessness remains

KEY TERMS

Deinstitutionalization—The process of moving people out of mental hospitals into treatment programs or halfway houses in local communities. With this movement, the responsibility for care shifted from large (often governmental) agencies to families and community organizations.

a national and international concern, particularly in urban areas, for the twenty-first century.

How to help the homeless mentally ill

There are many ways that Americans can support community and federal efforts to help homeless people living with mental illness. Some strategies include:

- support collective public and private efforts to build homes and provide health care for people with unmet medical needs.
- become educated about the challenges faced by homeless and mentally ill people in American society.
- stop the practice of equating people in poverty and with illness with their medical conditions, instead of recognizing them as human beings. Succeeding in this step could open doors for recovery of health and housing without demeaning the humanity of people in need.

Resources

BOOKS

Burt, M., L. Aron, and others. *Homelessness: Programs and the People They Serve*. Washington, D.C.: U.S. Department of Housing and Urban Development, 1999.

Daly, Gerald. *Homeless*. New York: Routledge, 2005.

Hombs, Mary E. *American Homelessness*. Santa Barbara, CA: ABC-CLIO, 2001.

ORGANIZATIONS

National Alliance for the Mentally Ill (NAMI). Colonial Place 3, 2107 Wilson Blvd., Suite 300, Arlington VA, 22201-3042. Telephone: (703) 524-7600 or (800) 950-6264. <http://www.nami.org>.

National Coalition for the Homeless. 2201 P Street, NW, Washington, DC 20037. Telephone: (202) 462-4822. <http://www.nationalhomeless.org/>.

National Coalition for Homeless Veterans. 333 1/2 Pennsylvania Ave., SE, Washington, DC 20003-1148. Telephone: (800) 838-4357. <http://www.nchv.org>.

National Health Care for the Homeless Council. P.O.Box 60427, Nashville, TN 37206-0427. Telephone: (615) 226-2292. <http://www.nhchc.org/>.

National Institute of Mental Health. 6001 Executive Boulevard, Rm. 8184, MSC 9663, Bethesda, MD 20892-9663. Telephone: (301) 443-4513. <http://www.nimh.nih.gov>.

Substance Abuse and Mental Health Services Administration (SAMHSA). 1 Choke Cherry Road, Rockville MD 20857. <http://www.samhsa.gov>.

U.S. Department of Housing and Urban Development. 451 7th Street S.W., Washington, DC 20410. Telephone: (202) 708-1112. <http://www.hud.gov>.

Michael Polgar, PhD
Stephanie N. Watson

Hospitalization

Definition

Hospitalization or inpatient care is the most restrictive form of treatment for a psychiatric disorder, addictive disorder, or for someone with more than one **diagnosis**. Whether treatment is voluntary or involuntary, the patient relinquishes the freedom to move about and, once admitted, becomes subject to the rules and schedule of a treatment environment. Hospitalization is necessary in cases where individuals are in imminent danger of harming themselves or others or have made a **suicide** attempt. Crisis stabilization, **behavior modification**, supervised **substance abuse-detoxification**, and medication management are compelling reasons to consider hospitalization. Ideally, hospitalization is at one end of a comprehensive continuum of services for people needing treatment for behavioral problems. It is generally viewed as a last resort after other less restrictive forms of treatment have failed.

Purpose

For a person to be admitted to a hospital, a medical doctor (in the case of mental health, most often a **psychiatrist**) must "admit" the patient or approve the patient's request to be admitted. Although hospitalization may be considered a drastic treatment **intervention**, it can be essential in keeping people safe, helping monitor and adjust medications, treating medication side effects, supervising alcohol and/or drug detoxification, and stabilizing a patient after an acute psychiatric episode.

Before an individual is hospitalized, an evaluation and a diagnosis must be made by a medical professional. This is required in order for the patient to receive maximum insurance coverage and to receive the most appropriate treatment.

Precautions

In the public mental health system, less restrictive forms of treatment other than hospitalization are strongly recommended first. In the late 1960s, the patients' rights movement led to reforms governing **involuntary hospitalization**. Today the criteria for admission, particularly in the case of involuntary hospitalization, are extremely narrow, reflecting a strong reluctance in the United States to infringe on any person's liberty. The unintended consequences of this public policy are often observed in the numbers of people with mental illnesses who are homeless. So long as they are not posing a danger to themselves or others, they are likely to remain outside the traditional treatment system.

Hospitalization has long been negatively characterized in the media, contributing to the **stigma** of seeking inpatient treatment, even when it is voluntary. Scenes from the 1975 movie *One Flew Over the Cuckoo's Nest* have defined the worst in psychiatric hospital treatment. Such conditions cannot exist long in today's more sophisticated mental health, consumer-focused environment. A reputable facility will be accredited by the Joint Commission on Accreditation of Health Care Organizations, or by a similar governing body, which usually assures a minimum level of service. Most hospitals now have a Patient Advocate, usually an attorney who is on-site daily, or accessible by phone, and whose job is to investigate complaints and protect patients' rights. In addition, a federal law mandates that every state have a Protection and Advocacy Agency to handle complaints of abuse in hospitals. Although the effectiveness of these agencies varies from state to state, they can be helpful in explaining the rights of hospitalized patients. Some states have also implemented ombudsman programs to address patient complaints and to help people negotiate the mental health system.

Treatment facilities may be locked or unlocked. A locked unit will have tighter security to protect patient privacy and to keep patients from running away. In most cases when patients are voluntarily admitted, they may leave treatment at any time, invoking the right to do so against medical advice.

In the past, patients were often not part of their own treatment planning process. The rise of the patients' rights movement has led to more active patient involvement in all phases of treatment. They have the right to refuse certain forms of treatment.

Most hospitals now have a clearly posted Patient's Bill of Rights and may also have a patient's council or other body to represent their interests and recommend changes to the inpatient environment.

Confidentiality is paramount in a hospital setting, so much so that hospital staff seldom acknowledge that a specific patient has been admitted. **Group therapy** rules generally stress the importance of keeping members and the content of group sessions confidential.

Description

Most hospital rooms are similar to basic hotel rooms and are generally large enough for two people. In the case of public hospitals, the rooms may be larger and contain more beds. Men and women are in separate wings or on separate floors. If a treatment program is housed in a medical hospital, it may cover one or more floors.

Although there is wide variation in the quality of the physical surroundings and the resources available, most inpatient facilities are highly regimented. Patients get up, go to bed, eat, and take medication (if indicated) on a regular schedule. Days are filled with scheduled activities such as individual, family, or group therapy, expressive and occupational therapies, psychoeducation, recreation, and, in the case of children or adolescents, several hours of school.

Most hospital inpatient programs are based on a therapeutic milieu, which means that all the people involved in the patient's care and all the activities are designed to have a therapeutic function for the patient. For example, direct care workers are not simply aides; they are supportive of the patient and provide valuable feedback to the physician, **psychologist**, and social worker about the patient's conduct and progress.

Hospitalization statistics

For patients who enter the hospital because of substance abuse in the United States, a recent survey found that 9% of facilities offered inpatient care, and of these, almost half offered only detoxification facilities, without rehabilitation. About 74% offered programs for patients who had comorbidities. The majority of people who enter inpatient treatment do so in state and county hospitals. About 65 of every 100,000 people in the United States received treatment in an inpatient facility between 1969 and 2000.

Preparation

Even voluntary hospitalization can be overwhelming and anxiety-provoking. As a result, hospital staff will closely observe patients when they are first admitted. If the patients were admitted because of a suicide attempt or a violent episode, a "suicide watch" may be set up with more intensive staffing or in a room that can be monitored easily by nursing staff.

As patients adjust to the hospital routine, more privileges and freedom will be made available. For example, patients may earn privileges or rewards like outings with staff, a weekend pass to go home for a visit, or some other positive consequence if they follow hospital rules and engage in therapeutic activities.

An interdisciplinary treatment team made up of a psychiatrist, psychologist, social worker, nurse, direct care worker (sometimes called a psychiatric technician), and an expressive therapist usually oversees the care of patients while they are in the hospital. Treatment goals are developed by the team with patient input, and with discharge as a major objective.

Aftercare

Optimally, inpatient treatment prepares patients to deal with the realities of life outside the hospital. Emphasis is placed on how patients will behave differently in order to remain healthy and avoid future hospitalizations. During the discharge phase, patients may be scheduled for outpatient therapy and informed about various medications. Often times, patients experience **anxiety** at the thought of leaving the hospital, and this apprehension is addressed in therapy sessions as discharge nears.

Normal results

In the past, a patient might be admitted to a hospital for a minimum of 30 days. Today's rising health care costs and the prevalence of **managed care** have led to dramatically reduced hospital stays. An optimal outcome under these conditions is medication adjustment, monitoring, and the beginning of stabilization. Studies are under way to determine if shortened stays ultimately lead to more frequent hospitalizations later on.

Resources

ORGANIZATIONS

National Alliance for the Mentally Ill. Colonial Place Three, 2107 Wilson Boulevard, Suite 300, Arlington, VA 22201. Web site: <http://www.nami.org>.

National Association of Protection and Advocacy Systems. 900 2nd Street NE, Washington, DC 20001. Web site: <http://www.napas.org>.

National Mental Health Association. 1021 Prince Street, Alexandria, VA 22314. Web site: <http://www.nmha.org>.

National Mental Health Consumers' Self-Help Clearing-house. 1211 Chestnut Street, Suite 1207, Philadelphia, PA 19107. Web site <http://www.mhselfhelp.org>.

OTHER

Centers for Disease Control. "NCHS Data Definitions: Mental Health Organizations." Available online at: <http://www.cdc.gov/nchs/datawh/nchsdefs/mho.htm>.

Department of Health and Human Services. Drug and Alcohol Services and Information. "The DASIS Report: Facilities Offering Hospital Inpatient Care." Available online at: <http://www.oas.samhsa.gov/2k3/hospitalTX/hospitalTX.htm>.

O'Dea, Richard. "Moving from Coercion to Collaboration in Mental Health Services: State Hospital Perspective." U.S. Department of Health and Human Services, Substance Abuse and Mental Health Services Administration. National Mental Health Information Center. Available online at: <http://mentalhealth.samhsa.gov/publications/allpubs/sma04-3869/StateH.asp>.

U.S. Department of Health and Human Services, Substance Abuse and Mental Health Services Administration. "National Mental Health Statistics: 24-hour hospital and residential treatment residents." National Mental Health Information Center. Available online at: <http://mentalhealth.samhsa.gov/publications/allpubs/SMA04-3938/chp18table5.asp>.

Judy Leaver, MA
Emily Jane Willingham, PhD

House-tree-person test

Definition

The house-tree-person test (HTP) is a projective personality test, a type of exam in which the test taker responds to or provides ambiguous, abstract, or unstructured stimuli (often in the form of pictures or drawings). In the HTP, the test taker is asked to draw houses, trees, and persons, and these drawings provide a measure of self-perceptions and attitudes. As with other projective tests, it has flexible and subjective administration and interpretation.

Purpose

The primary purpose of the HTP is to measure aspects of a person's personality through interpretation of drawings and responses to questions. It is also sometimes used as part of an assessment of **brain** damage or overall neurological functioning.

The HTP was developed in 1948 by Buck, and later updated in 1969 by Buck and Hammer. Tests requiring human **figure drawings** were already being utilized as projective personality tests. Buck believed that drawings of houses and trees could also provide relevant information about the functioning of an individual's personality.

Precautions

Because it is mostly subjective, scoring and interpreting the HTP is difficult. Anyone administering the HTP must be properly trained. The test publishers provide a very detailed 350-page administration and scoring manual.

Description

The HTP can be given to anyone over the age of three. Because it requires test takers to draw pictures, it is often used with children and adolescents. It is also often used with individuals suspected of having brain damage or other neurological impairment. The test takes an average of 150 minutes to complete; it may take less time with normally functioning adults and much more time with neurologically impaired individuals.

During the first phase of the test, test takers are asked to use a crayon to draw pictures, respectively, of a house, a tree, and a person. Each drawing is done on a separate piece of paper and the test taker is asked to draw as accurately as possible. Upon completion of the drawings, they are asked questions about the drawings. There are a total of 60 questions created by Buck that examiners can ask. Examiners can also create their own questions or ask unscripted follow-up questions. For example, with reference to the house, Buck wrote questions such as, "Is it a happy house?" and "What is the house made of?" Regarding the tree, questions include, "About how old is that tree?" and "Is the tree alive?" Concerning the person, questions include, "Is that person happy?" and "How does that person feel?"

During the second phase of the test, test takers are asked to draw the same pictures with a pencil. The questions that follow this phase are similar to the ones in the first phase. Some examiners give only one of the two phases, choosing either a crayon, a pencil, or some other writing instrument.

One variation of test administration involves asking the individual to draw two separate persons, one of each sex. Another variation is to have test takers put all the drawings on one page.

Results

The HTP is scored in both an objective quantitative manner and a subjective qualitative manner. The

Kline, Paul. *The Handbook of Psychological Testing.* New York: Routledge, 1999.
Reynolds, Cecil R. *Comprehensive Clinical Psychology Volume 4: Assessment.* Amsterdam: Elsevier, 1998.

Ali Fahmy, PhD

Hypericum *see* **St. John's wort**

KEY TERMS

Projective test—A psychological test in which the test taker responds to or provides ambiguous, abstract, or unstructured stimuli, often in the form of pictures or drawings.

Reliability—The ability of a test to yield consistent, repeatable results.

Validity—The ability of a test to measure accurately what it claims to measure.

quantitative scoring scheme involves analyzing the details of drawings to arrive at a general assessment of intelligence, using a scoring method devised by the test creators. Research has shown this assessment of intelligence correlates highly with other **intelligence tests** such as the **Wechsler Adult Intelligence Scale** (WAIS).

The primary use of the HTP, however, is related to the qualitative scoring scheme in which the test administrator subjectively analyzes the drawings and the responses to questions in a way that assesses the test taker's personality. For example, a very small house might indicate rejection of one's home life. A tree that has a slender trunk but has large expansive branches might indicate a need for satisfaction. A drawing of a person that has a lot of detail in the face might indicate a need to present oneself in an acceptable social light.

Other methods of interpretation focus on the function of various parts in each of the drawings. In the house drawing, the roof might represent one's intellectual side, the walls might represent the test taker's degree of ego strength, and the doors and windows might represent the individual's relation to the outside world. In the tree drawing, the branches might indicate the test taker's relation to the outside world and the trunk might indicate inner strength.

As with other subjectively scored personality tests, there is little support for its reliability and validity. However, there is some evidence that the HTP can differentiate people with specific types of brain damage. More specifically, it has been shown to be effective when looking at the brain damage present in schizophrenic patients.

See also Figure drawings; Rorschach technique.

Resources

BOOKS

Groth-Marnat, Gary. *Handbook of Psychological Assessment.* 3rd edition. New York: John Wiley and Sons, 1997.

Hypersomnia

Definition

Hypersomnia refers to a set of related disorders that involve excessive daytime sleepiness.

Description

There are two main categories of hypersomnia: primary hypersomnia (sometimes called idiopathic hypersomnia) and recurrent hypersomnia (sometimes called recurrent primary hypersomnia). Both are characterized by the same signs and symptoms and differ only in the frequency and regularity with which the symptoms occur.

Primary hypersomnia is characterized by excessive daytime sleepiness over a long period of time. The symptoms are present all, or nearly all, of the time. Recurring hypersomnia involves periods of excessive daytime sleepiness that can last from one to many days and recur over the course of a year or more. The main difference between this and primary hypersomnia is that persons experiencing recurring hypersomnia will have prolonged periods where they do not exhibit any signs of hypersomnia, whereas persons experiencing primary hypersomnia are affected by it nearly all the time. One of the best documented forms of recurrent hypersomnia is **Kleine-Levin syndrome**, although there are other forms as well.

There are many different causes for daytime sleepiness that are not considered hypersomnia, and there are many diseases and disorders in which excessive daytime sleepiness is a primary or secondary symptom. Feelings of daytime sleepiness are often associated with the use of common substances such as caffeine, alcohol, and many medications. Other common factors that can lead to excessive daytime sleepiness that is not considered hypersomnia include shift work and **insomnia**. Shift work can disrupt the body's natural sleep rhythms. Insomnia can cause excessive daytime sleepiness because of lack of nighttime sleep and is a separate disorder.

Causes and symptoms

People experiencing hypersomnia do not get abnormal amounts of nighttime sleep. However, they often have problems waking up in the morning and staying awake during the day. People with hypersomnia nap frequently and do not feel refreshed upon waking from the naps. Hypersomnia is sometimes misdiagnosed as **narcolepsy**. In many ways the two are similar. One significant difference is that people with narcolepsy experience a sudden onset of sleepiness, while people with hypersomnia experience increasing sleepiness over time. Also, people with narcolepsy find daytime sleep refreshing, while people with hypersomnia do not.

People with Kleine-Levin syndrome have symptoms that differ from the symptoms of other forms of hypersomnia. These people may sleep up to 20 or more hours a day in episodes that last for several weeks. In addition, they are often irritable, sometimes to the point of violence. They can be sexually uninhibited (hypersexual) and make indiscriminate sexual advances. There may be some confusion and memory deficits, as well. People with Kleine-Levin syndrome often eat uncontrollably and rapidly gain weight, unlike people with other forms of hypersomnia. This form of recurrent hypersomnia is very rare, with only 27 cases described in the scientific literature between 1962 and 2004. The disorder, which most often starts in adolescence, generally lessens and resolves as a person ages.

The causes of hypersomnia remain unclear. There is some speculation that in many cases it can be attributed to problems involving the hypothalamus, but evidence supporting this idea is sparse. In the case of Kleine-Levin, there is some suggestion that onset of the disorder may in some cases be linked to certain viral illnesses.

Demographics

Hypersomnia is an uncommon disorder. In general, no more than 5% of adults complain of excessive sleepiness during the daytime. That does not mean all those who complain of excessive sleepiness have hypersomnia. There are many other possible causes of daytime sleepiness. Of all the people who visit sleep clinics because they feel they are too sleepy during the day, only about 5–10% are diagnosed with primary hypersomnia. Kleine-Levin syndrome is present in about four times more males than females, but it is a very rare syndrome.

Hypersomnia generally appears when the patient is between 15 and 30 years old. It does not begin

---

suddenly but becomes apparent slowly, sometimes over years.

Diagnosis

Hypersomnia is characterized by excessive daytime sleepiness, and daytime naps that do not result in a more refreshed or alert feeling. Hypersomnia does not include lack of nighttime sleep. People experiencing problems with nighttime sleep may have insomnia, a separate sleep disorder. In people with insomnia, excessive daytime sleepiness may be a side effect.

The *Diagnostic and Statistical Manual of Mental Disorders* (*DSM-IV-TR*), which presents the guidelines used by the American Psychiatric Association for **diagnosis** of disorders, states that hypersomnia symptoms must be present for at least a month, and must interfere with a person's normal activities. Also, the symptoms cannot be attributed to failure to get enough sleep at night or to another sleep disorder. The symptoms cannot be caused by another significant psychological disorder, nor can they be a side effect of a medicinal or illicit drug or a side effect of a general medical condition. For a diagnosis of recurrent hypersomnia, the symptoms must occur for at least three days at a time, and the symptoms have to be present for at least two years.

Treatments

There have been some attempts to use drugs for treating hypersomnia. No substantial body of evidence supports the effectiveness of these treatments. Stimulants are not generally recommended to treat hypersomnia because they treat the symptoms but do not address the cause. Some research suggests that treatments targeting the hypothalamus may be effective therapy for hypersomnia.

Prognosis

Kleine-Levin syndrome has been reported to occasionally resolve by itself around middle age. Except for

---

that syndrome, hypersomnia is considered both a lifelong disorder and one that can be significantly disabling. There is no body of evidence that concludes there is a way to successfully treat the majority of hypersomnia cases.

Resources

BOOKS

Aldrich, Michael S. *Sleep Medicines*. New York: Oxford University Press, 1999.

American Psychiatric Association. *Diagnostic and Statistical Manual of Mental Disorders*, 4th ed., Text rev. Washington, D.C.: American Psychiatric Association, 2000.

Chokroverty, Susan, ed. *Sleep Disorders Medicine: Basic Science, Technical Considerations, and Clinical Aspects*, 2nd ed. Boston: Butterworth-Heinemann, 1999.

Sadock, Benjamin J., and Virginia A. Sadock, eds.*Comprehensive Textbook of Psychiatry*, 7th ed., Vol. 2. Philadelphia: Lippincott Williams and Wilkins, 2000.

Thorpy, Michael J, ed. *Handbook of Sleep Disorders*. New York: Marcel Dekker, 1990.

PERIODICALS

Arnulf, I., J.M. Zeitzer, J. File, N. Farber, and E. Mignot. "Kleine-Levin Syndrome: A Systematic Review of 186 Cases in the Literature." *Brain* 128 (2006): 2763–76.

Boris, Neil W., Owen R. Hagina, and Gregory P. Steiner. "Case Study: Hypersomnolence and Precocious Puberty in a Child with Pica and Chronic Lead Intoxication." *Journal of the American Academy of Child and Adolescent Psychiatry* 35.8 (Aug. 1996): 1050–55.

Mahowald, Mark W., and Carlos H. Schenck. "Insights from Studying Human Sleep Disorders." *Nature* 43 (2005): 1279–85.

National Center on Sleep Disorders Research Working Group, Bethesda, Maryland. "Recognizing Problem Sleepiness in Your People." *American Family Physician* (Feb. 15, 1999): 937–38.

ORGANIZATIONS

American Academy of Sleep Medicine. 6301 Bandel Road NW, Suite 101, Rochester, MN 55901. Telephone: (507) 287-6006. Web site: <www.asda.org>.

National Organization for Rare Disorders (NORD). P.O. Box 1968/55 Kenosia Ave., Danbury, CT, 06813-1968. Telephone: (203) 744-0100. Web site: <http://www.rarediseases.org>

OTHER

NINDS Hypersomnia Information Page. (2007) Available online at: <http://www.ninds.nih.gov/disorders/hypersomnia/hypersomnia.htm>.

NINDS Kleine-Levin Syndrome Information Page. Available online at: <http://www.ninds.nih.gov/disorders/kleine_levin/kleine_levin.htm>.

Tish Davidson, AM
Emily Jane Willingham, PhD

Hypnotherapy

Definition

Hypnotherapy is the use of hypnosis as part of psychological or psychiatric treatment. Hypnotherapy may be used in short-term **psychotherapy** to help alleviate symptoms or as part of a long-term plan of psychotherapeutic **intervention** for personality change. Hypnotherapy may use any one or a combination of techniques administered by a trained professional who induces a hypnotic state in the patient and then presents therapeutic suggestions.

Purpose

Hypnosis, when used in conjunction with proven therapeutic procedures, can be a highly effective form of treatment for many mental, psychosomatic, and physical disorders. For example, through the use of regressive techniques, an adult patient may mentally travel back to a point in youth that was particularly troublesome, allowing the healing of old emotional wounds. Another patient can be led to understand that emotional pain has been converted to physical pain, and that the pain can be eliminated once the source has been addressed. Hypnotherapy can also be used to help persons with **chronic pain** to control the pain without use of medications. There are a number of techniques for correcting dysfunctional behaviors such as self-destructive habits, **anxiety disorders**, and even managing side effects of various medical treatments and procedures.

Hypnotherapy has been used to stop self-destructive and addictive habits like smoking. It has also been used to curb overeaters' urge to eat, to stem the disruptive actions of tics, cure **insomnia**, stop bed-wetting, and minimize **anxiety**. Excessive **stress** can be generated from any number of sources and can be the springboard for anxiety. Some of the more prominent sources of anxiety and stress for which people seek hypnotherapy are: public speaking, test taking, and job stress. Hypnotherapy also works well for other anxiety disorders such as phobias and has proven to be an effective treatment for mild to moderate **depression**. In one study, hypnotherapy was used in conjunction with traditional cognitive therapy to assist persons who had severe aversion to needles. The treatment was necessary, because it was essential that each participant receive periodic medical injections. However, the participants would have become noncompliant without the adjunct intervention of hypnotherapy. In another case, involving care for terminally ill cancer patients, it was concluded that hypnotherapy was more effective at enhancing

MILTON ERICKSON (1901–1980)

Erickson rose to prominence during the 1940's and 1950's as a pioneer in the medical, dental, and psychotherapeutic uses of hypnosis. He was considered the world's leading authority on the subject of hypnotherapy and was instrumental in establishing worldwide recognition and acceptance of hypnosis as a valid and effective therapeutic technique. He was frequently consulted by doctors and scientists, including anthropologist Margaret Mead, and during the 1950's he collaborated with author Aldous Huxley on research on hypnosis and other states of consciousness.

Erickson practiced psychiatry in Massachusetts and Michigan before moving to Arizona in the late 1940's. He was confined to a wheelchair following a bout with polio but continued to conduct teaching seminars from his Phoenix home. Erickson's teaching style was similar to his psychotherapeutic method–distraction by verbal communication and other forms of indirection disrupted the conscious set, providing access to the subject's unconscious mind. His orientation was eclectic, drawing on the widest range of schools of personality theory for the most useful elements of each. Erickson's books on the subject of hypnotherapy are geared toward health professionals and are, according to a *Psychology Today* reviewer, "written in a style…as original and personal as [Erickson's] technique."

quality of life and relieving anxiety and depressive symptoms, when compared to others who received traditional care.

Precautions

Confusion can occur when one seeks a hypnotherapist as a result of the various titles, certifications, and licenses in the field. Many states do not regulate the title "hypnotist" or "hypnotherapist," so care must be exercised when selecting someone to see. As a rule, it is best to consult a professional in the field of mental health or medicine, although alternative sources for hypnosis are available. Care must also be taken by the therapist to ensure adequate training and sufficient experience for rendering this specialized service. The therapist must be well-grounded in a psychotherapeutic approach before undertaking the use of hypnotherapy. Professionals should not attempt hypnotherapy with any disorder for which they would not use traditional therapeutic approaches. The patient seeking hypnotherapy is reminded that unskilled or amateur hypnotists can cause harm and should not be consulted for the purpose of implementing positive

change in an individual's life. The detrimental effects of being subjected to amateur or inadequately trained persons can be severe and long lasting.

Description

In order to understand hypnotherapy, it is necessary to understand the underlying concepts of hypnosis. A brief review of the history of hypnosis, description of hypnosis, and modern techniques follows.

History of hypnosis

It appears that hypnosis, under other names, has been used since the beginning of time. In fact, it has been insinuated that the earliest description of hypnosis may be portrayed in the Old Testament and in the Talmud. There is also evidence of hypnosis in ancient Egypt, some 3,000 years ago. However, the man credited with the development of what has become modern hypnosis is Friedrich Anton Mesmer. An Austrian physician, Friedrich Anton Mesmer one day watched a magician on a street in Paris demonstrate that he could have spectators do his bidding by touching them with magnets. Fascinated by the demonstration, Mesmer believed the magnets had power of their own and from this belief developed his theory of "animal magnetism." He also believed that good health depended on having correct magnetic flow and that the direction of one's magnetic flow could easily be reversed. He further believed that he could direct this magnetic flow into inanimate objects, which could then be used for the good health of others. The term "mesmerism" came to be applied to his mystical workings. He experienced much success in helping the people of Paris as well as visitors who came from other countries, upon hearing of his powers. Later he was completely discredited by a special commission of the French Academy appointed by the king, resulting in Mesmer's departure from France. Two of the more famous members of the French Academy at the time were chairman of the commission Benjamin Franklin, American ambassador to France, and Dr. Guillotine, the inventor of the execution device.

Later, around 1840, a patient in the office of Scottish physician James Braid accidentally entered a state of trance while waiting for an eye examination. Braid, aware of the disfavor of mesmerism and animal magnetism coined the term "hypnosis," and thus began the serious study of this altered state of awareness.

What is hypnosis?

It is far easier to describe what hypnosis is not than to describe what it is. For example, it is not one person controlling the mind of another. The patient is not unconscious and does not lose control of his or her faculties. People will not do things under hypnosis that they would be unwilling to do otherwise. The person being hypnotized is always in control. The hypnotized person decides how deep the trance will be, what suggestions will be accepted, and when to awaken. Therefore, a hypnotized person cannot be forever "lost" if the therapist should fall dead during an induction or while the patient is deep in trance.

Hypnosis is first and foremost a self-accepted journey away from the reality of the moment. Although the trance state is often referred to as if the patient is asleep, nothing could be further from the truth. The patient is fully awake at all times. The hypnotic subject is simply in a heightened, more receptive state of mind. This fact is proven with inductions called open-eye techniques, where the patient keeps his/her eyes open during the hypnotherapy. Full and deep trance is still achievable.

Trance is commonplace. People fall into traces many times without even being aware that it has happened. Examples of this include reaching the destination of a morning commute, but not recalling the passing of familiar landmarks; daydreaming while sitting in a college classroom; or that anxiety-free state achieved just before going to sleep. The difference between these altered states and clinically used hypnotherapy is that a professionally trained person is involved in helping the patient achieve the trance, which can be done in many ways.

A typical hypnotherapy session has the patient seated comfortably with their feet on the floor and palms on their lap. Of course, the patient could choose to lie down if that option is available and if that will meet the patient's expectation of hypnosis. The therapist can even set the stage for a favorable outcome by asking questions like, "Would you prefer to undergo hypnosis in this chair or on the sofa?" Once patients makes the choice, they are in effect agreeing to undergo hypnosis. Depending on the approach used by the therapist, the next events can vary, but generally will involve some form of relaxing the patient. Suggestions will lead the patient to an increasingly relaxed state. The therapist may wish to confirm the depth of trance by performing tests with the patient. For example, the therapist may suggest that when the eyes close that they will become locked and cannot be opened. The therapist then checks for this by having patients try to open their eyes. Following a successful trial showing the patient's inability to open the eyes, the therapist might then further relax them by using deepening techniques. Deepening techniques will vary for

each patient and depend largely on whether the patient represents information through auditory, visual, or kinesthetic means. If the patient is more affected by auditory suggestions, the therapist would use comments such as "You hear the gentle patter of rain on the roof;" or, "The sound of the ocean waves allow you to relax more and more." For the visual person, the therapist might use statements such as, "You see the beautiful placid lake, with trees bending slightly with the breeze." Finally, with the kinesthetic person phrases like, "You feel the warm sun and gentle breeze on your skin," could be used. It is important for the therapist to know if the patient has difficulty with the idea of floating or descending because these sensations are sometimes used to enhance the experience for the patient. However, if the patient has a fear of heights or develops a feeling of oppression with the thought of traveling downward and going deeper and deeper, suggestions implying the unwanted or feared phenomenon will not be taken and can thwart the attempt.

Modern techniques

In order for a hypnotherapist to convey positive suggestions for change, the patient must be in a receptive state. The state is called trance and the method of achieving a trance is through induction. Induction techniques are many and varied and involve the therapist offering suggestions that the patient follows. The formerly common "your eyes are getting heavy" suggestion may still exist, but other more reliable and acceptable (to the patient) forms of induction have come to the forefront. The artful hypnotherapist is always aware of the present condition of the patient and uses this information to lead him/her down the path of induction. In its lighter stages, trance can be noted by the relaxation of muscles. At this point, hands can levitate when given the suggestion, and paresthesia, a feeling of numbness, can be induced. In a medium trance, a patient can be led to experience partial or complete **amnesia**, or failure to recall events of the induction after the fact. A deep trance opens the patient to powerful auditory, visual, or kinesthetic experiences. The phenomenon of time distortion is experienced most profoundly at this level. Patients may believe they have been away briefly, and may react with disbelief when told they were away much longer. Although some work can be done in lighter states of trance, the best circumstance for implementing change is when the patient reaches a deep trance state. At this level, the patient is focused inwardly and is more receptive to positive suggestions for change. This is also the point at which the therapist can invoke posthypnotic suggestions, or instructions given to the patient so he/she will perform some act or experience some particular sensation following awakening from the trance. These suggestions, if accepted by the patient, can be formed to make foods or cigarettes taste bad, or to delay impulses, curb hunger, or eliminate pain, for example. However, it should be noted that posthypnotic suggestions given to a person which run counter to the person's value system, or are not something they are likely to do under ordinary circumstances, will not be accepted and therefore not implemented.

Neuro-Linguistic Programming (NLP) is the name given to a series of models and techniques used to enhance the therapist's ability to do hypnotherapy. NLP consists of a number of models, with a series of techniques based on those models. Sensory acuity and physiology is one model whose premise is that a person's thought processes change their physiological state. People recognize such a physiological change when startled. The body receives a great dose of **adrenaline**, the heart beats faster, the scare may be verbalized by shouting, and the startled person may sweat. Sensory acuity (i.e., being attuned to changes occurring in another person) will strengthen communication to a person in ways over and above simple verbal cues, therefore making the therapist more effective. A second model of NLP deals with representational systems. The idea behind this model is that different people represent knowledge in different sensory styles. In other words, an individual's language reveals that person's mode of representation. There are three basic modes of representation: auditory, visual, and kinesthetic. The same information will be expressed differently by each type. For example, the auditory person might say, "That sounds good to me," the visual person might offer, "I see it the same way," and the kinesthetic person would say, "I'm comfortable with it too."

Preparation

Before people subject themselves to hypnotherapy they are advised to learn as much about the process and about the chosen therapist as is necessary to feel comfortable. Rapport and trust are two key factors. Therapists should be open and willing to answer all questions regarding qualifications, expertise, and methods used. A well-qualified professional will not undertake the use of hypnosis without interviewing the patient to ascertain their level of understanding of the process. This is very important for two reasons. First, it allows the patient the opportunity to have questions answered and to develop some rapport with the therapist. Second, it is important for the therapist to know the patient's expectations since

meeting these expectations will enhance the likelihood of success.

Aftercare

Depending on the purpose of the hypnotherapy (i.e., **smoking cessation**, weight loss, improvement in public speaking, or addressing some deep emotional turmoil), follow-up may be advisable. When trying to eradicate unwanted habits, it is good practice to revisit the therapist, based upon a date prearranged between the therapist and the patient, to report progress and, if necessary, to obtain secondary hypnotherapy to reinforce progress made.

Risks

One obvious risk to patients is the insufficiently trained therapist. The inadequately trained therapist can cause harm and distort the normally pleasant experience of hypnotherapy. A second risk for patients is the unscrupulous practitioner who may be both inadequately trained and may have some hidden agenda. These rare individuals are capable of causing great harm to the patient and to the profession. As mentioned above, the patient should carefully scrutinize their chosen therapist before submitting themselves to this dynamic form of therapy.

Normal results

The result of hypnotherapy is overwhelmingly positive and effective. Countless success stories exist attesting to the benefits of this technique. Many people have stopped smoking, lost weight, managed pain, remembered forgotten information, stopped other addictions, or improved their health and well-being through its use.

Abnormal results

Abnormal results can occur in instances where amateurs, who know the fundamentals of hypnosis, entice friends to become their experimental subjects. Their lack of full understanding can lead to immediate consequences, which can linger for some time after the event. If, for example, the amateur plants the suggestion that the subject is being bitten by mosquitoes, the subject would naturally scratch where the bites were perceived. When awakened from the trance, if the amateur forgets to remove the suggestion, the subject will continue the behavior. Left unchecked, the behavior could land the subject in a physician's office in an attempt to stop the itching and scratching cycle. If the physician is astute enough to question the genesis of the behavior and hypnosis is used to remove the suggestion, the subjects may experience long-term negative emotional distress and anger once they understand exactly what happened. The lack of full understanding, complete training, and supervised experience on the part of the amateur places the subject at risk.

Resources

BOOKS

Barabasz, Arreed, and John G. Watkins. *Hypnotherapeutic Techniques,* 2nd ed. New York: Brunner-Routledge, 2004.

Flemons, Douglas. *Of One Mind: The Logic of Hypnosis, the Practice of Therapy.* New York: W. W. Norton, 2002.

Hawkins, Peter J. *Hypnosis and Stress: A Guide for Clinicians.* New York: Wiley, 2006.

Lynn, Steven Jay, and Irving Kirsch. *Essentials of Clinical Hypnosis: An Evidence-Based Approach.* Washington, D.C.: American Psychological Association, 2006.

Spiegel, Herbert, and David Spiegel. *Trance and Treatment: Clinical Uses of Hypnosis,* 2nd ed. Washington, D.C.: American Psychiatric Publishing, 2004.

Yapko, M.D, ed. *Hypnosis and Treating Depression.* New York: Routledge, 2006.

Zarren, Jordan I., and Bruce N. Eimer. *Brief Cognitive Hypnosis: Facilitating the Change of Dysfunctional Behavior.* New York: Springer Publishing, 2002.

PERIODICALS

Bamford, Candy. "A Multifaceted Approach to the Treatment of Phantom Limb Pain Using Hypnosis." *Contemporary Hypnosis* 23.3 (Sept. 2006): 115–26.

Bryant, Richard A., Michelle L. Moulds, Reginald D. V. Nixon, Julie Mastrodomenico, Kim Felmingham, and Sally Hopwood. "Hypnotherapy and Cognitive Behaviour Therapy of Acute Stress Disorder: A 3-Year Follow-Up." *Behaviour Research and Therapy* 44.9 (Sept. 2006): 1331–35.

Gay, Marie-Claire. "Effectiveness of Hypnosis in Reducing Mild Essential Hypertension: A One-Year Follow-Up." *International Journal of Clinical and Experimental Hypnosis* 55.1 (Jan. 2007): 67–83.

Kihslinger, Daun, and Marty Sapp. "Hypnosis and Diabetes: Applications for Children, Adolescents, and Adults." *Australian Journal of Clinical Hypnotherapy and Hypnosis* 27.1 (Fall 2006): 19–27.

Kraft, Tom, and David Kraft. "The Place of Hypnosis in Psychiatry: Its Applications in Treating Anxiety Disorders and Sleep Disturbances." *Australian Journal of Clinical and Experimental Hypnosis* 34.2 (Nov. 2006): 187–203.

Mende, Matthias. "The Special Effects of Hypnosis and Hypnotherapy: A Contribution to an Ecological Model of Therapeutic Change." *International Journal of Clinical and Experimental Hypnosis* 54.2 (Apr. 2006): 167–85.

Uccheddu, Ornella Manca, and Antonello Viola. "Descriptive Survey of Therapeutic Alliance in Hypnotherapy." *European Journal of Clinical Hypnosis* 7.1 (2006): 10–25.

ORGANIZATIONS

American Society of Clinical Hypnosis. 2250 East Devon Avenue, Suite 336, Des Plaines, IL 60018.

Society for Clinical and Experimental Hypnosis. 129-A Kings Park Drive, Liverpool, NY 13088.

Jack H. Booth, PsyD
Ruth A. Wienclaw, PhD

Hypoactive sexual desire disorder

Definition

Hypoactive sexual desire disorder (HSDD) is defined as the persistent or recurrent extreme aversion to, absence of, and avoidance of all, or almost all, genital sexual contact with a sexual partner. Synonyms for HSDD include sexual aversion, inhibited sexual desire, sexual **apathy**, and sexual anorexia. HSDD is not rare, occurring in both sexes. It is the most common of all female sexual disorders, occurring in at least 20% of women in the United States.

Description

The affected person has a low level of sexual interest and desire that is manifested by a failure to initiate or be responsive to a partner's initiation of sexual activity. HSD becomes a diagnosable disorder when it causes marked distress or interpersonal instability, according to the ***Diagnostic and Statistical Manual of Mental Disorders***, fourth edition, text revision (also known as the *DSM-IV-TR*), the handbook used by mental health professionals to diagnose mental disorders. HSDD may be either situational (solely oriented against one partner), or it may be general, in which case there is a lack of sexual interest in anyone. In the extreme form of HSDD, the patient not only lacks sexual desire, but may also find sex to be repulsive, revolting and distasteful. Phobic or panic responses may be present in extreme cases of HSD. HSDD may be the result of either physical or emotional factors.

Causes and symptoms

Causes

PRIMARY HSD. HSDD may be a primary condition in which the patient has never felt much sexual desire or interest, or it may have occurred secondarily when the patient formerly had sexual desire, but no longer has interest. If lifelong or primary, HSDD may be the consequence of sexual trauma such as incest, sexual abuse, or rape. In the absence of sexual trauma, there is often a repressive family attitude concerning sex that is sometimes enhanced by rigid religious training. A third possibility is that initial attempts at sexual intercourse resulted in pain or sexual failure. Rarely, HSDD in both males and females may result from insufficient levels of the male sex hormone, testosterone.

ACQUIRED HSD. Acquired, situational HSDD in the adult is commonly associated with boredom in the relationship with the sexual partner. **Depression**, the use of psychoactive or antihypertensive medications, and hormonal deficiencies may contribute to the problem. HSDD may also result from impairment of sexual function, particularly **erectile dysfunction** on the part of the male, or **vaginismus** on the part of the female. Vaginismus is defined as a conditioned voluntary contraction or spasm of the lower vaginal muscles resulting from an unconscious desire to prevent vaginal penetration. An incompatibility in sexual interest between the sexual partners may result in relative HSDD in the less sexually active member. This usually occurs in the presence of a sexually demanding partner.

PAINFUL INTERCOURSE. Painful intercourse (**dyspareunia**) is more common in women than in men, but may be a deterrent to genital sexual activity in both sexes. The causes are usually physical in nature and related to an infection of the prostate gland, urethra, or testes. Occasionally, an allergic reaction to a spermicidal preparation or condom may interfere with sexual intercourse. Painful erections may be a consequence of Peyronie's disease, which is characterized by fibrotic changes in the shaft of the penis that prevent attainment of a normal erection. In the female, dyspareunia may be caused by vaginismus or local urogenital trauma or inflammatory conditions such as hymenal tears, labial lacerations, urethral bruising, or inflammatory conditions of the labial or vaginal glands.

PRIAPISM. Priapism is the occurrence of any persistent erection of more than four hours duration occurring in the absence of sexual stimulation. It is not associated with sexual excitement and the erection does not subside after ejaculation. Priapism can occur at any age, but clusters of occurrence are common between the ages of five and 10 years and between the ages of 20 and 50. In children, priapism is commonly associated with leukemia and sickle cell disease, or occurs secondary to trauma. The most common cause in adults is the intrapenile injection of agents to correct erectile dysfunction. Priapism may also occur secondary to the use of psychotropic drugs, such as **chlorpromazine** and prazosin. The pain accompanying priapism may be a cause of HSDD.

PROLACTINOMA. A rare but important cause of HSDD is a functioning prolactin-secreting tumor of the pituitary gland, a prolactinoma. Men with this condition typically state that they can achieve an erection, but that they have no interest in sexual relations. In the female, prolactinomas are associated with galactorrhea (lactation in the absence of pregnancy), amenorrhea, symptoms of estrogen deficiency and dyspareunia. Although prolactinomas are benign tumors, they can cause visual disturbances by enlarging and causing pressure on the optic nerves within the confines of the *sella turcica*, the location of the pituitary gland at the base of the **brain**. Headaches and enlargement of the male breasts are fairly common in this condition. The **diagnosis** is confirmed by the finding of high levels of circulating prolactin in the blood. Enlargement of the pituitary gland area may be detected by the use of **magnetic resonance imaging** (MRI) or computerized axial tomography (CAT) scanning, also called **computed tomography**.

DELAYED SEXUAL MATURATION. Delayed sexual maturation is a potential cause of HSDD. It is present in boys if there is no testicular enlargement by age 13-and-a-half or if there are more than five years between the initial and complete growth of the genitalia. In girls, delayed sexual maturation is characterized by a lack of breast enlargement by age 13, or by a period greater than five years between the beginning of breast growth and the onset of menstruation. Delayed puberty may be the result of familial constitutional disorders, genetic defects such as Turner's syndrome in females and Klinefelter's syndrome in males, central nervous system disorders such as pituitary conditions that interfere with the secretion of gonadotropic hormones, and chronic illnesses such as diabetes mellitus, chronic renal failure, and cystic fibrosis.

SEXUAL ANHEDONIA. Sexual anhedonia is a rare variant of HSDD seen in the male, in which the patient experiences erection and ejaculation, but no pleasure from orgasm. The cause is attributed to penile anesthesia, due to psychogenic factors occurring in an hysterical or obsessive person. Psychiatric referral is indicated unless there is evidence of spinal cord injury or peripheral neuropathy. Loss of tactile sensation of the penis is unlikely to be organic in cause unless there is associated anesthetic areas in the vicinity of the anus or scrotum.

Symptoms

The HSDD patient complains of a lack of interest in sex even under circumstances that are ordinarily erotic in nature, such as pornography. Sexual activity is infrequent and eventually is absent, often resulting in serious marital discord. HSDD may be selective and focused against a specific sexual partner. When boredom with the usual sexual partner is the cause and frequency of sex with the usual partner decreases, real or fantasized sexual desire toward others may be normal or even increased.

If the cause of HSD falls into a detectable category such as abnormalities of the genitalia, or is due to a related condition such as a prolactinoma, chronic renal disease, diabetes mellitus, genetic disorder, or is familial in nature, the patient will manifest the signs and symptoms of the comorbid (co-occurring) condition. It is important to identify such causes, as their presence will usually dictate appropriate therapy.

Treatments

Currently, there is no approved drug or pharmacological treatment for HSDD and **psychotherapy** has proved to be only minimally effective. A primary goal of therapy is aimed at removal of the underlying cause of HSDD. The choice of medical therapy or behavioral or dynamic psychotherapy depends on the cause. If the cause is related to a medical condition, therapy is directed toward the cure or amelioration of that condition. Examples include cure or amelioration of underlying comorbid conditions such as genitourinary infections, improvement in diabetic control, avoidance of **substance abuse** and of medications that may be potentially responsible.

Therapy should also be directed towards other accompanying sexual disorders such as erectile dysfunction, which may be contributory. In cases where insufficient testosterone is suspected as a possible cause, serum androgen levels should be tested. A testosterone level less than 300 ng/dl in males and less than 10 ng/dl in females indicates a need for supplemental replacement therapy. If the cause is deemed to be of an interpersonal nature, **couples therapy** may be beneficial, in which case the support and understanding of the sexual partner is essential. Tricyclic **antidepressants** (TCAs) or monoamine oxidase inhibitors (MAOIs) may help in the treatment of accompanying depression or panic symptoms.

A recent study has reported that almost a third of nondepressed women with HSDD responded favorably to therapy with sustained release tablets of **bupropion** hydrochloride. The responders noted significant increases in the number of sexual arousals, sexual fantasies, and in the desire to engage in sexual activities. Bupropion hydrochloride (Wellbutrin) is currently approved by the FDA for the treatment of depression. Its favorable action on HSDD may be attributable to its enhancement of certain **neurotrans-**

mitters that affect sexual desire, principally norepinephrine and **dopamine**.

Prognosis

The prognosis for HSDD depends primarily on the underlying cause or causes. In certain medical conditions, the prognosis for development, or recovery of sexual interest, is good. Examples include therapy of hypogonadism with testosterone, or the appropriate treatment of a prolactin-secreting pituitary tumor. On the other hand, in certain genetic defects such as Turner's syndrome and Klinefelter's syndrome, attainment of sexual function is impossible. By far, however, the vast majority of HSDD cases are situational in nature, usually relating to dissatisfaction or loss of interest in the sexual partner. In cases of marital discord, significant assistance may be obtained by counseling given by a health professional trained in the field. Cases of dissatisfaction by both partners often do not respond to such therapy, and frequently culminate in separation, finding a new sexual partner, and divorce.

Prevention

Unfortunately, it is difficult or impossible to predict the occurrence of HSDD in situational cases that comprise the majority of patients. The patience, understanding and support of the sexual partner is essential in those cases of HSDD in which the cause is temporary or transient. Some therapists recommend a period of abstinence from genital sex and have emphasized the value of a period of concentration on non-genital sex in the treatment of HSD.

KEY TERMS

Comorbid—Having another disorder or condition simultaneously.

Dyspareunia—Painful sexual intercourse.

Galactorrhea—Lactation occurring in the absence of pregnancy

Hypogonadism—Abnormally decreased gonad function with retardation of sexual development.

Priapism—Painful involuntary penile erection persisting in excess of four hours.

Prolactin—A hormone that stimulates milk production and breast development.

Vaginismus—An involuntary tightening of the vaginal muscles that makes sexual intercourse painful, difficult, or impossible.

Resources

BOOKS

Borkow F., and A. J. Fletcher, eds. *The Merck Manual of Diagnosis and Therapy*. 16th edition. Rahway, NJ: Merck Research Laboratories, 1992.

Carnes, Patrick, Ph.D. *Sexual Anorexia*. Center City, MN: Hazelden Press, 1997.

Hawton, Keith. *Sex Therapy: A Practical Guide*. New York: Oxford University Press, 1985.

Lue, Tom F., F. Goldstein. "Impotence and Infertility." In *Atlas of Clinical Urology*. Volume 1. New York: Current Medicine, 1999.

PERIODICALS

Segraves R.T., Croft H., Kavoussi R., and others. "Bupropion sustained release (SR) for the treatment of Hypoactive Sexual Desire Disorder (HSDD) in nondepressed women." *Journal of Sex and Marital Therapy* 27 (May-June 2001): 303-16.

Ralph Myerson, MD

Hypochondriasis

Definition

Hypochondriasis is a mental disorder in which the individual is preoccupied with the thought of having a serious physical disease based on the incorrect or exaggerated interpretation of physical symptoms. This preoccupation continues for at least six months and interferes with the individual's social and occupational functioning even in the face of medical evidence to the contrary. Hypochondriasis is considered a somatoform disorder.

Description

The primary feature of hypochondriasis is excessive fear of having a serious disease. This fear is not relieved when a medical examination finds no evidence of disease. People with hypochondriasis are often able to acknowledge that their fears are unrealistic, but this intellectual realization is not enough to reduce their **anxiety**. In order to qualify for a **diagnosis** of hypochondriasis, preoccupation with fear of disease must cause a great deal of distress or interfere with a person's ability to perform important activities, such as work, school activities, or family and social responsibilities. Hypochondriasis is included in the category of somatoform disorders in the *Diagnostic and Statistical Manual of Mental Disorders* (*DSM-IV-TR*), which is the reference handbook that clinicians use to guide

the diagnosis of mental disorders. Some experts, however, have argued that hypochondriasis shares many features with **obsessive-compulsive disorder** or **panic disorder** and would be more appropriately classified with the **anxiety disorders**.

The fears of a person with hypochondriasis may be focused on the possibility of a single illness, but more often they include a number of possible conditions. The focus of the fears may shift over time as a person notices a new symptom or learns about an unfamiliar disease. The fears appear to develop in response to minor physical abnormalities, like **fatigue**, aching muscles, a mild cough, or a small sore. People with hypochondriasis may also interpret normal sensations as signs of disease. For instance, an occasional change in heart rate or a feeling of dizziness upon standing up will lead a person with hypochondriasis to fears of heart disease or **stroke**. Sometimes hypochondriacal fears develop after the death of a friend or family member, or in response to reading an article or seeing a television program about a disease. Fear of illness can also increase in response to **stress**. Individuals with hypochondriasis visit physicians frequently; and when told there is nothing physically wrong, they are likely to seek a second opinion since their fears are not soothed. Their apparent distrust of their physicians' opinions can cause tensions in doctor-patient relationships, leading to the patient's further dissatisfaction with health-care providers. Physicians who regularly see a patient with hypochondriasis may become skeptical about any reported symptom, increasing the danger that a real illness may be overlooked. People with hypochondriasis also run the risk of undergoing unnecessary medical tests or receiving unneeded medications. Although they are usually not physically disabled, they may take frequent sick days from work, or annoy friends and family with constant conversation or complaints about illness, reducing their ability to function effectively in some aspects of life.

Causes and symptoms

Causes

AMPLIFICATION OF SENSORY EXPERIENCE. One theory suggests that people with hypochondriasis are highly sensitive to physical sensations. They are more likely than most people to pay close attention to sensations within their bodies (heart rate, minor noises in the digestive tract, the amount or taste of saliva in the mouth, etc.), which magnifies their experience of these feelings. While many people fail to notice minor discomfort as they go about their regular activities, the individual with hypochondriasis pays constant attention to inner sensations and becomes alarmed when these sensations vary in any way. This heightened scrutiny may actually increase the intensity of the sensations, and the intensity of the experience fuels fears that the sensations signal an underlying illness. Once the fears are aroused, preoccupation with the symptom increases, further enhancing the intensity of sensations. The tendency to amplify may be either temporary or chronic; it may also be influenced by situational factors, which helps to explain why hypochondriacal fears are made worse by stress or by events that appear to justify concerns about illness. Some researchers have observed that heightened sensitivity to internal sensations is also a feature of panic disorder, and have suggested that there may be an overlap between the two disorders.

DISTORTED INTERPRETATION OF SYMPTOMS. Another theory points to the centrality of dysfunctional thinking in hypochondriasis. According to this theory, the internal physical sensations of the person with hypochondriasis are not necessarily more intense than those of most people. Instead, people with hypochondriasis are prone to make catastrophic misinterpretations of their physical symptoms. They are pessimistic about the state of their physical health and overestimate their chances of falling ill. Hypochondriasis thus represents a cognitive bias; whereas most people assume they are healthy unless there is clear evidence of disease, the person with hypochondriasis assumes he or she is sick unless given a clean bill of health. Interestingly, research suggests that people with hypochondriasis make more realistic estimations of their risk of disease than most people, and in fact underestimate their risk of illness. Most people simply underestimate their risk even more. Some studies indicate that people with hypochondriasis are more likely to have had frequent or serious illnesses as children, which may explain the development of a negative cognitive bias in interpreting physical sensations or symptoms.

Symptoms

The primary symptom of hypochondriasis is preoccupation with fears of serious physical illness or injury. The fears of persons with hypochondriasis have an obsessive quality; they find thoughts about illness intrusive and difficult to dismiss, even when they recognize that their fears are unrealistic. In order to relieve the anxiety that arises from their thoughts, people with hypochondriasis may act on their fears by talking about their symptoms, by seeking information about feared diseases in books or on the Internet, or by "doctor-shopping," going from one specialist to another for consultations. Others may deal with their fears through

avoidance, staying away from anything that might remind them of illness or death. Persons with hypochondriasis vary in their insight into their disorder. Some recognize themselves as "hypochondriacs," but have anxiety in spite of their recognition. Others are unable to see that their concerns are unreasonable or exaggerated.

Demographics

According to the *DSM-IV-TR*, hypochondriasis affects 1–5% of the general population in the United States. The rates of the disorder are higher among clinical outpatients, between 2% and 7%. One recent study suggests that full-blown hypochondriasis is fairly rare, although lesser degrees of worry about illness are more common, affecting as many as 6% of people in a community sample.

Hypochondriasis can appear at any age, although it frequently begins in early adulthood. Men and women appear to equally develop the disorder. The *DSM-IV-TR* notes that people from some cultures may appear to have fears of illness that resemble hypochondriasis, but are in fact influenced by beliefs that are traditional in their culture.

Diagnosis

Hypochondriasis is most likely to be diagnosed when one of the doctors consulted by the patient considers the patient's preoccupation with physical symptoms and concerns excessive or problematic. After giving the patient a thorough physical examination to rule out a general medical condition, the doctor will usually give him or her a psychological test that screens for anxiety or **depression** as well as hypochondriasis. If the results suggest a diagnosis of hypochondriasis, the patient should be referred for **psychotherapy**. It is important to note, however, that patients with hypochondriasis usually resist the notion that their core problem is psychological. A successful referral to psychotherapy is much more likely if the patient's medical practitioner has been able to relate well to the patient and work gradually toward the notion that psychological problems might be related to fears of physical illness.

Specific approaches that have been found useful by primary care doctors in bringing psychological issues to the patient's attention in nonthreatening ways include the following:

- drawing connections between the patient's current physical symptoms and recent setbacks or upsetting incidents in the patient's life. For example, the patient may come in with health worries within a few days of having a problem in other areas of life, such as their car needing repairs, a quarrel with a family member, an overdue bill, etc.

- asking the patient to keep a careful diary of his or her symptoms and other occurrences. This diary may be useful in guiding the patient to see patterns in his or her worries about health.
- scheduling the patient for regular but short appointments. It is also better to see the patient briefly than to prescribe medications in place of an appointment, because many patients with hypochondriasis abuse medications.
- conduct routine screening tests during a yearly physical for patients with hypochondriasis, while discouraging them from scheduling extra appointments each time they notice a minor physical problem.
- maintain a realistic but optimistic tone in his or her conversation with the patient. He or she may wish to talk to the patient about health-related fears and clarify the differences between normal internal body sensations and serious symptoms.

In order to receive a *DSM-IV-TR* diagnosis of hypochondriasis, a person must meet all six of the following criteria:

- the person must be preoccupied with the notion or fear of having a serious disease. This preoccupation is based on misinterpretation of physical symptoms or sensations.
- appropriate medical evaluation and reassurance that there is no illness present do not eliminate the preoccupation.
- the belief or fear of illness must not be of delusional intensity. Delusional health fears are more likely to be bizarre in nature—for instance, the belief that one's skin emits a foul odor or that food is rotting in one's intestines. The preoccupations must not be limited to a concern about appearance; excessive concerns that focus solely on defects in appearance would receive a diagnosis of body dysmorphic disorder.
- the preoccupation must have lasted for at least six months.
- the person's preoccupation with illness must not simply be part of the presentation of another disorder, including generalized anxiety disorder, obsessive-compulsive disorder, panic disorder, separation anxiety, major depressive episode, or another somatoform disorder.

The *DSM-IV-TR* also differentiates between hypochondriasis with and without poor insight. Poor insight is specified when the patient does not recognize that his or her concerns are excessive or unreasonable.

Treatments

Traditionally hypochondriasis has been considered difficult to treat. In the last few years, however, cognitive and behavioral treatments have demonstrated effectiveness in reducing the symptoms of the disorder.

Cognitive therapy

The goal of cognitive therapy for hypochondriasis is to guide patients to the recognition that their chief problem is fear of illness, rather than vulnerability to illness. Patients are asked to monitor worries and to evaluate how realistic and reasonable they are. Therapists encourage patients to consider alternative explanations for the physical signs they normally interpret as disease symptoms. Behavioral experiments are also employed in an effort to change the patient's habitual thoughts. For instance, a patient may be told to focus intently on a specific physical sensation and monitor increases in anxiety. Another behavioral assignment might ask the patient to suppress urges to talk about health-related worries with family members, then observe their anxiety level. Most people with hypochondriasis believe that their anxiety will escalate until they release it by seeking reassurance from others. In fact, anxiety usually crests and subsides in a matter of minutes. Cognitive therapy effectively reduces many symptoms of the disorder, and many improvements persist up to a year after treatment ends.

BEHAVIORAL STRESS MANAGEMENT. One study compared cognitive therapy to behavioral stress management. This second form of therapy focuses on the notion that stress contributes to excessive worry about health. Patients were asked to identify stressors in their lives and taught stress management techniques to help them cope with these stressors. The researchers taught the patients relaxation techniques and problem-solving skills, and the patients practiced these techniques in and out of sessions. Although this treatment did not focus directly on hypochondriacal worries, it was helpful in reducing symptoms. At the end of the study, behavioral stress management appeared to be less effective than cognitive therapy in treating hypochondriasis, but a follow-up a year later found that the results of two therapies were comparable.

EXPOSURE AND RESPONSE PREVENTION. This therapy begins by asking patients to make a list of their hypochondriacal behaviors, such as checking body sensations, seeking reassurance from physicians or friends, and avoiding reminders of illness. Behavioral assignments are then developed. Patients who frequently monitor their physical sensations or seek reassurance are asked not to do so, and to allow themselves to experience the anxiety that accompanies suppression of these behaviors. Patients practice exposing themselves to anxiety until it becomes manageable, gradually reducing hypochondriacal behaviors in the process. In a study comparing exposure and response prevention to cognitive therapy, both therapies produced clinically significant results. Although cognitive therapy focuses more on thoughts and exposure therapy more on behaviors, both appear to be effective in reducing both dysfunctional thoughts and behaviors.

Prognosis

Untreated hypochondriasis tends to be a chronic disorder, although the intensity of the patient's symptoms may vary over time. The *DSM-IV-TR* notes that the following factors are associated with a better prognosis: the symptoms develop quickly; are relatively mild; are associated with an actual medical condition; and are not associated with comorbid psychopathology or benefits derived from being ill.

Prevention

Hypochondriasis may be difficult to prevent in a health-conscious society, in which people are constantly exposed to messages reminding them to seek regular medical screenings for a variety of illnesses, and telling them in detail about the illnesses of celebrities and high-ranking political figures. Trendy new diagnostic techniques like full-body MRIs may encourage people with hypochondriasis to seek unnecessary and expensive medical consultations. Referring patients

with suspected hypochondriasis to psychotherapy may also help to reduce their overuse of medical services.

See also Exposure treatment.

Resources

BOOKS

American Psychiatric Association. *Diagnostic and Statistical Manual of Mental Disorders,* 4th ed., Text rev. Washington D.C.: American Psychiatric Association, 2000.

Asmundson, Gordon J. G., Steven Taylor, and Brian J. Cox, eds. *Health Anxiety: Hypochondriasis and Related Disorders.* New York: John Wiley and Sons, 2002.

Maj, Mario, Hagop S. Akiskal, Juan E. Mezzich, and Ahmed Okasha, eds. *Somatoform Disorders,* WPA Series. Evidence and Experience in Psychiatry, Volume 9. New York: John Wiley and Sons, 2005.

Walker, John R., and Patricia Furer. "Treatment of Hypochondriasis and Psychogenic Movement Disorders: Focus on Cognitive-Behavior Therapy." *Psychogenic Movement Disorders: Neurology and Neuropsychiatry.* Mark Hallett, Stanley Fahn, Joseph Jankovic, Anthony E. Lang, and C. Robert Cloninger, eds. Philadelphia: Lippincott Williams and Wilkins Publishers, 2006: 163–79.

VandenBos, Gary R., ed. *APA Dictionary of Psychology.* Washington D.C.: American Psychological Association, 2006.

PERIODICALS

Abramowitz, Jonathan S. "Hypochondriasis: Conceptualization, Treatment, and Relationship to Obsessive Compulsive Disorder." *Annals of Clinical Psychiatry* 17.4 (Oct.–Dec. 2005): 211–17.

Abramowitz, Jonathan S., and Autumn E. Braddock. "Hypochondriasis: Conceptualization, Treatment, and Relationship to Obsessive-Compulsive Disorder." *Psychiatric Clinics of North America* 29.2 (June 2006): 503–19.

Asmundson, Gordon J. G., and Michael J. Coons. "Current Directions in the Treatment of Hypochondriasis." *Journal of Cognitive Psychotherapy* 19.3 (Fall 2005): 285–304.

Avia, M. D., and M. A. Ruiz. "Recommendations for the Treatment of Hypochondriac Patients." *Journal of Contemporary Psychotherapy* 35.3 (Fall 2005): 301–13.

Bleichhardt, Gaby, Barbara Timmer, and Winfried Rief. "Hypochondriasis Among Patients with Multiple Somatoform Symptoms—Psychopathology and Outcome of a Cognitive-Behavioral Therapy." *Journal of Contemporary Psychotherapy* 35.3 (Fall 2005): 239–49.

Furer, Patricia, and John R. Walker. "Treatment of Hypochondriasis with Exposure." *Journal of Contemporary Psychotherapy* 35.3 (Fall 2005): 251–67.

Martínez, M. Pilar, and Cristina Botella. "An Exploratory Study of the Efficacy of a Cognitive-Behavioral Treatment for Hypochondriasis Using Different Measures of Change." *Psychotherapy Research* 15.4 (Oct. 2005): 392–408.

Monopoli, John. "Managing Hypochondriasis in Elderly Clients." *Journal of Contemporary Psychotherapy* 35.3 (Fall 2005): 285–300.

Noyes, Russell, Jr., Scott Stuart, David B. Watson, and Douglas R. Langbehn. "Distinguishing Between Hypochondriasis and Somatization Disorder: A Review of the Existing Literature." *Psychotherapy and Psychosomatics* 75.5 (Aug. 2006): 270–81.

Starcevic, Vladan. "Fear of Death in Hypochondriasis: Bodily Threat and Its Treatment Implications." *Journal of Contemporary Psychotherapy* 35.3 (Fall 2005): 227–37.

Stuart, Scott, and Russell Noyes, Jr. "Treating Hypochondriasis with Interpersonal Psychotherapy." *Journal of Contemporary Psychotherapy* 35.3 (Fall 2005): 269–83.

Danielle Barry, MS
Ruth A. Wienclaw, PhD

Hypomania

Definition

A hypomanic episode is a distinct period of time that lasts at least four days during which the individual's mood is consistently elevated, expansive, or irritable and is distinct from his or her usual nondepressed mood. Hypomanic episodes are characteristic of bipolar II disorder as well as features of **cyclothymic disorder**. They may also occur as a transitional phase from euthymia (feeling of well-being often associated with individuals with **bipolar disorder** when they are not having a manic or a depressive episode) to mania in cases of bipolar I disorder.

Description

Hypomanic episodes usually begin suddenly with the symptoms rapidly increasing over the course of a day or two. A hypomanic episode may last anywhere from four days to several months, although some clinicians are beginning to argue that hypomanic episodes may be as short as two days in duration. However, because such research is based on the self-reports of patients (who tend not to be aware of their symptoms at first), there is not widespread agreement about this change in diagnostic criteria.

Demographics

Hypomanic episodes associated with bipolar II disorder have the same demographics as that disorder. Hypomanic episodes can affect both adults and younger patients. In younger patients and adolescents, hypomania may be associated with such behaviors as school truancy, antisocial behavior, failure in school, or **substance abuse**.

Cultural differences can affect the experience and communication of the symptoms of hypomanic disorder, with different cultures interpreting such symptoms as irritability or inflated self-esteem in various ways. Some cultures and subcultures, for example, value such aspects of hypomania as decreased need for sleep, racing thoughts, or increased goal orientation as positive qualities of a productive individual, and do not regard them negatively.

Causes and symptoms

Hypomania is not a disorder in and of itself. The causes of hypomania vary depending on whether it is a characteristic of bipolar I disorder, bipolar II disorder, or cyclothymic disorder.

During a hypomanic episode, the individual's mood is consistently elevated, expansive, or irritable and distinct from his or her usual nondepressed mood. During this period, the individual must also display at least three of the following symptoms (or four if he or she is only irritable) to be diagnosed as hypomanic:

- inflated sense of self-esteem
- decreased need for sleep
- increased talkativeness or need to talk
- racing thoughts or flight of ideas
- easily distracted
- increased goal-oriented activity
- excessive involvement in pleasurable but high-risk activities (for example, buying sprees, sexual indiscretions, foolish investments)

In hypomania, these symptoms are associated with a clear change from the individual's normal behavior and are readily observable by others. Hypomanic symptoms, however, are not severe enough to noticeably affect the individual's functioning at work or in social situations, nor does their presence require **hospitalization**. To be classified as hypomanic, the individual's symptoms cannot contain psychotic features or be due to the direct physiological effects of a substance (such as drug **abuse** or medication) or a general medical condition (for example, hyperthyroidism).

Diagnosis

It is important to distinguish hypomania from euthymia in patients who are not used to a nondepressed mood state. In addition, although the two have the same list of diagnostic symptoms, hypomanic episodes are different from manic episodes. Hypomanic symptoms are less severe than manic symptoms and do not cause marked impairment of social or occupational functioning. However, approximately 5% to 15% of individuals experiencing hypomanic episodes will eventually develop a **manic episode**.

Many of the warning signs of a hypomanic episode such as increased goal-oriented behavior can also be normal and appropriate given the situation. Sometimes a patient's good mood is just that. Some of the signs of a normal good mood that could distinguish it from hypomania include:

- ability to enjoy reading for a significant period of time without becoming bored
- ability to listen more than talk in a social setting
- no need to do something risky just to shake things up
- ability to complete tasks without repeatedly being distracted
- experience of appropriate anxiety about demands of life such as responsibilities, deadlines, and financial obligations
- ability to enjoy times of peace and quiet
- ability to sleep well at night for an appropriate period of time
- ability to accept well-meaning, constructive criticism without undue irritation

Treatments

Cognitive-behavioral therapy

Cognitive-behavioral therapy (CBT) is regularly used to help patients test how realistic their thought processes and resultant behaviors are. The goal of such reality testing is to help patients weigh the facts more carefully than they would otherwise do and to seek the insights of others before acting on their beliefs. This approach can help patients be more independent in controlling their lives.

One of the tools used in CBT to assist patients in controlling their impulses during hypomanic episodes is keeping a daily journal of their thoughts. Such daily thought records are a structured method to help patients do a reality check on their thinking and actions. For example, patients can look for situations in which they overestimate their capabilities, rely on luck, underestimate risks, minimize problems, or overvalue immediate gratification.

Patients with hypomanic episodes can also be taught to test the validity of their thoughts and beliefs by consulting trusted others. By talking things through with a trusted and objective person, a patient

in a hypomanic episode can be helped to test the reality of his or her thoughts and beliefs.

Another method that can help hypomanic patients test reality is to have them rate the relative risks of the options that they are considering by listing the productive potential and destructive risks of their alternatives. If patients are unable to think of examples of destructive risks for their plans, the therapist or other objective outsider can help by giving them examples and helping them to develop their own list of potential risks. Similarly, lists can be made of the benefit to others versus the cost to oneself or the benefit to oneself versus the cost to others.

Patients can also be helped to more realistically evaluate their thoughts and plans through role playing or playing "devil's advocate." Such techniques can be used to do a hypothetical trial run to see what possible consequences might be incurred if an unreasonable risk is taken.

To help reduce impulsivity and recklessness in hypomanic patients, psychotherapists use various different techniques. One technique is to institute a "wait 48 hours before acting" rule to help the patient avoid spur-of-the-moment reckless actions. It is also sometimes helpful for the patient to try to foresee the possible negative consequences of their proposed actions through imagery by describing the bad things that could happen if they took their proposed course of action. Because hypomanic patients are often overly active, it is sometimes also helpful to have them schedule their activities to help them focus their attention on what is important so that they do not become overextended. Hypomanic patients can also be taught listening skills that can help them focus and break the vicious circle of constant activity and to listen to others. Similarly, patients can be taught anticipatory problem-solving skills that help them recognize the symptoms of a building hypomanic episode and to reduce the stressors that put them at risk. It is also helpful for hypomanic patients to minimize or completely avoid situations that are apt to trigger a hypomanic episode such as daredevil hobbies, exaggerated acts of generosity or intimacy with relative strangers, unsupervised expenditures of large amounts of money, or situations that require the use of a lethal weapon. Hypomanic patients can also be taught to help control or adjust their moods through relaxation techniques and breathing control exercises.

Biological treatments

In addition to CBT approaches in controlling hypomanic episodes, several biologic management strategies may help patients. These include:

- optimizing the dose of mood stabilizer or antimanic medication
- encouraging good sleep practices
- discontinuing antidepressants
- including lorazepam or clonazepam (1–6 mg/day) as clinically indicated
- including mood stabilizers such as lithium, divalproex, or caramazepine in the treatment regimen as appropriate

In most cases, such biologic treatments can be used on an outpatient basis.

Prevention

There are a number of warning signs of hypomania. If patients can be taught to recognize such early warning signs, they have a better chance of using various techniques to help lessen the possibility of acting out and the negative consequences of inappropriate actions that may be associated with hypomania. Attending to such warning signs also can give patients and their doctors more time to adjust medications or arrange for greater supervision to reduce the potential harm from inappropriate behavior.

Some of the typical early warning signs of an impending hypomanic episode include:

- disruption in sleep patterns (for example, decreased subjective need for sleep)
- decrease in anxiety without cause (such as ignoring a deadline or less concern about owing money)
- high levels of optimism without appropriate sound planning and problem-solving (for example, belief that everything will turn out all right even though nothing has been done to make that a reality)
- increased desire to be with others along with relatively poor listening skills (for example, talking at length to someone who is obviously anxious to leave)
- decreased mental concentration (such as difficulty following through or becoming more disorganized than usual)
- increased libido to the point where it affects other areas of life (for example, dressing more provocatively than usual, or inappropriate talk of or joking about sex)
- increased goal-directed behavior to the point where the individual appears driven

According to CBT, if the patient can be taught to recognize the signs of an impending hypomanic episode early enough, he or she will have the time necessary to put into practice the various techniques already

---

KEY TERMS

Bipolar II disorder—One of a group of mood disorders in which the individual has one or more major depressive episodes and at least one hypomanic episode.

Cognitive-behavioral therapy (CBT)—A form of psychotherapy used to help patients modify their behavior by testing their thought processes.

Cyclothymic disorder—A mood disorder in which hypomanic episodes and depressive episodes both occur over the course of at least two years during which time symptom-free periods last no more than two months.

Euthymia—A feeling of well-being often associated with individuals with bipolar disorder when they are not having a manic or a depressive episode,

Mania—Excitement, overactivity, and inappropriate physical and mental restlessness, often accompanied by impaired judgment.

Psychotic—Behavior characteristic of any of a number of severe mental disorders in which the accuracy of perceptions and thoughts is incorrectly evaluated despite of evidence to the contrary, affecting the individual's interaction with external reality.

Role playing—A technique used in psychotherapy in which the patient acts out a situation to test attitudes, relationships, actions, and their potential consequences.

---

discussed to help avoid the negative consequences of potential risky actions.

Resources

BOOKS

American Psychiatric Association. *Diagnostic and Statistical Manual of Mental Disorders.* 4th ed., text rev. Washington, D.C.: American Psychiatric Association, 2000.

Bowden, Charles L., Vivek Kusumakar, Frank P. MacMaster, and Lakshmi N. Yatham. "Diagnosis and Treatment of Hypomania and Mania." *Bipolar Disorder: A Clinician's Guide to Biological Treatments.* Eds. Lakshmi N. Yatham, Vivek Kusumakar, and Stanley P. Kutcher. New York: Brunner-Routledge, 2002.

Newman, Cory F., Robert L. Leahy, Aaron T. Beck, Noreen A. Reilly-Harrington, and Laszlo Gyulai. *Bipolar Disorder: A Cognitive Therapy Approach.* Washington, D.C.: American Psychological Association, 2002.

VandenBos, Gary R., ed. *APA Dictionary of Psychology.* Washington, D.C.: American Psychological Association, 2007.

PERIODICALS

Akiskal, Hagop S., and Franco Benazzi. "The DSM-IV and ICD-10 Categories of Recurrent [Major] Depressive and Bipolar II Disorders: Evidence that They Lie on a Dimensional Spectrum." *Journal of Affective Disorders* 92.1 (2006): 45–54.

Bauer, Michael, and others. "Self-Reported Data from Patients with Bipolar Disorder: Impact on Minimum Episode Length for Hypomania." *Journal of Affective Disorders* 96.1–2 (2006): 101–105.

Benazzi, Franco, and Hagop Akiskal. "The Duration of Hypomania in Bipolar-II Disorder in Private Practice: Methodology and Validation." *Journal of Affective Disorders* 96.3 (2006): 189–96.

Mansell, Warren. "The Hypomanic Attitudes and Positive Predictions Inventory (HAPPI): A Pilot Study to Select Cognitions that Are Elevated in Individuals with Bipolar Disorder Compared to Non-Clinical Controls." *Behavioural and Cognitive Psychotherapy* 34.4 (2006): 467–76.

Utsumi, Takeshi, Tsukasa Sasaki, Iwao Shimada, Mayuko Mabuchi, Takuro Motonaga, Toshiyuki Ohtani, Mamoru Tochigi, Nobumasa Kato, and Shinichiro Nanko. "Clinical Features of Soft Bipolarity in Major Depressive Inpatients." *Psychiatry and Clinical Neurosciences* 60.5 (2006): 611–15.

Ruth A. Wienclaw, PhD

Hypomanic episode *see* **Manic episode**

Illusion of doubles *see* **Capgras Syndrome**

Illusion of false recognition *see* **Capgras syndrome**

Imaginal desensitization *see* **Exposure treatment**

Imaginal exposure *see* **Exposure treatment**

Imaging studies

Definition

Imaging studies are tests performed with a variety of techniques that produce pictures of the inside of a patient's body.

Description

Imaging tests are performed using sound waves, radioactive particles, magnetic fields, or x rays that are detected and converted into images after passing through body tissues. Dyes are sometimes used as contrasting agents with x-ray tests so that organs or tissues not seen with conventional x rays can be enhanced. The operating principle of the various techniques is based on the fact that rays and particles interact differently with various types of tissues, especially when abnormalities are present. In this way, the interior of the body can be visualized and pictures are provided of normal structure and function as well as of abnormalities. In the fields pertaining to mental health including psychology and psychiatry, imaging is often used to help rule out other health problems that could be causing symptoms (such as **brain** tumors), and imaging studies are often used in research. Once a person's **diagnosis** has been established, various imaging techniques may help to confirm the diagnosis, and also serve as a way to study the disorder. The imaging techniques may shed new light on the way the disorder affects the brain, so that new treatment methods can be discovered.

Major imaging techniques in mental health

Computed tomography scan (CT scan)

Computed tomography, or computed axial tomography (CAT), scans show a cross-section of a part of the body, such as the brain. In this technique, a thin beam is used to produce a series of exposures detected at different angles. The exposures are fed into a computer which overlaps them, yielding a single image analogous to a slice of the organ or body part being scanned. A dye is often injected into the patient so as to improve contrast and obtain images that are clearer than images obtained with x rays.

Magnetic resonance imaging (MRI)

Magnetic resonance imaging also produces cross-sectional images of the body using powerful magnetic fields instead of radiation. MRI uses a cylinder housing a magnet which will induce the required magnetic field. The patient lies on a platform inside the scanner. The magnetic field aligns the hydrogen atoms present in the tissue being scanned in a given direction. Following a burst of radio-frequency radiation, the atoms flip back to their original orientation while emitting signals which a fed into a computer for conversion into a two- or three-dimensional image. Dyes can also be injected into patients to produce clearer images.

Positron emission tomography (PET)

Positron emission tomography uses a form of sugar that contains a radioactive atom which emits particles called positrons. The positrons are absorbed to a different extent by cells varying in their metabolic rate. PET scans are especially useful for brain imaging studies and are used to illustrate the differences between brains of people without mental disorders and brains of people with mental disorders. For example, because PET scans can detect brain activity, PET scans of the brains of depressed and non-depressed persons can show researchers where brain activity is decreased in depressed patients. Similar scans have been taken of brains affected by **schizophrenia** or Alzheimer's disease. Such research can help scientists discover new ways to treat these disorders.

Single photon emission computerized tomography(SPECT)

Single photon emission computerized tomography is used in research, and in diagnosing brain disorders such as Alzheimer's and Parkinson's diseases. As of 2002, research for Parkinson's disease at Harvard, for example, in the Division of Neurochemistry was focused on the diagnosis of the disease before motor control is compromised signalling the advancing degeneration. It uses a radio-labeled compound that targets key proteins responsible for regulating brain **dopamine** levels to determine neural changes before problems with motor symptoms begin to occur. This research is also being used to improve PET imaging in the diagnosis and consequent treatment of these neurological disorders.

Resources

BOOKS

Seeram, E. *Computed Tomography: Physical Principles, Clinical Applications and Quality Control.* Philadelphia: W. B. Saunders and Co., 2001.

von Schulthess, G. K., ed. *Clinical Positron Emission Tomography.* Philadelphia: Lippincott, Williams and Wilkins, 1999.

Westbrook, C. *Handbook of MRI Techniques.* Malden, MA: Blackwell Science, 1999.

OTHER

Alzheimer Society of British Columbia. "What is Alzheimer Disease?" (cited June 2002) <http://www.alzheimerbc.org/>.

Harvard Medical School, Harvard University, Parkinson's Disease.rdquo; (cited June 2002) <http://www.hms.harvard.edu/nerprc/parkinson/>.

Monique Laberge, Ph.D.

Imaging techniques *see* **Imaging studies**

Imipramine

Definition

Imipramine is a tricyclic antidepressant. It is sold under the brand name Tofranil in the United States.

Purpose

Imipramine is used to relieve symptoms of **depression**. It is also used in the treatment of **enuresis** (bedwetting) in people between the ages of six and 25.

Description

Imipramine hydrochloride was the first tricyclic antidepressant to be discovered. Tricyclic **antidepressants** act to change the balance of naturally occurring chemicals in the **brain** that regulate the transmission of nerve impulses between cells. Mental well-being is partially dependent on maintaining a correct balance of these brain chemicals. Imipramine is thought to act primarily by increasing the concentration of norepinephrine and serotonin (both chemicals that stimulate nerve cells) and, to a lesser extent, by blocking the action of another brain chemical, acetylcholine. Imipramine shares most of the properties of other tricyclic antidepressants, such as **amitriptyline, amoxapine, clomipramine, desipramine, nortriptyline, protriptyline,** and **trimipramine.**

The therapeutic effects of imipramine, like other antidepressants, appear slowly. Maximum benefit is often not evident for two to three weeks after starting the drug. People taking imipramine should be aware of this and continue taking the drug as directed even if they do not see immediate improvement.

Recommended dosage

Imipramine is usually started with a total dosage of up to 100 mg per day divided into several smaller doses. This is generally increased to a total of 200 mg per day divided into several doses. Total dosages for patients who are not hospitalized should be no more than 200 mg per day. The recommended maximum dosage for the drug for all patients is 250 to 300 mg per day. Before dosages greater than 200 mg per day are taken, an electrocardiogram (ECG) should be done. This should be repeated at regular intervals until a steady-state dosage is reached. Lower dosages are recommended for adolescents (see also the warning detailed below) and older people (over age 60). The lowest dosage that controls symptoms of depression should be used.

Imipramine should be withdrawn gradually, rather than abruptly discontinued. This will help reduce the possibility of a **relapse** into depression.

Precautions

There is a warning that accompanies patient information about antidepressants such as imipramine. It states that some studies have shown that children and teenagers who take antidepressants such as imipramine may have an increased likelihood of thinking about self-harm or killing themselves, or of attempting **suicide**. If a child is prescribed the drug, parents or caregivers should closely monitor the child because serious symptoms can develop suddenly. Any signs that a child is considering self-harm or suicide warrants an immediate call to the doctor. These signs might include worsening depression, panic attacks, difficulty falling asleep, irritability, planning to engage in self-harm or to attempt suicide, or abnormal excitement.

Like all tricyclic antidepressants, imipramine should be used cautiously and with close physician supervision in people, especially the elderly, who have benign prostatic hypertrophy, urinary retention, and glaucoma, especially angle-closure glaucoma (the most severe form). Before starting treatment, people with these conditions should discuss the relative risks and benefits of treatment with their doctors to help determine if imipramine is the right antidepressant for them.

A common problem with tricyclic antidepressants is sedation (drowsiness, lack of physical and mental alertness). This side effect is especially noticeable early in therapy. In most patients, sedation decreases or disappears entirely with time, but until then patients taking imipramine should not perform hazardous activities requiring mental alertness or coordination. The sedative effect is increased when imipramine is taken with other central nervous system depressants, such as alcoholic beverages, sleeping medications, other **sedatives**, or antihistamines. It may be dangerous to take imipramine in combination with these substances.

Imipramine may increase heart rate and **stress** on the heart. It may be dangerous for people with cardiovascular disease, especially those who have recently had a heart attack, to take this drug or other antidepressants in the same pharmacological class. Older people and people with a history of heart disease may develop heart arrhythmias (irregular heartbeat), heart conduction abnormalities, congestive heart failure, heart attack, abnormally rapid heart rates, and strokes.

Until a therapeutic dosage has been determined, people starting imipramine should be closely watched for signs of suicide. The risk of suicide is increased when imipramine is taken in overdose or combined with alcohol.

Manic episodes and the emergence of symptoms of preexisting psychotic states have been reported when imipramine therapy is started.

Side effects

Imipramine shares side effects common to all tricyclic antidepressants. The most frequent of these are dry mouth, constipation, urinary retention, increased heart rate, sedation, irritability, dizziness, and decreased coordination. As with most side effects associated with tricyclic antidepressants, the intensity is highest at the beginning of therapy and tends to decrease with continued use.

Dry mouth, if severe to the point of causing difficulty speaking or swallowing, may be managed by dosage reduction or temporary discontinuation of the drug. Patients may also chew sugarless gum or suck on sugarless candy in order to increase the flow of saliva. Some artificial saliva products may give temporary relief.

Imipramine usage has been linked to both increases and decreases in blood pressure and heart rate. Heart attacks, congestive heart failure, and strokes have been reported.

Confusion, disorientation, **delusions**, **insomnia**, and **anxiety** have also been reported as side effects in a small percentage of people taking imipramine. Problems associated with the skin (loss of sensation, numbness and tingling, rashes, spots, itching, and puffiness),

KEY TERMS

Acetylcholine—A naturally occurring chemical in the body that transmits nerve impulses from cell to cell. Generally, it has opposite effects from dopamine and norepinephrine; it causes blood vessels to dilate, lowers blood pressure, and slows the heartbeat. Central nervous system well-being is dependent on a balance among acetylcholine, dopamine, serotonin, and norepinephrine.

Anticholinergic—Related to the ability of a drug to block the nervous system chemical acetylcholine. When acetylcholine is blocked, patients often experience dry mouth and skin, increased heart rate, blurred vision, and difficulty urinating. In severe cases, blocking acetylcholine may cloud thinking and cause delirium.

Anticonvulsant—A medication used to control abnormal electrical activity in the brain that causes seizures.

Electrocardiogram (EKG)—A test that measures the electrical activity of the heart as it beats. An abnormal EKG can indicate possible cardiac disease.

Enuresis—The inability to control urination; bedwetting.

Hypertension—High blood pressure, often brought on by smoking, obesity, or other causes; one of the major causes of strokes.

Manic—Referring to mania, a state characterized by excessive activity, unwarranted euphoria, excitement, or emotion.

Methylphenidate—A mild central nervous system stimulant that is used to treat hyperactivity.

Tachycardia—A pulse rate above 100 beats per minute.

seizures, and ringing in the ears have also been reported. Nausea, vomiting, loss of appetite, diarrhea, and abdominal cramping are all side effects associated with imipramine usage in a small number of people.

Interactions

Methylphenidate may increase the effects of imipramine. This is usually avoided by reducing the dosage of imipramine.

Imipramine may increase the depressant action of alcohol. For this reason, people taking imipramine should not drink alcoholic beverages.

Dangerously high blood pressure has resulted from the combination of tricyclic antidepressants, such as imipramine, and members of another class of antidepressants known as monoamine oxidase (MAO) inhibitors. Because of this, imipramine should never be taken in combination with MAO inhibitors. Patients taking any MAO inhibitors, for example Nardil (**phenelzine** sulfate) or Parnate (**tranylcypromine** sulfate), should stop the MAO inhibitor, then wait at least 14 days before starting imipramine or any other tricyclic antidepressant. The same holds true when discontinuing imipramine and starting an MAO inhibitor.

The sedative effects of imipramine are increased by other central nervous system depressants such as alcohol, sedatives, sleeping medications, or medications used for other mental disorders such as **schizophrenia**. The anticholinergic (drying out) effects of imipramine are additive with other anticholinergic drugs such as **benztropine**, **biperiden**, **trihexyphenidyl**, and antihistamines.

Resources

BOOKS

Adams, Michael, and Norman Holland. *Core Concepts in Pharmacology*. Philadelphia: Lippincott-Raven, 1998.

Foreman, John C., and Torben Johansen. *Textbook of Receptor Pharmacology*. 2nd ed. Boca Raton, FL: CRC Press, 2002.

Page, Clive P., and Michael Murphy. *Integrated Pharmacology*. St. Louis: Mosby-Year Book, 2002.

Von Boxtel, Chris J., Budiono Santoso, and I. Ralph Edwards. *Drug Benefits and Risks: International Textbook of Clinical Pharmacology*. New York: John Wiley and Sons, 2001.

PERIODICALS

Juarez-Olguin, Hugo, and others. "Clinical Evidence of an Interaction Between Imipramine and Acetylsalicylic Acid on Protein Binding in Depressed Patients." *Clinical Neuropharmacology* 25.1 (2002): 32–36.

Jain A. K., N. S. Thomas, and R. Panchagnula. "Transdermal Drug Delivery of Imipramine Hydrochloride. I. Effect of Terpenes." *Journal of Controlled Release* 19.79 (2002: 93–101.

ORGANIZATIONS

American Academy of Clinical Toxicology. 777 East Park Drive, P.O. Box 8820, Harrisburg, PA 17105-8820. Telephone: (717) 558-7750. Web site: <http://www.clintox.org/index.html>.

American Academy of Family Physicians. 11400 Tomahawk Creek Parkway, Leawood, KS 66211-2672. Telephone: (913) 906-6000. Web site: <http://www.aafp.org/>.

American Medical Association. 515 N. State Street, Chicago, IL 60610. Telephone: (312) 464-5000. Web site: <http://www.ama-assn.org/>.

American Psychiatric Association. 1400 K Street NW, Washington, DC 20005. Telephone: (888) 357-7924. Web site: <http://www.psych.org/>.

American Society for Clinical Pharmacology and Therapeutics. 528 North Washington Street, Alexandria, VA 22314. Telephone: (703) 836-6981.

American Society for Pharmacology and Experimental Therapeutics. 9650 Rockville Pike, Bethesda, MD 20814-3995. Telephone: (301) 530-7060. Web site: <http://www.aspet.org/>.

OTHER

National Library of Medicine. National Institutes of Health. Imipramine. Available online at: <http://www.nlm.nih. gov/medlineplus/druginfo/medmaster/a682389.html>.

National Library of Medicine. National Institutes of Health. Daily Med Current Medication Information: Imipramine hydrochloride, injected. Available online at: <http://dailymed.nlm.nih.gov/dailymed/drugInfo. cfm?id=2039>.

United States Food and Drug Administration. "Class Suicidality Labeling Language for Antidepressants." <http:// www.fda.gov/cder/foi/label/2005/16792s024lbl.pdf.>

L. Fleming Fallon, Jr., M.D, Dr. P.H.
Emily Jane Willingham, PhD

Impulse-control disorders

Definition

Impulse-control disorders are characterized by the repeated inability to refrain from performing a particular action that is harmful either to oneself or to others.

Description

Impulse-control disorders are thought to have both neurological and environmental causes and are known to be exacerbated by **stress**. Some mental health professionals regard several of these disorders, such as compulsive gambling or shopping, as addictions. In impulse-control disorder, the impulse action is typically preceded by feelings of tension and excitement and followed by a sense of relief and gratification, often—but not always—accompanied by guilt or remorse.

The Fourth Edition Text Revision of the ***Diagnostic and Statistical Manual of Mental Disorders*** (a handbook that mental health professionals use to diagnose mental disorders, also known as the *DSM-IV-TR*) describes several impulse-control disorders:

- Pyromania. This disorder is diagnosed when a person has deliberately started fires out of an attraction to and curiosity about fire. To meet the criteria for this diagnosis, the firestarter cannot seek monetary gain or be trying to destroy evidence of criminal activity, or be trying to make a political statement or improve one his or her standard of living.

- Trichotillomania. This disorder is characterized by compulsive hair pulling.

- Intermittent explosive disorder. This diagnosis is indicated when a person cannot resist aggressive impulses that lead to serious acts of assault or property destruction.

- Kleptomania. The recurrent failure to resist the urge to steal, even though the items stolen are not needed for personal use or for their monetary value, is required for diagnosis of this disorder.

- Pathological gambling. This form of persistent gambling disrupts the affected individual's relationships or career.

- Impulse-control disorders not otherwise specified. This category is reserved for clinicians' use when the clinician has established that a patient's disorder is caused by lack of impulse control, but does not meet the criteria for the disorders listed above or the criteria for any other disorder listed in the *DSM-IV-TR*.

Process or behavioral **addiction** may also ultimately be classified as an impulse-control disorder, or even provide the umbrella classification for impulse-control disorders. Behavioral addiction has been suggested as the unifying theme of a number of other impulse disorders, including those in which the act or behavior is preceded by a feeling of tension or even eager anticipation. Individuals with these addictions cannot resist the behavior, even if they are aware it will cause harm to themselves or others. Once they have engaged in the behavior, there may be a feeling of pleasure or relief. For any impulsive behavior that **process addiction** may underlie, there is a consistent pattern of urge, anticipation or tension building, engaging in the behavior, release, and recurrence.

The behaviors now classified as impulse-control disorders may also fall into this category of behavioral addictions. These classifications include pathological gambling, kleptomania, pyromania, trichotillomania, compulsive buying, and compulsive sexual behavior. Another disorder that has arisen with the growing availability of the Internet is compulsive Internet/ computer use, which studies are increasingly treating as a real and growing problem. It has been proposed that these disorders be grouped in the *DSM-V* into a new category of Substance and Behavioral Addictions. Compulsive buying and impulsive-compulsive sex behavior would fall into the category of Impulsive-Compulsive Behaviors Not Otherwise Specified under this construct.

Resources

BOOKS

American Psychiatric Association. *Diagnostic and Statistical Manual of Mental Disorders,* 4th ed., Text rev. Washington, D.C.: American Psychiatric Association, 2000.

Koziol, Leonard F., Chris E. Stout, and Douglas H. Ruben, eds. *Handbook of Childhood Impulse Disorders and ADHD: Theory and Practice.* Springfield, IL: C.C. Thomas, 1993.

Stein, D.J., ed. *Impulsivity and Aggression.* Chichester, NY: Wiley, 1995.

PERIODICALS

Grant, Jon E., JD, MD, M.P.H., Judson A. Brewer, MD, PhD, and Marc N. Potenza, MD, PhD. "The Neurobiology of Substance and Behavioral Addictions." *CNS Spectrums* 11 (2006): 924–30.

Lobo, Daniela S.S., MD., PhD, and Kennedy, James L., MD, F.R.C.P.C. "The Genetics of Gambling and Behavioral Addictions." *CNS Spectrums* 11 (2006): 931–39.

Mick, Thomas M., MD, and Eric Hollander, MD. "Impulsive-Compulsive Sexual Behavior." *CNS Spectrum 11* (2006): 944–55.

Pallanti, Stefano, MD, PhD. "From Impulse-Control Disorders Toward Behavioral Addictions." *CNS Spectrums* 11 (2006): 921–22.

Pallanti, Stefano, MD, PhD, Silvia Bernardi, MD, and Leonardo Quercioli MD. "The Shorter PROMIS Questionnaire and the Internet Addiction Scale in the Assessment of Multiple Addictions in a High-School Population: Prevalence and Related Disability." *CNS Spectrums* 11(2006): 966–74.

ORGANIZATIONS

American Psychiatric Association, 1400 K Street NW, Washington, DC 20005. Web site; <http://www.psych.org>.

Gamblers Anonymous, International Service Office, P.O. Box 17173, Los Angeles, CA 90017. Telephone: (213) 386-8789. Web site: <http://www.gamblersanonymous.org/>.

Sex Addicts Anonymous, ISO of SAA, PO Box 70949, Houston, TX 77270. Web site: <http://saa-recovery.org/>

Emily Jane Willingham, PhD

Inderal *see* **Propranolol**

Informed consent

Definition

Informed consent is a legal document in all 50 states, prepared as an agreement for treatment, non-treatment, or for an invasive procedure that requires physicians to disclose the benefits, risks, and alternatives to the treatment, non-treatment, or procedure. It is the method by which a fully informed, rational patient may be involved in the choices about his or her health. Informed consent applies to mental health practitioners (psychiatrists, psychologists, etc.) in their treatment with their clients in generally the same way as physicians with their patients.

Description

Informed consent stems from the legal and ethical right the patient has to decide what is done to his or her body, and from the mental health provider's ethical duty to ensure that the patient is involved in decisions about his or her own health care. The process of ensuring informed consent for treatment involves five elements, all of which involve information exchange between doctor and patient and are a part of patient education. First, in words the patient can understand, the therapist must convey three things: (1) the details of a treatment or procedure, (2) its potential benefits and serious risks, and (3) any feasible alternatives. The patient should be presented with information on the most likely outcomes of treatment. Next, the practitioner must evaluate whether or not the person has understood what has been said, must ascertain that the risks have been accepted, and that the patient is giving consent to proceed with the treatment with full knowledge and forethought. Finally, the patient must sign the consent form, which documents in generic format the major points of consideration. The only exception to this is securing informed consent during extreme emergencies. It is critical that the patient receive enough information on which to base informed consent, and that the consent is wholly voluntary and has not been forced in any way.

Consent is generally not assumed or considered to be "implied" except in emergency cases where a patient's life is in danger, no prior wishes have been expressed, and a family member or guardian is not present to give consent. Furthermore, a person must possess the mental faculties to understand and give consent; people who are mentally retarded, intoxicated, or otherwise impaired due to lack of sleep may not be legally able to consent to treatment.

According to the Ethical Principles of Psychologists and Code of Conduct designed by the American Psychological Association, informed consent also applies when conducting research involving human subjects prior to their participation. Participants in the study should be informed in understandable language to three main points. First, the participant should be informed about the nature of the research. Secondly, participants should be informed that their participation is completely voluntary and that they are free to withdraw from or not participate in the study at any time. Consent must be made without pressure being put on the participant to engage in the study. Finally, the potential consequences of participating or withdrawing should be presented to the participant. This includes risks, discomfort, and limitations of confidentiality.

With regard to either therapy treatment or research participation, another member of the health care/research team may obtain the signed informed consent with the assurance that the provider has satisfied the requirements of informed consent.

The actual informed consent form is to document the process and protect the provider and the hospital. Legally, it is proof that things have been covered and the patient agrees to the procedure, risks, benefits, options, etc. The informed consent process is in place for the protection of the patient. The process is in place to ensure that everything is discussed with the patient: all of the options, all of the common risks, the worst case scenario, and other similar situations.

Viewpoints

There is a theory that the practice of acquiring informed consent is rooted in the post–World War II Nuremberg Trials. Following the war crimes tribunal in 1949, as a result of the Kaarl Brandt case, 10 standards were put forth regarding physician's requirements for experimentation on human subjects. This established a new standard of ethical medical behavior for the post–World War II human rights age, and the concept of voluntary informed consent was established. A number of rules accompanied voluntary informed consent within the realms of research. It could only be requested for experimentation for the gain of society, for the potential acquisition of knowledge of the pathology, and for studies performed that avoided physical and mental suffering to the fullest extent possible.

A crucial component of informed consent is that the person signing it is competent or able to make a rational decision and meaningfully give consent. This

situation gets more complicated when working with people who are unable to understand what has been explained or are unable to make a reasonable decision about their health care. According to the Code of Conduct for Psychologists designed by the American Psychological Association, if this is the case, informed permission from a "legally authorized person" should then be sought, if that is a legal alternative. The ethical guidelines are more stringent than legal guidelines in many states, where the informed consent of the parent or guardian is all that is required, whether or not the professional has attempted to explain the procedure to the client.

Although it is necessary to present the procedure or treatment formally to the patient, there is concern that this process could hurt the therapeutic relationship between the client and therapist. For example, if an informed consent is too detailed, it could frighten a new client who may be hesitant about therapy to begin with. In addition, informing patients about the risks of treatment might scare them into refusing it when the risks of non-treatment are even greater. There are however, advantages to the informed consent process. First, it can be empowering to the patient to understand that he/she plays an important role in their own treatment. They are encouraged to be active participants in the treatment process and know their options well enough to make the best treatment decisions for themselves. This also shifts the responsibility to patients to work with the therapist towards their mental health goals possibly increasing self-confidence and autonomy, and decreasing dependence on the therapist.

Professional implications

There are undoubtedly many issues regarding informed consent. As modern society continues to be litigious, the courts and/or government may take on a more active role in deciding the extent to which patients must be informed of treatments, procedures, and **clinical trials** in which they voluntarily become enrolled. Therefore, health care providers must become more educated as to what needs to be conveyed to patients, and to what extent.

Resources

BOOKS

Berg, Jessica W., and others. *Informed Consent: Legal Theory and Clinical Practice.* 2nd ed. New York: Oxford University Press, 2001.

PERIODICALS

Caplan, Arthur L. "Ethical Issues Surrounding Forced, Mandated, or Coerced Treatment." *Journal of Substance Abuse Treatment* 31.2, Sep. 2006: 117–20.

Dunn, Laura B., and others. "Assessing Decisional Capacity for Clinical Research or Treatment: A Review of Instruments." *American Journal of Psychiatry* 163.8, Aug. 2006: 1323–34.

Fallon, April. "Informed Consent in the Practice of Group Psychotherapy." *International Journal of Group Psychotherapy* 56.4, 2006: 431–53.

Jackson, Grace E. "Mental Health Screening in Schools: Essentials of Informed Consent." *Ethical Human Psychology and Psychiatry* 8.3, Fall–Winter 2006: 217–24.

OTHER

"Health Information for surgical procedures, family health, patient education." <http://www.docs4patients.com/informed-consent.asp>.

"Informed Consent." <http://www.nocirc.org/consent>.

"Informed Consent." The University of Washington. <http://eduserv.hscer.washington.edu/bioethics/topics/consntc1.html>.

"Informed Consent." *Risk Management Handbook*. Yale-New Haven Hospital & Yale University School of Medicine. <http://info.med.yale.edu/cim/risk/handbook/rmh_informed_consent.html>.

"Risk Management Issues: Improved Informed Consent." <http://www.rmf.harvard.edu/rmLibrary/rmissues/infconsent/body.html>.

Jenifer P. Marom, Ph.D.

A teenager huffing an inhalant from a plastic bag. *(James Marshall/Corbis)*

Inhalants and related disorders

Definition

The inhalants are a class of drugs that include a broad range of chemicals found in hundreds of different products, many of which are readily available to the general population. These chemicals include volatile solvents (liquids that vaporize at room temperature) and aerosols (sprays that contain solvents and propellants). Examples include glue, gasoline, paint thinner, hair spray, lighter fluid, spray paint, nail polish remover, correction fluid, rubber cement, felt-tip marker fluids, vegetable sprays, and certain cleaners. The inhalants share a common route of administration—that is, they are all drawn into the body by breathing. They are usually taken either by breathing in the vapors directly from a container (known as "sniffing"); by inhaling fumes from substances placed in a bag (known as "bagging"); or by inhaling the substance from a cloth soaked in it (known as "huffing").

Inhalants take effect very quickly because they get into the bloodstream rapidly via the lungs. The "high" from inhalants is usually brief, so that users often take inhalants repeatedly over several hours. This pattern of use can be dangerous, leading to unconsciousness or even death.

The latest revision of the manual that is used by mental health professionals to diagnose mental disorders is the ***Diagnostic and Statistical Manual of Mental Disorders*** published in 2000 (also known as *DSM-IV-TR*). It lists inhalant dependence and inhalant **abuse** as substance use disorders. In addition, the inhalant-induced disorder of inhalant intoxication is listed in the substance-related disorders section as well. Inhalant withdrawal is not listed in the *DSM-IV-TR* because it is not clear that there is a "clinically significant" withdrawal syndrome. In addition, withdrawal is not included as a symptom of inhalant dependence, whereas withdrawal is a symptom of dependence for all other substances.

Anesthetic gases (such as nitrous oxide, chloroform, or ether) and nitrites (including amyl or butyl nitrite) are not included under inhalant-related disorders in the

DSM-IV-TR because they have slightly different intoxication syndromes. Problems with the use of these substances are to be diagnosed under "Other Substance-Related Disorders." There is, however, a significant degree of overlap between the symptoms of disorders related to inhalants and these "other" substances.

Inhalant dependence

Inhalant dependence, or **addiction**, is essentially a syndrome in which a person continues to use inhalants in spite of significant problems caused by or made worse by the use of these substances. People who use inhalants heavily may develop tolerance to the drug, which indicates that they are physically dependent on it.

Inhalant abuse

Inhalant abuse is a less serious condition than inhalant dependence; in most cases, it does not involve physical dependence on the drug. Inhalant abuse refers essentially to significant negative consequences from the recurrent use of inhalants.

Inhalant intoxication

When a person uses enough of an inhalant, they will get "high" from it. The symptoms of intoxication differ slightly depending on the type of inhalant, the amount used, and other factors. There is, however, a predictable set of symptoms of inhalant intoxication. When too much of the substance is taken, an individual can overdose.

Description

Inhalant dependence

Dependence on inhalants involves problems related to the use of inhalants. It is often difficult for a person to stop using the inhalants despite these problems. Individuals dependent on inhalants may use these chemicals several times per week or every day. They may have problems with unemployment, with family relationships, and/or such physical problems as kidney or liver damage caused by the use of inhalants.

Inhalant abuse

People who abuse inhalants typically use them less frequently than those who are dependent on them. Despite less frequent use, however, a person with inhalant abuse suffers negative consequences. For example, the use of inhalants may contribute to poor grades or school truancy.

Inhalant intoxication

Intoxication from inhalants occurs rapidly (usually within five minutes) and lasts for a short period of time (from 5–30 minutes). Inhalants typically have a depressant effect on the central nervous system, similar to the effects of alcohol; and produce feelings of euphoria (feeling good), excitement, dizziness, and slurred speech. In addition, persons intoxicated by inhalants may feel as if they are floating, or feel a sense of increased power. Severe intoxication from inhalants can cause coma or even death.

Causes and symptoms

Causes

Because inhalants are readily available and inexpensive, they are often used by children (ages 6–16) and the poor. Factors that are associated with inhalant use include poverty; a history of childhood abuse; poor grades; and dropping out of school. The latter two factors may simply be a result of inhalant use, however, rather than its cause.

The use of inhalants is highly likely to be influenced by peers. Inhalants are often used in group settings. The solitary consumption of inhalants is associated with heavy, prolonged use; it may indicate that the person has a more serious problem with these substances.

Symptoms

INHALANT DEPENDENCE. The *DSM-IV-TR* specifies that three or more of the following symptoms must occur at any time during a 12-month period (and cause significant impairment or distress) in order to meet diagnostic criteria for inhalant dependence:

- Tolerance. The individual either has to use increasingly higher amounts of the drug over time in order to achieve the same effect, or finds that the same amount of the drug has much less of an effect over time than before. After using inhalants regularly for a while, people may find that they need to use at least 50% more than the amount they started with in order to get the same effect.

- Loss of control. The person either repeatedly uses a larger quantity of inhalant than planned, or uses the inhalant over a longer period of time than planned. For instance, someone may begin using inhalants on school days, after initially limiting their use to weekends.

- Inability to stop using. The person has either unsuccessfully attempted to cut down or stop using the inhalants, or has a persistent desire to stop using. Users may find that despite efforts to stop using inhalants on school days, they cannot stop.

- Time. The affected person spends large amounts of time obtaining inhalants, using them, being under the influence of inhalants, and recovering from their effects. Obtaining the inhalants might not take up much time because they are readily available for little money, but the person may use them repeatedly for hours each day.
- Interference with activities. The affected person either gives up or reduces the amount of time involved in recreational activities, social activities, and/or occupational activities because of the use of inhalants. The person may use inhalants instead of playing sports, spending time with friends, or going to work.
- Harm to self. The person continues to use inhalants in spite of developing either a physical (liver damage or heart problems, for example) or psychological problem (such as depression or memory problems) that is caused by or made worse by the use of inhalants.

INHALANT ABUSE. The *DSM-IV-TR* specifies that one or more of the following symptoms must occur at any time during a 12-month period (and cause significant impairment or distress) in order to meet diagnostic criteria for inhalant abuse:

- Interference with role fulfillment. The person's use of inhalants frequently interferes with his or her ability to fulfill obligations at work, home, or school. People may find they are unable to do chores or pay attention in school because they are under the influence of inhalants.
- Danger to self. The person repeatedly uses inhalants in situations in which their influence may be physically hazardous (while driving a car, for example).
- Legal problems. The person has recurrent legal problems related to using inhalants (such as arrests for assaults while under the influence of inhalants).
- Social problems. The person continues to use inhalants despite repeated interpersonal or relationship problems caused by or made worse by the use of inhalants. For example, the affected person may get into arguments related to inhalant use.

INHALANT INTOXICATION. The *DSM-IV-TR* specifies that the following symptoms must be present in order to meet diagnostic criteria for inhalant intoxication:

- Use. The person recently intentionally used an inhalant.
- Personality changes. The person experiences significant behavioral or psychological changes during or

shortly after use of an inhalant. These changes may include spoiling for a fight; assaultiveness; poor judgment; apathy ("don't care" attitude); or impaired functioning socially or at work or school.

- Inhalant-specific intoxication syndrome. Two or more of the following symptoms occur during or shortly after inhalant use or exposure: dizziness; involuntary side-to-side eye movements (nystagmus); loss of coordination; slurred speech; unsteady gait (difficulty walking); lethargy (fatigue); slowed reflexes; psychomotor retardation (moving slowly); tremor (shaking); generalized muscle weakness; blurred vision or double vision; stupor or coma; and euphoria (a giddy sensation of happiness or well-being).

Demographics

Inhalants are one of the few substances more commonly used by younger children rather than older ones. It has been estimated that 10%–20% of youths aged 12–17 have tried inhalants. About 6% of the United States population admits to having tried inhalants prior to fourth grade. The peak time for inhalant use appears to be between the seventh and ninth grades. Inhalants are sometimes referred to as "gateway" drugs, which means that they are one of the first drugs that people try before moving on to such other substances as alcohol, marijuana, and **cocaine**. Only a small proportion of those who have used inhalants would meet diagnostic criteria for dependence or abuse.

Males generally use inhalants more frequently than females. However, a National Household Survey on Drug Abuse has shown no gender differences in rates of inhalant use in youths between the ages of 12 and 17. Children younger than 12 and adults who use inhalants, however, are more likely to be male.

Diagnosis

People rarely seek treatment on their own for inhalant dependence or abuse. In some cases, the child or adolescent is brought to a doctor by a parent or other relative who is concerned about personality changes, a chemical odor on the child's breath, or other signs of inhalant abuse. The parent may also have discovered empty containers of the inhaled substance in the child's room or elsewhere in the house. In other cases, the child or adolescent's use of inhalants is diagnosed during a medical interview, when he or she is brought to a hospital emergency room after overdosing on the inhalant or being injured in an accident related to inhalant use. Although inhalants can be detected in blood or urine samples, laboratory tests may not always confirm the **diagnosis** because the inhalants do not remain in the system very long.

Inhalant dependence

Other substance use disorders are commonly seen among people diagnosed with inhalant dependence. The use of inhalants is usually secondary to the use of other substances, however; only occasionally are inhalants a person's primary drug of choice.

Inhalant abuse

The use of other substances is not uncommon among people who abuse inhalants.

Inhalant intoxication

Intoxication from the use of such other substances as alcohol, **sedatives**, hypnotics (medications to induce sleep), and anxiolytics (tranquilizers) can resemble intoxication caused by inhalants. Furthermore, people under the influence of inhalants may experience **hallucinations** (typically auditory, visual, or tactile); other perceptual disturbances (such as illusions); or **delusions** (believing they can fly, for example).

Treatments

Inhalant dependence and abuse

Chronic inhalant users are difficult to treat because they often have many serious personal and social problems. They also have difficulty staying away from inhalants; **relapse** rates are high. Treatment usually takes a long time and involves enlisting the support of the person's family; changing the friendship network if the individual uses with others; teaching coping skills; and increasing self-esteem.

Inhalant intoxication

Inhalant intoxication is often treated in a hospital emergency room when the affected person begins to suffer serious psychological (such as hallucinations or delusions) or medical consequences (difficulty breathing, headache, nausea, vomiting) from inhalant use. The most serious medical risk from inhalant use is "sudden sniffing death." A person using inhalants, especially if they are using the substance repeatedly in a single, prolonged session, may start to have a rapid and irregular heartbeat or severe difficulty breathing, followed by heart failure and death. Sudden sniffing death can occur within minutes. In addition, inhalant use can cause permanent damage to the **brain**, lung,

kidney, muscle, and heart. The vapors themselves cause damage, but there are also dangerously high levels of copper, zinc, and heavy metals in many inhalants.

People who use inhalants may also be treated for injuries sustained while under the influence of inhalants or while using inhalants. For example, individuals intoxicated by inhalants may fall and injure themselves, or they may drive while intoxicated and have an accident. People who use inhalants may also die from or require treatment for burns because many inhalants are highly flammable. They may also need emergency treatment for suffocation from inhaling with a plastic bag over the head, or for choking on inhaled vomit.

Prognosis

Inhalant dependence and abuse

The course of inhalant abuse and dependence differs somewhat depending on the affected person's age. Younger children who are dependent on or abuse inhalants use them regularly, especially on weekends and after school. As children get older, they often stop using inhalants. They may stop substance use altogether or they may move on to other substances. Adults who abuse or are dependent on inhalants may use inhalants regularly for years. They may also frequently "binge" on inhalants (i.e., using them much more frequently for shorter periods of time). This pattern of use can go on for years.

The use of inhalants and subsequent dependence on the substance occurs among people who do not have access to other drugs or are otherwise isolated (such as prison inmates). Also, as with other substance use disorders, people who have greater access to inhalants are more likely to develop dependence on them. This group of people may include workers in industrial settings with ready access to inhalants.

Prevention

Comprehensive prevention programs that involve families, schools, communities, and the media (such as television) can be effective in reducing **substance abuse**. The recurring theme in these programs is to stay away from drugs in the first place, which is the primary method of ensuring that one does not develop a substance use disorder.

Parents can help prevent the misuse of inhalants by educating their children about the negative effects of inhalant use. Both teachers and parents can help prevent inhalant abuse and dependence by recognizing the signs of inhalant use, which include chemical odors

KEY TERMS

Aerosol—A liquid substance sealed in a metal container under pressure with an inert gas that propels the liquid as a spray or foam through a nozzle.

Euphoria—A feeling or state of well-being or elation.

Gateway drug—A mood-altering drug or substance, typically used by younger or new drug users, that may lead to the use of more dangerous drugs.

Nystagmus—A persistent involuntary movement of the eyes from side to side. It is one of the symptoms of inhalant intoxication syndrome.

Sudden sniffing death—Death resulting from heart failure caused by heavy use of inhalants in a single lengthy session.

Syndrome—A group of symptoms that together characterize a disease or disorder.

Volatile solvent—A solvent (substance that will dissolve another substance) that evaporates at room temperature.

on the child's breath or clothes; slurred speech; a drunken or disoriented appearance; nausea or lack of appetite; and inattentiveness and lack of coordination.

See also Polysubstance abuse.

Resources

BOOKS

American Psychiatric Association. *Diagnostic and Statistical Manual of Mental Disorders*. 4th edition, text revised. Washington, DC: American Psychiatric Association, 2000.

Kaplan, Harold I., M.D., and Benjamin J. Sadock, M.D. *Kaplan and Sadock's Synopsis of Psychiatry: Behavioral Sciences, Clinical Psychiatry*. 8th edition. Baltimore: Williams and Wilkins.

ORGANIZATIONS

American Psychiatric Association. 1400 K Street, Washington, DC 20005. (202) 682-6000. <http://www.psych. org>.

American Psychological Association. 750 First Street, NE, Washington, DC 20002-4242. (800) 374-2721. <http://www.apa.org>.

National Clearinghouse for Alcohol and Drug Information. (800) 729-6686. <http://www.health.org>.

National Institute of Mental Health. 6001 Executive Boulevard, Room 8184, MSC 9663, Bethesda, MD 20892-9663. (301) 443-4513. <http://www.nimh.nih.gov>.

National Institute on Drug Abuse (NIDA). 5600 Fishers Lane, Room 10-05, Rockville, MD 20857. Nationwide Helpline: (800) 662-HELP. <http://www.nida.nih.gov>.

National Library of Medicine. 8600 Rockville Pike, Bethesda, MD 20894. <http://www.nlm.nih.gov/medlineplus/drugabuse.html >.

Jennifer Hahn, Ph.D.

Inkblot test *see* **Rorschach technique**

Insomnia

Definition

Insomnia is a condition that occurs when a person in unable to get long enough or refreshing enough sleep at night. An inability to fall asleep, an inability to stay asleep, or waking too early before having gotten enough sleep are all forms of insomnia

Description

Insomnia is a disorder in which people are unable to get enough, or enough restorative, sleep because of one or more factors. People with insomnia often have daytime symptoms related to a lack of sleep, such as daytime sleepiness, **fatigue**, and decreased mental clarity.

There are two main types of insomnia. One is acute insomnia (sometimes called transient insomnia). This type occurs when insomnia symptoms exist over a reasonably short period of time. The other type is chronic insomnia, which is diagnosed when the symptoms manifest themselves over a longer period (generally more than one month). Insomnia can also be classified as either primary or secondary. Primary insomnia is a disorder that cannot be attributed to another condition or disorder. Secondary insomnia can be traced back to a source, which may be a medical condition; the use of medications, alcohol, or other substances; or a mental disorder such as severe **depression**.

Not all disruptions in the normal pattern of sleeping and waking are considered insomnia. Such factors as jet lag, unusually high levels of **stress**, changing work shifts, or other drastic changes in the person's routine can all lead to sleep problems. Unless the problems are ongoing and severe enough that they are causing distress for the person in important areas of life, he or she is not considered to have insomnia.

Causes and symptoms

The symptoms of insomnia can vary greatly from person to person. Some people find that they have trouble falling asleep at night and can lie in bed for hours without being able to drift off. Others find that they fall asleep easily, but wake many times during the night. Other people awaken too early in the morning and are then unable to get back to sleep. Some people even get enough hours of sleep but find that they do not feel rested, often because their sleep is too light.

Not all people experiencing insomnia have symptoms that occur during the daytime, but many do. Some people experience such symptoms as reduced ability to concentrate or pay attention, decreased alertness, and mental sluggishness. Some people have trouble staying awake. More people think that they have these symptoms than actually do. Upon clinical examination, many people who think that they are excessively sleepy during the day actually are not.

Many different things are thought to cause or contribute to insomnia. Stressors, such as starting a new job, or changes in routine, such as beginning to work a different shift, can lead to temporary sleep problems. Sleep problems can become aggravated and persist after the worry or change causing the sleep problem has been resolved. This persistence is thought to be related to the **anxiety** created by attempting to go to sleep and not expecting to fall asleep. Anxiety about sleep loss can lead to a vicious circle in which the person has more and more concern about being able to fall asleep, making it increasingly difficult to do so. Some people even report that they are better able to fall asleep when they are not in their beds. This relative success is thought to occur because the new environment is not associated with the fear and anxiety of not being able to sleep, therefore making it easier to fall asleep.

Many other factors are thought to lead to or perpetuate insomnia. These include drinking tea or coffee, eating a large meal, taking certain medications or drugs of **abuse** (**cocaine**, **amphetamines**) that have a stimulating effect, or exercising heavily in the hours before attempting to sleep. Also, attempting to sleep in a room with too much light or noise can make it harder for some people to sleep. Doing activities in bed that are not associated with sleep, such as reading or watching television, can make it more difficult for some people to fall asleep when they finally want to. Sleep may be even more difficult if the television show or book was frightening or upsetting.

Demographics

There are many different opinions about how much of the general American population experiences insomnia. Estimates suggest that around 5–20% of the adult population suffers from some form of insomnia

or long-term sleeping problem. Nearly half report at least occasional sleeping problems. Accurate data is difficult to gather, as many people misperceive how much sleep they actually get and how many times they normally wake up during the night. It is generally agreed, however, that women are more likely than men to suffer from insomnia. As people get older, they are also are more likely to experience insomnia. People who are nervous or tense are more likely to have insomnia than those who are not. Lastly, people who live near airports or other sources of nighttime as well as daytime noise have higher rates of insomnia than the general population.

Diagnosis

According to the *Diagnostic and Statistical Manual of Mental Disorders-IV-TR(DSM-IV-TR)*, which presents the guidelines used by the American Psychiatric Association for **diagnosis** of disorders, in order to be diagnosed with primary insomnia, a person must experience the symptoms for at least a month, and the symptoms must cause them distress or reduce their ability to function successfully. The symptoms cannot be caused by a different sleep disorder, a medical condition, or be a side effect of medications or **substance abuse**.

Insomnia may also be comorbid with (occur together with) other psychiatric disorders, including mania, depression, and the **anxiety disorders**.

Insomnia is a disorder that is usually self-reported; that is, patients usually bring up the subject of sleep problems with their doctors rather than the doctor suggesting the diagnosis. There are no laboratory tests for insomnia, but the doctor may suggest keeping a sleep diary, in which the patient notes the time they went to bed, the time(s) at which they got up during the night, their activities before bed, etc. Sleep diaries can be helpful in uncovering specific factors related to the insomnia.

Treatments

Many treatments have been explored for treating insomnia in a number of different settings. The patient may wish to consider consulting a sleep clinic or a doctor who specializes in the treatment of **sleep disorders** as well as their family doctor.

Behavioral and educational therapies are usually tried first, because they do not have side effects and cannot create a chemical dependence the way some sleep medications can. Many different approaches have been designed to help patients whose insomnia is linked to particular factors.

Behavioral treatments

One common behavioral therapy involves changing any pre-bedtime activities or behaviors that might interfere with sleep. Avoiding large meals, alcohol or caffeinated beverages, or intensive exercise in the hours before bedtime may help the patient to fall asleep.

Another non-medicinal treatment for insomnia involves controlling the patient's mental associations with the bedroom. The patient is trained to associate the bed only with sleep, not with the frustration of trying to fall asleep or with such waking activities as reading or watching television. As part of this training, if the patient cannot sleep after a certain amount of time, he or she is instructed to get out of bed and spend time somewhere else in the house doing an activity that they find relaxing. The patient lies down again only when sleepy. This technique helps to prevent frustration from trying to sleep.

Another common technique that does not involve medication is sleep restriction therapy. During this therapy, the amount of time that patients are allowed to spend in bed is limited to only slightly more time than they believe that they already sleep at night. Gradually the amount of time patients are allowed to spend in bed is increased until they are getting a full night's sleep. Unfortunately, many people find this treatment difficult to stick with, because they often become mildly sleep-deprived. The resultant fatigue can be useful, however, as it may help them fall asleep more easily and to stay asleep longer at night.

Teaching relaxation techniques that help patients concentrate on relaxing thoughts or images can also help patients experiencing insomnia. Most of these therapies also include setting times for waking and having the patient stick to them even if he or she has not gotten a full night of sleep. The elimination of all daytime napping can help to facilitate sleep at night. These treatments are effective by themselves, but may also be combined with other approaches. The course of treatment depends on the patient's specific symptoms.

Treatment with medications

Many different medicines, which are called hypnotics, are used to treat insomnia. These are usually not recommended for use for longer than a week because they may cause dependence. In addition, there is always the risk of side effects. There are many different types of hypnotics, and choosing one for a patient depends on the patient's symptoms, other drugs that he or she may be taking, any medical or psychological conditions, and other health factors. Medication treatment is best used in coordination with a behavioral therapy program.

Recently, two drugs have been approved by the US Food and Drug Administration for long-term use. A drug called ramelteon (brand name Rozerem) has shown no evidence of potential for abuse, dependence or withdrawal in clinical studies. Eszopiclone (brand name Lunesta) is also approved for long-term use. Rozerem and Lunesta are currently available by prescription only.

Alternative remedies

Alternative remedies for insomnia, particularly herbal preparations, should be mentioned because they are among the most popular nonprescription treatments for sleep problems. According to *Prevention* magazine, insomnia is the sixth most common condition treated with herbal formulas in the United States; it accounts for 18% of all use of herbal preparations. Some herbs used for insomnia are safer than others. Persons who are using alternative remedies, whether to treat insomnia or other conditions, should always tell their doctor what they are taking, how much, and how often. This warning is important because some herbal preparations that are safe in themselves can interact with prescription medications.

Prognosis

Untreated insomnia has potentially serious consequences, including an increased risk of motor vehicle accidents, impaired school or job performance, and a high rate of absenteeism from work. Fortunately, insomnia can be treated very effectively in most patients. Treatment using a combination of approaches is usually most effective. Patients who have had insomnia once are at an increased risk for recurrent insomnia.

See also Caffeine-related disorders; Chamomile; Passionflower; Valerian.

Resources

BOOKS

American Psychiatric Association. *Diagnostic and Statistical Manual of Mental Disorders*. 4th ed. text revised. Washington DC: American Psychiatric Association, 2000.

Currie, Shawn R. "Sleep Dysfunction." *Clinicians's Handbook of Adult Behavioral Assessment*, Ed. Michel Hersen. San Diego, CA: Elsevier Academic Press, 2006: 401–430.

Lee-Chiong, Teofilo L. Ed. *Sleep: A Comprehensive Handbook*. New York: Wiley-Liss, 2006.

Neubauer, David N. *Understanding Sleeplessness: Perspectives on Insomnia*. Baltimore: The Johns Hopkins University Press, 2003.

Pelletier, Kenneth R. *The Best Alternative Medicine*. New York: Simon and Schuster, 2002.

Spinella, Marcello. *Concise Handbook of Psychoactive Herbs: Medicinal Herbs for Treating Psychological and Neurological Problems*. New York: The Haworth Herbal Press, 2005.

Szuba, Martin P., Kloss, Jacqueline D., and Dinges, David F., eds. *Insomnia: Principles and Management*. New York: Cambridge University Press, 2003.

PERIODICALS

Irwin, Michael R. and Cole, Jason C. "Comparative Meta-Analysis of Behavioral Interventions for Insomnia and Their Efficacy in Middle-Aged Adults and in Older Adults 55+ Years of Age." *Health Psychology*, 25(1), Jan 2006: 3–14.

Jansson, Markus and Linton, Steven J. "The Role of Anxiety and Depression in the Development of Insomnia: Cross-Sectional and Prospective Analyses." *Psychology and Health*, 21(3), Jun 2006: 383–397.

Jansson, Markus and Linton, Steven J. "Psychosocial Work Stressors in the Development and Maintenance of Insomnia: A Prospective Study." *Journal of Occupational Health Psychology*, 11(3), Jul 2006: 241–248.

Manber, Rachel and Harvey, Allison. "Historical Perspective and Future Directions in Cognitive Behavioral Therapy for Insomnia and Behavioral Sleep Medicine." *Clinical Psychology Review*, 25(5), Jul 2005: 535–538.

Smith, Michael T. and Perlis, Michael L. "Who Is a Candidate for Cognitive-Behavioral Therapy for Insomnia?" *Health Psychology*, 25(1), Jan 2006: 15–19.

ORGANIZATIONS

American Academy of Sleep Medicine. 6301 Bandel Road NW, Suite 101, Rochester, MN 55901. (507) 287-6006. <www.asda.org>.

Tish Davidson, A.M.
Ruth A. Wienclaw, Ph.D.

Intake evaluation *see* Assessment and diagnosis

Intelligence tests

Definition

Intelligence tests are psychological tests that are designed to measure a variety mental functions, such as reasoning, comprehension, and judgment.

Purpose

The goal of intelligence tests is to obtain an idea of the person's intellectual potential. The tests center around a set of stimuli designed to yield a score based on the test maker's model of what makes up intelligence. Intelligence tests are often given as a part of a battery of tests.

Precautions

There are many different types of intelligence tests and they all do not measure the same abilities. Although the tests often have aspects that are related with each other, we should not expect that scores one intelligence test, that measures a single factor, will be similar to scores on another intelligence test, that measures a variety of factors. Also, when determining whether or not to use an intelligence test, a person should make sure that the test has been adequately developed and has solid research to show its reliability and validity. Additionally, psychometric testing requires a clinically trained examiner. Therefore, the test should only be administered and interpreted by a trained professional.

A central criticism of intelligence tests is that psychologists and educators use these tests to distribute the limited resources of our society. These test results are used to provide rewards such as special classes for gifted students, admission to college, and employment. Those who do not qualify for these resources based on intelligence test scores may feel angry and as if the tests are denying them opportunities for success. Unfortunately, intelligence test scores have not only become associated with a person's ability to perform certain tasks, but with self-worth.

Many people are under the false assumption that intelligence tests measure a person's inborn or biological intelligence. Intelligence tests are based on an individual's interaction with the environment and never exclusively measure inborn intelligence. Intelligence tests have been associated with categorizing and stereotyping people. Additionally, knowledge of one's performance on an intelligence test may affect a person's aspirations and motivation to obtain goals. Intelligence tests can be culturally biased against certain minority groups.

Description

When taking an intelligence test, a person can expect to do a variety of tasks. These tasks may include having to answer questions that are asked verbally, doing mathematical problems, and doing a variety of tasks that require eye hand coordination.

A student checks their work during an SSAT camp. *(Jen Hulshizer/Star Ledger/Corbis)*

Some tasks may be timed and require the person to work as quickly as possible. Typically, most questions and tasks start out easy and progressively get more difficult. It is unusual for anyone to know the answer to all of the questions or be able to complete all of the tasks. If a person is unsure of an answer, guessing is usually allowed.

The four most commonly used intelligence tests are:

- Stanford-Binet Intelligence Scales
- Wechsler-Adult Intelligence Scale
- Wechsler Intelligence Scale for Children
- Wechsler Primary & Preschool Scale of Intelligence

Advantages

In general, intelligence tests measure a wide variety of human behaviors better than any other measure that has been developed. They allow professionals to have a uniform way of comparing a person's performance with that of other people who are similar in age. These tests also provide information on cultural and biological differences among people.

Intelligence tests are excellent predictors of academic achievement and provide an outline of a person's mental strengths and weaknesses. Many times the scores have revealed talents in many people, which have lead to an improvement in their educational opportunities. Teacher, parents, and psychologists are able to devise individual curriculum that matches a person's level of development and expectations.

Disadvantages

Some researchers argue that intelligence tests have serious shortcomings. For example, many intelligence tests produce a single intelligence score. This single score is often inadequate in explaining the multidimensional aspects of intelligence. Another problem with a single score is the fact that individuals with similar intelligence test scores can vary greatly in their expression of these talents. It is important to know the person's performance on the various subtests that make up the overall intelligence test score. Knowing the performance on these various scales can influence the understanding of a person's abilities and how these abilities are expressed. For example, two people have identical scores on intelligence tests.

Although both people have the same test score, one person may have obtained the score because of strong verbal skills while the other may have obtained the score because of strong skills in perceiving and organizing various tasks.

Furthermore, intelligence tests only measure a sample of behaviors or situations in which intelligent behavior is revealed. For instance, some intelligence tests do not measure a person's everyday functioning, social knowledge, mechanical skills, and/or creativity. Along with this, the formats of many intelligence tests do not capture the complexity and immediacy of real-life situations. Therefore, intelligence tests have been criticized for their limited ability to predict non-test or nonacademic intellectual abilities. Since intelligence test scores can be influenced by a variety of different experiences and behaviors, they should not be considered a perfect indicator of a person's intellectual potential.

Results

The person's raw scores on an intelligence test are typically converted to standard scores. The standard scores allow the examiner to compare the individual's score to other people who have taken the test. Additionally, by converting raw scores to standard scores the examiner has uniform scores and can more easily compare an individual's performance on one test with the individual's performance on another test. Depending on the intelligence test that is used, a variety of scores can be obtained. Most intelligence tests generate an overall intelligence quotient or IQ. As previously noted, it is valuable to know how a person performs on the various tasks that make up the test. This can influence the interpretation of the test and what the IQ means. The average of score for most intelligence tests is 100.

See also Stanford-Binet Intelligence Scales; Wechsler Adult Intelligence Scale; Wechsler Intelligence Scale for Children.

Resources

BOOKS

Kaufman, Alan, S., and Elizabeth O. Lichtenberger. *Assessing Adolescent and Adult Intelligence*. Boston: Allyn and Bacon, 2001.

Matarazzo, J. D. *Wechsler's Measurement and Appraisal of Adult Intelligence*. 5th ed. New York: Oxford University Press, 1972.

Sattler, Jerome M. "Issues Related to the Measurement and Change of Intelligence." In *Assessment of Children: Cognitive Applications*. 4th ed. San Diego: Jerome M. Sattler, Publisher, Inc., 2001.

Sattler, Jerome M. and Lisa Weyandt. "Specific Learning Disabilities." In *Assessment of Children: Behavioral and Clinical Applications*. 4th ed. Written by Jerome M. Sattler. San Diego: Jerome M. Sattler, Publisher, Inc., 2002.

Keith Beard, Psy.D.

Intermittent explosive disorder

Definition

Intermittent explosive disorder (IED) is a disorder characterized by impulsive acts of aggression, as contrasted with planned violent or aggressive acts. The aggressive episodes may take the form of "spells" or "attacks," with symptoms beginning minutes to hours before the actual acting-out. The **Diagnostic and Statistical Manual of Mental Disorders**, fourth edition, text revision (2000), also known as *DSM-IV-TR*, which is the basic reference work consulted by mental health professionals in determining the **diagnosis** of a mental disorder, classifies IED under the general heading of "Impulse-Control Disorders Not Elsewhere Classified." Other names for IED include rage attacks, anger attacks, and episodic dyscontrol.

Description

Intermittent explosive disorder was originally described by the eminent French **psychiatrist** Esquirol as a "partial insanity" related to senseless impulsive acts. Esquirol termed this disorder *monomanies instinctives*, or *instinctual monomanias*. These apparently unmotivated acts were thought to result from instinctual or involuntary impulses, or from impulses related to ideological obsessions.

People with intermittent explosive disorder have a problem with controlling their temper. In addition, their violent behavior is out of proportion to the incident or event that triggered the outburst. Impulsive acts of aggression, however, are not unique to intermittent explosive disorder. Impulsive aggression can be present in many psychological and nonpsychological disorders. The diagnosis of intermittent explosive disorder (IED) is essentially a diagnosis of exclusion, which means that it is given only after other disorders have been ruled out as causes of impulsive aggression.

Patients diagnosed with IED usually feel a sense of arousal or tension before an outburst, and relief of tension after the aggressive act. Patients with IED believe that their aggressive behaviors are justified; however, they feel genuinely upset, regretful, remorseful, bewildered or embarrassed by their impulsive and aggressive behavior.

Causes and symptoms

Causes

Recent findings suggest that IED may result from abnormalities in the areas of the **brain** that regulate behavioral arousal and inhibition. Research indicates that impulsive aggression is related to abnormal brain mechanisms in a system that inhibits motor (muscular movement) activity, called the serotoninergic system. This system is directed by a neurotransmitter called serotonin, which regulates behavioral inhibition (control of behavior). Some studies have correlated IED with abnormalities on both sides of the front portion of the brain. These localized areas in the front of the brain appear to be involved in information processing and controlling movement, both of which are unbalanced in persons diagnosed with IED. Studies using **positron emission tomography** (PET) scanning have found lower levels of brain glucose (sugar) metabolism in patients who act in impulsively aggressive ways.

Another study based on data from electroencephalograms (EEGs) of 326 children and adolescents treated in a psychiatric clinic found that 46% of the youths who manifested explosive behavior had unusual high-amplitude brain wave forms. The researchers concluded that a significant subgroup of people with IED may be predisposed to explosive behavior by an inborn characteristic of their central nervous system. In sum, there is a substantial amount of convincing evidence that IED has biological causes, at least in some people diagnosed with the disorder.

Other clinicians attribute IED to cognitive distortions. According to cognitive therapists, persons with IED have a set of strongly negative beliefs about other people, often resulting from harsh punishments inflicted by the parents. The child grows up believing that others "have it in for him" and that violence is the best way to restore damaged self-esteem. He or she may also have observed one or both parents, older siblings, or other relatives acting out in explosively violent ways. In short, people who develop IED have learned, usually in their family of origin, to believe that certain acts or attitudes on the part of other people "justify" aggressive attacks on them.

Although gender roles are not a "cause" of IED to the same extent as biological and familial factors, they are regarded by some researchers as helping to explain why most people diagnosed with IED are males.

According to this theory, men have greater permission from society to act violently and impulsively than women do. They therefore have less reason to control their aggressive impulses. Women who act explosively, on the other hand, would be considered unfeminine as well as unfriendly or dangerous.

Symptoms

IED is characterized by violent behaviors that are impulsive as well as assaultive. One example involved a man who felt insulted by another customer in a neighborhood bar during a conversation that had lasted for several minutes. Instead of finding out whether the other customer intended his remark to be insulting, or answering the "insult" verbally, the man impulsively punched the other customer in the mouth. Within a few minutes, however, he felt ashamed of his violent act. As this example indicates, the urge to commit the impulsive aggressive act may occur from minutes to hours before the "acting out" and is characterized by the buildup of tension. After the outburst, the IED patient experiences a sense of relief from the tension. While many patients with IED blame someone else for causing their violent outbursts, they also express remorse and guilt for their actions.

Demographics

IED is apparently a rare disorder. Most studies, however, indicate that it occurs more frequently in males. The most common age of onset is the period from late childhood through the early 20s. The onset of the disorder is frequently abrupt, with no warning period. Patients with IED are often diagnosed with at least one other disorder—particularly **personality disorders**, **substance abuse** (especially alcohol **abuse**) disorders, and neurological disorders.

Diagnosis

As mentioned, IED is essentially a diagnosis of exclusion. Patients who are eventually diagnosed with IED may come to the attention of a psychiatrist or other mental health professional by several different routes. Some patients with IED, often adult males who have assaulted their wives and are trying to save their marriages, are aware that their outbursts are not normal and seek treatment to control them. Younger males with IED are more likely to be referred for diagnosis and treatment by school authorities or the juvenile justice system, or brought to the doctor by concerned parents.

A psychiatrist who is evaluating a patient for IED would first take a complete medical and psychiatric history. Depending on the contents of the patient's history, the doctor would give the patient a physical examination to rule out head trauma, epilepsy, and other general medical conditions that may cause violent behavior. If the patient appears to be intoxicated by a drug of abuse or suffering symptoms of withdrawal, the doctor may order a toxicology screen of the patient's blood or urine. Specific substances that are known to be associated with violent outbursts include **phencyclidine** (PCP or "angel dust"), alcohol, and **cocaine**. The doctor will also give the patient a mental status examination and a test to screen for neurological damage. If necessary, a neurologist may be consulted and **imaging studies** performed of the patient's brain.

If the physical findings and laboratory test results are normal, the doctor may evaluate the patient for personality disorders, usually by administering diagnostic questionnaires. The patient may be given a diagnosis of antisocial or **borderline personality disorder** in addition to a diagnosis of IED.

In some cases the doctor may need to rule out **malingering**, particularly if the patient has been referred for evaluation by a court order and is trying to evade legal responsibility for his behavior.

Treatments

Some adult patients with IED appear to benefit from cognitive therapy. A team of researchers at the University of Pennsylvania found that cognitive approaches that challenged the patients' negative views of the world and of other people was effective in reducing the intensity as well as the frequency of violent episodes. With regard to gender roles, many of the men reported that they were helped by rethinking "manliness" in terms of self-control rather than as something to be "proved" by hitting someone else or damaging property.

Several medications have been used for treating IED. These include **carbamazepine** (Tegretol), an anti-seizure medication; **propranolol** (Inderal), a heart medication that controls blood pressure and irregular heart rhythms; and lithium, a drug used to treat bipolar type II manic-depression disorder. The success of treatment with lithium and other mood-stabilizing medications is consistent with findings that patients with IED have a high lifetime rate of **bipolar disorder**.

Prognosis

Little research has been done on patients who meet *DSM-IV* criteria for IED, although one study did find that such patients have a high lifetime rate of comorbid (co-occurring) bipolar disorder. In some

KEY TERMS

Assaultive—An act with intent of causing harm.

Electroencephalograph—(EEG) An instrument that measures the normal and abnormal electrical activity in the brain.

Episodic dyscontrol—Another term for intermittent explosive disorder.

Malingering—Knowingly pretending to be physically or mentally ill to avoid some unpleasant duty or responsibility, or for economic benefit.

Monomania—A nineteenth-century term for a pathological obsession with one idea or one social cause. Nineteenth-century psychiatrists often associated explosive behavior with monomania. The word is no longer used as a technical term.

Serotonin—A widely distributed neurotransmitter that is found in blood platelets, the lining of the digestive tract, and the brain, and that works in combination with norepinephrine. It causes very powerful contractions of smooth muscle, and is associated with mood, attention, emotions, and sleep. Low levels of serotonin are associated with depression.

Toxicology screen—A blood or urine test that detects the presence of toxic chemicals, alcohol, or drugs in body fluids.

persons IED decreases in severity or resolves completely as the person grows older. In others the disorder appears to be chronic.

Prevention

As of 2002, preventive strategies include educating young people in parenting skills, and teaching children skills related to self-control. Recent studies summarized by an article in a professional journal of psychiatry indicate that self-control can be practiced like many other skills, and that people can improve their present level of self-control with appropriate coaching and practice.

See also Gender issues in mental health.

Resources

BOOKS

Baumeister, Roy F., PhD. Chapter 8, "Crossing the Line: How Evil Starts." In *Evil: Inside Human Violence and Cruelty*. New York: W. H. Freeman and Company, 1999.

Beck, Aaron T., M.D. *Prisoners of Hate: The Cognitive Basis of Anger, Hostility, and Violence.* New York: Harper-Collins, 1999.

Tasman, Allan, and others, eds. *Psychiatry.* 1st edition. Philadelphia: W. B. Saunders Company. 1997: 1249-1258.

PERIODICALS

Bars, Donald R., and others. "Use of Visual Evoked-Potential Studies and EEG Data to Classify Aggressive, Explosive Behavior of Youths." *Psychiatric Services* 52 (January 2001): 81-86.

McElroy, Susan L. "Recognition and Treatment of DSM-IV Intermittent Explosive Disorder." *Journal of Clinical Psychiatry* 60 (1999) [suppl. 15]: 12-16.

Strayhorn, Joseph M., Jr. "Self-Control: Theory and Research." *Journal of the American Academy of Child and Adolescent Psychiatry* 41 (January 2002): 7-16.

Laith Farid Gulli, M.D.
Bilal Nasser, M.D.

Internet addiction disorder

Definition

Internet **addiction** disorder refers to the problematic use of the Internet, including the various aspects of its technology, such as electronic mail (e-mail) and the World Wide Web. The reader should note that Internet addiction disorder is not listed in the mental health professional's handbook, the ***Diagnostic and Statistical Manual of Mental Disorders***, fourth edition, text revision (2000), which is also called the *DSM*. Internet addiction has, however, been formally recognized as a disorder by the American Psychological Association.

Description

In some respects, addictive use of the Internet resembles other so-called "process" addictions, in which a person is addicted to an activity or behavior (including gambling, shopping, or certain sexual behaviors) rather than a substance (mood-altering drugs, tobacco, food, etc.). People who develop problems with their Internet use may start off using the Internet on a casual basis and then progress to using the technology in dysfunctional ways. Many people believe that spending large amounts of time on the Internet is a core feature of the disorder. The amount of time by itself, however, is not as important a factor as the ways in which the person's Internet use is interfering with their daily functioning. Use of the Internet may interfere with the person's social life, school work, or job-related

tasks at work. In addition, cases have been reported of persons entering Internet chat rooms for people with serious illnesses or disorders, and pretending to be a patient with that disorder in order to get attention or sympathy. Treatment options often mirror those for other addictions. Although only a limited amount of research has been done on this disorder, the treatments that have been used appear to be effective.

Causes and symptoms

Causes

No one knows what causes a person to be addicted to the Internet, but there are several factors that have been proposed as contributing to Internet addiction. One theory concerns the mood-altering potential of behaviors related to process addictions. Just as a person addicted to shopping may feel a "rush" or pleasurable change in mood from the series of actions related to a spending spree—checking one's credit cards, driving to the mall, going into one's favorite store, etc.—the person with an Internet addiction may feel a similar "rush" from booting up their computer and going to their favorite web sites. In other words, some researchers think that there are chemical changes that occur in the body when someone is engaging in an addictive behavior. Furthermore, from a biological standpoint, there may be a combination of genes that make a person more susceptible to addictive behaviors, just as researchers have located genes that affect a person's susceptibility to alcohol.

In addition to having features of a **process addiction**, Internet use might be reinforced by pleasurable thoughts and feelings that occur while the person is using the Internet. Although researchers in the field of addiction studies question the concept of an "addictive personality" as such, it is possible that someone who has one addiction may be prone to become addicted to other substances or activities, including Internet use. People with such other mental disorders or symptoms as **depression**, feelings of isolation, **stress**, or **anxiety**, may "self-medicate" by using the Internet in the same way that some people use alcohol or drugs of **abuse** to self-medicate the symptoms of their mental disorder.

From a social or interpersonal standpoint, there may be familial factors prompting use of the Internet. For example, a person might "surf the Web" to escape family conflict. Another possibility is that social or peer dynamics might prompt excessive Internet use. Some affected persons may lack the social skills that would enable them to meet people in person rather than online. Peer behavior might also encourage Internet use if all one's friends are using it. **Modeling** may play a role—users can witness and experience how

Computer users in an Internet café, South Korea. *(AP Images)*

others engage in Internet use and then replicate that behavior. The interactive aspects of the Internet, such as chat rooms, e-mail, and interactive games like Multi-User Dungeons and Dragons (MUDS), seem to be more likely to lead to Internet addiction than purely solitary web surfing.

One question that has not yet been answered concerning Internet addiction is whether it is a distinctive type of addiction or simply an instance of a new technology being used to support other addictions. For example, there are gambling casinos on the Internet that could reinforce a person's pre-existing gambling addiction. Similarly, someone addicted to shopping could transfer their addiction from the local mall to online stores. Persons addicted to certain forms of sexual behavior can visit pornography sites on the Internet or use chat rooms as a way to meet others who might be willing to participate in those forms of behavior. Researchers may need to determine whether there is such a disorder as "pure" Internet addiction.

Symptoms

One symptom of Internet addiction is excessive time devoted to Internet use. A person might have difficulty cutting down on his or her online time even when they are threatened with poor grades or loss of a job. There have been cases reported of college students failing courses because they would not take time off from Internet use to attend classes. Other symptoms of addiction may include lack of sleep; **fatigue**; declining grades or poor job performance; **apathy**; and racing thoughts. There may also be a decreased investment in social relationships and activities. A person may lie about how much time was spent online or deny that they have a problem. They may be irritable when offline, or angry toward anyone who questions their time on the Internet.

Demographics

In the past, people reported to have an Internet addiction disorder were stereotyped as young, introverted, socially awkward, computer-oriented males. While this stereotype may have been true in the past, the availability of computers and the increased ease of access to the Internet are quickly challenging this notion. As a result, problematic Internet use can be found in any age group, social class, racial or ethnic group, level of education and income, and gender.

Diagnosis

As previously noted, Internet addiction disorder has not yet been added as an official **diagnosis** to the *DSM*. The following, however, is a set of criteria for Internet addiction that has been proposed by addiction researchers. The criteria are based on the diagnostic standards for pathological gambling.

The patient must meet all of the following criteria:

- He or she is preoccupied with the Internet (thinks about previous online activity or is anticipating the next online session).
- He or she needs to spend longer and longer periods of time online in order to feel satisfied.
- He or she has made unsuccessful efforts to control, cut back, or stop Internet use.
- He or she is restless, moody, depressed, or irritable when attempting to cut down or stop Internet use.
- He or she repeatedly stays online longer than he or she originally intended.

The person must meet at least one of the following criteria:

- He or she has jeopardized or risked the loss of a significant relationship, job, educational or career opportunity because of Internet use.
- He or she has lied to family members, a therapist, or others to conceal the extent of involvement with the Internet.
- He or she uses the Internet as a way of escaping from problems or of relieving an unpleasant mood (such as feelings of helplessness, guilt, anxiety, or depression).

Treatments

Since Internet addiction disorder is a relatively new phenomenon, there is little research on the effectiveness of treatment procedures. It may be unrealistic to have a person completely end all Internet use. As our society becomes more and more dependent on computers for business transactions, educational programs, entertainment, and access to information as well as interpersonal communication, it will be difficult for a computer-literate person to avoid using the Internet. Learning how to use the Internet in moderation is often the main objective in therapy, in a way analogous to the way that people with eating disorders need to come to terms with food. Many of the procedures that have been used to treat Internet addiction have been modeled after other addiction treatment programs and support groups.

If a person's Internet addiction disorder has a biological dimension, then such medication as an antide-

---

KEY TERMS

Carpal tunnel syndrome—A disorder of the hand and wrist characterized by pain, weakness, or numbness in the thumb and other fingers. It is caused by pressure on a nerve in the wrist. Carpal tunnel syndrome is frequently associated with heavy use of a computer, typewriter, or musical keyboard.

Denial—A psychological defense mechanism that reduces anxiety by excluding recognition of an addiction or similar problem from the conscious mind.

Process addiction—An addiction to a mood-altering behavior or series of behaviors rather than a substance.

Reinforcement—A term that refers to the ability of a drug, substance, or behavior to produce effects that will make the user want to take the substance or perform the behavior again.

Rush—The initial intensely pleasurable sensation experienced from injecting a narcotic or stimulant drug. The term has also been applied to the feeling of excitement experienced from the behaviors involved in process addictions.

---

pressant or anti-anxiety drug may help them with these aspects of the addiction. Psychological interventions may include such approaches as changing the environment to alter associations that have been made with Internet use, or decrease the **reinforcement** received from excessive Internet use. Psychological interventions may also help the person identify thoughts and feelings that trigger their use of the Internet. Interpersonal interventions may include such approaches as **social skills training** or coaching in **communication skills**. Family and couple therapy may be indicated if the user is turning to the Internet to escape from problems in these areas of life.

Relapsing into an addictive behavior is common for anyone dealing with addiction disorders. Recognizing and preparing for **relapse** is often a part of the treatment process. Identifying situations that would trigger excessive Internet use and generating ways to deal with these situations can greatly reduce the possibility of total relapse.

Prognosis

Although extensive studies have not yet been done, treatment appears to be effective in maintaining and changing the behavior of people drawn to excessive use of the Internet. If the disorder is left untreated, the person may experience an increased amount of conflict in his or her relationships. Excessive Internet use may jeopardize a person's employment or academic standing. In addition, such physical problems may develop as fatigue, carpal tunnel syndrome, back pain, and eyestrain.

Prevention

If a person knows that he or she has difficulty with other forms of addictive behavior, they should be cautious in exploring the types of applications that are used on the Internet. In addition, it is important for people to engage in social activities outside the Internet. Finally, mental health workers should investigate ways in which to participate in the implementation of new technology rather than waiting for its after effects.

See also Factitious disorder; Pathological gambling disorder.

Resources

BOOKS

Young, K. S. *Caught in the Net.* New York, NY: John Wiley and Sons, Inc., 1998.

PERIODICALS

Beard, K., and E. Wolf. "Modification in the Proposed Diagnostic Criteria for Internet Addiction." *Cyberpsychology & Behavior* 4 (2001): 377-383.

Beard, K. "Internet Addiction: Current Status and Implication for Employees." *Journal of Employment Counseling* 39 (2002): 2-11.

Griffiths, M. "Psychology of Computer Use: XLIII. Some Comments on 'Addictive Use of the Internet' by Young." *Psychological Reports* 80 (1997): 81-81.

Kraut, R., M. Patterson, V. Lundmark, S. Kiesler, T. Mukopadhyay, and W. Scherlis. "Internet Paradox: A Social Technology That Reduces Social Involvement and Psychological Well-Being?" *American Psychologist* 53 (1998): 1017-1031.

Keith Beard, Psy.D.

Internet-based therapy

Definition

Internet-based therapy is a form of **psychotherapy** conducted over the Internet rather than in face-to-face sessions. Therapeutic sessions may be conducted using instant messaging, chat rooms, or e-mail messages. Internet-based therapy is also called on-line therapy or e-therapy.

Description

As the Information Age progresses, more and more services are available over the Internet. We can buy not only books on-line but also electronics, clothes, and even groceries. In the business world, the requirement and expense of traveling to in-person meetings is often negated by the ability to teleconference. College degrees no longer need to be earned in the classroom but can be acquired in the comfort of one's own home at one's own pace. The wait for a technician on a manufacturer's help line is often replaced by the ability to search the company's database on one's own or to engage in on-line chat with the same technician to whom one once spoke. Even for medical problems, one can often chat with a physician or nurse practitioner by e-mail rather than going into the office.

There is little wonder, therefore, that there is a demand for psychological services over the Internet. Chatting with one's therapist on-line is more private than going to an office and waiting in a public waiting room. For those in rural areas where access to a therapist is exceedingly difficult, the Internet can provide a convenient alternative for getting the help that one needs.

There are pros and cons to both sides of the on-line versus face-to-face therapy issue. First, communicating through e-mail, on-line chat, or instant messages has the same drawbacks of any written-only communication: The non-verbal cues such as tone of voice, facial expression, and body language are missing, making interpretation of the message more problematic than in a face-to-face situation. On the other hand, the relative anonymity of on-line interactions make such therapeutic relationships more attractive to those who would hesitate to go into a therapist's office for fear of being found out by others, fear of embarrassment, or unwillingness or inability to get to the office. In addition, on-line therapy tends to be less expensive than in-office therapy, a consideration for many clients.

There are, of course, some things that cannot be done over the Internet. For example, psychologists and psychiatrists use a variety of tools and techniques to diagnose mental disorders so that they can prescribe the appropriate course of treatment. Some of the tools used in **diagnosis** include psychometric instruments such as the **Minnesota Multiphasic Personality Inventory** (MMPI), projective instruments such as the Rorschach test or the **Thematic Apperception Test** (TAT), and diagnostic interviews. The various tests and instruments used in diagnosis should ethically only be given by a credentialed professional in a controlled situation and cannot be given across the Internet where there is no control over who will see the test, how long the client takes to answer the questions, or even whether it was the client or someone else who took the test. In addition, it would be extremely difficult to diagnose a patient's problem without a face-to-face meeting for a diagnostic interview.

Research into the effectiveness of on-line therapy is only beginning. However, a number of disorders have been successfully treated electronically. For example, Internet-based therapy has been successful in the treatment of **panic disorder**, **social phobia**, child adjustment after traumatic **brain** injury, and complicated **grief**, among others.

Precautions

As with any service provided over the Internet, one must be an informed consumer not only before choosing an e-therapist, but even before deciding to use Internet-based therapy itself. Because Internet-based therapy is an emerging field, there are still many issues to be resolved. Obviously, one must check the professional credentials of a therapist to make sure that he or she is licensed, whether one is choosing a therapist for on-line or in-office therapy. In addition, it is unclear at this time whether it is legal for a therapist licensed in one state to treat a patient in another state. Choosing a therapist in one's own state makes this issue irrelevant, but requires research.

Client/therapist confidentiality is important in any therapeutic relationship. When choosing an on-line provider of psychological services, one must be certain not only that the therapist subscribes to a professional code of ethics, but also that any information—including personal data about the client—is kept confidential and not sold to or shared with third parties. Similarly, it is important to check that the Web site used in on-line therapy is secure and that conversations, instant messages, and e-mail transmissions between client and therapist are not recorded on the site's secured host computer.

Internet-based therapy shows promise for helping people who could not or would not otherwise engage in a therapeutic relationship. This potential is beginning to be tested in research. However, much of this research also recommends that Internet-based therapy be used in conjunction with face-to-face sessions. There are still many technical, logistical, and ethical questions to be answered regarding how the Internet best can be used for therapy.

KEY TERMS

Chat room—A space on a Web site or network server that allows multiple people to communicate by entering text messages at their individual computers. The messages are viewable by all in the virtual "room," and messages appear almost instantaneously once they are sent.

E-mail—Short for "electronic mail," a system for sending and receiving messages electronically through personal computers or other computer network. Usually, it takes only a few minutes or even seconds for an e-mail to be sent between computers.

Instant messaging (IM)—A method of electronic communication that allows two or more people to communicate nearly instantaneously without using a chat room. Instant messaging is much like a telephone conversation with text messages. The sender types a message at his or her computer, which is then sent to and received at the other person's computer. Instant messaging can be used in much the same way as a private chat room.

Resources

BOOKS

Goss, Stephen, and Kate Anthony, eds. *Technology in Counselling and Psychotherapy: A Practitioner's Guide.* New York: Palgrave Macmillan, 2003.

Hsiung, Robert C., ed. *E-Therapy: Case Studies, Guiding Principles, and the Clinical Potential of the Internet.* New York: W. W. Norton & Company, 2002.

Kraus, Ron, Jason Zack, and George Stricker. *Online Counseling: A Handbook for Mental Health Professionals.* New York: Academic Press, 2003.

VandenBos, Gary R., ed. *APA Dictionary of Psychology.* Washington, D.C.: American Psychological Association, 2007.

PERIODICALS

Andersson, Gerhard, Per Carlbring, Annelie Holmström, Elisabeth Sparthan, Tomas Furmark, and Monica Buhrman. "Internet-Based Self-Help with Therapist Feedback and In Vivo Group Exposure for Social Phobia: A Randomized Controlled Trial." *Journal of Consulting and Clinical Psychology* 74.4 (2006): 677–86.

Carlbring, Per, and Gerhard Andersson. "Internet and Psychological Treatment. How Well Can They Be Combined?" *Computers in Human Behavior* 22.3 (2006): 545–53.

Chester, Andrea, and Carolyn A. Glass. "Online Counselling: A Descriptive Analysis of Therapy Services on the Internet." *British Journal of Guidance & Counselling* 34.2 (2006): 145–60.

Gollings, Emma K., and Susan J. Paxton. "Comparison of Internet and Face-to-Face Delivery of a Group Body Image and Disordered Eating Intervention for Women: A Pilot Study." *Eating Disorders: The Journal of Treatment and Prevention* 14.1 (2006): 1–15.

Klein, Britt, Jeffrey C. Richards, and David W. Austin. "Efficacy of Internet Therapy for Panic Disorder." *Journal of Behavior Therapy and Experimental Psychiatry* 37.3 (2006): 213–38.

Lam, Raymond W. "Challenges in the Treatment of Anxiety Disorders: Beyond Guidelines." *International Journal of Psychiatry in Clinical Practice* 10.3 (2006): 18–24.

O'Kearney, Richard, Mal Gibson, Helen Christensen, and Kathy M. Griffiths. "Effects of a Cognitive-Behavioural Internet Program on Depression, Vulnerability to Depression and Stigma in Adolescent Males: A School-Based Controlled Trial." *Cognitive Behaviour Therapy* 35.1 (2006): 43–54.

Patten, Christi A., Ivana T. Croghan, Tracy M. Meis, Paul A. Decker, Suzanne Pingree, Robert C. Colligan, Ellen A. Dornelas, Kenneth P. Offord, Eric W. Boberg, Rhonda K. Baumberger, Richard D. Hurt, and David H. Gustafson. "Randomized Clinical Trial of an Internet-Based Versus Brief Office Intervention for Adolescent Smoking Cessation." *Patient Education and Counseling* 64.1–3 (2006): 249–58.

Przeworski, Amy, and Michelle G. Newman. "Efficacy and Utility Of Computer-Assisted Cognitive Behavioural Therapy for Anxiety Disorders." *Clinical Psychologist* 10.2 (2006): 43–53.

Pull, Charles B. "Self-Help Internet Interventions for Mental Disorders." *Current Opinion in Psychiatry* 19.1 (2006): 50–53.

Schultze, Nils-Günter. "Success Factors in Internet-Based Psychological Counseling." *CyberPsychology & Behavior* 9.5 (2006): 623–26.

Spence, Susan H., Jane M. Holmes, Sonja March, and Ottmar V. Lipp. "The Feasibility and Outcome of Clinic Plus Internet Delivery of Cognitive-Behavior Therapy for Childhood Anxiety." *Journal of Consulting and Clinical Psychology* 74.3 (2006): 614–21.

Wade, Shari L., JoAnne Carey, and Christopher R. Wolfe. "The Efficacy of an Online Cognitive-Behavioral Family Intervention in Improving Child Behavior and Social Competence Following Pediatric Brain Injury." *Rehabilitation Psychology* 51.3 (2006): 179–89.

Wagner, Birgit, and Christine Knaevelsrud. "Internet-Based Cognitive-Behavioral Therapy for Complicated Grief: A Randomized Controlled Trial." *Death Studies* 30.5 (2006): 429–53.

ORGANIZATIONS

American Psychological Association, 750 First Street NE, Washington, DC 20002-42427. Telephone: (800) 374-2721. <http://www.apa.org>.

Ruth A. Wienclaw, PhD

Interpersonal psychotherapy *see* **Interpersonal therapy**

Interpersonal therapy

Definition

Interpersonal therapy (IPT) is a short-term supportive **psychotherapy** that focuses on the connection between interactions between people and the development of a person'spsychiatric symptoms.

Purpose

Interpersonal therapy was initially developed to treat adult **depression**. It has since been applied to the treatment of depression in adolescents, the elderly, and people with Human Immunodeficiency Virus (HIV) infection. There is an IPT conjoint (couple) therapy for people whose marital disputes contribute to depressive episodes. IPT has also been modified for the treatment of a number of disorders, including **substance abuse**; bulimia and **anorexia nervosa**; **bipolar disorder**; and dysthymia. Research is underway to determine the efficacy of IPT in the treatment of patients with **panic disorder** or **borderline personality disorder**; depressed caregivers of patients with traumatic **brain** injuries; depressed pregnant women; and people suffering from protracted bereavement.

Interpersonal therapy is a descendant of psychodynamic therapy, itself derived from **psychoanalysis**, with its emphasis on the unconscious and childhood experiences. Symptoms and personal difficulties are regarded as arising from deep, unresolved personality or character problems. **Psychodynamic psychotherapy** is a long-term method of treatment, with in-depth exploration of past family relationships as they were perceived during the client'sinfancy, childhood, and adolescence.

There are seven types of interventions that are commonly used in IPT, many of which reflect the influence of psychodynamic psychotherapy: a focus on clients' emotions; an exploration of clients' resistance to treatment; discussion of patterns in clients' relationships and experiences; taking a detailed past history; an emphasis on clients' current interpersonal experiences; exploration of the therapist/client relationship; and the identification of clients' wishes and fantasies. IPT is, however, distinctive for its brevity and its treatment focus. IPT emphasizes the ways in which a person's current relationships and social context cause or maintain symptoms rather than exploring the deep-seated sources of the symptoms. Its goals are rapid symptom reduction and improved social adjustment. A frequent byproduct of IPT treatment is more satisfying relationships in the present.

IPT has the following goals in the treatment of depression: to diagnose depression explicitly; to educate the client about depression, its causes, and the various treatments available for it; to identify the interpersonal context of depression as it relates to symptom development; and to develop strategies for the client to follow in coping with the depression. Because interpersonal therapy is a short-term approach, the therapist addresses only one or two problem areas in the client's current functioning. In the early sessions, the therapist and client determine which areas would be most helpful in reducing the client's symptoms. The remaining sessions are then organized toward resolving these agreed-upon problem areas. This time-limited framework distinguishes IPT from therapies that are open-ended in their exploration. The targeted approach of IPT has demonstrated rapid improvement for patients with problems ranging from mild situational depression to severe depression with a recent history of **suicide** attempts.

Interpersonal therapy has been outlined in a manual by Klerman and Weissman, which ensures some standardization in the training of interpersonal therapists and their practice. Because of this standardized training format, IPT is not usually combined with other talk therapies. Treatment with IPT, however, is often combined with drug therapy, particularly when the client suffers from such mood disorders as depression, dysthymia, or bipolar disorder.

Precautions

Training programs in interpersonal therapy are still not widely available, so that many practicing therapists base their work on the manual alone without additional supervision. It is unclear whether reading the manual alone is sufficient to provide an acceptable standard of care.

While interpersonal therapy has been adapted for use with substance abusers, it has not demonstrated its effectiveness with this group of patients. Researchers studying patients addicted to opiates or **cocaine** found little benefit to incorporating IPT into the standard recovery programs. These findings suggest that another treatment method that offers greater structure and direction would be more successful with these patients.

Description

Since the interpersonal therapy model was developed for the treatment of depression and then modified for use with other populations and mental disorders, an understanding of IPT's approach to depression is

crucial. Interpersonal therapists focus on the functional role of depression rather than on its etiology or cause; and they look at the ways in which problematic interactions develop when a person becomes depressed. The IPT framework considers clinical depression as having three components: the development of symptoms, which arise from biological, genetic and/or psychodynamic processes; social interactions with other people, which are learned over the course of one's life; and personality, made up of the more enduring traits and behaviors that may predispose a person to depressive symptoms. IPT intervenes at the levels of symptom formation and social functioning, and does not attempt to alter aspects of the client's personality.

Subtypes of IPT

Interpersonal therapy offers two possible treatment plans for persons with **depressive disorders**. The first plan treats the acute episode of depression by eliminating the current depressive symptoms. This approach requires intervening while the person is in the midst of a depression. The acute phase of treatment typically lasts 2–4 months with weekly sessions. Many clients terminate treatment at that point, after their symptoms have subsided. Maintenance treatment (IPT-M) is the second treatment plan and is much less commonly utilized than acute treatment. IPT-M is a longer-term therapy based on the principles of interpersonal therapy but with the aim of preventing or reducing the frequency of further depressive episodes. Some clients choose IPT-M after the acute treatment phase. IPT-M can extend over a period of 2–3 years, with therapy sessions once a month.

Psychoeducation in IPT

Treatment with IPT is based on the premise that depression occurs in a social and interpersonal context that must be understood for improvement to occur. In the first session, the psychiatric history includes a review of the client's current social functioning and current close relationships, their patterns and their mutual expectations. Changes in relationships prior to the onset of symptoms are clarified, such as the death of a loved one, a child leaving home, or worsening marital conflict.

IPT is psychoeducational in nature to some degree. It involves teaching the client about the nature of depression and the ways that it manifests in his or her life and relationships. In the initial sessions, depressive symptoms are reviewed in detail, and the accurate naming of the problem is essential. The therapist then explains depression and its treatment and may explain to the client that he or she has adopted the "sick role." The concept of the "sick role" is derived from the work of a sociologist named Talcott Parsons, and is based on the notion that illness is not merely a condition but a social role that affects the attitudes and behaviors of the client and those around him or her. Over time, the client comes to see that the sick role has increasingly come to govern his or her social interactions.

Identification of problem areas

The techniques of IPT were developed to manage four basic interpersonal problem areas: unresolved **grief**; role transitions; interpersonal role disputes (often marital disputes); and interpersonal deficits (deficiencies). In the early sessions, the interpersonal therapist and the client attempt to determine which of these four problems is most closely associated with the onset of the current depressive episode. Therapy is then organized to help the client deal with the interpersonal difficulties in the primary problem area. The coping strategies that the client is encouraged to discover and employ in daily life are tailored to his or her individual situation.

UNRESOLVED GRIEF. In normal bereavement, a person experiences symptoms such as sadness, disturbed sleep, and difficulty functioning but these usually resolve in 2–4 months. Unresolved grief in depressed people is usually either delayed grief, which has been postponed and then experienced long after the loss; or distorted grief, in which there is no felt emotion of sadness but there may be nonemotional symptoms, often physical. If unresolved grief is identified as the primary issue, the goals of treatment are to facilitate the mourning process. Successful therapy will help the client re-establish interests and relationships that can begin to fill the void of what has been lost.

ROLE DISPUTES. Interpersonal role disputes occur when the client and at least one other significant person have differing expectations of their relationship. The IPT therapist focuses on these disputes if they seem stalled or repetitious, or offer little hope of improvement. The treatment goals include helping the client identify the nature of the dispute; decide on a plan of action; and begin to modify unsatisfying patterns, reassess expectations of the relationship, or both. The therapist does not direct the client to one particular resolution of difficulties and should not attempt to preserve unworkable relationships.

ROLE TRANSITIONS. Depression associated with role transitions occurs when a person has difficulty coping with life changes that require new roles. These may be such transitions as retirement, a career change, moving, or leaving home. People who are clinically depressed are most likely to experience role changes as losses rather than opportunities. The loss may be obvious, as when a marriage ends, or more subtle, as the loss of freedom people experience after the birth of a child. Therapy is terminated when a client has given up the old role; expressed the accompanying feelings of guilt, anger, and loss; acquired new skills; and developed a new social network around the new role.

INTERPERSONAL DEFICITS. Interpersonal deficits are the focus of treatment when the client has a history of inadequate or unsupportive interpersonal relationships. The client may never have established lasting or intimate relationships as an adult, and may experience a sense of inadequacy, lack of self-assertion, and guilt about expressing anger. Generally, clients with a history of extreme social isolation come to therapy with more severe emotional disturbances. The goal of treatment is to reduce the client's social isolation. Instead of focusing on current relationships, IPT therapy in this area focuses on the client's past relationships; the present relationship with the therapist; and ways to form new relationships.

IPT in special populations

ELDERLY CLIENTS. In translating the IPT model of depression to work with different populations, the core principles and problem areas remain essentially the same, with some modifications. In working with the elderly, IPT sessions may be shorter to allow for decreased energy levels, and dependency issues may be more prominent. In addition, the therapist may work with an elderly client toward tolerating rather than eliminating long-standing role disputes.

CLIENTS WITH HIV INFECTION. In IPT with HIV-positive clients, particular attention is paid to the clients' unique set of psychosocial stressors: the **stigma** of the disease; the effects of being gay (if applicable); dealing with family members who may isolate themselves; and coping with the medical consequences of the disease.

ADOLESCENTS. In IPT with adolescents, the therapist addresses such common developmental issues as separation from parents; the client's authority in relationship to parents; the development of new interpersonal relationships; first experiences of the death of a relative or friend; peer pressure; and single-parent families. Adolescents are seen weekly for 12 weeks with once-weekly additional phone contact between therapist and client for the first four weeks of treatment.

The parents are interviewed in the initial session to get a comprehensive history of the adolescent's symptoms, and to educate the parents as well as the young person about depression and possible treatments, including a discussion of the need for medication. The therapist refrains from giving advice when working with adolescents, and will primarily use supportive listening, while assessing the client for evidence of suicidal thoughts or problems with school attendance. So far, research does not support the efficacy of antidepressant medication in treating adolescents, though most clinicians will give some younger clients a trial of medication if it appears to offer relief.

CLIENTS WITH SUBSTANCE ABUSE DISORDERS. While IPT has not yet demonstrated its efficacy in the field of substance **abuse** recovery, a version of IPT has been developed for use with substance abusers. The two goals are to help the client stop or cut down on drug use; and to help the client develop better strategies for dealing with the social and interpersonal consequences of drug use. To meet these goals, the client must accept the need to stop; take steps to manage impulsiveness; and recognize the social contexts of drug purchase and use. **Relapse** is viewed as the rule rather than the exception in treating substance abuse disorders, and the therapist avoids treating the client in a punitive or disapproving manner when it occurs. Instead, the therapist reminds the client of the fact that staying away from drugs is the client's decision.

CLIENTS WITH EATING DISORDERS. IPT has been extended to the treatment of eating disorders. The IPT therapist does not focus directly on the symptoms of the disorder, but rather, allows for identification of problem areas that have contributed to the emergence of the disorder over time. IPT appears to be useful in treating clients with bulimia whose symptoms are maintained by interpersonal issues, including social **anxiety**; sensitivity to conflict and rejection; and difficulty managing negative emotions. IPT is helpful in bringing the problems underlying the bingeing and purging to the surface, such as conflict avoidance; difficulties with role expectations; confusion regarding needs for closeness and distance; and deficiencies in solving social problems. IPT also helps people with bulimia to regulate the emotional states that maintain the bulimic behavior.

Anorexia nervosa also appears to be responsive to treatment with IPT. Research indicates that there is a connection between interpersonal and family dysfunction and the development of anorexia nervosa. Therapists disagree as to whether interpersonal dysfunction causes or is caused by anorexia. IPT has been helpful because it is not concerned with the origin but rather seeks to improve the client's interpersonal functioning and thereby decreasing symptoms. IPT's four categories of grief, interpersonal disputes, interpersonal deficits, and role transitions correspond to the core issues of clients with anorexia. **Social phobia** is another disorder that responds well to IPT therapy.

Aftercare

Interpersonal therapy as a maintenance approach (IPT-M) could be viewed as aftercare for clients suffering from depression. It is designed as a preventive measure by focusing on the period after the acute depression has passed. Typically, once the client is in remission and is symptom-free, he or she takes on more responsibilities and has increased social contact. These changes can lead to increased **stress** and greater vulnerability to another episode of depression. IPT-M enables clients to reduce the stresses associated with remission and thereby lower the risk of recurrence. The goal of maintenance therapy is to keep the client at his or her current level of functioning. Research has shown that for clients with a history of recurrent depression, total prevention is unlikely, but that maintenance therapy may delay a recurrence.

In general, long-term maintenance psychotherapy by itself is not recommended unless there are such reasons as pregnancy or severe side effects that prevent the client from being treated with medication. IPT-M does, however, seem to be particularly helpful with certain groups of patients, either alone or in combination with medication. Women appear to benefit, due to the importance of social environment and social relations in female gender roles; the effects of the menstrual cycle on symptoms; and complications related to victimization by rape, incest, or battering. IPT is also useful for elderly clients who can't take **antidepressants** due to intolerable side effects or such medical conditions as autoimmune disorders, cardiovascular disorders, diabetes, or other general medical conditions.

Normal results

The expected outcomes of interpersonal therapy are a reduction or the elimination of symptoms and improved interpersonal functioning. There will also be a greater understanding of the presenting symptoms and ways to prevent their recurrence. For example, in the case of depression, a person will have been educated about the nature of depression; what it looks like for him or her; and the interpersonal triggers of a

KEY TERMS

Bereavement—The emotional experience of loss after the death of a friend or relative.

Bingeing—An excessive amount of food consumed in a short period of time. Usually, while a person binge eats, he or she feels disconnected from reality, and feels unable to stop. The bingeing may temporarily relieve depression or anxiety, but after the binge, the person usually feels guilty and depressed.

Dysthymia—Depression of low intensity.

Dysthymic disorder—A mood disorder that is less severe than depression but usually more chronic.

Etiology—The cause or origin of a disease or disorder. The word is also used to refer to the study of the causes of disease.

Psychosocial—A term that refers to the emotional and social aspects of psychological disorders.

Purging—Inappropriate actions taken to prevent weight gain, often after bingeing, including self-

induced vomiting or the misuse of laxatives, diuretics, enemas, or other medications.

Remission—In the course of an illness or disorder, a period of time when symptoms are absent.

Role—The set of customary or expected behavior patterns associated with a particular position or function in society. For example, a person's role as mother is associated with one set of expected behaviors, and her role as a worker with a very different set.

Role transition—Life changes that require an alteration in one's social or occupational status or self-image.

Stigma—A mark or characteristic trait of a disease or defect; by extension, a cause for reproach or a stain on one's reputation. Such sexually transmitted diseases as HIV infection carry a severe social stigma.

Supportive—An approach to psychotherapy that seeks to encourage the patient or offer emotional support to him or her, as distinct from insight-oriented or exploratory approaches to treatment.

depressive episode. A person will also leave therapy with strategies for minimizing triggers and for resolving future depressive episodes more effectively. While interpersonal therapy focuses on the present, it can also improve the client'sfuture through increased awareness of preventive measures and strengthened coping skills.

Abnormal results

Research has shown that IPT requires clients' commitment to therapy prior to starting the treatment. If clients are resistant to an educational approach, the results of IPT are generally poor. It has been found that when people do not accept IPT's methods and approach at the outset; they are unlikely to be convinced over the course of therapy and they receive little benefit from treatment. IPT clients appear to do better in therapy if they have confidence in their therapist; therefore, if the initial fit between therapist and client is not good, therapy will often be unsuccessful. A client should listen to his or her instincts early in treatment, and either seek out another interpersonal therapist or find a therapist who uses a different approach—such as **cognitive-behavioral therapy**, which was also developed specifically for the treatment of depression.

See also Bulimia nervosa; Gender issues in mental health; Grief; Major depressive disorder.

Resources

BOOKS

American Psychiatric Association. *Diagnostic and Statistical Manual of Mental Disorders*. 4th edition, text revised. Washington, DC: American Psychiatric Association, 2000.

Klerman, Gerald L., and others. *Interpersonal Psychotherapy of Depression*. New York: Basic Books, Inc., 1984.

Mufson, Laura, Ph.D. *Interpersonal Psychotherapy for Depressed Adolescents*. New York: Guilford Press, 1993.

Klerman, Gerald L., M.D., and Myrna M. Weissman, Ph.D., eds. *New Applications of Interpersonal Psychotherapy*. Washington, D.C.: American Psychiatric Press, Inc., 1993.

PERIODICALS

Apple, Robin F. "Interpersonal Therapy for Bulimia Nervosa." *JCLP/In Session: Psychotherapy in Practice* 55, no. 6 (1999): 715-725.

Barkham, Michael, and Gillian E. Hardy. "Counselling and interpersonal therapies for depression: towards securing an evidence-base." *British Medical Bulletin* 57 (2001): 115-132.

Frank, Ellen, Ph.D., and Michael E. Thase, M.D. "Natural History and Preventative Treatment of Recurrent Mood Disorders." *Annual Reviews Medicine* 50 (1999): 453-468.

House, Allan, D. M. "Brief psychodynamic interpersonal therapy after deliberate self-poisoning reduced suicidal ideation and deliberate self-harm." *ACP Journal Club* 136 (January/February 2002): 27.

McIntosh, Virginia V. "Interpersonal Psychotherapy for Anorexia Nervosa." *International Journal of Eating Disorders* 27 (March 2000): 125-139.

Mufson, Laura, Ph.D., and others. "Efficacy of Interpersonal Psychotherapy for Depressed Adolescents." *Archives of General Psychiatry* 56, no. 6 (June 1999): 573-579.

Weissman, Myrna M., Ph.D., and John C. Markowitz, M.D. "Interpersonal Psychotherapy: Current Status." *Archives of General Psychiatry* 51, no. 8 (August 1994): 599-606.

ORGANIZATIONS

International Society for Interpersonal Psychotherapy. c/o Myrna M. Weissman, Columbia University, 1051 Riverside Drive, Unit 24, New York, NY 10032. <http://interpersonalpsychotherapy.org>.

Holly Scherstuhl, M.Ed.

Intervention

Definition

A standard dictionary defines intervention as an influencing force or act that occurs in order to modify a given state of affairs. In the context of behavioral health, an intervention may be any outside process that has the effect of modifying an individual's behavior, cognition, or emotional state. For example, a person experiencing **stress** symptoms may find a variety of interventions effective in bringing relief. Deep breathing, vigorous exercise, talking with a therapist or counselor, taking an anti-anxiety medication, or a combination of these activities are all interventions designed to modify the symptoms and potentially the causes of stress-related discomfort.

The term is also used to describe a specific process designed to break through **denial** on the part of persons with serious addictive disorders. Interventions in this sense of the word involve carefully orchestrated confrontations in which friends, family members, and (in many cases) employers confront the person with the negative impact and consequences of his or her **addiction**. The goal of an intervention is to bring the addicted person to acknowledge that he or she suffers from a disorder and agree to treatment. This goal, however, is not always realized.

Description

According to the *Report of the Surgeon General on Mental Health* published in 1999, one in five Americans in a given year will experience behavioral health difficulties of sufficient magnitude and discomfort as to benefit from some form of therapeutic intervention. Unfortunately, only a small number of these persons seek help. The report goes on to state that the efficacy of mental health treatments is now well documented and a range of treatment interventions exists for even the most serious mental disorders.

There is no one-size-fits-all-intervention for behavioral health disorders. Recent research advances and greater understanding of behavioral health problems have provided an expanded range of treatments that promise better outcomes than those available in the past. For people who overcome the barriers of **stigma**, discrimination, and limited access, there is a broad variety of helpful interventions from which to choose. Both personal preference and the severity of discomfort may influence the choice of "talk therapy," the use of medications, participation in self-help or **support groups**, or even inpatient treatment. In most cases, a combination of different interventions has proven to be most effective. As a result, many therapists tend to be eclectic in their practice and use a combination of approaches to in order to be as effective as possible with a wide variety of people.

Psychotherapy or "talk therapy" involves face-to-face meetings with a therapist who may specialize in a certain approach to treatment.

- Psychoanalysis is the oldest form of "talk therapy." It is a long-term form of treatment intended to uncover a person'sunconscious motivations and early patterns in order to resolve present issues.

- Behavioral therapy is designed to change thinking patterns and behavior. Exposure therapy is a subtype of behavioral therapy that is useful in treating obsessive-compulsive disorder and post-traumatic stress disorder. The client is deliberately exposed to stimuli that trigger the painful thoughts or feelings under carefully controlled conditions that include support from the therapist. The individual is then taught techniques to avoid performing the compulsive behaviors or to work through the traumatic event.

- Cognitive therapy seeks to identify and correct dysfunctional thinking patterns that lead to troublesome feelings or behavior.

- Family therapy includes discussion and problem-solving sessions that include all members of the family.

- Group therapy takes place in a small group with the guidance of a therapist. The focus is on individual issues; group members assist each other in problem solving.
- Movement, art, and music therapists use these forms of creative expression to help people deal with strong emotions that are less easily handled in a "talk therapy" format.

Drug therapy involves the use of prescribed medications to treat the symptoms of certain mental or emotional disorders. It is important for patients to be aware of possible side effects of the medications; to inform the doctor of all other medications and alternative remedies that they are taking; and to have their blood, blood pressure, or other vital signs monitored regularly by the prescribing physician.

Electroconvulsive therapy (ECT) is used to treat **depression** and a few other specific conditions that have not responded to other interventions. It involves a controlled series of electric shocks to certain areas of the **brain**. It has been proven effective for some people despite the fact that it continues to be controversial. Patients should be fully aware of the side effects of ECT and assure themselves that the professional has been properly trained to administer ECT.

Psychosocial treatments may include **talk therapy** and medication in combination with social and vocational training to assist people recovering from severe mental illnesses. Psychosocial interventions may also include education about the illness itself, techniques for managing its symptoms, and ways in which friends and family members can help.

Psychoeducation is a word used to describe the process of teaching people about their illness, its treatment, and early warning signs of **relapse**, so that they can seek treatment before the illness worsens. Psychoeducation may also include learning about coping strategies, problem solving, and preparation of a crisis plan in the event of a relapse or future episode.

Self-help and support groups are another form of intervention that has become increasingly common in recent years. They exist for almost all disorders and are often based on the basic principles and values of the Alcoholics Anonymous movement founded in the 1930s. Although they are not led by professionals, these groups may be therapeutic because members give one another ongoing support and assistance. Group members share frustrations and successes, recommendations about specialists and community resources, and helpful tips about recovery. They also share friendship and hope for themselves, their loved ones, and others in the group. Unqualified acceptance by other people can be a powerful intervention for people recovering from a mental illness or addictive disorder.

Preparation

A common question about interventions concerns sources of help or further information. Many communities have a local hotline number that provides referrals and resources, or a mental health association that can direct callers to appropriate clinics, agencies, or groups. Helping resources may include the following:

- A community mental health center, usually a part of the state's department of mental health.
- Local mental health organizations with which the reader may be familiar.
- Family physicians.
- Clergy or spiritual counselors.
- Family service agencies, including charities and family or social services sponsored by various churches, synagogues, or other religious groups.
- High school or college guidance counselors.
- Marriage and family counselors.
- Child guidance counselors.
- Accredited psychiatric hospitals.
- Hotlines, crisis centers, and emergency rooms.

There are several categories of mental health professionals who have been specially trained to provide a range of interventions to relieve suffering, treat specific symptoms, or improve overall mental health. Competent professionals are licensed or certified by a particular specialty board or state licensing body. Their credentials imply a certain level of education, training, experience, and subscription to a code of ethics. Mental health professionals include:

- Psychiatrists. Psychiatrists are medical doctors with specialized training in the diagnosis and treatment of behavioral and emotional illnesses. They are qualified to prescribe medications. They may also specialize in certain fields within psychiatry, such as child/ adolescent or geriatric psychiatry.
- Psychologists. These professionals are counselors with a doctoral degree (Ph.D. or Psy.D.) and two or more years of supervised work experience. They are trained to make diagnoses, administer and interpret psychological tests, and provide individual, family and group therapy.
- Clinical social workers. Clinical social workers have completed a master's degree in social work from an accredited graduate program. They are trained to make diagnoses and provide individual, family and group therapy.

- Licensed professional counselors and mental health counselors also hold a master's degree with supervised work experience and are trained to make diagnoses and provide individual, family and group therapy.

- Certified alcohol and drug abuse counselors. These professionals have specialized training in the treatment of alcohol and drug abuse. They are able to diagnose and provide counseling to individuals, families and groups.

- Nurse psychotherapists. Nurse psychotherapists are registered nurses (RNs) with specialized training in psychiatric and mental health nursing. They can diagnose disorders and provide counseling to individuals, families and groups.

- Marital and family therapists. These counselors have completed a master'sor doctor'sdegree with specialized training in marital and family therapy. They are also trained to diagnose and provide individual, family and group counseling.

- Pastoral counselors. These counselors are ordained clergy with advanced training and certification in Level II clinical pastoral education as well as the master'sdegree in theology (M. Div.) required by most American denominations for ordination. In addition to offering psychological counseling to individuals, families and groups, pastoral counselors have been trained to offer spiritual and sacramental ministry to those who request it.

Resources

ORGANIZATIONS

American Psychological Association. 750 First Street, NE, Washington, DC 20002. (800) 374-2721. <www.apa.org>.

National Alliance for the Mentally Ill (NAMI). Colonial Place Three, 2107 Wilson Blvd., Suite 300, Arlington, VA 22201. <http://www.nami.org>.

National Mental Health Association. 1021 Prince St., Alexandria, VA 22314. <http://www.nmha.org >.

National Mental Health Consumers' Self-Help Clearinghouse. 1211 Chestnut St, Suite 1207, Philadelphia, PA 19107. <www.mhselfhelp.org >.

Judy Leaver, M.A.

Involuntary hospitalization

Definition

Involuntary **hospitalization** is a legal procedure used to compel an individual to receive inpatient treatment for a mental health disorder against his or her will. The legal justifications vary somewhat from state to state, but are generally based on a determination that a person is imminently dangerous to self or others; is gravely disabled; or clearly needs immediate care and treatment. Involuntary hospitalization is synonymous with involuntary commitment or involuntary treatment, and is an extremely controversial course of action. It is generally a last resort used in dealing with a person who is so ill that he/she is unable to use proper judgment or insight in deciding to refuse treatment.

Purpose

Civil commitment laws in the United States have been justified on the historical foundation of two fundamental powers and responsibilities of government. First, governments are responsible for protecting each citizen from injury by another. This power of protection is commonly called police powers. The second power, known as *parens patriae* (Latin for "parent of the nation") is based on the government's responsibility to care for a disabled citizen as a loyal parent would care for a child. A person with a significant mental illness may be civilly committed, or involuntarily hospitalized, under either of these powers. It is understood that the purpose of civil commitment is protecting the safety of the public or of the ill person.

Thirty-four states currently permit some type of involuntary commitment procedure. Most require proof of dangerousness, which can be interpreted in ambiguous ways but generally means the danger is imminent or provable. The legal process usually requires a court hearing within 24–72 hours after the emergency commitment procedure to assure due process.

Beyond safety issues, mental health professionals have thought that proper psychiatric treatment, even when administered against a person's wishes, is preferable to the continued worsening of a serious mental illness. There is some question currently about the effectiveness of forced treatment in the legal and mental health communities. Indeed "involuntary treatment" is considered by many patients' rights advocates and mental health consumers to be an oxymoron (a figure of speech that uses seeming contradictions). It may, in fact, protect public safety at the expense of the liberty, dignity and health of the person with a mental illness.

Precautions

The use of involuntary hospitalization or any other form of forced treatment is perhaps the most controversial issue in the wider mental health community, pitting family members, citizen advocacy groups, professionals and consumers against one another on the subject. In addition, legal advocates and the courts take very seriously the **denial** of a person's liberty. Involuntary hospitalization is one of the most extreme examples of denial of liberty in a democratic society.

Most people involved in the debate would agree that forced treatment is indicative of a failed treatment system. There is some evidence that forced treatment is generally harmful and counterproductive. Yet, many people with an intensely personal stake in such a decision may see the necessity of forced treatment to prevent harm to the person with an illness or to others. Outspoken advocates may believe that in the case of involuntary **intervention**, only custodial care should be provided. There is great concern, often based on experience, that a person who has been civilly committed to a treatment facility, will also receive such forced treatment as strong antipsychotic medications or **electroconvulsive therapy** (ECT). The issue of a person's ability to exercise **informed consent** about his/her treatment is clouded when the legal process of civil commitment has been initiated. In addition, there is concern that inpatient treatment will add to the **stigma** of being diagnosed with a mental illness. One research study found that persons who had been hospitalized (voluntarily or involuntarily) for treatment of a mental illness were even more likely to suffer discrimination in the job market than those who had received only outpatient treatment.

On the other hand, there are many mental health consumers who claim that an incident of involuntary hospitalization in their own treatment history may not only have saved their lives, but enabled them to receive treatment at a time when they were not capable of making a decision to do so. Family members sometimes consider involuntary hospitalization their only recourse to prevent the downward spiral of a loved one into a severe and debilitating mental illness, contact with the criminal justice system, or the devastation and dangers of **homelessness**.

Description

As of 2002, involuntary hospitalization is a complex process because of the legal requirements that have been put in place to protect citizens from being hospitalized because of a family quarrel or similar interpersonal issue. In the nineteenth century, for example, it was commonplace for husbands who wanted to end a marriage to have wives hospitalized against their will, or for parents to commit "disobedient" children. At present, however, most states require the person who thinks someone else should be hospitalized to call 911 or their local police department. A general summary of the events that may follow the call to 911 follows, but it should be noted that procedures vary from state to state and that the following is a general synopsis. In many cases, the department will send a patrol team rather than only one officer. If the person who has made the call is in the same house (or other location) as the person needing treatment, one officer will usually talk to the caller in one room while the other talks to the affected person in a different room (if circumstances permit). The officers may also interview other family members, neighbors, bystanders, or others who may know the affected person or have witnessed their behavior. Then the two police officers will compare their evaluations of the situation. In most jurisdictions the police officers can make one of three decisions: they can decide that the person who made the call has misjudged the situation (for example, the other person may simply be intoxicated); they can decide that the affected person is mentally ill but not necessarily dangerous; or they can take the affected person to the nearest hospital emergency room. They may ask the person who called them to accompany them to the hospital. In some states, however, the officers themselves must witness the affected person attempting to harm him- or herself or someone else before they can take him or her to the emergency room.

In the emergency room, the **psychiatrist** on duty will evaluate the affected person for dangerousness as well as the presence of mental illness. He or she will interview the police officers and anyone who accompanied them as well as the affected person. If the affected person has been receiving treatment for a mental disorder, the psychiatrist will usually contact the therapist. In some cases the affected person will need a medical evaluation, including assessment for **substance abuse** or withdrawal, before the doctor can proceed with a psychiatric assessment. The psychiatric assessment will be thorough, and documented as completely as possible; laboratory tests will be ordered if necessary. When the assessment is complete, the doctor is legally required to decide in favor of the least restrictive environment to which the patient can be safely discharged for continued care.

If the doctor decides that the person is dangerous but not mentally ill, he or she will turn the person over to law enforcement. If the person has threatened to kill themselves, but the psychiatrist does not consider the threat to be lethal, he or she may allow the patient to leave the emergency room after assessment. A decision to hospitalize the person involuntarily is based on three considerations: loss of emotional control; clear evidence of a psychotic disorder; evidence of impulsivity with serious thoughts, threats, or plans to kill self or others. In most cases the affected person will be reassessed the next day. Most states stipulate that the affected person is entitled to a hearing before a judge who specializes in mental health law within 72 hours of hospitalization. The judge can order the person released if he or she thinks the person is not dangerous.

Readers who are concerned about the mental health of a family member, roommate, or friend are advised to gather information about the legal requirements for involuntary hospitalization in their state ahead of time, because it is not easy to think clearly when someone is acting in a bizarre or frightening manner. It is also a good idea to write down the name and telephone number of the affected person's therapist (if they have one), and the names of any medications that the person is taking.

Risks

A number of factors in the early 1980s led to a trend toward declining use of involuntary hospitalization for people with significant mental illnesses. The development and effectiveness of a range of new medications meant that treatment in general was more successful. The continued move toward **deinstitutionalization**, or moving people out of hospitals and into their communities, contributed as well. Treating people in hospitals is inherently expensive and was being viewed as less effective, compared to more innovative and less costly forms of treatment in smaller community-based programs. Finally, a continuing concern about civil liberties led to closer court scrutiny, the right to a hearing and legal counsel, and laws establishing a person's rights to the least restrictive form of treatment.

Recently, however, after a number of tragic and highly publicized violent incidents involving people with severe untreated mental illness, there appears to be a trend toward modification of the criteria required for involuntary hospitalization, court-ordered treatment, and outpatient commitment. Those who advocate liberalizing the process would like a person's previous mental health history to be included in the court's consideration and the standard of dangerousness to be broadened.

Most persons involved in the mental health community believe that an adequately funded, community-based continuum of care and treatment would drastically reduce the number of cases in which involuntary treatment of any kind is necessary. The use of psychi-

KEY TERMS

Deinstitutionalization—The process of moving people out of mental hospitals into treatment programs or halfway houses in local communities. With this movement, the responsibility for care shifted from large (often governmental) agencies to families and community organizations.

Due process—A term referring to the regular administration of a system of laws that conform to fundamental legal principles and are applied without favor or prejudice to all citizens. In the context of involuntary commitment, due process means that people diagnosed with a mental illness cannot be deprived of equal protection under the laws of the United States on the basis of their diagnosis.

Oxymoron—A figure of speech that involves a seeming contradiction, as in the phrase "making haste slowly."

atric **advance directives** may have an effect on the use of involuntary treatment as well. A psychiatric advance directive is a clearly written statement of an individual's psychiatric treatment preferences or instructions, somewhat like a living will for medical conditions. Psychiatric advance directives have not yet been tested in the court system but are widely endorsed throughout the mental health community as an alternative to involuntary treatment.

See also Advance directives; Schizophrenia; Suicide.

Resources

BOOKS

Butler, Robert N., Myrna I. Lewis and Trey Sunderland. *Aging and Mental Health.* 5th ed. Needham Heights, MA: Allyn and Bacon, 1998.

"Psychiatric Emergencies Requiring Hospitalization or Other Institutional Support." Section 15, Chapter 194 in *The Merck Manual of Diagnosis and Therapy*, edited by Mark H. Beers, MD, and Robert Berkow, MD. Whitehouse Station, NJ: Merck Research Laboratories, 2001.

Wahl, Otto F. *Telling Is Risky Business: Mental Health Consumers Confront Stigma.* New Brunswick, NJ: Rutgers University Press, 1999.

PERIODICALS

Stavis, Paul F. "Involuntary Hospitalization in the Modern Era: Is Dangerousness Ambiguous or Obsolete?" *Quality of Care Newsletter* Issue 41, August-September 1989.

ORGANIZATIONS

Judge David L. Bazelon Center for Mental Health Law. 1101 15th St. NW, Suite 1212, Washington, DC 20005. <http://www.bazelon.org >.

National Alliance for the Mentally Ill (NAMI). Colonial Place Three, 2107 Wilson Blvd, Suite 300, Arlington, VA 22201. <http://www.nami.org >.

National Mental Health Association. 1021 Prince St. Alexandria, VA 22314. <http://www.nmha.org >.

National Mental Health Consumers' Self-Help Clearinghouse. 1211 Chestnut Street, Suite 1207, Philadelphia, PA 19107. <http://www.mhselfhelp.org >.

Judy Leaver, M.A.

Isocarboxazid

Purpose

Isocarboxazid (brand name Marplan) is an older-generation antidepressant drug. It is used to treat symptoms associated with **major depressive disorder**. Major depressive disorder refers to a long-lasting bout of depressed mood that is severe enough to interfere with basic life activities like work, relationships, sleeping, and eating. Feelings of self-worth, interest, motivation, and pleasure are typically absent while worthlessness, emptiness, being overwhelmed, and sadness are often reported.

Isocarboxazid is used for long-term maintenance of major **depression** and may be most useful for patients whose depression has atypical features. Unless effectiveness has already been established for a particular patient, isocarboxazid would not be the first drug of choice. Its use is limited to those patients who do not respond to first-line **antidepressants** and who are amenable to close supervision. Isocarboxazid's status as a drug of last resort (as is the case with other drugs in its class) is due to its potentially dangerous side effects and the dietary restrictions taking it requires.

The safety of isocarboxazid in children has not been established.

Description

Isocarboxazid belongs to the class of antidepressants known as monoamine oxidase inhibitors (MAOIs). The MAOIs inhibit the function of an enzyme in the body called monoamine oxidase; that enzyme breaks down monoamine neurotransmitters—namely serotonin, **dopamine**, and norepinephrine. Under normal conditions, monoamine oxidase halts the action of these **neurotransmitters**. With MAOIs, the neurotransmitters last longer and accumulate, and their action is enhanced. It is this enhancement of neurotransmitter action that is thought to contribute to isocarboxazid's therapeutic efficacy.

There are two types of monoamine oxidases; they are denoted MAO-A and MAO-B. Isocarboxazid acts on both types, as do other nonselective monoamine oxidase inhibitors such as **phenelzine** and tranylcypormine.

Monoamine oxidase inhibitors do not elevate mood in non-depressed people. In depressed patients, they are used when other, first-line antidepressants are ineffective.

Recommended dosage

Isocarboxazid is taken orally. As is the case with most antidepressant drugs, patients are started at one dose and medication is gradually increased to a so-called maintenance dose to achieve the best outcome. For isocarboxazid, the starting dose is 10 mg, twice a day. Whereas dosage can vary widely in individual patients, a typical progression would be to increase the dose gradually to 15–30 mg twice a day as a maintenance dose. Because of the delayed therapeutic response, at least one to two weeks should pass before increasing the dose.

Precautions

Patients taking isocarboxzaid must be warned about food interactions. Foods like aged cheese, beer, and red wine contain tyramine and in concert with MAOIs can result in hypertensive crisis. Other foods high in tyramine (or dopamine itself) are bananas, fava beans, figs, raisins, yogurt, sour cream, soy sauce, pickled herring, caviar, liver, and tenderized meats; these foods should not be consumed when taking isocarboxazid.

Hypertensive crisis can also occur with certain drug interactions (detailed below). Monoamine oxidase inhibitors should not be taken with asthma drugs, cold and allergy medications, or diet drugs. Patients taking isocarboxazid should inform their doctors and dentists of that fact to avoid being administered a contraindicated medication.

Isocarboxazid use may negatively interact with certain health conditions. It should not be used in patients with cardiovascaular disease, cerebrovascular disease, or liver disease, and great caution should be used if there is poor kidney function or a history of **seizures**.

KEY TERMS

Antidepressant—A medication taken to alleviate clinical depression.

Major depressive disorder—A clinical psychiatric diagnosis of chronic depressed mood that interferes with normal life activities.

Dopamine—A chemical messenger in the brain that regulates reward and movement.

Hypertensive crisis—A precipitous rise in high blood pressure that can lead to brain hemorrhage or heart failure.

Monoamine oxidase inhibitors (MAOIs)—A class of antidepressant drugs that work by enhancing the neurotransmitters dopamine, norepinephrine, and serotonin in the brain.

Neurotransmitters—Chemical messengers that transmit signals between nerves.

Norepinephrine—A chemical messenger in the brain that regulates arousal and attention.

Serotonin—A chemical messenger in the brain that regulates arousal and mood.

Worsening of depression and risk of **suicide** are relevant to isocarboxazid, as they are to all antidepressant drugs. The risk is especially high during the lag time until therapeutic efficacy can be achieved. Close monitoring of patients for the first four weeks of treatment is advised.

Side effects

Isocarboxazid, like the other MAOIs, can cause a variety of side effects apart from the food interactions described above. Common side effects include dizziness and fainting associated with low blood pressure when standing up (orthostatic hypotension), sexual dysfunction, **anxiety**, headache, nausea, sleep disturbances, edema, constipation, and weight gain. Serious but less common side effects include hepatic damage.

Interactions

A patient should not take isocarboxazid at the same time as other antidepressants. Two to five weeks of wash-out time must pass before switching from a non-MAOI antidepressant drug to isocarboxazid.

The following drugs should not be taken with MAOIs: Stimulants like amphetamine, **methylphenidate**, and epinephrine; dopaminergic drugs like levodopan, L-tryptophan, and phenylalanine; over-the-counter cold and allergy medications like pseudoephedrine and dextromethorphan; diet drugs like ephedrine and phenylpropanolamine; and analgesics like meperidine.

Resources

BOOKS

Charney, Dennis S., MD, and Charles B. Nemeroff, MD, PhD. *The Peace of Mind Prescription: An Authoritative Guide to Finding the Most Effective Treatment for Anxiety and Depression*. New York: Houghton Mifflin, 2004.

Morrison, Andrew L., MD, *The Antidepressant Sourcebook: A User's Guide for Patients and Families*. New York: Doubleday, 1999.

Beers, Mark H., ed. "Depressive Disorders." *The Merck Manual of Diagnosis and Therapy, Professional Edition.* 18th ed. Whitehouse Station, NJ: Merck, 2005.

McEvoy, Gerald K., ed. "Monoamine Oxidase Inhibitors." *AHFS Drug Information* Pharm.D. Bethesda: American Society of Health-System Pharmacists, 2006.

First, Michael B., MD, and Laura J. Fochtmann, MD, eds. "Treating Major Depressive Disorder: A Quick Reference Guide." *The American Psychiatric Association's Quick Reference Guides*. 2nd ed. Arlington: American Psychiatric Press, 2000.

Jill U. Adams

J

Jin Shin Jyutsu *see* **Bodywork therapies**

Journal therapy *see* **Creative therapies**

Juvenile bipolar disorder

Definition

Juvenile **bipolar disorder** (also called manic-depressive illness) is a chronic condition characterized by repeated swings in mood between mania (a state of elation and high energy) and **depression**. Early-onset bipolar disorder is manic depression that appears very early in life. Historically it was thought that children could not suffer the mood swings of mania or depression, but recent research has revealed that bipolar disorder (or early temperamental features of it) can occur in very young children, and that it is much more common than previously thought.

Although children with bipolar disorder have not been well studied, the condition is believed to occur as frequently as it does in adults, and it can affect children more severely. Adults typically experience abnormally intense moods for weeks or months at a time, but children can have rapid shifts of mood that commonly cycle many times within the day. This cycling pattern is called ultra-ultra rapid or ultradian cycling, and it is most often associated with low arousal states in the mornings followed by afternoons and evenings of increased energy. Bipolar disorder is often hard to diagnose in children, because its symptoms are difficult to distinguish from those of other mental disorders. If left untreated, bipolar disorder can significantly affect a child's relationships, overall functioning, and school performance. It also can lead to violence, drug and alcohol use, and **suicide** attempts.

Description

Juvenile bipolar disorder is a mental condition characterized by repeated episodes of depression, mania, or both symptoms. The child may experience extreme shifts in mood and behavior. For a child to be diagnosed with bipolar disorder, the condition must be severe enough to disrupt his or her normal functioning.

The fourth edition (revised text) of the *Diagnostic and Statistical Manual of Mental Disorders (DSM-IV)* identifies three types of bipolar mood episodes (these episodes were defined for adults, not children):

- Manic episodes: an elevated or irritable mood that lasts for a period of at least one week
- Hypomanic episodes: a distinct period of persistently elevated, expansive, or irritable mood that lasts for at least four days
- Mixed episodes: increased energy and agitation, coupled with feelings of sadness and worthlessness

Three major subtypes of bipolar disorder exist—bipolar I disorder (BP-I), bipolar II disorder (BP-II), and bipolar disorder not otherwise specified (BP-NOS). The *DSM-IV-TR* defines these bipolar disorder subtypes as follows:

- BP-I: the occurrence of a manic or mixed episode that lasts for at least one week
- BP-II: alternating depressive and hypomanic episodes
- BP-NOS: cases that do not meet the full criteria for the other two bipolar disorder subtypes but that involve an elevated or irritable mood, plus two or three bipolar symptoms (difficulty concentrating, sleep changes, and so on) that are severe enough to interfere with functioning

Evidence exists that juvenile bipolar disorder is a different and more severe form than adult-onset bipolar disorder. The child may cycle more rapidly from emotional highs (elation) to lows (anger and irritability). Bipolar disorder often can coexist with other emotional and behavioral problems, such as attention deficit hyperactivity disorder (ADHD), **conduct disorder** (CD), **schizophrenia**, and **anxiety disorders**.

Demographics

The lifetime prevalence of bipolar disorder is between 1% and 3%. However, considering borderline cases, the rate may be as high as 6%. Some research suggests that as many as 1% of children may have bipolar disorder. Although the condition affects males and females equally, in children under 13 the cases are predominantly male.

Causes and symptoms

Bipolar disorder has a strong genetic component. Studies suggest that the children or siblings of bipolar individuals have a four-to-six-fold increased risk of developing the disorder. Environmental factors, such as child maltreatment, also may play a role in the development of the condition.

Symptoms of bipolar disorder can be broken down into two categories—manic symptoms and depressive symptoms. Children with bipolar disorder may swing through cycles of these two different types of emotions. Manic symptoms include:

• Extreme shifts in mood, from anger to euphoria
• Bursts of rage
• Irritability
• Increased energy
• Over-inflated sense of self-esteem, grandiose behavior
• Decreased need for sleep, without any apparent drowsiness during the day
• Lack of attention, moving quickly from one topic or task to the next
• Increased sexuality inappropriate to age
• Agitation
• Willingness to engage in risky behaviors

Depressive symptoms are at the opposite end of the mood spectrum. They include:

• Persistent sadness (this can include unexplained crying episodes, reclusiveness, and increased sensitivity)
• Decreased energy
• Low self-esteem
• Sleepiness and increased desire to sleep
• Difficulty concentrating
• Lack of interest in school and other activities
• Persistent thoughts of death or suicide
• Unexplained aches and pains
• Alcohol or drug use

Children and adolescents with bipolar disorder may have difficulty regulating between these two types of moods. They may have explosive outbursts of anger lasting anywhere from a few minutes to a few hours, followed by periods of extreme happiness. Whereas adults can take months to cycle between mania and depression, children can cycle within weeks or even days, so they are more often symptomatic.

It is sometimes difficult to distinguish manic symptoms with those of ADHD, because hyperactivity and irritability can be hallmarks of both conditions, and both often occur simultaneously. Research suggests that more than half of children and adolescents with bipolar disorder also have ADHD. To distinguish bipolar disorder from ADHD, doctors look for symptoms that are unique to bipolar disorder, such as elated mood, decreased sleep, and grandiose behavior.

Diagnosis

Children with symptoms of bipolar disorder should see a **psychologist** or **psychiatrist** for evaluation, especially if a first-degree family member has a history of the condition. Evaluation is also important in children who are taking stimulant medications for ADHD and who are experiencing manic symptoms as a result. Children with bipolar disorder should be carefully monitored for associated problems, such as **substance abuse**, developmental delays, and suicide.

Diagnosis of children with bipolar disorder is often challenging, because the condition can present with other mental disorders, such as depression, and because symptoms (such as boasting and elation) can be difficult to distinguish from other childhood disorders and normal childhood emotions. Doctors often use *DSM-IV* guidelines to diagnose children with bipolar disorder, but these were developed for adults, and the symptoms can differ.

Assessment should include personal and family histories of depression and mood disorders, and identification of mood changes. Diagnostic interviews and questionnaires, such as the Diagnostic Interview for Children and Adolescents-revised (DICA-R), the Diagnostic Interview Schedule for Children (DISC), and the Kiddie Schedule for Affective Disorders and Schizophrenia for School-Age Children (K-SADS) can be useful for diagnosis. Clinical rating scales, such as the Mania Rating Scale, can help doctors initially identify illness severity and later assess the effects of treatment on the child's symptoms.

When diagnosing mania episodes, 2005 treatment guidelines from the Academy of Child and Adolescent Psychiatry (AACAP) suggest that doctors use Frequency, Intensity, Number, and Duration (FIND) as a guide:

- Frequency: Symptoms occur most days of the week
- Intensity: Symptoms are severe enough to cause extreme disturbance in one area of a child's life, or moderate disturbance in two areas
- Number: Symptoms occur three to four times per day
- Duration: Symptoms last for four hours a day (not necessarily contiguous)

Treatments

Most treatment recommendations for children with bipolar disorder are made based on adult research data, because little research has been done on the safety and efficacy of mood stabilizing medications in children. Doctors typically use two types of drugs to treat children with bipolar disorder: mood stabilizers (lithium, divalproex, **carbamazepine**, valproate) and atypical antipsychotics (**olanzapine, quetiapine, risperidone**). These drugs have only been approved by the U.S. Food and Drug Administration for bipolar disorder in adults, with the exception of lithium, which has been approved for children age 12 and older.

The AACAP panel recommends that doctors treat their patients with medication for a minimum of four to six weeks and reassess if there is a lack of response. Doctors should carefully monitor their patients who are taking these medications, because of the risks of side effects. According to the AACAP practice parameters, doctors should consider effectiveness, phase of illness, tolerability, and patient history of medication response, among other factors, when prescribing these medications. Atypical antipsychotics can cause marked weight gain in some children, which can lead to heart problems and diabetes later in life. They have also been linked to a rare but serious condition called **tardive dyskinesia**, which is characterized by abnormal movements (such as of the tongue).

Drugs used to treat other mental health conditions, such as **antidepressants** for depression and stimulant medications used to treat ADHD, may lead to manic symptoms. If a child becomes manic while taking antidepressants or stimulants, he or she may require treatment for bipolar disorder.

Some children with bipolar disorder may benefit from a combination of medication and **psychotherapy**, including **cognitive-behavioral therapy**, which

teaches children how to recognize and cope with the emotions that are leading to their condition.

Prognosis

Children with bipolar disorder will typically require ongoing treatment with medication to prevent a **relapse**, and some will require a lifetime of treatment. Even with medication, bipolar disorder can be chronic, with symptoms persisting for many months or even years. In adolescents, bipolar disorder tends to be more chronic and treatment-resistant than it is in adults. The rate of relapse in young people can be greater than 50%.

KEY TERMS

Attention deficit hyperactivity disorder (ADHD)—A behavioral disorder occurring during childhood that is characterized by poor concentration and hyperactivity.

Atypical antipsychotics—A class of newer generation antipsychotic medications that are used to treat schizophrenia, bipolar disorder, and other mental disorders.

Conduct disorder—A pattern of disruptive behaviors that violate rules or the rights of others. These behaviors can include bullying, lying, destroying property, and stealing.

Hypomania—A milder form of mania that involves increased mood and a decreased need for sleep.

Mania—A condition involving excessive elation or irritability, difficulty focusing, restlessness, and a decreased need for sleep.

Mixed episodes—Periods in which mania and depression coexist.

Rapid cycling—A condition that occurs with bipolar disorder, in which the person cycles rapidly between manic and depressive symptoms.

Schizophrenia—A mental disorder in which a person experiences hallucinations, delusions, and displays unusual behavior.

Tardive dyskinesia—Abnormal involuntary movements that can occur with the long-term use of certain antipsychotic medications.

Ultra-ultra rapid or ultradian cycling—Most often associated with low arousal states in the mornings followed by afternoons and evenings of increased energy.

Prevention

Although the initial onset of bipolar disorder is not preventable, there are strategies to help avoid a relapse. The family of the bipolar child can learn ways to identify relapse symptoms and how to avoid factors that may trigger relapse (such as substance **abuse**, **stress**, medication noncompliance, or sleep deprivation). Families also may be taught **communication skills** to improve their interpersonal relationships.

Resources

BOOKS

American Psychiatric Association. *Diagnostic and Statistical Manual of Mental Disorders*. 4th ed., text rev. Washington, D.C.: American Psychiatric Association, 2000.

Faedda, Gianni L., and Nancy B. Austin. *Parenting a Bipolar Child: What to Do and Why*. Oakland: New Harbinger Publications, 2006.

Lombardo, Gregory T. *Understanding the Mind of Your Bipolar Child: The Complete Guide to the Development, Treatment, and Parenting of Children with Bipolar Disorder*. New York: St. Martin's Press, 2006.

Mash, Eric J., and Russell A. Barkley, eds. *Treatment of Childhood Disorders*. 3rd ed. New York: The Guilford Press, 2006.

Suppes, Trisha, MD, PhD, and Ellen B. Dennehy, PhD. *Bipolar Disorder: The Latest Assessment and Treatment Strategies*. Kansas City: Compact Clinicals, 2005.

ORGANIZATIONS

Child & Adolescent Bipolar Foundation, 1000 Skokie Boulevard, Suite 570, Wilmette, IL 60091. (847) 256-8525. <http://www.bpkids.org>.

Depression and Bipolar Support Alliance, 730 N. Franklin Street, Suite 501, Chicago, IL 60610-7224. (800) 826-3632. < http://www.dbsalliance.org>.

Mental Health America, 2000 N. Beauregard Street, 6th Floor, Alexandria, VA 22311. (800) 969-6642. <http://www.nmha.org>.

National Alliance on Mental Illness, Colonial Place Three, 2107 Wilson Boulevard, Suite 300, Arlington, VA 22201-3042. (800) 950-6264. <http://www.nami.org>.

National Institute of Mental Health, 6001 Executive Boulevard, Room 8184, MSC 9663, Bethesda, MD 20892-9663. (866)615-6464. <http://www.nimh.nih.gov>.

Stephanie N. Watson

Juvenile depression

Definition

Depression is not confined to adulthood—it also can arise in childhood and adolescence. Depression in children can be triggered by a traumatic life experience, such as the death of a loved one, parents' divorce, difficulty in school, or illness. A **diagnosis** of depression is made when the feelings of sadness are severe enough to disrupt the child's daily life. Significant depression also can interfere with a child's development and can potentially lead to alcohol or drug use, or **suicide**. Children who experience depression are more likely to be depressed as adults.

Description

Research has indicated that rates of depression have risen in children and adolescents during the last few decades, although the reason for this rise is unclear. Just as in adults, depression in children can range in severity.

Major depressive disorder is the most severe form of depression. The ***Diagnostic and Statistical Manual of Mental Disorders***, fourth edition, text revised (*DSM-IV TR*), defines a major depressive episode as five or more symptoms (which can include depressed mood or irritability most of the day, markedly diminished interest in activities, significant weight loss without dieting, **insomnia** or **hypersomnia** nearly every day, agitation, **fatigue**, feelings of worthlessness or guilt, diminished ability to think or concentrate, and recurrent thoughts of death or suicide) within a two-week period.

Dysthymic disorder is a milder but chronic form of depression that persists for at least one year in children (episodes last between two and three years). It is characterized by symptoms of depression or irritability, as well as appetite changes, difficulty sleeping, low self-esteem, fatigue, poor concentration, or feelings of hopelessness. Dysthymia can interfere with a child's relationships, schoolwork, and self-esteem.

Demographics

Approximately 1% to 2% of children and 5% of adolescents experience symptoms of depression, and 3% to 5% of young people have major depressive disorder. The incidence of depression is lower in young children and rises after puberty. In childhood, the rates of depression are about equal in boys and girls, but, in adolescence, girls are more than twice as likely to be depressed as boys, possibly due to hormonal changes that occur during puberty. Additionally, girls tend to have an internal locus of control, which is related to self-blame versus the external locus of control experienced by many adolescent males.

About two-thirds of children with depression have a concurrent mental disorder, and so are at higher risk for developing depression again after receiving treatment. Children with depression have a two- to fourfold increased risk of being depressed as adults. Nearly three-quarters of children and adolescents with **depressive disorders** do not receive appropriate treatment.

Causes and symptoms

Although in some cases depression stems from a life event, in other situations it arises without apparent cause.

Causes

Doctors are unsure about the underlying causes of depression, but the problem may arise from neurotransmitter abnormalities in the **brain** as well as hormone perturbations. Changes in the prefrontal cortex have been noted in childhood depression. Hormones seem to play a role in depression, too.

Depression has both genetic and social components. The condition runs in families, and there is evidence that a child is more likely to develop depression if his or her parent is depressed. Studies have indicated that identical twins, who share the same genes, are about three times more likely to both have major depressive disorder than are fraternal twins, who share fewer of the same genes. It also may be possible that growing up with a parent who is depressed may make a child more prone to duplicating the behavior. Negative parenting tactics (such as rejection and lack of nurturing) also can influence the development of depression.

Stressful experiences, such as the death of a loved one, moving to a new city, living in poverty, or suffering sexual or physical **abuse**, can trigger depression, especially in children who are already vulnerable due to inherited factors. Depression can be distinguished from normal sadness during these experiences because its duration is disproportionate to the event.

In some cases, a medical condition, such as cancer, infectious mononucleosis, anemia, thyroid disease, or vitamin deficiency, can trigger depression. Some medications, such as isotretinoin (Accutane), may also lead to depressive symptoms. Depression stemming from illness or medication is referred to as secondary depressive mood disorder.

Symptoms

A child who is experiencing depression may have uncontrollable feelings of sadness. He or she may lose interest in friends, school, and activities. Other symptoms of depression include:

- Feelings of worthlessness or hopelessness
- Crying for no apparent reason
- Change in appetite
- Weight loss or gain
- Disrupted or prolonged sleep
- Lack of energy
- Difficulty concentrating
- Irritable, aggressive, or hostile behaviors
- Aches and pains that have no known medical cause (this is particularly common in children under age seven, who are less able to articulate their emotions)
- Alcohol or drug use
- Suicidal thoughts or actions

Depression often occurs together with other mental disorders, including **anxiety disorders**, attention-deficit/hyperactivity disorder, **substance abuse** disorder, and **oppositional defiant disorder**.

Diagnosis

Diagnosing depression may begin with the child's primary care doctor, who can make a referral to a child **psychiatrist** or **psychologist** if necessary. The doctor will typically start a depression evaluation by interviewing the child and his or her parents. The assessment may include a physical history and examination to rule out any conditions that can cause depression, such as thyroid disorders.

To diagnose depression, doctors sometimes used questionnaires or scales. The Children's Depression Inventory (CDI) is commonly used to diagnose children ages 7 to 17 years old. The results of this inventory are represented as a t-score. A t-score of greater than 20 on the long form or greater than 7 on the short form indicates a diagnosis of clinical depression.

Because patients with depression are at greater risk for attempting suicide (major depression increases the suicide risk 12-fold), doctors should assess the child's suicide risk during the initial visit.

Treatments

Treatment methods for children with depression include therapy and medication. Therapy may be conducted individually, in groups, or with the child's family. **Cognitive-behavioral therapy** (CBT) is the most thoroughly studied treatment for childhood depression, and research indicates that it is effective for treating mild to moderate depression. CBT involves changing the negative or distorted thoughts that are leading to the depression, and improving the child's coping skills. The therapist can help the child deal with grief and more appropriately handle his or her emotions, as well as educate the parents about developing healthier communication strategies and familial relationships. **Interpersonal therapy** (IPT), which is based on the belief that depression is triggered by interpersonal disputes, has also been shown to positively influence depressive symptoms in children and adolescents.

In moderate to severe cases of depression, doctors may prescribe antidepressant medications called **selective serotonin reuptake inhibitors** (SSRIs), such as **fluoxetine** (Sarafem) and **paroxetine** (Paxil). Presently, fluoxetine is the only SSRI approved by the U.S. Food and Drug Administration for treating depression in children 8 to 17 years of age. SSRIs work by restoring the correct balance of serotonin in the brain. However, because **antidepressants** have been linked to an increased risk of suicidal thoughts and behaviors in children and adolescents (the packaging of SSRIs carries a black-box warning regarding this risk), doctors should carefully monitor their young patients for any signs of suicidal tendencies during treatment. Due to their high risk of side effects and lack of effectiveness in a younger population, tricyclic antidepressants such as **imipramine** (Tofranil) are not recommended for children and adolescents.

The recommended treatment duration for children experiencing their first episode of depression is at least six months. Medication should be tapered off over a period of one to two months to prevent symptoms of withdrawal. Subsequent depressive episodes require at least one year of treatment, and children who have had more than three episodes should be treated indefinitely. More severe cases of depression may require a combination of medication and **psychotherapy**. Patients with treatment-resistant depression may require additional medication, such as lithium, as well as extended CBT.

Children or adolescents who are exhibiting suicidal behaviors may be hospitalized until it has been determined that they are no longer a danger to themselves.

Prognosis

Research indicates that starting treatment early can improve the outcomes for children and adolescents with depression. Children usually recover faster from major depressive episodes than adults. In most cases, children will recover from an initial depressive episode within one to two years, even if they have not been treated in some cases. However, children who have had at least one depressive episode face an increased risk of recurrence during adolescence and adulthood.

KEY TERMS

Cognitive behavioral therapy (CBT)—A treatment that helps patients control the negative thoughts that are leading to their depressive symptoms.

Dysthymic disorder (dysthymia)—A mood disorder characterized by feelings of sadness, as well as excessive fatigue, low energy, disturbed sleep, poor concentration, feelings of hopelessness and/or low self-esteem. Symptoms persist for more than two years but are not severe enough to qualify for a diagnosis of major depressive disorder.

Hypersomnia—Excessive sleepiness and the inability to stay awake during the day.

Interpersonal therapy (IPT)—A form of treatment for depression that focuses on improving the patient's relationships with friends and family members.

Neurotransmitter—A chemical that carries messages between nerve cells in the brain.

Oppositional defiant disorder—A type of behavior disorder characterized by defiant or disobedient behavior toward authority figures.

Selective serotonin reuptake inhibitors (SSRIs)—A class of antidepressant medications that help improve mood by increasing the amount of the neurotransmitter serotonin in the brain.

Tricyclic antidepressants—A class of medications that is used to treat depression.

Prevention

Although little research exists on the prevention of depression in children, there is some evidence that CBT can prevent the onset of major depression in children with depressive symptoms and/or **anxiety** disorders. Family dynamics also can have an impact on the development of depression. A stable, loving, and communicative family can decrease a child's vulnerability to the condition. Parents can help prevent potential problems by identifying depression earlier, when the treatment success odds are greatest. Early identification of depression involves looking for the warning signs, which may be more subtle in children than they are in adults. For example, a depressed child may appear bored, overly tired, withdrawn, or irritable. Children with depression also may experience aches and pains that are not associated with any obvious medical condition.

Resources

BOOKS

American Psychiatric Association. *Diagnostic and Statistical Manual of Mental Disorders*. 4th ed., text rev. Washington, D.C.: American Psychiatric Association, 2000.

Gillberg, Christopher, Richard Harrington, and Hans-Christoph Steinhausen, eds. *A Clinician's Handbook of Child and Adolescent Psychiatry*. Cambridge: Cambridge University Press, 2006.

Jongsma, Arthur E., Jr., L. Mark Peterson, and William P. McInnis. *The Child Psychotherapy Treatment Planner*. 4th ed. Hoboken, NJ: John Wiley & Sons, 2006.

Wilmshurst, Linda. *Essentials of Child Psychopathology* . Hoboken, NJ: John Wiley & Sons, 2005.

Zalsman, Gil, and David Brent. *Depression, An Issue of Child and Adolescent Psychiatry Clinics*. Philadelphia: Saunders, 2006.

ORGANIZATIONS

The American Academy of Child and Adolescent Psychiatry, 3615 Wisconsin Avenue N.W., Washington, D.C. 20016-3007. (202) 966-7300. <http://www.aacap.org>.

Families for Depression Awareness, 395 Totten Pond Road, Suite 404, Waltham, MA 02451. (781) 890-0220. <http://www.familyaware.org>.

National Alliance on Mental Illness, Colonial Place Three, 2107 Wilson Boulevard, Suite 300, Arlington, VA 22201-3042. (800) 950-6264. <http://www.nami.org>.

U.S. Department of Health & Human Services Substance Abuse and Mental Health Services Administration (SAMHSA), 1 Choke Cherry Road, Rockville, MD 20857. (240) 276-1310. <http://www.samhsa.gov>.

Stephanie N. Watson

Juvenile manic-depressive illness *see* Juvenile bi-polar disorder

K

K-ABC *see* **Kaufman Assessment Battery for Children**

K-SNAP *see* **Kaufman Short Neurological Assessment Procedure**

KAIT *see* **Kaufman Adolescent and Adult Intelligence Test**

Kaufman Adolescent and Adult Intelligence Test

Definition

The Kaufman Adolescent and Adult Intelligence Test (KAIT) is an individually administered general intelligence test appropriate for adolescents and adults, aged 11 to over 85 years.

Purpose

The KAIT is intended to measure both fluid and crystallized intelligence. Fluid intelligence refers to abilities such as problem solving and reasoning, and generally thought not to be influenced by one's cultural experience or education. Crystallized intelligence refers to acquired knowledge and is thought to be influenced by one's cultural experience and education.

The KAIT was developed by Alan S. Kaufman and Nadeen L. Kaufman as a method of measuring intelligence assuming broader definitions of fluid and crystallized abilities than assumed by other measures. Also, they wanted a test based on theories that accounted for developmental changes in intelligence. Although the Kaufmans had earlier designed a test for younger children, the **Kaufman Assessment Battery for Children** (K-ABC), they did not consider the KAIT to be an extension of this test. They believed that the developmental and neuropsychological changes specific to adults and

adolescents warranted a different testing approach than did the changes relevant to younger children. Thus, a different approach was used when developing the KAIT, although the K-ABC was also based somewhat on the split between fluid and crystallized intelligence.

Theoretically, the KAIT is most influenced by Horn and Cattell's formulation of the distinction between fluid and crystallized intelligence, sometimes referred to as Gf-Gc theory. Gf refers to general fluid abilities and Gc refers to general crystallized abilities. The KAIT is also influenced by Piaget's theory of cognitive development, specifically the formal operations stage experienced in adolescence. During this stage, adolescents begin to perform more complex mental operations and are better able to transform and manipulate information. Another theoretical influence of the KAIT is Luria's theory of planning ability. This theory attempted to explain developmental changes occurring in early adolescence that influence decision making and problem solving.

Precautions

There are very specific rules governing administration of the test that must be adhered to for scoring to be accurate. Thus, administrators must be properly trained to administer the KAIT. Specifically, for all subtests there is a discontinue rule, instructing administrators when to stop administering test items.

The KAIT is not appropriate for children younger than 11. A test more appropriate for younger children, such as the K-ABC, should be given instead. The K-ABC is appropriate for children up to the age of 12 years and six months, so there is some overlap between the two tests, specifically for children between 11 and 12 years and six months old.

Description

The KAIT includes two components, a core battery and an expanded battery. The core battery consists of a fluid scale, a crystallized scale, and six subtests, and takes about 65 minutes to complete. The expanded battery includes the core battery elements, as well as four additional subtests, and takes about 90 minutes to complete.

The following core battery subtests are related to fluid intelligence: logical steps, a test of sequential reasoning; mystery codes, a test measuring induction; and Rebus learning, a test of long-term memory. The following core battery subtests are related to crystallized intelligence: definitions, a test of word knowledge and language development; double meanings, a measure of language comprehension; and auditory comprehension, a test of listening ability.

The expanded battery also includes memory for block designs, a measure of visual processing related to fluid intelligence; famous faces, a test of cultural knowledge related to crystallized intelligence; auditory delayed recall; and Rebus delayed recall. The two delayed recall subtests provide a general measure of delayed memory.

There is also an optional supplemental mental status exam included in the KAIT battery. This subtest is only given to examinees with suspected mental impairment.

One strength of the KAIT is that most of the subtests are presented in both visual and auditory formats. This gives test takers more variety and allows for measurement of intelligence in different contexts. Also, the test was designed in a way to keep test takers active and engaged.

In contrast to other adult-specific or adolescent-specific **intelligence tests**, the KAIT is appropriate for a wider age range. This allows for more accurate tracking of intelligence changes between adolescence and adulthood.

Results

The KAIT yields several different kinds of scores, including raw scores, scaled scores, and intelligent quotient (IQ) scores. Raw scores and scaled scores are calculated for each subtest (six for the core battery; 10 for the expanded battery). Raw scores are calculated first, and simply refer to the number of points achieved by the examinee on a particular subtest. Raw scores are converted to scaled scores to ease comparison between subtests and between examinees. The subtest scaled scores are standardized to have a mean of 10 and a standard deviation of three.

Three IQ scores are obtained: composite intelligence, fluid intelligence, and crystallized intelligence.

The IQ scores have a mean of 100 and a standard deviation of 15. The fluid intelligence IQ score is based on the sum of the three fluid intelligence subtests (logical steps, mystery codes, and Rebus learning). The crystallized intelligence IQ score is based on the sum of the three crystallized intelligence subtests (definitions, double meanings, and auditory comprehension). The composite intelligence IQ score is based on all six core subtests. The expanded battery subtests are not utilized when computing the three IQ scores.

Overall, the KAIT has high reliability and validity. Studies have indicated that in relation to other general intelligence tests, the crystallized, fluid, and composite IQ scores are accurately and consistently measured. Data looking at trends related to age show that average subtest and IQ scores are fairly consistent across the age range in which the KAIT is administered.

The KAIT yields IQ scores in a relatively wide range, from much lower than average intelligence to much higher than average intelligence. Because of this, the KAIT is often used as an assessment of individuals with exceptional abilities, such as gifted children.

There have been factor analysis studies comparing the KAIT to the widely used Wechsler scales of intelligence, (the **Wechsler Intelligence Scale for Children** and the **Wechsler Adult Intelligence Scale**). The KAIT crystallized IQ has been shown to measure abilities similar to those measured by the Wechsler scales' verbal intelligence factor. However, the KAIT Fluid IQ has been shown to measure abilities considerably different from those measured by the Wechsler performance factor, which is thought to be a measure of fluid intelligence.

See also Stanford-Binet intelligence scales.

Resources

BOOKS

Groth-Marnat, Gary. *Handbook of Psychological Assessment.* 3rd edition. New York: John Wiley & Sons, 1997.

Kline, Paul. *The Handbook of Psychological Testing.* New York: Routledge, 1999.

Lichtenberger, Elizabeth O., Debra Y. Broadbooks, and Alan S. Kaufman. *Essentials of Cognitive Assessment with KAIT and Other Kaufman Measures.* New York: John Wiley and Sons, 2000.

McGrew, Kevin S., and Dawn P. Flanagan. *The Intelligence Test Desk Reference.* Needham Heights, MA: Allyn and Bacon, 1998.

Sternberg, Robert J. *Encyclopedia of Human Intelligence.* New York: Macmillan, 1994.

Ali Fahmy, Ph.D.

Kaufman Assessment Battery for Children

Definition

The Kaufman Assessment Battery for Children (K-ABC) is a standardized test that assesses intelligence and achievement in children aged two years, six months to 12 years, 6 months. The edition published in 1983 by Kaufman and Kaufman was revised in 2002 to expand its age range (to cover children ages three to eighteen) and enhance its usefulness. In addition, new subtests were added and existing subtests updated.

Purpose

The K-ABC was developed to evaluate preschoolers, minority groups, and children with learning disabilities. It is used to provide educational planning and placement, neurological assessment, and research. The assessment is to be administered in a school or clinical setting and is intended for use with English speaking, bilingual, or nonverbal children. There is also a Spanish edition that is to be used with children whose primary language is Spanish.

Precautions

The K-ABC is especially useful in providing information about nonverbal intellectual abilities. How-

ever, it has been criticized for not focusing on measures of verbal intelligence in the Mental Processing Composite score, which measures intelligence. Additionally, the separation of intelligence and achievement scores has been questioned by researchers who claim the two terms are misleading. For example, many subtests in the achievement composite are in fact measures of intelligence rather than achievement (knowledge acquired through school and/or home environment). The K-ABC should be used with caution as the primary instrument for identifying the intellectual abilities of children.

Administration and interpretation of results (as with all psychometric testing) requires a competent examiner who is trained in psychology and individual intellectual assessment—preferably a **psychologist**.

Description

Administration of the K-ABC takes between 35 and 85 minutes. The older the child, the longer the test generally takes to administer. It is comprised of four global test scores that include:

- sequential processing scales
- simultaneous processing scales
- achievement scales
- mental processing composite

There is an additional nonverbal scale that allows applicable subtests to be administered through gestures to hearing impaired, speech/language impaired, or children who do not speak English.

The test consists of 16 subtests—10 mental processing subtests and six achievement subtests. Not all subtests are administered to each age group, and only three subtests are administered to all age groups. Children ages two years, 6 months are given seven subtests, and the number of subtests given increase with the child's age. For any one child, a maximum of 13 subtests are administered. Children from age seven years to 12 years, 6 months are given 13 subtests.

The sequential processing scale primarily measures short-term memory and consists of subtests that measure problem-solving skills where the emphasis is on following a sequence or order. The child solves tasks by arranging items in serial or sequential order including reproducing hand taps on a table, recalling numbers that were presented. It also contains a subtest that measures a child's ability to recall objects in correct order as presented by the examiner.

The simultaneous processing scale examines problem-solving skills that involve several processes at once. The seven subtests comprising this scale are facial recognition, identification of objects or scenes in a partially completed picture, reproduction of a presented design by using rubber triangles, selecting a picture that completes or is similar to another picture, memory for location of pictures presented on a page, and arrangement of pictures in meaningful order.

The achievement scales measures achievement and focuses on applied skills and facts that were learned through the school or home environment. The subtests are expressive vocabulary; ability to name fictional characters, famous persons, and well known places; mathematical skills; ability to solve riddle; reading and decoding skills; and reading and comprehension skills.

The sequential and simultaneous processing scales are combined to comprise the mental processing composite. This composite measures intelligence on the K-ABC and concentrates on the child's ability to solve unfamiliar problems simultaneously and sequentially. The simultaneous processing scales have a greater impact on the mental processing composite score than do the sequential processing scales. The mental processing composite score is considered the global estimate of a child's level of intellectual functioning.

Results

The K-ABC is a standardized test, which means that a large sample of children in the two years, six months to 12 years, six months age range was administered the exam as a means of developing test norms. Children in the sample were representative of the population of the United States based on age, gender, race or ethnic group, geographic region, community size, parental education, educational placement (normal versus special classes), etc. From this sample, norms were established.

Based on these norms, the global scales on the K-ABC each have a mean or average score of 100 and a standard deviation of 15. For this test, as with most measures of intelligence, a score of 100 is in the normal or average range. The standard deviation indicates how far above or below the norm a child's score is. For example, a score of 85 is one standard deviation below the norm score of 100.

Test scores provide an estimate of the level at which a child is functioning based on a combination of many different subtests or measures of skills. A trained psychologist is needed to evaluate and interpret the results, determine strengths and weaknesses, and make overall recommendations based on the findings and behavioral observations.

See also Intelligence tests; Luria-Nebraska Neuropsychological Battery.

Resources

BOOKS

Sattler, Jerome. *Assessment of Children*. 3rd Edition. San Diego, CA: Jerome Sattler, Publisher Inc. 1992.

PERIODICALS

Cahan, S. and A. Noyman. "The Kaufman Ability Battery for Children Mental Processing Scale: A Valid Measure of 'Pure' Intelligence?" *Educational and Psychological Measurement* 61, no. 5 (2001): 827-840.

ORGANIZATIONS

The American Psychological Association. 750 First St., NE, Washington, DC 20002-4242. (202) 336-5500. <www. apa.org>.

The National Association of School Psychologists. 4340 East West Highway, Suite 402, Bethesda, MD 20814. (301) 657-0270. <www.nasponline.com>.

Jenifer P. Marom, Ph.D.

Kaufman Short Neurological Assessment Procedure

Definition

The Kaufman Short Neurological Procedure, often abbreviated as K-SNAP, is a brief test of mental functioning appropriate for adolescents and adults between the ages of 11 and 85 years. It is administered on an individual basis, and measures mental functioning at varying levels of cognitive complexity as well as addressing possible neurological damage.

Purpose

The K-SNAP is intended as a short measure of mental functioning and is sometimes preferable to other longer mental status and intelligence exams. Compared to the **Kaufman Adolescent and Adult Intelligence Test** (KAIT), which is given to people in the same age range and takes over an hour to complete, the K-SNAP takes only 20–30 minutes. The K-SNAP provides a measure of general mental status, as well as addressing specific mental abilities. It also allows for assessment of damage to the nervous system.

The K-SNAP was developed by Alan S. Kaufman and Nadeen L. Kaufman. Other Kaufman tests include the KAIT and the **Kaufman Assessment Battery for Children** (K-ABC). The Kaufmans based their tests on Horn and Cattell's formulation of the distinction between fluid and crystallized intelligence, sometimes referred to as the Gf-Gc Theory. Gf refers to such general fluid abilities as problem solving and reasoning. Fluid intelligence is thought not to be influenced by a person's cultural experience and education. Gc refers to such general crystallized abilities as acquired knowledge. Crystallized intelligence, unlike fluid intelligence, is thought to be shaped by a person's cultural experience and education.

Because the K-SNAP provides a measure of possible neurological impairment, it is often preferable to other measures of mental status and intelligence. If the doctor suspects that a patient may have a disorder of the nervous system, the doctor can use the K-SNAP as a short initial assessment. Depending on the results of the K-SNAP, the doctor can give more specific tests.

Precautions

One should be careful when using the results of the K-SNAP to assess neurological impairment. It should be used as a supplement to other more extensive and more specific measures of neuropsychological functioning.

The K-SNAP is primarily a test of mental and neuropsychological functioning. Although it measures cognitive skills, it should not be used to measure someone's overall intelligence.

Description

The K-SNAP consists of four subtests administered in the following order of complexity: Mental Status; Gestalt Closure; Number Recall; and Four-Letter Words. Each subtest contains between 10 and 25 items.

The Mental Status subtest assesses the test taker's alertness, attentiveness, and orientation to the environment. In this subtest, the examiner asks the examinee to answer verbal questions. It is the easiest and shortest of the four subtests, containing only 10 items.

The Gestalt Closure subtest provides an assessment of visual closure and simultaneous processing. In this subtest, the examinee is shown partially completed inkblot pictures and is asked to name the objects in the pictures.

The Number Recall subtest assesses sequential processing and short-term auditory memory. In this subtest, the examiner recites series of numbers and the examinee repeats the numbers.

The Four-Letter Words subtest measures the test taker's ability to solve problems and make plans. In this subtest, the examinee is asked to guess a secret word by analyzing a series of four-letter words that provide clues to the answer. It is the most complex of the subtests.

The K-SNAP is a relatively easy test to administer. Except for the Mental Status subtest, the test items are presented on an easel, which is visually appealing to many test takers. Also, because the test is brief and includes a variety of tasks, the test takers often find the test engaging and interesting.

The K-SNAP is considered to be useful in evaluating elderly people, especially with regard to decline in fluid intelligence. The Mental Status subtest can also detect possible age-related impairment in mental functioning.

Compared to other neurological and cognitive assessments, there are smaller than usual differences in K-SNAP performance between African-American and Caucasian individuals, especially with regard to fluid intelligence. This cultural neutrality makes the K-SNAP a preferred method for testing African-Americans.

Results

The K-SNAP yields several scores, including raw scores, scaled scores, a composite score, and an impairment index. Raw scores and scaled scores are calculated for each of the four subtests. Raw scores are calculated first; they refer simply to the number of points that the examinee scored on a particular subtest. The raw scores are converted to scaled scores to simplify comparisons between the subtests and between examinees. The subtest scaled scores are standardized to have a mean of 10 and a standard deviation of three.

One composite score is obtained on the K-SNAP. The composite score has a mean of 100 and a standard deviation of 15 and is based on the scores of the four subtests.

The results of the Mental Status subtest are primarily of interest when working with middle-aged or elderly people, as well as people with neurological or cognitive impairments. Most people find the mental Status subtest very easy, and they get most, if not all, of the items correct.

KEY TERMS

Gestalt—A German word that means "form" or "structure." The Gestalt Closure subtest on the K-SNAP measures a person's ability to identify a whole object from a partially completed drawing of its form.

Mean—The mathematical average of all scores in a set of scores. The K-SNAP Composite Score has been standardized to have a mean of 100. The K-SNAP subtests have been standardized to have a mean of 10. The means are based on a comparison to others in the same age group. Standardizing in this way then allows the scores to be comparable across age groups.

Orientation—In psychiatry, the ability to locate oneself in one's environment with respect to time, place and people.

Reliability—The ability of a test to yield consistent, repeatable results.

Standard deviation—A measure of variability in a set of scores. The K-SNAP Composite Score has been standardized to have a standard deviation of 15. The subtests have been standardized to have a standard deviation of three. The standard deviations are based on a comparison to others in the same age group. Standardizing in this way then allows the scores to be comparable across age groups.

Standardization—The administration of a test to a sample group of people for the purpose of establishing scoring norms. Prior to the publication of the K-SNAP, it was standardized in 1988 using a sample of 2,000 adults and adolescents.

Validity—The ability of a test to measure accurately what it claims to measure.

Some of the interpretation of the K-SNAP involves comparisons of performance on tasks of varying complexity. For example, Gestalt Closure is considered a less complex task than Number Recall. Someone who performs better on the more difficult Number Recall subtest may exhibit some kind of **brain** dysfunction. On the other hand, that person may simply prefer sequential processing tasks.

An impairment index is also calculated and provides an objective measure of cognitive and neurological impairment. The impairment index is based on the following four factors: the K-SNAP composite score; the test taker's performance on the Mental Status subtest; the difference between the scaled scores on the Number Recall and Gestalt Closure subtests; and the difference between the actual composite score and the predicted composite score based on the test taker's level of education. These four factors determine whether a more comprehensive assessment of impairment is necessary. For example, if an examinee has a composite score below 70, a low score on the Mental Status subtest, a large difference in performance in the Number Recall and Gestalt Closure subtests, and a difference of at least 24 points between the predicted and actual composite scores, there may be indications of impairment. One example of such impairment is damage to one hemisphere of the brain.

Overall, the K-SNAP has above-average to good reliability. As a mental status examination, it has been shown to have good validity as well. There have been no studies, however, demonstrating the K-SNAP's validity as a measure of neuropsychological impairment. Because the K-SNAP is based on similar theories and on the same standardization sample as other Kaufman tests, such as the KAIT, interpretation across the range of Kaufman tests is easier than comparing results from the K-SNAP to results from tests designed by other persons.

Resources

BOOKS

Groth-Marnat, Gary. *Handbook of Psychological Assessment*. 3rd edition. New York: John Wiley and Sons, 1997.

Kline, Paul. *The Handbook of Psychological Testing*. New York: Routledge, 1999.

Lichtenberger, Elizabeth O., Debra Y. Broadbooks, and Alan S. Kaufman. *Essentials of Cognitive Assessment with KAIT and Other Kaufman Measures*. New York: John Wiley and Sons, 2000.

McGrew, Kevin S., and Dawn P. Flanagan. *The Intelligence Test Desk Reference*. Needham Heights, MA: Allyn and Bacon, 1998.

Sternberg, Robert J. *Encyclopedia of Human Intelligence*. New York: Macmillan, 1994.

Ali Fahmy, Ph.D.

Kava kava

Definition

Kava kava is a dioecious (having male and female reproductive parts of the plant on different individuals) shrub native to the Pacific islands. Its botanical name is *Piper methysticum*; it is a member of the Piperaceae, or pepper, family. It is also known as asava pepper or intoxicating pepper. The narcotic drink made from the roots of this shrub is also called

Kava Kava leaf. *(bildagentur-online.com/th-foto/Alamy)*

kava kava. Kava kava has been widely recommended in recent years as a mild tranquilizer due to its pain-killing properties. As of 2002, however, kava kava has been the subject of official safety warnings from the U.S. Food and Drug Administration (FDA) and its counterparts in Canada, France, Germany, Switzerland, and Spain.

Captain James Cook is credited with introducing kava kava to Europeans when he visited the South Pacific in 1773. Previously, the inhabitants of the Pacific islands used kava kava as a ceremonial beverage. It was consumed at weddings, funerals, and birth rituals, and it was offered to honored guests. Kava kava was also drunk as part of healing rituals. The first commercial products containing kava kava were offered to European consumers around 1860.

As of 2001, kava kava ranked ninth in sales of all herbal dietary preparations sold in the United States through mainstream retailers, with total sales of $15 million. Health food stores, health professionals, and mail order firms accounted for another $15 million in sales of kava kava.

Purpose

The German Commission E, a panel of physicians and pharmacists that reviews the safety and efficacy of herbal preparations, at one time approved the use of kava kava as a nonprescription dietary supplement for the relief of nervous **anxiety**, **stress**, and restlessness. That approval was withdrawn in the fall of 2001.

In addition to relief of stress and anxiety, kava kava has also been recommended by health care providers for **insomnia**, sore or stiff muscles, toothache or

sore gums, attention-deficit/hyperactivity disorder, menstrual cramps, uncontrolled epilepsy, and jet lag.

Description

The beverage form of kava kava was traditionally prepared in the Pacific islands by chewing the roots of the kava plant and spitting them into a bowl. The active compounds, known as kavalactones and kava-pyrones, are found primarily in the root of the plant and are activated by human saliva. Contemporary Pacific islanders prepare kava kava by pounding or grinding the roots and mixing them with coconut milk or water. Modern Western manufacturers use alcohol or acetate in making liquid kava preparations. Kava kava is also available in capsules, tablets, powdered, or crushed forms. Experts in herbal medicine recommended the use of kava preparations standardized to contain 70% kavalactones.

Kavalactones are chemicals that affect the **brain** in the same way as **benzodiazepines** such as valium, which is prescribed for **depression** or anxiety. Kavalactones cause the tongue or gums to feel numb. Kava-pyrones are chemicals that have anticonvulsant and muscle relaxant properties.

Recommended dosage

Kava kava should never be given to children, particularly in view of recent health warnings concerning adults.

The usual dose of kava kava that has been recommended to relieve stress or insomnia in adults is 2–4 g of the plant boiled in water, up to three times daily. Alternately, 60–600 mg of kavalactones in a standardized formula could be taken per day.

Precautions

Before 2002, the usual precautions regarding kava kava stated that it should not be used at all by pregnant or lactating women, or by any individual when driving or operating heavy machinery. The American Herbal Products Association (AHPA) advised consumers in 1997 not to take kava kava for more than three months at a time, and not to exceed the recommended dosages. In light of more recent findings, however, it may be prudent to completely avoid preparations of or products containing kava kava.

Side effects

Prior to 2002, most reports of side effects from kava kava concerned relatively minor problems, such as numbness in the mouth, headaches, mild dizziness, or skin rashes. In the nineteenth-century, missionaries to the Pacific islands noted that people who drank large quantities of kava kava developed yellowish scaly skin. A recent study found the same side effect in test subjects who took 100 times the recommended dose of the plant.

As of 2002, kava kava has also been associated with causing damage to the liver, including hepatitis, cirrhosis, and liver failure. Most of the research on kava kava has been done in Europe, where the herb is even more popular than it is in the United States. By the late fall of 2001, there had been at least 25 reports from different European countries of liver damage caused by kava kava; French health agencies reported one death and four patients requiring liver transplants in connection with kava kava consumption. On December 19, 2001, the Medwatch advisory of the FDA posted health warnings about the side effects of kava kava; on January 16, 2002, Health Canada advised Canadians to avoid all products containing the herb. France banned the sale of preparations containing kava kava in February 2002. The U. S. National Center for Complementary and Alternative Medicine (NCCAM) has put two research studies of kava kava on hold while awaiting further action by the FDA. NCCAM advised consumers in the United States on January 7, 2002, to avoid products containing kava.

In addition to causing liver damage, kava kava appears to produce psychological side effects in some patients. A team of Spanish physicians has reported that beverages containing kava kava may cause anxiety, depression, and insomnia. In addition, kava kava may cause tremors severe enough to be mistaken for symptoms of Parkinson's disease.

Interactions

Kava kava has been shown to interact adversely with alcoholic beverages and with several categories of prescription medications. It increases the effect of **barbiturates** and other psychoactive medications; in one case study, a patient who took kava kava together with **alprazolam** (a benzodiazepine used to treat anxiety) went into a coma. It may produce dizziness and other unpleasant side effects if taken together with phenothiazines (used to treat **schizophrenia**). Kava kava has also been reported to reduce the effectiveness of levodopa, a drug used in the treatment of Parkinson's disease. To avoid potential reactions with prescription medications, people should inform their physician if they are taking kava kava.

KEY TERMS

Dioecious—A category of plants that reproduce sexually but have male and female reproductive organs on different individuals. Kava kava is a dioecious plant.

Kavalactones—Medically active compounds in kava root that act as local anesthetics in the mouth and as minor tranquilizers

Kavapyrones—Compounds in kava root that act as muscle relaxants and anticonvulsants.

Resources

BOOKS

Cass, Hyla, and Terrence McNally. *Kava: Nature's Answer to Stress, Anxiety, and Insomnia.* Prima Communications, Inc., 1998.

Schulz, V., R. Hänsel, and V. Tyler. *Rational Phytotherapy: A Physician's Guide to Herbal Medicine.* New York, NY: Springer-Verlag; 1998.

PERIODICALS

Almeida, J. C., and E. W. Grimsley. "Coma from the Health Food Store: Interaction Between Kava and Alprazolam." *Annals of Internal Medicine* 125 (1996): 940-941.

Ballesteros, S., S. Adan, and others. "Severe Adverse Effect Associated with Kava-Kava." *Journal of Toxicology: Clinical Toxicology* 39 (April 2001): 312.

Beltman, W., A. J. H. P van Riel, and others. "An Overview of Contemporary Herbal Drugs Used in the Netherlands." *Journal of Toxicology: Clinical Toxicology* 38 (March 2000): 174.

"France is Latest to Pull Kava Kava Products." *Nutraceuticals International* (February 2002).

Humbertson, C. L., J. Akhtar, and E. P. Krenzelok. "Acute Hepatitis Induced by Kava Kava, an Herbal Product Derived from *Piper methysticum.*" *Journal of Toxicology: Clinical Toxicology* 39 (August 2001): 549.

Kubetin, Sally Koch. "FDA Investigating Kava Kava." *OBGYN News* 37 (February 1, 2002): 29.

ORGANIZATIONS

NIH Office of Dietary Supplements. Building 31, Room 1B25. 31 Center Drive, MSC 2086. Bethesda, MD 20892-2086. (301) 435-2920. Fax: (301) 480-1845. <www.odp.od.nih.gov/ods>

OTHER

American Botanical Council (ABC). P.O. Box 144345, Austin, TX 78714-4345. (512) 926-4900. Fax: (512) 926-2345. <www.herbalgram.org>.

FDA Center for Food Safety and Applied Nutrition. <www.fda.gov/medwatch/safety/2001/kava.htm>.

NIH National Center for Complementary and Alternative Medicine (NCCAM) Clearinghouse. P. O. Box 8218, Silver Spring, MD 20907-8218. TTY/TDY: (888) 644-6226. Fax: (301) 495-4957. <www.nccam.nih.gov>.

Rebecca J. Frey, Ph.D.

Kleine-Levin syndrome

Definition

Kleine-Levin syndrome (also known as KLS) is a rare disorder. The most prevalent characteristic of the syndrome is recurring periods of excessive drowsiness and sleep (up to 20 hours per day) that can last weeks.

Description

KLS was first described in 1862 and is considered extremely rare, with only 27 cases reported from 1962 to 2004 in the United States. In addition to excessive drowsiness, an episode of KLS can also involve hypersexuality and compulsive behaviors, including compulsive eating. It usually first manifests in adolescence and appears to lessen and resolve on its own with age. Although cognitive and behavioral disturbances, including transient confusion and memory deficits, can accompany the disorder, there appear to be no lasting, permanent effects. In addition to other manifestations, KLS can be accompanied by mood disorders and an extreme irritability that translates into violent behaviors in atypical cases.

The average number of episodes of KLS among cases is seven, each lasting a median 10 days about every 3.5 months. The median length of time a person experiences the syndrome is eight years, although this time is longer in women and in people who experience less frequent episodes in their first year following onset.

Causes and symptoms

Most studies suggest that KLS is related to the hypothalamus, the organ in the **brain** that governs appetite, sleep, and hormone cycles, among other things. Researchers have failed to identify specific causes of KLS, although there are some apparent associations between events preceding the first episode of the disorder and its manifestation. The majority of cases are isolated, meaning that they do not appear to have a heritable basis.

Because many people with KLS experienced a viral illness just prior to their first episode, some experts propose that the causative agent is a type of viral or post-autoimmune encephalitis that affects the hypothalamus. Reported infections included tonsillitis, nonspecific flu-like fever, upper respiratory tract infection, and gastroenteritis. One study revealed that three of four autopsied patients with KLS had signs of inflammatory encephalitis in the hypothalamus.

Despite the suggested involvement of the hypothalamus, no association has been found clinically between a KLS episode and changes in hypothalamic hormones, cerebrospinal fluid, or other neurological signs. Similarly, in spite of symptoms such as hypersexuality, there have been no identified related changes in sex steroid hormones. One clinical association with KLS that has been found in 70% of patients is a nonspecific slowing of background brain activity on electroencephalogram testing. All **magnetic resonance imaging** (MRI) and cat scan (CT) imaging of the brain in KLS cases has been normal.

Symptoms can last weeks or even months. In addition to **hypersomnia** (excessive sleepiness), symptoms can include excessive eating without regard to content or quantity, extreme irritability, disorientation and confusion, low energy or no energy, hypersensitivity to noise, disconnection from reality, and blurred vision. A person experiencing a KLS episode may also report **hallucinations**. The abnormally uninhibited sex drive associated with some KLS episodes occurs more frequently in males and manifests in ways that can be alarming: those affected may expose themselves and make unwanted sexual advances. The disorder is episodic, and affected people behave normally between episodes. Intervals between episodes can sometimes last years.

Although an episode can come on without much warning, there are sometimes prodromal (pre-occurrence) signs that a KLS event is impending, especially a feeling of sudden, overwhelming tiredness. The excessive drowsiness of a KLS episode precludes normal participation in activities. In spite of the hypersomnia, a person experiencing a KLS episode is still able to wake to eat or void.

There may be some **depression** or **amnesia** after an attack. Depression can accompany KLS and an episode of KLS can occur with a recurring episode of depression. About half of patients report a depressive mood in conjunction with a KLS event.

KLS can occur as the primary disease, with onset in the teen years, or it can occur secondary to another disease or health problem, such as multiple sclerosis or brain trauma. Although fewer cases of secondary KLS occur compared to primary KLS, patients with secondary

Kleine-Levin syndrome

KEY TERMS

Hypersexuality—A clinically significant level of desire to engage in sexual behaviors.

Hypersomnia—Excessive sleepiness.

Hypothalamus—The hypothalamus is part of the brain that links the nervous and endocrine systems and also governs emotion, sexual activity, body temperature, hunger, thirst, and sleep cycles.

KLS may experience much longer and more frequent episodes.

Demographics

There are no published population-based studies reporting KLS incidence. Age at onset is usually in the late teens, and the syndrome is four times more common in males. The average age at onset is about 16.9 years, with a range from 4 to 82 years. About 81% of cases start in the preteen and teen years. Although it occurs more often in males, symptoms may be worse or the disease longer lasting in females.

Diagnosis

According to one source, diagnosing KLS is an difficult process and can result in an average delay of four years before a patient receives the correct **diagnosis**.

Treatments

No definitive treatment for KLS exists, and response to current treatments can be limited. A clinician can try to address the excessive sleepiness using orally administered stimulants (**amphetamines**, **methylphenidate**, modafinil). Because there are crossover characteristics between KLS and other mood disorders, lithium or **carbamazepine** are sometimes prescribed, and lithium appears to have some beneficial effect on **relapse** rates in a little less than half of the cases.

Prognosis

Excluding quality-of-life issues, KLS is a benign disorder that usually improves or resolves with age without permanent effects on intellect or physical function.

Prevention

Because the causes of KLS are undefined, prevention measures have not been identified.

Resources

PERIODICALS

Arnulf, I., J.M. Zeitzer, J. File, N. Farber, and E. Mignot, "Kleine-Levin syndrome: a systematic review of 186 cases in the literature." *Brain* 128(2006): 2763–2776.

ORGANIZATION

NINDS Kleine-Levin Syndrome Information Page. Available online at <http://www.ninds.nih.gov/disorders/kleine_levin/kleine_levin.htm> (accessed 01/07/07).

Kleine-Levin Syndrome Foundation, P.O. Box 5382, San Jose, CA, 95150-5382. (408) 265-1099. <http://www.klsfoundation.org/site/kls/>.

National Organization for Rare Disorders (NORD), P.O. Box 1968, 55 Kenosia Avenue, Danbury, CT, 06813-1968. (203) 744-0100. <http://www.rarediseases.org>.

National Sleep Foundation, 1522 K Street NW, Suite 500, Washington, D.C. 20005. (202) 347-3471. <http://www.sleepfoundation.org>.

Emily Jane Willingham, Ph.D.

Kleptomania

Definition

Kleptomania is an impulse control disorder characterized by a recurrent failure to resist stealing.

Description

Kleptomania is a complex disorder characterized by repeated, failed attempts to stop stealing. It is often seen in patients who are chemically dependent or who have a coexisting mood, **anxiety**, or eating disorder. Other coexisting mental disorders may include major **depression**, panic attacks, **social phobia**, **anorexia nervosa**, **bulimia nervosa**, **substance abuse**, and **obsessive-compulsive disorder**. People with this disorder have an overwhelming urge to steal and get a thrill from doing so. The recurrent act of stealing may be restricted to specific objects and settings, but the affected person may or may not describe these special preferences. People with this disorder usually exhibit guilt after the theft.

Detection of kleptomania, even by significant others, is difficult and the disorder often proceeds undetected. There may be preferred objects and environments where theft occurs. One theory proposes that the thrill of stealing helps to alleviate symptoms in persons who are clinically depressed.

Causes and symptoms

Causes

The cause of kleptomania is unknown, although it may have a genetic component and may be transmitted among first-degree relatives. There also seems to be a strong propensity for kleptomania to coexist with obsessive-compulsive disorder, bulimia nervosa, and clinical depression.

Symptoms

The handbook used by mental health professionals to diagnose mental disorders is the *Diagnostic and Statistical Manual of Mental Disorders*. Published by the American Psychiatric Association, the *DSM* contains diagnostic criteria and research findings for mental disorders. It is the primary reference for mental health professionals in the United States. The 2000 edition of this manual (fourth edition, text revision), known as the *DSM-IV-TR*, lists five diagnostic criteria for kleptomania:

- Repeated theft of objects that are unnecessary for either personal use or monetary value.
- Increasing tension immediately before the theft.
- Pleasure or relief upon committing the theft.
- The theft is not motivated by anger or vengeance, and is not caused by a delusion or hallucination.
- The behavior is not better accounted for by a conduct disorder, manic episode, or antisocial personality disorder.

Demographics

Studies suggest that 0.6% of the general population may have this disorder and that it is more common in females. In patients who have histories of obsessive-compulsive disorder, some studies suggest a 7% correlation with kleptomania. Other studies have reported a particularly high (65%) correlation of kleptomania in patients with bulimia.

Diagnosis

Diagnosing kleptomania is usually difficult since patients do not seek medical help for this complaint, and initial psychological assessments may not detect it. The disorder is often diagnosed when patients seek help for another reason, such as depression, bulimia, or for feeling emotionally unstable (labile) or unhappy in general (dysphoric). Initial psychological evaluations may detect a history of poor parenting, relationship conflicts, or acute stressors—abrupt occurrences that cause **stress**, such as moving from one home to

---

KEY TERMS

Anorexia nervosa—An eating disorder characterized by an intense fear of weight gain accompanied by a distorted perception of one's own underweight body.

Bulimia nervosa—An eating disorder characterized by binges in which large amounts of food are consumed, followed by forced vomiting.

Cognitive-behavioral therapy—An approach to psychotherapy that emphasizes the correction of distorted thinking patterns and changing one's behaviors accordingly.

Obsessive-compulsive disorder—Disorder in which the affected individual has an obsession (such as a fear of contamination, or thoughts he or she doesn't like to have and can't control) and feels compelled to perform a certain act to neutralize the obsession (such as repeated handwashing).

Panic disorder—An anxiety disorder in which an individual experiences sudden, debilitating attacks of intense fear.

Phobia—Irrational fear of places, things, or situations that lead to avoidance.

Rational emotive therapy—A form of psychotherapy developed by Albert Ellis and other psychotherapists based on the theory that emotional response is based on the subjective interpretation of events, not on the events themselves.

---

another. The recurrent act of stealing may be restricted to specific objects and settings, but the patient may or may not describe these special preferences.

Treatments

Once the disorder is suspected and verified by an extensive psychological interview, therapy is normally directed towards impulse control, as well as any accompanying mental disorder(s). **Relapse prevention** strategies, with a clear understanding of specific triggers, should be stressed. Treatment may include psychotherapies such as **cognitive-behavioral therapy** and **rational emotive therapy**. Recent studies have indicated that **fluoxetine** (Prozac) and **naltrexone** (Revia) may also be helpful.

Prognosis

Not much solid information is known about this disorder. Since it is not usually the presenting problem or chief complaint, it is frequently not even diagnosed. There are some case reports that document treatment success with antidepressant medications, although as with almost all psychological disorders, the outcomes vary.

Prevention

There is little evidence concerning prevention. A healthy upbringing, positive intimate relationships, and management of acutely stressful situations may lower the incidence of kleptomania and coexisting disorders.

Resources

BOOKS

Tasman, Allan, Jerald Kay, and Jeffrey A. Lieberman, eds. *Psychiatry*. 1st ed. Philadelphia: W. B. Saunders Company, 1997.

Laith Farid Gulli, M.D.

Klonopin *see* **Clonazepam**

L

Lamotrigine

Definition

Lamotrigine is an anticonvulsant drug commonly used to prevent **seizures**. It is also used as a mood stabilizer in some people with bipolar (manic-depressive) disorder. In the United States, lamotrigine is available under the trade name of Lamictal.

Purpose

Lamotrigine is used to prevent seizures in individuals with seizure disorders. It is also used as a mood stabilizer in people with **bipolar disorder**.

Description

The United States Food and Drug Administration (FDA) approved Lamotrigine in 1994. This drug appears to suppress the activity of neurons (nerve cells) in the **brain**. By stabilizing neurons, lamotrigine prevents seizure activity and may also stabilize abnormal mood swings.

Lamotrigine is available as both oral and chewable tablets. It is broken down in the liver.

Recommended dosage

The dosage of lamotrigine varies depending upon the age and weight of the patient, other medications that the patient is taking, and whether the patient has heart, liver, or kidney disease. It is common for patients to start with a low dosage of lamotrigine. The dosage is then increased slowly over several weeks to help pre-vent side effects. The dosage may be adjusted frequently by the prescribing physician.

A common dose for an adult who takes no other medications and has no other diseases is 150–250 mg taken twice daily.

Precautions

A serious and permanently disfiguring rash may occur as a result of lamotrigine. The rash, which is symptom of a systemic reaction to the drug, may be life-threatening. If a rash occurs, a doctor should be contacted immediately, and the drug stopped. People who have experienced any kind of rash while taking lamotrigine should never take the drug again.

Lamotrigine should be used with physician supervision after assessing the risks and benefits in people with heart, kidney, or liver disease. The dosage is usually reduced in these individuals.

Side effects

Side effects that occur in more than 10% of people taking lamotrigine are: headache, dizziness, unsteadiness while walking, blurred vision, double vision, nausea, cold-like symptoms involving runny noses or sore throats, and infections.

Although relatively rare, any rash that develops while taking lamotrigine should be evaluated by a health care professional, since life-threatening rashes may occur.

Other side effects include confusion, impaired memory, **sleep disorders**, nonspecific pain all over the body, and disruption of menstrual cycles.

Interactions

Some drugs can decrease the levels of lamotrigine in the body. This may make the drug less effective. Examples include **carbamazepine**, phenobarbital, primidone, phenytoin, and **valproic acid**. Interestingly, valproic acid

KEY TERMS

Bipolar disorder—A mental disorder characterized by dramatic, and sometimes rapid mood swings, resulting in both manic and depressive episodes; formerly called manic-depressive disorder.

Folic acid—An essential B-vitamin that humans obtain through diet.

Manic—Referring to mania, a state characterized by excessive activity, excitement or emotion.

Milligram (mg)—One-thousandth of a gram. A gram is the metric measure that equals approximately 0.035 ounces.

and its close relative, **divalproex sodium**, have also been reported to increase lamotrigine levels in some people, which could increase the side effects of the drug. When lamotrigine and valproic acid are used together, there is a greater chance that a serious rash may develop. Very specific dosage guidelines must be followed when these two drugs are used at the same time.

Lamotrigine may increase the levels of carbamazepine in the body, increasing adverse effects associated with carbamazepine.

An increased risk of certain side effects may occur if lamotrigine is used with drugs such as methotrexate, that inhibit folic acid synthesis.

Resources

BOOKS

Ellsworth, Allan J., and others, eds. *Mosby's Medical Drug Reference.* St. Louis, MO: Mosby, Inc, 1999.

Facts and Comparisons Staff. *Drug Facts and Comparisons.* 6th Edition. Saint Louis: Facts and Comparisons; Philadelphia: Lippincott Williams and Wilkins, 2002.

Medical Economics Co. Staff. *Physician's Desk Reference.* 56th edition. Montvale, NJ: Medical Economics Company, 2002.

Kelly Karpa, RPh, Ph.D.

Late-life depression

Definition

Late-life **depression** is depression occurring in older individuals. Although often associated with the **stress** and physical problems attendant with advancing age, depression is not a normal part of the aging process.

Description

Depression in the aging and the aged is a major public health problem. Many who suffer from late-life depression go undiagnosed. The insidious nature of depression in the elderly is that its symptoms are often obfuscated in the context of the multiple physical problems of many elderly people. As the body ages, it becomes less able to respond to stress and is at increased risk for disease. The hair grays, the skin wrinkles, and reaction times slow. In addition, disabilities resulting from external factors such as stress, trauma, chronic diseases, lifestyle limitations, financial factors, and isolation may accelerate the process, resulting in the symptoms we think of as defining old age. It would seem little wonder, then, that many seniors are depressed. Depression, however, is not a normal part of aging, nor is it inevitable.

The symptoms of late-life depression can be the same as they are for **depressive disorders** in younger people, whether they be **major depressive disorder**, a **bipolar disorder**, or subsyndromal depression. The individual may experience a profound and persistent feeling of sadness or despair or lose interest in things that were once pleasurable (anhedonia). Late-life depression can also exhibit itself in less obvious ways, including sleep disturbance, change in appetite, or disturbed mental functioning. In extreme cases, late-life depression can lead to **suicide**. Depression in late life, however, is treatable, not a condition to be suffered in silence.

Demographics

The percentage of Americans 65 years old and older who have clinical depression is significantly greater than for the general population. Whereas approximately 1% of Americans are clinically depressed, nearly 16% of those 65 years of age and older meet the criteria for clinical depression. Similarly, suicide rates for older adults are disproportionately high, particularly for white males.

A **diagnosis** of major depressive disorder is more likely in elderly patients who are also medically ill, older than 70 years of age, and are hospitalized or institutionalized. Depression in the elderly is more common when there is a history of depression earlier in life, chronic physical illness, **brain** disease, alcohol **abuse**, or stressful life events. Elderly women are more likely to become depressed than are elderly men, and single seniors are more likely to become depressed than are those who are married. It has been estimated that as many as 15% of widowed adults will have a serious depression for a year or more after the death of their spouse.

Subsyndromal depression (depression that is clinically significant but does not meet the criteria for major depressive disorder) is more common than major depressive disorder in elderly adults. It is estimated that 15% to 50% of older adults with subsyndromal depression will develop major depressive disorder within two years. Approximately 30% of nursing home residents have subsyndromal depression. As with major depressive disorder, elders with subsyndromal depression tend to be female.

Causes and symptoms

As opposed to younger individuals, older adults are more likely to have a medical condition in addition to depression. A number of medical conditions have commonly been associated with depression in the elderly. These include:

- Coronary artery disease (high blood pressure, history of heart attack, coronary artery bypass surgery, congestive heart failure)
- Neurologic disorders (stroke, Alzheimer's disease, Parkinson's disease, Lou Gehrig's disease, multiple sclerosis, Binswanger's disease, senile dementia)
- Metabolic disturbances (diabetes, hypoglycemia, hypothyroidism, hyperthyroidism, hyperparathyroidism, Addison's disease)
- Cancer (particularly of the pancreas)
- Other medical conditions (chronic obstructive pulmonary disease, rheumatoid arthritis, chronic pain, sexual dysfunction, renal dialysis, chronic constipation, viral pneumonia, hepatitis, influenza)

In addition, a number of medications routinely taken by elderly patients may cause depression. These include:

- Cardiovascular drugs (clonidine, digitalis, guanethidine, hydralazine, methyldopa, procainamide, propranolol, reserpine, thiazide diuretics)
- Chemotherapeutics (6-azauridine, asparaginase, azathioprine, bleomycin, cisplatin, cyclophosphamide, doxorubicin, mithramycin)
- Antiparkinsonian drugs (amantadine, bromocriptine, levodopa)
- Antipsychotic drugs (fluphenazine, haloperidol)
- Sedatives and antianxiety drugs (barbiturates, benzodiazepines, chloral hydrate, ethanol)
- Anticonvulsants (carbamazepine, ethosuximide, phenobarbital, phenytoin, primidone)
- Anti-inflammatory/anti-infective agents (ampicillin, cycloserine, dapsone, ethambutol, griseofulvin, isoniazid, metoclopramide, metronidazole, nalidixic acid, nitrofurantoin, nonsteroidal anti-inflammatory drugs [NSAIDs], penicillin G procaine, streptomycin, sulfonamides, tetracycline)
- Stimulants (amphetamines, caffeine, cocaine, methylphenidate)
- Hormones (adrenocorticotropin, anabolic steroids, glucocorticoids, oral contraceptives)
- Other medications (choline, cimetidine, disulfiram, lecithin, methysergide, phenylephrine, physostigmine, ranitidine, vinblastine, vincristine)

Because of concurrent medical problems and lowered expectations for functionality, elderly patients with depression are often undiagnosed. In addition, elderly patients often are reluctant to speak about psychological symptoms and consider depression to be a normal response to the aging process. Depressed older people may not report being depressed because they have no hope that anyone will intervene. These factors can make diagnosis difficult.

Depression in older adults does not necessarily present with the same symptoms as in the general population. Common symptoms in older people that can signify a problem with depression include:

- Unexplained physical complaints: Older adults are often reluctant to discuss psychological symptoms. As a result, symptoms of depression may be expressed in terms of a physical rather than a psychological complaint. For example, depression in older adults is often characterized by physical complaints for which no medical cause can be found or by physical symptoms that are out of proportion to the underlying medical illness.
- Hopelessness or helplessness: In older adults, it is hopelessness rather than sadness that tends to be associated with thoughts of suicide. Statements such as "I wish I were dead already," "I wish I would fall asleep and not wake up," or "what's the use in trying" are cause for immediate concern and should be responded to with psychological assessment rather than platitudes or meaningless assurances that everything is all right. Talk of suicide—even in jest—should always be taken seriously
- Anxiety and worries: Older adults often experience general feelings of worry and tension not associated with specific anxiety or panic disorders. Statements of anxiety and worry in older adults often are signs of depression in addition to or instead of an anxiety disorder. Treatment for an anxiety disorder, however, will not treat any underlying depression.
- Memory complaints: Depressed older adults may complain about memory loss with or without objective signs of cognitive impairment. Particularly when no demonstrable memory problems can be discerned

by simple tests, it is important that the patient also be assessed for depression and treated accordingly.

- Loss of feeling of pleasure (anhedonia): A common symptom of depression in older adults is the inability to experience pleasure from life and daily events. Expressions of anhedonia might include no longer deriving enjoyment from being with grandchildren; not wanting to read, listen to music, or participate in hobbies once found enjoyable; or feeling estranged from God or no longer being comforted by religion. Although it might seem that being less active and involved in life is a response to illness or decreased abilities associated with aging, research suggests that depression might in fact contribute to heart disease, diabetes, and arthritis.

- Slowed movement: "Slowing down" is often associated with old age. However, things such as stooped posture, slowed movements, or slowed speech may also be signs of depression. In particular, depression associated with vascular disease is often expressed in such symptoms.

- Irritability: Depression in older adults may also be expressed by excessive or easily provoked anger, annoyance, or impatience. Symptoms of irritability include fussiness, whining, or fretfulness even in the face of comforting. When such a pattern is persistent, assessment for depression should be considered.

- Lack of interest in personal care: Depressed older adults may believe that they are "not worth the trouble" and fail to follow instructions for taking medications or dietary guidelines as a result. Similarly, depressed older adults may display such symptoms as lack of care about personal appearance—including not getting dressed, bathing, or performing other hygiene activities. Individuals displaying such symptoms should be assessed for depression.

- Other symptoms: Sleep disturbance, decreased appetite, weight loss, difficulty concentrating, and fatigue are all common symptoms of late-life depression.

Diagnosis

According to the *Diagnostic and Statistical Manual of Mental Disorders (DSM-IV-TR)* of the American Psychiatric Association, there are nine criteria for major depressive disorder:

- Depressed mood
- Sleep disturbance
- Lack of interest or pleasure in activities
- Guilt and feelings of worthlessness
- Lack of energy
- Loss of concentration and difficult making decisions
- Anorexia or weight loss
- Psychomotor agitation or retardation
- Suicidal ideation (thoughts of suicide)

A diagnosis of depression requires at least five of these criteria to be present nearly every day during a two-week period, or a score of 10 or more on the **Beck Depression Inventory** (BDI) or on the **Geriatric Depression Scale**.

However, significant depression in older adults does not always meet the criteria for a *DSM-IV-TR* diagnosis of depression. As a result, although depression occurs more frequently in older adults than in the general population, it often goes undiagnosed in seniors. In addition to or instead of the classic diagnostic symptoms, older adults may exhibit such symptoms as discussed in the previous section, "Causes and symptoms." Such symptoms should also be considered when diagnosing depression in older adults.

Screening of an elderly patient for depression should include an electrocardiogram (ECG), urinalysis, general blood chemistry screen, complete blood count, and determination of the levels of thyroid-stimulating hormone, vitamin B12, folate, and medication in the blood.

Treatments

Treatment for depression in elderly patients may be done with medication and/or **psychotherapy** (including **talk therapy** and behavior therapy). Further, research has shown that a combination of the two treatment options is more effective than the use of medication or therapy alone. Although improvement may be seen as early as two weeks, the full effect of therapy may not be observable for several months. If the patient is having a major depressive episode, recovery may take from 6 to 12 months. This means that therapy for older adults is typically needed for longer periods of time than for the general population.

Medication for depression is generally well tolerated in older adults. Drugs used in treating depression in older adults include **selective serotonin reuptake inhibitors (SSRIs) (sertraline, fluoxetine, paroxetine, fluvoxamine, citalopram, escitalopram)**, secondary tricyclic **antidepressants (nortriptyline, protriptyline, desipramine, amoxapine)**, tertiary tricyclic antidepressants **(amitriptyline, imipramine, doxepin, trimipramine, clomipramine)**, monoamine oxidase inhibitors (MAOIs) **(phenelzine, tranylcypromine)**, and other antidepressants **(maprotiline, bupropion, trazodone, venlafaxine, nefazodone, mirtazapine)**. As with any medication, the patient should be monitored closely to determine how

KEY TERMS

Bipolar disorders—A group of mood disorders characterized by both depressive and manic or hypomanic episodes.

Major depressive disorder—Mental illness characterized by a profound and persistent feeling of sadness or despair and/or a loss of interest in things that were once pleasurable.

Seasonal affective disorder—A mood disorder in which major depressive episodes and/or manic episodes occur at predictable times of the year, with depressive episodes typically occurring during the fall and winter months. Seasonal affective disorder may be associated with a bipolar disorder, major depressive disorder, or subsyndromal depression.

Subsyndromal depression—Depressive episodes that do not meet the severity levels necessary for classification as major depressive episodes.

well he or she is reacting to the medication. If adverse reactions occur, another medication can be tried.

Prognosis

The general prognosis for recovery from depression in older adults is good, although recovery may take longer for older adults than for the general population.

Prevention

Increasingly, the literature is recognizing that although it is imperative to diagnose and treat depression in late life, it is equally important to prevent late-life depression in the first place. Researchers are currently investigating several models of prevention. These focus on individuals at high risk for depression in late life, including those with diseases that often occur with depression.

There are a number of steps that can be taken to help prevent depression. Eating a balanced diet and keeping regular meal times is important, particularly if one has problems with insulin or blood sugar levels. Getting regular exercise also helps stave off depression. If one's depression has a seasonal component, taking walks in the morning sunshine or using a light box can also help. Maintaining a regular sleep pattern is also helpful, as is avoiding drugs and alcohol. Those seniors living alone should also make an effort to

widen their social support network. Research has found that making friends at a senior center is an excellent way to do this. Additional steps that can be taken by those who have been diagnosed and are being treated for depression are to continue to take any antidepressant medications as prescribed until directed to stop by one's physician and to continue with therapy even after the medications have been stopped.

Researchers are continuing to investigate depression prevention for older adults in the hope that this too common and undiagnosed disorder can be not only successfully treated, but also prevented from occurring in the first place.

See also Seasonal affective disorder.

Resources

BOOKS

American Psychiatric Association. *Diagnostic and Statistical Manual of Mental Disorders.* 4th ed., text rev. Washington, D.C.: American Psychiatric Association, 2000.

Baldwin, Robert C.; Edmond Chiu, Cornelius Katona, and Nori Graham. *Guidelines on Depression in Older People: Practising the Evidence.* Oxford: Taylor and Francis, 2002.

Baldwin, Robert C., and Jane Garner. "Anxiety and Depression in Women in Old Age." *Mood and Anxiety Disorders in Women.* Eds. David J. Castle, Jayashri Kulkarni, and Kathryn M. Abel. New York: Cambridge University Press, 2006. 242–66.

Ellison, James E., and Sumer K. Verma, eds. *Depression in Later Life: A Multidisciplinary Psychiatric Approach.* London: Informa Healthcare, 2003.

Hinrichsen, Gregory A., and Kathleen F. Clougherty. *Interpersonal Psychotherapy for Depressed Older Adults.* Washington, D.C.: American Psychological Association, 2006.

Karel, Michele J., Suzann Ogland-Hand, and Margaret Gatz. *Assessing and Treating Late-Life Depression.* New York: Basic Books, 2002.

Roose, Steven P., and Harold A. Sackeim. *Late-Life Depression.* New York: Oxford University Press, 2004.

VandenBos, Gary R., ed. *APA Dictionary of Psychology.* Washington, D.C.: American Psychological Association, 2007.

PERIODICALS

Aday, Ronald H., Gayle C. Kehoe, and Lori A. Farney. "Impact of Senior Center Friendships on Aging Women Who Live Alone." *Journal of Women and Aging* 18.1 (2006): 57–73.

Antai-Otong, Deborah. "The Art of Prescribing: Antidepressants in Late-Life Depression: Prescribing Principles." *Perspectives in Psychiatric Care* 42.2 (2006): 149–53.

Baldwin, Robert C., Andrew Gallagley, Mhairi Gourlay, Alan Jackson, and Alistair Burns. "Prognosis of Late Life Depression: A Three-Year Cohort Study of

Outcome and Potential Predictors." *International Journal of Geriatric Psychiatry* 21.1 (2006): 57–63.

Bremmer, Marijke A., and others. "Depression in Older Age Is a Risk Factor for First Ischemic Cardiac Events." *American Journal of Geriatric Psychiatry* 14.6 (2006): 523–30.

Brenes, G. A., and others. "Treatment of Minor Depression in Older Adults: A Pilot Study Comparing Sertraline and Exercise." *Aging & Mental Health* 11.1 (2007): 61–68.

Burroughs, Heather, and others. "'Justifiable Depression': How Primary Care Professionals and Patients View Late-Life Depression? A Qualitative Study." *Family Practice* 23.3 (2006): 369–77.

Elderkin-Thompson, and others. "Executive Dysfunction and Memory in Older Patients with Major and Minor Depression." *Archives of Clinical Neuropsychology* 21.7 (2006): 669–76.

Hinton, Ladson, Mark Zweifach, Sabine Oishi, Lingqi Tang, and Jürgen Unützer. "Gender Disparities in the Treatment of Late-Life Depression: Qualitative and Quantitative Findings from the IMPACT Trial." *American Journal of Geriatric Psychiatry* 14.10 (2006): 884–92.

Holley, Caitlin, Stanley A. Murrell, and Benjamin T. Mast. "Psychosocial and Vascular Risk Factors for Depression in the Elderly." *American Journal of Geriatric Psychiatry* 14.1 (2006): 84–90.

Hybels, Celia F., David C. Steffens, Douglas R. McQuoid, and K. Ranga Rama Krishnan. "Residual Symptoms in Older Patients Treated for Major Depression." *International Journal of Geriatric Psychiatry* 20.12 (2005): 1196–1202.

Karp, Jordan F., Eric Lenze, Lalith Solai, Jules Rosen, and Charles F. Reynolds III. "Preventing Depression in Older Adults." *Clinical Neuropsychiatry: Journal of Treatment Evaluation* 3.1 (2006): 69–80.

Newberg, Andrew R., Dimitry S. Davydow, and Hochang B. Lee. "Cerebrovascular Disease Basis of Depression: Post-Stroke Depression and Vascular Depression." *International Review of Psychiatry* 18.5 (2006): 433–41.

Payne, Martha E., Celia F. Hybels, Connie W. Bales, and David C. Steffens. "Vascular Nutritional Correlates of Late-Life Depression." *American Journal of Geriatric Psychiatry* 14.9 (2006): 787–95.

Rainer, Michael K., and others. "Data From the VITA Study Do Not Support the Concept of Vascular Depression." *American Journal of Geriatric Psychiatry* 14.6 (2006): 531–37.

Schoevers, Robert A., and others. "Prevention of Late-Life Depression in Primary Care: Do We Know Where to Begin?" *American Journal of Psychiatry* 163.9 (2006): 1611–21.

Smit, Filip, Agnieska Ederveen, Pim Cuijpers, Dorly Deeg, Aartjan Beekman. "Opportunities for Cost-effective Prevention of Late-Life Depression: An Epidemiological Approach." *Archives of General Psychiatry* 63.3 (2006): 290–96.

Szanto, Katalin, Benoit H. Mulsant, Patricia R. Houck, Mary Amanda Dew, Alexandre Dombrovski, Bruce G. Pollock, and Charles F. Reynolds III. "Emergence, Persistence, and Resolution of Suicidal Ideation During Treatment of Depression in Old Age." *Journal of Affective Disorders* 98.1–2 (2007): 153–61.

Vaishnavi, Sandeep, and Warren D. Taylor. "Neuroimaging in Late-Life Depression." *International Review of Psychiatry* 18.5 (2006): 443–51.

von Gunten, Armin, Panteleimon Giannakopoulos, and René Duc. "Cognitive and Demographic Determinants of Dementia in Depressed Patients with Subjective Memory Complaints." *European Neurology* 54.3 (2005): 154–58.

Whyte, Ellen M., and Barry Rovner. "Depression in Late-Life: Shifting the Paradigm from Treatment to Prevention." *International Journal of Geriatric Psychiatry* 21.8 (2006): 746–51.

Yang, Yang. "How Does Functional Disability Affect Depressive Symptoms in Late Life? The Role of Perceived Social Support and Psychological Resources." *Journal of Health and Social Behavior* 47.4 (2006): 355–72.

ORGANIZATIONS

American Association for Geriatric Psychiatry (AAGP), 7910 Woodmont Avenue, Suite 1050, Bethesda, MD 20814-3004. (301) 654-7850. <http://www.AAGPonline.org>.

American Psychiatric Association, 1000 Wilson Boulevard, Suite 1825, Arlington, VA 22209-3901. (703) 907-7300. <http://www.psych.org>.

American Psychological Association, 750 First Street NE, Washington, D.C. 20002-4242. (800) 374-2721. TDD/TTY: (202) 336-6123. <http://www.apa.org>.

Depression and Bipolar Support Alliance (DBSA), 730 North Franklin Street, Suite 501, Chicago, IL 60610-7224. (800) 826-3632. <http://www.dbsalliance.org>.

Fuqua Center for Late-Life Depression, Wesley Woods Health Center, 4th Floor, 1841 Clifton Road NE, Atlanta, GA 30329. (404) 728-6302. <http://www.emoryhealthcare.org/departments/fuqua>.

Geriatric Mental Health Foundation, 7910 Woodmont Avenue, Suite 1050, Bethesda, MD 20814. (301) 654-7850. <http://www.gmhfonline.org/gmhf/consumer/depression.html>.

National Alliance on Mental Illness, Colonial Place Three, 2107 Wilson Boulevard, Suite 300, Arlington, VA 22201-3042. (703) 524-7600, (800) 950-6264. TDD: (703) 516-7227 <http://www.nami.org>.

Older Adult Consumer Mental Health Alliance (OACMHA), Bazelon Center for Mental Health Law, 1101 15th Street, NW, Suite 1202, Washington, DC 20005. (202) 467-5730 Ext. 140. <http://www.oacmha.com>.

Ruth A. Wienclaw, PhD

Lavender

Definition

Lavender is the shrub-like aromatic plant, *Lavandula officinalis*, sometimes called *Lavandula vera* or true lavender.

Purpose

Lavender is a mild sedative and antispasmodic. The essential oil derived from lavender is used in **aromatherapy** to treat **anxiety**, difficulty sleeping, nervousness, and restlessness. Other preparations of the plant are taken internally to treat sleep disturbances, stomach complaints, loss of appetite, and as a general tonic.

Description

Lavender is a shrubby evergreen bush that grows to about 3 feet (1 m) tall and 4 feet (1.4 m) in diameter. The plant produces aromatic spiky flowers from June to September. An essential oil used for healing and in perfume is extracted from the flowers just before they open.

Lavender is native to the Mediterranean region and is cultivated in temperate regions across the world. There are many species and subspecies. The preferred lavender for medicinal use is *L. officinalis* or true lavender. In Europe lavender has been used as a healing herb for centuries. It was a prominent component of smelling salts popular with women in the late 1800s.

Lavender is used both externally and internally in healing. Externally the essential oil is used in aromatherapy as a relaxant and to improve mood. Aromatherapy can be facilitated through massage, used in the bath, in potpouri jars, and burned in specially-dsigned oil burners. Lavender is also used to treat **fatigue**, restlessness, nervousness, and difficulty sleeping. Pillows stuffed with lavender have been used as a sleep aid in Europe for many years. Lavender oil applied to the forehead and temples is said to ease headache.

Researchers have isolated the active compounds in lavender. The most important of these is an aromatic volatile oil. Lavender also contains small amounts of coumarins, compounds that dilate (open up) the blood vessels and help control spasms. Some modern scientific research supports the claim that lavender is effective as a mild sedative and a calming agent. In one Japanese study, people exposed to the odor of lavender were found to show less mental **stress** and more alertness than those not exposed to the

French lavender flowers. *(Jim Allan/Alamy)*

fragrance when evaluated by psychological tests. In a peer-reviewed British study, when the sleeping room was perfumed with lavender, elderly nursing home residents with **insomnia** slept as well as they did when they took sleeping pills and better than they did when they were given neither sleeping pills nor exposed to lavender fragrance.

Other external uses of the essential oil of lavender are as an antiseptic to disinfect wounds. When used on wounds, lavender oil often is combined with other essential oil extracts to enhance its antiseptic and dehydrating properties. Lavender oil added to bathwater is believed to stimulate the circulation.

Taken internally as a tea made from lavender flowers or as a few drops of lavender oil on a sugar cube, this herb is used as a mild sedative and antispasmodic. The German Federal Health Agency's Commission E established to independently review and evaluate scientific literature and case studies pertaining to medicinal plants has approved the use of lavender tea or lavender oil on a sugar cube to treat restlessness and insomnia. Despite conflicting scientific claims, this organization has also endorsed the internal use of lavender for stomach upsets, loss of appetite, and excess gas. Animal research confirms that lavender oil has an antispasmodic effect on smooth muscle of the intestine and uterus. These results have not been confirmed in humans.

Recommended dosage

Lavender tea is made by steeping 1 to 2 teaspoons of flowers per cup of boiling water. One cup of tea can be drunk three times a day. Alternatively, 1 to 4 drops of lavender oil can be placed on a sugar cube and eaten once a day. Externally, a few drops of oil can be added to bath water or rubbed on the temples to treat headache. Like any herbal product, the strength of the active ingredients can vary from batch to batch, making it difficult to determine exact dosages.

Precautions

The use of lavender, either alone or in combination with other herbs, is not regulated by the United States Food and Drug Administration. Unlike pharmaceuticals, herbal and dietary supplements are not subjected to rigorous scientific testing to prove their claims of safety and effectiveness. The strength of active ingredients varies from manufacturer to manufacturer, and the label may not accurately reflect the contents.

Particular problems with lavender oil revolve around substitution of oil from species of lavender other than *Lavandula officinalis*, the preferred medicinal lavender. Most often true lavender oil is adulterated with less expensive lavadin oil. Lavadin oil comes from other species of lavender. It has a pleasant lavender odor, but its chemical compositions, and thus its healing actions, are different from true lavender oil. People purchasing lavender oil or tonics containing lavender should be alert to substitutions.

Side effects

When used in the recommended dosage, lavender is not considered harmful. Some people have reported developing contact dermatitis (a rash) when lavender oil is used directly on the skin.

Interactions

There are no studies on interactions of lavender with conventional pharmaceuticals. Traditionally lavender has been used in combination with other herbs such as tea oil and lemon balm without adverse interactions.

KEY TERMS

Antispasmodic—A medication or preparation given to relieve muscle or digestive cramps.

Resources

BOOKS

Medical Economics Staff. *PDR for Herbal Medicines.* Montvale, NJ: Medical Economics Company, 1999.

Peirce, Andrea. *The American Pharmaceutical Association Practical Guide to Natural Medicines.* New York: William Morrow and Company, 1999.

Weiner, Michael and Janet Weiner. *Herbs that Heal.* Mill Valley, CA: Quantum Books, 1999.

OTHER

"Lavender" Plants for the Future. 2000 (cited 12 March 2002) <http://www.comp.leeds.ac.uk/pfaf/database/commonL.html>.

Tish Davidson, A.M.

Learning disabilities *see* **Learning disorders**

Learning disorders

Definition

Learning disorders, or learning disabilities, are disorders that cause problems in speaking, listening, reading, writing, or mathematical ability.

Description

A learning disability, or specific developmental disorder, is a disorder that inhibits or interferes with the skills of learning, the ability to store, process, or produce information. Under federal law, public schools consider a child to be learning disabled if his or her level of academic achievement is two or more years below the standard for age and IQ level. The fourth edition, text revision, of the *Diagnostic and Statistical Manual of Mental Disorders* (*DSM-IV-TR*, a handbook that mental health professionals use to diagnose mental disorders) uses the term *learning disorder* and defines this as cognitive difficulties arising from **brain** dysfunction.

It is estimated that 15% of the U.S. population, or one in seven Americans, has some kind of learning disability. About six percent of school-age children,

A teacher works with a young female student. *(AP Images)*

or almost three million children, receive some kind of special education services in school as a result of learning disabilities, and this number does not include children in private or home schools. Often, learning disabilities appear together with other disorders, such as attention-deficit hyperactivity disorder (ADHD). Irregularities in the functioning of certain parts of the brain that can result in information processing problems are thought to cause learning disorders. Evidence suggests that these irregularities are often inherited (i.e., a person is more likely to develop a learning disability if other family members have them). Learning disabilities are also associated with certain conditions occurring during fetal development, birth, or infancy, including maternal use of alcohol, drugs, and tobacco; exposure to infection; injury during birth; low birth weight; and sensory deprivation, in addition to some socioeconomic factors.

The socioeconomic link to the development of learning disabilities manifests as a greater rate in certain ethnic groups. In 2001, 2.5 times as many non-Hispanic black children were receiving special education services related to a learning disability. This skewed incidence is attributable to increased risk of developmental exposure to substances known to cause neurological harm among people living in low-income communities.

The signs of the presence of a learning disorder can vary based on the type of disorder and a person's age. The factor of age can be important because what is normal in a preschool child can be a sign of a problem in a child of elementary school age. In addition to underachievement, signs can include overall lack of organization, forgetfulness, and taking unusually long amounts of time to complete assignments. In the classroom, the child's teacher may observe one or more of the following characteristics: difficulty paying attention, unusual sloppiness and disorganization, social withdrawal, difficulty working independently, and trouble switching from one activity to another. In addition to the preceding signs, which relate directly to school and schoolwork, certain general behavioral and emotional features often accompany learning disabilities. These include impulsiveness, restlessness, distractibility, poor physical coordination, low tolerance for frustration, low self-esteem, daydreaming, inattentiveness, and anger, or sadness. These signs also can be symptomatic of other disorders that are not learning

A learning disorder makes writing a challenge.. *(Will & Deni McIntyre/Science Source/Photo Researchers, Inc.)*

disorders, and only a professional evaluation can distinguish them.

Types of learning disabilities

Learning disabilities are associated with brain dysfunctions that affect a number of basic skills. Perhaps the most fundamental is sensory-perceptual ability—the capacity to take in and process information through the senses. Difficulties involving vision, hearing, and touch will have an adverse effect on learning. Although learning is usually considered a mental rather than a physical pursuit, it involves motor skills, and it can also be impaired by problems with motor development. Other basic skills fundamental to learning include memory, attention, and language abilities.

The three most common academic skill areas affected by learning disabilities are reading, writing, and arithmetic. Some sources estimate that between 60% and 80% of children diagnosed with learning disabilities have reading as their only or main problem area. Learning disabilities involving reading have traditionally been known as dyslexia; currently, the preferred term is "reading disorder." A wide array of problems is associated with **reading disorder**, including difficulty identifying groups of letters, problems relating letters to sounds, reversals and other errors involving letter position, chaotic spelling, trouble with syllabication (breaking words into syllables), failure to recognize words, hesitant oral reading, and word-by-word rather than contextual reading.

Writing disabilities, known as dysgraphia or **disorder of written expression**, include problems with letter formation and writing layout on the page, repe-

titions and omissions, punctuation and capitalization errors, "mirror writing" (writing right to left), and a variety of spelling problems. Children with dysgraphia typically labor at written work much longer than their classmates, only to produce large, uneven writing that would be appropriate for a much younger child.

Learning abilities involving math skills, generally referred to as dyscalcula (or dyscalculia) or **mathematics disorder**, usually become apparent later than reading and writing problems—often at about the age of eight. Children with dyscalcula may have trouble counting, reading and writing numbers, understanding basic math concepts, mastering calculations, and measuring. This type of disability may also involve problems with nonverbal learning, including spatial organization.

In order to meet the criteria established by the American Psychiatric Association (APA) for these various diagnoses, the child's skills in these areas must be significantly below that of their peers on standardized tests (taking age, schooling, and level of intelligence into account), and the disorders must significantly interfere with academic achievement and/or daily living.

Treatment for a learning disorder can depend on the specific disorder, the age of the person at **diagnosis**, the disorder severity, and the assumed underlying cause. For example, people with central auditory processing disorder (CAPD), a common underlying cause of some learning disorders that is centered on a person's inability to process heard language correctly, may undergo therapy with a speech-language pathologist and other experts may use different kinds of auditory therapies to improve the person's ability to process heard language.

Resources

BOOKS

American Psychiatric Association. *Diagnostic and Statistical Manual of Mental Disorders*. 4th ed., text rev. Washington D.C.: American Psychiatric Association, 2000.

Bowman-Kruhm, Mary, and Claudine G. Wirths. *Everything You Need to Know about Learning Disabilities*. New York: Rosen Publishing Group, 1999.

Tuttle, Cheryl Gerson, and Gerald A. Tuttle, eds. *Challenging Voices: Writings By, For, and About People with Learning Disabilities.* Los Angeles: Lowell House, 1995.

Wong, Bernice, ed. *Learning About Learning Disabilities.* San Francisco: Morgan Kauffman Publishers, 1998.

ORGANIZATIONS

Learning Disabilities Association of America (formerly ACLD, the Association for Children and Adults with Learning Disabilities). 4156 Library Road, Pittsburgh, PA 15234-1349. Telephone: (412) 341-1515. Web site: <http://www.ldanatl.org>.

National Center for Learning Disabilities. 381 Park Avenue South Suite 1401, New York, NY 10016. Telephone: (212) 545-7510, or (888) 575-7373. Web site: <http://www.ncld.org>.

National Institute of Child Health and Human Development (NICHD), National Institutes of Health, DHHS, 31 Center Drive, Rm. 2A32 MSC 2425, Bethesda, MD 20892-2425 Telephone: (301) 496-5133, Fax: (301) 496-7101. Web site: <http://www.nichd.nih.gov>

WEB SITES

American Speech-Language-Hearing Association. <http://www.asha.org/public/speech/disorders/Language-Based-Learning-Disabilities.htm>

"Developmental reading disorder." National Library of Medicine. <http://www.nlm.nih.gov/medlineplus/ency/article/001406.htm>.

National Library of Medicine. Resources for learning disorder. <http://www.nlm.nih.gov/medlineplus/learningdisorders.html>

National Institute on Deafness and Other Communication Disorders. <http://www.nidcd.nih.gov/health/voice/auditory.asp>

Emily Jane Willingham, Ph.D.

Librium *see* **Chlordiazepoxide**

Lidone *see* **Molindone**

Light therapy

Definition

Light therapy refers to two different categories of treatment, one used in mainstream medical practice and the other in alternative/complementary medicine. Mainstream light therapy (also called phototherapy) includes the use of ultraviolet light to treat psoriasis and other skin disorders, and the use of full-spectrum or bright light to treat **seasonal affective disorder** (SAD). Light therapy for SAD was first introduced in the 1980s and is now a widely approved form of treatment for the disorder.

Light therapy in alternative or complementary approaches includes such techniques as the use of colored light or colored gemstones directed at or applied to various parts of the body. In some alternative forms of light therapy, the person visualizes being surrounded by and breathing in light of a particular color.

Purpose

Mainstream light therapy

The purpose of light therapy in mainstream psychiatric treatment is the relief of seasonal affective disorder, a form of **depression** most often associated with shortened daylight hours in northern latitudes from the late fall to the early spring. It is occasionally employed to treat such sleep-related disorders as **insomnia** and jet lag. Recently, light therapy has also been found effective in the treatment of such nonseasonal forms of depression as **bipolar disorder**. Light therapy for SAD and nonseasonal forms of depression is thought to work by triggering the brain's production of serotonin, a neurotransmitter related to mood disorders. Other researchers think that light therapy may relieve depression or jet lag by resetting the body's circadian rhythm, or inner biological clock.

In dermatology, ultraviolet (UV) light therapy is used to treat rashes, psoriasis, other skin disorders, and jaundice. Outpatient treatment for psoriasis usually requires three treatment sessions per week until the skin clears, which takes about seven weeks.

Alternative light therapies

Alternative light therapies are generally used to treat energy imbalances in the seven major chakras. Chakras are defined in Eastern systems of traditional medicine as energy centers in the human body located at different points along the spinal column. Each chakra is thought to absorb a certain vibration of light in the form of one of the seven colors of the rainbow, and to distribute this color energy through the body. When a specific chakra is blocked, light in the color associated with that chakra can be used to unblock the energy center and balance the flow of energy in the body.

The seven major chakras in the body and their associated colors are:

- red: the root chakra, located at the base of the spine
- orange: the sacral chakra, located in the small of the back
- yellow: the solar plexus chakra
- green: the heart chakra

- blue: the throat or thyroid chakra
- indigo: the so-called "third eye," located in the head at the level of the pineal gland
- violet or white: the crown chakra, located at the level of the pituitary gland

Alternative forms of light therapy also use colored light to heal different parts of the body associated with the various chakras. For example, yellow light would be used to heal digestive disorders, green to treat the circulatory system, and so on. Concentrating colored light into a narrow beam or applying a colored gemstone is thought to stimulate the **acupuncture** or acupressure points that govern the various organ systems of the body. This application of light therapy is sometimes called chromatherapy.

Precautions

Patients with eye disorders should consult an ophthalmologist before being treated with any form of phototherapy. Patients who are taking medications that make their skin sensitive to UV rays or bright light should also consult their health care provider. Although there are no reports of permanent eye damage from either light box therapy or UV treatment for skin disorders, patients sometimes experience headaches, dry eyes, mild sunburn, or **fatigue**. These problems can usually be relieved by adjusting the length of time for light treatments and by using a sunscreen and nose or eye drops. Lastly, patients who should have UV treatment for skin disorders should receive it from a board-certified dermatologist or other licensed health care professional; they should not attempt to treat themselves with sunlamps or similar tanning appliances.

There are no precautions needed for alternative light therapies.

Description

Mainstream light therapy

Mainstream phototherapy for skin disorders involves the exposure of the affected areas of skin to ultraviolet light. It is most often administered in an outpatient clinic or doctor's office. Light therapy for seasonal affective disorder and other forms of depression can be self-administered at home or in a private room in the workplace. The patient sits in front of a light box mounted on or near a desk or table for a period of time each day ranging from 15 minutes to several hours, depending on the severity of the SAD symptoms. Some SAD patients may have two or three sessions of light therapy each day. Treatment typically begins in the fall, when the days grow noticeably shorter, and ends in the spring.

The light box itself may be equipped with full-spectrum bulbs, which do emit UV rays as well as visible light; or it may use bulbs that filter out the UV rays and emit bright light only. Most light boxes emit light ranging from 2500–10,000 lux, a lux being a unit of light measurement equivalent to 1 lumen per square meter. For purposes of comparison, average indoor lighting is 300–500 lux, and the sunlight outdoors on a sunny day in summer is about 100,000 lux. Patients are instructed to sit facing the light box but to avoid staring directly at it. They can read or work at their desk while sitting in front of the light box. Light boxes cost between $200 and $500, but can often be rented from medical supply companies.

Newer forms of light therapy for SAD include the light visor, which resembles a baseball cap with a light source attached underneath the front of the device, above the wearer's eyes. The light visor allows the patient to walk or move about while receiving light treatment. Another new treatment is dawn simulation, which appears to be especially helpful for SAD patients who have difficulty getting up in the morning. In dawn simulation, the lighting fixture is programmed to turn gradually from dim to brighter light to simulate the sunrise. Dawn simulation is started around 4:30 or 5 o'clock on the morning, while the patient is still asleep.

Alternative light therapies

Chromatherapy may be administered in several different ways. The first step is determining the source or location of the patient's energy imbalance. Some color therapists or chromapaths are sensitive to the colors in the aura, or energy field surrounding a person's physical body that is invisible to most people. Dark or muddy colors in the aura are thought to indicate the locations of energy imbalance. Another technique involves suspending a quartz crystal on a pendulum over each chakra while the patient lies on a table or on the floor. The crystal swings freely if the chakra is open and energy is moving normally, but stops or moves irregularly if the chakra is blocked.

In the second stage of treatment, colored light is directed at specific areas of the body. The chromapath may use either colored light bulbs or may filter white light through a colored plastic filter. The red, orange, and yellow rays are thought to enter the body more effectively through the soles of the feet; patients receiving these colors of light may be asked to sit on the floor with their bare feet 12–14 in from the light source. The green ray is thought to enter through the solar plexus and the blue, indigo, and violet rays through the crown of the head. Blue light can be used to irradiate the whole body for the relief of physical pain, and violet light can be similarly used to relieve nervous strain and mental disorders.

Another form of colored light therapy involves the use of gemstones in the colors appropriate to each chakra. The crystal structures of gemstones are thought to reflect and transmit energy vibrations, including color vibrations. In gemstone treatment, the chromapath first cleanses the patient's aura with a clear quartz crystal and then places colored gemstones (usually semiprecious rather than expensive precious stones) on the parts of the body corresponding to the location of the chakras while the patient is lying on his or her back or stomach. The colored stones are thought to both cleanse the aura and recharge the energy centers.

A third form of colored light therapy is called color breathing or color visualization. It can be self-administered at home or any other private space. The patient sits in a chair with both feet on the floor, or sits on the floor in the lotus position. He or she then breathes slowly and rhythmically while visualizing being surrounded by light of the appropriate color and breathing in that color. The patient may also repeat a verbal affirmation related to the color, such as "The orange ray is filling me with vitality and joy," or "The violet ray is healing every part of my being."

Preparation

Patients should consult their health care provider before mainstream phototherapy, in order to determine possible sensitivity to bright light and adjust medication dosages if necessary.

Holistic and alternative practitioners usually ask patients to bathe or shower before chromatherapy, and to wear loosely fitting white or neutral-colored clothing. Washing is considered necessary to remove any negative energies that the patient has picked up from other people or from the environment. Wearing light-colored loose clothing is thought to minimize interference with the vibrations from the colored light or gemstones. The final step in preparation is a brief period of **meditation** or creative visualization for the practitioner as well as the patient. This step helps to create an atmosphere of calm and relaxation for the treatment.

Aftercare

No aftercare is necessary for mainstream light treatments.

KEY TERMS

Aura—An energy field that is thought to emanate from the human body and to be visible to people with special psychic or spiritual powers.

Chakra—One of seven major energy centers in the body, according to traditional systems of Eastern medicine. The chakras are associated with the seven colors of light in the rainbow.

Chromatherapy—An alternative form of light therapy in which colored light is directed toward a specific chakra or part of the body in order to heal or to correct energy imbalances. Practitioners of chromatherapy are sometimes called chromapaths.

Dawn simulation—A form of light therapy in which the patient is exposed while asleep to gradually brightening white light over a period of an hour and a half.

Lux—The International System unit for measuring illumination, equal to one lumen per square meter.

Neurotransmitter—A chemical in the brain that transmits messages between neurons, or nerve cells.

Phototherapy—Another name for light therapy in mainstream medical practice.

Seasonal affective disorder (SAD)—A mood disorder characterized by depression, weight gain, and sleepiness during the winter months. An estimated 4–6% of the population of Canada and the northern United States suffers from SAD.

Serotonin—A widely distributed neurotransmitter that is found in blood platelets, the lining of the digestive tract, and the brain, and that works in combination with norepinephrine. It causes very powerful contractions of smooth muscle, and is associated with mood, attention, emotions, and sleep. Low levels of serotonin are associated with depression.

Practitioners of alternative light therapies recommend that patients sit or rest quietly for a few minutes after the treatment rather than returning abruptly to their daily routines. This brief rest is thought to maximize the benefits of the treatment.

Risks

As was previously mentioned, mainstream light therapies may produce minor side effects (headache, insomnia, mild sunburn or skin irritation, dry eyes) in some patients. In addition, some patients receiving phototherapy for SAD may experience **hypomania**, which is a feeling of euphoria or an exaggeratedly "upbeat" mood. As with the physical side effects, hypomania can usually be managed by adjusting the frequency or length of light therapy sessions.

There are no known risks associated with alternative light therapies.

Normal results

Normal results for mainstream light treatments are clearing of the skin disorder or a lifting of depressed mood or jet lag.

Normal results for alternative light therapies include a sense of heightened energy and relief from negative thoughts or preoccupations. Some chromapaths also consider relief of physical pain or symptoms to be normal results for chromatherapy.

See also Circadian rhythm sleep disorder.

Resources

BOOKS

American Psychiatric Association. *Diagnostic and Statistical Manual of Mental Disorders.* 4th ed, text revised. Washington, DC: American Psychiatric Press, Inc., 2000.

Chiazzari, Suzy. "Part Six: Healing with Color." *The Complete Book of Color: Using Color for Lifestyle, Health, and Well-Being.* Boston, MA: Element Books Ltd., 1998.

Lam, Raymond, ed. *Seasonal Affective Disorder and Beyond: Light Treatment for SAD and Non-SAD Conditions.* Washington, DC: American Psychiatric Press, 1998.

Partonen, Timo, and Andres Magnusson, eds. *Seasonal Affective Disorder: Practice and Research.* Oxford, UK: Oxford University Press, 2001.

Rosenthal, Norman. *Winter Blues: Seasonal Affective Disorder—What It Is and How to Overcome It.* New York: Guilford Press, 1998.

Stein, Diane. *All Women Are Healers: A Comprehensive Guide to Natural Healing.* Freedom, CA: The Crossing Press Inc., 1996. Includes a chapter on healing with colored crystals and gemstones.

PERIODICALS

Eagles, John M. "SAD—Help arrives with the dawn?" *Lancet* 358 (December 22, 2001): 2100.

Jepson, Tracy, and others. "Current Perspectives on the Management of Seasonal Affective Disorder." *Journal of the American Pharmaceutical Association.* 39 no. 6 (1999): 822–829.

Sherman, Carl. "Underrated Light Therapy Effective for Depression." *Clinical Psychiatry News* 29 (October 2001): 32.

ORGANIZATIONS

American Holistic Medicine Association. Suite 201, 4101 Lake Boone Trail, Raleigh, NC 27607.

Colour Therapy Association. P. O. Box 16756, London SW20 8ZW, United Kingdom.

International Society for the Study of Subtle Energies and Energy Medicine (ISSSEEM). 356 Goldco Circle. Golden, CO 80401. (303) 278-2228. <www.vitalenergy.com/ISSSEEM>.

National Depressive and Manic Depressive Association. 730 Franklin Street, Suite 501, Chicago, IL 60610. (800) 826-3632. <www.ndmda.org>.

National Institute of Mental Health. Mental Health Public Inquiries, 5600 Fishers Lane, Room 15C-05, Rockville, MD 20857. (301) 443-4513. (888) 826-9438. <www.nimh.nih.gov>.

Society for Light Treatment and Biological Rhythms. 824 Howard Ave., New Haven, CT 06519. Fax (203) 764-4324. <www.sltbr.org> E-mail: sltbr@yale.edu.

Rebecca J. Frey, Ph.D.

Limbic system *see* **Brain**

Lithium carbonate

Definition

Lithium is a naturally occurring element that is classified as an anti-manic drug. It is available in the United States under the brand names Eskalith, Lithonate, Lithane, Lithotabs, and Lithobid. It is also sold under its generic name.

Purpose

Lithium is commonly used to treat mania and bipolar **depression** (manic depression). Less commonly, lithium is used to treat certain mood disorders, such as **schizoaffective disorder** and aggressive behavior and emotional instability in adults and children. Rarely is lithium taken to treat depression in the absence of mania. When this is the case, it is usually taken in addition to other antidepressant medications.

Description

Lithium salts have been used in medical practice for about 150 years. Lithium salts were first used to treat gout. It was noted in the 1880s that lithium was somewhat effective in the treatment of depression, and in the 1950s lithium was seen to improve the symptoms of bipolar disease (manic depression). The way lithium works in the body is unclear, but its therapeutic benefits are probably related to its effects on other electrolytes such as sodium, potassium, magnesium, and calcium. Lithium is taken either as lithium carbonate tablets or capsules or as lithium citrate syrup.

The therapeutic effects of lithium may appear slowly. Maximum benefit is often not evident for at least two weeks after starting the drug. People taking lithium should be aware of this and continue taking the drug as directed even if they do not see immediate changes in mood.

Lithium is available in 300-mg tablets and capsules, 300-mg and 450-mg sustained-release tablets, and a syrup containing approximately 300 mg per teaspoonful.

Recommended dosage

Depending on the patient's medical needs, age, weight, and kidney function, doses of lithium can range from 600 to 2,400 mg per day, although most patients will be stabilized on 600 to 1,200 mg per day. Patients who require large amounts of lithium often benefit from the addition of another anti-manic drug, which may allow the dose of lithium to be lowered.

Generally, lithium is taken two or three times daily. However, the entire dose may be taken at once if the physician believes that a single daily-dose program will increase patient **compliance**. The single-dose schedule is especially helpful for people who are forgetful and may skip doses on a multiple-dose schedule. Additionally, evidence indicates that once-daily doses are associated with fewer side effects.

More than with any other drugs used in the treatment of mental disorders, it is essential to maintain lithium blood levels within a certain narrow range to derive the maximum therapeutic benefit while minimizing serious negative side effects. It is important that patients have their blood levels of lithium measured at regular intervals.

Precautions

Because lithium intoxication may be serious and even life-threatening, blood concentrations of lithium should be measured weekly during the first four weeks of therapy and less often after that.

Patients taking lithium should have their thyroid function monitored and maintain an adequate sodium (salt) and water balance. Lithium should not be used or used only with very close physician supervision in patients with kidney impairment, heart disease, and other conditions that affect sodium balance. Dosage reduction or complete discontinuation may be necessary during infection, diarrhea, vomiting, or prolonged fast. Patients who are pregnant, breast-feeding, those over age 60, and people taking diuretics ("water" pills) should discuss the risks and benefits of lithium treatment with their doctors before beginning therapy. Lithium should be discontinued 24 hours before a major surgery, but may be continued normally for minor surgical procedures.

Side effects

Tremor is the most common neurological side effect. Lithium tremor is an irregular, nonrhythmic twitching of the arms and legs that is variable in both intensity and frequency. Lithium-induced tremors occur in approximately half of people taking this medication. The chance of tremors decreases if the dose is reduced. Acute lithium toxicity (poisoning) can result in neurological side effects, ranging from confusion and coordination impairment, to coma, **seizures**, and death. Other neurological side effects associated with lithium therapy include lethargy, memory impairment, difficulty finding words, and loss of creativity.

About 30 to 35% of patients experience excessive thirst and urination, usually due to the inability of the kidneys to retain water and sodium. However, lithium is not known to cause kidney damage.

Lithium inhibits the synthesis of thyroid hormone. About 10 to 20% of patients treated with lithium develop some degree of thyroid insufficiency, but they usually do not require supplementation with thyroid hormone tablets.

Gastrointestinal side effects include loss of appetite, nausea, vomiting, diarrhea, and stomach pain. Weight gain is another common side effect for patients receiving long-term treatment. Changes in saliva flow and enlargement of the salivary glands may occur. An increase in tooth cavities and the need for dental care among patients taking lithium has been reported.

Skin reactions to lithium are common but can usually be managed without discontinuing lithium therapy. Lithium may worsen folliculitis (inflammation of hair follicles), psoriasis, and acne. Thinning of the hair may occur, and, less commonly, hair loss may be experienced. Swollen feet are an uncommon side effect that responds to dose reduction.

Electrocardiographic abnormalities may occur with lithium therapy, but significant cardiovascular effects are uncommon except as the result of deliberate or accidental overdose.

A mild-to-moderate increase in the number of white blood cells is a frequent side effect of lithium use. Conversely, lithium may slow the formation of red blood cells and cause anemia.

Increased risk of fetal cardiovascular disease may be associated with the use of lithium during pregnancy, especially during the first trimester (first three

KEY TERMS

Bipolar disease—A mental disorder characterized by periods of mania alternating with periods of depression.

Compliance—In medicine or psychiatry, cooperation with a treatment plan or schedule of medications.

Electrocardiograph (EKG)—A test that measures the electrical activity of the heart as it beats. An abnormal EKG can indicate possible cardiac disease.

Mania—An elevated or euphoric mood or irritable state that is characteristic of bipolar I disorder. This state is characterized by mental and physical hyperactivity, disorganization of behavior, and inappropriate elevation of mood.

Schizoaffective disorder—A mental disorder that shows a combination of symptoms of mania and schizophrenia.

Thyroid—A gland in the neck that produces the hormone thyroxine, which is responsible for regulating metabolic activity in the body. Supplemental synthetic thyroid hormone is available as pills taken daily when the thyroid fails to produce enough hormone.

months). For this reason, pregnant women should discontinue lithium use until the second or third trimester and should receive alternative treatments for their mania.

Interactions

Patients taking lithium should always be concerned that other medications they are taking may adversely interact with it; patients should consult their physician or pharmacists about these interactions. The following list represents just some of the medications that lithium may interact with to either (a) increase or decrease the effectiveness of the lithium or (b) increase or decrease the effectiveness of the other drug:

- angiotensin converting enzyme inhibitors such as captopril, lisinopril, or enalapril
- nonsteroidal anti-inflammatory drugs such as ibuprofen or naprosyn
- diuretics (water pills) such as hydrochlorothiazide, furosemide, or ethacrynic acid
- asthma drugs such as theophylline and aminophylline
- anticonvulsants such as phenytoin and carbamazepine

- calcium channel blockers such as verapamil or diltiazem
- muscle relaxants such as methocarbamol, carisoprodol, and cyclobenzaprine
- metronidazole, a commonly prescribed antibiotic used to treat infections
- antidiabetic therapy
- amiodarone, an antiarrhythmic drug
- antacids containing sodium bicarbonate
- antidepressants

Resources

BOOKS

American Society of Health-System Pharmacists. *AHFS Drug Information 2002.* Bethesda: American Society of Health-System Pharmacists, 2002.

Preston, John D., John H. O'Neal, and Mary C. Talaga. *Handbook of Clinical Psychopharmacology for Therapists.* 4th ed. Oakland, CA: New Harbinger Publications, 2004.

PERIODICALS

Baldessarini, Ross J., Maurizio Pompili, and Leonardo Tondo. "Suicide in Bipolar Disorder: Risks and Management." *CNS Spectrums* 11.6 (June 2006): 465–71.

Baldessarini, Ross J., and others. "Decreased Risk of Suicides and Attempts During Long-Term Lithium Treatment: A Meta-Analytic Review." *Bipolar Disorders* 8.5, part 2 (Oct. 2006): 625–39.

De Fruyt, Jürgen, and Koen Demyttenaere. "Bipolar (Spectrum) Disorder and Mood Stabilization: Standing at the Crossroads?" *Psychotherapy and Psychosomatics* 76.2 (Jan. 2007): 77–88.

El-Mallakh, Rif, and others. "Bipolar II Disorder: Current and Future Treatment Options." *Annals of Clinical Psychiatry* 18.4 (Oct.–Dec). 2006: 259–66.

Eyer, Florian, and others. "Lithium Poisoning: Pharmacokinetics and Clearance During Different Therapeutic Measures." *Journal of Clinical Psychopharmacology* 26.3 (June 2006): 325–30.

Gonzalez-Pinto, Ana, and others. "Suicidal Risk in Bipolar I Disorder Patients and Adherence to Long-Term Lithium Treatment." *Bipolar Disorders* 8.5, part 2 (Oct. 2006): 618–24.

Kellner, Charles H., and others. "Continuation Electroconvulsive Therapy vs Pharmacotherapy for Relapse Prevention in Major Depression." *Archives of General Psychiatry* 63.12 (Dec. 2006): 1337–44.

Livingstone, Callum, and Hagen Rampes. "Lithium: A Review of Its Metabolic Adverse Effects." *Journal of Psychopharmacology* 20.3 (May 2006): 347–55.

McElroy, Susan L., and others. "Antidepressants and Suicidal Behavior in Bipolar Disorder." *Bipolar Disorders* 8.5, part 2 (Oct. 2006): 596–617.

Ozcan, Mehmet Erkan, Geetha Shivakumar, and Trisha Suppes. "Treating Rapid Cycling Bipolar Disorder with Novel Medications." *Current Psychiatry Reviews* 2.3 (Aug. 2006): 361–69.

Patel, Nick C., and others. "Lithium Treatment Effects on Myo-Inositol in Adolescents with Bipolar Depression." *Biological Psychiatry* 60.9 (Nov. 2006): 998–1004.

Singh, Jaskaran B., and Carlos A. Zarate, Jr. "Pharmacological Treatment of Psychiatric Comorbidity in Bipolar Disorder: A Review of Controlled Trials." *Bipolar Disorders* 8.6 (Dec. 2006): 696–709.

Jack H. Raber, Pharm.D.
Ruth A. Wienclaw, PhD

Lithobid *see* **Lithium carbonate**

Lithonate *see* **Lithium carbonate**

Lithotabs *see* **Lithium carbonate**

Lobotomy *see* **Psychosurgery**

Lorazepam

Definition

Lorazepam, a mild tranquilizer in the class of drugs known as **benzodiazepines**, is sold in the United States under the brand names Alzapam, Ativan, or Loraz. It is also available generically.

Purpose

Lorazepam is used for management of **anxiety**, nausea and vomiting, **insomnia**, and **seizures** (the injectable form). Lorazepam is also used prior to surgery to produce sedation, sleepiness, drowsiness, relief of anxiety, and a decreased ability to recall the events surrounding the surgery.

Description

Lorazepam is a member of the benzodiazepine family. Benzodiazepines primarily work by enhancing the function of a certain naturally occurring **brain** chemical, gamma-aminobutyric acid (GABA), which is responsible for inhibiting the transmission of nervous impulses in the brain and spinal cord. At the same time, the enhancement of GABA in the brain decreases symptoms associated with anxiety. Lorazepam differs from drugs such as **diazepam** (Valium) and **chlordiazepoxide** (Librium) in that it is shorter-acting and does not accumulate in the body after repeated doses.

Lorazepam is available in 0.5-mg, 1-mg, and 2-mg tablets and in an injectable form.

Recommended dosage

Lorazepam is taken several times daily by mouth or injected to treat anxiety. Dosage ranges from 1–2 mg taken either every 12 or every eight hours. The maximum daily total dosage for anxiety is 10 mg given in two to three divided doses. For sleep, patients may take from 2 to 4 mg at bedtime. Doses taken before surgery range from 2.5 to 5 mg.

Between 0.5 mg and 1 mg of lorazepam may be taken every six to eight hours to help control treatment-related nausea and vomiting (nausea and vomiting that occur as a side effect of a drug or medical treatment). Two mg of lorazepam is often given half an hour before chemotherapy to help prevent stomach upset. An additional 2 mg may be taken every four hours as needed.

The usual dose to treat seizures is 4 mg given intravenously (through a vein). This dose may be increased to 8 mg in patients who do not respond to the 4-mg dose.

Precautions

Lorazepam, like other drugs of this type, can cause physical and psychological dependence. Patients should not increase the dose or frequency of this drug on their own, nor should they suddenly stop taking this medication. Instead, when stopping the drug, the dosage should gradually be decreased, and then discontinued. If the drug is stopped abruptly, patients may experience agitation, irritability, difficulty sleeping, convulsions, and other withdrawal symptoms.

Patients allergic to benzodiazepines should not take lorazepam. Those with narrow-angle glaucoma, preexisting **depression** of the central nervous system, severe uncontrolled pain, or severe low blood pressure should not take lorazepam. This drug should be used with caution in patients with a history of drug **abuse**. Children under age 12 should not take lorazepam. Children between the ages of 12 and 18 may take the drug by mouth, but not intravenously. Pregnant women and those trying to become pregnant should not take lorazepam. This drug has been associated with damage to the developing fetus when taken during the first three months of pregnancy. Patients taking this drug should not breast-feed.

Side effects

Drowsiness and sleepiness are common and expected effects of lorazepam. Patients should not drive, operate machinery, or perform hazardous activities that require mental alertness until they have a sense of how lorazepam will affect their alertness.

Patients over age 50 may experience deeper and longer sedation after taking lorazepam. These effects may subside with continued use or dosage reduction.

The effects of an injection may impair performance and driving ability for 24–48 hours. The impairment may last longer in older patients and those taking other central nervous system depressants, such as some pain medication.

Lorazepam may also make patients feel dizzy, weak, unsteady, or clumsy. Less frequently, they may feel depressed, disoriented, nauseous, or agitated while taking this drug. Other side effects include headache, difficulty sleeping, rash, yellowing eyes, vision changes, and **hallucinations**. Redness and pain may occur at the injection site.

Patients may experience high or low blood pressure and difficulty in breathing after an injection of lorazepam. Nausea, vomiting, dry mouth, and constipation may also occur. The patient's sex drive may decrease, but this side effect is reversible once the drug is stopped. Patients should alert their physician to confusion, depression, excitation, nightmares, impaired coordination, changes in personality, changes in urinary pattern, chest pain, heart palpitations, or any other side effects.

Interactions

Alcohol and other central nervous system depressants can increase the drowsiness associated with this drug. Some over-the-counter medications depress the central nervous system. The herbal remedies **kava kava** and **valerian** may increase the effects of lorazepam. Patients should check with their doctors before starting any new medications while taking lorazepam. People should not drink alcoholic beverages when taking lorazepam and for 24–48 hours before receiving an injection prior to surgery.

Resources

BOOKS

Lacy, Charles F. *Drug Information Handbook*. Lexi-Comp, 2002.

Preston, John D., John H. O'Neal, and Mary C. Talaga. *Handbook of Clinical Psychopharmacology for Therapists*. 4th ed. Oakland, CA: New Harbinger Publications, 2004.

PERIODICALS

Giersch, Anne, and others. "Impairment of Contrast Sensitivity in Long-Term Lorazepam Users." *Psychopharmacology* 186.4 (July 2006): 594–600.

Hung, Yi-Yung, and Tiao-Lai Huang. "Lorazepam and Diazepam Rapidly Relieve Catatonic Features in Major Depression." *Clinical Neuropharmacology* 29.3 (May–June 2006): 144–47.

Izaute, M., and E. Bacon. "Effects of the Amnesic Drug Lorazepam on Complete and Partial Information Retrieval and Monitoring Accuracy." *Psychopharmacology* 188.4 (Nov. 2006): 472–81.

Kamboj, Sunjeev K., and H. Valerie Curran. "Neutral and Emotional Episodic Memory: Global Impairment After Lorazepam or Scopolamine." *Psychopharmacology* 188.4 (Nov. 2006): 482–88.

Pomara, Nunzio, and others. "Dose-Dependent Retrograde Facilitation of Verbal Memory in Healthy Elderly After Acute Oral Lorazepam Administration." *Psychopharmacology* 185.4 (May 2006): 487–94.

Verster, Joris C., Dieuwke S. Veldhuijzen, and Edmund R. Volkerts. "Is It Safe to Drive a Car When Treated with Anxiolytics? Evidence from On-the-Road Driving Studies During Normal Traffic." *Current Psychiatry Reviews* 1.2 (June 2005): 215–25.

Yacoub, Adee, and Andrew Francis. "Neuroleptic Malignant Syndrome Induced by Atypical Neuroleptics and Responsive to Lorazepam." *Neuropsychiatric Disease and Treatment* 2.2 (2006): 235–40.

Debra Wood, RN
Ajna Hamidovic, Pharm.D.
Ruth A. Wienclaw, PhD

Loss *see* **Grief**

Loxapine

Definition

Loxapine is a prescription-only drug used to treat serious mental, nervous, and emotional disorders. Loxapine is sold under the brand name Loxitane in the United States. Loxapine is also available in generic form.

Purpose

Loxapine is used to treat a variety of mental disorders including **anxiety**, mania, **depression**, and psychotic disorders.

Description

Loxapine is in the class of drugs known as antipsychotic agents. The exact mode of action of loxapine has not been precisely determined, but this drug has a tranquilizing effect on patients with anxiety, mania, and other psychotic disorders. It is known that loxapine reduces the amount of **dopamine** transmitted within the **brain**. Loxapine is available in 5-, 10-, 25-, and 50-mg tablets.

Recommended dosage

Loxapine is available in oral solution, capsules, tablets, and injectable form. The typical starting dose for adults and children over the age of 16 years is 10 mg given two to four times daily. The maximum range after the initial period is between 60 mg and 100 mg given two to four times per day. After a period of time, the dose is usually lowered to 20–60 mg per day given in divided doses. Injections are usually given only during the initial phase and are delivered into muscle (IM) in doses ranging from 12.5 mg to 50 mg every four to six hours until a desired level of response is reached. Then, the patient is usually put on the oral (PO) form for maintenance therapy. Guidelines for use in people under the age of 16 years have not been established.

Precautions

People taking loxapine should not stop taking this medication suddenly. The dosage should be gradually decreased over time. Loxapine should not be combined with other agents that depress the central nervous system, such as antihistamines, alcohol, tranquilizers, sleeping medications, and seizure medications. Loxapine can cause the skin to become more sensitive to the sun. People taking this drug should use sunscreen with a skin protection factor (SPF) greater than 15.

Loxapine is typically not administered to people who are in severe drug-induced states or in a coma. People with a history of **seizures**, heart disease, prostate enlargement, glaucoma, or chronic obstructive pulmonary disorder should receive loxapine only after careful evaluation. Guidelines for use in children under the age of 16 years have not been established. Loxapine has not been thoroughly studied in pregnant and nursing women, but such women should exercise great caution when using loxapine.

Side effects

Rare side effects, but ones that need to be reported immediately to a doctor, include seizures, breathing

> ## KEY TERMS
>
> **Anticholinergic**—Related to the ability of a drug to block the nervous system chemical acetylcholine. When acetylcholine is blocked, patients often experience dry mouth and skin, increased heart rate, blurred vision, and difficulty in urinating. In severe cases, blocking acetylcholine may cloud thinking and cause delirium.
>
> **Chronic obstructive pulmonary disease**—A disorder characterized by the decreasing ability of the lungs to adequately ventilate.
>
> **Dopamine**—A chemical in brain tissue that serves to transmit nerve impulses (is a neurotransmitter) and helps to regulate movement and emotions.
>
> **Glaucoma**—A group of eye diseases characterized by increased pressure within the eye significant enough to damage eye tissue and structures. If untreated, glaucoma results in blindness.
>
> **Mania**—An elevated or euphoric mood or irritable state that is characteristic of bipolar I disorder. This state is characterized by mental and physical hyperactivity, disorganization of behavior, and inappropriate elevation of mood.
>
> **Neurotransmitter**—A chemical in the brain that transmits messages between neurons, or nerve cells.
>
> **Psychotic**—Having a mental disorder characterized by disturbances of personality and a loss of normal association with reality.
>
> **Respiratory depression**—A significant impairment of the respiratory system.

difficulties, irregular heartbeat, significant changes in blood pressure, increased sweating, severe stiffness, extreme weakness, and unusually pale skin. Patients who experience these symptoms should stop using the medication immediately, as these symptoms are considered an emergency. More common but less serious side effects include uncontrolled movement of the arms or legs, lip smacking, unusual movements of the tongue, puffing of the cheeks, and uncontrolled chewing movements. These symptoms should also be reported immediately to a doctor.

More common and even less serious side effects include difficulty in speaking or swallowing, restlessness, stiffness of arms and legs, trembling, and loss of balance. These symptoms also need to be reported to a doctor. Less common and not especially significant side effects include urination problems, muscle spasms, skin rash, and severe constipation. Rare and not particularly serious side effects include uncontrolled twisting and movement of the neck, fever, sore throat, unusual bleeding, yellowing of the eyes or skin, and changes in facial expression.

Overdose symptoms include significant drowsiness, severe dizziness, significant breathing difficulties, severe weakness, trembling muscles, and severe uncontrolled movements.

Interactions

Loxapine should not be combined with anticholinergic drugs because of the potential of decreased antipsychotic effects. Loxapine should not be combined with bromocriptine because the combination can decrease the effectiveness of bromocriptine in patients with pituitary tumors. The combination of loxapine with lithium increases the toxicity of both drugs significantly. Likewise, loxapine and **lorazepam** should not be combined because the combination of the two has produced very low blood pressure, severe drowsiness, and respiratory depression in rare cases.

See also Anxiety and anxiety disorders; Depression and depressive disorders.

Resources

BOOKS

Consumer Reports Complete Drug Reference. 2002 ed. Denver: Micromedex Thomson Healthcare, 2001.

Ellsworth, Allan J., and others. *Mosby's Medical Drug Reference.* 2001–2002. St.Louis: Mosby, 2001.

Preston, John D., John H. O'Neal, and Mary C. Talaga. *Handbook of Clinical Psychopharmacology for Therapists.* 4th ed. Oakland, CA: New Harbinger Publications, 2004.

PERIODICALS

Bourin, Michel, Olivier Lambert, and Bernard Guitton. "Treatment of Acute Mania—From Clinical Trials to Recommendations for Clinical Practice." *Human Psychopharmacology: Clinical and Experimental* 20.1 (Jan. 2005): 15–26.

Janowsky, David S., and others. "Minimally Effective Doses of Conventional Antipsychotic Medications Used to Treat Aggression, Self-Injurious and Destructive Behaviors in Mentally Retarded Adults." *Journal of Clinical Psychopharmacology* 25.1 (Feb. 2005): 19–25.

Reinblatt, Shauna P., and others. "Advanced Pediatric Psychopharmacology: Loxapine Treatment in an Autistic Child with Aggressive Behavior: Therapeutic Challenges." *Journal of Child and Adolescent Psychopharmacology* 16.5 (Oct. 2006): 639–43.

Mark Mitchell, MD
Ruth A. Wienclaw, PhD

Loxitane *see* **Loxapine**

LSD *see* **Hallucinogens and related disorders**

Ludiomil *see* **Maprotiline**

Luria-Nebraska Neuropsychological Battery

Definition

The Luria-Nebraska Neuropsychological Battery, also known as LNNB or Luria-Nebraska Battery, is a standardized test battery used in the screening and evaluation of neuropsychologically impaired individuals.

Purpose

The LNNB was developed in an attempt to combine the qualitative techniques of some neuropsychological tests with the quantitative techniques of others. However, the scoring system that most clinicians use is primarily quantitative. The battery measures specific neuropsychological functioning in several areas including motor skills, language abilities, intellectual abilities, nonverbal auditory skills, and visual-spatial skills.

The battery is used by clinicians as a screening tool to determine whether a significant **brain** injury is present or to learn more about known brain injuries. It is also used to determine what the patient is or is not able to do with regard to neuropsychological functioning. For example, the LNNB may be used to determine which intellectual or cognitive tasks a patient may or may not be able to complete. The battery can also be used to arrive at underlying causes of a patient's behavior. More specifically, information regarding the location and nature of the brain injury or dysfunction causing a patient's problems is collected.

The LNNB is also used to help distinguish between brain damage and functional mental disorders such as **schizophrenia**. Also, within the category of schizophrenia, the battery can be used to help distinguish between patients with normal neuropsychological functioning and those with clear deficits. Besides its specifically clinical use, the battery is sometimes used for legal purposes—the presence or severity of a brain injury may be measured as part of an evaluation used in the court system.

Precautions

Because of the length of the test and complexity in interpretation, the examiner must be competent and properly trained. Also, the fact that many patients are, indeed, brain damaged can make test administration difficult or frustrating.

Description

The LNNB is based on the work of A. R. Luria, a Russian neuropsychologist who performed pioneering theoretical and clinical work with regard to brain function. Luria believed in a primarily qualitative approach to assessment and was opposed to standardization. He did not believe that neuropsychological functioning could be measured quantitatively. Thus, although his name is part of the test itself, his contribution to the LNNB is entirely theoretical. Also, the LNNB is based, in part, on Luria's Neuropsychological Investigation, a measure developed by Christensen in 1975. This test included items asked by Luria in his clinical interviews, some of which are used in the LNNB.

The battery, written in 1981 by Charles Golden, is appropriate for people aged 13 and older and takes between 90 and 150 minutes to complete. It consists of 269 items in the following 11 clinical scales:

- reading
- writing
- arithmetic
- visual
- memory
- expressive language
- receptive language
- motor function
- rhythm
- tactile
- intellectual

Scores for three summary scales can also be calculated: pathognomonic, right hemisphere, and left hemisphere. A children's version of the battery, called the Luria-Nebraska Neuropsychological Battery for Children (LNNB-C), appropriate for children aged eight to 12, is also available.

Results

The probability of brain damage is assessed by comparing an individual's score on each of the battery's 11 clinical scales to a critical level appropriate

for that person's age and education level. For example, if a person has five to seven scores above the critical level, they most likely have some sign of neurological impairment. Eight or more scores above the critical level indicate a clear history of neurological disorder.

The battery has been criticized by researchers on the grounds that it overestimates the degree of neuropsychological impairment. In other cases, it has been found to fail to detect neuropsychological problems. Also, the intellectual processes scale has not been found to correspond well to other measures of intelligence, such as the **Wechsler Adult Intelligence Scale (WAIS)**.

Other research, however, has found it to be a useful measure. It has been found as effective as the **Halstead-Reitan Battery** in distinguishing between brain-damaged individuals and nonbrain-damaged individuals with psychiatric problems. Part of the inconsistencies in opinion regarding the LNNB may be due to the specific nature of the population being tested by the battery and the difficulties in administration and scoring that some clinicians experience.

See also Intelligence tests; Kaufman Assessment Battery for Children; Kaufman Short Neuropsychological Assessment; Neuropsychological testing.

Resources

BOOKS

Golden, Charles J., and Shawna M. Freshwater. "Luria-Nebraska Neuropsychological Battery" In *Understanding Psychological Assessment: Perspectives on Individual Differences,* edited by William I. Dorfman and Michael Hersen. New York: Kluwer Academic/Plenum Publishers, 2001.

Golden, Charles J., Shawna M. Freshwater, and Jyothi Vayalakkara. "The Luria-Nebraska Neuropsychological Battery." In *Neuropsychological Assessment in Clinical Practice: A Guide to Test Interpretation and Integration,* edited by Gary Groth-Marnat. New York: John Wiley and Sons, 2000.

Lezak, Muriel D. *Neuropsychological Assessment.* New York: Oxford University Press, 1995.

Moses, James A., Jr., Ph.D., Charles J. Golden, Ph.D., Rona Ariel, Ph.D., and John L. Gustavson, Ph.D. *Interpretation of the Luria-Nebraska Neuropsychological Battery.* Volume 1. New York: Grune and Stratton, 1983.

Strub, Richard L., M.D., and F. William Black, Ph.D. *The Mental Status Exam in Neurology.* Philadelphia: F. A. Davis, 2000.

Luvox *see* **Fluvoxamine**